W9-BMB-183

ELEMENTS OF

Writing

REVISED EDITION

Second Course

James L. Kinneavy

John E. Warriner

HOLT, RINEHART AND WINSTON

Harcourt Brace & Company

Austin • New York • Orlando • Atlanta • San Francisco
Boston • Dallas • Toronto • London

Critical Readers

Requests for permission to make copies of any part of the work should be mailed to: Permissions Department, Holt, Rinehart and Winston, 6277 Sea Harbor Drive, Orlando, Florida 32887-6777.

Portions of this work were published in previous editions.

Acknowledgments: See page 1004, which is an extension of the copyright page.

Printed in the United States of America

ISBN 0–03–050874–6   3 4 5 6 7 040 00 99 98

James L. Kinneavy, the Jane and Roland Blumberg Centennial Professor of English at The University of Texas at Austin, directed the development and writing of the composition strand in the program. He is the author of *A Theory of Discourse* and coauthor of *Writing in the Liberal Arts Tradition*. Professor Kinneavy is a leader in the field of rhetoric and composition and a respected educator whose teaching experience spans all levels—elementary, secondary and college. He has continually been concerned with teaching writing to high school students.

John E. Warriner developed the organizational structure for the Handbook of Grammar, Usage, and Mechanics in the book. He coauthored the *English Workshop* series, was general editor of the *Composition: Models and Exercises* series, and editor of *Short Stories: Characters in Conflict*. He taught English for thirty-two years in junior and senior high school and college.

Writers and Editors

Anthony Buckley has both a B.A. and an M. A. from Purdue University and a Ph.D. from Cornell University. He teaches communication and theater at East Texas State University. He has written educational materials in speech communication, theater, and literature.

Joseph Fitzgibbon has an M.A. in English from The University of Oklahoma. He teaches American literature and writing at Sunset High School in Beaverton, Oregon, and he also teaches composition at Portland Community College. In addition to writing educational materials, Fitzgibbon is a newspaper journalist.

Peter Harris has a Ph.D. in English literature from Texas Tech University. He teaches composition and technical writing at West Virginia Institute of Technology. He is a writer of educational material in literature and composition.

Mary Hynes-Berry has a Ph.D. in English from The University of Wisconsin-Madison. She is an educational consultant for public schools in Chicago, Illinois. She has been a writer of educational materials for over fifteen years.

Marsha Lippincott has an M.A. in English from Mississippi University for Women and has studied English at Oxford University. She is a teacher who has written educational materials for twelve years.

Mary Elizabeth Podhaizer has an M.Ed. from the University of Vermont. She has been a writer of educational materials in literature and composition for fifteen years. She is currently engaged in research on secondary students' responses to literature.

Staff Credits

Associate Director: Mescal K. Evler

Managing Editor: Steve Welch

Senior Editors: Lynda Abbott, Richard Blake, Suzanne Thompson

Editorial Staff: *Editors,* Cheryl Christian, Ed Combs, Adrienne Greer, Scott Hall, Colleen Hobbs, Eileen Joyce, Ginny Power, Laura Cottam Sajbel, Elizabeth Smith, Stephen Wesson; *Copyeditors,* Joel Bourgeois, Roger Boylan, Mary Malone, Michael Neibergall; *Editorial Coordinators,* Susan Grafton Alexander, Amanda F. Beard, Rebecca Bennett, Wendy Langabeer, Marie Hoffman Price; *Support,* Ruth A. Hooker, Christina Barnes, Kelly Keeley, Margaret Sanchez, Raquel Sosa, Pat Stover

Editorial Permissions: Catherine J. Paré, Janet Harrington

Production: *Pre-press,* Beth Prevelige, Simira Davis; *Manufacturing,* Michael Roche

Design: Richard Metzger, *Art Director;* Lori Male, *Designer*

Photo Research: Peggy Cooper, *Photo Research Manager;* Mavournea Hay, Mike Gobbi, Victoria Smith, *Photo Research Team*

Acknowledgments

We wish to thank the following teachers who participated in field testing of pre-publication materials for this series:

Susan Almand-Myers
Meadow Park Intermediate School
Beaverton, Oregon

Theresa L. Bagwell
Naylor Middle School
Tucson, Arizona

Ruth Bird
Freeport High School
Sarver, Pennsylvania

Joan M. Brooks
Central Junior High School
Guymon, Oklahoma

Candice C. Bush
J. D. Smith Junior High School
N. Las Vegas, Nevada

Mary Jane Childs
Moore West Junior High School
Oklahoma City, Oklahoma

Brian Christensen
Valley High School
West Des Moines, Iowa

Lenise Christopher
Western High School
Las Vegas, Nevada

Mary Ann Crawford
Ruskin Senior High School
Kansas City, Missouri

Linda Dancy
Greenwood Lakes Middle School
Lake Mary, Florida

Elaine A. Espindle
Peabody Veterans Memorial High School
Peabody, Massachusetts

Joan Justice
North Middle School
O'Fallon, Missouri

Beverly Kahwaty
Pueblo High School
Tucson, Arizona

Lamont Leon
Van Buren Junior High School
Tampa, Florida

Susan Lusch
Fort Zumwalt South High School
St. Peters, Missouri

Michele K. Lyall
Rhodes Junior High School
Mesa, Arizona

Belinda Manard
McKinley Senior High School
Canton, Ohio

Nathan Masterson
Peabody Veterans Memorial High School
Peabody, Massachusetts

Marianne Mayer
Swope Middle School
Reno, Nevada

Penne Parker
Greenwood Lakes Middle School
Lake Mary, Florida

Amy Ribble
Gretna Junior-Senior High School
Gretna, Nebraska

Kathleen R. St. Clair
Western High School
Las Vegas, Nevada

Carla Sankovich
Billinghurst Middle School
Reno, Nevada

Sheila Shaffer
Cholla Middle School
Phoenix, Arizona

Joann Smith
Lehman Junior High School
Canton, Ohio

Margie Stevens
Raytown Middle School
Raytown, Missouri

Mary Webster
Central Junior High School
Guymon, Oklahoma

Susan M. Yentz
Oviedo High School
Oviedo, Florida

We wish to thank the following teachers, who contributed student papers for the Revised Edition of *Elements of Writing, Second Course.*

Dana Humphrey
North Middle School
O'Fallon, Missouri

Annie Kornegay
Rochelle Middle School
Kinston, North Carolina

Judi Thorn
Jenks East Middle School
Tulsa, Oklahoma

Contents in Brief

Table of Contents

PROFESSIONAL ESSAYS

PART ONE WRITING

What's The Secret?

An Introduction to Writing by James L. Kinneavy 2

► CHAPTER 2 LEARNING ABOUT PARAGRAPHS

▶ CHAPTER 4 EXPRESSIVE WRITING: NARRATION

It is beautiful to see
the people got to love Papa through
all his sickness. While we were
carrying Papa's remains to
Washington we came past Princeton. The whole college was down
at the depot and had strewn
flowers all along the tracks,
and after the train had passed,

►CHAPTER 5 USING DESCRIPTION

CHAPTER 6 CREATIVE WRITING: NARRATION

►CHAPTER 7 WRITING TO INFORM: EXPOSITION

CHAPTER 8 WRITING TO PERSUADE

CHAPTER 9 WRITING ABOUT LITERATURE: EXPOSITION

▶ CHAPTER *11* **WRITING EFFECTIVE SENTENCES**

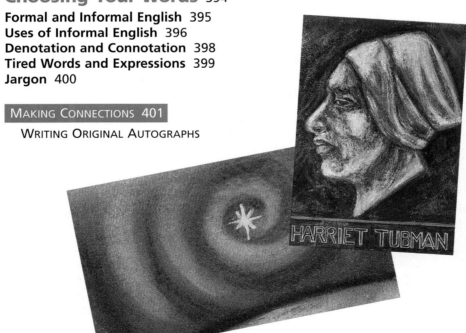

HARRIET TUBMAN

▶ CHAPTER *13* **THE SENTENCE**   404

Emblems, Roger De la Fresnaye
(c. 1913), © The Phillips Collection,
Washington, D.C.

CHAPTER **16** **COMPLEMENTS** 487

Direct and Indirect Objects, Subject Complements

► CHAPTER *20* AGREEMENT   572

Subject and Verb, Pronoun and Antecedent

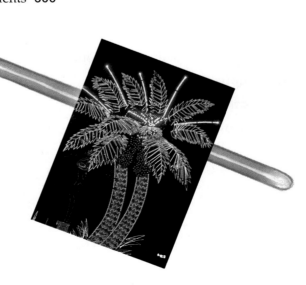

Principal Parts, Regular and Irregular Verbs

▶ CHAPTER 24 A GLOSSARY OF USAGE   680

Common Usage Problems

▶ CHAPTER 25 CAPITAL LETTERS   707

Rules for Capitalization

CHAPTER 28 SPELLING 798

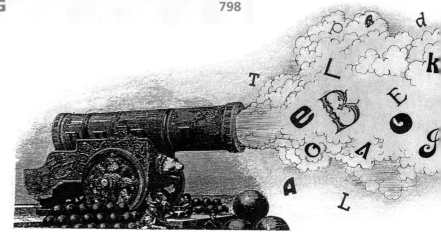

Improving Your Spelling

CHAPTER 29 CORRECTING COMMON ERRORS 828

Key Language Skills Review

PART THREE **RESOURCES**

▶ CHAPTER 30 **SPEAKING**   860

Skills and Strategies

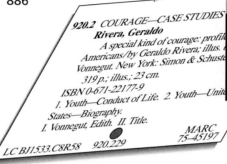

920.2 COURAGE—CASE STUDIES
  Rivera, Geraldo
    A special kind of courage: profile
  Americans/by Geraldo Rivera; illus.
  Vonnegut. New York: Simon & Schuster
    319 p.; illus.; 23 cm.
    ISBN 0-671-22177-9
    1. Youth—Conduct of Life. 2. Youth—Unite
  States—Biography.
    I. Vonnegut, Edith. II. Title.
                                    MARC
                                    75-45197
LC BJ1533.C8R58   920.229

Fiction

Toni Cade Bambara, "My Man Bovanne,"
  Gorilla My Love
Ernest Hemingway, "A Day's Wait," *The Short
  Stories of Ernest Hemingway*
Langston Hughes, "Thank You, M'am," *The
  Langston Hughes Reader*
Madeleine L'Engle, *A Wind in the Door*
David Low, "Winterblossom Garden,"
  Ploughshares
Anne McCaffrey, "The Smallest Dragonboy,"
  Science Fiction Tales
Lensey Namioka, "The All-American Slurp,"
  Visions
"The Sound of Flutes," told by Henry Crow Dog,
  The Sound of Flutes and Other Indian Legends
Karen Tei Yamashita, from *Brazil-Maru*

Nonfiction

Maya Angelou, *I Know Why the Caged Bird Sings*
"Animal Body Talk," *National Geographic World*
Dave Barry, "What to Do in a Wilderness Medical
  Emergency," *Dave Barry's Only Travel Guide
  You'll Ever Need*
Jean Bartenbach, *Rockhound Trails*
A. Scott Berg, *Max Perkins: Editor of Genius*
Bob Berger, "Road Warrior," *Omni*
Jennifer Cohen, "Disaster Hits Home," *Seventeen*
Stanley Crouch, "The Duke's Blues," *The
  New Yorker*
Kent Dannen, "Ban Dogs from Trails?"
  Dog Fancy
Gwen Diehn and Terry Krautwurst, *Science Crafts
  for Kids*
J. Frank Dobie, *A Vaquero of the Brush Country*
Gerald Durrell with Lee Durrell, *The Amateur
  Naturalist*
"Earth SOS," *Seventeen*
The EarthWorks Group, "Use It Again . . . and
  Again . . . and Again," *50 Simple Things Kids
  Can Do to Save the Earth*
Colin Fletcher, *The Secret Worlds of Colin Fletcher*
Anne Frank, "Becoming a Journalist," *The Diary
  of a Young Girl*
Michael Frome, *National Park Guide*
Mary Garfield, journal entry, in *Small Voices,* Josef
  and Dorothy Berger
Billy Goodman, "A Cautionary Tale," *A Kid's
  Guide to How to Save the Planet*
Bob Greene, "Cut," *Cheeseburgers—The Best of Bob
  Greene*

Judith E. Heumann, "Letter to the Editor," *USA
  Today*
Stephen King "Everything You Need to Know
  About Writing Successfully in Ten Minutes,"
  The Writer's Handbook
Nedra Newkirk Lamar, "Does a Finger Fing?,"
  The Christian Science Monitor
Barry Lopez, *River Notes: The Dance of Herons*
Elsa Marston, "Pictures of the Poor," *Highlights
  for Children*
N. Scott Momaday, *The Way to Rainy Mountain*
Pat Mora, "A Letter to Gabriela, A Young Writer,"
  English Journal
Kathleen Odean, "Review of Katherine
  Paterson's *Lyddie*," *School Library Journal*
Ann Petry, *Interviews With Black Writers*
Marian T. Place, *Mount St. Helens: A Sleeping
  Volcano Awakes*
Beatrix Potter, *The Journal of Beatrix Potter,
  1881–1897*
A.J.S. Rayl, "Making Fun," *Omni*
Tony Reichhardt, "Water World,"*Popular Science*
Dougal Robertson, *Survive the Savage Sea*
Sylvia Duran Sharnoff, "Beauties from a Beast:
  Woodland Jekyll and Hydes," *Smithsonian*
Laurel Sherman, "Energy: Powering a Nation,"
  Cobblestone
Scott Stuckey, *"A Home on the Martian Range,"
  Boys' Life*
Joyce Carol Thomas in *Speaking for Ourselves*
Elizabeth Vitton, "Paradise Lost," *3-2-1 Contact*
Geoffrey C. Ward and Ken Burns, "Alta Weiss,"
  Baseball: An Illustrated History
William Wise, "Strange and Terrible Monsters of
  the Deep," *Boys' Life*
Della A. Yannuzzi, "Billy Mills," *Highlights for
  Children*
William Zinsser, *On Writing Well*

Poetry

Ray Young Bear, "grandmother," *Winter of the
  Salamander*
Gwendolyn Brooks, "Robert, Who Is Often a
  Stranger to Himself"
Langston Hughes, "Dreams," *The Dream Keeper
  and Other Poems*
Shel Silverstein, "Jimmy Jet and His TV Set,"
  Where the Sidewalk Ends
Gary Soto, "October," *The Elements of San Joaquin*
Ernest Lawrence Thayer, "Casey at the Bat"

A Teacher's Guide to

ELEMENTS OF
WRITING

CONTENTS

DONALD MURRAY

**KAREN
GREENBERG**

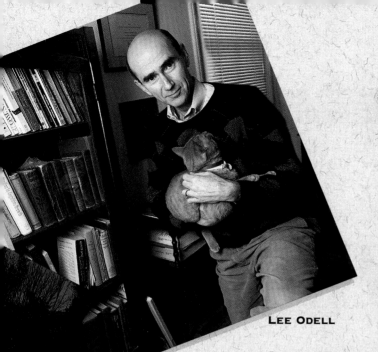

LEE ODELL

BARBARA
SHADE

MAXINE
HAIRSTON

NORBERT
ELLIOT

WANDA
SCHINDLEY

HOW DARE THEY?

. . . IN THE SPIRIT OF MAINTAINING THE LASTING VALUES AND STANDARDS OF THE SERIES . . .

Certainly when teachers saw a new name listed on *Elements of Writing* as a coauthor with John E. Warriner, some must have said, "How can the editors dare do this?" Warriner has been a legendary name in high school English composition and grammar books since 1941, the year of the first edition of his series. His high school textbooks have changed somewhat through the decades, but they have stood the test of half a century—despite many educational trends and fashions—because they have incorporated important values and standards. Warriner's texts have assumed an almost biblical authority.

But even the Bible is translated anew for different generations. So it is in the spirit of maintaining the lasting values and standards of the series that this new edition of the series is published with a new coauthor. I was properly flattered when Holt, Rinehart and Winston asked me to be the consultant for the composition sections of the books in the new series. But I was also in awe of this long tradition of excellence and can only hope that this tradition can be upheld.

Like John E. Warriner, I have a long and varied experience as a teacher. He taught in junior high, high school, and college. I have taught in elementary school, high school, and college. He taught for many years; I have been teaching since 1941 and continue to teach today. For the past twenty-five years I have given workshops to high school students involved in statewide competition in extemporaneous writing. Like Warriner, I have attempted to keep up with the profession and to reflect in my writings what we have learned and continue to learn about teaching the language arts. I have trained students to teach at all grade levels from elementary school through graduate school. I have also observed student teachers for years at the high school and college levels.

You will find in this series, therefore, an attempt to maintain the best values of the Warriner series and to add to it a few new features that teachers, administrators, and scholars think will make it an even better set of books.

THE TEACHER'S EDITION IS A *GREAT* HELP

I know that teaching school is incredibly time consuming: You're there at 8:00 and leave at 4:00; then you take on extra professional chores in the evening, and spend weekends correcting papers, read to keep up professionally, work on extracurricular activities, and attend conventions. Clearly you need all of the timesavers you can find.

You will find help in this series. On each page you will find that your objectives, your lesson plan, and your resources are involved with the student text. Questions for the students are provided with answers. Vocabulary items are defined. Adaptations for more-advanced students, less-advanced students, and ESL students are suggested. Opportunities for critical thinking and for cooperative learning are continually provided.

So, before spending hours looking up supplementary materials for a class, look in your teacher's edition. Someone else may have done your work already and saved you hours

Also, beginning teachers should exploit these thorough materials to avoid some all-too-common problems in the classroom.

RELATIONSHIP BETWEEN COMPOSITION AND GRAMMAR

Elements of Writing demonstrates the same close relationship between composition and grammar that has characterized the Warriner's series since its inception. You can see this by simply looking at the table of contents, which makes quite clear that primary attention is given to writing, and that grammar is a support to writing. Yet both are covered extensively.

Given the increasing importance of rhetoric in public schools and in college, you will find more depth in the composition section of this textbook. Lesson plans add more discernible structure to the chapters on writing. The chapters cover the kinds of writing students need to succeed in school and in life. Thus, there is a chapter devoted to each of the major purposes of writing—to inform or explain, to persuade, to entertain, and to express oneself. Strategies or modes of writing, such as narration, description, classification, and evaluation, are also discussed at each grade level.

In each chapter, the close relationship between composition and grammar is maintained. A relevant grammatical issue is covered in each writing chapter. Thus, a chapter on persuasion may consider fragments and a chapter on description may consider adjectives and adverbs. Finally, the composition chapters refer to the grammar chapters for coverage of issues that relate to the kind of writing under consideration.

Studies at all levels, from elementary school through college, confirm that grammar is learned best when taught in conjunction with composition, as well as with speaking and listening and literature. For instance, consistent fragments in a student's paper suggest a need for a lesson in the parts of the sentence. A mini-lesson about fragments should increase students' awareness of sentence structure. The mini-lesson would be followed with an activity in which students read peers' papers,

WHAT THIS TEXTBOOK DOES NOT WANT TO DO IS TO ENCOURAGE THE ISOLATED TEACHING OF GRAMMATICAL SKILLS IN A ROTE MANNER.

identify fragments, and resolve them with the writer. You will have reinforced a grammatical point and, more importantly, integrated grammar and composition. This textbook does not want to encourage the isolated teaching of grammatical skills in a rote manner. Most of the time, the grammar is linked to a writing assignment and even motivated by it.

THE PROCESSES OF COMPOSING

Elements of Writing consistently focuses on the processes of writing in every writing chapter. The stress on process is evident in the structuring of the chapters by the stages of the writing process—prewriting, writing, evaluating, revising, publishing, and finally reflecting.

A COOPERATIVE ATMOSPHERE

The idea that writing is a solitary, sedentary process, as a poet once said, is not at all adhered to in this textbook. Rather writing is viewed as a collaborative and cooperative action. Working cooperatively enables students to receive support from one another and from the teacher.

The students who work in *peer groups* of three or four help each other turn out better work. The members plan the papers, critique drafts, and provide a real audience for the final paper. The members of the group are like a team working toward a common goal.

The *teacher* moves from group to group, helping in the planning and discussing problems. Like the members of the peer groups, the teacher fulfills different functions:

at times the teacher is a motivator, a problem solver, a careful listener, a constructive critic, a sympathetic reader, and above all, a fellow writer.

With this view of the writing process, the teacher with a *heavy paper load* can be assisted by students. The teacher now is not the only person who reads and evaluates a student's paper. The support group also provides useful feedback to the author about mechanics, word choice, organization, ideas, and style. If the teacher trains peer groups to be constructively critical, a good deal of the drudgery of grading papers can be avoided.

The writing process often results in some kind of *publication,* such as a public speech, a performance, a class newspaper, or placement in a permanent portfolio that the student keeps of his or her progress as a writer.

The general structure of *Elements of Writing* places the composition chapters before grammar, usage, and mechanics chapters, thus mirroring the process in which students write rapidly and enthusiastically in their first plans, sketches, and drafts, without stopping to check spelling, word choice, or grammatical purity. The idea is to support the writing process as a creative surge in the beginning. The mechanical and stylistic matters are better addressed in revision with peers.

THE AIMS OR PURPOSES OF WRITING AND DIFFERENT LANGUAGE STYLES

Different levels of formality are suggested with the different pur-

poses of writing presented in *Elements of Writing*. In the chapters on expressive writing, a casual, personal, and familiar style is suggested. At the other extreme, in the chapters on information and proof, a more formal sense of grammar and word choice is expected. This is true in real life and in the classroom. In between self-expression and these types of expository writing, there are various shades of formality in persuasive, creative, and exploratory writing.

The model adopted here is that of Martin Joos, whose book *The Five Clocks* distinguishes five different levels of formality that nearly all of us use, depending on the circumstances. Joos calls these the intimate, the colloquial, the consultative, the formal, and the ritual levels. We speak to our family members in a familiar language. We speak to our friends in an ordinary conversation on the colloquial level. We adopt the consultative tone usually when we are teaching class. We use a formal level when we are giving speeches at a convention. And we use the ritual level of formality when we are at church or are graduating or are being initiated into a society.

But teachers are not the only people who have their five levels of formality. Teenagers also have their own colloquial, consultative, formal, and ritual levels as do middle-aged adults and older people.

WRITING AND LITERATURE

This series is permeated with reading and literature. Each writing chapter includes models of the type of writing that is being studied. Many samples are drawn from

the literary canon. In one grade level, for instance, an excellent poem by William Stafford illustrates the aims of writing. Nearly every writing chapter in the student's edition contains similar material. Of course, all of these selections used as writing models are annotated. Further, in the teacher's edition, are **Literature Links,** which take common literary selections and relate them to the material being studied.

Some writing chapters are almost completely devoted to literary writing, especially the chapters on creative writing, narration, and description. Thus writing and literature are highly integrated by a common underlying philosophy of language.

WRITING AND THE OTHER LANGUAGE ARTS

In addition to being highly integrated with literature, *Elements of Writing* is also integrated with reading, speaking and listening, and viewing.

Each chapter contains several reading samples of the type of writing being studied. These are carefully analyzed by the students by means of questions after each selection. These questions may be answered orally. The oral emphasis continues throughout the chapter as each stage of the writing process is carried out by means of peer discussion groups. Frequently, the publication of the paper takes an oral form as persuasive speeches are delivered to the class.

The peer group is also clearly a speaking and listening group. Students must learn to listen care-

fully to each other in order to make constructive suggestions for improvement.

Thus the four language arts are carefully interwoven into the structure of each chapter at each stage of the writing process.

WRITING AND NEW TECHNOLOGIES

Whenever possible, teachers should take advantage of the new technologies that are increasingly becoming available at the high school level. Consequently, throughout this edition there are continual reminders of these possibilities.

Networking with Computers

Many schools have computers available for use in teaching writing. Some are even networked to allow student interactions with each other, either with the entire class or with selected groups. The simultaneous writing reactions of all members of the class to a common reading assignment is one of the most effective methods to ensure one hundred percent participation in group discussions, especially if the right questions are asked. And the use of computers to set up small support groups for the different stages of the writing process is also an exceptionally efficient technique of using small groups in teaching writing.

Revising and Computers

Even without networking, however, the use of computers is to be commended whenever possible, particularly because of the manner in which revising is accomplished on computers. Students who formerly hated to revise now see revision as an easy and enjoyable manner to improve their work, not just at the level of vocabulary or mechanics, but even at the level of full discourse changes.

Computers also bring substantial help to the poor speller and to the student having trouble finding the right word. Nearly all word-processing programs have some type of spell-check feature that shows students which words are incorrectly spelled. Thus each student can keep a list of his or her own problem words. This is acknowledged by nearly all spelling research as the single best way to improve spelling. Most spell-check programs are accompanied by programs that properly hyphenate words at the end of a line. This is an additional bonus for students who use computers.

In addition, most word-processing programs now come with a thesaurus and grammar program. The first enables students to look for options in vocabulary, even while working at the computer.

The grammar programs can check tense, case, subject-verb agreement, fragments, and so forth.

Publishing and Word Processors

It is possible to use a computer as a desktop publisher to enable students to see some of their writings in elegant print and format. These can be put into portfolios for permanent records. Throughout the annotated teacher's edition there are reminders of this option of publishing.

A FINAL WORD

Possibly after reading this essay, which brings together many of the rather complex tasks of the writing teacher, you may be worried about the size of the task. But luckily you don't have to solve all of these problems overnight. The teaching of writing is a slow and cumulative process. Each chapter of this textbook focuses on a very specific issue and tries to address just that particular skill. Subsequent chapters build on the skill just learned. The students then slowly build up a range of abilities.

Just remember that your predecessors have worked with the students whom you now face, just as your colleagues will pick up where you leave off. And you are not alone at the present time: Your current colleagues are working with the same students in other classes.

In other words, just as writing is a cooperative endeavor for your students, so also is it a cooperative endeavor for you with the teachers from year to year and among a group of teachers one year at a time.

No One Does A More Important Job

Finally, you should be assured that your task is at the top of educational priorities. No one does a more important job than the teacher of writing. Such a person is also teaching students how to read, think, listen, and speak in ways that will enable them to contribute to a complex modern society as educated communicators.

By Donald M. Murray, Professor Emeritus of English, The University of New Hampshire

Use Genre as Lens

WE WRITE ABOUT WHAT WE DON'T KNOW ABOUT WHAT WE KNOW.

Students are usually introduced to each genre—essay, narrative, poem—in isolated units, as if one form of writing would contaminate another. But each genre is a lens, a way to observe, record, and examine the world. Students should be encouraged to use each genre to explore a single important experience.

Student writers and their teachers should begin the exploration with a personal experience—an event, a person, a place—that holds a significant mystery for them. Mystery is the starting place for most writing, what Grace Paley described when she said, "We write about what we don't know about what we know." Invite your students to explore a moment in their lives to which they keep returning in memory, the way the tongue seeks the missing tooth.

Encourage your students to play with the fragments of language connected with that experience in their minds and on paper to discover a line, a phrase, or a word that contains a tension or conflict within the experience. The "line" might be a word—*Christmas*—that

might have special implications for a student with a Catholic mother and a Jewish father. It might be a phrase—*the debts of Christmas*—to a person whose family spends too much money to make up for their true family feelings. The "line" could be a sentence—"Each Christmas I remember my sister who will never grow old."—for someone who lost a sister years before. Each "line" has a tension and mystery the writer needs to understand by writing.

Before your students begin, it is important to remind them that all writing is experimental, that experimentation implies failure, and that failure is instructive. It is not possible they will fail; it is imperative that they fail. We do not improve our writing by avoiding failure, but by making use of it.

To guarantee failure, urge students to write the first draft fast. Velocity is as important in writing as it is in bicycle racing. Speed will produce the accidents of language, connection, and insight that will propel the draft forward towards meaning. And velocity allows students to escape, for the moment,

the censor that demands premature correctness.

They should allow their drafts to instruct them. The evolving text will take its own course, exploring the experience as it is relived. If they are patient, receptive, and open to surprise, the text will tell them what they have to say. You may want to write two statements by E. M. Forster on the chalkboard:

Think before you speak is criticism's motto; speak before you think creation's.

and

How do I know what I think until I see what I say?

Students should write out loud, hearing the text as they write it. They may actually do this—it is your classroom—or read silently but *listen* to the text. As they tune their voices to the story being told, the voice—angry, nostalgic, humorous, sad, analytical, instructive, argumentative, poetic, even narrative—will reveal the meaning of the draft to the writer.

I invite you to stand beside me at my workbench and to observe me

as I use genre to explore an experience of mine.

THE ESSAY

I prefer the term *reflective essay* to *personal essay* because the writer reflects on personal experience, or on a topic of personal interest. The essay is neither a simple narrative of experience nor of thought unanchored by experience, but a combination of thought and experience, an effort to discover and share meaning in experience. The essay is a demonstration of critical thinking.

Some notes on the craft of the essay.
- Narrow the territory to be explored so you can achieve depth.
- Be specific. The specific will instruct. The more specific you are, the more universal your audience will be.
- Work locally; the paragraph you have just written contains the seed of the next paragraph. For example, if you have said the experience was important, show how it was important in the next paragraph.
- Answer the reader's questions. Writing is a conversation between reader and writer.
- When the draft surprises you, pay attention. Develop the surprise to discover its meaning.

On April 21, while visiting a daughter and her husband in their new home, I got up early without the alarm, as is my habit, and ended up sitting at the top of the stairs waiting for my family to wake, and I found mystery in the experience. It was a moment full of emotion, and I needed—not wanted, but needed—to explore that moment through writing.

I made a few notes in my daybook:

I can remember myself as a small boy in Doctor Denton's trying to be quiet sitting at the head of the stairs (night) waiting for the family to get up

I can remember my own daughter's impatient waiting

Sunday morning I sit at the head of the stairs a good place to read, a good place legs waiting, wife, behind me in the room, my wife

The next day I wrote the column that was published in *The Boston Globe,* April 30, 1991:

I am, once again a small boy in Dr. Denton's sitting at the top of the stairs waiting for the snoring to stop and another day to begin.

I am, at the same time, an old man sitting at the top of the stairs in the new home of a daughter and her husband, waiting once more for the snoring to stop and a new day to begin.

Minnie Mae and I, on our first visit, have taken their bed, and they sleep on the hide-a-bed in the living room. They work in the theatre and have agreed to get up early—at 9 o'clock on Sunday morning—because the old folks are here.

But I followed the custom of many old men and was up at 5:33 A.M. I tiptoed downstairs, went out to the car, explored Mount Kisco, sipped a cup of coffee at Dunkin Donuts—yes, and had a doughnut, and yes, juice to get down my six pills I take because of previous doughnuts—bought the Sunday *New York Times,* sat in the car reading it, and now, at 8 A.M. sit at the head of the stairs where I can stretch my legs, flex my football knee, and read my book and wait.

It has been a good morning, and I feel little guilt that I have not been able to sleep in. They will laugh at my compulsion to be up and doing, and I will tease them for their laziness, but they will not understand the joy I, like many over sixties, experience when I am up in the lonely hours of dawn.

I ruminate—early morning is ideal for rumination—on the fact that as a child I was always up early when I could lose myself in a book —no TV then—explore the backyard or the vacant lot where the morning glories grew.

Awake before the grown-ups, I could be what I needed to be: Lindbergh crossing the Atlantic alone, Admiral Byrd isolated in his tiny room under the Antarctic ice, the unnamed Indian scout watching the palefaces land on the Maine coast

As a teenager I bicycled my route for Gallagher's News Agency in Quincy finishing before the sun was up, drove Miller's grocery truck to market in Boston or cleaned the vegetables and laid them out in rows on the boxes balanced in front of the small store on Beach Street.

Only now I confess that when I nicked myself trimming the lettuce that was packed in ice, my hands numb and clumsy, I would turn that lettuce head so the blood did not show. I was apprentice to Miller's game: profit through deceit.

I still remember playing grown-up early in the morning, the grocer's apron twice tucked so it did not sweep the sawdust strewn floor. The profit would be Miller's not mine, but I anticipated the customers who might, this Depression Saturday, pay cash. That anticipation would last until midnight when Mr. Miller would go out and scan the street right and left and reluctantly, when no one was on the street, give the command to close.

In combat I preferred the early morning patrols, guard duty when I was alone to watch the theatre of morning's change from dark to light, the promise of a new day even when the landscape was littered with last night's dead.

After college I worked for a morning newspaper and liked the mystery and companionship of the night worker, enjoyed the coming home at dawn. Eventually I returned to days, and morning became my best writing time as it is for most writers.

Goethe advised, "Use the day before the day. Early morning hours have gold in their mouth." John Hersey testified that "To be a writer is to sit down at one's desk in the chill portion of every day, and to write." A few years ago poet Donald Hall said, "In summer I'll be up at 4:30, make coffee, let out the dog, go pick up *The Boston Globe.* Then I write."

In retirement I, like so many other over sixties, still get up early when there are no cows to milk, no commuter train to meet, no factory shift to join. It is habit, but for me a habit built not from compulsion but delight.

Sitting at the top of the stairs waiting for the young—and the not-so-young Minnie Mae—to wake, I try to define the strange emotion I feel. At last it comes to me. I am, after a lifetime of chasing the carrot, content.

I have another day to celebrate. Sitting here alone, I can enjoy the feeling of this house that is turning so quickly into a home. I am comfortable in this home and know that soon my wife will wake with a groan and a smile, and downstairs I will hear conversation and music, smell coffee and we will all make plans for the day not too far off when a grandchild will sit where I sit, perhaps beside me, waiting for another day to begin.

The grandchild has arrived. His name is Joshua. I have not yet sat beside him at the top of the stairs but I will.

THE NARRATIVE

There are many wonderful ways to tell stories, but I suggest student fiction writers begin with the scene. Conrad is supposed to have said that a novel is a series of scenes of confrontation. The writer experienced in nonfiction tells *about* the story; the fiction writer *reveals* the story. That is an enormous difference, and the writing of a scene is the best way to cross the divide. Students can draw on their experiences with TV and film. The reader observes a room with the fourth wall removed; the action within the room tells the story and the reader discovers its meaning. As the short-story writer Becky Rule points out, students

WE DO NOT IMPROVE OUR WRITING BY AVOIDING FAILURE, BUT BY MAKING USE OF IT.

think that fiction has no rules, but the rules come from the story, and they are established early; if Hamlet is an indecisive prince he can suddenly become a king but not a decisive one.

Some notes on the craft of narrative.

• Start with character, not theme. The story and its meaning are revealed through the interaction of the characters.

• Write in the third person. It gives you more room and detachment.

• Dialogue is action, what the characters do to each other. Joan Didion says, "I don't have a very clear idea of who the characters are until they start talking."

• Point of view is where the camera is positioned to record the scene. In the beginning, stick with one point of view, perhaps entering into one head but not jumping in and out of every head. If you are in one sister's head, you don't know Frank is in the freezer; in the other sister's head, you do.

• Kurt Vonnegut counsels, "Don't put anything in a story that does not reveal character or advance the action."

In writing a draft of my novel, I found myself stealing the experience from my own essay and began a scene:

Melissa found Iain sitting in the shadows at the top of the stairs, "It's 5:30 in the morning."

He nodded.

"On guard duty?"

"In a way. I often sit here in winter, watch the light just before dawn, the woods, the field that goes down to the lake."

She thought for a moment of what it would be like to be a spy to your life, always on guard and asked, "You said last night that wherever you are, you see a field of fire, are aware of where to dig in, put the machine guns, even after all these years?"

"I'm not proud of it, Melissa. It's just my geography, an infantryman's geography."

"Do you always see a geography of war?"

"Always first, then I can make it go away. Most times.

It's natural, just the way I see things. The doctor sees you as kidney or a colon; I'm an old soldier, I see a field of fire, where the attack would come from."

"That's sad."

"Tedd's a soldier too, Melissa."

They hear the key probe for the lock, at last find it, and hurried down the stairs....

That is just a small fragment of narrative, and yet you can see how the story is revealing itself dramatically to the writer and the reader.

THE POEM

Poetry is the most disciplined and difficult form of writing. It is also the most fun. Experience is distilled by the writing of poetry. Poetry is always play—play with image and language so that meaning is revealed directly without rhetoric getting between the writer and reader or between experience and reader. Inexperienced poets often write with adjectives and adverbs, trying to describe their own feelings. The experienced poet writes with information, revealing specifics, provocative details, and compelling images that make the reader feel and think. The meaning is rarely stated but always there. In the poem, even more than fiction, the meaning is implied. The poem is the stimulus to the reader's thinking.

Some notes on the craft of poetry.

• Forget, for the moment, rhyme, meter, and traditional verse forms.

• Brainstorm images and other specifics, creating a list that may become a poem.

• Draft lines—not sentences but fragments of language—that capture an event, person, or place.

• Rearrange the lines until they reveal a meaningful pattern.

• Pay attention to the line breaks, trying to end on a strong word that causes the reader to read on.

The morning I wrote the column, I also wrote, on the computer, what might become a poem for my poetry group that was meeting that Thursday evening. I pasted this in my daybook:

Sitting at the top of the stairs
I listen to the silences
to understand Grandma's war with Mother

Sitting at the top of the stairs
I tune
        train myself to 1 elinesss

Later that day I made a handwritten note I also cut out and pasted in the daybook:

I lived at the top of the stairs, behind the living room couch, under the dining room table, the tent of tablecloth—in the apple tree, under the porch,

And still later I drafted a poem that went through one radical and three or four extensive revisions (periods of word play) until it became the following completed poem:

Childhood Espionage

Spy to my life, I lived at the top of the stairs, recorded silence, mapped how hurt was done. Under the porch, at the bedroom door, behind living room

sofa, I filled notebooks with what was not said, not done, escaped to the sidewalk, tried to read the shades drawn against my life. It must be Mother's shadow

sitting on the edge of the double bed, must be father's kneeling to pray. I cannot be sure, circle the block, listen to the neighbor's opera of argument, stand under

an open window where conversation will pour over me Once I saw my friend's older sister. She never pulled the shade. The dogs learned my smell

and let me patrol back yard, alley, vacant lot, in silence. I found the room where the Beckers kept the boy with the enormous head, watched comfort flow

from a priest's dancing hands as he gave the last rites to Vinnie's grandma, swayed to the rhythm of the Mitchells' bedroom dancing, lying down. Late, I returned to the home

of closed doors where we passed each other without touching. We never raised our voices, never stood between light and shade, never let a secret fall out a window.

Students should be encouraged to take central experiences from their lives—Willa Cather said, "Most of the basic material a writer works with is acquired before the age of fifteen"—and explore them with an array of genre, using each lens—essay, narrative, poem—and then examining the subject through other genre, perhaps argument, report, screenplay, or news story, to discover the many meanings in their lives. ❧

POETRY IS THE MOST DISCIPLINED AND DIFFICULT FORM OF WRITING. IT IS ALSO THE MOST FUN.

❧❧❧❧❧

Sources quoted include Grace Paley, Joan Didion, and Kurt Vonnegut cited in the following work: Donald M. Murray, *Shoptalk: Learning to Write with Writers*, Boynton/Cook Publishers, Inc., 1990.

By James L. Kinneavy

Meet the Aims and Modes of Writing

The place to start (and end) the teaching of writing is to have students see what written language can do for them.

WHY WRITE? WHERE DO I BEGIN?

Writing is a very complex activity, and so is the teaching of writing. I admit these facts, and I have been teaching writing for fifty years. You may be teaching your first class this year, and you probably have the same problem: In the face of this complex process, where do you start?

Some teachers recommend what may seem to be a very simple and logical approach: Start with the simple building blocks of writing and gradually work up to more complex blocks. In other words, teach students some elementary things about words, then move up to phrases, afterwards teach sentences, eventually work up to paragraphs, and finally, have students write full themes. Some say this is how children learn to use language orally. At first blush this theory has a kind of plausible simplicity to it. Years of research, however, have shown that it doesn't work and that it isn't the way children learn language.

LANGUAGE GETS THINGS DONE

Babies see the family members around them accomplish things by using language, and they quickly learn to use it themselves to get food, drink, or attention. This is the motivation behind all language acquisition and usage, from cradle to grave—language gets things done.

Consequently, if we can keep this elementary driving force behind our attempts to teach writing (or any language art for that matter), we can draw on a basic incentive that even babies understand. But when language teaching is divorced from getting things done, students rightly find it boring and uninteresting.

For this reason, the place to start (and end) the teaching of writing is to have students see what written language can do for them. What can writing do? In one introductory chapter, we attempt to get students to look around and see what language is getting done. We call language-users the hidden agents behind many of the mir-

acles of our age, we say that language is where the action is, and we call language-users the movers and shakers of the world.

Using very concrete examples, we focus the student's attention on the different kinds of things that language accomplishes. But the principle is the same at every grade-level and on into the college educations, careers, and adult lives of our graduates: The central concept in the teaching of writing at every level is an awareness of the aims or purposes of writing.

THE FOUR MAJOR AIMS OR PURPOSES OF WRITING

Luckily for you as well as for the students, these aims are not infinite, unpredictable, and unmanageable. They can be reduced to a few basic categories, and both you and the students have a good deal of practical experience with the categories in general. For example, one kind of language experience with which you are very familiar has to do with attempts to explain to or inform an audience about something of which it is partially or totally ignorant. You do this daily in the classroom and the students are the targets of this use of language. Other examples of this kind of writing are news stories in newspapers and magazines, encyclopedia articles, reports, textbooks, discussions, proposed solutions to problems, and research studies. *The emphasis is always on the subject matter, considered more or less objectively.* This kind of writing is generically referred to as **expository writing.**

As a teacher, you are only too aware of a second kind of writing that places more emphasis on the writer. In this case, the writing reveals the feelings of the writer, allows the writer to voice his or her aspirations or reactions to something in a quite personal way, or gives the writer a chance to articulate important beliefs. Examples of this kind of writing are journals, diaries, myths, prayers, credos, and protests. Of course, some of this writing may also overlap with other kinds. *The major emphasis in this kind of writing is on the writer.* This kind of writing is often called **expressive writing.**

As a teacher, you often try to convince your students of the importance of an education and of their duties as citizens. As a matter of fact, in our culture we are bombarded with attempts to get readers

to vote a certain way, to change attitudes or beliefs, to buy certain products, to switch allegiances, etc. Examples of such writing are advertising, political speeches, legal oratory, editorials, and religious sermons. In all of these cases, *the focus of the use of language is on the receiver of the message.* Usually, this kind of writing is called rhetorical or **persuasive writing.**

A fourth kind of writing, probably your favorite, is literature. This type of writing is given an honored place in English classes. We read selections of literature. They are intended to delight us and sometimes to teach us lessons. Examples of literature range from simple jokes, funny stories, ballads, small poems, and TV sitcoms to serious dramas, movies, novels, and epics. We try to get students to write this way when we teach creative writing. *Although all writing involves originality, we usually reserve the term* **creative writing** *for this kind of writing.*

THE COMMUNICATION BASIS OF THE AIMS OF WRITING

As a perceptive reader, you may have noticed as we went through the four major aims of writing that each one emphasized a different element of the communication process. It is not accidental that the

major purposes of writing generally can be reduced to four. The structure of the written communication process is based on a writer, a reader, a language, and the subject matter.

To assist you to get students to see the different roles of each aim, the relationship between the elements of the communication process and those of the aims of discourse is expressed graphically below. (The major aims of writing and the main parts of the communication process).

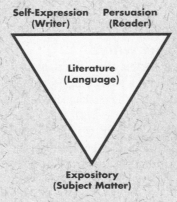

Self-Expression (Writer) Persuasion (Reader)

Literature (Language)

Expository (Subject Matter)

The major parts of the communication process and the aims of writing.

Consequently, from aim to aim, there is a continual shifting of roles in the communication process. The lead role determines the major purpose of the writing and the other roles become subordinate. Many teachers have found this simple diagram enables students to grasp the changing dynamics of language use.

DOMINANT AIMS AND OVERLAP

As a teacher, you have probably written one or two of these different kinds of writing, but you may not have written all of them. In your own writing you are certainly aware that most writing does not

attempt to achieve all of these aims at the same time. A specific piece of writing usually has a single dominant aim, subordinating the others to avoid conflicts and confusion. Though subordinate, the other aims are still present. Thus, movie ads in the newspaper contain important information about actors, actresses, directors, titles, and show times, but the information is there to persuade people to come to the movies.

Indeed, all the aims overlap each other.

WHY ARE THE BASIC AIMS IMPORTANT?

Despite overlaps, however, it is quite important to distinguish the various aims. As a teacher, you are very aware that the criteria by which one kind of discourse is judged are different from the criteria by which another kind of discourse is judged. You try to impress upon your students that expository writing is judged on the basis of objective evidence; the appeal of the writer as such is not relevant to the final proof or explanation, nor is the use of emotion or humor. For this reason, you know that when you teach expository writing, it is important to discourage the use of these other kinds of appeal—they are, in fact, considered inappropriate in news stories, scientific reports, or textbooks. Thus the pedagogy of expository writing follows from the nature of this kind of writing.

But when you teach other kinds of writing, these other appeals are important. In persuasion, for example, the emphasis is on the appeal of the writer and the appeal to the interests of the audience. **The differences among exposi-**

AS A TEACHER YOU OFTEN TRY TO CONVINCE YOUR STUDENTS OF THE IMPORTANCE OF AN EDUCATION . . .

tion, persuasion, literature, and self-expression force you to emphasize different criteria when teaching these different kinds of writing. There is no single criterion of aim which makes all writing good. That is why the different aims are taught separately.

THE MODES OF WRITING

After all this talk about the aims of writing, you, as a teacher, might ask, "Are you maintaining that if I get students to pay attention to the aims of their writing, all other problems will disappear? There are many other facets of the process of writing to which we teachers have to pay attention. Grammar is clearly a persistent concern, as are spelling, vocabulary, sentence structure, paragraphing, genres of writing (letter, report, story, poem, speech, ad, etc.), subject matter, and last but not least, the modes. What do you propose to do with all of these issues?"

I recognize all of these concerns and reply that they will be given close and continuous attention throughout the entire course, but I would like to stress the last dimension, that of the modes of writing.

JAMES L. KINNEAVY
AUTHOR OF
ELEMENTS OF WRITING

This dimension bridges the two mentioned just before it—genre and subject matter, and it implicates a major concern of all writing teachers—organization. More than any other aspect of writing, modes determine overall organization. This particular essay, for example, is a series of classifications and definitions.

At times in the history of writing, modes have been given almost as much attention as the aims, but most of the time they have been a serious second candidate. The modes are listed differently in vari-

ous books. In this textbook we call narration, description, classification, and evaluation the modes. They could be called the genres of writing, and they could be called ways of looking at subject matter.

When I want to introduce students to the modes, I use a newspaper. I ask students to find examples of news stories (narratives). I ask them to find classifications, especially in the classifieds, as they are called. I ask the students to examine individual items within each section of the classifieds and to tell me what the details are. It becomes clear to them that there are specific descriptions of cars, houses, lost dogs, or jobs in the classifieds. Finally, I have students check reviews of books, movies, television programs, or concerts. These are all evaluations.

Like the aims, the modes have to be taught separately. **What makes a good narrative is not what makes a good evaluation or a good description or a good classification.** Consequently, the modes are given careful consideration in this textbook. 🍃

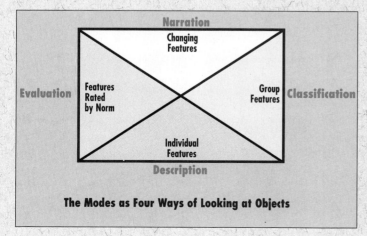

The Modes as Four Ways of Looking at Objects

BY DR. LEE ODELL, RENSSELAER POLYTECHNIC INSTITUTE

MODELING

MAKE US SEE WHAT YOU'RE TALKING ABOUT.

For some time now, teachers of writing have made a point of exhorting students to make their writing "show, not tell." Don't just tell us your reactions or opinions, we say to them. Make us see what you're talking about. If you're trying to describe a person, let us see facial expressions, details of clothing, mannerisms, actions; let us hear exactly what the person says. Or, if students are trying to write persuasively, we insist: Don't just give us your generalized conclusions. Give us some specific information that lets us see what you base your judgment on and that lets us decide for ourselves whether your judgement makes sense.

This advice is not an infallible, inflexible rule. Writers can't elaborate on everything. Furthermore, readers sometimes let a generali-zation pass unchallenged because it seems to ring true or because writers have sufficient authority for us simply to take their word on the matter. But if we are judicious in asking students to "show, not tell," the phrase constitutes good advice for writers and excellent advice for teachers. If we want students to make significant progress as writers, we will have to show them—not just tell them, *show*

LEE ODELL OPENS HIS CLASSROOM DOOR AT RENSSELAER POLYTECHNIC INSTITUTE.

them—what we mean. In effect, we need to make sure they have models, not just of the kinds of writing they will do but of the writing processes.

There is, of course, a long history to the practice of working with models. For centuries, teachers of rhetoric and writing have required students to study the works of great writers, sometimes having students copy model texts word for word or asking students to imitate the sentence structures they found in these works. Indeed, a version of this practice persisted through the middle 1980's in the form of sentence combining. This system did not ask students to emulate one specific writer, but it did show them frequently used sentence patterns in the works of highly admired professional writers so students could construct their own sentences based on a wide variety of these patterns.

Traditional approaches to using models have their uses, but these approaches are not what I'm talking about here. I'm suggesting that we depart from traditional practice in several ways. For one thing, the model should come not solely from famous authors but rather from books and magazines students read willingly and have readily accessible. Also, teachers don't have to provide all the models; students should be asked to bring in articles or excerpts from books that they personally find engaging and effective. Finally, these models should not be treated as though they are sacred; they are, instead, objects for analysis— for criticism as well as for praise. We and our students need to examine entire models where writers

have used successful strategies that students might incorporate into their own writing, as the occasion warrants. But we and our students also need to identify things that don't work and maybe even to collaborate on devising ways to improve the model.

There are several ways we might use models, but my favorite is to use them to help students solve their own writing difficulties. For example, a number of my students can't figure out how to begin a piece of writing, what Donald Murray would refer to as a "lead." When this is a problem, I ask students to bring in copies of the first pages of articles that they somehow found themselves reading, even though the topics might not normally have concerned them.

For example, one student brought in an article entitled "Hell on Wheels," which began this way:

Almost from the time the downtown No. 4 subway train began its 21-mile run below New York City at 11:38 p.m. on the night of Tuesday, Aug. 27, something seemed amiss. Heading from the Bronx to Manhattan, the train overshot the platform at a couple of stations. At times it slowed to a crawl and then accelerated to breakneck speeds. The conductor contacted the motorman, Robert Ray, 38, several times on the intercom to find out if everything was all right. Ray replied that he was fine. But that was clearly not the case....

This article begins of course, with a claim about a specific event ("something seemed amiss") and then illustrates this claim with a series of incidents. It mentions specific, troubling things that happened (for example, the train "slowed to a crawl and then accelerated to breakneck speeds"); it reports what people said to each other; and then it challenges what one of the people said ("But that clearly was not the case...."). In this last sentence, the author creates a conflict that engages the reader and lets the reader know what the rest of the article will be about (i.e., it will show how the driver's claim was "not the case").

Other articles brought in by the students began quite differently— by citing troubling statistics, for example, or by describing general trends in society that a reader was almost certain to know and be concerned about. These differences are important. I don't want students to think there is just one way to begin a piece of writing. Consequently, I photocopied a variety of examples and asked students to talk them through to identify the strategies writers had used to engage readers. My goal was to

help students recognize some of the options that are open to them in doing their own writing.

In addition to bringing in models written by professionals, it can be extremely useful for us to bring in copies of our own efforts to do the same kind of writing students are working on. And once we have developed an atmosphere of trust, it can be useful to bring in effective examples of student work, continually asking such questions as these: What did the writer do here? How did he or she go about capturing our interest and letting us know what to expect in the rest of the text? Is there anything that this writer is doing that you might profitably do? Again, the goal is not to provide recipes or rules chiseled on tablets of stone but to get students to see what is possible.

MODELING THE COMPOSING PROCESS

Thus far, I have been describing ways we might use written products as models. In addition, we also need models of the composing processes of writers. This modeling can be as sophisticated or as rudimentary as our students need. It can focus on the work of an individual writer as Donald Murray shows in his "Use Genre as Lens" essay or on the efforts of peers as they revise their initial drafts. That is, we need to let students see the processes professional writers and students go through in doing their own writing and even in responding to classmates' writing.

There are several activities teachers can use that allow students to observe their peers' writ-

I DON'T WANT STUDENTS TO THINK THERE IS JUST ONE WAY TO BEGIN A PIECE OF WRITING.

ing processes. For example, a colleague was concerned that her tenth-graders would have difficulty passing the state basic competency test that is required for high school graduation. Knowing that one of the questions on that test was likely to require students to report information in a well-organized form, she could have concentrated on paragraph form and the proper use of transitions. But suspecting that her students' difficulties were more profound than that, she decided that her students weren't paragraphing because they did not understand that certain kinds of expository paragraphs require writers to group facts by setting up categories that the paragraphs would be about.

Consequently, she asked students to watch a videotape of a movie that she was fairly certain they would find moving, an account of the difficulties encountered by a child who had been classified as mentally retarded but who had, nonetheless, a number of good traits and who was personally likable. After students had watched the videotape, she asked them to write down every fact they could remember from the movie and to collaborate as a class to make the list as complete as possible. That night she typed a complete list of facts, made an overhead transparency of them, and then cut the transparency into strips, each strip containing one fact.

The next day, she asked students to collaborate on ways to group these facts. For instance, students noticed that many of the facts pertained to ways people reacted to the young boy, while others could be grouped under such headings

as the boy's reactions to other people or his abilities. As students discussed ways of grouping facts, the teacher reflected what they were saying by moving the transparency strips around on the overhead projector. She was showing, not telling, her students about the basic process they needed to create one type of organized paragraph.

Another approach to modeling the composing process comes from a ninth-grade teacher concerned that her students' descriptive writing was bland. She believed their real problem was not a lack of descriptive adjectives and adverbs but that students weren't really looking closely at the people or objects they were describing.

She also knew that television programs routinely provide excellent examples of the process of observing. That is, as a rule, television cameras do not stay in one

spot to observe everything from the same angle and distance. Instead, the cameras change position to vary the angles and the distances from which they view things. For example, one detective program began with a close-up shot of a ringing phone. Then the camera moved back so that the viewers could see a well-dressed man hurrying across an elegant apartment toward the phone. Next the camera moved in to focus on the man's trembling hands as he nervously dried his sweaty palms on his handkerchief before picking up the phone. Finally, the camera shifted focus again, to show the head and shoulders of a burly, unshaven man speaking into a pay phone. These shifts in focus set the scene for the entire episode.

To help students understand this process of observing by shifting focus, the teacher asked students,

as part of their homework, to watch one of their favorite TV programs and to count the number of times the camera shifted its focus in a two-minute period. She also asked them to make notes about the different things they saw every time the camera shifted focus. The next day they discussed these episodes and concluded that a program in which the camera did not shift focus would almost certainly be dull.

To help students see how this process applied to writing, the teacher gave students the following description:

She probably has false teeth and wears glasses. She wears her hair up in a bun and wears dresses from the 1930's. She has a habit of tapping her pencil on her desk.

Students readily agreed that this passage was uninteresting. To help them see why, the teacher asked students to think of the grammatical subject of each sentence as the visual focus of the sentence. (In response to the predictable question, the teacher told students that, for this passage, they could think of the grammatical subject as "how the writer begins each sentence.") Students saw readily that this writer's "camera" was standing in one place, not shifting at all. So the teacher asked students to work in groups to revise the passage so that the grammatical focus reflected changes in visual focus.

As one group collaborated on revising the passage, the following discussion took place:

"OK. Let's start with her false teeth—yeah—write that down."

She has false teeth.

"No, dummy. We gotta start the sentence with 'her false teeth'."

Her false teeth

"OK, now what?"

"Oh, no. If we start with that we gotta add stuff. Like.... 'Her false teeth look funny'."

"Yeah, put that down."

"No, you gotta tell what 'funny' means. She'll [the teacher] only ask 'What's funny mean?'"

"I got it." Her false teeth look yellow. *"My grandma's are."*

"Yeah, 'cause they're old, like her."

"Hey. Who's writing?"

"I am." Her false teeth are yellow because they're old.

"That's good."

"OK, now the stuff on glasses. Oh, gosh. We're gonna have to add stuff to everything!"

Indeed, they would. And that was just the point. Their teacher wanted them to see that as they shifted visual focus, they would have to explore their subject further. Not only was their teacher showing these students a fundamental process of observing, but also she was showing them how the process of observing translated into the process of writing.

In addition to modeling the writing process, we also need to model the process of responding to writing. It is true that students can learn to make very helpful comments about their peers' writing. But the important phrase here is *learn to.* As Karen Spear has pointed out in her excellent book *Sharing Writing,* working in response groups is a complex process. It requires that students be able to go beyond uninformative, global comments ("Yeah, it's pretty good." "I guess it's OK.") and do two things: pay attention to specific words, phrases, or ideas and explain why and how they personally react to those things. The ninth-grade class I've just described illustrates one way to model the process of responding. When the teacher asked students to revise the bland description, she was showing them a process they could use in responding to each other's drafts. That is, she was helping them see that when they responded to a classmate's descriptive writing, they might consider whether the student had shifted focus and whether the shifts in focus helped give the reader a clearer visual picture of the person, object, or place being described. Indeed, the teacher made sure students worked as a class to give this sort of response to one or two students' subsequent drafts.

But modeling the response process may not be enough. It may also be necessary to model the processes of listening to and using those responses. Listening can be especially difficult when the response implies that a writer's work is unclear or in need of further effort. In such cases, any writer—and students are no exception—may well become defensive, more eager to prove that responses are invalid or irrelevant than to listen to those responses and consider the uses they might have. In other words, students may need to learn how to respond to responses.

If so, teachers may need to model the way we want student writers to react to their classmates' comments. Specifically, we should bring in our own efforts to do some of the same writing students are doing and ask students to respond to it. Where is it clear or unclear? What sort of personality or attitude is our writing conveying? At what points have we said things that seem appropriate or inappropriate for the audience we are addressing? My experience in doing this sort of work with students is that if they trust us, they can be very perceptive and painfully direct. If they don't get it, they can tell us so in no uncertain terms. In doing so, they give us a chance to show how a writer listens to readers, not by arguing but by attempting to find out why readers react as they do and then using that information to revise a subsequent draft.

❦

The process of modeling is, like everything else about teaching writing, a slow business. One example rarely does the trick. But if we are persistent in showing students what is involved in producing good writing through the writing process, we can usually count on results. But if we don't model, we should expect our distinction between *showing* and *telling* to fall on deaf ears. If we don't follow our own advice, why should they? ❦

*I*N ADDITION TO MODELING THE WRITING PROCESS, WE ALSO NEED TO MODEL THE PROCESS OF RESPONDING TO WRITING.

❦❦❦❦❦

BY DR. MAXINE HAIRSTON, FORMER DIRECTOR OF FRESHMAN ENGLISH, THE UNIVERSITY OF TEXAS

THE JOY OF WRITING

STUDENTS NEED TO GET SOME FUN OUT OF WHAT THEY'RE DOING.

MAXINE HAIRSTON TAKES A BREAK FROM CLASSES.

In recent years I have come to believe that the most important job I can do as a writing teacher is to help my students enjoy writing. I say this because I am convinced that unless students find some pleasure in their writing classes, most of them will not be willing to invest the time and energy required to turn out work that they—and we, as their teachers—can be proud of. Few adults are disciplined and determined enough to drudge away at some project—whether it's exercising or learning Spanish verbs—simply because someone else tells us that it will be good for us in the long run. We just won't stay with some projects unless there's some satisfaction in the process itself. How much harder it is, then, for youngsters to whom college or even next fall seems light years away to subject themselves to the hard work of learning to write if they get no pleasure from it at the time. Deficit motivation, working to avoid penalties or simply for a passing grade, isn't enough; students need to get some fun out of what they're doing. Fortunately, given what we now know about teaching the writing process, it's quite possible to create a writing classroom in which many students work from growth motivation; that is, they work at their writing because they enjoy doing it for its own sake.

Cognitive studies, ethnographic studies about writing, and the national projects argue that four characteristics define the congenial writing classroom, the kind in which students are likely to enjoy writing and to flourish as writers.

First, teachers provide a low-risk environment that encourages students to write without fear. Second, teachers have students develop their papers through a series of drafts and revisions. Third, teachers honor the students' right to their own writing, allowing students to choose their own topics and encouraging them to write about their interests. Fourth, teachers create and support a collaborative learning environment.

ESTABLISHING A LOW-RISK CLASSROOM

Creating a low-risk environment in the writing classroom may seem like a formidable challenge, and indeed it can be at the beginning of a new term when many students are as wary as stray cats. They're nervous for fear someone is going to try to trap them. In the first week of a writing class sometimes I feel as if I want to wear a banner across my chest, emblazoned with "Trust me! It's going to be all right!" But I can understand students' anxiety. Students who have come from writing courses with a heavy emphasis on rules and form, courses in which they did badly, have good reason to see a composition course as a high-risk situation. No wonder they start out by trying to stay in the safety zone of rules and formulas.

The humanistic psychologist Abraham Maslow theorizes that all people have two sets of forces operating within them: a need for safety and a fear of risk on one hand and an urge toward growth

and autonomy on the other hand. Maslow also believes that every individual has an innate urge to create, to grow, to discover new abilities and talents. I agree; I think all children want to communicate, to write something that catches the interest and attention of others, but most will hesitate if they think they will be punished for

IN THE FIRST WEEK OF A WRITING CLASS SOMETIMES I FEEL AS IF I WANT TO WEAR A BANNER ACROSS MY CHEST, EMBLAZONED WITH "TRUST ME! IT'S GOING TO BE ALL RIGHT!"

breaking rules. As Maslow points out, "Safety needs are prepotent over growth needs.... [and] in general, only a child who feels safe dares to grow forward healthily" (49). He adds, "Only the [teacher] who respects fear and defense can teach; . . ." (53).

The writing teacher's challenge is to foster the low-risk environment that will encourage creativity and expression but at the same time to work toward helping students master the writing conventions that they must know to be accepted as writers. There are several ways teachers can do this. First, of course, is to emphasize that we write in stages; we plan, we draft, we read and reread, and we revise. Final details matter when a writer gets ready to publish, but the most-productive writers learn how to suspend their error monitors in the early stages.

I have found it helps me to suspend my own error monitor when reading early drafts if I can put down my pencil and force myself to read strictly for content, good practice for trying to become a courteous reader. I ask myself, what is this writer trying to express? Why? How? Then I make only a large-scale response, focusing on being positive and on asking questions that could help the next draft. I emphasize that I hope to see substantial change and development in that draft. It would waste time even to mention error at this stage. When students realize that I really am not looking for mistakes in their drafts, they begin to relax and become more venturesome.

On second drafts, I still try to avoid writing on the paper, but focus on more specific suggestions for improvement. I also make checks in the margins to indicate potential trouble spots that the writers need to be aware of when they begin to polish their papers, sometimes adding a comment that the writer should be alert for problems with commas, subject-verb agreement, or whatever area seems most troublesome. This gives the writer specific areas to concen-

trate on at proofreading/editing time.

Probably one of the best ways to reduce risk in the writing classroom is to set up a portfolio system that allows students to draft a variety of papers over a period of time and then to choose a limited number to develop fully and submit for final evaluation. This method has become increasingly popular for a number of reasons. For one, student writers can work more as adult working writers do. They can attempt different kinds of writing, can stay with those projects that go well and, putting the others aside, they can invest as much as they like in them. It also gives students more control over the evaluation process. They decide which pieces they want evaluated; the teacher doesn't even have to see the others. There is considerable literature on the portfolio system if you find it an attractive option. (See also Elliot and Greenberg's essay "The Direct Assessment of Writing: Notes for Teachers.")

A final specific suggestion for reducing your students' anxieties is to establish a hierarchy of errors. We know from research that not all errors are created equal. Some are truly damaging: for instance, wrong verb forms, egregious sentence fragments, double negatives and faulty parallelism. Errors like these set off alarms for most readers. Others, such as split infinitives, comparison of absolutes, or misusing *lie* and *lay* cause scarcely a riffle with most audiences. We should be lenient about such lapses and reduce the number of things our students have to worry about.

We should also remember that the more a writer attempts, the more mistakes he or she is likely to make. But if we are encouraging growth, we need to let student writers know that we regard such mistakes as the natural accompaniment of growth and as less important than the students' fresh ideas.

TEACHING THE WRITING PROCESS THROUGH A SYSTEM OF DRAFTS

Because this textbook so strongly emphasizes that drafting, evaluating, and revising are essential parts of the writing process, I don't feel I need to build an elaborate case for having students develop their papers in drafts. Fortunately, with most writing teachers and curriculum supervisors embracing the concept of writing as a process, students accept drafting as a routine practice. I hope so, because students write more freely and more confidently when they know that their readers view their drafts as "work in progress," not as finished products to be critiqued and judged. Under such a system, knowing they're not irrevocably committed to what they've written, writers can afford experiments. Writing tentatively, they can count on getting help from their readers to help them work out their ideas. That's very reassuring, particularly to students who haven't written much and aren't sure they have anything to say.

The less articulate, inexperienced writers are probably those who get the most out of numerous drafts because they have the opportunity to improve first attempts substantially before they must submit the papers for evaluation. They also have the chance to get feedback *during* the writing process, feedback that is far more valuable than comments on a paper that has already been graded. We know that many students, perhaps even most, pay scant attention to comments written on graded papers, especially negative comments. But when they get comments—both written and oral—on drafts, they are likely to pay attention because they use them to real advantage.

Good students also benefit from drafts, although sometimes they may resist doing them because the system requires more work than they've usually had to do in order to get good grades. But for some good writers, developing a paper through drafts can be a heady experience as they tap into talent they didn't know they had and then earn new recognition from their peers. Writing can become a genuine joy for good writers working at their peak.

In my opinion the worst possible system for having students write papers is to give a fresh assignment each week, have everyone write the paper only once and turn it in for a grade, and then return the graded papers and repeat the process. Under such circumstances the anxiety level skyrockets for all but the most able

students, writers get no help during the process (when they need it most), and teachers never learn what most students can really do. Even when students write in class, those papers should be drafts that they can work on again during the next class periods. Only then are students likely to develop their potential.

LETTING STUDENTS CHOOSE THEIR OWN TOPICS FOR WRITING

After several years of having students choose their own writing topics, I am committed to the practice because it has several invaluable benefits. First, most students have never had an opportunity to write about matters they're genuinely interested in and can write about with authority. Too often they see traditional assignments that ask everyone to write on the same topic as meaningless exercises in which the teacher seems to be forgetting that students are individuals.

Second, students are more likely to put time and energy into their writing when they can explore topics that interest them. When students are writing on their own topics, they may also discover a potent truth: Writing is a powerful tool for learning, one that will serve them well.

Third, when students choose their own topics, a rich diversity can develop as they write about their own special interests. Some students may write about family rituals that come from their ethnic heritages or about unusual people in their families; others may write about living in another country or on a military base; others may write about hobbies—bicycling or scuba diving or canoeing. The possibilities are almost endless. In many schools, a rich multicultural tapestry can emerge as students from diverse backgrounds and cultures read each other's work and share stories.

Fourth, students will become more confident as writers because they have more control over their writing. As they develop their expertise in some area, they begin to realize how much they know about something, whether it's car stereos or cooking hamburgers. They can take on a new identity in the class and find that people pay attention to what they have to say. That's good for all of us.

Finally when students choose their own writing topics, the class simply becomes more interesting for everyone. Students may cover a remarkable range of subjects, and even those writing on similar topics bring different perspectives to them. Boredom drops quickly because everyone is constantly learning directly from other people's experiences. Perhaps the greatest bonus is to teachers, who not only garner a wealth of information about their students, but also over a period of years become mini-experts on numerous topics. Furthermore, they are spared trying to think up a good writing topic and then having to read fifty papers on that topic.

I BELIEVE STRONGLY IN PEER GROUPS AND COLLABORATIVE LEARNING IN WRITING CLASSES.

❦❦❦❦

It does take considerable class time to help select topics, since many students will protest that they have nothing to write about, but such obstacles can be overcome in a few days of brainstorming and group work in class. As teacher, you can come in with a list of possible topics and then work with the class to generate subtopics. Or ask everyone to bring in a list of fifteen things to write about, encouraging the concrete and specific rather than large, abstract categories.

I have had good success with asking students to choose a general topic to write on for the whole term and then to pick subtopics for individual papers. That way they get into their topics in some depth and eliminate the process of having to work through choosing a fresh topic for each paper. You may want to specify the kinds of papers students write within their topics—informative, expressive, persuasive, and so on—to focus the class within the formats they're learning from the textbook.

ESTABLISHING A COLLABORATIVE-LEARNING CLASSROOM

I believe strongly in peer groups and collaborative learning in writing classes. Perhaps their greatest advantage is that they give students an immediate sense of audience, something that's hard to achieve when the teacher is the only reader for the drafts. Usually they respect each other's opinions; in fact, they may take their peers' responses more seriously than they do the teacher's because they feel closer to peers and they genuinely want to communicate.

Students also begin to see how useful collaboration can be for generating ideas. Most students in writing groups readily admit how much their classmates have contributed to the final versions of their papers. Each class period when I hand back graded papers, I pick two or three of the best ones to read aloud and then ask the writer and the writer's group to comment on how the paper developed through drafts. Their accounts are revealing, and the investment they feel in each other's work is truly gratifying.

I favor randomly chosen groups of at least four students so if someone is absent, the discussion doesn't break down. I reorganize groups to allow working with as many writers as possible. This arrangement also enhances every student's exposure to diverse cultural experiences as they get to know other students more closely. Managing groups in the classroom may not be easy, although I suspect trained secondary teachers know considerably more about it than most college teachers do. For the teacher who doesn't feel comfortable with groups, there is considerable literature on the concept.

Ultimately, groups help to establish the whole class as a community of writers who work together, feel a common sense of purpose, and see writing as a shared enterprise that's important to everyone. We all know intuitively that the most important element for achieving a congenial writing classroom is the teacher's attitude, and for that reason it's important for the teacher to be a part of that community, not to be an outside authority and a judge. Teachers need to write with students during writing workshops and share writing with them—its joys and frustrations. With luck and time, I am convinced that both teachers and students will enjoy being in a writing classroom more than they might have thought possible. ❧

References

Maslow, Abraham. Toward a Psychology of Being, 2nd ed. New York: D. Van Nostrand Company. 1968.

TEACHERS NEED TO WRITE WITH STUDENTS DURING WRITING WORKSHOPS AND SHARE WRITING WITH THEM —ITS JOYS AND FRUSTRATIONS.

❦❦❦❦

By Dr. Barbara J. Shade, Professor and Dean, School of Education, The University of Wisconsin–Parkside

TEACHING FOR LEARNING'S SAKE

THIS APPROACH TO TEACHING WILL EMPOWER STUDENTS AS LEARNERS.

Helping students incorporate ideas, skills, and concepts that will improve their ability to perform tasks and to solve problems is the ultimate goal of teaching. Teachers who achieve this goal effectively find ways to accommodate students' different learning styles so that the teaching-learning process works more efficiently.

What do we mean by *learning styles?* Over the years, researchers have identified three dimensions in which students have specific learning preferences: (1) their preferences for various environmental factors that influence the learning climate; (2) their preferences about the ways they choose to engage in the learning process (motivational style); and (3) their preferences for the various ways in which they process information (cognitive style).

ENVIRONMENTAL PREFERENCES

Individual environmental preferences focus on the lighting, temperature, and furniture used in the learning process. For example, some individuals might prefer bright light while others prefer it muted; some might prefer a warm room while others like it cool. A variation in studying postures has also been noted, with some individuals preferring to sit in a traditional classroom desk while others prefer to stand or recline when engaged in a learning task.[1]

MOTIVATIONAL STYLE

The second dimension of learning style focuses upon the extent to which students take responsibility for their own learning. Teachers often incorrectly assume that students desire to engage in work is inherent. As with other aspects of learning, the extent to which individuals become involved in work depends upon how they have been socialized to respond to work. Some students, for example, have been taught to rely on others for assistance, to follow directions as given, and to perform the task as modeled. Others have been made more independent of others and have been taught to work alone, to find their own solutions, and to decide whether or not they can complete the work before asking for assistance. Corno and Mandinach refer to this stylistic dimension as a preference for resource management, and students tend to use the approach that makes them feel the most comfortable and the most competent.

The teaching-learning process involves human interaction, and students prefer different levels of involvement with others, depending upon the social and personality development that emanates from their families and communities. Families stressing prosocial behavior encourage children to help, to share, and to work toward benefiting others.

These students are more likely to give and receive assistance in the learning process and to like cooperative-learning ventures. Children trained to be highly individualistic and self-oriented are less likely to cooperate

---

[1] For a more detailed description of the social and physical environment preferences of students, the reader should examine the writings of Kenneth and Rita Dunn.

and offer help. Learners with this orientation function well in a competitive setting because they prefer to work alone and are less likely to enjoy cooperative-learning activities unless there is a reward or a method of accommodating their need for individuality.

COGNITIVE STYLE

The least discussed dimension of learning style—that of cognitive style—represents individually preferred ways of perceiving, organizing, and evaluating information so that it can be learned.

Three cognitive processes influence the way individuals acquire and produce knowledge. These are the perceptual, the conceptual, and the evaluative processes.

1. Perceptual Processes: The most recognized area in learning-style literature, this area focuses on the sensory modalities. Through cultural socialization, learners develop a preference for either the visual modality (photographs, graphs, art, texts); the aural modality (records, tapes, lectures); the haptic/kinesthetic modality (group discussions, interactive debates, drama); or some combination of these. Instruction delivered through the preferred modality establishes an instant rapport that allows students to process information more easily.

Different cultures socialize their children to attend to different cues in the environment; therefore, students have selective attention. Some students focus their attention on the task or idea being presented. For others, the people, their peers, their self-evaluation, or even the teacher's reaction to them are the most important

elements on which to focus. How children choose to attend to cues is an important dimension of learning, and teachers who wish to ensure cognitive engagement find ways to influence the perceptive focus of the students.

2. Conceptual Processes: Having focused on an idea that must be learned, students must then classify it based upon prior experiences. The techniques involved include assessing similarities and differences to prior knowledge, as well as determining how best to define or describe the concepts. Again, the extent to which students can manipulate various concepts depends upon whether or not the ideas can be communi-

cated to them using a common language with commonly accepted images.

Some students prefer to have ideas presented in a hierarchical manner, beginning with the big picture followed by the details involved (whole to part). Other

students prefer to have the information presented in a more sequential approach, beginning with the minute details and building toward the larger concept (part to whole). Regardless of the technique used, teachers must include methods of helping learners make connections with prior knowledge.

3. Evaluative Processes: The third aspect of cognitive style focuses on the processes of thinking about the information. *Thinking* is difficult to define, but many researchers define it as "comprehension monitoring." The major focus of thinking centers on the individual's ability to plan, monitor, and evaluate his or her learning and understanding about the information he or she is seeking to learn.

Again, teachers should look for variations in the way individuals approach thinking. On one hand, individuals may spend time using their imaginations to create ideas based upon personal views or

THE KEY TO A GOOD GROUP DISCUSSION IS A TEACHER WHO IS AN EXCELLENT QUESTIONER, WHO IS REFLECTIVE, WHO CAN LEAD STUDENTS TO REFLECT AND INQUIRE . . .

beliefs. On the other hand, some individuals will engage in a more formal logic, which requires familiarity with the rules in order to select the correct problem-solving strategies. In the first type of information processing, individuals seem to arrive at their decisions rather intuitively, using a process that seems to be generated from an internalized logic. In the second type, the one most influenced by instruction, students learn to organize and review their approach to information or problems through an analytical process.

ACCOMMODATING VARIATIONS IN LEARNING STYLES

When teachers are first introduced to the concept of learning styles, they immediately conjure up visions of having to construct thirty different learning plans to accommodate their students. *Learning styles* is not another euphemism for individually guided education. Instead, it is an entreaty to teachers to provide different approaches and strategies that individuals can use as they work at learning.

In today's classrooms, there are basically *two distinct modes of learning:* the *traditional orientation,* the one to which most instruction is geared; and the *community orientation,* the one more likely to be displayed by African American, Hispanic American, Native American and immigrant Asian students who identify closely with the culture of their ethnic communities.

Particular suggestions to enhance the instructional process for the community-oriented students who are often ignored in instructional delivery system include the following ones:

Environment Style Accommodation: For the community-oriented students, the classroom should become inviting and supportive as an experiential setting in which students can use various media to explore concepts that may be foreign to them because they are not prevalent in their communities or because their economic situation does not permit the type of travel or involvement in enrichment activities that is true of the more successful, economically affluent students. Being able to see an enlarged picture of the Eiffel Tower in the classroom can provide an important conceptual image that might be needed to foster comprehension. Because learning centers permit self-exploration, they should also become important aspects of the classroom design for all levels of students in all types of classes.

Motivational Style Accommodation: Having the opportunity to participate in a good class discussion on lesson content motivates community-oriented students, satisfying their needs to share information with others and to obtain feedback. Moreover, it provides them an opportunity to listen to different perspectives. Teachers should note, however, that group discussion is not the same as class recitation in which students are asked to recite facts and information to the teacher from a textbook. For example, it is not enough to discuss nouns as a part of speech without leading students through the concept of a complete sentence and the purpose of using nouns within sentences and paragraphs. Moreover, students need to be able to identify nouns within the framework of their own speech and written narratives as well as to determine how and why they have used a particular word as a noun.

The key to a good group discussion is a teacher who is an excellent questioner, who is reflective, who can lead students to reflect and inquire, and who has an excellent understanding of the broad structure and relationships within the lesson content.

Information Processing Style Accommodation: Teachers can facilitate the processing of information by students through the use of some of the following techniques:

1. Present concepts with multimedia using a variety of modalities.

2. Assist the students in identifying the relationships of concepts through cognitive mapping, brainstorming, or reciprocal teaching.

3. Take time to ensure there is a common understanding of words, concepts, or ideas. Bilingual students should be encouraged to interpret the words in their languages. Students should also be encouraged to develop art projects and to use new words orally.

4. Model the thinking processes needed to complete tasks successfully. Provide students time to think about a problem or to complete an assignment. Students learn best when they can perform when the teacher is available for feedback.

Teachers must remember that students have different perceptions of the world and teach to these perceptions. Assisting students in learning requires lots of talking— talking between students and teachers and between students.

When considering the use of learning styles, teachers must confront three important perceptions. First, teachers should understand that the identified style preference should not and cannot be used as evidence of deficiencies. Second, teachers should not think that the community-oriented style reflects all members of a group. It is merely behavior that is most likely to be found within the community. Third, teachers who use the concept of learning styles should do so as indicators of approaches to lesson design and to the selection of methods of instruction, not as the basis for judging intellectual potential.

A FINAL CAVEAT

Developing a successful learner is the ultimate goal of a successful teacher, and ensuring that children become successful learners requires that teachers see themselves not as the ultimate purveyors of knowledge, but as guides through the learning process. This approach to teaching will empower students as learners and will permit them to approach the learning process in their own words. When learners grasp the ideas, their sense of self-worth and confidence and their intellectual strength improve tremendously. It is at this point teachers know they, too, have been successful. What a great sense of accomplishment! ✾

MULTIPLE INTELLIGENCES AND THE WRITING CLASSROOM

WHAT ARE THE MULTIPLE INTELLIGENCES?

The theory of multiple intelligences was developed by Harvard psychologist Howard Gardner, who, in researching the function of the human brain in trauma, discovered that damage to one area of the brain, such as the speech center, does not necessarily incapacitate other areas of intelligence, such as appreciation of music or artistic ability. This discovery led to the proposal that the human brain does not operate with one single intelligence, but with seven.

Gardner labeled the seven intelligences logical-mathematical, linguistic, musical, bodily-kinesthetic, interpersonal, intrapersonal, and spatial.

Each intelligence operates both independently and cooperatively with the others in every human brain. Gardner contends that even though a certain intelligence may not be fully developed or even apparent in every person, the potential for that development exists and its expansion depends in large part on the environment in which the person lives or works.

IDENTIFYING STUDENTS' MULTIPLE INTELLIGENCES

The most immediate challenge for teachers is to identify students' intelligences and then to apply strategies and to create opportunities for students that will allow them to use and develop all their intelligences in the classroom. Discovering students' intelligences should

An overview of the seven intelligences

Intelligence	Characteristics	Possible vocation using this intelligence
Linguistic	Uses language effectively, orally or in writing	Writer, storyteller, editor
Logical-Mathematical	Uses numbers and figures effectively, reasons, identifies patterns, has organizing skills	Accountant, lawyer, journalist
Spatial	Observes or perceives relationships between real or imaginary objects	Artist, architect, nature guide
Bodily-Kinesthetic	Has sense of ease in movement of one's body to express ideas or to create or transform something	Dancer, mechanic, surgeon
Musical	Perceives and/or creates music, rhythm, pitch, or harmony	Musician, composer, disc jockey
Interpersonal	Interacts with the outside world, is sensitive to the feelings, actions and motivations of others	Social worker, politician, parent
Intrapersonal	Is sensitive to one's own thoughts, feelings, ideas, and place in the world	Poet, artist, singer

not be a time-consuming process. But it does require that teachers become better acquainted with their students so that they can learn **how students perform, what students prefer to do,** and **how students perceive themselves.**

Thomas Armstrong, the author of *Multiple Intelligences in the Classroom,* suggests several approaches.
- Consider preparing a questionnaire or checklist of the characteristics of the multiple intelligences for students and ask them to choose the items that apply to them.
- Give students an informal, oral survey that, with general questions about their likes and dislikes and talents, identifies which intelligences dominate the class.
- Use journal entries or personal narratives as an opportunity to evaluate the intelligences of students.

Keep in mind, though, that students usually have strengths in several areas. Armstrong also suggests that teachers identify their own intelligences and mention them to students as a way to explain their approaches to the subject matter so that students can see how their intelligences are compatible with their teachers'.

INSTRUCTIONAL STRATEGIES THAT TARGET THE MULTIPLE INTELLIGENCES

The next step for teachers is to target the kinds of strategies that facilitate students' multiple intelligences and to include those in their instruction. The following list gives samples of some strategies for each learning style. However, you should try to develop some of your own adaptations to address the needs of your classroom.

Stage of the Writing Process	Activities and Multiple Intelligences
Prewriting	**Brainstorming:** Linguistic, Interpersonal **Cluster/Diagramming:** Spatial, Intrapersonal, Interpersonal **Freewriting/Journaling:** Intrapersonal **Researching/Asking questions:** Logical-Mathematical **Observing/Imagining:** Spatial, Musical, Bodily-Kinesthetic **Reading with a Focus:** Linguistic, Logical-Mathematical, Intrapersonal **Listening with a Focus:** Musical, Interpersonal, Logical-Mathematical
Drafting	**Expressive/Creative Writing:** Interpersonal, Musical, Linguistic, Bodily-Kinesthetic **Informative Writing:** Logical-Mathematical **Writing to Explain:** Spatial, Logical-Mathematical, Interpersonal **Writing to Explore:** Logical-Mathematical **Writing about Literature:** Musical, Bodily-Kinesthetic, Spatial **Writing a Research paper:** Logical-Mathematical (depends also on the subject researched)
Evaluating and Revising	**Peer revision:** Interpersonal **Attention to details and organization:** Logical-Mathematical **Organization of text:** Bodily-Kinesthetic **Attention to images:** Spatial
Proofreading and Publishing	**Peer revision, public reading, performance:** Interpersonal **Polishing manuscript:** Intrapersonal **Reflecting:** Interpersonal, Linguistic

- **Spatial learners** benefit from watching videotapes or from drawing on overhead transparencies, a chalkboard, or a computer screen.
- **Interpersonal learners** thrive in discussion groups, especially if given opportunities to act as the group leader.
- **Intrapersonal learners** need individual goal-setting sessions and time for reflection in personal journals or portfolios.
- **Bodily-Kinesthetic learners** benefit from acting out concepts alone or in front of the class and from being able to physically manipulate things, such as a puzzle pieces, flashcards, index cards, or sections of a written draft.
- **Musical learners** are more productive if music is played during discussion sessions or while reading or writing, particularly if the music reflects the emotional content of the work.

- **Logical-mathematical learners** need a set of direct questions to work on and independent time to explore and research answers.
- **Linguistic learners** do well using tape recorders to record oral brainstorming sessions and having opportunities to discuss their ideas with their teacher or their peers.

It is important to remember that the activities mentioned here engage more than one intelligence at a time. Consider experimenting with different activities, and ask for student feedback.

APPLYING MULTIPLE INTELLIGENCES TO THE WRITING PROCESS

Being flexible and recursive, the writing process allows student writers to use their multiple intelligences at each of the four stages—prewriting; drafting; evaluating and revising; and proofreading, publishing, and reflecting.

Writing projects draw heavily on linguistic and intrapersonal intelligences, but consider the chart above for other possible intelligences that can be addressed at each stage in the writing process.

References

Armstrong, Thomas. *Multiple Intelligences in the Classroom.* Alexandria, VA: Association for Supervision and Curriculum Development. 1994.
Gardner, Howard. *Frames of Mind: The Theory of Multiple Intelligences.* 1983. NY: Basic Books. 1985.
Grow, Gerald. "Writing and Multiple Intelligences." June 1996. Online. Internet. 18 July 1996. Available HTTP://www.famu.edu/sjmga/ggrow/7In/7IntelIndex.html

DR. WANDA B. SCHINDLEY, NORTHEAST TEXAS COMMUNITY COLLEGE

INTEGRATING THE LANGUAGE ARTS

INTEGRATING THE TEACHING OF THE LANGUAGE ARTS CREATES THE MAGIC THAT HELPS STUDENTS LEARN.

Thirty-five years ago in a rural classroom, a creative woman integrated the teaching of reading, writing, speaking, listening, and even math. Her second-graders built a playhouse-size cardboard post office, made block-letter signs, wrote and read letters, counted tokens to buy and sell stamps, and spoke and listened as postmaster and customer. That teacher had not read research on the integration of skills or on using whole-language methodologies, but she knew intuitively what worked. I don't remember much about my experiences in kindergarten, first grade, third grade, or even fourth grade, but I remember well that second-grade classroom; I remember the magic of learning.

Integrating the teaching of the language arts creates the magic that helps students learn. It creates a context for developing language proficiency and relevancy for reading, writing, speaking, and listening activities. Students grow through active participation in language activities. Although categorizing the language arts may be necessary for describing curricula, in the classroom language skills are best learned through doing—through seeking meaning from texts, through writing and revising, and through sharing ideas and opinions.

WANDA SCHINDLEY IS A SPECIALIST FOR THE WORKPLACE PARTNERSHIP.

SUGGESTIONS FOR INTEGRATING THE LANGUAGE ARTS

• Involve students in prereading activities such as discussion, writing, research, and sometimes, vocabulary development. Creating a context for reading involves discussing themes and related issues, making predictions, recalling prior knowledge and related experiences, and searching out related information.

• Involve students in prewriting activities such as discussion of possible topics and details, reading model essays, searching out and reading informative pieces, reading literary writing, interviewing others, and sentence-combining or sentence-revision activities. Like the writing process itself, development of language proficiency involves a recursive practice in reading, writing, thinking, speaking, and listening.

• Make writing assignments relevant by having students write for and share with real audiences for meaningful purposes. Have students share their writing with peers.

• Relate correctness—development of conventional usage, spelling, grammar, and punctuation—

to the revising and proofreading stages of the writing process. Correctness becomes important to students when it helps them communicate their ideas clearly. Class review of grammar, usage, and mechanics can be done with sentences from student papers and with sentence-combining, sentence manipulation, and vocabulary activities.

• Approach standard usage in speech as appropriate for use in business and academic situations, not as a replacement for all vernacular expression.

• Encourage student involvement in class discussion, team study groups, cooperative research projects and presentations, group creative writing, and role playing.

• Foster an atmosphere in which students feel free to respond to, to evaluate, and to critique literature.

• Act as facilitator in students' discovery processes through activities that encourage creative and critical thinking—decision making and problem solving—and allow students to take more responsibility for their own learning.

Create an atmosphere of cooperation, caring, and high expectations.

*L*IKE THE WRITING PROCESS ITSELF, DEVELOPMENT OF LANGUAGE PROFICIENCY INVOLVES A RECURSIVE PRACTICE IN READING, WRITING, THINKING, SPEAKING, AND LISTENING.

USING THE TEXTBOOK IN AN INTEGRATED APPROACH

Literature selections are provided in each chapter to give students opportunities to read before writing. However, this book can be used in a literature-driven approach as the springboard to writing by incorporating into the study of each chapter ample readings from literature anthologies, magazines, and student papers. The features in each chapter of the *Teacher's Edition* contain suggestions for integrating additional literature selections (**Integrating the Language Arts: Literature Link**), using a variety of group activities (**Cooperative Learning**), and encouraging students to use higher-level thinking skills to contribute to class discussion (**Critical Thinking**).

The **Common Error** and **Integrating the Language Arts** features in each chapter of the *Teacher's Edition* contain suggestions for integrating the teaching of grammar, usage, and mechanics into the stages of the writing process, as do the suggestions for integrating the language arts in the introduction of each composition chapter.

Sample Integrated Lesson Plan

A lesson on creative writing might begin with a class discussion about stories and poems.

Guiding questions encourage students to share attitudes: What kinds of stories/poems do you like?
—to recall prior knowledge about the structure of stories: What happened toward the end of a favorite story? How did you feel as you

read? What name do we use for the most exciting or scary part of the story?
—to synthesize knowledge about fiction: What characteristics do stories and poems have in common? What other forms might a writer use to tell about an event or to express an idea?

Teachers can use group stories and poems as guided practice and as a non-threatening introduction to creative writing. A group activity in which students write noun poems might begin informal grammar instruction. Small groups can then choose from the list of topics for noun-metaphor poems.

Example: Dreams are
    Envelopes of hope,
    Fluffy clouds that
      disappear in daylight,
    Stars to reach for.

As groups begin to revise and proofread their poems for class presentation, teachers might focus on the use of commas and end marks.

When students begin the creative writing assignments, they are again given opportunities to write, discuss, read, think, talk, revise, and so on. Instruction in usage and mechanics can be provided to the class as the need arises, to partners as they debate an issue of correctness, and to individuals in one-on-one conferences.

Finally, students share their work with the class—perhaps anonymously at first, but eventually as accomplished and proud authors who share a firsthand knowledge of the creation of literature and a greater understanding of language. ❧

DR. JUDITH IRVIN, FLORIDA STATE UNIVERSITY

BECOMING A STRATEGIC READER

BECOMING A PROFICIENT READER AND WRITER IS A LIFE-LONG PROCESS.

In the past, reading was viewed as a simple task of decoding words. Educators generally emphasized the strategies of sounding out words, recognizing words out of context by sight, and reproducing content by answering comprehension questions. Research has led to a new conceptualization of the reading process—that, as writing is, reading is a complex learning process. In this new view, readers construct meaning from a text, not simply by decoding words, but by using reading strategies that incorporate and expand their prior knowledge. Prior knowledge includes not only readers' knowledge of the definition of a word, but also their responses to the context of the word—the entire text. Careful reading of a text using strategies like those explained in the following pages will allow readers to use their prior knowledge to create meaning and to extend their understanding of a text. As students become more involved in developing and reflecting on their reading and learning processes, meaning may now be defined as "something that is actively created rather than passively received" (Buehl, 1995, p. 8).

As will be explained, the process of constructing meaning both in writing and in reading is not linear, but recursive and interactive and helps to create a richer, more productive experience.

THE READER

Former models of reading focused on whether or not students had acquired specific skills. Recent models of reading allow that students come to learning with previous information about particular topics, with definite attitudes about reading, writing, and school in general, and with varying motivations for reading and learning. It is the interaction of what is in reader's minds with what is on the page within a particular context that helps them to comprehend what they read.

SCHEMA THEORY

It is impossible for readers to learn anything new without making connections to their prior knowledge or schemata. The schemata are like the components of an elaborate filing system inside every reader's head. If the reader's mind is the filing system, the schemata, then, are the ideas contained in the file folders within the system. For example, you probably have a schema for a computer, a mental picture of what a computer is and what it does. You probably also bring to that basic picture many other associations, ideas, and feelings. If you use computers regularly, your schema may include positive feelings about their limitless applications. If the computer revolution has left you yearning for the days of yellow note pads and typewriters, then you may have feelings of anxiety as you approach a computer manual. For teachers, it is important to remember that readers encountering new ideas must often be shown how the new material fits into their existing filing system.

THE TEXT

The content, format, and organization of a text are factors that make a text easy or difficult for students to understand. If students' schemata tell them that a particular assignment will be difficult or unrelated to their personal experiences, they will probably be reluctant to read it and will most likely not make much meaning of it. The students know with one look that they will read and respond to a poem differently than they will to a chapter in a science book. A teacher should be prepared to exercise flexibility and sensitivity in presenting the text so as to encourage students to use their schemata to enhance their reading experiences.

THE CONTEXT

Readers and writers approach texts differently, and they also vary their processes according to their purposes. If they are reading for pleasure, students may skip over a difficult word or read an exciting passage more than once. But if they are reading for class, skipping a word might mean not understanding an important concept needed in class the next day. A reader's purpose for reading also dictates how attentive he or she is to details and how much effort will be put into remembering what is read. Similarly, when and where the reading is done affects the reading process. Readers will make less meaning from texts they read on the bus or with thoughts of a sick relative in the backs of their minds than they might make if they had a quiet space and clear thoughts.

STRATEGIC LEARNING

Suppose that during a racquetball game you hit a straight shot down the right side of the court, and your opponent misses the ball. The point is yours. This well-placed shot may have been a lucky one, or it may have been the result of a strategy. Before you hit the ball, you may have noticed that your opponent was standing in the middle of the court, and you remembered that she is left-handed with a weak backhand. You hit the ball to exactly the right spot deliberately and strategically. The analogy of planning your shots in a game can be applied to learning.

Strategic learning involves analyzing the reading task, establishing a purpose for reading, and then selecting strategies for making meaning. A strategy is a conscious effort by the reader to attend to comprehension while reading. Weinstein explains that "learning strategies include any thoughts or behaviors that help us to acquire new information in such a way that the new information is integrated with our existing knowledge" (Weinstein, p. 590). Strategies occur before reading when readers activate prior knowledge by thinking and discussing the title and topic and by identifying a purpose for reading. They also occur during reading as readers use context to figure out unknown words and monitor their understanding, and beyond the reading when readers summarize or evaluate the main ideas of the text.

METACOGNITION

Reading is often referred to as a cognitive event. It is also a metacognitive event. Cognition refers to a person's using the knowledge and skills he or she possesses; metacognition refers to a person's awareness and understanding of that knowledge and conscious control over those skills. It is essentially, thinking about one's way of thinking. Metacognition, then, is knowing how and when to use strategies to solve problems in understanding. It develops as a reader matures, usually during adolescence, but it can be taught and strengthened by explicit instruction and practice.

Becoming a proficient reader and writer is a life-long process. Accepting the premise that meaning is constructed in the mind of the learner implies that metacognitive abilities must be operational for learning to occur. Adolescents are just beginning to be able to consider their own thinking in relation to the thoughts of others. The middle and high school level years are an ideal time to develop the metacognitive abilities that will serve them throughout life.

STRATEGIC READING

Good readers are strategic, and being strategic involves the metacognitive abilities to think, plan, and evaluate their understanding of a text.

Adolescence is partially characterized by a new capacity for thought. Students are moving from the concrete stage (able to think logically about real experiences) to the formal stage (able to consider "what ifs," think reflectively, and reason abstractly). This intellectual change is gradual and may occur in different contexts at different times for different students.

Formal thinking is just developing during the middle school years, so concrete examples and step-by-step modeling are necessary to move students to the more abstract metacognitive thinking. The following concepts help students to focus on their own reading strategies:

- activating schema (prior knowledge) and building background information
- predicting and confirming
- organizing information
- drawing conclusions
- making inferences
- text differences
- retelling/summarizing

As strategic readers, before they read, students use their prior knowledge by making predictions about the content of a selection, to establish a clear purpose for reading, and to think about reading strategies they might use as they read. During the reading process, students use context to connect what they are reading with what they already know and to continue to monitor and evaluate their comprehension. And after completing their reading, students review their reading through peer discussion, class discussion, preparing entries in Reader's Logs, and using graphic organizers.

New research and practice in literacy learning reflects a more holistic view of understanding text. Students need opportunities to apply reading strategies to a variety of texts in a meaningful manner. ❧

References
Buehl, D. *Classroom Strategies for Interactive Learning*.
Schofield, WI: Wisconsin State Reading Association, 1995.
Weinstein, C.E. "Fostering Learning Autonomy Through the Use of Learning Strategies." *Journal of Reading* 30 (1987): 590-595.

JOYCE ARMSTRONG CARROLL, DIRECTOR, THE NEW JERSEY WRITING PROJECT IN TEXAS

SHOW DON'T TELL: THE ORIGINAL VIRTUAL REALITY

GOOD WRITING THAT SHOWS TAKES US THROUGH THE EXPERIENCE . . .

Perhaps one of the oldest pieces of advice offered by master writers to neophytes is "show don't tell." Likewise, one of the most frequent pieces of advice offered by teachers to fledgling student writers is "show don't tell."

The truth is the old "show don't tell" adage lives as the original virtual reality and makes sense to students if presented that way. Think about it. Our brains receive and process sensory signals from our environment through our five senses in order to make sense of our world, our experiences. Good writing that shows takes us through the experience; it excites the brain by wrapping pictures and sounds, tastes, smells and movements around its readers and immersing their senses in such a way that the writing actually creates another world. Catherine Drinker Bowen, biographer and writer on musical subjects, puts it more poetically, "Writing, I think, is not apart from living. Writing is a kind of double living."

Phrased in the positive, this "showing," this "going through the experience" causes the reader to feel an immediacy, a vitality, and an authenticity. When we're finished reading writing that shows, we often think, "I wish this wouldn't end." Flip-flopping to the negative, writing devoid of this "showing" reads flat, seems plastic, and bores the brain. If we even finish reading writing that tells, we find ourselves yawning and asking, "What did I just read?"

But there's an irony in "show don't tell." The maxim itself tells. It's right up there with "develop your writing" and "liven those verbs." There is no doubt about it—the advice is sound—it's just too abstract. Therein lies the rub. What can we teachers do to make "show don't tell" more concrete, more understandable for students? I'd like to share five ways to involve students in learning this concept. Students

• Analyze the work of published authors
• Compare telling writing to showing writing
• Identify telling parts in their own writing
• Replace the telling parts of their writing with showing passages
• Recognize and use "show don't tell" as an elaboration technique

ANALYZING THE WORK OF PUBLISHED AUTHORS

When examining the work of published authors, I start with Mark Twain's words, "Don't say the old lady screamed. Bring her on and let her scream." It's a great quote that begs great questions, "What does Twain mean?" "How might we describe her?" "Where is she?" "What words could we use to hear her scream?" "Why is she screaming?" It's fun to divide the room—half tells about the old lady, while the other half shows. Students of all ages delight in the comparison and begin their move toward understanding.

Will Hobbs, noted YA author, says it this way, "Let's say I almost drowned last summer, when a rip tide was taking me out to sea, and I'm trying to tell a reader what it was like: 'I was drowning. It was really bad. I thought I was going to die...' Now, is my writing coming to life? Does the reader feel what it was like? Not really. Did I tell, or did I show? I told. I didn't use the five senses. Where's the taste of salt water, the powerful tug of the rip

T67

tide, the voices at the shore dimming, the squawk of a gull?" (Hobbs, 19).

Now what Hobbs suggests is pure virtual reality. No one really wants to experience drowning, but if the writer crafts the experience by showing not telling then the reader experiences the virtual reality of drowning. It works this way because of the sensory signals the words conjure; the brain makes a connection and consequently makes meaning. Since our senses are the primary information gatherers, constantly sending signals to the brain, Hobbs invites student writers to stimulate all five senses through the power of words. That way, after the brain has reconstructed and synthesized the signals, it makes an identification and the reader understands. Helping that connection equals good writing.

Once students awaken to "show don't tell" in their writing it becomes an excellent technique for literary analysis. Imagine students quibbling over colonist Edward Winslow's letter to a friend in England, pointing out how much more powerful it would have been had he taken his friend through the experience of the "harvest being gotten in" instead of just telling him. Or picture a group of students eagerly identifying examples of showing not telling in *The Red Badge of Courage.* After reading, "One of the wounded men had a shoeful of blood. He hopped like a schoolboy in a game. He was laughing hysterically...." (Crane, 44), it is unlikely they would settle for, "One man was shot in the foot. He was in pain."

COMPARE TELLING WRITING TO SHOWING WRITING

One of the attributes of showing writing is specificity and concern for detail. Using comparisons of different versions of the same story helps students see this. For example, take the passage that first describes Baba Yaba in the Russian, Romania, Yugoslavian, Polish folktale called by titles such as "The Doll," "The Doll in Her Pocket," "Vasalisa the Wise," "Vassilisa the Wise," "Vasilisa the Beautiful," "Baba Yaga and Vasilisa the Brave," or simply "Vasilisa."

Version One: "When they had entered the hut the old witch threw herself down on the stove, stretched out her bony legs and said. . ." (Sierra, 97).

Version Two: "When Vasilisa entered the hut, Baba Yaga was already sitting in her chair by the fire. Her black eyes sparkled as she fixed them on the girl" (Mayer).

Version Three: "Suddenly the forest was filled with a terrible noise, and Baba Yaga came flying through the trees. She was riding in a great iron mortar and driving it with a pestle, and as she rode, she swept away her trail with a kitchen broom" (Winthrop, 17).

Finally we come to Version Four. This version is embedded in the penetrating psychological study *Women Who Run With the Wolves: Myths and Stories of the Wild Woman Archetype* by Clarissa Pinkola Estes.

Now the Baba Yaga was a very fearsome creature. She traveled not in a chariot, not in a coach, but in a cauldron shaped like a mortar which flew along all by itself. She rowed this vehicle with an oar

shaped like a pestle, and all the while she swept out the tracks of where she'd been with a broom made of long-dead persons' hair.

And the cauldron flew through the sky with Baba Yaga's own greasy hair flying behind. Her long chin curved up and her long nose curved down, and they met in the middle. She had a tiny white goatee and warts on her skin from her trade in toads. Her brown-stained fingernails were thick and ridged like roofs, and so curled over she could not make a fist (Estes, 77).

Juxtaposing these versions (or versions of other literary pieces) illuminates the power of "show don't tell." While the first three versions, taken from children's literature, rely on pictures to convey most of the detail, even the slowest student will see how ably Estes crafted her showing of Baba Yaga from the opening, somewhat telling statement, through the layers of detail, calling upon each of the reader's senses to prove Baba Yaga's fearsomeness.

Again, after an exercise such as this, students no longer write, "She was ugly." They are no longer satisfied with "She was a witch." Their journey into the lushness of writing and literature is enriched.

IDENTIFYING TELLING PARTS IN THEIR OWN WRITING

Armed now with clearly concrete experiences between telling and showing in writing, the students are better able to assess their own writing with new eyes and finding parts to improve is an awesome cognitive task, especially for adolescents.

As students reread their work,

they simply highlight the telling statements, share and discuss them with peers or teacher, and ultimately decide if each is fine as it is (some telling is inevitable in any piece of writing) or if it needs reworking. This process not only invites higher-level thinking and decision-making, but it also paves the way by patterning the brain for the day-to-day coping of considerations based on importance, need, aptness, and priority.

REPLACE THE TELLING PARTS OF THEIR WRITING WITH SHOWING PASSAGES

This represents the pith of the showing/telling dichotomy. When students become facile enough to enliven their writing with powerful passages that show not tell, they have learned the concept. Following is an example from Adrian's writing. He highlighted his first three sentences:

I stayed over at Robert's house last Friday. We were going camping. That was our favorite thing to do even though we only pretended.

On his next draft he replaced those telling with this showing passage:

I was spending Friday night at Robert's house, so our camping gear was strewn across the backyard. We pretended we had pitched camp in the outback of Australia, so we called each other "mate" alot.

"Ay, mate," I'd call even though we were pretty close to each other in that backyard. "Let's take a walkabout." (I had seen a movie about that.)

"Ay, mate," he'd call back louder. "Let's throw some shrimp on the barbee." (I knew he saw that commercial on T.V.)

Finally, we went to bed. Robert had asthma and was lying in the tent on his cot wheezing like a water pump gone dry. My buddy did many things better than me, but I envied his asthmatic wheeze the most. That night he wheezed out a little tune in his sleep and I accompanied him on the drums by playing my stomach and cot.

While Adrian did some throat clearing first, the passage about Robert's asthma takes us through what Adrian went through. It shows promise and a grasp of the "show don't tell" concept.

RECOGNIZE AND USE "SHOW DON'T TELL" AS AN ELABORATION TECHNIQUE

I opened the novel in full view of the class. "Take out some paper and write down these sentences," I invited.

I remember the day Claire Louise started first grade.... She had on a red dress.... Mother made all our clothes.... She had a book satchel my grandmother bought for her.... That was a Saturday (Arnold, 7–8).

"What do you think about that writing?" I asked.

Students, who typically want to please the teacher, began by tenta-tively, and without much enthusi-asm, saying, "It's O.K." But then they quickly pulled the turn-about and asked, "Who is Claire Louise?" "Why are you reading this?"

I continued to probe. "She's a character in this novel, but I really want to know what you think of the writing."

Eventually a brave soul admit-ted, "It sounds dull." Another agreed and collectively they deter-mined it was definitely telling not showing.

At this point I wrote ELABORA-TION on the board. I explained how showing helps the writer achieve an elaborated piece, one that reveals depth of thought. Under "elaboration" I wrote D.I.D. I told the students that although there are many ways to achieve this depth, these letters stood as a mnemonic device to remember at least three of them.

Their first response was "dia-logue," which we had worked on previously and which is one way to achieve elaboration. We talked about that, but I wanted them to explore further. After some nudges and discussion, they came up with DESCRIPTION, ILLUSTRATION, DETAIL.

Together we defined DESCRIP-TION by comparing it to a camera shot in movies. It's the long shot as in "the gray house sitting way up on the hill in the distance." Following that analogy, we defined DETAIL as a close-up as in "the run-down gray house squatted on a crumbling foundation. Its paint puckered and peeled as one shut-ter banged against the wood like some large, slow-witted wood-pecker. Weeds marked flower beds and masked a stone walkway lead-ing to the discolored, stained back door." ILLUSTRATION gave us a tussle. What finally worked was in-serting the phrase "for instance" as a reminder that an illustration serves as an example, a support for a telling sentence.

Then I told them I would read the passage from the novel exact-ly as it was written and cautioned them to listen for D.I.D.

I remember the day Claire Louise started first grade. Everyone claims I'd have been too young to remember that, that at two years old I couldn't possi-bly remember Claire Louise starting school. But I do remember. She had on a red dress. Red was always my favorite color, still is for that matter. The dress was red checks and had a starched white collar and puffy white sleeves with white cuffs on them. And the belt that went with the dress my mother bought from the store to go with it, the dress she made herself. Mother made all our clothes. Mostly she made Claire Louise's clothes and I wore them four years later. And Claire Louise even had red socks to go with her dress and she wore her black and white saddle oxfords that my mother bought to be her school shoes. She had a book satchel my grandmoth-er bought for her, and all the school supplies the drugstore had printed on the first-grade list on the lowest shelf. She had those in the book bag. She had carefully printed her name on everything that went in her bag. We watched her do it, my mother and me. I sat in my mother's lap and watched Claire Louise get ready for her first day at school. That was a Saturday, I'm sure, because I can remember the sound of the lawn mower as Claire Louise carefully wrote her name, and my father only mowed on Saturday morning.

The students caught the big picture, the description of the nar-rator on her mother's lap. They rev-eled in all the details of color of collar, belt, and satchel. They real-ized the moving proved to be an illustration, a proof. (This tech-nique can be used with any rich piece of writing.)

They were ready, once again, to reenter their writing. They added some description and lots of detail. One young man asked, "Now what's illustration again?" I told him to find a telling sentence in his writing. He offered, "My little broth-er loves me." I asked him to insert "for instance" and give me an ex-ample. After some thought, he said, "For instance, he runs down the sidewalk to meet me after school and gives me a high-five."

"Perfect," I said. Although none of us really saw his little brother running to meet him, hand ex-tended, we did see it in the virtual reality of writing that shows. 🍎

References

Arnold, Janis. *Daughters of Memory.* Chapel Hill, NC: Algonquin Books, 1991.

Crane, Stephen. *The Red Badge of Courage.* New York: W.W. Norton & Co., 1962.

Estes, Clarissa Pinkola. *Women Who Run With the Wolves: Myths and Stories of the Wild Woman Archetype.* New York: Ballantine Books, 1992.

Hobbs, Will. "Bringing Your Words to Life." *R & E Journal.* (Spring, 1996): 19-21.

Mayer, Marianna. *Baba Yaga and Vasilisa the Brave.* New York: Morrow Junior Books, 1994.

Sierra, Judy. *The Oryx Multicultural Folktale Series: Cinderella.* Phoenix, AZ: The Oryx Press, 1992.

Winthrop, Elizabeth. *Vasilissa the Beautiful.* New York: Harper Collins, 1991.

BLOCK SCHEDULING

WHAT IS BLOCK SCHEDULING?

A block schedule arranges classes into longer time periods of approximately ninety minutes. Classes may meet every day for one semester—called the A/B or the rotating block. Or, they may meet every other day for a full year—called the 4 x 4 or semester block.

WHAT ARE ITS BENEFITS?

There are several advantages to implementing block scheduling, both for the teacher and for the students. Block scheduling

• Is economical, allowing teachers to teach more students and requiring fewer textbooks and other materials.

• Allows more time for instruction and for more personalized student-teacher interaction.

• Promotes teaching a concept or skill in more depth.

• Affords more time for teachers to identify and respond to student needs and performances.

• Provides the opportunity for structuring interdisciplinary coordination.

• Provides for greater opportunities for multiple and creative teaching strategies and for use of more resources during a given class period (library resources, laboratory space, computers).

• Allows for varied assessment strategies.

• Reduces the number of classes students must prepare for each day.

• Allows students to earn more credits each year.

• Decreases the number of teachers students must adjust to.

HOW DOES BLOCK SCHEDULING AFFECT TEACHING?

In preparing for a block scheduling classroom, teachers should carefully examine their curriculum and be prepared for adjustments. Consider the following guidelines:

• Pare down the curriculum rather than padding it to fill an extended teaching period. Don't try to teach twice as much. This practice will frustrate you and your students. Covering less material can actually be more effective in block scheduling classes. The key phrase has been "more is less" because teachers have taught fewer concepts but have taught them in more depth.

• Concentrate on a few key skills or concepts that you want students to master at the end of the course and plan your units and lessons around these skills.

• Think about the class period in terms of smaller time segments. Most adults can maintain focus for only twenty to thirty minutes. The average students are no different, so plan to their advantage—base your lessons on shorter, attention-getting activities and allow students to work in groups on longer, more enriching assignments.

• Use authentic assessments such as portfolios; peer groups and peer evaluation; and displays of student products. Allow students to learn and demonstrate mastery of their learning in ways that are successful for them.

HOW DOES A TYPICAL BLOCK-SCHEDULE CLASS PERIOD WORK?

The following is a general format that suggests the flexibility and variety that a teacher can explore in a block scheduling classroom.

By varying activities, a teacher can maintain students' attention, increase students' motivation, and create an environment that encourages learning.

HOW DOES BLOCK SCHEDULING AFFECT THE LANGUAGE ARTS CLASSROOM?

Block scheduling is particularly conducive to the teaching of language arts.

- The ninety-minute class period allows for a more seamless blending of reading, writing, language, and speaking and listening.
- Because the lessons are less fragmented, the connections between the strands can be seen more readily. For example, if literature is used as a springboard for writing, there is an opportunity for a more immediate shift from literature to writing.
- Also, for teaching the writing process in a block schedule, a watchful teacher can tailor the time spent on each stage of the process to fit the needs of the students. If students need more time revising than they do brainstorming, that is figured into a schedule that allows for more flexibility. If students need periodic mini-lessons on the uses of quotation

marks, the block schedule allows for that, too.

EXPECTATIONS FOR TRANSITION/ TROUBLESHOOTING

Achieving a successfully balanced learning experience in a block schedule may take some time. However, keeping careful records of planning and daily activities and a file of ideas for varying instruction can help. Consider establishing a support group with other teachers. Sharing common problems and success stories will help the transition.

In the classroom, some regularity will help students adjust to the longer time period. Consider the following ideas for instruction:

- Begin class quickly.
- Deliver short lectures only.
- Allow some student movement/ interaction.
- Monitor student responses well.
- Vary activities every 15-20 minutes on average.
- State expectations very clearly before students begin any activity.

For classroom management, try some of the following suggestions:

- Devote a portion of team meetings to discussion of the block.
- Color code class rosters, student files, gradebook by day.
- Keep a notebook to record after class the basics of each lesson.
- Fill in only the dates in your gradebook on which classes actually meet to help avoid confusion regarding dates students were in class.
- Consider allowing students a short break from time to time during a longer class period.

CONCLUSION

Although it is a fairly new concept in education, block scheduling seems to be popular with educators because it provides them with the opportunity to control the time factor in learning. In schools that have instituted block scheduling, no longer are students racing from one 50-minute class to another, attending as many as seven classes in a single day. Teachers are not having to rush to get through the period's objectives before the bell.

In general, teachers and students seem to like longer classes. According to John O'Neil in his article "Finding Time to Learn," most teachers don't want to return to traditional scheduling—not because things are easier in block scheduling, but because they think they have been more successful in working with their students. 🍎

*B*LOCK SCHEDULING SEEMS TO BE POPULAR WITH EDUCATORS BECAUSE IT PROVIDES THEM WITH THE OPPORTUNITY TO CONTROL THE TIME FACTOR IN LEARNING.

BY HILVE FIREK, COLLEGE OF EDUCATION AND ALLIED PROFESSIONS, UNIVERSITY OF NORTH CAROLINA AT CHARLOTTE

TECHNOLOGY IN THE LANGUAGE ARTS CLASSROOM

IF WE'VE LEARNED ONE THING FROM TECHNOLOGY, IT IS THAT WE EXIST IN A STATE OF FLUX.

If we've learned one thing from technology, it is that we exist in a state of flux. What is cutting-edge today may be obsolete tomorrow. What the following day will bring is anybody's guess. But regardless of the frenetic changes, the need to communicate effectively in writing remains constant.

So, how do we teach composition in the glare of the bright lights, pulsating sounds, and moving images that are everywhere in today's technologically-fascinated society? Simple. We use the lights, sounds, and images to build bridges between popular culture and the culture of the classroom. We use what is familiar to teach what is new. *In essence, we use technology to inspire students to want to learn to write.*

TELEVISION AND VIDEOS

Let's begin with a technology your students know extremely well— television. If you doubt the intimate relationship our young people have with TV, listen to them talk about the characters and situations on the latest sitcoms, soaps, or prime-time dramas. Or eavesdrop on a discussion of the most popular music videos on MTV or BET. Without their even knowing it, these young adults have developed for themselves a rather complex understanding of plot, characterization, symbolism, and other literary devices used by the most skilled writers. The challenge for educators is to help students span the distance between what television has already taught them and what we, as facilitators of the language arts, are attempting to teach them.

Let's examine ways we might use television to reach students in teaching the writing process. If you spend an hour or two watching the shows your students watch, chances are you will encounter any number of situations that reflect the human condition. In a single segment, a program may explore the emotions of love, hate, jealousy, and desire through the dramatic elements of conflict and complications or through such devices as irony and satire. For the most part, the plot has a discernible beginning, middle, and end. Of course, setting plays a critical role in establishing tone; for example, a love affair set against the backdrop of a hospital emergency room differs from a summer romance on the beaches of California. Further, devices common in television, such as laugh and music tracks, steer viewers to specific responses.

The problem is that adolescents process this information that they see on TV without necessarily being cognizant of how each part contributes to the whole. Using this popular medium, teachers can help students recognize the numerous means by which messages are conveyed. Once they learn the tools that are utilized on television, students can build on this learning to understand the tools writers employ in their craft. In essence, by becoming critical viewers, students may more readily learn to see themselves as critical writers. For instance, if your students decide to change the format of a popular show from a situational comedy to a dramatic miniseries, what writing devices would they utilize? How would the dialogue change? How would the setting change? Would the characters develop differently?

By envisioning what they might see on the small screen, students can envision what they must put down on paper or key into their word-processing programs.

WORD PROCESSING AND DESKTOP PUBLISHING

Though most of us tend to think of word-processing software as an elementary tool that permits us to correct typos easily, most programs now offer features that serve to engage spatial learners in the written word. Simply by changing font styles and sizes and by incorporating such options as bold, italics, and underline, students can add a visual flair to their compositions impossible with a blue ball-point pen. Additionally, many word-processing programs interface easily with desktop publishing software, thus providing users with the means to import clip art, digitized photos, charts, and graphs into their documents. The paintbrush feature found on many programs allows students to create their own illustrations, giving spatial learners the opportunity to express their thoughts in visual terms before embarking on the writing process.

The ample features of today's desktop publishing software encourage writers to experiment with eclectic blends of text and images to create new and ever-changing forms of communication where style conveys every bit as much as content. The increasing popularity among adolescents of alternative publications, known as *zines,* reflects this interest in multi-layered combinations of words, type styles, and graphics. Armed with computers, printers, and copiers, students turned off by the rigid structure of the five paragraph essay are using zines to experiment with voice, to share ideas, and to create unique products via a medium heretofore available only to professional writers (Williamson). By utilizing software commonly loaded on computers, young adults can begin to understand the connection between how messages are presented and how they are received. We teachers of the language arts can help our students incorporate this understanding.

AUTHENTIC COLLABORATION AND PUBLICATIONS: THE INTERNET

Netzines

As more and more schools across the country obtain Internet access, teens are establishing for themselves a writing-centered subculture that revolves around electronic versions of alternative publications, or *netzines.* Traditionally a forum for free expression, the Internet provides adolescents with the opportunity to share ideas through a creative blending of words, art, animation, sound, and video with little or no interference, or criticism, from adults. Jon Katz, in his article "The Rights of Kids in the Digital Age," asserts that America's youth is finding its identity tied inextricably to the digital world and the information age (122). Netzines created by and for kids are everywhere on the World Wide Web, and their often-uncensored formats may concern some parents and teachers.

Still, Internet access has ignited in many young people a desire, even a compulsion, to write. Since they have the freedom to play with words, young adults take risks with expression, experimenting with style, spelling, diction, capitalization, and punctuation in ways that proclaim a message of artistic experimentation. For example, young women who create electronic publications often refer to their creations as *gurl-* or *grrrl-zines;* in doing so, they have used alternative spellings to define themselves in a way other teens immediately recognize.

Netzines also give adolescents a chance to explore, in writing, topics of their own choosing, topics that are rarely addressed in the language arts classroom. Of course, kids discuss among themselves the issues frequently considered taboo in schools, but they also write untiringly about topics that may be considered too frivolous for the academic classroom or too embarrassing to share with a teacher, such as friends, dating, parents, fashion, cars, skating, and music.

Traditional Writing and Netzines

The idea of students writing and publishing their own magazines via computer technology is exciting, but most language arts teachers are expected, if not required, to teach standard methods of composition using standard rules of the English language. Describing a potential date as a wAy2KoOl chick may be acceptable in the underground press, but a similar statement on a job application might give a potential employer an excuse to join the education bashing that is so popular in this country. How then, might caring educators teach the rigors of composition without crushing the fervor teens show for writing?

The answer may reside in the zines themselves. If language arts teachers use zines, either the electronic or paper variety, to introduce written communication, they offer their students a chance to begin their writing journeys by learning to express themselves honestly and for real purpose. Interestingly, at least one study suggests that the writing young people do for their peers via the Net is often actually better than the writing they produce in traditional classroom assignments. In 1989, two researchers from the University of California at San Diego compared compositions written for teachers with those addressed to peers in other countries linked by the Internet. The compositions written and transferred by way of the Internet received distinctly better grades than those written for the teachers (Leslie 20).

EDUCATIONAL MULTIMEDIA PROGRAMS

There is also a whole new world of CD-ROM programs that address a variety of needs in the language arts classroom. These multimedia products capture the imaginations of even the most reluctant learners because of their dynamic nature and visual appeal. For example, Holt, Rinehart and Winston's CD-ROM software *Writer's Workshop* uses an environmental interface to engage students who might otherwise be completely disinterested in writing. It also includes music, a media center, author interviews, video clips, graphic organizers, photos, and online chat features to inspire students during prewriting, writing, or revising.

To involve students when teaching grammar, usage, and mechanics, Holt, Rinehart and Winston also offers *Language Workshop.* This award-winning CD-ROM program offers interactive instruction with options for on-screen self-assessment through performance-based practice. Along with these features for the student, *Language Workshop* has monitoring and assessment features exclusively for the teacher.

ON-LINE RESOURCES

Those of us who have attempted to teach research writing know that the struggle to engage young people in a systematic process of research can be tough. The Internet not only offers students the means by which they can publish their work, but also serves as a resource tool on topics of interest and on writing itself. Students who wouldn't be caught dead with a copy of Strunk's *Elements of Style* might not think twice about accessing the online version of the book.

Also, Net aficionados form a community of people, so that there is always an expert to be found on any subject, including composition. If students have World Wide Web access from home, they can do a keyword search for grammar and find a site that lists a state-by-state Grammar Hotline Directory. Or if they are too shy to speak aloud in class, they can post questions to tutors at several writing labs available through e-mail. Teachers just need to be aware that because these resources are sometimes public forums, the content on them can be unpredictable.

The Internet also serves as a resource for those of us who teach composition. If you access any major search engine, you will find a link to education-related sites; from there you can narrow your search as needed. On the World Wide Web teachers can find lesson plans, collaborative project ideas, supplementary materials, and even a netzine or two. And since teaching is all too often an isolated activity, many educators find reward in discussing their chosen field with colleagues in chat groups or on such e-mail discussion lists as the Dead Teachers Society.

Regardless of the position we take on the humans versus machines conflict, we cannot deny that technological innovations are now a part of everyday life. What still seems magical to us is commonplace to children who grow up expecting more than a hundred channels on their television sets and instant information from their computers. As concerned teachers, we can use technology to our own advantages—to incite interest, to simulate reality, and to open the world to our students. And if one of our goals as teachers of composition is to instill a love of writing—a need to write—then we owe it to our students to foster this love using all the tools we can find. ❦

References

Katz, Jon. "The Rights of Kids in the Digital Age." *Wired* July 1996: 120+

Leslie, Jacques. "Connecting Kids: On-line Technology Can Reform Our Schools." *Wired* Nov. 1993: 20-23.

Williamson, Judith. "Engaging Resistant Writers through Zines in the Classroom." College Composition and Communication Conference. Nashville, TN. March 1994.

By Dr. Norbert Elliot, Writing Program Director, New Jersey Institute of Technology & Dr. Karen Greenberg, Associate Professor, Hunter College of the City University of New York

THE DIRECT ASSESSMENT OF WRITING:

Notes For Teachers

HOW CAN ASSESSMENT STRATEGIES BE MODIFIED TO HELP BOTH TEACHERS AND STUDENTS?

Teachers spend a great deal of time assessing students' writing: They correct errors, offer suggestions, and assign grades. This process can be exhausting to teachers and discouraging for students. How can assessment strategies be modified to help both teachers and students?

Instruction and assessment can be aligned so that the two work together. To enable instruction and assessment to complement each other, teachers have turned to two relatively new methods of direct assessment: holistic scoring and portfolio assessment.

HOLISTIC SCORING

One of the most common methods of scoring writing samples is holistic scoring, a procedure based on the responses of con-

cerned readers to a meaningful whole composition. Holistic scoring involves reading a writing sample for an overall impression of the writing and assigning the sample a score based on a set of consistent scoring criteria. Most holistic scoring systems use a scoring scale, or guide, that describes papers at six or eight different levels of competence.

Holistic scoring has many advantages:

1. It communicates to students that writing is a process leading to a unified, synergistic piece of writing.

2. Writing samples that have been holistically scored provide students with clear information about the quality of their writing, but they are less intimidating than grades or written critiques.

NORBERT ELLIOT, DIRECTOR OF THE WRITING PROGRAM AT THE NEW JERSEY INSTITUTE OF TECHNOLOGY.

3. Holistic scoring is rapid. Readers spend only minutes judging the total effect of a paper.

4. The criteria on a holistic scoring scale give teachers a vocabulary to use in discussing essays with students and their parents.

5. The process of developing holistic scoring guides and scoring writing samples enables teachers to share their unique responses to writing, as well as their evaluative criteria. If an entire department uses the same scoring guide, students will realize that effective writing has definable features upon which all of their English teachers agree.

Nevertheless, there are weaknesses to this method. It alone cannot, for instance, provide diagnostic information about specific writing proficiencies and deficiencies. The score cannot substitute for a teacher's detailed responses to an essay—the provocative notes in the margin, the encouraging comments at the end, etc. This weakness, however, can be overcome if teachers review papers with their students in light of the scoring criteria.

Another weakness is more serious. Using holistic scoring, teachers often consider only one piece of writing during assessment. If only one sample of writing is evaluated, then teachers may not get a representative idea of students' writing ability, because this ability does not exist in a vacuum but varies from day to day and across the aims and modes of writing. In response to this concern, teachers have investigated a second method of direct assessment.

KAREN GREENBERG, DIRECTOR OF THE NATIONAL TESTING NETWORK IN WRITING.

PORTFOLIO ASSESSMENT

Portfolio assessment allows writing teachers to evaluate various samples of students' work, taken at various times under various conditions. Consequently, portfolio assessment can provide a fuller portrait of writing abilities.

To begin portfolio assessment, teachers develop a series of writing assignments that express the goals of a course. For instance, a group of teachers might require their students to write papers based on each of James Kinneavy's aims: expressive writing (a journal entry), informative writing (a summary of a news article), literary writing (a short story), and persuasive writing (an editorial). Over time, students work on these papers both at home and in class. Portfolios can include other forms of communication that students have produced, such as artwork, audio recordings, or videotapes.

Teachers need not assess everything that is included in a portfolio. In fact, it is often preferable not to evaluate every piece of a student's writing. This strategy allows teachers to separate instruction and response from formed evaluation. Portfolio assessment, therefore, can be based on samples that the teacher, the student, or both consider to be the student's best writing.

Clearly, there are advantages to this method:

1. Because multiple samples are assessed, portfolio assessment is a valid, authentic evaluation.

2. Because the authenticity of the assessment is increased, the curriculum becomes enriched.

As teachers plan tasks, they debate curricular values and strategies, devise workable instructional schemes for the classroom, and design thoughtful evaluative criteria for assignments.

With portfolio assessment, students gain a more positive attitude toward writing. Because they invest in their writing, students seek both teacher and peer response, create multiple drafts, and revise

for their readers. Over time, a school's entire writing program can become an exciting adventure in communication and critical thinking.

CONCLUSION

There is still much to be investigated about the evaluation of writing. What kind of assessment best suits the multiple literacies on which our democratic society rests? What kind of local assessments will best supplement large-scale assessment? How can assessment reveal more about effective teaching? Answers will have to come from those who know students best: their teachers. ❦

PORTFOLIO ASSESSMENT ALLOWS WRITING TEACHERS TO EVALUATE VARIOUS SAMPLES OF STUDENTS' WORK, TAKEN AT VARIOUS TIMES UNDER VARIOUS CONDITIONS.

❦❦❦❦❦

To the Teacher

A new feature in the Annotated Teacher's Edition *for* Elements of Writing *is the Chapter Planning Guide. Located at the beginning of each of the writing chapters, this four-page guide includes the features listed below.*
Within each guide, we have included lesson plans for you to use in customizing your instruction. The instructional choices and lesson pacing in these plans are only suggestions. *We recognize that any determination of lesson planning must be based on the needs of your individual classrooms.*

Objectives
Identifies the major objectives covered in the chapter.

Writing-in-Process Assignments
Provides an overview of the cumulative writing assignments that culminate in the main writing assignment of the chapter. Also outlines the developmental skills addressed in the chapter exercises.

Cross-Curriculum feature
Workplace Writing feature

Vary with each writing chapter in the Pupil's Edition. These features suggest ways to tailor the writing instruction addressed in the chapter to either a cross-discipline writing activity or to a form of writing used in the workplace.

Integrating the Language Arts Chart
Offers a convenient overview of the different strands of the language arts curriculum as they are incorporated in the activities provided in the Pupil's Edition.

Suggested Integrated Unit Plan
Appears only with chapters that address a particular kind of writing, such as a personal narrative or the research paper. Provides teachers with a unit plan that addresses reading; writing; listening and speaking; and language.

Chapter Planning Guide—Pupil's Edition
Suggests lesson plans and pacing for the instructional material, writing assignments, and exercises in each writing chapter in the Pupil's Edition. Outlines plans for students at three levels of learning—**developmental, core, and accelerated**.

Suggested pacing can be used to develop lesson plans for either a block or a traditional schedule.

Chapter Planning Guide—Program Resources
Provides an overview of the many program resources that support the instruction for each segment of the chapter.

These resources include various blackline masters for practice and assessment, transparencies for reinforcement, and writing and language CD-ROMs for instruction and practice.

Elements of Writing: Curriculum Connections
Identifies the activities at the end of each writing chapter that incorporate a cross-disciplinary approach.

Assessment Options
Identifies the assessment materials that accompany *Elements of Writing*. Addresses summative, portfolio, on-going, and self-assessment opportunities for evaluation.

ELEMENTS OF *Writing*

THE WRITING PROCESS COMES *Alive!*

If you're going to teach writing, *Elements of Writing* is *the* program to use. With *Elements of Writing,* students explore the writing process through unique lessons that take the puzzle and perplexity out of the experience and put the excitement of discovery back in.

A Pupil's Edition that Shows *and* Explains

This student book opens up the process of writing with an easy-to-follow, interactive style that hones students' writing skills and that talks to students in a friendly, encouraging tone. The program includes

- Brief, accessible segments of instruction immediately followed by practice
- Four writing models in *every* chapter to accommodate different learning styles
- Specific revision strategies for each major chapter
- A superb grammar handbook for reference and practice
- **NEW TO THIS EDITION!** More workplace writing; more grammar, usage, and mechanics; more student models; and even more attention to the revision process.

A Teacher's Edition at Work for You

In addition to pacing charts, program managers, and ideas for integrating workplace writing and reading skills, the *Elements of Writing* Annotated *Teacher's Edition* includes

Instructional Strategies to help you meet the needs of your students in efficient, effective, and creative ways.

- *Visual Connections*
- *Meeting Individual Needs*
- *Using the Selection*
- *A Different Approach*
- *Timesaver*
- *Critical Thinking*
- *Integrating the Language Arts*
- *Cooperative Learning*

Lesson Plans that provide clear and easy suggestions for managing the program at each step in the lesson.

- *Objectives*
- *Teaching the Lesson*
- *Guided* and *Independent Practice*
- *Assessment*
- *Reteaching*
- *Closure*
- *Motivation*
- *Extension*

Elements of Writing Supplements—
The *joy* of Following Through

Every teacher knows the importance of following through. With *Elements of Writing,* you get a comprehensive array of support materials to help students follow through with a piece of writing and succeed in the writing process. Practice sheets, technology, instructional transparencies, activity booklets, and a whole lot more let your class discover just how joyful and relevant the writing process can be.

Teaching Resources Outstanding materials reinforce
concepts and strategies for students and provide teachers with support for reteaching and assessment. Supplements include

Academic and Workplace Skills

Practice for Assessment in Reading, Vocabulary, and Spelling

Practicing the Writing Process

Strategies for Writing

Word Choice and Sentence Style

Language Skills Practice and Assessment

Holistic Scoring: Prompts and Models

Portfolio Assessment

Fine Art and Instructional Transparencies
Transparencies for each major writing chapter, including teacher's notes and graphic organizers, prompt students to generate and organize ideas.

Available separately are other invaluable resources that will add an extra dimension to your instruction. These include **Merriam-Webster Middle School** and **High School Dictionaries, Holt Complete School Atlas, English Workshop,** and **Vocabulary Workshop.**

Multimedia and Technology

HRW Multimedia and Technology opens doors, expands options, and turns possibilities into realities. Connections that begin in the textbook move to a new level—a level that motivates students to get involved, to look farther, deeper, and beyond the page. **HRW Multimedia and Technology** also gives you the flexibility to teach the way you want, whether you have only a few computers or a writing lab for 30 students.

TEST GENERATOR A software package that allows you to revise, edit, or re-sort existing worksheets, quizzes, or tests for each grammar, usage, and mechanics chapter in the *Pupil's Edition.*

LANGUAGE WORKSHOP CD-ROMs for Macintosh® and Windows® A software program for your students that gives additional instruction and practice with grammar, usage, and mechanics, while engaging students with lively, interactive examples, prompts, and exercises.

WRITER'S WORKSHOP 1 AND 2 CD-ROMs for Macintosh® and Windows® Writing process software that provides visual and spoken prompts to guide students through the eight most common assignments, such as writing a story, an informative report, or a persuasive essay.

HOLISTIC SCORING WORKSHOP An effective teacher-tutorial program in integrated performance assessment that instructs you in the use of holistic scoring of student reading and writing and that gives you practice with actual student papers.

ELEMENTS OF

Writing

REVISED EDITION

Second Course

James L. Kinneavy

John E. Warriner

HOLT, RINEHART AND WINSTON

Harcourt Brace & Company

Austin • New York • Orlando • Atlanta • San Francisco
Boston • Dallas • Toronto • London

Critical Readers

The following critical readers reviewed pre-publication materials for this book:

John Algeo
University of Georgia
Athens, Georgia

Alice Bartley
Byrd Middle School
Henrico County, Virginia

Wilma Bell
Fairfield Middle School
Highland Springs, Virginia

Anthony Buckley
East Texas State University
Commerce, Texas

Norbert Elliot
New Jersey Institute
   of Technology
Newark, New Jersey

Elaine A. Espindle
Peabody Veterans
   Memorial High School
Peabody, Massachusetts

Maxine M. Long
Genesee Community
   College
Batavia, New York

James Lynch
Van Buren Junior High
   School
Tampa, Florida

Jeri McInturff
Chattanooga School
   for the Liberal Arts
Chattanooga, Tennessee

Judy Olliff
Dallas School District 2
Dallas, Oregon

Cecilia Owen
Flagstaff Junior High School
Flagstaff, Arizona

Staff Credits

Associate Director: Mescal K. Evler
Executive Editors: Kristine E. Marshall, Robert R. Hoyt
Editorial Staff: Managing Editor, Steve Welch; *Editors,* Cheryl Christian,
A. Maria Hong, Constance D. Israel, Kathryn Rogers Johnson, Karen Kolar,
Christy McBride, Laura Cottam Sajbel, Patricia Saunders, Michael L. Smith,
Amy Strong, Suzanne Thompson, Katie Vignery; *Copyeditors,* Michael Neibergall,
Katherine E. Hoyt, Carrie Laing Pickett, Joseph S. Schofield IV, Barbara Sutherland;
Editorial Coordinators, Amanda F. Beard, Rebecca Bennett, Susan G. Alexander,
Wendy Langabeer, Marie H. Price; *Support,* Ruth A. Hooker, Christina Barnes,
Kelly Keeley, Margaret Sanchez, Raquel Sosa, Pat Stover
Permissions: Catherine J. Paré, Janet Harrington
Production: Pre-press, Beth Prevelige, Simira Davis; *Manufacturing,* Michael Roche
Design: Richard Metzger, *Art Director;* Lori Male, *Designer*
Photo Research: Peggy Cooper, *Photo Research Manager;* Tim Taylor, Sherrie Cass,
Victoria Smith, *Photo Research Team*

ISBN 0-03-050863-0

3 4 5 6 7   040   00 99 98

Authors

James L. Kinneavy, the Jane and Roland Blumberg Centennial Professor of English at The University of Texas at Austin, directed the development and writing of the composition strand in the program. He is the author of *A Theory of Discourse* and coauthor of *Writing in the Liberal Arts Tradition*. Professor Kinneavy is a leader in the field of rhetoric and composition and a respected educator whose teaching experience spans all levels—elementary, secondary, and college. He has continually been concerned with teaching writing to high school students.

John E. Warriner developed the organizational structure for the Handbook of Grammar, Usage, and Mechanics in the book. He coauthored the *English Workshop* series, was general editor of the *Composition: Models and Exercises* series, and editor of *Short Stories: Characters in Conflict*. He taught English for thirty-two years in junior and senior high school and college.

Writers and Editors

Ellen Ashdown has a Ph.D. in English from the University of Florida. She has taught composition and literature at the college level. She is a professional writer of educational materials and has published articles and reviews on education and art.

Jan Freeman has an M.A. in English from New York University. She has taught college composition classes. A published poet, she is a contributing editor to *The American Poetry Review* and the editor of Paris Press.

Madeline Travers-Hovland has a Master of Arts in Teaching from Harvard University. She has taught English in elementary and secondary school and has been an elementary school librarian. She is a professional writer of educational materials in literature and composition.

Elizabeth McCurnin majored in English at Valparaiso University. A professional writer and editor, she has over twenty-five years' experience in educational publishing.

John Roberts has an M.A. in Education from the University of Kentucky. He has taught English in secondary school. He is an editor and a writer of educational materials in literature, grammar, and composition.

Alice M. Sohn has a Ph.D. in English Education from Florida State University. She has taught English in middle school, secondary school, and college. She has been a writer and editor of educational materials in language arts for seventeen years.

PART ONE

WRITING

PART ONE: WRITING
The following **Teaching Resources** booklets contain materials that may be used with this part of the Pupil's Edition.

WRITING HANDBOOK
- *Practicing the Writing Process*
- *Portfolio Assessment*
- *Practice for Assessment in Reading, Vocabulary, and Spelling* (for Ch. 3)

AIMS FOR WRITING
- *Strategies for Writing*
- *Holistic Scoring: Prompts and Models*
- *Portfolio Assessment*
- *Practice for Assessment in Reading, Vocabulary, and Spelling*

LANGUAGE AND STYLE
- *Word Choice and Sentence Style*
- *Portfolio Assessment*

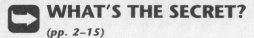

WHAT'S THE SECRET?
(pp. 2–15)

OBJECTIVES

- To explore the ways that writers and writing affect the world
- To identify and analyze the aims of writing
- To compare and contrast the aims of writing

INTRODUCTION TO WRITING

WHAT'S THE SECRET?

James L. Kinneavy

USING THE INTRODUCTION TO WRITING

This introduction to writing is just that—an introduction. It starts by talking briefly about the power of writing in people's lives rather than by talking about writing as schoolwork. Next, it touches upon the two central focuses of the writing chapters in the book—the "how" of writing (modes) and the "why" of writing (aims).

The communication triangle graphically reflects the four major aims of Kinneavy's theory of discourse. For more information, refer to the essay in the front of this book, **"Meet the Aims and Modes of Writing,"** or to Dr. Kinneavy's two books, *A Theory of Discourse* and *Writing in the Liberal Arts Tradition.* ■

Your everyday life isn't mysterious, is it? You get up, get dressed, eat breakfast, and go through your day. There's no mystery to it.

But wait!

Why did you pick that pair of jeans to wear? Why do all your friends want the same kind of jeans? And why did you choose that brand of cereal to eat for breakfast? **What's the secret?**

It's pouring down rain in the morning, but the weather forecasters say it will be sunny later on. How do they know? What's their secret?

Yesterday, your best friend won the election for student council president. You're glad she won, but how did she do it?

It's just another ordinary day, but things are happening all around you. And all these things—and more—share one great secret.

What is it? What's the secret?

©Jay Maisel

3

The Secret Is . . .

The secret is a power that's so strong it affects almost everything you do. It's the power of communication!

It's the magazine ad that convinces you that those jeans are "right" for you. It's the clever TV commercial that encourages you to choose that brand of cereal and not some other. It's the scientific knowledge that results in an accurate weather report. It's the posters and the speech that convince students to vote for your friend as student council president.

Who has this power? The planners and the talkers and the doers have it. They may be artists, businesspeople, teachers, composers, writers, or scientists. They write the manuals that explain how to repair a bike or program a VCR. They write the scripts that make you laugh or cry or scream during a movie. They design your computer games and write everything you read, even the messages on cereal boxes. They're all the people who communicate ideas to you.

And you're one of them. Every time you talk to someone, jot down a telephone message, scribble a note to a friend, or write an essay in class, you're using the power of communication.

The Key to the Mystery

All these *writers* who influence your life share the same secret. They know how to communicate. They have something to say (a *subject*), someone to say it to (an *audience*), and a way to say it (a *language*).

Think of these elements as a triangle. Language—both written and spoken—is at the center.

How Writers Write

The Writing Process

Effective communication doesn't just happen. A great deal of thinking and planning goes into it—deciding what ideas to convey and how to get them across to an audience.

Most writers say that their powers of communication work best when they follow a *writing process.* Writers may vary in the way they work through the process, but they all use the following basic steps.

Prewriting	Thinking and planning—choosing a subject, a purpose, and an audience; thinking up ideas; planning how to present the ideas
Writing	Writing a first draft—putting ideas into sentences and paragraphs; following the plan for presenting ideas
Evaluating and Revising	Looking over the draft—deciding what's good and what needs to be changed; making changes to improve the writing
Proofreading and Publishing	Finding and fixing errors; making a final copy; sharing the writing with an audience

Why Writers Write

The Aims of Writing

What reason do you have for writing? Writers always have some purpose, or aim, in mind. All writing has at least one of these four basic aims: to inform, to persuade, to express oneself, to be creative.

To Inform	Writers often aim to give facts and other kinds of information or to explain something.
To Persuade	Writers may want to convince people of something—to buy a product or to vote for someone—or to take some action.
To Express Themselves	Writers may simply want to express their thoughts and feelings.
To Be Creative	Writers sometimes create stories, poems, songs, and plays.

On the following pages are four models. They are all about the same topic—a ballplayer named Casey—but each one has a different aim. As you read, notice how the writing changes as the aim changes.

INFORMATIVE WRITING

Casey strikes out

Five thousand Mudville fans were in attendance yesterday at Sandtown Field when the Mighty Casey took three straight strikes to lose the game for Mudville.

Mudville was down 4–2, with two out, in the ninth inning when Flynn hit a single and landed safely on first base. He was followed by Jimmy Blake, who blasted out a double, driving Flynn to third base.

With the tying runs on second and third, Casey was next in the lineup. The first pitch was straight across the plate, but Casey didn't swing. Strike one. Casey signaled the pitcher, who threw the second pitch. Again, Casey didn't swing, and the umpire called the second strike.

Casey swung hard at the third pitch. He missed. The Mighty Casey had struck out. Sandtown won, 4–2.

ANSWERS

Reader's Response

Responses will vary.

1. Some students will say that although the article is informative, many questions are left unanswered. Students might have questions about who got hits, who the winning and losing pitchers were, how Casey had done in previous at-bats, and so on.

2. Students may mention that Sandtown beat Mudville 4–2, five thousand fans went to the game at Sandtown Field, Flynn hit a single, Blake hit a double, and Casey struck out.

READER'S RESPONSE

1. Suppose the Mudville players were your school baseball team. What else would you want to know about the game?
2. Informative writing gives facts and other kinds of information. What are some important facts that you learn about the Mudville game from this article?

PERSUASIVE WRITING

Dear Editor:

I've been a fan of the Mighty Casey for many years. After his poor showing last week, it's time for him to hang up his bat. He acts tough, but his performance in recent games has been disappointing, and last week was the final straw.

Casey let two perfectly good pitches go by. His eyesight must be gone. He can still swing a bat, but what good is that if he can't connect? He's stubborn, and he uses bad judgment. Those things cost us the game.

Mudville has depended on Casey for too long. We need some new, young players who perform well all the time. We need to give old Casey a rest. He's been a great player, but he's long past his prime.

Casey needs to retire. If enough fans speak out, he'll have no choice. Let him know how you feel. Let's get Mudville back in the playoffs again!

Sincerely,

Lyndsey Denis

Lyndsey Denis

READER'S RESPONSE

1. If you were one of Casey's fans, would this letter convince you that Casey should retire? Explain why or why not.
2. What reasons does the writer give for needing to get rid of Casey?

ANSWERS
Reader's Response

Responses will vary.

1. Some students may say a good player who has earned a reputation as "Mighty Casey" should not be replaced after one poor performance. Others may feel the editorial is correct—a player who cannot perform well should retire to keep the team in the playoffs.

2. The writer states that Casey apparently has poor eyesight, is stubborn, uses bad judgment, and is long past his prime. His performance in recent games has been disappointing and the team needs a new, young player to replace him.

EXPRESSIVE WRITING

Today, I took the longest walk of my life back to the dugout. It wasn't the first tim I've struck out, but it was the worst. I don't know if the fans'll ever trust me ag Maybe it's time to hang it up. I don't fe a lot of the time, and I know my

Today, I took the longest walk of my life—back to the dug-out. It wasn't the first time I've struck out, but it was the worst. I don't know if the fans'll ever trust me again.

Maybe it's time to hang it up. I don't feel good a lot of the time, and I know my running ain't what it used to be. My eyes ain't either. I was showing off some when I let the first one go, but I never should've missed that third pitch! I've always taken chances, and the fans've loved it, but I found out today they don't like me taking chances and failing. I'm too old to change my ways, I guess. But not connecting with a perfect pitch. That's as bad as it gets.

I overheard some people saying I should retire. Maybe I ought to see about managing a team. Baseball's all I know. It scares me to think about quitting.

READER'S RESPONSE

1. Think about a time you didn't perform well, perhaps on a test or in a contest. How did you feel?
2. The article on page 8 gives you facts about Casey. What do you learn about him from this letter to an old teammate?

ANSWERS
Reader's Response

Responses will vary.

1. Students will express a variety of feelings—anger, disappointment, fear, frustration, embarrassment, and similar emotions.

2. The journal entry shows that Casey is dismayed at his strikeout and worried that his fans won't trust him again. He is contemplating retirement and is concerned about his health problems. He has learned that the fans don't like for him to take chances if he fails. But he feels he is too old to change his ways. He feels perhaps managing a team is his next job because baseball is all he knows. He is frightened to think about retiring.

CREATIVE WRITING

CASEY AT THE BAT

by Ernest Lawrence Thayer

The outlook wasn't brilliant for the Mudville nine that day;
The score stood four to two, with but one inning more to play;
And so, when Cooney died at first, and Burrows did the same,
A sickly silence fell upon the patrons of the game.

A straggling few got up to go in deep despair. The rest
Clung to the hope which springs eternal in the human breast;
They thought, if only Casey could but get a whack, at that,
They'd put up even money now, with Casey at the bat.

But Flynn preceded Casey, as did also Jimmy Blake,
And the former was a pudding, and the latter was a fake;
So upon that <u>stricken</u> <u>multitude</u> grim <u>melancholy</u> sat,
For there seemed but little chance of Casey's getting to the bat.

But Flynn let drive a single, to the wonderment of all,
And Blake, the much-despised, tore the cover off the ball;
And when the dust had lifted, and they saw what had occurred,
There was Jimmy safe on second, and Flynn a-hugging third.

Then from the gladdened multitude went up a joyous yell;
It bounded from the mountaintop, and rattled in the <u>dell</u>;
It struck upon the hillside, and recoiled upon the flat;
For Casey, mighty Casey, was advancing to the bat.

There was ease in Casey's manner as he stepped into his place;
There was pride in Casey's bearing, and a smile on Casey's face;
And when, responding to the cheers, he lightly <u>doffed</u> his hat,
No stranger in the crowd could doubt 'twas Casey at the bat.

Ten thousand eyes were on him as he rubbed his hands with dirt;
Five thousand tongues applauded when he wiped them on his shirt;
Then while the <u>writhing</u> pitcher ground the ball into his hip,
<u>Defiance</u> gleamed in Casey's eye, a sneer curled Casey's lip.

And now the leather-covered <u>sphere</u> came hurtling through the air,
And Casey stood a-watching it in <u>haughty grandeur</u> there;
Close by the sturdy batsman the ball <u>unheeded</u> sped.
"That ain't my style," said Casey. "Strike one," the umpire said.

From the benches, black with people, there went up a muffled roar,
Like the beating of the storm waves on a stern and distant shore;
"Kill him! Kill the umpire!" shouted someone on the stand;
And it's likely they'd have killed him had not Casey raised his hand.

With a smile of Christian charity great Casey's <u>visage</u> shone;
He stilled the rising <u>tumult</u>; he <u>bade</u> the game go on;
He signaled to the pitcher, and once more the <u>spheroid</u> flew;
But Casey still ignored it, and the umpire said, "Strike two."

"Fraud!" cried the maddened thousands, and the echo answered, "Fraud!"
But a scornful look from Casey, and the audience was awed;
They saw his face grow stern and cold, they saw his muscles strain,
And they knew that Casey wouldn't let that ball go by again.

The sneer is gone from Casey's lips, his teeth are clenched in hate,
He pounds with cruel violence his bat upon the plate;
And now the pitcher holds the ball, and now he lets it go,
And now the air is shattered by the force of Casey's blow.

Oh! somewhere in this favored land the sun is shining bright;
The band is playing somewhere, and somewhere hearts are light;
And somewhere men are laughing, and somewhere children shout,
But there is no joy in Mudville—mighty Casey has struck out!

READER'S RESPONSE

1. This is a famous poem about baseball. Why do you think
it's a popular poem? What do you like about it?
2. Words like *a joyous yell* and *a muffled roar* help you "hear"
the crowd when Casey is at bat. What are some words that
help you "see" Casey at bat?

ANSWERS
Reader's Response

Responses will vary.

1. Students may think the poem is popular because baseball is a popular national pastime. In addition, they may like it because it involves the reader in a play-by-play of the game and makes the reader root for the Mudville team, even though they lose. Students may also think it is popular because it gives a vivid, lyrical description.

2. Words that help the reader visualize Casey at bat include "advancing to the bat," "stepped into his place," "pride in Casey's bearing," "a smile on Casey's face," "lightly doffed his hat," "rubbed his hands with dirt," "wiped them on his shirt," "a sneer curled Casey's lip," "Casey raised his hand," "signaled to the pitcher," "scornful look from Casey," "his face grow stern and cold," "his muscles strain," "sneer is gone from Casey's lips," and "teeth are clenched in hate."

ANSWERS

Writing and Thinking Activities

1a. The second example tries to convince readers to do something.

b. The last example, **"Casey at the Bat,"** makes you feel you're at the game.

c. The first example mostly states facts about a baseball player striking out.

d. The third model mostly describes the writer's thoughts and feelings.

Questions 2 and 4 might be journal activities. Question 3 is a group activity. You might want to save these projects to work on at a later date.

Writing and Thinking Activities

1. Get together with two or three other students. Look over the four models you've just read about the baseball game and then discuss the following questions.
   a. Which model tries to convince readers to do something?
   b. Which one makes you feel that you're actually there?
   c. Which one mostly states facts about a baseball player striking out?
   d. Which model mostly describes the writer's own thoughts and feelings?

2. Do you know how you communicate? Pick a day to find out. For two hours, keep a record of each time you read, speak, write, and listen. Try to decide what your aim is each time you communicate. Is it to inform, to persuade, to express yourself, or to be creative? Can you see a pattern? Do you have some aims more often than others? Then, get together with a few classmates, and exchange notes. Is their pattern of communication like yours? Or is it different?

3. What aim do you find most in what you read? Bring a magazine or newspaper to class. Meet with two or three classmates to find examples of the four aims of writing—informative, self-expressive, creative, and persuasive. What aim seems to be used most?
4. Creative writing is usually thought of as novels, short stories, poems, and plays. Do you think other kinds of writing are also creative? What about scientific papers and book reports, for example? How might they be creative?

"The bat flashes, there is a new, louder sound, and suddenly we see the ball streaking wild through the air..."

Roger Angell

SELECTION AMENDMENT
Description of change: excerpted
Rationale: to focus on the writing theme presented in this chapter

WRITING AND THINKING

OBJECTIVES

- To use prewriting techniques to find ideas for writing
- To analyze a composition's audience
- To arrange ideas in a logical order appropriate for the purpose, audience, and topic of a composition
- To evaluate and revise a paragraph for content, organization, and style

WORKPLACE writing

"How Will the Writing Process Help Me in the Real World?"

To help students understand that writing is not just a classroom activity, allow the class to learn from outside sources how the writing experience is a vital part of an active community life.

- **Prewriting** Suggest the class invite a panel of outside experts to speak on the role of writing in their daily lives. Have students brainstorm a list of potential panel members. Students may wish to use a cluster diagram such as the one that follows to help organize their thoughts.

As students study this chapter and learn the writing process, ask them to work as a class to compose a general letter of invitation for potential panel mem-

bers. Be sure that students realize that in composing this letter they will be using the writing process. Their prewriting has already included clustering. Now they may use brainstorming for the letter's contents. The brainstorming session may include why they are issuing the invitations and what they hope to learn from the panelists invited. Intrapersonal learners may wish to try freewriting or journal writing as an organizational tool.

- **Writing** If some students feel that a form letter is too impersonal, have them use the form letter as a basis to develop a more personal letter to the potential panelist of their choice. Visualizing may help students to see their finished product—their panel members in action—and to imagine what specifics to include in the letters' instructions to the panelist.

- **Evaluating and Revising** For evaluation and revision of letters, suggest that students exchange drafts for peer input. Emphasize that their letters will be a major factor in whether or not the person invited will accept the invitation, so their revision and later their proofreading are vital.

- **Proofreading and Publishing** Students may want to publish their letters for their classmates' input before they send the invitations.

INTEGRATING THE LANGUAGE ARTS

SELECTION	READING AND LITERATURE	WRITING AND CRITICAL THINKING	LANGUAGE AND SYNTAX	SPEAKING, LISTENING, AND OTHER EXPRESSION SKILLS
• "**An Interview with Ann Petry**" from ***Interviews with Black Writers*** pp. 18–20 • ***National Park Guide*** by Michael Frome p. 35	• Using inferential comprehension skills p. 21 • Analyzing passages and applying strategies such as self-questioning for comprehension p. 21	• Analyzing audience pp. 23, 35 • Writing a journal entry pp. 25, 26 • Using brainstorming to generate ideas for writing p. 27 • Generating ideas by using clustering p. 28 • Using critical-thinking skills to ask relevant questions pp. 29–31 • Using an encyclopedia to find information p. 30 • Using and analyzing cause-and-effect relationships p. 32 • Writing and revising persuasion p. 35 • Identifying organizational scheme pp. 37–39 • Writing an initial draft with emphasis on content p. 42 • Evaluating drafts alone and with peers pp. 43–45, 49 • Revising a draft for content clarity p. 49 • Editing and proofreading for grammatical, mechanical, and usage errors p. 51 • Writing and revising using a computer p. 55	• Adjusting language to suit audience p. 35 • Proofreading to avoid nonstandard usage p. 51 • Editing for capitalization, punctuation, spelling, and usage errors pp. 50, 51	• Contributing ideas in a small group discussion pp. 27, 35 • Speaking in a group p. 27 • Listening with a focus p. 31 • Distinguishing between communication purposes of informing and persuading p. 35 • Organizing ideas by making a chart to show information p. 40 • Making lists to show information p. 54 • Reporting research findings to class p. 55

CHAPTER 1: WRITING AND THINKING

Use this guide for creating an instructional plan that addresses the individual needs of your students. Assignments accompanied by the following symbol (✻) may be completed out of class. Times given for pacing lessons are estimated.

CHAPTER PLANNING GUIDE—PUPIL'S EDITION

| LESSONS | LITERARY MODEL pp. 18–20 An interview with Ann Petry from *Interviews with Black Writers* | PREWRITING pp. 24–40 | |
		Generating Ideas	Gathering/Organizing
DEVELOPMENTAL PROGRAM	🕐 **20–25 minutes** • Read model aloud in class and work with students to answer questions on p. 21 orally.	🕐 **90–95 minutes** • Main Assignment: Looking Ahead p. 21 • "Why" and "How" pp. 22–23 • Finding Ideas for Writing pp. 24–31 • Exercises 1–8 pp. 25–31 • Purpose and Audience p. 33	🕐 **35–40 minutes** • Arranging Ideas pp. 36–39 • Arranging Ideas Chart p. 36 • Critical Thinking pp. 37–38 • Exercises 9–10 p. 40✻
CORE PROGRAM	🕐 **15–20 minutes** • Assign students to read the model and answer questions on p. 21 in pairs.	🕐 **30–35 minutes** • Main Assignment: Looking Ahead p. 21 • Finding Ideas for Writing pp. 24–31✻ • Exercises 1–2, 5, 7, 8 pp. 25, 26, 29, 31✻ • Purpose and Audience p. 33 • Critical Thinking pp. 32, 33–35✻	🕐 **25–30 minutes** • Charts pp. 36, 38 • Critical Thinking pp. 37–38 • Exercise 10 p. 40✻
ACCELERATED PROGRAM	🕐 **10–15 minutes** • Assign students to read model independently.	🕐 **20–25 minutes** • Main Assignment: Looking Ahead p. 21 • Prewriting Techniques Chart p. 24 • Exercises 6, 7, 8 pp. 30, 31✻ • Purpose and Audience p. 33 • Critical Thinking pp. 32, 33–35✻	🕐 **15–20 minutes** • Charts pp. 36, 38 • Critical Thinking pp. 37–38

CHAPTER PLANNING GUIDE—PROGRAM RESOURCES

	LITERARY MODEL	PREWRITING
PRINT	• Reading Master 1, *Practice for Assessment in Reading, Vocabulary, and Spelling* p. 1	• Freewriting and Brainstorming; Clustering and Questioning; Reading and Imagining; Purpose and Audience; Organizing Ideas; Charts and Tree Diagrams, *Practicing the Writing Process* pp. 1–6 • Prewriting: Finding Ideas for Writing, Prewriting: Asking Questions, Prewriting: Arranging Ideas, *English Workshop* pp. 1–4
MEDIA		• Graphic Organizer 1: Aim: The "Why" of Writing, *Transparency Binder* • Graphic Organizer 2: Process: The "How" of Writing, *Transparency Binder*

WRITING pp. 41–42	EVALUATING AND REVISING pp. 43–49	PROOFREADING AND PUBLISHING pp. 50–54

🕐 15–20 minutes
• Writing a First Draft
  pp. 41–42
• Writing Note p. 42
• Exercise 11 p. 42*
	🕐 40–45 minutes
	• Evaluating/Revising
	  pp. 43–44, 46–47
	• Guidelines pp. 44, 48
	• Critical Thinking
	  pp. 44–45*
	• Exercise 12 p. 49
		🕐 40–45 minutes
		• Guidelines pp. 50, 53
		• Exercise 13 p. 51 in pairs
		• Critical Thinking
		  pp. 52–53*
		• Exercise 14 p. 54
		• Symbols p. 54

🕐 10–15 minutes
• Writing a First Draft
  pp. 41–42*
• Writing Note p. 42
• Exercise 11 p. 42*
	🕐 35–40 minutes
	• Tips p. 43
	• Guidelines pp. 44, 48
	• Critical Thinking
	  pp. 44–45*
	• Revising Chart p. 46
	• Exercise 12 p. 49
		🕐 20–25 minutes
		• Guidelines pp. 50, 53
		• Exercise 13 p. 51*
		• Critical Thinking
		  pp. 52–53*
		• Exercise 14 p. 54
		• Symbols p. 54

🕐 5–10 minutes
• Writing Note p. 42
• Exercise 11 p. 42*
	🕐 15–20 minutes
	• Tips p. 43
	• Guidelines pp. 44, 48
	• Critical Thinking
	  pp. 44–45*
	• Revising Chart p. 46
		🕐 15–20 minutes
		• Guidelines pp. 50, 53
		• Critical Thinking
		  pp. 52–53*
		• Exercise 14 p. 54
		• Symbols p. 54

 Computer disk or CD-ROM   Overhead transparencies

WRITING	EVALUATING AND REVISING	PROOFREADING AND PUBLISHING

• Writing: Two Approaches,
  *Practicing the Writing
  Process* p. 7
• Writing a First Draft,
  English Workshop p. 5
	• Evaluation, Revising,
	  *Practicing the Writing
	  Process* pp. 8, 10
	• Evaluating and Revising,
	  English Workshop
	  pp. 6–7
		• Using a Proofreading
		  Checklist, Manuscript
		  Form, *Practicing the
		  Writing Process* pp. 11–12
		• *English Workshop*
		  pp. 8–10, 59–70,
		  159–220, 231–276

	• Revision Transparencies
	  1–2, *Transparency*
	  Binder
		• *Language Workshop:*
		  Lessons 10–15, 17–20,
		  34–38, 40–50, 45–49,
		  57–60

ASSESSMENT OPTIONS

Reflection
Portfolio forms, *Portfolio Assessment* pp. 5–24

Peer Evaluation
Peer Evaluation, *Practicing the Writing Process* p. 9

Summative Assessment
Review: The Aim and Process of Writing, *Practicing the Writing Process* p. 13

LOOKING AT THE PROCESS

OBJECTIVES

- To analyze personal feelings toward writing
- To analyze personal habits of writing
- To interpret a professional writer's statements regarding her writing

TEACHING THE LESSON

One way to introduce this lesson is to have students read a short story by Ann Petry or an excerpt from her biography of Harriet Tubman. Ask students to describe their impressions of the author.

You may want to ask a volunteer to read the introductory material. Then have two volunteers read the interview, with one

---

PROGRAM MANAGER

CHAPTER 1

- **Computer Guided Instruction**
  Writer's Workshop 1 CD-ROM
  Applied instruction about specific types of writing is cross-referenced, where appropriate, in subsequent chapters beginning with **Chapter 4.**

- **Practice** To help less-advanced students who need additional practice with concepts and activities related to this chapter, see **Chapter 1** in *English Workshop, Second Course,* pp. 1–10.

- **Reading Support** For help with the reading selection, pp. 18–20, see **Reading Master 1** in *Practice for Assessment in Reading, Vocabulary, and Spelling,* p. 1.

VISUAL CONNECTIONS
Introspection

About the Artist. Will Barnet was born in Beverly, Massachusetts, in 1911. While studying in the Art Students League in New York, he developed innovative techniques in lithography and printing. Throughout his career as an artist and an instructor, Barnet has emphasized composition by focusing not only on the figures in a painting, but also on the way they fit into the space of the picture.

continued on next page

1 WRITING AND THINKING

student reading the part of the interviewer and another the part of Ann Petry. After the reading, ask students to describe any changes in their impressions of Ann Petry.

Looking at the Process

People aren't born knowing how to play a guitar or a piano. First, they go through a **process** of learning how. Then they have to practice. This is true of writing, too. Becoming a better writer starts with learning and practicing the writing process.

Writing and You. Do you like to write? Is writing easy for you, or do you have to struggle with every word? Believe it or not, even professional writers run into trouble. They can't think of a new idea, they get stuck looking for the right word, or they know something is wrong but they're not sure how to fix it. What part of writing causes you the most trouble?

As You Read. As you read the following interview with novelist Ann Petry, notice what she says about where she gets her ideas.

William Barnet, *Introspection* ©1998 William Barnet/Licensed by VAGA, New York, NY.

a discussion. Some leading questions might include "How does Petry's biographical information help clarify the statement?" and "How does your experience as a writer help you understand what Petry says?"

Students should be able to answer independently the first, second, and fourth questions of the **Reader's Response** feature. Encourage students to give well-developed answers by requiring examples of the points they make.

18

FROM *INTERVIEWS WITH BLACK WRITERS*

AN INTERVIEW WITH ANN PETRY

USING THE SELECTION
from Interviews With Black Writers

1

Ann Petry wrote the fictionalized young-adult biography *Tituba of Salem Village* (1964).

2

The Narrows examines life within the black ghetto and relationships between members of that community and the white community.

INTERVIEWER: Have you ever been unable to write a story which you would have liked to write?

PETRY: I've never abandoned a story or a novel once I started working on it. I've abandoned many ideas before I ever put a pen to paper. I once planned or thought about writing a book for young people about Daniel Drayton and Edward Syres, two ships' captains imprisoned for attempting to help slaves escape from the District of Columbia on the schooner *Pearl*. I didn't
1 write that particular book because I became interested in—actually fascinated by—a slave, Tituba, who was one of three women charged with witchcraft at the beginning of the trials for witchcraft in Salem, Massachusetts. . . .

INTERVIEWER: Is there a part of a novel which is more difficult for you to write than any other?

2 **PETRY:** Sometimes. I had great difficulty writing the chapter (*The Narrows*) in which Link is murdered.

INTERVIEWER: Is there some point in the novel where you feel that you have everything in hand and the rest will fall into place?

You can use students' written or oral responses to the questions at the end of the interview to evaluate how well they have analyzed their personal feelings about writing. If you used the third **Reader's Response** question as guided practice, ask students to write sentences summarizing the discussion.

Have students write brief paragraphs comparing their feelings about writing with Ann Petry's feelings. ■

19

PETRY: I never have a novel "in hand" until it is completed.

INTERVIEWER: Do you ever experience any conflict between meaning and form, or between what you might like to do in a novel and what you think your reader will be able to understand? Or does the form of a novel develop on its own?

PETRY: The form finds itself.

INTERVIEWER: Do you remember how old you were when you first started to write?

PETRY: Fourteen.

INTERVIEWER: Were you anxious to show your work to people?

PETRY: I rarely ever told anyone that I was writing. And I still don't talk about what I write if I can avoid it.

INTERVIEWER: Do you think of your fiction as autobiographical?

"...everything I write is filtered through my mind, consciously or unconsciously. The end product contains everything

I know,

have experienced,

thought about,

dreamed about,

talked about,

lived for."

VISUAL CONNECTIONS

Exploring the Subject. In addition to short stories and several adult novels, Ann Petry (1908–   ), a well-known African American writer, wrote for young adults the fictionalized biography *Tituba of Salem Village.* Her biography *Harriet Tubman: Conductor on the Underground Railroad* (1955) was also written for young readers.

With the publication of her 1946 novel, *The Street,* Petry became the first African American woman writer to write about the problems of African American women who live in inner-city neighborhoods.

MEETING *individual* NEEDS

LEARNING STYLES

Kinetic Learners. Some students may find that physical position affects the way they write. Share with students that Ernest Hemingway liked to write while standing up and Mark Twain preferred to write while lying down. Emphasize that each writer must decide what works best for him or her.

SELECTION AMENDMENT
Description of change: excerpted and modified
Rationale: to focus on the concept of a writer's process presented in this chapter

PETRY: I could say that none of my work is <u>autobiographical</u>, or that all of it is—everything I write is filtered through my mind, <u>consciously</u> or <u>unconsciously</u>. The end product contains everything I know, have experienced, thought about, dreamed about, talked about, lived for. And so in that sense I am any of the characters that I create, all of them, some of them, or none of them.

INTERVIEWER: Could you say something about your writing habits? When do you work? How much revising do you do? Are you subject to moods during the time you are working on a novel?

PETRY: When I'm writing I work in the morning from 8:00 A.M. to about noon. If I'm going to do any revising I do it in the afternoon. The first draft is in longhand. The planning and the writing go hand in hand for the most part. I revise endlessly. And yet the first chapter of *The Street* was written in one sitting and that first draft was the final one—no changes. And there were no changes in a story entitled "Like a Winding Sheet" or in "Sole on the Drums." I do not work at night if I can avoid it. I am not subject to moods. I doubt if my family or anyone else can tell when I'm thinking about writing.

READER'S RESPONSE

1. Do you, like Ann Petry, sometimes abandon ideas before you ever start to write about them? What are your reasons for dropping those ideas in favor of some others?
2. Ann Petry says she started to write when she was fourteen, but she has never liked to talk about her writing with anyone else. How do you feel about your own writing? Do you like to share it, or do you want to keep it to yourself?
3. What do you think Ann Petry means when she says "I could say that none of my work is autobiographical, or that all of it is . . ."?
4. Ann Petry says she writes in the mornings and revises in the afternoons. When do you write best? Do you think your writing is better when you come back later and revise it?

LOOKING AHEAD

In this chapter, you'll learn some techniques that you can work into your own writing process. You'll practice these techniques through all the stages of the writing process—from choosing a topic to publishing. As you work through the chapter, remember that

- writing and thinking work together in the process
- the writing process can be bent or shaped to fit your own style

ANSWERS
Reader's Response

Responses will vary. Answers to the first, second, and fourth questions should include specific examples from students' experiences. The third question requires inferential reading and thinking. Students will probably come to the conclusion that although Petry does not write about herself, her writing reflects her experience and so is, in a way, autobiographical.

LESSON 2 *(pp. 22–23)*
THE "WHY" AND "HOW" OF WRITING
TEACHING AIM AND PROCESS

After students read the **Why People Write** chart, write the following list on the chalkboard and ask students to match each item with the appropriate aim (given in brackets):

1. a short story [literary]
2. a letter to the editor [persuasive]
3. a journal entry [expressive]
4. a news story [informative]

If students have examples of any of these kinds of writing, have them share the topics the samples addressed.

MEETING *individual* NEEDS

LEARNING STYLES

Kinetic Learners. To help students who might have difficulty reading the pie chart, copy the chart and cut each copy into four pieces for students to work with. These smaller pieces will allow students to focus on one aspect of the process at a time. Students can practice putting the pieces together in the order they belong. Remind students, however, that the process differs depending on the writer.

AT-RISK STUDENTS

To some extent, most students experience anxiety about writing. You can help relieve some of this anxiety by explaining that every student has special needs and that your goal is for your students to develop their skills as writers to the best of their ability. Remind students that writing isn't a competitive activity and that there aren't any limits on how far or how fast they can progress.

22

Aim—The "Why" of Writing

People have a number of different reasons for writing. They talk for the same reasons that they write—because they have something to say, they have some purpose for saying it, and they have somebody they want to say it to.

But these are general reasons for why people communicate. What are the specific purposes that people have when they write? There aren't as many of these purposes as you might think. Look at the following chart.

WHY PEOPLE WRITE	
To express themselves	To get to know themselves, to find meaning in their own lives
To share information	To give other people information that they need or want; to share some special knowledge
To persuade	To convince other people to do something or believe something
To create literature	To be creative, to say something in a unique way

Process—The "How" of Writing

Good writing doesn't just happen. For most writers, it comes from following stages in a process. And the stages are all linked to thinking. In the first stage, prewriting, you'll probably do more thinking than writing. Later, when you're writing your first draft, you may do more writing than thinking.

The following diagram shows the stages that writers usually follow. However, the process differs for every writer. You may spend more time thinking up ideas than your classmates, or you may write down your ideas faster.

Then have students look at the pie chart while you explain the four stages of the writing process. Ask volunteers to share their ideas about which stage is the most important or which stage they think takes the most time. The varying opinions will illustrate how differently each writer views the process. ■

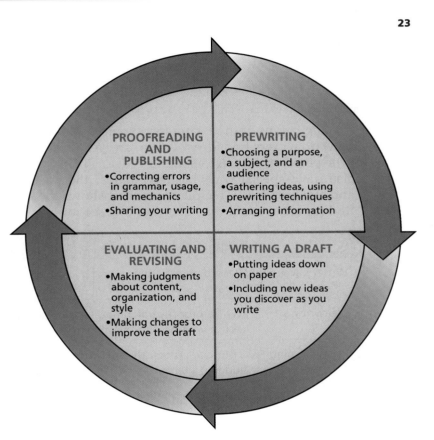

As the diagram shows, at any stage you can return to an earlier one (even to the beginning) if you need to. For example, your ecology club plans to start a recycling project at school. You agree to write a letter to the recycling center to ask for recycling bins. Then you realize you don't know how many bins the school will need. So you go back to the prewriting stage to find ideas and take notes about the information you need.

Topic, purpose, and *audience* are also important in the writing process. Sometimes they come together naturally. The topic (recycling), purpose (requesting bins), and audience (adults) determine what goes into your letter. In school, your teacher may assign topics, purposes, and audiences to give you practice for the important writing you do for your own reasons.

OBJECTIVES

- To find ideas for writing by using a writer's journal, freewriting, brainstorming, clustering, the *5W-How?* questions, and imagining
- To read and listen with a focus
- To organize information by using a chart and a tree diagram

PROGRAM MANAGER

PREWRITING

- **Heuristics** To help students generate ideas, see **Freewriting and Brainstorming, Clustering and Questioning,** and **Reading and Imagining** in *Practicing the Writing Process,* pp. 1–3.

- **Analyzing** To help students analyze and organize ideas, see **Purpose and Audience, Organizing Ideas,** and **Charts and Tree Diagrams** in *Practicing the Writing Process,* pp. 4–6.

- **Instructional Support** See **Graphic Organizers 1** and **2.** For suggestions on how to tie the transparencies to instruction, review teacher's notes for transparencies in *Fine Art and Instructional Transparencies for Writing,* pp. 47, 49.

QUOTATION FOR THE DAY

"It is odd that we never question the feasibility of a football team practicing long hours for one game; yet in writing we rarely give ourselves the space for practice." (Natalie Goldberg, American teacher and writer)

Have students freewrite responses to the quotation. Explain that prewriting allows writers to gather ideas to formulate writing plans, which will help lead to successful finished products.

24

Finding Ideas for Writing

Writing begins with looking for something to write about. How do writers find ideas? Often, an everyday experience or a personal interest sparks an idea. But many writers also have special ways, or techniques, they use to find and explore ideas. The following chart shows the ways for finding ideas you'll read about in this section.

PREWRITING TECHNIQUES		
Writer's Journal	Recording experiences and ideas	Page 25
Freewriting	Writing for several minutes about whatever comes to mind	Page 25
Brainstorming	Listing ideas quickly, without judging them	Page 27
Clustering	Brainstorming ideas and connecting the ideas with circles and lines	Page 28
Asking Questions	Asking the *5W–How?* questions	Page 29
Reading and Listening with a Focus	Reading and listening to find specific information	Pages 30–31
Imagining	Using your imagination to think of details	Page 31

For most of your writing assignments, you'll use more than one way to find ideas. For example, you get the idea to write a character sketch of your grandfather from a note in your writer's journal. Then you might use freewriting to recall specific details about him. Feel free to experiment with different ways to find ideas.

Ask volunteers to describe something unusual they saw on the way to school. Then ask students to tell you what they ate for breakfast or lunch yesterday, what they did after school yesterday, and what they plan on doing this afternoon. Write a list of all responses on the chalkboard.

Go through the list and point out how each item could be used as a topic for writing. Emphasize that finding topics for writing need not be a difficult chore.

☞

Writer's Journal

Many writers keep a *writer's journal* in a notebook or computer file to record their experiences, feelings, and ideas. When keeping a journal, try to follow these guidelines:

- Write daily, keeping your journal handy.
- Let your imagination run free. Write down dreams, songs, poems, story ideas. Include drawings.
- Forget about grammar and punctuation. Only your thoughts matter.

EXERCISE 1 ▶ **Keeping a Writer's Journal**
Journal entries will vary. Evaluate students' entries on completion rather than on content.

If you haven't already started a journal, why not do it now? What's on your mind today? Write a journal entry about whatever it is.

COMPUTER NOTE: If you keep your journal on a computer or a floppy disk, you may be able to keep it private by using a password. A password lets you protect a document, so that only people who know your password can read it.

Freewriting

Freewriting means writing whatever pops into your head. You don't judge ideas or worry about wording or punctuation. Freewriting can loosen you up for later writing or can give you ideas for topics. When you freewrite, follow these guidelines:

- Set a time limit of three to five minutes, and keep writing until the time is up.
- Start with a subject that's important to you.
- If you get stuck, just write anything. The important thing is to keep your pen moving.

Another form of freewriting is called *focused freewriting* or *looping*. Here, you choose a word or phrase from your freewriting to use as a starting point. Then you freewrite all over again, using that word or phrase as your subject. This practice helps you to focus your ideas for writing.

MEETING individual NEEDS

LEP/ESL

General Strategies. Although students might feel comfortable with their ability to communicate verbally, chances are good that many are anxious about their writing abilities in English. Having them work with peers in small groups may ease their transition into this area of study.

AT-RISK STUDENTS

Many students have a greater-than-average need to experience success in school work. The prewriting techniques, especially keeping the writer's journal and using freewriting and imagining, provide good opportunities for success.

TECHNOLOGY TIP

Encourage students who use passwords to create passwords that they will be certain to remember. You can suggest they use the name of a person or place or a date that has special meaning, a meaning that others wouldn't be likely to associate with that word or date.

Give students an overview of the lesson by having them read the **Prewriting Techniques** chart on p. 24. Explain that you will cover the material slowly and that there will be plenty of chances to practice the skills.

For some of the prewriting techniques—especially brainstorming, clustering, questioning, and imagining—you may want to model each technique on the chalkboard.

The three **Critical Thinking** features in the lesson are integral parts of the lesson. As you work through these features and the prewriting techniques, you may want to refer students to the writing process pie chart on p. 23 to remind them how the steps of prewriting are linked to the entire writing process.

INTEGRATING THE LANGUAGE ARTS

Literature Link. If your literature textbook contains the selection, you may want to have students read "Crossing" by Philip Booth and speculate about the poet's prewriting. Name each technique listed in the **Prewriting Techniques** chart on p. 24, and have students discuss how Booth might have used these methods to gather information. Be sure to point out, however, that the effect of the poem is achieved by how the poet groups the gathered information. The use of rhythm, rhyme, onomatopoeia, alliteration, and repetition creates the effect of the quickening tempo of a moving train.

ANSWERS
Exercise 2

You will probably want to evaluate students' freewriting on completion rather than on content. However, you could check to see that each student has included both a time and a place.

Here's an example of freewriting notes about pioneers.

Pioneers. Worked hard outside. Kids worked hard, too. Remember pictures of Abe Lincoln splitting logs as a child. Simple life. Families close. Good. Close to nature, but hard life. People died young—too hard. No doctors. Kids died, too. Pioneers. Going across plains. Oxen and horses. Wild animals. Built own houses. Wish I was a pioneer. Snakes. Wolves. Glad I wasn't a pioneer.

EXERCISE 2 ▶ **Using Freewriting**

Think of a specific time and place that's important to you—perhaps your kitchen on Thanksgiving morning or the school parking lot at 3:00 P.M. Write it on your paper. Now, freewrite for three or four minutes about the place. Just put down whatever comes to mind.

You can proceed through the lesson by asking a student volunteer to read the material or by reading it aloud yourself. Encourage students to study the material carefully and to ask questions if they don't understand.

Sometimes exercises such as **Exercise 4** on p. 28 build on previous exercises, so you probably will want students to save their work from day to day. Encourage students to keep completed exercises in their notebooks as ideas for future writing assignments.

Brainstorming

In *brainstorming,* say what comes to mind in response to a word without stopping to judge what's said. You can brainstorm alone, but group or partner brainstorming is more fun because hearing other people's ideas helps you think of even more ideas. When you brainstorm:

- Write down a subject at the top of a piece of paper. (In a group, use the chalkboard.)
- List every idea about the subject that comes to mind. (In a group, have one person list the ideas.)
- Keep going until you run out of ideas.

Here are some brainstorming notes about teen culture.

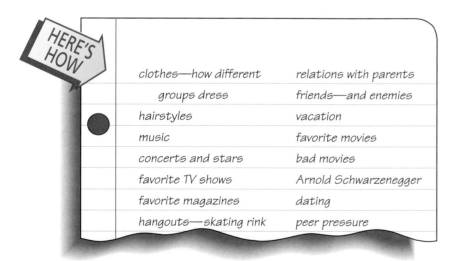

clothes—how different	relations with parents
groups dress	friends—and enemies
hairstyles	vacation
music	favorite movies
concerts and stars	bad movies
favorite TV shows	Arnold Schwarzenegger
favorite magazines	dating
hangouts—skating rink	peer pressure

EXERCISE 3 ▶ **Using Brainstorming**

Get together with a partner and have a brainstorming session. Use one of the topics listed below or make up your own. Make a list of your ideas.

1. fads
2. true adventures
3. bicycling
4. summer camps
5. space exploration
6. scary movies

COOPERATIVE LEARNING

To ensure that all members of brainstorming groups contribute to the total effort, you may want to have students initial each contribution. A good way to encourage participation is to require that each student in the group be responsible for at least two items in the final list.

ADVANCED STUDENTS

After partners choose topics in **Exercise 3,** suggest that the partners briefly research the topics before brainstorming. This will give students a wider base of information from which to gather ideas.

ANSWERS
Exercise 3

Lists will vary. You may want to evaluate students' brainstorming on completion rather than on content.

Students might benefit from guided practice on the prewriting techniques and on constructing charts and tree diagrams. Select a topic of interest to students and ask volunteers to work at the chalkboard while the other students provide ideas. Using the same topic for all of the prewriting techniques should make it easier for students to compare the techniques. As students make suggestions, you can guide their work and point out other ways of handling the ideas.

CRITICAL THINKING

Analysis. The clustering technique often involves perceiving cause-and-effect relationships among items in the cluster. For example, in the **Here's How** model cluster diagram, there is a causal link between the item *followed buffalo* and the items *how they lived* and *clothes made from skins.*

Remind students to watch for cause-and-effect links among their ideas. Also, as they generate ideas, suggest that they think about the effect a particular fact might have.

ANSWERS

Exercise 4

Responses will vary, but clusters should show clearly how ideas are related.

Clustering

In *clustering,* sometimes called *webbing,* you brainstorm ideas and connect them with circles and lines that show how the ideas are related. To make a cluster diagram, follow these guidelines:

- Write your subject on your paper and circle it.
- Around the subject, write whatever ideas about it occur to you. Circle these ideas. Draw lines connecting them with the subject.
- When your ideas make you think of related ideas, connect them with circles and lines.

Here's a cluster diagram on the lives of Plains Indians in the eighteenth and nineteenth centuries. The two main ideas are *where they lived* and *how they lived.*

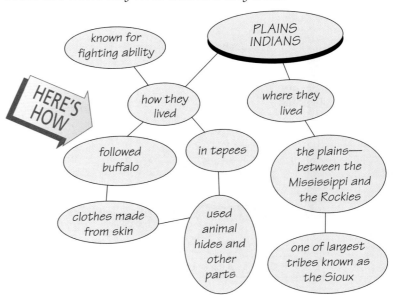

EXERCISE 4 ▶ **Using Clustering**

Turn your brainstorming notes from Exercise 3 into a cluster diagram. Or pick another topic important to you. You can model your cluster diagram after the one above.

INDEPENDENT PRACTICE

Most of the exercises in this lesson can be done independently, but **Exercises 3** (p. 27), **4** (p. 28), and **10** (p. 40) are probably best handled in class so you can monitor students' work.

ASSESSMENT

You can assess students' understanding of prewriting techniques by evaluating their responses to the exercises or by checking the prewriting stage of previous writing assignments.

☛

Prewriting **29**

Asking Questions

Reporters often get information for news stories by asking the *5W-How? questions: Who? What? Where? When? Why?* and *How?* Not every question word applies to every subject. And sometimes you'll think of more than one question for a particular question word. If you were writing a report for your local environmental club, you could ask these questions. The notes in parentheses tell how you might look for the answers.

HERE'S HOW

> TOPIC: How Gorillas Might Be Saved from Extinction
>
> WHO?   Who is working on the effort to save gorillas from extinction? (Check at the library for names and addresses of groups.)
>
> WHAT?   What is needed to save the gorillas? (Read books and articles; interview a zoo director.)
>
> WHAT?   What is done with money given to save gorillas? (Contact groups working to save gorillas.)
>
> WHERE? Where do gorillas live? (Check in an encyclopedia.)
>
> WHY?   Why are gorillas in danger? (Read books and articles; interview a zoo director.)
>
> HOW?   How can we save gorillas? (Check in a book, or call the education department at a zoo.)

EXERCISE 5 ▶ Asking the *5W-How?* Questions

You're a reporter for your town newspaper, and you're writing a feature article about the local skating rink. Write

A DIFFERENT APPROACH

Most news stories begin with a lead paragraph that incorporates the answers to the *5W-How?* questions in order of their importance to the story. For example, if the story is about a person, the question *Who?* usually will be answered first and the name of the person will be given. If the story is about a fire, the question *What?* is most important and the fire will be mentioned first. Bring a few news stories to class to show students how the questions are used. Tell students the basic topic of the story and ask them to predict which of the questions will be answered first.

ANSWERS
Exercise 5

Responses will vary, but students should include at least one of each kind of the *5W-How?* questions.

Reversing the process might help students grasp the concept of how prewriting techniques can provide ideas for writing. You may want to write various paragraphs on an overhead transparency and help students analyze the prewriting techniques that the writers might have used. You could use the same paragraphs to demonstrate the organizational techniques mentioned in this chapter.

INTEGRATING THE LANGUAGE ARTS

Reading Link. Many students never learn how to vary their reading rate to suit specific purposes. In addition to providing a prewriting technique, focused reading is an opportunity to encourage students to vary their reading speed.

You may want to make up an exercise on using the parts of this book. Ask students to use the index, table of contents, and other book parts to locate specific information. Your questions might include the following examples:

1. On what page would you find a rule for using commas to separate items in a series?
2. How many pages deal with using the library?
3. What are the main headings in the chapter on writing effective sentences?

ANSWERS

Exercise 6

Responses will vary. You may want to have students list the sources of their information.

down some *5W-How?* questions that would help you gather the information you need. Your purpose is to inform parents that the skating rink is a safe place for teens to be.

Reading and Listening

Sometimes you'll write about things outside your own experience. So how do you get the information you need? You can read and listen.

Reading.   Reading sources include books, magazines, newspapers, and brochures. It saves time to look for your topic by checking the tables of contents and indexes to find the exact pages you need to read. You don't need to read everything. You can skim the pages until you find something about your topic. Then slow down and take notes on the main ideas and important details.

EXERCISE 6 ▶ **Reading with a Focus**

Which of the following American Indian peoples interests you most: Mohawk, Seminole, Navajo, Cherokee, or Nez Perce? Look in an encyclopedia or another book to find the answers to the following questions.

1. Where did the tribe originally live?
2. What did they build to live in?
3. What foods did they eat?
4. What kinds of clothes did they wear?
5. Are they known for some kind of art, such as beadwork, pottery, jewelry, or basket making?

CLOSURE

Ask students how they might use the prewriting techniques to generate ideas for a special assembly program at school. Point out that the kind of thinking involved in planning a piece of writing is the same kind they might use in other aspects of their lives.

Cont. on p. 35

Listening.   By listening, you can get a lot of information from speeches, radio and TV programs, interviews, audiotapes, or videotapes. To prepare, make a list of questions about your topic. Then, while you listen, take notes on the main ideas and important details.

EXERCISE 7 ▶   **Listening with a Focus**

Responses will vary according to the broadcasts students choose.

Listen to a radio broadcast of the top songs of the week (pop, rock, country, or gospel), then answer the following questions. Compare lists with your classmates if you listen to different countdowns.

1. Of the songs you heard, which three do you like best?
2. Who recorded each of these three songs? What number in the countdown is each?
3. What radio station was the countdown on?
4. Who is the host of the show?

Imagining

Can you imagine that you're someone else or somewhere else? Imagining gives you creative ideas for your writing. Trigger your imagination with *"What if?" questions.* "What if?" questions can be silly or serious. Here are examples.

1. What if I became a grown-up overnight?
2. What if something in my life—like TV—didn't exist?
3. What if people could fly like birds?
4. What if everyone looked exactly alike?

EXERCISE 8 ▶   **Using Imagining**

You're developing the plot of a mystery story for a class magazine. The story is about two eighth-graders on a camping trip with their families. Use your imagination and write five "What if?" questions that will help you work out a plot.

EXAMPLES   *What if one of the campers disappears?*
What if strange tracks are found by the river?

ANSWERS
Exercise 8

Encourage students to write questions pertaining to the aspects of plot such as characters, conflict, and setting.

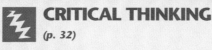

TEACHING *ANALYZING "WHAT IF?" ANSWERS*

Before students begin the **Critical Thinking Exercise,** help them develop criteria for determining the value of answers to "What if?" questions. Have the groups complete the exercise and share their answers. To close, have a volunteer explain how "What if?" questions are useful in writing.

MEETING *individual* NEEDS

LEP/ESL

General Strategies. Recent immigrants to the United States might come from cultures in which plastic packaging is uncommon. By sharing experiences from their cultures, they might help put the issue of packaging materials in perspective for American students who are familiar with the commercial packaging used in this country.

COOPERATIVE LEARNING

You could have students work in groups of three to complete the **Critical Thinking Exercise.** One of the first things the groups should do is to decide how they will make their decisions about keeping or discarding answers. They should start out with some simple criteria such as practicality and feasibility. They also should decide if they are going to operate on a majority-rule basis or if they will keep an answer even if only one member thinks it's worthwhile. You may want to monitor closely the early stages of the group work to prevent farfetched answers from becoming the norm in any group.

ANSWERS
Critical Thinking Exercise

Responses will vary. Check the practicality of answers that students list to be sure each is suitable for a report.

CRITICAL THINKING
Analyzing "What if?" Answers

When you ask "What if?" questions for creative writing, you might use any answer, no matter how unusual. But you can also use "What if?" questions to help you explore possibilities for other types of writing—such as reports. These answers need to be more practical, however. For instance, possible answers to *What if stores no longer bag items people buy?* could include these:

1. People could bring their own bags to stores to carry out items purchased.
2. People could make or buy cloth bags to be used over and over.
3. People could hand-carry all the items that they buy in the store.
4. People could fasten helium balloons to items and float them home.

Thinking about these answers, you might decide that answers 1 and 2 would be practical and could help you develop a report on recycling. Answer 3 would work only if people purchased just one or two items. Answer 4 is creative but not practical.

CRITICAL THINKING EXERCISE:
Analyzing Useful Answers

Now it's your turn. Think about all the items you buy that are enclosed in plastic—in department stores, drugstores, grocery stores, and fast-food restaurants. Use the question *What if no plastic could be used for packaging?* Or make up another "What if?" question. On your own or with a partner or small group, give some answers to the question. Then look over your answers and make a list of the ones that could be used for a report.

OBJECTIVES

- To analyze a particular audience to determine how best to persuade that audience
- To rewrite a professional model to persuade a particular audience

TEACHING *ANALYZING AUDIENCE*

You may want to start the lesson by asking students if they always act the same no matter where they are or whom they're with. [Most will probably say that they adjust their speech and mannerisms accordingly.] Explain that in this same way, writers adapt their material depending on their audiences and purposes.

 *Prewriting*

Thinking About Purpose and Audience

Most people want to know why they're doing something. *Why* can't I watch this TV program? *Why* do I have to go to bed so early? In the same way, ask yourself, *Why am I writing?* This chart shows the basic purposes you might have for writing and the forms of writing you might use for these different purposes.

MAIN PURPOSE	FORMS OF WRITING
To express your feelings	Journal entry, letter, personal essay
To be creative	Short story, poem, play
To explain or inform	Science or history writing, news story, biography, autobiography, travel essay, office memo
To persuade	Persuasive essay, letter to the editor, advertisement, political speech

Before you write, also ask yourself, *Who will read my writing?* Consider your audience—the readers.

CRITICAL THINKING

Analyzing Audience

Why do you need to think about your audience? Because you're writing to tell them something. You want them to understand what you're saying. You don't want to tell them what they already know—that's boring, like seeing a movie you've already seen.

INTEGRATING THE LANGUAGE ARTS

Speaking Link. One way to make students aware of the need to tailor what and how they write to a particular audience is to have them role-play situations involving different audiences. Ask volunteers to act out scenarios in which a student loses a valuable watch. First, have the student explain the loss to his or her parents. Next, have students role-play the same situation, this time substituting the parents' role with that of a friend.

Discuss how the two situations differed in terms of the student's vocabulary, tone of voice, selection of details, and body language. Remind students that the audience controls much of what a speaker (and writer) says and does.

After students read the text, discuss with them how the audience and purpose dictated what the writer would include in the examples about trains. Guide students in using the three questions to evaluate both examples.

Before students rewrite the paragraph in the **Critical Thinking Exercise** on p. 35, encourage them to list the objections that sponsors might have to considering the trip. Addressing these objections in their letters indicates that they are keeping their audience in mind.

You may want to have the groups read their letters aloud to the rest of the class. As closure, ask a volunteer to summarize the importance of considering audience and purpose when writing.

MEETING *individual* NEEDS

LEP/ESL

Spanish and French. Speakers of Spanish and French have a bit of an advantage when it comes to audience analysis because these languages have a sense of audience built into their pronoun systems. In both languages, one set of second person pronouns is used with audiences composed of family members, close friends, and children. A second set, consisting of more-formal pronouns, is used in all other situations. Thus, speakers of these languages intuitively learn how to adjust their speech to suit their audience.

Take advantage of this fact by pointing out that just as the Spanish and French adapt pronouns to the audience, English adapts tone and words to the audience.

For example, your hobby is trains. Here's an example of how you might analyze two different purposes and audiences for writing about your hobby.

HERE'S HOW

AUDIENCE:	eighth-graders
PURPOSE:	to inform
WHAT THEY NEED TO KNOW:	different trains I've ridden
	why I like steam trains best
	where they still run
	how steam engines work
	the difference between steam and diesel engines
	the oldest steam train I've seen

AUDIENCE:	fifth-graders
PURPOSE:	to describe
WHAT THEY NEED TO KNOW:	how I became interested in trains
	what I like about trains
	my trip to the Green Bay Railroad Museum
	my most exciting steam-train ride
	nearby train trips the students could take

Before you write, ask yourself these questions about your audience—your readers.

- Why is my audience reading my writing? Do they expect to be entertained, informed, or persuaded?
- What does my audience already know about my topic? (You don't want to bore your readers by telling them things they already know.)
- What does my audience want or need to know about my topic? What vocabulary and type of language should I use?

Cont. from p. 31

EXTENSION

Challenge students to create analogies for the writing process with an emphasis on the prewriting stage. For example, the writing process could be compared to making a stew. The gathering of ingredients and equipment is the prewriting stage. Cooking the stew is the writing stage. Tasting and adjusting flavors is the evaluating and revising stage. Serving the stew for all to enjoy is the publishing stage.

 CRITICAL THINKING EXERCISE:
Analyzing Audience

The following paragraph is from a chapter in a travel guide about Zion National Park in Utah. The author's purpose is to tell about his experiences as a park guest and to inform readers about the park's challenges and beauty.

> It took me a little more than half a day to cover the five-mile round-trip hike from the trailhead on Zion Canyon Road to Angels Landing; parts of it were fairly tough going. It's almost 1,500 feet uphill, and the final stretch involves holding on to handrails along a steep, narrow path, but the time and energy were more than worth it. Every step of the way opened a new vista of the "Land of Rainbow Canyons" in southern Utah. I traced the vertical walls of red sandstone as they gradually merged upward into white, while beneath them shales of purple, pink, orange, and yellow revealed what surely must be some of the most brilliantly colored rock in the world.
>
> Michael Frome, *National Park Guide*

You want to persuade a parent, the leader of your scout troop, or another adult sponsor to take you to Zion National Park. The adult you want to persuade knows very little about the park and may be reluctant to even consider the trip. In a small group, discuss ways to change this paragraph for your purpose and audience. Then, rewrite the paragraph in the form of a letter to the adult.

ANSWERS
Critical Thinking Exercise

Letters will vary, but students should choose tone and vocabulary to suit their audiences.

INTEGRATING THE LANGUAGE ARTS

Literature Link. If the selections are contained in your literature textbook or are available in your library, you could show students how audience and purpose can influence a writer's presentation by having them read *The Diary of Anne Frank* by Frances Goodrich and Albert Hackett and "A Tragedy Revealed: A Heroine's Last Days" by Ernst Schnabel. Both works are about Anne Frank. The first work is a play and the second is an article published in *Life* magazine.

After students have read both selections, have them offer suggestions about why the authors chose that genre to present their ideas. [Students might say that Schnabel's primary aim is to inform; however, informing is the secondary aim for Goodrich and Hackett. As a reporter, Schnabel's audience expects accurate, factual information. However, because theater audiences expect to be entertained, some of the facts are generally changed or expanded for dramatization.]

SELECTION AMENDMENT
Description of change: excerpted
Rationale: to focus on the concept of audience presented in this chapter

35

ARRANGING IDEAS

Before students arrange their ideas in a particular type of order, they need to select the details that they are going to include in their compositions. Remind students that after prewriting, they should look over the information they have generated to eliminate the ideas that don't fit their purposes and audiences. This will help keep the writing unified, and it will make the process of arranging information easier.

 *Prewriting*

Arranging Ideas

Once you have gathered ideas to write about, the next step in the writing process is arranging them. You always need to arrange your ideas so that readers can follow them.

Types of Order

The following chart shows four common ways of arranging ideas. The right-hand column gives examples of types of writing that arrange ideas in each way.

ARRANGING IDEAS		
TYPE OF ORDER	DEFINITION	EXAMPLES
Chronological	Narration: order that presents events as they happen in time	Story, narrative poem, explanation of a process, history, biography, drama
Spatial	Description: order that describes objects according to location	Descriptions (near to far; left to right; top to bottom)
Importance	Evaluation: order that gives details from least to most important or the reverse	Persuasive writing; description; explanation (main idea and supporting details); evaluative writing
Logical	Classification: order that relates items and groups	Definitions; classifications; comparisons and contrasts

 REFERENCE NOTE: For more information on arranging ideas, see page 98.

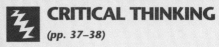

CRITICAL THINKING
(pp. 37–38)

OBJECTIVE

- To analyze the order of development used in paragraphs

TEACHING *ARRANGING IDEAS*

Before assigning the **Critical Thinking Exercise,** discuss with students the **Arranging Ideas** chart on the previous page. You could use the first paragraph of the **Critical Thinking Exercise** to guide students through the process of identifying order. Then have students complete the second paragraph as independent practice. As a

CRITICAL THINKING

Arranging Ideas

How do you know how to arrange your ideas when you write? Sometimes the order you use depends on the kind of information you want to present. For example, your class schedule is printed in the order in which your classes are held (*chronological order*) because class times are most important. Your teacher's list of students is in alphabetical order because it's easier to locate names that way. Sometimes it makes sense to describe items close to you, then those a little further away, and end with items in the distance (*spatial order*). Or you might choose to list your reasons for an opinion with the most important one last because you think this arrangement focuses the reader's attention on your final, best argument (*order of importance*). When you write, your topic, purpose, and audience help you decide which order is best.

CRITICAL THINKING EXERCISE:
Analyzing the Order of Ideas

Use your new skills to assess how the ideas in the following paragraphs are organized. With two or three classmates, figure out the type of order used in each paragraph. Then, discuss how you identified the order.

1. Some people really want to be rich. Money is nice, and I want to have enough. But being happy seems more important to me. I know some rich, miserable people, so money must not always make people happy. Okay, so I want to be happy. Next, I want to have time to do things I like to do, like read and be with my friends. I don't like to be rushed all of the time. Then, I guess getting along better with my family would be great.

LESS-ADVANCED STUDENTS

Before assigning the **Critical Thinking Exercise,** you may want to provide models of the different types of order. These models should help students better understand the various possibilities of organization.

ANSWERS
Critical Thinking Exercise

1. order of importance; writer gives details from most important to least important

2. spatial order; description moves from outer edges to the main focus in the center of the yard

2.   Getting a trampoline really changed the way our yard looked. My little brother's swing set had to be moved from the middle of the yard to the southeast corner. The birdbath was moved to the front yard. The two planters filled with petunias were moved from beside the swing set to near the west fence. The trampoline takes up the whole center of the yard now. Everything else kind of lurks around the edges.

Using Visuals to Organize Ideas

It's hard to understand anything unless it's put in some kind of order—as you know if you've ever tried to find a pair of socks under your bed. The same is true with writing. Visuals—such as charts, diagrams, or other graphic layouts—can help you bring order to your writing.

Charts. To create a chart, think about the different types of information you have. For example, if you gather ideas for a report on gorillas in the wild, you might organize it by making a chart like the following one. You might plan to discuss how many of each kind of gorilla remain in the wild.

Kind	Location	Number in the Wild
Western lowland gorilla	Western Africa	35,000–45,000
Eastern lowland gorilla	Eastern Zaire	3,000–5,000
Mountain gorilla	Rwanda, Zaire, Uganda	3,000–5,000

MEETING individual NEEDS

LEARNING STYLES

Kinetic Learners. Some students might need help using charts to organize ideas. One way to help students is to have them write the cells of their charts on individual index cards and then to practice arranging them in the proper order. You can have students start with one horizontal line of the chart at first and then work up to including the other lines as they gain confidence with the idea.

38

Tree Diagrams.   A tree diagram is another way of organizing main ideas and details. Here is a tree diagram for a report on Matthew Henson, an explorer with Admiral Peary on the first expedition to reach the North Pole.

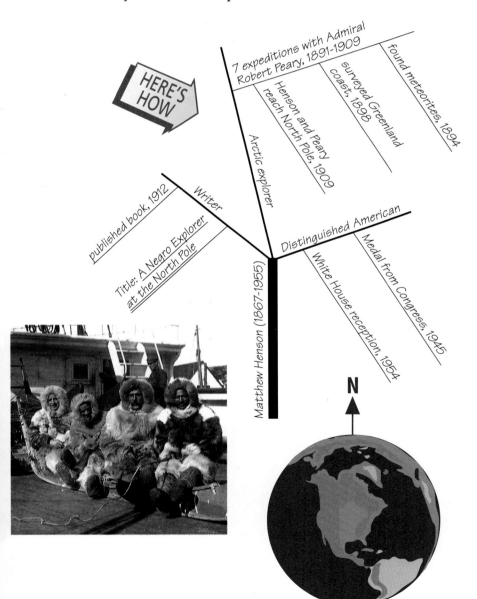

HERE'S HOW

7 expeditions with Admiral Robert Peary, 1891-1909

found meteorites, 1894

surveyed Greenland coast, 1898

Henson and Peary reach North Pole, 1909

Arctic explorer

published book, 1912

Writer

Title: A Negro Explorer at the North Pole

Distinguished American

Medal from Congress, 1945

White House reception, 1954

Matthew Henson (1867-1955)

N

MEETING *individual* NEEDS

LESS-ADVANCED STUDENTS

To simplify **Exercise 9** and to help students feel more comfortable with charting, provide the chart's headings and let students fill in the information. You can similarly simplify **Exercise 10** by drawing the tree and strategically placing some of the answers on the diagram.

COOPERATIVE LEARNING

Because classifying details requires higher-level thinking skills, you may want to have students work in groups of three or four for both **Exercises 9** and **10**. Make sure the groups are balanced, with advanced and less-advanced students in each group.

ANSWERS
Exercise 10

Responses will vary, but diagrams should show clearly how the ideas are related.

EXERCISE 9   **Making a Chart**

With a little practice, charts become easy to create. Try your hand at it. Make a chart to organize the following notes about the advantages and disadvantages of having school year-round.

a   Students don't forget skills over long summer vacation.
d   Students can't take long vacations in the summer.
a   Students can learn more.
d   Students can't earn money at summer jobs.
d   Kids can't go to summer camps.
a   School schedules could more nearly match parents' work schedules.
a or d   Schools are used year-round.

EXERCISE 10   **Making a Tree Diagram**

Tree diagrams help you "see" the structure of ideas. Make a tree diagram using the following notes on the sources of income for eighth-graders. You'll have three sources—parents, outdoor jobs, and indoor jobs.

pet care	kitchen help	running errands
yardwork	gifts of money	posting signs or
allowance	baby-sitting	notices
delivering papers or fliers	pay for extra jobs at home	washing cars

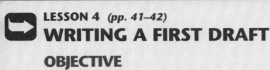
WRITING A FIRST DRAFT

OBJECTIVE

- To write the first draft of a paragraph

TEACHING THE LESSON

The assignment in **Exercise 11** on p. 42 is independent of the work students have done in the prewriting lesson of the chapter, so you may want to remind them that they should use one or more prewriting techniques to generate ideas. Students might find ideas in their writing journals, but if not, they will have to spend some time prewriting.

Writing a First Draft

You've done your prewriting by identifying a topic, purpose, and audience, and by organizing your information. Now it's time to start writing.

There's no one right way to write a paper. Some people write their first drafts quickly, just trying to get their ideas on paper. Others go slowly, carefully shaping each sentence and paragraph. These tips may help you.

- Use your prewriting plans as a guide.
- Write freely. Focus on expressing your ideas clearly.
- As you write, you may discover new ideas. Include these ideas in your draft.
- Don't worry about spelling and grammar errors. You can correct them later.

Here's a first draft of a personal essay. You'll find that there are mistakes in it. First drafts always need some corrections. Notice that the writer makes a note to check on something. The writer will replace the note with the proper information and will correct mistakes in a later stage of the writing process.

Last year, my family went to the Yucatán Peninsula of Mexico. We stayed in Mérida, which is an ancient city that has many neat buildings. There are big arches and sculptures and parks. The best part of our trip, though, was going to the Chichén Itzá ruins to see the pyramids. I used to think that pyramids were only in Egypt. [Note: look up name] is the biggest pyramid in Chichén Itzá. It has nine levels, and has a temple on top. It was built a thousand years ago over a smaller, older pyramid. Inside the smaller pyramid is a big cat carved out of limestone. After we came home, we all wanted to go back. The cat statue has green jade eyes. I've never seen such interesting things before. We didn't have enough time to see everything.

PROGRAM MANAGER

WRITING A FIRST DRAFT

- **Instructional Support** For practice on writing a rough draft, see **Writing: Two Approaches** in *Practicing the Writing Process,* p. 7.

QUOTATION FOR THE DAY

"That is a good book which is opened with expectation and closed with profit." (Louisa May Alcott, 1832–1888, American author)

Initiate a discussion of books students have recently read. Ask how students feel they might have profited from what they read. [Students might say that they've learned lessons, gained insight, or entertained themselves.] Remind students that when they read, they also view the way another writer works with language.

They will also have to figure out how to organize the material they want to use in their paragraphs. You could have students prewrite in class under your supervision and assign the drafts as homework. Collect the drafts to assess students' understanding.

CLOSURE

On the day the drafts are due, you may want to spend some time in class talking about how students feel about the writing process so far. ■

MEETING *individual* NEEDS

LEP/ESL

General Strategies. In asking students to write the first drafts, you could give them an alternative topic to the one suggested in **Exercise 11** (which has students consider the one thing they would like to change about themselves). As a confidence builder, they might decide what they like best about themselves. Ask them to give concrete examples of this behavior or trait.

ANSWERS
Exercise 11

Responses will vary. You probably will not want to penalize the students for errors in spelling and grammar at this stage.

WRITING NOTE

When your friends call you on the telephone, you almost always recognize their voices. That's because each friend speaks in a different way—loudly or softly, with a different accent. And each friend has certain words that he or she uses. That makes your friend's voice almost like a fingerprint—no two are exactly alike. And when you write, you have a voice, too. It's made up of the words and kinds of sentences that you use. In your writing, work very hard to have a natural voice—one that sounds like you. Don't use big words or long sentences just because they sound "important." Even when your writing is formal—like a research report—let your natural voice come through.

EXERCISE 11▶   **Writing a First Draft**

If you could change one thing about yourself, what would it be? Do you daydream about being a better athlete, a talented piano player, or a computer wizard? Think about what you'd like to change. Then write a first draft of a paragraph telling what you'd like to change and why.

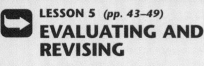

MOTIVATION

Tell students that there are times, such as in test taking and in impromptu speaking when evaluating and revising are not possible. Discuss with students the importance of being able to rethink the content and form of a first draft.

Cont. on p. 46

Evaluating and Revising

Evaluating and revising are two different steps in improving your writing, but you usually do them at the same time.

> Evaluating—deciding on the strengths and weaknesses of your paper
>
> Revising—making the necessary changes to improve your paper

Evaluating

You evaluate writing all the time, whether you think about it or not. You like some books and hate others. You find some written directions easy to follow and others hard. You enjoy certain comic strips but not others.

Self-Evaluation. Because you're so close to your own writing, evaluating it is harder than judging someone else's work. These tips may help make the process easier.

Tips for Self-Evaluation

1. **Reading Carefully.** Read your paper more than once. First, read for *content* (what you say). Next, read for *organization* (how you order ideas). Finally, read for *style* (how you use words and sentences).

2. **Listening Carefully.** Read your paper aloud to yourself. *Listen* to what you've said. You may notice that the ideas don't flow smoothly or that some sentences sound awkward.

3. **Taking Time.** Set your draft aside. Come back to it later and read through it. You'll find it's easier to be objective about it after a little time away.

Peer Evaluation. Most writers, even people who make a living by writing, have someone else read and eval-

PROGRAM MANAGER

EVALUATING AND REVISING

- **Reinforcement/Reteaching** See **Revision Transparencies 1** and **2.** For suggestions on how to tie the transparencies to instruction, review teacher's notes in *Fine Art and Instructional Transparencies for Writing,* pp. 85, 87.

- **Ongoing Assessment** To help students apply evaluation techniques and identify the main ways to revise, see **Evaluation, Peer Evaluation,** and **Revising** in *Practicing the Writing Process,* pp. 8–10.

- **Assessment/Reflection** To assess student work and evaluate progress, see **Portfolio Forms** in *Portfolio Assessment,* pp. 5–17.

QUOTATION FOR THE DAY

"Wisely, and slow; they stumble that run fast." (William Shakespeare, 1564–1616, English playwright and poet)

Ask students how this statement from Shakespeare's play *Romeo and Juliet* could apply to the evaluating and revising stage of the writing process. [At this stage the writer should slow down to carefully evaluate and revise to ensure a clear and interesting final product.]

OBJECTIVE

• To evaluate a paragraph using standards for good writing

TEACHING *EVALUATING WRITING*

This feature gives five standards for good writing and refers students to a more extensive list. Before assigning the **Critical Thinking Exercise,** you'll probably want to discuss the five standards to make sure students understand what each item means. For example, to extend the third standard, explain chronological order, spatial order,

LEP/ESL

General Strategies. At this critical stage of the writing process, you may want to spend a short amount of time with each of your English-language learners to emphasize the positive aspects of their drafts. Your individual attention should bolster their confidence and help minimize confusion. Most students want to know if they are headed in the right direction; however, they may feel too shy to ask for guidance.

AT-RISK STUDENTS

Some students miss a great deal of school and are thus unable to profit much from group activities. You may want to emphasize self-evaluation with these students to make sure they have sufficient skills to independently evaluate their writing.

44 WRITING HANDBOOK   *Process*

uate their work. You can get advice from others by sharing your writing with your classmates in a peer-evaluation group. In the group, you'll sometimes be the writer whose work is evaluated. Other times you'll be the evaluator.

EVALUATION GUIDELINES

Guidelines for the Writer
1. Make a list of questions for the peer evaluator. Which parts of your paper worry you?
2. Keep an open mind. Don't take your evaluators' suggestions as personal criticism.

Guidelines for the Peer Evaluator
1. Tell the writer what's good about the paper. Give the writer some encouragement.
2. Focus on content and organization. The writer will catch spelling and grammar errors when proofreading.
3. Be sensitive to the writer's feelings. State your suggestions as questions, such as "What does this mean?" and "Can you give an example?"

After your classmates evaluate your paper, think about the comments. Which comments are most helpful? Remember that the final decisions about changes are yours.

CRITICAL THINKING

Evaluating Writing

When you *evaluate* writing, you judge it against a set of standards. You decide whether or not the writing meets each standard. Here are some standards you might use to evaluate your writing. (More detailed standards for evaluating writing appear on page 48.)

and order of importance. You could discuss the transitional words and phrases that help ideas flow smoothly, as mentioned in the fourth standard. You can assess students' understanding by evaluating how well they handle the exercise.

To close the lesson, ask students to take another look at the standards and to pick out the one standard they think is most important for good writing. [Most of them will probably say that the fifth standard—that the writing is interesting—is most important.] Ask students to give their ideas about what's interesting. ⚡

1. The writing has a clear main idea.
2. The main idea is supported with details.
3. The order of the ideas makes sense.
4. The ideas flow smoothly.
5. The writing is interesting.

⚡ CRITICAL THINKING EXERCISE:
Evaluating a Paragraph

Do you like true-life adventure stories? Read the following paragraph. Then evaluate it, using the standards listed above. Write two comments on what's good about the paragraph. Write two comments on what needs to be improved.

> Can you imagine being lost? That's what happened to Steven Callahan, and he wrote about it in the book *Adrift*. He was finally rescued by some fishermen. Callahan's boat sank in the Atlantic Ocean, and he survived in an inflatable raft. He was lost at sea for 76 days. He survived storms, shark sightings, and a diet of raw fish. And, oh, yes, there's something I need to tell you. He spotted ships, but they passed him by. No one else ever survived so long at sea in an inflatable raft. His story is a great one.

⚡

MEETING *individual* NEEDS

LEP/ESL

General Strategies. Students who don't read English well might need help reading the paragraph in the **Critical Thinking Exercise** to evaluate it effectively. You may want to pair them with other students who can read the paragraph aloud. Because students might be shy about having a peer read to them, another alternative is to tape the reading of the paragraph and furnish individual tape players and headphones for privacy.

ANSWERS
Critical Thinking Exercise

Answers may vary. Students will probably comment positively on the paragraph's clear ideas and interesting details. The negative comments might include that not all of the ideas are presented in an order that makes sense. (The sentence "He was finally rescued by some fishermen" is out of place.) In addition, all of the ideas don't flow smoothly.

Cont. from p. 43
TEACHING THE LESSON

First, you may want to refer students to the pie chart on p. 23 as an introduction to how evaluating and revising fit into the writing process. Then have students read **Evaluating** starting on p. 43, and discuss with them the pros and cons of self evaluation and peer evaluation. The **Critical Think-** ing feature focuses on an important point that you may want to emphasize—that a set of standards is used to evaluate writing. As students read **Revising**, point out the importance of their familiarity with the symbols for proofreading and revising that are given on p. 54. Spend time carefully discussing the handwritten revisions of the model paragraph on p. 47. Discussing the **Guidelines**

A DIFFERENT APPROACH

If you have access to tape recorders, you may want to have students tape readings of their drafts by other students. They can then listen to the reading as they follow along in their text. If you decide to have students use this technique, emphasize to the readers that they should read the drafts exactly as they are written. Students should not mentally edit the work as they read.

Revising

Many writers consider revising the most important stage in writing. They have their first ideas down on paper, and now they can add finishing touches. They may revise their work five or more times before they're satisfied with it.

When you revise, you make handwritten corrections on your paper. You then write or type a new copy. If you have a word processor, you'll find revising easier. You can make changes directly on the draft file and print out a new copy. Use the following techniques to revise.

REVISING	
TECHNIQUE	EXAMPLE
1. **Add.** Add new information. Add words, sentences, and whole paragraphs.	Many of the Amish still live much as they did ^when they came to the United States more than 250 years ago.
2. **Cut.** Take out repeated or unnecessary information and unrelated ideas.	~~They haven't changed much.~~ The women wear long dresses and bonnets; the men wear dark suits and wide-brimmed hats.
3. **Replace.** Take out weak or awkward wording. Replace with precise words or details.	Many Amish use no ~~new things~~ (modern conveniences,) not even ~~like~~ electricity or telephones.
4. **Reorder.** Move information, sentences, and paragraphs for logical order.	They use mostly horse-drawn machinery and make their living by farming.

Here's the personal essay from page 41. It has been revised, using the four revision techniques. To understand the changes, see the chart of proofreading and revision symbols on page 54. Notice how the writer has answered the note in the rough draft.

Last year, my family went to the Yucatán Peninsula of Mexico. We stayed in Mérida, which is an ancient city that has many ~~neat~~ ^beautiful^ buildings. There are big arches and sculptures and parks. ^(in the city)^ The best part of our trip, though, was going to the Chichén Itzá ruins to see the pyramids. ~~I used to think that pyramids were only in Egypt. [Note: look up name]~~ ^El Castillo^ is the biggest pyramid in Chichén Itzá. It has nine levels, and has a temple on top. It was built a thousand years ago over a smaller, older pyramid. Inside the smaller pyramid is a ~~big cat~~ ^jaguar^ carved out of limestone. ⟨After we came home, we all wanted to go back.⟩ The cat statue has green jade eyes. I've never seen such interesting things before. We didn't have enough time to see everything.

You'll learn more about evaluating and revising different kinds of writing in later chapters. But the following general guidelines apply to all kinds of writing.

RETEACHING

Using the **Guidelines for Evaluating and Revising** chart as a guide, conference with students about the paragraphs they wrote in **Exercise 11.** Although this procedure takes time, it guarantees that each student will get the guidance that he or she needs.

CLOSURE

Discuss with students how the evaluating and revising process can differ for writers. Many writers evaluate and revise as they write. Others write freely and evaluate later. Most professional writers evaluate and revise many times before publishing.

48 WRITING HANDBOOK *Process*

COOPERATIVE LEARNING

Peer evaluation provides one of the best opportunities for cooperative learning, but students need time to get used to the process. Don't be alarmed if the peer-evaluation groups don't seem to have a great deal to offer each other at first. One way you can help students feel comfortable with peer evaluation is to participate in the process yourself. Write the same assignment the students do and join one of the groups. Be careful not to dominate the group (students will naturally look to you for leadership), but do model for students how a group member should work within the group. After you work with all of the groups in the class in this way, you'll probably notice considerable improvement in how students evaluate each other's work.

GUIDELINES FOR EVALUATING AND REVISING

EVALUATION GUIDE	REVISION TECHNIQUE
CONTENT	
1 Is the writing interesting?	**Add** examples, an anecdote (brief story), dialogue, and details. **Cut** repeated or boring details.
2 Does the writing achieve its purpose?	**Add** explanations, examples, or details to achieve the purpose.
3 Are there enough details?	**Add** details, facts, or examples to support the main idea.
4 Are there unrelated ideas that distract the reader?	**Cut** the unrelated ideas.
ORGANIZATION	
5 Are ideas and details arranged in an effective order?	**Reorder** ideas and details to make the meaning clear.
6 Are the connections between ideas and sentences clear? (See pages 71–73.)	**Add** transitional words to link ideas: *because, for example,* and so on.
STYLE	
7 Is the meaning clear?	**Replace** unclear wording. Use precise, easy-to-understand words.
8 Does the language fit the audience and purpose?	**Replace** slang and contractions to create a formal tone. **Replace** formal words with less formal ones to create an informal tone.
9 Do sentences read smoothly?	**Reorder** words to vary sentence beginnings. **Reword** to vary sentence structure.

You could have students evaluate a portion of this book or one of their other textbooks. Because both audience and purpose are obvious, ask students to determine how well the book does what it's supposed to do. How would they revise it? ■

EXERCISE 12 ▶ **Evaluating and Revising a Paragraph**

Now it's your turn to evaluate and revise. The following paragraph is the first draft of a paper written to describe a frightening experience. It's aimed at an audience of eighth-graders. With a partner, evaluate and then revise the paragraph. Use the Guidelines for Evaluating and Revising on page 48.

Ever since The Wonderful Wizard of Oz was read to me when I was little, I've wanted to see a tornado. I also liked books about dinosaurs. Maybe I thought that a tornado would take me to some magical place. Tornados are violent circular windstorms that have winds that whirl around and around. When I was eleven, I visited my aunt and uncle in Texas. They live in Texas. We saw black clouds swirling in the sky. It ripped up some big trees. A tornado dropped down out of the clouds and started coming toward the house. It really scared all of us. We and were very lucky. It went back up into the clouds before it because damaged any buildings. I've seen a tornado. I never want to see another one! No one was hurt, either.

ANSWERS
Exercise 12

Revisions will vary.

1. Cut "I also liked books about dinosaurs" because it is unrelated to the topic.

2. Remove the sentence describing tornadoes because it is inappropriate for the audience.

3. Cut "They live in Texas" because it repeats information.

4. Move "It ripped up some big trees" because the sentence refers to the tornado and not to the clouds. Combine the moved sentence with the sentence that follows to avoid choppiness.

5. Add "because" to join "We were very lucky" and "It went back up into the clouds before it damaged any buildings."

6. Move the last sentence to follow "before it damaged any buildings." It reinforces why the people were lucky.

PROOFREADING AND PUBLISHING

OBJECTIVES

- To proofread a paragraph
- To compile a booklet of possible publishers of student writing

TEACHING THE LESSON

You may want to make some long-range plans about how to cover the material referred to in the **Guidelines for Proofreading** chart (below). Some of your students might need only a spot review of a few grammar, usage, and mechanics rules. Others might need extensive teaching and review. It is probably not a good idea to try

PROGRAM MANAGER

PROOFREADING AND PUBLISHING

- **Instructional Support** For practice with proofreading and using a manuscript checklist, see **Using a Proofreading Checklist** and **Manuscript Form** in *Practicing the Writing Process*, pp. 11–12.

- **Review** For a review of the writing process, see **The Aim and Process of Writing** in *Practicing the Writing Process*, p. 13.

- **Assessment/Reflection** To assess student work and evaluate progress, see **Portfolio Forms** in *Portfolio Assessment*, pp. 18–21.

- **Computer Guided Instruction** For additional practice with grammar, usage, and mechanics concepts as referred to in the **Guidelines for Proofreading**, see **Lessons 10–15, 17–20, 40, 50,** and **57–60** in *Language Workshop CD-ROM*.

- **Practice** To help less-advanced students with additional instruction and practice with related grammar, usage, and mechanics concepts, see **Chapters 8, 17–20,** and **22–25** in *English Workshop, Second Course*, pp. 59–70, 159–220, and 231–296.

Proofreading and Publishing

After you've revised your paper, most of your work is done. You can relax—now you're in the home stretch of the writing process.

Proofreading

When you proofread, you carefully reread your paper. You correct mistakes in grammar, spelling, capitalization, and punctuation. Again, it's helpful to put your paper aside for awhile. Then focus on one line at a time and read slowly, one word at a time. If you're not sure what's correct, look it up. Afterward, exchange papers with a classmate and proofread each other's paper to try to find errors that need to be corrected.

The following guidelines will remind you what to look for as you review your writing one last time.

GUIDELINES FOR PROOFREADING

1. Is every sentence a complete sentence, not a fragment? (See pages 360–362.)
2. Does every sentence begin with a capital letter and end with the correct punctuation mark? (See pages 708–710 and pages 737–740.)
3. Do plural verbs have plural subjects? Do singular verbs have singular subjects? (See pages 575–588.)
4. Are verbs in the right form? Are verbs in the right tense? (See pages 604–623.)
5. Are adjective and adverb forms used correctly in making comparisons? (See pages 657–664.)
6. Are the forms of personal pronouns used correctly? (See page 437.)
7. Does every pronoun agree with its antecedent (the word it refers to) in number and in gender? Are pronoun references clear? (See pages 594–595.)
8. Are all words spelled correctly? Are the plural forms of nouns correct? (See pages 798–827.)

to cover the entire list of grammar, usage, and mechanics skills as part of this lesson because that would slow down the introduction to the writing process. You may want to concentrate on one set of skills and postpone the other skills for later composition chapters.

EXERCISE 13▶   Proofreading a Paragraph

See how sharp your proofreading eyes are. The following paragraph has five mistakes. See if you can find and correct the errors. Refer to the **Handbook** on pages 402–827 and to a dictionary to correct the errors.

> For the past two weeks, we've had repeated ice storms. On all the sidewalks and on the ground, the ice is now over six inches thick⊙The main roads are clear, but the side roads are still ice-covered. The main hazard, though, is walking. No one can clear the ice, so the outside is one huge ice-skating rink. ˍschools are closed because the bus drivers don't dare to go off the main roads. School officials are also concerned about students falling and seriously hurting themselves on school property. Most people ˄is simply staying indoors completely.
>   are

Publishing

After you proofread, you're ready to publish, or share your writing. You've worked hard, and you can be proud of your writing. Here are some ways of publishing your work.

- Read what you've written to the class or to a group of friends.
- Illustrate or decorate a copy of your creative writing, and give it to a friend or relative.

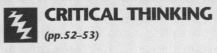
OBJECTIVE
• To write a reflection on the student's personal writing process

TEACHING *REFLECTING ON YOUR WRITING*

Begin by having a volunteer read the text material up to the **Critical Thinking Exercise.** Explain how the portfolios will be managed.

You may wish to give students the option of writing a paragraph based on the questions in the text instead of answering

■ Post book and movie reviews on a bulletin board.
■ Keep a folder of your writing.
■ Enter a writing contest. Some award prizes.
■ Send your writing to a newspaper or magazine. Find out which magazines publish student writing.

CRITICAL THINKING

Reflecting on Your Writing

After you've explored some ways to communicate with an audience, take some time to look at yourself, the writer. One way to do this is by creating a portfolio.

A **portfolio** is a collection that represents different types of your writing and shows your growth as a writer. As you complete writing assignments, choose the pieces that you think say something interesting about you as a writer, and put them in your portfolio. Remember to date each piece so that you and your teacher can trace the development of your writing over time.

By the end of the school year, your portfolio will contain a range of writing types—short stories, reports, and poems, for example—that fulfill a variety of purposes. You will use a variety of thinking skills and writing strategies to create these different types of writing. Therefore, you may sometimes choose pieces for your portfolio that don't completely satisfy you but that do show your progress with different techniques. When considering whether or not to include a piece in your portfolio, be honest but don't be too hard on yourself. One of the challenges of writing is figuring out how to evaluate your work without being overly critical, so that you grow as a writer.

As you reflect on your writing, think about how you used the writing process to create your pieces. By thinking about your writing process, you can identify your strengths and set goals for areas that need work.

MEETING *individual* NEEDS

LEP/ESL

General Strategies. Some English-language learners might benefit from composing their reflections orally before they write them. You can allow students to compose orally into a tape recorder and later have students transcribe the tape. Also, some students may be more comfortable writing in a language other than English and then translating their work into English when they're finished writing.

INTEGRATING THE LANGUAGE ARTS

Vocabulary Link. Have students look up *portfolio* in a dictionary. Ask them to read the etymology that follows the pronunciation and part of speech. Then ask students how a portfolio might be easy to carry. [Everything is in one place and bound together in some way.] Then ask them to suggest as many other words as they can that contain *port* as a root word. [Examples: *port, portable, porter,* but not *portrait* or *portion*]

the questions directly. If you give them this option, emphasize that their paragraphs should address all of the questions.

Discuss the first question, and model how you would answer it for your own writing. Then let students work independently. Assess their understanding of the reflection process by determining how thoroughly they answered each question.

CRITICAL THINKING EXERCISE:
Reflecting on Your Writing

Think about the writing you have done recently for different classes. If you still have some of your papers, take them out and reread them. Then, reflect on your writing process by answering the following questions. Date your answers and save them in your portfolio.

1. Which part of the writing process generally goes most smoothly for you? Which part do you find the most challenging? Why?
2. Which part of each paper are you most pleased with and why? Which part would you handle differently the next time you write that type of paper? Do you notice any patterns in your writing? What types of writing do you most enjoy doing?
3. What have you discovered about your writing process? What have you discovered about yourself by reflecting on your writing?

You've worked hard on your writing and should give yourself a pat on the back. Before you share your writing with others, however, follow these guidelines to make sure your paper looks as good as it can.

GUIDELINES FOR MANUSCRIPT FORM

1. Use only one side of a sheet of paper.
2. Write in blue or black ink, type, or use a word processor.
3. Leave margins of about one inch at the top, sides, and bottom of each page.
4. Follow your teacher's instructions for putting your name, the date, your class, and the title on your paper.
5. If you write, do not skip lines. If you type, double-space the lines.
6. Indent the first line of each paragraph.

ANSWERS
Critical Thinking Exercise

Answers to the questions will vary. They should be written in complete sentences, and they should address completely the ideas in the questions. Students should use the terms for the stages of the writing process that are used in the textbook.

TIMESAVER

Even though **Guidelines for Manuscript Form** says that students should not skip lines in handwritten work, you may want to have them skip lines to provide you with room for writing comments. This procedure could help eliminate the search for room in the margins.

Exercise 14

Responses will vary.

Addresses of Magazines:

1. *Seventeen*
   850 Third Avenue
   New York, NY 10022

2. *Scholastic Scope*
   Scholastic Magazines, Inc.
   730 Broadway
   New York, NY 10003

3. *Odyssey*
   21027 Crossroads Circle
   P.O. Box 1612
   Waukesha, WI 53187

Writing Awards and Contests for Young People:

1. Scholastic Writing Awards
   Scholastic Magazines, Inc.
   730 Broadway
   New York, NY 10003

2. Achievement in Writing Program
   National Council of Teachers of English
   1111 Kenyon Road
   Urbana, IL 61801

Addresses of Newspapers:
These should be local ones.

A DIFFERENT APPROACH

The handwritten proofreading symbols are the basic ones that students will use throughout their school years. You may want to have the class memorize the symbols and their meanings. You can give a quick matching quiz to verify that students have learned the symbols.

Shoe, by Jeff MacNelly, reprinted by permission: Tribune Media Services.

EXERCISE 14 ▶ **Publishing Your Writing**

Can you think of other ways to publish your writing? Get together with two or three classmates to find information about publishers who print student writing. Two reference books to check are the *Market Guide for Young Writers* and *Writer's Market*. Ask the librarian for other sources of information. Then, compile a class booklet of possible publishers.

SYMBOLS FOR REVISING AND PROOFREADING

SYMBOL	EXAMPLE	MEANING OF SYMBOL
≡	at Waukeshaw lake	Capitalize a lowercase letter.
/	a gift for my Uncle	Lowercase a capital letter.
∧	cost cents (fifty)	Insert a missing word, letter, or punctuation mark.
⌐	by their house (our)	Replace something.
⌐	What day is is it?	Leave out a word, letter, or punctuation mark.
∩	recieved	Change the order of letters.
¶	¶ The last step is	Begin a new paragraph.
⊙	Please be patient	Add a period.
⌃	Yes that's right.	Add a comma.

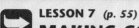

TEACHING THE LESSON

Since there will be references to the use of computers throughout this book, you might want to take this opportunity to review basic concepts about using a computer for writing. At a minimum, remind students that virtually all software has a "help" file they can turn to for information on how to perform particular tasks.

MAKING CONNECTIONS

Writing with a Computer

Pens and pencils will always be required tools for writers, even those who type their finished work. You can carry a pen or pencil anywhere, and whenever a new idea strikes you, you can jot it down while it's still fresh in your mind—even if the only thing you can find to write on is a table napkin or the back of an envelope.

Even though pens and pencils are great for scribbling notes, there are several reasons to switch to a computer when you actually start *drafting*. Computers let you type words and sentences as you think of them, without worrying about putting them in order. If you write in pen and need to rearrange many parts of your draft, you'll have to do a lot of rewriting or retyping. With a computer, you can use your word-processing program's Cut and Paste commands to reorder just the parts you want to move—without doing any retyping at all.

Most computers also let you use special formatting options such as bold, italic, underline, strike through, and different-colored type. You need to follow standard rules when you use these options in your final paper, but when you're drafting, you can use them any way you want.

Computers make it easy to create and change line spacing, paragraph indents, margins, and tabs, too. When you need to make a change, you just change your format settings and print out another copy.

Type and format your next writing assignment on a computer. Attach to the assignment a short note explaining how the computer helped you during drafting. If you don't have a computer at home or in your classroom, check to see if your school library or computer lab has computers you can use, and find out what software is installed on them. Report your findings to the class.

Chapter

2

LEARNING ABOUT PARAGRAPHS

OBJECTIVES

- To identify main ideas, topic sentences, sensory details, and transitions
- To identify sentences that destroy unity
- To classify details
- To establish criteria for evaluation
- To follow the writing process to write paragraphs with the four strategies of paragraph development

CROSS CURRICULUM

Paragraphs and Fine Arts—Connected?

Students interested in the fine arts may recognize that the parts of a painting are often similar to the parts of a paragraph. To help students recognize this similarity, provide small groups with narrative pictures such as Winslow Homer's *Snap the Whip,* Carmen Lomas Garza's *Tamalada,* Francis Blackbear Bosin's *Prairie Fire,* or Henry Ossawa Tanner's *The Banjo Lesson* from the *Transparency Binder.* Then, ask them to describe the picture in one sentence that could serve as a topic sentence for a paragraph discussing the artwork.

Example: Winslow Homer's *Snap the Whip* illustrates two themes: rural life and carefree boyhood in the nineteenth-century United States.

- **Order** Ask students if they recognize a type of order in *Snap the Whip.* They may say that spatial order is dominant in this picture as it might be in a description of a room and that chronological order is common in historical murals and comic strips as well as in most narratives and process pieces. Have students bring in examples of artwork to illustrate various types of order.

- **Sensory Details** Have groups find sensory details in *Snap the Whip.* They may want to create a chart like the following one.

Theme	Senses	Details
rural life	sight	flowers, trees, clouds, sky, village, boys
rural life	smell	flowers, playing children, summer air
carefree boyhood	touch	boys touching in whip game, boys falling, grass on bare feet, scratch of wool clothes on hot skin
carefree boyhood	sound	possible shouts of children at play, possible tolling of church bell, possible summons by parents, possible sound of insects or birds
nineteenth century	touch	clothes, summer heat without air conditioning
nineteenth century	sight	clothes, buildings

You may want students to find sensory details in other transparencies.

INTEGRATING THE LANGUAGE ARTS

SELECTION	READING AND LITERATURE	WRITING AND CRITICAL THINKING	LANGUAGE AND SYNTAX	SPEAKING, LISTENING, AND OTHER EXPRESSION SKILLS
• *Beauties from a Beast: Woodland Jekyll and Hydes* pp. 58–60 • *The Secret Worlds of Colin Fletcher* pp. 63–64 • *The Way to Rainy Mountain* p. 64 • *I Know Why the Caged Bird Sings* p. 65 • *A Wind in the Door* p. 66 • *Mount St. Helens: A Sleeping Volcano Awakes* p. 67 • "Animal Body Talk" p. 68 • "Strange and Terrible Monsters of the Deep" p. 69 • "Earth SOS" pp. 72–73 • "Survive the Savage Sea" p. 73 • *Winterblossom Garden* p. 75 • "Making Fun" p. 76 • *Rockhound Trails* p. 77 • *River Notes* pp. 77–78 • "Road Warrior" p. 80 • *The Amateur Naturalist* p. 80 • "The Duke's Blues" pp. 82–83	• Analyzing information and making judgments on the basis of information given p. 61 • Determining main idea p. 61 • Identifying topic sentences pp. 64–65 • Identifying specific facts that support the main idea p. 67 • Identifying sentences that destroy unity in a paragraph p. 70 • Identifying transitional words and phrases p. 73 • Making inferences and forming generalizations and conclusions supported with facts pp. 86–87	• Writing details to support a main idea pp. 68, 83 • Using narration to develop a main idea p. 78 • Using evaluation to develop a main idea p. 83 • Selecting topics of personal interest and exploring personal experience and knowledge p. 84 • Using prewriting techniques such as listing, clustering, and brainstorming to generate ideas for writing p. 84 • Prewriting, writing, revising, editing, and proofreading a paragraph pp. 84–89 • Creating a setting for a short story pp. 88–89	• Identifying transitional words and phrases p. 73	• Demonstrating principles of good listening and speaking in group situations p. 83 • Making critical judgment as a listener and viewer p. 83 • Hearing and sharing personal experiences, stories, and drama p. 83 • Evaluating and generating statements of opinion, personal preference, and values p. 83

CHAPTER 2: LEARNING ABOUT PARAGRAPHS

Use this guide for creating an instructional plan that addresses the individual needs of your students. Assignments accompanied by the following symbol (*) may be completed out of class. Times given for pacing lessons are estimated.

CHAPTER PLANNING GUIDE—PUPIL'S EDITION

LESSONS	LITERARY MODEL pp. 58–60 *Beauties from a Beast: Woodland Jekyll and Hydes* by Sylvia Duran Sharnoff	WHAT MAKES A PARAGRAPH pp. 62–68
DEVELOPMENTAL PROGRAM	🕐 **30–35 minutes** • Read model aloud in class and have students in small groups answer questions on p. 61 orally.	🕐 **45–50 minutes** • Main Assignment: Looking Ahead p. 61 • The Main Idea p. 62 • The Topic Sentence pp. 63–64 • Exercise 1 in pairs pp. 64–65 • Supporting Sentences pp. 66–68 • Exercise 2 in pairs p. 68
CORE PROGRAM	🕐 **20–25 minutes** • Assign to student pairs reading of model and discussion of questions on p. 61.	🕐 **30–35 minutes** • Main Assignment: Looking Ahead p. 61 • The Main Idea p. 62 • The Topic Sentence pp. 63–64* • Exercise 1 pp. 64–65* • Supporting Sentences pp. 66–68 • Exercise 2 p. 68*
ACCELERATED PROGRAM	🕐 **10–15 minutes** • Assign model for independent reading.	🕐 **10–15 minutes** • Main Assignment: Looking Ahead p. 61 • The Topic Sentence pp. 63–64* • Sensory Details p. 66

CHAPTER PLANNING GUIDE—PROGRAM RESOURCES

	LITERARY MODEL	WHAT MAKES A PARAGRAPH
PRINT	• Reading Master 2, *Practice for Assessment in Reading, Vocabulary, and Spelling* p. 2	• Main Ideas and Topic Sentences, Using Sensory Details, Using Facts and Examples, *Practicing the Writing Process* pp. 17–19 • Main Ideas and Topic Sentences, *English Workshop* pp. 11–12
MEDIA		• Graphic Organizer 3: Developing a Paragraph: Supporting Details, *Transparency Binder*

UNITY AND COHERENCE pp. 69–73	WAYS OF DEVELOPING PARAGRAPHS pp. 74–83
50–55 minutes • Unity p. 69 • Exercise 3 pp. 70–71 in pairs • Coherence pp. 71–73 • Transitional Words and Phrases Chart p. 72 • Exercise 4 in pairs p. 73	**70–75 minutes** • Ways of Developing Paragraphs Chart p. 74 • Writing Notes pp. 74, 76 • Description/Narration/Classification/ Evaluation (read sample paragraphs aloud) pp. 74–83 • Exercises 5, 8 pp. 75, 83* • Exercises 6, 7 pp. 78–79, 81 in pairs
20–25 minutes • Unity p. 69 • Exercise 3 pp. 70–71* • Coherence pp. 71–73* • Transitional Words and Phrases Chart p. 72 • Exercise 4 p. 73*	**30–35 minutes** • Ways of Developing Paragraphs Chart p. 74 • Writing Notes pp. 74, 76 • Sample paragraphs pp. 75, 76, 77–78, 80, 82–83* • Exercises 5–7 pp. 75, 78–79, 81* • Exercise 9 p. 83
5–10 minutes • Unity p. 69 • Exercise 3 pp. 70–71* • Transitional Words and Phrases Chart p. 72	**20–25 minutes** • Ways of Developing Paragraphs Chart p. 74 • Writing Notes pp. 74, 76 • Exercises 5–7 pp. 75, 78–79, 81* • Exercise 9 p. 83

Computer disk or CD-ROM   Overhead transparencies

UNITY AND COHERENCE	WAYS OF DEVELOPING PARAGRAPHS
• Achieving Unity, Transitional Words and Phrases, Using Transitions, *Practicing the Writing Process* pp. 20–22 • Unity and Coherence, *English Workshop* pp. 13–14	• Description: Using Spatial Order; Narration: Explaining a Process; Comparing and Contrasting; Evaluation, *Practicing the Writing Process* pp. 23–26 • Using Description and Narration, Using Comparison/Contrast and Evaluation, *English Workshop* pp. 15–18
	• Revision Transparency 3, *Transparency Binder*

ELEMENTS OF WRITING: CURRICULUM CONNECTIONS

Making Connections
• Writing a Paragraph to Express Yourself pp. 84–85
• Writing a Paragraph to Inform pp. 85–86
• Writing a Paragraph to Persuade pp. 86–88
• Writing a Paragraph That Is Creative pp. 88–89

ASSESSMENT OPTIONS

Portfolio Assessment
Revision Checklist, *Portfolio Assessment* p. 10

Summative Assessment
Review: Transitional Words and Phrases, *Practicing the Writing Process* p. 27

Reflection
Self-assessment Record, *Portfolio Assessment* p. 15

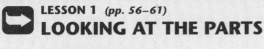

LESSON 1 *(pp. 56–61)*

LOOKING AT THE PARTS

OBJECTIVES

- To give personal responses to a literary model
- To identify the main idea of a literary selection
- To analyze the strategies used in different paragraphs

PROGRAM MANAGER

CHAPTER 2

- **Practice** To help less-advanced students who need additional practice with concepts and activities related to this chapter, see **Chapter 2** in *English Workshop, Second Course,* pp. 11–18.
- **Reading Support** For help with the reading selection, pp. 58–60, see **Reading Master 2** in *Practice for Assessment in Reading, Vocabulary, and Spelling,* p. 2.

VISUAL CONNECTIONS

Exploring the Subject. The three large images on this page show all of the parts of an orange, yet the combination does not result in a picture of the whole fruit. You can use these images as an illustration of the importance of organization in paragraph structure. A student might have all of the sentences necessary for a paragraph, but if they are not written in order, they will not work together to form a complete idea. Also point out that, just as each section of an orange is connected to its core, each sentence in a paragraph should relate directly to the main idea.

continued on next page

2 LEARNING ABOUT PARAGRAPHS

56

MOTIVATION

Give each student two copies of the same composition—one with paragraph indentations and one without. Ask students to comment on how paragraphing affects the meaning and clarity of the composition. Explain that this chapter will help them add to what they already know about paragraphs.

TEACHING THE LESSON

After students have read the introductory material, have one or two students summarize the ideas. Then ask a volunteer to read aloud the professional model. Explain to students that all paragraphs are not of equal length and that most of the time, as in the model, paragraphs introduce topics that are different from ones

Looking at the Parts

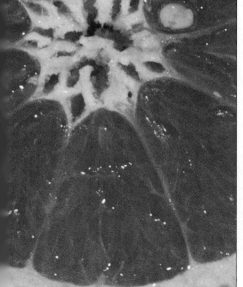

When directors cast a movie, they decide who will play each part. Some actors will have big parts. Others will have only one word to say. Yet, each **part** is important if the movie is to come out right. Paragraphs are like this. Some are big, some are small, but they are all important.

Writing and You. Paragraphs can stand alone, and many do. But most are like links in a chain. They work together to create a longer piece of writing—a magazine article, a short story, a novel, or a letter. Paragraphs separate ideas and yet, at the same time, join them in some way. Why do you think paragraphs come in different sizes?

As You Read. On the pages that follow, you'll find selected paragraphs from a magazine article. As you read, notice how the paragraphs work together to discuss unusual living creatures called slime molds.

Ideas for Writing. To help students plan for prewriting, have them use diagrams that are shaped like the cross-section of an orange. Have each student draw a large circle, draw a smaller circle in the center, and draw lines from the core to the outer edge to form wedge-shaped spaces. Ask students to write their main ideas in the smaller circles and their supporting sentences in the wedges. Remind them to verify that each sentence relates directly to the main idea.

QUOTATION FOR THE DAY

"All words are pegs to hang ideas on." (Henry Ward Beecher, 1813–1887, American preacher)

Write the quotation on the chalkboard and ask students to freewrite for a few minutes about what the quotation means.

MEETING *individual* **NEEDS**

LEP/ESL

General Strategies. Before having students read "Beauties from a Beast: Woodland Jekyll and Hydes," you may want to discuss the general notion of aliens from outer space and how these "creatures" have been depicted in movies and comic books.

that have gone before them. Point out, though, that sometimes in a long piece of writing, paragraphing is used to break up the material in smaller units.

You may want to guide students through the first question of the Reader's Response and allow them to answer orally. Also, discuss the Writer's Craft questions as a class activity. This discussion will allow students to practice locating and identifying main ideas.

58

f r o m

BEAUTIES
from a
BEAST:
WOODLAND JEKYLL AND HYDES

by Sylvia Duran Sharnoff

During the final stage of their life cycle, slime molds can look like beautiful, minute coral.

INDEPENDENT PRACTICE

Have students independently answer the rest of the questions in the **Reader's Response.** Because the lesson focuses on paragraphs, ask each student to write one paragraph that includes not only a response to the question, but also a main idea.

ASSESSMENT

Ask students to underline the main ideas in their paragraphs. You can then quickly assess students' comprehension of main idea.

☛

1 It had been a wet spring. Now, in the summer of 1973, panic was spreading in the Dallas suburbs, on Long Island, around Boston. Pulsating yellow blobs were crawling across people's lawns and even up onto their porches. The blobs broke apart when they were blasted with water, but the pieces continued to crawl and grow—reinforcing fears that they were indestructible aliens from outer space or, at the very least, menacing mutant bacteria.

In due time, scientists assured the public that the "unidentified growing objects" were merely a stage in the bizarre life cycle of remarkable but terrestrial creatures called slime molds. Alarming as they can be to those who come across them unexpectedly, slime molds in the crawling stage are so entertaining that some people keep them as pets. In their spore-bearing stage, many slime molds are astonishingly beautiful, overlooked natural treasures.

Early botanists first noticed slime molds in the spore-bearing stage and mistakenly believed they were puffballs, those spherical fungi that sometimes release smoky clouds of spores. Hence, slime molds have traditionally been the province of mycologists, people who study mushrooms and other fungi. The experts who identified the mysterious invaders in 1973 were mycologists. While slime molds are studied by mycologists, and while they may resemble fungi during a part of their life, they take on the appearance of other living things during other portions of their life cycle. They sometimes appear as slimy blobs capable of

> "Pulsating yellow blobs were crawling across people's lawns and even up onto their porches."

2 moving as fast as slugs; in an earlier stage, they take the form of microscopic protozoans. Because of this Jekyll-and-Hyde devel-
3 opment, slime molds have been a difficult group to pigeonhole.

Plasmodia, the "blobs from outer space" that so alarmed those homeowners, are typically fan-shaped with a delicate, open network of veins and a ruffled leading edge. In some species, they stay microscopic and colorless. Others are large

USING THE SELECTION
from Beauties from a Beast: Woodland Jekyll and Hydes

1
What kind of relationship do the first two sentences imply between the wet spring and the panic of the summer of 1973? [a cause-effect relationship, that somehow the wet spring caused the panic]

2
protozoans: a large group of mostly aquatic, microscopic animals

3
Jekyll-and-Hyde: containing good and evil in the same creature. In Robert Louis Stevenson's 1886 novella, *The Strange Case of Dr. Jekyll and Mr. Hyde,* the good Dr. Henry Jekyll swallows a potion that turns him into the evil Edward Hyde.

RETEACHING

Try explaining paragraph structure by comparing it to a tree. The trunk is the main idea, and it grows branches—specific details. Use a volunteer's paper to illustrate this analogy on the chalkboard. Write the supporting sentences on the branches and write the main idea on the trunk.

CLOSURE

Ask students to define the characteristics of a paragraph. [A paragraph has a main idea and can stand alone or work together with other paragraphs to create a longer piece of writing.]

CRITICAL THINKING

Synthesis. Ask students to imagine that they are the mayor of a town that has been invaded by slime mold before scientists have figured out what it is, and that the people of the town are beginning to panic. Working in groups of four, have students design a campaign to reassure the people and to help them cope with their fears. The campaign can include radio and TV public service announcements, posters, speeches, newspaper articles, and other means of disseminating information. You can let each group present the results of their work to the whole class.

TIMESAVER

You may want to ask students to underline or highlight the main idea in any writing you assign. The highlighting will help you scan the paragraphs quickly and assess students' comprehension of main idea.

4

What does this paragraph imply about the state of the scientific knowledge about slime molds? [scientists still don't agree on how to classify them, as plants or as animals]

SELECTION AMENDMENT
Description of change: excerpted and modified
Rationale: to focus on the concept of paragraph structure presented in this chapter

and colorful: violet, pink or red, but most come in shades of yellow. A few species occasionally grow very large, more than three feet across. One mentioned in the scientific literature covered an entire decaying log that was a yard in diameter and ten yards long.

Plasmodia creep about, eating bacteria, fungi, protozoans, and algae, and sometimes cannibalizing sibling slime molds.

Plasmodia transform themselves into dry fruiting bodies called sporophores that can be seen with a magnifying glass.

They generally live under leaf litter on the forest floor or inside rotting logs, where they can squeeze through narrow spaces in search of food.

Aside from the occasional, frightening encounter with large plasmodia, most people have little knowing contact with slime molds: the exceptions are the scientists who study them and the <u>aficionados</u> who keep them as pets. In the early 1900s, an eccentric Japanese folklorist and biological collector named Kumagusu Minakata kept slime molds in his garden. At first he reportedly had to get up every two hours during the night to protect his pets from garden slugs, but then he trained a succession of cats to drive away the <u>vermin</u>.

Forty years ago, a woman named Ruth Nauss kept a "garden" of slime molds in jars and dishes in the living room of her home. She fed them ground oatmeal flakes, their usual diet in laboratories. When she went on vacation, she took the most delicate along with her, tucking them in with a "warm water bottle" on cold nights. She withheld moisture from the hardier ones for several weeks before a vacation to induce them to harden into <u>sclerotia</u>, so she could leave them unattended. At the time she wrote about them, her oldest plasmodium had been crawling around in its dish for more than nine years.

A scientist who studied slime molds wrote in 1892: "Personally, it is not a matter of prime importance whether it be eventually shown that I have been a botanist or a zoologist." A hundred years later, their place in the great chain of life is still imperfectly resolved.

4

EXTENSION

Have students work together to survey the ways writers use paragraphs. You could suggest the following categories:

1. to develop a main idea
2. To emphasize a point
3. to show a transition from one idea to another
4. to indicate a change in speakers
5. to create visual appeal

Have students look at sources such as magazine and newspaper articles; ads; CD and album cover notes; movie, book, and restaurant reviews; novels; and "how-to" manuals. Have students draw conclusions about the relationship between sources and uses of paragraphs. ■

READER'S RESPONSE

1. Do you think slime molds are more like plants or animals? Why?
2. What were your reactions to the people who have kept slime molds as pets? Would you want to keep them as pets?
3. Did reading the selection make you want to find some slime molds to look at? Why or why not?

WRITER'S CRAFT

4. What main idea is the writer trying to convey in these paragraphs?
5. Which paragraphs describe something? Which ones tell a story?

LOOKING AHEAD

In this chapter, you'll study the form and structure of paragraphs. Even though most paragraphs are part of a larger piece of writing, keep in mind that

- most paragraphs have a central, or main, idea
- sensory details, facts, and examples can be used to support the main idea
- description, narration, classification, and evaluation are ways of developing paragraphs

ANSWERS

Reader's Response

Answers may vary.

1. Students might say slime molds act more like animals because they can move on their own and because they eat other living things.

2. Students might have favorable reactions to keeping slime molds as pets and would be willing to do so themselves because of the unusual nature of this "pet." Others might think it's eccentric and unrewarding since they can't interact with slime molds.

3. Some students might be curious to see slime molds because they are so unusual. Other students might find the idea repulsive and scary.

Writer's Craft

4. The main idea is that slime molds are remarkable and highly unusual creatures.

5. Describe: paragraphs 4 and 5; tell a story: paragraphs 1, 2, 3, 6, 7, and 8

WHAT MAKES A PARAGRAPH

OBJECTIVES

- To identify main ideas and topic sentences in paragraphs
- To provide supporting details for specific main ideas

MOTIVATION

Have students consider the steps in planning a meal. Generally, a main dish is decided on first, and then complementary side dishes are chosen. Lead students to see that a paragraph resembles a meal: the main idea is like the main dish, and the supporting details are like side dishes.

PROGRAM MANAGER

WHAT MAKES A PARAGRAPH

- **Independent Practice** For practice and reinforcement, see **Main Ideas and Topic Sentences, Using Sensory Details,** and **Using Facts and Examples** in **Practicing the Writing Process,** pp. 17–19.

- **Instructional Support** See **Graphic Organizer 3.** For suggestions on how to tie the transparency to instruction, review teacher's notes for transparencies in *Fine Art and Instructional Transparencies for Writing,* p. 51.

QUOTATION FOR THE DAY

"You can observe a lot just by watching." (Yogi Berra, 1925–   , American baseball player and manager)

Write the quotation on the chalkboard and tell students that although Berra's message may seem obvious at first, it could have a deeper meaning. Just as one can watch without really observing details, one can read without being very conscious of the writing. Encourage students to be aware of the way writers create paragraphs and to notice what ingredients make a good paragraph the next time they read a story or book.

What Makes a Paragraph

The Main Idea

Have you ever met some of your friends for a game of baseball? You don't always have enough players, but you always have a pitcher and a catcher. You don't have a baseball game without a pitcher and a catcher.

Paragraphs are like that, too. They may not have a topic sentence and a summary sentence, but they have to have a main idea. You don't have a paragraph without a main idea.

The *main idea* is the big idea around which the entire paragraph is organized. Look back at the second paragraph (page 58) in the opening selection. What is the main idea? It is that slime molds are remarkable creatures. The other sentences in the paragraph give specific details about the characteristics that make slime molds unusual and interesting.

Peanuts reprinted by permission of United Feature Syndicate, Inc.

Although students probably will be familiar with the concept of main idea, you may want to have a volunteer read aloud the expository material. Then guide students through the information about the topic sentence. Point out that a topic sentence is not always in the obvious position of the first sentence in the paragraph. Note that purpose often influences the choice of location for the topic sentence. Writers who want to inform frequently place the topic sentence near the beginning of a paragraph. This placement helps readers understand the significance of each supporting detail. Writers who want to entertain sometimes place the topic sentence near the end of a paragraph to build a dramatic effect or to add an unexpected twist. ☞

The Topic Sentence

The *topic sentence* states the main idea of the paragraph. It can occur anywhere in the paragraph, but it's usually either the first or second sentence. (Sometimes the topic sentence is made up of two sentences.) Look again at the second paragraph of the opening selection (page 58). The topic sentence occurs first. Can you see how it helps the reader understand the paragraph's main idea?

Sometimes a topic sentence comes later in the paragraph, or even at the end. In these paragraphs the topic sentence pulls the ideas together and helps the reader see how they are related. Sometimes it summarizes, as in the following paragraph.

> Gray clouds ran a mad race across the sky. The wind howled through the hills, ripping the last of the leaves from the trees. Throughout the morning, the temperature continued to drop, and by noon the puddles along the road were beginning to freeze over. It was the first day of winter.

Many paragraphs have no topic sentence. This is especially true of narrative paragraphs that tell about a series of events. The reader has to add the details together to figure out what the main idea is. Look at the following paragraph. What's the main idea?

> When the coyote had finished drinking it trotted a few paces, to above the stepping-stones, and began to eat something. All at once it looked up, directly at me. For a moment it stood still. Then it had turned and almost instantly vanished, back into the shadows

MEETING *individual* NEEDS

LESS-ADVANCED STUDENTS

Using a graphic organizer might help students assess whether supporting details relate to the topic sentence. Each student could write the main idea as a topic sentence and draw a square around it. Then she or he could draw a circle stemming from this main idea and fill it with a specific detail. Students can add as many details as necessary, but they should aim for three to five.

Finally, guide students through the excerpts and information about supporting sentences, including sensory details, facts, and examples in the paragraphs.

As guided practice, you could help students find the main idea and topic sentence of the first excerpt in **Exercise 1** below. Likewise, have the class work together to generate details to support the main idea in the first sentence of **Exercise 2** on p. 68.

Then assign the remaining excerpts in **Exercise 1** and the last two sentences in **Exercise 2** for students to complete independently.

INTEGRATING THE LANGUAGE ARTS

Listening Link. Tell students that when they listen to lectures, news reports, or even friends' conversations, they are probably listening for main ideas. By identifying a speaker's main ideas, the listener is more able to evaluate the information. Remind students that speakers often use certain verbal clues such as *most importantly, first, second, next,* and *remember that* to emphasize main points.

You may want to read aloud several paragraphs and have students listen for the main ideas. Or if the school's daily announcements are broadcast, you could have students jot down the main idea of each announcement.

AMENDMENTS TO SELECTIONS
Description of change: excerpted
Rationale: to focus on the concepts of topic sentence and main idea presented in this chapter

that underlay the trees. From behind the trees, a big black hawklike bird with a red head flapped out and away. Up in the lake, the herons took wing. They, too, circled away from me, angled upriver.

Colin Fletcher, *The Secret Worlds of Colin Fletcher*

Each sentence in this paragraph describes a separate action. But if you put them all together, they suggest the main idea: Colin Fletcher disturbed the animals and they fled.

EXERCISE 1 ▶ **Identifying Main Ideas and Topic Sentences**

All your life you'll be asked to read something and figure out what the main idea is. Sharpen your skills by identifying the main idea in the following paragraphs. If the paragraph has a topic sentence, tell what it is. If there isn't a topic sentence, summarize the main idea in your own words.

1.　　There were always dogs about my grandmother's house. Some of them were nameless and lived a life of their own. They belonged there in a sense that the word "ownership" does not include. The old people paid them scarcely any attention, but they should have been sad, I think, to see them go.

N. Scott Momaday, *The Way to Rainy Mountain*

To assess whether students understand main idea, topic sentences, and supporting details, you could check their answers to **Exercises 1** and **2.** In addition, you may want to evaluate the topic sentences and supporting details of paragraphs students have written.

CLOSURE

Ask students to define *main idea* and *topic sentence.* Then ask a volunteer to list the various ways to supply supporting evidence in a paragraph [sensory details, facts, examples].

2.   <u>In March of 1996, the Justice Department and the state of California announced a plan to improve emergency telephone service for Californians who are deaf or hard of hearing.</u> Under the agreement, the state will install text telephones known as TTYs or TDDs in 475 emergency telephone centers. A text telephone has a small screen and a keyboard that allow callers to type and receive text messages over telephone lines. Before the agreement, people who were deaf or hard of hearing had to call special 911 centers to get emergency help, and they often had to wait to be transferred to those centers. The Justice Department decided that this two-step procedure was no longer acceptable. Under the Americans with Disabilities Act of 1990, cities must provide telephone emergency services to everyone, including people with disabilities.

3.   I arrived in San Francisco, leaner than usual, fairly unkempt, and with no luggage. Mother took one look and said, "Is the rationing that bad at your father's? You'd better have some food to stick to all those bones." She, as she called it, turned to, and soon I sat at a clothed table with bowls of food, expressly cooked for me.   M.I.: Because the writer looked thin when she arrived, her mother fed her.   Maya Angelou, *I Know Why the Caged Bird Sings*

CRITICAL THINKING

Synthesis. When students sort through details to determine the main idea, they are using the thinking skill of generalizing. You might give students copies of paragraphs in which you have omitted the topic sentences and have students generalize to discover the main idea.

SELECTION AMENDMENT
Description of change: excerpted
Rationale: to focus on the concepts of topic sentence and main idea presented in this chapter

You could have each student evaluate a paragraph from one of his or her writing assignments. Tell students to identify their main ideas and topic sentences and to determine whether they used sensory details, facts, or examples as supporting details.

Suggest that students create photo essays. Have students choose themes and collect photographs or pictures from magazines to support their themes. Tell students to think of their themes as the main ideas and to think of their pictures as supporting details. You may want to use the photo essays as prompts for writing

A DIFFERENT APPROACH

You could suggest that, before students develop paragraphs with sensory details, they make prewriting charts with each of the five senses as headings. Using such charts might keep students from relying mainly on visual details.

INTEGRATING THE LANGUAGE ARTS

Literature Link. Writers often use sensory details to enliven descriptive passages. For example, in *A Christmas Carol*, Charles Dickens uses sensory details to help his readers feel the dampness of the fog, taste the thinness of the gruel, see the gas lamps, and hear the clanking of Marley's chains. If your literature textbook contains it, ask students to read part of *A Christmas Carol* and to fill in sensory detail charts containing the following headings: "Sight," "Sound," "Touch," "Taste," and "Smell." You could use the charts as the basis for a discussion about the effects of sensory details in Dickens's writing.

SELECTION AMENDMENT
Description of change: excerpted
Rationale: to focus on the concept of sensory details presented in this chapter

Supporting Sentences

In addition to a main idea and a topic sentence, paragraphs may also have *supporting sentences*. **Supporting sentences** give specific details that explain or prove the main idea. These sentences may use sensory details, facts, or examples.

Sensory Details. When you use words that appeal to one of your five senses—sight, hearing, touch, taste, and smell—you are using *sensory details.* Vivid sensory details help your reader clearly imagine what you're writing about.

Notice the sensory details in this paragraph from *A Wind in the Door.* In the first two sentences, for example, you can "see" Meg move along the wall, you can "smell" the apples, and you can "feel" the cold wind. What other sensory details can you find?

> She moved slowly along the orchard wall. The cidery smell of fallen apples was cut by the wind which had completely changed course and was now streaming across the garden from the northwest, sharp and glittery with frost. She saw a shadow move on the wall and jumped back: Louise the Larger, it must be Louise, and Meg could not climb that wall or cross the orchard to the north pasture until she was sure that neither Louise nor the not-quite-seen shape was lurking there waiting to pounce on her. Her legs felt watery, so she sat on a large, squat pumpkin to wait. The cold wind brushed her cheek; corn tassels hished like ocean waves. She looked warily about. She was seeing, she realized, through lenses streaked and spattered by raindrops blowing from sunflowers and corn, so she took off her spectacles, felt under the poncho for her kilt, and wiped them. Better, though the world was still a little wavery, as though seen under water.
>
> Madeleine L'Engle, *A Wind in the Door*

paragraphs. Each paragraph should include the main idea written in a sentence and three to five supporting sentences that include sensory details, examples, or facts suggested by individual pictures. ■

Facts.   Supporting sentences may also contain *facts*. A *fact* is a statement that can be proved true by direct observation or by checking a reliable reference source. For example, if you say that Washington, D.C., is the capital of the United States, that's a fact. It can be proved. But if you say that it's the best city in the world, that's an opinion. Opinions can't be proved. (For more information on facts and opinions, see pages 261–262.)

Look at how the facts in the following paragraph support the main idea that a volcano was erupting. Many of the facts are statistics, or numbers. In the first sentence, for example, facts include the date and time of the boom, as well as the height of the peak. Can you find other facts?

> Those who camped overnight on March 28 atop 3,926-foot-high Mitchell Peak were wakened about 2:00 A.M. by a loud boom and whistling sounds. In the brilliant moonlight they watched a great plume of steam rise from the crater. Another eruption at 3:45 A.M. blew ash three miles into the sky and was followed by three quakes registering 4.0 on the Richter intensity scale. Later observers learned the volcano had blown out a second crater. Three small mudflows, not lava, dribbled a thousand feet down the slope. The east and south slopes turned gray from the ash projected by gases <u>roiling</u> from the <u>magma</u> far below the surface.
>
> Marian T. Place, *Mount St. Helens: A Sleeping Volcano Awakes*

INTEGRATING THE LANGUAGE ARTS

Test-Taking Link. The information on using supporting sentences might be helpful to students when they are asked to develop answers to essay questions. Remind students that an essay response includes a main idea and the development of the main idea. To reinforce this concept for students, ask each student to bring in an essay question from a previous exam in another class. Have the class discuss ways that each student might develop an essay answer for his or her question. Or you could work with a teacher in another department to provide students with essay questions to practice developing main ideas.

SELECTION AMENDMENT
Description of change: excerpted
Rationale: to focus on the use of facts as supporting details presented in this chapter

TIMESAVER

You could save time and encourage student involvement by asking students to label all supporting sentences as facts, examples, or sensory details. You will readily see how many details students have included in a paragraph, and students will be practicing application of terms in their own writing. In addition, ask students to circle the main idea in each paragraph so you can check their comprehension of main idea.

ANSWERS

Exercise 2

Responses will vary. Here are some possibilities:

1. Not smoking cuts a person's chance of lung cancer by 80%. One can help lessen the incidence of heart and vascular problems by exercising aerobically at least three times a week.

2. I hear shouts, laughter, and the squeaking of rubber-soled shoes as my friends shoot baskets. I smell freshly cut grass, and an amplifier barks as a neighbor's band tunes up to practice.

3. Students might mention unusual hobbies, possessions, or family customs. Or they might focus on the way they view life, friends, or school.

SELECTION AMENDMENT
Description of change: excerpted
Rationale: to focus on the use of examples as supporting details presented in this chapter

Examples. *Examples* are a third kind of supporting detail. They are specific instances or illustrations of a general idea. Soccer and football are examples of team sports played with a ball. Getting grounded is an example of what might happen if you disobey your parents.

In the following paragraph the author gives examples of how animals behave when they're angry.

When animals are angry, they use a different kind of body language. If one animal invades another's territory, the first animal threatens it. Animals may threaten by displaying their teeth or claws. Some try to make their bodies look bigger. Birds fluff up their feathers. Fish stick their back fins straight up and open their gill covers outward. Angry cats arch their backs and make their hair stand on end. These messages say, "I'm a BIG angry animal. Don't come any closer!"

"Animal Body Talk,"
National Geographic World

EXERCISE 2 **Collecting Supporting Details**

Have you ever collected baseball cards, sea shells, or stamps? You search and choose only the ones you think are best. Now you're going to collect supporting details for topic sentences. Think up at least two details to support each of the following main ideas. With each idea, a type of support—sensory details, facts, or examples—is suggested.

1. Staying alive and healthy is at least partly under your control. (facts and statistics—for example, diet, smoking, or exercise)
2. When I walk around my neighborhood (or city), there's always something going on. (sensory details)
3. No one in my class is just like me. (examples)

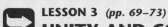

LESSON 3 *(pp. 69–73)*
UNITY AND COHERENCE

OBJECTIVES

• To identify sentences that destroy unity in a paragraph
• To identify transitional words and phrases in a paragraph

MOTIVATION

You may want to introduce this lesson in a humorous way to get students' attention. Add a bizarre item of clothing or a funny hat to your outfit. Point out to students that not only does the item look out of place, but also your entire outfit is overshadowed by the item that does not match or does not belong. Tell students

Unity and Coherence

A paragraph may have a main idea, topic sentence, and supporting sentences. But the reader may still not understand it fully. What may be missing is unity or coherence.

Unity

When a paragraph has *unity,* all the sentences relate to the main idea. For example, in a paragraph explaining the origin of baseball, every sentence should give some information about baseball's beginnings. Including a sentence about this year's best team will ruin the paragraph's unity. That sentence isn't about the paragraph's main idea—how baseball began.

As you read the following paragraph, notice how each sentence is directly connected to the main idea: how sailors once believed in mermaids.

> Another monster that was equally dreaded by sailors was the beautiful mermaid. Like the sirens, mermaids were thought to be half woman and half fish. Such creatures were said to carry a mirror in one hand and a comb in the other, and from time to time they would run the comb through their long seagreen hair. Most sailors were convinced that it was very bad luck to see a mermaid. At best, it meant that someone aboard their ship would die soon afterward. At worst, it meant that a terrific storm would arise, the ship would sink, and many of the crew would drown.
>
> William Wise, "Strange and Terrible Monsters of the Deep"

**PROGRAM MANAGER**

UNITY AND COHERENCE

■ **Instructional Support** To help students determine unity in paragraphs and identify appropriate transitional words and phrases, see **Achieving Unity, Transitional Words and Phrases,** and **Using Transitions** in *Practicing the Writing Process,* pp. 20–22.

QUOTATION FOR THE DAY

"The way to be a bore, for an author, is to say everything." (William F. Fleming's translation of François Marie Arouet de Voltaire, 1694–1778, French author)

Ask students to recall times when they were bored by conversations or books. Challenge the class to brainstorm some elements that made these experiences annoying or uninteresting, and note their responses on the chalkboard. Lead students to understand that unity and coherence in writing not only create compositions that are easy to read and understand but also make the written work more likely to hold a reader's interest.

SELECTION AMENDMENT
Description of change: excerpted
Rationale: to focus on the concept of unity presented in this chapter

that, similarly, a sentence that does not relate to the main idea in a paragraph can cause distractions. The reader is left wondering "What's that doing there?" Tell students that for a paragraph to have unity, all sentences must relate to the main idea.

You may want to define *unity* and *coherence* for students, or ask a volunteer to give the class a dictionary definition for each word. Then have a student read aloud William Wise's paragraph on p. 69, and discuss how each sentence supports the main idea. You may also want to have students suggest sentences that would not

MEETING *individual* NEEDS

LEP/ESL

General Strategies. The placement of transitions within sentences varies with some languages. For example, in Japanese, Korean, and Turkish languages, transitional words customarily follow the ideas that are connected. You could reinforce the placement of transitions in English sentences by having students underline transitions and identify the ideas that the transitions connect.

LEARNING STYLES

Auditory Learners. You could have students read the paragraphs in **Exercise 3** into a tape recorder and play them back. Hearing the paragraphs could help students locate the sentences that destroy the unity.

VISUAL CONNECTIONS

Exploring the Subject. Amelia Earhart made several solo flights across the United States, including a flight across the Pacific from Hawaii to California in 1935. Earhart worked with the Luddington airline, an early East Coast passenger service. In 1931 she married publisher George Palmer Putnam, who wrote her biography *Soaring Wings* in 1939.

EXERCISE 3 ▶ **Identifying Sentences That Destroy Unity**

In each of the following paragraphs, one sentence should make you say, "What's *that* doing there?" Find the sentence that destroys the unity of each paragraph. [Remember: In a unified paragraph, all details are directly related to the main idea or the sequence of actions.]

1. The disappearance of Amelia Earhart remains a mystery. Earhart, who was the first woman pilot to fly across the Atlantic Ocean, crashed in the Pacific while attempting to fly around the world. She was born in Atchison, Kansas, in 1897. Some searchers believe that she survived the crash into the Pacific, because radio distress calls were received. An intensive search for the source of the signals was made. Searchers were not able to find her, however. Finally, the distress signals ceased. In spite of continued searches by airplane and ship, no clue to what became of Amelia Earhart has yet been found.

directly relate to the main idea of the paragraph. After going over the **Transitional Words and Phrases** chart on p. 72, discuss with students how the transitions add coherence to the "Earth SOS" paragraph that follows.

GUIDED PRACTICE

Guide students through the first paragraph of **Exercise 3** on p. 70 and identify the main idea before having students identify the sentence that destroys unity. Then you could use **Exercise 4** on p. 73 to guide students through the process of identifying transitions.

☞

2. One reason the mountain bike is popular is because it's built to help the rider keep control even when riding it off paved roads. The extra-wide handlebars improve the rider's balance. <u>Jeremy has a mountain bike, but he only rides on city streets.</u> With its wide tires the mountain bike will roll right over small obstacles that would trip up the skinny tires of a racer. And because the tires are knobby, riders can keep going even if the ground is muddy or sandy. That helps riders keep their balance. Because of these features, mountain bike riders can go almost anywhere.

COOPERATIVE LEARNING

You could have students work in pairs to add unrelated sentences to paragraphs. Have each pair of students choose a paragraph from available sources such as magazines, newspapers, textbooks, and encyclopedias. Then ask each pair to rewrite the paragraph and add one or two sentences that destroy the paragraph's unity. Finally, have the pairs exchange paragraphs and see if they can identify the unrelated sentences.

Coherence

In addition to having unity, a paragraph needs to be coherent. When a paragraph has *coherence,* the reader can easily see how ideas are related. One way to create coherence is to use *transitional words and phrases.* These are words or phrases that show that ideas are connected and how they are connected. The following chart lists some common transitions. Notice that the transitions you use depend, in part, on the kind of paragraph you're writing.

Assign the second paragraph of **Exercise 3** as independent practice. Then choose one of the excerpts from this chapter or write an anonymous paragraph on the chalkboard and have students list the transitional words and phrases.

To assess comprehension of paragraph unity, check students' responses to **Exercise 3** and their lists of transitions. To determine whether students understand unity and coherence, you will probably want to evaluate writing samples.

CRITICAL THINKING

Evaluation. Give students newspaper or magazine articles and ask students to critique the articles in terms of unity and coherence. You may want to have students answer the following questions and give reasons for their answers:

1. Does the article have clear transitions? Give at least three examples to support your opinion.
2. Do all sentences relate to the main idea? If so, explain how. If not, give specific examples that show unrelated sentences.
3. Rate this article on a scale from one to ten. How could the writer increase this score? Give at least two suggestions for improvement.

TRANSITIONAL WORDS AND PHRASES

Comparing Ideas/Classification and Definition		
also	another	similarly
and	moreover	too
Contrasting Ideas/Classification and Definition		
although	in spite of	on the other hand
but	instead	still
however	nevertheless	yet
Showing Cause and Effect/Narration		
as a result	for	so that
because	since	therefore
consequently	so	
Showing Time/Narration		
after	eventually	next
at last	finally	then
at once	first	thereafter
before	meanwhile	when
Showing Place/Description		
above	beyond	into
across	down	next to
around	here	over
before	in	there
behind	inside	under
Showing Importance/Evaluation		
first	mainly	then
last	more important	to begin with

Notice how the underlined transitions help show how ideas are related.

Doesn't the earth sometimes seem like one big mess? That's <u>because</u> it is. Think about how much trash you make in one day. Where does it go? The garbageman picks it up <u>and</u> it's gone. <u>But</u> where?

If students are having difficulty with paragraph unity and coherence, give them sentences on strips of paper from two different paragraphs. Then help students to arrange the sentences in a logical order and to discard any sentences that detract from unity in either paragraph.

To close this lesson, you could ask students to explain how a writer can add unity and coherence to a paragraph. [The writer can add related information and transitions or delete unrelated information.] ■

Unity and Coherence **73**

Sometimes trash is burned, releasing harmful pollutants into the air—not a smart idea. Other times it goes to a dump or a landfill, where it's buried with dirt. Not a great idea either, but it doesn't matter anymore, because we're fast running out of space for landfills—so where to next?

"Earth SOS," *Seventeen*

EXERCISE 4 ▶ **Identifying Transitional Words and Phrases**

Lists will vary.

Can you find the words and phrases that connect the writer's ideas? Make a list of all the transitional words and phrases you can find in this paragraph about a family adrift on the ocean in a rubber raft and dinghy.

The rain continued all night long, and as we bailed the warm sea water out of the raft we were glad not to be spending this night in the dinghy at least. I went over to the dinghy twice in the night to bail out, for the rain was filling her quite quickly, and I shivered at the low temperature of the rain water. The raft canopy offered grateful warmth when I returned, and the puddles of salt water in the bottom of the raft seemed less hostile after the chill of the dinghy. We all huddled together on top of the flotation chambers, our legs and bottoms in the water, and although we did not sleep, we rested, for the work of blowing and bailing now went on around the clock, the bailer passing back and forth between the two compartments.

Dougal Robertson, "Survive the Savage Sea"

AMENDMENTS TO SELECTIONS
Description of change: excerpted and modified
Rationale: to focus on the use of transitions presented in this chapter

LESSON 4 *(pp. 74–75)*

DESCRIPTION

OBJECTIVE

- To list sensory details for a descriptive essay

TEACHING THE LESSON

Have students identify the sensory details in David Low's paragraph. Then guide students in listing descriptive details for an appropriate subject before assigning **Exercise 5.** Assessment and closure can be combined by having each student read aloud one descriptive detail. ∎

PROGRAM MANAGER

DESCRIPTION

- **Analyzing** To help students analyze and organize ideas, see **Description: Using Spatial Order** in *Practicing the Writing Process,* p. 23.

QUOTATION FOR THE DAY

"Nothing ever becomes real till it is experienced . . ." (John Keats, 1795–1821, English poet)

Ask students to recall times when they were younger and they heard descriptions of junior high school. Now that they have experienced being in junior high school, how do their experiences compare with the descriptions they heard?

MEETING *individual* NEEDS

LEP/ESL

General Strategies. Students with limited English vocabularies may have difficulty choosing appropriate descriptive adjectives and adverbs. Providing guided practice with a thesaurus would be helpful to students. In addition, bring pictures to class and describe them to provide examples of adjectives and adverbs that students might use in writing.

Ways of Developing Paragraphs

You've learned about the parts of a paragraph and some ways to give a paragraph unity and coherence. Now think about how you plan to develop your main ideas. Here is a list showing four different strategies for developing your main idea. They're really four different ways of looking at a subject or topic, and they also help create coherence.

WAYS OF DEVELOPING PARAGRAPHS	
Description	Describing parts of a person, place, or thing
Narration	Telling how a person or situation changes over time
Classification	Showing relationships between items
Evaluation	Deciding on the value of an item or making a judgment about its importance

WRITING NOTE   Often, you'll use more than one strategy in a paragraph. You may, for example, describe a person and also narrate a story about the person. This blend of strategies will give your writing variety and interest.

Description

What's the sound a rock makes when it is dropped into a bucket of water? What does the Vietnam Veterans Memorial look like? How can you recognize a rattlesnake?

You use *description* to tell what something is like or what it looks like. You use mostly sensory details to tell about what you can see, hear, smell, taste, or touch.

Descriptions are usually organized by *spatial order*—how they are arranged in space. In the following paragraph, the writer uses spatial order to describe part of his family's restaurant.

NARRATION

OBJECTIVE

- To use narration as a strategy to develop specific details

MOTIVATION

To introduce narration and chronological order, perform a process such as making a paper airplane in front of the class. After you have finished, ask students to list in order the steps you took to make the airplane. Emphasize the importance of chronological order in narrative paragraphs. ☞

Ways of Developing Paragraphs **75**

> In a glass case near the cash register, cardboard boxes overflow with bags of fortune cookies and almond candies that my father gives away free to children. The first dollar bill my parents ever made hangs framed on the wall above the register. Next to that dollar, a picture of my parents taken twenty years ago recalls a time when they were raising four children at once, paying mortgages and putting in the bank every cent that didn't go toward bills.
>
> David Low, *Winterblossom Garden*

EXERCISE 5 ▶ **Using Description as a Strategy**

How would you describe your favorite movie star, your sneakers, or the inside of your locker? Choose one of these subjects or one of the five in the following list. List or cluster the details you would use to describe it. Try to appeal to the senses by listing things you can see, hear, smell, taste, or touch. Observe the subject if you can or brainstorm some details. (See page 66.)

1. an amusement park or city park
2. the moment just after a touchdown at a football game
3. a garbage truck or garbage dump
4. your favorite place in the whole world
5. a monster in a late-night, grade-B TV movie

Narration

What happened after Old Yeller died? How do you repair a flat on a bicycle? What caused the Civil War?

To answer any of these questions, you *narrate.* In other words, you tell how a person or how a situation changes over a period of time. You can narrate to tell a story, explain a process, or explain causes and effects.

Paragraphs that use narration are often organized in ***chronological order.*** That is, events are told in the order in which they occur.

TEACHING THE LESSON

Most students have written stories or explained processes; therefore, narration should be a familiar developmental strategy. As students read through the models that illustrate telling a story, explaining a process, and explaining cause and effect, have them identify the transitional words and phrases that indicate chronological order.

To guide students in using the three strategies, list the following subjects on the chalkboard:

1. a frightening experience
2. how to conserve water
3. how your day is affected when your alarm doesn't go off

MEETING individual NEEDS

LESS-ADVANCED STUDENTS

To help students more smoothly explain a process, suggest that they begin all of their sentences with transitional words and phrases such as *then, remember to, proceed on to, include the, next,* and *finally.* Once students become more familiar with chronological order, many of the transitions can be omitted.

ADVANCED STUDENTS

Because students are focusing on narrative writing, you may want to introduce the narrative perspective. Discuss first-person, third-person, third-person omniscient, and third-person limited omniscient points of view. Then give each student the same picture from a book or magazine. Have each student choose a different point of view and write a short story about the picture. Have students compare their completed stories.

SELECTION AMENDMENT
Description of change: excerpted
Rationale: to focus on the concept of telling a story presented in this chapter

WRITING NOTE   Many narrative paragraphs do not have a topic sentence. Because they are about a series of events, they begin with an action. The other sentences tell about additional actions.

Telling a Story.   You're probably very familiar with one kind of narrating—telling a story. When you tell a story, you tell what happened. The story may be about either imaginary or real events.

Here is a narrative paragraph that tells what happens during a ride in a theme park. You are about to meet a very angry gorilla.

Transporting his passengers on the Roosevelt Island tramway, the operator suddenly announces that King Kong has escaped and is wreaking havoc on Manhattan. Suddenly a wall of water breaks from mains and floods the streets below. Fires rage. Then Kong appears in all his terror, hanging from the Queensboro Bridge. He swats at a police helicopter and sends it crashing to the ground. Then the six-ton, four-story-tall gorilla turns his attention to you, grabbing the tram as if it were a Tonka toy. Twisting and turning the vehicle, he picks it up, blasts you with his banana-scented breath, and hurls you to the ground. Falling at 12 feet per second with 1.75 g's of acceleration, the tram is saved from certain disaster by a single cable.

A.J.S. Rayl, "Making Fun"

Ask a volunteer to respond to the first topic as you list on the chalkboard the actions described. Do the same with the second and third subjects, explaining to students that they are narrating in each instance. Then assign **Exercise 6** as independent practice.

ASSESSMENT

To evaluate students' comprehension, ask several students to read aloud their lists from **Exercise 6** on p. 78. This procedure should help you to assess students' performance, and it will also allow students to hear additional examples of narrative prewriting.

Explaining a Process. Whenever you tell someone how something works or how to do something, you're explaining a process. To help readers follow the steps in the process, you once again use chronological order.

In this paragraph, the writer explains how to pan for gold. Once the gold pan is filled with rock and sand, the panning begins.

> Swirl your pan around and around just below the surface of the water. The water will cause the light sand and gravel to rise to the top. Pour off the sand, pick out the pebbles and repeat the process. When the top dirt is stripped off, you will see black streaks in the bottom of your pan. These are tiny grains of iron magnetite. This is the "pay dirt." Be careful not to wash it away. Magnetite is heavy, but gold is heavier. Your gold, if it is there, will be under the black sand.
>
> Jean Bartenbach, *Rockhound Trails*

Explaining Cause and Effect. Narrating is also used to explain how one event causes another event. To make the cause-and-effect connections clear, events are often narrated in the order in which they happened.

In the following paragraph, the cause is an October storm. The effects of the storm are what happens to the people, the trees, the animals, and the buildings.

Cause
> A storm came this year, against which all other storms were to be measured, on a Saturday in October, a balmy afternoon....
> It built as it came up the valley as did every fall storm, but the steel-gray thunderheads, the first sign of it anyone saw, were higher, much higher, too high. In the stillness before it hit, men looked at each other as though a fast and wiry man had pulled a knife in a bar. They felt the trees falling

Effect
> before they heard the wind, and they

MEETING
individual
NEEDS

STUDENTS WITH SPECIAL NEEDS

Some students may best understand a paragraph that explains a process if they think of it as a "how-to" paragraph. Begin by analyzing familiar routines or procedures such as tying a shoe or making a sandwich. Working in groups, students can analyze the steps, act them out, and have other students guess the situations.

LEARNING STYLES

Visual Learners. Encourage students to use time lines, outlines, or other visual devices to help them understand that narration describes changes over a period of time.

SELECTION AMENDMENT
Description of change: excerpted
Rationale: to focus on the concept of explaining a process presented in this chapter

RETEACHING

You may want to bring in videotaped samples of narration. For example, an episode of a TV sitcom tells a story; a segment from a "how-to" program explains a process; and a segment from a documentary (on global warming, for example) illustrates cause-and-effect relationships.

CLOSURE

Ask students to explain the terms *chronological order, process,* and *cause-and-effect relationships.* Then ask students to write down three circumstances in which narrative writing would be necessary [for example, instructions on how to assemble a bicycle]. ∎

INTEGRATING THE LANGUAGE ARTS

Literature Link. You may want to have students analyze Daniel Keyes's effective use of narration in *Flowers for Algernon.* Suggest that students look for examples of all three narrative strategies—telling a story, explaining a process, and explaining cause and effect. You could also have students discuss how the main character and his situation change over a period of time.

ANSWERS

Exercise 6

Responses will vary, but students should include three actions in chronological order to tell their stories, list four steps to explain a process, and list three causes or three effects.

SELECTION AMENDMENT
Description of change: excerpted and modified
Rationale: to focus on the concept of cause and effect presented in this chapter

---

Effect

dropped tools and scrambled to get out. The wind came up suddenly and like a scythe, like piranha after them, like seawater through a breach in a dike. The first blow bent trees half to the ground, the second caught them and snapped them like kindling, sending limbs raining down and twenty-foot splinters hurtling through the air like mortar shells to stick quivering in

Effect

the ground. Bawling cattle running the fences, a loose lawnmower bumping across a lawn, a stray dog lunging for a child racing by. The big trees went down screaming,

Effect

ripping open holes in the wind that were filled with the broken-china explosion of a house and the yawing screech of a pickup rubbed across asphalt, the rivet popping and twang of phone and electric wires.

Barry Holstun Lopez, *River Notes*

EXERCISE 6 ▶ **Using Narration as a Strategy**

When you tell a joke—or any kind of story—you start at the beginning and tell what happens next until you get to the punch line, or ending. Read the directions and then use narration to develop each of the following items.

1. Choose one of the following subjects and list at least three actions that took place.
   A. the funniest thing that ever happened to me (Make up a story, if you like.)
   B. what happened at the Boston Tea Party (Check an encyclopedia or history book.)
2. Choose one of the following subjects and list at least four steps in the process.
   C. how to apply for a job
   D. how to ask someone for a date

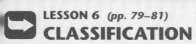
CLASSIFICATION

OBJECTIVE

- To list details about specific subjects by using the strategy of comparison and contrast and the strategy of definition

TEACHING THE LESSON

You could begin by drawing four traffic signs on the chalkboard: "stop," "yield," "speed limit," and "one way." Explain classification by having students define the large group to which the subjects belong [traffic signs] and compare and contrast the individual signs.

3. Choose one of the following subjects and list at least three causes or effects. You may need to do some research on your selected subject.
   E. getting a part-time job after school (the effects)
   F. water pollution (the causes)

Classification

What's country music? What are the differences between a piano and an electronic keyboard?

In answering either of these questions, you would be *classifying.* That is, you'd tell how the specific subject relates to other subjects that belong to the same group. Country music, for example, belongs to the group *music,* which includes rock, jazz, blues, rap, folk, gospel, classical, opera, and other types of music. When you classify, you define (*country music*) or compare and contrast (*piano and electronic keyboard*).

When you write a paragraph to classify, you usually arrange your ideas in *logical order.* Something is called logical because it makes sense; its meaning is clear. When you classify, it makes sense to group or arrange related ideas together.

Defining.   When you tell about a subject that's new to your reader, you may have to give a definition. Usually, a *definition* has two parts. First, it identifies the large group, or general class, that the subject belongs to. Second, it tells how the subject is different from all other members that belong to this general class.

Here is a one-sentence definition of tae kwon do. The general class that the subject, tae kwon do, belongs in is italicized. Notice how the other details in the sentence tell how tae kwon do is different from other martial arts.

EXAMPLE   Tae kwon do is an ancient form of *martial art* from Korea that uses kicks and punches in a hard style.

Now here's a paragraph that defines tae kwon do. As you read, think about how the paragraph goes beyond the one-sentence definition.

PROGRAM MANAGER

CLASSIFICATION

- **Analyzing** To help students analyze and organize ideas, see **Comparing and Contrasting** in *Practicing the Writing Process,* p. 25.

QUOTATION FOR THE DAY

"Actually, male or female, what a writer has to have are an extraordinary memory, a marvelous ear, and a passion for bringing disparities together." (John Cheever, 1912–1982, American author)

After explaining that *disparities* means "differences," have students brainstorm lists of reasons why each characteristic in Cheever's quotation might be important to writers. End the activity by explaining that, using the classification strategy, students have opportunities to display the three traits Cheever cites.

After you guide students through the literary examples of defining and the literary example of comparing and contrasting, write the following headings on the chalkboard: "Comparisons (Similarities)"; "Contrasts (Differences)." Then hold up two shoes, perhaps a high-heeled shoe and a tennis shoe. As students offer similarities and differences, list them on the chalkboard under the correct heading. This procedure should prepare students to respond independently to the first question in **Exercise 7**. Then holding up only the tennis shoe, have students define the subject and list all the characteristics that distinguish it from other shoes. This procedure should prepare students to respond independently to the second question in **Exercise 7**.

MEETING *individual* NEEDS

AT-RISK STUDENTS

You may want to personalize **Exercise 7** to make it more relevant for students. For example, have students compare and contrast two careers they are interested in and have them define a hobby or familiar sport.

LEARNING STYLES

Kinetic Learners. Students could write their details for **Exercise 7** on large pieces of posterboard or paper. This will provide students freedom to move around as they list their details. Encourage them to share their lists with the class.

Visual Learners. Students may benefit from writing the columns for comparison and contrast in two different colors. This will allow students to envision the differences and help them remember to categorize.

AMENDMENTS TO SELECTIONS
Description of change: excerpted
Rationale: to focus on the concept of classification presented in this chapter

Tae kwon do is a martial art more than 2,000 years old. An assortment of kicks and punches that focus power with deadly effectiveness, it's a so-called hard style. Hard style? I ask Master Son. "Punch, side kick, roundhouse," Son replies. "One kick, fight finished."

Bob Berger, "Road Warrior"

Comparing and Contrasting. When writing about two or more subjects, you may want to compare and contrast them. *Compare* them by explaining how they're alike. *Contrast* them by telling how they're different. In a single paragraph, you'll probably do one or the other, not both.

Read this paragraph and decide which creature in the drawing below is a moth and which is a butterfly. See if you can find the major differences as you read.

There are three main differences between butterflies and moths. Butterflies are out by day while moths usually fly at night, but this is not an infallible guide since some moths fly by day. Second, moths spread their wings sideways at rest whereas butterflies hold them together over their backs, though again there are exceptions. Third, the butterfly's antennae are long and slender with clubbed ends, whereas a moth's are shorter and feathery.

Gerald Durrell with Lee Durrell,
The Amateur Naturalist

You could assess students' understanding of using classification as a strategy
by checking their responses to **Exercise 7**.

Close the lesson by asking students
to identify the two ways to develop classifi-
catory writing [defining; comparing and
contrasting]. ■

EXERCISE 7 ▶ Using Classification as a Strategy

What is it? What makes it different? How is it like or different from something else? All of these questions involve
the strategy of classification. Follow the directions below
to develop each main idea.

Main Idea	Classification Strategy
1. Japanese schools are very different from American schools.	Compare and contrast the two subjects: Japanese schools and American schools. List some details about each kind of school to support the main idea. (You may need to do some reading about Japanese schools.)
2. Even if you don't know much about dogs, you can't possibly mistake a Saint Bernard for a Siamese cat.	Define the subject. Tell its general class. Then, list all the characteristics that distinguish it from other breeds. (If you need some information about the animal, use an encyclopedia or talk to an owner.)

 COMPUTER NOTE: Create
charts or tables within your
word-processing program,
and use them to organize
details about a topic. These charts
may be particularly helpful when
you're comparing and contrasting
different subjects.

ANSWERS
Exercise 7

Responses will vary. Because the main
idea of the first question is how different
the schools are, check to see that students
list only contrasting details. Because
students are defining rather than
comparing and contrasting in the second
question, check to be sure that all details
are about the Saint Bernard.

OBJECTIVES

- To write an evaluative statement and to list reasons to support it
- To work cooperatively to establish criteria for evaluation

TEACHING THE LESSON

Begin by asking for a show of hands from students who like country music and from those who don't. Explain that when students make such a decision, they are evaluating. As a volunteer reads aloud the excerpt about Duke Ellington, point out the reasons on which the writer's final evaluation is based. Then, on the chalkboard,

---

Evaluation

Did you like the last movie you saw? What didn't you like? Would you recommend the movie to a friend?

In writing a paragraph to answer these questions, you'd be *evaluating.* This is the process of deciding whether something is good or bad—how valuable it is. Remember, though, it's not enough just to give your opinion. You also have to give reasons, or support, for your opinion.

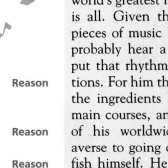

When you write an evaluation, you'll often give the reasons for your opinion in the *order of importance.* That is, you'll tell the most important reason first, the next most important reason next, and so on. Or you may decide to reverse the process and tell the least important reason first. Here is the opening paragraph of an article about the legendary composer and musician Duke Ellington. Notice the reasons the writer gives to support his evaluation.

Reason

Reason

Reason

Evaluation

Duke Ellington considered himself "the world's greatest listener." In music, hearing is all. Given the two or three thousand pieces of music Ellington wrote, he could probably hear a flea scratching itself and put that rhythm into one of his compositions. For him the sounds of the world were the ingredients he mixed into appetizers, main courses, and desserts for the appetite of his worldwide audience. He wasn't averse to going out in a boat to catch the fish himself. He would raise the fowl and the livestock and slaughter them all himself if there was no one else to do it. But when

---

PROGRAM MANAGER

EVALUATION

- **Analyzing** To help students analyze and organize ideas, see **Evaluation** in *Practicing the Writing Process,* p. 26.
- **Reinforcement/Reteaching** See **Revision Transparency 3.** For suggestions on how to tie the transparency to instruction, review teacher's notes in *Fine Art and Instructional Transparencies,* p. 89.
- **Review** For a review of transitional words and phrases, see **Transitional Words and Phrases** in *Practicing the Writing Process,* p. 27.

QUOTATION FOR THE DAY

"There is no book so bad . . . but something good may be found in it." (Miguel de Cervantes, 1547–1616, Spanish author)

LEP/ESL

General Strategies. To teach students the kind of functional speech necessary to express their opinions politely in English, give them the following list to

continued on next page

guide students through **Exercise 8** (below), having them choose subjects, form opinions, and suggest reasons to support their evaluations. You may want to develop a set of criteria for evaluation based on students' reasons. Students should then be prepared to complete **Exercise 9** (below) independently. You could assess understanding by checking each group's reasons and criteria developed in **Exercise 9.** Close the lesson by having students suggest how they might use evaluation throughout the course of a day. ■

that musical meal appeared before you none of the drudgery showed. It seemed perfectly natural, as if it had all appeared from behind an invisible door in the air.
                          Stanley Crouch, "The Duke's Blues"

EXERCISE 8 ▶ Using Evaluation as a Strategy

What's your evaluation—good, bad, or somewhere in between? What are your reasons for your evaluation? Pick two of the following topics and write a sentence expressing your evaluation. Then give two or three reasons to support your opinion.

EXAMPLE   *Evaluation: This pizza is delicious.*
           Reasons: (1) It has lots of cheese.
           (2) It has a crisp, crunchy crust.
           (3) The toppings are fresh and plentiful.

1. a recent recording you've listened to or a concert you've attended
2. last week's episode of your favorite TV series
3. a sporting event you attended or watched on TV
4. a new fad or fashion for teenagers

EXERCISE 9 ▶ Speaking and Listening: Evaluating a Movie

Of all the movies you've seen lately, which one is the best? Why? Think of at least three reasons to support your choice of best movie. Jot down your evaluation and your reasons. Then meet with a small group and give your evaluation and your reasons. Listen carefully as others present their evaluations. See if your group can agree on some criteria, or standards, for good movies. How important, for example, is suspense? believable characters and plot? good actors? You may find that the criteria have to be different for different types of films—for example, science fiction, action, drama, and mysteries.

use in verbal or written statements of evaluation:

1. In my opinion, . . .
2. It seems to me . . .
3. I think . . .
4. I believe . . .

ADVANCED STUDENTS

You could have students keep evaluation diaries for a week to evaluate foods and merchandise they encounter. Explain to students that, as consumers, they have the right to voice opinions based on facts. After a week, have students share their diaries in small groups.

ANSWERS
Exercise 8

Sentences will vary. Be sure students use facts, rather than opinions, to support their evaluative sentences.

ANSWERS
Exercise 9

Responses will vary. You may want to assign students to groups according to the types of films they have evaluated. Then groups could compare criteria and make a master list to go on a bulletin board or in a class notebook.

SELECTION AMENDMENT
Description of change: excerpted
Rationale: to focus on the concept of evaluation presented in this chapter

MAKING CONNECTIONS

WRITING A PARAGRAPH TO EXPRESS YOURSELF
OBJECTIVE
- To write an expressive paragraph, by following the steps of the writing process

WRITING A PARAGRAPH TO EXPRESS YOURSELF
Teaching Strategies
Explain to students that to write expressively, they must have emotions to express. Without such emotions, the writing will lack conviction, and it probably won't appeal to the reader. You may want to model the writing process for students by sharing a personal emotional experience that you are comfortable revealing.

GUIDELINES
You could assess these paragraphs on effort, but keep in mind that inexperienced writers often have difficulty expressing emotions on paper. You might ask students to share their paragraphs with each other in the revising stage. If details need clarifying, ask students to help each other come up with more precise sentences.

MAKING CONNECTIONS

WRITING PARAGRAPHS FOR DIFFERENT PURPOSES

In this chapter, you've studied the form and structure of paragraphs. Now you can try applying what you've learned as you write paragraphs. Remember that all writing has one or more of the following purposes: self-expression, information, persuasion, and creativity.

Writing a Paragraph to Express Yourself

What makes you feel angry or happy or frightened? What do you think about everyday things that happen to you or that you observe? Personal writing, or *expressive writing,* can help you get in touch with your thoughts and feelings. You may keep these written thoughts to yourself, but perhaps you share them with others.

Write a paragraph expressing how you think or what you feel about a specific subject. Here are some ideas.

- You've just learned that your family will be moving to a distant state next month.
- You just saw something that's made you furious.
- You're at a school dance. Someone you like but have never talked to before asks you to dance.
- You're thinking about a person who's made a big difference in your life. You want to tell that person how he or she has changed your life.

 Prewriting. Thoughts and feelings aren't neat; they come "boinging" through your brain the way a pinball travels in a pinball game. You may want to sort them out a bit before you start writing. Try listing or clustering or brainstorming to make some notes. (See pages 24–31 for a review of prewriting techniques.)

- To write an informative paragraph, by following the steps of the writing process

If you don't like any of the ideas listed above, look through your journal or diary. Try to recall an event or idea that you felt strongly about.

 Writing, Evaluating, and Revising. Write one paragraph explaining what you think and feel. If you're writing only for yourself, just leave your first draft the way you wrote it. But if you want to share your paragraph—and read what others have written—look over your draft carefully. Will your reader be able to follow your ideas?

Proofreading and Publishing. If you plan to share your paragraph, correct all mistakes in usage, spelling, and punctuation. (See the **Guidelines for Proofreading** on page 50.)

Writing a Paragraph to Inform

You take in a great deal of information every day from people, TV, radio, newspapers, and books. But you also give information to your friends and family. You may give directions for playing racquetball, advice on how to care for a pet, or information about the latest styles in clothes.

Write a paragraph using the information in the following chart. It gives statistics (facts stated in numbers) about how junior high students in the United States and in Japan spend their time. The numbers in the chart are hours per week.

Don't try to use all of the chart's information in one paragraph. Focus on what you think is most interesting or important. You can use the topic sentence suggested below or make up one of your own. In your paragraph, focus on differences (as in the topic sentence below) or on similarities. Think of your audience as readers of your school newspaper.

Topic sentence: If you were a junior high student in Japan, you'd be spending the 168 hours in every week differently than a junior high student in the United States.

**WRITING A PARAGRAPH
TO INFORM**
Teaching Strategies

Before students write, you could have them read some articles in their school newspaper to give them a better sense of audience and tone. Remind students that strong informative writing provides the reader with precise details.

GUIDELINES

You may want to use a focused holistic scale for assessment. Check that each paragraph includes a topic sentence, includes at least three supporting details, considers the audience, and communicates accurate information clearly.

- To write a persuasive paragraph, by following the steps of the writing process

TIME SPENT PER WEEK BY JUNIOR HIGH STUDENTS		
Activities	**United States**	**Japan**
Household work	4.6	3.3
School work	31.9	62.8
In school	28.7	46.6
Studying	3.2	16.2
Reading	1.2	2.6
Television	17.5	15.4
Playing games and sports	8.3	3.4
Sleep	59.6	56.6
Other	44.9	13.9

Institute for Social Research, University of Michigan, 1990

Prewriting and Writing. Start with a topic sentence, and add three to five supporting sentences. You can use specific numbers from the chart as well as conclusions based on the chart. (Sample conclusion: "Junior high students in Japan spend almost twice as much time on school work as American students.") Write so clearly that no one could possibly misunderstand what you're saying.

Evaluating and Revising. Would a seventh-grader understand your ideas? As you look for ways to improve your first draft, you might use easier words, reorder sentences, and reword your clincher sentence. Remember unity: Get rid of details that stray from the main idea.

Proofreading and Publishing. Give your paragraph a final polish by correcting mistakes in usage, punctuation, and spelling. Consult your classmates and choose one or two paragraphs to submit to your school paper.

Writing a Paragraph to Persuade

Both in speaking and in writing, persuasion aims to convince someone to take a specific action or to think in a certain way. How persuasive are you? Can you convince

WRITING A PARAGRAPH TO PERSUADE

Teaching Strategies

Point out to students that the key to being a successful persuasive writer is convincing readers that they will benefit from something. As Earth Educators, students should point out to their audience how reducing garbage will benefit readers personally. It might be helpful to suggest that students include words like *should, ought,* or *must* in their topic sentences to help them write persuasively instead of informatively.

people to volunteer to clean up a local park? Can you try to persuade local restaurants to stop using polystyrene cups and plates?

When seen from outer space, the planet Earth looks very beautiful. However, when you look closely, you can see that Earth has many problems.

You've just been appointed Earth Educator in your school. Use some of the facts in the chart below to write one paragraph persuading middle school students to take some action. In your topic sentence, identify the action you want them to take. Don't try to use all of the information in the chart. Just make sure you support your topic sentence with convincing facts and reasons. Here's a suggestion for a topic sentence that you might use.

Topic sentence: Unless we take action now, our beautiful Earth may not be beautiful much longer.

PROBLEM: Too much garbage

THINGS YOU CAN DO:
  Recycle glass, aluminum, plastic, newspaper.
  Don't buy products with a lot of packaging.
  Don't buy polystyrene at all.

FACTS:
1. Americans average four pounds of garbage per day per person.
2. Landfills (where garbage is deposited) are filling up.
3. A third of all our garbage is packaging waste.
4. Almost one tenth of every dollar spent on food goes for packaging that is thrown out.
5. Littered aluminum cans will still be there in five hundred years. Glass bottles last twice as long.
6. Polystyrene doesn't biodegrade at all. It kills turtles and other sea animals.
7. It takes nine times as much energy to make an aluminum can from raw materials as it takes to make an aluminum can from recycled aluminum.
8. Recycling glass and aluminum greatly lessens air pollution and water pollution from glass and aluminum factories.

GUIDELINES

To assess these paragraphs you will need to look at the topic sentences and supporting information. You might ask students to underline their supporting arguments so they will be easy to identify. Students should have convincing supporting details for each argument presented.

WRITING A PARAGRAPH
THAT IS CREATIVE
OBJECTIVE

• To write a creative paragraph, by
  following the steps of the writing
  process ■

88

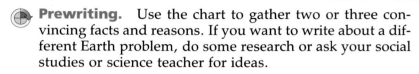 **Prewriting.** Use the chart to gather two or three convincing facts and reasons. If you want to write about a different Earth problem, do some research or ask your social studies or science teacher for ideas.

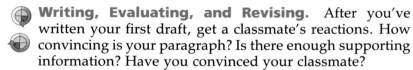 **Writing, Evaluating, and Revising.** After you've written your first draft, get a classmate's reactions. How convincing is your paragraph? Is there enough supporting information? Have you convinced your classmate?

Proofreading and Publishing. Correct any errors in usage and mechanics. Brainstorm ways of sharing your paragraphs with people in your school and community. You might compile a booklet that you can distribute to adults in your community.

Writing a Paragraph That Is Creative

In 1899, an American artist named Winslow Homer created the painting on page 89 and called it *The Gulf Stream*. Homer knew what the sea and sky looked like because he'd sailed across the Gulf Stream ten times. But how did he imagine the man, the boat, and the sharks?

Your assignment is to imagine a story based on Homer's painting. As in most stories, the main character is involved in some kind of ***conflict***, or struggle. Think of a beginning, middle, and end for the story of the man in the boat. Then, write the opening paragraph that describes the story's ***setting***, the time and place where the events occur. To develop your paragraph, you'll use description (pages 74–75).

Prewriting. Think through the story first.

- Who is the man in the boat? How did he get there?
- What is he thinking? What will happen to him?
- What part do the sharks and the sailboat on the horizon play in the story?

Jot down some sensory details. If you were on the boat, how would you describe the sky and sea? What would you smell and feel? What sounds would you hear?

WRITING A PARAGRAPH THAT IS CREATIVE
Teaching Strategies

This writing assignment requires students to place themselves in a picture and to tell a story. You could spend a few minutes asking students to imagine the sounds and smells of the sea. You might also explain to students that because this writing is creative, it will be based on their own knowledge, and because their experiences in life vary from their peers', everyone will have a different paragraph. Explain to students that style and life experiences are what make writing unique and interesting.

Winslow Homer, *The Gulf Stream* (1899). The Metropolitan Museum of Art, Catherine Lorillard Wolfe Collection, Wolfe Fund, 1906. (06.1234) Photograph © 1995 The Metropolitan Museum of Art.

 Writing, Evaluating, and Revising. Write the story's opening paragraph. Try to describe precisely how the sea looks, feels, sounds, and smells. You might use the first-person point of view with the man in the boat telling the story, using the pronoun *I.* Share your first draft with a classmate, and add or change details to make your description more interesting.

 Proofreading and Publishing. Correct any errors in usage and mechanics. In a small group, read your paragraph aloud. Discuss how others imagine the beginning of the man's story and its end. If you want to, work alone or with a partner to write the rest of your story.

 Reflecting on Your Writing

If you plan to include one or more of these paragraphs in your **portfolio,** date each one and use the following questions to include a brief reflection:

■ Which type of paragraph writing did you find easier, the persuasive paragraph or the creative one? Why?
■ Explain how you organized your ideas in each paragraph. Did you plan how to organize your ideas before you began writing?
■ Did writing only one paragraph on each subject seem just right, or did you want to write more?

 VISUAL CONNECTIONS
The Gulf Stream

About the Artist. Winslow Homer (1836–1910) was an American artist whose most famous paintings depicted the daily lives of fishermen and the power of the wind and the sea. Most of his sea paintings were done at his home on the Maine coast. However, he often traveled to the Adirondack Mountains and to Florida and the West Indies, where he found inspiration for some of his finest water colors.

GUIDELINES

Because creative writing is the most difficult to assess, you may want to grade this assignment holistically. For example, two plus signs (++) indicate clear and precise sensory details and developed setting and conflict; one plus sign (+) indicates that sensory details are present and that the setting and conflict are at least somewhat developed; and a minus sign (–) indicates that students need to work on developing sensory details, setting, or conflict. Additional feedback might include models so students can see the difference.

TEACHING NOTE

Evaluate students' answers to the questions listed under **Reflecting on Your Writing** based on whether they have analyzed their writing processes effectively.

LEARNING ABOUT COMPOSITIONS

OBJECTIVES

- To identify the structure of a composition (statement of main idea, introduction, body, and conclusion)
- To write a main idea statement for a composition
- To group and order details for a composition
- To use effective techniques to introduce, develop, and conclude a composition
- To use transitional words to ensure coherence in a composition

WORKPLACE writing

Writing a Letter of Inquiry

As students study the parts of a composition, have them keep a list of times in out-of-school situations when they would write using an introduction, body, and conclusion. Suggest that business letters have parts corresponding to these. Refer students to Chapter 35 "Letters and Forms" and suggest that a letter's heading, inside address, and salutation compare to the introduction while the closing and signature correspond to the conclusion. In the case of electronic mail, the address corresponds to the introduction and the identification of the sender to the conclusion.

Remind students that finding information is something they will do throughout their lives. They read newspaper ads to find information about what is on sale. They may write letters or send e-mail to request more information on a topic.

- **Prewriting** Have students list in their journals some things they might want information on. After students have completed their journaling, have them share in small groups what they have written and how they might most easily find the information they want. Students may want to create a graphic organizer like the following to help them organize their ideas.

Information Sought	Possible Source
the cost and availability of a shar-pei dog	• American Kennel Club • local pet shop • home pages
the date my favorite musical group will be performing in this area	• record company the group performs for • concert venues in this area • home pages

If students find the information they want without writing a letter, challenge them to expand their inquiry and send a letter or e-mail to request more information. If students have e-mail connections available to them, assign a computer-knowledgeable person to each group to help with using search engines and home pages.

- **Evaluating and Revising** If students are working on e-mail, have them print out their queries to share with their groups before sending their messages.

INTEGRATING THE LANGUAGE ARTS

SELECTION	READING AND LITERATURE	WRITING AND CRITICAL THINKING	LANGUAGE AND SYNTAX	SPEAKING, LISTENING, AND OTHER EXPRESSION SKILLS
• **"Does a Finger Fing?"** by Nedra Newkirk Lamar pp. 92–94 • from **Speaking for Ourselves** by Joyce Carol Thomas p. 105 • from **"Water World"** by Tony Reichhardt p. 106 • from **"Disaster Hits Home"** by Jennifer Cohen pp. 106, 111 • from **"Energy: Powering a Nation"** by Laurel Sherman p. 106 • from **"A Home on the Martian Range"** by Scott Stuckey p. 107 • from **"Billy Mills"** by Della A. Yannuzzi p. 107 • from **"Pictures of the Poor"** by Elsa Marston p. 111	• Using inferential comprehension skills when reading a passage p. 95 • Identifying main idea pp. 95, 100 • Using evaluative comprehension skills when reading a passage p. 95 • Identifying the conclusion of a selection p. 95 • Identifying the structure of a passage introduction pp. 106, 107	• Writing sentences to express the main idea clearly p. 100 • Using listing as a prewriting technique to generate ideas for writing pp. 101, 114 • Using logical thought patterns such as chronological order p. 101 • Using appropriate transitions p. 109 • Rewriting a conclusion based on an evaluation of a sample p. 112 • Analyzing information to make inferences p. 113 • Creating a product based on information pp. 113–115 • Arranging supporting details and facts in a logical, coherent order pp. 113–115 • Writing a draft with emphasis on content pp. 113–115 • Revising a draft for unity and coherence pp. 113–115 • Writing essays with topic sentences, details, organization, and closing statements pp. 113–115	• Proofreading for spelling, capitalization, punctuation, and usage errors p. 115	• Contributing to small group discussions pp. 106–107 • Organizing ideas pp. 113–114 • Asking questions to obtain information p. 115 • Providing constructive criticism based on critical judgments p. 115 • Responding to the writing of peers during the writing process p. 115

CHAPTER 3: LEARNING ABOUT COMPOSITIONS

Use this guide for creating an instructional plan that addresses the individual needs of your students. Assignments accompanied by the following symbol (∗) may be completed out of class. Times given for pacing lessons are estimated.

CHAPTER PLANNING GUIDE—PUPIL'S EDITION

LESSONS	LITERARY MODEL pp. 92–94 "Does a Finger Fing?" by Nedra Newkirk Lamar	WHAT MAKES A COMPOSITION pp. 96–103
DEVELOPMENTAL PROGRAM	🕐 **20–25 minutes** • Read model aloud in class and work with students to answer questions on p. 95 orally.	🕐 **40–45 minutes** • Main Assignment: Looking Ahead p. 95 • Read aloud "What Makes a Composition" pp. 96–99 • Exercise 1 p. 100∗ • Exercise 2 p. 101∗ • Read aloud "A Writer's Model" pp. 101–103
CORE PROGRAM	🕐 **20–25 minutes** • Assign student pairs to read model and answer questions on p. 95.	🕐 **20–25 minutes** • Main Assignment: Looking Ahead p. 95 • What Makes a Composition pp. 96–99 • Exercises 1, 2 pp. 100, 101∗ • A Writer's Model pp. 101–103∗
ACCELERATED PROGRAM	🕐 **10–15 minutes** • Assign students to read model independently.	🕐 **5–10 minutes** • Main Assignment: Looking Ahead p. 95 • What Makes a Composition pp. 96–99∗ • Exercises 1, 2 pp. 100, 101∗

CHAPTER PLANNING GUIDE—PROGRAM RESOURCES

	LITERARY MODEL	WHAT MAKES A COMPOSITION
PRINT	• Reading Master 3, *Practice for Assessment in Reading, Vocabulary, and Spelling* p. 3	• Planning a Composition, Grouping and Organizing Ideas, Writing a Formal Outline, *Practicing the Writing Process* pp. 31–33 • Planning a Composition, *English Workshop* pp. 19–20
MEDIA		

THE INTRODUCTION pp. 104–107	THE BODY pp. 108–110	THE CONCLUSION pp. 110–112
⏱ **35–40 minutes** • Read "The Introduction" pp. 104–106 in pairs • Exercise 3 pp. 106–107	⏱ **20–25 minutes** • The Body pp. 108–109 • Writing Note p. 108 • Exercise 4 pp. 109–110 in pairs	⏱ **15–20 minutes** • The Conclusion pp. 110–111 • Exercise 5 p. 112*
⏱ **20–25 minutes** • The Introduction pp. 104–106* • Exercise 3 pp. 106–107	⏱ **5–10 minutes** • The Body pp. 108–109* • Writing Note p. 108 • Exercise 4 pp. 109–110*	⏱ **5–10 minutes** • Ways to Write Conclusions pp. 110–111 • Exercise 5 p. 112*
⏱ **10–15 minutes** • Exercise 3 pp. 106–107	⏱ **5–10 minutes** • Writing Note p. 108 • Unity p. 108* • Coherence p. 109*	⏱ **5–10 minutes** • Ways to Write Conclusions pp. 110–111 • Exercise 5 p. 112*

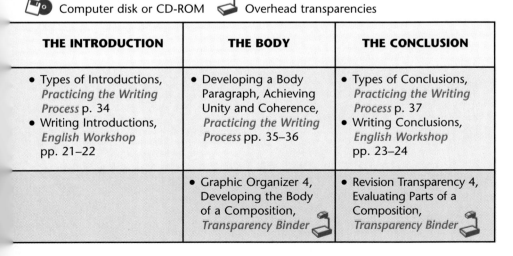 Computer disk or CD-ROM Overhead transparencies

THE INTRODUCTION	THE BODY	THE CONCLUSION
• Types of Introductions, *Practicing the Writing Process* p. 34 • Writing Introductions, *English Workshop* pp. 21–22	• Developing a Body Paragraph, Achieving Unity and Coherence, *Practicing the Writing Process* pp. 35–36	• Types of Conclusions, *Practicing the Writing Process* p. 37 • Writing Conclusions, *English Workshop* pp. 23–24
	• Graphic Organizer 4, Developing the Body of a Composition, *Transparency Binder*	• Revision Transparency 4, Evaluating Parts of a Composition, *Transparency Binder*

 **ELEMENTS OF WRITING: CURRICULUM CONNECTIONS**

Making Connections
• Writing an Informative Composition pp. 113–115

ASSESSMENT OPTIONS

Portfolio Assessment
Evaluating a Paper, Analytic Scale for Evaluation, Simplified Analytic Scales, Proofreading Checklist, *Portfolio Assessment* pp. 11–14, 18–19

Summative Assessment
Review: Revising and Proofreading, *Practicing the Writing Process* p. 38

Reflection
Self-assessment Record, Proofreading Record, *Portfolio Assessment* pp. 15, 20–21

LOOKING AT THE WHOLE

OBJECTIVES

- To respond personally to a professional writing model
- To analyze a professional model for main idea, content, and completeness

MOTIVATION

Ask students if they have ever talked with friends whose conversations rambled. Was it sometimes hard to understand what they were trying to say? Tell students that rambling compositions result in the same confusion. If the writing isn't clear, the reader doesn't understand.

PROGRAM MANAGER

CHAPTER 3

- **Practice** To help less-advanced students who need additional practice with concepts and activities related to this chapter, see **Chapter 3** in *English Workshop, Second Course,* pp. 19–24.
- **Reading Support** For help with the reading selection, pp. 92–94, see **Reading Master 3** in *Practice for Assessment in Reading, Vocabulary, and Spelling,* p. 3.

VISUAL CONNECTIONS

Exploring the Subject. The threads of this spider's web all support the structure and relate, directly or indirectly, to the central point. You could use this picture as a visual metaphor for composition structure, describing the central hub as the main idea, the radial spokes as supporting paragraphs, and the crossthreads as sentences that develop the paragraphs and tie them together. Remind students that just as the spider's web exists within specific boundaries, a good composition covers only ideas that belong within the topic.

3 LEARNING ABOUT COMPOSITIONS

TEACHING THE LESSON

Tell students that the model composition on the next page has some words they might not know. Write *tinker, clabber, sock-dolager, adjuster,* and *fruiterer* on the chalkboard and help students define each word. Choose a volunteer to read **"Does a Finger Fing?"** to the class. If students are confused by unfamiliar words, pause to pronounce and define them. Ask students how the author uses humor in her composition. Do they agree with her point of view? The author gives many examples of *-er* words that don't mean someone or something does anything. Have students think of *-er* words that follow the normal pattern.

Looking at the Whole

Who's the most important player on a softball team? The pitcher who strikes out the side? Or the batter who gets a hit every time? They're both important because they help make up a whole team. Words, sentences, and paragraphs are also team players. Together, they make up a **whole composition.**

Writing and You. A *TV Guide* article says that one day you'll be able to talk back to your TV set. A science magazine reports that a fossil of a whale has been found deep in the desert. In the newspaper, you read a review of a new movie. These are all compositions. They all explore one idea about a single topic. Where else might you read a composition?

As You Read.   In the following article, Nedra Newkirk Lamar uses basic composition form to have fun with the English language.

QUOTATION FOR THE DAY

"English is a funny language. A fat chance and a slim chance are the same thing." (Jack Herbert, American author)

Ask half of the class to write sentences or dialogues using the expression *fat chance* and the other half to write sentences or dialogues using the expression *slim chance.* After they compare their sentences, ask volunteers to draw conclusions about peculiarities in our language.

MEETING *individual* NEEDS

LEP/ESL

General Strategies. Students should read the article that begins on the next page without using their dictionaries to look up every nonsense word of the selection. Because the body of the article is a long list of word jokes, understanding just two or three of the jokes can lead students to understand the point of the article.

GUIDED PRACTICE

To model answers to the **Reader's Response** questions, you might list specific examples of word tricks on the chalkboard, such as using the same word as different parts of speech. For analysis questions, you could model finding the main idea of a sample paragraph from **A Writer's Model** on pp. 101–103.

INDEPENDENT PRACTICE

For the **Reader's Response** questions, students might brainstorm in small groups to write down additional examples of unusual language that they feel is tricky. To ensure that you get thoughtful answers to the **Writer's Craft** questions, have students give examples.

USING THE SELECTION
Does a Finger Fing?

1

Lamar introduces her composition with a series of questions. Is this an effective way to capture the reader's attention?
[Responses will vary. Most students will find the introduction effective.]

DOES A FINGER FING?

by Nedra Newkirk Lamar

1 Everybody knows that a tongue-twister is something that twists the tongue, and a skyscraper is something that scrapes the sky, but is an <u>eavesdropper</u> someone who drops eaves? A thinker is someone who thinks but is a <u>tinker</u> someone who tinks? Is a <u>clabber</u> something that goes around clabbing?

Somewhere along the way we all must have had an English teacher who gave us the fascinating information that words that end in ER mean something or somebody who *does* something, like trapper, designer, or stopper.

> " . . . a skyscraper is something that scrapes the sky, but is an eavesdropper someone who drops eaves? "

93

VISUAL CONNECTIONS
Related Expression Skills.
After students have read the essay, have them brainstorm together to make a list of occupational titles that end in –*er* or –*or,* such as *teacher, doctor, navigator,* and so on. Have students make a collage that depicts people acting out varied occupational tasks. You may want to call students' attention to the sourcebook *Dictionary of Occupational Titles* to increase their awareness of occupational titles.

A stinger is something that stings, but is a finger something that fings? Fing fang fung. Today I fing. Yesterday I fang. Day before yesterday I had already fung.

You'd expect eyes, then, to be called seers and ears to be hearers. We'd wear our shoes on our walkers and our sleeves on our reachers. But we don't. The only parts of the body that sound as if they might indicate what they're supposed to do are our fingers, which we've already counted out, our livers, and our shoulders. And they don't do what they sound as if they might. At least, I've never seen anyone use his shoulders for shoulding. You shoulder your way through a crowd, but you don't should your way. It's only in slang that we follow the pattern, when we smell with our smellers and kiss with our kissers.

The animal pattern seems to have more of a feeling for this formation than people do, because insects actually do feel with their feelers. But do cats use their whiskers for whisking?

I've seen people mend socks and knit socks, but I've never seen anyone dolage a sock. Yet there must be people who do, else how could we have <u>sock-dolagers</u>?

Is a <u>humdinger</u> one who dings hums? And what is a hum anyway, and how would one go about dinging it? Maybe Winnie the Pooh could have told us. He was always humming hums, but <u>A. A. Milne</u> never tells us whether he also was fond of dinging them. He sang them but do you suppose he ever dang them?

2

Why does the author write "Fing, fang, fung"? [She shows in a humorous way that *fing* isn't a verb and that it can't be conjugated.]

Ask the class to identify the components of a composition. Next, have students give two examples of writing that would not follow the structure of a composition [poem, dialogue]. Then have students name two examples of writing that would be in composition form [news article, book review].

Challenge students to paint or draw humorous artwork illustrating words that are exceptions to the regular -er pattern. As an example, hold up a ruler and ask students if it follows the pattern. Suggest that students draw the ruler as a king. ■

3

Although all the paragraphs relate to the main idea of the composition, many of the individual paragraphs have main ideas. This paragraph focuses on occupational names.

4

How does the author begin her conclusion? [She closes with a definitive statement that sums up the points in the rest of her article.]

MEETING *individual* NEEDS

STUDENTS WITH SPECIAL NEEDS

Students who have difficulties with written language generally need practice analyzing selections with several paragraphs. To assist the students, you might analyze short selections on an overhead projector. Have students identify the title of the selection and the number of paragraphs it contains. Have students identify and highlight the main idea of each paragraph. After reading the entire selection, have them state the writer's point. Then they can analyze how each paragraph supports the main idea.

SELECTION AMENDMENT
Description of change: excerpted
Rationale: to focus on the main idea of the literary model presented in this chapter

3 Sometimes occupational names do reveal what the worker does, though. Manufacturers manufacture, miners mine, adjusters adjust—or at least try to. But does a grocer groce? Does a fruiterer fruiter? Does a butler buttle?

4 No, you just can't trust the English language. You can love it because it's your mother tongue. You can take pride in it because it's the language Shakespeare was dramatic in. You can thrill to it because it's the language Browning and Tennyson were poetic in. You can have fun with it because it's the language Dickens and Mark Twain and Lewis Carroll were funny in. You can revere it because it's the language Milton was majestic in. You can be grateful to it because it's the language the Magna Carta and the Declaration of Independence were expressed in.

But you just can't trust it!

"These are but wild and whirling words..."

—**Shakespeare**
Hamlet, Act 1, Scene 5

READER'S RESPONSE

1. The writer's point is that the English language is tricky. You can't trust it. What do you think? What tricks has English played on you?
2. If English is your second language, think about your first language for a minute. Is it tricky? What are some examples of rules that are irregular or hard to follow?

WRITER'S CRAFT

3. In this article, the writer includes several paragraphs with examples to support her main idea. What is the main idea?
4. The last two paragraphs bring the article to an end. What has the writer done to let you, the reader, know that it's the end?

LOOKING AHEAD

As you work through this chapter, you'll learn about the parts of a composition. You'll learn that most compositions

- have one main idea
- have three main parts: an introduction, a body, and a conclusion
- have unity and coherence so that readers can clearly follow ideas

ANSWERS

Reader's Response

Responses will vary.

1. Most students will agree that English is tricky. In addition to -er words, they might point out irregular verbs, idiomatic expressions, peculiar pronunciations and spellings, puns, and other oddities.

2. Answers will depend upon the first languages of your English-language learners.

Writer's Craft

3. The main idea is that English is tricky; you can't trust it to work logically.

4. The author states her main idea, "No, you just can't trust the English language." Then she names famous authors and the positive attributes of the English language (drama, humor, majesty). Her concluding sentence then restates the main idea.

WHAT MAKES A COMPOSITION

OBJECTIVES

- To write a sentence that states the main idea of a composition
- To analyze, group, and arrange details for a composition

MOTIVATION

Have a student read the first three paragraphs of **What Makes a Composition.** Then ask students if they have ever forgotten to take something important to school or on a trip. Have several describe their experiences. Ask what they learned about planning ahead.

PROGRAM MANAGER

WHAT MAKES A COMPOSITION

■ **Analyzing** To help students analyze and organize ideas, see **Planning a Composition, Grouping and Organizing Ideas,** and **Writing a Formal Outline** in *Practicing the Writing Process,* pp. 31–33.

QUOTATION FOR THE DAY

"Of all those arts in which the wise excel,/Nature's chief masterpiece is writing well." (John Sheffield, 1648–1721, Duke of Buckingham and Normanby)

You could use the quotation to initiate a discussion of writing. Ask students to brainstorm in small groups and to list ways that knowing how to write well might help someone. [They might mention the benefits good writing provides a student, an employee, a consumer, a friend, or a relative.] Explain that in this lesson students will learn some elements of a well-written composition.

What Makes a Composition

You probably remember a time in elementary school when you stood before a class, knees quaking, to read a composition like "My Dog Spot" or "How I Spent My Summer Vacation." You may not have realized it then, but you were practicing skills that you will use for the rest of your life.

Someday an employer may ask you to write a short composition, or essay, on your goals and interests in life. This composition may help decide whether you get the job. And you'll use these same composition skills throughout school. On a history test, you might write a composition to explain the causes of the American Revolution. In science, you might compose a short composition to explain how a tadpole becomes a frog.

In this chapter, you'll learn the basic parts of the composition form. In later chapters, you'll use that form to explain a process, to write a persuasive essay, to write about literature, and to write a research report.

" 'What I Did This Summer.' This summer, I went to camp. I hated it. I hated every minute of it. I hated my counsellor. I hated the food. I hated the woods. I hated the nature walks and the nature talks. I hated the outings. I hated the campfires. I hated the overnights. I hated . . ."

Drawing by H. Martin; © 1985 The New Yorker Magazine, Inc.

TEACHING THE LESSON

Guide students in a discussion of the material in **The Composition Plan** to help them realize the importance of planning when writing compositions. You might list on the chalkboard the steps of planning a composition so that students have a visual representation of how each step leads to the next.

Include the following steps:
1. Choose a topic.
2. Narrow the focus with a main idea statement.
3. List all details the main idea suggests.
4. Arrange details in groups.
5. Name the groups of ideas.
6. Select the best order to present ideas.

The Composition Plan

Imagine planning spring vacation and looking at an empty suitcase. What will you pack? Well, you might say, that depends on several things. *Where am I going? How long will I be gone? Where will I stay?* You ask these questions so you can plan.

Without planning, you might end up at the beach with your favorite jeans but no bathing suit. Writing compositions takes planning, too. And the more planning you do, the easier your job will be.

The Main Idea Statement

Just like every article you read, every composition has a *main idea.* And that's where you begin your planning. For example, after some thought, you've chosen "movies" as the topic of your composition. What point will you make about movies? This point, or idea, is what your composition will be about. Every detail and each paragraph you write will tie into this main idea. After brainstorming, you might decide to limit the topic of movies to "what makes a good movie." This would become the main idea of your composition.

Early Plans

An early plan, also called an *informal outline,* is one way of sorting your ideas to make your job of writing easier. You put items into groups and then arrange your groups in order.

Grouping.   First, list all the details you can think of on your topic. Look them over, and ask yourself: *Which items are the most alike? What do they have in common? Which items don't fit at all?* (You can cross these out.) Then, arrange all the items into groups. Finally, write a heading for each group that shows how the items in it are related. Here's how one writer grouped and labeled items for a composition with the main idea "what makes a good movie."

Emphasize to students the importance of narrowing their topics to one main idea statement. That statement usually involves a specific claim or opinion that the rest of the composition will support.

Tell students that if they choose to plan their compositions with formal outlines, they will combine several steps of the **Early Plans** process. Explain that formal outlines are especially helpful for longer compositions because they are more structured and show the relationships of ideas.

—STRONG PLOT—
interesting beginning, high interest level

—STRONG CHARACTERS—
real and interesting people, sympathetic to viewers

—SPECIAL FEATURES—
special effects, unusual settings, different time periods, music

Ordering.   You also have to think about how to order, or arrange, your ideas so that they will make sense. What should you tell your readers about first? second? last?

Sometimes, your ideas will fall right into place. If you're explaining to readers how to program a VCR, a step-by-step process, you would use *chronological* (time) *order.* For the composition on what makes a good movie, on pages 101–103, it made sense to the writer to use *order of importance* (from most important to least important characteristic: plot, characters, special features. Of course, you could also do it in reverse order if it suited your purpose.) If you were describing an old haunted house, however, you would probably want to use *spatial* (space or location) *order.*

You can use any order that makes sense. Sometimes the topic itself suggests the order. Other times, you simply begin at the beginning with important background information and then cover the material in an order that makes sense. With whatever order you use, ask yourself: *Will my readers be able to follow my thoughts easily? Does each group of details make sense from what comes before?*

INTEGRATING THE LANGUAGE ARTS

Literature Link. Newspaper and magazine articles often use chronological order to arrange events. But longer news features that are written in essay form sometimes use order of importance to switch from past events to reflections about them. In "A Tragedy Revealed: A Heroine's Last Days," reporter Ernst Schnabel tells Anne Frank's story in the order in which his research about her life progressed. If both selections are contained in your literature textbook or are available in your library, students might contrast this kind of order with the order used in *The Diary of Anne Frank.*

Library Link. Take students to the library and teach or review the use of the *Readers' Guide* to find current articles on topics students are considering. Have students think of topics to look up as a class. Locate the articles to give students practice finding sources including microfiche and microfilm. If the material is on microfiche or microfilm, teach students how to load the film, how to find the appropriate pages, and how to copy them. Consider requiring that students use at least one current source each when writing the papers.

GUIDED PRACTICE

To help prepare students to write main idea statements, pull the important details from a selection in a science or social studies textbook and read them orally. See if students can state the main idea of the selection by listening to the details.

Then prepare students for grouping details. Find varied facts about a country (languages, resources, foods, and so on) and list the facts on the chalkboard or on a handout. With your students, group the facts and name the groups.

 REFERENCE NOTE: See page 36 for more information about ordering ideas.

Formal Outlines

Another way to plan your composition is to make a *formal outline.* It's similar to the early plan, except it's more structured. It uses letters and numbers to show the relationships of ideas. You won't need to make a formal outline for every composition, but in most cases, a formal outline can help you plan.

There are two kinds of formal outlines. A *topic outline* states ideas in words or brief phrases. A *sentence outline* states ideas in complete sentences.

Here is the topic outline that the writer prepared when planning the composition on what makes a good movie.

Title: Good Movies: Two Thumbs Up
Main Idea: Good movies share certain qualities that make them winners.
  I. Plot
    A. Strong beginning
    B. Interesting plot developments
  II. Characters
    A. Real and interesting
    B. Sympathetic in some way
  III. Special features
    A. Special effects
    B. Interesting or unusual settings
    C. Historical time periods
    D. Music

 REFERENCE NOTE: To learn more about formal outlines, see pages 342–343.

 COMPUTER NOTE: If your word-processing program has a built-in outlining function, you can use it to help create an outline. An outlining function allows you to move whole sections of the outline at once, as you decide how you want to arrange your ideas.

COOPERATIVE LEARNING

List several possible topics for papers on the chalkboard. Have students form groups of five or six based on their interest in a topic.

Students can then brainstorm for main idea statements and details to include in their papers. Students might want to use reference materials for more information. Have students group and order the details to make formal outlines.

MEETING *individual* **NEEDS**

AT-RISK STUDENTS

To help students better understand how formal outlines can help them organize their papers, make copies of the outline and the composition on what makes a good movie. Have small groups of students label each part of the composition from the outline. Point out how the supporting details strengthen the author's main points.

TECHNOLOGY TIP

Encourage students to explore the outline function of their word-processing program, if it is available. Typically, these functions do not use traditional Roman numerals and letters to indicate divisions, but you can quickly and effectively use outlines produced on computers to teach the more traditional outline format.

Have students work independently on **Exercises 1** and **2** to create main idea statements and to group details under two headings for these main ideas.

Assess students' ability to state the main ideas and to organize details by evaluating their performances on **Exercises 1** and **2**.

ANSWERS

Exercise 1

Responses will vary. Here is a possibility: Many changes have taken place since the Olympic games first began.

A DIFFERENT APPROACH

Have students analyze existing compositions to understand better how they are organized. You could copy magazine articles and have students highlight the main idea of each article. Then have students find and highlight related ideas by using different colors for each main point.

TECHNOLOGY TIP

You may wish to take students to a library and to ask a librarian to demonstrate the use of a CD-ROM index. This computerized version of the *Readers' Guide* will be very useful to students when they search for information on current topics.

EXERCISE 1   **Writing the Main Idea**

You've been magically transported back in time to the first Olympic Games. After you have watched the original version of the Olympic competition, you're transported to the 2002 Olympic Games in Salt Lake City, Utah. You jot down the following facts that you learned from your journeys. Ask yourself what point or idea is suggested by these facts, and write a sentence that states the main idea.

* *Modern athletes compete for gold, silver, or bronze medals and can make money from endorsements.*
* *First Olympic games took place in Olympia, Greece, in 776 B.C.*
* *Modern athletes train for years before competing.*
* *Now both men and women compete in more than twenty-five different sports.*
* *Ancient athletes received wreaths of laurel leaves as prizes for Olympic victories.*
* *Millions watch the modern games in person and through TV.*
* *Winter sports events were not a part of the ancient Greek games.*
* *In the Greek games, only men could compete.*
* *Ancient athletes trained under professional coaches for ten months before the games.*
* *Today's competitors receive great recognition and lots of attention.*
* *Tens of thousands of spectators gathered at the ancient games.*

If students are having trouble determining the main idea of a selection, try giving them a choice of main idea statements.
First, have students read a selection. Then,
offer three statements that apply to the
subject; only one should directly state the
main idea. You may want to do this with a
selection that states the main idea as a topic sentence and with a selection that
has an implied main idea.

☞

The Composition Plan **101**

EXERCISE 2 ▶ Creating an Early Plan

You're still working on your composition about your experiences at the 776 B.C. and the 2002 Olympic Games. With the main idea written, it's time to create an early plan. First, read over the details in Exercise 1 again. Then, group common details under two headings. Finally, arrange the details in each group into an order that you think would make sense to your readers. [Hint: You might want to use chronological order.]

A WRITER'S MODEL

Here's a composition on what makes a good movie. After you read it, look to see how it follows both the early plan and the formal outline. Also, notice how each paragraph topic supports the main idea throughout the composition.

Good Movies: Two Thumbs Up

INTRODUCTION

You are slumped in your seat, jumbo-sized popcorn in your hand. The lights dim, and you're ready for another escape into the world of movies. Maybe you'll find adventure, comedy, romance, or suspense. But maybe you won't. In fact, you may

Main idea

enjoy your popcorn more than the movie. What makes the difference? What makes a good movie?

BODY
Main topic:
Plot

First of all, a good movie draws you into the action quickly. The excitement begins early in Apollo 13, for example, as it dramatizes the thirteenth Apollo space mission. When an oxygen tank in the spacecraft explodes on the way to the moon, the astronauts on board must turn the ship around to try to get back to Earth alive. Who could resist such a suspenseful plot?

A good movie also fulfills the promise of early thrills. Apollo 13 does this by showing the obstacles

CLOSURE

Ask students what they should do after choosing a topic. [Narrow the focus of the topic by stating the main idea.] Ask students what they need to do after stating the main idea. [They should list and group the details they will include in their papers.]

EXTENSION

Have students read various poems to compare the treatment of main ideas in poetry to the treatment of main ideas in compositions. Begin the discussion by choosing a poem and asking what the main idea is. Is it overtly stated or does the reader have to deduce it? ■

◆ INTEGRATING THE LANGUAGE ARTS

Literature Link. A screenplay or teleplay reveals the main idea through the characters' words and actions. The screenwriter includes stage directions to help present details that will be incorporated into the movie. If the teleplay is contained in your literature textbook or is available in your library, you might have students analyze the stage directions of a movie such as *Let Me Hear You Whisper,* screenwritten by Paul Zindel. Have students look at how the directions present visual or sound images to help create the main idea.

102 | WRITING HANDBOOK | *Compositions*

the astronauts have to overcome on their way back to Earth. With their oxygen running out, the astronauts must direct the spacecraft to reenter the Earth's atmosphere at precisely the right angle, or it will either be incinerated or bounced off into space forever. This plot keeps you riveted, because you want the astronauts to make it home safely.

Main topic: Characters

A good movie also has characters who catch your interest or your sympathy. Jo March, one of the main characters in Little Women, does both. Jo is one of four daughters in the March family, who live in Concord, Massachusetts, during the Civil War. Jo captures your interest because she is so lively and assertive—a tomboy who wants to be a writer, she stages family plays in which everyone, including the cat, has to play a role. But you also feel sympathy for Jo and her sisters as they try to fulfill their dreams in a world that doesn't encourage girls to act like independent individuals. When Jo moves to New York to pursue a writing career, she shows her excitement about her new adventure, even as she struggles with questions about work and love.

Main topic: Special features

Finally, a really good movie has special features. It has something extra that sets it apart from other movies. One of these extras might be

102

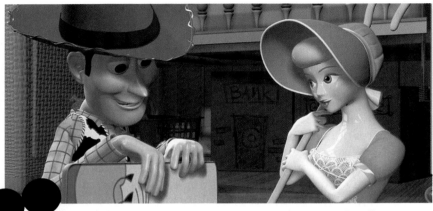

INTEGRATING THE LANGUAGE ARTS

Test-taking Link. Tell students that they probably will be required to complete essay tests all through their school years. Emphasize that planning is especially important on these tests because time is limited. Planning will help students to include all their main points and to avoid rambling about unimportant details. You may want to have timed practices in which students write main idea statements and outlines. (Choose topics that students already know about.)

great special effects. For example, <u>Toy Story</u> uses computer technology to create realistic animation that seems three-dimensional. Another special feature might be the setting. <u>The Secret of Roan Inish</u>, for example, draws you into the magical world of a seal-populated island on the western coast of Ireland. A beautiful, unusual setting makes a good story even better.

A historical setting, especially one based on actual events, can also make a good movie. <u>Glory</u> tells the true account of the first African American company to fight for the Union army. This gives the plot a special edge. You just can't help thinking that this is about real soldiers facing real bullets.

Finally, music is another special feature that can improve a movie. Think of <u>The Sound of Music</u>. Without its songs, it wouldn't be nearly as interesting.

CONCLUSION

By the time the lights come up in the theater, you know which was better—the popcorn or the movie. If you're lucky, the movie won out. But if you're not, there are always new movies to see. Maybe the next one will get it right—both the popcorn and the movie will be two thumbs up!

THE INTRODUCTION

OBJECTIVE

- To identify three effective techniques used to introduce compositions

Have a student read the first paragraph of **The Introduction.** Ask students to think of someone who made a favorable first impression on them. Ask them why they were impressed.

Remind students that an introduction in a composition is the reader's first impression. For the impression to be favor-

---

PROGRAM MANAGER

THE INTRODUCTION

- **Analyzing** To help students analyze and organize ideas, see **Types of Introductions** in *Practicing the Writing Process,* p. 34.

QUOTATION FOR THE DAY

"Self-confidence is the first requisite to great undertakings." (Samuel Johnson, 1709–1784, English lexicographer, essayist, and poet)

Ask students to imagine that Johnson's dog has chewed up the rest of this quotation and have them write one or two sentences to complete it. Have them consider what the second and third requisites might be.

LESS-ADVANCED STUDENTS

Students may discover that finding an interesting way of writing an introduction slows them down in getting their ideas down on paper. Suggest that they skip their introductions and come back to them later. Explain that the process of putting down words on paper sometimes brings other words to mind.

The Parts of the Composition

You have a topic, a main idea, and an early plan or outline. Now you need to think about the three parts of a composition: the introduction, the body, and the conclusion.

The Introduction

Think about a time when you met someone who made a great first impression. Didn't you instantly like him or her and want to get to know that person better? Compositions also make first impressions with their introductions. A lively introduction hooks its readers and makes them eager to read more. A dull introduction runs the risk of boring its readers, who might stop reading.

Capturing the Reader's Interest. In the composition on good movies, the writer could have written the following introduction.

> Some movies are fun to watch. Some aren't. But good movies do have things in common.

Does this introduction make a good impression? You'd probably agree that it doesn't. It does do one thing—it tells what the composition is about. But it's so boring that most people might not read any further.

Now, take another look at the introduction in the model on page 101. The writer begins by describing a scene familiar to most moviegoers. The writer then encourages the reader to think: What *does* make a good movie?

Presenting the Main Idea. You'll usually want to include your main idea statement in your introduction. This keeps both you and your readers on track. It's your way of saying, "This is what I'm going to talk about." Do you see how the writer stated the main idea in the last sentence of the introduction on page 101? Even though it's a question, there's no doubt what this composition is about.

able, it must grab the reader's interest. Read the remainder of the page with your students. Remind them of the importance of the main idea statement and explain why it needs to be near the beginning of the composition. Then read and discuss the three types of introductions.

To prepare students to identify types of introductions, find examples of the three types: questions, anecdotes, and startling facts. Read the examples to the class, and help students to identify the types of introductions.

Ways to Write Introductions

Writers use a variety of techniques to grab their readers' attention with interesting introductions. Here are three.

1. **Ask a question.** The writer of the composition on good movies ends the introduction by asking a question: *What makes a good movie?* By starting this way, the writer does a couple of things: quickly gets the reader's attention and involves the reader in the paper. Most people would want to read more.

2. **Tell an anecdote.** An anecdote is a short, interesting story. Since most people like a good story, an anecdote is a good way to begin your composition. Notice how the author Joyce Carol Thomas uses an anecdote to introduce an autobiographical sketch.

I was reluctant to leave Ponca City, Oklahoma, where I was born. As we boarded the train to California in 1948, I celebrated my tenth birthday, enjoying the traveling adventure but longing to be back in the place I knew. When I look at my books, I suddenly realize that I have never really left Oklahoma. *Marked by Fire* is set in Ponca City, and so are *Bright Shadow* and *The Golden Pasture*. Going to a new place held its own excitement, too, and the California landscape became the setting of *Water Girl* and *Journey*.

Joyce Carol Thomas, *Speaking for Ourselves*

LEARNING STYLES

Visual Learners. You could visually show students how some introductions start with a broad topic and narrow to a specific main idea. Draw on the chalkboard the following inverted triangle. Then help students determine whether their topics can be narrowed using an inverted triangle.

Soccer

Positions

Skill needed to be a goalie

VISUAL CONNECTIONS
Ideas for Writing. Students might be interested in reading more about Joyce Carol Thomas and in preparing outlines of pertinent information about her life and writing. They could save their notes and outlines to use in **Chapter 10: "Writing a Research Report."**

SELECTION AMENDMENT
Description of change: excerpted
Rationale: to focus on the concept of introductions presented in this chapter

INDEPENDENT PRACTICE

Have students work independently in groups of three to identify the introductions in **Exercise 3**.

ASSESSMENT

Assess students' ability to recognize different types of introductions by evaluating their performances on **Exercise 3**.

![icon] **COOPERATIVE LEARNING**

Have students work in small groups to find examples of all three types of introductions. You may want to have newspapers, magazines, and collections of essays on hand for students to look through. Have students share the introductions with the rest of the class and explain which ones they prefer.

AMENDMENTS TO SELECTIONS
Description of change: excerpted
Rationale: to focus on the concept of introductions presented in this chapter

3. **State an intriguing or startling fact.** A surprising or unusual fact can get your readers' attention right away. The fact can be an eye-opening statement, or it can refer to a surprising statistic. Either way, readers are curious. They can't wait to read on.

> The surfaces of Venus and Mars have been mapped more thoroughly than the oceans that cover 70 percent of Earth's surface.
>
> Tony Reichhardt, "Water World"

EXERCISE 3 ▶ **Identifying Types of Introductions**

You've learned about three types of introductions. Can you recognize them? Working with two or three classmates, read the following introductions. Identify the technique used for each. (To make things interesting, one technique is used more than once.) If you disagree on the technique, discuss your reasons with your classmates.

1. anecdote

1.
> The other day I spotted a T-shirt for sale on the side of the road that read, "I survived Hurricane Hugo, but the aftermath is killing me." I laughed when I saw it, but now it saddens me. Around my neighborhood trees are uprooted, homes destroyed—the debris is everywhere. The hurricane left sixty-five thousand people in South Carolina homeless and eighteen people dead. The hurricane also left millions of changed lives behind it, mine included.
>
> Jennifer Cohen, "Disaster Hits Home"

2. question

2.
> Sometimes you feel as though you are full of energy. Other times you are so tired you say, "I don't feel like playing; I don't have the energy." What is this mysterious thing we call energy?
>
> Laurel Sherman, "Energy: Powering a Nation"

CLOSURE

Have students name each of the three types of introductions presented in this lesson [questions, anecdotes, startling facts]. Ask students what should be included near the beginning of a composition [the main idea statement]. ∎

VISUAL CONNECTIONS

Ideas for Writing. Ask students to speculate on what it would be like to visit Mars in their lifetimes. First, have them freewrite their reactions to Martian travel. Then have them use one of the techniques explained in the text to write an attention-grabbing introduction.

3. If you are between 7 and 16 years old, you may stand on the surface of planet Mars by the time you are 40.

    Scott Stuckey, "A Home on the Martian Range"

3. fact   4. anecdote

4. Billy Mills enjoyed running across the countryside on the Pine Ridge Sioux Indian Reservation in South Dakota. His legs would fly like the wind as he leaped over logs and chased scurrying rabbits. Running was good training for the boxing matches Billy had with his father, who was an amateur boxer. Little did he know that running, and not boxing, would one day earn him an Olympic medal.

    Della A. Yannuzzi, "Billy Mills"

AMENDMENTS TO SELECTIONS
Description of change: excerpted
Rationale: to focus on the concept of introductions presented in this chapter

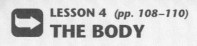

TEACHING THE LESSON

You may want to expand on the teamwork metaphor used in **The Body** to emphasize the importance of unity and coherence. Compare the introduction, body, and conclusion to three runners in a relay race.

Guide students through the first question of **Exercise 4** before assigning the

QUOTATION FOR THE DAY

". . . the art of writing has for backbone some fierce attachment to an idea." (Virginia Woolf, 1882–1941, English novelist and critic)

Lead students in discussing whether it is important to write from conviction. To emphasize the influence of conviction, ask students if they would rather write about their school or about schools in general.

The Body

Think of the parts of the composition as a team. The introduction's job is to grab the reader's attention and announce the main idea. Then the body develops that idea with paragraphs. Each paragraph supports or proves a main point by developing it with supporting ideas.

☞ REFERENCE NOTE: See pages 74–83 for information on strategies of paragraph development.

The body's job is very important, and teamwork is crucial. Maybe you've read compositions that lack teamwork. They might go off on tangents, ramble on and on, or seem disjointed. What's missing is unity and coherence.

WRITING NOTE

Like any long form of writing, compositions are made up of paragraphs. And each paragraph can be made up of several sentences or even just one sentence. What's most important is how each paragraph, no matter how long or how short, helps the writer to support the main idea of the whole composition.

Unity. You know you have **unity** in your composition when all your body paragraphs develop a point about the *main idea* that you wrote in your introduction. Look at the model on pages 101–103. Do you see how each paragraph has its own main idea (topic)? In every case, the paragraph topic relates to or supports the main idea.

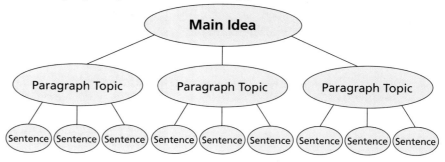

remaining three questions for independent practice.

Assess students' ability to use appropriate transitional words to tie paragraphs together by evaluating their performances on **Exercise 4.** You could also assess their use of transitions in a writing assignment.

CLOSURE

Ask students how they can achieve unity in their papers. [Each paragraph should support the main idea of the paper.] Then ask how they can make their papers coherent. [Use transitional words or phrases to connect ideas.] ■

Coherence.   Remember connect-the-dots pictures? By following numbered dots in order with your pencil, you created a picture. The ideas in your paragraphs should be as easy to follow as numbered dots. When they are, your paragraphs have *coherence.* Every sentence leads easily to another. Every paragraph leads to the next.

How can you work on coherence? First, arrange your ideas in an order the reader will understand. Then, make it easy for the reader to see how your ideas are connected.

You can make it easy for readers by using *transitional words and phrases,* such as *next, first, however, in addition to,* and *finally.* They are like the numbered dots. They help readers connect the ideas in your composition. Then readers can see the big picture you've developed.

☞ REFERENCE NOTE: See pages 71–73 for more information and examples of transitional words and phrases.

EXERCISE 4 ▶ **Using Transitions**

It's time to connect the ideas! The following list of transitional words or phrases are your dots. Read the four pairs of sentences that show the end of one paragraph and the beginning of the next. Then choose the transitional word or phrase that best ties together the two paragraphs. Some pairs might have more than one right answer. (You won't use all the choices.)

Next	Furthermore
Otherwise	At the last minute
Afterward	First of all
However	Later

1. Of all the annoying people on Earth, my little brother leads the list.   **1.** First of all
   _____, he uses his age to get his own way.
2. Chen didn't listen to the music. He concentrated on counting the nails in the floor backstage.
   _____, he knew he'd get so nervous that he'd never be able to play his recital piece.   **2.** Otherwise

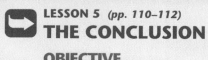

THE CONCLUSION

OBJECTIVE

- To revise a conclusion for a composition using one of three techniques

TEACHING THE LESSON

Ask students if they have ever felt disappointment at the end of a movie or a book and have them discuss why. Then ask students if they have ever had trouble ending papers.

Guide the class in reading **Ways to Write Conclusions.** To give students practice identifying techniques for concluding

---

QUOTATION FOR THE DAY

"The p'int of good writing is knowing when to stop." (L. M. Montgomery, 1874–1942, Canadian writer of children's stories)

Explain to students that the word *p'int* is an abbreviated form of the word *point.* Ask students whether or not they agree with the quotation. Then ask them if they could add to the quotation, "and how to stop." Have them discuss what makes *how* to stop the difficult part of knowing *when* to stop.

---

3. When you ask your parents if you can stay out past curfew, explain your reasons carefully. 3. Afterward
____, be prepared to answer any objections they might have.

4. I was convinced that all Mexican food was too spicy for me to enjoy.   4.However
____, I discovered that real Mexican food is delicious and fun to eat after eating at Luisa's house.

The Conclusion

After you've worked so hard to keep your readers interested, you certainly don't want to leave them hanging in the end. When a composition ends suddenly, readers can feel dissatisfied, let down. Your goal when writing the conclusion is to let your readers know that your composition has come to an end. Here are some of the ways you can do this.

Ways to Write Conclusions

1. **Refer to your introduction.** A favorite technique used by writers is to refer to something in their introduction. This is what the writer of "Good Movies: Two Thumbs Up" (page 101) did. The introduction describes a scene at the movie theater. The conclusion comes back to that scene. The last line also ties the title, introduction, and conclusion together.

> "Maybe the next one will get it right—both the popcorn and the movie will be two thumbs up!"

This statement has a finality to it. It lets the reader know that the paper has come to an end.

2. **Restate the main idea.** One of the most direct ways to end a composition is to restate your main idea *in different words.* In the following example, the writer uses different words to describe the importance of one artist's drawings.

ASSESSMENT

Assess students' ability to write effective conclusions by evaluating their performances on **Exercise 5**.

The Parts of the Composition   **111**

However, Käthe Kollwitz did what few other artists have done—and especially artists who portray children. She would not let us forget the children of the poor and miserable, or the very old, or the overworked mothers struggling for their children. *Their* lives are important, too, she told us in her pictures.

Elsa Marston, "Pictures of the Poor"

3. **Close with a final idea.** Leaving the reader with one last thought can pull your composition together. Here, the teenage writer explaining some of the devastating effects of Hurricane Hugo points to some hope in the crisis.

Yesterday I saw another T-shirt. This one read: HUGO 1, CHARLESTON 0. I thought to myself how wrong that was. The people here have all worked together to rise above defeat. Right now it's HUGO 1, CHARLESTON 1. And gaining.

Jennifer Cohen, "Disaster Hits Home"

CLOSURE

Ask students to name three effective techniques for concluding a paper [refer to the introduction, restate the main idea, close with a final idea]. ■

ANSWERS
Exercise 5

Conclusions will vary. Here is a possibility:

The ancient and modern Olympics are similar in some ways. The modern Olympics, however, with more events and female as well as male competitors, are markedly different.

EXERCISE 5 ▶ **Writing Conclusions**

Remember your trips to the 776 B.C. and the 2002 Olympic Games? Here's a possible conclusion for a composition about the two events. As you can see, it's weak. Rewrite the conclusion to make it more memorable. If you wish, start over completely. (You may also want to refer to the notes on page 100.)

> I learned many things about how the Olympic games have changed since the first ones in 776 B.C. I also realized that some things haven't changed that much.

MAKING CONNECTIONS

- To organize and draft an informative composition with an interesting introduction, coherent body, and effective conclusion
- To proofread an informative composition

113

MAKING CONNECTIONS

WRITING AN INFORMATIVE COMPOSITION

As you know, you write for different reasons. You might write to express your feelings, to be creative, to persuade, or to provide information. And you can use the composition form you've been studying in this chapter for any of these purposes.

Now it's time for you to put what you've learned into action. Following are notes on the subject of African American cowboys who helped shape the Old West during the frontier days. (Some of these notes were gathered from an article titled "Black Cowboys" by Suzanne Sobell.) Review the following information. Then, write a short composition to inform your classmates about these African American adventurers.

> Main idea: African American cowboys played an important role in the Wild West.
>
> 1. Diaries, newspapers, and government reports of the day recorded the accomplishments of several cowboys who were black.
> 2. Bill Pickett, an African American cowboy, invented the cowboy sport of bulldogging.
> 3. After the Civil War, about 8,000 former slaves went West and became cowboys.
> 4. Pickett once survived a five-minute ride on a bucking bull in a Mexico City arena.
> 5. At least one quarter of all cowboys from the 1860s to the 1890s were black.
> 6. The legendary African American cowboy Henry Harris became foreman of a cattle ranch in Nevada.
> 7. Some African American cowboys were broncobusters, cowhands, and wranglers.

MEETING *individual* NEEDS

LEP/ESL

General Strategies. You may want to provide English-language learners with some specific transitional words that would work well for this composition. Possible transitions are *specifically, in fact, that is, in particular, one such,* and *for example.*

TIMESAVER

Ask students to highlight the main idea sentences, the main points of paragraphs, any transitional words, and the conclusions in different colors to make assessment easier for you.

You may want to allow students to plan and write their essays in groups of two or three. You might review with students the techniques for introductions and conclusions before they begin. Remind students to use transitional words to tie their ideas together. Refer them to the **Main Idea** diagram on p. 108 as they begin arranging their ideas.

When students answer the third question, ask them to think about why their introductions were interesting. Also ask them to think about other subjects that would go with the type of introduction they used.

VISUAL CONNECTIONS

Exploring the Subject. Refer students who wish to read more non-fiction about African American cowboys on the frontier to *The Black West* and *Black People Who Made the Old West* by William Loren Katz, *Black Heroes of the Wild West* by Ruth Pelz, or *Blacks in the West* by William Sherman Savage. For historical fiction about black pioneers, refer them to *Bring Home the Ghost* by K. Follis Cheatham. This is the story of a master and a slave who grow up together on an Alabama plantation and then travel west to the frontier in the 1830s.

114

8. Pickett was elected to the Cowboy Hall of Fame in 1971, years after his death.
9. A Nevada railroad stop, Henry, is named after Harris.
10. Other black cowboys were popular singers, musicians, and songwriters.
11. One of the most famous of all African American cowboys was Nat Love, who recounted his interesting life in an autobiography.
12. Some African American cowboys were cooks, foremen, and trail bosses.

Prewriting. Look over all the information you've been given. Keeping the main idea in mind, divide and arrange the notes into groups that make sense. Then create an early plan for your paper as shown on pages 97–98. You may not want to use all the ideas.

Writing, Evaluating, and Revising. Begin by putting yourself in your audience's place. How can you capture their attention? What can you say that will get them interested and make them want to read further? As a help, you may want to use one of the ways to write introductions on pages 105–106. Remember to include your main idea in the introductory paragraph.

ASSESSMENT

As the basis of your assessment, use a checklist composed of the aspects of a composition: main idea, introduction, conclusion, unity, and coherence. You might post students' papers so students can evaluate the strengths of each composition.

CLOSURE

Ask students to identify the purpose of an informative essay. Have them recall how they went about all the steps in the writing process as they wrote their essays. ■

115

Next, write your body paragraphs. Make sure that each body paragraph makes a point that ties into your main idea. Use transitions to move easily from one idea to the next.

Finally, write a conclusion that brings your composition to a satisfying, obvious end. You may want to use one of the ways to write conclusions on pages 110–111.

After you've finished writing your first draft, look it over to see how you can improve it. Consider exchanging papers with another student for peer review. Ask the peer-evaluator questions on page 44.

 Proofreading and Publishing. At this point, you may want to take a break from your paper. Come back to it when you're fresh. Then look over your paper one more time. Check for and correct any misspelled words and mistakes in grammar and mechanics. Write or print out a clean copy.

Once you have a clean, corrected copy, think about how you can share it with others. You and your classmates might simply post your compositions on the bulletin board for others to read. Or you may want to use them as the beginning of a booklet on other pioneers of the Old West.

 Reflecting on Your Writing

To add your paper to your **portfolio,** date it and include a brief reflection by answering the following questions:

- How did you decide which ideas to include in your paper?
- How helpful was it to you to make an early plan?
- Which technique did you use to create an interesting introduction? Why did you choose this technique over others?

Chapter 4

EXPRESSIVE WRITING: NARRATION

OBJECTIVES

- To analyze purpose, audience, and organization of expressive writing
- To gather and arrange details
- To write a draft of a narrative
- To evaluate and revise the content and organization of a narrative
- To proofread a narrative and prepare it for publication

WRITING-IN-PROGRESS ASSIGNMENTS

Major Assignment: Writing a personal narrative
Cumulative Writing Assignments: The chart below shows the sequence of cumulative assignments that will guide students as they write a personal narrative. These Writing Assignments form the instructional core of Chapter 4.

PREWRITING

WRITING ASSIGNMENT
- Part 1: Exploring Possible Topics p. 124
- Part 2: Choosing a Topic p. 124
- Part 3: Recalling and Arranging Details p. 129

WRITING YOUR FIRST DRAFT

WRITING ASSIGNMENT
- Part 4: Writing a First Draft p. 137

EVALUATING AND REVISING

WRITING ASSIGNMENT
- Part 5: Evaluating and Revising Your Personal Narrative p. 140

PROOFREADING AND PUBLISHING

WRITING ASSIGNMENT
- Part 6: Proofreading and Publishing Your Personal Narrative p. 142

In addition, exercises 1–3 provide practice in noting details about events, analyzing the organization of a personal narrative, and analyzing a writer's revisions.

WORKPLACE writing

Personal Narratives—in the Real World?

Remind students that if they tell what happened at a party or in class, they are relating personal narratives. If they write friendly letters or send e-mail about a personal experience, they are writing personal narratives.

Tell students that composing a personal narrative is a life skill they may need for more serious reasons. Various application processes may call for oral or written personal narratives. Some organization, scholarship, or camp applications, as well as college and job applications, may require these.

- **Prewriting** Adapt Chapter 4 to help students understand the concept of audience for narratives. Assign small groups to role-play the scholarship administrator or camp official preparing the topic prompts. Students should consider what qualities the group wants in a student or participant and then write topics to display these traits.

  For example:

  - **Persistence** Describe an experience to demonstrate your persistence in seeking a goal.
  - **Ingenuity** Tell of an incident where your incentive and quick planning saved the day.

  After students create a list of topics, give them an opportunity to freewrite or create a graphic organizer about the topic. Students will need to consider the material on pp. 123–129 as they prewrite and on pp. 130, 133, and 135 as they write their narratives.

- **Evaluation** Have students take turns acting as students and as interviewers to submit and evaluate narratives.

- **Proofreading and Publishing** After students have revised their papers based on this input, refer them to pp. 141–142 for proofreading and publishing ideas.

INTEGRATING THE LANGUAGE ARTS

SELECTION	READING AND LITERATURE	WRITING AND CRITICAL THINKING	LANGUAGE AND SYNTAX	SPEAKING, LISTENING, AND OTHER EXPRESSION SKILLS
• **"Becoming a Journalist"** by Anne Frank pp. 118–120 • **"Cut"** by Bob Greene pp. 130–132 • from ***The Journal of Beatrix Potter, 1881–1897*** pp. 144, 145 • **Journal Entry** by Mary Garfield p. 148	• Reading analytically pp. 121, 133 • Analyzing author's purpose p. 121 • Finding details pp. 121, 133, 144 • Making inferences pp. 121, 144 • Formulating a personal response to literature pp. 121, 133, 144, 145 • Demonstrating evaluation and comprehension skills p. 133 • Determining cause-and-effect relationships p. 136	• Analyzing a narrative pp. 121, 129, 133–136, 144 • Evaluating and choosing topics p. 124 • Identifying and taking notes on supporting details p. 129 • Recalling and arranging details p. 129 • Analyzing and evaluating revisions p. 140 • Revising a narrative p. 140 • Applying proofreading skills pp. 140, 142 • Writing a reflection for portfolio selection p. 142 • Journaling pp. 145–146 • Writing a skit about a humorous situation p. 147 • Writing a paper in the expressive aim from a historical perspective pp. 148–149	• Using first-person pronouns p. 133 • Using adjectives p. 141 • Proofreading for spelling, capitalization, punctuation, and usage errors pp. 141–142	• Discussing and expressing ideas in a small group pp. 124, 136, 140 • Giving a short talk to classmates p. 129 • Identifying relevant supporting details and examples p. 136 • Sharing a personal narrative in an oral presentation p. 142 • Presenting a humorous skit to the class p. 147

SUGGESTED INTEGRATED UNIT PLAN

This unit plan suggests how to integrate the major strands of the language arts with this chapter.

If you begin with this chapter on personal narrative or with the suggested autobiographical literature selections, you should focus on the common characteristics of autobiographical writing. You can then integrate speaking/listening and language concepts with both the writing and the literature.

Common Characteristics

- Frequent use of first person—*I, me, us, we*
- Figurative language that evokes a mood and appeals to the senses
- Content that is self-expressive and conveys emotion and attitudes
- Rhythmic repetition of words and phrases
- Usually chronological organization
- Use of dialogue

Writing
Expressive Writing: Narration

**UNIT FOCUS
AUTOBIOGRAPHY**

Speaking/Listening

- Give and take notes on short talks based on details of an event
- Identify relevant supporting details and examples
- Dramatize a personal experience

Language
Grammar, Usage

- Case of pronouns
- Position of adjectives
- Transitional words

Literature
Autobiographical selections, such as

- "One More Lesson" Judith Ortiz Cofer
- *Once Upon a Time When We Were Colored* Clifton Taulbert
- "A Book-Writing Venture" Kim Yong Ik

CHAPTER 4: EXPRESSIVE WRITING: NARRATION

Use this guide for creating an instructional plan that addresses the individual needs of your students. Assignments accompanied by the following symbol (*) may be completed out of class. Times given for pacing lessons are estimated.

CHAPTER PLANNING GUIDE—PUPIL'S EDITION

LESSONS	LITERARY MODEL pp. 118–120 from "Becoming a Journalist" by Anne Frank	PREWRITING pp. 123–129	
		Generating Ideas	**Gathering/Organizing**
DEVELOPMENTAL PROGRAM	🕐 **20–25 minutes** • Read model aloud in class and have students answer questions on p. 121 orally.	🕐 **35–40 minutes** • Ways to Express Yourself p. 122 • Main Assignment: Looking Ahead p. 122 • Choosing an Experience to Write About p. 123 • Writing Assignment: Part 1 p. 124 • Writing Assignment: Part 2 p. 124*	🕐 **40–45 minutes** • Planning Your Narrative pp. 125–129 • Reminder p. 128 • Exercise 1 p. 129 • Writing Assignment: Part 3 p. 129*
CORE PROGRAM	🕐 **15–20 minutes** • Assign students to read model independently and to discuss answers to Reader's Response p. 121.	🕐 **25–30 minutes** • Ways to Express Yourself p. 122 • Main Assignment: Looking Ahead p. 122 • Choosing an Experience p. 123* • Writing Assignment: Part 1 p. 124 • Writing Assignment: Part 2 p. 124*	🕐 **25–30 minutes** • Planning Your Narrative pp. 125–129* • Reminder p. 128 • Exercise 1 p. 129 • Writing Assignment: Part 3 p. 129*
ACCELERATED PROGRAM	🕐 **10–15 minutes** • Assign students to read model and in pairs to discuss Writer's Craft questions p. 121.	🕐 **20–25 minutes** • Ways to Express Yourself p. 122 • Main Assignment: Looking Ahead p. 122 • Writing Assignment: Part 1 p. 124 • Writing Assignment: Part 2 p. 124*	🕐 **15–20 minutes** • Planning Your Narrative pp. 125–129* • Reminder p. 128 • Writing Assignment: Part 3 p. 129*

CHAPTER PLANNING GUIDE—PROGRAM RESOURCES

	LITERARY MODEL	PREWRITING
PRINT	• Reading Master 4, *Practice for Assessment in Reading, Vocabulary, and Spelling* p. 4	• Prewriting, *Strategies for Writing* p. 2
MEDIA	• Fine Art Transparency 1: *Snap the Whip, Transparency Binder* 🖥	• Graphic Organizers 5 and 6, Recalling Specific Details and Recalling and Arranging Details, *Transparency Binder* 🖥 • *Writer's Workshop 1:* Autobiographical Incident 💽

WRITING pp. 130–137	EVALUATING AND REVISING pp. 138–140	PROOFREADING AND PUBLISHING pp. 141–143
⏱ **30–35 minutes** • Understanding the Basic Parts of a Personal Narrative p. 130 • Writing Note p. 133 • A Writer's Model pp. 134–135 • Framework p. 135 • Writing Assignment: Part 4 p. 137*	⏱ **35–40 minutes** • Evaluating and Revising p. 138 • Chart p. 139 • Reminder p. 139 • Exercise 3 p. 140* • Writing Assignment: Part 5 p. 140	⏱ **50–55 minutes** • Proofreading and Publishing pp. 141–142 • Grammar Hint p. 141 • Writing Assignment: Part 6 p. 142 • Reflecting p. 142 • A Student Model pp. 142–143
⏱ **25–30 minutes** • A Magazine Column pp. 130–132* • Exercise 2 pp. 132–133 • Framework p. 135 • Critical Thinking pp. 136–137* • Writing Assignment: Part 4 p. 137*	⏱ **25–30 minutes** • Evaluating and Revising Chart p. 139 • Reminder p. 139 • Writing Assignment: Part 5 p. 140	⏱ **40–45 minutes** • Publishing pp. 141–142 • Grammar Hint p. 141 • Writing Assignment: Part 6 p. 142 • Reflecting p. 142 • A Student Model pp. 142–143*
⏱ **10–15 minutes** • A Magazine Column pp. 130–132* • Framework p. 135 • Writing Assignment: Part 4 p. 137*	⏱ **20–25 minutes** • Evaluating and Revising Chart p. 139 • Writing Assignment: Part 5 p. 140	⏱ **30–35 minutes** • Publishing pp. 141–142 • Grammar Hint p. 141 • Writing Assignment: Part 6 p. 142 • Reflecting p. 142*

 Computer disk or CD-ROM   Overhead transparencies

WRITING	EVALUATING AND REVISING	PROOFREADING AND PUBLISHING
• Writing, *Strategies for Writing* p. 3 • Pronouns, *English Workshop* pp. 91–92	• Evaluating and Revising, *Strategies for Writing* p. 4	• Proofreading/Revising Practice, *Strategies for Writing* p. 6 • *English Workshop* pp. 93–94
• *Language Workshop:* Lessons 17–18	• Revision Transparencies 5–6, *Transparency Binder*	• *Language Workshop:* Lesson 3

ELEMENTS OF WRITING: CURRICULUM CONNECTIONS

Writing Workshop
• A Personal Journal pp. 144–146

Making Connections
• Dramatizing a Personal Experience p. 147
• Social Studies pp. 148–149

ASSESSMENT OPTIONS

Summative Assessment
Holistic Scoring: Prompts and Models pp. 3–8

Portfolio Assessment
Portfolio forms, *Portfolio Assessment* pp. 5–24, 38–43

Reflection
Writing Process Log, *Strategies for Writing* p. 1

Ongoing Assessment
Proofreading, *Strategies for Writing* p. 5

DISCOVERING YOURSELF

OBJECTIVES

- To respond personally to literature
- To analyze the expressive qualities of a literary model

MOTIVATION

Ask students to recall times of intense feeling such as anger, joy, sadness, or fear. Ask if they shared those feelings with others or if they kept their feelings to themselves. Explain that some people choose to express their emotions in the form of diaries or journals.

PROGRAM MANAGER

CHAPTER 4

- **Computer Guided Instruction** For a related assignment, see **Autobiographical Incident** in *Writer's Workshop 1 CD-ROM.*

- **Practice** To help less-advanced students, see **Chapter 4** in *English Workshop, Second Course,* pp. 25–32.

- **Summative Assessment** For a writing prompt, including grading criteria and student models, see *Holistic Scoring: Prompts and Models,* pp. 3–8.

- **Extension/Enrichment** See **Fine Art Transparency 1**, *Snap the Whip* by Winslow Homer. For suggestions on how to tie the transparency to instruction, review teacher's notes in *Fine Art and Instructional Transparencies for Writing,* p. 3.

- **Reading Support** For help with the reading selection, pp. 118–120, see **Reading Master 4** in *Practice for Assessment in Reading, Vocabulary, and Spelling,* p. 4.

4 EXPRESSIVE WRITING: NARRATION

Have a volunteer read aloud the introduction to the chapter. If you prefer to place Anne Frank in a historical context, present the following background information before having students read the model: Anne Frank was a Jewish girl, born in 1929 in Frankfurt, Germany. When she was four, her family fled to Holland to escape harsh anti-Jewish laws created under Hitler and the Nazis. But in 1940, the German army took over Holland, and soon Jews were rounded up and placed in concentration camps, where millions were murdered. For two years, from 1942 to 1944, the Frank family (Anne had an older sister Margot) and four other people hid from the Nazis in the "Secret Annexe," and it was there that Anne

Discovering Yourself

To excel, athletes reach deep inside themselves for strength and commitment. In the same way, every now and then we need to take a good look inside ourselves. This is how we **discover** who we really are, and how we feel about things.

Writing and You. Writing about your thoughts and experiences helps you pry loose your deepest feelings. If you want to keep your feelings private, you can write about them in a diary or journal. If you want to share them with others, you might write a personal narrative. Either way, you'll be discovering who you are and how you feel. How well do you think you know yourself?

As You Read. In the following selection from *The Diary of a Young Girl*, Anne Frank writes in her diary about wanting to become a journalist. As you read, notice how honest Anne is about herself and her feelings.

Olympic Hurdler, Bart Forbes © 1993.

QUOTATION FOR THE DAY

"Writing was/is an act of discovery." (Toni Cade Bambara, 1939–1995, African American novelist and lecturer)

Lead students in a discussion of how people sometimes discover unrecognized feelings such as anger or hidden fears when they talk out problems with friends or even with strangers. Then ask students how those discoveries might also be made by writing.

VISUAL CONNECTIONS
Olympic Hurdler

About the Artist. Art Forbes, the son of an Air Force officer, was born in Altus, Oklahoma. He graduated from the University of North Carolina before going to the Art Center College of Design in Los Angeles. In his career as a freelance artist, Forbes has published in several magazines and designed many commemorative postage stamps. The artist was also named the Official Artist of the Olympic Games in 1988 by the Korean Olympic Committee. A major theme of Forbes' work is athletics, and in 1986 the United States Sports Academy chose him as Artist of the Year.

Exploring the Subject. Just as writers use words and papers as tools of expression, athletes use their bodies. Discuss with the class the ways sports allow people to express themselves. You might ask some athletic students, for example, why they participate in sports or what feelings they have when they are participating in sports activities.

Frank wrote her diary. In August 1944, the Nazi police discovered them, and they all were sent to concentration camps. Anne died of typhus in Bergen-Belsen three weeks before the British liberated the camp. Her diary was discovered in the annexe and presented to her father, the only one of the eight people in hiding to survive.

Before students read the model, explain that Anne Frank wrote this expressive piece for herself alone, and it was published after her death. Because it is an emotional and private piece without much difficult vocabulary, you could have students read it silently. You may want to point out to students the expressive qualities of the writing—the use of first person and the emphasis on feelings.

USING THE SELECTION
Becoming a Journalist

1

The conversational tone is characteristic of expressive writing.

2

Point out the author's use of first-person pronouns, an important characteristic of expressive writing. (She uses over eighty in this short excerpt.)

3

Words that show feelings are characteristic of expressive writing.

Becoming a

Journalist

by Anne Frank

1
2 For a long time I haven't had any idea of what I was working for any more; the end of the war is so terribly far away, so unreal, like a fairy tale. If the war isn't over by September I shan't go to school any more, because I don't want to be two years behind. Peter filled my days—nothing but Peter, dreams and thoughts
3 until Saturday, when I felt so utterly miserable; oh, it was terrible. I was holding back my tears all the while I was with Peter, then laughed with Van Daan over lemon punch, was cheerful and excited, but the moment I was alone I knew that I would have to cry my heart out. So, clad in my nightdress, I let myself go and slipped down onto the floor. First I said my long prayer very earnestly, then I cried with my head on my arms, my knees bent up, on the bare floor, completely folded up. One large sob brought me back to earth again, and I quelled my tears because I didn't want them to hear anything in the next room. Then I

To model responding personally to literature, guide students through the first **Reader's Response** question. Then guide students through the process of analyzing literature with the first **Writer's Craft** question.

Have students independently answer the remaining **Reader's Response** and **Writer's Craft** questions. Encourage students to answer with specifics from the selection. Use an evaluation of students' answers as your assessment of students' understanding.

☛

4
began trying to talk some courage into myself. I could only say: "I must, I must, I must . . ." Completely stiff from the unnatural position, I fell against the side of the bed and fought on, until I climbed into bed again

5
just before half past ten. It was over!

And now it's all over. I must work, so as not to be a fool, to get on, to become a journalist, because that's what I want! I know that I can write, a couple of my stories are good, my descriptions of the "Secret Annexe" are humorous, there's a lot in my diary that speaks, but— whether I have real talent remains to be seen.

"Eva's Dream" is my best fairy tale, and the queer thing about it is that I don't know where it comes from. Quite a lot of "Cady's Life" is good too, but, on the whole, it's nothing.

I am the best and sharpest critic of my own work. I know myself what is and what is not well written. Anyone who doesn't write doesn't know how wonderful it is; I used to <u>bemoan</u> the fact that I couldn't draw at all, but now I am more than happy that I can at least write. And if I haven't any talent for writing books or newspaper articles, well, then I can always write for myself.

I want to get on; I can't imagine that I would have to lead the same

4
What does the author feel she "must" do? [Students should connect their answers with the following paragraph in which Anne Frank says she "must work . . . to become a journalist."]

5
Exclamation points indicate emphatic thoughts.

VISUAL CONNECTIONS

Exploring the Subject. For her thirteenth birthday, Anne Frank's father gave her a diary. Anne named her diary "Kitty" and treated it like a friend. She wrote in the diary for the two years that she and her family were in confinement in the "Secret Annexe." The diary has been adapted for the stage and for film.

CLOSURE

Ask students to consider how Anne Frank lives on in her writing. [Her writing reflects her goals, feelings, experiences, and self-analysis; it also reflects her evaluations of others; she lives on when people read her writing, reflect on her, and share her self-discoveries.]

ENRICHMENT

Many people have chronicled their lives. Suggest that each student read a journal, diary, or autobiography of an author and share interesting information with the rest of the class. Some students might want to read *The Diary of A Young Girl* in its entirety. ■

6

The author is referring to the work of raising a family and maintaining a home.

SELECTION AMENDMENT

Description of change: excerpted and modified
Rationale: to focus on the concept of expressive writing presented in this chapter

"*A*nyone who 6 doesn't write doesn't know how wonderful it is...."

sort of life as Mummy and Mrs. Van Daan and all the women who do their work and are then forgotten. I must have something besides a husband and children, something that I can devote myself to!

I want to go on living even after my death! And therefore I am grateful to God for giving me this gift, this possibility of developing myself and of writing, of expressing all that is in me.

I can shake off everything if I write; my sorrows disappear, my courage is reborn. But, and that is the great question, will I ever be able to write anything great, will I ever become a journalist or a writer? I hope so, oh, I hope so very much, for I can recapture everything when I write, my thoughts, my ideals and my fantasies.

I haven't done anything more to "Cady's Life" for ages; in my mind I know exactly how to go on, but somehow it doesn't flow from my pen. Perhaps I never shall finish it, it may land up in the wastepaper basket, or the fire . . . that's a horrible idea, but then I think to myself, "At the age of fourteen and with so little experience, how can you write about philosophy?"

So I go on again with fresh courage; I think I shall succeed, because I want to write!

READER'S RESPONSE

1. What did you learn about Anne Frank from reading this selection? Do you have anything in common with her?
2. Would you be interested in reading "Eva's Dream" or "Cady's Life"? How do you feel about Anne Frank's criticism of her own works?
3. Do you agree with Anne that fourteen-year-olds are too young to write about philosophy?

WRITER'S CRAFT

4. What evidence is there in the diary entry that Anne Frank would have been a successful writer if she had lived?
5. Anne Frank addressed her diary entries to an imaginary friend called Kitty. Why might she have included so many details about her life in these diary entries?
6. What reasons does Anne Frank give for wanting to write?

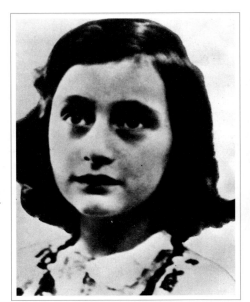

Dit is een foto, zoals
ik me zou wensen,
altijd zo te zijn.
Dan had ik nog wel
een kans om naar
Holywood te komen.

Anne Frank.
10 Oct. 1942

(translation)
"This is a photo as I would wish myself to look all the time. Then I would maybe have a chance to come to Hollywood."

Anne Frank, 10 Oct. 1942

ANSWERS

Reader's Response

Responses will vary.

1. Students might say they learned that Anne is frustrated with life in the "Secret Annexe"; she thinks often of Peter; she wants to become a journalist; she knows she can write; she is passionate and determined.

2. Encourage students to give reasons for their opinions.

3. Students might feel that fourteen is too young for considering the purpose of life. However, others might think of fourteen as mature.

Writer's Craft

Responses will vary.

4. Anne seems to have both talent and determination; she writes constantly in the form of diary entries and stories.

5. Anne's writing was solely for self-expression. She needed to express thoughts and feelings and chose to express those through her diary.

6. She knows she has talent; she wants something to devote herself to—something more than raising a family; she longs for immortality through writing; writing gives her courage and peace.

SELECTION AMENDMENT
Description of Change: excerpted
Rationale: to focus on the concept of expressive writing presented in this chapter

INTEGRATING THE LANGUAGE ARTS

Literature Link. If these selections are available in your literature textbook or library, you may want to refer students to the following texts.

1. "Broken Chain" by Gary Soto
2. "I Have a Dream" by Martin Luther King, Jr.
3. "Refugee in America" by Langston Hughes
4. "Mrs. Flowers" from *I Know Why the Caged Bird Sings* by Maya Angelou

---

122   *Expressive Writing*

Ways to Express Yourself

Personal expression can occur in different forms and different places: letters to friends, magazine articles, or newspaper columns. A piece of writing is a personal expression when it emphasizes what the writer experiences, feels, and thinks. There are several ways that you can develop an expressive message. Here are some examples.

- in a letter to a friend, writing about an event that was especially important to you
- in your journal, writing your autobiography
- in an article for the school newspaper, defining the word *strong* and explaining what it means to you
- in an essay for social studies class, describing your reactions to past fashions and hairstyles
- in your journal, writing about a visit to the workplace of an adult you know
- in a personal narrative, telling about a job such as baby-sitting or delivering newspapers
- in a letter to a friend, describing the summer camp you're going to
- in an essay for science class, writing about your fascination with a certain type of insect

LOOKING AHEAD

In this chapter, you'll use narration to develop a personal experience narrative. As you work through the writing assignments, keep in mind that an effective personal narrative

- tells about events in the order that they occurred
- uses details about the experience, including sensory details
- shows what meaning the experience had for the writer

LESSON 3 *(pp. 123–129)*

PREWRITING

OBJECTIVES

- To evaluate possible topics for a personal narrative
- To select an appropriate topic for a personal narrative
- To gather details for speaking and listening purposes
- To gather and organize details for a personal narrative

Writing a Personal Narrative

Choosing an Experience to Write About

Like Anne Frank, you have had personal experiences worth sharing—personal experiences worth writing about. What was your happiest day? your most exciting moment? your biggest disappointment?

Tap into your personal store of memories. Perhaps you won a big race or took an interesting trip. You can probably recall a number of experiences that had special value for you. Chances are you learned something about yourself on these occasions.

A personal narrative is a good way to explore an important event in your life. As you think about a topic for such a narrative, keep these three questions in mind:

1. **How important was the experience to you? What did you learn about yourself from it?** Don't get the idea that only an earthshaking adventure will do. The smallest incident—important only to *you*—may have taught you a valuable lesson about life.
2. **Do you remember the experience clearly?** You don't have to recall every detail, but you should have a vivid memory of the event.
3. **Are you willing to share the experience with others?** A personal narrative is just that: personal. But it isn't private. Avoid choosing a topic you'd rather keep secret.

"Writing is an exploration. You start from nothing and learn as you go."
E.L. Doctorow

PROGRAM MANAGER

PREWRITING

- **Self-Assessment** Before beginning instruction of the writing process, see **Writing Process Log** in *Strategies for Writing*, p. 1.
- **Heuristics** To help students generate ideas, see **Prewriting** in *Strategies for Writing*, p. 2.
- **Instructional Support** See **Graphic Organizers 5** and **6.** For suggestions on how to tie the transparencies to instruction, review teacher's notes in *Fine Art and Instructional Transparencies for Writing*, pp. 55, 57.

QUOTATION FOR THE DAY

"Above all, let who you are, what you are, what you believe shine through every sentence you write, every piece you finish." (John Jakes, American writer)

Write this quotation on the chalkboard and have students write journal entries explaining how the quotation relates to personal expression.

SELECTION AMENDMENT
Description of change: excerpted
Rationale: to focus on the concept of expressive writing presented in this chapter

MOTIVATION

Ask students to think of something that recently made them feel especially happy, angry, or proud. You could ask volunteers to share some of their experiences. Then explain that because expressive writing deals with feelings, possible topics surface easily.

TEACHING THE LESSON

Tell students that their narratives will differ from Anne Frank's diary entry. She wrote down thoughts and feelings as they came to her, and one idea or event quickly led to another, as is generally the case with journals and diaries. When the students write their narratives, they should each describe only one important experience.

MEETING *individual* NEEDS

LESS-ADVANCED STUDENTS

Some students might need additional guidelines for choosing experiences to write about. You could try having them focus on their feelings to brainstorm experiences that are funny, frightening, suspenseful, or inspiring. You could also try suggesting some exciting situations or events (a fire, a storm, a camping trip, a fair, an amusement park) that could prompt ideas. If these approaches do not work, talking individually with students may draw out experiences that would serve as good topics.

AT-RISK STUDENTS

You might find that some students are reluctant to share their feelings. Others might feel that their experiences are not worth writing about. Allowing students to work through the writing assignments with trusted partners may help them realize that their feelings and experiences are important and related to others' situations.

124

124   *Expressive Writing*

WRITING ASSIGNMENT

PART 1:
Exploring Possible Topics

It's often helpful to talk over possible topics with others. Think of two topics you might like to explore—for example, "when I forgot Mom's birthday," or "how I won a photo contest." Get together with two or three classmates and share your ideas. What do they think of your possible topics? What do you think of theirs?

WRITING ASSIGNMENT

PART 2:
Choosing a Topic

In Writing Assignment, Part 1 (above), you discussed two possible topics with your classmates. Review those topics here, and make a final decision about the topic for your personal narrative. Use these questions to help you decide.

1. Which experience was more important in your life? A good personal narrative has meaning for *you*.
2. Which experience do you remember more clearly? The more details you can include, the more interesting your narrative will be.
3. Which experience do you feel more comfortable about sharing? Don't write about anything you'd prefer not to share.

As students read **Choosing an Experience to Write About** on p. 123, call their attention to the three questions to consider when choosing a topic.

As students consider purpose and audience, they will begin to examine their thoughts and feelings about their topics. They probably will also start worrying about others' reactions. Discussing some guidelines for how readers should respond to expressive writing can help relieve anxiety. Remind students that readers of expressive writing in a classroom context need to value kindness as much as they do correctness.

Have a volunteer read aloud each subsection of **Recalling Details,** and follow up with discussion. Although the text focuses on memory as a source for details, suggest

 *Prewriting*

Planning Your Narrative

Even though you're writing about yourself, you need to plan your personal narrative. Since other people will read it, you need to make sure it's clear and interesting.

Thinking About Purpose and Audience

When you write, you do so for a reason, a *purpose.* You also expect someone to read what you have written. That someone is your *audience.*

Think about your purpose for writing. Your first thought might be, *It's to get a high grade in English.* That's a worthy goal, but it isn't your true *writing* purpose. When you write a personal narrative, your purpose is to express yourself on paper—and to discover something about yourself in the process. You examine your thoughts and feelings about an event. Then you share your experience with others so that they will understand what you thought and felt.

Who is the audience for a personal narrative? You can always be sure of one reader—yourself. In addition, your teacher will probably read your narrative, and so may your classmates, or a friend, or an adult you trust with your personal feelings. Keep the audience in mind when you write. Include enough background facts and information to make the events in your narrative clear.

Recalling Details

When you write your personal narrative, you'll try to show readers exactly what happened. If you saw a deer, for example, describe the deer in writing so that your readers will *see* it. The way to do this is by including details.

Details are the small, specific parts of an experience. In a personal narrative, they come from your memory. You remember, for example, that the deer you saw was a

 INTEGRATING THE LANGUAGE ARTS

Speaking and Listening Link. Students might benefit from working in pairs to interview each other about their topics. Students can ask a series of questions about their partners' topics and write down the answers. Encourage students to ask questions about specific details and sensory impressions. After the interviews, students can exchange their notes so they can use the information for their writing assignments.

A DIFFERENT APPROACH
As students read **Recalling Details,** they are likely to begin thinking of details that relate to their own topics. If you present **Writing Assignment: Part 3** on p. 129 before students work through **Recalling Details,** students can prepare charts for organizing details and start taking notes as ideas come to mind. This procedure will help students retain ideas that are generated during reading, will reduce students' frustration at having to repeat trains of thought, and will save class time.

other sources that can refresh students' memories: photo albums, mementos, and conversations with people who shared the experiences.

Guide students through the prewriting chart on p. 128. Point out the topic stated at the top, the three column headings, and the four row designations.

Before students begin arranging details for their narratives, review sequencing skills.

MEETING *individual* NEEDS

LEARNING STYLES

Visual Learners. Suggest that students use graphic organizers to record sensory details. You could draw the following diagram on the chalkboard and discuss its use:

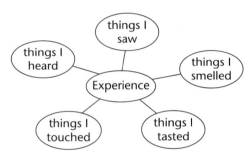

Auditory Learners. Students might recall more details if they talk aloud about their experiences and take notes as new details come to mind. They can do this with peers or, to maintain privacy, they can use tape recorders.

buck with large antlers and a white tail. When you came near it, the buck stood still for a moment in a clearing in the woods. It stared at you with wide, curious eyes and then bounded away. You heard nothing but the rustling of brush as it fled. You remember the clean smell of the pine trees.

Those are details. They add information about the deer and your experience with it. In this case, they're *sensory details,* because they're based on one or more of the senses—sight, hearing, smell, taste, touch. Details can come from any area of your experience: from events, people, places, or thoughts and feelings.

Events. Details about events are just what you'd expect them to be. They're the small actions that occurred. Suppose you rode on a float in the last Martin Luther King Day parade. Your details of that event might include (1) breaking both shoestrings in your haste to get ready, (2) helping your younger sister climb onto the float, and (3) waving at people along the street until your arms just ached.

People. Although you're the center of your own personal narrative, there may be other people in it, too. You observed them at the time. You heard them. When you

You may want to share several personal narrative topics that you would choose for this type of assignment. You could mention your first day of teaching or your high school graduation. Then guide students through the prewriting steps for a personal narrative. First, select the topic by using the three suggested questions in **Writing**

Assignment: Part 2 on p. 124. Then model the planning stage by completing a chart on the chalkboard to clarify chronological order and sensory details.

☞

Prewriting **127**

write, you'll draw on your memories of them to add life to your narrative. Details about people can be anything from the color of their hair (*sight*) to the tone of their voice (*sound*) to the texture of their skin (*touch*).

Places. Your experience happened in a certain place. It may have been in your house or your neighborhood or your city. The location itself may not have been very exciting. That doesn't matter. Your aim is to make the place, wherever it was, seem real to readers. Once again, sensory details are the key. Remember your sighting of the deer? How did the woods feel? Do you remember "the clean smell of the pines"? What noise did the deer make? Do you remember hearing "nothing but the rustling of brush" as the deer fled?

Thoughts and Feelings. Finally, look back at your thoughts and feelings about the experience. Were you happy? scared? surprised? There are two ways to share your thoughts and feelings. One way is by stating them directly: "I was scared." Another way is to show your thoughts and feelings through action and dialogue: "I crept forward cautiously. My friend clutched my arm. 'There's something strange floating out there,' she said."

Using a chart like the one on the next page can help you recall and record details of your experience.

INDEPENDENT PRACTICE

Students should be prepared to complete **Writing Assignment: Parts 1–3.** Although **Exercise 1** provides practice for gathering details, it is not specific to the narrative that students will write. Therefore, you could assign it after the three parts of the **Writing Assignment.**

ASSESSMENT

To check for mastery in choosing a topic and gathering and organizing details, have students turn in their charts from **Writing Assignment: Part 3.** You may want to devise a rating scale that listeners can use to evaluate the short talks given in **Exercise 1.**

MEETING individual NEEDS

LESS-ADVANCED STUDENTS

Some students might have difficulty using charts to structure the details of their experiences. You could have them start with time lines marked *Background, Beginning, Middle,* and *End* to establish the narrative flow. Then have students transfer the information to the chart and complete the *Sensory details* and the *Thoughts and feelings* columns. This procedure should help reduce the task to manageable proportions.

HERE'S HOW

Topic: My experience in trying to win a crafts contest			
	What happened	Sensory details	Thoughts and feelings
Background	eight years old; playground coach announced a crafts contest; I told everyone I'd win	blazing sun; playground felt like a hot stove	excited by the contest; sweaty
Beginning	drew picture of a jet airplane; made a clay bowl; strung macaroni into a necklace	kids shouting as they worked; cool, soft feel of clay	confident about winning
Middle	saw other crafts; some were nice; realized materials could be combined	beauty of Luz's cactus-flower drawing; smooth surface of Adela's vase	worried; not bragging
End	did frantic last-minute project—clay bookends; finished third; stayed for picnic	pleased voice of coach announcing winners; smell of picnic for contestants	proud of being third; enjoyed tostadas and lemonade

If you need help remembering specific details about your experience

- brainstorm, cluster, or freewrite for ideas (see pages 25–28 of Chapter 1, Writing and Thinking)
- look through your journal for details
- talk to other people who were also part of the experience
- to spur your memory, put the details you can remember in a chart

RETEACHING

Provide students with copies of a short piece of expressive writing, perhaps a magazine article. Ask students to prepare prewriting charts, like the one in the textbook, for the article. Then work through the chart on the chalkboard, having volunteers provide the details.

CLOSURE

To help students recall the main points of the lesson, write vertically on the chalkboard the acronym *SEND ACE.* Go over the points as you fill in the meaning for each letter as follows: **S**elect **E**xperience; **N**ote **D**etails; **A**rrange **C**hart **E**ntries. ■

Prewriting **129**

Arranging the Details of Your Narrative

Most personal narratives begin with important background information. Then writers put events in *chronological order.* This means that you write the first thing that happened, then the second, then the third, and so on. To help your reader follow this time order, you may use transitional words and phrases such as *first, second, then, at last,* and *finally.*

☞ REFERENCE NOTE: For more help with chronological order and transitions, see pages 75–78 and 71–73.

Speaking and Listening: Noting Details About Events

How good are you at noting details about events? Think of *five* details to show what *one* of the following events might be like. Prepare a short talk to give in class or to a small group about the event based on the five details. Tell your classmates to listen for the details and take notes on them. Do your classmates feel that they are sharing in the event because of your details?

1. going to an auto race
2. shopping on a major sale day at the mall
3. attending a football game
4. entering a pet in a pet show
5. taking a final exam

PART 3:
Recalling and Arranging Details

For the personal narrative you plan to write, make a chart like the one on page 128. Under *What happened,* list the events or actions that made up your experience. Under *Sensory details,* list some of the things you saw, heard, smelled, tasted, or touched. Under *Thoughts and feelings,* list how you thought and felt about what happened.

ANSWERS
Exercise 1

Explain to students that organization will give their talks more coherence than if they just pick five details and try to string them together. Review with students various ways to organize details. For example, students might narrate, outlining a beginning, a middle, and an ending. Or, they might use spatial order to describe the events.

 INTEGRATING THE LANGUAGE ARTS

Vocabulary Link. Have students list all of the common sensory words like *noisy* or *pretty* from their charts in **Writing Assignment: Part 3.** Then have the class brainstorm in small groups or use thesauruses to compile word banks for their writing.

OBJECTIVES

- To analyze the organization of a personal narrative
- To organize and write a first draft of a personal narrative

TEACHING THE LESSON

Have students look back at the charts they completed for **Writing Assignment: Part 3** on p. 129. Tell students that the first column on the chart can provide the organization for the main part of their personal narratives. Then have them read independently the introduction to the professional model "Cut."

PROGRAM MANAGER

WRITING YOUR FIRST DRAFT

- **Instructional Support** For help with writing a paragraph about one event, see **Writing** in *Strategies for Writing,* p. 3.

QUOTATION FOR THE DAY

"I like to write the first draft quickly, to do it in one sitting if it were only possible . . ." (Eudora Welty, 1909–   , American writer of fiction)

Use the quotation as a springboard for a discussion about students' writing preferences. Do they like to draft quickly and spend time revising, or do they prefer to concentrate their efforts in the writing stage?

USING THE SELECTION
Cut

1

What clues immediately identify this as an expressive piece? [first-person pronouns, reference to crying—an emotional reaction]

130

---

130   *Expressive Writing*

Writing Your First Draft

Understanding the Basic Parts of a Personal Narrative

You already know that a personal narrative

- tells about an important experience that happened to you
- describes important events, people, and places that are part of the experience
- explains the importance of the experience to you

There is no one best way to put together a personal narrative. One writer may begin by describing the story's setting and then tell about events. Another may begin with background and hint at what he or she learned from the experience. Then the writer may go on to tell about events. Two good ways to grab the reader's interest at the outset are with a startling statement or a quotation.

The middle of most personal narratives tells about the experience itself—the details of the event. The conclusion, or ending, usually explains the importance of the experience to the writer. As you read "Cut" by Bob Greene, notice how he has used the basic elements of the personal narrative.

A MAGAZINE COLUMN

Cut
by Bob Greene

INTRODUCTION
Background information

EVENT 1

1

I remember <u>vividly</u> the last time I cried. I was twelve years old, in the seventh grade, and I had tried out for the junior high school basketball team. I walked into the gymna-

Because the model is expressive, it will gain power if you read it aloud. You could introduce the difficult vocabulary (covered in the annotations and the glossary) prior to reading aloud. You may want to save discussion of the model until after students have completed **Exercise 2** on p. 132.

Divide the class into small groups to complete **Exercise 2.** You could have students write individual answers to the questions after the group discussion, or you could have the groups turn in cooperative work. As the groups carry on their discussions, move through the room to provide assistance as necessary.

After students read **"Catch of the Day "** on pp. 134–135, have them compare it to **"Cut"** and the **Framework for a Personal** ☛

Additional background

sium; there was a piece of paper tacked to the bulletin board.

It was a cut list. The seventh-grade coach had put it up on the board. The boys whose names were on the list were still on the team; they were welcome to keep coming to practices. The boys whose names were not on the list had been cut; their presence was no longer desired. My name was not on the list.

EVENT 2
Sensory details

I had not known the cut was coming that day. I stood and I stared at the list. The coach had not composed it with a great deal of <u>subtlety</u>; the names of the very best athletes were at the top of the sheet of paper, and the other members of the squad were listed in what appeared to be a descending order of

Thoughts and feelings

2 | talent. I kept looking at the bottom of the list, hoping against hope that my name would miraculously appear there if I looked hard enough.

2
The best player was listed first, the second best was listed second, and so forth.

EVENT 3
Thoughts and feelings

I held myself together as I walked out of the gym and out of the school, but when I got home I began to sob. I couldn't stop. For the first time in my life, I had been told officially that I wasn't good enough. Athletics meant everything to boys that age; if you were on the team, even as a substitute, it put you in the desirable group. If you weren't on the team, you might as well not be alive.

Additional background

Additional background

I had tried desperately in practice, but the coach never seemed to notice. It didn't matter how hard I was willing to work; he didn't

Thoughts and feelings

3 | want me there. I knew that when I went to school the next morning I would have to face the boys who had not been cut—the boys whose names were on the list, who were still on the team, who had been judged worthy while I had been judged unworthy.

All these years later, I remember it as if I

3
How do you think the author expected the boys who hadn't been cut to react to him? [with ridicule]

Narrative chart on p. 135. This comparison will give students an idea of the range of organizations available to them.

If you modeled the completion of the **Here's How** chart during the prewriting stage, you may want to guide students through the organization and writing of the first draft of a personal narrative based on the chart. Because some students might feel apprehensive about sharing something personal, continuing to write your narrative publicly will serve two purposes: As the topic is one of personal value to you, you will be showing students your willingness to open up and share your thoughts and feelings with them; in addition, you will be modeling the organizational strategies for writing a first draft.

4

inordinately large proportion: too many; far more than you would expect normally

MEETING *individual* NEEDS

LEP/ESL

General Strategies. Students' cultural perspectives might become particularly apparent in the writing of personal narratives; therefore, individual student conferences could serve two purposes. You could be alerted to any potentially sensitive topics, and you could help students see the value of their cultural points of view. In addition, an awareness of students' topics could be helpful in grouping students for cooperative learning and peer revision.

SELECTION AMENDMENT
Description of change: excerpted
Rationale: to focus on the basic elements of the personal narrative

---

EVENT 4

4

CONCLUSION
Meaning
of experience

were still standing right there in the gym. And a curious thing has happened: in traveling around the country, I have found that an <u>inordinately</u> large proportion of successful men share that same memory—the memory of being cut from a sports team as a boy.

I don't know how the mind works in matters like this; I don't know what went on in my head following that day when I was cut. But I know that my <u>ambition</u> has been enormous ever since then; I know that for all of my life since that day, I have done more work than I had to be doing, taken more assignments than I had to be taking, put in more hours than I had to be spending. I don't know if all of that came from a determination never to allow myself to be cut again—never to allow someone to tell me that I'm not good enough again—but I know it's there.

EXERCISE 2 ▶ **Analyzing the Organization of a Personal Narrative**

After reading Bob Greene's narrative, get together with some classmates and discuss the following questions.

ASSESSMENT

Students should turn in their group answers to **Exercise 2**. Mastery of **Writing Assignment: Part 4** can be determined from observation and conferencing, or the assignment could be turned in for a more thorough check. If you require students to create outlines, checking these will ☛

1. Have you ever had a disappointment like Greene's? Are you willing to share it? If so, tell about it.
2. How does the author grab your attention at the beginning? How does he make his personal experience seem real to you?
3. What order does Greene use to organize most of the events of his narrative?
4. What thoughts and feelings does Greene have about being cut? Give examples of his thoughts and feelings in this selection.
5. Personal narratives often reveal the writer's sense of how the experience affected his or her life. How does Greene think the cut affected his life?

WRITING NOTE
For some types of writing, such as research reports, you leave out your thoughts and feelings. Instead, you develop the paper with outside sources such as facts and expert opinions. With a personal narrative, however, you *are* the center of attention. You speak directly to your readers, using the words *I, me, we,* and *us.* Your reader sees the experience through your eyes and gets a glimpse inside the personal you. Notice how Bob Greene addresses you—his readers—directly and how the writer of the following narrative does also.

Following a Basic Framework for a Personal Narrative

Bob Greene is a professional writer. His personal narrative deals with an experience that he looks back on as an adult. Still, he includes background information, thoughts and feelings, and sensory details to make the experience real to his readers. In learning to write a personal narrative, you may find it helpful to follow a simpler model, like the personal narrative that follows.

ANSWERS
Exercise 2

Responses will vary.

1. If no student is willing to share a disappointment, you may want to do so. Emphasize, as Greene does, that one can benefit from disappointment.
2. Most students will probably say that they wanted to know what made the author cry. The experience seems real because it is one most people can relate to.
3. He uses chronological order.
4. He is disappointed and crushed and indicates that by not being able to quit sobbing. He is embarrassed thinking about how hard he has tried in practice and how he'll have to face the boys who have made the team. He feels as though he has failed.
5. He believes it made him more ambitious. He has always worked harder to keep himself from ever being cut again.

give you an additional chance to evaluate students' work.

CLOSURE

Make sure that students are aware that everyone has a different way of writing and putting drafts together. Ask students what difficulties they encountered when writing their first drafts. Then ask what went smoothly.

A WRITER'S MODEL

"**Catch of the Day**" illustrates the use of quotations in personal narratives. Examine how the quotations help make the narrative more vivid and interesting. You may want to review rules governing the use of quotation marks in **Chapter 27: "Punctuation."**

⬧ TIMESAVER

You could have students use colored markers in their drafts to differentiate the structural parts of their personal narratives and to identify in the margins, as the model did, the various information and details they have used. As you confer with students or take up their drafts, you can quickly see if their drafts contain the essential components.

134

A WRITER'S MODEL

Catch of the Day

INTRODUCTION

Background information

Thoughts and feelings

EVENT 1

Sensory details

Thoughts and feelings

Sensory details

EVENT 2

Sensory details

One Saturday last spring, my friend Kazutaka said, "Let's go fishing." His plan called for a trip to Catherine Creek, which is a great trout stream. People come from far away to catch rainbow trout in the rippling waters of Catherine Creek. Kaz and I are lucky. We live just a short bicycle ride away.

A light rain stung our faces as we pedaled along the narrow country road toward our favorite spot. By the time we got there the rain had stopped, but the sky was still gray. We walked our bikes to the edge of the creek. We were all alone. The only sound we heard besides the running water was the distant cawing of a crow.

What we saw upset us. Three or four people had had a picnic at our fishing spot. They had thrown their trash on the ground and left it there—cans, bottles, napkins, orange peels. What a mess! We put down our fishing poles and began to pick up. We stuffed everything into the plastic bag Kaz had brought for trout. It was a big bag. Kaz is an optimist.

No sooner had we picked up the very last crumpled napkin than Kaz pointed downstream.

EVENT 3	Beneath a large willow tree there was more trash. We walked over and picked that up, too. Then I spotted a plastic ice chest across the
EVENT 4	creek. Someone had thrown it away. We waded over to it. "It'll make a good garbage can," Kaz said. "I can strap it on the back of my bike."
EVENT 5	And so it went. We spent more than six hours picking up trash along the creek, all the way to
Sensory details **EVENT 6**	Montour Falls. By afternoon the sun was shining. As we left, loaded down with trash, we saw a tall man with gray hair standing near a car with out-of-state license plates. We waved to him. He
CONCLUSION Meaning of experience	shouted, "Beautiful creek you've got here!" That remark alone made us feel that our day's work was worthwhile.

FRAMEWORK FOR A PERSONAL NARRATIVE

Introduction • • • • • ▶	Attention grabber; Background information
Event 1 • • • • • • • ▶	Details—event, people, places; Thoughts and feelings
Event 2 • • • • • • • ▶	Details—event, people, places; Thoughts and feelings
Event 3 • • • • • • • ▶	Details—event, people, places; Thoughts and feelings
Possibly more events • ▶	More details about more events; Thoughts and feelings
Conclusion • • • • • ▶	Meaning of the experience for narrator

COOPERATIVE LEARNING

Have students work in pairs to compare their prewriting charts to the **Framework for a Personal Narrative** chart. Students might find that the background information on the charts will correspond with the **Introduction**, while the beginning, middle, and end will correspond to **Events 1, 2,** and **3.** For some students, however, this might not be the most appropriate way to organize their work, and they might require your assistance in addition to the help of their peers. Attention to this matter should make **Writing Assignment: Part 4** on p. 137 easier to complete.

A DIFFERENT APPROACH

Artistic students and those who are visual learners might wish to develop their narratives initially in cartoon frames. Students could sketch a scene for each of the important parts of their papers.

INTEGRATING THE LANGUAGE ARTS

Literature Link. Although it is fiction, "Raymond's Run" by Toni Cade Bambara is written like a personal narrative—it is in the first person and relates a personal experience. For this reason, it may be used as an additional model of expressive writing.

CRITICAL THINKING
(pp. 136–137)

OBJECTIVE
• To analyze causes and effects

TEACHING *ANALYZING CAUSES AND EFFECTS*

Tell students that while chronological order provides the overall order for a narrative, cause-and-effect relationships provide some of the links between the events. After students have read the introductory information, group students to complete the **Critical Thinking Exercise.** Then have groups share

136   *Expressive Writing*

CRITICAL THINKING

Analyzing Causes and Effects

When you analyze causes, you ask yourself *Why did that happen?* When you analyze effects, you ask yourself *What happened as a result?*

When you write a narrative, recognizing causes and effects plays an important part. You need to think about how one thing is related to something else.

In the Writer's Model on pages 134–135, two friends set out for a fishing trip, but they end up cleaning up the creekside. The friends themselves may have caused this to happen. If one of them had said, "Oh, leave the mess! We came here to fish!" the trash wouldn't have been picked up. The place itself also affected the boys' behavior. The mess at the creek caused them to change their plans from fishing to cleaning up the environment.

As you write your narrative, think about the causes and effects of people, places, and actions. These are the important details that you should include in your narrative.

CRITICAL THINKING EXERCISE:
Analyzing Causes and Effects

What details are important enough to include in a personal narrative? Which have a cause-and-effect relationship? Get together with several classmates and decide which of the following sets of details have a cause-and-effect relationship by determining whether or not detail *a* caused detail *b*. Then, discuss which sets of details are important enough to include in a narrative about how an argument with a friend started.

1. **a.** My friend wanted to play a joke on me.
   b. She told me the hair on the back of my head looked green today.

their answers with the rest of the class. While students are still in groups, you may want to have them analyze the relationships among the events on their prewriting charts.

2.
  a. We were standing outside by the water fountain.
  b. As usual, the fountain wasn't working.
3.
  a. The bell rang for class.
  b. We had plenty of time to get to class.
4.
  a. I asked another friend if it was true and he said no and laughed.
  b. I was angry with my friend and told her so.

Kudzu by Doug Marlette. By permission of Doug Marlette and Creators Syndicate.

WRITING ASSIGNMENT

PART 4:
Writing a First Draft

Are you ready to write? If not, you may want to spend some time quietly jotting down notes or making a simple outline. Then, begin your first draft. Keep the framework on page 135 in mind as you write. Remember to use the chart you made in Writing Assignment, Part 3 (page 129).

COMPUTER NOTE: When writing your first draft, you can use boldface, italic, or underline styling to mark words, sentences, and sections that you might want to replace or revise later.

ANSWERS
Critical Thinking Exercise

Responses will vary. The details included in 1 and 4 have a cause-and-effect relationship and are important enough to be used in a narrative about an argument with a friend. The details included in 2 and 3 do not have a cause-and-effect relationship.

MEETING *individual* **NEEDS**

ADVANCED STUDENTS

You may want to explain to students that although a personal narrative focuses on the writer, it is still crucial to give value to the reader. Giving value to the reader requires analyzing the audience and using illustrations and examples that a particular audience can relate to. In other words, the writer should try to make readers feel the experience and to make them identify with the writer through similar experiences of their own. Ask students to analyze their personal narratives to decide if they have given value to their readers.

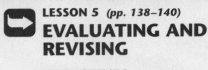

LESSON 5 (pp. 138–140)
EVALUATING AND REVISING

OBJECTIVES

- To analyze the revisions of a model
- To work collectively on evaluating and revising a personal narrative

TEACHING THE LESSON

Recall with students Bob Greene's feeling in **"Cut"** when he was told officially that he wasn't good enough and the profound effect this experience had on his life. Remind students that in their expressive writing, they have each exposed some personal feelings and experiences. If students evaluate each other's work, they should keep

PROGRAM MANAGER

EVALUATING AND REVISING

- **Reinforcement/Reteaching** See **Revision Transparencies 5** and **6**. For suggestions on how to tie the transparencies to instruction, review teacher's notes in *Fine Art and Instructional Transparencies for Writing,* p. 93.

- **Ongoing Assessment** For a rubric to guide assessment, see **Evaluating and Revising** in *Strategies for Writing,* p. 4.

- **Assessment/Reflection** To assess student work and evaluate progress, see **Portfolio Forms** in *Portfolio Assessment,* pp. 5–17.

QUOTATION FOR THE DAY

"The difference between the right word and the almost right word is the difference between lightning and the lightning-bug." (Mark Twain, 1835–1910, American novelist and humorist)

After discussing with students the relevance of Twain's metaphor, suggest that as students evaluate their own or their partners' first drafts, they circle five words that could be replaced with more effective words.

138

138 *Expressive Writing*

Evaluating and Revising

For many students, revising is a chore that won't go away. For professional writers, revising is a natural part of writing. If you dread revising, don't feel alone. Even great writers face tough revising problems, as cartoonist Gary Larson, creator of "The Far Side," shows in the following cartoon.

The Far Side copyright 1988 FarWorks, Inc. Distributed by Universal Press Syndicate. Reprinted with permission. All rights reserved.

Edgar Allan Poe in a moment of writer's block.

If possible, let your writing "cool off" for a while before you begin to evaluate and revise. Then use the chart on the following page to improve your narrative. Ask yourself each question in the left-hand column. If you find a weakness, revise your paper, using the technique suggested in the right-hand column.

"Cut" in mind as they decide what to say and how to say it.

Have a volunteer read the introduction and allow students time to examine the cartoon. As students read the **Evaluating and Revising Personal Narratives** chart, point out that questions 3 and 5 are the easiest to check. Questions 1, 2, and 4 require looking at the narrative from the chosen audience's point of view.

You could guide students through the questions in **Exercise 3** to prepare students for **Writing Assignment: Part 5**. As students evaluate and revise in pairs, you could assess their understanding while circulating throughout the room.

☞

EVALUATING AND REVISING PERSONAL NARRATIVES

EVALUATION GUIDE	REVISION TECHNIQUE
1 Does the beginning of the narrative grab the reader's attention?	Rethink the beginning; **add** a startling statement or a quotation.
2 Does the narrative include enough background information?	**Add** information or facts that the reader needs to understand events.
3 Are the events arranged in chronological order?	**Reorder** events, putting them in the order in which they happened.
4 Does the narrative include details that make the people, places, and events seem real?	**Add** details based on the five senses: sight, hearing, smell, taste, and touch.
5 Are the writer's thoughts and feelings included in the narrative?	**Add** specific details about thoughts and feelings.

As you evaluate and revise your personal narrative

- use transitions like *first, next, then,* and *later* to make the order of events clear
- use vivid and specific words to help people, places, and events come alive for your readers

MEETING *individual* **NEEDS**

LEP/ESL

General Strategies. Some students might at first feel uncomfortable with peer revision. You could either confer with students individually or carefully place them in groups of patient and understanding peers.

ANSWERS
Exercise 3

1. The addition clarifies for the reader who Kazutaka is. The use of *my* is characteristic of expressive writing.

2. The second sentence is about the result of a day's work and should not interrupt the chronological order of events.

3. The writer added a specific detail.

4. The writer probably moved the sentence to improve the narrative flow. He decided to tell first that people traveled from afar to fish in the creek. Then he explained that he and Kaz lived a short bicycle ride away, which also led smoothly into the next paragraph about the bicycle ride to the creek.

◆ INTEGRATING THE LANGUAGE ARTS

Speaking and Listening. You may want to introduce some alternative methods of evaluation for **Writing Assignment: Part 5.** For example, writers might read their work aloud and evaluators could give holistic responses followed by suggestions. Or, writers might begin by talking about what the experiences meant to them so that evaluators can read the drafts in context. Techniques that focus on the overall work rather than on details are probably best for this assignment.

EXERCISE 3 ▶ **Analyzing a Writer's Revisions**

Prepare for evaluating and revising your own paper. Analyze the writer's revisions of the first paragraph of the personal narrative on pages 134–135. Then answer the questions that follow.

One Saturday last spring, ⎡my friend⎤ Kazutaka   **add**

said, "Let's go fishing." ~~You'd never guess~~   **cut**

~~what we "caught"!~~ His plan called for a

trip to Catherine Creek, which is a ~~famous~~ *great*   **replace**

trout stream. ⎡Kaz and I live just a short   *are lucky. We*   **reorder/add**

bicycle ride away.⎤ People come from far

away to catch ~~fish~~ *rainbow trout* in the rippling waters   **replace**

of Catherine Creek.

1. Why did the writer add *my friend* in the first sentence?
2. How did the second sentence—cut in the revised version—damage chronological order?
3. Why did the writer replace *fish* with *rainbow trout* in the last sentence?
4. Why did the writer move the next-to-last sentence to the end?

WRITING ASSIGNMENT   PART 5:
Evaluating and Revising Your Personal Narrative

Now it's time to evaluate and improve your own personal narrative. Exchange personal narratives with another student. Then, evaluate each other's writing, using the chart on page 139. When you evaluate your partner's writing, give specific suggestions for improvement, and ask for these in return. When you get your paper back, read it carefully. Which suggestions seem good? Which seem off the mark? Finally, revise your paper to correct any weaknesses you and your partner have discovered.

PROOFREADING AND PUBLISHING

OBJECTIVES

- To use proofreading to prepare a personal narrative for publication
- To share a personal narrative with an audience

TEACHING THE LESSON

You may want to reproduce an anonymous personal narrative on an overhead transparency and guide students through the proofreading stage. If peer proofreading seems appropriate, students could share their narratives before making a final copy.

☞

 # *Proofreading and Publishing*

Proofreading. Perhaps more than any other form of writing, your personal narrative reflects you. So make it as error-free as you can. Proofread carefully by checking spelling, capitalization, punctuation, and usage.

GRAMMAR HINT

Varying the Position of Adjectives

In narratives you often use adjectives to describe people, places, and events. For interest, learn to vary their position in your sentences. Adjectives often appear before the words they describe.

EXAMPLE   The *only* sound we heard besides the *running* water was the *distant* cawing of a crow.

Sometimes, however, adjectives can appear after the word they describe.

EXAMPLES   The sneakers, old and smelly, were sitting on the doorstep.

As in the sentence above, when adjectives follow the noun they modify, they need to be set off with commas.

☞ REFERENCE NOTE: For more information on placing adjectives in sentences, see page 447.

Publishing. When you wrote your personal narrative, you had an audience in mind—your classmates, the school community, or a friend or family member. Now is

---

 ## PROGRAM MANAGER

PROOFREADING AND PUBLISHING

- **Instructional Support** For a chart students may use to evaluate their proofreading progress, see **Proofreading** in *Strategies for Writing*, p. 5.

- **Independent Practice/ Reteaching** For additional practice on language skills, see **Proofreading/Revising Practice: Varying the Position of Adjectives** in *Strategies for Writing*, p. 6.

- **Assessment/Reflection** To assess student work and evaluate progress, see **Portfolio Forms** in *Portfolio Assessment*, pp. 18–21.

- **Computer Guided Activity** For writing and storing journal entries, use the **Journal** feature in *Writer's Workshop 1 CD-ROM*.

QUOTATION FOR THE DAY

"Proofreading is like the quality-control stage at the end of an assembly line." (John R. Trimble, American writer and teacher)

Write this quotation on the chalkboard and ask students to freewrite about its meaning.

MEETING *individual* NEEDS

STUDENTS WITH SPECIAL NEEDS

You may want to guide students in taking a careful and methodical approach when they proofread. You could provide them with a checklist of a manageable number of items. Suggest the following steps:

1. Use a ruler or piece of paper to cover all but the sentence being read.
2. Read through the selection orally, checking for words that have been left out or that don't sound right. Repeat the procedure to check first for capitalization and then for punctuation.
3. Have a peer read your selection.

QUOTATION FOR THE DAY

"Give yourself a lot of space in which to explore writing. A cheap spiral notebook lets you feel that you can fill it quickly and afford another." (Natalie Goldberg, American writer, poet, and teacher)

Encourage students to decorate their writing journals or notebooks with drawings, quotations, photographs, ads, and anything else that will personalize the notebooks.

142

---

the time to reach out to that audience and share your experience. Here are two ways to do it:

- Give a copy of your personal narrative to a friend or trusted adult who is aware of your experience.
- Present your personal narrative as a dramatic monologue to your class. Use appropriate tone and gestures to add zest to your monologue.

WRITING ASSIGNMENT

PART 6:
Proofreading and Publishing Your Personal Narrative

Proofread your personal narrative carefully, and correct any errors. Then, use one of the suggestions above or an idea of your own to share your narrative.

Reflecting on Your Writing

If you want to put your personal narrative in your **portfolio,** date it and include a brief reflection by responding to the questions below.

- What factors made you choose this subject over others to write about in your personal narrative?
- Which techniques did you use to spur your memory about specific details? How helpful were they?
- Did you learn anything about yourself in the process of writing the narrative?

A STUDENT MODEL

Going through a tough experience can sometimes teach us something important. Lindi Martin, who attends Jenks East Middle School in Tulsa, Oklahoma, describes such an experience in the following passages from her personal narrative.

Conquering Your Fears
by Lindi Martin

I was only eight, but I remember it like yesterday. I was sitting in the doctor's office when they gave my parents and me the shocking news. "I'm sorry to tell you this, but your daughter's condition is getting worse. The only way to fix it is by surgery."

Those words ripped into me like a serrated knife into a crisp, cold apple. It was a horrible sinking feeling that seemed to possess my whole body—a feeling so terrifying, even the bravest person alive could not possibly endure it.

I knew I had been "sick" and I knew it had been serious, but never, even in my nightmares, did I think of surgery. You see, I was born with a condition that affects your kidneys; it is called Bilateral Reflux. The only way I would live was to have reconstructive surgery.

. . . It was now time for surgery. They sent a surgical nurse down to my room with a gurney. Being the scared little girl that I was, I thought the moment I got up on it, they would hurt me. So I decided that my teddy bear, Rainbow, and I would follow along behind it, very defiantly, with my parents. When the doctors saw me walk in, they started to laugh, and I realized that everyone else who had seen me probably had laughed too. What was comic relief to them was no comedy at all to me. So I simply put my nose into the air and kept walking.

The nurse prepped me and had me lie down on the operating table. The doctor asked me what "flavor" of anesthesia I wanted; I thought for a while and answered, "Strawberry." He then asked me to count backward from one hundred as he lifted the mask over my face. I woke up a few hours later, feeling woozy and very sore. I saw my parents and drifted back to sleep. . . .

My experience has taught me a lot. I discovered that in order to conquer your fears, you must face them first. In a way I am thankful for my surgery, because I conquered a lot of my fears.

A STUDENT MODEL
Evaluation

1. Lindi's introduction grabs readers' attention, especially by using the quotation, which makes readers want to know more about the experience.
2. The details Lindi includes about her need for surgery provide enough background for readers to follow the story, and the other details make the people, places, and situation seem real.
3. Lindi arranges events in chronological order, and her thoughts in the conclusion show the significance of the experience to her life.

WRITING WORKSHOP

OBJECTIVES

- To analyze journal writing as a form of personal expression
- To use the writing process in journal writing

TEACHING THE LESSON

Ask students if they have ever tried to write secret messages in code. Explain that some famous people—including Italian artist Leonardo da Vinci and British children's writer Beatrix Potter—kept journals in code.

Discuss why people might choose to keep coded journals. [to protect privacy]

WRITING WORKSHOP

A Personal Journal

A personal narrative is meant to be shared with others—perhaps your classmates or a trusted adult. But some kinds of expressive writing are more private. The personal journal, for example, is usually written for yourself alone. You can use it to discover and to explore important things about your thoughts and feelings.

One woman who kept a personal journal is Beatrix Potter, who wrote and illustrated *Peter Rabbit* and other famous stories for children. One unusual thing about Potter's journal was that she kept it in code, which made it absolutely private. She started keeping the journal in 1881, when she was fifteen years old, and the code wasn't even translated until 1958. Here's what the journal looked like before it was translated.

SELECTION AMENDMENT
Description of change: excerpted
Rationale: to focus on coded writing in a personal journal

Have students independently read **A Personal Journal,** and discuss with the class the answers to the questions that follow. Then have students write their own journal entries. Because you will probably not want to formally assess this writing assignment, you could informally evaluate participation while circulating throughout the room as students write.

CLOSURE

Ask students to analyze how writing journal entries was similar to and different from writing their personal narratives. Encourage students to discuss aspects of the writing process, the results of their writing, and their feelings of satisfaction. ■

All her life, Beatrix Potter was interested in animals, especially rabbits. Her pet rabbit was named Mr. Benjamin Bunny. She writes about him in this translated entry from her journal.

> Rabbits are creatures of warm volatile temperament but shallow and absurdly transparent. It is this naturalness, one touch of nature, that I find so delightful in Mr. Benjamin Bunny, though I frankly admit his vulgarity. At one moment amiably sentimental to the verge of silliness, at the next, the upsetting of a jug or tea-cup which he immediately takes upon himself, will convert him into a demon, throwing himself on his back, scratching and spluttering. If I can lay hold of him without being bitten, within half a minute he is licking my hands as though nothing has happened.
>
> * * *
>
> Benjamin once fell into an Aquarium head first, and sat in the water which he could not get out of, pretending to eat a piece of string. Nothing like putting a face upon circumstances.
>
> from *The Journal of Beatrix Potter, 1881–1897*

Thinking It Over

1. What does Beatrix Potter like about Mr. Benjamin Bunny?
2. What details tell you that Benjamin isn't the easiest pet in the world to get along with?
3. What does Beatrix Potter mean by "Nothing like putting a face upon circumstances"? How would people today express the same idea?

Writing a Personal Journal

Prewriting. Animals and drawing were Beatrix Potter's greatest interests through her whole life. What are yours? Music? Computer games? Books? Write a journal entry where you, like Beatrix Potter, describe an experience about

MEETING individual NEEDS

LEP/ESL

General Strategies. Students who are adapting to a new culture might welcome a private outlet for writing down their thoughts and venting their feelings. A journal is a good place for students to share these ideas and concerns. Emphasize to students, however, that their entries need not always include all stages of the writing process, as suggested in the **Writing Workshop.**

ANSWERS
Thinking It Over

Responses will vary.

1. She likes the way he responds so naturally to situations.
2. Upsetting something can turn him into a demon; he tries to bite.
3. To keep from looking foolish or awkward, one sometimes pretends that there are reasons for his or her actions. Today people might say "saving face."

SELECTION AMENDMENT
Description of change: excerpted and modified
Rationale: to focus on the concept of a personal journal presented in this chapter

TECHNOLOGY TIP

Some word-processing programs include fonts that replace each letter of the alphabet with a tiny graphic. If such programs are available, students could use these fonts to code their journal entries.

VISUAL CONNECTIONS

Exploring the Subject. Beatrix Potter's code is actually a substitution cipher in which a symbol is substituted for each letter. She seems to have used a combination of numerals, standard English letters, Greek letters, and original symbols.

SELECTION AMENDMENT
Description of change: excerpted
Rationale: to focus on coded writing in a personal journal as presented in this chapter

your greatest interest. You might want to write your journal in a code, like Beatrix Potter's. The following diagram shows a "translation" of that code. You can use her code or make up one of your own.

The Code Alphabet					
ɑ	a	ɧ	k	ʊ	ü
Ⳑ	b	t	l	η	v
𝔞	c	n	m	ɱ	w
ơ	d	m	n	x	x
k	e	e	o	ɳ	y
c	f	Ɑ	p	3	z
σ	g	q	q	2	to, too, two
ⱶ	h	ɯ	r	3	the, three
ι	i	ɤ	s	4	for, four
ι	j	1	t	✛	and

Writing, Evaluating, and Revising. Some people, like Beatrix Potter, know very early what their interests are; others don't develop their interests until later in life. Remember that Albert Einstein—who won a Nobel Prize in physics—didn't do well in some high school science courses. If you're not sure yet what your interests are, try brainstorming or freewriting to generate some ideas.

Proofreading and Publishing. If you don't intend to share your journal, especially if it's written in code, there's no need to proofread it, since it's written just for you. If you do want to share it, it might be interesting to see if a friend can break your code and understand what you've written.

You may also want to include your journal entry in your **portfolio.** If so, date the entry and attach a note of reflection on your writing. How does this piece differ from the other writings you have put in your portfolio so far? Did writing this journal entry make you want to keep a journal on a regular basis?

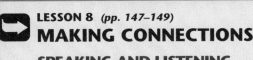

SPEAKING AND LISTENING
OBJECTIVE
• To create and present a comic scene

MAKING CONNECTIONS

SPEAKING AND LISTENING

Dramatizing a Personal Experience

Have you ever thought of a television comedy as a form of personal expression? Many sitcoms are just that. They're based on things that actually happened to the writer or to people the writer knew. Of course, the writer stretches the truth—and then stretches it some more.

With a partner, think of a personal experience that could be the basis for a comic scene. Perhaps one of you did something that had unexpected results. Or maybe you made a mistake that now seems amusing. Write the scene with your partner. Add humorous elements. Make the dialogue funny. Exaggerate! You'll probably find it helpful to act out the scene with your partner as you write. If you like, present your comic scene to the class. Here are some practical suggestions to get you started.

1. Your dog—who eats shoes, plants, and books—ate the science project that's due today from you and your partner. Explain the problem to your teacher.
2. You've just started helping out in your family's fast-food restaurant. You're slow because it's your first day, and a long line of customers stretches before you. Now you're faced with an angry customer who claims you gave him the wrong change.
3. Reluctantly, you agreed to play the role of Abraham Lincoln in the class play. Your first lines are, "Four score and seven years ago our fathers brought forth on this continent a new nation, conceived in liberty, and dedicated to the proposition that all men are created equal." On opening night, you can't remember a single word. A friend prompts you from the wings.

SPEAKING AND LISTENING
Teaching Strategies

Encourage students to use the stages of the writing process when collaborating to write their comic scenes. You may want to make the groups larger to allow scenes with more than two people.

TECHNOLOGY TIP

If video-recording equipment is available, have students videotape their dramatic scenes. Encourage students to bring or create props, costumes, and scenery. After students choose a location, they will probably want to run through the scene first for camera placement and for lighting.

GUIDELINES

The dramatization should be appropriate for a comic scene, and the presentation itself should be amusing. Both students should have a share in the creation and production of the scene. You may wish to collect the written product, but if you intend to grade it, inform students beforehand.

PERSONAL EXPRESSION ACROSS
THE CURRICULUM
OBJECTIVE

• To write a composition by using the
expressive aim from a historical
perspective

PERSONAL EXPRESSION ACROSS THE CURRICULUM

Teaching Strategies

Read aloud the excerpt from Mary Garfield's diary and ask students to note the characteristics of personal expression. Then let each student choose one of the three historical moments on p. 149 as the subject for a piece of expressive writing. Assist students in figuring out how to adapt the writing process to this assignment. If time permits, you could ask volunteers to share their writing.

VISUAL CONNECTIONS

Exploring the Subject. In 1880 James Garfield was elected twentieth President of the United States. He was assassinated only a few months after taking office. Before becoming President, he had been a professor, a college president, a Civil War general, and a U.S. Congressman. He and his wife, Lucretia, had seven children, two of whom died as infants.

SELECTION AMENDMENT
Description of change: excerpted
Rationale: to focus on the concept of personal expression presented in this chapter

---

PERSONAL EXPRESSION ACROSS THE CURRICULUM

Social Studies

Different forms of personal expression—letters, journals, speeches, narratives—may become important historical documents. This happens when they leave a record of some important moment in history. For example, on July 2, 1881, President James Garfield was shot; he died eighty days later. His teenage daughter kept a journal describing what happened after his death. Now, more than one hundred years later, readers can relive this moment in history. Imagine that you were a witness to the scene that Mary Garfield describes. What might you have thought or felt?

It is beautiful to see how much the people got to love Papa through all his sickness. While we were carrying Papa's remains to Washington we came past Princeton. The whole college was down at the depot and had strewn flowers all along the tracks, and after the train had passed, the boys rushed on the tracks and gathered up the flowers to keep as mementos. At every town and crossing the people were standing, some bareheaded. In Baltimore people had come from miles around with their children, even their babies, hardly expecting to see anything but the train.

Now, imagine that you have been taken forward or backward in time to one of the following historical moments. Or, if you like, you can choose your own historical moment. Then, write a brief speech, journal entry, or narrative about the experience. Before you write, you might want to do some research on the topic.

GUIDELINES

With the help of the class, you could devise a rating scale to be used for assessing students' writing. You will probably want to include characteristics of expressive writing—first person and the sharing of thoughts and feelings—as well as the effectiveness of communicating the experience.

1. You're John Glenn, the first U.S. astronaut to orbit the earth. Alone in space, you look back and see the earth hanging in its beauty below you.

2. The year is 2005, and the first woman President of the United States is being sworn in to office. You're in the audience, witnessing the event.

3. The year is 1974. You're Hank Aaron, and you've just broken the home run record Babe Ruth set in 1935. (Babe Ruth hit his 714th home run that year.) The crowd goes wild.

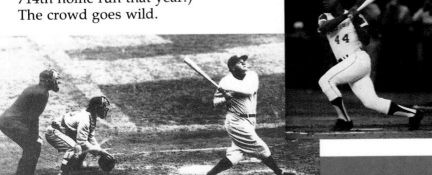

USING DESCRIPTION

OBJECTIVES

- To identify the descriptive mode and to analyze the characteristics of descriptive writing
- To select an appropriate topic for a description
- To generate a list of sensory and factual details for a description by observing, recalling, imagining, and researching
- To organize details in spatial order or order of importance
- To write a draft of a description
- To evaluate and revise and proofread and publish a description

WRITING-IN-PROGRESS ASSIGNMENTS

Major Assignment: Writing a description
Cumulative Writing Assignments: The chart below shows the sequence of cumulative assignments that will guide students as they use description. These Writing Assignments form the instructional core of Chapter 5.

PREWRITING

WRITING ASSIGNMENT
- Part 1: Starting Your Description p. 158
- Part 2: Collecting Details p. 162
- Part 3: Selecting and Arranging Details p. 163

WRITING YOUR FIRST DRAFT

WRITING ASSIGNMENT
- Part 4: Writing a First Draft p. 170

EVALUATING AND REVISING

WRITING ASSIGNMENT
- Part 5: Evaluating and Revising Your Description p. 174

PROOFREADING AND PUBLISHING

WRITING ASSIGNMENT
- Part 6: Proofreading and Publishing Your Description p. 176

In addition, exercises 1–4 provide practice in gathering sensory and factual details, collecting details for speaking and listening, analyzing a description, and analyzing a writer's revisions.

cross CURRICULUM

Writing Descriptions for Social Studies

In your team teaching situation, develop a combination social studies/descriptive writing assignment. Work with the social studies teacher to create a list of topics for descriptions based on specific time periods or events from American history, or allow students to brainstorm topics they might like to develop themselves. Suggest that students place themselves as teenagers in the time period and describe their lives. Students might brainstorm a list like the following.

Time/Place	Descriptive Possibilities
• colonial America	work, clothing, food, housing, schooling, politics, religion
• crossing the Atlantic on the *Mayflower*	possessions, purpose, attitude of passengers, living conditions, food
• Appomattox Court House, April 9, 1865	participants in surrender, appearance, attitudes, atmosphere, events

- **Visualizing** If students have difficulty visualizing the life and time period, refer them to their history books or other resources.

- **Audience, Purpose, Tone** Suggest that the standard essay form is not the only way to present material. Students could write their descriptions as letters to family members, as journal entries, or as eyewitness articles for a local newspaper. Remind students that in another time period, today's expressions and slang are inappropriate. To get a feel for the language, students might read documents or stories from the time period they are investigating.

- **Assessment** Advise students that their social studies teacher will assess the content of their papers while you will be concerned with style, development, and language.

INTEGRATING THE LANGUAGE ARTS

SELECTION	READING AND LITERATURE	WRITING AND CRITICAL THINKING	LANGUAGE AND SYNTAX	SPEAKING, LISTENING, AND OTHER EXPRESSION SKILLS
• "October" by Gary Soto p. 152 • "The Smallest Dragonboy" by Anne McCaffrey p. 157 • from *Brazil-Maru* by Karen Tei Yamashita pp. 166–168 • "grandmother" by Ray Young Bear p. 179	• Responding to selections p. 153 • Identifying imagery pp. 153, 168 • Recognizing and interpreting figurative language pp. 153, 180 • Determining the author's purpose and attitude in a selection p. 168 • Identifying elements of poetry p. 180 • Identifying examples of major types of figurative language p. 180 • Using encyclopedias and reference materials p. 183	• Analyzing a poem p. 153 • Identifying sensory details pp. 159, 168, 180 • Listing and brainstorming as prewriting pp. 160, 180 • Organizing appropriately for audience and purpose p. 163 • Using literary devices appropriately pp. 168, 170 • Writing and revising for clarity, coherence, economy, and unity pp. 170, 171, 174 • Analyzing word function in sentences and in a writer's revision p. 173 • Proofreading for spelling, grammar, capitalization, and usage errors p. 175 • Writing reflection for portfolio selection p. 176 • Writing a classified advertisement pp. 182–183 • Writing a riddle p. 183	• Choosing correct words from synonyms p. 174 • Identifying word connotations p. 174 • Using advanced dictionaries to determine word meaning p. 174	• Developing an awareness of personal uniqueness p. 151 • Making charts to show information pp. 158, 162 • Contributing ideas in brainstorming in a group pp. 160–161 • Composing visuals to communicate information p. 176 • Participating in oral reading p. 176

SUGGESTED INTEGRATED UNIT PLAN

This unit plan suggests how to integrate the major strands of the language arts with this chapter.

If you begin with this chapter on using description or with literature selections, like the ones listed below, you should focus on the common characteristics of descriptive writing. You can then integrate speaking/listening and language concepts with both the writing and the literature.

Common Characteristics

- Content that contains both facts and personal impressions
- Precise language that helps readers form clear images
- Sensory details to add clarity
- Clear, easy-to-follow, often spatial, organization

Writing
Description

Language
Grammar, Style, Figurative Language

- First-person pronouns
- Sensory details and figures of speech

UNIT FOCUS
USING DESCRIPTION

Speaking/Listening

- Describe and listen to ways to collect details
- Contribute to group discussion
- Read description to class

Literature
Nonfiction/Fiction/Poetry such as

- "Camp Harmony" Monica Sone
- "I Like to See It Lap the Miles" Emily Dickinson
- *An American Childhood* Annie Dillard
- "The Dinner Party" Mona Gardner

CHAPTER 5: USING DESCRIPTION

Use this guide for creating an instructional plan that addresses the individual needs of your students. Assignments accompanied by the following symbol (∗) may be completed out of class. Times given for pacing lessons are estimated.

CHAPTER PLANNING GUIDE—PUPIL'S EDITION

LESSONS	LITERARY MODEL p. 152 "October" by Gary Soto	PREWRITING pp. 155–163	
		Generating Ideas	Gathering/Organizing
DEVELOPMENTAL PROGRAM	⏱ **20–25 minutes** • Read model aloud in class and have students answer questions 1, 3, 4 on p. 153 orally and write the answer to question 2.	⏱ **30–35 minutes** • Uses of Description p. 154 • Main Assignment: Looking Ahead p. 154 • Finding a Focus pp. 155–157 • Writing Note p. 157 • Writing Assignment: Part 1 p. 158∗	⏱ **50–55 minutes** • Planning Your Description pp. 159–163 • Exercises 1, 2 pp. 159–160, 161–162 • Reminder p. 163 • Writing Assignments: Parts 2, 3 pp. 162, 163∗
CORE PROGRAM	⏱ **15–20 minutes** • Assign student to read model independently • Have students write answer to question 2 on p. 153 and share responses with the class.	⏱ **20–25 minutes** • Uses of Description p. 154 • Main Assignment: Looking Ahead p. 154 • Finding a Focus pp. 155–157∗ • Writing Note p. 157 • Writing Assignment: Part 1 p. 158∗	⏱ **10–15 minutes** • Planning Your Description pp. 159–163∗ • Reminder p. 163 • Writing Assignments: Parts 2, 3, pp. 162, 163∗
ACCELERATED PROGRAM	⏱ **10–15 minutes** • Assign students to read model independently and freewrite answers to question 2 on p. 153.	⏱ **15–20 minutes** • Main Assignment: Looking Ahead p. 154 • Thinking About Subject, Purpose, and Audience pp. 155–157∗ • Writing Assignment: Part 1 p. 158∗	⏱ **5–10 minutes** • Planning Your Description pp. 159–163∗ • Reminder p. 163 • Writing Assignments: Parts 2, 3, pp. 162, 163∗

CHAPTER PLANNING GUIDE—PROGRAM RESOURCES

	LITERARY MODEL	PREWRITING
PRINT	• Reading Master 5, *Practice for Assessment in Reading, Vocabulary, and Spelling* p. 5	• Prewriting, *Strategies for Writing* p. 9 • *English Workshop* pp. 193–198
MEDIA	• Fine Art Transparency 2: *Tamalada, Transparency Binder*	• Graphic Organizers 7 and 8: *Transparency Binder* • *Writer's Workshop 1:* Firsthand Biography • *Language Workshop:* Lesson 15

WRITING pp. 164–170	EVALUATING AND REVISING pp. 171–174	PROOFREADING AND PUBLISHING pp. 175–177
40–45 minutes • Exact Words and Figures of Speech pp. 164–166 • Writing Note p. 166 • A Writer's Model pp. 169–170 • Writing Assignment: Part 4 p. 170*	**40–45 minutes** • Evaluating and Revising p. 171 • Chart p. 172 • Exercise 4 in pairs pp. 172–173 • Writing Assignment: Part 5 p. 174	**40–45 minutes** • Proofreading and Publishing pp. 175–176 • Grammar Hint p. 175 • Writing Assignment: Part 6 p. 176 • Reflecting p. 176 • A Student Model p. 177
30–35 minutes • Exact Words pp. 164–165 • Writing Note p. 166 • A Passage from a Novel pp. 166–168* • Exercise 3 p. 168 • Writing Assignment: Part 4 p. 170*	**30–35 minutes** • Evaluating and Revising Description Chart p. 172 • Critical Thinking pp. 173–174* • Writing Assignment: Part 5 p. 174	**30–35 minutes** • Grammar Hint p. 175 • Publishing p. 176 • Writing Assignment: Part 6 p. 176 • Reflecting p. 176 • A Student Model p. 177*
10–15 minutes • Figures of Speech pp. 165–166 • Writing Note p. 166 • A Passage from a Novel pp. 166–168* • Writing Assignment: Part 4 p. 170*	**25–30 minutes** • Evaluating and Revising Description Chart p. 172 • Writing Assignment: Part 5 p. 174	**25–30 minutes** • Grammar Hint p. 175 • Publishing p. 176 • Writing Assignment: Part 6 p. 176 • Reflecting on Your Writing p. 176

Computer disk or CD-ROM   Overhead transparencies

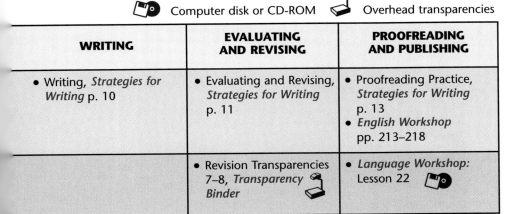

WRITING	EVALUATING AND REVISING	PROOFREADING AND PUBLISHING
• Writing, *Strategies for Writing* p. 10	• Evaluating and Revising, *Strategies for Writing* p. 11	• Proofreading Practice, *Strategies for Writing* p. 13 • *English Workshop* pp. 213–218
	• Revision Transparencies 7–8, *Transparency Binder*	• *Language Workshop:* Lesson 22

ELEMENTS OF WRITING: CURRICULUM CONNECTIONS

Writing Workshop
• A Free Verse Poem pp. 178–181

Making Connections
• A Classified Ad pp. 182–183
• Biology Riddles p. 183

ASSESSMENT OPTIONS

Summative Assessment
Holistic Scoring: Prompts and Models pp. 9–14

Performance Assessment
Assessment 1 *Integrated Performance Assessment, Level C* For help with evaluation, see *Holistic Scoring Workshop.*

Portfolio Assessment
Portfolio forms, *Portfolio Assessment* pp. 5–24, 38–43

Reflection
Writing Process Log, *Strategies for Writing* p. 8

Ongoing Assessment
Proofreading, *Strategies for Writing* p. 12

CREATING PICTURES AND IMAGES

OBJECTIVES

- To use sensory details in description
- To identify and analyze descriptive details in poetry

TEACHING THE LESSON

Tell students to think about a dramatic weather scene—a storm, a blistering-hot day, or a first snow. Have them close their eyes and imagine how it looks, feels, sounds, and smells. You may want to have a few volunteers describe their scenes to the class.

 PROGRAM MANAGER

CHAPTER 5

- **Computer Guided Instruction** For a related assignment that students may use for additional instruction and practice, see **Firsthand Biography** in *Writer's Workshop 1 CD-ROM.*

- **Summative Assessment** For a writing prompt, including grading criteria and student models, see *Holistic Scoring: Prompts and Models,* pp. 9–13.

- **Performance Assessment** Use **Assessment 1** in *Integrated Performance Assessment, Level C.* For help with evaluating student writing, see *Holistic Scoring Workshop, Level C.*

- **Extension/Enrichment** See **Fine Art Transparency 2,** *Tamalada* by Carmen Lomas Garza. For suggestions on how to tie the transparency to instruction, review teacher's notes in *Fine Art and Instructional Transparencies for Writing,* p. 9.

- **Reading Support** For help with the reading selection, p. 152, see **Reading Master 5** in *Practice for Assessment in Reading, Vocabulary, and Spelling,* p. 5.

5 USING DESCRIPTION

Then have a volunteer read aloud the introductory paragraphs of the chapter. Point out that in description a writer often focuses on what is unique about the subject. Students might jot down in their writing journals descriptions that uniquely suit them. Or they might try describing another individual to the class.

As you guide students through the poem, elicit personal responses. Use the annotations to help students analyze the writer's style. Then assign the **Reader's Response** and **Writer's Craft** questions for independent practice. To assess understanding, evaluate students' personal responses and answers to the **Writer's Craft** questions.

Creating Pictures and Images

Have you ever read or heard a story so scary that you couldn't sleep that night? You never actually saw them, but you have a very clear **image** of the horrors. The **pictures** you imagine were created with words—words that grabbed and played on your senses.

Writing and You. Writers often use words to paint a picture in your mind. Their words cause you to imagine sights, sounds, smells, textures, and tastes. Their vivid language helps you "see" what they want you to see—a woman's face, a crumbling building, a boat in a swirling, stormy sea. What kind of words might a writer use to describe you?

As You Read. As you read the following poem, look for the words that help you "see" the beginning of winter in the mountains.

Clifford Faust, *Jamaica* (1989).

Ask students to close their eyes and recall trees, flowers, or plants they have seen. Encourage students to create vivid pictures in their minds by concentrating on how the plants looked, felt, smelled, and so on. Have students recreate the images by writing one or two sentences describing the pictures they created.

VISUAL CONNECTIONS
Jamaica

About the Artist. Clifford Faust was born in Vinita, Oklahoma, in 1944, and he grew up in Corvallis, Oregon. He graduated from the Art Center College of Design and studied with Jack Potter at the School of Visual Arts in New York. Faust's main influences were the artists Degas, Van Gogh, and David Hockney, but he was also inspired by Walt Disney's animation art.

About the Artwork. Inspired by a trip to the Caribbean, *Jamaica* is a colorful portrayal of the island. The artist used mixed media—cut paper collage with bits of watercolor and pastel—to achieve this vibrant, tropical effect.

CLOSURE

Ask the class to give a brief definition of *description*. Then ask what two characteristics of description Gary Soto has used in his poem **"October"** [sensory details, comparisons].

EXTENSION

For most people, vision and hearing are the primary means of receiving information; therefore, most description uses visual and auditory images. Challenge students to increase their descriptive powers by preparing a description for a blind or deaf person. What words could students use to

USING THE SELECTION
October

1

Writers often use vivid verbs to bring their imagery into sharp focus. Identify vivid verbs and participles in the poem and describe their overall effect. [Answers may include *grayed, hardened, steamed, spread, lifted, shuffled, flapping, gathered, slipped, squatted,* and *tilting.* These verbs give a picture of exactly what happened.]

2

A simile compares two unlike things using the words *like* or *as.*

3

The metaphor comparing the image of a lizard in the owl's mouth to a black tassel flapping emphasizes visual descriptions rather than the violent, physical aspects of nature.

MEETING *individual* NEEDS

LEP/ESL

General Strategies. Emphasize to students that, in poetry, punctuation is often used in different ways. For example, in **"October,"** poet Gary Soto uses several commas at the end of complete sentences where a period would normally be used. Tell students that this is acceptable only in poetry; in all other forms of written English, complete sentences require periods.

152

152

October
by Gary Soto

A cold day, though only October,
1   And the grass has grayed
Like the frost that hardened it
This morning.

    And this morning
After the wind left
With its pile of clouds
The broken fence steamed, sunlight spread
2   Like seed from one field
To another, out of a bare <u>sycamore</u>
Sparrows lifted above the ridge.

In the ditch an owl shuffled into a nest
Of old leaves and cotton,
3   A black <u>tassel</u> of lizard flapping
From its beak. Mice
And ants gathered under the flat ground
And slipped downward like water,
A coyote squatted behind granite,
His ears tilting
Toward a rustle, eyes dark
With winter to come.

describe colors to someone who doesn't see
or to describe music to someone who does
not hear? ■

READER'S RESPONSE

1. After reading the poem, what feeling do you have about the coming of winter in the mountains?
2. Write a short journal entry about an especially hot or cold day where you live. Tell how the animals behave.

WRITER'S CRAFT

3. In this poem, Gary Soto uses many sight words to describe how the animals move as winter comes on. What are some of these words?
4. Writers of description sometimes compare a familiar object with an unfamiliar one. What does Soto compare the way sunlight spreads across the field with? What does he compare mice and ants going underground with?

ANSWERS

Reader's Response

Responses will vary.

1. Some students may believe that the poem's feeling about the coming of winter is one of peacefulness and serenity in the natural cycle of life. Others may feel it is bleak or foreboding with expectations of change. Students will bring their experiences into their interpretations.
2. Responses should include specific sensory details.

Writer's Craft

3. Answers may vary. The visual imagery used includes these descriptions of animal movement: sparrows flew from a sycamore, an owl "shuffled into a nest," "A black tassel of lizard flapping," mice and ants "slipped downward like water," a coyote squats "behind granite."
4. Soto compares the way the sunlight spreads with the way seeds spread from one field to another. He compares the mice and ants with water flowing downward.

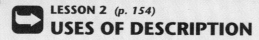
After having a volunteer read aloud **Uses of Description,** tell students that the examples in the textbook can be grouped as four general purposes for writing. These purposes are self-expression (examples 1 and 2), persuasion (examples 3 and 4), information (examples 5, 6, and 7), and creative writing (examples 8 and 9). Then ask students to write down additional examples of ways to use descriptive writing for each purpose. Make a list of these on the chalkboard. Assess students' understanding of the purposes for writing by checking the examples they write.

COOPERATIVE LEARNING

Examples of different ways to use description according to the purpose intended are given in the textbook. You may want to have students experiment with the sample topics in small groups. Group students according to the topics they are interested in and have the groups brainstorm to produce lists of sensory details.

Uses of Description

Writers of description want you mentally to see, hear, touch, taste, and smell what they describe. However, they may have different purposes for their descriptions. Here are some examples of possible uses of description.

- in a postcard, describing the mountain town you are visiting
- in a journal entry, describing your reaction to a friend's comment
- in an electronic bulletin board posting, describing some guinea pigs that you want to give away
- in a newspaper ad, describing a summer internship available to students
- in a police report, giving a detailed description of your stolen bicycle
- in a recipe, telling how to make enchiladas
- in an office memo, describing a photocopier that needs to be repaired
- in a poem, re-creating the sound of water splashing in a pool
- in a play, describing the setting of a scene

If you read a travel brochure about China or a history chapter about the ancient Maya, you'll find description. You'll also find it in ads on buses and in magazines and enjoy it in stories, poems, plays, and novels. No matter what the writer's purpose or where you find it, all good description forms pictures and images in the reader's mind.

LOOKING AHEAD

In this chapter, you'll use the writing process to write a description. Your basic purpose will be literary. Keep in mind that a good description

- has sensory details that help the reader form clear images of the subject
- uses precise words
- is clearly organized and easy to follow

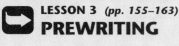
PREWRITING

OBJECTIVES

- To choose a subject, purpose, and audience for a description
- To brainstorm and list sensory details and factual details
- To collect details by observing, recalling, researching, and imagining
- To organize details in spatial order or order of importance
- To select details that create a main feeling

Writing a Description

Finding a Focus

"Focus your attention on the hat," the magician says, and before your eyes a rabbit appears!

In writing a good description, you become a magician of sorts, too. Focusing your attention on a specific subject, a particular audience, and a clear purpose is the first step in making the subject you are writing about "appear like magic" in print before the very eyes of your readers.

Thinking About Subject, Purpose, and Audience

Description is part of almost every kind of writing you do. You usually don't have to think of a subject to write about. The subject is just a natural part of the writing you're doing. For example, you might describe last week's pep rally to a friend in a letter. And, if your collie wanders away, you'll describe it in notices that you put up around the neighborhood.

When the choice of a subject is yours, however, select something or someone familiar. For example, a teacher might ask you to write a description of a person. A good choice might be your favorite neighbor or your best

PROGRAM MANAGER

PREWRITING

- **Self-Assessment** Before beginning instruction of the writing process, see **Writing Process Log** in *Strategies for Writing*, p. 8.
- **Heuristics** To help students generate ideas, see **Prewriting** in *Strategies for Writing*, p. 9.
- **Instructional Support** See **Graphic Organizers 7** and **8**. For suggestions on how to tie the transparencies to instruction, review teacher's notes in *Fine Art and Instructional Transparencies for Writing*, pp. 59, 61.

QUOTATION FOR THE DAY

"The real composer thinks about his work the whole time; he is not always conscious of this, but he is aware of it later when he suddenly knows what he will do." (Igor Stravinsky, 1882–1971, Russian composer)

You may wish to tell students that Stravinsky's quotation about music composers could also apply to writers. Explain that spending time thinking about the work one wants to create is an essential part of the prewriting stage. Lead students to understand that observing, recalling, and imagining are worthwhile activities that take time.

MOTIVATION

Begin by listing these topics on the chalkboard: a favorite notebook, my funniest friend, the best dinner, the scariest ride. Ask students to brainstorm for sensory details that could describe each topic. Remind students to use words that appeal to each of the senses.

TEACHING THE LESSON

Have students read the material in **Finding a Focus**, p. 155, and ask a volunteer to read aloud the objective description of the dragon. Then have students suggest other writing situations that call for objective descriptions [science writing, news articles, reports, manuals, textbooks, encyclopedia articles, advertising].

MEETING *individual* NEEDS

LESS-ADVANCED STUDENTS

You may want to work individually with students to help them select topics of special interest. Help them limit their topics to something specific. If the topic selected is an object, encourage the student to bring the object to class as he or she works on the assignment.

156   *Using Description*

friend. It's also a good idea to limit your subject. You can describe the Statue of Liberty more thoroughly than you could describe all of New York City.

Your purpose for writing helps you to decide whether to write an objective or subjective description. When your purpose is to inform, you usually write an *objective description.* An objective description gives a factual, realistic picture of a subject without revealing your feelings about it. Notice the factual, realistic details in this objective description of a dragon.

> A dragon is a large, imaginary, cold-blooded creature that has a bony skeleton and a body covered with scales or horny plates. It usually has a large tail, claws, and wings that enable it to fly. It also has the ability to breathe fire and smoke.

When your purpose is to be creative, you'll usually write a *subjective description.* This type of description creates a clear picture of the subject with details that also reveal your thoughts and feelings about it. Its details may also create a mood, or main feeling. In this subjective description of a dragon, a boy named Keevan learns that a newly hatched dragon will be his. As you read, compare this description with the objective description of the dragon above. How do you think Keevan feels about his dragon?

Have another volunteer read aloud the subjective description of the dragon and then have students suggest other writing situations that call for subjective descriptions [journals, letters, short stories, plays, political speeches, novels].

After students have read **Planning Your Description** on p. 159, discuss the

Here's How chart on p. 161 as a method of keeping track of details. You could also share another way to collect and organize sensory details: ask each student to make five columns on a page for each of the five senses and to list sensory details under each heading.

After students have read **Selecting and Organizing Details** on p. 163, point

Why? asked the dragon again. *Don't you like me?* His eyes whirled with anxiety, and his tone was so piteous that Keevan staggered forward and threw his arms around the dragon's neck, stroking his eye ridges, patting the damp, soft hide, opening the fragile-looking wings to dry them, and assuring the hatchling wordlessly over and over again that he was the most perfect, most beautiful, most beloved dragon in the entire weyr, in all the weyrs of Pern.

Anne McCaffrey, "The Smallest Dragonboy"

WRITING NOTE In subjective description, you may want to speak directly to your reader, using the words *I* and *me*. And you usually write in a relaxed way, as though you were speaking with good friends.

No matter what kind of description you're writing, think about your audience. Ask yourself these questions:

1. What details do my readers already know about my subject?
2. What details do my readers need to know about my subject?
3. How do I want my readers to feel about my subject?

INTEGRATING THE LANGUAGE ARTS

Vocabulary Link. Anne McCaffrey's story about a dragonboy uses the word *weyr* to describe a group of dragons. Point out that fiction writers sometimes coin new words to enliven their stories. Writers don't necessarily define the new words, but they often give contextual clues. You could select other examples of new words from science fiction or fantasy works for students to identify. Or have students write sentences containing made-up words for their classmates to define from the context.

SELECTION AMENDMENT
Description of change: excerpted
Rationale: to focus on the concept of description presented in this chapter

157

out that occasionally chronological order is used in description, as in the first paragraph of the excerpt from *Brazil-Maru* on p. 166.

You may want to model choosing a subject as students will be asked to do in **Writing Assignment: Part 1** below. Then use the subject selected to model collecting details for **Writing Assignment: Part 2** on p. 162. Have the class help you choose sensory and factual details as you write them on the chalkboard. Emphasize using the four

INTEGRATING THE LANGUAGE ARTS

Literature Link. In "The Legend of Sleepy Hollow," Washington Irving skillfully uses subjective detail. His descriptions create a feeling (atmosphere) as powerful as the visual images. Refer students to passages in the story that use sensory details and subjective descriptions, and that create feeling. [The daytime atmosphere or feeling is one of quiet calmness. Nighttime is restless and scary.]

A DIFFERENT APPROACH

Encourage students to think about places that are rich with sensory impressions and have each student choose one place as a topic. Examples include a school cafeteria, a pizza shop, a locker room, a kitchen, a cosmetic counter, a woodworking shop, a hairdresser's salon, and a fishing boat. Have students spend time observing the places they choose. They should take their notebooks and make notes of sensory and factual details at the site.

158

158 *Using Description*

PART 1:
Starting Your Description

Who or what stands out in your mind? a grandparent? a pop star? a stuffed animal from long ago? a favorite pair of tennis shoes? In this chapter, you'll write a subjective description. To begin, choose a subject (a specific person, place, or object). Then, focus your writing by filling out a chart like the one below.

A pop star?

A stuffed animal?

SUBJECT: my tennis shoes
PURPOSE: to express my feelings
TYPE: subjective
AUDIENCE: my classmates and teacher

A grandparent?

methods of collecting details. This should prepare students for **Exercises 1,** below, and **2,** p. 161. Then show students how to select and organize the details to create a main feeling, as suggested in **Writing Assignment: Part 3** on p. 163.

INDEPENDENT PRACTICE

Students should be able to complete **Exercises 1** and **2** and **Writing Assignment: Parts 1–3** independently. You may want to circulate through the class, having brief conferences about topics as necessary.

☞

 *Prewriting*

Planning Your Description

To explore your subject further, you'll need to gather specific details. This means you'll need to know what to look for, where to look, and how to use what you find.

Identifying Descriptive Details

As you describe your subject, look for different kinds of specific details. These include both sensory details and factual, realistic details.

Sensory Details. You gather information through all five of your senses—sight, hearing, touch, smell, and taste. Include details that appeal to all your senses. The fastest way to create a clearer description is to add more sensory details. For example, you can write that the dog *whimpered pleadingly* (sound) and that it had a *soft, silky coat* (touch) and a *faint, perfumy scent* (smell) after its bath.

Factual, Realistic Details.
Sometimes your sensory details will need to be very precise. These factual, realistic details create an exact image that can't be misunderstood. They can be tested or checked for accuracy by your readers. For example, you can write about a missing dog that it's a *cream-colored collie, thirty inches high.*

EXERCISE 1 ▶ **Gathering Sensory and Factual Details**

How many sensory and factual details can you imagine about a subject? With two or three classmates, choose one

ASSESSMENT

Assess students' ability to generate and categorize details by evaluating their lists from **Exercises 1** and **2**. For **Writing Assignment: Part 3**, students might exchange their numbered lists for peer evaluation. Have students place stars above all details that create precise pictures.

RETEACHING

Supply students with examples of excellent descriptive writing and help them to identify sensory and factual details. Then help students determine the main feeling that each detail evokes.

ANSWERS

Exercise 1

Responses will vary. Students should include details that appeal to all five senses in their lists of sensory details. Their factual details should be precise and should create exact images that could be tested or checked for accuracy.

MEETING *individual* **NEEDS**

LEP/ESL

General Strategies. You may need to clarify the terms *observe, recall, research,* and *imagine.* Create four columns on the chalkboard and ask students to suggest examples of each.

Have them find examples from daily life in which one observes [combing one's hair in front of the mirror, window shopping in the mall], recalls [taking a test, trying to remember someone's name], researches [reading a bus schedule to decide which bus to take, looking up a number in the telephone book], and imagines [thinking about the future, thinking about a dream vacation]. Help students see that they will apply these familiar skills in a new way.

---

160 *Using Description*

of the subjects below. Then make two lists. Label them *Sensory Details* and *Factual Details.* Now brainstorm with your classmates, and write down as many sensory and factual details as you can think of about your subject.

1. a school assembly
2. the beach or the woods
3. a thunderstorm
4. a frog or snake
5. a new car
6. a baseball or soccer game

Collecting Details

Depending upon your subject, you can collect specific details for your description in one or more ways. You can *observe, recall, research,* or *imagine* details.

Observing.   Real observation requires planting yourself in front of your subject and tuning up all your senses. As you observe, ask yourself, "What sensory details do I notice?" "What factual, realistic details can I include?"

Recalling.   You can collect details by tapping into your memories. Close your eyes and try to recall how your subject looked, smelled, felt, sounded, or tasted. Check your details with others who shared the experience with you. Try to remember if your subject reminded you of something else. What was it? Why did you make the connection?

Researching.   Books, magazines, pictures, audiovisual materials, online sources, and knowledgeable people expand your horizons. They give you a way to go beyond the limits of your specific time and place. You may live in a warm climate, but by searching the Internet for images of and information on Alaska, you can gather details about a blizzard.

CLOSURE

Ask a student to describe a favorite place on campus to the class. Encourage him or her to give descriptive details that will help the class to visualize the place. Ask students to tell which details are subjective and which are objective.

EXTENSION

Ask students to concentrate on a strong emotion such as love, hate, joy, sadness, or anger for a few minutes. Have them write a subjective description of how that emotion personally affects them. Challenge them to use sensory details and comparisons. With a few prodding questions to

Prewriting **161**

Imagining. To imagine your subject, close your eyes and focus on it. Ask the same kinds of questions you ask when you observe directly. Whether your subject is real or imaginary, your readers will need specific details to re-create it in their "mind's eye." (For more on imagining, see page 31.) For real subjects, you might imagine how you'd *like* the subject to be.

As you collect details, a chart can help you keep track of them. For example, if you're collecting details about your school bus, you might make a chart like the following one. This writer focused on recalling, observing, and imagining details. For other subjects, you might find it helpful to use different methods of collecting details.

> *What I recall:* Face of Mr. Deal—the driver—scowls and smiles; 25 rows of torn brown vinyl seats; litter on floor; number 672 on bus; laughter; squealing brakes; bounces on bumpy roads; hot seats in summer; wet wool coats
>
> *What I observe:* Mr. Deal's county bus license; safety rules and fire extinguisher; squishy feel of foam under ripped vinyl; sticky seats; strong smell of cleaner used on floors every Monday
>
> *What I imagine:* Small TVs and CD players installed on seat backs; soft, padded seats that recline; air conditioning; bus attendants serving snacks

EXERCISE 2 ▶ **Speaking and Listening: Collecting Details**

In groups of four, practice using different methods of collecting details. Have one person, the speaker, choose one of the following situations and describe which method (or methods) of collecting details is best. Then use that method to gather details for your group. The rest of the

INTEGRATING THE LANGUAGE ARTS

Vocabulary Link. After students have generated lists of details, have them find synonyms for words that describe size, shape, color, or some other attribute. It would be helpful if students worked in groups of three or four and suggested words to each other. Suggest that students use thesauruses for this activity.

CRITICAL THINKING

Analysis. You may want to have students find examples of each of the different purposes of writing in magazines and newspapers to analyze the descriptive details. They should find examples of self-expression [first-person feature story, letter to the editor]; persuasion [advertisement, editorial]; information [news article, science article]; and literary [short story, poem].

Have students analyze the selections for the use of sensory and factual details. Ask them to determine which writing purpose uses more description. They could work in groups of three or four to discuss their conclusions and use their examples as evidence.

inspire them, many students will be able to develop rich metaphors. ■

group—the listeners—should try to think of details to add to the speaker's description. Take turns until each group member has had a chance to be speaker. Have a volunteer list the details.

1. Look out the window, wherever you are. Describe the view to a movie director who's looking for a place to film a new movie. **1.** observing
2. You're talking on an intergalactic phone hookup to an alien teenager. Describe the nearest shopping mall on a Saturday afternoon. **2.** recalling
3. You've been asked to design a float that would represent your school in a national parade. Describe how it would look. **3.** imagining
4. Describe Mount Rushmore to an exchange student from India. **4.** researching

ANSWERS

Exercise 2

You might want to have students first decide which method would work best for each situation. Then have them form groups to choose one of the situations to describe.

VISUAL CONNECTIONS

Exploring the Subject. Mount Rushmore is a massive carving of the faces of four Presidents—George Washington, Thomas Jefferson, Theodore Roosevelt, and Abraham Lincoln. Drilled and blasted with dynamite from a granite cliff in the Black Hills, the carving rises more than 500 feet above a valley in South Dakota. George Washington's head is as tall as a five-story building.

PART 2:
Collecting Details

Have a contest with yourself. See how many details you can collect for the subject you chose in Writing Assignment, Part 1. Make a chart such as the one on page 161. Collect as many details as you can, although you probably won't use all of them in your description.

Selecting and Organizing Details

Movie directors control what their audience "sees." To create a main feeling for readers, you'll include certain details and leave out others. For example, if you're describing the "chaos" of your afternoon bus ride, you'd include "litter on floor," "laughter," and "squealing brakes." But you might omit "safety rules" and "fire extinguisher."

After you've selected your details, think about arranging them in a way that makes sense to readers. You usually arrange details in a description in one of two ways:

- *spatial order*—arranges details in the way you see them
- *order of importance*—puts the most important details either first or last

 REFERENCE NOTE: For more on arranging details, see pages 36–39.

 *Reminder*

To develop your subject for description

- think about your purpose and your audience
- collect both sensory and realistic details by observing, recalling, researching, or imagining
- choose details that create a main feeling
- arrange details in a way that makes sense

 **WRITING** ASSIGNMENT

PART 3:
Selecting and Arranging Details

What do you want your readers to feel about your subject? Suspense—like on a stormy night when the lights go out? Excitement—like during a Chinese New Year's celebration? Review your lists of details for your subject. Select details that create one main feeling. Then, arrange your details in a reasonable order, and number them.

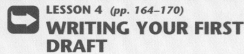
OBJECTIVES

- To analyze a description by considering details, feelings, and order
- To write a subjective description

MOTIVATION

Write these phrases on the chalkboard: (1) gentle as a _____ ; (2) mad as a _____ ; (3) mean as a _____.

Remind students that similes lose power with overuse, so they will want to find fresh analogies for their writing and speaking. Challenge students to create three new similes from the phrases on the chalkboard.

PROGRAM MANAGER

WRITING YOUR FIRST DRAFT

■ **Instructional Support** For help with writing descriptions, see **Writing** in *Strategies for Writing*, p. 10.

QUOTATION FOR THE DAY

"Being specific sometimes involves no more than choosing the right word or phrase." (Ronald Munson, American author and teacher)

You may wish to ask students to brainstorm in small groups. Have them list words, phrases, or descriptive details that make a vague sentence more specific. (You may wish to assign sentences such as "The woman enjoyed her work," "The dog came home," or "The man walked down the road.") As students evaluate and revise their descriptive papers, encourage them to add sensory details and to exchange more vivid words for dull or overused subjects, verbs, and objects.

Writing Your First Draft

Exact Words and Figures of Speech

The basic elements of good description that you've studied so far are

- sensory and factual details
- a main feeling, or main impression
- an arrangement of details that makes sense

When you add *exact words* and *figures of speech* as you write your first draft, your description will leap off the pages into your reader's mind.

Exact Words.   What's the difference between *walking* or *slithering* across the room? *Walking* is such a general word that it gives a weak, fuzzy picture. *Slithering*, on the other hand, is precise—slinky, sneaky, snaky.

In your descriptions, avoid vague, general words. Choose precise nouns, verbs, adjectives, and adverbs. Add to your supply of precise words by developing your own **word bank.** As you read or hear vivid, specific words, collect them. Write them down in a special section of your notebook or journal. Organize them into useful groups, as in the following word bank.

A SENSORY WORD BANK			
SIGHT WORDS			
oblong	twisted	aqua	vivid
four-sided	flat	mulberry	canary
SOUND WORDS			
roar	hum	rasp	thunder
twitter	blast	scrape	rumble
TASTE WORDS			
sour	bitter	nutty	bland
spicy	sweet	salty	hot

(continued)

Before students read the professional model on pp. 166–168, have them read **Exact Words and Figures of Speech,** pp. 164–166, independently. Tell students to keep these points in mind as they read the model. The professional model can be read independently, or you could have volunteers prepare oral readings for the class.

You may want to allow time for students to work on their word banks. They could work in groups to generate rich word lists.

A Writer's Model on pp. 169–170 may also be read independently. After students have finished reading, use the annotations to direct a discussion of how the writer uses details and figures of speech to create a central feeling. ☛

Writing Your First Draft **165**

A SENSORY WORD BANK *(continued)*			
SMELL WORDS			
sweet	rotten	mildewed	moldy
spicy	stale	musty	fresh
TOUCH WORDS			
smooth	icy	slippery	cool
slimy	wet	dry	rough

Figures of Speech. Figures of speech are "special-effects" language that is not meant to be taken literally. When you say, for example, that it's raining cats and dogs, you don't *really* mean that animals are falling from the sky. *Figures of speech* (*similes, metaphors,* and *personification*) are imaginative comparisons that create striking images. (See pages 178–181 for more about using figurative language in writing poems.)

- A *simile* compares two basically unlike things, using the word *like* or *as.*

    The pep band's *sound* hit us *like a tidal wave.*

- A *metaphor* makes a direct comparison without using the word *like* or *as.* A metaphor says that something *is* something else.

    The missing dog's *wagging tail was a white flag of surrender.*

A DIFFERENT APPROACH
The **Exact Words** section gives students an opportunity for pantomime. Have students work in groups of four or five to brainstorm and list more precise synonyms for vague words such as *walked, said, asked, large, nice,* and *a lot.* Have them work quietly so other groups won't overhear their ideas. Then students can dramatize their stronger, more exact words. The class can guess each group's synonyms. Students may wish to add these words to their word banks.

165

GUIDED PRACTICE

After students have read the lesson, have them write their answers to **Exercise 3** on p. 168 before they discuss the questions in groups. Have each group share the responses with the class.

INDEPENDENT PRACTICE

Students should be ready to write first drafts of their descriptions in **Writing Assignment: Part 4,** p. 170, independently. Use student-teacher conferences if students need help structuring their descriptions.

MEETING *individual* NEEDS

LEP/ESL

General Strategies. The **Writing Note** deals with clichés. The examples provided may not be useful guides for students because clichés are closely tied to the cultures that produce them. Ask students to tell about clichés that are used in their cultures.

INTEGRATING THE LANGUAGE ARTS

Literature Link. If the selection is contained in your literature textbook or is available in your library, have students analyze *A Christmas Carol* by Charles Dickens for its use of vivid descriptions. Tell students to divide a sheet of paper into five parts labeled *sight, hearing, touch, taste,* and *smell.* Then they can identify words that appeal to each sense. Explain that sensory details bring the literature to life. A good passage to use is the scene describing Scrooge's school the day Fan comes to take him home.

You could also encourage students to read aloud favorite descriptions from books they enjoyed and to identify sensory details in the passages.

166

---

166 *Using Description*

- *Personification* gives human characteristics to nonhuman things.

  The *heat swallowed* my energy.

When used well, figures of speech can make your subject come alive for readers.

WRITING NOTE

Clichés are overused and worn-out figures of speech. You probably know hundreds: "fresh as a daisy," "cold as ice," "eager beaver." Try to avoid clichés when you write. Instead, use your imagination to think of a new comparison.

In the following passage, a character named Ichiro Terada describes a Japanese Brazilian farming community, Esperança, established by pioneers in the 1920s. Look for the precise details that bring an imaginary scene to life.

A PASSAGE FROM A NOVEL

from Brazil-Maru
by Karen Tei Yamashita

Realistic details

When Okumura first went out to show my father the boundaries of our new land, I went along. He pointed out the measurements across the front of the land along the road. The lots were all measured out in long strips of sixty acres, each lot having access to one of several roads which crisscrossed Esperança. Now we were only a handful of families, but soon there would be over two hundred of us. Our lot was several miles from the long house which marked what became the center of Esperança with its co-op offices, store, ware-

ASSESSMENT

At this stage in the writing process, stress the positive aspects of students' writing. You may want to evaluate only the first paragraph by placing a check mark above each well-written descriptive detail.

RETEACHING

If you find that students are having difficulty with description, ask them to volunteer a few descriptive sentences to show on an overhead projector. In a group discussion, let students suggest ways the descriptions could be improved.

☞

Writing Your First Draft   **167**

houses, and eventually a school and church. Okumura's house was located in this center, and soon, so were the houses of others who worked at the co-op.

Sensory details— sight

My father and I looked at the acreage. It was a green wall of dense forest, trees and vines and brush rising high into the sky. We could not see farther than several meters in from the road. What might be behind that wall of green life, we could not say. When we set fire to the forest, <u>droves</u> of yellow and green parakeets and clattering orange-beaked <u>toucans</u> swept up in great clouds above the

Sensory detail— sound

1

flames, while small animals, armadillos, snakes, and lizards stumbled and scurried from the smoke. From time to time, wild boars and even a panther might be seen. When the fires died down and the earth was only warm to the touch, the men took long saws and hatchets

Sensory detail— touch

and cut down the large trees that had not succumbed to the fire. Across the road could be seen the results of the labor of other settlers further along in this enterprise — the charred stumps of enormous trees now hidden in a field of green rice. Soon everything would be very different.

Realistic details

When I think about the old forest, I invariably think about the incredible variety of insects in those days. Along with the occasional appearance of some unusual bird, the great variety of insects that yet remain are a reminder of the wonderfully complex living space the forest once was. When the forest was still <u>intact</u>, you could not light a candle or a lamp at night without being visited by a small dense cloud of moths, butterflies, beetles, mosquitoes, flies, crickets, and spiders of every color and description. They flew and crept through our open windows and doors in

USING THE SELECTION
from **Brazil-Maru**

1

armadillo: a small mammal that has armorlike plates covering its body. An armadillo tries to escape danger by running to its burrow, digging into the ground, or curling itself into a tight ball.

CLOSURE

Ask students to discuss what they found easiest about writing their drafts. What did they find most difficult? List responses in two columns on the chalkboard. Have volunteers suggest strategies for overcoming their difficulties.

EXTENSION

Students probably won't have much experience using figures of speech in their writing. You can prepare them to use this more vivid imagery by suggesting two unlike things and asking them to write a comparison as either a simile or a metaphor. You might use words from the following list: flowers—ideas; talent—faucet; age—seasons;

2

One centimeter corresponds to .394 of an inch. Have students convert the spiders' measurements to inches. [5.91 to 7.88 inches]

ANSWERS

Exercise 3

1. She uses spatial order.

2. Words that appeal to the sense of touch include *warm, lighting,* and *burned.* The images help create a clear description. The details relating to the insects help the reader identify with the families in Esperança.

3. The details make the forest seem vast and dense. They show that the forest is a complex ecosystem. Reader responses to the details will vary. Some may say that they better understand the complexity of the Brazilian forest and how important it is to keep it intact.

4. Students may suggest that the narrator's main feeling about Esperança is nostalgia or wonder. The narrator describes how Esperança used to look. He catalogs "the incredible variety of insects" and the types of animals that emerged from the forest when it was burned.

SELECTION AMENDMENT
Description of change: excerpted
Rationale: to focus on the concept of description presented in this chapter

168

---

168   *Using Description*

Sensory details— touch and sound

the hot evenings or congregated near the seeping lights on the walls of our houses. They seemed to us a terrible nuisance, lighting on our bodies to suck our blood or buzzing frantically around, falling into our food and clothing. In the mornings, my mother was forever sweeping out their brittle carcasses. As more and more of the forest was cleared, the number and variety of insects slowly diminished....

Realistic details

It's not possible here to name all the strange bugs we had never before seen. There were the giant *sauva* ants, who came in small armies and could destroy in one evening an entire crop of anything we might have planted.

Sensory details— sight and touch

There were poisonous caterpillars whose furry bodies burned our skin. There were giant hairy spiders, sometimes as large as fifteen or twenty centimeters across. There were large ticks whose hard bodies were the size of large watermelon seeds. Those insects that could find food despite the clearing of the forest can still be encountered today, but the strangest and most interesting of them have disappeared with the trees.

2

EXERCISE 3   **Analyzing a Description**

After reading the passage from *Brazil-Maru,* discuss the following questions with your class or in a small group.

1. What type of order does the writer use in the description of the settlement in the first paragraph?
2. Identify three words in this passage that appeal to the sense of touch. What do these images have in common?
3. How do the factual and sensory details in the third and fourth paragraphs contribute to the portrait of the forest? How do the sensory details make you feel?
4. What is the narrator's main feeling about the place he describes? Which words convey this feeling?

emotions—volcano; teeth—china; traffic—bee hive; pearls—the moon; and diamonds—grapes.

A Writer's Model for You

In the passage from *Brazil-Maru*, Karen Tei Yamashita imagines the sensory details—of sight, touch, and sound—in an unusual community. When you write, your subject may be closer to home than hers. Whatever your subject, it can become "real" for your readers if it has the elements of good description.

Notice how the writer in the following model states her subject and main feeling near the beginning. Then she develops these with specific details presented in a clear order. By the end, readers would recognize these shoes anywhere. You may want to follow this writer's model as you write your own description.

A WRITER'S MODEL

INTRODUCTION

Sensory detail—smell

Main feeling

My mom complains that they're glued to my feet and that I only take them off to go to bed. My dad complains that they're raggedy-looking. My sister complains that they stink of sweat and my feet. They're my size 8 1/2 well-worn sneakers. Like a faithful old horse, they've seen me through all my adventures—good and bad—during the past six months.

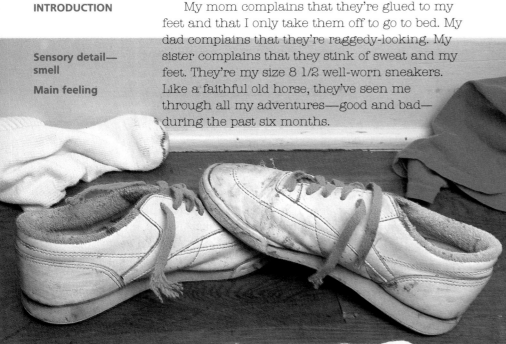

169

MEETING *individual* NEEDS

STUDENTS WITH SPECIAL NEEDS

Some students might have difficulty turning the details they have collected into subjective descriptions. Review the idea that subjective description conveys how a writer feels about a subject, and give them an example.

An objective description of a tennis shoe might describe it as musty smelling. But a subjective description gives the shoe personal associations as in "The tennis shoe smelled musty from the sweat of victories."

First, have students determine how they feel about their subjects. Then help students to make associations with their subjects and to add words to the collected details that show those associations.

A DIFFERENT APPROACH

Select three or four papers written by previous students. The papers should exhibit a range of quality. Show them on an overhead projector and let students see the language, understand the topics, note the details, and determine the main feelings.

BODY
Spatial order—
top to bottom

Sensory detail—
touch

Once when they were new, the tops of my sneakers used to be sparkling white leather with crisply rolled, neatly stitched trim. Now they're dim and gray with dirt in all the crinkles. The top stitching's coming unstitched in parts, and there are rough places where the shiny, soft leather's been totally scuffed off. My glow-in-the-dark orange shoelaces were once bright and cheerful, but now they're all dirty with frayed edges. Their shiny plastic tips are long gone, which makes it hard for me to lace the shoes if they ever get unlaced.

Realistic
details

Simile

Sensory detail—
touch

Sensory detail—
sight

CONCLUSION

If you turn them over, you'll see that the sneakers' thick gray soles are made up of hundreds of raised dots. They're huddled together like a crowd squeezed into a subway car at rush hour. The dots on the heel and front of the sole are worn totally smooth. And where I drag my right foot when I serve in tennis, the sole is completely worn through. This one-inch hole goes from the bottom of the shoe under my right big toe all the way through to the inside of my shoe. I'd be able to recognize my sneakers anywhere because of this hole.

WRITING ASSIGNMENT

PART 4:
Writing a First Draft

You have a list of details about your subject, and you've put them in the order you want to use them. Now write a first draft of your description. As you turn your notes into sentences and paragraphs, concentrate on using sensory and factual details, precise words, and figures of speech. To create a main feeling for readers, carefully choose suitable details.

EVALUATING AND REVISING

OBJECTIVES

- To analyze a writer's revisions of a description
- To evaluate and revise a description following specific guidelines

TEACHING THE LESSON

Ask students if they've ever wanted to change or take back something they've said. Explain that while speakers seldom have the luxury of deleting or revising, writers can revise until they've expressed themselves in the most effective way.

Emphasize to students that there is a revision process, just as there is a prewriting

Evaluating and Revising

Revising is cleaning up after yourself, but it means more than just correcting mechanical errors in your writing. It means finding weaknesses in content and organization and then correcting them.

To help you evaluate and revise your own description, use the chart on the following page. Begin by asking yourself each question in the left-hand column. If you find a weakness, use the revision technique suggested in the right-hand column. You can use these guidelines for your own or for a classmate's writing.

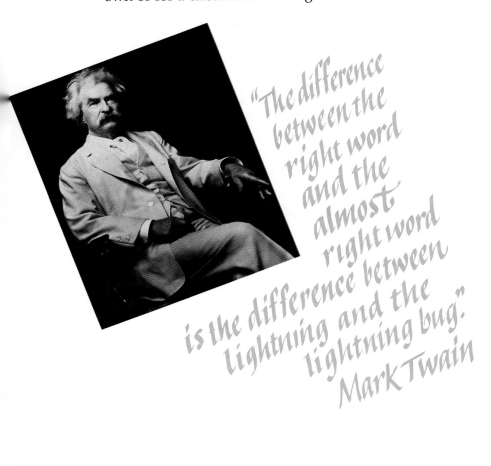

"The difference between the right word and the almost, right word is the difference between lightning and the lightning bug." Mark Twain

PROGRAM MANAGER

EVALUATING AND REVISING

- **Reinforcement/Reteaching** See **Revision Transparencies 7** and **8.** For suggestions on how to tie the transparencies to instruction, review teacher's notes in *Fine Art and Instructional Transparencies for Writing,* p. 97.

- **Ongoing Assessment** For a rubric to guide assessment, see **Evaluating and Revising** in *Strategies for Writing,* p. 11.

- **Assessment/Reflection** To assess student work and evaluate progress, see **Portfolio Forms** in *Portfolio Assessment,* pp. 5–17.

QUOTATION FOR THE DAY

"A word fitly spoken is like apples of gold in pictures of silver." (Proverbs 25:11)

Finding exactly the right words to form word pictures is a task of all writers and speakers. Challenge students to come up with another simile for choosing appropriate words for writing.

SELECTION AMENDMENT
Description of change: excerpted
Rationale: to focus on the concept of description presented in this chapter

process and a writing process. Discuss the **Evaluating and Revising Description** chart (below) with students, and write on the chalkboard examples of each revision technique. Using the questions in **Exercise 4** below, discuss why the revisions were necessary. Then assign **Writing Assignment: Part 5** on p. 174. Have students revise at least one of their paragraphs in class so you can assess their strengths and revision techniques. To close, ask volunteers to share with the class the revision techniques they used. ■

MEETING *individual* NEEDS

LEP/ESL

General Strategies. If possible, meet with your students individually and walk them through the evaluation guidelines. Photocopy students' descriptions so that both of you have a copy to refer to. Use examples from students' papers to help them evaluate whether they are meeting the guidelines. Instead of correcting, call attention to problem areas. Have students make written notations concerning sections that need revising.

TIMESAVER

If you prefer to read drafts before evaluating final essays, you may find it helpful to make copies of the evaluation chart and attach a copy to each draft. You then can quickly read a draft and answer the evaluation questions.

Have students underline all descriptive details to speed up your evaluations and to encourage them to further analyze their work.

EVALUATING AND REVISING DESCRIPTION

EVALUATION GUIDE	REVISION TECHNIQUE
1 Is the subject clearly identified?	**Add** an opening sentence that clearly identifies the subject.
2 Do sensory and factual details create a clear picture of the subject? Are figures of speech and precise words included?	**Add** figures of speech and details, especially those appealing to senses other than sight. **Replace** general words with precise ones.
3 Are the writer's thoughts and feelings a part of the description?	**Add** sentences that express the writer's thoughts and feelings.
4 Do all specific details help create the main feeling?	**Cut** details that don't support the main feeling. **Add** some that do.
5 Are the details organized in a way that makes sense?	**Reorder** details in a way that makes sense to the reader.

EXERCISE 4 ▶   **Analyzing a Writer's Revisions**

Here's part of an early draft of the description on page 170. Study the writer's revisions, then answer the questions.

> If you turn them over, you'll see that the
> sneakers' thick soles are made up of lots of   add/replace
>   gray   hundreds
> raised dots. They're huddled together like a
> crowd squeezed into a subway car at rush
> hour. The dots on the heel and front of the

OBJECTIVE

- To select the most precise words for sentences and to explain reasons for choices

TEACHING *EVALUATING WORD CHOICE*

Students often misuse words when they are stretching to improve their writing skills (or to impress their teachers). Encourage students to broaden their vocabularies by using dictionaries as guides. You may want to have students look up *shift* and *transfer* and discuss how the definitions can

---

(totally smooth)

sole are worn. And where I drag my right   **add**

foot when I serve in tennis, the sturdy,   **cut**

~~cushioned~~ sole is completely worn through.

I'd be able to recognize my sneakers   **reorder**

anywhere because of this hole. This

one-inch hole goes from the bottom of the

shoe under my right big toe all the way

through to the inside of my shoe.

1. Why did the writer add *gray* to the first sentence and *totally smooth* to the third sentence? How do these changes improve the paragraph?
2. Why did the writer replace *lots* with *hundreds* in the first sentence?
3. Why did the writer cut *sturdy, cushioned* from the fourth sentence? [Hint: What main feeling does the writer want to give about the sneakers?]
4. Why did the writer rearrange the order of the last two sentences?

CRITICAL THINKING

Evaluating Word Choice

Is your precise word the right word? No two words have exactly the same meaning.

Some words are used with specific situations. For example, *shift* and *transfer* both mean "move." *Shift* usually suggests changing position. But *transfer* more often describes changing from something like one vehicle to another. You might *shift* nervously from one foot to the other, but you would *transfer* from one bus to another.

Specific words may also call up specific feelings. *Murmur* and *mutter* both mean "a low flow of words or sounds," but *mutter* usually suggests anger. An unhappy

---

ANSWERS

Exercise 4

1. The words are precise and improve the visual image the reader gets. The words *totally smooth* also add detail appealing to touch.
2. *Hundreds* is a more precise word.
3. The main feeling the writer wants to give about the sneakers is that they are worn. These two words contradict the impression.
4. Reordering improves the paragraph because it places all the specific details together and ends with a general comment.

LEP/ESL

General Strategies. Being able to detect nuance of meaning is a skill that requires a broad and continuous exposure to English. You may want to present the **Critical Thinking Exercise** as a whole-class activity to offer support for English-language learners. Ask the class to suggest other sentences that use the words in parentheses and write the new sentences on the chalkboard. Encourage students to enter all new vocabulary (along with a short definition and model sentence) in their word banks.

help them make the correct distinction. Have students go through the same process with *murmur* and *mutter*.

Guide students through the first question in the **Critical Thinking Exercise**, and have them complete the remaining sentences independently. To assess, go over the correct word choices in class, discussing dictionary definitions. ⚡

customer would probably *mutter* about a bill, but a happy mother would *murmur* (not *mutter*) to her baby.

To help you decide if you've got the right word, check a dictionary. After a word's definitions, look for a list of synonyms. There you'll find the differences between the closely related words.

ANSWERS
Critical Thinking Exercise

1. roosted—suggests settled in and comfortable
2. blurted—suggests sudden outburst
3. slumped—suggests suddenly or heavily
4. ingenious—associated with inventive skill
5. bland—suggests tasteless

⚡ CRITICAL THINKING EXERCISE:
Evaluating Word Choice

What's your choice for the most precise word? For each of the following sentences, select the word in parentheses that best fits the situation and the feeling. Explain your choice. Use a dictionary to help you if you wish.

1. In the middle of watching her favorite television program, my sister (*roosted, perched*) on the sofa.
2. Unable to contain her ideas any longer, she (*sputtered, blurted*) out her plan.
3. Totally exhausted, he (*slumped, slouched*) into the chair.
4. Fashioned from discarded car parts, his invention was a(n) (*ingenious, cunning*) solution to our problem.
5. Without salt, the stew left a (*bland, dull*) taste in my mouth.

INTEGRATING THE LANGUAGE ARTS

Vocabulary Link. In addition to discussing the examples in the textbook, you may want to suggest other word pairs for students to consider. Have students look the words up in a dictionary and use the pairs in sentences. Possible examples include *discover, find; hint, suggest; hide, disguise;* and *shut, slam.*

PART 5:
Evaluating and Revising Your Description

You've learned that revision is a natural part of writing. Now apply the guidelines on page 172 to your first draft. Exchange papers with a partner and comment on each other's descriptions. Based on your evaluation and your partner's, make any changes you feel are needed. Evaluate and revise your word choice where necessary.

PROOFREADING AND PUBLISHING

OBJECTIVES

- To proofread and prepare a description for publication
- To share a description with an audience

TEACHING THE LESSON

You may want to focus students' attention on one or two specific problem areas in grammar, usage, or mechanics. The **Grammar Hint** (below) on misplaced modifiers is a good place to start. Have a volunteer read the **Grammar Hint.** If you think students need more examples or practice, use the cross-reference to locate explanations and exercises.

Proofreading and Publishing **175**

 Proofreading and Publishing

Proofreading. Before you consider your paper finished, read it again for mistakes in spelling, capitalization, grammar, and usage. When others read your description, you want them to *see* your subject, not your careless errors!

GRAMMAR HINT

Misplaced Modifiers

As you write description, you'll often include phrases that describe words in your paper. When a sentence has a modifying phrase, you should usually place the phrase right next to the word it modifies. A misplaced modifier may have comic results.

MISPLACED Buried beneath a huge pile of oak leaves, Elena found a five dollar bill.

CORRECTED Elena found a five dollar bill buried beneath a huge pile of oak leaves.

☞ REFERENCE NOTE: For more information on placement of modifiers, see pages 668–673.

PROGRAM MANAGER

PROOFREADING AND PUBLISHING

- **Instructional Support** For a chart students may use to evaluate their proofreading progress, see **Proofreading** in *Strategies for Writing,* p. 12.

- **Independent Practice/ Reteaching** For additional practice with language skills, see **Proofreading Practice: Misplaced Modifiers** in *Strategies for Writing,* p. 13.

- **Assessment/Reflection** To assess student work and evaluate progress, see **Portfolio Forms** in *Portfolio Assessment,* pp. 18–21.

- **Computer Guided Instruction** For additional instruction and practice with misplaced modifiers as noted in the **Grammar Hint,** see **Lesson 22** in *Language Workshop CD-ROM.*

- **Practice** To help less-advanced students who need additional practice with misplaced modifiers, see **Chapter 20** in *English Workshop, Second Course,* pp. 213–218.

QUOTATION FOR THE DAY

"What is written without effort is in general read without pleasure." (Samuel Johnson, 1709–1784, English lexicographer, essayist, and poet)

You may want to provide a proof-reading checklist with specific items for students to focus on. Guide students through the proofreading procedure by using a sample description on an overhead transparency. Then assign **Writing Assignment: Part 6** (below). When students write their reflections, ask them to focus in particular on the second question. The answers they give to it can be helpful to them in future writing assignments.

To close, have volunteers suggest additional publishing ideas or share some of their reflections with the class.

COOPERATIVE LEARNING

Organize the class into groups of five. Provide the groups with copies of a model student description that has many errors in grammar, usage, and mechanics. The groups should find and correct as many errors as they can in five minutes. Before passing out the descriptions, allow group members to discuss strategies for finding the most errors. They may appoint a leader and a recorder, divide the paper into segments, or work independently and then combine their results. The group correcting the most errors wins.

INTEGRATING THE LANGUAGE ARTS

Spelling Link. Students who have difficulty with spelling often become discouraged and don't develop any proofreading strategies for spelling. Point out that few people are perfect spellers. The goal should be to become careful spellers. This means that students should learn to question words that may be incorrect and to check them in a dictionary or with the spell-check feature of a word-processing program. This process may be quicker if, when they proofread, they circle questionable words, marking them *sp.* They can then look them all up at once. Spell-check features eliminate much of the tedium of this task.

Publishing. Here are two suggestions for sharing descriptions with an audience:

- Take turns reading your descriptions aloud in class. Keep a list of vivid, precise words that you hear. Use your lists to create a class word bank.
- Make a class anthology. Illustrate your description with a photo, cartoon, or drawing. Collect the illustrated descriptions in a special notebook. Save your class anthology to be used as a model for a similar project that can be compiled by later classes.

 COMPUTER NOTE: You can use your word-processing program's Border and Box tools to create eye-catching pages when preparing to publish your description.

 PART 6:
Proofreading and Publishing Your Description

Proofread your description carefully, correcting any errors you discover. Publish or share your final version with your classmates.

 Reflecting on Your Writing

If you plan to include your description in your **portfolio,** date it and use the following questions to write a brief reflection to accompany your description.

- Which method of collecting details—observing, recalling, researching, or imagining—did you find most helpful?
- Were you able to convey the feeling you wanted about your subject? What might you do differently the next time you write a description?
- In writing this description, did you learn anything new about your feelings or attitude toward your subject?

After publishing their descriptions, students might select their favorites and write short critiques. They could set up personal evaluation scales to help explain why they like the descriptions. Students might include the following criteria: interest in the subject; aspects of description such as focus, feeling, sensory and factual details, order, word choice, and figures of speech; grammar; mechanics; and presentation (including handwriting and illustration). ■

A STUDENT MODEL

Sometimes, descriptions of the people or places closest to you turn out to be especially memorable. Alyssa Reynolds, who attends Paris Gibson Middle School in Great Falls, Montana, paints a vivid picture of her brother David.

The Thing That Lives in My House
by Alyssa Reynolds

"Oh, how sweet he looks. You are so lucky to have a brother like him," they tell me. I suppose he looks sort of sweet and innocent. Strawberry-blond hair and blue eyes with dirty shoes and holey jeans certainly don't hurt his impression on people. He might even come across ... . cute?

When I see the dirt, I know better. He has either dug up the flower garden or buried my TV. To me his smile looks sneaky and superficial, and his answers to questions sound guilty and evasive. I grab him and pull him from the room. His arm feels gritty and sweaty. "David, what did you do this time?" I ask.

"Nothing . . . except dig a few holes for Jack." He turns and goes back into the living room. (Jack is our neighbor boy.)

David whines a little more to my mother and then goes back outside, slamming the door loudly. I know him. He is a sneaky little liar who plays up to anyone who listens. If he doesn't get his way, he runs to his room, slams the door at least twice, and then cries like a baby. He is obstinate and does anything he wants, no matter what the consequences. Sometimes, it's true, he can be pretty decent and usually isn't as bad as I've just described. I still am going to look for my television set.

A STUDENT MODEL
Evaluation

1. Alyssa clearly identifies her subject in the second sentence.
2. Alyssa's description includes numerous sensory details about her brother. For example, she includes "strawberry-blond hair," "holey jeans," "gritty and sweaty," and "slamming the door loudly."
3. Throughout her description, Alyssa includes her thoughts and feelings about her brother. She gives examples to support her belief that he is not as sweet and innocent as people think.
4. Alyssa includes specific details that support her main idea. For example, "If he doesn't get his way, he runs to his room, slams the door at least twice, and then cries like a baby."

WRITING WORKSHOP

OBJECTIVES

- To analyze a free verse poem
- To use the writing process to create a free verse poem

TEACHING THE LESSON

You may want to begin by reading students a favorite descriptive poem and discussing its strengths with them. Point out ways that the poet uses details to create vivid images by showing what is unique.

Have a volunteer read the introduction. You may want to read the poem aloud or have a student do so. Have students listen

QUOTATION FOR THE DAY

"Prose,—words in their best order; poetry,—the best words in their best order." (Samuel Taylor Coleridge, 1772–1834, English poet, essayist, and critic)

Use the quotation to initiate a discussion about the differences between prose and poetry.

MEETING *individual* NEEDS

LEP/ESL

General Strategies. The rarely used subjunctive mood may cause problems for less-proficient speakers of English. Ray Young Bear uses the subjunctive mood past tense repeatedly in "**grandmother.**" Because many students learn to associate past tense with past events, you may want to explain the circumstances that these conditional phrases establish.

WRITING WORKSHOP

A Free Verse Poem

The writer of the model on pages 169–170 includes many specific details in her description. For example, she mentions details that tell you about her old tennis shoes' size, their smell, what material they're made of, and how they looked when they were new contrasted with how they look now.

But notice that these details are not what make the writer's tennis shoes distinctly individual. Although the writer's description of these general details help give us a clear picture of her well-worn sneakers, there is one special detail that she mentions that she believes makes her shoes unique—the hole in the sole underneath the big toe of the right shoe. This special detail about her shoes makes the writer feel that she could recognize them anywhere.

Sometimes when you are writing a shorter description, such as a short free verse poem, you may decide to focus only on those special details that make your subject "stand out from the crowd." While they may not give your readers a complete picture, these few details can still create a powerful image.

In "grandmother," Ray Young Bear uses only a few details to describe his subject. Still, these details are enough to give readers a unique feeling about her. Like other free verse poetry, this poem doesn't have a regular pattern of rhyme or rhythm. Instead, it creates a pattern with repeated phrases and uses the rhythms of everyday speech.

for the few unique details that characterize the grandmother. Guide the students in discussing the questions that follow.

Depending on students' abilities, you could use several class periods to guide students through the writing process, or you could have students write free verse poems as independent assignments. Evaluate their use of description.

Ask students to explain the similarities and differences of a description and a descriptive poem. ■

grandmother

by Ray Young Bear

if i were to see
1 her shape from a mile away
i'd know so quickly
that it would be her.
the purple scarf
and the plastic
shopping bag.
if i felt
hands on my head
i'd know that those
2 were her hands
warm and damp
with the smell
of roots.
if i heard
a voice
coming from
a rock
i'd know
3 and her words
would flow inside me
like the light
of someone
stirring ashes
from a sleeping fire
at night.

USING THE SELECTION
grandmother

1

Her shape, the purple scarf, and the plastic shopping bag give brief but unique visual images of the grandmother.

2

The phrase "hands warm and damp with the smell of roots" creates the sensation of someone who loves the earth in addition to loving her grandson.

3

The passage "her words would flow inside me like the light" creates the feeling of warmth at hearing the grandmother's voice.

MEETING individual NEEDS

ADVANCED STUDENTS

Allow students to write one poem based on the model and one following a different format. Let them read their poems to the class and have them discuss the power of the images created.

LEARNING STYLES

Auditory Learners. Arrange for students to talk-write their rough drafts to partners. One person could describe his or her subject aloud while the other person writes down words and phrases. Students could then trade roles. This process can help students gain confidence in their ability to write poetry.

Visual Learners. Students may benefit from drawing or bringing to class pictures of the subjects of their poems to help in prewriting. They can also use the pictures when they publish their poems.

Thinking It Over

1. What two details of sight would make it possible for the person who speaks in the poem to recognize his grandmother from a great distance?
2. A *simile* uses the word *like* or *as* to compare two different things. What is the simile in this poem?
3. How do you think the speaker in this poem feels about his grandmother?
4. The poem begins "if i were to see." Where else in the poem does Ray Young Bear repeat this pattern of words? How does the pattern change each time?

Writing a Free Verse Poem

Prewriting. Now you try it. Write a free verse poem describing a person you know well, perhaps a relative, a neighbor, or a friend. After you've chosen a subject, jot down your answers to these questions.

1. How would you recognize this person from a great distance? List two or three details of sight that would cause you to recognize him or her.
2. How would you recognize this person's touch? List two or three details of touch.
3. How would you recognize the person by sound? List two or three sound details.
4. What main feeling does this person give you? What else gives you the same feeling?

Writing, Evaluating, and Revising. In your poem, loosely follow the pattern of images Ray Young Bear uses: two sight images + one touch image + one sound image + one figure of speech that gives your feeling about this person.

Use repeated phrases to introduce and develop each image. Begin your poem with "When I see (the person)/I recognize (two sight images)." Then, repeat "When I" and "I recognize" as you introduce the other images in your poem. Or, if you wish, use other repeated phrases.

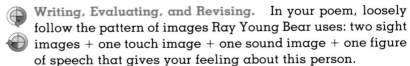

To decide where lines should end, read your poem aloud. Listen for places where the thought seems to break naturally.

Proofreading and Publishing. Make sure that your poem looks as good as it sounds. Proofread carefully before making your final copy. With your classmates, create a bulletin board display showcasing your work. Include a photograph or drawing of your subject with your poem.

If you want to add your poem to your **portfolio,** first date it. Then, reflect on your writing process by answering the following questions, remembering to save your answers in your portfolio. Which type of sensory detail—sight, touch, or sound—was the hardest to come up with? Why? Did reading your poem aloud help you to decide where lines should end? Was writing a poem about this particular person the best way to describe her or him? Or would you prefer to write a story or essay about this person instead?

TEACHING NOTE

Remind students that their portfolios should contain a variety of different types of writing, including poetry. You can have them answer the questions directly or address the ideas from the questions in a short paragraph. Some students might even enjoy writing their reflections as a poem.

MAKING CONNECTIONS

MASS MEDIA
OBJECTIVE

- To work with a group to write classified ads using objective and subjective details

MASS MEDIA
Teaching Strategies

Ask students to consider what classified ads would be like if they weren't classified. [The ads would be jumbled: used cars alternating with free kittens, garage sales, and so on.] If you have any examples of local papers in which the ads are not classified, show students how a reader has to scan all the ads to find a needed item. Then, using a local newspaper, point out the index of classifications.

Before students write their ads, provide them with examples of classified ads from newspapers and magazines to read. Have students do this preliminary study in their writing groups so they can point out to each other the special strengths in the ads they read.

GUIDELINES

Ads will vary but should include both objective and subjective details. The ads also should conform to the three-line format. You may want to have the class vote for the three most appealing ads.

MAKING CONNECTIONS

MASS MEDIA

A Classified Ad

PUPS! Boston terriers, 6 mos., all shots. Need loving home. $10! 555-0098

Two-person tent, excel cond, blue, mesh window and door. $25. Mike—555-3379 eves.

Ordinary people trying to sell cars, houses, furniture, bicycles, and pets sometimes place a classified advertisement in a newspaper. Because newspapers charge by the line, sellers try to give information in just a few lines. A classified ad gives realistic details about the object (such as its price, size, and age) and tells how to reach the seller. Advertisers may also try to attract buyers by expressing their feelings about an object's appearance or condition.

How good a salesperson or advertiser are you? Work with two or three classmates and write a three-line (twenty-two letters per line) classified ad for three of the following objects. Make up any details you need and use abbreviations to save space. Remember that you want to sell the item. Make it appealing to readers!

1. a skateboard
2. a ten-speed bicycle
3. a CD player
4. a pet python
5. a collection of baseball cards
6. a Siamese kitten

WRITING ACROSS THE CURRICULUM

Biology Riddles

What living creature does this riddle describe?

> **RIDDLE**
> It lives in the water and breathes through gills. With no legs, it moves from place to place by moving its tail. It feeds on algae. In the spring, it hatches from an egg. By fall, it has disappeared into something else. What is it?

The riddle describes a tadpole, the early stage of a frog.

Riddles like these are a fun way to review or learn about plants and animals. With your classmates, create a set of riddles on index cards. Write a riddle like the tadpole example on one side of a card and your answer (the name of the plant or animal you're describing) on the back. You may need to do some research on your animal in an encyclopedia or field guide.

WRITING ACROSS THE CURRICULUM

Teaching Strategies

Before students work on this activity, you may want to provide other riddles as examples or have students share any riddles they have heard.

One way to organize the activity is to divide the class into groups of three or four and give each group a volume of an encyclopedia or another reference book to work from in case students need help with research. After groups have finished writing their riddles, have them pass the riddles around so the other groups can try to figure them out.

GUIDELINES

Riddles will vary, but each should contain accurate details about the animal or plant it describes. You may wish to have the class vote to select the most clever riddle.

CREATIVE WRITING: NARRATION

OBJECTIVES

- To identify the literary aim and to analyze the characteristics of literary writing
- To determine the appropriate purpose and audience for a story
- To select point of view, characters, setting, and plot for a story
- To write a draft of a short story using appropriate story elements
- To evaluate and revise the content, organization, and style of a story
- To proofread a story and prepare it for publication

WRITING-IN-PROGRESS ASSIGNMENTS

Major Assignment: Writing a short story

Cumulative Writing Assignments: The chart below shows the sequence of cumulative assignments that will guide students as they write a story. These Writing Assignments form the instructional core of Chapter 6.

PREWRITING

WRITING ASSIGNMENT
- Part 1: Finding a Story Idea p. 196
- Part 2: Gathering Details for Characters and Setting pp. 198–199
- Part 3: Creating a Story Map p. 200
- Part 4: Speaking and Listening: Choosing a Point of View p. 200

WRITING YOUR FIRST DRAFT

WRITING ASSIGNMENT
- Part 5: Writing Your First Draft p. 211

EVALUATING AND REVISING

WRITING ASSIGNMENT
- Part 6: Evaluating and Revising Your Story p. 214

PROOFREADING AND PUBLISHING

WRITING ASSIGNMENT
- Part 7: Proofreading and Publishing Your Story p. 216

In addition, exercises 1–2 provide practice in exploring story ideas and analyzing the elements of a short story.

CROSS CURRICULUM

Social Studies and Setting

Inexperienced writers are often told to write about what they know, but they need not limit their writing to their firsthand experience. Suggest that students having trouble choosing a setting tap into their social studies experiences by freewriting lists of time periods and places they find interesting. Then, have them use a chart like the following to record their comments or queries about the era.

Time or Place	Comments or Queries
1960s	I wonder how the civil rights movement might have affected someone my age.
2098	I'm curious what the world will be like at the end of the next century if global warming continues.
Poland during WW II	I wonder what life would have been like in an Axis-occupied country for an American teenager stranded there.

After students complete their charts, have them use a two-column organizer like the following to list questions that the time and place suggest.

Situation	Questions
1960s, March on Washington	What would teenagers have been wearing? What kind of food would people gathered on the mall have been eating? What hopes and fears might the participants have had?

Now, assign students to small groups based on time or place choices to brainstorm with each other the answers to their questions. Next, have students research answers to any remaining relevant questions using history and geography books, almanacs, encyclopedias, and online sources. Students are now ready to use their research in their short stories.

Chapter 6

CREATIVE WRITING: NARRATION

OBJECTIVES

- To identify the literary aim and to analyze the characteristics of literary writing
- To determine the appropriate purpose and audience for a story
- To select point of view, characters, setting, and plot for a story
- To write a draft of a short story using appropriate story elements
- To evaluate and revise the content, organization, and style of a story
- To proofread a story and prepare it for publication

WRITING-IN-PROGRESS ASSIGNMENTS

Major Assignment: Writing a short story
Cumulative Writing Assignments: The chart below shows the sequence of cumulative assignments that will guide students as they write a story. These Writing Assignments form the instructional core of Chapter 6.

PREWRITING

WRITING ASSIGNMENT
- Part 1: Finding a Story Idea p. 196
- Part 2: Gathering Details for Characters and Setting pp. 198–199
- Part 3: Creating a Story Map p. 200
- Part 4: Speaking and Listening: Choosing a Point of View p. 200

WRITING YOUR FIRST DRAFT

WRITING ASSIGNMENT
- Part 5: Writing Your First Draft p. 211

EVALUATING AND REVISING

WRITING ASSIGNMENT
- Part 6: Evaluating and Revising Your Story p. 214

PROOFREADING AND PUBLISHING

WRITING ASSIGNMENT
- Part 7: Proofreading and Publishing Your Story p. 216

In addition, exercises 1–2 provide practice in exploring story ideas and analyzing the elements of a short story.

Cross Curriculum: Social Studies and Setting

Inexperienced writers are often told to write about what they know, but they need not limit their writing to their firsthand experience. Suggest that students having trouble choosing a setting tap into their social studies experiences by freewriting lists of time periods and places they find interesting. Then, have them use a chart like the following to record their comments or queries about the era.

Time or Place	Comments or Queries
1960s	I wonder how the civil rights movement might have affected someone my age.
2098	I'm curious what the world will be like at the end of the next century if global warming continues.
Poland during WW II	I wonder what life would have been like in an Axis-occupied country for an American teenager stranded there.

After students complete their charts, have them use a two-column organizer like the following to list questions that the time and place suggest.

Situation	Questions
1960s, March on Washington	What would teenagers have been wearing? What kind of food would people gathered on the mall have been eating? What hopes and fears might the participants have had?

Now, assign students to small groups based on time or place choices to brainstorm with each other the answers to their questions. Next, have students research answers to any remaining relevant questions using history and geography books, almanacs, encyclopedias, and online sources. Students are now ready to use their research in their short stories.

1. a skateboard
2. a ten-speed bicycle
3. a CD player
4. a pet python

5. a collection of baseball cards
6. a Siamese kitten

WRITING ACROSS THE CURRICULUM

Biology Riddles

What living creature does this riddle describe?

> RIDDLE
>
> It lives in the water and breathes through gills. With no legs, it moves from place to place by moving its tail. It feeds on algae. In the spring, it hatches from an egg. By fall, it has disappeared into something else. What is it?

The riddle describes a tadpole, the early stage of a frog.

Riddles like these are a fun way to review or learn about plants and animals. With your classmates, create a set of riddles on index cards. Write a riddle like the tadpole example on one side of a card and your answer (the name of the plant or animal you're describing) on the back. You may need to do some research on your animal in an encyclopedia or field guide.

WRITING ACROSS THE CURRICULUM

Teaching Strategies

Before students work on this activity, you may want to provide other riddles as examples or have students share any riddles they have heard.

One way to organize the activity is to divide the class into groups of three or four and give each group a volume of an encyclopedia or another reference book to work from in case students need help with research. After groups have finished writing their riddles, have them pass the riddles around so the other groups can try to figure them out.

GUIDELINES

Riddles will vary, but each should contain accurate details about the animal or plant it describes. You may wish to have the class vote to select the most clever riddle.

INTEGRATING THE LANGUAGE ARTS

SELECTION	READING AND LITERATURE	WRITING AND CRITICAL THINKING	LANGUAGE AND SYNTAX	SPEAKING, LISTENING, AND OTHER EXPRESSION SKILLS
• from *The Sound of Flutes* told by Henry Crow Dog pp. 186–192 • "Thank You, M'am" by Langston Hughes pp. 203–208 • from "A Letter to Gabriela, A Young Writer" by Pat Mora p. 212 • "Jimmy Jet and His TV Set" by Shel Silverstein pp. 218–219	• Responding to literature creatively pp. 192, 209 • Identifying conflict pp. 192, 209 • Finding and analyzing author's purpose and theme p. 192 • Analyzing and distinguishing point of view p. 200 • Analyzing story elements p. 209 • Reading and analyzing a narrative poem pp. 218–219 • Finding poet's purpose and theme pp. 218–219	• Writing a journal entry p. 192 • Using brainstorming and note taking as prewriting techniques p. 196 • Gathering details for character and setting pp. 198–199 • Creating and arranging plot, conflict, characters, and point of view p. 200 • Writing a draft of a story p. 211 • Analyzing a revision of a short story p. 214 • Applying proofreading skills p. 216 • Writing a reflection for portfolio selection p. 216 • Writing a narrative poem by using the writing process p. 220 • Writing a myth p. 221 • Writing a story based on a photograph p. 221	• Proofreading for errors in spelling, usage, and mechanics p. 215	• Talking to others about story ideas p. 196 • Taking notes on group discussions p. 196 • Reading to a group of classmates p. 200 • Conversing with a partner about a writer's revisions p. 214 • Brainstorming about publishing stories p. 215 • Brainstorming orally to generate ideas for narrative poems p. 220 • Reading a poem aloud p. 220 • Creating a story from a photograph p. 221

SUGGESTED INTEGRATED UNIT PLAN

This unit plan suggests how to integrate the major strands of the language arts with this chapter.

If you begin with this chapter on creative writing or with short story selections for analysis, you should focus on the common characteristics of short stories. You can then integrate speaking/listening and language concepts with both the writing and the literature.

Common Characteristics

- Content choices are consistent with choice of form and style
- Content often presents readers with something they didn't expect
- Effective choice and use of point of view

Writing
Short Story

Speaking/Listening

- Reading and listening to selections written from two points of view
- Conversing with a partner about a writer's revisions
- Participating in a rap about a book, movie, or play

UNIT FOCUS
SHORT STORY

Language
Usage, Mechanics, Style

- Pronoun case
- Punctuating dialogue
- Precise words reflecting time period

Literature
Short Stories such as

- "There Will Come Soft Rains" Ray Bradbury
- "The Gift of the Magi" O. Henry
- "Gentleman of Río en Medio" Juan A. A. Sedillo
- "Raymond's Run" Toni Cade Bambara

CHAPTER 6: CREATIVE WRITING: NARRATION

Use this guide for creating an instructional plan that addresses the individual needs of your students. Assignments accompanied by the following symbol (∗) may be completed out of class. Times given for pacing lessons are estimated.

CHAPTER PLANNING GUIDE—PUPIL'S EDITION

LESSONS	LITERARY MODEL pp. 186–192 from *The Sound of Flutes* by Henry Crow Dog	PREWRITING pp. 194–200	
		Generating Ideas	Gathering/Organizing
DEVELOPMENTAL PROGRAM	20–25 minutes • Assign students to read the model in a popcorn reading, to answer questions 1, 3, 4 p. 192 orally, and to write the answer to question 2.	30–35 minutes • Ways to Write Creatively p. 193 • Main Assignment: Looking Ahead p. 193 • Finding a Story Idea pp. 194–196 • Reminder p. 196 • Exercise 1 p. 196 • Writing Assignment: Part 1 p. 196∗	40–45 minutes • Planning Your Story pp. 197–200 • Writing Assignments: Parts 2–3 pp. 198, 200∗ • Writing Assignment: Part 4 p. 200
CORE PROGRAM	15–20 minutes • Assign students to read the model and work with them to answer questions 1, 3, 4 p. 192 orally. Encourage students to share written responses to question 2.	15–20 minutes • Ways to Write Creatively p. 193 • Main Assignment: Looking Ahead p. 193 • Finding a Story Idea pp. 194–196∗ • Reminder p. 196 • Writing Assignment: Part 1 p. 196∗	25–30 minutes • Thinking About Character, Setting, Plot pp. 197–199∗ • Writing Assignments: Parts 2–3 pp. 198, 200∗ • Writing Assignment: Part 4 p. 200
ACCELERATED PROGRAM	15–20 minutes • Assign students to read model independently and write answer to question 2 on p. 192.	10–15 minutes • Ways to Write Creatively p. 193 • Main Assignment: Looking Ahead p. 193 • Reminder p. 196 • Writing Assignment: Part 1 p. 196∗	20–25 minutes • Choosing a Point of View p. 200 • Writing Assignments: Parts 2–3 pp. 198, 200∗ • Writing Assignment: Part 4 p. 200

CHAPTER PLANNING GUIDE—PROGRAM RESOURCES

	LITERARY MODEL	PREWRITING
PRINT	• Reading Master 6, *Practice for Assessment in Reading, Vocabulary, and Spelling* p. 6	• Prewriting, *Strategies for Writing* pp. 16–19
MEDIA	• Fine Art Transparency 3: *Prairie Fire, Transparency Binder*	• Graphic Organizers 9 and 10, *Transparency Binder* • *Writer's Workshop 1:* Story

WRITING pp. 201–211	EVALUATING AND REVISING pp. 212–214	PROOFREADING AND PUBLISHING pp. 215–217
🕐 **20–25 minutes** • Basic Elements of a Story pp. 201–202 • Writing Note p. 202 • A Writer's Model pp. 210–211 • Writing Assignment: Part 5 p. 211*	🕐 **40–45 minutes** • Evaluating and Revising p. 212 • Chart p. 213 • Critical Thinking pp. 213–214 • Writing Assignment: Part 6 p. 214	🕐 **40–45 minutes** • Proofreading and Publishing pp. 215–216 • Mechanics Hint p. 215 • Writing Assignment: Part 7 p. 216 • Reflecting p. 216 • A Student Model pp. 216–217
🕐 **20–25 minutes** • Making Your Characters Seem Real p. 201* • A Short Story pp. 203–208* • Exercise 2 p. 209 • Writing Assignment: Part 5 p. 211*	🕐 **30–35 minutes** • Evaluating and Revising Short Stories Chart p. 213 • Critical Thinking pp. 213–214 • Writing Assignment: Part 6 p. 214	🕐 **40–45 minutes** • Mechanics Hint p. 215 • Publishing pp. 215–216 • Writing Assignment: Part 7 p. 216 • Reflecting p. 216* • A Student Model pp. 216–217*
🕐 **10–15 minutes** • A Short Story pp. 203–208* • Writing Assignment: Part 5 p. 211*	🕐 **20–25 minutes** • Evaluating and Revising Short Stories Chart p. 213 • Writing Assignment: Part 6 p. 214	🕐 **40–45 minutes** • Mechanics Hint p. 215 • Publishing pp. 215–216 • Writing Assignment: Part 7 p. 216 • Reflecting p. 216

ELEMENTS OF WRITING: CURRICULUM CONNECTIONS

Writing Workshop
• A Narrative Poem pp. 218–220

Making Connections
• A Legend or Myth p. 221
• Visual Stories p. 221

ASSESSMENT OPTIONS

Summative Assessment
Holistic Scoring: Prompts and Models pp. 15–20

Portfolio Assessment
Portfolio forms, *Portfolio Assessment* pp. 5–24, 38–43

Reflection
Writing Process Log, *Strategies for Writing* p. 15

Ongoing Assessment
Proofreading, *Strategies for Writing* p. 22

 Computer disk or CD-ROM   Overhead transparencies

WRITING	EVALUATING AND REVISING	PROOFREADING AND PUBLISHING
• Writing, *Strategies for Writing* p. 20	• Evaluating and Revising, *Strategies for Writing* p. 21	• Proofreading Practice, *Strategies for Writing* p. 23 • Quotation Marks, *English Workshop* pp. 269–272
	• Revision Transparencies 9–10, *Transparency Binder*	• *Language Workshop:* Lesson 54

LESSON 1 *(pp. 184–192)*

IMAGING OTHER WORLDS

- To analyze conflict, purpose, and details in a story

OBJECTIVES

- To respond personally to literature
- To write a journal entry about a response to music

PROGRAM MANAGER

CHAPTER 6

- **Computer Guided Instruction** For a related assignment that students may use for additional instruction and practice, see **Story** in *Writer's Workshop 1 CD-ROM.*

- **Summative Assessment** For a writing prompt, including grading criteria and student models, see *Holistic Scoring: Prompts and Models*, pp. 15–20.

- **Additional Information** To help less-advanced students who need additional practice with concepts and activities related to this chapter, see **Chapter 5** in *English Workshop, Second Course*, pp. 33–44.

- **Extension/Enrichment** See **Fine Art Transparency 3**, *Prairie Fire* by Francis Blackbear Bosin. For suggestions on how to tie the transparency to instruction, review teacher's notes in *Fine Art and Instructional Transparencies for Writing*, p. 15.

- **Reading Support** For help with the reading selection, pp. 186–192, see **Reading Master 6** in *Practice for Assessment in Reading, Vocabulary, and Spelling*, p. 6.

6 CREATIVE WRITING: NARRATION

MOTIVATION

Ask students to imagine that they are living on the plains of North America hundreds of years ago. How would they as young people meet and get to know one another? What kinds of recreational activities would they have? How would music and musical instruments be created? At night as they sat around the campfire, what would young people talk about? Would they tell stories? What kinds of stories would they tell?

Give students opportunities to respond. Then explain that the Lakota people may have become storytellers in the same way. Explain that the story they are about to read was most likely told not only to entertain, but also to explain how the flute came to be and ☛

Imagining Other Worlds

Living in this **world** is often fun and exciting. But when it isn't, all we have to do is open the escape hatch of our imagination. Our **imaginations** can take us to past worlds, future worlds, or worlds that can never be.

Writing and You. Writers use their imaginations to come up with ideas for stories, novels, poems, plays, and movie and TV scripts. They create hairy monsters in horror movies, domed cities in science fiction stories. They write poems that look at parrots, or snow, or spiders in imaginary ways. They imagine people and places so real that you feel you know them. Imagine a world of your own. What would it be like?

As You Read. As you read this story, notice how people can also use their imagination to explain the world around them.

John Ross, detail of *Homage to the City* (1984).

QUOTATION FOR THE DAY

"Imagination . . . in truth,/Is but another name for absolute power/And clearest insight" (William Wordsworth, 1770–1850, English poet)

Ask students to freewrite about the power of the imagination. How can imagination create new worlds and change ordinary ones? How does it affect understanding? Why is imagination important for a writer?

VISUAL CONNECTIONS
Homage to the City

About the Artist. John Ross was born in New York City in 1921. His artwork focuses mainly on cityscapes, in which the artist explores the environments that people create for themselves. In 1964 Ross became a professor of art at Manhattanville College in New York.

Ideas for Writing. Ask students to imagine that they live in the city shown here, or have them create characters for this setting. Then have each student write a short story that gives the reader a sense of life in the city. Encourage students to choose any time periods and locations for their fictional cities. For example, a story could be set in Atlantis or on Mars.

how it became an expression of a young man's love.

After you have interested your students in storytelling, emphasize that stories such as **"The Sound of Flutes"** were passed down orally for generations before they were recorded by editors like Richard Erdoes.

Oral reading may help students better enjoy and understand the myth. It may also accentuate the oral tradition of mythology.

186

f r o m

The Sound of Flutes

told by Henry Crow Dog

USING THE SELECTION
from **The Sound of Flutes**

1

What does the beginning "Once, untold generations ago, . . ." suggest about the story? [It is like a fairy tale or folktale—another kind of myth.]

2

bull-roarer: a sacred wooden instrument attached to a cord; it creates sounds representing wind, thunder, and lightning when it is twirled above the head

3

The Lakota are Plains Indians. They used to live a nomadic lifestyle, tracking elk and hunting buffalo and other game, across the Great Plains.

4

obsidian: a black volcanic glass used to make blades for spear points and arrow points

186

1
2

nce, untold generations ago, the people did not know how to make flutes. Drums, rattles, bull-roarers, yes—but no flutes. In these long-past days, before the white man came with his horse and firestick, a young hunter went out after game. Meat was scarce, and the people in

3 his village were hungry. He found the tracks of an elk and followed them for a long time. The elk is wise and swift. It is the animal that possesses the love-charm. If a man has elk medicine, he will win the one he loves for his wife. He will also be a lucky hunter.

Our poor young man had no elk medicine. After many hours, he finally sighted his game. The young hunter had a fine new bow and a quiver made of otterskin full of good, straight

4 arrows tipped with points of obsidian—sharp, black, and shiny like glass. The young man knew how to use his weapon—he was the best shot in the village—but the elk always managed to stay just out of range, leading the hunter on and on. The young man was so intent on following his prey that he hardly took notice of where he went.

At dusk the hunter found himself deep inside a dense forest of tall trees. The tracks had disappeared, and so had the elk. The

As you read the myth, use the annotations to guide your discussion. Emphasize the story framework and the elements of myth. There are several Lakota words in the story that are explained in context. Students may need guidance with pronunciations. Most words are pronounced as they look.

GUIDED PRACTICE

Use the annotations to guide your discussion of the story and to prepare students to answer the **Writer's Craft** questions. You might want to discuss other myths, folktales, or fables that explain something before students begin the **Reader's Response** group activity. Before students begin their journal writing, as requested in the second ☛

Before students begin their journal writing, as requested in the second ☛

MEETING individual NEEDS

LEP/ESL

General Strategies. People from all cultures have folktales and myths that explain the world around them. Students whose primary languages aren't English might become more interested in reading and writing stories if they could share with other students folktales from their cultures.

"**He** dreamed that a bird called *Wagnuka*, the redheaded woodpecker, appeared to him, singing the strangely beautiful new song, saying, 'Follow me and I will teach you.' "

Reader's Response question, you might play a piece of popular music and describe your responses.

INDEPENDENT PRACTICE

Students can work independently on the **Reader's Response** questions. Question 1 is a group activity and question 2 is a journal activity. Answers to the **Writer's Craft** questions may be discussed or written.

188

ASSESSMENT

Assess students' responses to the **Writer's Craft** questions. Have students judge the most interesting stories from their group discussions. You may want to have students make informal comments about one another's writing journal entries.

RETEACHING

If students have trouble understanding the explanatory purpose of this myth, you might read another, such as the Blackfoot myth "The Orphan Boy and the Elk Dog," which explains the origin of horses on the Great Plains. Point out the elements of myth as you read.

☞

189

5 young man had to face the fact that he was lost and that it was now too dark to find his way out of the forest. There was not even a moon to show him the way. Luckily, he found a stream with clear, cold water to quench his thirst. Still more luckily, his sister had given him a rawhide bag to take along, filled with

6 *wasna*—pemmican—dried meat pounded together with berries and kidney fat. Sweet, strong wasna—a handful of it will keep a man going for a day or more. After the young man had drunk and eaten, he rolled himself into his fur robe, propped his back against a tree, and tried to get some rest. But he could not sleep.

7 The forest was full of strange noises—the eerie cries of night animals, the hooting of owls, the groaning of trees in the wind. He had heard all these sounds before, but now it seemed as if he were hearing them for the first time. Suddenly there was an entirely new sound, the kind neither he nor any other man had ever experienced before.

It was very mournful, sad, and ghostlike. In a way it made him afraid, so he drew his robe tightly about him and reached for his bow, to make sure that it was properly strung. On the other hand, this new sound was like a song, beautiful beyond imagination, full of love, hope, and yearning. And then, before he knew it, and with the night more than half gone, he was suddenly

8 asleep. He dreamed that a bird called *Wagnuka*, the redheaded

9 woodpecker, appeared to him, singing the strangely beautiful new song, saying, "Follow me and I will teach you."

When the young hunter awoke, the sun was already high, and on a branch of the tree against which he was leaning was a redheaded woodpecker. The bird flew away to another tree and then to another, but never very far, looking all the time over its shoulder at the young man as if to say "Come on!" Then, once more the hunter heard that wonderful song, and his heart yearned to find the singer. The bird flew toward the sound, leading the young man, its flaming red top flitting through the leaves, making it easy to follow. At last the bird alighted on a cedar tree and began tapping and hammering on a dead branch, making a noise like the fast beating of a small drum. Suddenly there was a gust of wind, and again the hunter heard that beautiful sound right close by and above him.

5
The fact that the young hunter is lost helps to illustrate the archetypal pattern of a hero's separation from home. His search has begun.

6
pemmican: meat, usually deer, dried in the sun or over a slow fire and then packed into skin bags to keep for four or five years

7
The storyteller uses vivid sensory descriptions to depict the sounds of the forest in the night and to show the fear of the hunter. This use illustrates another device of myth—the hero's test or initiation.

8
The appearance of the woodpecker with its cryptic message helps to build suspense.

9
Heroes in myths often encounter protective figures who help lead them to their destinies. The woodpecker, Wagnuka, is such a guide.

CLOSURE

Ask students to list two reasons for telling stories [to entertain and to explain one's world].

EXTENSION

Have students read other myths to find relationships between the stories. For example, ask students to look for related purposes in explanatory myths such as the American Indian "Great Medicine Makes a Beautiful Country" and the Greek "Phaëthon." Or have students compare and

190

10

belaboring: working away at something persistently

11

This young man, like many mythical heroes, returns from his quest with something of value for his people. Although the hero has returned with a boon for his people, he does not yet know its use or its value.

12

tipi: a movable dwelling place (tepee)

13

sweatlodge: a small, round house made of sod, sticks, or hide, and filled with hot rocks and water to cause steam; used for religious purposes and for purification

14

Transformations like the one in this dream are often a part of myths. Only as a man can Wagnuka show the young man how to make the flute sing.

15

The American Indian custom of smoking objects involves blessing or purifying them with the smoke from burning sacred plants—in this case, sage and sweet grass.

16

itancan: leader of any kind of group

17

wincincala: a girl a warrior is in love with

10 Then he discovered that the song came from the dead branch which the woodpecker was belaboring with its beak. He found, moreover, that it was the wind which made the sound as it whistled through the holes the bird had drilled into the branch. "*Kola*, friend," said the hunter, "let me take this branch 11 home. You can make yourself another one." He took the branch, a hollow piece of wood about the length of his forearm, and full of holes. The young man walked back to his village. He had no meat to bring to his tribe, but he was happy all the same.

12 Back in his tipi, he tried to make the dead branch sing for him. He blew on it, he waved it around—but no sound came. It made the young man sad. He wanted so much to hear that won- 13 derful sound. He purified himself in the sweatlodge and climbed to the top of a lonely hill. There, naked, resting with his back against a large rock, he fasted for four days and four nights, crying for a dream, a vision to teach him how to make the branch sing. In the middle of the fourth night, Wagnuka, the bird with the flaming red spot on his head, appeared to him, saying, 14 "Watch me." The bird turned into a man, doing this and that, always saying, "Watch me!" And in his vision the young man watched—very carefully.

When he awoke he found a cedar tree. He broke off a branch, and working many hours hollowed it out delicately with a bowstring drill, just as he had seen Wagnuka do it in his vision. He whittled the branch into a shape of a bird with a long neck and an open beak. He painted the top of the bird's head red with *washasha*, the sacred vermilion color. He prayed. He 15 smoked the branch with incense of burning sage and sweet grass. He fingered the holes as he had watched it done in his dream, all the while blowing softly into the end of his flute. Because this is what he had made—the first flute, the very first *Siyotanka*. And all at once there was the song, ghostlike and beautiful beyond words, and all the people were astounded and joyful.

16 In the village lived an *itancan*, a big and powerful chief. This itancan had a daughter who was beautiful, but also very haughty. Many young men had tried to win her love, but she had turned them all away. Thinking of her, the young man 17 made up a special song, a song that would make this proud *winc-*

contrast American tall tales about characters like Paul Bunyan and Pecos Bill.

191

incala fall in love with him. Standing near a tall tree a little way from the village, he blew his flute.

All at once the wincincala heard it. She was sitting in her father's, the chief's, tipi, feasting on much good meat. She
18 wanted to remain sitting there, but her feet wanted to go outside; and the feet won. Her head said, "Go slow, slow," but her feet said, "Faster, faster." In no time at all she stood next to the young man. Her mind ordered her lips to stay closed, but her heart commanded them to open. Her heart told her tongue to speak.

"*Koshkalaka, washtelake,*" she said. "Young man, I like you." Then she said, "Let your parents send a gift to my father. No matter how small, it will be accepted. Let your father speak for you to my father. Do it soon, right now!"

18
This description of the wincincala's feet, head, lips, and heart acting in contradiction illustrates how love can make people act peculiarly.

Another activity students might enjoy is creating a mural to accompany the myth. You could provide a long sheet of white butcher paper on which students can depict the story's characters and events.

You could also have students prepare a reader's theater presentation of **"The Sound of Flutes."** They could draw a setting on white butcher paper and improvise props such as a flute and a woodpecker with items available in the classroom. ■

19

Because it explains how the flute came to be, this story may be called an explanatory myth.

ANSWERS

Reader's Response

1. Help students get started by suggesting some of the stories they have read earlier in the year before the class divides into small groups for discussion. Have groups report their favorites to the class.

2. Remind students to include details about their responses to music when writing in their journals. Did the music include romance as this tale did?

Writer's Craft

Answers may vary.

3. This story explains the way flutes came to be and how flute music came to be the expression of love.

4. The problem that sets the main character in motion is that meat is scarce and people in the village are hungry. The young man must leave to hunt elk.

5. The hunter's arrows are straight and tipped with obsidian, which is sharp, black, and as shiny as glass. His food is *wasna*, or pemmican—a mixture of dried meat, kidney fat, and berries pounded together. It is sweet and strong and just a handful will keep a man going for a day or more. The flute has a mournful, sad sound, one the hunter has never heard before. It is ghostlike and makes him afraid, but it also is a beautiful sound, full of love and hope.

SELECTION AMENDMENT
Description of change: excerpted
Rationale: to focus on the concept of creative writing presented in this chapter

192

And so the old folks agreed according to the wishes of their children, and the chief's daughter became the young hunter's wife. All the other young men had heard and seen how it came about. Soon they, too, began to whittle cedar branches into the shapes of birds' heads with long necks and open beaks, and the beautiful haunting sound of flutes traveled from tribe to tribe until it filled

19 the whole prairie. And that is how Siyotanka the flute came to be—thanks to the cedar, the woodpecker, the wind, and one young hunter who shot no elk but who knew how to listen.

transcribed and edited by Richard Erdoes

READER'S RESPONSE

1. What other stories have you heard or read that explain something in the world—questions about nature, the earth, early inventions? In a small group, share the stories you remember. What's the most unusual or the most interesting one?

2. The hunter and the chief's daughter are strongly affected by the music they hear. In your journal, write about a time music affected you.

WRITER'S CRAFT

3. Legends and myths tell stories to explain the world. What is explained in this legend?

4. In most stories, a problem or conflict sets the characters in motion. What is it in this story?

5. A good story has many specific details. What details can you find about the hunter's arrows? his food? the sound of the music?

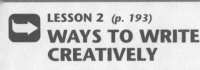

TEACHING *WAYS TO WRITE CREATIVELY*

Tell students that there are four basic methods of development that writers use in creative writing. They are narration, description, comparison/contrast, and evaluation. Have students identify passages in **"The Sound of Flutes"** that illustrate these methods.

For example, the myth primarily uses narration. But it also contains descriptive passages, such as the description of the bow and arrows on p. 186 and the description of the strange noises in the forest on p. 189. ■

Ways to Write Creatively

A story, the main kind of writing you're going to do in this chapter, is one kind of creative writing. A poem, which you may also write in this chapter, is another kind of creative writing. When people write creatively, they use their imagination and their skill with language to make something unique. They might write novels, plays, television scripts, or song lyrics. Here are some specific ways writers develop their creative writing.

- in a poem, telling about a girl who hits her first home run
- in a story, telling what happens to astronauts lost in space
- in a science fiction story, describing what a town would look like twenty years from now
- in a play, describing how a character acts during her first day at a new job
- in a poem, recalling the memory of a favorite meal
- in a children's story, telling about an otter that tries to figure out what a pomegranate is
- in a movie script, showing how two brothers are alike yet different
- in a story, telling how a fourteen-year-old helps his Danish cousin learn English
- in a novel, having a character decide whether an action would help others

LOOKING AHEAD

In the main assignment in this chapter, you'll use narration to create a story. Keep in mind that an effective short story

- entertains the reader
- develops a conflict, or problem
- holds the reader's interest through well-developed characters, setting, and plot

MEETING individual NEEDS

LEP/ESL

General Strategies. Explain to students the four ways that writers develop their creative writing by discussing with them the kinds of words that help identify each method: narration—action verbs; description—adverbs and adjectives; classification—quantifiers and qualifiers; evaluation— comparative and superlative modifiers.

◆ INTEGRATING THE LANGUAGE ARTS

Literature Link. While one work of literature can employ all four methods of development, one method is often dominant. To illustrate the different methods used, ask students to read poems that emphasize the different methods. Possible poems are Edna St. Vincent Millay's "The Ballad of the Harp-Weaver" (narration); Sara Teasdale's "Stars" (description); Victor M. Valle's "Food" (classification); and Langston Hughes's "Refugee in America" (evaluation).

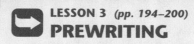
OBJECTIVES

- To brainstorm and formulate story ideas
- To plan and develop a story's characters, setting, plot, and point of view
- To create a story map

MOTIVATION

You might interest students in a contest for the best story idea by proposing an award for the winner. Explain that students will be learning how to find good ideas and develop them into interesting stories. Reassure students that they will all be able to think of good ideas.

PROGRAM MANAGER

PREWRITING

- **Self-Assessment** Before beginning instruction of the writing process, see **Writing Process Log** in *Strategies for Writing*, p. 15.
- **Heuristics** To help students generate ideas, see **Prewriting** in *Strategies for Writing*, pp. 16–19.
- **Instructional Support** See **Graphic Organizers 9** and **10**. For suggestions on how to tie the transparencies to instruction, review teacher's notes in *Fine Art and Instructional Transparencies for Writing*, pp. 63, 65.

QUOTATION FOR THE DAY

"O reader! had you in your mind/ Such stores as silent thought can bring,/ O gentle reader! you would find/A tale in every thing." (William Wordsworth, 1770–1850, English poet)

Write the excerpt from Wordsworth's poem on the chalkboard and ask students what the poet means by "Such stores as silent thought can bring." Then have students write journal entries about how their stored ideas can be turned into tales or stories.

Writing a Short Story

Prewriting

Finding a Story Idea

Some scientists actually study creative people, and they've learned some things about how creativity works. Big ideas often come to artists and thinkers when they're relaxed and *not* searching for brilliant thoughts. So relax. Let your imagination react to the people, places, and events around you.

Shoe reprinted by permission: Tribune Media Services.

Thinking About Purpose and Audience

Your main *purpose* in writing a story is to give your imagination some exercise—to be creative. But your purpose is also to entertain your readers, whether with humor, suspense, exciting action, or a heartbreaking drama. Your story may even have a message, or theme. For instance, the story of an injured hockey star will really hold readers in suspense. Yet it may also show them that dealing with a physical disability takes courage and patience.

Who will be your *audience*? You may write a story for very young readers, your classmates, or adults. Keep your audience in mind as you plan your story. A story about cheating on final exams just won't work for preschoolers, and fairy tales probably won't interest your classmates.

Explain that many story ideas and many ways of developing story ideas are possible. You may even be able to use the students' responses to Wordsworth's poem in the **Quotation for the Day** as an effective lead-in for discussing the story elements in this lesson.

Explain to students that story ideas must be developed with purpose and audience in mind, and then have a volunteer read to the class **Thinking About Purpose and Audience,** p. 194. Remind students that their classmates will be the audience for the stories they write.

As you discuss **Starting with Characters and Situations,** below, you could

Starting with Characters and Situations

What do all good stories have in common? Two things: a main character (an interesting one, of course!) and a *conflict,* or problem, to be solved. The character has to want something, or be confused, or face a threat—any *situation* that makes the reader wonder what's going to happen.

Characters.   Sometimes the character suggests the conflict. Maybe a girl gets on your bus—a girl who has the longest hair you've ever seen. Does someone else have to untangle it? Doesn't it get caught in things? You're on your way to a situation with conflict.

Situations.   Sometimes a situation, or conflict, suggests a character. Maybe you come across a newspaper article on spelunking (cave exploring). Don't people get afraid in caves—or lost? How could it happen? What kind of person would get into that fix? You're on your way to a main character with a definite problem.

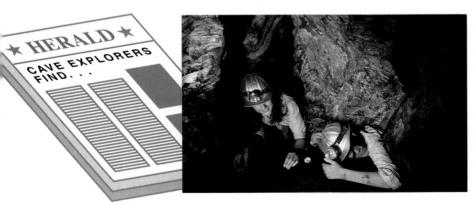

Here are some examples of story ideas that include characters in situations with conflict.

STORY IDEAS

- Alicia, who came to the United States from Mexico when she was nine, has to go to a school where no one speaks Spanish.

LEP/ESL

General Strategies. To help students with ideas for characters with conflicts, encourage them to recall their experiences learning about a new culture. Suggest that they replace themselves with fictional characters and embellish or expand upon their experiences to make them more entertaining and to follow a story format.

LESS-ADVANCED STUDENTS

If some students have trouble thinking of story ideas independently, you may want to allow them to develop one of the suggested examples from **Story Ideas.**

INTEGRATING THE LANGUAGE ARTS

Literature Link. Have students work in pairs to identify the essence of the story ideas in two or three short stories such as "Too Soon a Woman" by Dorothy M. Johnson or "The Ransom of Red Chief" by O. Henry. Who is the major character, and what is the situation that gets the story started?

ask students about some of their favorite characters in literature. List some of their choices on the chalkboard and have the class mention traits that make the characters likable. Then have students explain the situations or problems that the characters deal with so students will begin to understand the relationship of character and situation in a story. You might discuss **Story Ideas** by asking students if they can envision what might happen next in the examples.

When you teach **Planning Your Story,** pp. 197–200, work with the class to create a story map, as illustrated on p. 199. First, have the class decide on a character or characters. Someone might start by suggesting a name, and others could add details by asking and responding to "What if?" questions. Then

A DIFFERENT APPROACH

To help students develop their major characters, have them role-play the characters in small groups. One student might role-play a girl who doesn't speak the same language as her classmates, while another might role-play a visitor from outer space, and so on. Encourage students to concentrate on how the characters would feel and act and what the characters would say and do.

To help students visualize their settings, have the students illustrate them. A student writing about a computer whiz who taps into a dangerous spy ring could draw exactly how the computer room is arranged.

ANSWERS
Exercise 1

You may want to post lists so that students can share ideas.

- A boy discovers that a visitor from outer space has eaten his bicycle.
- An eighth-grader's chess team, the Rooks, wins the city championship, but the school doesn't have enough money to send the team to the state finals.
- A girl must decide what to do when she sees a friend cheat on a test.

As you search for story ideas, try

- brainstorming story ideas in a small group
- using your own experience, newspapers, and TV
- asking yourself some "What if?" questions
(See pages 24–31 for more help with these prewriting techniques.)

EXERCISE 1 ▶ **Exploring Story Ideas**

Who would be fun to write about? What real or imaginary situations might make good stories? With a small group, brainstorm ideas for characters and situations with a conflict. Have one person take notes, keeping two separate lists for characters and situations.

PART 1:
Finding a Story Idea

Loosen up and let your imagination soar. You can use ideas from Exercise 1 or think up an altogether different main character and situation. In two or three sentences, write your idea for a story. Identify the main character and the story situation. Be sure the situation involves a conflict.

have the class place the character or characters in a setting. Have students suggest a time and a place as you record their suggestions on the chalkboard. Next, work with the class to devise a plot. Reassure students that in the process of developing a plot they can change the characters and setting.

After students have read **Choosing a Point of View** on p. 200, discuss how point of view determines what the reader will know about events in the story. For example, first-person reveals only what the narrator thinks. A mystery might be narrated from the point of view of the detective or from the point of view of the criminal being tracked down. ☞

Prewriting

Planning Your Story

As you gather material for your story, you'll need to develop your characters, setting, and plot.

Thinking About Characters, Setting, Plot

Characters. A story holds the reader's interest when the *characters* seem so real they could walk right off the page. To get them walking, you can use realistic details from the people around you as well as from your imagination. One character may have your brother's curly hair and your next-door neighbor's funny laugh. Another character may sneeze like your science teacher or walk like your Aunt May. To develop your characters, you might make a list, a cluster, or a chart of details. Start by asking yourself these questions:

- How old is the character? What does he or she look like?
- How does the character dress? move?
- What are the character's personality traits (patient, bossy, stubborn, kind, and so on)?

Setting. The time and place of your story is its **setting.** Setting can be just a backdrop for the action, or it can be very important. Henry, for example, may be descending in a hot-air balloon right into a Civil War battle.

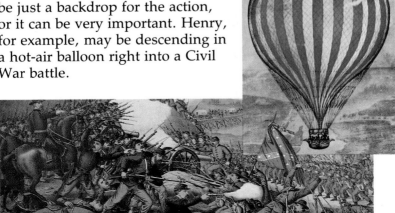

Remind students that third-person allows the reader to know what several characters think, and it can show different perspectives. In a story about a disagreement between a mother and a daughter, the reader would know how both characters feel.

INDEPENDENT PRACTICE

If you have developed a character, a setting, and a plot with your class as a group, you might want to circulate throughout the class while students brainstorm in groups on **Exercise 1**, p. 196.

Writing Assignments: Parts 1–4 (pp. 196, 198, 200) may be completed independently. However, students could work in

Setting can also help create a mood, or atmosphere. As Jem walks alone through misty woods, the darkness and forest noises create a mood of mystery and suspense. To think about your story's setting, try listing, clustering, or using a chart to gather details. Use the following questions to get started.

- How important is the setting to the story's action? Is it just a backdrop that helps create a feeling? Or does the setting help put events in motion?
- Can I use the setting to create a mood?
- What places, weather, or times of day will I need to describe? What sensory details (smells, sights, and sounds) will I use?

 COMPUTER NOTE: Use your word-processing program's thesaurus to help you brainstorm ideas and generate words to describe your characters, setting, and plot.

 **WRITING ASSIGNMENT**

PART 2:
Gathering Details for Characters and Setting

Can you see your characters in your mind's eye? Can you hear them? Are they short, muscle-bound, fidgety, or loud? And *where* are they? Are they seeking shelter from a sandstorm or snorkeling underwater? Is it the year 4002 or a winter night in the present? Use the questions on pages 197 and 198 to spark your imagination, and jot down your ideas.

Plot. What happens in the story is its *plot*. Some stories are fast-moving and action-packed. Others focus on one or two important events. To develop an effective plot, think about the following main elements.

- **Conflict.** Your story situation must hold a conflict or problem. Does the main character want something badly or face a tough decision? Or must the character struggle against something—nature or another person?

 **COOPERATIVE LEARNING**
Divide the class into four or five groups and have each group develop a setting for a story. Assign each group a different era (or time period), climate, time of day, and mood. Have each group list words and phrases that could develop a setting. Have the groups share their collected details. You might want to have students vote on the most convincing setting.

TECHNOLOGY TIP
Remind students that thesauruses can help jog their memories of words they already know, but they should never use a word from a thesaurus unless they are familiar with the word and know it fits the context.

INTEGRATING THE LANGUAGE ARTS

Literature Link. You may want to explain to students how in some stories the setting becomes a principal force and actually creates the conflict or problem in the story. If the selection is available in your literature textbook, have students read "To Build a Fire" by Jack London to determine whether the setting or the character is more important in the story. [Most students will recognize that the author uses very little characterization; the man and the dog are not even given names. On the other hand, the setting plays an integral part: The conflict of the story is between the man and the elements of nature.]

pairs to select story ideas and then to develop characters, settings, and plots that will serve as plans for writing their complete stories.

ASSESSMENT

While you probably will not make a formal assessment of students' writing at this stage, it may be helpful to circulate among your students to read and comment on their writing as they work. Praise passages that are particularly well developed.

☞

- **A Series of Events.** One action should lead to another as the character struggles to solve the problem or conflict. Do you have a chain of events that keeps the action moving?
- **High Point.** You need a moment in the story, the high point, when the reader feels great interest and suspense about how the problem will be settled. Do you have a scene in your story when things will be decided, one way or another?
- **Outcome.** Following the high point, there are usually a few final details to work out. Do you tie up loose ends so that readers aren't left with questions?

Creating a Story Map. When you plan your story plot, you can put it into a story map. A *story map* outlines your characters, setting, and plot all at once.

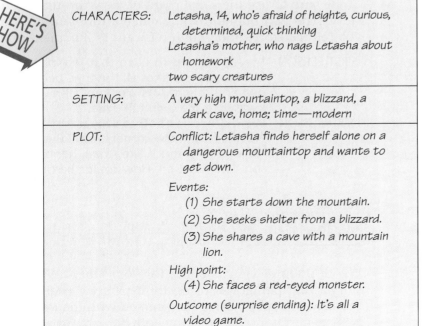

CHARACTERS:	Letasha, 14, who's afraid of heights, curious, determined, quick thinking Letasha's mother, who nags Letasha about homework two scary creatures	
SETTING:	A very high mountaintop, a blizzard, a dark cave, home; time—modern	
PLOT:	Conflict: Letasha finds herself alone on a dangerous mountaintop and wants to get down. Events: (1) She starts down the mountain. (2) She seeks shelter from a blizzard. (3) She shares a cave with a mountain lion. High point: (4) She faces a red-eyed monster. Outcome (surprise ending): It's all a video game.	

CRITICAL THINKING

Analysis. To help students understand the plot elements of conflict, series of events, high point, and outcome more fully, draw the following diagram on the chalkboard:

Then have students analyze plot structure by applying this diagram to **"The Sound of Flutes."**

[**Background and setting:** The story occurs in and around a Sioux village during a young man's hunt for elk.
Conflict: The hunter becomes lost and hears frightening sounds in the forest.
Series of events: The hunter dreams of Wagnuka, the redheaded woodpecker; the woodpecker appears to lead him; the woodpecker taps on a cedar branch and a beautiful sound is heard; the young man takes the branch to his tribe; the bird appears in a dream to show the young man how to use the flute; the young man writes a song to woo the chief's daughter with his flute music.
High point: The chief's daughter hears the music and is attracted to it.
Outcome: The chief's daughter becomes the young hunter's wife, and young men use flutes to romance their sweethearts.]

Ask students what two questions they should ask themselves before they begin their stories. [What is my purpose? Who is my audience?] Then ask students to list the four elements of a story [characters, setting, plot, and point of view]. ■

TIMESAVER

Have groups of four students share their completed maps. Group members should check the maps to be sure that each map contains characters that are clearly identified and described, a stated point of view, a clearly described setting, and a plot with a logical sequence of events, a high point, and an outcome.

Encourage students to discuss their maps with you when the groups identify problems.

200

---

200   *Creative Writing*

WRITING ASSIGNMENT

PART 3:
Creating a Story Map

Pull your ideas together and create a story map like the one on page 199. Take time to flesh out your plot. What will be your story's events, conflict, and outcome? Be sure to include characters and the setting, too.

Choosing a Point of View

Who will tell your story? If you use the ***first-person point of view,*** the narrator (or storyteller) is a character in the story. The narrator uses the first-person pronoun *I* and speaks directly to the reader. First-person can make a story more believable.

If you use the ***third-person point of view,*** the narrator is *not* a character in the story. Characters are referred to with third-person pronouns, such as *he, she,* and *they.*

Be sure to use the same point of view throughout the story. The two points of view make a difference in how you tell the story, and you don't want to mix them up.

FIRST PERSON	**I** really needed to keep that job in the cafe, but **I** made mistakes all the time because the owner, grouchy Mrs. Yu, kept staring at **me.** **I** was sure she didn't like **me.**
THIRD PERSON	Wing dropped another cup, as Mrs. Yu watched from the corner. **She** sighed. **He** looked so much like Arlan, **her** only son—**her** lost son. How could **she** fire **him**?

WRITING ASSIGNMENT

PART 4:
Speaking and Listening: Choosing a Point of View

Which point of view is better for your story? Write your story's first paragraph using third-person. Then rewrite the same paragraph using first-person with the main character as narrator. After reading both paragraphs aloud to a small group, ask them which version they like better.

WRITING YOUR FIRST DRAFT

OBJECTIVES

- To identify and analyze character, setting, and plot in a short story
- To write a draft of a short story using a story map

MOTIVATION

Read aloud the first sentence of "The Tell-Tale Heart" from **Making the Plot Interesting** (below). Discuss with students how the sentence sets the mood and arouses curiosity about the story. Then read an introduction from another story such as Shirley Jackson's "Charles" and ask students what ☞

Writing Your First Draft

Keep your story map in front of you as you write your first draft. But let your imagination take charge. As your story takes shape, feel free to make changes.

Combining the Basic Elements of a Story

Professional writers know the essential ingredients of a good short story: a strong beginning and ending, interesting characters, dialogue, and suspense.

Making the Plot Interesting. Use a zesty or teasing beginning to hook your reader's attention. Here's Edgar Allan Poe's first sentence in "The Tell-Tale Heart": "True!—nervous—very, very dreadfully nervous I had been and am; but why *will* you say that I am mad?"

A suspenseful story keeps the readers guessing about what will happen next. Give your story a strong high point and resolve the conflict in a satisfying and believable way.

Making Your Characters Seem Real. You can *tell* the reader directly what a character is like. (For example, "María is determined and hard-working.") But it's always better to *show*, not tell.

- **Show what the character says.** "No matter what you say," María repeated, "I won't give up. I'm sure I have a chance to win this meet."

- **Show what the character does.** María got to the gym at 6 A.M., just as she had every day for a year. She dove into the water and started swimming laps— 10, 25, 40, 75, 100. After school she was back at the gym swimming another 50 laps.

- **Show what others say about the character.** "Poor María," Janice sighed. "She hasn't got a life. All she does is practice, practice, practice."

PROGRAM MANAGER

WRITING YOUR FIRST DRAFT

- **Instructional Support** For help with creating dialogue, see **Writing** in *Strategies for Writing*, p. 20.

QUOTATION FOR THE DAY

"I am of those who believe that a story, of whatever length, should have a beginning, a middle, and an ending. Indeed, I have never yet begun to write a short story or a novel when I did not see in advance, . . . the ending of that story." (Christopher LaFarge, 1897–1956, American poet and novelist)

Ask students to write journal entries comparing their own creative writing processes with LaFarge's. Do they know how their stories are going to end before they begin writing?

SELECTION AMENDMENT
Description of change: excerpted
Rationale: to focus on the concept of creating interesting story beginnings presented in this chapter

they know from the introduction. Ask if the introduction grabbed their attention.

After showing students how the beginning of a story gets the reader involved, you could discuss with the class **Combining the Basic Elements of a Story**, p. 201. You may want to demonstrate the three ways to make characters seem real by using characters from the prewriting story map the class developed. You could also

MEETING individual NEEDS

LEP/ESL

General Strategies. You might instruct students to write their stories in English, but if they don't know a particular English word or phrase, have them use words from their native languages. In the evaluating and revising stage, they can replace those words with English words or phrases.

 ### INTEGRATING THE LANGUAGE ARTS

Vocabulary Link. You may want to extend the **Writing Note** with practice using specific vocabulary. Give students a list of words and ask them to write more-specific sensory words to express the same ideas. You might use words like *walked, said, went,* and *wrote.*

---

202   *Creative Writing*

Good storytellers use vivid word pictures so their readers can "see" the story's characters and events in their mind's eye. Be sure to make the verbs and sensory details in your story as specific and lively as possible.

VAGUE (telling)   For a long time Jim didn't write anything. He just listened to noises in the room and felt sick.

SPECIFIC (showing)   Jim stared at his paper. Around him, he could hear the other students coughing, turning pages, scratchily writing. His stomach felt knotted, and his hands were sweaty. But his brain stayed horribly empty.

☞ REFERENCE NOTE: See pages 457–468 for more about verbs and page 66 for help with using sensory details.

Creating Dialogue. Which of these two sentences would you rather read in a story?

SUMMARY   Angela hates her new haircut.

DIALOGUE   "I look like I was just attacked by a crazy lawn mower!" Angela hollered.

Writers use *dialogue* (the words that characters say) to help reveal a character's personality. To make your dialogue sound natural, use short sentences, fragments, and contractions. Use informal language, the kind people actually use when they talk. And don't always write *he said* or *she said.* Try to use dialogue tags that give a better idea of *how* a character speaks (*she murmured, yelled, complained, laughed,* and so on).

Looking at a Short Story

No two stories emphasize exactly the same elements. The writer of a mystery may choose to emphasize plot. The writer of a love story may devote more time to character. Notice how the writer of the following story gets right into the action—bam!—and also creates a memorable character.

have volunteers suggest dialogue for the characters as you write the suggestions on the chalkboard.

Then read aloud and discuss **"Thank You, M'am"** or have volunteers take turns reading it. As you read the short story, use the side glosses and the annotations to discuss and analyze the elements of a story. After students finish reading and discussing

the professional model, assign **Exercise 2, p. 209,** for independent practice.

Next, you might read and discuss **A Writer's Model** on p. 210 with the class. Use the side glosses to point out details relating to character development and setting. Have students identify the conflict, the series of events, the high point, and the outcome. You may want to use this story to reinforce ☞

A SHORT STORY

Thank You, M'am
by Langston Hughes

BEGINNING *1*
Character and setting details

Event 1/ Conflict

2

Appearance and action details

3

Event 2

Dialogue— character development *4*

5

6

7

She was a large woman with a large purse that had everything in it but hammer and nails. It had a long strap and she carried it slung across her shoulder. It was about eleven o'clock at night, and she was walking alone, when a boy ran up behind her and tried to snatch her purse. The strap broke with the single tug the boy gave it from behind. But the boy's weight, and the weight of the purse combined, caused him to lose his balance so, instead of taking off full blast as he had hoped, the boy fell on his back on the sidewalk, and his legs flew up. The large woman simply turned around and kicked him right square in his blue-jeaned sitter. Then she reached down, picked the boy up by his shirt front, and shook him until his teeth rattled.

After that the woman said, "Pick up my pocketbook, boy, and give it here."

She still held him. But she bent down enough to permit him to stoop and pick up her purse. Then she said, "Now ain't you ashamed of yourself?"

Firmly gripped by his shirt front, the boy said, "Yes'm."

The woman said, "What did you want to do it for?"

The boy said, "I didn't aim to."

She said, "You a lie!"

By that time two or three people passed, stopped, turned to look, and some stood watching.

USING THE SELECTION
Thank You, M'am

1
The first sentence provides direct and indirect characterization: The woman is large and prepared for anything.

2
From this scene, what can you infer about the size and strength of the woman and the boy? [The woman is much stronger than the boy, who must be small and somewhat weak.]

3
The reversal of expectation in this scene and the term "blue-jeaned sitter" set a humorous mood.

4
pocketbook: an old-fashioned term for a purse

5
The characters speak naturally using authentic dialect.

6
The boy is so stunned that his reaction is polite and honest about his attempt to rob the woman.

7
The woman seeks a motive from the boy; his response seems to be an excuse, but it may be the truth.

the use of a story map. Review the story map on p. 199 and discuss how the characters, setting, and plot were developed in the story from the outline in the story map.

Now that students have analyzed two story models, they should be ready to begin **Writing Assignment: Part 5** on p. 211. Remind students to refer to their prewriting notes and story maps while writing their rough drafts. Tell the class not to worry about grammatical correctness at this stage.

8
The boy remains honest even though it means he will remain captive.

9
The boy's dirty physical appearance might lead the reader to wonder about whether the boy is well cared for.

10
The direct physical description of the boy as frail confirms the earlier scene in which the woman was able to subdue him.

8

Appearance—
details   9

MIDDLE
Event 3

Appearance—
details   10

Dialogue—
character
development

"If I turn you loose, will you run?" asked the woman.

"Yes'm," said the boy.

"Then I won't turn you loose," said the woman. She did not release him.

"I'm very sorry, lady, I'm sorry," whispered the boy.

"Um-hum! And your face is dirty. I got a great mind to wash your face for you. Ain't you got nobody home to tell you to wash your face?"

"No'm," said the boy.

"Then it will get washed this evening," said the large woman starting up the street, dragging the frightened boy behind her.

He looked as if he were fourteen or fifteen, frail and willow-wild, in tennis shoes and blue jeans.

The woman said, "You ought to be my son. I would teach you right from wrong. Least I can do right now is to wash your face. Are you hungry?"

"No'm," said the being-dragged boy. "I just want you to turn me loose."

"Was I bothering *you* when I turned that corner?" asked the woman.

Although you will assess students' understanding of the elements of a story by discussion and analysis of the models, you probably will not want to make a formal evaluation of their drafts at this stage. However, you may want to have students read and comment on one another's drafts in small groups. After advising students to make notes on the comments, discuss the notes with students, either in groups or individually.

☛

"No'm."

"But you put yourself in contact with *me*," said the woman. "If you think that that contact is not going to last awhile, you got another thought coming. When I get through with you, sir, you are going to remember Mrs. Luella Bates Washington Jones."

11

Action details/ Suspense 12

Sweat popped out on the boy's face and he began to struggle. Mrs. Jones stopped, jerked him around in front of her, put a half-nelson about his neck, and continued to drag him up the street. When she got to her door, she dragged the boy inside, down a hall, and into a large kitchenette-furnished room at the rear of the house. She switched on the light and left the door open. The boy could hear other roomers laughing and talking in the large house. Some of their doors were opened, too, so he knew he and the woman were not alone. The woman still had him by the neck in the middle of her room.

Setting details

She said, "What is your name?"

"Roger," answered the boy.

13

Action and setting details/ Suspense

Event 4

Dialogue— character development

"Then, Roger, you go to that sink and wash your face," said the woman, whereupon she turned him loose—at last. Roger looked at the door—looked at the woman—looked at the door—*and went to the sink.*

"Let the water run until it gets warm," she said. "Here's a clean towel."

"You gonna take me to jail?" asked the boy, bending over the sink.

"Not with that face, I would not take you nowhere," said the woman. "Here I am trying to get home to cook me a bite to eat and you snatch my pocketbook! Maybe you ain't been to your supper either, late as it be. Have you?"

11
The woman has not been identified by name until this point, but the reader knows that she is strong, courageous, determined, and kind.

12
The boy reacts in fear and tries to escape.

13
The boy admits his identity and makes a conscious choice not to try to run away again.

If your students have trouble writing their story drafts from their story maps, try having them work in small groups to analyze where the difficulties occurred. Students might compare their story maps to the stories they wrote to see what elements need improvement. You might even set up review groups, each of which could analyze characters, setting, plot, theme, or point of view. Each group could analyze one element of a story and pass the story to the next group for suggestions. You might want to be available to answer questions as they arise.

14

This response shows that the boy has no supervision and no one to cook for him—perhaps no one to care for him.

15

Mrs. Jones looks for a motive in Roger's actions and thinks he must be hungry.

16

Mrs. Jones offers an alternative to stealing to get blue suede shoes; Roger is shocked at her solution.

17

Roger makes a final commitment not to run away from Mrs. Jones.

18

Mrs. Jones understands the boy's feelings, and she doesn't lecture.

14

"There's nobody home at my house," said the boy.

15

"Then we'll eat," said the woman. "I believe you're hungry—or been hungry—to try to snatch my pocketbook."

"I wanted a pair of blue suede shoes," said the boy.

16

"Well, you didn't have to snatch *my* pocketbook to get some suede shoes," said Mrs. Luella Bates Washington Jones. "You could of asked me."

"M'am?"

Action and *17* **setting details**

The water dripping from his face, the boy looked at her. There was a long pause. A very long pause. After he had dried his face and not knowing what else to do dried it again, the boy turned around, wondering what next. The door was open. He could make a dash for it down the hall. He could run, run, run, run, *run!*

HIGH POINT

The woman was sitting on the daybed. After a while she said, "I were young once and I wanted things I could not get."

There was another long pause. The boy's mouth opened. Then he frowned, but not knowing he frowned.

Dialogue— *18* **character development**

The woman said, "Um-hum! You thought I was going to say *but,* didn't you? You thought I was going to say, *but I didn't snatch people's pocketbooks.* Well, I wasn't going to say that." Pause. Silence. "I have done things, too, which I would not tell you, son—neither tell God, if He didn't already know. So you set down while I fix us something to eat. You might run that comb through your hair so you will look presentable."

Setting details

In another corner of the room behind a screen was a gas plate and an icebox. Mrs.

Event 5

Jones got up and went behind the screen.

To close, ask the following questions about the story elements discussed in this lesson:

1. How can you make the plot interesting? [Use a suspenseful opener, keep the reader guessing about what will happen next, have a strong high point, and resolve the conflict in a believable way.]

2. How can you make characters seem real? [Show what they say and do and what others say about them.]

3. How can you make your writing interesting? [Use specific words and realistic dialogue.]

☞

Writing Your First Draft **207**

19

The woman did not watch the boy to see if he was going to run now, nor did she watch her purse which she left behind her on the daybed. But the boy took care to sit on the far side of the room where he thought she could easily see him out of the corner of her eye, if she wanted to. He did not trust the woman *not* to trust him. And he did not want to be mistrusted now.

20

OUTCOME
Dialogue—
character
development

"Do you need somebody to go to the store," asked the boy, "maybe to get some milk or something?"

"Don't believe I do," said the woman, "unless you just want sweet milk yourself. I was going to make cocoa out of this canned milk I got here."

"That will be fine," said the boy.

21

Action and
setting details

She heated some lima beans and ham she had in the icebox, made the cocoa, and set the table. The woman did not ask the boy anything about where he lived, or his folks, or anything else that would embarrass him. Instead, as they ate, she told him about her job in a hotel beauty shop that stayed open late, what the work was like, and how all

19
Mrs. Jones shows her trust.

20
Roger's experience has changed him. He now wants and needs her trust.

21
sweet milk: a Southern term used to distinguish milk from buttermilk or clabbered milk

EXTENSION

To get your students even more involved with the characters from **"Thank You, M'am,"** stage a mock trial to try Roger for the crime of attempted theft. Select a judge, a defense attorney, a prosecuting attorney, and a jury. Allow the defendant Roger and the witness Mrs. Jones to state their versions of what occurred from each character's point of view.

22

Mrs. Jones reinforces the mother-son feeling that has developed.

23

Mrs. Jones turns the experience into a memorable lesson for Roger.

24

The boy realizes the significance of his experience with Mrs. Jones but can only express his thanks simply.

25

Why do you think Mrs. Jones helped Roger? [Responses will vary. Students might mention that Mrs. Jones's economic condition is similar to Roger's or that she remembers what it was like to be young or that despite his attempted theft, Mrs. Jones likes his manner.]

INTEGRATING THE LANGUAGE ARTS

Speaking and Listening. Because it relies heavily on dialogue, this story is excellent for reader's theater. Have students prepare a presentation with two students reading the dialogue for Mrs. Jones and Roger, and a third reading the narration. Remind students to read the dialogue as they think the characters would sound and to show the emotions of the characters as they read.

---

kinds of women came in and out, blondes, redheads, and Spanish. Then she cut him a half of her ten-cent cake.

"Eat some more, son," she said.

22

Event 6/   23
Final details

When they were finished eating she got up and said, "Now, here, take this ten dollars and buy yourself some blue suede shoes. And next time, do not make the mistake of latching onto *my* pocketbook *nor nobody else's* — because shoes come by devilish like that will burn your feet. I got to get my rest now. But I wish you would behave yourself, son, from here on in."

She led him down the hall to the front door and opened it. "Goodnight! Behave yourself, boy!" she said, looking out into the street.

Character   24
development

Action details

The boy wanted to say something else other than, "Thank you, m'am," to Mrs. Luella Bates Washington Jones, but he couldn't do so as he turned at the barren stoop and looked back at the large woman in the door. He barely managed to say, "Thank you," before she shut the door. And he never saw

25

her again.

You can further enrich your students' understanding of Langston Hughes's work by giving them some biographical details about Hughes's life or by bringing to class other stories and poems that he has written. For example, you could read to your students Hughes's poem "Mother to Son" and have students discuss the characters of the mother and the absent son. Students might even use this poem to generate a story about the mother and her son. ■

> **EXERCISE 2** ▶ **Analyzing the Elements of a Short Story**

Think about the basic elements of "Thank You, M'am," and answer the following questions with a partner.

1. Did this story hold your interest? make you laugh? keep you guessing? What was your reaction? Why?
2. In this story Roger and Mrs. Jones have a conflict with each other: He wants to steal her purse and escape. She doesn't want him to. How is the conflict settled?
3. Both Roger and Mrs. Jones are vivid characters. For each one, find an example of actions and dialogue that helps make the character seem real.
4. Setting details in Mrs. Jones's apartment are sometimes very important in this story. Explain with an example.
5. After Roger decides he wants to stay with Mrs. Jones, there's quite a bit of story left. What do you learn in the outcome?

Using a Story Framework

Your story won't be exactly like Langston Hughes's. It may have less dialogue. It may have a more suspenseful high point or more action. But even with these differences, your story can be just as entertaining.

As a beginning story writer, you may find it helpful to use a framework like the one the writer used in the following story. Notice how the story gets right to a conflict and has a clear chronological framework.

"It's the little details that do it, that bring a character or a scene alive in the reader's mind."

Jean Auel

ANSWERS
Exercise 2

Responses will vary.

1. Most students will find that the story holds their interest and keeps them guessing. Many will find it humorous. Students should support their opinions.

2. The conflict is settled when Mrs. Jones treats Roger with kindness and empathy and he responds by becoming trustworthy.

3. The story is rich with actions and dialogue that portray the characters, so details will vary. Ask students to explain their choices.

4. The details illustrate that Mrs. Jones has very little money. She lives in one large room with a screen separating it into parts and cooks on a gas plate instead of on a stove. The description also implies that she lives alone.

5. In the outcome the reader learns that Roger is open to the influence of a good person like Mrs. Jones. The reader also learns that although Roger never sees her again, Mrs. Jones makes an impression on him, and he is truly thankful to her for her kindness.

SELECTION AMENDMENT
Description of change: excerpted
Rationale: to focus on the concept of creative writing presented in this chapter

CRITICAL THINKING

Analysis. Remind students that writers often indirectly tell their readers about characters. The reader must infer the characters' qualities from what the characters say and do.

To give your students practice in making inferences, write this conversation on the chalkboard and ask students to describe the character qualities shown by Felicia, Sheba, and Marsha below:

"I just know I will make the starting lineup for the basketball team," Felicia said with a smug smile. [happiness, pride]

"I don't know whether I will or not," responded Sheba. "I thought I might, but then I missed those two free throws. Now I just don't know." [nervousness, insecurity, shyness]

"Well, I don't really care if I make the team or not," grumbled Marsha as she threw her jacket over her arm and walked out of the gym. "Watching Nelda and Lucha playing up to Coach, I know they already have the places I might have gotten." [anger, jealousy, discontent]

A WRITER'S MODEL

The Final Problem

BEGINNING

Conflict and setting

Background/ Setting

For someone afraid of heights, I'm in a fine mess. Here I am alone on a mountaintop who-knows-how-many miles high. Last night I went to bed in the room I share with my sister. And now, suddenly, I'm thousands of miles from nowhere, and it's twenty below zero—at least.

Dialogue— character development

"Now calm down, Letasha." (I always talk to myself when I'm nervous.) "You have two choices. You can try to get down off this mountain. Or you can stay here and just wait for everything to get better." ("Are you crazy?" the other voice inside me shouts. "If you don't <u>act</u>, there's no hope.")

Event 1

What's this? Mountain-climbing stuff! And a backpack with a tent! OK. I'm going down.

MIDDLE

Setting

My heart's thumping and my knees feel squishy, but I inch myself downward. Suddenly an angry-looking black cloud surrounds me, and the wind picks up like in <u>The Wizard of Oz</u>.

Dialogue— character development

"Now, think, Letasha, think," I say to myself as I try to come up with a plan. I can't pitch the tent in this wind, but I <u>can</u> go into that cave.

Event 2

So I hurry into the cave. It's so dark I can't see a thing, but I'm safe from that storm . . . I think.

Suspense

Whose yellow eyes aren't blinking at me from over there on the far side of the cave? And—oh, oh—what's that roar?

Dialogue

"Now, Letasha. You can either run out of this cave into the worst blizzard you've ever imagined, or you can stay here and hope your cave buddy is already full and feeling friendly." (Right.)

Suspense

Event 3

I stay, staring at those yellow eyes that stare right back at me. Finally, the storm stops, and I rush outside.

MEETING *individual* **NEEDS**

STUDENTS WITH SPECIAL NEEDS

Some students are distracted and frustrated by spelling difficulties during the writing process. The fluency and creativity of their stories may be improved by recording their first drafts on tape. Students can use their story maps to help them get started and stay on track during the recording.

Suspense	I gasp. Right there in the fresh snow gigantic footprints walk past my cave and around a curve.
Dialogue	"OK, Letasha, do you follow these footprints to see who made them? Or do you run for it in the opposite direction—and down? Or is it back to the cave with the Yellow-Eyed Roaring Thing?"
Character development/ Suspense	Mom always says I'm too curious for my own good. Scared to death, I follow the footprints round the curve. Suddenly, a huge monster with an ugly head, angry red eyes, and hairy arms with sharp claws is reaching toward me—
HIGH POINT	
OUTCOME Dialogue	"Letasha, haven't you finished your math yet?" Mom yells from the kitchen.
Surprise ending	Hurriedly I switch off the video game. "Almost, Mom. This last problem is kind of hard."

WRITING ASSIGNMENT

PART 5:
Writing Your First Draft

Both "Thank You, M'am" and "The Final Problem" give you good ideas for writing. But don't think that you have to make your story like them. Just begin following your story map—but, of course, feel free to make changes. Start writing now, and see what happens.

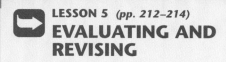
TEACHING THE LESSON

Tell students that evaluating and revising is like polishing silver or waxing a car—it can make their writing shine. Read and discuss the excerpt from Pat Mora's letter. Then read aloud the **Evaluating and Revising Short Stories** chart on p. 213.

You could use a volunteer's story to model the evaluating and revising tech-

---

QUOTATION FOR THE DAY

"The novelist's—any writer's—object is to whittle down his meaning to the exactest and finest possible point." (Elizabeth Bowen, 1899–1973, British author)

Ask students to restate the meaning of Bowen's phrase "whittle down his meaning to the exactest and finest possible point." You may need to define the meaning of *whittle.*

SELECTION AMENDMENT
Description of change: excerpted and amended
Rationale: to focus on the concept of revision presented in this chapter

212

 Evaluating and Revising

The hardest part is over, but you've still got important work to do. How can you make your story better? Is the conflict really interesting? Are the characters believable? If something doesn't work, either fix it or get rid of it. Here's what writer Pat Mora has to say about revising.

Do you know the quotation that says that learning to write is like learning to ice-skate? You must be willing to make a fool of yourself. Writers are willing to try what they can't do well so that one day they can write a strong poem or novel or children's book.

After writers gain some confidence, writers begin to spend more and more time revising just as professional ice-skaters create and practice certain routines until they have developed their own, unique style. You probably don't like rewriting now. I didn't either until a few years ago. . . .

It's important . . . not to fall in love with the words you write. Pick your words or phrases, and then stand back and look at your work. Read it out loud.

Pat Mora, "A Letter to Gabriela, A Young Writer"

The following guidelines will help you pinpoint weak spots in your draft. If you answer *no* to any question in the left-hand column, use the revision technique suggested in the right-hand column.

niques. As students revise their stories, circulate throughout the room to evaluate students' use of revision techniques. To close, have students list the five evaluation questions on the chalkboard. ■

CRITICAL THINKING
(pp. 213–214)

OBJECTIVE
• To analyze a writer's revisions of a paragraph from a short story

EVALUATING AND REVISING SHORT STORIES

EVALUATION GUIDE	REVISION TECHNIQUE
1 Does the beginning present a main character in an interesting conflict?	**Add** sentences that show the main character and a clear conflict or problem.
2 Does the plot have a strong high point and satisfying outcome?	**Add** a tense scene that solves the conflict. **Add** details that explain how everything works out.
3 Are the characters lifelike and believable?	**Add** details about what the characters look like, what they do, and how they feel. **Add** dialogue that sounds natural.
4 Is the setting clear? If possible, does it help set a mood?	**Add** specific details of time and place. **Add** vivid sensory details.
5 Is the point of view the same throughout the story?	**Cut** or **replace** statements that change the point of view.

LEP/ESL

General Strategies. The papers of English-language learners tend to be shorter in length than those of more proficient speakers. To encourage students to write more details, ask them to imagine that they are using movie cameras instead of pencils and paper. Have they left out any film shots or scenes?

LESS-ADVANCED STUDENTS

Less-advanced students often have difficulty evaluating their writing. Encourage them to follow closely the **Evaluating and Revising Short Stories** guide and to focus on only one task at a time. They should read their stories through each time they need to answer an evaluation question.

CRITICAL THINKING
Analyzing the Parts of a Short Story

When you *analyze* something, you look closely at its separate parts and see how they work together. That's just what writers do when they revise. They look at charac-

Remind students that the three major revisions are to add, to cut, and to replace information. Tell students that to determine which technique is appropriate, they must analyze each sentence carefully.

Then tell students to use the questions from the **Critical Thinking Exercise** to analyze the writer's revisions with partners. Have the class read and discuss their analyses. Close by having students summarize the major revision methods and their uses.

MEETING *individual* NEEDS

LEP/ESL

General Strategies. English-language learners may be hesitant to contribute revision ideas. Have them work in pairs with more-proficient speakers so that they can become familiar with the language and understand the revision analysis.

ANSWERS

Critical Thinking Exercise

Responses will vary.

1. The writer has made a change from third-person to first-person point of view to maintain consistency.

2. The word change immediately lets the reader see Letasha's reaction. It involves the reader with the character.

3. Yes, they make the description more vivid.

4. The phrase sounds more convincing because the dialogue seems more natural.

5. It is better because it shows rather than tells. The combination of the details and the uncertainty are more frightening than *animal*.

---

214   *Creative Writing*

ters, plot, setting, and dialogue to see if changes can make them stronger and more entertaining for the reader. When the writer of "The Final Problem" analyzed one paragraph of her story, she made these revisions.

> Right there in the snow ^fresh ^gigantic footprints   **add**
>
> walk past my cave and around a curve.
>
> ~~Letasha gasps.~~ I gasp. "OK, Letasha, do you follow   **replace/reorder**
>
> these footprints to see who made them?
>
> Or do you run for it in the opposite
>
> direction—and down? Or ~~would you prefer~~ *is it back*   **replace**
>
> ~~to return~~ to the cave with the ^*Yellow-Eyed Roaring Thing* animal?"   **replace**

 CRITICAL THINKING EXERCISE:
Analyzing a Writer's Revisions

Analyzing the changes the writer made can help you with your own revision. Working with a partner, first read aloud the draft paragraph and then the revision. Then, use the following questions to guide your analysis.

1. Why does the writer change *Letasha* to *I*?
2. What's the effect of moving *I gasp* to the beginning?
3. Are the words *fresh* and *gigantic* good additions? Why?
4. Why does the writer replace *would you prefer to return* with *is it back*? [Hint: See page 202.]
5. Is *Yellow-Eyed Roaring Thing* better than *animal*? Why?

 **WRITING ASSIGNMENT**   PART 6:
Evaluating and Revising Your Story

Now evaluate and revise your own story, using the guidelines on page 213. Swap drafts with a classmate for feedback and additional suggestions.

PROOFREADING AND PUBLISHING

OBJECTIVES

- To proofread a story for errors
- To publish a story or to share it with an audience

You may want to begin this lesson by explaining that the proofreading and publishing stage of writing is like serving a dinner to special company. You want to be sure that your manners and appearance are just right.

The **Mechanics Hint** (below) suggests an emphasis for proofreading by presenting

Proofreading and Publishing

Proofreading. Double-check your story carefully to correct errors in spelling, usage, and mechanics.

MECHANICS HINT

Punctuating Dialogue

Punctuating dialogue can be especially tricky. Here are some rules that will help you figure out two things: what to put in quotation marks and how to punctuate what your characters say.

1. Enclose a character's words in quotation marks.

EXAMPLE   **"Get off that phone!" Mark demanded.**

2. Commas and periods always go inside a quotation mark. Question marks and exclamation marks go inside when the quotation itself is a question or an exclamation.

EXAMPLES   "OK, Mark. The phone's all yours."
"It's about time, Larry," Mark scowled.
"Don't snap at me!" Larry barked.
"How would you like to wait so long?" Mark grumbled.

 REFERENCE NOTE: For more information on punctuating dialogue, see pages 772–777.

Publishing. With two or three classmates, brainstorm some ideas for publishing your stories or sharing them with others. Here are two possibilities.

 **PROGRAM MANAGER**

PROOFREADING AND PUBLISHING

- **Instructional Support** For a chart students may use to evaluate their proofreading progress, see **Proofreading** in *Strategies for Writing*, p. 22.

- **Independent Practice/ Reteaching** For additional practice with language skills, see **Proofreading Practice: Punctuating Dialogue** in *Strategies for Writing*, p. 23.

- **Assessment/Reflection** To assess student work and evaluate progress, see **Portfolio Forms** in *Portfolio Assessment,* pp. 18–21.

- **Computer Guided Instruction** For additional instruction and practice with punctuating dialogue as noted in the **Mechanics Hint,** see **Lesson 54** in *Language Workshop CD-ROM.*

- **Practice** To help less-advanced students who need additional practice with punctuating dialogue, see **Chapter 24** in *English Workshop, Second Course,* pp. 269–272.

rules for punctuating dialogue. You may want to use some of the exercises in **Chapter 27: "Punctuation"** before students begin proofreading their work.

Allow students to work in pairs to proofread their stories. Have each student use a different color pen than his or her partner to make comments on the other's story. Have students publish their final products after they decide on publication choices.

The third reflection question offers an opportunity for students to review character-development techniques. Close the lesson by asking volunteers to read their answers to this question to the class.

- Illustrate your story with drawings or magazine photos, make a classroom short story collection, and give it to the school library.
- Volunteer to read your story aloud to someone who does not read or see well.

WRITING ASSIGNMENT

PART 7:
Proofreading and Publishing Your Story

Carefully proofread your revised story, and give your final copy a once-over, too. Share your story with friends and family, or find another way to publish it.

 Reflecting on Your Writing

Your story will make a good addition to your **portfolio.** To include it, write a brief reflection by responding to the questions below. Remember to date your story and reflection.

- Which aspect of your story did you decide on first: characters, setting, or plot? Why?
- Did you use a story map? Why or why not?
- Which techniques did you use to make your characters seem real? What else could you do to make the characters more realistic?

A STUDENT MODEL

Imagining can get you everywhere and anywhere, as Amey Horse Looking shows in the following passages from her story. A student at Dakota Junior High School in Rapid City, South Dakota, Amey says her ideas come from her imagination and that "once I get started I can't stop."

QUOTATION FOR THE DAY

"Heedless of grammar, they all cried, 'That's him!'" (Rev. R. H. Barham, 1788–1845, English humorist)

Remind students that people speak more informally than they write and that to make dialogue sound realistic they can use what people actually say—even if it is grammatically incorrect.

COOPERATIVE LEARNING

You may want to have your students meet in small groups to plan how they want to publish their work. Each group could make different publishing decisions and be responsible for planning their publications or oral readings.

TECHNOLOGY TIP

Tell students to make notes about artwork while they are getting ready to publish their stories. After they have finished writing their final revisions, let them experiment with a graphics program on a computer to add an artistic flair to their papers.

TEACHING NOTE

Tell students that the reflection process will provide them with insights that may also be helpful for peer-review sessions. Reflection also gives students experience in asking the same types of questions that professional writers ask as they write stories.

Evaluate the mechanical correctness of your students' proofread stories, focusing on their punctuation of dialogue. Assess the final drafts before students publish their stories.

Ask students what they should look for when they proofread [errors in mechanics, grammar, and usage]. Then ask them to name at least two ways to publish their stories [illustrate and publish a collection, read the story orally]. ■

Proofreading and Publishing   **217**

The Dream
by Amey Horse Looking

The wind blew through her hair while she was walking in the meadow. The flowers were so irresistible that she picked some and then she heard a sound like someone saying something but the person was running. She could hear the heavy footsteps coming. She looked around frantically and started to run until she entered the forest and looked around her.

. . . As she ventured deeper and deeper in the forest, she saw a little cabin with a light on and smoke coming out of the chimney. She knew she must go somewhere safe because she felt that something or someone was following her.

Just then, she felt cold, cold hands running up her shoulders. She was so horrified she did not think to look around and she fainted. It was hours before she awoke; she was not harmed or hurt—she was lying in a strange bed.
. . . As she turned around, she saw a kind old man sitting in a rocking chair. His hair was very stringy with streaks of gray. The wrinkles of his face were like ripples of water. His eyes were a majestic gray. The lips of his face were faded pink. The weird thing that she could not understand was what a kind old man was doing in the deep part of the forest.

As the day passed, she decided to stay with the man until he drove into town the next day. That night, she lay in her bed. Suddenly, she heard a chopping sound, the strange noise she had heard in the meadow. Then she heard a lot of racket and the sound of heavy feet walking toward the door, frightening her. She called for the old man but could not find him. When she opened the back door, she was surprised because she saw the old man moving toward her in a fierce way. Just then, she woke up from her dream as her mother called her for breakfast.

As she was eating, she pushed the bowl of oatmeal back and looked out the window and saw the same man walking by and looking at her while laughing. She figured her dream was true.

A STUDENT MODEL
Evaluation

1. Amey presents in her opening paragraph a main character in an interesting conflict.
2. Amey's "dead, gray, and foggy" forest helps to set the mood. Her use of vivid sensory details, such as "crackling of twigs" and "cold, cold hands running up her shoulders," adds to the suspense.
3. The characters Amey has created seem believable in her setting of fantasy.
4. Amey uses the third-person point of view throughout her story.

A DIFFERENT APPROACH
This chapter began with an emphasis on storytelling as both an oral and a written art. To bring the experience of hearing, reading, and writing stories full circle, give students an opportunity to read their stories to an audience. The audience might be a group of four or five students, an entire class, or an assembly of two or three classes. Remind students to use appropriate voice tones and gestures (verbal and nonverbal language) to show how characters feel. You may want to refer students who are planning to present their stories orally to **Chapter 30: "Speaking."**

WRITING WORKSHOP

OBJECTIVES

- To analyze a narrative poem
- To use the writing process to write a narrative poem

TEACHING THE LESSON

Ask students if they think all poetry is serious and formal. Do they realize that poetry can be written for fun or to tell a story? Explain that a narrative poem like this one tells a story.

Then read **"Jimmy Jet and His TV Set"** to students and use the annotations and the **Thinking It Over** questions to guide

WRITING WORKSHOP

A Narrative Poem

Poems can tell stories, too, and when they do, they're called *narrative poems.* In fact, narrative poems may be one of the first ways stories were passed around—before writing and books—because poetry's rhythms make memorization easier. (Have you noticed how people say even the Pledge of Allegiance in a singsong way?)

Like stories, narrative poems can have characters, conflict, setting, and theme. Unlike stories, poems may have musical rhythm (whether a regular or loose beat) and rhyme (but poems don't have to rhyme). Poems also usually have very strong word-pictures (poets love sensory words!).

Here's a narrative poem that builds, line by line, an unusual picture. Where do you think the poet got his idea for this story?

Jimmy Jet and His TV Set
by Shel Silverstein

1 I'll tell you the story of Jimmy Jet—
2 And you know what I tell you is true.
   He loved to watch his TV set
3 Almost as much as you.

4 He watched all day, he watched all night
   Till he grew pale and lean,
   From "The Early Show" to "The Late Late Show"
   And all the shows between.

USING THE SELECTION
Jimmy Jet and His TV Set

1

The poem is narrated in the first-person point of view.

2

By addressing the reader as *you,* the speaker implies a connection between the reader and Jimmy; thus, the narrative of what happens to Jimmy is a lesson for the reader.

3

In this stanza, the rhyme scheme is *abab.*

4

Here and elsewhere in the poem, the poet uses exaggeration and absurd imagery to achieve humor.

your discussion of Silverstein's poem. As guided practice for the writing assignment, you may want to work with the class to write a few lines of a narrative poem.

Have students independently write their poems. You will probably want to circulate among your students to answer questions and make suggestions as they work.

ASSESSMENT

Because criticism can often destroy students' interest in writing poetry, take care when evaluating their work. You may want to try a contract system for creative writing and base grades on completion.

☞

219

5 He watched till his eyes were frozen wide,
And his bottom grew into his chair.
And his chin turned into a tuning dial,
And antennae grew out of his hair.

And his brain turned into TV tubes,
And his face to a TV screen.
And two knobs saying "VERT." and "HORIZ."
Grew where his ears had been.

And he grew a plug that looked like a tail
6 So we plugged in little Jim.
And now instead of him watching TV
We all sit around and watch him.

Thinking It Over

1. Well, Jimmy Jet is certainly a character with a problem. What is it? (What causes the narrative's events?) What do you think of the poem's outcome?
2. At which line did you suspect something fantastic was happening?
3. In each group of lines (called a *stanza*), which lines rhyme? How many beats do you hear in each line? How would you describe the feeling, or tone, that the rhyme and rhythm give the poem?
4. In this poem, the narrator is a character. How can you tell? Make a guess about who he (or she) is.
5. Does this funny poem have a message? Explain.

5
The poet begins to create a strong visual picture of the transformation.

6
The use of *we* clarifies that the speaker is a member of Jimmy's family.

ANSWERS
Thinking It Over

Answers may vary.

1. Jimmy watches television all the time. Students may find the outcome amusing.
2. The second line hints that something fantastic will happen. The ninth line makes it obvious.
3. The first and third and the second and fourth lines rhyme in the first stanza. After that, only the second and fourth lines rhyme. The rhythm of the poem is not uniform. It ranges from three to four feet per line. The rhyme and rhythm give the poem a humorous tone.
4. The narrator uses first person. The last line implies that the narrator is a family member.
5. Yes, one shouldn't watch too much television.

SELECTION AMENDMENT
Description of change: modified
Rationale: to focus on the concept of creative writing presented in this chapter

220

MEETING individual NEEDS

LEP/ESL

General Strategies. The musical rhythm and word sounds of poetry might be easier for students to write in their first languages than in English, so you may want to let students decide for themselves which language they prefer for their narrative poems. Allow students with the same first languages to consult with one another.

INTEGRATING THE LANGUAGE ARTS

Literature Link. Writing narrative poems is a good way to reintroduce students to reading narrative poems. Assign poems such as Henry Wadsworth Longfellow's "Paul Revere's Ride" or Ernest Lawrence Thayer's "Casey at the Bat."

COOPERATIVE LEARNING

Allow students to work in groups of three to evaluate, revise, and proofread their poems.

220

Writing a Narrative Poem

Prewriting. What you learned about story ideas holds true for narrative poems. They can be fantastic or about everyday life. Choose a story about yourself or someone you know or have heard or read about. Then, in a small group, brainstorm narrative poem ideas. Choose the idea you like best, and jot down details to develop your plot and characters.

Writing, Evaluating, and Revising. You can write with rhyme or without it—whichever seems comfortable. And you also have choices in rhyme patterns (look at a few different poems). The rhythm can use regular beats or be more free: Just make it pleasing to your ears.

Remember to show rather than tell, using specific nouns, lively verbs, and descriptive modifiers. Break your poem into lines and stanzas where breaks seem natural.

Read your poem aloud to see how it sounds. Then, swap poems with a classmate, and give each other suggestions.

Proofreading and Publishing. Correct all spelling, and check to see that your punctuation helps readers pause and stop in the right places. Hold a "Storyteller's Day" in class, but practice reading aloud first.

To add your narrative poem to your **portfolio,** date it and attach a note of reflection that answers the following questions. Did you write a fantastic poem or a realistic one? Why? How did you choose the rhyme and rhythm patterns you used?

LESSON 8 *(p. 221)*
MAKING CONNECTIONS

A LEGEND OR MYTH OBJECTIVE

• To write a myth or legend that explains the origin of something

VISUAL STORIES OBJECTIVE

• To write a story based on a photograph

221

MAKING CONNECTIONS

A Legend or Myth

Myths and *legends* are traditional stories that explain something about the world. They usually involve gods or other supernatural beings. For example, because people everywhere have similar questions about nature, most cultures have myths that explain the cycles of sun and moon, the presence of stars in the sky. "The Sound of Flutes" (pages 186–192) is a traditional Native American legend. It has a bird that communicates with a man, and it explains how the Plains Indians invented the flute.

Try writing a myth that explains why something is the way it is. Start by thinking about the world around you, and brainstorm some questions you'd like to explain in a fun and imaginative way. For example:

- Why do cats chase mice?
- Why do flowers smell sweet?
- Why do people kiss?

Visual Stories

There is an old saying that one picture is worth a thousand words. But maybe that isn't so—maybe one picture can *stimulate* a thousand words! For this activity, begin by finding a photograph or a painting that grabs your imagination. (The photograph can be one you've taken yourself or one you find in a newspaper or magazine.) What story can you write about the moment captured in the picture? Here are some questions to help you plan.

- Who is in the picture? And why?
- What can you tell about the character(s) from the setting?
- What happens to the character(s)? What's the conflict?

A LEGEND OR MYTH
Teaching Strategies

You might review the details of the beginning story, **"The Sound of Flutes,"** and discuss the elements of a myth that it contains. If time allows, read myths from other cultures that explain things from nature.

Remind students to include a hero or heroine, a guide or supernatural figure, and an explanation about nature or some common object as they create their myths. You might also point out that because many myths involve quests, students might base their plots upon similar searches.

GUIDELINES

Myths will vary, but the best ones will have creative settings, interesting plots, and vivid characters. They should begin with trying problems that set the characters in motion and end by explaining something about nature.

VISUAL STORIES
Teaching Strategies

Have students work in groups to discuss pictures and share ideas. After students complete their stories, post the stories on a bulletin board for others to read.

GUIDELINES

Stories should have strong character development and conflict.

Chapter 7

WRITING TO INFORM: EXPOSITION

OBJECTIVES

- To identify the characteristics and appropriate uses of a "how-to" process essay
- To list steps and materials for explaining a process
- To arrange information in chronological order and evaluate details for explaining a process
- To organize and draft a "how-to" process essay
- To evaluate and revise, proofread and publish a process essay

WRITING-IN-PROGRESS ASSIGNMENTS

Major Assignment: Writing to inform
Cumulative Writing Assignments: The chart below shows the sequence of cumulative assignments that will guide students as they write an informative essay. These Writing Assignments form the instructional core of Chapter 7.

PREWRITING

WRITING ASSIGNMENT
- Part 1: Choosing a Topic to Explain p. 230
- Part 2: Planning Your Instructions p. 235

WRITING YOUR FIRST DRAFT

WRITING ASSIGNMENT
- Part 3: Writing a Draft of Your Set of Instructions p. 244

EVALUATING AND REVISING

WRITING ASSIGNMENT
- Part 4: Evaluating and Revising Your "Instructions" Paper p. 247

PROOFREADING AND PUBLISHING

WRITING ASSIGNMENT
- Part 5: Proofreading and Publishing Your Paper p. 248

In addition, exercises 1–7 provide practice in matching topic and audience, exploring possible topics, listing steps and materials, arranging information in chronological order, analyzing a set of instructions, analyzing a writer's revisions, and explaining instructions.

cross CURRICULUM

"How-to" Create a Work of Art

Invite teachers from the art department to join with you in a shared art/language arts project for which students will create both a work of art and a video explaining to their classmates how to create a specific work of art. Tell students they are to present, with their art teachers' input, a demonstration—such as tie-dyeing, throwing a pot, designing a holiday card on the computer, or making batik or candles.

- **Cooperative Learning** Assign students to groups of three to create three four-minute video demonstrations. Until each person has worked in each position, students will take turns as
  - scriptwriter
  - artist
  - camera person

Once the artists have worked out the process, they must work with the writers to create a clear, time-limited script that will include all the necessary directions and explanations. The artist must then decide how much time can be allotted to demonstrating each part of the process and exactly what should be filmed. The artists may choose to speak as they demonstrate or, if that is impractical, to provide voice-over instructions.

- **Assessment** Explain to students that their art teachers will assess the actual artwork, but that you will evaluate how effectively they have explained and demonstrated the process.

- **Publishing** After the videos have been shown in your class, ask students' permission to add the tapes to the school or art class film library to be used as lessons for future art projects or as examples of "how-to" demonstrations for the language arts classes.

INTEGRATING THE LANGUAGE ARTS

SELECTION	READING AND LITERATURE	WRITING AND CRITICAL THINKING	LANGUAGE AND SYNTAX	SPEAKING, LISTENING, AND OTHER EXPRESSION SKILLS
• **What to Do in a Wilderness Medical Emergency** by Dave Barry pp. 224–226 • from **Science Crafts for Kids** by Gwen Diehn and Terry Krautwurst pp. 238–241 • **"A Cautionary Tale"** by Billy Goodman pp 250–251	• Identifying purpose p. 226 • Identifying supporting details pp. 226, 251 • Recognizing elements of style p. 241 • Identifying order of events p. 241 • Locating and interpreting information p. 241 • Interpreting author's intention p. 251 • Distinguishing cause from effect p. 251 • Identifying probable cause and effects p. 251	• Selecting topics of personal interest pp 229–230 • Writing a thesis statement geared to a specific audience p. 230 • Explaining a procedure p. 233 • Assembling information in chronological order pp. 233, 234, 241 • Identifying relevant details p. 235 • Evaluating and revising a draft of an essay pp. 244, 246, 252 • Participating in peer editing conferences p. 247 • Analyzing a writer's revisions pp. 246, 247 • Using clustering and mapping as prewritng techniques in a cause-effect paper p. 252	• Analyzing sentence structure p. 246 • Using prepositional phrases effectively p. 247 • Proofreading for spelling, punctuation, and usage errors p. 248	• Contributing ideas in brainstorming and speaking in a group pp. 229, 233 • Listening to others carefully pp. 229, 246, 247 • Using charts and available information to solve problems pp. 244, 245, 247 • Making an oral presentation to a small group pp. 246–247 • Writing reflections for portfolio selections p. 248 • Role-playing and using process analysis p. 253 • Taking and giving messages with completeness and accuracy p. 253

SUGGESTED INTEGRATED UNIT PLAN

This unit plan suggests how to integrate the major strands of the language arts with this chapter.

If you begin with this chapter on writing to inform or with literary selections like the following, you should focus on the common characteristics of process writing. You might point out that the process, whether it involves escaping from slavery or saving endangered animals, can be found in all types of literature because step-by-step processes are part of daily living. You can then integrate speaking/listening and language concepts with both the writing and the literature.

Common Characteristics

- Content is mainly factual and comprehensive.
- Precise language is neutral and unbiased.
- Possibly technical terms with definitions
- Chronological or step organization
- Likely use of second person

Writing
"How-to" Process

**UNIT FOCUS
PROCESS WRITING**

Language
Usage, Style

- Imperative sentences
- Transitional words
- Varied sentences

Literature:
Fiction/Nonfiction/Poetry

- "The Dogs Could Teach Me" Gary Paulsen
- "Birdfoot's Grampa" Joseph Bruchac
- "Brer Possum's Dilemma" Jackie Torrence
- "They Call Her Moses" Ann Petry

Speaking/Listening

- Oral explanation and demonstration of process
- Role-playing and using process analysis
- Taking and giving messages accurately

CHAPTER 7: WRITING TO INFORM: EXPOSITION

Use this guide for creating an instructional plan that addresses the individual needs of your students. Assignments accompanied by the following symbol (*) may be completed out of class. Times given for pacing lessons are estimated.

CHAPTER PLANNING GUIDE—PUPIL'S EDITION

| LESSONS | LITERARY MODEL pp. 224–226 from "What to Do in a Wilderness Medical Emergency" by Dave Barry | PREWRITING pp. 228–235 | |
		Generating Ideas	Gathering/Organizing
DEVELOPMENTAL PROGRAM	🕐 **20–25 minutes** • Have students do a pop-corn reading of the model and answer questions p. 226 orally.	🕐 **40–45 minutes** • Ways to Inform p. 227 • Main Assignment: Looking Ahead p. 227 • Choosing a Product or Procedure to Explain p. 228 • Exercises 1, 2 p. 229 in groups • Writing Assignment: Part 1 p. 230*	🕐 **30–35 minutes** • Gathering and Organizing Your Information pp. 231–234 • Exercise 3 p. 233 • Reminder p. 234 • Exercise 4 p. 234* • Writing Assignment: Part 2 p. 235*
CORE PROGRAM	🕐 **30–35 minutes** • Assign student pairs to read model and discuss answers to questions p. 226.	🕐 **20–25 minutes** • Ways to Inform p. 227 • Main Assignment: Looking Ahead p. 227 • Choosing a Product or Procedure to Explain p. 228* • Exercise 2 p. 229 • Writing Assignment: Part 1 p. 230*	🕐 **25–30 minutes** • Gathering and Organizing Your Information pp. 231–234* • Reminder p. 234 • Critical Thinking p. 235* • Writing Assignment: Part 2 p. 235*
ACCELERATED PROGRAM	🕐 **10–15 minutes** • Have students read model independently.	🕐 **10–15 minutes** • Ways to Inform p. 227 • Main Assignment: Looking Ahead p. 227 • Choosing a Product or Procedure to Explain p. 228* • Writing Assignment: Part 1 p. 230*	🕐 **15–20 minutes** • Reminder p. 234 • Critical Thinking p. 235* • Writing Assignment: Part 2 p. 235*

CHAPTER PLANNING GUIDE—PROGRAM RESOURCES

	LITERARY MODEL	PREWRITING
PRINT	• Reading Master 7, *Practice for Assessment in Reading, Vocabulary, and Spelling* p. 7	• Prewriting, *Strategies for Writing* p. 26
MEDIA	• Fine Art Transparency 4: *The Banjo Lesson, Transparency Binder*	• Graphic Organizers 11 and 12: *Transparency Binder* • *Writer's Workshop 1:* Cause and Effect

WRITING pp. 236–244	EVALUATING AND REVISING pp. 245–247	PROOFREADING AND PUBLISHING pp. 248–249
🕐 **25–30 minutes** • Instructions pp. 236–237 • A Writer's Model pp. 242–243 • Writing Note p. 243 • Framework p. 244 • Writing Assignment: Part 3 p. 244*	🕐 **40–45 minutes** • Evaluating and Revising Instructions Chart p. 245 • Exercises 6*, 7 pp. 246–247 • Grammar Hint p. 247 • Writing Assignment: Part 4 p. 247	🕐 **40–45 minutes** • Proofreading and Publishing p. 248 • Writing Assignment: Part 5 p. 248 • Reflecting p. 248 • A Student Model p. 249
🕐 **30–35 minutes** • Instructions pp. 236–237 • A Passage from a Book pp. 238–241* • Writing Note p. 241 • Exercise 5 p. 241* • Framework p. 244 • Reminder p. 244 • Writing Assignment: Part 3 p. 244*	🕐 **30–35 minutes** • Evaluating and Revising Instructions Chart p. 245 • Grammar Hint p. 247 • Writing Assignment: Part 4 p. 247	🕐 **20–25 minutes** • Proofreading and Publishing p. 248 • Writing Assignment: Part 5 p. 248 • Reflecting p. 248 • A Student Model p. 249*
🕐 **20–25 minutes** • Instructions pp. 236–237 • A Passage from a Book pp. 238–241* • Writing Note p. 241 • Framework p. 244 • Writing Assignment: Part 3 p. 244*	🕐 **20–25 minutes** • Evaluating and Revising Instructions Chart p. 245 • Writing Assignment: Part 4 p. 247	🕐 **20–25 minutes** • Proofreading and Publishing p. 248 • Writing Assignment: Part 5 p. 248 • Reflecting p. 248

 Computer disk or CD-ROM   Overhead transparencies

WRITING	EVALUATING AND REVISING	PROOFREADING AND PUBLISHING
• Writing, *Strategies for Writing* p. 27 • *English Workshop* p. 261	• Evaluating and Revising, *Strategies for Writing* p. 28 • *English Workshop* pp. 213–214	• Proofreading Practice: Using Prepositional Phrases, *Strategies for Writing* p. 30
• *Language Workshop:* Lesson 40	• Revision Transparencies 11–12, *Transparency Binder*	• *Language Workshop:* Lesson 6

 **ELEMENTS OF WRITING: CURRICULUM CONNECTIONS**

Writing Workshop
• The Cause-and-Effect Essay pp. 250–252

Speaking and Listening
• Health: Emergency Directions p. 253

ASSESSMENT OPTIONS

Summative Assessment
Holistic Scoring: Prompts and Models
pp. 21–26

Performance Assessment
Integrated Performance Assessment Level C
For help with evaluating student
writing, see *Holistic Scoring Workshop 2.*

Portfolio Assessment
Portfolio forms, *Portfolio Assessment*
pp. 5–24, 38–43

Reflection
Writing Process Log, *Strategies for Writing*
p. 25

Ongoing Assessment
Proofreading, *Strategies for Writing* p. 29

WORKING AND PLAYING

OBJECTIVES

- To evaluate the use of humor in a set of instructions
- To identify elements that signal an author's purpose

MOTIVATION

Have each student write instructions explaining how to get from school to a store, movie theater, or playground. Then, pair students and ask them to take turns giving their instructions to their partners. Partners should tell each other whether they think they could find the way by following the instructions.

PROGRAM MANAGER

CHAPTER 7

- **Computer Guided Instruction** For a related assignment that students may use for additional instruction and practice, see **Cause and Effect** in *Writer's Workshop 1 CD-ROM.*

- **Practice** To help less-advanced students who need additional practice with concepts and activities related to this chapter, see **Chapter 6** in *English Workshop, Second Course,* pp. 45–52.

- **Summative Assessment** For a writing prompt, including grading criteria and student models, see *Holistic Scoring: Prompts and Models,* pp. 21–26.

- **Performance Assessment** Use **Assessment 2** in *Integrated Performance Assessment, Level C.* For help with evaluating student writing, see *Holistic Scoring Workshop, Level C.*

- **Extension/Enrichment** See **Fine Art Transparency 4,** *The Banjo Lesson* by Henry Ossawa Tanner. For instructional suggestions, review teacher's notes in *Fine Art and Instructional Transparencies for Writing,* p. 21.

- **Reading Support** For help with the reading selection, pp. 224–226, see **Reading Master 7** in *Practice for Assessment in Reading, Vocabulary, and Spelling,* p. 7.

7 WRITING TO INFORM: EXPOSITION

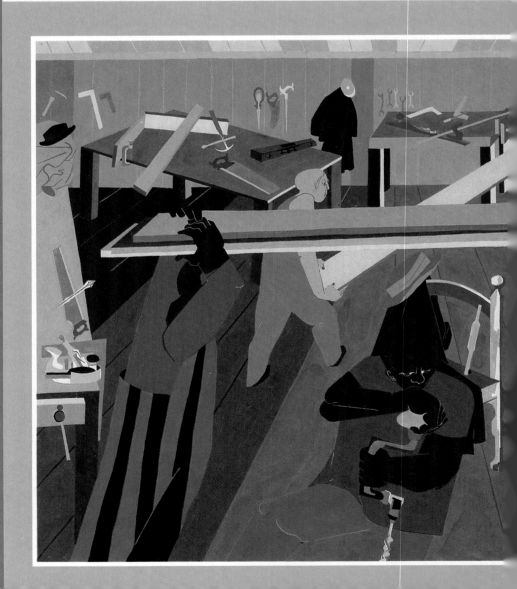

After a volunteer reads the opening paragraphs, have the class list what instructions others have given them, such as how to do a dance, ride a bicycle, or play a sport. Ask what directions they anticipate needing in the future. [Possibilities include how to drive a car, schedule classes, apply for a job, and plan a budget.]

Have a volunteer read aloud "**What to Do in a Wilderness Medical Emergency**" by Dave Barry on pp. 224–226. Point out to students that although this is a humorous essay, it does give step-by-step instructions. Much of its humor comes from the fact that people recognize what instructions look like.

☞

Working and Playing

When was a big INFORMATION sign a great relief for you? Were you in a subway station, a sports arena, a museum? People couldn't get through life without information, and that's why we're always sharing it—everything from world news to baseball scores. And because **working and playing** are such big parts of life, we often give instructions for how to use something or how to do something.

Writing and You. Everywhere you look, writers are giving you instructions. In a magazine, you learn how to save money on clothes. On television, you learn how to build a birdhouse. Have you followed any instructions today?

As You Read. In the following essay, humorist Dave Barry tells you how to deal with a medical emergency in the wilderness. Do you think he wants you to take his directions seriously?

Jacob Lawrence, *The Builders No.1* (1970). Henry Art Gallery, University of Washington, Seattle. Gift of the artist.

VISUAL CONNECTIONS
The Builders No. 1

About the Artist. Jacob Lawrence was born on September 7, 1917, in Atlantic City, New Jersey. He is an African American painter whose art portrays the life and history of African Americans. When he was thirteen, Lawrence moved to Harlem in New York City. In free art classes, he developed a talent for making lively colored masks. Lawrence is noted for his use of stylized patterns, abstract designs, and bright colors. He uses browns and black for outlines in an otherwise vibrant palette. Like *The Builders No. 1*, most of Lawrence's paintings have human subjects.

Lawrence has painted several historical series consisting of a number of paintings put together to depict a broad topic. These series include the 40-panel *The Life of Harriet Tubman* and the 60-panel *The Migration of the Negro*. Many people have seen in Lawrence's paintings the theme of the perseverance of the human spirit in the face of adversity.

GUIDED PRACTICE

Guide students through the first question in **Reader's Response** and the second question in **Writer's Craft.**

INDEPENDENT PRACTICE

Assign the second question in **Reader's Response** and the first question in **Writer's Craft** as independent practice. Encourage students to give strong supporting evidence for each of their ideas about the **Writer's Craft** question.

MEETING *individual* NEEDS

LEP/ESL

General Strategies. Humor is so culture-bound that it is rare for members of various cultures to enjoy the same jokes. Dave Barry's article might seem quite humorless to some students. To give both English-language learners and English-proficient speakers insight into American culture, discuss the humor in Barry's article.

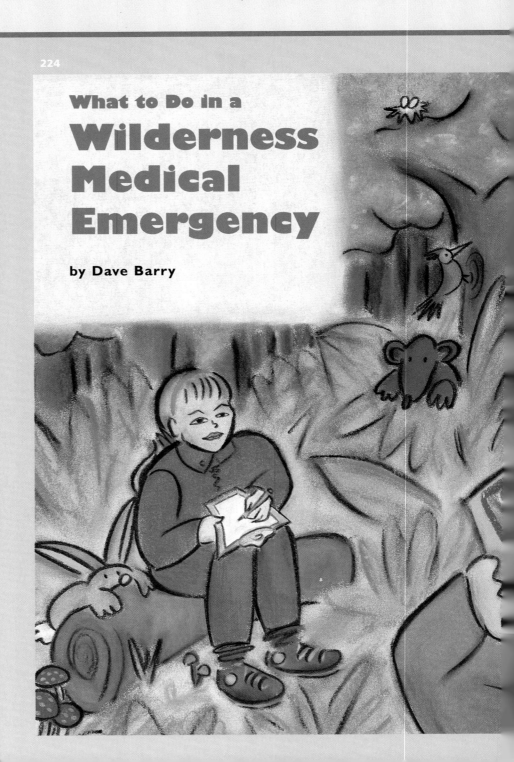

224

What to Do in a Wilderness Medical Emergency

by Dave Barry

ASSESSMENT

Evaluate students' answers to the **Writer's Craft** questions to assess students' ability to identify elements that establish and support the writer's purpose. Volunteers can share their lists of situations and settings from the second question in **Reader's Response**.

RETEACHING

Give students a sample of instructions published in a local newspaper or a "how-to" magazine. Guide them through identifying the steps given in the instructions and any helpful hints that are included.

☛

225

1 **E**xperts agree that the most important rule in a wilderness medical emergency is: *Keep your head down on the follow-through.* No! My mistake! That's the most important rule in *golf*. The most important rule in a wilderness medical emergency is: *Don't panic.* To prevent the victim from going into shock, you must reassure him, as calmly as possible, that everything's going to be fine:

> VICTIM (*clearly frightened*): Am I going to be okay?
>
> YOU (*in a soothing voice*): Of course you are! I'm sure we'll find your legs around here someplace!
>
> VICTIM (*relieved*): Whew! You got any Cheez-Its?

2 Once the victim has been calmed, you need to obtain pertinent information by asking the following Standard Medical Questions:

3 1. Does he have medical insurance?
   2. Does his spouse have medical insurance?
   3. Was he referred to this wilderness by another doctor?
   4. How much does he weigh?
   5. Does that figure include legs?

Write this information down on a medical chart; then give the victim a 1986 copy of *Fortune* magazine to read while you
4 decide on the correct course of treatment. This will depend

USING THE SELECTION
What to Do in a Wilderness Medical Emergency

1

Why does Barry open his essay the way he does? [to establish a humorous tone that lets readers know the title shouldn't be taken literally]

2

The writer begins giving the steps in the order in which they are to be done.

3

What is ironic about the "Standard Medical Questions"? [The first three have nothing to do with medicine or the patient but everything to do with the health-care system. The last two are irrelevant and absurd.]

4

Why does Barry specify an old magazine? [He pokes fun at those who think doctors only have old magazines in their waiting rooms.]

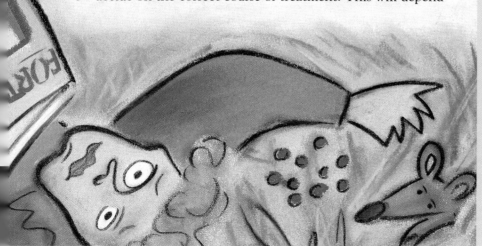

225

CLOSURE

Ask students to enumerate the steps Barry describes that are involved in a wilderness medical emergency.

ENRICHMENT

You may want to have students make drawings, cartoons, or collages to illustrate Barry's **"What to Do in a Wilderness Medical Emergency."** ■

226

on the exact nature of the injury. For example, if it's mushroom poisoning or a broken limb, you'll need to apply a tourniquet. Whereas if it's a snake bite, then you need to determine whether the snake was poisonous, which will be indicated by tiny markings on the snake's stomach as follows:

WARNING: POISON SNAKE!

ACHTUNG! SCHLANGE SCHNAPPENKILLEN!

In this case, you need to apply a tourniquet to the snake, as shown in Figure 1.

Figure I. Putting a tourniquet on a snake

1. Have snake lie down.

wrong

right

2. Apply tourniquet to snake's body.

wrong

right

from *Dave Barry's Only Travel Guide You'll Ever Need*

ANSWERS

Reader's Response

Responses will vary.

1. Have students explain their preferences.

2. Situations or settings should be described in enough detail that the humor in them comes through.

Writer's Craft

Answers may vary.

3. Barry confuses medicine with sports, signaling that he is no authority on wilderness medical emergencies and that the instructions he will give are not to be taken seriously.

4. He uses expressions that are often found in real first-aid instructions, such as "the most important rule . . . is . . .," what to do after "the victim has been calmed," how to handle the information that is gleaned from the "Standard Medical Questions," and how to decide on a "course of treatment."

SELECTION AMENDMENT
Description of change: excerpted
Rationale: to focus on the concept of informative writing presented in this chapter

226

READER'S RESPONSE

1. Which step in "What to Do in a Wilderness Medical Emergency" do you think is the funniest? the least funny? Why?
2. What other situations or settings can you think of that could be turned into a funny story?

WRITER'S CRAFT

3. Dave Barry's purpose isn't really to inform, but to use his imagination to entertain you. How does Barry's first sentence signal that he is not going to provide serious instructions?
4. Although you know early on that Barry is not being serious, what words and phrases does he use that make his instructions sound like real ones you have read?

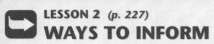

You may want to have a volunteer read aloud the material that gives an overview of the different ways to share information. Then, explain that the examples deal with five different methods students can use to present information. These methods are narration (examples 1 and 2), description (examples 3 and 4), comparison/contrast (example 5), definition (example 6), and evaluation (examples 7 and 8).

Then, ask students to look through their literature books to find some examples of writing to inform, and ask them to identify the methods used. Reiterate that instructions are written using narration. ∎

227

Ways to Inform

In this chapter, you'll focus on a way of writing to inform: giving instructions. But this is only one of many ways to share information. Here are some examples of how you can write to inform.

- in a presentation to a photography club, telling how to take good pictures with a specific camera model
- in a note to your younger brother, telling how to buy clothes on a budget
- in a notice on a bulletin board, describing your lost jacket so that teachers and fellow students will recognize it
- in a paper for science class, describing the inside of a beehive
- in a letter to a friend, explaining the differences between writing with a word processor and writing with a typewriter
- in an essay, writing about the meaning of *self-reliance*
- in a movie review, evaluating how well a film's music fits the action
- in a report to the school board, explaining how a computer lab will benefit students

LOOKING AHEAD

In this chapter's main assignment, you'll use narration to give instructions. You will write about how to use or do something. As you work, keep in mind that a paper giving instructions

- tells readers how to use a product or follow a procedure
- discusses all necessary materials and steps
- defines any terms the audience may not understand

A DIFFERENT APPROACH

To demonstrate how an informative essay could be written in different ways, give your students the following list of topics. Ask them to identify the method of development in each case.

1. describing a set of in-line skates to a friend [description]
2. explaining the differences and similarities between two brands of in-line skates [comparison/contrast]
3. explaining how to purchase a pair of in-line skates [narration]
4. explaining to a parent why in-line skates are a good form of transportation [evaluation]

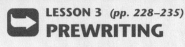

LESSON 3 *(pp. 228–235)*
PREWRITING

OBJECTIVES

• To match topic and audience
• To explore possible topics
• To choose a topic for a set of instructions
• To list steps and materials
• To arrange information in chronological order
• To gather and organize information for a paper giving instructions for a product or procedure

PROGRAM MANAGER

PREWRITING

■ **Self-Assessment** Before beginning instruction of the writing process, see **Writing Process Log** in *Strategies for Writing,* p. 25.

■ **Analyzing** To help students analyze and organize ideas, see **Prewriting** in *Strategies for Writing,* p. 26.

■ **Instructional Support** See **Graphic Organizers 11** and **12**. For suggestions on how to tie the transparencies to instruction, review teacher's notes in *Fine Art and Instructional Transparencies for Writing,* pp. 67, 69.

 QUOTATION FOR THE DAY

"In a very real sense, the writer writes in order to teach himself." (Alfred Kazin, 1915–   , literary critic)

Tell students that as they explain a process, they will probably learn more about it. Explain that in teaching others, one also makes discoveries.

Writing Instructions

 *Prewriting*

Choosing a Product or Procedure to Explain

Instructions explain a process—how to use something or how to do something. A set of instructions may be a few lines on a package of frozen food that explain how to cook it. Or they may form a thousand-page manual that accompanies a powerful computer. For many people in the workplace, writing instructions is a regular part of the job. But you don't have to be an expert to write instructions. Do you know how to perform basic dives from a springboard, operate a VCR, or use a computer? Can you take especially good pictures, make spaghetti, or change a bicycle tire? Brainstorm a list of things you know how to do, or products you know how to use. Then, to narrow down your list, think about your purpose and audience.

Thinking About Purpose

Remember that your purpose is to inform readers about how to use a product or perform a procedure. If your paper succeeds, your readers will learn a new skill. If you explain how to whittle a duck out of wood, for instance, your readers should come away knowing how to make a wooden duck.

Thinking About Audience

Make sure your topic fits your audience. If you're writing for wilderness explorers, don't waste time telling them how to follow trail markers. Think of something your audience might not know and may want to learn how to do.

Ask students to think of times when they have taught people how to do things. Maybe a student taught a younger sibling how to ride a bike, showed a friend how to do French braiding, or showed someone how to hook up a stereo system. Tell students that any time someone explains how to do something, he or she is explaining a process. The reason for giving instructions is usually to share information about something.

☞

Reminder

To choose a topic for your set of instructions

- brainstorm (see page 27) a list of products you know how to use or things you like to do
- pick something you know or do well
- make sure your topic and your audience are a good match

EXERCISE 1 ▶ **Matching Topic and Audience**

Decide which topics are <u>suitable</u> or unsuitable for each audience. (More than one topic may work for some of the audiences.) Be ready to explain your choices.

1. Audience: Eighth-grade students
   Topics: How to repair a machine that stamps out plastic forks
   <u>How to get ready for school quickly</u>
   <u>How to fix a flat bicycle tire</u>
   How to tell time

2. Audience: Readers of a science fiction magazine
   Topics: How to arrange flowers
   <u>How to predict advances in transportation technology</u>
   How to join the Loyal Order of Moose
   <u>How filmmakers create fantasy characters and settings for movies</u>

EXERCISE 2 ▶ **Exploring Possible Topics**

Get together with three or four classmates to talk about what each of you might teach the others. Using the prompt, "One thing I do really well is _____," try to come up with at least three ideas for each person in the group. Now review your ideas: Which ones would you most like to learn? Which ones could you explain in a paragraph or short paper?

ANSWERS
Exercise 1

1. Suitable: How to get ready for school quickly; How to fix a flat tire (relevant to eighth-graders' lives)
   Unsuitable: How to repair a machine that stamps out plastic forks (for a specialized audience); How to tell time (for a younger audience)

2. Suitable: How to predict advances in transportation technology (something science fiction readers are interested in); How filmmakers create fantasy characters and settings for movies (something science fiction readers are interested in)
   Unsuitable: How to arrange flowers (not related to science fiction); How to join the Loyal Order of Moose (not related to science fiction)

ANSWERS
Exercise 2

Students should choose products or procedures that are interesting but fairly simple. Topics might be selected from students' hobbies or daily activities or from current events.

TEACHING THE LESSON

Have a volunteer read aloud the material on **Choosing a Topic to Explain** (below). Then, guide students through the first question in **Exercise 1**, p. 229, and assign the second question as independent practice. Divide the class into mixed-ability groups to work on **Exercise 2**, p. 229, and circulate among the groups to offer guidance as they explore possible topics. Then, assign **Writing Assignment: Part 1** as independent practice.

Read aloud the material on **Listing Steps and Materials**, p. 231, and have students discuss steps, materials, other information sources, and possible drawings for their set of instructions. Guide students through one process in **Exercise 3**, p. 233, and

COOPERATIVE LEARNING

Ask students to compile two lists of topics using the following categories:

1. things I know about (hobbies, sports, travel, jobs, school, and home)
2. things I want to know about

Compile a master list of responses on kraft paper and point out to students that in some cases they can serve as resources for each other. If one student knows how to do something that another student wants to learn, the second student could interview the first.

WRITING ASSIGNMENT

PART 1:
Choosing a Topic to Explain

You can explain how to use a product or to do a procedure that your group listed, or you can choose another one that you know or do well. Can you apply clown makeup? Can you tell young children how to use basic computer functions? Can you explain how to give a party? After you've picked your topic, write a sentence telling what you will explain. Also identify the audience for your paper.

Garfield copyright 1986 Paws, Inc. Distributed by Universal Press

Have students read **Organizing Your Information,** p. 233. Help students decide which is the first step in **Exercise 4,** p. 234, and have them complete the arranging as independent practice. After they finish the **Critical Thinking Exercise,** students should be well prepared to complete

Writing Assignment: Part 2 on p. 235 as independent practice.

Gathering and Organizing Your Information

Before you start writing, plan what you will say. Organized notes make writing much easier.

Listing Steps and Materials

A set of instructions gives two kinds of information. It tells readers, step by step, how to use a product or do a procedure; and it tells them what materials and equipment they need.

The amount and kind of information you give depend on your audience. Suppose that you want to explain how to make quesadillas. Are you writing for classmates preparing food for a school fair? Are you writing for people who think that cooking means microwaving a frozen dinner? Or are you writing for experienced cooks? Each audience knows different things about cooking and will need different information.

Drawing from Experience. Since you've done the process, you can draw most of your information from experience. Picture yourself going through the procedure or using the product. In your mind, break the task down into specific steps. What do you do first, second, and so on? What is the result of going through the process?

As you mentally "do" each step, think about the materials you're using. Take notes about any tools and supplies that you need. Also, jot down special terms—for example, *joystick, greasepaint, Phillips screwdriver*—so you'll remember to define them later.

You can use a three-column chart to record your information. Write each step in the first column, materials in the second, and terms in the third. Here's a chart one writer made for a paper giving instructions.

INTEGRATING THE LANGUAGE ARTS

Literature Link. If the selection is available in your literature textbook, have students read "To Build a Fire" by Jack London, in which the author explains a procedure in detail. Have them list the steps and materials for the procedure of building a fire as described in the story. Ask students how the procedure figures in the plot of the story. [The main character's life depends on his ability to successfully complete the procedure of building a fire.] How do the details of the procedure contribute to the tension in the story? [Suspense builds over whether he can light a match, light the birch bark, light the grass and twigs, and keep a fire going.]

You may want to have groups exchange papers for **Exercises 1, 3,** and **4.** Hold individual conferences to check **Writing Assignment: Part 1.** Use **Writing Assignment: Part 2** to assess students' mastery of the prewriting steps.

Bring in a recipe, a newspaper article, or a magazine article explaining a procedure. Ask students how each succeeds or fails as a set of instructions. Have them note the opening and closing, chronological steps, details, purpose, and audience appeal.

MEETING *individual* NEEDS

LEARNING STYLES

Auditory and Visual Learners. Challenge students to integrate auditory and visual elements into the preparation of their instructions. These elements might include music, brochures, charts, graphs, or drawings.

VISUAL CONNECTIONS

Exploring the Subject. The gymnast runs toward the horse vault and jumps up and forward from a springboard. After placing both hands on the horse for support, the gymnast can twist in the air, do a somersault, or execute any one of several movements. The horse vault resembles a pommel horse but has no handles (pommels).

232

---

232   *Writing to Inform*

How to Compost Garbage		
Steps	Materials	Terms
1. Collect garbage	Plastic jug	Organic garbage
2. Dig hole	Spade	
3. Dump garbage in hole		
4. Cover with fertilizer	Fertilizer	
5. Cover with dirt		
6. Spray with water	Garden hose	

Using Other Information Sources. As you take notes, you may find gaps in your knowledge. The library is the best place to do research. You may even find a "how-to" video on your topic. People can help, too. If you don't know anyone who can answer your question, look for an expert in the Yellow Pages. A plumber, for example, can tell you what tools to use to fix a leaky faucet.

Drawing Pictures to Show Steps. You can make some activities clearer by drawing diagrams of important steps. Look at common instructions (for model building or sewing, for instance), and you'll see how diagrams can help. As you go through your steps, decide whether pictures would help readers. (And if your procedure needs many pictures to be clear, pick another one. It's too hard!) Here's a diagram on performing a horse vault.

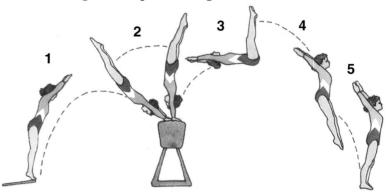

CLOSURE

Have students list the prewriting steps for a set of instructions. [Choose a product or procedure, determine audience, list steps and materials, do research, draw pictures, and organize information in chronological order.]

ENRICHMENT

Have each student pick a poem from a literature book and imagine that as the poet, he or she must explain how the work was written. Encourage students to explain the purpose of and audience for the poem and to describe the experience of writing the poem. ■

Prewriting **233**

EXERCISE 3 ▶ **Listing Steps and Materials**

You breeze through dozens of everyday procedures on automatic pilot. It sounds easy, right? But can you break them into clear steps? Get together with a group of classmates and break each of the following procedures into steps. Also list materials and any necessary equipment, and decide if you need drawings.

1. blow-drying or moussing your hair
2. changing a bicycle tire
3. making a grilled cheese sandwich
4. packing clothes and personal belongings for a move

Organizing Your Information

What's wrong with these directions for painting a room?

> Paint the ceiling first. Then do the walls. Keep the floor from getting paint on it. Use dropcloths to protect the furniture. Move the furniture away from the walls. Wear old clothes that you don't mind getting paint on.

Readers who followed these steps in order would have as much paint on floors, furniture, and clothes as on the walls. To keep readers on the right track (and clean), plan how you'll arrange your information—before you begin to write. To explain most processes, you begin by telling what materials will be needed. Then you put the steps in *chronological order*—the order in which the steps occur in time.

ANSWERS
Exercise 3

Responses will vary. Lists of steps and materials should be complete, and steps should be in chronological order. You may want to have groups exchange lists and evaluate each other's lists.

TIMESAVER

For a quick assessment of the groups' efforts for **Exercise 3**, appoint a student in each group to list all comments made. Reading through these lists will help you determine group progress.

MEETING individual NEEDS

LEP/ESL

General Strategies. English-language learners might take the textbook's instructions quite literally and list each step in a separate sentence. To help students achieve a readable style, show them how to write categorizing sentences or phrases that group steps. For example, the steps of washing a car could be grouped into washing steps and drying steps.

And once you start explaining how to do something, stay focused on the task. Include only the information that your audience needs to do the procedure or use the product. Unnecessary details distract and confuse readers. Cross out facts, examples, and descriptions that don't relate to the procedure or product.

Reminder

To plan a set of instructions

- list the steps readers should follow
- as you list steps, jot down materials and/or equipment, and terms to explain
- put the steps into chronological order
- cross out unnecessary information

 **EXERCISE 4** ▶ **Arranging Information in Chronological Order**

A ranger made some quick notes for campers about how to build a campfire. See if you can put these steps in the most efficient chronological order.

Set fire to newspaper.
Gather dead twigs for kindling.
● Buy newspaper at camp store.
Make twigs lean together like tepee poles over newspaper.
Crumple newspaper.
Sweep ground clear of anything that might burn.
Buy wood at camp store.
● When fire gets going, lay wood over kindling.

CRITICAL THINKING
(p. 235)

OBJECTIVE
• To evaluate details for a set of instructions

TEACHING *EVALUATING DETAILS*
Ask students to evaluate lists of details for a set of instructions and to provide a rationale for each choice. What criteria do they use in choosing some details and ignoring others? [Possible criteria include audience's prior knowledge, availability of materials, and similar cultural interests.]

Prewriting **235**

CRITICAL THINKING
Evaluating Details

Sometimes, too much detail in a set of instructions can overwhelm and confuse the reader. To decide if a detail is necessary in your instructions, ask yourself *Is this information that my audience already knows? Without this detail, could readers make a mistake?*

CRITICAL THINKING EXERCISE:
Evaluating Details

Here are some notes a writer jotted down about recording a message for a telephone answering machine. The audience is a class of eighth-graders. What information isn't needed in the instructions?

> *A telephone answering machine answers the telephone for you.*
>
> *My brother taught me how to use my answering machine.*
>
> *These instructions will show you how to record an outgoing message on your answering machine.*
>
> *First, press and hold the ANNOUNCE button.*
>
> *The ANNOUNCE button is located on the inside compartment of your machine.*
>
> *As you record the message, do not pause more than two seconds.*
>
> *The president signed a new bill that affects the telephone, TV, and cable industries.*

MEETING *individual* NEEDS

LEP/ESL
General Strategies. English-language learners who come from cultures where independent thinking is not taught in classrooms may require more encouragement to think critically. To keep them involved, pair English-language learners with English-proficient speakers to work on answers to the exercises. Then, call on English-language learners to express the answers the two of them have agreed upon.

TIMESAVER
You may want to have students work in mixed-ability groups of three to check and evaluate the charts they complete for **Writing Assignment: Part 2.** Have them use the guidelines given in the assignment to make sure all the information is included in the proper order and all unnecessary information is deleted.

ANSWERS
Critical Thinking Exercise
The first, second, and last items are not needed.

PART 2:
Planning Your Instructions

Make a chart like the one on page 232, and list steps, materials, equipment, and terms to define. Make sure steps are chronological, and cross out unnecessary information.

235

WRITING YOUR FIRST DRAFT

OBJECTIVES

- To analyze a professional model of a set of instructions
- To write a draft of a set of instructions

MOTIVATION

You may want to give the class a mystery story without the solution. Have students work in groups to solve the mystery by asking questions and noting clues. Discuss the importance of giving details and complete information.

PROGRAM MANAGER

WRITING YOUR FIRST DRAFT

■ **Instructional Support** For help with writing a set of instructions, see **Writing** in *Strategies for Writing*, p. 27.

QUOTATION FOR THE DAY

"All you have to do is write one true sentence. Write the truest sentence that you know." (Ernest Hemingway, 1899–1961, American novelist and winner of the 1954 Nobel Prize for literature)

Introduce the idea that students might want to begin writing at the easiest, clearest points in their processes. For instance, they might write the steps of their instructions first and then write their introductions.

236

Writing Your First Draft

The Parts of a Set of Instructions

A set of instructions includes these parts:

- an introduction that catches the reader's attention
- a body that includes a description of the product, a list of materials and equipment, and the steps in the procedure
- a conclusion that summarizes the steps or discusses problems and what to do about them

With some instructions, you do not need every one of these parts. For example, if you are explaining how to use a digital clock radio, you will not have to describe materials and equipment other than the radio itself.

The Introduction. How many times have you put down a set of instructions after reading only a sentence or two? A good introduction catches your readers' attention and motivates them to read the instructions. The introduction tells what the instructions will help them to achieve, for example: *This manual explains in simple steps how to install, use, and care for your new telephone answering system.*

The introduction may also state

- how the product or procedure benefits you
- how the instructions are organized
- what you'll need to know in order to follow the instructions

The Body. If you are explaining how to use a product—for example, how to program a remote control or how to use an electronic "invisible fence" to keep your dog in the yard—include a description of the product. Tell how it works and what its special features are. If, on the other hand, your instructions explain how to do something—how to be a champion in-line skater or how to deflea a dog, for example—you do not have to describe a product.

Have a volunteer read aloud the introductory material. After discussing the criteria for an effective introduction, body, and conclusion, ask students to keep these elements in mind as they read the passage from **Science Crafts for Kids**. After they have completed **Exercise 5** on p. 241 and have read **A Writer's Model** on pp. 242–243, have students compare the structure of the two essays in this lesson.

☞

The body also includes a list of materials and equipment. In this part, you describe the items the reader will need to use the product or do the procedure, for example: *To program this remote-control device, you will need the all-in-one remote-control device and 4 AAA alkaline batteries.*

The steps are the heart of the body in a set of instructions. They explain the sequence for carrying out the process—how to use the product or perform the procedure. As you list steps in the instructions, remember to

- list steps in the order they're actually done
- supply background information and helpful hints
- include warnings with steps that might be unsafe
- define unfamiliar terms

As you write, remember that you're a guide, not a drill sergeant. A friendly tone will be helpful to your audience.

The Conclusion.   The conclusion usually sums up the steps the reader follows to use the product or do the procedure. It may also include a trouble-shooting guide to help readers with problems that might arise. Trouble-shooting guides typically appear in chart form, as illustrated by the following example.

PROBLEM	CAUSE	SOLUTION
TV does not respond to remote control.	Remote control batteries might be weak.	Replace batteries.

Calvin & Hobbes copyright 1986 Watterson. Distributed by Universal Press Syndicate. Reprinted with permission. All rights reserved.

MEETING *individual* NEEDS

LEARNING STYLES

Visual Learners. Students might benefit from seeing an outline of the material in **The Parts of a Set of Instructions.** You can create this outline on the chalkboard as student volunteers read the text aloud. For example, after a student reads **The Introduction,** you can write the following:

I. Introduction
  A. Catches readers' interest
  B. Motivates readers to continue
  C. Tells what instructions will help readers achieve
  D. Provides optional information
    1. how the product or procedure benefits readers
    2. how the instructions are organized
    3. what readers will need to know to follow instructions

You can continue through the rest of the material and create an outline in the same manner.

TECHNOLOGY TIP

Remind students that most word-processing programs allow them to create tables and charts within documents. Most also allow tables and charts that have been created in other programs to be imported into documents.

MEETING *individual* **NEEDS**

LEP/ESL

General Strategies. The **Reminder** suggests that students define unfamiliar terms, and some students who are learning English may not be sure which terms would be unfamiliar to proficient speakers of English. You might want to suggest that students define any terms they are unsure of. Later, when they evaluate and revise their papers, they can ask English-proficient students whether all of these terms need to be defined.

USING THE SELECTION
from Science Crafts for Kids

1

What purpose does this statement serve in the passage? [It motivates readers to continue reading and to carry out the procedure the authors describe.]

---

238   *Writing to Inform*

To write a set of instructions

- tell readers what the instructions will do for them
- describe the product or procedure
- list materials and equipment readers will need
- give directions in the order the steps should be completed
- tell readers what to do if things go wrong

The writers of the following instructions explain how to build a hot air balloon. As you read, ask yourself if you would be able to follow their instructions.

A PASSAGE FROM A BOOK

from Science Crafts for Kids

by Gwen Diehn and Terry Krautwurst

Hot Air Balloon

INTRODUCTION *1*

This is a tricky project but well worth the fine-tuning it takes to get your balloon aloft. The trick is to be sure the air outside the balloon is much cooler than the air you put into the balloon.

LIST OF EQUIPMENT AND MATERIALS

What You'll Need

12 pieces of colored tissue paper, each 20 by 30 inches	A ruler or yardstick
	Sharp scissors
White craft glue	Old newspaper
A stapler	A hair dryer
A marker	

ASSESSMENT

Ask each student to label the intro-duction, body, and conclusion of his or her paper and to number the steps of the procedure. Use the drafts students write for **Writing Assignment: Part 3** to assess their mastery of the material in this lesson.

CLOSURE

Have students explain the framework for a set of instructions. They can refer to the chart on p. 244, if necessary.

Writing Your First Draft **239**

What to Do

BODY Steps **2**

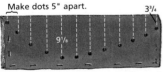
Figure 1

3

Explanation

Make dots 5" apart.   3³⁄₄
9¹⁄₈
Figure 2

Figure 3

Figure 4

1. Run a thin bead of glue along the short edge of a piece of tissue paper, 1/4 inch from the edge. Overlap a second piece of paper over the glue so that the two pieces are joined and make one long piece of tissue paper 20 inches wide and about 5 feet long.

2. Repeat Step 1 five more times until you have six long sheets of paper.

3. Fold each long sheet of paper in half lengthwise, and stack the six sheets exactly on top of one another. Keep all folded edges on the same side.

4. Be sure all edges are even; then, staple the stack together along the unfolded edges and at the top and bottom. (See Figure 1.) Put the staples about 10 inches apart, and be sure not to put any staples on the folded edge. (The staples will make it easier to cut the pieces of paper all at one time.)

5. Use the marker and ruler to mark the top sheet of tissue paper like Figure 2.

6. Join the dots with a curving line. (See Figure 3.) You should have a gentle curve. Carefully cut through the whole stapled stack of paper at once along the curved line. You will have cut off the stapled pieces and will be left with a stack of folded papers.

7. Put the first folded piece of paper on top of some sheets of old newspaper. Put a piece of newspaper between the two layers of tissue, to keep the glue from seeping through. Run a thin bead of glue along the curved edge of the top sheet. (See Figure 4.)

8. Place the second piece of folded tissue paper on top of the first, gluing the curved edges together.

2

All but one of the instructions begin with an imperative verb. Using parallel structure makes the steps easy to follow.

3

The authors provide a helpful hint in their directions. They also explain why it is important to include this step.

239

4

Authors use a simile to help readers visualize the project.

SELECTION AMENDMENT
Description of change: excerpted
Rationale: to focus on the concept of informative writing presented in this chapter

240

Figure 5

Hint

Figure 6

Figure 7

4

9. Slip newspaper between the two layers of tissue paper on piece number two.

10. Repeat Steps 7, 8, and 9 for the rest of the six sheets of tissue paper. You should end up with a stack of tissue paper sheets folded on one edge and glued together like an accordion on the other, curved edge. (See Figure 5.)

11. When the glue is dry, carefully take out all of the newspaper. Some of it will be stuck to the tissue paper, and you will have to peel it away in the stuck spots.

12. Open the bottom piece of tissue.

13. Put a thin bead of glue all along the curvy edge, just as you did in Step 7.

14. Unfold the top piece of tissue paper, and press its curvy edges all along the bead of glue. (See Figure 6.) The balloon pieces are now all joined.

15. Wait for the glue to dry completely before inflating the balloon. (See Figure 7.) While you are waiting for the glue to dry, you can glue tissue paper streamers to the bottom edge for decoration if you like.

16. Ask a friend to help you hold the balloon upright while you carefully place a hair dryer just inside the open bottom of the balloon. When the balloon is inflated and all puffed out, it should rise to the ceiling.

Tip to avoid problems

CONCLUSION

> **17.** If you want to fly your balloon outside, you can do so successfully only on dry, cool or cold days when there is no breeze.
>
> When you fly your balloon inside, try to find a cool room with a high ceiling so you can watch the balloon lift as if by magic. *Happy flying!*

WRITING NOTE

Notice that the writers of this essay keep their sentences short and to the point. Simple, straightforward language will help readers understand and follow your instructions.

EXERCISE 5 ▶ **Analyzing a Set of Instructions**

1. How do the authors introduce their set of instructions? Does their introduction make you want to construct a balloon? Explain.
2. Where is the list of equipment and materials? Why do you think it appears here rather than in the body of the essay?
3. What determines the order in which the authors give steps?
4. Could you follow the authors' instructions and create your own balloon? Explain.
5. The authors' last step hints at one problem the reader might have. What do you think are some other problems a reader might have building or flying a hot air balloon?

A Basic Framework for a Set of Instructions

Building a hot air balloon—even one that can't carry people—is a complicated project. Your instructions will probably require fewer steps. Here is a writer's model that shows you a basic framework for a set of instructions.

ANSWERS
Exercise 5

Answers may vary.

1. The authors introduce their instructions by stating that the project is worth the effort it takes to get a hot air balloon aloft. They also encourage readers by stating at the outset what conditions are necessary to successfully fly the balloon. Students should provide reasons for their answers to the second question.

2. The list appears before the start of the text of the passage. It probably appears there so readers can assemble what they need to follow the instructions as they read them.

3. The order of the steps is determined by what needs to be done before other steps can be taken.

4. Most students will answer yes, largely because the authors are so specific.

5. Responses will vary. One possible problem is that it may be difficult to control the glue. People who try the procedure will have to accurately gauge weather or indoor conditions.

MEETING individual NEEDS

LEP/ESL

General Strategies. You may need to provide students with a few concrete ideas about what is considered to be an attention-getting introduction. Here are some examples:

1. Begin with a question such as "Did you know that you could freeze to death in the middle of summer?"
2. Provide facts and figures as in "Eleven hikers died in the Rockies last summer."
3. Put the subject in historical perspective as in "Since time began, people have died on mountains; this weekend history repeated itself."

LEARNING STYLES

Kinetic Learners. Students might benefit from the hands-on experience of demonstrating processes to a classmate before writing out the steps.

Auditory Learners. You may want to have auditory learners dictate their explanations into a tape recorder before writing their drafts. Another possibility would be to pair students with partners and have them talk through their processes while their fellow students take notes.

A WRITER'S MODEL

INTRODUCTION
Attention grabber

DESCRIPTION OF PRODUCT

Benefits of learning the process

Isn't it time you gave something back to Mother Earth? Here's a gift she'll really appreciate: a compost pile that turns your household garbage into rich soil. And you can make it yourself.

Just think how much garbage goes out of your house every year. If your family is like most in America, in a year's time your garbage can be measured in tons! We're even running out of places to put our garbage. Composting is one little thing you can do to help. These instructions will teach you how to make your own compost.

BODY

LIST OF MATERIALS AND EQUIPMENT
Helpful hint/ Explanation

To compost garbage, you need a yard, and it has to have a corner that you don't use. You also need a plastic jug, a shovel, a bag of fertilizer, and a garden hose. You can use a one-gallon milk jug, but cut off the top to make a wider opening. You'll find fertilizer at garden stores.

STEPS
Step 1
Definition of term

Explanation

Composting is pretty simple. Begin by collecting your organic garbage in the plastic jug. What is organic garbage, you ask? It's anything that comes from a plant or many other living things. You can put egg shells, coffee grounds, and vegetable peels into your compost jug. But

Helpful hint

you can't put cans, bottles, and paper in there. Also, don't put meat or fat into your compost, because they will attract unwanted animals and insects.

Step 2

Explanation

Step 3

As soon as you begin to collect organic garbage, go out to your yard and dig a hole where you want your compost. Make it about two feet deep and three feet across. Then, when your jug is full, empty it into the hole and pour a thin layer of fertilizer over it. Shovel a layer of dirt over the fertilizer. Wet it down with the hose, and you're finished for the day. The next time your jug is full, repeat the process.

Step 4

Step 5

CONCLUSION

That's all there is to it: a layer of organic garbage, a thin layer of fertilizer, a layer of dirt, and a little water. In a year or so, the hole in your yard will be full of rich, crumbly brown garden soil. You'll have the satisfaction of knowing you've done something that helps the earth. And when you taste the vegetables grown in the soil you've made, you'll know it was worth the trouble.

Restatement of benefits

New benefit

![WRITING NOTE]

The writer of the essay about composting uses transitional words and phrases like *after, then,* and *in a year or so.* These words help the reader know when each step takes place. (For more information on transitions, see pages 71–73.)

INTEGRATING THE LANGUAGE ARTS

Library Link. Writing a set of instructions provides an opportunity to reinforce library skills. You could invite the school librarian to talk to your class about using periodicals, pamphlets, audiovisual materials, and books that demonstrate processes.

You may find it helpful to use this framework for your essay. The essay about composting describes a procedure, not a product. Otherwise, it follows the framework.

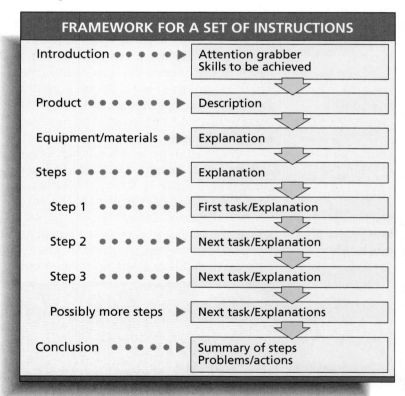

FRAMEWORK FOR A SET OF INSTRUCTIONS

Introduction • • • • • ▶	Attention grabber Skills to be achieved
Product • • • • • • • ▶	Description
Equipment/materials • ▶	Explanation
Steps • • • • • • • • ▶	Explanation
Step 1 • • • • • • ▶	First task/Explanation
Step 2 • • • • • • ▶	Next task/Explanation
Step 3 • • • • • • ▶	Next task/Explanation
Possibly more steps ▶	Next task/Explanations
Conclusion • • • • • ▶	Summary of steps Problems/actions

WRITING ASSIGNMENT

PART 3:
Writing a Draft of Your Set of Instructions

You've got all the information you need to write a first draft of your set of instructions. To help you stay on track as you write, keep looking back at the basic framework on this page. Also, be sure to use the chart you made in Writing Assignment, Part 2 (page 235).

 REFERENCE NOTE: For help in writing introductions and conclusions, see pages 104–106 and 110–111.

OBJECTIVES

- To analyze a writer's revisions
- To explain a process orally
- To evaluate and revise a set of instructions

MOTIVATION

Ask students if anyone ever gave them directions that were confusing and hard to follow. Tell them that a disorganized essay has the same effect and that in this lesson they will work on revising their drafts to make them clear.

Evaluating and Revising

Use the following chart to evaluate and revise your paper. If you answer no to a question in the left-hand column, use the revision technique in the right-hand column.

EVALUATING AND REVISING INSTRUCTIONS

EVALUATION GUIDE	REVISION TECHNIQUE
1 Does the introduction catch the reader's interest and tell what skills the instructions teach?	**Add** interesting details in your opening sentence. **Add** a sentence that tells what skills readers will learn.
2 If the essay involves a product, is the product described?	**Add** descriptive details about the product.
3 Does the essay list needed equipment and materials before giving the steps?	**Add** a list of all the necessary equipment and materials before giving the steps.
4 Are the steps given in the order in which they should be done? Are all the details related to the process?	**Reorder** the steps so they are in chronological order. **Cut** unnecessary details.
5 Are all unfamiliar terms clearly defined?	**Add** definitions of terms the audience may not know.
6 Does the conclusion summarize the steps? Does it discuss problems and possible solutions for readers to try?	**Add** a sentence that summarizes the steps. **Add** information on possible problems and possible solutions for readers to try.

PROGRAM MANAGER

EVALUATING AND REVISING

- **Reinforcement/Reteaching** See **Revision Transparencies 11** and **12.** For suggestions on how to tie the transparencies to instruction, review teacher's notes in *Fine Art and Instructional Transparencies for Writing,* p. 105.

- **Ongoing Assessment** For a rubric to guide assessment, see **Evaluating and Revising** in *Strategies for Writing,* p. 28

- **Assessment/Reflection** To assess student work and evaluate progress, see **Portfolio Forms** in *Portfolio Assessment,* pp. 5–17.

QUOTATION FOR THE DAY

"I can't write five words but that I change seven." (Dorothy Parker, 1893–1967, writer of short stories and witty verse)

Ask students what Parker meant by this exaggeration. Obviously, if she changed seven words out of every five, she would never finish. Suggest that as long as a writer has ideas about how to improve the writing, he or she is making progress.

Go over the chart on p. 245 with students, and then guide them through the first question in **Exercise 6**. Assign the rest of **Exercise 6** and all of **Exercise 7** as independent practice. As students work cooperatively on **Exercise 7,** you could circulate around the room and encourage students to stay focused and to make their comments as positive as possible.

Assign **Writing Assignment: Part 4,** p. 247, as independent practice. Have students refer to the chart on p. 245 as they revise their papers.

MEETING individual NEEDS

LEP/ESL

General Strategies. You may want to group less-advanced English-language learners with one another rather than with English-proficient speakers or advanced English-language learners. Because they have similar levels of grammatical knowledge, less-advanced English-language learners are able to read each other's papers for content without overemphasizing grammatical errors. English-proficient students may tend to focus too much on correcting the surface errors and not give enough feedback on content.

LESS-ADVANCED STUDENTS

Students often respond well to peer coaching in which students with similar interests talk through some of their revisions. Encourage students to be positive and attentive when it is their turn to coach.

ANSWERS
Exercise 7

The speaker should retell the process as described by the writer, not as the speaker would describe it. If the speaker does not retell the process adequately, the author must determine whether the fault is with the speaker or the essay. Usually, changes involve clarifying terms and rearranging and adding material.

---

246   *Writing to Inform*

EXERCISE 6 ▶ **Analyzing a Writer's Revisions**

Study the writer's revisions of a paragraph from the model on pages 242–243. Then, answer the questions that follow the paragraph.

To compost garbage, you need a yard, and it has to have a corner that you don't use. ~~You might want to put a fence~~ **cut** ~~around the corner that you're going to use~~ ~~for composting. A picket fence or one~~ ~~made out of wire mesh would look nice,~~ ~~but you don't really need one.)~~ However, **cut**

also
you do need a plastic jug, a shovel, a bag **replace**
of fertilizer, and a garden hose. Watering **cut** ~~is the last step.~~ You can use a one-gallon milk jug, but cut off the top to make a wider opening. *You'll find fertilizer at* **add** *garden stores.*

1. Why did the writer cut the second and third sentences? **1. not directly concerned with process**
2. Why did the writer change the beginning of the fourth sentence? **2. *However* is unnecessary because of earlier cut**
3. Why did the writer remove the sentence about watering? **3. it belongs at end of process, not in introduction**
4. Why did the writer add the sentence about fertilizer? **4. tells reader where to obtain one of the necessary materials**

EXERCISE 7 ▶ **Speaking and Listening: Explaining Instructions Orally**

Here's a way to find out if your instructions make sense to other people. Work in groups of three. Read your draft to one person only. Then, listen as he or she explains the instructions to the third student. Does the speaker understand your instructions? Take notes about any

To assess students' mastery of evaluating and revising, have them work with partners after they have completed their evaluations and revisions. Have each partner explain his or her changes. Remind students that they won't always agree with each other.

Ask students to answer these questions about their essays:
1. What was the most difficult part of writing the essay?
2. What comments did others make about your paper?
3. What are your goals for the final draft of the essay? ■

problems. Keep trading places so that everyone has a turn as reader, speaker, and listener.

GRAMMAR HINT

Using Prepositional Phrases

When you write instructions, it's often very important to show clear relationships between objects. Otherwise your instructions could be very confusing. Prepositional phrases can help you show those relationships.

UNCLEAR	Move the candle.
CLEAR	Move the candle **to the table.**

UNCLEAR	Twist the cap.
CLEAR	Twist the cap **off the bottle.**

UNCLEAR	Pack essential repair tools and mount the bag securely.
CLEAR	Pack essential repair tools **in a saddlebag** and mount the bag securely **under the bicycle seat.**

 REFERENCE NOTE: For more information on prepositional phrases, see pages 506–509.

PART 4:
Evaluating and Revising Your Set of Instructions

Build on the notes you took for Exercise 7 by trading your written instructions with another student. Use the questions from the chart on page 245 to evaluate each other's paper. Listen without arguing to your partner's evaluation of your work. Now it's up to you to evaluate your own paper and revise the weaknesses you find.

GRAMMAR HINT

Ask students to circle the prepositional phrases in their essays. If students do not find any prepositional phrases, suggest that they add some. Then, have students evaluate whether or not the prepositional phrases make their explanations clearer.

INTEGRATING THE LANGUAGE ARTS

Vocabulary Link. Students could use thesauruses or brainstorm lists of action words to replace or supplement common verbs such as *get, do, take, go,* and *tell.*

COOPERATIVE LEARNING

You might want to establish editing groups of five students each. Provide students with a checklist using information from the chart on p. 245 and have them take turns reading their essays aloud to the group. Ask listeners to use the checklists to evaluate individual papers.

PROOFREADING AND PUBLISHING

OBJECTIVE

- To proofread and publish a set of instructions

TEACHING THE LESSON

Model the proofreading process by rewriting an excerpt from a published set of instructions and adding errors. Guide students through proofreading the excerpt. Then, assign **Writing Assignment: Part 5** as independent practice. When students write their reflections, ask them to pay special attention to the second question.

PROGRAM MANAGER

PROOFREADING AND PUBLISHING

- **Instructional Support** For a chart students may use to evaluate their proofreading progress, see **Proofreading** in *Strategies for Writing*, p. 29.
- **Independent Practice/ Reteaching** For additional practice with language skills, see **Proofreading Practice: Using Prepositional Phrases** in *Strategies for Writing*, p. 30.
- **Assessment/Reflection** To assess student work and evaluate progress, see **Portfolio Forms** in *Portfolio Assessment,* pp. 18–21.

QUOTATION FOR THE DAY

"Of course no writers ever forget their first acceptance. . . ." (Truman Capote, 1924–1984, novelist and author of *In Cold Blood*)

Ask your students to imagine where their essays might be read if they were published professionally. Would they reach a magazine reader on the other side of the country? Would they reach readers in Europe? Would they be recorded on microfilm at the Library of Congress to be saved for the next fifty or one hundred years?

Proofreading and Publishing

Proofreading. A tiny error can ruin a set of instructions. If you write about how to get into *The Guinness Book of World Records,* an incorrect address could mean that readers would never see their new records published!

COMPUTER NOTE: Spell-checking programs can be real time-savers. Remember, though, that they can't tell the difference between homonyms such as *their, there,* and *they're.*

Publishing. Now you need to communicate your instructions to the audience you had in mind. Here are two suggestions.

- Glue your essay on cardboard, framed with a border. Hang it in a workshop or other place suitable to your topic.
- Send your paper to a hobby magazine. You can find addresses in directories at your local library.

WRITING ASSIGNMENT	PART 5: **Proofreading and Publishing Your Paper**

Correct any errors you find in your essay. Use one of the ideas above or one of your own to share your paper.

 Reflecting on Your Writing

If you want to put your instructions in your **portfolio,** date them. Include the answers to these questions.

1. How did you choose a product or procedure to explain?
2. How did you grab your readers' attention at the beginning of the instructions?
3. Did you have problems in giving step-by-step directions? Explain.

If you have each student identify an appropriate audience and publishing forum, you can use that information as part of your assessment criteria.

Ask students to answer the following questions:

1. How did you feel about sharing your paper with others?
2. What did you look for most when you were proofreading papers? ■

A STUDENT MODEL

Michael Hutchison's paper offers what nearly every student needs at one time or another: instructions on how to get organized for school in the morning. Michael, who is a student at North Middle School in O'Fallon, Missouri, suggests that writers of instructions "just think of how you would normally go about doing" a procedure. Here is the first part of Michael's paper.

Starting the School Day Right
by Michael Hutchison

Are you tired of always rushing around trying to get ready for school in the mornings? Would you like to know how to get to school without missing your bus or panicking because you did not wake up early enough? Just follow this simple plan and you will never be late again.

The first thing you might want to do is take your bath or shower the night before, instead of in the morning. This can save a lot of time! Also, go ahead and decide what you are going to wear the following day and lay it out so you won't have to spend time looking for your belt or shoes.

Finally, gather all your books and anything else you need to take to school the next morning and place it close to the door along with your coat. If you have to look for these things, it takes up valuable time. You will be in a good mood in the morning, because you have not had to rush around looking for your things.

A STUDENT MODEL
Evaluation

1. Michael begins his instructions by grabbing readers' attention, and he tells readers what skills the instructions teach.
2. In the second and third paragraphs, Michael tells what is needed (bath or shower, clothes, books), and he gives an order in which to accomplish the tasks he specifies.

CRITICAL THINKING
Analysis. Have students randomly exchange papers and read their classmates' instructions, predicting what difficulties a reader might encounter in attempting to follow the steps. Some of the instructions could then be tested, and students could verify the accuracy of their predictions.

INTEGRATING THE LANGUAGE ARTS
Mechanics Link. In a set of instructions, students should use transitional words and phrases such as *next, first, after, finally, in conclusion,* and *before.* When these transitional words or phrases come at the beginning of a sentence, they are followed by a comma. You may want to present this rule to your students and have them pay particular attention to its use as they proofread their instructions.

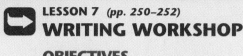

LESSON 7 *(pp. 250–252)*
WRITING WORKSHOP
OBJECTIVES
- To analyze cause-and-effect elements in a literary model
- To write, revise, proofread, and publish a cause-and-effect essay

TEACHING THE LESSON
After they have read the introductory paragraphs, ask students to name ten important news stories of the past month having to do with politics, entertainment, sports, business, the community, or school. Discuss the causes and the immediate and long-term effects of each. Determine which topics would be appropriate for papers.

QUOTATION FOR THE DAY
"Every why hath a wherefore." (William Shakespeare, 1564–1616, English playwright and poet)

You may want to explain that *wherefore* in this quotation from *A Comedy of Errors* means a "reason, a cause." Ask pairs of students to list several causes and effects. Start them with an example such as "Mothers Against Drunk Driving was formed as a result of . . ."

USING THE SELECTION
A Cautionary Tale

1

Which does the author immediately present the reader with, a cause or an effect? [effect]

2

Acid rain is formed when water vapor in the air collects chemical compounds given off by automobiles, factories, and power plants and deposits them through rain, snow, or sleet into rivers and lakes.

250

WRITING WORKSHOP

The Cause-and-Effect Essay

Instructions are a kind of informative writing that answer the question *How do you do or use that?* A similar kind of informative writing is the *cause-and-effect essay*. It answers the question *Why does that happen?* or *What is the result?* A cause-and-effect essay begins with an event or situation and then helps readers understand its causes (*Why?*) or its effects (*What's the result?*).

Let's suppose a new school fad is wearing banana necklaces. You could explore its causes (someone really cool did it for a joke). Or you could write about its effects (a new club—the Necklace Squashers).

Sometimes causes and effects are very clear and simple, but events worth writing about usually aren't. They may have more than one cause or effect—and sometimes we simply can't know them all. Here's an essay about a mysterious decline in frogs and toads. Notice how the writer first discusses possible causes but then focuses on effects.

A Cautionary Tale
by Billy Goodman

1   In many parts of the United States, and indeed the world, frogs and toads are becoming less and less common. The once-loud chirping and croaking of huge numbers of these animals is getting quieter, as their numbers decline. Why?

Scientists don't have an answer. It probably has something to do with the destruction of frogs' habitats. Some scientists

2 have suggested that acid rain—rain that's more acidic than normal because of air pollution—might be the culprit. Many frogs and toads are easily harmed by acidity in water where they lay their eggs. The decline may have nothing to do with humans.

As students read "**A Cautionary Tale,**" help them to recognize the causes and the immediate and long-term effects. Use the questions following the model to guide a discussion of the essay.

You may want to guide students through the prewriting steps, assign the first draft for independent practice, and have students work in groups for evaluating, revising, and proofreading their papers.

☛

Whatever the reason, a decline in frog and toad populations could have far-reaching effects. Since frogs and toads normally eat lots of insects, fewer of the amphibians could lead to an insect population explosion. The larger number of insects will devour more plant food—including crops—than usual. In response, farmers may increase their use of pesticides.

Many fish eat tadpoles. So if there are fewer tadpoles, there will be less food for some fish. So fish populations might decline. That would be bad news for fish-eating birds or for people who like to fish.

The moral of this story is "You can't do just one thing." Something that affects one species is bound to affect others up and down the food chain.

from A Kid's Guide to How to Save the Planet

3
What might be the effects of an increase in the use of pesticides? [One effect might be more pollution of the earth and its atmosphere.]

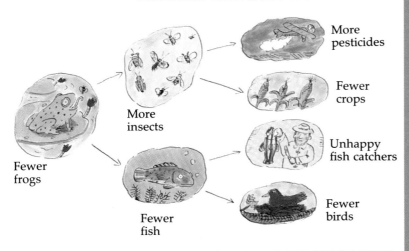

Fewer frogs

More insects

More pesticides

Fewer crops

Unhappy fish catchers

Fewer fish

Fewer birds

Thinking It Over

1. What does the writer say about possible causes for the decline in frogs and toads?
2. The writer tells about effects that go on to produce other effects. This is called a **cause-and-effect chain.** What are all the effects of fewer frogs?
3. A "cautionary tale" is a story that gives a warning. What is the writer's warning?

ANSWERS
Thinking It Over
Answers may vary.

1. The decline is probably related to the destruction of habitats and possibly to acid rain, but it may not even be connected with people.

2. Possible effects include less chirping by frogs, increased growth of insect populations, more plant consumption by insects, increased pesticide use by farmers, less food for fish, and fewer fish for birds and people to eat.

3. Since what affects one species affects other species, people should carefully consider all the effects of their actions.

SELECTION AMENDMENT
Description of change: excerpted
Rationale: to focus on the concept of informative writing presented in this chapter

CLOSURE

Have students name the two questions that a cause-and-effect essay can answer. [*Why does that happen?* or *What is the result?*] ■

252

MEETING *individual* NEEDS

LEP/ESL

General Strategies. Many English-language learners omit modal auxiliaries (*may, might, could,* and *should*), an omission that makes their writing sound too absolute. In **"A Cautionary Tale,"** the author uses many modals so that both causes and effects are presented as possibilities rather than actualities ("acid rain . . . *might be* the culprit; a decline in frog and toad populations *could have* . . . effects; fewer . . . *could lead* to an insect population explosion; farmers *may increase* their use of pesticides"). To master this style, English-language learners will need to have such structural devices clearly described.

◆ INTEGRATING THE LANGUAGE ARTS

Literature Link. Have students read "Charles" by Shirley Jackson and list the effects of Charles's behavior on others in the classroom. Then, ask students what causes his mischievousness. What causes him to lie to his mother, and what is the effect?

Writing a Cause-and-Effect Essay

Prewriting. For this paper, just focus on the causes or the effects of an event. You don't have to explain both. Think of something that makes you want to explore *Why?* or *What's the result?*—perhaps a real fad at your school or being the oldest child in your family. Don't tackle a vast question such as *What caused the Vietnam War?* Use a diagram like the one on page 251 to map your paper. Write your event in a circle (you don't have to draw), and then use more circles and arrows to connect causes and effects.

Writing, Evaluating, and Revising. In your introduction, clearly identify the event or situation. Then you can use order of importance—from most to least important, or the opposite—to organize causes or effects. For a cause-and-effect chain, use chronological order. Make sure you have some facts and examples that help support your explanation.

Proofreading and Publishing. Check for errors in your final copy, and think about who might want to read your paper. A paper on teen centers could go to the city council, one on reducing concert ticket prices to the newspaper, and one on fads to the school paper.

If you want to include your cause-and-effect essay in your **portfolio,** date it. Then, include the essay with a reflection on your writing based on these questions. How did you choose the topic for your essay? How difficult (or easy) was it to find facts and examples to support your explanation?

253

SPEAKING AND LISTENING

Health: Emergency Directions

Workers who answer the 911 emergency number operate under a great deal of stress. They often have to explain a complicated procedure over the phone to someone who's in a panic and screaming for help. Could you give life-saving instructions over the phone? You never know until you try. Get together with a group of four or more classmates. Each group member should learn a separate emergency medical procedure from a first-aid manual. For example, you might learn how to deal with a bad cut or what to do if someone's choking on a piece of food.

Then, take turns being the 911 emergency worker, the injured person, the helper, and an observer. Position yourselves so that the 911 speaker can't see or be seen by the others. As the helper tries to follow the speaker's directions, the observer should take notes. After each "emergency," discuss what happened, especially anything that went wrong and how to correct it.

SPEAKING AND LISTENING
Teaching Strategies
You may want to give students some time to study first-aid manuals and to decide on a procedure to learn. Tell students that it's important in life to know some basic first-aid information.

GUIDELINES
When it is his or her turn to play the 911 worker, each student should demonstrate knowledge of a first-aid procedure. After each role-playing situation, students in each group should evaluate the effectiveness of the procedure.

WRITING TO PERSUADE

OBJECTIVES

- To select an appropriate topic for a persuasive essay and to write a statement of opinion about that topic
- To gather information that supports an opinion statement
- To organize and draft a persuasive essay
- To evaluate and revise the content and organization of a persuasive essay
- To proofread a persuasive essay and to prepare it for publication

WRITING-IN-PROGRESS ASSIGNMENTS

Major Assignment: Writing to persuade
Cumulative Writing Assignments: The chart below shows the sequence of cumulative assignments that will guide students as they write a persuasive essay. These Writing Assignments form the instructional core of Chapter 8.

PREWRITING
WRITING ASSIGNMENT
- Part 1: Choosing an Issue to Write About p. 263
- Part 2: Finding Support for Your Opinion p. 269

WRITING YOUR FIRST DRAFT
WRITING ASSIGNMENT
- Part 3: Writing A Draft of Your Persuasive Paper p. 276

EVALUATING AND REVISING
WRITING ASSIGNMENT
- Part 4: Evaluating and Revising Your Persuasive Paper p. 279

PROOFREADING AND PUBLISHING
WRITING ASSIGNMENT
- Part 5: Proofreading and Publishing Your Paper p. 280

In addition, exercises 1–5 provide practice in distinguishing fact from opinion, exploring possible issues, analyzing audience, analyzing a persuasive editorial, and analyzing a writer's revisions.

WORKPLACE writing ▶ Advertising Is Persuasion

Remind students that when they create a pep banner, a student council campaign poster, or a bake sale ad, they aim to persuade an audience by creating ad copy. Before students tackle their essays, have them concentrate on persuasion techniques for ads.

- **Prewriting** Have students in small groups brainstorm times they might need to write a type of ad and who their audience might be. Students may produce a list like the following.

Aims	Audience
• to sell skis in the want ads	• skiers
• to advertise to cut grass	• homeowners
• to sell seeds	• people with gardens
• to promote a school play, band concert, soccer game	• students, faculty, boosters, parents, graduates

Students might create a chart like the following to organize types of appeal for each ad and the type of ad they want to produce.

ad	type of appeal	type of ad
school event	emotional appeal	poster
job wanted	reasons, evidence	want ad

- **Writing** Then, have students create copy for their ads.
- **Evaluating and Revising** Have groups exchange ads to get a buyer's input.
- **Proofreading and Publishing** Have students create actual posters or other advertisements to post in the school or to publish in the school newspaper.

INTEGRATING THE LANGUAGE ARTS

SELECTION	READING AND LITERATURE	WRITING AND CRITICAL THINKING	LANGUAGE AND SYNTAX	SPEAKING, LISTENING, AND OTHER EXPRESSION SKILLS
• "Use It Again . . . and Again . . . and Again" by The EarthWorks Group pp. 256–258 • from "Ban Dogs from Trails?" by Kent Dannen pp. 271–273 • from *On Writing Well* by William Zinsser p. 277	• Identifying and evaluating stated and implied main ideas and supporting details pp. 259, 273, 283 • Identifying why and where emotional language is used pp. 259, 283 • Distinguishing between fact and opinion pp. 262–263 • Demonstrating evaluation and comprehension skills p. 273	• Writing a statement of opinion p. 263 • Using brainstorming and listing as prewriting techniques p. 263 • Analyzing audience pp. 265, 273 • Using and writing reasons for opinions pp. 269, 283 • Providing accurate support through examples, details, and appeals pp. 269, 283 • Analyzing organization of a persuasive editorial p. 274 • Revising and evaluating drafts of a persuasive essay and a speech pp. 279, 283 • Evaluating reasoning p. 283 • Gathering support for an opinion p. 283 • Analyzing an advertisement for persuasive techniques pp. 286–287 • Writing an advertisement p. 287	• Proofreading for spelling, punctuation, and usage errors p. 280 • Using a variety of sentence structures p. 284	• Contributing ideas in brainstorming and speaking in a group p. 262 • Distinguishing between fact and opinion pp. 262–263 • Evaluating and generating statements of opinion, personal preference, and values p. 263 • Analyzing propaganda techniques pp. 267–268 • Using charts and available information to solve problems p. 279 • Preparing and delivering a speech p. 284 • Sharing information in an oral presentation pp. 286–287

SUGGESTED INTEGRATED UNIT PLAN

This unit plan suggests how to integrate the major strands of the language arts with this chapter.

If you begin with this chapter on writing to persuade or with the following literature selections, you should focus on the common characteristics of persuasive writing. You can then integrate speaking/listening and language concepts with both the writing and the literature.

Common Characteristics

- Content that is mainly evidence and explanation mixed with emotional appeal
- A purpose that is to convince a specific audience
- Repetition of key words and sentence and paragraph structures
- Language geared to the intended audience
- Organization that can vary with purpose

Writing
Persuasion

Language
Style, Usage

- Controlling emotional language
- Stating an opinion
- Using active voice

UNIT FOCUS NONFICTION

Speaking/Listening

- Work in groups to analyze audience
- Discuss emotional appeals
- Videotape ad

Literature
Nonfiction

- "Gettysburg Address" Abraham Lincoln
- "I Have a Dream" Martin Luther King, Jr.
- "The First Americans" The Grand Council Fire of American Indians

CHAPTER 8: WRITING TO PERSUADE

Use this guide for creating an instructional plan that addresses the individual needs of your students. Assignments accompanied by the following symbol (∗) may be completed out of class. Times given for pacing lessons are estimated.

CHAPTER PLANNING GUIDE—PUPIL'S EDITION

| LESSONS | LITERARY MODEL pp. 256–258 "Use It Again and Again and Again" by The EarthWorks Group | PREWRITING pp. 261–269 | |
		Generating Ideas	Gathering/Organizing
DEVELOPMENTAL PROGRAM	🕐 **20–25 minutes** • Read model aloud in class and have students answer questions on p. 259 orally.	🕐 **45–50 minutes** • Ways to Persuade p. 260 • Main Assignment: Looking Ahead p. 260 • Choosing a Topic pp. 261–263 • Exercises 1, 2 pp. 262–263 • Writing Assignment: Part 1 p. 263∗	🕐 **40–45 minutes** • Planning for Persuasive Writing pp. 264–267 • Writing Note p. 265 • Critical Thinking pp. 267–269 • Writing Assignment: Part 2 p. 269∗
CORE PROGRAM	🕐 **30–35 minutes** • Assign students to read model and answer questions p. 259 independently.	🕐 **25–30 minutes** • Ways to Persuade p. 260 • Main Assignment: Looking Ahead p. 260 • Identifying and Stating Your Opinion pp. 261–262 • Reminder p. 262 • Exercise 2 p. 263 • Writing Assignment: Part 1 p. 263∗	🕐 **30–35 minutes** • Planning for Persuasive Writing pp. 264–267∗ • Writing Note p. 265 • Exercise 3 p. 265 • Critical Thinking pp. 267–269 • Writing Assignment: Part 2 p. 269∗
ACCELERATED PROGRAM	🕐 **20–25 minutes** • Have students read model independently and discuss their responses to questions p. 259.	🕐 **10–15 minutes** • Ways to Persuade p. 260 • Main Assignment: Looking Ahead p. 260 • Identifying and Stating Your Opinion pp. 261–262 • Reminder p. 262 • Writing Assignment: Part 1 p. 263∗	🕐 **20–25 minutes** • Thinking About Purpose and Audience p. 264∗ • Writing Note p. 265 • Critical Thinking pp. 267–269 • Writing Assignment: Part 2 p. 269∗

CHAPTER PLANNING GUIDE—PROGRAM RESOURCES

	LITERARY MODEL	PREWRITING
PRINT	• Reading Master 8, *Practice for Assessment in Reading, Vocabulary, and Spelling* p. 8	• Prewriting, *Strategies for Writing* pp. 33–34 • Persuading Others, *English Workshop* pp. 53–58
MEDIA	• Fine Art Transparency 5, *Transparency Binder*	• Graphic Organizers 13 and 14, *Transparency Binder* • *Writer's Workshop 1:* Evaluation

WRITING pp. 270–276	EVALUATING AND REVISING pp. 277–279	PROOFREADING AND PUBLISHING pp. 280–281
35–40 minutes • Elements of Persuasion pp. 270–271 • A Writer's Model p. 274 • Framework p. 275 • Grammar Hint p. 276 • Writing Assignment: Part 3 p. 276*	**40–45 minutes** • Evaluating and Revising p. 277 • Evaluating and Revising Persuasive Papers Chart p. 278 • Exercise 5 p. 279* • Writing Assignment: Part 4 p. 279	**40–45 minutes** • Proofreading and Publishing p. 280 • Writing Assignment: Part 5 p. 280 • Reflecting p. 281 • A Student Model p. 281
30–35 minutes • Elements of Persuasion pp. 270–271 • Writing Note p. 271 • A Magazine Editorial pp. 271–273* • Exercise 4 p. 273* • Framework p. 275 • Grammar Hint p. 276 • Writing Assignment: Part 3 p. 276*	**30–35 minutes** • Evaluating and Revising Persuasive Papers Chart p. 278 • Reminder p. 278 • Writing Assignment: Part 4 p. 279	**30–35 minutes** • Proofreading and Publishing p. 280 • Writing Assignment: Part 5 p. 280 • Reflecting p. 281* • A Student Model p. 281*
20–25 minutes • Writing Note p. 271 • A Magazine Editorial pp. 271–273* • Framework p. 275 • Writing Assignment: Part 3 p. 276*	**25–30 minutes** • Evaluating and Revising Persuasive Papers Chart p. 278 • Reminder p. 278 • Writing Assignment: Part 4 p. 279	**20–25 minutes** • Writing Assignment: Part 5 p. 280 • Reflecting p. 281* • A Student Model p. 281*

 Computer disk or CD-ROM   Overhead transparencies

WRITING	EVALUATING AND REVISING	PROOFREADING AND PUBLISHING
• Writing, *Strategies for Writing* p. 35 • Sentence Sense, *English Workshop* pp. 77–78	• Evaluating and Revising, *Strategies for Writing* p. 36	• Proofreading Practice, *Strategies for Writing* p. 38
• *Language Workshop:* Lesson 39	• Revision Transparencies 13–14, *Transparency Binder*	

ELEMENTS OF WRITING: CURRICULUM CONNECTIONS

Writing Workshop
• A Campaign Speech pp. 282–284

Making Connections
• Persuasive Letters pp. 285–286
• Presenting Solutions for Problems p. 286
• Persuasion in Advertising p. 287

ASSESSMENT OPTIONS

Summative Assessment
Holistic Scoring: Prompts and Models pp. 27–32

Performance Assessment
Assessments 3 and 4, *Integrated Performance Assessment, Level C* For help with evaluation, see *Holistic Scoring: Prompts and Models.*

Portfolio Assessment
Portfolio forms, *Portfolio Assessment* pp. 5–24, 38–43

Reflection
Writing Process Log, *Strategies for Writing* p. 32

Ongoing Assessment
Proofreading, *Strategies for Writing* p. 37

LESSON 1 *(pp. 254–259)*

TAKING A STAND

OBJECTIVES

- To identify and analyze the characteristics of persuasion
- To evaluate the persuasive qualities of a literary model

MOTIVATION

Begin a class discussion of persuasion by having students argue for opposing maxims. One might take "He who hesitates is lost," while another might choose "Look before you leap." Ask students to consider how they could convince others that their side has more merit.

PROGRAM MANAGER

CHAPTER 8

- **Practice** To help less-advanced students who need additional practice with concepts and activities related to this chapter, see **Chapter 7** in *English Workshop, Second Course,* pp. 53–58.

- **Summative Assessment** For a writing prompt, including grading criteria and student models, see *Holistic Scoring: Prompts and Models,* pp. 27–32.

- **Performance Assessment** Use **Assessment 4** in *Integrated Performance Assessment, Level C.* For help with evaluating student writing, see *Holistic Scoring Workshop, Level C.*

- **Extension/Enrichment** See **Fine Art Transparency 5,** *Paradise, #1* by Suzanne Duranceau. For suggestions on how to tie the transparency to instruction, review teacher's notes in *Fine Art and Instructional Transparencies for Writing,* p. 27.

- **Reading Support** For help with the reading selection, pp. 256–258, see **Reading Master 8** in *Practice for Assessment in Reading, Vocabulary, and Spelling,* p. 8.

8 WRITING TO PERSUADE

TEACHING THE LESSON

Have a volunteer read the introductory material in the chapter orally. Emphasize that for persuasion to be effective, writers must know exactly what audience they want to convince. In the model on p. 256, the writers address young people as their primary target.

Students should benefit from listening to someone read the excerpt aloud since it was written with a young audience in mind. As students read, discuss the information in the annotations. Help students look for aspects of persuasion in the model.

Use the **Reader's Response** questions to guide your discussion. Lead students in discovering what makes the arguments

Taking a Stand

Taking a stand is our way of telling people that we feel strongly about something. Persuasion means trying to bring others around to our way of thinking.

Writing and You.   Someone is always trying to persuade someone else to act or think a certain way. Advertisers do whatever they can to get you to buy everything from T-shirts to tennis rackets. Your parents try to convince you to do more homework. You do it yourself. You try to persuade your best friend to go to a ballgame. Do you think it's important to take a stand when you feel strongly about something?

As You Read.   Here is an excerpt from a book that takes a stand on recycling. As you read, think about what you are being asked to do. Are you convinced you should do it?

Bernie Boston, *Flower Power* (1967).

QUOTATION FOR THE DAY

"I dearly love to persuade people. There can hardly be a greater pleasure (of a selfish kind) than to feel you have brought another person around to your way of thinking." (James Hinton, 1822–1875, English philosopher)

Have students discuss occasions when they have changed people's minds. What kinds of arguments did they use? What was most effective?

VISUAL CONNECTIONS
Flower Power

About the Artist. Bernie Boston, born in Washington, D.C., in 1933, has been a photojournalist since 1963. Boston has won numerous awards for his work and also has taught young photographers about photojournalism in photography classes.

Exploring the Subject. This photograph was taken in 1967 in Washington, D.C., during the antiwar march at the Pentagon. The protestor in this picture takes a stand by placing flowers—symbols of peace and love during the antiwar movement—into the barrels of guns.

Related Expression Skills. Discuss with the class the effectiveness of this gesture. Ask students to think of issues that concern them today, such as the environment. Ask students what positive actions they would take to persuade someone to feel as they do about an issue. Volunteers might act out or pantomime their ideas for the class.

RETEACHING

Provide students with copies of a news story and a letter to the editor, ideally on the same topic. Guide students in comparing and contrasting the two selections for the purposes and methods of writing. [A news story is informative with objective facts. A letter to the editor is persuasive with convincing evidence and emotional appeals.]

MEETING *individual* NEEDS

LEP/ESL

General Strategies. The word *convince* is used throughout the chapter and is a key to understanding the text. Before students begin reading, you may want to write a definition of the word on the chalkboard to make sure they understand:

convince—to overcome the doubts of or to persuade by arguments and evidence; to make one feel sure

USING THE SELECTION
Use It Again and Again and Again

1
What technique does the writer use to catch the reader's attention? [The writer uses a question.]

2
What kind of background information is provided and why? [Fifty years ago people did not have the disposable items that are common today. The writer is probably trying to show that the United States has not always been a throwaway society; the writer is comparing and contrasting the past and present ways of life.]

3
Notice the writer's opinion that natural resources are being thrown away as trash.

256

256

USE IT AGAIN AND AGAIN AND AGAIN

by The EarthWorks Group

Take A Guess.

1 *How many disposable plastic bottles do we use in four days?*
A) Enough to fill a truck B) Enough to fill a warehouse
C) As many as there are people in the whole U.S.

2 Long before you were born, back when your grandparents were kids, there was no such thing as a paper towel or a paper napkin. People used cloth. Back then, everything was used again and again. In fact, most people would never have imagined throwing something away after using it just once.

But today, we have lots of things that are made especially to be tossed in the garbage after one use; we call them "disposable." Aluminum foil, plastic bags, paper bags, plastic food wrap, and other products are all considered "disposable."

3 **What's going on? Our Earth's treasures are being thrown out as trash.** Wouldn't it be wonderful if everyone did a little something to stop this waste? Just imagine what a difference it would make!

Discuss the characteristics of persuasion. Then ask students to think of times that they might need to be persuasive. List their responses on the chalkboard. [Possible examples include asking for permission to go to a party, negotiating a raise in allowance, and talking a friend into going to a particular movie.] ■

257

Did You Know

4 ■ We use millions of feet of paper towels every year. That's a lot of trees!
■ Americans use 35 million paper clips every day.
■ Americans buy 500 million disposable lighters every year. That's millions of pounds of plastic made by factories just so grown-ups can throw it away.

What You Can Do

5 ■ Keep a cloth towel by the sink. Next time you rinse your hands or need to wipe up a spill, grab the cloth towel instead of a paper one.
■ Keep a "rag bag" handy. Put your old, torn clothes in it, and you'll have a supply of rags to help you out with messy chores or art projects.
■ Save plastic bags—you can use them again. If they're dirty, turn them inside out, rinse them and hang them up to dry.
■ Aluminum foil is reusable. Wash it off, let it dry, and put it away. When it can't be used again, recycle it.

4
What kind of information does the article include? [The article includes statistics that help to support the main idea. The information covers recorded facts from several operations, and it can be verified.]

5
How would you describe these suggestions? [Responses will vary. The writer proposes practical solutions to the problems posed by the factual data. The ideas are practical, easy to carry out, and involve items everyone uses.]

INTEGRATING THE LANGUAGE ARTS

Literature Link. Analyzing a speech can help students see how important language is to persuasive speaking. If the selection is available in your literature textbook, have students examine Dr. Martin Luther King, Jr.'s speech, "I Have a Dream." Dr. King skillfully uses repetition, parallelism, and metaphor to motivate and inspire his audience.

Students might analyze and evaluate the effectiveness of the repetition, parallelism, and metaphor in heightening the impact of the message. They could also identify the most inspirational passages in the speech and give specific evidence and reasons for their opinions.

SELECTION AMENDMENT
Description of change: modified
Rationale: to focus on the concept of persuasion presented in this chapter

"Take a plastic bag or plastic wrap and try to see it as oil – or even better, a prehistoric creature."

- Have you got some reusable food containers in your kitchen? (You know, the kind with snap-on tops.) Use them instead of just covering or wrapping food with plastic wrap.
- Start an Earth-positive lunchtime <u>trend</u>—use a lunchbox to carry your food to school. Or if you take a bag lunch, bring home the paper and plastic bags so you can reuse them.

See For Yourself

Look around your house for some "disposable" things. Try to picture where they come from. Hold up a roll of paper towels and imagine it's a tree. Take a plastic bag or plastic wrap and try to see it as oil—or even better, a prehistoric creature. See aluminum foil as a precious metal from underground. They seem a lot more important now, don't they? They are!

from *50 SIMPLE THINGS KIDS CAN DO TO SAVE THE EARTH*

Answer: C. 240 million! Incredible!

READER'S RESPONSE

1. The writers want to convince you that people are wasteful *and* to change your behavior. Will you try any suggestions listed under "What You Can Do"? Which ones, and why?
2. What do you think is the most convincing part of this piece of writing? Why? Take a few minutes to respond in your journal. Do you feel you should try any of the writers' suggestions?

WRITER'S CRAFT

3. The writers give one main reason why we should use things again and again. What is it?
4. What is some of the evidence—proof—that supports this reason?
5. Where do you think the writers are appealing to your emotions, not just to your mind?

"You have to figure out what you think because you're taking a stand."

—ELLEN GOODMAN

ANSWERS
Reader's Response
Responses will vary.

1. Some students might say they already do many of these things. Some will find the most practical ideas to be cloth towels, rag bags, and reusable food containers.
2. Many students will say that the statistics provide the most convincing evidence for adopting the suggestions. The facts can be verified.

Writer's Craft
Responses will vary.

3. The writer says that natural treasures are being thrown away as trash.
4. The writer mentions several disposable items made from oil and trees. Also, the writer lists facts about wasted resources.
5. Students might suggest that using the word *treasures* to describe natural resources appeals to the desire to save things that are valuable. Others might suggest the last paragraph where the reader is told to imagine that everyday products are the limited natural resources they once were.

SELECTION AMENDMENT
Description of change: excerpted
Rationale: to focus on the concept of persuasion presented in this chapter

The examples in the textbook can be grouped under five methods of development of writing: narration (1 and 2), description (3 and 8), comparison-contrast (4), definition (5), and evaluation (7 and 8). Write these terms in random order on the chalkboard and review their meaning. Then ask students where each example fits best as they read them.

Assess students' understanding by asking them to suggest other examples of persuasive writing that use each of these methods of development. ∎

MEETING *individual* NEEDS

LEP/ESL

General Strategies. To prepare students to use evaluation as a method of persuasion, hold a small group debate. Have each group member draw one strip of paper from a hat. Each strip should have a word written on it such as *clocks, trees, oil, wheel, colors,* or *numbers.* To win the debate, a student must persuade the group that the object has been more important for the world than other objects. English-language learners may benefit from hearing the structures that English-proficient students use.

INTEGRATING THE LANGUAGE ARTS

Literature Link. You may want to have students look for the methods of development in a novel such as *Flowers for Algernon* by Daniel Keyes. Students should note that pieces of literature often depend on a mixture of all the methods—a page of description and then a page of narration. Students might also determine which method occurs least frequently in the novel.

Ways to Persuade

Any writer trying to persuade has the same goal as the writers of "Use It Again . . .": to make readers believe or act in a certain way. But writers can present their persuasive messages in many ways. Here are some examples.

- in a personal essay, writing about your experiences to persuade more girls to study science
- in a poster, describing a Cinco de Mayo celebration to encourage people to come to it
- in a newspaper opinion piece, describing your local library to convince readers that it's not truly accessible to people who use wheelchairs
- in an office memo, contrasting two types of software to persuade your supervisor that one type is better
- in a letter to the city council, defining the word *compassion* to convince council members to support a program to help people who are homeless
- in a multimedia review, evaluating a World Wide Web site to encourage people to visit it
- in a letter to school administrators, weighing the pros and cons of a lunch policy to persuade them to change it
- in an e-mail message to a friend, describing a band to convince him to go to a show

LOOKING AHEAD

In this chapter, you'll use evaluation to develop a persuasive composition and a campaign speech. As you work on your writing in this chapter, keep in mind that effective persuasion

- states a clear opinion on the topic
- gives convincing support for the opinion
- may appeal to the reader's emotions

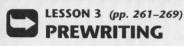
OBJECTIVES

- To distinguish between a statement of fact and a statement of opinion
- To list topics collaboratively for persuasive essays
- To select a suitable topic for a persuasive essay and to compose a clear statement of opinion
- To analyze the concerns and interests of an audience
- To list reasons and evidence that support an opinion

Writing a Persuasive Paper

 Prewriting

Choosing a Topic

You've learned that your old elementary school is about to be renamed. Its present name is the Shady Lawn School. The Board of Education wants to call it the Roderick O. Terwilliger School, after a former principal. You don't know much about Mr. Terwilliger, since he retired before you attended. But you think that changing the name of the school would be a mistake.

If you decide to say what you think, you'll be trying to persuade. And the school name is an ideal persuasion topic: an issue you feel strongly about, and one that matters to others.

Finding an Issue That Matters.   When you write persuasion, you focus on issues you really care about. After all, if you're not interested, how can you be convincing? But your own interest is just the starting point. The issue (the topic or problem you're concerned about) shouldn't matter *only* to you. It should also be an issue that your audience will find of interest and importance.

Identifying and Stating Your Opinion.   Obviously, you have to know what you think before you can write about it. That requires asking, "What is my opinion about this issue?" An *opinion* is how you feel or what you think about a topic. It's what you believe. Of course, someone else may have an opposing opinion on the issue.

An opinion is not the same as a *fact.* You can check the truth of a fact. For example, it's a fact that the northern spotted owl is on the endangered species list. But whether the government should ban logging in certain areas to protect the spotted owl is a matter of opinion.

 **PROGRAM MANAGER**

PREWRITING

- **Self-Assessment** Before beginning instruction of the writing process, see **Writing Process Log** in *Strategies for Writing,* p. 32.
- **Analyzing** To help students analyze and organize ideas, see **Prewriting** in *Strategies for Writing,* pp. 33–34.
- **Instructional Support** See **Graphic Organizers 13** and **14.** For suggestions on how to tie the transparencies to instruction, review teacher's notes in *Fine Art and Instructional Transparencies for Writing,* pp. 71, 73.

QUOTATION FOR THE DAY
"All men have a reason, but not all men can give a reason." (John Henry Cardinal Newman, 1801–1890, English theologian and writer)

Use the quotation as a springboard for a discussion about using reasons to support a belief. Ask students if they can think of times when this quotation could have applied to them.

MOTIVATION

You may want to begin by showing students a transparency of several headlines that focus on controversial issues. The headlines could be reproduced from the local newspaper. Ask students what makes these issues controversial and why people might have strong opinions about them.

TEACHING THE LESSON

Guide students through the information in **Choosing a Topic** on p. 261 by having several volunteers read sections aloud. Help students become aware of the decision-making process involved in selecting an issue.

After students have read and discussed the information, have them list the

MEETING individual NEEDS

STUDENTS WITH SPECIAL NEEDS

Some students have trouble organizing their ideas on paper, and many times they need help before they start writing. You might design a planning sheet that incorporates the charts in this chapter. Include places for several opinions and possible audiences for each. Use the same individual chart to include support later. When students begin the writing process, have them refer to the charts for reminders of what to include for a particular audience.

LEP/ESL

General Strategies. Many cultures place a greater value on collective, cooperative efforts than on individual, competitive ones. To capitalize on this cooperative spirit and to increase the strength of students' persuasive arguments, have students work in two groups to develop opposing viewpoints on a given topic. Have the groups compare reasons to see if they can generate stronger reasons after listening to opposing sides. This might help less-advanced writers contribute and develop ideas.

262 *Writing to Persuade*

When you choose an issue to write about, it's a good idea to write a *statement of opinion.* That's a single sentence expressing your opinion about the topic. For example, here are some statements of opinion you might write on a variety of topics.

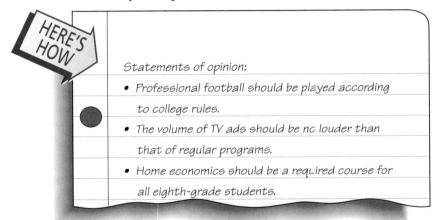

HERE'S HOW

Statements of opinion:

• Professional football should be played according to college rules.

• The volume of TV ads should be no louder than that of regular programs.

• Home economics should be a required course for all eighth-grade students.

Reminder

When choosing a topic for a persuasive composition

- find an issue that concerns you by brainstorming, talking to other people, listening to radio and television, or looking through newspapers and magazines
- recognize opposing opinions, and be ready to deal with them
- write a sentence that clearly states your topic and your opinion about it

EXERCISE 1 ▶ **Distinguishing Fact from Opinion**

With a small group, identify each of the following statements as either a *fact* or an *opinion.* Remember that a fact can be checked for truth, while an opinion is a belief or an attitude.

prewriting steps for writing to persuade: explore suitable issues, choose an issue that matters to the writer, write a thesis statement, analyze purpose and audience, and gather support for the thesis statement.

Students often benefit from a model, so if you have a sample paper, you may want to demonstrate these prewriting steps.

GUIDED PRACTICE

To prepare students for answering questions about facts and opinions in **Exercise 1**, p. 262, have them practice distinguishing between the two by using examples such as "Cars are a means of transportation" [fact] and "Cars are the best means of transportation" [opinion].

☞

Prewriting **263**

1. Persian cats have longer hair than Siamese cats.   **1. fact**
2. Horror movies are a waste of money.   **2. opinion**
3. The sport of baseball is so well liked by Americans that it is often called the "national pastime."   **3. fact**
4. John F. Kennedy deserves a national holiday in his honor.   **4. opinion**

E X E R C I S E **2** ▶   **Exploring Possible Issues**

Working with a small group, make a list of five issues you think you could write about. Use your imagination, but discuss whether the topics will work for short papers. You can suggest issues involving your school, your community, your state, the nation, or the world.

PART 1:
Choosing an Issue to Write About

To choose an issue, remember: How much you care really counts. You can choose an issue from Exercise 2 or make up a new one. If an item in today's news caught your attention—and you have a definite opinion about it—you may have a ready-made topic. When you've decided, write a statement of opinion: a sentence that names the topic or issue and tells your opinion about it.

MEETING *individual* NEEDS

LESS-ADVANCED STUDENTS

Some students may have trouble writing thesis statements. Have them work in pairs to ask each other questions such as "What do you want me to think or do?" and "Why should I think or do that?" Help them ensure that their reasons adequately support their opinions.

ANSWERS
Exercise 2

Answers may vary. Help students choose topics that have opposing viewpoints. If a student lists a topic like "crime," have him or her limit it to an arguable issue—few people favor crime. Explain that if the topic is narrowed to laws governing juvenile offenders, there are several possible points of view.

Before you assign **Writing Assignment: Part 1** (p. 263), students might need to discuss how to choose issues that are not too broad or too narrow. Students should not choose topics that are difficult to address in short papers or that are too obscure for a variety of opinions.

To prepare students for **Exercises 2** (p. 263) and **3** (p. 265) and **Writing Assignment: Part 2** (p. 269), work with the class to choose a topic, develop a thesis, and list supporting details. Students might practice listing opposing arguments so that they see how important the audience and the opposing viewpoints are to persuasive writing.

A DIFFERENT APPROACH

Students might make up questionnaires as a way of analyzing audience reaction to their thesis proposals. They might use the following attitudes: strongly in favor, slightly in favor, neutral, uninformed, slightly against, and strongly against. Students could distribute the questionnaires to the class, tabulate the results, and then use the results to support their theses.

SELECTION AMENDMENT
Description of change: excerpted and modified
Rationale: to focus on the concept of persuasion presented in this chapter

264

 Prewriting

Planning for Persuasive Writing

"True ease in writing," wrote the poet Alexander Pope, "comes from art, not chance." Part of the art lies in careful planning. Let's take a look at how to plan a paper that will persuade your readers.

Thinking About Purpose and Audience

Purpose is clear and strong in a persuasion paper: You want to convince your readers to think as you do—and perhaps to make them act. To succeed, you'll have to understand the people you're writing for: your audience. Who are they? What do they already know about your topic? And, most important, what are *their* opinions on it? If you can answer those questions, you're off to a solid start.

Suppose, for example, you belong to a club that would like to hold a hayride. You'll probably have to convince several different groups that a hayride is a good idea. Think about the interests and concerns of these people.

HERE'S HOW

AUDIENCE	INTERESTS AND CONCERNS
Other club members	Having fun, having a long ride in a wagon pulled by a horse
Parents of club members	Transporting members to the hayride, having chaperones, ensuring safety
Club sponsor	Figuring costs, organizing the hayride, finding chaperones, preventing accidents

INDEPENDENT PRACTICE

Have students work in groups on **Exercise 1** to distinguish fact from opinion. **Exercise 2** is also a cooperative activity and the same groups could complete it. These two exercises lead to **Writing Assignment: Part 1**, which students can begin independently.

Exercise 3 requires group participation in an analysis of audiences. Students might need time in the library or outside class to gather evidence for **Writing Assignment: Part 2.**

WRITING NOTE
You don't have to be the ultimate expert on your topic. However, you should know enough about it to make a persuasive case. If you don't have all the information you need, make sure you can get it from the library or from other people.

EXERCISE 3 ▶ **Speaking and Listening: Analyzing Audience**

Two questions will help you analyze your audience: (1) *What person or group in my audience will disagree most strongly with my opinion?* (2) *Why will they disagree?* Practice using these questions in a small group. Here's how to do it.

- One person chooses one of the following opinions.
- He or she names an audience that might disagree with it (like the club sponsor for the hayride).
- The other group members become the "disagreers." They each give one reason for disagreeing. (The sponsor might say, "It's just too dangerous.")

1. Our school week should be four days instead of five.
2. Our community should create one or more parks ✓ entirely for the use of teenagers.
3. The United States should ban professional boxing. ✓

COOPERATIVE LEARNING

Ask pairs of students to find several different advertisements in a newspaper and to label each one according to the appeal it uses. Is the ad based purely on emotion? Or does the ad use reasons and evidence? Is there a combination of approaches? Students might also consider the source credibility. Students could share their ads with the class, explaining their decisions for each ad.

ANSWERS
Exercise 3

Answers may vary. Because **Exercise 3** includes three statements of opinion, you might have students work in groups of three. Students could follow the bulleted steps suggested and then change roles, thus giving each the chance to choose an audience that would disagree. Students should be aware that different audiences could disagree for different reasons.

Cont. on p. 269

Supporting Your Opinion

Few readers will accept your opinion merely because you tell them you're right. To be convincing, you have to give your readers *reasons* and *evidence*.

Reasons. *Reasons* answer the question "Why?" If you write "We need a larger budget for the school library," the question "Why?" immediately arises. You give reasons: "Many books need to be replaced. Students can't always find the materials they need."

But reasons alone aren't always enough to persuade your audience. Readers usually want proof that your reasons are good ones.

Evidence. *Evidence* is the proof that your opinion and reasons for it are sound. It can consist of facts or expert opinion. A *fact* is information that can be checked by testing, by observing firsthand, or by reading reference materials. Some facts consist of **data,** or information that may lead to conclusions. Facts may also consist of **statistics,** or numerical information. For example, you examine fifty books in the school library. You find that fourteen have pages missing and three have no covers. These are facts—in the form of statistics—that you can use to support your opinion that the library needs more money.

Expert opinion consists of statements by people who are recognized as authorities on the subject. You ask your school librarian about the budget. She replies, "Yes, we need more money if we're going to provide students with the services they need." That's an expert opinion.

Using Appeals to the Emotions

You know what an emotion is. It's a lump in your throat, a sense of belonging, a rush of sympathy. When you make an emotional appeal, you try to cause such feelings.

Writers often make powerful emotional appeals through examples. For instance, you may want to persuade readers to give money for the relief of flood victims.

TEACHING *EVALUATING YOUR REASONING*

Before students examine the material, explain that advertising is the persuasive writing that people encounter most often. Ads play on emotions and try to make people feel a certain way so that they will buy products. Provide examples of ads and have students discuss what emotions the ads appeal to.

A vivid description of one suffering family—their home destroyed, their belongings washed away—will pull strongly at your readers' sympathy.

So consider how you want your audience to *feel* about your topic. If you do, then you can choose an example that appeals to their emotions. Your own experiences can help. An experience that made you angry will probably make your readers feel the same way. But remember: Don't overdo it—you need to balance your emotional appeals with reasons and evidence. Most people will want to see data, statistics, or expert opinions backing up a passionate statement before they accept it as being true.

LEP/ESL

General Strategies. When students don't know the meaning of a term like *bandwagon*, examples can be more helpful than definitions. Point out key words that help identify both the type of appeal and the term associated with it. Use examples such as these to help them categorize appeals:

1. bandwagon—"All across America . . ." "Why not do what most people do?"
2. flattery—"You know a good X when you see one." "Buy X because you're worth it."
3. testimonial—"As a doctor and a parent, I . . ." "As John F. Kennedy once said . . ."

CRITICAL THINKING

Evaluating Your Reasoning

Emotional appeals can be powerful. They're important in persuasion. But watch out! They can be used in ways that weaken your case instead of strengthening it. As you plan your paper, it's good to know some common types of appeals so that you can *evaluate,* or judge, the support you'll use.

EMOTIONAL APPEALS THAT MAY BACKFIRE		
APPEAL	EMOTION/NEED	EXAMPLE
Bandwagon	Desire to join the crowd, to be on the winning side	Buy Apple Zingers cereal! Everyone is eating Apple Zingers—for breakfast and for healthful snacks.
Flattery	Desire to think highly of oneself	You're young, stylish, practical—so of course you shop at Uchida's.

Then lead students in a discussion of the **Emotional Appeals That May Backfire** chart (below). Ask students if they can give more examples of advertisements that use the three types of appeals.

Students can work in groups on the **Critical Thinking Exercise** (pp. 268–269) as you circulate through the room. To conclude, have students suggest other examples of emotional appeals they've encountered.

EMOTIONAL APPEALS THAT MAY BACKFIRE *(continued)*		
APPEAL	**EMOTION/NEED**	**EXAMPLE**
Testimonial	Desire to identify with those who seem more important, more knowledgeable, or more famous than we are	As a pro football coach, I know how important a healthful diet is. That's why I start every day with Health-Aid Orange Juice.

 CRITICAL THINKING EXERCISE:
Evaluating Support

You've seen and heard many emotional appeals like the three in the chart. Now you know their names and what they're supposed to do. With a small group, read the following opinion and the three emotional appeals that support it. Identify each appeal as *bandwagon*, *flattery*, or *testimonial*. Discuss whether you think the appeal works well or backfires. Be sure you can explain your answers to other groups.

Opinion: All baseball stadiums should have playing fields of real grass.

RETEACHING

On a transparency copy a letter to the editor from a local newspaper. Guide students in identifying the thesis statement plus the facts the writer uses. Help them to evaluate the strength of the arguments and determine how well the writer considers opposing viewpoints.

CLOSURE

Have students recall the prewriting steps they used in planning persuasive writing. Have them discuss choosing a topic, thinking about a purpose and an audience, supporting an opinion, and using emotional appeals. What was the most difficult prewriting step for students? What did they find was easiest? ∎

Emotional Appeals

1. "You're a real baseball fan—not one of those people who watch the World Series and nothing else. So you *know* that real grass is the only surface for baseball."
2. "As Phillies star Dick Allen put it, 'If my horse can't eat it, I don't want to play on it.'"
3. "Artificial turf has few defenders. Everybody from the baseball commissioner on down prefers green grass to a green rug."

PART 2:
Finding Support for Your Opinion

Read over your opinion statement, and ask yourself "Why?" That's what readers will do. Start listing reasons *and* evidence to support the reasons. Remember that facts, data, statistics, and expert opinions make the best evidence, but also consider emotional appeals that could help. A chart like this one is a good organizer.

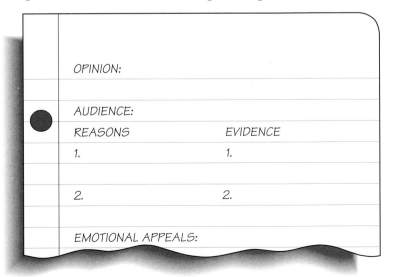

OPINION:

AUDIENCE:

REASONS	EVIDENCE
1.	1.
2.	2.

EMOTIONAL APPEALS:

ANSWERS
Critical Thinking Exercise

Responses will vary.

1. This statement uses flattery, but not very effectively. It could backfire. Real baseball fans have differing opinions about playing surfaces and might resent the implication.
2. This idea uses testimonial. The quotation is illogical, but Dick Allen is an expert in the field. The humor might keep it from backfiring.
3. This is a bandwagon appeal. It tries to sound factual, but "everybody" does not make the same decision.

MEETING *individual* NEEDS

LEP/ESL

General Strategies. What constitutes effective persuasion is often a cultural matter. A highly impassioned argument is sometimes considered more convincing because it shows the depth of the writer's or speaker's conviction. At the same time, a more reasoned argument may be considered less convincing because the writer or speaker is perceived as being less sincere.

SELECTION AMENDMENT
Description of change: excerpted
Rationale: to focus on the concept of persuasion presented in this chapter

WRITING YOUR FIRST DRAFT

OBJECTIVES

- To analyze the principles of organization and the basic elements of an effective persuasive essay
- To write a persuasive essay

MOTIVATION

You may want to have students think of discussions they have had in which someone tried to convince them of something or they tried to persuade another person. Ask them if they ever thought of better arguments or ways to present their positions afterwards. Explain that writing their persuasive argu-

PROGRAM MANAGER

WRITING YOUR FIRST DRAFT

- **Instructional Support** For help with writing the body of a composition, see **Writing** in *Strategies for Writing*, p. 35.
- **Computer Guided Instruction** For additional instruction and practice with types of sentences as noted in the **Grammar Hint** on p. 276, see **Lesson 39** in *Language Workshop CD-ROM*.
- **Practice** To help less-advanced students who need additional practice with types of sentences, see **Chapter 10** in *English Workshop, Second Course*, pp. 77–86.

QUOTATION FOR THE DAY

"You don't write because you want to say something; you write because you've got something to say." (F. Scott Fitzgerald, 1896–1940, American novelist and essayist)

Write the quotation on the chalkboard and ask students to respond to it orally or in their journals. How does the quotation relate especially to persuasive essays? After prewriting and writing first drafts do students find that they have something to say?

Writing Your First Draft

Now that you've gathered support for your opinion, it's time to put everything together and write.

Combining the Basic Elements of Persuasion

Always keep in mind what a persuasive paper does. It

- states an opinion about a topic
- aims to convince an audience to think or act as the writer suggests
- uses reasons, evidence, and sometimes emotional appeals to convince the audience

But how do you get this onto paper? Here are some guiding ideas for writing your draft.

A Good Beginning. You have to grab your readers' attention right away. Perhaps you can begin with a startling fact: "Texas has the legal right to divide itself into five states." That's exactly what your paper recommends doing—but the fact itself is eye-catching enough to be a good beginning. Or you might start with an interesting anecdote. Then, when you have your readers' attention, state your opinion clearly.

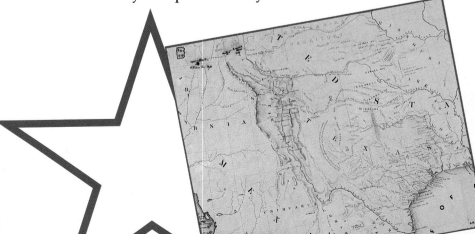

ments gives them the opportunity to organize their thoughts first.

Before students read the model, ask them to examine **Combining the Basic Elements of Persuasion** on p. 270 and to refer to this information as they read the editorial. Ask a student to read aloud the editorial for the class. Then use the side glosses and the annotations to conduct a discussion of the essay's organization. ☞

WRITING NOTE
You might need to include some background information in your introduction. This will help your readers understand what's behind the issue—what all the excitement is about. For example, you might believe that people in your neighborhood should donate money to help your local animal shelter to expand. Some background information is that your neighborhood has doubled in size in the last five years. That will help readers understand your opinion.

Clearly Organized Support. In a persuasive paragraph, you might have a sentence to support each reason. In a composition, you might need a paragraph for each reason. In arranging reasons, you may want to put them in order of importance: from the most important to the least important or vice versa.

A Good Ending. A persuasive paper needs a strong ending. You may find that a summary of reasons works well. Or you may want to repeat your opinion in forceful words. Or you may end with a call to action. You tell readers what they should do as a result of being persuaded.

Here's a chance to see how a professional writer combines the basic elements of persuasion.

A MAGAZINE EDITORIAL

from Ban Dogs from Trails?
by Kent Dannen

Emotional appeal

Issue

The "dogs-shouldn't-be-allowed" people are pressuring the U.S. Forest Service to ban all dogs from Indian Peaks Wilderness in Colorado for two reasons: A significant

---

MEETING *individual* **NEEDS**

LEP/ESL

General Strategies. To write persuasive essays, students need to know how to use words that introduce concessions, such as *although* or *even though.* You may want to point out that *although* or *even though* introduces a clause, and a clause must contain a subject and a verb. (Although snakes are not popular, they are my favorite pets.)

LESS-ADVANCED STUDENTS

Some students might be anxious about writing because they are still unsure of their opinions. Assure students that any opinion that can be supported by facts is valid. Remind them that prewriting helps provide them with ideas for starting. Also assure them that it is okay to change their ideas or even their topics if they feel stifled.

ADVANCED STUDENTS

Advanced students might feel limited by the format outlined in the chapter. Allow them to experiment with other organizational patterns for their essays.

LEARNING STYLES

Kinetic Learners. Allow students who find it difficult to sit still and write [271-273] lengthy time the opportunity to m about to collect their ideas. Kinetic le ers might also benefit from composing on computers.

After students have read the model, have them work in groups to answer the questions in **Exercise 4,** p. 273. Then have groups share and compare their responses. As a visual cue, you may want to introduce the **Framework for a Persuasive Paper** on p. 275 before students read **A Writer's Model** on p. 274.

GUIDED PRACTICE

To prepare students to write their first drafts, use one of the sample thesis statements and supporting reasons you developed as a class in the prewriting lesson to show how the framework is used.

You may need to show students how to choose introductions for theses. Write an example thesis on the chalkboard. Then have

USING THE SELECTION
from **Ban Dogs from Trails?**

1

Why does the writer use a question? [This is a rhetorical question—the writer does not expect an answer. However, he wants the audience to think about the issue in a very personal manner.]

VISUAL CONNECTIONS
Exploring the Subject. Many historians agree that the dog was the first animal to be domesticated. About 12,000 years ago, when human beings were nomadic hunters and gatherers, dogs were attracted to garbage around camps and dwellings because they found it easier to feed there than to hunt for themselves. Soon people tamed the dogs and valued them because they kept the areas clean and warned of approaching danger. Dogs perform these same functions today in many societies.

Background/
Emotional
appeal

Reason

Explanation/
Emotional
appeal

1

Emotional
appeal

Statement of
opinion

<u>minority</u> of dog owners do not obey the rule to leash their dogs on wilderness trails; and some people just do not like dogs. . . .

Banning dogs from Indian Peaks trails affects me and every other responsible American dog owner because these national paths through <u>unsurpassed</u> beauty belong to us. Even if you do not or cannot use your right to enjoy Indian Peaks with your dog at present, do you want this right taken away from you? Don't you want this right preserved for other dog owners? . . .

Banning dogs from wilderness trails is a remedy far worse than the <u>ailment</u>. . . .

Reason

Evidence/
Facts

Numerical
data

Wilderness managers and users need to recognize that dogs greatly <u>enhance</u> the wilderness experience for humans. As burden bearers and companions, domestic dogs have been in Indian Peaks and other North American wilderness areas for some 10,000 years. Dogs share their senses with humans to point out things we otherwise would over-

students suggest ways to introduce that statement. Try several strategies suggested in **A Good Beginning** on p. 270. Students could choose the strategies they like best when they write. Then they could write original introductions and thesis statements.

INDEPENDENT PRACTICE

Students can work on their drafts independently for **Writing Assignment: Part 3** on p. 276. You may want to use mini-conferences with students when they have questions about their writing. At this stage, address only the content of the essays.

☞

Writing Your First Draft **273**

Emotional appeal	2	look. Dogs are the best bridge between humans and the nonhuman aspects of nature and, thus, greatly broaden our viewpoint of the world. Hiking with dogs is fun.
Evidence/ Expert opinion		Many famous writers about the wilderness, such as John Muir, Aldo Leopold and Bob Marshall, have testified to the value of
Call to action	3	dogs on the trail. Now you need to do the same. Please write to the Forest Service in Colorado.

Dog Fancy

2

What emotion does this idea appeal to? [It appeals to an appreciation of nature's marvels.]

3

Note the use of imperative sentences in the call to action, which adds to the power of the conclusion.

ANSWERS
Exercise 4

Answers may vary.

1. The author uses surprising facts and begins by pointing out the opposing side. The writer does not directly state his opinion until the third paragraph. The background information leads to the statement of opinion.

2. The author states that the ban affects all responsible dog owners who have a right to enjoy Indian Peaks with their animals. The second reason is that dogs enhance the wilderness experience. The evidence includes that they have been in the area for 10,000 years as burden bearers and companions, and they share their senses and bridge the gap between man and nature.

3. Dannen's support fits his audience. Readers of *Dog Fancy* might want to include dogs in their travels.

4. Dannen's ideas are clear and straightforward and provide adequate evidence and valid emotional appeals—a convincing argument for action.

EXERCISE 4 ▶ **Analyzing a Persuasive Editorial**

After you have read Kent Dannen's editorial, discuss it with some other students. How would you answer these questions?

1. How does the author grab your attention at the beginning of the editorial? Do you learn the author's opinion in the first paragraph? Explain.
2. What two reasons does Dannen give for opposing the ban on dogs on the trail? What specific evidence does he offer to support his second reason?
3. Kent Dannen's audience is readers of *Dog Fancy* magazine. Do you think his support fits this audience? Explain.
4. Dannen ends with a call to action. Does he persuade you to write to the Forest Service? Why?

A Simple Framework for a Persuasive Paper

The editorial on pages 271–273 shows you that persuasion doesn't have to be organized in a single way. But until you're a professional persuader (as an editor is), you'll find the following framework useful for your own writing.

SELECTION AMENDMENT
Description of change: excerpted and modified
Rationale: to focus on the concept of persuasion presented in this chapter

273

ASSESSMENT

Students might read their first drafts orally to small groups of classmates for peer evaluation. Assess understanding of this stage of the writing process with student-teacher conferences. Have students turn in their responses to **Exercise 4** for evaluation.

CLOSURE

Ask students to evaluate the processes they used in writing their first drafts. You may want to put a chart on the chalkboard and have a student volunteer list the responses. Discuss the successes and strengths as well as the problems and weaknesses.

COOPERATIVE LEARNING

Find several persuasive essays or speeches and reproduce them. Scramble the sentences and distribute the scrambled essays to small groups of students.

Students can then hunt for thesis statements and the reasons, evidence, and emotional appeals that belong to each thesis statement.

After groups have put their essays back together, they can compare their arrangements to the originals and draw conclusions about their efforts.

TIMESAVER

Have each student color-code the first draft by underlining the attention grabber in red, the thesis statement in blue, the reasons in green, and the concluding idea or call to action in yellow. At a glance, both the student and you can evaluate the organization of the draft.

A WRITER'S MODEL

Video Games Yes, Violence No

INTRODUCTION
Attention grabber

"Explosions so real you should warn the neighbors!" "Smash somebody's face in the comfort of your own home!" "The most violent karate game available!" Those are real quotes from the boxes of real video games. No wonder parents think video games are all violence and death-defying danger. Fortunately, they're wrong.

Statement of opinion

Plenty of exciting, nonviolent video games exist. Those are the ones worth playing.

Reason
Evidence/Facts

Violence in video games is just as wrong as violence anywhere else. It's true that on-screen guided missiles don't kill real people. And some studies have concluded that video games don't breed violence among kids. But even makers of video games have acknowledged that video-game violence can have harmful effects like frightening young children. For instance, in 1993, video-game companies began rating games for violence to warn consumers about violent content.

Data

Reason
Explanation
Evidence/Facts

With violent games, the violence is all there is. You don't have to use your brain, only your reflexes. You don't have to know anything except the game's basic rules. Despite all the explosions and phony danger and near-disasters, these games are boring to people who want mental challenge. Give me a quest or a mystery any day.

Emotional appeal

CONCLUSION
Statistics

Violence in video games affects many people. Half the households in the United States—and 80 percent of those with eight- to fourteen-year-old boys—have video games. Let's not spend any more money on death and destruction packaged as fun. The next time you play a video game, why not choose a brainteaser over brute force?

Restatement of opinion and call to action

Have students find copies of *Consumer Reports* or similar publications. Ask each student to choose a type of product (such as home video games) that he or she is interested in and to read an article about it. Then have each student write a personal endorsement for a specific brand, giving reasons and facts to support the endorsement.

Have students exchange endorsements. Students can then write whether or not they would buy the products in response.

☞

Here is the writer's framework in visual form.

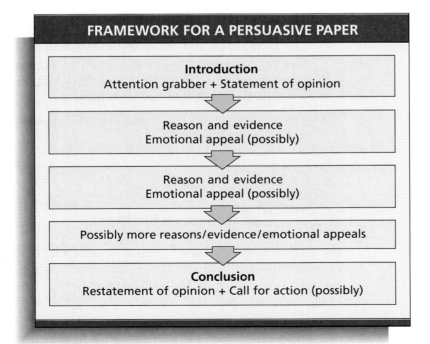

FRAMEWORK FOR A PERSUASIVE PAPER

Introduction
Attention grabber + Statement of opinion

Reason and evidence
Emotional appeal (possibly)

Reason and evidence
Emotional appeal (possibly)

Possibly more reasons/evidence/emotional appeals

Conclusion
Restatement of opinion + Call for action (possibly)

A DIFFERENT APPROACH

As students organize and write their first drafts, help them learn to rank their reasons according to the strengths of their evidence and emotional appeals. They can rank the reasons from most important to least important as suggested in the textbook, or they can rank them from the strongest reason with the best support to the weakest reason with the least support (especially if they find they lack evidence for some of their reasons).

Another option is for students to organize the drafts by beginning with the second best reason, placing the weakest reason(s) in the middle, and ending with the strongest argument. You may want to remind students of the old saying "Save the best for last."

GRAMMAR HINT

Students might need to review the types of sentences and to practice using them before beginning their drafts. Additional practice may be found in **Chapter 13: "The Sentence."** After reviewing, students might find ideas from their prewriting lists and experiment with the various sentence types. You may want students to identify these sentence types in the models so that they can see how other writers use variety to strengthen their essays.

GRAMMAR HINT

Types of Sentences

Part of being persuasive is keeping your audience's attention. One way to do that is by writing interesting sentences—by using sentence variety. There are four basic types of sentences: *declarative, interrogative, imperative,* and *exclamatory.* For instance, to convince your readers that Mary McLeod Bethune should be studied in history class, you could use sentences like these.

EXAMPLES   *Declarative* **(makes a statement):** Mary McLeod Bethune was an early leader in the struggle for racial justice.

Interrogative **(asks a question):** Have you ever heard of Mary McLeod Bethune?

Exclamatory **(expresses strong emotion):** What an impressive leader she was!

Imperative **(gives a command):** Sign the petition today if you think Mary McLeod Bethune should not be forgotten.

 REFERENCE NOTE: For more information about types of sentences, see pages 422–423.

WRITING ASSIGNMENT

PART 3:
Writing a Draft of Your Persuasive Paper

You know your opinion. You've gathered evidence. You're committed! Now let others know it. Write the first draft of your composition, and as you write, keep the **Framework for a Persuasive Paper** (see page 275) in mind.

EVALUATING AND REVISING

OBJECTIVES

- To analyze credibility
- To evaluate the strengths and weaknesses of a persuasive essay
- To revise a persuasive essay

TEACHING THE LESSON

Ask students if they have ever listened to an insincere sales pitch. The salesperson may have presented a product with vague or ambiguous language, no concrete data, or exaggerated information. Tell the class that in persuasion, ideas and their organization must be double-checked and revised when needed.

Evaluating and Revising

You know what the word *incredible* means. In persuasive writing, you want to be the opposite of incredible. You want to be *credible,* or believable. Credibility is something you should evaluate carefully in your draft. One professional writer has made this point clear:

> Credibility is just as fragile for a writer as for a President. Don't inflate an incident to make it more outlandish than it actually was. If the reader catches you in just one bogus [phony] statement that you are trying to pass off as true, everything you write thereafter will be suspect. It's too great a risk, and not worth taking.
>
> William Zinsser, *On Writing Well*

That's good advice, and the chart on the following page gives you more. Answer the questions in the left-hand column. If you find a weakness, use the revision technique suggested in the right-hand column.

Peanuts reprinted by permission of United Feature Syndicate, Inc.

PROGRAM MANAGER

EVALUATING AND REVISING

- **Reinforcement/Reteaching** See **Revision Transparencies 13** and **14.** For suggestions on how to tie the transparencies to instruction, review teacher's notes in *Fine Art and Instructional Transparencies for Writing,* p. 109.

- **Ongoing Assessment** For a rubric to guide assessment, see **Evaluating and Revising** in *Strategies for Writing,* p. 36.

- **Assessment/Reflection** To assess student work and evaluate progress, see **Portfolio Forms** in *Portfolio Assessment,* pp. 5–17.

QUOTATION FOR THE DAY

"I have rewritten—often several times—every word I have ever published. My pencils outlast their erasers." (Vladimir Nabokov, 1899–1977, Russian-born author)

Ask students to write this quotation in their journals with their opinions on revising essays. They might consider the need for revision when writing is to be published.

SELECTION AMENDMENT
Description of change: excerpted and modified
Rationale: to focus on the concept of persuasion presented in this chapter

Have students read the first part of the lesson, which deals with credibility. Have a volunteer read the paragraph by William Zinsser on p. 277. Then discuss with the class the paragraph's relevance to essay writing. Remind students that, at this stage, they should be concerned with what they have written and how they have presented it.

Point out that the textbook offers guidelines to use when students examine their drafts for weaknesses. Analyze the **Evaluating and Revising Persuasive Papers** chart (below) with students and use **Exercise 5** on p. 279 as guided practice. Have a student read the writer's revisions aloud before reading and discussing the questions that follow.

MEETING individual NEEDS

LESS-ADVANCED STUDENTS

Less-skilled writers often have trouble with circular thinking. Instead of supporting their opinions, they repeat the opinions in different words. Pair less-advanced students with advanced ones who can question the evidence presented.

TIMESAVER

Stronger writers, especially those who have a good grasp of the elements of persuasion, might save you some time on one-to-one conferences by becoming peer revisionists or editors.

A DIFFERENT APPROACH

Each student might take one paragraph of his or her essay and, on a transparency, write the first draft version, and then below it or on another transparency provide the revised version. Then each student can present the revisions to the class and give explanations of changes.

EVALUATING AND REVISING PERSUASIVE PAPERS

EVALUATION GUIDE	REVISION TECHNIQUE
1 Do the first one or two sentences grab the reader's attention?	**Add** a startling fact or **replace** the present sentences with an anecdote.
2 Is the writer's opinion stated clearly and quickly?	**Add** a sentence (or **replace** an existing sentence) to make your opinion clear.
3 Are there enough reasons and evidence to make the opinion convincing?	**Add** more reasons, facts, data, statistics, or expert opinions to the paper.
4 Are the emotional appeals effective?	**Cut** any statements that rely too much on the band-wagon approach, flattery, or nonexpert testimonials.
5 Is the conclusion strong?	**Add** a sentence that restates your opinion in strong words, or **add** a call to action.

Reminder

When you evaluate and revise your persuasive paper, make sure you have

- clearly connected your ideas by using transitions
- arranged your ideas logically so your readers can follow your thinking
- used sentence variety to keep your readers' attention

When students revise their drafts in **Writing Assignment: Part 4** (below), remind them to use the chart and the feedback from their peers in evaluating. Mini-conferences will help you assess mastery of the revision process.

Make transparencies of two student essays. Choose one weak and one strong persuasive essay. Have students apply the **Evaluation Guide** questions on p. 278 to the essays to determine their strengths and weaknesses.

Ask students to recall some evaluation and revision strategies for persuasive essays and list these on the chalkboard. Then have students check the chart to see if they have included everything. ■

EXERCISE 5 ▶ **Analyzing a Writer's Revisions**

Study the revisions of the paragraph from the composition on page 274. Then, answer the questions that follow.

> With violent games, the violence is all *↲only your reflexes⊙*
> there is. You don't have to use your brain.   **add**
> ~~These are games for the stupid.~~ You don't   **cut**
> *the game's basic rules⊙*
> have to know anything except ~~what the~~   **cut/replace**
> ~~game is about~~. Despite all the explosions
> and phony danger and near-disasters, *↲to people who want mental challenge⊙*
> these games are boring. Give me a quest,   **add/cut**
> ~~or a great battle~~, or a mystery any day.   **cut**

1. Why did the writer add *only your reflexes* to the second sentence?
2. Why did the writer cut the third sentence?
3. Why is *the game's basic rules* better support than *what the game is about*?
4. Why would adding *to people who want mental challenge* help the writer convince the audience?
5. Why did the writer cut *or a great battle*?

 COMPUTER NOTE: Use your word-processing program's Find command to help you look for overused words to replace.

 **WRITING ASSIGNMENT**

PART 4:
Evaluating and Revising Your Persuasive Paper

Exchange papers with a classmate, and use the questions from the chart on page 278 to evaluate your classmate's paper. Then, make any changes you have decided are necessary.

ANSWERS
Exercise 5

Responses will vary.

1. The phrase contrasts mental and physical responses and emphasizes the mindlessness of violent video games.
2. The sentence might offend a reader. The word *stupid* is a loaded term with strong negative overtones.
3. The first attempt is vague and general, while the revised version is concrete and specific.
4. The phrase qualifies *boring* and suggests that people want to improve their mental capabilities—a convincing emotional argument.
5. The phrase implies violence, which undercuts the central point of the paragraph.

TECHNOLOGY TIP
Students might benefit from using computers in the revision stage. Have the class input their first drafts to evaluate and revise. They can then move sentences and words around and make additions and deletions as necessary. Remind students when they revise on-screen to make a printout before revising. Some programs have a "Save As" function that allows the user to save the original and subsequent versions for comparison.

PROOFREADING AND PUBLISHING

OBJECTIVES

- To proofread and prepare an essay for publication
- To share an essay with an audience

TEACHING THE LESSON

Ask students if they have ever gone shopping and been impressed with merchandise because it was well made and had no defects. Point out that writing for publication is much the same. To impress an audience, writers must produce well-written essays that readers will appreciate for their quality.

PROGRAM MANAGER

PROOFREADING AND PUBLISHING

- **Instructional Support** For a chart students may use to evaluate their proofreading progress, see **Proofreading** in *Strategies for Writing*, p. 37.

- **Independent Practice/ Reteaching** For additional practice with language skills, see **Proofreading Practice: Types of Sentences** in *Strategies for Writing,* p. 38.

- **Assessment/Reflection** To assess student work and evaluate progress, see **Portfolio Forms** in *Portfolio Assessment,* pp. 18–21.

Proofreading and Publishing

Proofreading. When your purpose is to persuade, you want your paper to be convincing in every way. That means careful proofreading—getting rid of any errors you've made in spelling, capitalization, punctuation, and usage. Check to be sure you haven't overused exclamation marks. Strong feelings about a topic can lead to too many *!!!!!!!*'s.

Publishing. Finally the time has come to reach out to your audience. They won't be persuaded if they don't know about your paper. Here are some possible ways to publish it.

- If you've written on a school issue or an issue of concern to teens, ask for permission to photocopy and hand out your paper before school.
- If you've written on a broader issue, send your paper to the local newspaper as a letter to the editor.
- If several members of your class have written on the same issue, have a debate. Each person can present his or her side, and your classmates can discuss both sides of the issue. Or, you can just have an "opinion forum," in which everyone has a chance to present his or her paper to the class.

 PART 5:
Proofreading and Publishing Your Paper

You've worked hard on your paper. You don't want any errors to distract your readers. Take care now to proofread your paper and to correct any errors. Then publish or share your paper with others. You can use one of the ideas given above.

Have a volunteer read **Proofreading** and **Publishing** on p. 280. Concentrate on a few kinds of errors, when students begin proofreading, by giving mini-lessons on the problems students should look for. Find a well-developed persuasive essay with the kinds of errors you want the class to identify and transfer it onto a transparency. Have students find and correct the errors. When students proofread their essays, have them designate where they might publish them. Keep their decisions in mind as you evaluate.

The answers to the first two reflection questions can offer guidance in future persuasive writing. Encourage students to think through their answers carefully before writing them. ■

Reflecting on Your Writing

To add your paper to your **portfolio,** date it and use the following questions to write a reflection to accompany your paper.

- Did you use evidence such as statistics to support your opinion? What type of evidence might you add to make the paper more persuasive?
- Do your ideas seem to flow in a natural manner? Could you rearrange and reword your sentences to express your ideas more smoothly?
- What did you learn about your ability to persuade by writing this paper?

A STUDENT MODEL

LaKeesha Fields, a student at Nottingham Middle School in St. Louis, Missouri, takes a stand on a personal issue in her persuasive paper. As you read LaKeesha's persuasive paragraph, notice how naturally she presents her reasons for owning a pet.

Everyone Should Own a Pet
by LaKeesha Fields

Loneliness is a painful state of being. This is why people need the companionship of animals when there is no one else around. For example, you can talk to pets. Although they don't respond, it seems as if they always understand. You can snuggle up with your pet to watch TV. When you go for a walk, your pet can protect you from danger, and your pet can also be a friend when you're in need of one. Pets can be very helpful when you're home alone, because they can be very alert and sense things that you can't. Although pets can't talk or respond, they give unconditional love. They're an antidote for loneliness, because they can cure your desire for company.

LEP/ESL

General Strategies. English-language learners often have difficulty understanding the change in tone implied by connecting words and phrases such as *although, even though, however, in spite of,* and *despite.* They also may miss the nuances between the words. Have them proofread for the correct use of words that introduce opposing points of view. If they are in doubt, have them check with an English-proficient speaker.

ADVANCED STUDENTS

Students might compile their essays to produce a newsmagazine. The class could design the layouts and include artwork, photographs, or ads relevant to their issues.

A STUDENT MODEL
Evaluation

1. LaKeesha uses a startling observation—loneliness is painful—to grab the reader's attention.
2. At the beginning of her paper, LaKeesha clearly states her opinion that pets help cure loneliness.
3. She lists several reasons to support her opinion, such as talking to pets and snuggling up with pets.
4. She includes the emotional appeal of love.
5. Her conclusion restates her belief that having pets is a cure for loneliness.

WRITING WORKSHOP

TEACHING THE LESSON

Begin by showing or reading a campaign speech of a famous person. (Speeches can be obtained from *Vital Speeches of the Day* or by contacting local legislative representatives.) Discuss the purpose and form of the speech. Ask a volunteer to read the sample speech, and use the questions as a springboard for further discussion. You may choose

QUOTATION FOR THE DAY

"The moment we want to believe something, we suddenly see all the arguments for it, and become blind to the arguments against it." (Bernard Shaw, 1856–1950, Irish dramatist, critic, and essayist)

Use this quotation as a basis for a class discussion of persuasive speaking. Students might interpret Shaw's ideas and then apply his opinion to campaign speaking. Ask students if they agree with Shaw that once people feel a need to believe something they are more easily persuaded.

MEETING *individual* NEEDS

LEP/ESL

General Strategies. To help students understand the purpose and tone of campaign speeches, invite English-proficient speakers to give short impromptu campaign speeches to the class.

TIMESAVER

To evaluate student essays, use a holistic scoring guide that includes the criteria in the textbook for organization and content. Add to those criteria your expectations for mechanics and usage. Or allow students to create their own scoring guides. When they know how they will be evaluated, students might try harder to meet those expectations.

282

WRITING WORKSHOP

A Campaign Speech

Politics is the art of persuasion. New laws need backers. Candidates need supporters. One key goal of a politician is to attract votes, and a good campaign speech can go a long way toward doing that.

Why not use what you've learned about persuasion to write a campaign speech for someone in your class? Read the following speech, and then answer the questions.

When next Friday's election is over, Latricia Gonzalez will be our new vice-president. Yes, Latricia will win the second-highest office in our student government at Montoya Middle School. She'll win because she clearly deserves to. She knows that the vice-presidency is more than just a title. It's a challenge she can meet.

The vice-president has a job to do. She has to step in when the president is absent. That happened four times last year. It's likely to happen again this year. In addition, the vice-president has a major responsibility for fund-raising for student projects.

Who could handle this job better than Latricia Gonzalez? No one. Period. That's because Latricia is a take-charge person--a born leader. Last year she co-chaired the program for Health Awareness Month. She has served as co-captain of the Glee Club and as president of the Girls Sports Club. And fund-raising is one of her specialties. Last year she helped raise nearly a thousand dollars for the all-club banquet.

Latricia Gonzalez is well qualified for the vice-presidency--as she's proved again and again. She's eager to serve, and she'll make things happen. Vote for Latricia Gonzalez on May 4. Latricia for Leadership!

to allow students to work several class days on their speeches, or you could assign the campaign speeches as homework. Be sure to assess students' progress periodically. Before students write final drafts, use peer conferences so that students can assess the effectiveness of their presentations.

CLOSURE
Have students compare the techniques used in writing a persuasive essay to the strategies used in writing a campaign speech. ■

Thinking It Over

1. Why does the writer begin by saying that Latricia is going to win?
2. What two specific duties of the vice-presidency does the writer name?
3. What reasons does the writer give for thinking Latricia will be a good vice-president?
4. What specific evidence does the writer give to support the reasons?
5. Are any of the writer's appeals emotional? Explain.

Writing a Campaign Speech

Prewriting. What elections go on at your school? Choose one (and if it's happening now that's even better), and write a campaign speech for someone you really believe would do a good job. Like the writer of the sample speech, you need to know the duties of the office. Then list all the reasons you can think of why someone would support your candidate. Also think about the voters (people at your school). Which of the reasons will they find most convincing? What do they care about? Choose the two or three reasons most likely to persuade the audience.

ANSWERS
Thinking It Over

Answers may vary.

1. The writer uses a strong positive statement as an attention grabber. Listeners tend to remember what they hear first and last.

2. The vice-president fills in when the president is absent, and the vice-president is responsible for fund-raising.

3. Latricia is a take-charge person, a born leader who has experience with the duties of vice-president.

4. Latricia co-chaired the program for Health Awareness Month, served as co-captain of the Glee Club and president of the Girls Sports Club, and helped raise nearly $1,000 for the all-club banquet.

5. The writer appeals to the audience's emotions by using vivid words to paint Latricia as a competent, take-charge person who is eager for a chance to serve her school.

INTEGRATING THE LANGUAGE ARTS

Listening Link. In persuasive campaign speeches the speaker often becomes impassioned about his or her subject. This emotion is not only conveyed in content, but also in body language. Remind students that when they are listening to rousing speeches, they should tune out the emotional distractions and evaluate the content—both the facts and the arguments.

TIMESAVER

Because campaign speeches are just that—speeches—save grading time by having students deliver their speeches orally. You and the student audience can evaluate the campaign speeches. Use a critique sheet that can be returned to students for feedback.

  Writing, Evaluating, and Revising. Most people like speeches to be brief and to the point. Think of a way to grab the audience's attention and to hold it while you make your points. Short sentences are usually more forceful than long sentences.

When evaluating the speech, be sure to read it aloud. A speech is written to be spoken, so pay attention to rhythm and word choice. The speech should be clear, convincing, and lively. You may even want to invent a slogan like *Latricia for Leadership!*

Proofreading and Publishing. Make all necessary corrections and then practice. Give your speech to the class with a strong, confident voice. And even if you don't speak publicly, show your written speech to the candidate you chose.

If you want to include your speech in your **portfolio,** date it and attach a note of reflection on your writing. Did you keep your audience of peers in mind when you were writing your speech? How might you change the speech to emphasize the concerns of people in your school? Which part of your speech do you think delivers the most impact?

LESSON 8 *(pp. 285–287)*
MAKING CONNECTIONS

PERSUASION IN ACTION
OBJECTIVE

- To write a persuasive letter to the editor

MAKING CONNECTIONS

PERSUASION IN ACTION

Persuasive Letters

When you want to persuade someone, a letter can be the best way. Teachers write letters of recommendation, consumers write letters of complaint, and many people write persuasive letters to the editors of newspapers and magazines. Here's an example of a letter to the editor.

> Dear Editor:
>
> As one who has used a wheelchair all my life, I have seen the vast increases in educational opportunities for children and youth with disabilities since passage of the Individuals with Disabilities Education Act (IDEA). Contrary to <u>alarmist</u> views, in its twenty years IDEA has brought students with disabilities out of the scholastic Dark Ages. Before IDEA, most such students—including myself—were either excluded from public schools or received an inadequate education. Too many of us were ill-prepared for employment and had to depend on public funds. With IDEA, more students with disabilities are graduating from high school, entering college, getting jobs, and paying taxes.
>
> The IDEA does not require that children with disabilities get a "better" or "fancier" education than others. It does guarantee they will receive the education they need to fulfill their potential. America can't afford to go back to pre-IDEA days when the contributions of those with disabilities were wasted through the lack of granting them an adequate education.
>
> Judith E. Heumann
> Washington, D.C.

PERSUASION IN ACTION
Teaching Strategies

Provide students with copies of a newspaper editorial section and have them examine the kinds of issues covered. Then have a volunteer read the introduction and the sample from the textbook. Students can discuss how the writers use reasons, evidence, and emotional appeals to support their opinions. They might compare the letters to see which is most effective and why.

When students turn in their letters for evaluation, have them include their articles. Encourage students to send their letters so that they are aware there is an audience other than you.

GUIDELINES

Letters will vary. Each letter should have the basic ingredients of a persuasive essay: the appropriate format as dictated by the publication, an attention grabber, a thesis statement, sound reasons and evidence, and perhaps some suitable emotional appeal, organized in the most effective manner to express the opinion.

SELECTION AMENDMENT
Description of change: modified
Rationale: to focus on the concept of persuasion presented in this chapter

WRITING ACROSS THE CURRICULUM

Teaching Strategies

Ask students what they can recall from last night's news reports. What problems in the community are mentioned daily? As students mention problems, write their ideas on the chalkboard. Then, have students select one of the problems as the topic for their persuasive essays or letters.

Remind students to use the steps listed to present their solutions and to organize the reasons, facts, and examples so their solutions will stand out and their audience may respond.

GUIDELINES

Students might set up a mock consumer-opinion television forum and read their solutions to the audience. They could respond to one another's opinions with brief notes about the reasoning used.

286

Look through a magazine or newspaper that you read regularly. Starting with a topic or issue that interests you, find an article with which you strongly agree or disagree. Then, write a persuasive letter to the editor about it. Send or e-mail your letter to the magazine or newspaper. If it's published, bring the clipping to class.

WRITING ACROSS THE CURRICULUM

Presenting Solutions for Problems

Sometimes persuasion involves offering solutions to problems. For example, you think that you have a solution for the problem of tardiness to classes in your junior high school. You could write a letter or essay to persuade the school administration that your solution is a good one. When you need to persuade someone to accept your solution to a problem, you can follow these steps:

- **Identify and explain the problem.** For example, you might explain how many students are late to class in a typical day and how long it takes to get from a first-floor class to a second-floor class.
- **Explain the solution you are recommending.** For example, you could explain that adding ten minutes to the school day would allow the time students have between classes to be increased from three minutes to five minutes.
- **Show why your solution will work. Use reasons, facts, data, statistics, and examples.** For example, you could explain that 80 percent of teachers, parents, and students support this solution.

Now, think of a problem in your school or community. If you haven't already thought of a solution, brainstorm or research ideas. Then, write an essay or letter to persuade your audience to accept your solution to the problem.

SPEAKING AND LISTENING

Persuasion in Advertising

Television advertising shows you that words *and* images are tools of persuasion. Most ads use emotional appeals, but they may also refer to facts or statistics. Here are two examples:

- A narrator explains that a man with a stomach-ache who has used the wrong antacid could have gotten relief in "2.2 seconds."
- A pink, drum-beating, mechanical bunny wanders across the screen because its batteries keep on "going and going and going."

Can you use words and images to persuade someone to buy a product in *30 seconds*? First, watch some TV ads, making notes about visuals, words, and the audience you think the ads are meant for.

Then, work with a partner to make up an ad for a real or invented product. Write and sketch your ad idea in two columns: **Words** and **Images.** Be ready to present your ad to the class or—if you can—videotape it.

SPEAKING AND LISTENING
Teaching Strategies

This activity is a good opportunity to discuss the pervasive influences of the mass media on society. Select some popular ad slogans and ask if students can name the products or companies associated with the slogans. Explain that this quick connection is part of the power of advertising.

To help students analyze the powerful effects of these slogans, videotape some television commercials to show the class. Students could analyze and evaluate the commercials for the effects the pictures and words exert.

Explain that before an ad is filmed, artists and scriptwriters plan their presentation on storyboards that show both the images and the language needed; students will be doing the same thing by choosing pictures and words. Remind them to choose an audience and to gear their words and pictures to the interests of that audience.

GUIDELINES

Responses will vary. On presentation day, students might turn in all their planning work after they have presented their ads to the class. They could perform their ads on videotape or in skit form. Students can evaluate each ad for effective word and picture choice and for audience appeal.

WRITING ABOUT LITERATURE: EXPOSITION

OBJECTIVES

- To analyze the characteristics of informative writing about literature
- To read, respond to, analyze, and draw a conclusion about a story
- To gather evidence about a story to support a conclusion
- To organize, draft, evaluate, and revise an evaluation of a story
- To proofread a story evaluation and prepare it for publication

WRITING-IN-PROGRESS ASSIGNMENTS

Major Assignment: Writing an evaluation of a story
Cumulative Writing Assignments: The chart below shows the sequence of cumulative assignments that will guide students as they write a literary evaluation. These Writing Assignments form the instructional core of Chapter 9.

PREWRITING

WRITING ASSIGNMENT
- Part 1: Choosing a Story for Response p. 299
- Part 2: Looking at a Story Closely p. 301
- Part 3: Evaluating and Drawing a Conclusion p. 305
- Part 4: Gathering Support for Your Conclusion p. 306

WRITING YOUR FIRST DRAFT

WRITING ASSIGNMENT
- Part 5: Writing a Draft of Your Story Evaluation p. 309

EVALUATING AND REVISING

WRITING ASSIGNMENT
- Part 6: Evaluating and Revising Your Story Evaluation p. 313

PROOFREADING AND PUBLISHING

WRITING ASSIGNMENT
- Part 7: Proofreading and Publishing Your Story Evaluation p. 315

In addition, exercises 1–4 provide practice in responding to a story, acting out a story, thinking about story elements, and analyzing a writer's revisions.

Cross Curriculum

How Is a Biography like a Story?

Remind students that fiction is not the only material to look at with a critical eye. Set up a cooperative assignment with a teacher from another discipline, such as social studies, and have students evaluate nonfiction material, such as a biographical sketch of a historical figure or of a newsmaker.

- **Brainstorming** Work with social studies teachers to come up with a list of possible biographical selections, or ask the teachers to share periodicals, like *American Heritage,* that would feature appropriate sketches. After they have selected biographical material to evaluate, place students in small groups based on similarity of topics. Then, have them brainstorm how the characteristics to be evaluated would change between fiction and nonfiction. They may want to develop a set of questions like the following as a guide for evaluating biography. Ask the social studies teachers to add input specific to their discipline.

Evaluation of a Biographical Sketch
- Is the depiction of the person believable?
- In what ways is the character worth learning about?
- Does the sketch document factual material about the character?
- Are opinions adequately supported?
- Is the development based on hearsay or on facts?
- Is the presentation objective? Does it show both positive and negative qualities of the character?
- What might the author's agenda be for depicting the person in a particular way?

- **Evaluating** Have students submit their evaluations to the cooperating teacher for content input before publishing the paper.

INTEGRATING THE LANGUAGE ARTS

SELECTION	READING AND LITERATURE	WRITING AND CRITICAL THINKING	LANGUAGE AND SYNTAX	SPEAKING, LISTENING, AND OTHER EXPRESSION SKILLS
• "A Review of Katherine Paterson's *Lyddie*" by Kathleen Odean pp. 290–291 • "A Day's Wait" by Ernest Hemingway p. 294–298 • "Everything You Need To Know About Writing Successfully in Ten Minutes" by Stephen King pp. 310–311 • "Robert, Who Is Often a Stranger to Himself" by Gwendolyn Brooks p. 320	• Finding main idea pp. 291, 301, 318 • Finding supporting examples p. 291 • Making predictions based on story content p. 299 • Analyzing story elements p. 301 • Evaluating and drawing a conclusion about a story pp. 304–306 • Identifying supporting details pp. 306, 317, 318 • Gathering supporting evidence and details in a comparison of two stories pp. 317, 318 • Analyzing a character analysis pp. 321–322	• Analyzing a literary review p. 291 • Drawing and writing conclusions about a story pp. 304–306 • Gathering support for a conclusion p. 306 • Analyzing a writer's revisions for clarity and unity p. 312 • Writing a paragraph to compare two stories pp. 318–319 • Responding to a poem p. 320 • Writing a character analysis p. 322 • Comparing and contrasting two historical figures p. 323	• Proofreading in spelling, grammar, punctuation, and capitalization pp. 315, 319	• Sharing a paper pp. 299, 304, 313, 314, 318 • Using available information to solve new problems pp. 301, 303 • Responding to the writing of peers during the writing process p. 318

SUGGESTED INTEGRATED UNIT PLAN

This unit plan suggests how to integrate the major strands of the language arts with this chapter.

If you begin with this chapter on writing about literature or with the short stories suggested for evaluation, you should focus on the elements of fiction to be evaluated. You can then integrate speaking/listening and language concepts with both the writing and the literature.

Common Characteristics

- Fact-supported content
- Precise language that is neutral and unbiased
- Possibly documentation of facts
- Avoidance of first person whenever possible to retain a sense of objectivity and factuality
- Organization of ideas usually from least to most important
- Explicitness and detail

Writing
Evaluation

UNIT FOCUS
ELEMENTS OF A SHORT STORY

Speaking/Listening
- Share a paper
- Discuss an opinion
- Act out a scene

Language
Style, Mechanics
- Point-by-point development
- Quotation marks

Literature
Short Story
- "The Monkey's Paw"—plot—W. W. Jacobs
- "Dancer"—character—Vickie Sears
- "The Gift"—theme—Ray Bradbury
- "The Treasure of Lemon Brown"—setting—Walter Dean Myers

CHAPTER 9: WRITING ABOUT LITERATURE: EXPOSITION

Use this guide for creating an instructional plan that addresses the individual needs of your students. Assignments accompanied by the following symbol (∗) may be completed out of class. Times given for pacing lessons are estimated.

CHAPTER PLANNING GUIDE—PUPIL'S EDITION

LESSONS	LITERARY MODEL pp. 290–291 "A Review of Katherine Paterson's *Lyddie*" by Kathleen Odean	PREWRITING pp. 293–306	
		Generating Ideas	**Gathering/Organizing**
DEVELOPMENTAL PROGRAM	⏱ **20–25 minutes** • Have students read model aloud in class and answer questions on p. 291 orally.	⏱ **75–80 minutes** • Purposes p. 292 • Main Assignment: Looking Ahead p. 292 • Personal Response p. 293 • A Short Story pp. 294–298 • Exercises 1∗–3 pp. 299, 301 • Looking at a Story pp. 300–301 • Writing Assignment: Parts 1, 2 pp. 299, 301∗	⏱ **30–35 minutes** • Planning a Story Evaluation pp. 302, 305–306 • Characteristics Chart p. 302 • Writing Note pp. 304–305 • Writing Assignments: Parts 3, 4 pp. 305, 306∗ • Reminder p. 306
CORE PROGRAM	⏱ **20–25 minutes** • Assign student pairs to read model aloud and discuss answers to questions p. 291.	⏱ **25–30 minutes** • Purposes p. 292 • Main Assignment: Looking Ahead p. 292 • Response Chart p. 293 • A Short Story pp. 294–298∗ • Elements Chart pp. 300–301 • Writing Assignment: Parts 1, 2 pp. 299, 301∗	⏱ **25–30 minutes** • Characteristics Chart p. 302 • Critical Thinking pp. 303–304 • Writing Note pp. 304–305 • Writing Assignments: Parts 3, 4 pp. 305, 306∗ • Reminder p. 306
ACCELERATED PROGRAM	⏱ **10–15 minutes** • Assign students to read model independently.	⏱ **20–25 minutes** • Purposes p. 292 • Main Assignment: Looking Ahead p. 292 • A Short Story pp. 294–298∗ • Charts pp. 293, 300–301 • Writing Assignments: Parts 1, 2 pp. 299, 301∗	⏱ **20–25 minutes** • Characteristics of a Good Story Chart p. 302 • Writing Note pp. 304–305 • Writing Assignments: Parts 3, 4 pp. 305, 306∗ • Reminder p. 306

CHAPTER PLANNING GUIDE—PROGRAM RESOURCES

	LITERARY MODEL	PREWRITING
PRINT	• Reading Master 9, *Practice for Assessment in Reading, Vocabulary, and Spelling* p. 9	• Prewriting, *Strategies for Writing* pp. 41–42
MEDIA	• Fine Art Transparency 6: *Forward, Transparency Binder* 📽	• Graphic Organizers 15 and 16, *Transparency Binder* 📽 • *Writer's Workshop 1:* Evaluation 💾📽

WRITING pp. 307–309	EVALUATING AND REVISING pp. 310–313	PROOFREADING AND PUBLISHING pp. 314–316
25–30 minutes • Parts of a Story Evaluation p. 307 • A Writer's Model p. 308 • Basic Framework p. 309 • Writing Assignment: Part 5 p. 309*	**40–45 minutes** • Evaluating and Revising pp. 310–311 • Evaluation Chart p. 311 • Exercise 4 pp. 312–313 • Writing Assignment: Part 6 p. 313	**50–55 minutes** • Proofreading and Publishing p. 314 • Mechanics Hint p. 314 • Writing Assignment: Part 7 p. 315 • Reflecting p. 315* • A Student Model pp. 315–316
15–20 minutes • Parts of a Story Evaluation p. 307 • A Writer's Model p. 308* • Framework Chart p. 309 • Writing Assignment: Part 5 p. 309*	**30–35 minutes** • Evaluation Chart p. 311 • Writing Assignment: Part 6 p. 313	**30–35 minutes** • Publishing p. 314 • Mechanics Hint p. 314 • Writing Assignment: Part 7 p. 315 • Reflecting p. 315* • A Student Model pp. 315–316*
10–15 minutes • A Writer's Model p. 308* • Framework Chart p. 309 • Writing Assignment: Part 5 p. 309*	**30–35 minutes** • Evaluation Chart p. 311 • Writing Assignment: Part 6 p. 313	**20–25 minutes** • Publishing p. 314 • Mechanics Hint p. 314 • Writing Assignment: Part 7 p. 315 • Reflecting p. 315*

 Computer disk or CD-ROM   Overhead transparencies

WRITING	EVALUATING AND REVISING	PROOFREADING AND PUBLISHING
• Writing, *Strategies for Writing* p. 43	• Evaluating and Revising, *Strategies for Writing* p. 44	• Proofreading Practice, *Strategies for Writing* p. 46 • Quotation Marks, *English Workshop* pp. 269–272
	• Revision Transparencies 15–16, *Transparency Binder*	• *Language Workshop:* Lesson 54

ELEMENTS OF WRITING: CURRICULUM CONNECTIONS

Writing Workshop
• Comparing and Contrasting Stories pp. 317–318
• Writing a Paragraph About Two Stories pp. 318–319

Making Connections
• Responding to Poetry p. 320
• A Character Analysis pp. 321–322
• Comparing and Contrasting Historical Figures pp. 322–323

ASSESSMENT OPTIONS

Summative Assessment
Holistic Scoring: Prompts and Models pp. 33–38

Portfolio Assessment
Portfolio forms, *Portfolio Assessment* pp. 5–24, 38–43

Reflection
Writing Process Log, *Strategies for Writing* p. 40

Ongoing Assessment
Proofreading, *Strategies for Writing* p. 45

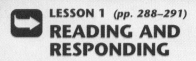
OBJECTIVE

- To analyze and personally respond to a literary review

MOTIVATION

Tell students that when they tell a friend, "That story stunk" or "That movie was great!" they are responding to the story or movie. When they explain why they like or don't like the story or movie, they are giving brief oral reviews.

PROGRAM MANAGER

CHAPTER 9

- **Computer Guided Instruction** For a related assignment that students may use for additional instruction and practice, see **Evaluation** in *Writer's Workshop 1 CD-ROM.*

- **Summative Assessment** For a writing prompt, including grading criteria and student models, see *Holistic Scoring: Prompts and Models,* pp. 33–38.

- **Performance Assessment** Use **Assessment 3** in *Integrated Performance Assessment, Level C.* For help with evaluating student writing, see *Holistic Scoring Workshop, Level C.*

- **Extension/Enrichment** See **Fine Art Transparency 6,** *Forward* by Jacob Lawrence. For suggestions on how to tie the transparency to instruction, review teacher's notes in *Fine Art and Instructional Transparencies for Writing,* p. 33.

- **Reading Support** For help with the reading selection, pp. 290–291, see **Reading Master 9** in *Practice for Assessment in Reading, Vocabulary, and Spelling,* p. 9.

9 WRITING ABOUT LITERATURE: EXPOSITION

TEACHING THE LESSON

Read Odean's review of *Lyddie* aloud to your students. Then use the annotations and the **Reader's Response** and **Writer's Craft** questions to develop your students' understanding of the purpose and content of a literary review. Explain to students that there are no right or wrong answers to the questions in **Reader's Response**—students should respond according to what they think and how they feel.

You may want students to write rough answers to the questions in **Writer's Craft** and to discuss the answers in small groups.

Reading and Responding

Do you like every book, every comic strip, every magazine article you **read?** Of course not. Nobody does. But, whether you like them or not, chances are you'll **respond.** Reading does that to us. It makes us laugh, fires us up, gives us gooseflesh, or makes us yawn.

Writing and You. Some writers make a living by telling us what they think about books, movies, plays, and TV shows. Their opinions have turned so-so movies into blockbusters. Their discoveries of little known authors have led to delightful hours of reading for the rest of us. Have you ever read a book that you liked so much you couldn't wait to tell a friend about it?

As You Read. Here's a response to Katherine Paterson's book *Lyddie.* As you read, think about the reviewer's opinion. Do you think she likes the book?

Roger de la Fresnaye, detail of *Emblems* (c. 1913). © The Phillips Collection, Washington, D.C.

 QUOTATION FOR THE DAY

"Some books are undeservedly forgotten; none are undeservedly remembered." (W.H. Auden, 1907–1973, British poet)

You may wish to write the quotation on the chalkboard and tell students that any book they remember reading or from which they remember a line, word, or character was probably worth reading. Students might write reading histories in their writing journals by recording the very first books they remember reading and their favorites since then.

VISUAL CONNECTIONS
Emblems

About the Artist. Roger de la Fresnaye was born in 1885 in Le Mans, France. After years of traditional studies, the artist moved on to the Académie Ransom, where he was exposed to the work of contemporary artists such as Gauguin and Picasso. He adopted elements of cubism in his paintings and created a distinctive style of his own.

Ideas for Writing. Discuss the title of this painting with the class. Point out that an emblem is a visible symbol of an ideal. Ask students to respond to this painting by freewriting about the objects depicted and their symbolic meanings.

ASSESSMENT

Use students' responses to **Reader's Response** and **Writer's Craft** to assess their understanding of the review of *Lyddie*.

RETEACHING

If students have trouble understanding the purpose or content of Odean's review, you may want to have them read some reviews of recent popular movies. Then guide the class through answering questions similar to the ones in **Reader's Response** and **Writer's Craft**.

290

MEETING *individual* NEEDS

LEP/ESL

General Strategies. In the review of *Lyddie,* the author tells of an important event in the life of the main character— learning to read. Before students read this review, you may want to have them freewrite about their own experiences of learning how to read.

USING THE SELECTION
A Review of Katherine Paterson's *Lyddie*

1

Odean's first sentence states her main idea; she briefly summarizes the book and expresses her approval.

2

The review states the setting of the book—the Vermont mountains.

3

"Metaphorical" bears refers to the problems that Lyddie faces.

4

From the mid-nineteenth century until 1916 (when child labor laws were passed in the United States), it was common for children to work long hours in factories with poor safety conditions.

5

A quality of Lyddie's character is described and supported with a specific example.

6

Here the reviewer supports her main idea with specific details about how learning to read changes Lyddie's life.

A Review of Katherine Paterson's

LYDDIE
by Kathleen Odean

1
2

I n this superb novel, Paterson <u>deftly depicts</u> a Lowell, Massachusetts fabric mill in the 1840s and a factory girl whose life is changed by her experiences there. Readers first meet 13-year-old Lyddie Worthen staring down a bear on her family's debt-ridden farm in the Vermont mountains. With

3 her fierce spirit, she stares down a series of <u>metaphorical</u> bears in her year as a servant girl at an inn and then in her months under

4 <u>grueling</u> conditions as a factory worker. Lyddie is far from perfect, "close with her money and her friendships," but she is always trying. She suffers from loneliness, illness, and loss at too

5 early an age, but she survives and grows. An encounter with a runaway slave brings out her generosity and starts her wondering about slavery and inequality. Try as she might to focus on making money to save the farm, Lyddie cannot ignore the issues

6 around her, including the inequality of women. One of her roommates in the company boarding house awakens Lyddie to the wonder of books. This dignity brought by literacy is mov-

CLOSURE

To conclude this lesson, ask students to recall where Odean states her main idea— her opinion about Paterson's book [first sentence; restated in last sentence]. Then ask students how Odean supports her opinion. [She uses specific examples.] ■

291

ingly <u>conveyed</u> as she improves her reading and then helps an Irish fellow worker learn to read. The importance of reading is just one of the threads in this tightly woven story in which each word serves a purpose and each figure of speech, drawn from the farm or the factory, adds to the picture. Paterson has brought a troubling time and place <u>vividly</u> to life, but she has also given readers great hope in the spirited person of Lyddie Worthen.

READER'S RESPONSE

1. Does *Lyddie* sound like a book you'd like to read? Explain why or why not.
2. If you've already read this book, tell why you think it's a good story.

WRITER'S CRAFT

3. What does the reviewer think of *Lyddie*? What sentences tell you her opinion?
4. What examples does the reviewer use to support her opinion? In other words, what evidence does she give for liking or disliking the book?

ANSWERS

Reader's Response

Responses will vary.

1. Students should state their preferences and explain them by citing details from the review that helped form their opinions.
2. Students who have read the book should explain why they do or do not like it by giving specific examples of what they do or do not like.

Writer's Craft

3. The reviewer likes *Lyddie*. In the first sentence, she uses the words *superb* and *deftly*. In the ninth sentence she says Lyddie's dignity is "movingly conveyed." In the tenth sentence, she speaks of "this tightly woven story in which each word serves a purpose and each figure of speech . . . adds to the picture." In the last sentence, the reviewer says "Paterson has brought a . . . time and place vividly to life."
4. The reviewer likes the story partly because it is well written. Odean likes the character Lyddie because of Lyddie's "fierce spirit"; because she suffers, survives, and grows; and because of her generosity. Odean also finds the time and place interesting.

PURPOSES FOR WRITING ABOUT LITERATURE

TEACHING *PURPOSES FOR WRITING ABOUT LITERATURE*

Explain to students that writers have four basic purposes for writing: expressing themselves, persuading, giving information, and being creative. Have students decide which example in the textbook goes with each of these purposes. [1 and 2 go with self-expression, 3 and 4 go with persuasion, 5 goes with information, and 6 and 7 go with creative writing.] Assess students' understanding of the purposes by asking them to tell what is meant by each purpose. ∎

COOPERATIVE LEARNING

Divide the class into groups of four. Have each group pick a movie or television program to write about. Then have each group brainstorm topics for four different paragraphs about the movie or show, each paragraph written with a different purpose. Each student could write one of the paragraphs, and then the members of the group could work together to evaluate and revise all of the paragraphs. Finally, have groups exchange papers to identify the purpose of each paragraph from the other group.

MEETING *individual* NEEDS

LEP/ESL

General Strategies. When it is time to choose stories for evaluation, students may be interested in reading stories about their native countries or their cultures. Explain that there are published bibliographies of stories in specific categories. The librarian or media-center specialist may be able to help students locate stories of specific types.

---

292 *Writing About Literature*

Purposes for Writing About Literature

A review discusses the strengths and weaknesses of a book or film or other creative work. Sometimes a review's purpose is just to inform the reader. At other times, the purpose is to persuade the reader that a work is or is not worth reading or seeing. Remember, though, that reviews are not the only way to write about literature. You can write about books and other creative works in many other ways, for a variety of purposes. Here are a few examples.

- in your journal, writing about a monster movie that kept you from sleeping
- in a letter, telling a friend about your favorite movie
- in a letter to television network executives, trying to persuade them not to cancel your favorite show
- in a book jacket blurb, describing the book in order to persuade people to read it
- in a message for a company bulletin board, telling your coworkers about a book you think they'd enjoy
- in a script, recording a dialogue between similar characters from stories by two different authors
- in an epilogue for a novel you've read, imagining what happens to the characters after the novel ends

LOOKING AHEAD

In this chapter, you will be writing an informative evaluation of a story. Keep in mind that an effective evaluation

- evaluates at least one element from the story
- gives quotations and details from the story to support the evaluation

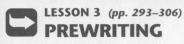
OBJECTIVES

- To read and respond to a story
- To write an additional scene for a story and to act it out
- To choose, read, analyze, and personally respond to a story
- To analyze a story to identify its elements
- To evaluate and draw a conclusion about a story and to find evidence to support the conclusion

Prewriting　**293**

Writing a Story Evaluation

Starting with Personal Response

No one feels and thinks exactly the way you do about a piece of literature. You may laugh out loud when a character does something silly. At the same time, your friend may be annoyed because he thinks the character is dumb. You may find a scene so spooky you forget to breathe, but someone else may think it's boring. There is no right or wrong personal response to a story or poem. Each person responds differently. That's why anyone's response is called a *personal* response.

WAYS TO RESPOND PERSONALLY
■ Write a journal entry about how a poem or story makes you feel. Is it scary like the one you tell around a campfire right before bedtime? Do you feel it says something about you and your life? Is it fun just because it leads you to imagine fantastic people, places, and situations?
■ Imagine what happens to a character after a story or poem ends. What's going on in the character's life a year later? five years later?
■ Pretend you're a character in the story or poem. As this character, write a letter to a friend. Tell about something that's important to the character.

Here's a story about a boy who is sick with the flu. Before the story begins, the boy has lived in France and gone to school there. As you read, start with your personal response. Can you understand the boy's feelings?

293

Read to the class a short, simple poem that expresses an image or an experience, such as Walter de la Mare's "Silver" or Robert Francis's "The Base Stealer." Before you read the poem, tell students that afterward you will want them to respond to the poem by telling whether they like or dislike it, and by describing how it makes them feel or what memories it triggers. After students have responded to the poem, explain that their personal responses are the starting point for literary evaluations.

USING THE SELECTION
A Day's Wait

1

The story raises some questions that are never answered. In particular, throughout the story Hemingway gives contradictory clues about the relationship of the narrator to the boy. Here the boy comes in to shut the windows in the narrator's room—a routine duty that probably would not be performed by a son.

2

We would seem to imply the narrator and his wife, but a woman is never mentioned, and this point is never clarified.

3

Schatz is a German term of endearment. The use of this nickname implies an affectionate relationship.

4

Here the narrator's reference to Schatz as "the boy" is rather formal or impersonal.

5

This fact indicates that the setting is somewhere where the Fahrenheit temperature scale is used.

6

Schatz does not hear the doctor's explanation.

A SHORT STORY

A Day's Wait
by Ernest Hemingway

1
2   He came into the room to shut the windows while we were still in bed and I saw he looked ill. He was shivering, his face was white, and he walked slowly as though it ached to move.

3   "What's the matter, Schatz?"
"I've got a headache."
"You better go back to bed."
"No. I'm all right."
"You go to bed. I'll see you when I'm dressed."

But when I came downstairs he was dressed, sitting by the fire, looking a very sick and miserable boy of nine years. When I put my hand on his forehead I knew he had a fever.

"You go up to bed," I said, "you're sick."
"I'm all right," he said.

4   When the doctor came he took the boy's temperature.
"What is it?" I asked him.

5   "One hundred and two."

6   Downstairs, the doctor left three different medicines in different colored capsules with instructions for giving them. One was to bring down the fever, another a purgative, the third to overcome an acid condition. The germs of influenza can only exist in an acid condition, he explained. He seemed to know all about influenza and said there was nothing to worry about if the fever did not go above one hundred and four degrees. This was a light epi-

To prepare students to read Ernest Hemingway's **"A Day's Wait"** (pp. 294–298), discuss with them the introductory material on personal response. You may want to introduce an additional technique for personal response, the reading log. Explain to students that this method differs from other personal-response techniques in that it requires them to record their questions, comments, and feelings about the story as they read it rather than afterward. This process gives students a stage-by-stage record of their reactions to the story by highlighting significant points of response that they might miss if they respond only after the whole story has unfolded for them. ☞

demic of flu and there was no danger if you avoided pneumonia.

Back in the room I wrote the boy's temperature down and made a note of the time to give the various capsules.

7 "Do you want me to read to you?"

"All right. If you want to," said the boy. His face was very white and there were dark areas under his eyes. He lay still in the bed and seemed very detached from what was going on.

8 I read aloud from Howard Pyle's *Book of Pirates*; but I could see he was not following what I was reading.

"How do you feel, Schatz?" I asked him.

"Just the same, so far," he said.

I sat at the foot of the bed and read to myself while I waited for it to be time to give another capsule. It would have been natural for him to go to sleep, but when I looked up he was looking at the foot of the bed, looking very strangely.

"Why don't you try to go to sleep? I'll wake you up for the medicine."

"I'd rather stay awake."

9   After a while he said to me, "You don't
10 have to stay in here with me, Papa, if it bothers you."

7
The narrator's behavior towards the boy is concerned and fatherly.

8
In the late nineteenth century, American writer and illustrator Howard Pyle published popular adventure books about King Arthur, Robin Hood, and other heroes.

9
In this exchange, the narrator and the boy misunderstand each other. They both refer to *it*, but each of them has a different antecedent in mind. The boy is referring to his dying, while the narrator is referring to the illness or, possibly, to staying in the room.

10
The boy calls the narrator *Papa*, which seems to imply a father/son relationship, but *Papa* may simply be a name or nickname and not a synonym for *father*. Although some interpreters assume that these characters are father and son, in fact, their relationship is never defined.

Explain that keeping a reading log is a form of freewriting—no particular format is necessary, and grammar and punctuation are unimportant. To show students how the process works, model for them your responses to the first page of "A Day's Wait."

If you do not want to use reading logs, you could have a volunteer read Hemingway's story aloud. You may want to tell students that although the story is fiction, it was based on an incident in Hemingway's life in which his son contracted influenza.

To prepare students for **Writing Assignment: Part 1** on p. 299, lead a discussion based on the questions in **Exercise 1** (p. 299) rather than having students write journal entries. If students keep reading logs,

"It doesn't bother me."

"No, I mean you don't have to stay if it's going to bother you."

I thought perhaps he was a little light-headed and after giving him the prescribed capsules at eleven o'clock I went out for a while.

11

It was a bright, cold day, the ground covered with a sleet that had frozen so that it seemed as if all the bare trees, the bushes, the cut brush and all the grass and the bare ground had been varnished with ice. I took the young Irish setter for a little walk up the road and along a frozen creek, but it was difficult to stand or walk on the glassy surface and the red dog slipped and slithered and I fell twice, hard, once dropping my gun and having it slide away over the ice.

11
Here the wintry landscape is described.

12

We <u>flushed</u> a <u>covey</u> of quail under a high clay bank with overhanging brush and I killed two as they went out of sight over the top of the bank. Some of the covey lit in trees, but most of them scattered into brush piles and it was necessary to jump on the ice-coated mounds of brush several times before they would flush. Coming out while you were <u>poised</u> unsteadily on the icy, springy brush they made difficult shooting and I killed two,

12
The narrator's pleasant recreational outing contrasts sharply with Schatz's agonizing ordeal.

ask volunteers to share some of their entries. **Exercise 2** on p. 299 offers students the opportunity to extend the story; students might need some guidance in preparing their performance.

At this point in the lesson, you might want to prepare students for what lies ahead by previewing the following steps of the prewriting stage:

1. Choose and respond to a story.
2. Analyze the elements of the story.
3. Evaluate and draw a conclusion about the story.
4. Gather details to support your conclusion.

Assign **Writing Assignment: Part 1** as independent practice. Students could use the reading-log method for their personal responses. ☞

Prewriting **297**

missed five, and started back pleased to have found a covey close to the house and happy there were so many left to find on another day.

At the house they said the boy had refused to let any one come into the room.

"You can't come in," he said. "You mustn't get what I have."

I went up to him and found him in exactly the position I had left him, white-faced, but with the tops of his cheeks flushed by the fever, staring still, as he had stared, at the foot of the bed.

I took his temperature.

"What is it?"

13 | "Something like a hundred," I said. It was one hundred and two and four tenths.

"It was a hundred and two," he said.

"Who said so?"

"The doctor."

"Your temperature is all right," I said. "It's nothing to worry about."

"I don't worry," he said, "but I can't keep from thinking."

"Don't think," I said. "Just take it easy."

"I'm taking it easy," he said and looked straight ahead. He was evidently holding tight onto himself about something.

"Take this with water."

"Do you think it will do any good?"

"Of course it will."

I sat down and opened the *Pirate* book and commenced to read, but I could see he was not following, so I stopped.

"About what time do you think I'm going to die?" he asked.

"What?"

"About how long will it be before I die?"

"You aren't going to die. What's the matter with you?"

13

Sensing Schatz's anxiety, he tries to ease the boy's mind by telling him his temperature is lower than it actually is.

Then discuss with students **Elements of Stories** on pp. 300–301. You could use the questions in **Exercise 3, p. 301**, as guided practice and assign **Writing Assignment: Part 2** on p. 301 as independent practice.

Carefully discuss with students **Characteristics of a Good Story** on p. 302. Have students review their personal responses from **Writing Assignment: Part 1** (and readers' logs, if applicable) for any specific comments about characters, setting, plot, or theme. Guiding students through the evaluative questions in **Critical Thinking** (pp. 303–304) should prepare them to complete **Writing Assignment: Part 3** on p. 305 as independent practice.

298   *Writing About Literature*

14

In this conversation between the narrator and the boy, the conflict of the story is resolved.

14

"Oh, yes, I am. I heard him say a hundred and two."

"People don't die with a fever of one hundred and two. That's a silly way to talk."

"I know they do. At school in France the boys told me you can't live with forty-four degrees. I've got a hundred and two."

He had been waiting to die all day, ever since nine o'clock in the morning.

"You poor Schatz," I said. "Poor old Schatz. It's like miles and kilometers. You aren't going to die. That's a different thermometer. On that thermometer thirty-seven is normal. On this kind it's ninety-eight."

"Are you sure?"

"Absolutely," I said. "It's like miles and kilometers. You know, like how many kilometers we make when we do seventy miles in the car?"

"Oh," he said.

But his gaze at the foot of the bed relaxed slowly. The hold over himself relaxed too, finally, and the next day it was very <u>slack</u> and he cried very easily at little things that were of no importance.

To prepare students for the final prewriting step, write on the chalkboard the example conclusion in **Writing Assignment: Part 3.** Model for students the process of finding details from the story to support the conclusion. Then assign **Writing Assignment: Part 4** on p. 306 as independent practice.

RETEACHING
If analyzing story elements is a problem for some students, give them photocopies of **"A Day's Wait"** and guide them through the parts of the story that reveal each of the elements. Have students highlight the different parts in different colors.
If drawing conclusions is difficult for some students, remind them that the

EXERCISE 1 ▶ **Responding to a Story**

What was your personal response to the story? Were you surprised at the end? Did you know that Schatz thought he was going to die? Do you think you would act the same way Schatz did? Choose one of the personal response ideas on page 293. Write your thoughts in your journal or share them with a classmate.

EXERCISE 2 ▶ **Speaking and Listening: Acting Out a Story**

Think about what Schatz might do a week after this story ends. Get together with a classmate or two and write a scene that might happen one week later. Here are some suggestions for writing your scene.

1. Decide where Schatz will be and who will be with him.
2. Decide what actions will take place. Will Schatz still think he's going to die? Will he be proud of his experience or embarrassed by it? Will he want to play all the time or just sit and think?
3. Write down what Schatz and any other characters will say.

After you've written your scene, act it out for the rest of your class.

PART 1:
Choosing a Story for Response

Find a story in your literature book or ask your teacher or media center specialist for a suggestion. Read the story for fun and then write your personal response to it in your journal. In addition to writing about your feelings, try writing a new ending for the story. How else might it have turned out?

ANSWERS
Exercise 1

Responses will vary. Students should use one of the modes in the **Ways to Respond Personally** chart on p. 293 to express their feelings or thoughts.

ANSWERS
Exercise 2

Scenes should demonstrate that students have considered and answered the questions in the exercise. In evaluating presentations, consider participation, originality, and relevance to the story.

MEETING *individual* **NEEDS**
STUDENTS WITH SPECIAL NEEDS

Students with low reading levels need guidance in selecting stories that can be read fairly easily. Look for concise language, short sentences, and brevity. If the story is available on videotape, a student could view it and then start his or her evaluation by comparing the written story to the film.

basic question is whether or not they think the story is good. Have them talk about their evaluations of the story and help them to see that the conclusion follows naturally.

The highlighting technique can also work for students who have trouble finding support for their conclusions. You could guide them through finding and highlighting supporting details in "**A Day's**

Wait" and then have them go through the same process on their own with their chosen stories.

Prewriting

Looking at a Story More Closely

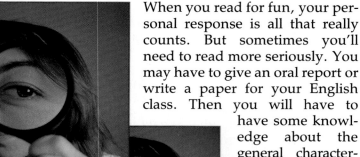

When you read for fun, your personal response is all that really counts. But sometimes you'll need to read more seriously. You may have to give an oral report or write a paper for your English class. Then you will have to have some knowledge about the general characteristics, or elements, of literature.

The following chart explains the main elements, or features, of stories.

ELEMENTS OF STORIES
CHARACTERS: *Characters* are the individuals in the story. They may be people, animals, or even things. For example, in a folk tale the characters may be animals. In a science fiction fantasy, they may be robots.
SETTING: The *setting* is where and when a story takes place. It may be the sidewalks and streets of Harlem, or it may be the muddy waters of a creek in the South. It may even be an imaginary city in a distant galaxy.

(continued)

LESS-ADVANCED STUDENTS

For **Exercise 3**, less-advanced students might learn to identify story elements more easily if the process is modeled for them by advanced students. Organize groups of five, with each group containing both advanced students and less-advanced students. Have less-advanced students do questions 1 and 2 while advanced students do questions 3, 4, and 5. Then each student should share his or her answer with the group and explain how the answer was deduced. Finally, have each student write answers to all five questions.

CLOSURE

Ask students to list the four prewriting steps for writing a story evaluation [(1) Select and respond to a story; (2) look closely at the elements of character, setting, plot, and theme; (3) draw a conclusion about the story; and (4) find support for the conclusion].

ENRICHMENT

The introduction of the idea of personal responses to literature opens doors for personal responses to other artistic forms. Ask your students to respond to each of two or three varied aesthetic experiences that you describe. You might show copies or slides of a work of art; play part of a symphony; or show a clip from a ballet, opera, or ☞

Prewriting **301**

ELEMENTS OF STORIES *(continued)*

PLOT: *Plot* is what happens in the story. It's a chain of events. One thing causes another thing to happen, and so on. A plot is centered around a *conflict* that must be resolved (solved or ended) by the end of the story.

THEME: *Theme* is the meaning of the story. Some stories are meant purely to entertain. The writer is not trying to make a point about life or human nature. In other stories, however, the actions and the way they turn out have some meaning or messages for the reader.

EXERCISE 3 ▶ **Thinking About Story Elements**

Review the story "A Day's Wait." This time, think about the elements of stories. Then, use your knowledge about stories to answer these questions.

1. Who is the main character?
2. Where does the story take place?
3. What is the basic plot of the story? How does one event lead to another?
4. What is the conflict in this story? How is the conflict resolved at the end of the story?
5. Does this story have a theme or message? If so, how would you state it in your own words?

WRITING ASSIGNMENT

PART 2:
Looking at a Story Closely

Now that you've given yourself a chance to respond personally to your story, take a closer look. Try to see how it works and what makes it work that way. Use the questions in Exercise 3 as a guide for your thinking. Write down your answers to the questions and save them to use later.

ANSWERS
Exercise 3

Answers may vary.

1. Schatz, a nine-year-old boy, is the main character.

2. The setting is only vaguely defined. It could be a home, an inn, or a hotel. It is in a rural area in a country where the Fahrenheit temperature scale is used and where the winters are cold.

3. The basic plot concerns the boy's illness, his misunderstanding of its meaning, and his fear of death. One event leads to another chronologically.

4. The conflict revolves around Schatz's misunderstanding of the meaning of his temperature. The resolution occurs when the narrator explains the difference between Fahrenheit and Celsius and the boy relaxes.

5. Possible themes are the pain that can be caused by a simple misunderstanding and the bravery of a child facing what he believes to be his death.

301

play. The point is to enrich your students' aesthetic experiences and to provide students an opportunity to respond to and discuss these experiences. ■

MEETING *individual* NEEDS

LEARNING STYLES

Auditory and Visual Learners. You may want to have students view a videotape of a short story from the *American Short Story* series. Possibilities include Katherine Anne Porter's "The Jilting of Granny Weatherall" and Richard Wright's "Almos' a Man." You could then have students analyze the story by following the steps from the textbook for responding to and evaluating a story.

A DIFFERENT APPROACH

Allow students to evaluate a new video game in class. You can have students make up their own questions or guidelines, or you can use these:

1. Is the purpose of the game clear?
2. Are the instructions clearly stated? What parts, if any, need more explanation?
3. Are the graphics clear and interesting?
4. Does the game hold your attention?

After students evaluate the games, ask them to draw conclusions. Have each student tell whether the game he or she evaluated is worth buying or renting.

Prewriting

Planning a Story Evaluation

Movie critics evaluate movies. Experts on video games evaluate new games. (Perhaps you've read evaluations of movies and video games in magazines or seen them on television.) And people who know literature evaluate stories, poems, and novels. When you evaluate literature, you start with two things: your personal response and your understanding of the elements of literature. Then you plan your evaluation.

Evaluating a Story

You evaluate things all the time. When you evaluate, you judge something against a set of standards. Standards are the characteristics that a good story or movie or video game will have. For example, all video games have graphics, but not all graphics are alike. They may be terrific, terrible, or somewhere in between. Here are some standards that are often used to make judgments about stories. Notice that they're based on the elements you reviewed on pages 300–301.

CHARACTERISTICS OF A GOOD STORY
1. The **characters** are believable. Even when the characters are animals or fantasy creatures, they seem natural and real.
2. The **setting** seems realistic. It helps the story along and doesn't get in the way.
3. The chain of events (**plot**) seems natural and possible but includes some surprises.
4. The story presents a **theme** or message that many readers care about.

OBJECTIVE

• To draw a conclusion about a story and to compare conclusions with classmates

TEACHING
DRAWING CONCLUSIONS

You may want to guide students through an analysis of a movie or story that is familiar to everyone in the class. Use the **Critical Thinking** questions to prompt the class discussion. Then discuss the examples in the **Writing Note** to show students how information about the elements of the story is

Prewriting   **303**

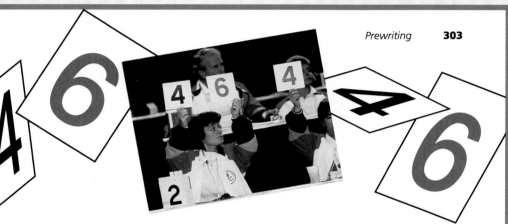

CRITICAL THINKING

Drawing Conclusions

You know what the conclusion to a story or movie is. It's the ending. But a *conclusion* can also be a way of thinking. After you evaluate something, you have to make a judgment about the meaning of your evaluation. That's called ***drawing a conclusion.***

You draw conclusions from your evaluations all the time. You look at a pair of jeans you might buy and ask questions about them. Are they in style? Are they made well? Do they cost too much? After you've finished the evaluation, you draw a conclusion. *I shouldn't buy these jeans because they aren't made well and they're too expensive.*

You evaluate and draw conclusions about a story the same way. You look at the elements and decide whether they're working well. Then you draw a conclusion—whether or not it's a good story. Usually your conclusion will determine whether you recommend the story to anyone else.

Here are some questions that will help you evaluate stories. (You'll see that these questions are related to the characteristics of a good story, page 302). Your answers will enable you to draw your own conclusion.

■ Are the characters believable? Does what they say and do seem natural and real?

MEETING individual NEEDS

LEP/ESL

General Strategies. You could point to the sample conclusions in the **Writing Note** on p. 304 to show how writers avoid using the words *I, me, my, you,* and *your* when they draw conclusions. Explain that even though they are expressing personal opinions and recommendations, good writers avoid using personal pronouns in situations when they want to achieve a formal tone.

incorporated in the conclusion. After students have drawn conclusions about **"A Day's Wait,"** have them compare conclusions in small groups, and then give them an opportunity to revise their conclusions after the discussions.

- Does the setting seem realistic? Is it important to the plot and the conflict?
- Does the plot seem possible? Does it include at least one surprise?
- Does the story have meaning for you? Will you remember anything about it a few weeks or months from now?

If you answer *yes* to all the questions, your conclusion is that the story is good—one you'd recommend. If you answer *no,* you wouldn't recommend it. If your answers are mixed, you may be able to recommend just parts of it.

 CRITICAL THINKING EXERCISE:
Drawing a Conclusion About a Story

Look at "A Day's Wait" again and use the questions above and on page 303 to evaluate it. Then, draw a conclusion about the story. Now, get together with some classmates and compare your conclusions. Would you recommend this story? Why?

WRITING NOTE

The conclusion you draw about a story may be based on one or more of the elements. For example, here's a sample conclusion about one story element.

In the story "_____ ," the main character's words, thoughts, and actions make her seem like a real person facing real problems.

Here's an example of a conclusion about all four of the elements you've studied.

In the story "_____ ," the elements of character, setting, plot, and theme work together to create a lively and meaningful story.

ANSWERS
Critical Thinking Exercise

Students' conclusions should follow the form of the sample conclusions in the **Writing Note.** Each conclusion should be a statement containing the title of the story, the name of the author, and specific judgments about one or more of the four elements. If students like some elements but not others, they should mention both judgments.

LEARNING STYLES

Visual Learners. To encourage students to take a close look at elements of character, setting, plot, and theme in their evaluations, have students illustrate one or two of these elements, as the pictures in the textbook illustrate "A Day's Wait."

Of course, your conclusion doesn't have to be positive. Here's one for a story that's not very good.

> In the story "_____ ," the plot is a series of dull actions that have no suspense or meaning.

PART 3:
Evaluating and Drawing a Conclusion

Now you're ready to evaluate the story you're going to write about. Evaluate it by writing down the answers to the questions listed under Critical Thinking (pages 303–304). What conclusion can you draw from your answers? Write a sentence or two stating your conclusion. Here's an example conclusion about "A Day's Wait": *"A Day's Wait" is a good story because the plot is believable yet surprising, and the characters seem like real people.*

Finding Support for Your Conclusion

You could just tell your readers your conclusion and stop there. But they might not accept it. They might say, "I'm not going to read this story unless you show me that the plot is surprising." You need to give your readers some evidence to prove your conclusion is true.

The place to find evidence is in the story itself. You need to read the story again. This time look for details that will prove your conclusion is right.

The kinds of details you can use are description, actions, and dialogue. Here are some examples of these kinds of details from "A Day's Wait."

Description:	"His face was very white and there were dark areas under his eyes."
Actions:	"At the house they said the boy had refused to let any one come into the room."
Dialogue:	"'You don't have to stay in here with me, Papa, if it bothers you.'"

CRITICAL THINKING

Evaluation. Have students work in pairs to evaluate the support gathered for **Writing Assignment: Part 4.** Here are some questions they might use to perform the evaluation:

1. Do the supporting items fall into the categories of description, action, or dialogue?
2. Is each item a specific detail rather than a general statement?
3. Do the details relate directly to the conclusion?

Here's the way one writer took notes on details to support her conclusion about the story.

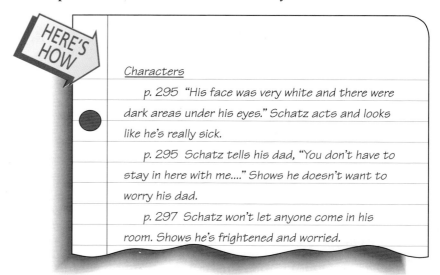

Characters

p. 295 "His face was very white and there were dark areas under his eyes." Schatz acts and looks like he's really sick.

p. 295 Schatz tells his dad, "You don't have to stay in here with me...." Shows he doesn't want to worry his dad.

p. 297 Schatz won't let anyone come in his room. Shows he's frightened and worried.

WRITING ASSIGNMENT PART 4:
Gathering Support for Your Conclusion

Read your story again. Look for descriptions, actions, or dialogue to support the conclusion you wrote in Writing Assignment, Part 3 (page 305). Keep reading until you find at least three pieces of evidence.

To plan a story evaluation

- look closely at the story
- judge the elements of the story against the characteristics of a good story
- draw a conclusion about one or more elements of the story
- find details in the story to support your conclusion

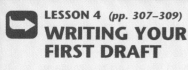
TEACHING THE LESSON
You may want to begin this lesson by reading aloud **The Basic Parts of a Story Evaluation** (below). Have a student volunteer write the parts (introduction: author and title, brief summary, and main idea; body; and ending) on the chalkboard for students to refer to during the writing, revising, and proofreading stages.

Writing Your First Draft

You've done quite a bit. You've evaluated a story, drawn a conclusion about it, and found evidence to support your ideas. Now it's time to create a written evaluation.

The Basic Parts of a Story Evaluation

An evaluation paper is one kind of composition. It has three basic parts.

The Introduction. The introduction is usually one paragraph and it contains three things:

- **The Author and Title of the Story**—Your readers need to know what you're writing about.
- **A Brief Summary of the Story**—You just need a tiny bit of information to help the reader understand what you'll say later.
- **The Main Idea**—You already have your paper's main idea: It's the conclusion you drew when you evaluated your story.

The Body. This is where you put the evidence you've gathered to support your conclusion, or main idea. You might have one or two paragraphs on each story element you're evaluating. For example, you might have one paragraph about character and another about theme.

The Ending. The last part of your paper has to bring things to a close. All you have to do is restate your main idea in slightly different words. For more information on composition form, look at Chapter 3.

A Writer's Model for You

Here's a model paper based on the writer's conclusion about the plot and characters of "A Day's Wait." The writer could have drawn a conclusion about the story's theme and written a different paper.

PROGRAM MANAGER

WRITING YOUR FIRST DRAFT
- **Instructional Support** For help with writing an evaluation, see **Writing** in *Strategies for Writing*, p. 43.

QUOTATION FOR THE DAY
"To note an artist's limitations is but to define his talent." (Willa Cather, 1873–1947, American author)
You may wish to write the quotation on the chalkboard and tell students that writing about literature involves assessing its weak points as well as its strong points.

Using the annotations, analyze **A Writer's Model** (below) with your students and discuss the **Framework for a Story Evaluation** chart (p. 309). Students should then be ready to begin writing their first drafts. Let them do some of the writing in class so you will be available to answer questions and make suggestions.

ASSESSMENT

Evaluate drafts to make sure each student has included the name of the author, the title, a main idea, and a summary of the story in her or his introduction. The body paragraphs should contain statements evaluating specific story elements with details from the stories to support students' judgments.

SELECTION AMENDMENT
Description of change: excerpted
Rationale: to focus on the concept of literary evaluation presented in this chapter

308   *Writing About Literature*

A WRITER'S MODEL

Evaluation of "A Day's Wait"

Information about story, author, title, main idea

In Ernest Hemingway's "A Day's Wait," a young boy is convinced that he's going to die. He has confused American and French thermometers and thinks his temperature is extremely high. This is a good story because the plot is believable and the characters seem like real people.

Evaluation of plot

Details from story

Quotations from story

One reason the plot works so well is that Schatz's conflict could have really happened. Schatz has heard the doctor say he has a temperature of one hundred two degrees, but he didn't hear the doctor explain "there was no danger." Also, in France, Schatz had heard " 'you can't live with forty-four degrees.' " It seems natural that he would worry about dying from a fever of one hundred two degrees. Also, the conflict is solved in a believable way. " 'About how long will it be before I die?' " Schatz asks. Then the father realizes what has been bothering Schatz and explains the difference between the thermometers. That solves Schatz's problem.

Quotation from story

Details from story

Evaluation of character

Quotation from story

Details from story

Hemingway makes Schatz and the father seem like real people. The reader can really "see" that Schatz is sick. "He was shivering, his face was white, and he walked slowly as though it ached to move." Schatz also has a headache and a fever. The father acts real. He puts his hand on Schatz's forehead to see if he has a fever and gives him his medicine. At the end, he realizes what's been bothering Schatz and feels sorry about it. He says, " 'You poor Schatz.' " Then, without making Schatz feel dumb, he explains about the thermometers.

Quotation from story

Restatement of main idea

The realistic characters and plot of "A Day's Wait" work well together. They make this story both memorable and enjoyable.

Writing Your First Draft   **309**

A Basic Framework for a Story Evaluation

It may be helpful for you to follow a framework when you're writing an evaluation. Here's the framework for the model evaluation of "A Day's Wait."

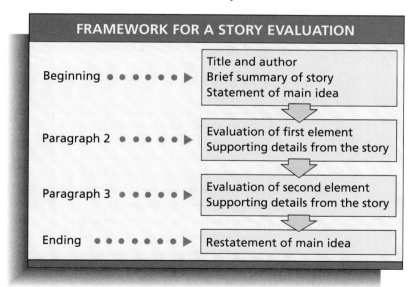

FRAMEWORK FOR A STORY EVALUATION

Beginning ● ● ● ● ● ● ▶	Title and author Brief summary of story Statement of main idea
Paragraph 2 ● ● ● ● ● ▶	Evaluation of first element Supporting details from the story
Paragraph 3 ● ● ● ● ● ▶	Evaluation of second element Supporting details from the story
Ending ● ● ● ● ● ● ▶	Restatement of main idea

WRITING ASSIGNMENT

PART 5:
Writing a Draft of Your Story Evaluation

Now it's time for you to try to pull it all together. Write your first draft of your story evaluation. You might follow the framework above. Don't worry about making this draft perfect. You'll get another chance to make it better.

VISUAL CONNECTIONS

Exploring the Subject. The material normally used in a thermometer is mercury, a metal that is a liquid at ordinary temperatures. The mercury expands inside a glass tube when heated and contracts when cooled.

The most common temperature scales for thermometers are Fahrenheit and Celsius (or centigrade). On the Fahrenheit scale, water freezes at 32 degrees and boils at 212 degrees. On the Celsius scale, 0 degrees is freezing and 100 degrees is boiling. The Fahrenheit scale was named for German physicist Gabriel Daniel Fahrenheit (1686–1736), who improved the accuracy of thermometers by substituting mercury for alcohol. The Celsius scale received its name from its inventor, Anders Celsius (1701–1744).

TIMESAVER

Have students annotate their first drafts by using the annotations beside **A Writer's Model** as a guide. Each student should identify and label the introduction and its parts, evaluative statements about story elements, supporting details, quotations from the story, and the ending.

309

OBJECTIVES
- To analyze a writer's revisions
- To evaluate and revise a story evaluation

MOTIVATION
Read aloud Stephen King's anecdote at the beginning of the lesson. Knowing that professional writers such as King must rewrite their work might help students feel more confident about beginning the process of evaluating and revising.

PROGRAM MANAGER

EVALUATING AND REVISING

- **Reinforcement/Reteaching** See **Revision Transparencies 15** and **16.** For suggestions on how to tie the transparencies to instruction, review teacher's notes in *Fine Art and Instructional Transparencies for Writing*, p. 113.
- **Ongoing Assessment** For a rubric to guide assessment, see **Evaluating and Revising** in *Strategies for Writing*, p. 44.
- **Assessment/Reflection** To assess student work and evaluate progress, see **Portfolio Forms** in *Portfolio Assessment*, pp. 5–17.

QUOTATION FOR THE DAY
"Intelligence is the effort to do the best you can at your particular job. . . ." (J.C. Penney, 1875–1971, American merchant and philanthropist)

You may wish to use the quotation to encourage students to be conscious of creating work that shows they have given their best effort. Explain that evaluation and revision are two ways to make sure they have done the best jobs they can do on their papers.

Evaluating and Revising

Stephen King has become one of our most popular writers. One of his first experiences as a writer happened when he was a sports writer for a small-town newspaper. King says that John Gould, an editor who worked on his first piece, taught him all he ever needed to know.

I wish I still had the piece—it deserves to be framed, editorial corrections and all—but I can remember pretty well how it looked when he had finished with it. Here's an example:

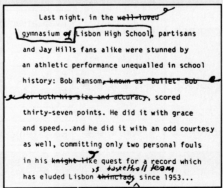

When Gould finished marking up my copy in the manner I have indicated above, he looked up and must have seen something on my face. I think *he* must have thought it was horror, but it was not: it was revelation.

"I only took out the bad parts, you know," he said. "Most of it's pretty good."

"I know," I said, meaning both things: yes, most of

Go over the **Evaluating and Revising Story Evaluations** chart (below) and apply the questions and solutions to the model draft on p. 312. Have students work in groups to analyze the model and to answer the questions in **Exercise 4,** pp. 312–313.

You may want to supervise as students exchange papers for evaluation. Making suggestions and answering questions, monitor the progress of the pairs. Then have students work independently to revise their drafts as suggested in **Writing Assignment: Part 6** on p. 313.

☞

it was good, and yes, he had only taken out the bad parts. "I won't do it again."

"If that's true," he said, "you'll never have to work again. You can do *this* for a living."

Stephen King, "Everything You Need to Know About Writing Successfully in Ten Minutes"

Like Stephen King, it's time to take out the bad parts of your paper and leave the good. To begin, ask yourself the questions in the left-hand column of the chart below. Then use the revision ideas suggested in the right-hand column to correct any problems.

EVALUATING AND REVISING STORY EVALUATIONS

EVALUATION GUIDE	REVISION TECHNIQUE
1 Does the beginning give the author and title of the story and summarize the plot?	**Add** the author and title of the story. **Add** a sentence or two summarizing the story.
2 Does the beginning state the main idea of the paper?	**Add** a sentence or two stating your main idea (the conclusion you drew from your evaluation of the story).
3 Does the writer support the main idea with evidence from the story?	**Add** information from the story to show why you drew your conclusion. Use descriptive details, action details, and dialogue to prove your main idea.
4 Does the ending bring the paper to a close without leaving the reader hanging?	**Add** a sentence or sentences (or **replace** one you have) that restate your main idea in different words.

MEETING *individual* NEEDS

LEP/ESL

General Strategies. You could have students consult with partners on different possible arrangements of the sentences or paragraphs in their essays. Remind students that the orderly and logical development of ideas is important and that if they rearrange the ideas, the original transitional words they used will probably have to be changed.

SELECTION AMENDMENT
Description of change: excerpted
Rationale: to focus on the concept of literary evaluation presented in this chapter

ASSESSMENT

Although you will not want to give a final grade on students' essays until the essays have been proofread and published, you could review the revisions to assess students' mastery of evaluation and revision techniques.

CLOSURE

Ask students to answer in their writing journals the following questions:

1. What is my essay's greatest strength?
2. What is my essay's greatest weakness? ■

 ## INTEGRATING THE LANGUAGE ARTS

Usage Link. Tell students to bracket the first four words of each sentence in their drafts and to count the total number of sentences. Then ask them to count the sentences that have the subject and verb of the main clause within the brackets. To create more variety in their sentence beginnings, students could change the beginnings of half the sentences that have subjects and verbs within the brackets. Suggest that they can start sentences with single-word modifiers, phrases, or subordinate clauses.

SELECTION AMENDMENT
Description of change: excerpted
Rationale: to focus on the concept of literary evaluation presented in this chapter

---

EXERCISE 4 ▶ Analyzing a Writer's Revisions

Here's the rough draft of the first two paragraphs from the evaluation of "A Day's Wait" (page 308). Work with one or two classmates to try to figure out why the writer made the changes shown here. Then, answer the questions that follow. The evaluating and revising chart on page 311 may help you decide.

In Ernest Hemingway's "A Day's Wait,"

A young boy is convinced that he's **add**
going to die. He has confused American
and French thermometers and thinks his
temperature is extremely high. This is a
good story because the plot is believable
and the characters seem like real people.

One reason the plot works so well is
that Schatz's conflict could have really
happened. Schatz has heard the doctor
say he has a temperature of one hundred
two degrees, but he didn't hear the doctor
"there was no danger."
explain it. Also, in France, Schatz had **replace**
heard " 'you can't live with forty-four
degrees.' " It seems natural that he would
worry about dying from a fever of one
hundred two degrees. Also, the conflict is
solved in a believable way. " 'About how
long will it be before I die?' " Schatz asks.
Then the father realizes what has been
and explains the difference between the thermometers.
bothering Schatz. That solves Shatz's **add**
problem. Then the father goes out **cut**
hunting.

1. In the first sentence, why did the writer add the words *In Ernest Hemingway's "A Day's Wait"*?
2. In the fifth sentence, why did the writer replace *it* with *"there was no danger"*?
3. Why did the writer add *and explains the difference between the thermometers* to the next-to-last sentence?
4. Why did the writer cut the last sentence? [Hint: Does this line give evidence to support the writer's main idea? Is it true to the story?]

Calvin & Hobbes copyright 1987 Watterson. Distributed by Universal Press Syndicate. Reprinted with permission. All rights reserved.

 **WRITING ASSIGNMENT**

PART 6:
Evaluating and Revising Your Story Evaluation

You've seen one writer's evaluation and revision. Now, exchange papers with a classmate and use the questions from the evaluating and revising chart on page 311 to evaluate each other's papers. (See the Peer-Evaluation Guidelines on page 44 for help.) Be ready to suggest ways of fixing any problems you find. Then, use your partner's comments and your own evaluation to revise your paper.

ANSWERS
Exercise 4

1. The author and title should be identified in the first sentence.

2. The antecedent for *it* was not clear. The revision makes clear what the doctor explained.

3. The addition is needed to explain how Schatz's problem is solved.

4. The last sentence needs to be cut because it does not support the main idea about Schatz's conflict. In addition, it is out of chronological order.

TEACHING THE LESSON

Discuss the **Mechanics Hint,** and then have pairs of students proofread their evaluations. If time allows, have students expand their audience by reading their evaluations to the class.

Remind students that their portfolios should contain a variety of writing and that their reflections will help show their growth.

 PROGRAM MANAGER

PROOFREADING AND PUBLISHING

- **Instructional Support** For a chart students may use to evaluate their proofreading progress, see **Proofreading** in *Strategies for Writing,* p. 45.

- **Independent Practice/ Reteaching** For additional practice with language skills, see **Proofreading Practice: Using Quotation Marks** in *Strategies for Writing,* p. 46.

- **Computer Guided Instruction** For additional instruction and practice with using quotation marks as noted in the **Mechanics Hint,** see **Lesson 54** in *Language Workshop CD-ROM.*

QUOTATION FOR THE DAY

"If you do not write for publication there is little point in writing at all." (Bernard Shaw, 1856–1950, Irish playwright, critic, and social reformer)

Have students write brief writing journal entries recording their reactions to this quotation. Then have students share their opinions in a class discussion.

SELECTION AMENDMENT
Description of change: excerpted
Rationale: to focus on the concept of literary evaluation presented in this chapter

---

314   *Writing About Literature*

 Proofreading and Publishing

Proofreading. You're ready to share your evaluation with the world. Proofread it carefully for errors in spelling, grammar, punctuation, or capitalization.

COMPUTER NOTE: Your word-processing program may allow you to add character names from the story to a user dictionary so the names won't be flagged as errors during a spelling check.

MECHANICS HINT

Using Quotation Marks

Be sure to put double quotation marks around any words taken directly from the story. If the words you quote include dialogue, enclose the dialogue in a set of single quotation marks within the existing double quotation marks.

EXAMPLES   *Words from Story.* "He was shivering, his face was white, and he walked slowly as though it ached to move."

Dialogue from Story. " 'You go up to bed,' I said, 'you're sick.' "

REFERENCE NOTE: For more information about using quotation marks, see pages 772–777.

Publishing. Plan a way to share your story evaluation with your classmates. Here is one idea.

- Get together with your classmates and gather your evaluations into booklets, organized by story titles. File the booklets in your classroom or library.

ASSESSMENT

You may want to give one point for each paragraph that is free from errors in grammar, usage, and mechanics. You could also give points for publishing.

CLOSURE

In a class discussion, have students respond to these questions:

1. How do you feel about sharing your evaluations with others?
2. Do you think it is important to find an audience for your essays? If so, why, and if not, why not?

Proofreading and Publishing **315**

WRITING ASSIGNMENT

PART 7:
Proofreading and Publishing Your Story Evaluation

You've just about completed your assignment. Now, proofread your final draft carefully, make changes to improve it, and then share it with others.

 Reflecting on Your Writing

If you plan to add your evaluation to your **portfolio,** date it and attach your answers to the following questions.

- What kinds of changes did you make during the revision stage? Why did you make the changes?
- Was it harder to express your main idea or to find story details to support it? Why?

A STUDENT MODEL

Nicci Ferrari, a student at Andrew Jackson Junior High School in Cross Lanes, West Virginia, offers some good ideas for writing about literature. She says, "I would take my time reading the story. I would make sure I understood the story first before I wrote anything."

"Up the Slide"
by Nicci Ferrari

Jack London's short story "Up the Slide" is an exciting and mysterious story about a young man named Clay who has to climb an almost impossible snow-covered slope. Clay and Swanson, his traveling partner, are headed down the Yukon Territory to get the mail. While Swanson is cooking dinner, Clay goes after firewood. What he thinks is going to

COOPERATIVE LEARNING

Divide the class into groups of three or four students and have each student proofread all the papers in the group for a particular aspect of grammar, usage, or mechanics. For example, you could have one student in a group check spelling, another subject-verb agreement, and another standard punctuation of direct quotations.

A STUDENT MODEL
Evaluation

1. In the first sentence, Nicci gives the author and title of the story, summarizes the plot, and states her main idea.
2. In her supporting evidence, Nicci uses descriptive details ("snow-covered slide") and action details ("climbs up and slides many times," and "falls, slides, and even rolls").
3. Nicci supports her conclusion about mystery with details such as "What he thinks is going to be a half hour trip turns out to be much more . . ." and "too steep . . . shoes are so slick . . . he cannot depend on them. . . ."
4. Nicci's final sentence restates her main idea.

CRITICAL THINKING

Analysis. Make copies of the student model, **"Up the Slide,"** and have students bracket and label the following elements:

1. Introduction
   a. title and author of story ["Up the Slide" by Jack London]
   b. summary ["a young man named Clay . . . . has to climb an almost impossible snow-covered slope."]
   c. main idea [" 'Up the Slide' is an exciting and mysterious story . . ."]
2. Support [details such as "half hour trip turns out to be much more than that"; "he realizes he cannot make it down the same way"; "he falls, slides, and even rolls . . . before he reaches the bottom"; and so on]
3. Ending ["The excitement and mystery in 'Up the Slide' is not knowing if Clay will actually make it down the slope."]

be a half hour trip turns out to be much more than that. Clay finds just the wood he wants, but it is up high on a snow-covered slide. He studies the cliff and decides on the correct way to reach the tree. He climbs up and slides many times, but he does manage to get to the tree and cut it down. When Clay is ready to leave, he realizes he cannot make it down the same way. It is too steep and his shoes are so slick that he cannot depend on them to dig in the snow. He decides on another route down the slide. When he starts out, he falls, slides, and even rolls many times before he reaches the bottom. At times the reader isn't sure he will make it down alive. When he is down, he is a long way from where he left the sled dogs, but he takes the river trail back. Here he also finds Swanson, who has a fire going, waiting for him to come down. Even though Swanson laughs at Clay, they have firewood to sell a week later. The excitement and mystery in "Up the Slide" is not knowing if Clay will actually make it down the slope.

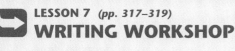

WRITING WORKSHOP

OBJECTIVES

- To analyze a comparison/contrast evaluation of two stories
- To write a paragraph that compares and contrasts two stories

TEACHING THE LESSON

You may want to read the sample comparison-and-contrast evaluation of "Poison" and "The Dinner Party" aloud to the class. Then use the questions in **Thinking It Over** to guide a class discussion.

Have students draw Venn diagrams of their stories similar to the ones on p. 319 to help them visualize the relationships among

WRITING WORKSHOP

Comparing and Contrasting Stories

Just as you've evaluated one story, you can evaluate two stories. Then you have a basis to compare or contrast them. When you **compare,** you show how things are alike. When you **contrast,** you show how they are different. Usually you compare or contrast only one element in the stories. For example, you might compare the characters or the setting, but probably not both.

Depending upon what you find when you evaluate, you may compare the two stories, contrast them, or both compare and contrast. Here's a paper that compares and contrasts the way the main characters from two different stories deal with a similar conflict—a poisonous snake. Notice that the writer begins by naming the author and title of each story and by stating the main idea. As you read, look for reasons and evidence the writer uses to support the likenesses and differences.

> Roald Dahl's story "Poison" and Mona Gardner's story "The Dinner Party" both take place in India, where the main characters have to deal with the same conflict—the threat of a poisonous snake. The way they deal with this conflict is very different. In "Poison," a man named Harry Pope thinks that a deadly poisonous snake is in his bed. Harry's terror makes him sweat horribly. He depends on his friend Timber to save him. But, because of his fear, Harry treats Timber rudely, saying things like " 'Don't be a fool' " and " 'Why don't you shut up then?' " At the end, the characters discover there actually wasn't a snake in the bed after all. In "The Dinner Party," a cobra is crawling across the foot of Mrs. Wynnes, the hostess of a dinner party. Only one other guest at the dinner table realizes a snake is present. The other guests remain unaware.

elements in the two stories. Then guide students through writing, evaluating, revising, proofreading, and reflecting on their essays. For assessment, consider content as well as organization.

CLOSURE

To close your lesson on comparing and contrasting stories, ask students to draw Venn diagrams in their notebooks. Then ask a volunteer to explain how the diagrams illustrate the principles of comparing and contrasting.

ANSWERS

Thinking It Over

1. The main idea—that the two main characters deal very differently with the same conflict—is stated in the first sentence.

2. The writer compares the setting (India) and the conflict (threat of a poisonous snake). Details that support the comparison are the fact that one snake is identified as a cobra (indicating India); Harry thinks a poisonous snake is in his bed; and a cobra crawls across Mrs. Wynnes's foot.

3. The writer contrasts the characters' reactions to the threat. Harry sweats in terror and treats Timber rudely; Mrs. Wynnes is calm and in control. The writer also contrasts the endings. In "Poison," the threat is false, but in "The Dinner Party," the snake is real.

4. Students' endings should summarize the similarities and differences between the stories and directly or implicitly restate the main idea.

SELECTION AMENDMENT
Description of change: excerpted
Rationale: to focus on the concept of literary evaluation presented in this chapter

Unlike Harry, Mrs. Wynnes does not sweat and snap at her friends. Instead she stares "straight ahead, her muscles contracting slightly." Calmly, and in perfect control, she instructs a servant to put a bowl of milk, bait for the snake, on the veranda. Her reaction is brave and unexpected, because earlier in the story, the colonel says that a woman's " 'unfailing reaction in any crisis is to scream.' "

Thinking It Over

1. Where does the writer state the main idea of the paper? What is it?
2. What does the paper compare? What details does the writer give from each story to support this comparison?
3. What does the paper contrast? What details does the writer give to show these differences?
4. This paper doesn't have an ending, or conclusion. Try writing a one- or two-sentence ending. Share it with two or three of your classmates and decide which one is best.

Writing a Paragraph About Two Stories

 Prewriting. Find a story that has something in common with the story you evaluated in this chapter. Perhaps the characters face similar struggles (like the stories compared above), or perhaps both stories have settings that create suspense. Look for key elements that the stories share. Next, jot down differences. Use a Venn diagram like the one below to record your notes. Notice how the similarities fall in the area where the ovals overlap.

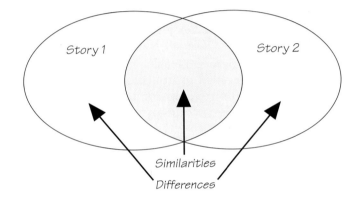

 Writing, Evaluating, and Revising. Begin by telling how the elements in the two stories are similar. Then, give details about one story, followed by details about the other story. Emphasize the likenesses or differences in the element. Remember that transitional words and phrases can help signal likenesses and differences and move the reader from one point to the next. When you finish, have a classmate read your paragraph to find unclear comparisons and suggest other supporting details. Then revise.

Proofreading and Publishing. Proofread to find mistakes in spelling, grammar, and punctuation. Then, share your paragraph with classmates. Get together with students who are familiar with both stories to discuss similarities and differences you may have missed.

You may decide to include this paper in your **portfolio.** If you do, date the paper and write a brief reflection that responds to these questions: Which was more interesting— comparing and contrasting two stories, or evaluating one story at a time? Why? Which took more time? Why?

RESPONDING TO POETRY
OBJECTIVE

- To respond to a poem by writing a poem, a letter, or a journal entry

RESPONDING TO POETRY
Teaching Strategies

To allow students to give personal responses that are not influenced by their classmates' opinions, have them read "**Robert, Who Is Often a Stranger to Himself**" and respond to one of the writing prompts before having a class discussion. If students want to write poems, but have difficulty beginning, give them these phrases: "I wish . . .," "I believe . . . ," or "I dream. . . ." For the second prompt, encourage students to write and mail letters. Discuss the poem with the class after they have completed their written responses.

USING THE SELECTION
Robert, Who Is Often a Stranger to Himself

1

The word *stranger* suggests that the child in the poem experiences alienation and conflict. The looking-glass can be a metaphor for the child's self-image.

2

The poem's format uses questions to explore a child's feelings about himself.

GUIDELINES

Responses to the first prompt should demonstrate evidence of some introspection on the students' part. Responses to the second and third prompts should show that students recognize a difference between public and private self-images.

SELECTION AMENDMENT
Description of change: excerpted
Rationale: to focus on the concept of literary evaluation presented in this chapter

---

MAKING CONNECTIONS

Responding to Poetry

Here is a poem that asks two questions. The questions may be addressed to an actual person named Robert, to all of the poem's readers, or to both. Read the poem, and then think about your own personal response.

Robert, Who Is Often a Stranger to Himself
by Gwendolyn Brooks

Do you ever look in the looking-glass
And see a stranger there?   *1*
A child you know and do not know,
Wearing what you wear?   *2*

What do you think of this poem? Did you like it? Have you ever looked in the mirror and been surprised at what you saw? Here are some ways you can respond to this poem. Try one of them.

- Write a journal entry describing what you see when you look at your reflection in a mirror.
- In a paragraph, explain how a person's self-image can sometimes differ from his or her outward appearance.
- Using the form of a poem, write a few questions that you would like to ask one of your friends, or someone you don't know very well. Give your poem a title that says something about the person to whom the questions are addressed.

A Character Analysis

When you evaluate story characters, like Schatz and his father or Harry Pope and Mrs. Wynnes, you look closely at the details that the writer uses to make the characters seem real. You study what the characters say, think, and do. You study the way the characters look and how other characters respond to them. But besides helping you to evaluate a character, these details also suggest the kind of person the character is.

You can use the same kind of information to analyze the character or personality of a real person. For example, here's a character analysis of Joseph, chief of the Nez Perce.

> Chief Joseph of the Nez Perce was an outstanding leader of his people. He was a brave, fierce warrior when he had to be, but also gentle and kind and loved by his people. He cared deeply for their individual welfare, showing concern when one of his people was sick. Each morning, he rode through the camp shouting a speech, giving thanks that the men, women, and children were alive and well. He tried all peaceful means to gain justice for his people before having to fight the soldiers. When he did fight the U.S. cavalry, he surrendered for the good of his people with the famous words, "I will fight no more forever."

A CHARACTER ANALYSIS
Teaching Strategies

Tell students that, if possible, they should choose characters about whom they have strong feelings, either positive or negative. Students will have to maintain some emotional distance to write their analyses, but the strong emotions will give their essays more power.

You may want to have students work in groups to evaluate, revise, and proofread their character analyses. For publishing, you could have the whole class put their analyses, together with pictures of the characters they have analyzed, in a binder.

VISUAL CONNECTIONS
Chief Joseph

Exploring the Subject. In 1877 the U.S. government ordered Chief Joseph and his people to leave their lands in Oregon for a reservation in Idaho. Chief Joseph's band fought the troops and, sensing defeat, retreated toward Canada where they hoped to join forces with some Sioux who had already retreated. Chief Joseph managed a retreat of one thousand miles before having to surrender just forty miles away from the Canadian border. Chief Joseph was first sent to Indian Territory (present-day Oklahoma) but lived his final years on a reservation in Washington.

GUIDELINES

After students read the assignment (but before they start writing) have the class determine the grading criteria. Students should decide which specific parts of the process and of the assignment will be evaluated and assign point values to each.

WRITING ACROSS THE CURRICULUM

Teaching Strategies

Have your students read the comparison of Sojourner Truth and Harriet Tubman and then have them outline the similarities and differences using a Venn diagram.

Students may want to select figures who relate to what they are currently studying in history class. After they have gone through the selection process, give students time to research before they begin writing their papers.

Choose a character to analyze. It may be a character from a novel or a story. It may be a movie character or a character from a favorite television program. Or it may be a real person—a friend, a relative, or even yourself.

Jot down notes about how the person looks, talks, and acts. Do any of these things give you a clue about the kind of person this is? Write a character analysis of the person. Begin with a statement that gives the overall qualities of the person and then list details and examples to support your statement. The notes you jotted down should help you.

WRITING ACROSS THE CURRICULUM

Comparing and Contrasting Historical Figures

History tests often have essay questions that ask you to compare two historical figures. Here, for example, is a comparison of two famous African American women who fought against the practice of slavery.

Sojourner Truth and Harriet Tubman were courageous African American women who devoted their lives to the fight against slavery during the 1800s. Both women were born as enslaved people; but their different backgrounds and distinct personalities led them to separate paths. Sojourner Truth was raised in New York and freed from slavery under a New York law. She had a deep, unshakable faith in God. Her quick wit and deep voice became famous as she preached against slavery throughout New England and the Midwest. Harriet Tubman was a bold, brave woman from Bucktown, Maryland. Her determination and resourcefulness helped her escape slavery. She also became the most famous leader of the Underground Railroad, guiding many slaves to freedom.

Use the skills that you learned in the Writing Workshop on pages 317–319 to compare and contrast two people from history. First, select two people that you have studied who have something in common. Then, use what you know about their thoughts, actions, and words to compare and contrast them. (You may want to do some research first.) Here are some suggestions.

- General Robert E. Lee and General Ulysses S. Grant
- The writers Maya Angelou and Alice Walker
- The conductors Seiji Ozawa and Leonard Bernstein

GUIDELINES

If you want to evaluate students' processes as well as their final products, check their prewriting and have peer-evaluation groups review drafts. Each essay should clearly state differences and similarities between the two figures being compared and contrasted.

VISUAL CONNECTIONS
Related Expression Skills. Students might extend the idea of this collage by creating a mural collage composed of representatives of the various historical figures compared by class members.

Chapter 10

WRITING A RESEARCH REPORT: EXPOSITION

OBJECTIVES

- To analyze the characteristics of an informative research report
- To plan an informative research report with both audience and purpose in mind
- To select and write a report about an appropriate topic that is sufficiently narrow
- To evaluate the sources and list them correctly
- To evaluate, revise, proofread, and publish a report

WRITING-IN-PROGRESS ASSIGNMENTS

Major Assignment: Writing a research report
Cumulative Writing Assignments: The chart below shows the sequence of cumulative assignments that will guide students as they write a research report. These Writing Assignments form the instructional core of Chapter 10.

PREWRITING

WRITING ASSIGNMENT
- Part 1: Choosing a Topic for Your Report p. 332
- Part 2: Making an Early Plan and Asking Questions p. 335
- Part 3: Finding and Listing Sources for Your Report p. 341
- Part 4: Taking Notes for Your Report p. 342
- Part 5: Writing an Outline for Your Report p. 343

WRITING YOUR FIRST DRAFT

WRITING ASSIGNMENT
- Part 6: Writing Your First Draft p. 348

EVALUATING AND REVISING

WRITING ASSIGNMENT
- Part 7: Evaluating and Revising Your Report p. 351

PROOFREADING AND PUBLISHING

WRITING ASSIGNMENT
- Part 8: Proofreading and Publishing Your Report p. 352

In addition, exercises 1–3 provide practice in thinking about audience and purpose, interviewing, and analyzing a writer's revisions.

WORKPLACE writing ▶ Surfing the Net

Since the workplace is becoming more and more linked to the information highway and since students may prefer using the Internet for research to using traditional resources, you may want to integrate this information source into your lesson plans. If you fear the potholes of the information highway, attend a workshop to familiarize yourself with materials found online or on CD-ROMs or learn the basics of using on-line catalogs and databases from your school or city librarian.

- **Information Highway Hazards** Remind students that while cutting and pasting information found online is tempting, doing so is plagiarism. To ensure that students use the information as a source only, require them to turn in highlighted hard-copy printouts with their first drafts.

- **Students as Resources** Establish knowledgeable students as resources for those new to computer searches. Have students make lists of information they hope to find through the computer and submit these to the resource person who can help them make a list of search engines or CD-ROMs to use.

- **Online Workshop** Use knowledgeable computer people—such as the director of multimedia, computer teachers, members of computer clubs, parents or students who are experienced surfers—to teach an online workshop. Assign a resource person to each computer station, and assign each student a set amount of time at the computer. Be sure the instructors realize that they are teaching students to access information, not just finding it for them.

INTEGRATING THE LANGUAGE ARTS

SELECTION	READING AND LITERATURE	WRITING AND CRITICAL THINKING	LANGUAGE AND SYNTAX	SPEAKING, LISTENING, AND OTHER EXPRESSION SKILLS
• from **"Paradise Lost"** by Elizabeth Vitton pp. 326–328 • from *Max Perkins: Editor of Genius* by A. Scott Berg p. 349 • from *Baseball: An Illustrated History* by Geoffrey C. Ward and Ken Burns pp. 357–358	• Determining the author's purpose p. 328 • Using information from text to clarify or refine understanding of contemporary issues or events p. 328 • Forming generalizations based on new information pp. 328, 356 • Identifying source material p. 328	• Evaluating possible topics p. 332 • Identifying, collecting, or selecting information pp. 333, 358 • Synthesizing information pp. 335, 337, 343, 348, 358 • Evaluating sources p. 338 • Taking notes from selected materials pp. 341, 342 • Analyzing model revisions p. 351 • Evaluating and revising a first draft p. 351 • Evaluating a model book report p. 353 • Synthesizing information to write a book report p. 355 • Synthesizing information to write a biographical report p. 358 • Evaluating current events for a news program p. 358	• Proofreading for errors in spelling, capitalization, usage, and punctuation p. 352	• Interviewing a classmate p. 337 • Writing notes to reflect the content of an oral discussion p. 337 • Interviewing potential sources to record pertinent information p. 341 • Listening to suggestions for revision p. 351 • Using print and nonprint sources to create an audiovisual presentation p. 358 • Presenting reports on effects on mass media pp. 358–359

SUGGESTED INTEGRATED UNIT PLAN

This unit plan suggests how to integrate the major strands of the language arts with this chapter.

You may begin this chapter with writing a research paper or with suggested biographies to focus on the common characteristics of researched writing. You can then integrate speaking/listening and language concepts with both the writing and the literature.

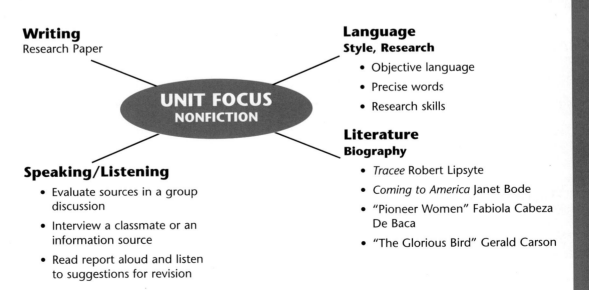

Common Characteristics

- Content that is mainly factual and comprehensive
- Precise language that is neutral and unbiased
- Third-person point of view to retain a sense of objectivity and factuality
- Organization often in order of importance or chronological

Writing
Research Paper

UNIT FOCUS
NONFICTION

Language
Style, Research

- Objective language
- Precise words
- Research skills

Literature
Biography

- *Tracee* Robert Lipsyte
- *Coming to America* Janet Bode
- "Pioneer Women" Fabiola Cabeza De Baca
- "The Glorious Bird" Gerald Carson

Speaking/Listening

- Evaluate sources in a group discussion
- Interview a classmate or an information source
- Read report aloud and listen to suggestions for revision

CHAPTER 10: WRITING A RESEARCH REPORT: EXPOSITION

Use this guide for creating an instructional plan that addresses the individual needs of your students. Assignments accompanied by the following symbol (∗) may be completed out of class. Times given for pacing lessons are estimated.

CHAPTER PLANNING GUIDE—PUPIL'S EDITION

LESSONS	LITERARY MODEL pp. 326–328 from "Paradise Lost" by Elizabeth Vitton	PREWRITING pp. 330–343	
		Generating Ideas	Gathering/Organizing
DEVELOPMENTAL PROGRAM	🕐 20–25 minutes • Read model aloud in class and have students answer questions p. 328 orally.	🕐 25–30 minutes • Ways to Develop a Report p. 329 • Main Assignment: Looking Ahead p. 329 • Choosing and Narrowing a Subject pp. 330–331 • Writing Assignment: Part 1 p. 332∗ • Writing Note p. 332	🕐 70–75 minutes • Planning Your Report pp. 333–343 • Exercises 1∗, 2 pp. 333–334, 337 • MLA Guide pp. 339–340 • Writing Assignments: Parts 2–5 pp. 335, 341, 342, 343∗
CORE PROGRAM	🕐 20–25 minutes • Assign students to read model and answer questions p. 328 in small groups.	🕐 20–25 minutes • Ways to Develop a Report p. 329 • Main Assignment: Looking Ahead p. 329 • Choosing and Narrowing a Subject pp. 330–331∗ • Writing Assignment: Part 1 p. 332∗ • Writing Note p. 332	🕐 40–45 minutes • Planning Your Report pp. 333–343∗ • Critical Thinking pp. 337–338 • MLA Guide pp. 339–340 • Reminder p. 335 • Writing Assignments: Parts 2–5 pp. 335, 341, 342, 343∗
ACCELERATED PROGRAM	🕐 15–20 minutes • Read model independently.	🕐 15–20 minutes • Ways to Develop a Report p. 329 • Main Assignment: Looking Ahead p. 329 • Choosing and Narrowing Your Subject pp. 330–331∗ • Writing Assignment: Part 1 p. 332∗ • Writing Note p. 332	🕐 35–40 minutes • Planning Your Report pp. 333–343∗ • Critical Thinking pp. 337–338 • MLA Guide pp. 339–340 • Writing Assignments: Parts 2–5 pp. 335, 341, 342, 343∗

CHAPTER PLANNING GUIDE—PROGRAM RESOURCES

	LITERARY MODEL	PREWRITING
PRINT	• Reading Master 10, *Practice for Assessment in Reading, Vocabulary, and Spelling* p. 10	• Prewriting, *Strategies for Writing* pp. 49–52 • *English Workshop* pp. 267–268, 271–272
MEDIA	• Fine Art Transparency 7: *Washington Crossing the Delaware, Transparency Binder* 📖	• Graphic Organizers 17 and 18: *Transparency Binder* 📖 • *Writer's Workshop 1:* Report of Information 💾📖 • *Language Workshop:* Lesson 53 💾

WRITING pp. 344–348	EVALUATING AND REVISING pp. 349–351	PROOFREADING AND PUBLISHING pp. 352–353
🕐 **30–35 minutes** • Writing Your First Draft pp. 344–345 • A Writer's Model pp. 345–348 • Writing Assignment: Part 6 p. 348*	🕐 **40–45 minutes** • Evaluating and Revising p. 349 • Evaluating and Revising Chart p. 350 • Exercise 3 p. 351* • Writing Assignment: Part 7 p. 351	🕐 **40–45 minutes** • Proofreading and Publishing p. 352 • Mechanics Hint p. 352 • Writing Assignment: Part 8 p. 352 • Reflecting p. 352* • A Student Model p. 353
🕐 **20–25 minutes** • Understanding the Parts of a Report pp. 344–345 • A Writer's Model pp. 345–348* • Writing Assignment: Part 6 p. 348*	🕐 **30–35 minutes** • Evaluating and Revising Chart p. 350 • Writing Assignment: Part 7 p. 351	🕐 **40–45 minutes** • Mechanics Hint p. 352 • Writing Assignment: Part 8 p. 352 • Reflecting p. 352* • A Student Model p. 353*
🕐 **15–20 minutes** • Understanding the Parts of a Report pp. 344–345* • A Writer's Model pp. 345–348* • Writing Assignment: Part 6 p. 348*	🕐 **30–35 minutes** • Evaluating and Revising Chart p. 350 • Writing Assignment: Part 7 p. 351	🕐 **40–45 minutes** • Mechanics Hint p. 352 • Writing Assignment: Part 8 p. 352 • Reflecting p. 352*

 Computer disk or CD-ROM   Overhead transparencies

WRITING	EVALUATING AND REVISING	PROOFREADING AND PUBLISHING
• Writing, *Strategies for Writing* p. 53	• Evaluating and Revising, *Strategies for Writing* p. 54	• Proofreading Practice: *Strategies for Writing* p. 56 • *English Workshop* pp. 239–240
	• Revision Transparencies 17–18, *Trans- parency Binder* 📄	• *Language Workshop:* Lesson 57 💿

ELEMENTS OF WRITING: CURRICULUM CONNECTIONS

Writing Workshop
• A Book Report pp. 354–356

Making Connections
• Biographical Report pp. 357–358
• Studying the Influence of the Mass Media
pp. 358–359

ASSESSMENT OPTIONS

Summative Assessment
Holistic Scoring: Prompts and Models
pp. 39–44

Portfolio Assessment
Portfolio forms, *Portfolio Assessment*
pp. 5–24, 38–43

Reflection
Writing Process Log, *Strategies for Writing*
p. 48

Ongoing Assessment
Proofreading, *Strategies for Writing* p. 55

LESSON 1 *(pp. 324–328)*
EXPLORING YOUR WORLD

OBJECTIVES

- To respond personally to a literary model
- To identify and analyze the techniques used in writing a research report

TEACHING THE LESSON

Ask students to read the selection from Elizabeth Vitton's **"Paradise Lost,"** pp. 326–328. Then, lead a discussion of the work by using the notes in the margins and by asking students how the writer introduced the topic, what the main idea is in each paragraph, how the ideas are connected, and how the writer concluded the selection.

PROGRAM MANAGER

CHAPTER 10

- **Computer Guided Instruction** For a related assignment, see **Report of Information** in *Writer's Workshop 1 CD-ROM.*

- **Summative Assessment** For a writing prompt, including grading criteria and student models, see *Holistic Scoring: Prompts and Models,* pp. 39–44.

- **Extension/Enrichment** See **Fine Art Transparency 7,** *Washington Crossing the Delaware* by Emmanuel Gottlieb Leutze. For suggestions on how to tie the transparency to instruction, review teacher's notes in *Fine Art and Instructional Transparencies for Writing,* p. 39.

- **Reading Support** For help with the reading selection, pp. 326–328, see **Reading Master 10** in *Practice for Assessment in Reading, Vocabulary, and Spelling,* p. 10.

VISUAL CONNECTIONS
We the People: The Land-Grant College Heritage

About the Artwork. This historical mural by Billy Morrow Jackson pays tribute to the Morrill Act, or Land-Grant Act of 1862, which provided federal aid to higher education in the form of grants of land to state colleges.

10 WRITING A RESEARCH REPORT: EXPOSITION

To give students guidance on the process of personal response, have a class discussion of question 1 in **Reader's Response.** Then, to model a response to the **Writer's Craft** questions, guide students through question 5. Assign the rest of the questions in **Reader's Response** and **Writer's Craft** as independent practice.

ASSESSMENT

Use students' responses to the questions in **Reader's Response** and **Writer's Craft** to assess their ability to respond to and analyze the literary model.

☞

Exploring Your World

There are many ways to explore your world. You can travel by rickshaw in China or by camel in Saudi Arabia. You can explore the sea from a submarine, or view the earth from a spaceship. But you can also **explore your world** without ever leaving home.

Writing and You. Written reports help you explore the world through the writer's eyes. Employees share information with their co-workers in workplace reports. Historians let you visit the exciting people and events of yesterday. Magazine, newspaper, and TV writers explore the world of today. Can you think of other kinds of reports?

As You Read. Use your imagination as you read the following report about the rain forests of the equator. You can explore a world you've probably never seen.

Billy Morrow Jackson, *We the People: The Land-Grant College Heritage* (1986–1987). Krannert Museum of Art, University of Illinois, Champaign.

QUOTATION FOR THE DAY
"We shall not cease from exploration/And the end of all our exploring/Will be to arrive where we started/And know the place for the first time." (T. S. Eliot, 1888–1965, American-born British author)
You may wish to ask students to freewrite for a few minutes about what it means to explore. Then, have several volunteers read from their responses. Lead students to understand that exploration plays an important part in researching and writing reports. Just as travelers explore new lands or astronauts explore space, writers explore by finding information.

MEETING individual NEEDS

LEP/ESL

General Strategies. To illustrate vocabulary terms that describe the rain forest, draw a simple sketch of a forest on the chalkboard and label the different areas with the terms *timber, trunks, logs, jungle, topsoil,* and *leaves.*

325

CLOSURE

Ask students to summarize the lesson by telling Vitton's purpose and the sources she cited.

ENRICHMENT

To get students to think about different uses of research, have them bring in published materials for which the writers have done research. Explain that most articles in newspapers and magazines are informative and require research. Persuasive writing such as an editorial may be partly informative and may require research. Expressive writing

326

USING THE SELECTION

from **Paradise Lost**

1

The first sentence poses the question quickly and tells the reader the main idea.

2

The writer introduces one of her expert sources by paraphrasing a fact he supplied.

3

After posing the problem, the writer explains the seriousness of the loss of trees by quoting an expert.

4

topsoil: rich surface layer of soil that has most of the materials needed by plants to grow

326

F R O M

PARADISE

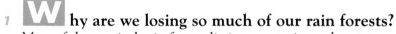

1 **W**hy are we losing so much of our rain forests? Most of the tropical rain forests lie in poor nations whose popu-
2 lations are growing very quickly. Since they have no big industries, Dr. [Stuart] Strahl [of Wildlife Conservation International] says, they make money by using the resources in the forest.

3   "It takes minutes for a chain saw to topple a seven-foot-wide tree, but it will take five centuries for another tree to grow to the same size," says Matthew Hatchwell. He works to help save the Earth's rain forests. The crashing timber destroys small trees lying in its path. Tractors flatten more forest when they drag the trunks to loading areas.

   As roads are cut to get the logs to market, it opens up the area to a flood of people who burn parts of the jungle to make room for farms and ranches. The problem is that most of the
4 nutrients are in the living trees—not in the topsoil. So if the forest is cut down and burned, there is a very thin layer of rich

does not require research, but creative writing sometimes requires research for accuracy of details in background and setting.

Have students share with the class the titles and topics of their articles. Discuss with students the ways research is used in the articles and have the class speculate on how the writers conducted their research. ■

L O S T

BY ELIZABETH VITTON

ash which can grow crops for a few years. But once the nutrients have been used up by the crops or been washed away by the warm rains, the land becomes almost worthless. "When the soil gives out," according to Hatchwell, "it forces farmers to clear more and more land."

RAIN FORESTS ARE THE "LUNGS" OF THE PLANET.

---

5   Destroying rain forests as far away as Brazil and Indonesia has serious consequences for all of us. For example, the world needs trees to recycle carbon dioxide (CO_2), an odorless gas. Rain forests are the "lungs" of the planet. They suck the CO_2 out of
6   the atmosphere through their leaves. The trees then "breathe" oxygen back into the atmosphere and pump it with moisture that falls as rain.

5
The writer explains the long-term effects of the loss of trees, including the consequences for the whole world.

6
atmosphere: mixture of gases surrounding the earth

327

But trees are about 50 percent carbon. If they are burned, the CO_2 trapped inside them is released. "It's a double whammy," explains Dr. Russell Mittermeier, a <u>conservationist</u>. "The burning itself releases huge amounts of CO_2. And it reduces the trees available to absorb the gas."

"WE NEED RAIN FORESTS TO HELP CONTROL OUR CLIMATE."

Carbon dioxide is a "greenhouse" gas. Like a greenhouse, carbon dioxide lets the sun's incoming rays through, but blocks reflected rays from leaving the atmosphere. It traps the sun's heat. But many scientists believe that too much carbon dioxide
7 could cause the Earth to heat up. The "greenhouse effect" would do more than just cause the temperature to rise, says Dr. Strahl. "It would also affect winds, rainfall, sea levels and storms. We need rain forests to help control our climate."

READER'S RESPONSE

1. Do you think that destroying rain forests is a bad idea? If so, what do you think we should do about it?
2. What did you learn from this report? In your own words, summarize or explain an interesting statement or fact from the report to a small group of your classmates.

WRITER'S CRAFT

3. The purpose of a report may be to inform or persuade. What do you think the purpose of this report was? Why?
4. Reports should contain facts that are new to the audience. What facts in this report were new to you?
5. The writer tells us the sources of some of her information. What are they?

7
The writer concludes with a thought-provoking statement.

ANSWERS
Reader's Response
Responses will vary.

1. Students should be able to give reasons for their opinions and suggestions.
2. Students may say they learned about forestry practices, ecology, or the Earth's atmosphere. For the second question, they should be able to cite specific examples from the report.

Writer's Craft

3. While the primary purpose of the report is to inform, it is also persuasive, as it presents only one side of the story.
4. Students could elaborate on their answers by telling what effect these new facts had.
5. Three of the writer's sources are Dr. Stuart Strahl of Wildlife Conservation International; Matthew Hatchwell, a conservationist; and Dr. Russell Mittermeier, a conservationist.

SELECTION AMENDMENT
Description of change: excerpted and modified
Rationale: to focus on the concept of writing a research report presented in this chapter

LESSON 2 (p. 329)
WAYS TO DEVELOP A REPORT

TEACHING WAYS TO DEVELOP A REPORT

Point out that there are four basic ways to develop a report that informs. These are narration, description, classification, and evaluation. Then, have a volunteer read the examples in the textbook. Draw on the chalkboard a chart with four columns headed by each of the methods of development. Ask students to give examples for each method, and write these in the columns.

329

Ways to Develop a Report

Each year, publishers release hundreds of books reporting on everything from popular video games to new exercise trends. Monthly and weekly magazines offer reports on new products and current topics of interest. Newspapers and TV networks provide daily news. And reports of all kinds are posted continuously on the Internet.

What all these reports have in common is that they give information. But they may be developed in different ways. The report on the rain forest was developed mostly by description. Here are some other ways to develop a report.

- in a history report, explaining how the Iroquois League of American Indian nations was formed
- in a report on a museum exhibit, describing how Egyptian mummies were prepared
- in a report for hikers, describing the plants on Mount Washington
- in a report for a life science class, describing how a giant anaconda snake feeds
- in a report on the need for recycling, classifying the types of garbage that make up a typical landfill
- in a workplace report, estimating how long it will take to complete a project, and explaining possible delays

LOOKING AHEAD

In the main assignment for this chapter, you'll choose a subject, gather information on it from several sources, and then write a short report. Your report should

- draw on information from a variety of sources
- present the information in an interesting way
- list all of the sources you used

CRITICAL THINKING

Analysis. Ask students to bring their history books to class. Explain that, in a way, history books are long research reports.

Divide the class into groups of three or four. Ask each group to choose any chapter in the history book and to analyze it by identifying the methods of development used to give information. Ask them to look for examples of narration, description, classification, and evaluation.

Give the groups fifteen minutes to work. If they need more time, extend the work period; however, it isn't necessary for each group to finish an entire chapter. The objective is for the students to realize that most writers use each of the four methods regularly.

After the work period, ask a representative from each group to report on what the group found.

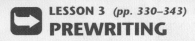

LESSON 3 *(pp. 330–343)*
PREWRITING

OBJECTIVES

• To choose a topic for a research report
• To adjust to audience and purpose
• To make an early plan and to ask questions

• To conduct an interview
• To find and list sources and to take notes
• To write an outline for a report

Writing a Report

 *Prewriting*

Choosing and Narrowing a Subject

How do hurricanes form? Do electric eels really give off shocks? Is it true cats were treated like royalty in ancient Egypt? Writing a report gives you a chance to find the answers to interesting questions.

Choosing Your Subject

What do you wonder about? What's important to you? Do you like to climb rocks or collect them? Do you play a musical instrument or a sport? What have you read or seen lately that you'd like to know more about? Answering these questions can help you decide on a subject for a report.

Here are some broad subjects. Think of some others that interest you.

snakes	Cuba	space labs
hairstyles	animals	holiday customs
robots	games	lasers

Narrowing Your Subject

You can find information on these subjects in books and articles, on videotapes, and on the World Wide Web. In fact, you'll find far too much information for a short report. But each broad subject contains many smaller *topics*, or parts, that are suitable for short reports. So you can narrow your subject by focusing on just one part of it. You may need to narrow your subject more than once, depending on the length of your report and how much information is available. Here's how the subjects you've just read about can be narrowed.

Several days before you begin this lesson, ask students to create lists of topics they want to know more about. Ask each student to write each topic on a sheet of paper and to post it on the bulletin board. Preliminary ideas should generate other ideas that can fill the bulletin board by the time you begin the lesson on prewriting.

On the day you begin this lesson, read several possible topics from the bulletin board and emphasize that the possibilities are endless.

☛

rattlesnakes	Havana	space labs in
men's hairstyles	greyhounds	the year 2000
of the past sixty	the origins	Cinco de Mayo
years	of lacrosse	lasers for dentistry
robots for the home		

Remember that each subject contains many topics. For example, here's a map of the subject "holidays."

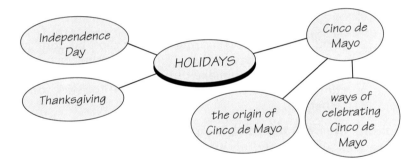

Independence Day — HOLIDAYS — Cinco de Mayo

Thanksgiving

the origin of Cinco de Mayo

ways of celebrating Cinco de Mayo

Before deciding on your topic, ask yourself these questions:

1. Can I find enough facts about this topic? Where?
2. Is my topic too broad for a short report? (Or, if the topic is too narrow, you won't be able to find enough information.)
3. Do I have time to get the information I need? (If you have to send away for information, how long will it take to get it?)
4. How can I make the topic interesting?

A DIFFERENT APPROACH
Students might need some prompting to decide on topics that interest them. A listing activity might help. Ask students to write two or three answers to a series of questions. Here are some example questions:

1. What places would you like to visit?
2. What cultures would you like to know more about?
3. What kinds of animals interest you?

VISUAL CONNECTIONS
Exploring the Subject. El Cinco de Mayo (the fifth of May) is the day the Republic of Mexico celebrates a victory over the French. In 1862 the French army had invaded Mexico and was marching on Mexico City. At Puebla they encountered the Mexican army, led by Texas-born General Ignacio Zaragoza. Zaragoza routed the French in one of the great military victories in Mexican history. Cinco de Mayo is celebrated by Mexican Americans and others in many parts of the United States.

TEACHING THE LESSON

This lesson is made up of ten mini-lessons. Prepare the students for the length of the prewriting period by reminding them that for professional writers, prewriting usually takes about 40 percent of the total time spent on a piece of writing. Good writers prepare carefully.

Write the following ten steps of prewriting on the chalkboard. Leave the list up throughout this lesson.

1. choosing a topic
2. determining audience and purpose
3. writing an informal outline
4. asking questions

MEETING individual NEEDS

STUDENTS WITH SPECIAL NEEDS

Some students will likely need extra assistance at several points during the prewriting process. Encourage them to choose topics they know something about so they will already be familiar with some of the information. To keep their reports concise, assist students in narrowing their topics. In the outline stage, you could work with students individually to assist them in organizing their main headings.

LEP/ESL

General Strategies. To ensure that students choose topics on which information is available, have them browse through the subject headings in the *Readers' Guide to Periodical Literature.* They can see what topics are currently in the media and how narrow or broad the topics are by observing the number of subtopics in each category.

332 *Writing a Research Report*

PART 1:
Choosing a Topic for Your Report

What would you like to know about? Think of a subject that interests you. Then, narrow it to a topic for your report. Before making a final decision, review the questions on page 331.

A well-written report can't be done in just a day or two. Think about the time you have, and make out a schedule that will give you time to do the following six things. Then, stick to your schedule.

1. Find information about your topic.
2. Take notes about the information.
3. Organize your information.
4. Write a first draft.
5. Evaluate and revise your first draft.
6. Proofread and publish your report.

5. finding sources
6. evaluating sources
7. listing sources
8. taking notes
9. organizing and outlining information
10. writing an outline

For each of the prewriting steps, ask the students to read the relevant pages. Then, lead a discussion of the material.

Because this writing project requires library work, you may want to ask the librarian to come to the class while the students are deciding on their topics. The librarian can answer questions about the availability of information on topics. The next day you could take the students to the library for a tour so they will know where to find sources such as the card catalog and the *Readers'* ☞

Prewriting

Planning Your Report

Have you ever gone camping or helped to give a party for someone? You probably planned ahead so that you'd have everything you needed. Planning ahead for your report will help you have what you need for it, too.

Thinking About Audience and Purpose

Why are you writing a report? The main *purpose* of a report is to give information. The information consists mostly of facts and the opinions of experts.

Who is your audience? Probably your first *audience* will be your teacher and classmates, but reports might be for different audiences. (On pages 33–35, you'll find suggestions for other audiences.) Always ask yourself these questions about your audience:

- What does my audience already know about my topic?
- What does my audience need to know?
- What new or unusual information will interest my audience? What will surprise them?

You don't want to bore your readers by telling them what they already know. But you don't want to confuse them by not telling enough, either. If you use a word they may not know, define it. If they need to know how or why about something, explain it.

| EXERCISE 1 ▶ | Thinking About Audience and Purpose |

You're planning a report on killer whales to read to your class. Here are some sentences about whales. Which information would you use in your report? Why wouldn't you use the rest of the information?

Guide. Then students should be able to begin looking for sources on their topics. You will probably want to schedule library days at several stages in the writing process.

After most of the students have chosen their topics, have a session in which students tell their topics to the class. Sometimes a student who hasn't found a good topic will get an idea from the topics the other students have selected. After the students have written short plans and have asked themselves questions, conduct another group discussion. Ask students to discuss their short plans and to explain what questions they are interested in answering. After each student's presentation, ask the rest of the class to

The numbers of the sentences to be used are circled.

1. Whales live in water. **1. audience would know material**
2. Killer whales are the fastest members of the dolphin family and can swim for short distances at 25 knots.
3. A knot is a measure of speed, equal to 1.15 miles per hour. **4. does not inform readers about whales**
4. A friend of mine saw a killer whale in a marine park.
5. Killer whales travel in groups, called pods.

Making an Early Plan

What do you want to know about your topic? What does your audience need to know? Before you begin your research, make an *early plan* for your report by listing the main ideas that you want to cover. An **early plan,** sometimes called an *informal outline,* is a list of headings that will guide your research. Here is a writer's early plan for a report on men's hairstyles.

HERE'S HOW

Report topic: men's hairstyles of the past sixty years

when hairstyles have changed the most

what these hairstyles were like

people who influenced the hairstyles

what the hairstyles have meant

VISUAL CONNECTIONS

Exploring the Subject. Killer whales, or orcas, actually are dolphins and are the largest members of the dolphin family. Predators equipped with forty to fifty large, conical teeth, they feed on a variety of fish and squid. They also eat birds, seals, or even whales. Orcas live in groups ranging in number from only a few up to as many as fifty. They swim in formation and hunt in packs.

MEETING *individual* NEEDS

ADVANCED STUDENTS

You may want to have advanced students collaborate on a longer, more involved report. They could do more extensive research such as contacting and interviewing experts, visiting museums, going through files at a newspaper office, consulting specialized reference sources, ordering information from businesses, and so on.

respond by suggesting other information the writer might want to consider when researching his or her report.

After the students have listed their sources, ask them to discuss their topics and the sources found so far. Ask the other students to suggest any other sources on the topics. The other students might be especially helpful with ideas for interviews.

After the students have completed their notes and have written outlines, divide students into groups of two or three so that all members of each group can see the same paper. Then, ask each student to explain his or her outline to the others in the group. Ask the others in the group to listen and to respond by telling the writer what more they want to know or by asking questions about

Asking Questions

The next step is to ask yourself questions that will help you find the information in your early plan. Like your early plan, the questions will help to guide your research and keep you focused on your topic.

You can start with the *5W-How?* questions: *Who? What? When? Where? Why? How?* These questions will often make you think of other questions you can ask. For the report on "men's hairstyles of the past sixty years," the writer began research with the following questions:

> *Who* has influenced hairstyles?
> *What* have been some of the most popular hairstyles?
> *What* have different hairstyles meant to men?
> *When* have hairstyles changed the most?
> *Where* do styles change first?
> *Why* do styles change?
> *How* are men wearing their hair now?

 PART 2:
Making an Early Plan and Asking Questions

What do you and your readers want to know about your topic? Write down the main points you want to cover in your report. This is your early plan. Then, make a list of *5W-How?* questions that will help you to find the information you need. Save your early plan and questions to guide your later research.

If you don't know much about your topic, you may want to do some general reading first. Then you can make your early plan. Encyclopedia articles or magazines or World Wide Web sources can give you a good overview of your topic. You might also talk to people who know about the topic.

INTEGRATING THE LANGUAGE ARTS

Literature Link. Explain that to include accurate and vivid detail in a short story or a novel, a writer often must do considerable research. If a description of a time period, place, or profession contains inaccurate details, readers will find the work less credible.

If the selection is available in your literature textbook, have students read "The Medicine Bag" by Virginia Driving Hawk Sneve, in which the author describes the lives of the Sioux with accurate and vivid detail. Have each student pick out at least one detail from several categories such as geography, history, flora, fauna, and so on. Then, have the student locate the Rosebud Reservation in South Dakota in an atlas, almanac, encyclopedia, or other reference work to check the accuracy of Sneve's details.

the way the writer has organized the material.

The idea is to provide students with multiple opportunities to talk about their writing and to provide support and help all the way through the process. At the end of the lesson, each student should have a topic, source cards, note cards, and an outline for the first draft of the report.

Cont. on p. 339

Finding Sources

Use at least three sources of information for your report. Check the library for both print sources (encyclopedias, books, magazines, newspapers, booklets, pamphlets) and nonprint sources (videotapes, audiotapes, CD-ROMs).

Also, search the World Wide Web for pages or sites containing keywords associated with your topic, and check radio and TV guides for related programs. Depending on your topic, you might also ask for information at museums, bookstores, colleges, or government offices.

☞ REFERENCE NOTE: For help with finding information using online catalogs, online databases, and the Internet, see pages 882–886.

Interviewing.   If you know of an expert on your topic, arrange to talk with him or her. The expert might be a teacher, a parent, a businessperson, or another student. For example, if your topic is the effect of the Beatles on later music, you might talk with a music teacher who knows about the group's history and influence.

☞ REFERENCE NOTE: For information on interviewing, see pages 873–874.

TECHNOLOGY TIP

Students can use one of the search engines that are available on the Internet to perform a keyword search. Encourage students to be as precise as possible in the word they search for, and suggest that they not be discouraged if the search yields a huge number of sites. They might want to limit their work to a search engine that provides a summary of each site so they can learn more about the site without having to go to it.

A DIFFERENT APPROACH

You may want to write a research report with your students. As they help you make decisions or discuss your work, you will be able to tell whether or not they understand the steps in the process. This also enables you to model each step of the prewriting process with more focus.

INTEGRATING THE LANGUAGE ARTS

Literature Link. Have students read a piece of journalistic writing such as Ernst Schnabel's "A Tragedy Revealed: A Heroine's Last Days" to show them the importance of good interviewing skills. Point out to students how interesting direct quotations are and how they provide a personal point of view about the events reported.

CRITICAL THINKING
(pp. 337–339)

OBJECTIVE

• To evaluate sources

TEACHING EVALUATING SOURCES

Read each evaluation question and its explanation in sequence. Ask the students to express the information in their own words and to give examples of strong and weak sources.

EXERCISE 2 ▶   **Speaking and Listening: Interviewing**

Practice interviewing with a classmate. Give each other a topic of interest: a favorite sport, hobby, movie, and so on. Then, write some *5W-How?* questions for gathering information when you interview your classmate about this interest. After the interview, organize your notes and prepare a two- or three-minute oral report. Tell the class about the person you interviewed.

CRITICAL THINKING

Evaluating Sources

When you evaluate, you make judgments about quality or value. When you're researching a topic, it's important to evaluate the sources of information. Not all your sources will be equally useful. Here are some questions that will help you evaluate, or judge, the usefulness of a source.

1. **Is the source nonfiction?** You're looking for facts, so don't use print or nonprint sources that are fiction, such as stories and novels.
2. **Is the information current?** Some topics, such as those about modern science, technology, and medicine, need the latest available information. However, if your topic is "the origin of hot-air balloons," your information doesn't need to be as up-to-date. You can find the publication date on the copyright page of a book or magazine.
3. **Can you trust the information?** Some sources can be trusted more than others. Usually, reference books, textbooks, books by experts, and respected magazines and newspapers are reliable. Papers and magazines that focus on scandals or bizarre events probably aren't. Evaluate TV programs, videotapes, and World Wide Web sources the same way. Use only those that actually present verifiable facts about your topic.

ANSWERS
Exercise 2

Each student should have at least one question beginning with each of the *5W-How?* keywords. Here are some sample questions for the topic of amateur photography: Who taught you to use a camera? What do you like to photograph? When did you begin taking pictures? Where do you usually go to take photographs? Why do you enjoy photography? How do you decide on subjects for pictures?

LEP/ESL

General Strategies. To understand the fourth evaluation criterion presented on p. 338, some students will need examples of biased and objective statements. You could write the following pairs of statements on the chalkboard and explain why one statement in each pair is biased and the other is not:

1. The band played to more than 10,000 people. [objective]
   The band played to more than 10,000 joyous fans. [biased]
2. Some people were disappointed in their team's performance. [objective]
   Some people were disappointed in their team's half-hearted performance. [biased]

After the discussion, ask students to rewrite each question in their own words on a note card or on a sheet of notebook paper to keep handy for reference as they look for sources.

Then, ask students to do the **Critical Thinking Exercise** (below) by evaluating each possible source and stating briefly why a source would or would not be a good one.

Be sure that students understand that they should evaluate each of the sources for their research reports using these criteria.

COOPERATIVE LEARNING

You may want to have the students work through the **Critical Thinking Exercise** in groups so they can benefit from a discussion about each source.

Divide the class into mixed-ability groups of three or four. Ask each group to discuss the sources in the exercise, to decide which ones should be used, and to give reasons for their decisions. Have each group appoint a recorder to document why each source should or should not be used. After the groups have finished, go over the exercise with the class and discuss which sources should or should not be used. Have volunteers explain the reasons.

ANSWERS
Critical Thinking Exercise

1a. This source should not be used because it is fiction.

b. This source should be used because it is from a reliable reference book.

c. This source should not be used because it is probably an outdated work on a topic about which knowledge is constantly changing.

338   *Writing a Research Report*

4. Is the information objective? Sometimes information is biased. That is, only one side of a topic is presented, and you don't get a realistic view.

 CRITICAL THINKING EXERCISE:
Evaluating Sources

How good are you at evaluating sources? With a classmate or a small group, evaluate the sources for each topic in the left-hand column by choosing the best source in the right-hand column. Use the four evaluation questions on page 337 and above. Discuss why the sources in the right-hand column should or should not be used.

Topic	*Sources*
1. Harmful and helpful spiders 	a. *Arachnophobia,* a movie about spiders that invade a town b. An article about spiders in the latest edition of *The World Book Encyclopedia* c. A book, written by a medical doctor in 1915, on the treatment of spider bites
2. Recent trends in video games 	a. An article on video games in the latest issue of *Scientific American* b. A TV interview with the inventor of a video game c. An article in a newspaper on sale at the supermarket checkout stand about someone who was captured by a video game and taken to Mars

338

GUIDED PRACTICE

After discussing each step of prewriting, you may want to model the activities in **Writing Assignment: Parts 1–5.** Use the same topic each time, making sure the students understand the procedure. Guide students through **Exercise 1,** p. 333. To prepare students for **Exercise 2** on p. 337,

select a topic that no students are using and develop some sample interview questions.

☞

Listing Sources

Finding sources is like going on a treasure hunt. Start your search at the library or at one of the other places mentioned on page 336. To keep track of the sources you find, create *source cards*. Source cards are index cards, half-sheets of paper, or computer files. Use a separate card, sheet, or computer file for each source. Put a *source number* at the top right of each source card. If you have four sources, for example, number them 1, 2, 3, 4. Source cards save you time, and you'll use the information from them at the end of your report.

There are several ways to list sources. The following way is recommended by the Modern Language Association (MLA). You should use whatever form your teacher recommends. No matter what form you use, follow the capitalization, punctuation, and order of information exactly. (Notice that the author's last name is first, followed by a comma and his or her first name.)

MLA Guide for Listing Sources

1. **Books:** author, title, city, publisher, and year.
   Nunn, Joan. Fashion in Costume, 1200–1980. New York: Schocken, 1984.

2. **Magazines and Newspapers:** author (if any), title of article, name of magazine or newspaper, date, and page numbers.
   Katz, Jane. "The Haircut That Changed My Life." Redbook July 1996: 25.

3. **Encyclopedia Articles:** author (if any), title of article, name of encyclopedia, year and edition (ed.).
   Sassoon, Vidal. "Hairdressing." The World Book Encyclopedia. 1995 ed.

4. **Interviews:** expert's name, the words *Personal interview* or *Telephone interview,* and date.
   Mullens, Sean. Telephone interview. 19 June 1996.

(continued)

2a. This source should be used because it is from a current issue of a respected periodical.

b. This source must be carefully evaluated. It may be biased, but it may be objective and therefore usable.

c. This source should not be used because the source is sensational and therefore unreliable.

⬥ INTEGRATING THE LANGUAGE ARTS

Mechanics Link. When students are learning to make source cards, remind them of the following punctuation rules:

1. Titles of books and periodicals are italicized or underlined.
2. Titles of articles from periodicals and entries in encyclopedias are placed inside quotation marks.
3. The first word and all important words in a title are capitalized.

💾 TECHNOLOGY TIP

The *Writer's Workshop CD-ROM* composition program provides a **Bibliography Maker** that will automatically arrange the student's bibliographical source information into a standard bibliography format. If students enter their source information early in their research, the form on the computer screen will serve as a reminder should they forget to note important data. Students will still have time, then, to collect the missing information and complete their final bibliography listings.

INDEPENDENT PRACTICE

Assign **Writing Assignment: Parts 1–5** and **Exercise 2** as independent practice.

ASSESSMENT

As students share their work with the rest of the class or with a small group, you can walk around the room to check on the progress of each student. To evaluate students' mastery of the prewriting process, assign point values for the completion of each stage and use the total as the grade for the prewriting process. Here's a plan that

340   *Writing a Research Report*

MLA Guide for Listing Sources *(continued)*

5. **Television or Radio Programs:** title, network, station call letters and city (if any), and date of broadcast.
   The Beatles Anthology. ABC. KVUE, Austin.
           19, 22, 23 Nov. 1995.

6. **Electronic Materials:** author (if any), title (include print publisher, date of print publication, and page numbers if material was originally in a print source), date of electronic posting or publication (if given, for online sources), title of CD-ROM or title of database (if any, for online sources), type of source (*CD-ROM* or *Online*), location of source (*Internet,* online service, or city, if given, for CD-ROMs), name of vendor or distributor (CD-ROMs), date of publication (CD-ROMs) or date of access, and Internet address (if any).
   "50 Years of Hairstyles." Ebony Magazine
           Nov. 1995: 222B. Middle Search. CD-ROM.
   EBSCO Publishing. May 1996.

MEETING *individual* NEEDS

LESS-ADVANCED STUDENTS

You may want to have each student make five sample source cards based on the **MLA Guide for Listing Sources.**

Have students work in pairs, exchanging source cards and proofreading them for errors. Students then should ask their partners what each word means and what each number means. The answers are in the textbook above each example.

TEACHING NOTE

Although MLA style requires listing a city of publication for CD-ROM databases, you may want to allow students to omit the city when the information is not readily available. For example, the city name may be printed on the box that the CD-ROM came in, but the city name and other copyright information may not be available from within the database itself.

Students may be confused when a sentence ends with an Internet address and a period follows the address. Remind students that the final period in such a listing is punctuation for the sentence; the period is not part of the Internet address. Although the mark for a period looks the same as the mark used to separate parts of an Internet address, that mark is called a *dot* when it appears in an Internet address.

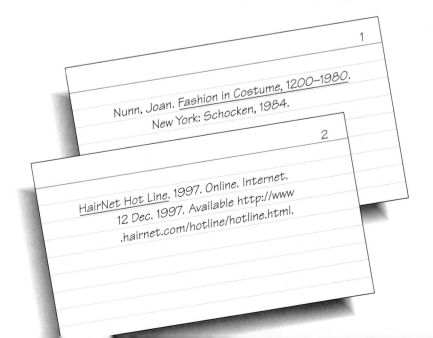

1
Nunn, Joan. Fashion in Costume, 1200–1980.
New York: Schocken, 1984.

2
HairNet Hot Line. 1997. Online. Internet.
12 Dec. 1997. Available http://www
.hairnet.com/hotline/hotline.html.

gives a total possible of 100:

    10 points—topic, audience, purpose
    10 points—making an early plan
    10 points—asking questions
    10 points—finding and evaluating
          sources
    10 points—listing sources correctly
    30 points—making note cards
    20 points—writing an outline

RETEACHING

Students who have difficulty gathering information for their reports might benefit from a discussion of each step. You can work with these students while the other students continue their work. Ask students to talk about the assignment and to tell you what they understand. Guide each student to apply that understanding to the research ☞

WRITING ASSIGNMENT

PART 3:
Finding and Listing Sources for Your Report

Where can you find the information you need? Start with a library, but check other places as well. Do you know of someone you can interview? Try to find at least one non-print source. Find three or four sources of information, and then create your source cards.

Taking Notes

You've found your information, but you can't use it all. How do you decide what to use? Let your early plan and questions about your topic guide you (see pages 334–335). Scan through your sources for information that relates to your headings and your questions. Don't be afraid to add new, interesting information you find, but add headings to your early plan that reflect these new ideas. These tips can help you take efficient notes:

- Use a separate 4″ × 6″ note card, sheet of paper, or computer file for each source and for each note.
- Use abbreviations and short phrases. You can also make lists of ideas. You don't need to write complete sentences.
- Put quotation marks around exact words from sources, and name your sources. *Plagiarism*—copying without using quotation marks or naming sources—is a type of cheating or lying, as bad as stealing answers for a test.
- Label the top of each card, sheet, or file with a key word or phrase that tells what it is about. These words and phrases can come from your early plan.
- Put the source number at the top, also.
- At the bottom of each card, sheet, or file, write the page number where you found the information.
- Take notes from each of your sources.

On the following page you'll find an example of a note taken from *Fashion in Costume, 1200–1980* by Joan Nunn.

MEETING individual NEEDS

report. After talking about a step, students may find it easier to perform.

Some students might forget instructions. Refer them to the proper place in the textbook. You can also reinforce instructions by making posters that display samples of source entries and note cards.

CLOSURE

With the class ready to begin writing, you may want to ask the students to look back on what they have done to get to this point. As they list the steps they have gone through, write the steps on the chalkboard or on an overhead transparency to give a visual review as well as an oral review. ■

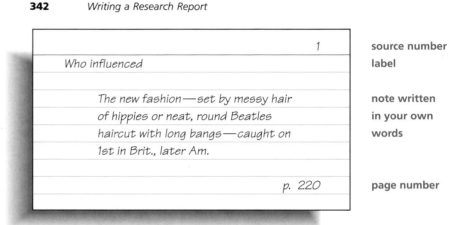

 REFERENCE NOTE: For more information on taking notes, see pages 917–918.

WRITING ASSIGNMENT

PART 4:
Taking Notes for Your Report

What interesting things have you found out about your topic? Using note cards, half-sheets of paper, or computer files, take notes from the sources you listed in Writing Assignment, Part 3 (page 341). You'll use your notes when you write your paper.

Organizing and Outlining Your Information

Now that you have most of your information, you need to organize it. You may make some changes as you write and revise, but the outline you make now will be a useful guide. Here are some steps you can take to organize your information.

1. Separate your note cards, sheets, or computer files into sets with the same or similar labels.
2. Think of a heading to identify each set. It will be similar to the labels on your cards, sheets, or files.
3. Decide on the order of your main headings—perhaps order of importance or chronological (time) order.

MEETING *individual* NEEDS

LEARNING STYLES

Kinetic Learners. Have students work on the floor or on a large table to go through the steps in **Organizing and Outlining Your Information.** Students can lay out the source cards and move them around until they are in a logical order. The students then can copy the outlines onto paper. They might find that what they thought was a main heading will turn out to be support for a main point.

ORGANIZING AND OUTLINING YOUR INFORMATION

Explain to students that to make their reports interesting and complete, they must properly develop each of the main ideas. When they sort their note cards to make outlines, they should have two or more subheadings for each main heading. If they find they have any main headings with fewer than two subheadings, they should either eliminate those main headings or gather more information.

4. Sort the cards, sheets, or files in each set to make subheadings for your outline.
5. Create an outline from your main headings and subheadings.

👉 REFERENCE NOTE: For more information on formal outlines, see page 99.

Below is an example of a formal outline. After you've finished organizing your notes, you can create an outline like this and use it as a plan for writing your first draft.

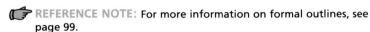

Sixty Years of Haircuts

I. Changes in the forties and fifties
   A. Forties: crew cuts
   B. Fifties: ducktails
      1. Influence of Tony Curtis
      2. Influence of Elvis Presley
II. Changes in the sixties and seventies
   A. Sixties: long hair
      1. Influence of the Beatles
      2. Influence of African ancestry
   B. Seventies: group identification
      1. Shaved heads
      2. Mohawks: now and long ago
III. Changes in recent decades
   A. Eighties: outrageous statements
   B. Nineties and today: personal style

PART 5:
Writing an Outline for Your Report

Now, use the information from your notes to write your outline. You don't have to put everything in the notes into the outline. Use just the headings and subheadings that will guide you when you write your report.

MEETING *individual* NEEDS

LESS-ADVANCED STUDENTS

You may want to allow students leeway in the matter of a formal outline. Some students are not sequential thinkers and will have difficulty making formal outlines. Suggest that they employ a cluster technique: The main idea is written in the center of the page and each main heading branches out from it. Additional branches hold supporting information. This whole-picture approach will make more sense than a traditional outline to some students. After the clusters are completed, each student can decide on the order of presentation for the information.

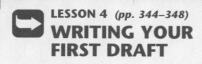
TEACHING THE LESSON
Ask a student volunteer to read aloud **Understanding the Parts of a Report** (below) and **Writing Your Report**, p. 345. Answer any questions students have.

To teach students how to do a Works Cited list, have them turn to the sample Works Cited list on p. 348. Guide them through the process of making a Works Cited

WRITING YOUR FIRST DRAFT

■ **Instructional Support** For help with writing a report, see **Writing** in *Strategies for Writing*, p. 53.

 QUOTATION FOR THE DAY

"[As a reporter] I act as a sponge. I soak it up and squeeze it out in ink . . ." (Janet Flanner, American journalist)

Ask students to explain Flanner's quotation. Lead them to understand that during prewriting, they soaked up information, and as they write their first drafts, they'll be squeezing it out in ink.

LEP/ESL

General Strategies. In some cultures, copying without using either quotation marks or citations is allowed and even respected. You may want to emphasize how important it is in English to either quote or paraphrase and to always give credit to the source. Give students some methods for paraphrasing such as changing the grammar, dividing a long sentence, joining two short sentences, and using synonyms. Guidelines for paraphrasing are given on p. 922.

344

---

344   *Writing a Research Report*

Writing Your First Draft

Is writing a report different from writing other compositions? It isn't in some ways. A report has an introduction, a body, and a conclusion, just like much of the other writing you've done. But the information in a report consists of facts from outside sources. At the end of a report you list your sources so that your readers know where your information comes from.

Understanding the Parts of a Report

Introduction.   The *introduction* of a report isn't mentioned in the outline, so what's it doing in your paper? It's a short beginning paragraph that's there to grab your reader's attention. It tells in an interesting way what your report is about. In the model report on page 345, the writer uses startling facts about what people do to their hair, followed by a surprising statement, to catch the reader's interest. The reader can tell what the main idea (or point) of the report is from this statement.

Body.   The *body* of the report is where the information from your note cards goes. Each of the main headings from your outline can be discussed in one or more paragraphs. Some of your subtopics may need separate paragraphs, too, if you have enough information about them. Or, you may combine some subtopics in a single paragraph. Just make sure each paragraph tells enough to make its main idea clear.

Conclusion.   The *conclusion* of a report sums up your main points in an interesting way. Your conclusion may be short, but it should give a finished feeling to your paper. Notice that the model report ends with a question, yet lets the reader know that it's the end.

If your readers want to know more about your topic, they can refer to your list of sources. Here's the way to make your list of sources.

list including one interview, one book, one magazine article, and one film. **The MLA Guide for Listing Sources** on p. 339 gives information not included in the sample Works Cited list on p. 348, so tell students they may need to refer to both models when they do the Works Cited lists for their reports.

Have students read **A Writer's Model** (below), and lead them in a discussion of organization of the report by using the notes to the left of the report.

To help students begin writing, model for them the process of writing a paragraph based on the information on one note card. Tell them they can write their introductions at any point, not necessarily before they write the body paragraphs.

☞

1. Put the title *Works Cited* at the top of a new page. (You might use *Bibliography* instead, but most style guides suggest using that word for a list of print sources only.)
2. List your sources in alphabetical order by the author's last name. (When there is no author, alphabetize by the first word of the title.)
3. Use the same style you used for your source cards.

Use the sample Works Cited list on page 348 as a model.

 COMPUTER NOTE: Most word-processing programs have features to help automatically format and alphabetize a Works Cited list.

Writing Your Report

Except for direct quotations, write your report in your own words. Although your outline helps to guide you, you don't have to follow it strictly. As you're writing, you may decide to rearrange parts of your draft, or to cut or add something. Keep referring to your notes and go back to your sources if you need more information.

You can use the following sample report as a model. As you read, notice how the report follows the outline on page 343. Remember that your report may not be this long. Writing a good report is what's important.

A WRITER'S MODEL

Sixty Years of Haircuts

INTRODUCTION
Interest grabber

Main idea

During the past sixty years, men's haircuts have gone through big changes--from crew cuts and moptops to Mohawks, flattops, and beyond. Over the decades, though, one thing has stayed the same: Hairstyles have been a way for men to show who they are and what they stand for.

BODY
1940s and 1950s

For many years before 1940, most men wore a standard hairstyle. It was parted on the

---

TECHNOLOGY TIP
If computers are available, have students use word-processing software with hanging paragraph capability to format their Works Cited lists. After the first line, subsequent lines in an entry are automatically indented five spaces. Entering a hard return takes the cursor flush left to start a new entry.

 **MEETING** *individual* **NEEDS**

LESS-ADVANCED STUDENTS
Because writing a first draft is an extensive project to complete as one assignment, you may want to divide the task into more manageable parts. For example, have students write introductions and put the students in small groups to read their introductions aloud. The groups can then provide feedback. You can follow the same procedure with each major idea in the body and the conclusion. The group process will be supportive, and the shorter assignments will be easier to complete.

You may want to have students write in class for at least one class period so you can help them when necessary. The rest of the writing could be assigned as independent practice.

ASSESSMENT

To make the assessment process easier, have students label the parts of their reports in the left margin and have them put the headings from their outlines next to the parts of the essay to which they pertain. They can use **A Writer's Model** as a guide. Use their margin notes to assess whether or not they have correctly organized their drafts.

A DIFFERENT APPROACH

Because students often rely too heavily on the exact language of their sources, you may want to have students start their papers in a different way. Give the students ten minutes to read over their note cards. Then, have them put the cards away and use only their outlines to write first drafts. If there is a direct quotation a student wants to use, he or she can leave a blank space to fill in later. Emphasize that students should write what they remember in their own words and that they will be able to go back to their notes later. They may be surprised at how much they know, and without the note cards they will write in their own voice instead of rewording someone else's writing.

Influence of Tony Curtis

Influence of Elvis Presley

1960s

Influence of the Beatles

left and tapered at the back. With the outbreak of the Second World War, U.S. Army and Navy men adopted the crew cut. It was a short-all-over style that was easy to keep clean. During the early fifties, the crew cut became the "in" fashion on college campuses. Whether men knew it or not, their crew cuts announced that they were clean-cut, athletic, and patriotic.

Crew-cut men laughed at men brave enough to try a new style, the ducktail, but many eventually wore it. The film star Tony Curtis was one of the first to comb and oil his curly hair to a flipped-up point at the back. A ducktail suggested that its wearer was romantic, healthy (so much hair!), and carefree.

Elvis Presley copied the Tony Curtis look and took it to new heights. Elvis's own hair was mousy brown, but he dyed it blue-black. Then he teased it into a high wave in front and used gel and spray to make it look as lush as possible on top. Elvis attracted attention by combing and stroking his long wooly sideburns on stage.

The true revolution in hairstyles began in the sixties with the Beatles. Their haircut, the "moptop," was cut in a bowl shape, with bangs over the eyebrows. The moptop looked completely different from other styles because it was so natural and childlike. Many American men

RETEACHING

Students who have difficulty writing first drafts may lack confidence even though they have done the preparatory work. To get them started, you could have them work in pairs to talk/write their drafts by having one student act as a scribe for the other.

CLOSURE

Ask students what they have learned about writing research reports. List what the students say on the overhead transparency or on the chalkboard. ■

Writing Your First Draft   **347**

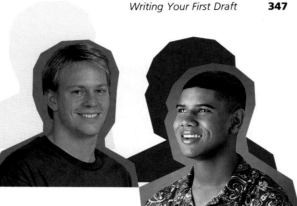

Influence of African ancestry

1970s

Shaved heads

Mohawks

1980s

quickly copied the Beatles. It was the first time they had let their hair grow long and natural since the 1780s.

In the late sixties, a hairstyle became a symbol of racial pride and the civil rights movement. To emphasize their African ancestry and distinctive culture, black men and women let their hair grow out in an "Afro." It was a round, naturally curly hairstyle.

Men's hairstyles during the seventies continued to identify the groups men belonged to. Men who wanted to look responsible returned to shorter hairstyles. To show their scorn of long-haired "idealists," some people shaved off all their hair.

Wild-looking, spiked hair saw a rebirth in the seventies. Some versions of this were called "Mohawks," but it was more like a style worn long ago by the Huron, Osage, and Omaha nations. As a way of daring their enemies to scalp them, some Native Americans used to arrange their hair in a row of long spikes. They used bear grease to stiffen the spikes and shaved the rest of their heads to emphasize the frightening effect.

In the eighties and early nineties, trendsetters wanted to look different from everyone else. They thought the more outrageous

COOPERATIVE LEARNING

Provide frequent opportunities for students to read aloud in small groups what they have written so they can get feedback from fellow students. Change the grouping each day so that the writers will receive feedback from different sets of listeners.

Here are some possible questions to guide students in giving each other feedback:

1. Is anything unclear?
2. Is the information interesting?
3. Does the introduction make you want to read the rest of the report?
4. Is there anything else you want to know about the main points presented?
5. Do you have any suggestions for the writer about additional information from other sources?

MEETING individual NEEDS

LESS-ADVANCED STUDENTS

You may want to schedule individual conferences with students at different stages in the writing process. Ask each student to read what he or she has drafted and to tell you what problems exist. After discussing the problems, close the conference with a discussion of what the student will do next on the assignment.

WORKS CITED

The MLA calls for a five-space indent in a Works Cited list. In the sample Works Cited list on this page, the indent appears to be about six and one-half spaces. Explain to students that for the typeface used in this book, the five-space indent translates into a printer's measure that is slightly different.

For examples of how to list articles from newspapers, magazines, or encyclopedias, refer students to the **MLA Guide for Listing Sources** on p. 339. For examples of how to list other sources such as computer software, refer students to the **MLA Guide for Listing Sources** on p. 340.

---

the better. One unisex style, called the "buzz" or "flattop," had closely cut or shaved sides like a Mohawk. However, the top hair of a flattop was clipped into a geometric shape and stood up straight--like Bart Simpson's hair. Neon colors emphasized the effect.

Styles today

Professional hairstylist Sean Mullens says that most men today want a short, easy-to-care-for hairstyle. He adds that many of his customers ask for a style that allows them to "get out of the shower, run their fingers through their hair, and be done with it."

Direct quotation

CONCLUSION Summary of main ideas

As you have seen, men's hairstyles can have political, social, and personal meanings. The journey from crew cut to flattop and beyond has taken sixty years. As the journey continues, what new hairstyles will men wear to show who they are and what they stand for?

Works Cited

The Beatles Anthology. ABC. KVUE, Austin. 19, 22, 23 Nov. 1995.

Corson, Richard. Fashions in Hair: The First Five Thousand Years. London: Owen, 1971.

"50 Years of Hairstyles." Ebony Magazine Nov. 1995: 222B. Middle Search. CD-ROM. EBSCO Publishing. May 1996.

Mullens, Sean. Telephone interview. 19 June 1996.

Sassoon, Vidal. "Hairdressing." The World Book Encyclopedia. 1995 ed.

 **WRITING ASSIGNMENT**

PART 6:
Writing Your First Draft

You've done a great deal of preparation, and now it's time to write your first draft. Use your notes and outline as guides. Remember to list your sources on a separate Works Cited page at the end of your report.

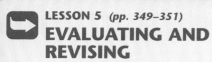
OBJECTIVES
- To analyze and evaluate revisions of a writer's model
- To evaluate and revise the first draft of a research report

TEACHING THE LESSON

Using the example about Marjorie Kinnan Rawlings in the first paragraph of this lesson, impress upon students the fact that good writers usually spend as much time on revision as on prewriting.

Go over the evaluation chart and then use it to evaluate **A Writer's Model** (pp. 345–348) with the class. This process

Evaluating and Revising

Sometimes it's surprising to learn how much time published writers spend revising their work. Marjorie Kinnan Rawlings, for example, worked on *The Yearling* for a year and then started all over again. Rawlings even spent a great deal of time revising the title itself. A book about her editor (a man named Maxwell Perkins) tells how the title of the novel changed.

> Six months into the writing, Marjorie Rawlings was still hunting for a title. She sent a list of alternatives to Perkins and asked for his opinion. He did not care much for *The Flutter Mill.* Of *Juniper Island* he said: "I do not think place names are good for a book. There is not enough human suggestion in them." Of her third title he wrote, "I would think one which carried the meaning of *The Yearling* was probably right." The more he spoke of it, the better it sounded to him. He wrote her in the spring of 1937, "It seems to have a quality even more than a meaning that fits the book." It stuck.
>
> A. Scott Berg, *Max Perkins: Editor of Genius*

You may like your title as it is, but every piece of writing can benefit from revision. After you write the first draft of your report, set it aside. After a day or two, use the following chart to help you evaluate and revise your writing. Begin by asking yourself the questions in the left-hand column. If your answer to any question is *no*, use the technique on the right to correct the problem.

 QUOTATION FOR THE DAY

"Blessed is the man who, having nothing to say, abstains from giving us wordy evidence of the fact." (George Eliot, 1819–1880, British author)

Ask students to think of times when they received more information than they wanted or needed to know and became bored or frustrated. Remind them that to keep their audience's interest, their reports should be concise and to the point.

SELECTION AMENDMENT
Description of change: excerpted
Rationale: to focus on the concept of writing a research report presented in this chapter

will serve as guided practice for **Writing Assignment: Part 6** on p. 348. Explain that this type of external evaluation addresses content more than style.

Guide students through the first two questions in **Exercise 3**, p. 351. Explain that these revisions are internal and deal with writing style. Then, assign the rest of **Exercise 3** and **Writing Assignment: Part 7**, p. 351, as independent practice.

MEETING *individual* NEEDS

LEP/ESL

General Strategies. To ensure variety in attributions, students will need an inventory of conventional expressions for citing what others have said. Here are a few suggested expressions:

1. Dr. Blake observed that . . .
2. According to Dr. Blake, . . .
3. In Dr. Blake's opinion, . . .

COOPERATIVE LEARNING

Divide the class into groups of three or four and have each student read aloud his or her first draft to the rest of the group. Have group members respond by writing answers to the following questions:

1. Does the introduction interest you in the topic?
2. Can you find the main idea of the report? What is it?
3. Can you find the main supporting ideas? What are they?
4. Do you want more information about anything?
5. Does the conclusion leave you feeling satisfied that the report is complete?

EVALUATING AND REVISING REPORTS

EVALUATION GUIDE	REVISION TECHNIQUE
1 Does the report use several different sources?	**Add** sources. Try to find and use at least one nonprint source.
2 Does the report consist of facts and the opinions of experts?	**Add** facts or an expert's opinion. **Cut** your own thoughts and feelings.
3 Is the report in the writer's own words? If someone else's words are used, are they in quotation marks?	**Replace** with your own words, or **add** quotation marks where you've used someone's actual words.
4 Is the information well organized?	**Reorder** sentences or paragraphs in order of importance or chronological order.
5 Is the introduction interesting? Does it tell what the report is about?	**Add** attention-getting details. **Add** a sentence that tells the main idea.
6 Does the conclusion bring the report to a close?	**Add** a sentence that summarizes the main idea.
7 Is the list of sources on a separate sheet at the end of the report? Is the form correct?	**Add** the list of sources in the correct form.

ASSESSMENT

Ask students to turn in the first drafts with notations indicating the revisions they plan to make. You can scan these quickly to see whether or not each student has understood what to do.

CLOSURE

Lead a brief discussion of what needs to be considered when evaluating and revising. You may also want students to discuss what helped them most at this stage of the process. ■

Evaluating and Revising **351**

EXERCISE 3 ▶ **Analyzing a Writer's Revisions**

Here are the changes the writer made in one paragraph while revising "Sixty Years of Haircuts." Look at the changes carefully. Then answer the questions that follow.

> In the eighties and early nineties, trendsetters wanted to look different from everyone else. They thought the ~~funnier~~ *more outrageous* the better. Neon colors emphasized the effect. One unisex style, called the "buzz" or "flattop," had closely cut or shaved sides like a Mohawk. ~~It's my favorite style.~~ However, the top hair of a flattop was clipped into a geometric shape and stood up straight *– like Bart Simpson's hair.*

replace
reorder
cut
add

1. Why did the writer replace the word *funnier* with the words *more outrageous* in the second sentence? [Hint: Which word expresses the correct fact?]
2. Why did the writer move (reorder) the third sentence to the end of the paragraph? How does this change help the organization of the paragraph?
3. Why did the writer cut the sentence *It's my favorite style*? [Hint: Review page 333.]
4. Why did the writer add the phrase *like Bart Simpson's hair* to the last sentence?

WRITING ASSIGNMENT

PART 7:
Evaluating and Revising Your Report

Read your report to two or three classmates. Listen to their suggestions and take notes on what seems helpful. Then go over your draft, using the evaluating and revising chart (page 350) and your classmates' suggestions.

ANSWERS
Exercise 3

Answers may vary.

1. *More outrageous* expresses the correct fact. *Funnier* is not accurate because many people thought their outrageous hairstyles were not at all funny.
2. The order of information is clearer. First comes a description of the hairstyle itself; then comes additional information about colors.
3. This sentence states an opinion and is not necessary. The writer's purpose is to inform about hairstyles, not about his or her own preferences.
4. The phrase adds a fact that makes the description clearer.

OBJECTIVE

- To proofread and publish a research report

TEACHING THE LESSON

Write on the chalkboard a paragraph containing several errors in grammar, usage, and mechanics. Guide students through the process of proofreading it before having them proofread their reports. To close, have students write the rule from the **Mechanics Hint** (below) on capitalizing titles. ∎

QUOTATION FOR THE DAY

"Any man can make mistakes, but only an idiot persists in his error." (Cicero, 106–43 B.C., Roman orator, statesman, and man of letters.)

Proofreading and Publishing

Remember, **proofreading** is reading carefully and correcting mistakes. **Publishing** is sharing your work. Here's a publishing idea: Offer your report to your school librarian as a resource that other students can consult later.

MECHANICS HINT

Capitalizing Titles

In titles, capitalize the first word and all important words. Unless one of them is the first word of a title, do not capitalize *a, an, the,* coordinating conjunctions, or prepositions with fewer than five letters.

EXAMPLES   Book: *Ambush in the Amazon*
Story: "Beware of the Dog"
Poem: "The Boy and the Wolf"

👉 REFERENCE NOTE: See pages 726–727 for more help.

WRITING ASSIGNMENT	PART 8: **Proofreading and Publishing Your Report**

Proofread your revised paper, and share it with others. Give a copy to anyone you interviewed, too.

Reflecting on Your Writing

To add your report to your **portfolio,** date it and include your answers to the following questions.

- How did you choose your topic?
- If you were just starting a report on the same topic, what would you do differently? Why?

A STUDENT MODEL

Alexis M. Webster attends school in Kinston, North Carolina. Notice the specific facts she provides in the following excerpt from her report on carnivorous plants.

Carnivorous Plants
by Alexis M. Webster

Carnivorous plants are plants that eat insects or animals to get their nutrients. These plants are most likely to be found in very moist or very nutrient-poor places. Unlike other plants, these plants capture their food. While the green leaves on the plants produce carbohydrates, the insects and animals they catch provide nutrients such as nitrogen.

Carnivorous plants have special organs that capture the insects. Some carnivorous plants have flowers that look or smell from a distance like old smelly meat. This smell and color attracts the insects and animals. Pitcher plants, sundews, bladderworts, butterworts, and Venus's-flytraps all are types of carnivorous plants.

Pitcher plants capture insects in order to get enough nutrients to stay alive. They have interesting ways of trapping their own insects. The pitcher plants grow leaves that look like pitchers with open lids (the pitchers are leaves, not flowers). The inner part of the pitcher has a sweet juice that attracts lots of insects. Once an insect gets into the pitcher, it cannot climb its way out. Therefore the prey is most likely to drown in the pool of digestive liquid inside the pitcher.

Some types of pitcher plants are found in the wilds of tropical Asia, Malaysia, New Caledonia, and northern Australia. Also, the American pitcher plant, which belongs to the genus Sarracenia, is found in North America, mainly in swampy places in the east. The pitchers of some of these plants contain downward pointing hairs. This makes it even more difficult for the insect to crawl out of the pitcher.

A STUDENT MODEL
Evaluation

1. Although the references have been omitted to conserve space, Alexis's paper is based on several sources.
2. Alexis uses many facts and details, and she states them in her own words.
3. Alexis's paper is well organized, moving from general information about carnivorous plants to details about one specific carnivorous plant.
4. The introduction of Alexis's paper grabs the reader's interest, and it tells what the report is about.

TEACHING THE LESSON

Read aloud the introductory material on the parts of a book report and then ask students to read silently **"The Secret Artist."** Have them note the parts of the report. Then have a class discussion based on the questions in **Thinking It Over.**

Go over the prewriting suggestions in the textbook and then allow students to

QUOTATION FOR THE DAY

"Education . . . has produced a vast population able to read but unable to distinguish what is worth reading." (George Macaulay Trevelyan, 1876–1962, British historian and writer)

Have students brainstorm two lists of books: those that they feel are worth reading and those that are not. Explain that writing book reports allows students to give their opinions about the value of particular books, and in the reports students can encourage or discourage others from reading the books.

354

WRITING WORKSHOP

A Book Report

You've already written one kind of report: a research report in which you presented information from a number of sources. Here's a chance for you to write another kind of report: a book report in which you evaluate a single work.

A book report is a lot like a movie review. The writers of both—often following a standard outline—evaluate a work, describe what they like or dislike about it, and give reasons for their opinions. A book report about a novel, for example, should include the features outlined below.

- the title of the book and the author's name
- an introduction that gets the reader interested
- a brief description of the setting and main character(s)
- a brief summary of the plot that doesn't ruin the suspense for the reader
- an evaluation of the book—why the audience should or should not read it

The following book report is an evaluation of the novel *I, Juan de Pareja*. Does the writer think the book is worth reading? What does the writer say is good or bad about the book? Does the writer give enough information about the book for you to understand the evaluation?

The Secret Artist

Juan de Pareja's mother dies when he is just five. A young black boy, Juan is a slave and totally dependent on the kindness of his owners. Then they both die, and he finds himself in the cruel grip of a muleteer (a person who drives mule teams). He runs away, but the muleteer finds him. Will his life now be one of slavery and cruelty?

go to the library to look for books.

Have students write, evaluate, and revise their book reports. Then, suggest that the book reports be published in folders and made available to other students. Knowing that other students will read their reports may encourage students to do their best work.

ASSESSMENT

You may want to give the students a grading scale at the beginning of this lesson. A grading scale could include these areas for assessment: 10 points for title of book and author; 15 points for interesting introduction; 25 points for setting and for main characters; 25 points for plot summary; 25 points for evaluation of the book. ☞

The answer is both yes and no. The life story of the young boy is told in the novel I, Juan de Pareja by Elizabeth Borton de Treviño. Juan's story is set in Spain during the 1600s. After his owners die, he is sent to Madrid to become the slave of Diego Velázquez, the great artist.

Velázquez trains Juan to be his assistant, and soon Juan is caught up in the beauty of his art. He learns to stretch a canvas, mix paints, clean brushes, and adjust the light. He watches and admires Velázquez, a quiet, hard-working man who is dedicated to his art. Juan yearns to paint, too, but Spanish law forbids slaves to learn the arts. Velázquez's fame grows, and Juan goes with him on trips to Italy. There Juan can no longer resist his yearning to paint. He paints in secret, learning and improving.

Through the years both Juan and his master's talent and their friendship grow. But still Juan hides his secret from the great artist. On one trip to Italy, he vows he will not keep his painting a secret any longer. The surprise ending is both sad and joyful.

This is a historical story of two painters, one the master, the other his slave. But the real enjoyment comes from seeing how the affection and kindness between the two men changes both of their lives. It's a story you won't easily forget.

I, Juan de Pareja
Elizabeth Borton de Treviño

MEETING *individual* NEEDS

LEP/ESL

General Strategies. The experience of reading and understanding a book written in English is a very satisfying experience for students with limited English proficiency. If students have difficulty finding books for their book reports, you may want to use some of the simplified literature books for English-language learners such as *Longman American Structural Readers: Horizontal Readers*.

VISUAL CONNECTIONS

Exploring the Subject. Elizabeth Borton de Treviño has written many novels for young people. She was born in 1904 in California. A musician as well as a writer, Treviño was at one time first violinist in the Vivaldi Orchestra. In 1935 she married Luís Treviño Gomez, and she now lives with her husband in Mexico. Treviño won the Newbery Medal for *I, Juan de Pareja* in 1966.

ANSWERS
Thinking It Over

Answers may vary.

1. The writer tries to create interest by creating suspense in the last sentence of the first paragraph. Most students will feel that the writer succeeds.

2. To reveal the ending would destroy much of the book's impact. It would detract from the reader's pleasure in reading the book.

3. The evaluation is positive. The final paragraph makes this fact absolutely clear.

4. Students will react in different ways. Those interested in painting and historical fiction will probably want to read the book and so will those wanting to find out how the book ends.

356

Thinking It Over

1. How does the writer try to get you interested in reading the report? Does the writer succeed?
2. Why doesn't the writer reveal the ending of the book?
3. Is the writer's evaluation positive? How do you know?
4. Does the report inspire you to read the book? Explain.

Writing a Book Report

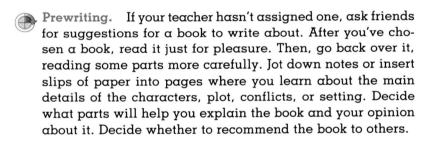

Prewriting. If your teacher hasn't assigned one, ask friends for suggestions for a book to write about. After you've chosen a book, read it just for pleasure. Then, go back over it, reading some parts more carefully. Jot down notes or insert slips of paper into pages where you learn about the main details of the characters, plot, conflicts, or setting. Decide what parts will help you explain the book and your opinion about it. Decide whether to recommend the book to others.

Writing, Evaluating, and Revising. As you write your report, keep in mind the features that are common to most book reports. Try to include some basic information about the setting, characters, and plot, without spoiling the suspense for anyone who might read the book. Finally, share your opinion of the book. Do you think other people should take the time to read the book?

Proofreading and Publishing. Since other people will be reading your book report, take the time to proofread it carefully. Clean up any errors in spelling, mechanics, and capitalization. If your school newspaper has a book review section, think about submitting your report for publication.

If you decide to include your book report in your **portfolio,** date it and attach a note responding to these questions: How did you decide which information from the book to include, and which to leave out? How was this paper different from others you've written?

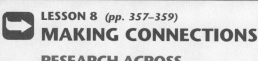

MAKING CONNECTIONS

• To write a biographical report

357

MAKING CONNECTIONS

RESEARCH ACROSS THE CURRICULUM

Biographical Report

Would you like to know more about some historical person or someone in your family? You can use your research and report-writing skills to prepare a biographical report.

For a biographical report, you'll need at least three sources. If books and articles have been written about the person, use them. If you research the life of a family member, interview the person and people who know him or her. Here are some things you'll want to find out.

1. When and where was the person born? If the person is no longer living, when and where did he or she die?
2. What is interesting and special about the person?
3. What are the person's achievements? Has the person received special recognition for something?

The following is an example of a biographical report written for a book. Notice how the writer uses facts and quotations that emphasize the uniqueness of his subject.

Alta Weiss

Alta Weiss was a doctor's daughter from Ragersville, Ohio, who began to pitch for boys' teams at the age of fourteen. At sixteen, she joined a men's semiprofessional
1 team, the nearby Vermilion Independents. Twelve hundred people turned out to see her make her debut: she gave up only four hits and a single run in five innings. "Miss Weiss," said the Lorain *Times Herald* in 1907, "can easily lay claim to being the only one who can handle the ball from the

RESEARCH ACROSS THE CURRICULUM
Teaching Strategies

You can direct the students' attention to how interesting a biography can be by telling them something interesting about yourself that you are sure they don't know. Then, ask for volunteers to share something about themselves that most other people don't know such as special skills, hobbies, trips, or unusual experiences. Then, ask each student to make a list of people he or she would like to know about and have the student select one person as a topic. You may want to encourage students who write about other students to submit their biographical reports to the school newspaper or to the local newspaper.

USING THE SELECTION
Alta Weiss

1

semiprofessional team: a team that gets paid for playing but that doesn't play baseball as a full-time job

2

What does the expression "fan the atmosphere" mean as it's used here? [strike out]

3

Why were special trains being run? [to accommodate the large number of people who wanted to see Alta Weiss play]

4

bloomers: loose trousers once worn by women

pitcher's box in such style that some of the best semi-pros are made to fan the atmosphere."

2

Soon, special trains were being run out from Cleveland whenever she pitched. When she appeared in the Cleveland Naps' park, more than 3,000 people paid their way in to see her. "I found that you can't play ball in skirts," she told reporters. "I tried. I wore a skirt over my bloomers—and nearly broke my neck. Finally I was forced to discard it, and now I always wear bloomers—but made so wide that the fullness gives a skirtlike effect."

3

4

Her baseball skills were good enough to put her through medical school. Even after she began to practice as a physician, she continued to play off and on into the 1920s.

Geoffrey C. Ward and Ken Burns,
from *Baseball: An Illustrated History*

Choose a person to write about, just as you chose a topic earlier for your report. Take careful notes as you read or interview. Then follow the same steps you followed for your research report.

SPEAKING AND LISTENING

Studying the Influence of the Mass Media

On the radio, you listen to an interview of the coach of the Buffalo Bills ten minutes after the Super Bowl is over. On television, you watch the president's State of the Union speech and, five minutes later, a comedian pretending he is the president.

Today the mass media bring information and entertainment to us the moment it happens, no matter where it occurs around the world. Have you ever thought about how the mass media affect your life? how much they influence you and your world? To find out, try one of the

SELECTION AMENDMENT
Description of change: excerpted
Rationale: to focus on the concept of writing a research report presented in this chapter

following research projects. Then share what you have discovered about the media in an oral report to your class.

A. Think of something, a product you have seen or heard advertised, that you or your family has bought recently. It might be sneakers, a CD or audiotape, a television, or even a food item you bought in a grocery store or at a health food restaurant. After you've thought of the product, you can use the following questions to study the influence of the media.

- Where was this product advertised—TV? radio? newspapers? magazines?
- What technique did the ad(s) use to sell the product—humor? a famous personality? facts? a comparison with another product?
- Would you or your family have purchased this product if it had not been advertised? Why?
- What does this research tell you about the way the media influence your buying habits?

B. Study how the media's handling of the news influences you and your world.

1. Begin by watching the evening edition of a nationally televised news program. Note one or two stories that the program highlights. What facts are given? How much time does the program give to each story?
2. Look for the same stories in your local newspaper the next day. How much space are they given? Are they on the front page or further back in the paper? Is the information the same, or has it been changed? How?
3. Check the paper's editorial page several days in a row. If you find the story, what's the writer's point of view? If there is more than one editorial about the story, how are they different?
4. Look for the story in the next issue of a weekly newsmagazine like *Time* or *Newsweek*. Is there more or less information? different information?
5. How do you think the media affected your thinking about this story? the thinking of other people you know?

OBJECTIVES

- To identify and revise sentence fragments and run-on sentences
- To combine sentences by inserting words or phrases, by creating compound subjects and verbs, by creating a compound sentence, and by using subordinate clauses
- To identify and revise stringy and wordy sentences

Fragments: Forbidden Forever?

While students need to realize that fragments are not usually acceptable in formal expository writing and are often a result of carelessness, they may notice that they do often use fragments to communicate clear ideas.

- **Brainstorming** Have students brainstorm in what situations and for what types of messages they might use incomplete sentences. You might want to use a two-column organizer like the following.

Situations	Messages
• in conversation	• exclamations
• in making lists	• direct address
• in writing dialogue	• yes-no answers
• in composing ads	• conversational fragments
	• greetings
	• attention getters

- **Real-Life Fragments** Provide students with magazines or ask them to bring in newspapers or circulars with advertising. Have students in small groups examine the ads and note their use of fragments. Then, ask them to analyze why the fragment was used.

Possible Reason for Use

- Brevity
- Space constraints

- Attention getter
- Clever wording
- Memorable
- Catchy

- **Creating Ads** Ask students to work in groups to come up with a product to advertise. The product may be imaginary or based on something that already exists. Students might create an ad for practical personal use such as for a garage sale or for services like lawn mowing. You may want to establish a set number of words or space constraints as newspapers would. Allow students to see if they are using sentences or fragments and if their writing is communicating their message. Then, allow students to produce the ad to post in a classroom display or to place in a classroom newspaper.

- **Reflecting** After the material has been published, allow the class to discuss the fragments' effectiveness. Ask if students would make any wording changes if the situation or audience changed.

- **Freewriting** Allow students time to freewrite samples of these changes and to share them with the class.

INTEGRATING THE LANGUAGE ARTS

SELECTION	READING AND LITERATURE	WRITING AND CRITICAL THINKING	LANGUAGE AND SYNTAX	SPEAKING, LISTENING, AND OTHER EXPRESSION SKILLS
	• Using context clues to aid in comprehension p. 364 • Making judgments about clarity p. 367 • Evaluating the effectiveness of sentences pp. 378, 382, 383	• Editing for sentence fragments and run-on sentences pp. 363, 364, 366–367 • Writing complete sentences p. 364 • Correcting fragments and run-on sentences pp. 364, 366–367 • Combining sentences pp. 366–367, 369–370 • Combining sentences by using conjunctions and phrases pp. 366, 371–372, 373 • Making subjects and verbs agree when there is a compound subject pp. 373, 374 • Producing well-formed compound sentences pp. 374–375 • Using sentence combining to develop coordination, subordination, and variety in structure and to improve style and coherence pp. 373, 374–375, 377, 378, 379, 380, 382 • Producing well-formed complex sentences p. 377 • Revising writing for correctness and clarity pp. 383, 384	• Identifying complete and incomplete sentences pp. 363, 364 • Using commas correctly after introductory subordinate clauses pp. 371–372, 377 • Making subjects and verbs agree in number p. 373	

CHAPTER 11: WRITING EFFECTIVE SENTENCES

Use this guide for creating an instructional plan that addresses the individual needs of your students. Assignments accompanied by the following symbol (∗) may be completed out of class. Times given for pacing lessons are estimated.

CHAPTER PLANNING GUIDE—PUPIL'S EDITION

LESSONS	WRITING CLEAR SENTENCES Sentence Fragments pp. 361–364	WRITING CLEAR SENTENCES Run-on Sentences pp. 364–367
DEVELOPMENTAL PROGRAM	🕐 **40–45 minutes** • Main Assignment: Looking Ahead p. 360 • Sentence Fragments pp. 361–362 • Writing Note p. 362 • Exercise 1 p. 363 in pairs • Exercise 2 p. 364∗	🕐 **40–45 minutes** • Run-on Sentences pp. 364–366 • Mechanics Hint p. 365 • Exercise 3 pp. 366–367 in pairs
CORE PROGRAM	🕐 **20–25 minutes** • Main Assignment: Looking Ahead p. 360 • Sentence Fragments pp. 361–362 • Writing Note p. 362 • Exercises 1, 2 pp. 363, 364∗	🕐 **15–20 minutes** • Mechanics Hint p. 365 • Revising Run-on Sentences pp. 365–366 • Exercise 3 pp. 366–367∗
ACCELERATED PROGRAM	🕐 **15–20 minutes** • Main Assignment: Looking Ahead p. 360 • Writing Note p. 362 • Exercise 2 p. 364∗	🕐 **5–10 minutes** • Mechanics Hint p. 365 • Exercise 3 pp. 366–367∗

CHAPTER PLANNING GUIDE—PROGRAM RESOURCES

	WRITING CLEAR SENTENCES Sentence Fragments	WRITING CLEAR SENTENCES Run-on Sentences
PRINT	• Sentence Fragments, *Word Choice and Sentence Style* p. 1 • Sentence Fragments, *English Workshop* pp. 59–60	• Run-on Sentences, *Word Choice and Sentence Style* p. 2 • Run-on Sentences, *English Workshop* pp. 61–62
MEDIA	• *Language Workshop:* Lesson 40	• *Language Workshop:* Lesson 41

COMBINING SENTENCES pp. 368–378	IMPROVING SENTENCE STYLE pp. 378–383
40–45 minutes • Inserting Words p. 369 • Writing Notes pp. 369, 374 • Exercises 4–8 pp. 369–370, 371–372, 373, 374–375, 377* • Inserting Phrases pp. 370–371 • Using *And, But,* or *Or* pp. 372–374 • Grammar Hint p. 373 • Using a Subordinate Clause pp. 375–376 • Mechanics Hint p. 377	**40–45 minutes** • Revising Stringy Sentences pp. 378–379 • Mechanics Hint p. 379 • Exercise 9 pp. 379–380* • Revising Wordy Sentences p. 381 • Writing Note p. 382 • Exercise 10 p. 382 in pairs
30–35 minutes • Writing Notes pp. 369, 374 • Inserting Phrases pp. 370–371 • Using a Subordinate Clause pp. 375–376 • Mechanics Hint p. 377 • Exercises 5, 8 pp. 371–372, 377*	**30–35 minutes** • Revising Stringy Sentences pp. 378–379* • Mechanics Hint p. 379 • Revising Wordy Sentences p. 381* • Exercises 9, 10 pp. 379–380, 382* • Writing Note p. 382
20–25 minutes • Writing Notes pp. 369, 374 • Using a Subordinate Clause pp. 375–376 • Mechanics Hint p. 377 • Exercise 8 p. 377*	**20–25 minutes** • Mechanics Hint p. 379 • Exercise 9 pp. 379–380* • Revising Wordy Sentences p. 381 • Writing Note p. 382 • Exercise 10 p. 382*

 Computer disk or CD-ROM

COMBINING SENTENCES	IMPROVING SENTENCE STYLE
• Combining Sentences; Combining by Using *And, But,* or *Or;* Adding Subordinate Clauses, *Word Choice and Sentence Style* pp. 3, 4, 5 • *English Workshop* pp. 63–68, 83–84, 125–130, 133–134, 139–140, 145–150, 153–156, 159–160, 169–170	• Stringy and Wordy Sentences, *Word Choice and Sentence Style* p. 6 • Improving Sentence Style; Commas with Compound Sentences; Introductory Words, Phrases, and Clauses *English Workshop* pp. 67–68, 249–250, 255–256
• *Language Workshop:* Lessons 10-12, 42–44, 49	• *Language Workshop:* Lessons 45–46

ELEMENTS OF WRITING: CURRICULUM CONNECTIONS

Making Connections
• Filling in the Missing Pieces p. 384

ASSESSMENT OPTIONS

Summative Assessment
Reviews A, B, C *Elements of Writing,* Pupil's Edition pp. 367, 378, 383
Review A: Writing Effective Sentences,
Review B: Writing Effective Sentences, *Word Choice and Sentence Style* pp. 7–8, 9–10
Review Exercises, *English Workshop* pp. 69–70, 85–86, 131–132, 141–142, 151–152, 157–158

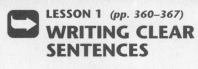

LESSON 1 *(pp. 360–367)*

WRITING CLEAR SENTENCES

OBJECTIVES

- To identify and revise sentence fragments
- To identify and revise run-on sentences

MOTIVATION

To help students see that fragments and run-ons create confusion, write the following directions on the chalkboard:

If you are sitting in the first row. The students in the second row are on another team the remaining students will judge. Might win a prize.

PROGRAM MANAGER

FOR THE WHOLE CHAPTER

- **Review** For exercises on chapter concepts, see **Review Form A** and **Review Form B** in *Word Choice and Sentence Style*, pp. 7–10.

PROGRAM MANAGER

WRITING CLEAR SENTENCES

- **Independent Practice/ Reteaching** For practice and reinforcement, see **Sentence Fragments** and **Run-on Sentences** in *Word Choice and Sentence Style*, pp. 1–2.
- **Computer Guided Instruction** For additional instruction and practice with sentence fragments and run-on sentences, see **Lessons 40** and **41** in *Language Workshop CD-ROM*.
- **Practice** To help less-advanced students with additional instruction and practice with sentence fragments and run-on sentences, see **Chapter 8** in *English Workshop, Second Course*, pp. 59–70.

11 WRITING EFFECTIVE SENTENCES

LOOKING AHEAD

This chapter will give you some practice at writing clear, effective sentences. As you work through the chapter, you will learn how to

- write complete sentences
- combine sentences
- revise sentences for style

Writing Clear Sentences

Whether you are writing for school or for the workplace, you want your writing to be clear and understandable. One of the easiest ways to make your writing clear is to use complete sentences. A complete sentence is a word group that

- has a subject
- has a verb
- expresses a complete thought

Ask students if they would know what to do from reading these directions. Point out how the use of the two sentence fragments and the one run-on sentence affects clear writing.

TEACHING THE LESSON
Have students examine the examples of the three kinds of sentence fragments. This careful look should help prepare students for using the three-part test mentioned in **Exercise 1** on p. 363 and for revising fragments in **Exercise 2** on p. 364. In the discussion of run-on sentences, call students' attention to the tip on p. 365 about reading ☞

Writing Clear Sentences　　**361**

EXAMPLES　Dolphins communicate with one another by making clicking and whistling sounds.
　　　　　When a dolphin is in trouble, it can give off a distress call.
　　　　　Help!

Each of these examples meets all the requirements of a sentence. At first glance, the third example may not appear to have a subject. The subject, *you,* is understood in the sentence even though it isn't stated: "(You) help!"

There are two stumbling blocks to the development of clear sentences: *sentence fragments* and *run-on sentences.* Once you learn how to recognize fragments and run-ons, you can revise them to create clear, complete sentences.

Sentence Fragments

A *sentence fragment* is a part of a sentence that has been punctuated as if it were a complete sentence. Like a fragment of a painting or photograph, a sentence fragment is confusing because it doesn't give the whole picture.

FRAGMENT　Looked something like a sewing machine. [The subject is missing. *What* looked like a sewing machine?]

SENTENCE　The first typewriter looked something like a sewing machine.

FRAGMENT　Christopher Sholes the typewriter in 1867. [The verb is missing. What did Sholes *do* in 1867?]

SENTENCE　Christopher Sholes helped design the typewriter in 1867.

QUOTATION FOR THE DAY
"Even though an unclear and imprecise style obviously does not bar a good many writers from getting into print, a person who can write clearly and gracefully goes out into the world with an uncommon skill." (Joseph M. Williams, 1933–　, American writer and teacher)

You could use this quotation as a basis for discussion. Ask students if they have ever read unclear writing. If so, can they explain why it was unclear? Remind students that fragments and run-on sentences add confusion to writing.

LEP/ESL

General Strategies. Sentences without stated subjects may seem perfectly acceptable to some students. They might be accustomed to conversations that use sentences such as "Had to wake up too early this morning" or "Could talk to my sister about it." Such sentences imply the subject *I* but don't directly state it. Remind students that although such fragments are acceptable in informal speaking and conversation, complete sentences should be used in formal speaking and writing.

361

aloud what they've written to listen for natural pauses that indicate the ends of sentences. Although the text gives examples of ways to revise run-on sentences, you could list other examples on the chalkboard.

GUIDED PRACTICE

You may wish to guide students through **Exercise 1** and have them practice the three-step test to distinguish between complete sentences and sentence fragments. To help students identify and revise run-on sentences, work through the revision process for the first sentence in **Exercise 3**, pp. 366–367.

362

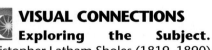

VISUAL CONNECTIONS
Exploring the Subject.
Christopher Latham Sholes (1819–1890) was an inventor, a newspaper editor, and a Wisconsin state legislator. His typewriter evolved from a page-numbering device into a letter-printing machine with the help of fellow inventors Samuel W. Soulé and Carlos Glidden. Even though he sold his patent rights to E. Remington and Sons in 1873, Sholes remained devoted to improving the typewriter until the end of his life.

FRAGMENT	After Mark Twain typed one of his manuscripts on a Sholes typewriter. [This group of words has a subject and a verb, but it does not express a complete thought. *What happened* after Mark Twain typed one of his manuscripts on a Sholes typewriter?]
SENTENCE	After Mark Twain typed one of his manuscripts on a Sholes typewriter, the invention began to attract public attention.

WRITING NOTE

Often, fragments are the result of writing in a hurry or being a little careless. For example, you might accidentally chop off part of a sentence by putting in a period and a capital letter too soon. In the following example, notice that the fragment in dark type is actually a part of the sentence that comes before it.

> We laughed at the clowns. **When they rode around on gigantic tricycles.**

You can correct the fragment by attaching it to the sentence it belongs with.

> We laughed at the clowns when they rode around on gigantic tricycles.

WRITING NOTE

Tell students that a special method of proofreading can help them eliminate the kind of sentence fragment mentioned in the **Writing Note**. Recommend that each student first read the last sentence of his or her composition and then work backward, reading the first sentence last. This method will break up the narrative flow and will make sentence fragments easier to recognize.

INDEPENDENT PRACTICE

You could have students work independently on **Exercises 2** and **3** to identify and revise sentence fragments and run-ons. You could also give students a short writing assignment that gives them practice using complete sentences.

ASSESSMENT

An evaluation of **Exercises 2** and **3** should indicate students' competence to revise sentence fragments and run-ons. If writing samples are available, assess them for sentence completeness.

Writing Clear Sentences   **363**

E X E R C I S E 1 ▶   **Identifying Sentence Fragments**

Use this simple three-part test to find out which of the following word groups are sentence fragments and which are complete sentences.

1. Does the group of words have a subject?
2. Does it have a verb?
3. Does it express a complete thought?

If the group of words is a complete sentence, write *S*. If it is a fragment, write *F*. [Remember: A complete sentence can have the unstated subject *you*.]

1. The English clown Lulu was one of the first female clowns to gain attention in the United States. **1. S**
2. When John Ringling North discovered her. **2. F**
3. Performed for the Ringling Brothers and Barnum & Bailey Circus. **3. F**
4. Lulu had entertained the British royal family in England. **4. S**
5. Lulu's grandmother a tightrope walker. **5. F**
6. While she and her husband performed as a clown team. **6. F**
7. Lulu used a gigantic fake hand to shake hands with children. **7. S**
8. The funny handshake Lulu's special trick. **8. F**
9. Lulu in this country in 1939. **9. F**
10. Was the wife of clown Albertino Adams. **10. F**

COOPERATIVE LEARNING

If students need more practice revising fragments, bring in classified ads and have students work in groups of two or three to revise the ads to create complete sentences.

INTEGRATING THE LANGUAGE ARTS

Literature Link. You may want to find a selection such as Robert Cormier's "The Moustache" in which the author intentionally uses sentence fragments. First, discuss what effect the author creates by using fragments. [The fragments convey emotion and help both the external and internal dialogue sound more realistic.] Then, have students revise some or all of the fragments and discuss the effects of the changes. [Students might say the dialogue sounds stilted or that the characters seem less real.]

363

EXERCISE 2 ▶ **Finding and Revising Fragments**

Some of the following groups of words are sentence fragments. Revise each fragment by (1) adding a subject, (2) adding a verb, or (3) attaching the fragment to a complete sentence. You may need to change the punctuation and capitalization, too. If the word group is already a complete sentence, write *S*.   Revisions will vary.

EXAMPLE   **1.** After the sun rose.
          1. *We walked to the beach after the sun rose.*

1. People near the water.   **1.** live
2. Two little children were playing in the wet sand.   **2.** S
3. Whenever the waves broke.   **3.** We got our faces wet
4. My sister and I on a red inflatable raft.   **4.** floated
5. Tried to ride the waves as they came in.   **5.** We
6. A huge wave flipped over the raft.   **6.** S
7. Because we were good swimmers,   **7.** , we made it to the shore.
8. We were ready to go back in the water after we rested in the sun for a while.   **8.** S
9. Ran by and kicked sand on our blanket.   **9.** Some children
10. The family next to us a sand sculpture of a dragon.
                                              10. made

Run-on Sentences

If you run together two complete sentences as if they were one sentence, you get a ***run-on sentence***. Run-ons are confusing because the reader can't tell where one idea ends and another one begins.

RUN-ON   Margaret Bourke-White was a famous news photographer she worked for *Life* magazine during World War II.

CORRECT   Margaret Bourke-White was a famous news photographer. She worked for *Life* magazine during World War II.

RUN-ON   Bourke-White traveled all over the world taking photographs, she went underground to photograph miners in South Africa.

fragments—might help emphasize the concept of sentence completeness.

You could use a similar tactic by having students incorrectly combine two sentences to form a run-on sentence.

CORRECT   Bourke-White traveled all over the world taking photographs. She went underground to photograph miners in South Africa.

To spot run-ons, try reading your writing aloud. A natural, distinct pause in your voice usually marks the end of one thought and the beginning of another. If you pause at a place where you don't have any end punctuation, you may have found a run-on sentence.

MECHANICS HINT

Using Correct End Punctuation

A comma does mark a brief pause in a sentence, but it does not show the end of a sentence. If you use just a comma between two complete sentences, you create a run-on sentence.

RUN-ON   Our dog finally came home late last night, she was dirty and hungry.
CORRECT   Our dog finally came home late last night. She was dirty and hungry.

☞ REFERENCE NOTE: For more about commas, see pages 741–755.

Revising Run-on Sentences

There are several ways you can revise run-on sentences. Here are two of them.

1. You can make two sentences.

RUN-ON   Kite building is an ancient art the Chinese made the first kites around three thousand years ago.
CORRECT   Kite building is an ancient art. The Chinese made the first kites around three thousand years ago.

A DIFFERENT APPROACH

Have students write coded messages in which the meanings of their sentences are masked by surrounding fragments and run-ons. To understand the message, their partners must eliminate all fragments and run-ons. The sentences that remain will provide the message.

You could make copies of several anonymous compositions that contain fragments and run-ons, and have students revise them. Students could then work in pairs to check each other's revisions. ■

TECHNOLOGY TIP

Some word-processing programs include a grammar-checker that functions similarly to a spell-checker. Encourage students to explore the use of this feature, if they have access to it, but remind them that devices of this sort aren't foolproof and that they will have to make decisions about needed changes when the grammar-checker detects a possible problem.

2. You can use a comma and the coordinating conjunction *and, but,* or *or.*

| RUN-ON | The Chinese sometimes used kites in religious ceremonies, they usually used them for sport. |
| CORRECT | The Chinese sometimes used kites in religious ceremonies, **but** they usually used them for sport. |

COMPUTER NOTE: Use your word-processing program when you revise your draft for fragments, run-on sentences, or style. The Cut and Paste commands can help you find the best place for words or phrases within a sentence and for sentences within your draft.

EXERCISE 3   **Identifying and Revising Run-ons**

Decide which of the following groups of words are run-ons. Then, revise each run-on by (1) making it into two separate sentences or (2) using a comma and a coordinating conjunction. If the group of words is already correct, write C. Revisions may vary.

1. The Louvre is the largest museum in the world‚it is also one of the oldest. 1. , and
2. The first works of art in the Louvre were bought by the kings of France‚each ruler added more treasures.
3. King Francis I was a great supporter of the arts‚he bought the *Mona Lisa.*
4. As other French rulers made additions, the collections grew. 4. C
5. The Louvre is now a state-owned museum‚ its new pieces are either bought or received as gifts. 5.

Writing Clear Sentences **367**

6. Each year, about one and a half million people from all over the world come to see the artwork at the Louvre. **6.** C

7. The buildings of the Louvre form a rectangle$_\wedge$there are courtyards and gardens inside the rectangle. **7.** , **and**

8. The Louvre covers about forty acres,$_\wedge$it has about eight miles of gallery space. **8. and**

9. Over one million works of art are exhibited in the Louvre. **9.** C

10. Many of the buildings of the Louvre have been expanded and modernized$_\odot$this photograph shows how the Louvre looks today.

REVIEW A ▶ **Revising to Correct Fragments and Run-ons**

The following paragraph is confusing because it contains some fragments and run-ons. First, identify the fragments and run-ons. Then, revise each fragment and run-on to make the paragraph clearer. **Revisions will vary.**

Godzilla$_\wedge$a movie about a huge reptile. Godzilla looks **is** like a dinosaur$_\wedge$he breathes fire like a dragon. He comes , **but** up out of the ocean.$_\wedge$After an atomic bomb wakes him up. Godzilla can melt steel with his atomic breath$_\wedge$he is big , **and** enough to knock down huge buildings. In the film he destroys the city of Tokyo$_\wedge$he gets killed at the end. , **but**

VISUAL CONNECTIONS

Exploring the Subject. In 1546 the Louvre became the royal residence of a French king, Francis I, who was an art collector. Louis XIV was the last king to live in the Louvre, as Versailles became the royal residence in 1682. It was not until 1793, after the French Revolution in 1789, that the Louvre became a public museum. In addition to European art, the museum houses ancient treasures from Greece, Egypt, and Russia.

ANSWERS

Review A

Sentences 1 and 4 are fragments; 2, 5, and 6 are run-ons; 3 needs no revision.

LESSON 2 *(pp. 368–378)*
COMBINING SENTENCES

OBJECTIVES

- To combine sentences by inserting words and phrases
- To combine sentences by creating compound subjects and verbs, by creating compound sentences, and by using subordinate clauses

Combining Sentences

Sometimes a short sentence can express your meaning perfectly. But a long, unbroken series of short sentences will make your writing sound choppy. For example, read the following paragraph, which is made up of short sentences:

> George Lucas's films are famous. They are famous for their plots and special effects. The plots are suspenseful. The special effects are thrilling. Star Wars became a success in the late 1970s. Lucas wrote and directed it. Its success was international. Lucas later teamed up with director Steven Spielberg. They created Raiders of the Lost Ark. The movie was popular.

Now read the revised version. To make the paragraph more interesting, the writer combined some of the short, choppy sentences into longer, smoother ones. Notice how *sentence combining* has helped to eliminate some repeated words and ideas.

> George Lucas's films are famous for their suspenseful plots and thrilling special effects. Star Wars, which Lucas wrote and directed, became an international success in the late 1970s. Lucas later teamed up with director Steven Spielberg to create the popular Raiders of the Lost Ark.

Students need to understand that short sentences can be useful for effect, but if overused, they can disrupt a fluid style. Sentence combining not only aids in smooth writing, but also increases clarity when repeated elements are eliminated.

In the lesson on inserting phrases, a potential problem for students is knowing when to use commas. Also, with the introduction of verb revision should come a review of irregular verbs to circumvent incorrect revisions by students. To model creating compound subjects, compound verbs, and compound sentences, you could prepare a transparency of a recipe written in extreme detail. It could be as simple as an explanation of how to make a peanut butter ☞

Combining by Inserting Words

One way to combine short sentences is to pull a key word from one sentence and insert it into the other sentence. Sometimes you'll need to change the form of the key word before you can insert it.

INSERTING WITHOUT A CHANGE	
ORIGINAL	Louis Armstrong was a famous musician. He was a jazz musician.
COMBINED	Louis Armstrong was a famous **jazz** musician.

INSERTING WITH A CHANGE	
ORIGINAL	Armstrong was an easygoing person. He was a friend to many people.
COMBINED	Armstrong was an easygoing, **friendly** person.

WRITING NOTE

When you change the forms of words, you often add endings such as *–ed, –ing,* and *–ly* to make adjectives and adverbs.

EXAMPLES
need ⟹ need**ed**
sing ⟹ sing**ing**
fortunate ⟹ fortunate**ly**

EXERCISE 4 ▶ Combining Sentences by Inserting Words

Combine each of the following sentence pairs by taking the italicized word from the second sentence and inserting it into the first sentence. Follow the hints in parentheses for changing the forms of words.

EXAMPLE 1. Young Louis Armstrong first showed his talent on the streets of New Orleans. His talent was for *music.* (Add *–al.*)
   1. *Young Louis Armstrong first showed his musical talent on the streets of New Orleans.*

sandwich. Have students work with you to make the recipe more concise by using combining techniques.

When students study **Combining by Using a Subordinate Clause** on p. 375, they will need to be able to differentiate between subordinate and independent clauses. Reviewing the ways to recognize fragments may prove helpful.

GUIDED PRACTICE

You may want to combine the first sentence set of **Exercise 4** on p. 369. To show them how to incorporate the *–ed* prompt into the combined sentence, write the following sentence on the chalkboard:

If you receive acclaim, you become acclaimed.

ANSWERS

Exercise 4

1. He became an acclaimed jazz musician.
2. Louis Armstrong had a deep, rough voice.
3. Louis Armstrong sang jazz brilliantly.
4. Louis started playing cornet at a New Orleans night spot.
5. He became internationally famous as a solo trumpet player.

VISUAL CONNECTIONS

Exploring the Subject. Louis Daniel Armstrong (1901–1971), called Satchmo, started his career playing the trumpet in marching bands and on Mississippi riverboats. He became a band leader, a composer, and a film and recording star. Armstrong is credited with popularizing jazz through his brilliance as a musician and through his engaging performances.

1. He became a jazz musician. He received *acclaim* for his music. (Add *–ed* and change *a* to *an*.)
2. Louis Armstrong had a deep voice. His voice was *rough*.
3. Louis Armstrong sang jazz. His jazz singing was *brilliant*. (Add *–ly*.)
4. Louis started playing at a New Orleans night spot. He played *cornet*.
5. He became famous as a solo trumpet player. He was famous on an *international* level. (Add *–ly*.)

Combining by Inserting Phrases

A *phrase* is a group of words that doesn't have a subject and a verb. You can combine sentences by taking a phrase from one sentence and inserting it into the other sentence.

ORIGINAL   Brown bears gather in groups. They gather around river banks.

COMBINED   Brown bears gather in groups **around river banks.**

Sometimes you will need to put commas around the phrase you are inserting. Ask yourself whether the phrase renames or explains a noun or pronoun in the sentence. If it does, use a comma or commas to set off the phrase from the rest of the sentence.

Then, write the combined sentence using *acclaimed.*

You could use the example sentences in **Exercise 5** on p. 371 to guide students through the combining process of inserting phrases. Write each set of sentences on the chalkboard and have the students close their books. Begin by circling the identical or similar elements, and then identify which word group in the second sentence could serve to combine the sentences. Before combining each set of sentences, ask students if the inserted phrase needs commas.

To guide students through the process of creating compound verbs, you could work through number 1 of **Exercise 6** (p. 373) on the chalkboard. Circle the similar components *Australia* and *many cattle products.*

ORIGINAL   Alaska is home to the big brown bears. The big brown bears are the largest kind of bear.
COMBINED   Alaska is home to the big brown bears, **the largest kind of bear.**

Often, you can change the verb in a sentence to make a phrase. You change the verb by adding *–ing* or *–ed* or by putting the word *to* in front of it. You can then use the phrase to modify a noun or pronoun in another sentence.

ORIGINAL   The bear prepares his winter retreat. He digs a burrow in a bank.
COMBINED   **Digging a burrow in a bank,** the bear prepares his winter retreat.

ORIGINAL   Bears dig in the ground. This is how they find roots and sweet bulbs.
COMBINED   Bears dig in the ground **to find roots and sweet bulbs.**

☞ REFERENCE NOTE: For more information about verb forms using *–ing, –ed,* or *to,* see pages 513–523.

 **Combining Sentences by Inserting Phrases**

Combine each pair of sentences by taking the italicized words from the second sentence and inserting them into the first sentence. The hints in parentheses tell you when to change the forms of words. Add commas where needed.

EXAMPLE   **1.** Television networks have made professional tennis a popular sport. They *show all the major tournaments.* (Change *show* to *showing.*)
   1. *Showing all the major tournaments, television networks have made professional tennis a popular sport.*

1. of the wealthy.

1. During the first fifty years of its history, tennis was largely a pastime‚ ~~It was a pastime~~ *~~of the wealthy.~~*

2. ‚Prominent players competed in professional promotions. ~~They~~ *~~toured with their managers.~~* (Change *toured* to *touring.*)   **2.** Touring with their managers,

LESS-ADVANCED STUDENTS
Students might be unsure of where to place the key words when they combine sentences in **Exercise 4.** You may want to monitor their progress, and if necessary, ask leading questions to help them position the words they are inserting. For example, in the first sentence you could ask what kind of jazz musician he became. In the second sentence, you could ask what kind of deep voice he had. This procedure could also prove helpful in the insertion of phrases in **Exercise 5.**

STUDENTS WITH SPECIAL NEEDS
Because some students often use run-on sentences and stringy sentences, you may want to downplay sentence combining. Instead, have students focus on including only one complete thought in each sentence.

TIMESAVER
For ease in grading, have students underline or highlight the phrases they inserted when combining sentences in **Exercise 5.**

Students should see that only the verbs are different. Combine the sentences using the compound verb *produces* and *consumes*. If you feel students need to see this process repeated in creating a compound subject, work through the second sentence.

Before working on **Exercise 7** (p. 374) as independent practice, students need to know when to choose *and, but,* or *or* in sentence combining. As you show them how to create compound sentence structures, point out that *and* is used for connecting similar ideas, *but* is used for contrasting ideas, and *or* is used when a choice is offered between ideas.

To prepare students for independent practice, work through number 1 in **Exercise 8** on p. 377. Put both sentences on the

3. Rod Laver‸won the Wimbledon men's singles title in 1961. ~~Rod Laver was~~ *an Australian*.   **3.** , an Australian,
4. Nonprofessional tennis declined‸as a major attraction. ~~It declined~~ *in a short time.*   **4.** in a short time
5. Women players organized themselves‸ ~~They did this so they could~~ *demand equal prize money.* (Add *to* in front of *demand*.)   **5.** to demand equal prize money.

Combining by Using *And, But,* or *Or*

You can also combine sentences by using the conjunctions *and, but,* or *or.* With one of these connecting words, you can form a *compound subject,* a *compound verb,* or a *compound sentence.*

Compound Subjects and Verbs

Sometimes two sentences have the same verb with different subjects. You can combine the sentences by linking the two subjects with *and* or *or.* When you do this, you create a **compound subject.**

ORIGINAL   Kangaroos carry their young in pouches. Koalas carry their young in pouches.
COMBINED   **Kangaroos and koalas** carry their young in pouches.

If two sentences have the same subject with different verbs, you can link the verbs with *and, but,* or *or* to form a **compound verb.**

MEETING *individual* NEEDS

LEARNING STYLES

Visual Learners. To help students link subjects and verbs, write sample sentences to be combined on the chalkboard and bracket the repeated information. Then, combine the sentences using *and, but,* or *or.*

chalkboard. Circle the subject *it* in the second sentence and ask students what the pronoun's antecedent is [religion]. Create a subordinate clause by replacing *it* with the given word *that* and combine the sentences. Remind students that by circling, underlining, or highlighting similar sentence components, they can often determine which word or group of words should be replaced by the prompt. If there are no clearly similar components, students should look for less-vital words, such as articles, that could be replaced.

☞

ORIGINAL	Kangaroos can hop on their hind legs. They can walk on all four legs.
COMBINED	Kangaroos **can hop** on their hind legs **or walk** on all four legs.

GRAMMAR HINT

Checking for Subject–Verb Agreement

When you form a compound subject, make sure that it agrees with the verb in number.

ORIGINAL	Tasmania is in Australia. Queensland is in Australia.
REVISED	**Tasmania and Queensland are** in Australia. [The plural subject takes the verb *are.*]

☞ REFERENCE NOTE: For more information about agreement of subjects and verbs, see pages 575–588.

GRAMMAR HINT

You may need to explain to students that a compound subject does not always take a plural verb. For example, when using the conjunctions *either . . . or* and *neither . . . nor,* one part of the compound subject can be singular and one part can be plural. Remind students that the verb always agrees with the subject that is closer.

1. Neither yeast nor <u>nuts were</u> used in the bread.
2. Neither nuts nor <u>yeast was</u> used in the bread.

EXERCISE 6 ▶ **Combining by Forming Compound Subjects and Compound Verbs**

Combine each of the following sentence pairs by forming a compound subject or a compound verb. Make sure your new subjects and verbs agree in number.

1. Australia produces∧many cattle products. ~~Australia consumes many cattle products.~~　**1.** and consumes
2. Beef∧is popular in Australia. ~~Lamb is popular in Australia.~~　**2.** and lamb are
3. Australians grill∧their meat. ~~Australians also roast their meat.~~　**3.** and roast
4. Potatoes∧are often served with the meat. ~~Other vegetables are often served with the meat, too.~~　**4.** and other vegetables
5. Italian∧cooking∧is becoming popular in Australia. ~~Greek cooking is also becoming popular.~~　**5.** and Greek/are

373

INDEPENDENT PRACTICE

After you have guided students through the combining process for each exercise, assign **Exercises 4–8** for independent practice.

ASSESSMENT

You can use **Exercises 4** and **5** to judge students' comprehension of word and phrase insertion. Students' performance on **Exercises 6, 7,** and **8** should indicate their level of mastery in sentence combining using compound subjects, compound verbs, and compound sentences. The true test,

INTEGRATING THE LANGUAGE ARTS

Mechanics Link. Remind students not to use a comma before the conjunction when combining two verbs. Commas are used when two sentences are combined to create a compound sentence. Write the following sentences on the chalkboard to illustrate the difference between compound verbs and compound sentences:

1. Juan went to the store but forgot the grocery list.
2. Juan went to the store, but he forgot the grocery list.

You may want to have students write several pairs of sentences modeled from those on the chalkboard.

Literature Link. If the selection is available in your literature textbook, have students read and discuss "The Tell-Tale Heart" by Edgar Allan Poe. Then, have them note the short, choppy sentences in the beginning of the story. Ask students to describe the effect of this technique. [They might say that it makes the storyteller seem breathless and anxious, or that it adds credibility to his maddened state of mind.] Point out to students that when the narrator actually begins telling the story, he starts combining sentences.

---

374   *Writing Effective Sentences*

Compound Sentences

Sometimes you may want to combine two sentences that express equally important ideas. You can connect the two sentences by using a comma and the conjunction *and, but,* or *or.* When you link sentences in this way, you create a *compound sentence.*

ORIGINAL   Many nations throughout the world use the metric system. The United States still uses the old system of measurement.

COMBINED   Many nations throughout the world use the metric system**, but** the United States still uses the old system of measurement.

WRITING NOTE   Before you create a compound sentence out of two simple sentences, make sure the thoughts in the sentences are closely related to each other. If you combine two sentences that are not closely related, you will confuse your reader.

UNRELATED   Kim chopped the vegetables, and I like soup.
RELATED   **Kim chopped the vegetables,** and **I stirred the soup.**

EXERCISE 7 ▶ **Combining Sentences by Forming a Compound Sentence**

The sentences in each of the following pairs are closely related. Make each pair into a single compound sentence by adding a comma and the connecting word *and, but,* or *or.*   Revisions may vary.

EXAMPLE   1. The kilogram is the basic unit of weight in the metric system. The meter is the basic unit of length.
1. *The kilogram is the basic unit of weight in the metric system, and the meter is the basic unit of length.*

CLOSURE

Ask students to help you list the sentence-combining strategies they have practiced and to give examples of each.

☞

Combining Sentences **375**

1. The metric system was developed in France.∧It became popular in many countries. **1.** **, but**
2. We can keep the old system of measurement.∧We can switch to the metric system. **2.** **, or**
3. The old system of measurement has more than twenty basic units of measurement.∧The metric system has only seven. **3.** **, but**
4. A meter equals ten decimeters.∧A decimeter equals ten centimeters. **4.** **, and**
5. Counting by tens is second nature to most people.∧Many people still find the metric system difficult to learn. **5.** **, but**

Combining by Using a Subordinate Clause

A *clause* is a group of words that contains a verb and its subject. An *independent clause* can stand alone as a sentence. A *subordinate clause* can't stand alone as a sentence because it doesn't express a complete thought.

INDEPENDENT CLAUSE **Henry David Thoreau was living alone in the woods.** [can stand alone as a sentence]

SUBORDINATE CLAUSE **when he wrote *Walden*** [can't stand alone as a sentence]

If two sentences are closely related but unequal in importance, you can combine them by using a subordinate clause. Just turn the less-important idea into a subordinate clause and attach it to the other sentence (the independent clause). The subordinate clause will give additional information about an idea expressed in the independent clause.

ORIGINAL **For two years, Thoreau lived in a simple hut. He built the hut at Walden Pond.**

COMBINED **For two years, Thoreau lived in a simple hut that he built at Walden Pond.**

☞ REFERENCE NOTE: For more information about sentences that contain subordinate clauses, see pages 562–565.

TECHNOLOGY TIP

Remind students that they can combine sentences quickly and efficiently using word-processing software. Large blocks of text can be easily moved around, and word endings can be added with just a few keystrokes.

COOPERATIVE LEARNING

To help your students understand the link between sentence complexity and maturity level, bring a few children's books to class and have students work in groups of two or three to combine simple sentences from the stories. Then the groups can take turns reading their revised stories to the class. Be sure that the books you bring to class reflect the cultural and ethnic diversity of your community.

Clauses Beginning with *Who*, *Which*, or *That*

You can make a short sentence into a subordinate clause by inserting *who*, *which*, or *that* in place of the subject.

ORIGINAL   The Aztecs were an American Indian people. They once ruled a mighty empire in Mexico.

COMBINED   The Aztecs were an American Indian people **who once ruled a mighty empire in Mexico.**

Clauses Beginning with Words of Time or Place

You can also make a subordinate clause by adding a word that tells time or place. Words that tell time or place include *after, before, where, wherever, when, whenever,* and *while.*

ORIGINAL   The capital city of the Aztec empire was in central Mexico. Mexico City stands in that spot today.

COMBINED   The capital city of the Aztec empire was in central Mexico, **where Mexico City stands today.**

VISUAL CONNECTIONS

Exploring the Subject. When the Spanish troops captured the Aztec capital of Tenochtitlán in 1521, they destroyed the temples and all other traces of the Aztec religion. They wiped out the capital and built Mexico City on the ruins. Archeologists have since excavated and rebuilt some Aztec buildings and temples and have uncovered four sides of the Great Temple in downtown Mexico City.

MECHANICS
HINT

Using Commas with Introductory Clauses

If you put your time or place clause at the beginning of the sentence, you'll need to put a comma after the clause.

ORIGINAL   The Aztec empire grew. Aztec warriors conquered nearby territories.

COMBINED   **When Aztec warriors conquered nearby territories,** the Aztec empire grew.

☞ REFERENCE NOTE: For more information about using commas after time or place clauses, see pages 752–753.

EXERCISE 8 ▶ **Combining Sentences by Using a Subordinate Clause**

Combine each of the following sentence pairs by making the second sentence into a subordinate clause and attaching it to the first sentence. The hints in parentheses will tell you what word to use at the beginning of the clause. To make a smooth combination, you may need to delete one or more words in the second sentence of each pair.

1. The Aztecs practiced a religion. ~~It~~ affected every part of their lives. (Use *that*.) **1.** that
2. Aztec craftworkers made drums and rattles. ~~Drums and rattles~~ were their main musical instruments. (Use a comma and *which*.) **2.** , which
3. Aztec cities had huge temples. ~~The~~ people held religious ceremonies ~~there~~. (Use *where*.) **3.** where
4. Their empire was destroyed by the Spanish. ~~The Spanish~~ conquered it in 1521. (Use *who*.) **4.** who
5. There was very little left of the Aztec civilization. ~~The~~ Spanish invaders tore down all the Aztec buildings. (Use *after*.) **5.** after

The Granger Collection, New York.

ANSWERS
Review B

Revisions will vary. Here is a possibility:

    The Arctic, a cold region around the North Pole, seems barren, but berries and vegetables actually grow in a few places. The area also has rich mineral deposits that have attracted people to the region. Mines in Alaska and Canada produce gold and copper, and mines in arctic Russia produce tin. Revealing that the Arctic is far from worthless, early explorers discovered many natural resources in the area.

PROGRAM MANAGER

IMPROVING SENTENCE STYLE

- **Independent Practice/ Reteaching** See **Stringy and Wordy Sentences** in *Word Choice and Sentence Style,* p. 6.

- **Computer Guided Instruction** For practice with revising sentences, see **Lesson 45** in *Language Workshop CD-ROM.* For practice with punctuating compound sentences as noted in the **Mechanics Hint** on p. 379, see **Lesson 49** in *Language Workshop CD-ROM.*

- **Practice** For practice with revising stringy and wordy sentences, see **Chapter 8** in *English Workshop, Second Course,* pp. 67–68. For practice with punctuating compound sentences, see **Chapter 16** in *English Workshop, Second Course,* pp. 153–154.

R E V I E W B ▶   **Revising a Paragraph by Combining Sentences**

The following paragraph sounds choppy because it has too many short sentences. Use the methods you've learned in this section to combine some of the sentences. You'll notice the improvement when you're finished.

> The Arctic is a cold region. It is around the North Pole. The Arctic seems like a barren place. But berries actually grow in a few places. Vegetables actually grow in a few places. The area also has rich mineral deposits. These deposits have attracted people to the region. Mines in Alaska and Canada produce gold and copper. Mines in arctic Russia produce tin. Early explorers revealed that the Arctic is far from worthless. They discovered many natural resources in the area.

Improving Sentence Style

You've learned how to improve choppy sentences by combining them into longer, smoother sentences. Now you'll learn how to improve *stringy* and *wordy sentences* by making them shorter and more precise.

Revising Stringy Sentences

Stringy sentences just ramble on and on. They have too many independent clauses strung together with words like *and* or *but*. If you read a stringy sentence out loud, you'll probably start to run out of breath. You won't have a chance to pause before each new idea.

> I dreamed I was in a big castle and I turned a corner and I could see a young princess and she waved at me but then she ran up the stairs and she ran into the darkness.

OBJECTIVES

- To identify and revise stringy sentences
- To identify and revise wordy sentences

TEACHING THE LESSON

Just as students should avoid sentence structures that are too simplistic, they must also avoid wordy or stringy construction, which is often the result of students' overcompensating for the short, choppy sentences that they have been told to avoid. The need to revise stringy construction can be related to the lesson about run-ons.

Improving Sentence Style **379**

As you can see, stringy sentences are confusing because they don't show the relationships between the ideas. To fix a stringy sentence, you can

- break the sentence into two or more sentences
- turn some of the independent clauses into phrases or subordinate clauses

Now read the revised version of the stringy sentence. Notice how the writer turned one independent clause into a subordinate clause and another into a phrase.

> I dreamed I was in a big castle. When I turned a corner, I could see a young princess. She waved at me, but then she ran up the stairs into the darkness.

MECHANICS HINT

Punctuating Compound Sentences

When you revise a stringy sentence, you may decide to keep *and* or *but* between two independent clauses. If you do, be sure to add a comma before the *and* or *but* to show a pause between the two thoughts.

ORIGINAL   She waved at me but then she ran up the stairs into the darkness.

REVISED   She waved at me, but then she ran up the stairs into the darkness.

EXERCISE 9 ▶ **Revising Stringy Sentences**

Some of the following sentences are stringy and need improving. First, identify the stringy sentences. Then, revise them by using the methods you've learned. If a numbered item doesn't need to be improved, write *C*.

QUOTATION FOR THE DAY

"Style is the dress of thoughts." (Philip Dormer Stanhope, fourth earl of Chesterfield, 1694–1773, English statesman)

Discuss the meaning of the quotation and explain that writing reflects style just as clothing does. Tell students that revising stringy sentences and reducing wordy sentences are two ways to improve writing style.

MEETING *individual* NEEDS

LEP/ESL

General Strategies. This lesson in the chapter contains new information that may be especially challenging. First of all, students need to understand on as concrete a level as possible what is intended by the words *choppy*, *stringy*, and *wordy*. On the one hand, students are encouraged to use conjunctions to make sentences less choppy. On the other hand, they are warned that conjunctions may result in stringy sentences. Unless these instructions are presented with deliberate clarity and with multiple examples, students might be perplexed by what seems to be a contradiction.

Ask a volunteer to read aloud the textbook's example of a stringy sentence. After discussing the various ways to fix a stringy sentence, have a volunteer read aloud the revision. You may want to point out the specific methods used in the revision. As students read the examples for revising wordy sentences, have them identify words that are omitted in each revision.

Guide students through the process of revising a stringy sentence by using the first sentence in **Exercise 9**, pp. 379–380. Work through the revision on the chalkboard so that students will have a model as they complete the exercise. Guiding students through the revision of the first sentence,

ANSWERS
Exercise 9

Revisions will vary. Here are some possibilities:

1. Harriet Ross grew up as a slave on a plantation in Maryland. In 1844 she married John Tubman, a freed slave.

2. Believing that people should not be slaves, Harriet Tubman decided to escape. Late one night she began her dangerous trip to the North.

3. C

4. New friends told her about the Underground Railroad, a secret group of people who helped runaway slaves get to the North.

5. Tubman decided she would rescue more slaves from the South. Using the North Star as her guide, she led groups of slaves along the road to freedom. She made nineteen trips in twelve years.

6. C

7. Although Tubman never learned to read or write, she was a powerful speaker who spoke at many antislavery meetings.

8. When the Civil War broke out, Tubman volunteered to help the Union army. She served as a cook and a nurse and later became a spy.

9. When the war ended, Tubman settled in Auburn, New York, where she started a home for elderly black men and women.

10. C

1. Harriet Ross grew up as a slave in Maryland, and she worked on a plantation there, but in 1844 she married John Tubman, and he was a freed slave.

2. Harriet Tubman did not believe that people should be slaves, and she decided to escape, and late one night she began her dangerous trip to the North.

3. Traveling at night, she made the long journey to Philadelphia, Pennsylvania.

4. New friends told her about the Underground Railroad, and it was a secret group of people, and they helped runaway slaves get to the North.

5. Tubman decided she would rescue more slaves from the South, and she used the North Star as her guide, and she led groups of slaves along the road to freedom, and she made nineteen trips in twelve years.

6. The slaves hid during the day and continued their journey at night.

7. Tubman never learned to read or write, but she was a powerful speaker, and she spoke at many antislavery meetings.

8. The Civil War broke out, and Tubman volunteered to help the Union army, and she served as a cook and a nurse, and later she became a spy.

9. The war ended, and Tubman settled in Auburn, New York, and she started a home for elderly black men and women.

10. The people of Auburn built Freedom Park in memory of Tubman.

HARRIET TUBMAN

ASSESSMENT

Exercises 9 and **10** should be helpful in determining whether or not students have a sufficient grasp of the material. Evaluating writing samples can also help you determine which students use stringy and wordy sentences.

☞

Revising Wordy Sentences

Sometimes you may use more words than you really need. Extra words don't make writing sound better. They just get in the reader's way. You can revise *wordy sentences* in three different ways.

1. Replace a group of words with one word.

WORDY   Our snowman was the biggest and best on the block due to the fact that we had spent over three hours making it.

REVISED   Our snowman was the biggest and best on the block **because** we had spent over three hours making it.

WORDY   With great suddenness, our beautiful snowman began to melt.

REVISED   **Suddenly,** our beautiful snowman began to melt.

2. Replace a clause with a phrase.

WORDY   When the play had come to an end, we walked to a restaurant and treated ourselves to pizza.

REVISED   **After the play,** we walked to a restaurant and treated ourselves to pizza.

WORDY   I ordered a slice with mozzarella cheese, which is my favorite topping.

REVISED   I ordered a slice with mozzarella cheese, **my favorite topping.**

3. Take out a whole group of unnecessary words.

WORDY   What I mean to say is that Carlos did not go to the movie with us.

REVISED   Carlos did not go to the movie with us.

WORDY   We all liked the movie because it had some very funny scenes that were the kinds of scenes that make you laugh.

REVISED   We all liked the movie because it had some very funny scenes.

MEETING *individual* **NEEDS**

ADVANCED STUDENTS

As most legal documents are purposefully wordy, you could bring in contracts (a lease agreement or a contract for hire) and have students revise the contracts to eliminate excessive wordiness. Encourage students to use dictionaries to help them understand the legal terminology.

COOPERATIVE LEARNING

To show students that there is more than one correct way to revise a sentence, have them work in groups of three to revise stringy and wordy sentences. Groups should have the same set of sentences to revise. After they have completed their revisions, have a representative from each group write the revised sentences on the chalkboard. Then, have the members of the class compare the revisions and vote on those that they think are best.

CRITICAL THINKING

Evaluation. You may want to have your students make a density analysis of the **Review C** paragraph. First, have them count the total number of words. Next, they should count the total number of essential words. (Prepositions, conjunctions, articles, pronouns, vague references, and trite expressions are not considered essential in terms of density analysis.)

When students have these two totals, they should divide the essential count by the total count to arrive at a percentage. After they have revised the paragraph, have them do the analysis again and compare the percentages. The second percentage should be higher.

If this type of analysis proves helpful for your students, you may want to have them apply it to their writing during future revision assignments.

382   *Writing Effective Sentences*

WRITING NOTE   Extra words and phrases tend to make writing sound awkward and unnatural. As you revise your writing, try reading your sentences aloud to check for wordiness or a stringy style. If a sentence sounds like a mouthful to you, chances are it is stringy, wordy, or both.

EXERCISE 10 ▶   **Revising Wordy Sentences**

Decide which of the following sentences are wordy and need improving. Then revise each of the wordy sentences. You can (1) replace a phrase with one word, (2) replace a clause with a phrase, or (3) take out an unnecessary group of words. If the sentence is effective as it is, write *C*.   **Revisions may vary.**

1. Most wasps are helpful to humanity because ~~of the fact that~~ they eat harmful insects.
2. ~~What I want to say is that~~ <u>w</u>asps do far more good than harm.
3. Social wasps ~~are the type that~~ live together as groups and work as a team to build their nests.
4. Social wasps make their nests from old wood and tough plant fibers.   **4. C**
5. They chew ~~and chew~~ the wood and fiber until the mixture becomes pasty and mushy.
6. The mixture ~~becomes a material that~~ is called wasp paper.
7. According to some historians, the Chinese invented paper after watching wasps make it.   **7. C**
8. A wasp colony lasts only through the summer.   **8. C**
9. ˰The queen wasp⁒ ~~being the only member of the colony to survive~~ the winter⁒ comes out of hibernation in the spring.   **9. Only/survives/and**
10. The queens start new colonies by ~~means of~~ building nests and laying eggs.

REVIEW C

OBJECTIVE

- To improve a paragraph by revising stringy and wordy sentences

REVIEW C ▶ **Revising Stringy and Wordy Sentences**

The following paragraph is hard to read because it contains stringy and wordy sentences. First, identify the stringy and wordy sentences. Then, revise them to improve the style of the paragraph. **Revisions will vary.**

On Halloween night in 1938, an amazing event took place that was very surprising. Many families were gathered around their radios, and they were listening to music, and then they heard that Martians had invaded **when** Earth. Actually, the fact is that the news report was a radio version of H. G. Wells's novel The War of the Worlds. But Orson Welles, who was the producer of this famous hoax, made the show very realistic. Thousands of Americans were frightened and upset, and many people jumped in their cars to escape from the aliens, and some people even reported seeing the Martians and their spaceships.

1982 Larson

"Yeeeeeeeeeeeha!"

ANSWERS
Review C

Stringy: 2, 5; Wordy: 1, 3, 4

 VISUAL CONNECTIONS

About the Artist. Gary Larson (1950–   ), once a Humane Society investigator and jazz musician, is creator of *The Far Side.* Larson says he didn't know where he got ideas for cartoons. Some came as he stared at a sheet of paper or while he doodled. Sometimes an idea didn't come out the way he envisioned it.

Related Expression Skills. You may want to have a class discussion about the sources of creative ideas. Ask students what they do to get ideas for a story, a poem, or a drawing. Where are they when they get ideas? Do they have special places that are conducive to creativity?

▶ LESSON 4 (p. 384)
MAKING CONNECTIONS

FILLING IN THE MISSING PIECES
OBJECTIVE
- To rewrite fragments in complete sentences to reconstruct newspaper articles ■

FILLING IN THE MISSING PIECES

Teaching Strategies

You may want to read the first article aloud and work with students to revise the sentence fragments. Then, assign the rest of the articles for independent practice.

ANSWERS

Revisions will vary. Possible responses are underlined.

LIMITS ON TEXAS CATTLE

However, a dreaded Texas fever among cattle <u>has destroyed</u> some herds. <u>Ranchers</u> have begun to lobby in both state and national legislatures.

Cowboys' wages continue to grow

However, <u>their wages</u> continue to grow. Last month's survey <u>showed</u> the average cowhand's wages at <u>$25 to $30</u> a month.

WESTWARD HO!

Eastern <u>farmers</u> are continuing to homestead on the high plains. Last month record numbers of farmers <u>settled</u> near Dodge City, Kansas, an area previously reserved for ranchers. Settlers <u>are moving</u> with equal speed into Nebraska.

Billy the Kid <u>dead</u> at the hand of Pat Garrett

RAILROAD STATIONS PROVIDE MANY SERVICES

Railroad stations from South Dakota to Missouri <u>have become</u> the center for town activity and business. Union Station in St. Louis now <u>has</u> telegraph and mail service as well as <u>a</u> full schedule of passenger and freight trains.

384

MAKING CONNECTIONS

Filling in the Missing Pieces

You're searching through an old trunk in an attic, hoping to find some treasures from the past. In a string-tied bundle of papers, you discover a yellowed newspaper that's dated exactly one hundred years from the day you were born. What luck! You anxiously unfold the front page and begin reading. However, every time you get really excited about an article, a tear or smudge in the newspaper keeps you from finding out what happened.

Read through each article a few times, and try to guess what words are missing. Rewrite the fragments in complete sentences to reconstruct the original articles. [Hint: If you can't puzzle out the original sentences, use your imagination.]

The Lincoln Reporter

LIMITS ON TEXAS CATTLE

Western ranchers are trying to improve their herds with breeding stock from the East. However, a dreaded Texas fever among cattle _____ some herds. Northern plains ranchers are demanding that limits be set on the number of cattle being brought in from Texas. _____ have begun to lobby in both state and national legislatures.

Cowboys' wages continue to grow

There may be no such thing as a rich cowboy. However, _____ continue to grow. Last month's survey _____ the average cowhand's wages at $25 to $30

WESTWARD HO!

Eastern _____ are continuing to homestead on the high plains. Last month record numbers of farmers _____ near Dodge City, Kansas, an area previously reserved for ranchers. Settlers _____ with equal speed into Nebraska.

Billy the Kid _____ at the hand of Pat Garrett
(Story on page 2)

RAILROAD STATIONS PROVIDE MANY SERVICES

Railroad stations from South Dakota to Missouri _____ the center for town activity and business. Union Station in St. Louis now _____ telegraph and mail service as well as a full schedule of passenger and freight trains. The station has also recently added a cafe and a saloon.

Chapter
12

ENGLISH: ORIGINS AND USES

OBJECTIVES

- To match modern English words to their Old English equivalents
- To research word origins and words derived from names
- To identify the appropriate level of language for given situations and to use appropriate language to write specific documents
- To listen for and list tired words and clichés

CROSS CURRICULUM

Remind students that a particular word may take on an uncommon meaning when it is used by a specialist in a given field. For example, to many students a *base* may be something that is touched in a ballgame; to a student of physical science it might refer to household ammonia, milk of magnesia, or lye.

- **Prewriting** Divide students into groups based on interests in specific areas of science such as ecology or space travel. Have groups brainstorm a list of terms specific to their subject matter that they would use to introduce someone to this specialty.

  Sample

  Discipline: physical science
  Terms: element
                compound
                mixture
                farsightedness

  If the subject is a very broad one, students might want to limit their dictionary to a specific aspect such as water pollution or components of a spacecraft.

- **Writing** Assign group members to work together to create a suitable definition for the words and to

compile a dictionary defining the terms and including parts of speech. Provide dictionaries, glossaries, or textbooks to help them arrive at suitable definitions. If the words are ones that are familiar in a more general sense, students might want to offer a genre-specific definition first and then a general definition.

Sample

gravity *n.* attraction of the earth for a given object; generally, seriousness

Students may include sample sentences using the words defined and illustrations.

- **Evaluation** For evaluation of definitions, allow students to play a game in which one team offers one correct and two bogus definitions for a jargon word and the other team tries to choose the correct definition. Teams score one point for stumping the opposition or one point for a correct answer.

- **Publication** Have group members compile a dictionary to be donated to the school library or appropriate science classroom for use by students learning the new jargon.

CHAPTER 12: ENGLISH: ORIGINS AND USES

Use this guide for creating an instructional plan that addresses the individual needs of your students. Assignments accompanied by the following symbol (∗) may be completed out of class. Times given for pacing lessons are estimated.

CHAPTER PLANNING GUIDE—PUPIL'S EDITION

LESSONS	A CHANGING LANGUAGE pp. 385–390	AMERICAN ENGLISH pp. 391–400
DEVELOPMENTAL PROGRAM	⏲ **60–65 minutes** • Main Assignment: Looking Ahead p. 385 • A Family of Languages/The Growth of English/Changes in English/English Builds Its Vocabulary pp. 386–390 • Exercises 1, 2 pp. 387, 388 in pairs • Exercises 3, 4 p. 390∗	⏲ **60–65 minutes** • Dialects of American English pp. 392–393 • Exercise 5 p. 393 in small groups • Choosing Your Words pp. 394–400 • Exercises 6, 8 pp. 397, 400∗ • Style Notes pp. 397, 398 • Exercise 7 p. 399
CORE PROGRAM	⏲ **40–45 minutes** • Main Assignment: Looking Ahead p. 385 • The Growth of English pp. 386–387 • Changes in Pronunciation p. 388 • Exercise 2 p. 388∗ • Looking at Language p. 389 • English Builds Its Vocabulary pp. 389–390 • Exercises 3, 4 p. 390∗	⏲ **20–25 minutes** • Choosing Your Words pp. 394–396, 398–400∗ • Style Notes pp. 397, 398 • Exercises 6, 8 pp. 397, 400∗ • Exercise 7 p. 399
ACCELERATED PROGRAM	⏲ **15–20 minutes** • Main Assignment: Looking Ahead p. 385 • Looking at Language p. 389 • English Builds Its Vocabulary pp. 389–390 • Exercises 3, 4 p. 390∗	⏲ **15–20 minutes** • Standard American English p. 394∗ • Style Notes pp. 397, 398 • Formal and Informal English pp. 395–396∗ • Exercises 6, 8 pp. 397, 400∗ • Denotation and Connotation p. 398 • Jargon p. 400

CHAPTER PLANNING GUIDE—PROGRAM RESOURCES

	A CHANGING LANGUAGE	AMERICAN ENGLISH
PRINT	• Old and Modern English, Word Origins, *Word Choice and Sentence Style* pp. 15–16	• Dialect in Writing, Formal and Informal English, Denotation and Connotation, Clichés and Jargon, *Word Choice and Sentence Style* pp. 17–20 • Language Workshops, *English Workshop* pp. 71–74

ELEMENTS OF WRITING: CURRICULUM CONNECTIONS

Making Connections

• Writing Original Autographs p. 401

ASSESSMENT OPTIONS

Summative Assessment
Review A: English: Origins and Uses; Review B: English: Origins and Uses, *Word Choice and Sentence Style* pp. 21–22, 23–24
Chapter Review, *English Workshop* pp. 75–76

INTEGRATING THE LANGUAGE ARTS

SELECTION	READING AND LITERATURE	WRITING AND CRITICAL THINKING	LANGUAGE AND SYNTAX	SPEAKING, LISTENING, AND OTHER EXPRESSION SKILLS
• from **"Gorilla, My Love"** by Toni Cade Bambara p. 393 • from **A Vaquero of the Brush Country** by J. Frank Dobie p. 395 • from **"The All-American Slurp"** by Lensey Namioka p. 396	• Identifying author's use of style and tone p. 395	• Analyzing words pp. 387, 388 • Using formal and informal language appropriately p. 397 • Avoiding clichés and trite expressions p. 399 • Comparing and combining lists to compile a writing guide p. 399 • Writing original autographs p. 401	• Understanding how the English language has developed, changed, and survived because it is adaptable to new times p. 387 • Demonstrating basic word-attack skills such as phonic analysis p. 388 • Using dictionary skills to find etymologies of words p. 390 • Studying the contributions of various cultures to American English (dialect, idioms, social context) p. 393 • Understanding and applying knowledge of the differences between standard and nonstandard English p. 393 • Using formal and informal English appropriately p. 397 • Identifying tired words and clichés p. 399 • Demonstrating knowledge of vocabulary as determined by a specific word list p. 400 • Using dictionary skills to find word meanings p. 400 • Identifying jargon p. 400	• Reading aloud a passage in dialect pp. 393–394 • Listening for tired words and clichés p. 399

OBJECTIVES

- To match modern English words to their Old English equivalents
- To spell words as they sound
- To research word origins
- To research origins of words from names

TEACHING THE LESSON

Have a volunteer read aloud the paragraph under **A Family of Languages** on p. 386. Have the class repeat aloud the words for *mother.* Point out that language is filled with these similarities, and ask students if they know of any other examples [English *blue*/French *bleu*].

12 ENGLISH: ORIGINS AND USES

FOR THE WHOLE CHAPTER

- **Review** For exercises on chapter concepts, see **Review Form A** and **Review Form B** in *Word Choice and Sentence Style,* pp. 21–24.

A CHANGING LANGUAGE

- **Independent Practice/ Reteaching** For practice and reinforcement, see **Old and Modern English** and **Word Origins** in *Word Choice and Sentence Style,* pp. 15–16.

LOOKING AHEAD

As you work through this chapter, you will learn

- where English comes from
- how English has grown and changed
- what varieties of English people use today
- how to choose appropriate words when you speak and write

QUOTATION FOR THE DAY

"A living language is like a man suffering incessantly from small haemorrhages, and what it needs above all else is constant transactions of new blood from other tongues. The day the gates go up, that day it begins to die." (H. L. Mencken, 1880–1956, American writer, editor, and critic)

Explain that the contributions of borrowed words from other languages are like transfusions that keep a language alive. Ask students what language changes they have experienced, such as new computer terms and slang.

A Changing Language

Did you know that the word *nice* originally meant "foolish," or that the word *prince* comes from French? Have you ever wondered how "teddy" bears got their name? Like people, words have histories. The story behind each English word is part of a much larger history—the history of English itself.

Have the volunteer read aloud **The Growth of English** (below). Guide students through the first two words in **Exercise 1** on p. 387 and assign the rest as independent practice. Ask students how they made their choices—through sounds, spellings, or both. Point out that English spelling and pronunciation continue to change to accommodate the needs of speakers and writers. Have students read **Changes in English** (p. 387) and **Changes in Pronunciation** (p. 388). Guide students through two words from **Exercise 2** on p. 388, and assign the other eight words as independent practice.

Read aloud **Changes in Meaning, Looking at Language,** and **English Builds Its Vocabulary,** pp. 388–390. Before students begin working on **Exercises 3** and **4,**

MEETING *individual* NEEDS

LEP/ESL

General Strategies. Hearing that English has over 600,000 words (p. 389) may be intimidating to students who are just learning English. Explain that while this statistic is accurate, an average American college freshman understands only 60,000–100,000 words, and most English-proficient speakers use only about 2,000 words for everyday conversation. You may want to have English-language learners research the number of words in their native languages and report the information to the class.

386

---

386   *English: Origins and Uses*

A Family of Languages

If you look at photographs in a family album, you can usually see a resemblance among people from different generations. Languages show family resemblances, too. English and dozens of other languages have the same ancestor, a language that was spoken over six thousand years ago in Europe. You can still see similarities among languages that come from this early language.

ENGLISH	FRENCH	GERMAN	SPANISH
mother	mère	Mutter	madre

The Growth of English

No one can say exactly when English began. But we do know that it was being written about 1,300 years ago and was being spoken long before that. Over the centuries, the language has gradually grown and changed along with the people who use it. This change and growth is divided into three major stages: *Old English*, *Middle English*, and *Modern English.*

Following are Old, Middle, and Modern English versions of a line from the Lord's Prayer (Matthew 6:9–13). Notice how the language gradually developed into the English we use today.

OLD ENGLISH	Urne gedæg hwamlican hlaf syle us to dæg.
MIDDLE ENGLISH	Oure iche-dayes-bred gif us to-day.
MODERN ENGLISH	Give us this day our daily bread.

both on p. 390, review the structure of a dictionary entry as explained in **Chapter 33: "The Dictionary,"** and show students the etymological information. Using different dictionaries to see if their findings are consistent, students should work in groups to research the words *moccasin, moose, pecan, raccoon,* and *squash.* Circulate among the groups and offer guidance. With this preparation

students should be ready to do **Exercises 3** and **4** as independent practice. Remind students that their answers for **Exercise 3** should not only cite the languages from which the words were borrowed but should also give the original meanings.

☞

English has changed so much in 1,300 years that only language scholars can understand Old English without a translation. Yet we can still see the resemblance between present-day English words and their Old English ancestors.

OLD ENGLISH	modor	sunne	steorra	meolc
MODERN ENGLISH	mother	sun	star	milk

EXERCISE 1 ▶ **Matching Present-Day and Old English Words**

See if you can match each present-day English word in the left-hand column with its Old English ancestor in the right-hand column. [Hint: Look at the beginning consonants, and use the process of elimination.]

1. blue   1. b   **a.** catt
2. green   2. h   **b.** blaewen
3. cat   3. a   **c.** docga
4. bright   4. g   **d.** muth
5. black   5. e   **e.** blaec
6. lip   6. j   **f.** regn
7. white   7. i   **g.** bryht
8. mouth   8. d   **h.** grene
9. rain   9. f   **i.** hwit
10. dog   10. c   **j.** lippa

Changes in English

As you can see from the examples at the top of this page, the spellings of words have changed since Old English times. English has changed in other ways, too. Pronunciations of words have changed, and some words have taken on meanings different from their original ones. English also has a much larger and richer vocabulary than it did 1,300 years ago.

INTEGRATING THE LANGUAGE ARTS

Listening Link. To give students a better idea about the extent to which English has changed, obtain recordings or audiocassettes of *Beowulf,* Chaucer's *Canterbury Tales,* and a play by Shakespeare. Play brief selections from each without telling students what they are hearing. Have students guess in each case what language is being spoken. Then distribute transcripts of the recordings along with modern translations of the Old English and Middle English. Lead a class discussion on the similarities and differences among these three different stages of English.

Literature Link. If your literature textbook contains it, you may want to incorporate the literary selection *Beowulf* during this lesson. Have students compare a portion of the Old English version with the modern English version. Give students a pronunciation guide, have them work in pairs, and have each student learn to speak a short phrase in Old English. Then each student could share a phrase and its translation with the class.

387

MEETING *individual* NEEDS

STUDENTS WITH SPECIAL NEEDS

To help students with **Exercise 2**, choose ten words and pronounce each word for them. Students may be very adept at phonetic spelling. If they enjoy this exercise, you may want to let them spell additional words phonetically.

ANSWERS

Exercise 2

Students should create phonetic spellings for ten words. Easier prediction of phonetic spelling is the main reason such a change would succeed. The main reason it would not succeed is that all the people who already read and write English have learned the old way and would have to relearn much of written language.

Changes in Pronunciation

Users of Old and Middle English pronounced words differently from the way we do. Pronunciation changes help explain why many present-day English words aren't spelled as they sound. For example, the word *knight* used to be pronounced with a *k* sound at the beginning. The *k* eventually became silent, but the spelling never caught up with the pronunciation.

The major pronunciation changes have been changes in vowel sounds. In the 13th century, *meek* would have sounded like *make*, *boot* like *boat*, and *mouse* like *moose*.

EXERCISE 2 ▶   **Spelling Words As They Sound**

You've been elected to a committee to update the spellings of English words. Choose ten words that aren't spelled as they sound. Then respell each word to reflect the way you pronounce it. Do you think your new spellings could catch on? Why or why not?

Changes in Meaning

Over time, words take on new meanings as people use them in different ways. Here are some examples of gradual changes in the meanings of words.

CHANGES IN MEANING

	Old English	Middle English	Modern English
	450	1100	1500 PRESENT
SILLY	happy, blessed	harmless	foolish
GLAMOUR		enchantment	charm, fascination
COMPUTER		a person who computes or calculates	an electronic machine

CLOSURE

Have students summarize the lesson by restating its main points. [Responses will vary but should include the following points:

1. English is part of a family of languages derived from a language that was spoken over six thousand years ago in Europe.

2. Words change in form, use, meaning, spelling, and pronunciation.

3. Only about 15 percent of the words used today come from Old English. The rest have been borrowed or invented.] ■

LOOKING AT Language

The Glamour of Grammar

Glamour and *grammar* may not seem to have much in common, but the two words are actually close cousins. Both come from the Middle English word *gramer,* which had two very different meanings: "grammar" and "enchantment." Eventually *glamour* was used only with the second meaning. As shown in the time line on the previous page, the meaning of *glamour* has changed over time to the one we're familiar with today.

English Builds Its Vocabulary

The large vocabulary of English (over 600,000 words!) makes it a rich and flexible language. But English wasn't always as expressive as it is today. For example, users of Old English never heard of the words *beauty, sketch,* or *key.* Only about 15 percent of the words we use come from Old English. The rest have been borrowed or invented over the centuries.

Borrowed Words

Thousands of our everyday words were borrowed from the vocabularies of other languages. Norse, Latin, French, and Spanish are just a few of the languages that have left their mark on English.

NORSE	*sky*	ENGLISH	*sky*
LATIN	*papyrus*	ENGLISH	*paper*
FRENCH	*faceon*	ENGLISH	*fashion*
SPANISH	*cañón*	ENGLISH	*canyon*

A DIFFERENT APPROACH

Explain to students that borrowed words sometimes fit into general categories. For example, many words pertaining to music are borrowed from Italian. Put the following three lists on the chalkboard, and have students categorize the words according to whether they are borrowed from Spanish, Italian, or French. Have students use dictionaries if necessary.

1. lariat, rodeo, mustang, stampede [Spanish]

2. allegro, largo, andante, piano [Italian]

3. attorney, captain, soldier, lieutenant, chancellor [French]

Have students research the question of why these borrowed words fit into these categories and then have them report their findings to the class. [The Spanish settled the southwestern region of what is now the United States and influenced cattle ranching. The practice of indicating speed and dynamics in musical scores was developed in Italy in the seventeenth century. During the Norman conquest of England, the French held all administrative, legal, and military positions.]

Words from Names

Proper names are another source of new words in English. Many objects are named after the people who invented or inspired them. Others are named after the places they come from.

EXAMPLES　　*graham cracker:* from Sylvester Graham, the American clergyman who invented this type of cracker

cologne: from Cologne, a city in Germany

sardines: from Sardinia, an island in the Mediterranean Sea

teddy bear: from Theodore ("Teddy") Roosevelt, twenty-sixth President of the United States

---

EXERCISE 3　　　　Researching Word Origins

Answers may vary according to the dictionary used.

Using a dictionary that gives word origins, find out what language each of the following words was borrowed from. Give the meaning of the original foreign word if your dictionary lists it.　These answers are from *Webster's New World College Dictionary,* Third Edition

1. noble　　1. French – "well-known"　　4. ghoul　　4. Arabic – "demon of the desert"
2. chigger　　2. Wolof (African) – "insect"　　5. tortilla
3. jungle　　　　　　　　　5. Spanish – "little cake"
3. Hindi – "desert forest"

EXERCISE 4　　　　Researching Words from Names

Use a dictionary to find out what name each of the following words comes from. Then choose one of the words and research it further in an encyclopedia. In two or three sentences, explain how and when the word came into English.

1. cashmere　　　　4. pasteurize
2. sandwich　　　　5. watt
3. diesel

TIMESAVER

If students master **Exercise 3,** you may want to have them each look up only three of the five words in **Exercise 4.**

ANSWERS
Exercise 4

Answers may vary.

1. In 19th century England, fine carded wool from goats of Kashmir and Tibet became popular. Wool and the cloth made from it took the name *cashmere* (old spelling of *Kashmir*).

2. The British Fourth Earl of Sandwich (1718–1792) popularized this food.

3. The German inventor Rudolf Diesel (1858–1913) gave his name to the engine he invented in 1898 and to the heavy fuel it requires.

4. Frenchman Louis Pasteur (1821–1890) developed a heat process to kill undulant fever germs (Bangs disease) in milk.

5. This unit of electrical power was named for Scottish engineer and inventor James Watt (1736–1819).

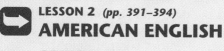
TEACHING THE LESSON

Begin by reading the introductory paragraphs and by pointing out that English changed as the colonists began developing their culture apart from England.

Discuss the types of dialects and emphasize that all dialects are equally valid. Use the examples to show students regional differences among dialects and words from

American English

When English colonists first settled in the New World, they used the same form of English that their relatives in England used. But the colonists began to develop their own form of English—*American English.* Gradually, colonists and settlers adopted new pronunciations and spellings of words. They also kept some old forms of words that people in England began to change.

Speakers of American English have borrowed words from many different languages. The languages of American Indian peoples, of African peoples, and of immigrants from around the world have helped shape the American English we use today. Here are just a few examples of words American English has borrowed from other languages.

AMERICAN INDIAN	chipmunk, moose, totem
AFRICAN	gumbo, okra
SPANISH	avocado, patio, tamale
DUTCH	boss, sleigh, waffle

The Granger Collection, New York.

PROGRAM MANAGER

AMERICAN ENGLISH

- **Independent Practice/ Reteaching** For practice and reinforcement, see **Dialect in Writing** in *Word Choice and Sentence Style*, p. 17.

QUOTATION FOR THE DAY

"The foreign language which has most affected English in our own time is contemporary American." (Ernest Weekley, 1865–1954, British linguist and author)

Ask students if they think British English sometimes seems like a foreign language. Do they ever have trouble understanding people in movies or TV shows who speak with British accents? Ask students if they can name any differences between British and American English in the names of things. [Some examples are *petrol* for *gasoline, lift* for *elevator, flat* for *apartment,* and *lorry* for *truck.*] Do students know any differences in the spellings of words? [Some examples are *honour/honor, theatre/theater, kerb/curb,* and *defence/defense.*]

ethnic dialects that have become part of general American vocabulary.

Introduce the section on ethnic dialects by asking a student to read Toni Cade Bambara's passage aloud. Ask students to paraphrase what they have heard. Then give other interested students the chance to read the passage aloud.

Discuss the differences between Bambara's usage and their own dialects. Have them write journal entries paraphrasing the passage into their own dialects.

Finally, have a volunteer read aloud **Standard American English,** p. 394.

MEETING *individual* NEEDS

LEP/ESL

General Strategies. To give students a better idea of the nature of American dialects, show the thirty-minute videotape *Yeah You Rite!* It features speakers from the old city neighborhoods of New Orleans whose dialects derive from a confluence of English, French, Spanish, Irish, Italian, and various African languages.

A DIFFERENT APPROACH

Have students use the chart of regional dialects from the textbook as a starting point for researching dialects of American English. Students should compare some features of two ethnic or regional dialects by considering variables such as word choice, syntax, and pronunciation. You may want to have students present their findings to the class.

392

Dialects of American English

Different groups of people speak different forms of American English. These special forms are called *dialects.* Dialects vary from one another in vocabulary, grammar, and pronunciation. You are already familiar with standard American English, the variety of English most often used in books and newspapers, in schools and businesses, and on radio and television. In addition to standard English, Americans speak two kinds of dialects: *regional dialects* and *ethnic dialects.*

Regional Dialects

You've probably noticed that people from a particular region of the country tend to talk alike. That's because they use the same *regional dialect.* There are three major regional dialects in the United States: *Northern, Midland,* and *Southern.* Here are some examples of the differences between them.

	NORTHERN	MIDLAND	SOUTHERN
Vocabulary	johnnycake	corn bread	corn pone
Grammar	ten pound	ten pounds	ten pound
Pronunciation	*greasy* with an s sound	*greasy* with an s or a z sound	*greasy* with a z sound

It's important to know that not everyone in a region must use that region's dialect. Also, people in one region may use words and expressions that are considered part of another group's dialect.

Ethnic Dialects

Your cultural heritage can also make a difference in how you speak. The English used by a particular cultural

ASSESSMENT

Use students' participation in class discussion and their journal entries to assess their ability to analyze and paraphrase dialect.

group is called an ***ethnic dialect.*** Like a regional dialect, an ethnic dialect is a shared language that many (but not all) members of a group have in common.

The most widely spoken American ethnic dialects are the Black English of many African Americans and the Spanish-influenced English of many people from Mexico, Central America, Cuba, and Puerto Rico. Many words from these dialects have become part of the general American vocabulary. For example, *jazz* and *jukebox* come from African American dialect, and *bronco* and *mesa* come from Hispanic English.

EXERCISE 5 ▶   **Hearing a Dialect**

When writers use dialect, they help you hear a character's speech. In the following passage, the speaker is an African American girl who is riding in a car with her family. She decides to ask her uncle a straightforward question—whether or not he is going to get married. In this passage, she explains why she is inclined to "speak-up" about what's on her mind. Read the passage aloud, pronouncing the words as the author has spelled them. Is the character's dialect different from the way you speak? How would you express the same thoughts in your own dialect?

> So there I am in the navigator seat. And I turn to him and just plain old ax him. I mean I come right on out with it. No sense goin all around that barn the old folks talk about. And like my mama say, Hazel—which is my real name and what she remembers to call me when she bein serious—when you got somethin on your mind, speak up and let the chips fall where they may. And if anybody don't like it, tell em to come see your mama. And Daddy look up from the paper and say, You hear your mama good, Hazel. And tell em to come see me first. Like that. That's how I was raised.
>
> Toni Cade Bambara, "Gorilla, My Love"

Literature Link. Have students read "Thank You, M'am" by Langston Hughes (pp. 203–208) and analyze Hughes's use of dialect to portray vivid characters. Hughes's story provides several examples of Black English, slang, and idiomatic phrasing. The story is short enough that students might enjoy reading it orally as a class or in small groups.

A DIFFERENT APPROACH

In the PBS series *The Story of English,* the sections "The American Plantations," "Black on White," and "Pioneers! O Pioneers!" focus on American dialects. You may want to show these episodes to your class.

ANSWERS

Exercise 5

Students might point out differences in pronunciation and word choice. If students write paraphrases in their own dialects, the paraphrases should be written phonetically unless the dialect is standard American English.

SELECTION AMENDMENT
Description of change: excerpted
Rationale: to focus on the use of dialects presented in this chapter

CHOOSING YOUR WORDS

OBJECTIVES

- To identify the appropriate levels of language for given situations
- To use appropriate language to write a letter, a writing journal entry, or a conversation
- To identify tired words and clichés
- To translate jargon

QUOTATION FOR THE DAY

"Slang is a language that rolls up its sleeves, spits on its hands and goes to work." (Carl Sandburg, 1878–1967, American poet)

Ask students to cite examples of current slang. Then ask if Sandburg's description fits these examples.

394

Standard American English

Many Americans use more than one variety of English. They speak a regional or ethnic dialect at home and use *standard American English* at school or work. Standard English is the most widely used and accepted variety of American English. Because it's commonly understood, it allows people from many different regions and cultures to communicate with one another clearly. It is the variety of English you read and hear most often in books and magazines, on radio and television. It is the kind of English people are expected to use in most school and business situations.

Standard English has rules and guidelines that help you to recognize and use it. Some of these rules and guidelines are presented for you in the **Handbook** in this textbook. To identify the differences between standard American English and other varieties of English, the **Handbook** uses the labels *standard* and *nonstandard.* *Nonstandard* doesn't mean wrong language. It means language that is inappropriate in situations where standard English is expected.

☞ REFERENCE NOTE: For more information about standard and nonstandard English, see page 682.

Choosing Your Words

Because English has such a large vocabulary, you can say the same thing in many different ways. For example, the following sentences have basically the same meaning:

> I am leaving, but I will return in a short period of time.
> I'm going out, but I'll be back in a spell.

Words communicate much more than basic meanings. They also express attitudes and feelings. That's why it's important to choose your words with care, adapting your language to suit different purposes, audiences, and situations.

Tell students that you are going to present part of the lesson in two different ways and that you want them to make notes on your speech patterns. Then present the first part of the lesson as you normally would. Next, present the same information in an informal style by using slang and collo-quialisms. Give students some time after your presentation to compare and contrast the two different styles. Ask students which one was more suitable for a classroom teacher. Which one was more understand-able? What effect did each presentation have on them as listeners?

Choosing Your Words **395**

Formal and Informal English

Look again at the example sentences on page 394. Just a few words have been changed from the first sentence to the second, but the effect of each sentence is different. One is written in *formal English* and the other in *informal English*.

Formal English is the language you would use for dig-nified occasions such as public speeches, graduation cere-monies, and serious papers and reports. It often includes long sentences and extremely precise words. It usually doesn't include contractions such as *don't* or *isn't*.

The following paragraph about cowboys is written in formal English. Notice the author's word choice and the length of the sentences.

> Many a cowboy has spread his bandanna, perhaps none too clean itself, over dirty, muddy water and used it as a strainer to drink through; sometimes he used it as a cup towel, which he called a "drying rag." If the bandanna was dirty, it was probably not so dirty as the other apparel of the cowboy, for when he came to a hole of water, he was wont to dismount and wash out his handkerchief, letting it dry while he rode along, holding it in his hand or spread over his hat. Often he wore it under his hat in order to help keep his head cool. At other times, in the face of a fierce gale, he used it to tie down his hat. The bandanna made a good sling for a broken arm; it made a good bandage for a blood wound.
>
> J. Frank Dobie, *A Vaquero of the Brush Country*

Informal English is used in most everyday speaking and writing. For example, you probably use informal English when you talk with family members or friends and when you write personal letters or journal entries. Informal English usually has short sentences that are easy to understand. It also includes contractions and conversa-tional expressions.

SELECTION AMENDMENT
Description of change: excerpted
Rationale: to focus on the use of formal English presented in this chapter

395

You may want to introduce this lesson by asking a volunteer to read aloud J. Frank Dobie's passage on cowboys. Then have another volunteer read the excerpt from Lensey Namioka's "The All-American Slurp." Initiate a discussion on formal and informal English by analyzing the differences between the two passages and by listing the kinds of situations for which each type of English is appropriate.

Discuss the material that explains slang and colloquialisms, and then work with students to categorize the topics in **Exercise 6** on p. 397. Pick one of the situations and model it for students by writing in the appropriate form of English. Then assign **Exercise 6** as independent practice.

CRITICAL THINKING

Evaluation. Have students consider the following scenario: A young woman has submitted an audition tape to a radio station, and she is being called in to interview for a job as a disc jockey. Ask students what form of language (formal or informal, standard or nonstandard) they think would be most appropriate to use in the interview. [Responses will vary. Because the station has already listened to her tape, they are familiar with her radio persona and with her ability to use slang and informal English. In the interview she should probably use a mixture of levels, less formal than for an interview with a law firm, but formal enough to impress her interviewer with her maturity and responsibility. Standard English would be most appropriate, and some slang or colloquialisms would probably be fine.]

SELECTION AMENDMENT
Description of change: excerpted
Rationale: to focus on the use of informal English presented in this chapter

In the following passage, a teenage girl is speaking. How does the writer's language differ from J. Frank Dobie's?

> The first time I visited Meg's house, she took me upstairs to her room, and I wound up trying on her clothes. We were pretty much the same size, since Meg was shorter and thinner than average. Maybe that's how we became friends in the first place. Wearing Meg's jeans and T-shirt, I looked at myself in the mirror. I could almost pass for an American—from the back, anyway.
>
> Lensey Namioka, "The All-American Slurp"

Uses of Informal English

There are two uses of informal English that you should be familiar with: *colloquialisms* and *slang*.

Colloquialisms are the colorful, widely used expressions of conversational language.

EXAMPLES   That movie **gave me the creeps.**
            Bernice is a **real sport.**
            The children were **acting up** at bedtime.

Slang consists of made-up words and old words used in new ways. Most slang expressions are a special vocabulary for a particular group of people, such as teenagers, musicians, or military recruits. Because slang has a limited use, it usually lives a short life.

The following words, when used with the given meanings, are all considered slang. Although these expressions were once current, they probably seem out-of-date to you now. What slang words do you and your friends use to express the same meanings?

cool: pleasing, excellent
hang out: spend time at a place
get into: enjoy, be interested in
grub: food

To teach the section on denotation and connotation, you could list pairs of synonyms on the chalkboard. Possibilities include *house/home, economical/cheap, skinny/thin, perspiration/sweat, old/antique,* and *spontaneous/impulsive*. Read aloud the material in the textbook on denotation and connotation, and discuss with students the connotations of the synonym pairs you have listed.

Discuss the material on tired words and clichés and assign **Exercise 7** on p. 399 as independent practice. Because **Exercise 7** is to be done over a few days' time, you may want to check students' lists each day to ensure that they stay on task.

Luann reprinted by permission of United Feature Syndicate, Inc.

STYLE NOTE   You may want to use slang sometimes in journal entries, letters to friends, and other writing that's highly informal. However, don't use slang in formal writing such as essays, test answers, or reports. Notice how inappropriate slang sounds in an otherwise formal sentence:

> We toured the elegant, stately rooms of Monticello, Thomas Jefferson's *cool pad.*

EXERCISE 6   **Using Formal or Informal English**

What kind of language would you use in each of the following situations? Choose one of the situations and do the writing described. Use the formal or informal English that you think is appropriate for the situation.

1. a letter to a mail-order company complaining about a faulty product **1. formal**
2. a note to a friend's parents thanking them for taking you on a weekend trip **2. formal**
3. a journal entry describing something funny that happened at school **3. informal**
4. a conversation between two teenagers in a mall **4. informal**

ANSWERS
Exercise 6

Responses will vary, but each student should choose one of the writing assignments suggested and use formal or informal language as appropriate.

Discuss the material on jargon and guide students through finding in a dictionary the specialized meaning of one of the words in **Exercise 8** on p. 400. Assign the rest of **Exercise 8** as independent practice. You may want to suggest that students use the library to research the examples of jargon in **Exercise 8** because some of the definitions may not be in a standard dictionary.

398

Denotation and Connotation

Would you rather be described as *thrifty* or *stingy*? The words have the same basic meaning, or **denotation,** but they have very different effects on a reader or listener. They have different emotional associations, or **connotations.** You might be pleased if someone described you as *thrifty,* since the word suggests the positive quality of being economical. But you would probably be offended if someone described you as *stingy,* since the word has negative associations of selfishness and penny-pinching.

Think about the connotations of a word before you use it. If you use a word without taking into account its emotional effect, you may send the wrong message to your audience.

STYLE NOTE

It's especially important to think about connotations when you are choosing among *synonyms*—words that have similar meanings. For example, suppose you've written the following sentence in a classified advertisement for a yard sale. You decide that you need to replace the word *selective.* Which of the words in parentheses is the best replacement?

> Attention, selective shoppers: we have a great selection of records, clothing, lawn tools, and toys. (*picky, choosy*)

Picky and *choosy* are both synonyms for *selective,* but they have very different connotations. *Picky* is a negative word that suggests your customers are overly fussy. *Choosy* is a positive word that suggests they are particular about what they buy. Which word is appropriate for your ad?

CLOSURE

When closing, ask students in what situations they might use formal and informal English. Ask students to define *slang* and *colloquialism* and to give an example of each. Have students explain the difference between *denotation* and *connotation*. Finally, ask students to define *jargon*.

ENRICHMENT

Provide students with graph paper and ask them to create word searches by using jargon terms associated with a certain sport, hobby, or profession.

After students are finished, their classmates can find the hidden words. Here is an ☞

Choosing Your Words   **399**

Tired Words and Expressions

You would probably get annoyed if you heard the same song being played every time you turned on the radio. After a while, the song would lose its appeal. The same thing happens to words when they are overused. They become tired, and they lose their freshness and force. *Nice, fine, great,* and *wonderful* are good examples of tired words. They may be acceptable in conversation, but they are too vague to be effective in writing.

Tired expressions, or **clichés,** are also vague and bland. Here are some examples of clichés.

(keep your) nose to the grindstone
bright and early
few and far between
light as a feather
on top of the world

EXERCISE 7 ▶   **Identifying Tired Words and Clichés**

Make a list of all the tired words and expressions you can think of. Spend a few days watching and listening for them, jotting down words and expressions in a notebook as you hear them. Then, compare your list with those of your classmates. By combining lists, you'll have a handy collection of words and expressions to avoid when you write.

COMPUTER NOTE: Once you have made a list of tired words and clichés, use your word-processing program's Find command to search for each of them in your draft. Then, use the thesaurus tool to choose appropriate synonyms.

example of a word search with a filmmaking theme:

Jargon

Jargon is special language that is used by a particular group of people, such as people who share the same profession, occupation, sport, or hobby. A word can be used as jargon by several groups, with each group giving it a different meaning. For example, the word *hold* is used by lawyers to mean "to bind by contract" and by musicians to mean "a pause" or "to prolong a tone or rest."

Jargon can be practical and effective because it reduces many words to just one or two. However, jargon is inappropriate for a general audience, who may not be familiar with the special meanings of the words.

☞ **REFERENCE NOTE:** For an example of how dictionaries label special uses of words, see pages 890–891.

EXERCISE 8 ▶   Translating Jargon

Like many other groups, television and movie crews have their own jargon. Look up each of the following words in a dictionary to find out what special meaning it has for filmmakers.

1. cut
2. dolly
3. dub
4. fade
5. frame

6. pan
7. scene
8. tracking shot
9. wipe
10. zoom

INTEGRATING THE LANGUAGE ARTS

Library Link. Students could conduct personal studies of jargon by researching the words associated with hobbies or possible future professions for themselves. They could then create their own jargon minidictionaries.

ANSWERS
Exercise 8

1. to change scenes quickly or to stop filming

2. movable platform for a studio camera

3. to insert sounds into a soundtrack

4. the gradual disappearance of a film image from the screen

5. a single shot from a strip of film; to compose a shot with elements at the edges to contrast with the subject

6. to move a camera from left to right or from right to left to cause a panoramic effect

7. a section of film that doesn't have any changes in time or setting

8. a shot in which the camera follows a moving subject

9. to change images by pulling the new one horizontally across the screen behind a vertical line

10. to move from a wide shot to a close-up of an image within a wide shot

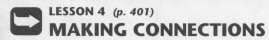

* To write original, creative autographs

401

MAKING CONNECTIONS

Writing Original Autographs

It's the last day of the school year, and your classmates are passing around autograph books in the cafeteria. You're about to sign a friend's book when you notice that everyone has written the same tired, boring expressions around the page. Instead of saying the same things everyone else has, you decided to write a lively, original message for each of your friends to remember you by.

Here are some of the autographs that you *don't* want to write. Use your imagination to express the same thoughts and feelings in more interesting ways. Write each autograph in any form you like—as a poem, a short letter, or just an attention-grabbing sentence or two.

WRITING ORIGINAL AUTOGRAPHS
Teaching Strategies
After a volunteer has read aloud the material from the textbook, lead a class discussion analyzing the problems with the autographs in the illustration. Rewrite one of the given autographs with the class to model the process. You may want to make a thesaurus available to students as they write their autographs.

GUIDELINES
Autographs should be inventive and should avoid the use of tired expressions and clichés.

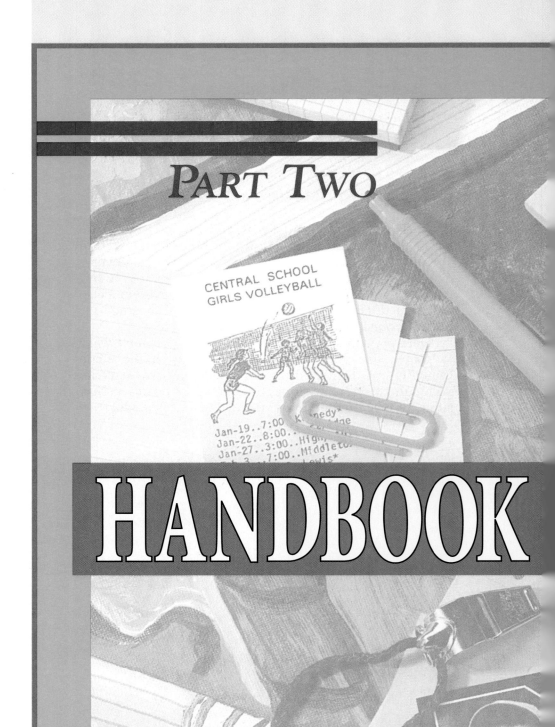

PART TWO

HANDBOOK

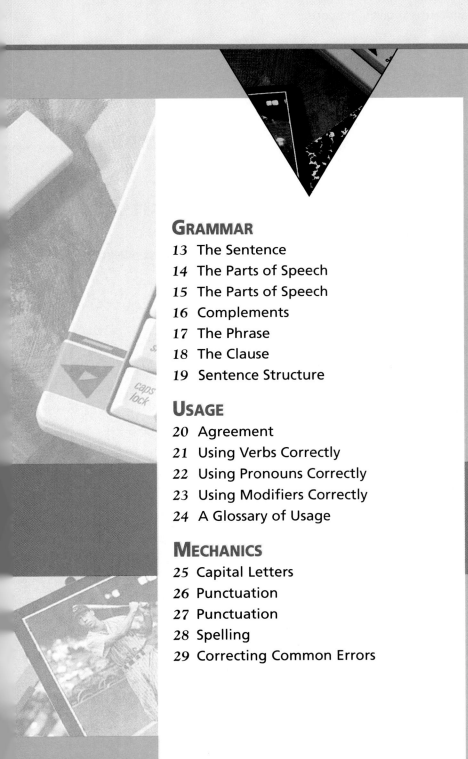

GRAMMAR

USAGE

MECHANICS

PART TWO: HANDBOOK

The following **Teaching Resources** booklets contain materials that may be used with this part of the Pupil's Edition.

- *Language Skills Practice and Assessment*
- *Portfolio Assessment* (for Ch. 28)
- *Practice for Assessment in Reading Vocabulary, and Spelling* (for Ch. 28)

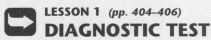
OBJECTIVES

- To identify complete sentences and sentence fragments
- To revise sentence fragments to form complete sentences
- To identify complete subjects, simple subjects, complete predicates, and verbs in given sentences

PROGRAM MANAGER

FOR THE WHOLE CHAPTER

■ **Review** For exercises on chapter concepts, see **Review Form A** and **Review Form B** in *Language Skills Practice and Assessment,* pp. 19–22.

■ **Assessment** For additional testing, see **Grammar Pretests** and **Grammar Mastery Tests** in *Language Skills Practice and Assessment,* pp. 1–8 and pp. 103–110.

GRAMMAR

CHAPTER OVERVIEW

The first part of this chapter explains the difference between complete sentences and sentence fragments. The chapter also covers subjects and predicates—simple and compound. The **Writing Application** concentrates on using subjects and predicates to express complete thoughts. The last part of the chapter deals with the different kinds of sentences.

You may want to refer students to this chapter throughout the year, especially during the revision stage of writing assignments. Once students have a working knowledge of the basics of a complete sentence, they can be more easily encouraged to add variety to their writing.

GRAMMAR

13 THE SENTENCE

Subject and Predicate, Kinds of Sentences

Diagnostic Test

A. Identifying Sentences and Sentence Fragments

Identify each group of words as a *sentence* or a *sentence fragment*. If the word group is a sentence fragment, correct it by adding words to make a complete sentence.

Revisions of sentence fragments will vary.

EXAMPLES **1.** Although I know your first name.
　　　　　1. *sentence fragment—Although I know your first name, I don't know your last name.*

　　　　　2. You may call me by my given name or by my surname.
　　　　　2. *sentence*

1. While it may seem strange to go by one name.   **1.** frag.
2. People had only first names for thousands of years.
3. Calling people by one name.   **2.** sent.   **3.** frag.

404

- To classify sentences as declarative, interrogative, imperative, or exclamatory
- To provide the correct end punctuation for given sentences

4. The ancient Romans sometimes gave people second names. **4.** sent.
5. Last names became common in the thirteenth century in Italy. **5.** sent.

B. Identifying Subjects and Predicates

Label each italicized group of words as the <u>*complete subject*</u> or the <u>*complete predicate*</u> of the sentence. Then, identify the <u>simple subject</u> or the <u>verb</u> in each word group.

EXAMPLES
  1. *The mean dog next door* barks fiercely.
  1. *complete subject; simple subject—dog*

  2. The mean dog next door *barks fiercely.*
  2. *complete predicate; verb—barks*

          6. comp. pred.
6. Mr. Adams *<u>gave</u> me his old croquet set.* **7.** comp. subj.
7. Why did *that large new <u>boat</u>* sink on such a clear day?
8. *<u>Trees</u> and <u>bushes</u> all over the neighborhood* had been torn out by the storm. **8.** comp. subj. **9.** comp. pred.
9. Walking to school, Bill *<u>was splashed</u> by a passing car.*
10. *My old <u>bicycle</u> with the ape-hanger handlebars* is rusting away in the garage now. **10.** comp. subj.
11. *The <u>creek</u> behind my house* rises during the summer rains. **11.** comp. subj.
12. Sandy's little sister *bravely <u>dived</u> off the high board at the community pool.* **12.** comp. pred.
13. *<u>Does</u> Max <u>want</u> another serving of pie?* **13.** comp. pred.
14. My cousins and I *<u>played</u> basketball and <u>walked</u> over to the mall yesterday.* **14.** comp. pred.
15. *<u>Fridays</u> and other test <u>days</u>* always seem longer than regular school days. **15.** comp. subj.

C. Classifying Sentences

Classify each of the following sentences as *declarative*, *interrogative*, *imperative*, or *exclamatory*. Then, write the <u>last word</u> of each sentence and supply the correct end punctuation.

USING THE DIAGNOSTIC TEST

Use the **Diagnostic Test** to gauge students' familiarity with sentence completeness, subjects and predicates, and the kinds of sentences. In addition, an evaluation of sentences in writing samples could suggest areas where students need more practice or extra guidance.

GRAMMAR

OBJECTIVES
- To identify sentences and sentence fragments
- To revise sentence fragments to form complete sentences

GRAMMAR

PROGRAM MANAGER

THE SENTENCE

■ **Independent Practice/ Reteaching** For instruction and exercises, see **Sentences and Fragments** in *Language Skills Practice and Assessment,* p. 13.

■ **Computer Guided Instruction** For additional instruction and practice with sentence fragments, see **Lesson 40** in *Language Workshop CD-ROM.*

■ **Practice** To help less-advanced students with additional instruction and practice with sentence sense, see **Chapter 10** in *English Workshop, Second Course,* pp. 77–78.

QUICK REMINDER

Write the following groups of words on the chalkboard:

1. Likes loud music.
2. A popular musician.
3. Because we know the drummer.

Ask students why the groups of words look like sentences but are not. [They begin with capital letters and have end punctuation but don't express complete thoughts.] Ask students to add words to each fragment to form complete sentences.

GRAMMAR

406 *The Sentence*

EXAMPLE   **1. Please tell me if the seahorse is a fish**
    1. *imperative—fish.*

16. The sea horse is a very unusual kind of <u>fish</u>.   **16.** decl.
17. What a beautiful butterfly that <u>is</u>!   **17.** excl.
18. Can you believe that most polar bears don't <u>hibernate</u>?   **18.** int.
19. Daniel, find out how many miles per hour a rabbit can <u>hop</u>.   **19.** imp.
20. Some jack rabbits can hop forty miles per <u>hour</u>.   **20.** decl.

The Sentence

13a.   A *sentence* is a group of words that expresses a complete thought.

A sentence begins with a capital letter and ends with a period, a question mark, or an exclamation point.

EXAMPLES   **Sean was chosen captain of his soccer team.**
    Have you read the novel *Shane*?
    What a dangerous mission it must have been!

When a group of words looks like a sentence but does not express a complete thought, it is a *sentence fragment.*

SENTENCE FRAGMENT   **The music of Scott Joplin.** [This is not a complete thought. What about the music of Scott Joplin?]

SENTENCE   **The music of Scott Joplin has been recorded by many musicians.**

SENTENCE FRAGMENT   **After watching Rita Moreno.** [The thought is not complete. Who watched Rita Moreno? What happened afterward?]

SENTENCE   **After watching Rita Moreno, Carol decided to become an entertainer.**

13a

GRAMMAR

| SENTENCE FRAGMENT | Even though she had worked a long time. [The thought is not complete. What happened even though she had worked a long time?] |
| SENTENCE | Louise Nevelson had not completed the sculpture even though she had worked a long time. |

☞ **REFERENCE NOTE:** For more information about sentence fragments, see pages 361–362.

▶ EXERCISE 1 **Identifying Sentences and Revising Sentence Fragments**

Tell whether each group of words is a *sentence* or a *sentence fragment*. If the word group is a sentence, correct it by adding a capital letter and end punctuation. If the word group is a sentence fragment, correct it by adding words to make a complete sentence. **Revisions of sentence fragments will vary.**

EXAMPLES **1.** classes in mountain climbing will begin soon
    1. *sentence—Classes in mountain climbing will begin soon.*

    2. living alone in the mountains
    2. *sentence fragment—Living alone in the mountains, the couple make their own furniture and clothes.*

1. catching the baseball with both hands   **1.** frag.
2. in the back of the storeroom stands a stack of boxes.   **2.** sent.
3. a long, narrow passage with a hidden trapdoor at each end   **3.** frag.
4. after waiting for six hours   **4.** frag.
5. the gymnasium is open.   **5.** sent.
6. last night there were six television commercials every half-hour.   **6.** sent.
7. instead of calling the doctor this morning about her sore throat   **7.** frag.
8. beneath the tall ceiling of the church   **8.** frag.
9. are you careful about shutting off unnecessary lights?   **9.** sent.
10. doing the multiplication tables   **10.** frag.

General Strategies. If students are having trouble recognizing the differences between complete sentences and sentence fragments, you may want to provide more oral examples. Some students are better at hearing the differences than they are at recognizing them in print. For example, you could read aloud "a picture of the city at night" and "A picture of the city at night won first prize in the photography contest." Ask students which one sounds complete.

EXERCISE 2

Identifying Sentences and Sentence Fragments

Tell whether each group of words is a *sentence* or a *sentence fragment*.

EXAMPLES [1] Can you name the famous American woman in the picture below?
1. *sentence*

[2] A woman who made history.
2. *sentence fragment*

1. sent.
2. frag.
3. sent.
4. frag.

5. sent.
6. frag.
7. frag.
8. sent.

9. sent.
10. sent.
11. frag.
12. frag.
13. sent.
14. frag.
15. sent.
16. frag.

[1] One of the best-known women in American history is Sacagawea. [2] A member of the Lemhi band of the Shoshones. [3] She is famous for her role as interpreter for the Lewis and Clark expedition. [4] Which was seeking the Northwest Passage. [5] In 1800, the Lemhis had encountered a war party of the Hidatsa. [6] Who captured some of the Lemhis, including Sacagawea. [7] Later, with Charbonneau, her French Canadian husband, and their two-month-old son. [8] Sacagawea joined the Lewis and Clark expedition in what is now North Dakota. [9] Her knowledge of many languages enabled the explorers to communicate with various peoples. [10] Sacagawea also searched for plants that were safe to eat. [11] And once saved valuable instruments during a storm. [12] As they traveled farther. [13] The explorers came across the Lemhis. [14] From whom Sacagawea had been separated years before. [15] The Lemhis helped the explorers. [16] By giving them guidance.

VISUAL CONNECTIONS
Related Expression Skills.
Have groups of three create dialogues between Sacagawea and some other member of the Lewis and Clark expedition. One student could write down the group's ideas, and the other two students could perform the dialogue.

Brainstorm with your students before they begin, and list on the chalkboard ideas for possible conversational topics. Remind students that people often speak in sentence fragments. You may want to have each group identify the sentence fragments in its dialogue.

408

The Granger Collection, New York.

LESSON 3 (pp. 409–417)
THE SUBJECT AND
THE PREDICATE Rules 13b–13d

OBJECTIVES
- To identify complete subjects and complete predicates in sentences
- To create sentences with given subjects and predicates

The Subject and the Predicate **409**

13b

17. frag. **18.** sent.

[17] After they returned from the expedition. [18] Clark tried to settle Sacagawea and Charbonneau in St. Louis. [19] However, the couple moved back to Sacagawea's native land. [20] Where this famous woman died in 1812.

19. sent. **20.** frag.

 EXERCISE 3 **Writing Interesting Sentences**

Revise each sentence fragment by adding words to make an interesting sentence.

EXAMPLE **1.** At the last minute.
    1. *At the last minute, her parachute opened*.

1. on the last day of summer
2. found only in the country
3. a graceful ballerina
4. burning out of control
5. the old building by the lake

The Subject and the Predicate

A sentence consists of two parts: a *subject* and a *predicate*.

13b. A *subject* tells whom or what the sentence is about. The *predicate* tells something about the subject. A complete subject or a complete predicate may be only one word or more than one word.

EXAMPLES
comp. subj. | comp. pred.
Christopher | ran the mile in record time.

comp. subj. | comp. pred.
Three jars on the shelf | exploded.

comp. subj. | comp. pred.
A large silver poodle | won first prize.

Usually, the subject comes before the predicate. Sometimes, however, the subject may appear elsewhere in the sentence. To find the subject of a sentence, ask *Who?* or *What?* before the predicate.

GRAMMAR

GRAMMAR

ANSWERS
Exercise 3
Revises will vary, but be sure students have written complete sentences. Check for capital letters and end punctuation.

PROGRAM MANAGER

THE SUBJECT AND THE PREDICATE
- **Independent Practice/ Reteaching** For instruction and exercises, see **Complete Subjects and Predicates** and **Simple Subjects and Predicates** in *Language Skills Practice and Assessment,* pp. 14–15.
- **Computer Guided Instruction** For additional instruction and practice with the subject and the predicate, see **Lessons 32** and **33** in *Language Workshop CD-ROM.*
- **Practice** To help less-advanced students with additional instruction and practice with the subject and the predicate, see **Chapter 10** in *English Workshop, Second Course,* pp. 79–82.

QUICK REMINDER
Write the following sentences on the chalkboard. Have students tell whether the underlined group of words is the complete subject or the complete predicate.

1. A strong, agile running back <u>charged through the defensive line.</u> [predicate]
2. During half time, <u>our marching band</u> performed. [subject]
3. Julio <u>made a touchdown in the final ten seconds.</u> [predicate]

409

- To distinguish between simple subjects and complete subjects of sentences
- To distinguish between complete predicates and verbs in sentences
- To identify the verbs or verb phrases in sentences

ADVANCED STUDENTS

Challenge students to find examples of sentences in which the order of the subject and verb is inverted. Suggest that students explore various media—newspapers, magazines, novels, and books of poetry. Remind students that reversing the order of the subject and the verb is a good way to add variety to their sentences.

STUDENTS WITH SPECIAL NEEDS

Students with visual-perceptual problems often have difficulty copying blocks of material. You could simplify **Exercise 4** by transferring the paragraph to individual sheets on which students can write. If possible, double-space between the lines of text to make the paragraph easier to read. Then students can draw the horizontal lines to separate the subjects and predicates without wasting time laboriously copying the sentences.

LEARNING STYLES

Visual Learners. You may want to introduce diagraming to help students see the relationship between subjects and predicates in sentences. Refer students to the diagraming information in the **Appendix.**

GRAMMAR

410 *The Sentence*

EXAMPLES **A bird's nest** sat at the top of the tree. [What sat at the top of the tree? A bird's nest sat there.]
Laughing and running down the street were **two small boys.** [Who were laughing and running down the street? Two small boys were.]
Can **horses** and **cattle** swim? [What can swim? Horses and cattle can swim.]

EXERCISE 4 **Identifying Subjects and Predicates**

Write the following sentences. Separate the complete subject from the complete predicate with a vertical line.

EXAMPLE [1] Legends and folk tales have been repeated and enjoyed throughout the Americas.
1. *Legends and folk tales | have been repeated and enjoyed throughout the Americas.*

[1] The Chorotega people|lived in Nicoya, Costa Rica, hundreds of years ago. [2] One Chorotega folk tale|tells the story of the Chorotegan treasure and praises Princess Nosara for protecting it from the Chirenos. [3] Chireno warriors|landed, according to the story, on the Nicoya Peninsula and attacked the Chorotegas. [4] The Chorotegas|were surprised but reacted quickly. [5] Princess Nosara| grabbed the treasure and ran to her friend's house for help. [6] Nosara and he|took a bow and some arrows and fled into the woods. [7] The couple|ran from the enemy all night and at last reached a river. [8] The brave girl|dashed into the mountains alone, hid the treasure, and returned to the river. [9] Chireno warriors|attacked shortly after her return, however, and killed the princess and her friend. [10] The murderous Chirenos|searched for the treasure but never found it.

EXERCISE 5 **Identifying Complete Subjects and Complete Predicates**

When you were younger, did you ever play mix-and-match animal games? In those games, players combine pictures of the head and upper body of one animal with the lower body and feet of another animal to make funny-looking creatures. You can play the same kind of mix-and-match game with sentence parts. Here are five complete subjects and five complete predicates that are all mixed up. Match each subject with a predicate to create sentences. Use any combination you want, but use each one only once. Be sure to capitalize and punctuate each sentence correctly. Then, draw a line between the complete subject and the complete predicate.

EXAMPLE **1.** a blue whale feeling happy
  likes to sing and dance
  1. *A blue whale feeling happy* |*likes to sing and dance.*

the purple elephant in the airport
screeched to a stop in front of the school
looked at my brother and sneezed
three opossums standing perfectly still
ate our telephone book and asked for more
a bird with wings twice as long as your arms
a noisy snail named Speedy
is sitting on my sandwich
the red and black frogs on the table
was reading the Help Wanted ads in the newspaper

The Simple Subject

13c. A *simple subject* is the main word in the complete subject.

EXAMPLES **My date** for the dance | arrived late. [The complete subject is *My date for the dance.*]
  The long, hard **trip** across the desert | was finally over. [The complete subject is *The long, hard trip across the desert.*]
  Pacing back and forth in the cage was | a hungry **tiger.** [The complete subject is *a hungry tiger.*]

ANSWERS
Exercise 5

Responses will vary. Here are some possibilities:

1. The purple elephant in the airport | was reading the Help Wanted ads in the newspaper.

2. A noisy snail named Speedy | screeched to a stop in front of the school.

3. Three opossums standing perfectly still | looked at my brother and sneezed.

4. The red and black frogs on the table | ate our telephone book and asked for more.

5. A bird with wings twice as large as your arms | is sitting on my sandwich.

COMMON ERROR

Problem. Students might mistake the object of a preposition for the subject of a sentence.

Solution. Suggest to students that the first step in analyzing a sentence should be to put brackets around all of the prepositional phrases. The brackets indicate that the phrases are modifiers and do not contain essential parts of the sentence. This procedure should remind students to look for the subject of the sentence outside the brackets. You may want to refer students to the list of prepositions on p. 474.

COOPERATIVE LEARNING

Divide the class into groups of three and set a time limit in which each group must compose the longest complete simple sentence they can. Tell students to add modifiers and prepositional phrases but to include only one subject and one verb.

When the time is up, have someone from each group write the sentence on the chalkboard. Have other members of the class identify the simple subject and the verb.

412

The simple subject may consist of more than one word.

EXAMPLES **Stamp collecting** is my father's hobby.
Looney Tunes is my favorite cartoon show on television.
Ann Richards was elected governor of Texas.

The simple subjects in these examples are all compound nouns.

☞ REFERENCE NOTE: For more information on compound nouns, see page 432.

NOTE: In this book, the term *subject* refers to the simple subject unless otherwise indicated.

▶ EXERCISE 6 **Identifying Complete Subjects and Simple Subjects**

Identify the *complete subject* and the *simple subject* in each sentence of the following paragraph.

EXAMPLE [1] The teams in the picture on the next page compete in the Caribbean Baseball Leagues.
1. complete subject—*The teams in the picture on the next page;* simple subject—*teams*

[1] People throughout Latin America enjoy going out to a ballgame. [2] The all-American sport of baseball has been very popular there for a long time. [3] In fact, fans in countries such as Cuba, Panama, and Venezuela go wild over the game. [4] As a result, the Caribbean Baseball Leagues were formed more than fifty years ago. [5] Each year the teams in Latin America play toward a season championship. [6] That championship is known as the Caribbean World Series. [7] A total of more than one hundred players compete in the series. [8] Many talented Latin American players are recruited by major United States teams each year. [9] The list of these players includes such baseball greats as Fernando Valenzuela, Ramón Martinez, and José Canseco. [10] In addition, a number of U.S. players train in the Latin American winter leagues.

The Simple Predicate, or Verb

13d. A *simple predicate,* or *verb,* is the main word or group of words in the complete predicate.

In the following examples, the vertical lines separate the complete subjects from the complete predicates.

EXAMPLES   comp. subj.   comp. pred.
The popular movie star | **signed** autographs for hours.

comp. subj.   comp. pred.
The trees | **sagged** beneath the weight of the ice.

A simple predicate may be a one-word verb, or it may be a verb phrase. A *verb phrase* consists of a main verb and its helping verbs.

EXAMPLES   comp. subj.   comp. pred.
Our class | **is reading** the famous novel *Frankenstein.*

comp. subj.   comp. pred.
The musicians | **have been rehearsing** since noon.

comp. subj.   comp. pred.
Those books | **will** not **be** available in the media center until next week.

INTEGRATING THE LANGUAGE ARTS

Literature Link. Consider giving students different examples of subject-verb order from literature. For example, have the class read and discuss Shakespeare's "When Icicles Hang by the Wall" from *Love's Labor's Lost*. The first five lines of each stanza follow a common subject-verb order. The sixth line reverses the pattern ("Then nightly sings the staring owl").

Other examples of poetry with reversed order are John Greenleaf Whittier's "Barbara Frietchie" and Henry Wadsworth Longfellow's "The Song of Hiawatha." Discuss with students the effect that reversed word order has. [It produces rhythm and variety, and it shifts the emphasis to different words.]

The words *not* and *never*, which are frequently used with verbs, are not part of a verb phrase. Both of these words are adverbs.

EXAMPLES She | **did** not **believe** me.
The two cousins | **had** never **met.**

☞ REFERENCE NOTE: For more information about verb phrases, see pages 464–465.

A *complete predicate* consists of a verb and all the words that describe the verb and complete its meaning. Sometimes the complete predicate can appear at the beginning of a sentence.

EXAMPLE **On the tiny branch perched** | a chickadee.

Part of the predicate may appear on one side of the subject and the rest on the other side.

EXAMPLE **Before winter** many birds **fly south.**

NOTE: In this book, the term *verb* refers to the simple predicate unless otherwise indicated.

▶ EXERCISE 7 **Identifying Complete Predicates and Verbs**

Identify the <u>complete predicate</u> and the <u>verb</u> in each of the following sentences. Keep in mind that parts of the complete predicate may come before and after the complete subject.

EXAMPLE 1. A ton and a half of groceries may seem like a big order for a family of five.
1. *complete predicate—may seem like a big order for a family of five; verb—may seem*

1. Such a big order <u>is possible in the village of Pang</u>.
2. This small village <u>is located near the Arctic Circle</u>.
3. The people of Pang <u>receive their groceries once a year</u>.
4. A supply ship <u>can visit Pang only during a short time each summer</u>.

OBJECTIVES
- To identify the subjects and verbs in sentences
- To write complete sentences with given subjects or predicates

5. <u>In spring</u>, families <u>order their year's supply of groceries by mail</u>.
6. The huge order <u>is delivered to Pang a few months later</u>.
7. The people <u>store the groceries in their homes</u>.
8. Frozen food <u>is kept outdoors</u>.
9. <u>Too costly for most residents is</u> the air-freight charge for a grocery shipment to Pang.
10. Villagers <u>also must hunt and fish for much of their food</u>.

▶ EXERCISE 8   **Identifying Verbs and Verb Phrases**

Identify the *verb* or *verb phrase* in each of the following sentences.

EXAMPLE   [1] Samuel Pepys (pēps) was an English government worker.
　　　　　1. *was*

[1] Between 1660 and 1669, Samuel Pepys <u>kept</u> a diary. [2] He <u>wrote</u> the diary in a secret shorthand. [3] This secret shorthand <u>was</u> finally <u>decoded</u> after many years of hard work. [4] In 1825, *The Diary of Samuel Pepys* <u>was published</u>. [5] <u>Presented</u> in the diary <u>is</u> a personal look at life in England during the seventeenth century. [6] In many entries Pepys <u>told</u> about his family and friends. [7] Some of these accounts <u>are</u> quite humorous. [8] In other entries Pepys <u>described</u> very serious events. [9] For example, in entries during 1666, Pepys <u>gave</u> a detailed account of the Great Fire of London. [10] What other events <u>might be described</u> in the diary?

▶ REVIEW A   **Identifying Subjects and Verbs**

Identify the *subject* and the *verb* in each of the following sentences.

EXAMPLE   [1] In Greek mythology, Medusa was a horrible monster.
　　　　　1. *subject—Medusa; verb—was*

[1] On Medusa's head <u>grew</u> <u>snakes</u> instead of hair. [2] According to Greek myth, a <u>glance</u> at Medusa <u>would turn</u> a mortal into stone. [3] However, one proud <u>mortal</u>, named Perseus, <u>went</u> in search of Medusa. [4] Fortunately, <u>he</u> <u>received</u> help from the goddess Athena and the god Hermes. [5] From Athena, <u>Perseus</u> <u>accepted</u> a shiny shield. [6] With Hermes as his guide, <u>Perseus</u> soon <u>found</u> Medusa. [7] <u>He</u> <u>knew</u> about Medusa's power. [8] Therefore, <u>he</u> <u>did</u> not <u>look</u> directly at her. [9] Instead, <u>he</u> <u>saw</u> her reflection in the shiny shield. [10] The <u>picture</u> below <u>shows</u> Perseus's victory over the evil Medusa.

VISUAL CONNECTIONS
Exploring the Subject. Medusa wasn't always the horrible monster she is famous for being. According to Greek myth, she was once a beautiful woman who made Athena, one of the Greek deities, angry. It was Athena who turned Medusa into the most famous of the monsters known as Gorgons.

▶ REVIEW B   **Writing Sentences**

Some of the following word groups are complete subjects and some are complete predicates. Write each word group, adding the part needed to make a sentence. Then, underline the <u>subject</u> once and the <u>verb</u> twice.

Completed sentences will vary.

EXAMPLE   **1.** marched for five hours
          1. *The <u>members</u> of the band <u>marched</u> for five hours.*

1. <u>should</u> not <u>be left</u> alone   **1.** comp. pred.
2. the vacant <u>lot</u> down the street   **2.** comp. subj.
3. <u>danced</u> across the floor   **3.** comp. pred.
4. <u>looked</u> mysteriously at us   **4.** comp. pred.
5. their best <u>player</u>   **5.** comp. subj.
6. the famous <u>movie star</u>   **6.** comp. subj.

OBJECTIVES

- To write detailed sentences from given sentence bases
- To identify subjects, verbs, compound subjects, and compound verbs in sentences
- To write descriptive sentences, some with compound subjects or compound verbs

The Subject and the Predicate **417**

7. <u>is going</u> to the game   7. comp. pred.
8. <u>one</u> of the Jackson twins   8. comp. subj.
9. <u>could have been left</u> on the bus   9. comp. pred.
10. the neighborhood watch <u>group</u>   10. comp. subj.

GRAMMAR

The Sentence Base

Because a subject and a verb are the essential parts of a sentence, they are called the *sentence base.* All the other words in a sentence are attached to the sentence base.

Sentence base: **Dogs play.**
Sentence base with other words attached: Every day two frisky **dogs** named Bison and Stark **play** for hours on our lawn.

The additional words give informative details, but they would be meaningless without the sentence base.

 EXERCISE 9   **Using the Sentence Base to Write Complete Sentences**

How would you send an urgent message to someone? Today, you might use a facsimile (fax) machine, a telephone, or a computer. You could also send a telegram. In 1837, Samuel F. B. Morse invented the first telegraph machine for sending messages electronically. Telegraph messages, called telegrams, are usually short because the number of words in a message determines the cost of sending it.

Your family has just received this telegram from your uncle who is coming to visit. Add words to each sentence base in this message to fill in details about what happened.   Responses will vary. Encourage students to add specific details.

CAR BROKE DOWN. DOG FAINTED. HELP ARRIVED. CAR REPAIRED. WE ARRIVE SUNDAY.

EXAMPLE   **1.** BAD LUCK CONTINUES.
   1. *Our bad luck on this vacation continues to cost us time and money.*

PROGRAM MANAGER

THE SENTENCE BASE

- **Independent Practice/ Reteaching** For instruction and exercises, see **Expanding Sentence Bases** and **Compound Subjects and Verbs** in *Language Skills Practice and Assessment,* pp. 16–17.

- **Computer Guided Instruction** For additional instruction and practice with compound subjects and compound verbs, see **Lessons 32** and **33** in *Language Workshop CD-ROM.*

- **Practice** To help less-advanced students with additional instruction and practice with compound subjects and compound verbs, see **Chapter 10** in *English Workshop, Second Course,* pp. 83–84.

QUICK REMINDER

Write the following sentence base on the chalkboard and have students add details:

Sparks flashed.

Remind students that the verb *flashed* can have an additional subject [Lightning and sparks from the fireworks flashed at the same time.] and that the subject can have more than one verb [Sparks flashed and danced before our eyes.]. Ask volunteers to share their sentences with the class.

GRAMMAR

417

GRAMMAR

GRAMMAR

The Compound Subject

13e. A *compound subject* consists of two or more connected subjects that have the same verb. The usual connecting words are *and* and *or*.

EXAMPLES **Keshia** and **Todd** worked a jigsaw puzzle.
Either **Carmen** or **Ernesto** will videotape the ceremony tomorrow.
Among the guest speakers were an **astronaut,** an **engineer,** and a **journalist.**

 EXERCISE 10 **Identifying Compound Subjects and Their Verbs**

Identify the <u>compound subject</u> and the <u>verb</u> in each of the following sentences.

EXAMPLE **1.** Festivals and celebrations are happy times throughout the world.
1. *compound subject—Festivals, celebrations; verb—are*

1. <u>Children</u> and <u>nature</u> <u>are honored</u> with their own festivals in Japan.
2. Among Japanese nature festivals <u>are</u> the <u>Cherry Blossom Festival</u> and the <u>Chrysanthemum Festival</u>.
3. Fierce <u>dragons</u> and huge <u>ships</u> <u>fly</u> in the sky during Singapore's Kite Festival.
4. Elaborate <u>masks</u> and <u>costumes</u> <u>are</u> an important part of the Carnival Lamayote in Haïti.
5. <u>Flowers</u> and other small <u>gifts</u> <u>are presented</u> to teachers during Teacher's Day in the Czech Republic.
6. Brave <u>knights</u> and their <u>ladies</u> <u>return</u> each year to the medieval festival at Ribeauvillé, France.
7. During Sweden's Midsommar (midsummer) Festival, <u>maypoles</u> and <u>buildings</u> <u>bloom</u> with fresh flowers.
8. <u>Wrestling</u> and pole <u>climbing</u> <u>attract</u> crowds to the Tatar Festival of the Plow in Russia.

9. <u>Games</u>, <u>dances</u>, and <u>feasts</u> <u>highlight</u> the Green Corn Dance of the Seminole Indians of the Florida Everglades.
10. In Munich, Germany, <u>floats</u> and <u>bandwagons</u> <u>add</u> color to the Oktoberfest Parade.

The Compound Verb

13f. A *compound verb* consists of two or more verbs that have the same subject.

A connecting word—usually *and, or,* or *but*—is used between the verbs.

EXAMPLES The dog **barked** and **growled** at the stranger.
We **can go** forward, **go** back, or **stay** right here.
The man **was convicted** but later **was found** innocent of the crime.

EXERCISE 11 **Identifying Subjects and Compound Verbs**

Identify the *subject* and the *compound verb* in each of the following sentences.

EXAMPLE **1.** The hikers loaded their backpacks and studied the map of the mountain trails.
1. *subject—hikers; compound verb—loaded, studied*

1. <u>Linda</u> <u>wrote</u> her essay and <u>practiced</u> the piano last night.
2. <u>Miami</u> <u>is</u> the largest city in southern Florida and <u>has been</u> a popular resort area since the 1920s.
3. According to Greek mythology, <u>Arachne</u> <u>angered</u> Athena and <u>was changed</u> into a spider.
4. <u>Martina Arroyo</u> <u>has sung</u> in major American opera halls and <u>has made</u> appearances abroad.
5. This year the <u>Wildcats</u> <u>won</u> seven games and <u>lost</u> five.

A DIFFERENT APPROACH

This activity gives students extra practice using compound subjects and compound verbs. It might appeal to students who follow the lives of popular entertainers.

Have the class brainstorm a list of television, movie, and music stars. Then have each student write ten sentences of dialogue in which entertainers interact. Encourage students to use compound subjects and compound verbs in their dialogues. You may need to review the punctuation rules for direct quotations in **Chapter 27: "Punctuation."**

EXERCISE 12

Teaching Note. You may want to remind students that some verbs are combined with other words to form idiomatic phrases often referred to as phrasal verbs. For example, *make up* in the first sentence and *grew up* in the sixth sentence are considered phrasal verbs. If students have questions, encourage them to consult dictionaries.

6. During special sales, <u>shoppers</u> <u>arrive</u> early at the mall and <u>search</u> for bargains.
7. <u>Maria Montessori</u> <u>studied</u> medicine in Italy and <u>developed</u> new methods for teaching children.
8. <u>Jim Rice</u> <u>autographed</u> baseballs and <u>made</u> a short speech.
9. <u>General Lee</u> <u>won</u> many battles but <u>lost</u> the war.
10. In the summer many <u>students</u> <u>go</u> to music camps or <u>take</u> music lessons.

Both the subject and the verb of a sentence may be compound. In such a sentence, each subject goes with each verb.

EXAMPLE   The **captain** and the **crew battled** the storm and

hoped for better weather. [The captain battled and hoped, and the crew battled and hoped.]

EXERCISE 12   **Identifying Compound Subjects and Compound Verbs**

Identify the *subjects* and the *verbs* in each sentence in the following paragraph.

EXAMPLE   [1] In the picture on the next page, Aaron Neville and his brothers are performing at the New Orleans Jazz Festival.
1. *subjects—Aaron Neville, brothers; verb—are performing*

[1] <u>Aaron</u> and his <u>brothers</u> (Art, Charles, and Cyril) <u>make up</u> the Neville Brothers. [2] The four <u>brothers</u> <u>play</u> different instruments and <u>have</u> their own individual styles. [3] <u>They</u> <u>formed</u> their act and <u>started</u> singing together in 1977. [4] Before then, the <u>brothers</u> <u>performed</u> and <u>toured</u> separately. [5] <u>New Orleans</u> <u>is</u> their hometown and <u>has influenced</u> their music. [6] <u>They</u> <u>grew up</u> hearing music at home and <u>found</u> it everywhere. [7] New Orleans gospel <u>sounds</u> and jazz <u>rhythms</u> <u>fill</u> the brothers' songs. [8] The four <u>brothers</u> <u>have</u> strong opinions and often <u>sing</u>

WRITING APPLICATION

OBJECTIVE

- To write a journal entry with complete sentences

The Subject and the Predicate **421**

about social issues. [9] *Yellow Moon* and *Brother's Keeper* are two of their most popular albums. [10] The children and grandchildren of the Neville Brothers have now joined in this family's musical tradition.

EXERCISE 13 **Writing Sentences and Identifying Subjects and Verbs**

Write ten sentences describing the major characters and actions in your favorite book or movie. Include at least two compound subjects and two compound verbs. Underline each subject once and each verb twice.

EXAMPLE **1.** *Bilbo Baggins and the dwarves travel to the Lonely Mountain in* The Hobbit.

WRITING APPLICATION

Using Subjects and Predicates to Express Whole Thoughts

Peanut butter and jelly, socks and shoes—what do they have in common? They are pairs of things that work together. A subject and a predicate are another working pair. You've got to use both of them to form a sentence that clearly expresses a whole thought.

SUBJECT	Alvin's new hamster
PREDICATE	ran in its exercise wheel all night long.
SENTENCE	Alvin's new hamster ran in its exercise wheel all night long.

MEETING individual NEEDS

AT-RISK STUDENTS

Cooperative learning has proven to be an effective instructional method for at-risk students. Therefore, you may want to have students work in pairs to complete **Exercise 13.** Encourage students to share ideas and to exchange papers for proofreading.

ANSWERS
Exercise 13

Sentences will vary. Students will be writing about books and movies, so look for correct punctuation of titles.

WRITING APPLICATION

This assignment asks students to write journal entries about real or imagined experiences with pets. Before students write, you may want to remind them that the point of view used in expressive writing is first person. In addition, natural language and words that express feelings are characteristics of expressive writing.

421

OBJECTIVES
- To classify and punctuate sentences according to purpose
- To write the four kinds of sentences and to punctuate the sentences correctly

GRAMMAR

CRITICAL THINKING
Synthesis. As students revise their paragraphs, have them check to see that they have arranged the events in a logical order. The most obvious choice is chronological order, but dramatic effect or humor may be achieved by stating the outcome at the beginning and then filling in the preceding events. Students should be able to explain the logic of their sequence of events.

TIMESAVER
To save time grading the writing assignment, you could provide the following peer-evaluation guidelines:

1. Underline simple subjects once.
2. Underline verbs twice.
3. Circle any spelling or punctuation errors.
4. Place a check (√) beside the best point or idea.
5. Place a question mark (?) beside a confusing idea.

Have students exchange papers to complete the five evaluative steps.

PROGRAM MANAGER

KINDS OF SENTENCES

- **Independent Practice/ Reteaching** For instruction and exercises, see **Kinds of Sentences** in *Language Skills Practice and Assessment,* p. 18.

- **Computer Guided Instruction** For additional instruction and practice, see **Lesson 39** in *Language Workshop CD-ROM.*

- **Practice** To help less-advanced students, see **Chapter 10** in *English Workshop, Second Course,* pp. 77–78.

422

GRAMMAR

422 *The Sentence*

▶ WRITING ACTIVITY
Your best friend is on vacation, and you are pet-sitting. Write a paragraph in your journal about your experiences taking care of your friend's pet.

Prewriting   You could write about a pet you know or one that is unfamiliar to you. Jot down notes about the pet you choose. Then, think about what you might do or what might happen while you're taking care of the pet.

Writing   As you write your first draft, think about how to organize your notes and your thoughts. Tell about your experiences in a logical order, and use complete sentences. Your tone can be humorous or serious.

Evaluating and Revising   Read through your paragraph to be sure that each sentence has a subject and a predicate. Does your paragraph tell about your experience in an interesting way? Add, delete, or rearrange details to make your paragraph more entertaining or informative.

Proofreading   Read over your paragraph once more, looking for errors in punctuation, spelling, and capitalization. The names of kinds or breeds of domestic animals aren't capitalized unless they contain a proper noun or adjective, as in *English setter.*

Kinds of Sentences

13g.   A *declarative sentence* makes a statement. It is followed by a period.

EXAMPLES   Miriam Colón founded the Puerto Rican Traveling Theatre**.**
Curiosity is the beginning of knowledge**.**

13
g–j

GRAMMAR

13h. An *interrogative sentence* asks a question. It is followed by a question mark.

EXAMPLES   **What do you know about glaciers?**
Was the game exciting?

13i. An *imperative sentence* gives a command or makes a request. It is followed by a period. A strong command is followed by an exclamation point.

EXAMPLES   **Do your homework each night.**
John, please close the door.
Watch out!

If an imperative sentence does not have a subject, the "understood" subject is always *you.*

> **(You) Do your homework each night.**
> **John, (you) please close the door.**
> **(You) Watch out!**

13j. An *exclamatory sentence* shows excitement or expresses strong feeling. It is followed by an exclamation point.

EXAMPLES   **What a sight the sunset is!**
Sarah won the VCR!

NOTE: Many people overuse exclamation points. In your own writing, save exclamation points for sentences that really do show strong emotion. When it is overused, this mark of punctuation loses its impact.

▶ EXERCISE 14   **Classifying Sentences**

Classify each of the following sentences according to its purpose.   decl. = declarative   excl. = exclamatory
int. = interrogative   imp. = imperative

EXAMPLE   **1. Let no man pull you so low as to make you hate him.**
Booker T. Washington, from *I Have a Dream*
1. *imperative*

GRAMMAR

OBJECTIVE

- To classify and punctuate sentences according to purpose

A DIFFERENT APPROACH

Have students bring in the comics from their Sunday papers, or keep a collection of your own for this and future assignments. Ask each student to collect comic strips that illustrate the four kinds of sentences. You may want to display these on a bulletin board if students collect many good examples of the different types of sentences.

MEETING individual NEEDS

LEARNING STYLES

Auditory Learners. Because voice inflection can indicate a sentence's purpose, you may want to read the sentences in **Review C** aloud.

AMENDMENTS TO SELECTIONS
Description of change: excerpted
Rationale: to focus on the concept of the kinds of sentences presented in this chapter

---

424 *The Sentence*

1. decl.   **1.** If all the beasts were gone, men would die from great loneliness of spirit, for whatever happens to the beasts also happens to the man.
> Chief Seattle, from his statement of surrender

2. decl.   **2.** No one can make you feel inferior without your consent.
> Eleanor Roosevelt, *This Is My Story*

3. int.   **3.** What happens to a dream deferred?
> Langston Hughes, "Harlem"

4. excl.   **4.** I know not what course others may take; but as for me, give me liberty or give me death!
> Patrick Henry, speech in the Virginia Convention of 1775

5. excl.   **5.** Look! Up in the sky! It's a bird! It's a plane! It's Superman!
> ™DC Comics Inc. All rights reserved. Used by permission of DC Comics Inc.

6. imp.   **6.** Join the union, girls, and together say *Equal Pay for Equal Work.*
> Susan B. Anthony, *The Revolution* (October 8, 1868)

7. int.   **7.** Why must everything work the same way for everybody?
> Denise Chávez, *The Flying Tortilla Man*

8. decl.   **8.** Peace is respect for the rights of others.
> Benito Juárez, from *The Kaleidoscopic Air*

9. decl.   **9.** The history of every country begins in the heart of a man or woman.
> Willa Cather, *O Pioneers!*

10. excl.   **10.** He who has courage and faith will never perish in misery!
> Anne Frank, *Anne Frank: The Diary of a Young Girl*

▶ REVIEW C   **Classifying Sentences**

Choose the appropriate end punctuation for each sentence. Classify each sentence according to its purpose.

EXAMPLE   **1.** Turn left at the corner   decl. = declarative
             1. *period—imperative*   int. = interrogative
                                    excl. = exclamatory
                                    imp. = imperative

1. Alana bought some angelfish for her aquarium   **1.** decl.

2. How many times has our track team won the state championship**?**   **2.** int.
3. Imagine a ride in the space shuttle.   **3.** imp. [3. *or* ! excl.]
4. Because of its ruffled "collar," the frilled lizard looks like a comical monster.   **4.** decl.
5. Can you give me directions to the post office**?**   **5.** int.
6. How fresh the air feels after a storm**!**   **6.** excl.
7. Think about both sides of the problem.   **7.** imp.
8. Many large museums in the United States display pottery made by Maria Martinez.   **8.** decl.
9. What teams are playing in the World Series**?**   **9.** int.
10. What a fantastic world lies beneath the waves**!**   **10.** excl.

PICTURE THIS

You are a member of the City Improvement Committee. Each month the committee awards a prize to the person who has done the most to improve the city's appearance. Your job is to rate this sculpture and report back to the rest of the committee. Miriam Schapiro designed this large, outdoor sculpture called *Anna and David.* The two dancing figures are made of painted stainless steel and aluminum. Write five sentences about the sculpture, giving your opinion of it. Use each of the four kinds of sentences at least once, and punctuate them correctly.

Miriam Schapiro, *Anna and David* (1987).
Painted stainless steel and aluminum,
35' × 31' × 9". Courtesy Steinbaum-Krauss
Gallery, NYC.

GRAMMAR

PICTURE THIS
Before students write, you may want to have the class develop a set of criteria by which to evaluate the sculpture. After students have completed the assignment, ask volunteers to share their opinions of the sculpture with the rest of the class.

 ## VISUAL CONNECTIONS
Anna and David
About the Artist. Miriam Schapiro was born in Toronto, Canada, in 1923. Her works have appeared in the nation's top galleries and museums, including the National Gallery of Art in Washington, D.C.

GRAMMAR

425

LESSON 6 *(pp. 426–428)*

REVIEW: POSTTESTS 1 and 2

OBJECTIVES

- To identify complete sentences and sentence fragments
- To revise sentence fragments to form complete sentences
- To identify complete subjects, complete predicates, simple subjects, and verbs in sentences

426 *The Sentence*

Subject:	outdoor sculpture
Audience:	City Improvement Committee members
Purpose:	to give your comments and opinions

Review: Posttest 1

A. Identifying Sentences and Sentence Fragments

Identify each group of words as a *sentence* or a *sentence fragment*. If the word group is a sentence fragment, correct it by adding words to make a complete sentence.

Revisions of sentence fragments will vary.

EXAMPLES
1. Do you like the U.S. Postal Service's special postage stamps?
   1. *sentence*

   2. When my parents buy stamps.
   2. *sentence fragment—When my parents buy stamps, they ask for new commemorative ones.*

1. Commemorative stamps are issued to give special recognition to someone or something.   **1.** sent.   **2.** frag.
2. Stamps with pictures of animals or famous people.
3. A block of four different stamps that commemorate Earth Day.   **3.** frag.
4. All four of the winning designs for the Earth Day 1995 stamp were created by young people.   **4.** sent.
5. Since I like "Love" stamps and holiday stamps.   **5.** frag.

B. Identifying Subjects and Predicates

Label each italicized group of words as the *complete subject* or the *complete predicate* of the sentence. Then, identify the <u>simple subject</u> or the <u>verb</u> in each word group.

426

- To classify and punctuate sentences according to purpose
- To write sentences based upon given guidelines

EXAMPLES **1.** *Anyone searching for the world's highest mountains* must look on land and in the sea.
1. *complete subject; simple subject—Anyone*

2. Anyone searching for the world's highest mountains *must look on land and in the sea.*
2. *complete predicate; verb—must look*

6. <u>*Much of the earth's surface*</u> is mountainous. **6.** comp. subj.

7. <u>*Can*</u> you <u>*name*</u> the world's highest mountain? **7.** comp. pred.

8. <u>*Mount Everest*</u>, which is in the Himalayas, claims that title. **8.** comp. subj.

9. In fact, <u>*seven of the world's highest mountains*</u> are in the Himalayan mountain range. **9.** comp. subj.

10. Mount Everest <u>*towers*</u> to a height of 29,028 feet above sea level. **10.** comp. pred.

11. *The* <u>*Alps*</u> *in Europe, the* <u>*Rockies*</u> *in North America, and the* <u>*Andes*</u> *in South America* are other high mountain ranges. **11.** comp. subj.

12. Many high mountains *also* <u>*have been discovered*</u> under the ocean. **12.** comp. pred.

13. Down the middle of the Atlantic Ocean floor runs *the earth's longest continuous* <u>*mountain range*</u>. **13.** comp. subj.

14. The peaks of some undersea mountains <u>*rise*</u> above the surface of the water and <u>*form*</u> islands. **14.** comp. pred.

15. In the Pacific Ocean, *the* <u>*islands*</u> *of Hawaii* are actually the peaks of submerged mountains that are part of a 1,600-mile-long chain. **15.** comp. subj.

C. Classifying Sentences

Classify each of the following sentences as <u>*declarative*</u>, <u>*interrogative*</u>, <u>*imperative*</u>, or <u>*exclamatory*</u>. Then, write the <u>last word</u> of each sentence and provide the appropriate end punctuation.

EXAMPLE **1.** Write your name and the date at the top of your paper
1. *imperative—paper.*

INTEGRATING THE LANGUAGE ARTS

Literature Link. You may want to assign parts and have students read aloud a play such as *The Monkey's Paw*, dramatized by Louis N. Parker. Ask students to note the different kinds of sentences the playwright uses. Ask students why end punctuation is so important to the actors. [End punctuation dictates voice inflection.] Then have students discuss what a play comprising only declarative sentences might be like. [It would probably seem monotonous, with little excitement or feeling.]

16. Juana plans to study architecture at the state university after she <u>graduates</u>. **16.** decl.
17. This isn't the right answer, is <u>it</u>? **17.** int.
18. No, it definitely is <u>not</u>! **18.** excl.
19. Clean up your room this morning, and be sure to put your dirty clothes in the laundry <u>hamper</u>. **19.** imp. [19. or <u>hamper</u>!
20. I can't right now, Mom, because everybody is waiting for me at Andy's <u>house</u>. **20.** decl. [20. *or* <u>house</u>! excl.]

Review: Posttest 2

Writing a Variety of Sentences

Write your own sentences according to the following guidelines. Make the subjects and verbs different for each sentence.

EXAMPLE **1. an interrogative sentence with a single subject and a single verb**
1. *Is Danielle bringing dessert?*

1. a declarative sentence with a compound subject
2. an imperative sentence with a compound verb
3. a declarative sentence with a single subject and a single verb
4. an interrogative sentence with a compound subject
5. an interrogative sentence with a compound verb
6. an exclamatory sentence with a single subject and a single verb
7. an imperative sentence with a single subject and a single verb
8. a declarative sentence with a compound verb
9. an exclamatory sentence with a compound verb
10. a declarative sentence with a compound subject and a compound verb

---

MEETING *individual* NEEDS

LESS-ADVANCED STUDENTS

You could provide an alternative for **Review: Posttest 2** by including only one directive for each sentence students must write. For example:

1. Write a declarative sentence.
2. Write a sentence with a compound verb.

ANSWERS
Review: Posttest 2

Sentences will vary. Here are some possibilities:

1. Toni Morrison and Zora Neale Hurston are excellent modern writers.

2. Open the window and enjoy the fresh air.

3. My grandmother paints beautiful landscapes.

4. Have you or your friends ever seen the intriguing paintings of Frida Kahlo?

5. Does the museum open at noon and offer guided tours?

6. What a fabulous exhibit we saw!

7. Look at the pastels in this watercolor.

8. The storm began as expected and ended quickly.

9. The sky poured rain and thundered like never before!

10. Karla and her brother ran for cover and found shelter in a bus stop.

OBJECTIVE

• To identify nouns, pronouns, and adjectives in sentences

PROGRAM MANAGER

FOR THE WHOLE CHAPTER

■ Review For exercises on chapter concepts, see **Review Form A** and **Review Form B** in *Language Skills Practice and Assessment*, pp. 33–36.

■ Assessment For additional testing, see **Grammar Pretests** and **Grammar Mastery Tests** in *Language Skills Practice and Assessment*, pp. 1–8 and pp. 103–110.

GRAMMAR

GRAMMAR

14 THE PARTS OF SPEECH

Noun, Pronoun, Adjective

Diagnostic Test

Identifying Nouns, Pronouns, and Adjectives

Identify each <u>italicized word</u> in the following sentences as a *noun*, a *pronoun*, or an *adjective*.

EXAMPLE **1.** The biplane had two *wings* and a *wooden* propeller.
  1. *wings—noun; wooden—adjective*

1. Sometimes I don't feel well when <u>*it*</u> gets cloudy and the <u>*dark*</u> sky threatens rain. **1.** pro./adj.
2. My little sister, <u>*afraid*</u> of <u>*thunder*</u> and lightning, hid under the bed. **2.** adj./n.
3. Inger's mother gave <u>*each*</u> of us a glass of <u>*cold*</u> milk. **3.** pro./adj.
4. One by one, <u>*each*</u> husky ventured out into the <u>*cold*</u>. **4.** adj./n.
5. <u>*Who*</u> went to the movie <u>*Saturday*</u> night? **5.** pro./adj.
6. When <u>the *Neville Brothers*</u> came to town, we went to <u>*their*</u> concert. **6.** n./pro. [or adj.]

CHAPTER OVERVIEW

This chapter covers three of the eight parts of speech: nouns, pronouns, and adjectives. In the **Writing Application,** students are asked to write personal adventure stories by using a variety of pronouns.

You may want to refer to this chapter throughout the year because knowledge of the parts of speech can help students add variety to their writing. The section on adjectives may prove especially helpful with **Chapter 5: "Using Description."**

USING THE DIAGNOSTIC TEST

The **Diagnostic Test** consists of twenty sentences in which students are asked to identify nouns, pronouns, and adjectives. The results of the test will help you determine the needs of individual students and the areas that require teaching or review.

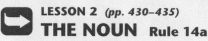

OBJECTIVES
- To identify nouns in sentences
- To identify compound nouns in sentences

430 *The Parts of Speech*

7. The house across the street has been up for *sale* since *Tuesday*. **7.** n./n.
8. *Diego Rivera* painted many *large* murals. **8.** n./adj.
9. *That* rifle doesn't belong to *anyone*. **9** adj./pro.
10. *That* is an *Aleut* mask. **10.** pro./adj.
11. Give me *some* iced *tea*, please. **11.** adj./n.
12. *Somebody* said that there would be no more *discount* movie tickets. **12.** pro./adj.
13. I got a *discount* on *our* tickets, though. **13.** n./pro. [*or* adj.]
14. *Mr. Taylor* donated the *sports* equipment. **14.** n./adj.
15. In high school, Carl Lewis excelled in *track* and several *other* sports. **15.** n./adj.
16. *Everyone* liked one painting or the *other*. **16.** pro./pro.
17. Juana went to the *mall* by *herself*. **17.** n./pro.
18. Hobbies take up so *much* time that they often become *work*. **18.** adj./n.
    19. adj./pro.
19. My aunt's *work* schedule often takes *her* out of town.
20. *This* parakeet screeches if he doesn't get *enough* seed.
    20. adj./adj.

	The Eight Parts of Speech		
noun	pronoun	verb	conjunction
adverb	adjective	preposition	interjection

The Noun

14a. A *noun* is a word used to name a person, a place, a thing, or an idea.

PERSONS	Alice Walker, Dr. Lacy, children, architect, team
PLACES	desert, neighborhood, outer space, New York City
THINGS	money, wind, animals, *Voyager 2*, Statue of Liberty
IDEAS	courage, love, freedom, luck, equality

PROGRAM MANAGER

THE NOUN

- **Independent Practice/ Reteaching** For instruction and exercises, see **The Noun** and **Types of Nouns** in *Language Skills Practice and Assessment,* pp. 27–28.

- **Computer Guided Instruction** For additional instruction and practice with nouns, see **Lesson 1** in *Language Workshop CD-ROM.*

- **Practice** To help less-advanced students with additional instruction and practice with nouns, see **Chapter 11** in *English Workshop, Second Course,* pp. 87–90.

QUICK REMINDER

Making four columns, write the following headings on the chalkboard.

Persons   Places   Things   Ideas

Have each student make a list of ten nouns that includes examples from each of the four categories.

Then ask volunteers to read nouns from their lists. Write the nouns in the proper column on the chalkboard. Some may fit into more than one category.

▶ EXERCISE 1   **Identifying Nouns**

Identify all of the <u>nouns</u> in each of the following sentences.

EXAMPLE   **1. Many Native American chiefs are known for their courage and wisdom.**
            1. *chiefs, courage, wisdom*

1. <u>Chief Joseph</u> of the <u>Nez Perce</u> was a wise <u>leader</u> whose American Indian <u>name</u> means "<u>Thunder Traveling over the Mountains</u>."
2. He was an educated <u>man</u> and wrote that his <u>people</u> believed in <u>speaking</u> only the <u>truth</u>.
3. In this <u>photograph</u>, <u>Satanta</u>, a Kiowa <u>chief</u>, wears a silver <u>medal</u> with the <u>profile</u> of <u>President James Buchanan</u> on it.
4. He wore the <u>medal</u> during a famous <u>council</u> for <u>peace</u> at <u>Medicine Lodge Creek</u> in <u>Kansas</u>.
5. In a moving <u>speech</u>, <u>Satanta</u> described the <u>love</u> that his <u>people</u> had for the <u>Great Plains</u> and the <u>buffalo</u>.
6. *<u>The Autobiography of Black Hawk</u>* is an interesting <u>book</u> by the Sauk <u>chief</u> who fought for <u>lands</u> in the <u>Mississippi Valley</u>.
7. Sitting Bull's <u>warriors</u> soundly defeated <u>General George A. Custer</u> and his <u>troops</u> at the <u>Battle of the Little Bighorn</u>.

MEETING *individual* NEEDS

LEP/ESL

General Strategies. Many languages have writing systems without capital letters. Because capital letters are one way to distinguish proper nouns from common nouns, speakers of these languages might have difficulty with this convention. Write nouns one at a time on the chalkboard and ask English-language learners to distinguish between proper and common nouns. Have students give reasons for their choices.

◉ VISUAL CONNECTIONS

Ideas for Writing. Have students work individually to compile lists of at least ten nouns that come to mind when they look at this picture. [Some examples are *strength, dignity, face, expression, medal, sadness, intelligence, uniform, gaze,* and *history*.] Then have students use these nouns to write expressive/descriptive paragraphs about the picture. Remind students that specific nouns help create vivid descriptions.

EXERCISE 1

Teaching Note. You may want to explain that the way a word is used in a sentence dictates its part of speech. For example, in the seventh sentence, *Sitting Bull* looks like a noun; however, when the *'s* is added, *Sitting Bull's* functions as an adjective.

EXERCISE 1

Teaching Note. In Sentence 8, some students may identify *leading* as a noun. You probably will not want to penalize such students. Instead, take the opportunity to explain to students that *leading* is a verbal—a verb form used as another part of speech. Specifically, *leading* is a gerund. For more information on verbals, see **Chapter 17: "The Phrase."**

INTEGRATING THE LANGUAGE ARTS

Grammar and Dictionary Skills. You may want to give your students more practice in identifying the three forms of compound nouns. Have each student look through a dictionary to find five compound nouns that are written as single words, five compound nouns that are written as separate words, and five compound nouns that are written as hyphenated words.

If time permits, have volunteers read compound nouns from their lists and have the rest of the class try to write the nouns correctly.

8. After <u>years</u> of leading the <u>Sioux</u> in <u>war</u>, <u>Sitting Bull</u> toured with <u>Buffalo Bill</u> and his <u>Wild West Show</u>.
9. <u>Red Cloud</u> of the <u>Oglala Sioux</u> and <u>Dull Knife</u> of the <u>Cheyennes</u> were other mighty <u>chiefs</u>.
10. <u>Chief Washakie</u> received <u>praise</u> for his <u>leadership</u> of the <u>Shoshones</u>, but he was also a noted <u>singer</u> and <u>craftsman</u>.

Compound Nouns

A *compound noun* is two or more words used together as a single noun. The parts of a compound noun may be written as one word, as separate words, or as a hyphenated word.

ONE WORD	seafood, filmmaker, footsteps, videocassette, grasshopper, daydream, Passover, Iceland
SEPARATE WORDS	compact disc, police officer, John F. Kennedy, House of Representatives, *The Call of the Wild*
HYPHENATED WORD	self-esteem, great-grandparents, fund-raiser, fourteen-year-old, sister-in-law

NOTE: When you are not sure how to write a compound noun, look in a dictionary.

EXERCISE 2 **Identifying Compound Nouns**

Identify the <u>compound noun</u> in each sentence of the following paragraph.

EXAMPLE [1] Did you know that the most famous alphabet used by people with visual impairments was invented by a fifteen-year-old?
1. *fifteen-year-old*

[1] In 1824, <u>Louis Braille</u>, a visually impaired French boy, decided to create an alphabet. [2] With talent, hard

work, and <u>self-discipline</u>, Braille developed the basics of his alphabet by the time he was fifteen years old. [3] His first version used a series of dots and dashes, but that system had <u>drawbacks</u>. [4] As a young teacher at the <u>National Institute for Blind Children</u> in Paris, Braille perfected an alphabet of raised dots. [5] Today, a machine called the <u>braillewriter</u> is used to write braille.

Collective Nouns

A *collective noun* is a word that names a group.

EXAMPLES   faculty   family   herd   team   congress
              audience   flock   crew   jury   committee

Common Nouns and Proper Nouns

A *common noun* names any one of a group of persons, places, things, or ideas. A *proper noun* names a particular person, place, thing, or idea. Proper nouns always begin with a capital letter. Common nouns begin with a capital letter only at the beginning of a sentence.

COMMON NOUNS	PROPER NOUNS
poem	"The Raven," *I Am Joaquín*
nation	Mexico, United States of America
athlete	Joe Montana, Zina Garrison-Jackson
ship	*Mayflower*, U.S.S. *Constitution*
newspaper	*The New York Times*, *USA Today*
river	Rio Grande, Congo River
street	Market Street, University Avenue
day	Friday, Independence Day
city	Los Angeles, New Delhi
organization	National Forensic League, Girl Scouts of America

INTEGRATING THE LANGUAGE ARTS

Grammar and Vocabulary. You may want to show your students how some things that have been named for their discoverers or inventors have been accepted into usage as common nouns. Direct students' attention to **Exercise 2** in which Louis Braille (proper noun) is credited with the invention of braille (common noun).

Then write the common nouns *pasteurization, sandwich, watt,* and *bowie knife* on the chalkboard. Ask students to look up the words in a dictionary to identify the people for whom they were named [Louis Pasteur, Earl of Sandwich, James Watt, James Bowie]. Perhaps students can suggest other proper nouns that have become common nouns.

COMMON ERROR

Problem. Students are often unsure about when to capitalize names of relatives.

Solution. Refer students to **Rule 25g(2)** in **Chapter 25: "Capital Letters,"** which reads "Capitalize a word showing a family relationship when the word is used before or in place of a person's name." To demonstrate the rule, write the following sentences on the chalkboard:

1. Is that your grandpa?
2. I need some help with my bike, Grandpa.
3. How old is Grandpa Joe?

Discuss with your students how the noun *grandpa* is used differently in each sentence. [In the first sentence *grandpa* is a common noun because it is preceded by a possessive pronoun. In the next two sentences, *Grandpa* is a proper noun because it is being used as a person's name.]

REVIEW A

OBJECTIVE

• To identify nouns and classify them as common or proper

434 *The Parts of Speech*

▶ EXERCISE 3   **Identifying Nouns**

Identify the <u>nouns</u> in each numbered sentence in the following paragraph. [Note: *One* and *their* are not nouns.]

EXAMPLE   **[1]** Forests provide a home for insects, mammals, birds, and reptiles.
     1. *Forests, home, insects, mammals, birds, reptiles*

[1] <u>Forests</u> exist in many <u>shapes</u>, <u>sizes</u>, and <u>kinds</u>. [2] Boreal <u>forests</u> grow in <u>regions</u> that have cold <u>winters</u> and short <u>springs</u>. [3] The <u>word</u> <u>*boreal*</u> means "located in northern <u>areas</u>." [4] For <u>example</u>, the boreal <u>forests</u> in <u>Canada</u> contain mostly <u>evergreens</u>, which grow well in a cold <u>climate</u>. [5] <u>Rain forests</u>, on the other <u>hand</u>, are usually located in tropical <u>regions</u>. [6] However, one <u>rain forest</u> is found on a <u>peninsula</u> in the northwestern <u>state</u> of <u>Washington</u>. [7] This <u>rain forest</u> is able to grow in a northern <u>climate</u> because the <u>area</u> is extremely damp. [8] <u>Forests</u> throughout most <u>areas</u> of the <u>United States</u> have both <u>evergreens</u> and deciduous <u>trees</u>, such as <u>oaks</u>, <u>beeches</u>, and <u>maples</u>. [9] Pacific coastal <u>forests</u> extend from central <u>California</u> to <u>Alaska</u>. [10] Two <u>types</u> of <u>trees</u> that grow in these <u>forests</u> are the famous <u>redwoods</u> (the tallest <u>trees</u> in the <u>world</u>) and the giant <u>Douglas fir</u>.

▶ REVIEW A   **Classifying Nouns**

Identify the nouns in the following paragraph. Classify each noun as *common* or *proper*.

EXAMPLE   **[1]** One of the most popular tourist attractions in the United States is the monument that commemorates Abraham Lincoln.
     1. *attractions—common; United States—proper; monument—common; Abraham Lincoln—proper*

[1] Each <u>day</u> huge <u>crowds</u> of <u>people</u> visit the <u>Lincoln Memorial</u> in <u>Washington, D.C.</u> [2] The <u>monument</u> was designed by <u>Henry Bacon</u> and was dedicated on <u>Memorial</u>

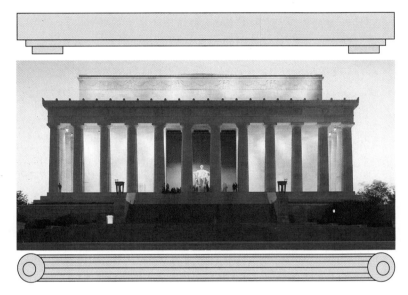

GRAMMAR

GRAMMAR

COOPERATIVE LEARNING
You may wish to have students invent proper names that describe professions or jobs. Have students work in groups of three. Ask each group to think of five different jobs and then create names that are puns related to these jobs. Remind students to write the names as proper nouns.

You may want to write the following examples on the chalkboard and read them aloud to help students get started.

1. dentist—Dr. U. R. Gumms
2. florist—Miss Ima Flower
3. lawyer—Ms. Sue N. Court
4. actor—B. A. Hamm
5. astronomer—Professor C. D. Starr

Day. [3] As you can see in the photograph, the Lincoln Memorial consists of a large marble hall that encloses a gigantic lifelike statue of Abraham Lincoln. [4] The figure, which was carved out of blocks of white marble, is sitting in a large armchair as if in deep meditation. [5] On the north wall is found a famous passage from an inaugural address by Lincoln, and on the south wall is inscribed the Gettysburg Address.

Concrete Nouns and Abstract Nouns

A *concrete noun* names a person, place, or thing that can be perceived by one or more of the senses (sight, hearing, taste, touch, or smell). An *abstract noun* names an idea, a feeling, a quality, or a characteristic.

CONCRETE NOUNS	hummingbird, telephone, teacher, popcorn, ocean, Golden Gate Bridge, Jesse Jackson
ABSTRACT NOUNS	knowledge, patriotism, love, humor, beliefs, beauty, competition, Zen Buddhism

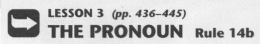

LESSON 3 *(pp. 436–445)*

THE PRONOUN Rule 14b

OBJECTIVES

- To identify pronouns and their antecedents in sentences
- To identify and classify forms of pronouns
- To use pronouns correctly in writing

GRAMMAR

THE PRONOUN

- **Independent Practice/ Reteaching** For instruction and exercises, see **The Pronoun** and **Types of Pronouns** in *Language Skills Practice and Assessment,* pp. 29–30.
- **Computer Guided Instruction** For additional instruction and practice with pronouns, see **Lesson 2** in *Language Workshop CD-ROM.*
- **Practice** To help less-advanced students with additional instruction and practice with pronouns, see **Chapter 11** in *English Workshop, Second Course,* pp. 91–92.

QUICK REMINDER

Write the following sentences on the chalkboard. Ask students to rewrite the sentences to eliminate repetitive nouns.

1. Mario read Mario's report aloud. [Mario read his report aloud.]
2. Josh and Tony played soccer with Josh and Tony's brothers. [Josh and Tony played soccer with their brothers.]

Remind students that a word that substitutes for a noun in a sentence is a pronoun.

GRAMMAR

436 *The Parts of Speech*

The Pronoun

14b. A *pronoun* is a word used in place of one noun or more than one noun.

EXAMPLES When Kelly saw the signal, Kelly pointed the signal out to Enrique.
When Kelly saw the signal, **she** pointed **it** out to Enrique.

Lee and Pat went fishing. Lee and Pat caught six bass.
Lee and Pat went fishing. **Both** caught six bass.

The word that a pronoun stands for is called its *antecedent.*

EXAMPLES
antecedent pronoun
Elena read the **book** and returned **it** to the library.

antecedent pronoun
The **models** bought **themselves** new dresses.

antecedent pronoun pronoun
Catherine told **her** father **she** would be late.

pronoun antecedent
"Do **you** know the answer?" Ms. Rios asked **Chen.**

Sometimes the antecedent is not stated.

pronoun
EXAMPLES **Who** invented the telephone?

pronoun
No one could solve the riddle.

pronoun pronoun pronoun
I thought **you** said that **everybody** would help.

EXERCISE 4 **Identifying Pronouns**

Identify the pronoun or pronouns in each sentence in the following paragraphs. After each pronoun, write the antecedent that the pronoun refers to. If a pronoun does not refer to a specific antecedent, write *unidentified.* [Note: The antecedent may appear before or after the pronoun or even in a previous sentence.]

436

14b

EXAMPLE   [1] When the luggage cart fell on its side, the bags and their contents scattered everywhere.
     1. *its—cart; their—bags*

[1] The passengers scrambled to find their luggage and even got down on hands and knees to pick up their belongings. [2] In no time, the travelers found themselves quibbling over toothbrushes, combs, and magazines.

[3] One salesperson shouted, "The brown bag belongs to me! [4] It has my name on it."

[5] "Are you sure the blue socks are yours?" asked another traveler. [6] "I have a pair just like them."

[7] A young couple asked, "Who owns a pink and yellow shirt? [8] This isn't ours."

[9] "Those are the birthday presents I bought for a friend of mine!" yelled an angry man in a blue suit.

[10] As a crowd of people gathered, many just laughed, but several offered to help.

Personal Pronouns

A *personal pronoun* refers to the one speaking (*first person*), the one spoken to (*second person*), or the one spoken about (*third person*).

PERSONAL PRONOUNS	
FIRST PERSON SECOND PERSON THIRD PERSON	I, me, my, mine, we, us, our, ours you, your, yours he, him, his, she, her, hers, it, its, they, them, their, theirs
FIRST PERSON SECOND PERSON THIRD PERSON	During spring break, **I** visited **my** relatives. Did **you** say that this pen is **yours?** The coach gathered the players around **her** and gave **them** a pep talk.

NOTE: Some authorities prefer to call possessive forms of pronouns (such as *my, his,* and *their*) adjectives. Follow your teacher's instructions regarding possessive forms.

GRAMMAR

ANSWERS
Exercise 4

1. their—passengers; their—passengers
2. themselves—travelers
3. me—salesperson
4. It—bag; my—salesperson; it—bag
5. You—unidentified; yours—unidentified
6. I—traveler; them—socks
7. Who—unidentified
8. This—shirt; ours—couple
9. Those—presents; I—man; mine—man
10. many—people; several—people

INTEGRATING THE LANGUAGE ARTS

Literature Link. If your literature textbook contains the selection, have students read and discuss "The Ransom of Red Chief," by O. Henry. Then have them analyze the story for the author's use of first-person point of view. [The story is told in the first person as though the author were speaking to his audience. The use of pronouns adds to the conversational tone.]

GRAMMAR

Reflexive and Intensive Pronouns

A *reflexive pronoun* refers to the subject and directs the action of the verb back to the subject. An *intensive pronoun* emphasizes a noun or another pronoun. Notice that reflexive and intensive pronouns have the same form.

REFLEXIVE AND INTENSIVE PRONOUNS	
FIRST PERSON	myself, ourselves
SECOND PERSON	yourself, yourselves
THIRD PERSON	himself, herself, itself, themselves

REFLEXIVE   Juan wrote **himself** a note as a reminder.
            The rescuers did not consider **themselves** heroes.
INTENSIVE   Amelia designed the costumes **herself.**
            I **myself** sold more than fifty tickets.

If you are not sure whether a pronoun is reflexive or intensive, try omitting the pronoun. If the meaning of the sentence stays the same, the pronoun is intensive. If the meaning changes, the pronoun is reflexive.

EXAMPLES   Rachel painted the fence herself.
           Rachel painted the fence. [Without *herself*, the meaning stays the same. The pronoun is intensive.]

           They treated themselves to a picnic.
           They treated to a picnic. [Without *themselves*, the sentence doesn't make sense. The pronoun is reflexive.]

▶ EXERCISE 5   **Identifying Pronouns and Antecedents**

Identify the pronoun or pronouns in each of the following sentences as *personal, reflexive,* or *intensive*. After each pronoun, write the antecedent that the pronoun refers to. If a pronoun does not refer to a specific antecedent, write *unidentified*. [Note: The antecedent may appear before or after the pronoun or even in a previous sentence.]

EXERCISE 5

Teaching Note. After students read the **Note** on p. 437, you will probably tell them whether you want possessive pronouns to be labeled as pronouns or as adjectives. Your decision will affect some of the answers in **Exercise 5:** *his* in the first and fifth sentences and *their* in the seventh sentence could be labeled as pronouns or as adjectives.

EXAMPLE **1.** Italian explorer Marco Polo traveled to China, where he and Emperor Kublai Khan became friends.

1. *he—personal—Marco Polo*

1. British explorer Sir Richard Burton himself wrote many books about his adventures in Africa.
2. We watched the movie about Robert O'Hara Burke's trip across Australia in the 1800s.
3. Queen Isabella of Spain herself gave approval for the famous voyages of Christopher Columbus.
4. Matthew Henson prided himself on being the first person actually to reach the North Pole.
5. He wrote *A Negro Explorer at the North Pole* about his expeditions with Commander Robert E. Peary.
6. I myself just read about Dutch explorer Abel Tasman's voyages on the South Seas.
7. Lewis and Clark surely considered themselves lucky to have Sacagawea, a Shoshone woman, as their guide.
8. President Thomas Jefferson sent them to explore the land west of the Mississippi River.
9. Do you think that the Spanish explorer Francisco Coronado really pictured himself finding the Seven Cities of Gold?
10. Our teacher told us about Samuel de Champlain's founding of the colony of Quebec.

GRAMMAR

ANSWERS
Exercise 5

1. himself—intensive—Sir Richard Burton
   his—personal—Sir Richard Burton
2. We—personal—unidentified
3. herself—intensive—Queen Isabella
4. himself—reflexive—Matthew Henson
5. He—personal—Matthew Henson
   his—personal—Matthew Henson
6. I—personal—unidentified
   myself—intensive—unidentified
7. themselves—reflexive—Lewis, Clark
   their—personal—Lewis, Clark
8. them—personal—Lewis, Clark
9. you—personal—unidentified
   himself—reflexive—Francisco Coronado
10. Our—personal—unidentified
    us—personal—unidentified

GRAMMAR

Berry's World reprinted by permission of Newspaper Enterprise Association, Inc.

MEETING *individual* NEEDS

LESS-ADVANCED STUDENTS

Which, who, whom, and *whose* are used as both interrogative and relative pronouns. Remind students that an interrogative pronoun always introduces a question. This explanation will help them classify pronouns in **Exercise 6** on p. 441 and in **Review B** on p. 444.

You may want to write the following sentences on the chalkboard and ask students to find the interrogative pronouns:

1. Who wrote Romeo and Juliet? [Who]
2. Which scene did you like best? [Which]
3. Whose families were quarreling? [Whose]

Demonstrative Pronouns

A *demonstrative pronoun* points out a person, a place, a thing, or an idea.

Demonstrative Pronouns			
this	that	these	those

EXAMPLES   **This** is the most valuable baseball card I have.
These are the names of **those** who volunteered.

NOTE: When the words *this, that, these,* and *those* are used before a noun, they are adjectives, not pronouns.

Interrogative Pronouns

An *interrogative pronoun* introduces a question.

Interrogative Pronouns				
what	which	who	whom	whose

EXAMPLES   **What** is the largest planet in our solar system?
Who scored the most points in the game?

Relative Pronouns

A *relative pronoun* introduces a subordinate clause.

Relative Pronouns				
that	which	who	whom	whose

EXAMPLES   The Bactrian camel, **which** has two humps, is native to central Asia.
Ray Charles is one of several blind performers **who** have had a number of hit recordings.

☞ REFERENCE NOTE: For more information about subordinate clauses, see pages 535–548.

EXERCISE 6

Identifying Demonstrative, Interrogative, and Relative Pronouns

Identify the <u>dem</u>onstrative, <u>int</u>errogative, and <u>rel</u>ative <u>pronouns</u> in each of the following sentences.

EXAMPLE
1. Which of you has heard of *The Mustangs of Las Colinas,* a sculpture that is located in Irving, Texas?
   1. *Which—interrogative; that—relative*

1. <u>This</u> is a picture of the sculpture, <u>which</u> suggests its larger-than-life size. **1. dem./rel.**
2. The nine mustangs <u>that</u> make up the work appear to gallop across Williams Square in the Las Colinas Urban Center. **2. rel.**
3. The horses, <u>whose</u> images are cast in bronze, form the world's largest equestrian (horse) sculpture. **3. rel.**
4. <u>That</u> is an amazing sight! **4. dem.**
5. <u>What</u> is the name of the sculptor <u>who</u> created the mustangs? **5. int./rel.**
6. Robert Glen, <u>who</u> was born in Kenya, is the artist <u>whom</u> you mean. **6. rel./rel.**
7. Looking at this work, you can imagine the amount of time <u>that</u> Glen has spent studying wildlife. **7. rel.**
8. The Mustang Sculpture Exhibit, <u>which</u> is housed in a building near the statue, provides more information about Glen and the mustangs. **8. rel.**
9. <u>Who</u> told me mustangs are descended from horses brought to the Americas by the Spanish? **9. int.**
10. Horses like <u>these</u> roamed wild over Texas and other western states in the 1800s. **10. dem.**

EXERCISE 6

Teaching Note. You may not want to penalize students who become confused and identify *this* in Sentence 7 as a demonstrative pronoun. Explain to students that words such as *this, that, these,* and *those* can be used as demonstrative pronouns when they take the place of a noun; when they come before another word that they modify, however, these words are called demonstrative adjectives. In Sentence 7, *this* modifies *work* and is an adjective. If students have difficulty recognizing that *this* in Sentence 7 is an adjective, not a pronoun, remind them that an adjective modifies a noun and a pronoun takes the place of a noun.

ANSWERS
Exercise 7

Paragraphs will vary. You could evaluate the effectiveness of students' paragraphs by how easily classmates guess the persons' names. You may want to more closely check students' papers for the correct use of pronouns.

 ## INTEGRATING THE LANGUAGE ARTS

Grammar, Speaking, and Writing. Have students formulate some interview questions that use interrogative pronouns. Ask students to survey a group of friends about music groups, food choices in the cafeteria, clothing styles, or another topic of interest.

When students have completed the surveys, have them write their results in informative paragraphs. Require the use of at least five indefinite pronouns. [For example: No one in my survey liked squash, but everyone liked pizza.]

 EXERCISE 7   **Writing Sentences with Pronouns**

Write a paragraph about a well-known person from public life, the entertainment field, or sports. By using pronouns, describe this person without revealing his or her name until the end of the paragraph. Read your paragraph aloud, and have the class guess who the person is.

Indefinite Pronouns

An *indefinite pronoun* refers to a person, a place, or a thing that is not specifically named.

Common Indefinite Pronouns				
all	both	few	nobody	several
another	each	many	none	some
any	either	more	no one	somebody
anybody	everybody	most	nothing	someone
anyone	everyone	much	one	something
anything	everything	neither	other	

EXAMPLES   **Everyone** completed the test before the bell rang.

Neither of the actors knew what costume the **other** was planning to wear.

Many indefinite pronouns can also serve as adjectives.

EXAMPLES   Look in **both** cabinets. [*Both* is an adjective modifying *cabinets.*]

Both contain winter clothing. [*Both* is an indefinite pronoun.]

Each player took **one** cap. [*Each* is an adjective modifying *player; one* is an adjective modifying *cap.*]

Each of the players took **one** of the caps. [*Each* and *one* are indefinite pronouns.]

EXERCISE 8   **Using Indefinite Pronouns**

Have you ever thought about who writes billboards? What you read is written by advertising copywriters. Their goal is to persuade you to do something or to buy something. Try creating your own billboard ads. First, think up five products, services, or places to advertise on billboards (you can make up items if you wish). Then, write at least one sentence to advertise each one. In each ad, use an indefinite pronoun, and underline it. If you like to draw, you might sketch the layout of the billboard and show where your ad's slogan should go.

EXAMPLES   Product: *Everybody should try new Super Comb Hair Styler Wand!*
Service: *No one likes to clean doghouses— except us!*
Place: *Be one of the few in your town to visit Zambia this year!*

GRAMMAR

WRITING APPLICATION

Using Pronouns in a Story

Just try writing about yourself or someone else without using pronouns! You'll soon find that it's awkward to keep using your own name or others' names over and over. That's where pronouns can help you.

AWKWARD   Yoshi returned to get Yoshi's book.
CORRECTED   Yoshi returned to get his book.

▶ **WRITING ACTIVITY**
You've just read a magazine article describing a boy's wild adventure while camping with his family. His story sparks your imagination. Write your own personal adventure story. In it, use a variety of pronouns.

CRITICAL THINKING

Analysis. Explain how the plot of an adventure story is developed around a conflict that is resolved at the conclusion. Have volunteers summarize the nature of the conflicts and resolutions in stories they have read. Ask them to share why those particular stories were memorable. [The stories may have been exciting or mysterious, or they may have included characters who were interesting or with whom the reader could identify.]

MEETING *individual* NEEDS

STUDENTS WITH SPECIAL NEEDS

When you grade students' stories, you may want to give one grade for content and another grade for mechanics. This type of grading will positively reinforce students' good ideas and divorce content from mechanical shortcomings.

REVIEW B

Teaching Note. As mentioned in the **Note** on p. 437, possessive forms of pronouns are sometimes called adjectives. Such possessive pronouns appear twice in **Review B:** *his* in the first sentence and *their* in the ninth sentence.

REVIEW B

OBJECTIVE

- To identify and classify pronouns

---

444   *The Parts of Speech*

Prewriting   First, you'll need to decide if you're going to write a true adventure story or a fictional one. Write down some details of your real or imagined adventure. Include specific details about the people or characters that you are writing about. You may also want to describe the setting.

Writing   As you write your first draft, be sure that your story follows a logical order.

Evaluating and Revising   Ask a friend to read your first draft. Are the actions and characters clear? Revise any parts of your story that confuse your reader. Make sure that the antecedent for each pronoun is clear.

Proofreading   After revising your story, set it aside for a while. Read through it again later, looking for errors in grammar, punctuation, and spelling. The order of events is important in a story, so be sure that verbs are in the right tense. Also, check that pronouns are in the right form.

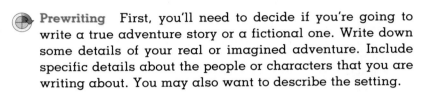

▶ REVIEW B   **Identifying Kinds of Pronouns**

Identify each of the <u>pronouns</u> in the following sentences as *personal*, *reflexive*, *intensive*, *demonstrative*, *interrogative*, *relative*, or *indefinite*.

EXAMPLE   **1.** Can you name some of the many famous Hispanic entertainers that have their stars on Hollywood's Walk of Fame?
   1. *you—personal; some—indefinite; that—relative; their—personal*

1. dem./its./ pers.   **1.** <u>This</u> is Tito Puente <u>himself</u> at the ceremony to install <u>his</u> star.

2. ind./pers.   **2.** <u>Many</u> refer to <u>him</u> as the "King of Latin Music" or the "King of Salsa."

3. int./pers.   **3.** <u>Who</u> is the woman kneeling beside <u>him</u>?

OBJECTIVES

- To add appropriate and interesting adjectives to sentences
- To identify adjectives and proper adjectives and the words they modify
- To write a descriptive paragraph using adjectives effectively

The Adjective **445**

14c

GRAMMAR

4. <u>She</u> is Celia Cruz, the Cuban salsa singer, and <u>you</u> can see for <u>yourself</u> <u>both</u> of <u>them</u> are very happy and proud.   4. pers./pers./refl./ind./pers.
5. <u>Everybody</u> has heard of <u>some</u> of the entertainers   5. ind./ind. honored with bronze stars on Hollywood Boulevard.
6. One musician <u>whom</u> <u>you</u> might know appeared on the old *I Love Lucy* TV show, <u>which</u> is still shown.
7. Of course, <u>that</u> was Desi Arnaz, <u>who</u> was a Cuban bandleader.   6. rel./pers./pers./rel.   7. dem./rel.
8. <u>Which</u> Hispanic singers can <u>you</u> name <u>who</u> have stars on the Walk of Fame?   8. int./pers./rel.
9. <u>All</u> of the following singers have <u>their</u> stars there: Julio Iglesias, Tony Orlando, Ritchie Valens, and José Feliciano.   9. ind./pers.
10. Actors José Ferrer, Cesar Romero, and Ricardo Montalbán are other Hispanics <u>whose</u> stars <u>you</u> will find there.   10. rel./pers.

The Adjective

14c.   An *adjective* is a word used to modify a noun or a pronoun.

PROGRAM MANAGER

THE ADJECTIVE

- **Independent Practice/ Reteaching** For instruction and exercises, see **Adjectives and Articles** and **Nouns and Pronouns Used as Adjectives** in *Language Skills Practice and Assessment*, pp. 31–32.

- **Computer Guided Instruction** For additional instruction and practice with adjectives, see **Lesson 3** in *Language Workshop CD-ROM.*

- **Practice** To help less-advanced students with additional instruction and practice with adjectives, see **Chapter 11** in *English Workshop, Second Course*, pp. 93–96.

QUICK REMINDER

Tell students to think of a visible object in the room and to write five adjectives that describe the object. Remind students that adjectives can tell *what kind, which one, how much,* or *how many*. Then ask volunteers to read their descriptive words and have other students guess their objects.

GRAMMAR

445

MEETING *individual* **NEEDS**

LEP/ESL

General Strategies. In English, adjectives usually precede the nouns they modify, as in *fast car.* In some languages, adjectives usually follow the noun, as in *car fast.* If students who speak these languages try to identify adjectives in English by their position, they might think *fast* is the noun and *car* is the adjective. You may wish to stress the adjective-noun order in English by writing adjective-noun pairs on the chalkboard and by having students identify the parts of speech and the order.

LESS-ADVANCED STUDENTS

Some students might have problems deciding when to use the article *a* and when to use the article *an.* To help students understand the difference, review vowels and consonants. Remind students that *a* precedes a word beginning with a consonant sound and *an* precedes a word beginning with a vowel sound.

Write the following words on the chalkboard. Have students read the words aloud with you and stress the beginning sounds. Then ask for volunteers to tell which words should be preceded by the article *a* and which by the article *an.*

orange	family
newspaper	airplane
watermelon	egg
umbrella	jar
icicle	heir

To **modify** a word means to describe the word or to make its meaning more definite. An adjective modifies a word by telling *what kind, which one, how much,* or *how many.*

WHAT KIND?	WHICH ONE?	HOW MUCH? or HOW MANY?
tall woman	*another* one	*less* time
steep mountain	*this* year	*more* money
long hike	*last* answer	*many* mistakes
eager clerk	*those* people	*several* others
tired dog	*that* dress	*few* marbles
exciting story	*middle* row	*larger* share

Articles

The most frequently used adjectives are *a, an,* and *the.* These adjectives are called *articles.*

The adjectives *a* and *an* are ***indefinite articles.*** Each one indicates that the noun refers to someone or something in general. *A* is used before a word beginning with a consonant sound. *An* is used before a word beginning with a vowel sound.

EXAMPLES   How is **a** gerbil different from **a** hamster?
An accident stalled traffic for **an** hour.

The adjective *the* is a ***definite article.*** It indicates that the noun refers to someone or something in particular.

EXAMPLE   **The** key would not open **the** lock.

▶ EXERCISE 9   **Using Appropriate Adjectives**

Revise the following sentences, replacing the italicized questions with adjectives that answer them.

EXAMPLE   **1.** They sold *how many?* tickets for the *which one?* show.
1. *They sold fifty tickets for the first show.*

1. Even though we had run *how many?* laps around the track, we still had to run *how many?* others.
2. *Which one?* weekend, *how many?* hikers went on a *what kind?* trip to the *what kind?* park.
3. We rode in a *what kind?* van that carried *how many?* people and drove *how many?* miles to the game.
4. There was *how much?* time left when I started to answer the *which one?* question on the test.
5. During the *what kind?* afternoon we washed more than *how many?* cars and earned *how many?* dollars.

Adjectives in Sentences

An adjective may come before or after the word it modifies.

> **Each** one of us brought **used** books for the auction.
>
> The map, although **old** and **worn,** proved to be **useful.**
>
> **These rare** coins are extremely **valuable.**

▶ EXERCISE 10   **Identifying Adjectives and the Words They Modify**

Identify the <u>adjectives</u> and the <u>words they modify</u> in the following paragraph. Do not include *a, an,* and *the.*

EXAMPLE   **[1] Many people considered the old man unlucky.**
        1. *Many—people; old—man; unlucky—man*

[1] For <u>eighty-four days</u>, Santiago, an <u>old Cuban fisherman</u>, had not caught a <u>single fish</u>. [2] Despite his <u>bad luck</u>, <u>he</u> remained <u>hopeful</u>. [3] On the <u>eighty-fifth day</u>, he caught a <u>ten-pound albacore</u>. [4] Soon after <u>this catch</u>, he hooked a <u>huge marlin</u>. [5] For nearly <u>two days</u>, the <u>courageous fisherman</u> struggled with the <u>mighty fish</u> and finally harpooned it. [6] <u>Exhausted</u> but <u>happy</u>, <u>Santiago</u> sailed toward shore. [7] Within an hour, however, his <u>bad</u>

ANSWERS
Exercise 9

Adjectives will vary. As reinforcement for the kinds of questions that adjectives answer, you may want to have students underline and label the adjectives they add to the sentences.

EXERCISE 10
Teaching Note. If you have instructed students to label possessive pronouns as adjectives, you will need to include *his* as an adjective in the second, seventh, and eighth sentences.

<u>luck</u> returned. [8] What happened to the <u>old</u> <u>fisherman</u> and his <u>big</u> <u>catch</u>? [9] Does the story have a <u>happy</u> <u>ending</u>? [10] You can find the answers in <u>Ernest Hemingway's novel</u> *The Old Man and the Sea.*

▶ EXERCISE 11 **Revising Sentences**

In each sentence, add interesting adjectives to modify the nouns and pronouns.

EXAMPLE   **1. The children took a nap.**
            1. *The five grumpy children took a long nap.*

1. Carolyn gave a cat to her aunt.
2. Luís donated books and jeans for the sale.
3. We watched the parade pass under our window.
4. The fielder caught the ball and made a throw to the catcher.
5. The dancer leaped across the stage.
6. The hikers took shelter in the cabin.
7. The actor played the role of a detective.
8. The explorers could not find a way out of the cave.
9. The lawyer questioned the witness.
10. The knight fought the dragon and rescued the princess.

Proper Adjectives

A *proper adjective* is formed from a proper noun and begins with a capital letter.

PROPER NOUN	PROPER ADJECTIVE
Africa	**African** nations
China	**Chinese** calendar
Shakespeare	**Shakespearean** drama
Islam	**Islamic** law
Rio Grande	**Rio Grande** valley

ANSWERS
Exercise 11

Adjectives will vary. Guide students away from overused adjectives such as *good, nice,* and *big.* Encourage students to use thesauruses to find interesting adjectives.

TIMESAVER

To minimize grading time, have students underline or highlight the adjectives they add to the sentences in **Exercise 11.**

▶ EXERCISE 12 **Identifying Proper Adjectives**

Identify the <u>proper adjectives</u> and the <u>words they modify</u> in the following sentences.

EXAMPLE **1.** In recent years many American tourists have visited the Great Wall in China.
1. *American—tourists*

1. The early <u>Spanish</u> <u>explorers</u> built several forts along the <u>Florida</u> <u>coast</u>.
2. The professor of <u>African</u> <u>literature</u> gave a lecture on the novels of Camara Laye, a writer who was born in Guinea.
3. Which <u>Arthurian</u> <u>legend</u> have you chosen for your report?
4. The program about the <u>Egyptian</u> <u>ruins</u> was narrated by an <u>English</u> <u>scientist</u> and a <u>French</u> <u>anthropologist</u>.
5. Aeolus was the god of the winds in ancient <u>Greek</u> <u>mythology</u>.
6. The society of <u>Victorian</u> <u>England</u> was the subject of many <u>British</u> <u>novels</u> in the late 1800s.
7. During last night's press conference, the president commented on the <u>Mideast</u> <u>situation</u>.
8. My friend from Tokyo gave me a <u>Japanese</u> <u>kimono</u>.
9. We saw a display of <u>Appalachian</u> <u>crafts</u> in the public library.
10. Marian McPartland, a jazz pianist from New York City, played several <u>Scott Joplin</u> <u>songs</u>.

PICTURE THIS

You are a scribe, an official writer, in ancient Egypt. The family in the painting on the next page has hired you to keep a record of their activities. Now your job is to record this scene of the children bringing gifts to their parents. Write a paragraph describing what you see. Use at least twenty adjectives to give an accurate description.

GRAMMAR

 INTEGRATING THE LANGUAGE ARTS

Literature Link. Explain to students that specific adjectives can be used to describe sensory details—how something looks, smells, sounds, feels, and tastes. To show students the effective use of descriptive adjectives, have them read Arthur Gordon's "The Sea Devil" if the selection is available in your literature textbook or library. First, ask students to identify the adjectives that Gordon uses to describe the sights and sounds of his setting in the first two paragraphs [*glowing, neat, orderly, dark, green, tiny, ebbing, silent,* and *breathless*]. Then have students finish the story and ask them to notice the effective use of adjectives as they read. When students come to the description of the sea devil, have them jot down specific details about its appearance and about its movements.

PICTURE THIS

Suggest to students that an Egyptian scribe might be compared to a modern journalist. When describing the scene, students should follow journalistic procedures. Ask students to study the scene in the picture and to pay close attention to details such as makeup, hair, clothing, and jewelry. Remind them to use adjectives that help the reader get a sense of being on the scene.

GRAMMAR

449

TECHNOLOGY TIP
If students compose their **Picture This** paragraphs on computers, remind them that some word-processing programs have thesauruses. Students could use the electronic thesaurus to locate specific, descriptive adjectives.

VISUAL CONNECTIONS
About the Artwork. Ancient Egyptian sculpture and wall paintings were created in accordance with strict rules that were rarely departed from. One facet of those rules was the stereotyped portrayal of the human figure. Heads were always in profile, with shoulders squared to the front. Hips and legs were also in profile, with one foot usually advanced.

450 *The Parts of Speech*

Subject: children bringing gifts to parents
Audience: a family in ancient Egypt
Purpose: to keep a family record

Egyptian Expedition of The Metropolitan Museum of Art, Rogers Fund, 1930.

Changing Parts of Speech

The way that a word is used in a sentence determines what part of speech it is. Some words may be used as nouns or adjectives.

NOUN	How often do you watch **television?**
ADJECTIVE	What is your favorite **television** program?
NOUN	Return these books to the **library.**
ADJECTIVE	These **library** books are overdue.
NOUN	Would you like to attend **school** year-round?
ADJECTIVE	The meeting will be held in the **school** cafeteria.

Some words may be used as pronouns or adjectives.

PRONOUN	**Each** did the assignment.
ADJECTIVE	**Each** person did the assignment.

PRONOUN	**Some** have gone to their dressing rooms.
ADJECTIVE	**Some** actors have gone to their dressing rooms.

PRONOUN	**Whose** are these?
ADJECTIVE	**Whose** gloves are these?

Shoe reprinted by permission: Tribune Media Services.

EXERCISE 13   Identifying Adjectives

Identify the <u>adjectives</u> in the following paragraph. Do not include the articles *a, an,* and *the.* [Note: If a word is capitalized as part of a name, it is part of a proper noun and is not an adjective, as in *New York* and *White House.*]

EXAMPLE   [1] Have you heard of the Heidi Festival, a popular event in New Glarus, Wisconsin?
   1. *popular*

[1] For <u>geography</u> class, I wrote a <u>short</u> paper about New Glarus. [2] It was founded by <u>adventurous</u> <u>Swiss</u> settlers in 1845, and people call it "Little Switzerland." [3] As you can see on the <u>next</u> page, <u>colorful</u> reminders of the <u>town's</u> <u>Swiss</u> heritage are everywhere. [4] The <u>special</u> emblems of <u>Switzerland's</u> cantons, or states, are on <u>street</u>

GRAMMAR

REVIEWS C and D

OBJECTIVE

- To identify nouns, pronouns, and adjectives in sentences

452 *The Parts of Speech*

signs and buildings. [5] Many of the women make <u>beautiful</u> lace, and there's even an <u>embroidery</u> factory. [6] Dairying is <u>big</u> business, too, and the townsfolk make <u>delicious</u> cheeses. [7] In a <u>historical</u> village, visitors can see <u>reconstructed</u> buildings, such as a schoolhouse, a <u>blacksmith</u> shop, a church, and the <u>cheese</u> factory shown below. [8] In this village, <u>pioneer</u> tools and belongings are on display. [9] New Glarus also has a museum in a <u>mountain</u> lodge, called a *chalet*. [10] Someday, I hope to see one of the <u>summer</u> festivals, such as the Heidi Festival, the Volksfest, or the Wilhelm Tell Pageant.

VISUAL CONNECTIONS

Ideas for Writing. You may want to have students use the pictures as a prompt for a writing journal entry. Students could focus on historical festivals they've been to or read about. Perhaps their county, city, or neighborhood holds such a celebration.

 REVIEW C

Identifying Nouns, Pronouns, and Adjectives

Identify the <u>italicized word</u> in each sentence of the following paragraph as a <u>*noun*</u>, a <u>*pronoun*</u>, or an <u>*adjective*</u>.

EXAMPLE   [1] Don't let *anyone* tell you that the age of exploration is over.
1. *pronoun*

1. n.
2. n.
3. pro.
4. adj.

[1] Two brothers, Lawrence and Lorne Blair, went on an amazing *adventure* that began in 1973. [2] For ten years they traveled among the nearly 14,000 *islands* of Indonesia. [3] *Each* of them returned with remarkable tales about the people, animals, and land. [4] Their *adventure* story began when some pirates guided them through the Spice

Islands. [5] There, they located *one* of the world's rarest   **5.** pro.
and most beautiful animals—the greater bird of paradise.   **6.**
[6] Another *island* animal that the brothers encountered   adj.
was the frightening Komodo dragon. [7] *Some* Komodo   **7.**
dragons are eleven feet long and weigh more than five   adj.
hundred pounds. [8] *Each* day brought startling discover-   **8.**
ies, such as flying frogs and flying snakes. [9] On *one*   adj.
island, Borneo, they found a tribe of people thought to be   **9.**
extinct. [10] To *some*, the brothers' stay with the cannibals   adj.
of West New Guinea is the strangest part of their trip.   **10.**
   pro.

GRAMMAR

> REVIEW D **Identifying Nouns, Pronouns, and Adjectives**

Identify each *noun*, *pronoun*, and [*adjective*] in the following
sentences. Do not include the articles *a*, *an*, and *the*.

EXAMPLE   **1.** Charles Drew was an American doctor.
   1. *Charles Drew—noun; American—adjective;
   doctor—noun*

1. <u>Charles Drew</u> developed <u>techniques</u> <u>that</u> are used in
   the <u>separation</u> and <u>preservation</u> of <u>blood</u>.
2. During <u>World War II</u>, <u>Dr. Drew</u> was the <u>director</u> of
   [donation] <u>efforts</u> for the <u>American Red Cross</u>.
3. <u>He</u> established [blood bank] <u>programs</u>. **4.** *or* [His]
4. <u>His</u> <u>research</u> saved [numerous] <u>lives</u> during the <u>war</u>.
5. <u>Dr. Drew</u> set up <u>centers</u> in <u>which</u> <u>blood</u> could be
   stored.
6. The [British] <u>government</u> asked <u>him</u> to develop a
   [storage] <u>system</u> in <u>England</u>.
7. Shortly before the <u>beginning</u> of <u>World War II</u>,
   <u>Dr. Drew</u> became a <u>professor</u> of <u>surgery</u> at
   <u>Howard University</u>.
8. After the <u>war</u>, <u>he</u> was appointed [chief] <u>surgeon</u> at
   <u>Freedman's Hospital</u>.
9. [This] <u>physician</u> and <u>researcher</u> made [important]
   <u>contributions</u> to [medical] <u>science</u>.
10. [Many] <u>people</u> <u>who</u> have needed <u>blood</u> owe <u>their</u>
    <u>lives</u> to <u>his</u> <u>methods</u>. **10.** *or* [their] *and* [his]

MEETING *individual* NEEDS

LESS-ADVANCED STUDENTS
   You may want to simplify **Review
D.** Tell students how many nouns,
pronouns, and adjectives are in each
sentence.

REVIEW: POSTTESTS 1 and 2

OBJECTIVES

- To identify nouns, pronouns, and adjectives in sentences
- To write sentences using the same word as two different parts of speech

Review: Posttest 1

A. Identifying Nouns, Pronouns, and Adjectives

Identify each <u>italicized word</u> in the following sentences as a *noun*, a *pronoun*, or an *adjective*.

EXAMPLE **1.** *Each* student is required to take a foreign *language.*
1. *Each*—adjective; *language*—noun

1. *Each* of the clubs decorated a float for the Cinco de Mayo *parade*. **1.** pro./n.
2. Jenna prepared breakfast *herself* this *morning*. **2.** pro./n.
3. *Everybody* says that *high school* will be more work but more fun, too. **3.** pro./n.
4. *This* is the greatest year the *team* has ever had. **4.** pro./n.
5. *Who* can tell me *whose* bicycle this is? **5.** pro./pro.
6. That *German shepherd* puppy is a *lively* rascal. **6.** adj./adj.
7. This is their fault because *they* ignored all the *danger* signals. **7.** pro./adj.
8. We received word *that* they aren't in *danger*. **8.** pro./n.
9. *That* drummer is the *best*. **9.** adj./adj.
10. Runner *Carl Lewis* won several Olympic *medals*. **10.** n./n.

B. Identifying Nouns, Pronouns, and Adjectives

Identify each numbered italicized word in the following paragraph as a *noun*, a *pronoun*, or an *adjective*.

EXAMPLE The [1] *president* has a [2] *private* airplane known as *Air Force One.*
1. *president*—noun
2. *private*—adjective

11. adj.   [11] *American* presidents have used many different types of transportation. President Thomas Jefferson's way
12. adj.   of getting to his first inauguration was [12] *simple*. [13] *He*
13. pro.   walked there and then walked home after taking the

[14] *oath* of office. President Zachary Taylor rode the
[15] *same* horse throughout the **[16]** *Mexican War* and later
during his term of office. James Monroe had the **[17]** *honor*
of being the first president to ride aboard a steamship. In
1899, William McKinley became the **[18]** *first* president to
ride in an automobile. President Theodore Roosevelt,
[19] *whose* love of adventure is famous, rode in a submarine in 1905. Probably **[20]** *nobody* was surprised when
the president himself took over the controls.

14. n.
15. adj.
16. n.
17. n.
18. adj.
19. pro.
20. pro.

GRAMMAR

Review: Posttest 2

Writing Sentences with Nouns, Pronouns, and Adjectives

Write two sentences with each of the following words.
Use each word as two different parts of speech—*noun* and
adjective or *pronoun* and *adjective*. Write the part of speech
of the word after each sentence.

EXAMPLE   **1.** this
        1. *This bicycle is mine.—adjective*
           This cannot be the right answer.—pronoun

1. game
2. some
3. American
4. right
5. that

6. green
7. more
8. Saturday
9. one
10. water

ANSWERS
Review: Posttest 2

Sentences will vary. Here are some
possibilities:

1. Let's play a game.—noun
   We saw some beautiful birds and
   animals at the game
   preserve.—adjective

2. Some think he is a hero.—pronoun
   Some people work long
   hours.—adjective

3. I am an American.—noun
   We fly an American flag.—adjective

4. Turn to the right.—noun
   Make a right turn here.—adjective

5. That is her mother.—pronoun
   You can wear that coat.—adjective

6. Her favorite color is green.—noun
   She put on her green plaid
   skirt.—adjective

7. Give me more.—noun
   We need more rain.—adjective

8. Tomorrow is Saturday.—noun
   We played soccer on Saturday
   afternoon.—adjective

9. I found the right one.—pronoun
   They have one child.—adjective

10. The water seemed polluted.—noun
    We enjoyed sliding down the water
    slide.—adjective

GRAMMAR

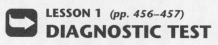

DIAGNOSTIC TEST

OBJECTIVES

- To identify specified parts of speech as verbs, adverbs, prepositions, conjunctions, and interjections
- To classify verbs as action, linking, or helping verbs

PROGRAM MANAGER

FOR THE WHOLE CHAPTER

- Review For exercises on chapter concepts, see **Review Form A** and **Review Form B** in *Language Skills Practice and Assessment*, pp. 49–50.
- Assessment For additional testing, see **Grammar Pretests** and **Grammar Mastery Tests** in *Language Skills Practice and Assessment*, pp. 1–8 and pp. 103–110.

CHAPTER OVERVIEW

This chapter focuses on identifying and using verbs, adverbs, prepositions, conjunctions, and interjections. In the **Writing Application**, students are asked to use fresh, lively action verbs to write stories.

Students might find this chapter useful when they are evaluating and revising writing assignments. You may also want to refer to this chapter when focusing on style in composition and in literature.

GRAMMAR

15 THE PARTS OF SPEECH

Verb, Adverb, Preposition, Conjunction, Interjection

Diagnostic Test

Identifying Verbs, Adverbs, Prepositions, Conjunctions, and Interjections

Write the <u>italicized word or word group</u> in each of the following sentences. Label each as an *<u>action verb</u>*, a *<u>linking verb</u>*, a *<u>helping verb</u>*, an *<u>adverb</u>*, a *<u>preposition</u>*, a *<u>conjunction</u>*, or an *<u>interjection</u>*.

EXAMPLE **1.** That girl has *traveled* widely with her family.
          1. *traveled—action verb*

1. Rosie <u>*hit*</u> a home run and tied up the score. **1.** a.v.
2. <u>*Wow*</u>, that's the best meal I've eaten in a long time! **2.** itj.
3. School can <u>*be*</u> fun sometimes. **3.** l.v.
4. Neither Carlos nor Jan wanted to go <u>*very*</u> far out into the water. **4.** adv.

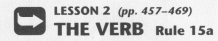

THE VERB Rule 15a

OBJECTIVES

- To identify action verbs in sentences
- To identify and use transitive and intransitive verbs
- To identify the objects of transitive verbs
- To use and identify linking verbs in sentences

GRAMMAR

5. That dog looks mean *in spite of* his wagging tail. **5.** prep.
6. *Have* you ever celebrated Cinco de Mayo? **6.** h.v.
7. If Ken will *not* help us, then he cannot share in the rewards. **7.** adv.
8. My older sister was a cheerleader *during* her senior year. **8.** prep.
9. The road that runs *close* to the railroad tracks is usually crowded. **9.** adv.
10. Several of my friends *enjoy* the music of Quincy Jones. **10.** a.v.
11. No one could do much to help, *for* the damage had already been done. **11.** conj.
12. *Where* have you been putting the corrected papers? **12.** adv.
13. *Oh*, I didn't know he had already volunteered. **13.** itj.
14. Jodie *was* taking in the wash for her mother. **14.** h.v.
15. Surely Ms. Kwan doesn't *expect* us to finish by today. **15.** a.v.
16. May I have a glass of milk and a combination sandwich *without* onions? **16.** prep.
17. James *became* impatient, but he waited quietly. **17.** l.v.
18. My uncle always brings us presents *when* he visits during Hanukkah. **18.** conj.
19. The car swerved suddenly, *yet* the driver remained in control. **19.** conj.
20. The rose *smells* lovely. **20.** l.v.

The Verb

15a. A *verb* is a word used to express action or a state of being.

Action Verbs

An *action verb* may express physical action or mental action.

USING THE DIAGNOSTIC TEST

The **Diagnostic Test** asks students to identify verbs, adverbs, prepositions, conjunctions, and interjections and to classify the verbs as action, linking, or helping verbs. You may want to use this test to assess your students' knowledge of the parts of speech. The assessment should help you group students to meet individual needs or to make special assignments.

GRAMMAR

PROGRAM MANAGER

THE VERB

- **Independent Practice/ Reteaching** For instruction and exercises, see **Transitive and Intransitive Verbs, Action Verbs and Linking Verbs,** and **The Verb Phrase** in *Language Skills Practice and Assessment,* pp. 41–43.

- **Computer Guided Instruction** For additional instruction and practice with verbs, see **Lesson 4** in *Language Workshop CD-ROM.*

- **Practice** To help less-advanced students with additional instruction and practice with verbs, see **Chapter 12** in *English Workshop, Second Course,* pp. 99–104.

- To differentiate between action and linking verbs
- To identify the words that linking verbs connect
- To identify verb phrases in sentences

QUICK REMINDER

Write the following verbs and verb phrases on the chalkboard and have students use them in sentences. Ask students to identify whether they have used each as an action verb or as a linking verb.

1. will be sleeping [The baby will be sleeping for hours. (action)]
2. tastes [The soup tastes delicious. (linking)]
3. is [Elayne is the captain of the team. (linking)]
4. have thought [I have thought about you all day. (action)]

MEETING *individual* NEEDS

STUDENTS WITH SPECIAL NEEDS

Because this lesson includes many terms, you may want to repeat important ideas frequently and to begin each lesson with a summary of material covered the previous day. This repetition should help students who have poor recall.

ADVANCED STUDENTS

Explain to students that verbs of mental action are often followed by noun clauses consisting of the word *that* and a subject and a verb, as in "I believe that someone is following me" or "I worry that I'll be late." Such a noun clause is used as the direct object of the sentence. The word *that* is often deleted, as in "I believe someone is following me" or "I worry I'll be late." You may want to have students work in pairs to brainstorm other examples of this pattern.

458

---

458 *The Parts of Speech*

PHYSICAL ACTION	*jump, shout, search, carry, run*
	Langston Hughes **wrote** volumes of poetry.
	A distinguished cinematographer, James Wong Howe, **filmed** the movie.
MENTAL ACTION	*worry, think, believe, imagine, remember*
	The scientist **studied** the ant colony.
	Mario **knew** the answer to every question on the test.

▶ EXERCISE 1   **Identifying Action Verbs**

Identify the <u>action verb</u> in each sentence in the following paragraph.

EXAMPLE   [1] Dr. Antonia Novello visited with children at a hospital.
  1. *visited*

[1] President Bush <u>named</u> Dr. Novello Surgeon General of the United States in 1990. [2] This position <u>made</u> her the nation's chief medical officer. [3] It also <u>gave</u> her authority over many health programs. [4] Dr. Novello, the first female Surgeon General, <u>trained</u> as a pediatrician.

[5] As the Surgeon General, she <u>directed</u> much of her attention to children's well-being. [6] She <u>has</u> often <u>referred</u> to her own childhood experiences in a close-knit Puerto Rican family. [7] She <u>believes</u> strongly in the rights of all children. [8] Dr. Novello <u>stresses</u> the importance of children's home lives. [9] She <u>urges</u> adult involvement with children's daily activities. [10] She also <u>promotes</u> volunteer participation in all sorts of child welfare organizations.

Transitive and Intransitive Verbs

A ***transitive verb*** is an action verb that expresses an action directed toward a person or thing.

EXAMPLES   Joel **held** the baby. [The action of *held* is directed toward *baby.*]

Loretta **brought** flowers. [The action of *brought* is directed toward *flowers.*]

With transitive verbs, the action passes from the doer—the subject—to the receiver of the action. Words that receive the action of a transitive verb are called ***objects.***

EXAMPLES   Our scout troop made a **quilt.** [*Quilt* is the object of the verb *made.*]

The voters elected **him.** [*Him* is the object of the verb *elected.*]

☞ REFERENCE NOTE: For more information about objects and their uses in sentences, see pages 491–493.

An ***intransitive verb*** expresses action (or tells something about the subject) without passing the action to a receiver.

EXAMPLES   Samuel Ramey **sang** beautifully in the opera *Don Giovanni.*

The Evans twins **played** quietly indoors the whole afternoon.

A verb may be transitive in one sentence and intransitive in another.

EXAMPLES   Janet **swam** ten laps. [transitive]
Janet **swam** well. [intransitive]

The teacher **read** a poem. [transitive]
The teacher **read** aloud. [intransitive]

☞ REFERENCE NOTE: Like intransitive verbs, linking verbs (*be, seem, feel,* etc.) never take direct objects. See page 461 for more information about linking verbs.

GRAMMAR

LESS-ADVANCED STUDENTS

To keep students from confusing objects of prepositions and objects of verbs, have students bracket the prepositional phrases in **Exercise 2** before they classify the verbs.

GRAMMAR

ANSWERS
Exercise 3

Sentences will vary. Here are some possibilities. The first sentence in each pair uses a transitive verb.

1. Juan won the <u>race</u>.
   He won easily.

2. Help your <u>sister</u> with her homework.
   Can I help?

3. Tani plays a <u>clarinet</u>.
   He plays well.

4. Ana ran a <u>marathon</u> last month.
   Don't run in the halls.

5. I will freeze the <u>leftovers</u>.
   Our garden froze last night.

GRAMMAR

▶ EXERCISE 2   **Identifying Transitive and Intransitive Verbs**

In the following paragraph, identify each italicized verb as *transitive* or *intransitive*. Be prepared to identify the (object) of each transitive verb.

EXAMPLE   Whether you [1] *know* it or not, about twenty percent of America's cowboys were African Americans.
   1. *transitive*

During the years following the Civil War, thousands of African American cowboys [1] *rode* the cattle (trails) north from Texas. They [2] *worked* alongside Mexican, Native American, and Anglo trail hands. All the members of a cattle drive [3] *slept* on the same ground, [4] *ate* the same (food) and did the same hard jobs. When day was done, they [5] *enjoyed* each other's (company) as they swapped stories and [6] *sang* around the campfire. When they finally [7] *reached* their (destinations) with their herds, they all [8] *celebrated* by having rodeos, parades, and shooting contests. Nat Love, one of the most famous African American cowboys, [9] *wrote* about his experiences on the range. In his book, he [10] *recalls* the (times) that he and his trailmates looked out for one another, regardless of skin color.

▶ EXERCISE 3   **Writing Sentences with Transitive and Intransitive Verbs**

For each verb given below, write two sentences. In one sentence, use the verb as a *transitive* verb and underline its object. In the other, use the verb as an *intransitive* verb. You may use different tenses of the verb.

EXAMPLE   **1. read**
   1. *For tomorrow, read the <u>chapter</u> about Taiwan that begins on page 441. (transitive)*
   I think I'll read this evening instead of watching television. (intransitive)

1. win   **2.** help   **3.** play   **4.** run   **5.** freeze

Linking Verbs

A *linking verb* links, or connects, the subject with a noun, a pronoun, or an adjective in the predicate.

EXAMPLES The star's name **is** Whoopi Goldberg. [name = Whoopi Goldberg]

Marie Curie **became** a famous scientist. [Marie Curie = scientist]

Tranh **is** one of the finalists. [Tranh = one]

Wild animals **remain** free on the great animal reserves in Africa. [free animals]

The watermelon **looks** ripe. [ripe watermelon]

COMMONLY USED LINKING VERBS				
Forms of *Be*	am are	be been	being is	was were
Other Verbs	appear become feel	grow look remain	seem smell sound	stay taste turn

NOTE: The forms of the verb *be* are not always used as linking verbs. When followed by a word or a group of words that tells *when* or *where*, a form of *be* is a *state-of-being verb*.

EXAMPLES Geraldo **is** here now.

Your roller skates **are** in the attic.

EXERCISE 4   **Using Linking Verbs**

Insert a different linking verb for each blank in the following sentences. Then, identify the <u>words that each verb links</u>. Linking verbs will vary.

EXAMPLE **1.** Judith Jamison _____ calm during the première of the dance.

1. *Judith Jamison remained calm during the première of the dance.*
Judith Jamison—calm

INTEGRATING THE LANGUAGE ARTS

Literature Link. If your literature textbook contains the selection, have students read and discuss Walt Whitman's poem "O Captain! My Captain!" Then have them compare the effects created by the linking verbs with those of the action verbs, such as *rise, hear,* and *trills.* [The action verbs are more forceful and direct. When linking verbs are used, emphasis is placed on the words connected with the subject rather than on any kind of action.]

A DIFFERENT APPROACH

Ask each student to write "action verb" or "linking verb" on a sheet of paper. Then begin to tell the nonsense story of "Weary Wanda and the Weird Wand" by repeating the sentence "My name is Weary Wanda of Wands Unlimited." Have each student contribute a sentence to the story. Each student should use the kind of verb he or she wrote on the sheet of paper at the beginning of the activity. Continue this procedure until you feel the story is complete. You may want students to switch verb categories after the first couple of rounds.

GRAMMAR

GRAMMAR

CRITICAL THINKING

Synthesis. You could integrate the study of linking verbs with that of similes and metaphors. Explain to students that a simile compares two unrelated things by using *like* or *as,* often with a form of the verb *be,* while a metaphor makes a direct comparison without using *like* or *as.* You may want to point out that a simile may be used with an action verb, as in "Amy whistles like a tea kettle" or "Leslie snores as loud as a bull." Read the two following sentences aloud and have students identify each as a simile or a metaphor:

1. Her eyes are like candles in the dark. [simile]
2. Her eyes are candles in the dark. [metaphor]

Ask students to create metaphors and similes using the nouns *heart, city,* and *wind.* Have them underline the verbs they use.
[**1.** My heart is like the ocean's steady tide.
2. The city is a ravenous wolf.
3. The wind is as soft as a kiss.]

1. The first <u>day</u> ____ <u>long</u>.   **1.** seems
2. Your <u>suggestion</u> ____ <u>good</u> to me.   **2.** sounds
3. Our <u>room</u> ____ <u>festive</u> after we decorated it for the party.   **3.** looked
4. The <u>orange</u> ____ a little too <u>sweet</u>.   **4.** tastes
5. In the novel the main <u>character</u> ____ a <u>doctor</u>, and he returns home to set up a clinic.   **5.** is
6. Before a storm the <u>air</u> ____ <u>wet</u> and <u>heavy</u>.   **6.** turns
7. Did <u>she</u> ____ <u>happy</u> about living in Florida?   **7.** appear
8. The <u>diver</u> ____ more <u>confident</u> with each dive she made.   **8.** felt
9. <u>They</u> ____ <u>quiet</u> as the theater lights dimmed.   **9.** became
10. The <u>lilacs</u> ____ <u>lovely</u>.   **10.** smelled

All the linking verbs except the forms of *be* and *seem* may also be used as action verbs. Whether a verb is used to link words or to express action depends on its meaning in a sentence.

LINKING   The tiger **looked** tame.
ACTION   The tiger **looked** for something to eat.

LINKING   The soup **tasted** good.
ACTION   I **tasted** the soup.

LINKING   She **grew** tired of playing.
ACTION   She **grew** into a fine woman.

▶ EXERCISE 5   **Identifying Action Verbs and Linking Verbs**

Identify the <u>verb</u> and its <u>subject</u> in each of the following sentences. If the verb is a linking verb, identify also the [word or words that the verb links to its subject].

EXAMPLES   **1.** The people in the picture on the next page are enjoying the International Championship Chili Cook-off in Terlingua, Texas.
1. *are enjoying, people*

2. The event, first held in 1967, is extremely popular.
2. *is, event—popular*

463

GRAMMAR

GRAMMAR

1. Chili <u>cook-offs</u> throughout the Southwest <u>attract</u> devoted chili fans.
2. Real <u>fans</u> <u>grow</u>[hungry]at the mention of any dish containing chili peppers and chili powder.
3. <u>These</u> <u>are</u> important[ingredients]in Mexican cooking.
4. Chili <u>cooks</u> <u>start</u> with their favorite chili powder.
5. Basic <u>chili powder</u> <u>consists</u> of ground, dried chilies blended with other spices.
6. The most common <u>chili</u> <u>is</u>[chili con carne].
7. <u>This</u> <u>is</u> a thick, spicy meat[stew], often including beans.
8. <u>Chili</u> <u>varies</u> from somewhat spicy to fiery hot.
9. <u>You</u> also <u>find</u> many recipes for chili without meat.
10. Regardless of the other ingredients in a batch of chili, the <u>chili powder</u> <u>smells</u>[wonderful]to chili fans.

▶ EXERCISE 6   **Identifying Verbs**

Identify the <u>verb or verbs</u> in each sentence in the following paragraph. If the verb is a linking verb, identify also the <u>words that the verb links</u>.

EXAMPLE   [1] Do you know Tomás Herrera?
    1. *Do know*

    [2] He is a friend of mine, who lives next door to me.
    2. *is, He—friend; lives*

[1] <u>Tomás</u> <u>is</u> a young <u>musician</u> who <u>loves</u> all kinds of music. [2] No one <u>knows</u> how many hours he <u>plays</u> each week, although many people <u>guess</u> at least twenty. [3] His parents <u>worry</u> about him, yet <u>he</u> <u>seems</u> <u>happy</u>.

[4] One afternoon <u>Tomás</u> <u>became</u> <u>restless</u>. [5] The <u>notes</u> <u>sounded</u> <u>wrong</u>, and <u>none</u> of his music <u>seemed</u> <u>right</u> to him. [6] He <u>grabbed</u> several sheets of music paper and then <u>wrote</u> some notes. [7] After a little careful revision, he <u>formed</u> the notes into an original harmony.

[8] That night he <u>performed</u> his song for some of his friends. [9] Cristina <u>exclaimed</u>, "Tomás, <u>that</u> <u>was</u> <u>excellent</u>! [10] <u>Is</u> <u>that</u> really your first original <u>song</u>?"

Verb Phrases

A *verb phrase* consists of a main verb preceded by at least one *helping verb* (also called an *auxiliary verb*).

The following sentences contain verb phrases.

> Seiji Ozawa **will conduct** many outstanding orchestras. [The main verb is *conduct.*]
> He **has been praised** for his fine conducting. [The main verb is *praised.*]
> His recordings **should be heard** by anyone interested in classical music. [The main verb is *heard.*]
> He **will be leading** the orchestra tonight. [The main verb is *leading.*]

COMMONLY USED HELPING VERBS				
Forms of *Be*	am are	be been	being is	was were
Forms of *Do*	do	does	did	
Forms of *Have*	have	has	had	
Other Helping Verbs	can could	may might	must shall	should will	would

---

COOPERATIVE LEARNING
You may want to give students extra practice with verb phrases. First, write on the chalkboard a base sentence such as "Ana drinks juice." Divide the class into groups of three and tell the groups that they will add helping verbs to the main verb in the base sentence to create as many new sentences as possible in five minutes. Remind students that the form of the main verb will change as they vary the helping verbs. At the end of five minutes, have the group with the most sentences read theirs aloud.

Some helping verbs may also be used as main verbs.

EXAMPLES   Did he **do** his homework?
She will **be** here soon.
We do not **have** enough time.

Sometimes the verb phrase is interrupted by another part of speech. In most cases, the interrupter is an adverb. In a question, however, the subject often interrupts the verb phrase.

EXAMPLES   People **may** someday **communicate** with dolphins.
How much **do** you **know** about Lucy Stone, the suffragist?
Because of the fog, we **could** not [*or* couldn't] **see** the road.

Notice in the last example that the word *not* is never part of a verb phrase.

☞ REFERENCE NOTE: For more information about contractions, see pages 783–784.

▶ EXERCISE 7   **Identifying Verb Phrases**

Identify the <u>verb phrases</u> in the sentences in the following paragraph. Some sentences contain more than one verb phrase.

EXAMPLE   **[1] What unusual jobs can you name?**
1. *can name*

[1] Many people <u>are earning</u> a living at unusual jobs. [2] Even today people <u>can find</u> positions as shepherds, inventors, and candlestick makers. [3] It <u>might seem</u> strange, but these people <u>have decided</u> that ordinary jobs <u>have become</u> too boring for them. [4] Some people <u>have been working</u> as messengers. [5] You <u>may have seen</u> them when they <u>were wearing</u> clown makeup or costumes such as gorilla suits. [6] Other people <u>have been finding</u> work as mimes. [7] They <u>can be seen</u> performing at circuses, fairs, and festivals. [8] Chimney sweeps <u>do</u> still <u>clean</u> chimney flues for people. [9] Some chimney sweeps,

COMMON ERROR

Problem. When a participle follows a linking verb, some students might identify the participle as an adjective and not as part of the verb phrase.

Solution. Write the following rule and examples on the chalkboard:

When a verb phrase contains a participle, the participle is considered part of the verb and not an adjective.

1. The class was listening.
2. The price was reduced by half.

Ask volunteers to write sentences on the chalkboard that use participles in verb phrases. [Some examples are "The car was stolen" and "Children were dancing."]

MEETING *individual* **NEEDS**

AT-RISK STUDENTS

Because of various social and economic pressures, some students might not see the value of staying in school. You could use **Exercise 7** as a springboard to discuss looking to the future. You may want to introduce students to books such as the *Occupational Outlook Handbook* that provide job descriptions, salary scales, and educational requirements for many professions. Lead students to see that the amount of education they have will greatly influence their future job prospects.

GRAMMAR

GRAMMAR

466

like the one in this picture, <u>may</u> even <u>wear</u> the traditional, old-time clothes of the trade. [10] With a little imagination, anyone <u>can find</u> an unusual job.

 REVIEW A

Labeling Linking Verbs and Action Verbs

Identify the verbs and the verb phrases in the following paragraph. Label each verb or verb phrase as an *action verb* or a *linking verb*.

EXAMPLE   [1] Who were the Vikings, and where did they live?
1. *were—linking verb; did live—action verb*

[1] The Vikings <u>were</u> Norsemen who <u>roamed</u> the seas from A.D. 700–1000. [2] The term *Vikings* <u>applies</u> to all Scandinavian sailors, whether they <u>were</u> Norwegians, Swedes, or Danes. [3] People in other countries <u>considered</u> the Vikings the terror of Europe. [4] They <u>worshiped</u> such fierce gods as Thor and Odin. [5] Viking warriors <u>hoped</u> that they <u>would die</u> in battle. [6] They <u>believed</u> that when they <u>died</u> in battle, they <u>went</u> to Valhalla. [7] In Valhalla, they <u>could</u> always <u>enjoy</u> battles and banquets. [8] Each day, the warriors in Valhalla <u>would go</u> out to the battlefield and <u>would receive</u> many wounds. [9] Then, in spite of their injuries, at the end of the day they <u>would</u> all <u>meet</u> back at the banquet hall. [10] Their wounds <u>would</u> promptly <u>heal</u>, and they <u>could boast</u> about their great bravery in battle.

WRITING APPLICATION

Using Verbs to Make Your Writing Fresh and Lively

You've probably heard the old saying "Actions speak louder than words." In your writing, action verbs "speak louder" than many other words. Well-chosen action words help your reader picture what you're writing about. They make your writing lively and interesting and catch your readers' attention.

DULL   Mississippi State won the championship last night.
LIVELY   Mississippi State seized the championship last night.

What are some other verbs you could use instead of *won*?

WRITING ACTIVITY

Your little sister likes for you to tell her exciting stories. You've told her so many stories that you've run out of new ones. To get ideas for new stories, you think about events you've read about or seen. Write a summary of an exciting incident from a book, a movie, or a television show. Use action verbs that are fresh and lively. Underline these verbs.

Prewriting   Think about books that you've read recently or movies and television shows that you've seen. Choose an exciting incident from one of these works. Freewrite what you remember about that incident.

Writing   As you write your first draft, think about how you're presenting the information. When telling a story, you should usually use chronological order (the order in which events occurred). This method would be easiest for your young reader to follow, too. Try to use fresh, lively action verbs.

Evaluating and Revising   Imagine that you are a young child hearing the story for the first time. Look over your summary and ask yourself these questions.

GRAMMAR

WRITING APPLICATION

In directing students through this exercise, remind them to pick a single incident from a book, movie, or television show. Students often have a tendency to retell the entire story rather than to focus on one incident. You may want to give students some examples of incidents from popular movies or from works read in class.

CRITICAL THINKING

Synthesis. To give students practice with chronological order, scramble the order of the following story and write it on the chalkboard or on an overhead transparency. Have students use chronological order to rewrite the story.

This morning I jumped out of bed as my mother shouted, "You're going to miss the bus!" As I pulled on my clothes, I stepped on my sister's jacks. Screaming with pain, I stumbled downstairs to eat breakfast. I was gulping my oatmeal when I spotted the bus turning the corner. I flew out the door and raced to the bus stop. As I leapt onto the bus, I tripped and dropped my books. Finally seated, I gazed out the bus window and remembered Mother calling to me, "Have a nice day!"

GRAMMAR

TECHNOLOGY TIP

Remind students who are composing their summaries on computers that many word-processing programs have thesauruses. Students could use the thesauruses to replace dull verbs with lively action verbs.

REVIEW B

OBJECTIVE

• To identify verbs as action or linking verbs

■ Would I be able to understand what happened?
■ Would the verbs I have used in the story help me picture what happened?
■ Would I think the story is exciting?

Revise your summary if any of your answers is "no." Replace dull verbs with lively action verbs.

Proofreading Look over your summary to be sure that each verb you use is in the correct form and tense. (See pages 604–616.) Be sure that you have used action verbs rather than linking verbs.

▶ REVIEW B   **Labeling Verbs**

Identify each verb in the following paragraph as an *action verb* or a *linking verb*. Treat verb phrases as single words. Some sentences contain more than one verb.

EXAMPLE   [1] She dedicated her life to helping young people.
1. *dedicated—action verb*

[1] Mary McLeod Bethune <u>is</u> a major figure in American history. [2] Bethune <u>taught</u> school after she <u>completed</u> her education in South Carolina. [3] In 1904, she <u>moved</u> to Florida and <u>opened</u> a school of her own. [4] This school eventually <u>became</u> Bethune-Cookman College, and Mary Bethune <u>served</u> as its president. [5] In 1930, Bethune <u>was invited</u> to a presidential conference on child health and protection. [6] Then, during Franklin Roosevelt's administration, she and others <u>founded</u> the National Youth Administration. [7] Her outstanding efforts <u>impressed</u> Roosevelt, and he <u>established</u> an office for minority affairs. [8] This office <u>gave</u> money to serious students so that they <u>could continue</u> their education. [9] In 1945, Bethune <u>was</u> an observer at the conference that <u>organized</u>

OBJECTIVES

- To identify adverbs and the verbs, adjectives, and adverbs they modify
- To choose adverbs to modify adjectives

the United Nations. [10] Throughout her life, Bethune <u>remained</u> interested in education, and her efforts <u>earned</u> her national recognition.

The Adverb

15b.	An *adverb* is a word used to modify a verb, an adjective, or another adverb.

An adverb tells *where, when, how,* or *to what extent (how much* or *how long).*

WHERE?	WHEN?
The forest fire started **here.** The couple was married **nearby.**	The police arrived **promptly. Then** the suspects were questioned.
HOW?	**TO WHAT EXTENT?**
The accident occurred **suddenly.** The prime minister spoke **carefully.**	We should **never** deceive our friends. She has **scarcely** begun the lesson.

Adverbs Modifying Verbs

Adverbs may come before or after the verbs they modify.

EXAMPLES **Slowly** the man crawled **down.** [The adverb *Slowly* tells how the man crawled, and the adverb *down* tells where he crawled.]
I **seldom** see you **nowadays.** [The adverb *seldom* tells to what extent I see you, and the adverb *nowadays* tells when I see you.]

PROGRAM MANAGER

THE ADVERB

- **Independent Practice/ Reteaching** For instruction and exercises, see **Adverbs That Modify Verbs** and **Adverbs That Modify Adjectives and Adverbs** in *Language Skills Practice and Assessment,* pp. 44–45.
- **Computer Guided Instruction** For additional instruction and practice with adverbs, see **Lesson 5** in *Language Workshop CD-ROM.*
- **Practice** To help less-advanced students, see **Chapter 12** in *English Workshop, Second Course,* pp. 105–106.

QUICK REMINDER

Write the following adverbs on the chalkboard and ask students to write a sentence with each. Have students label the word each adverb modifies as a verb, an adjective, or an adverb.

always	pleasantly
everywhere	quite
occasionally	really
often	well

GRAMMAR

GRAMMAR

COMMON ERROR

Problem. Overuse of the adverb *there* to start sentences produces unimaginative, weak writing. Starting a sentence with *there* takes the emphasis away from the subject of the sentence and may confuse the reader because of its vagueness.

Solution. Have students look through their papers for sentences that begin with *there*. They might circle these beginnings and decide which of the sentences need to be rewritten to emphasize the subject or to make the statement clearer.

INTEGRATING THE LANGUAGE ARTS

Literature Link. If your literature textbook contains the selection, ask one of the better speakers in the class to read aloud Martin Luther King, Jr.'s speech "I Have a Dream." Tell students to pay close attention to the adverbs that show time and to analyze the effect created by the deliberate repetition of many of these adverbs. [Adverbs give the speech a historical framework as well as a sense of history in the making. *Ago, later,* and *still* link the past (1863) to the time the speech was presented (1963). *Today* grounds the ideals of equality and justice to the time of the speech (1963). *Never* and *forever* link these ideals to the future.

The repetition of *later, still, never,* and *today* creates a sense of outrage that racial injustice continues and a sense of urgency to correct this injustice.]

Adverbs may come between the parts of verb phrases.

EXAMPLES   **Keisha has already completed her part of the project.** [The adverb interrupts and modifies *has completed.*]
Many students did not understand all of the directions. [The adverb interrupts and modifies *did understand.*]

Adverbs are sometimes used to ask questions.

EXAMPLES   **Where are you going?**
How did you do on the test?

▶ EXERCISE 8   **Identifying Adverbs That Modify Verbs**

Identify the <u>adverbs</u> and the <u>verbs they modify</u> in the following sentences.

EXAMPLE   **1. How can I quickly learn to take better pictures?**
1. *how—can learn; quickly—can learn*

1. You <u>can listen</u> <u>carefully</u> to advice from experienced photographers, who <u>usually</u> <u>like</u> to share their knowledge with beginners.
2. Nobody <u>always</u> <u>takes</u> perfect pictures, but some tips <u>can help</u> you <u>now</u>.
3. <u>First</u>, you <u>should</u> <u>never</u> <u>move</u> when you take pictures.
4. You <u>should stand</u> <u>still</u> and <u>hold</u> your camera <u>firmly</u>.
5. Some photographers suggest that you <u>keep</u> your feet <u>apart</u> and <u>put</u> one foot <u>forward</u>.
6. Many beginners <u>do</u> <u>not</u> <u>move</u> <u>close</u> to their subjects when they take pictures.
7. As a result, the subjects <u>frequently</u> <u>are lost</u> in the background, and the photographers <u>later</u> <u>wonder</u> what happened.
8. A good photographer <u>automatically</u> <u>thinks</u> about what will be in a picture and <u>consequently</u> <u>avoids</u> disappointment <u>afterward</u>.
9. <u>Nowadays</u>, cameras <u>have</u> built-in light meters, but you <u>should</u> <u>still</u> <u>check</u> the lighting.

10. You <u>may</u> <u>already</u> <u>have heard</u> the advice to stand with your back to the sun when taking pictures, and that tip <u>is</u> <u>often</u> a good one.

Adverbs Modifying Adjectives

EXAMPLES   An **unusually** fast starter, Karen won the race.
[The adverb *unusually* modifies the adjective *fast*, telling *how fast* the starter was.]
Our committee is **especially** busy at this time of year. [The adverb *especially* modifies the adjective *busy*, telling *how busy* the committee is.]

 EXERCISE 9   **Identifying Adverbs That Modify Adjectives**

Identify the <u>adverbs</u> and the <u>adjectives they modify</u> in the following sentences.

EXAMPLE   **1.** Because so many bicycles have been stolen, the principal hired a guard.
        1. *so, many*

1. The team is <u>extremely</u> <u>proud</u> of its record.
2. All frogs may look <u>quite</u> <u>harmless</u>, but some are poisonous.
3. The class was <u>unusually</u> <u>quiet</u> today.
4. The Mardi Gras celebration in New Orleans is <u>very</u> <u>loud</u> and <u>colorful</u>.
5. The coach said we were <u>too</u> <u>careless</u> when we made the routine plays.
6. I waited <u>nearly</u> <u>two</u> hours to get tickets to *Sarafina*.
7. When kittens are with their mother, they look <u>thoroughly</u> <u>contented</u>.
8. Weekends are <u>especially</u> <u>hectic</u> for me when all of my teachers assign homework.
9. Those *fajitas* seem <u>much</u> <u>spicier</u> than these.
10. The new exchange student who comes from Norway is <u>surprisingly</u> <u>fluent</u> in English.

INTEGRATING THE LANGUAGE ARTS

Grammar and Speaking. Have students prepare short persuasive speeches that focus on some things they would like to change. Perhaps students feel that a school policy is unfair, or they might have alternative ways to deal with issues in the news. Have students jot down their thoughts and arrange them in a logical order. You could refer students to the organizational strategy presented in the **Framework for a Persuasive Paper** on p. 275. Students will need to choose their words carefully and to use strong, specific adverbs to be convincing. Have students pair off to take turns giving their speeches. Some students might want to present their arguments to the entire class.

ANSWERS

Exercise 10

Adverbs will vary. Here are some possibilities:

1. surprisingly
2. terribly
3. extremely
4. incredibly
5. consistently
6. exceptionally
7. tremendously
8. quite
9. especially
10. breathtakingly

COOPERATIVE LEARNING

To help students expand their vocabulary, have the class play a game of Opposites with adverbs. Assign students to groups of three or four. After calling out an adverb such as *gracefully, noisily, happily,* or *suddenly,* let each group think of an antonym to use in a sentence. Then let the class decide which group has the best response.

EXERCISE 10 **Choosing Adverbs to Modify Adjectives**

The adverb *very* is used far too often to modify adjectives. Choose an adverb other than *very* to modify each adjective below. Use a different adverb with each adjective.

EXAMPLE **1.** strong
 1. *incredibly strong*

1. cheerful	4. messy	7. heavy	9. calm
2. sour	5. honest	8. long	10. graceful
3. wide	6. timid		

Adverbs Modifying Other Adverbs

EXAMPLES **Elena finished the problem more quickly than I did.** [The adverb *more* modifies the adverb *quickly*, telling *how quickly* Elena finished the problem.]
 Our guest left quite abruptly. [The adverb *quite* modifies the adverb *abruptly*, telling *how abruptly* our guest left.]

EXERCISE 11 **Identifying Adverbs That Modify Other Adverbs**

For each of the following sentences, identify the <u>adverb</u> that modifies another adverb. Then write the <u>adverb that it modifies</u>.

EXAMPLE **1.** Condors are quite definitely among the largest living birds.
 1. *quite—definitely*

1. The California condor and the Andean condor are <u>almost</u> <u>entirely</u> extinct.
2. <u>Only</u> <u>very</u> few California condors exist today, and nearly all of them live in captivity.
3. Andean condors are <u>slightly</u> <u>more</u> numerous, and more of them can still be seen in the wild.

REVIEW C

OBJECTIVE

- To identify adverbs and the words they modify in sentences

INTEGRATING THE LANGUAGE ARTS

Grammar and Vocabulary. Have each student write an adverb and a word for it to modify (verb, adjective, or other adverb) beginning with each letter of the alphabet. For example: *anxiously awaits, boastfully broadcasts,* and *carefully catches.* Encourage students to use dictionaries and to be creative.

You may want to have students combine their lists on poster board to display in the classroom as word banks for writing assignments.

4. You can see from this photograph why some people think that condors are <u>most</u> <u>assuredly</u> the ugliest birds.
5. Yet, once in the air, condors soar <u>so</u> <u>gracefully</u> that they can look actually beautiful.

▶ REVIEW C **Identifying Adverbs**

Identify the adverbs in the order that they appear in each sentence in the following paragraph. After each adverb, write the word or phrase that the adverb modifies. Some sentences have more than one adverb.

EXAMPLE **[1] Sherlock Holmes solved the case very quickly.**
 1. *very—quickly; quickly—solved*

[1] I have been a fan of mystery stories since I was quite young. [2] Some stories are incredibly exciting from start to finish. [3] Others build suspense very slowly. [4] If I like a story, I almost never put it down until I finish it. [5] In many cases, I can scarcely prevent myself from peeking at the last chapter to see how the story ends. [6] I never start reading a mystery story if I have tons of homework because then it is more tempting to read the story than to do my homework. [7] My favorite detectives are ones who cleverly match wits with equally clever villains. [8] I especially like detectives who carefully look around, hunting for clues. [9] The clues that they uncover are almost always found in unexpected, spooky places. [10] It's amazing how detectives can use these clues to solve the most complicated cases.

ANSWERS
Review C

1. quite—young
2. incredibly—exciting
3. very—slowly; slowly—build
4. almost—never; never—put; down—put
5. scarcely—can prevent; how—ends
6. never—start; then—is; more—tempting
7. cleverly—match; equally—clever
8. especially—like; carefully—look; around—look
9. almost—always; always—are found
10. how—can use; most—complicated

GRAMMAR

GRAMMAR

GRAMMAR

PROGRAM MANAGER

THE PREPOSITION

- **Independent Practice/ Reteaching** For instruction and exercises, see **Prepositions and Their Objects** in ***Language Skills Practice and Assessment,*** p. 46.
- **Computer Guided Instruction** For additional instruction and practice with prepositions, see **Lesson 6** in ***Language Workshop CD-ROM.***
- **Practice** To help less-advanced students with additional instruction and practice with prepositions, see **Chapter 12** in ***English Workshop, Second Course,*** pp. 109–110.

QUICK REMINDER

Write the following sentences on the chalkboard and ask students to fill in each blank with an appropriate word:

1. The moon shone ____ the clouds. [through, above, below]
2. The squirrel scurried ____ the tree. [up, around, to]
3. Tea roses grew ____ the walkway. [along, beside, near]

Point out that the only words that will make sense to use in the blanks are prepositions.

LESSON 4 *(pp. 474–478)*

THE PREPOSITION Rule 15c

OBJECTIVES

- To identify prepositions, compound prepositions, and prepositional phrases in a passage
- To write a tall tale with similes expressed in prepositional phrases
- To write sentences using words as adverbs, then as prepositions

GRAMMAR

The Preposition

15c. A ***preposition*** is a word used to show the relationship of a noun or a pronoun to another word in the sentence.

Notice how a change in the preposition changes the relationship between *package* and *tree* in each of the following examples.

The package **under** the tree is mine.
The package **in** the tree is mine.
The package **near** the tree is mine.
The package **behind** the tree is mine.
The package **next to** the tree is mine.
The package **in front of** the tree is mine.

Prepositions that consist of more than one word, such as *in front of,* are called ***compound prepositions.***

Commonly Used Prepositions

aboard	before	in	over
about	behind	in addition to	past
above	below	in front of	since
according to	beneath	inside	through
across	beside	in spite of	throughout
after	besides	instead of	to
against	between	into	toward
along	beyond	like	under
along with	but (meaning *except*)	near	underneath
amid		next to	until
among	by	of	unto
around	down	off	up
aside from	during	on	upon
as of	except	on account of	with
at	for	out	within
because of	from	out of	without

15c

EXERCISE 12   **Identifying Prepositions**

Identify the <u>prepositions</u> in each sentence in the following paragraph. Be sure to include all parts of any compound prepositions you find.

EXAMPLE   **[1] Throughout the centuries people have read about the legend of Romulus and Remus.**
   1. *Throughout, about, of*

[1] <u>According to</u> legend, Mars, the god <u>of</u> war <u>in</u> Roman mythology, was the father <u>of</u> the twin brothers Romulus and Remus. [2] When the twins were infants, an evil ruler had them placed <u>in</u> a basket and cast <u>into</u> the Tiber River. [3] Fortunately, they safely drifted <u>to</u> the bank <u>of</u> the river. [4] There they were rescued <u>by</u> a wolf. [5] Later they were found <u>by</u> a shepherd and his wife. [6] When the twins grew up, they wanted to build a city <u>on</u> the site where they had been rescued. [7] <u>Instead of</u> working together, however, the twins fought <u>against</u> each other. [8] <u>During</u> the quarrel Romulus killed Remus. [9] Then, the legend continues, Romulus founded the city <u>of</u> Rome <u>about</u> 753 B.C. [10] <u>Out of</u> hundreds <u>of</u> legends <u>about</u> the founding <u>of</u> Rome, this one has remained <u>among</u> the best known.

The Prepositional Phrase

A preposition is usually followed by a noun or a pronoun. This noun or the pronoun following the preposition is called the *object of the preposition.* All together, the preposition, its object, and the modifiers of the object are called a *prepositional phrase.*

EXAMPLE   **The wagon train slowly traveled across the dusty prairie.** [The prepositional phrase consists of the preposition *across,* its object *prairie,* and two adjectives modifying the object—*the* and *dusty.*]

☞ REFERENCE NOTE: For more information about prepositional phrases, see pages 506–509 and 670.

GRAMMAR

INTEGRATING THE LANGUAGE ARTS

Literature Link. If your literature textbook contains it, have students read Abraham Lincoln's Gettysburg Address. Then have them take a closer look at the prepositions *of, by,* and *for* in the final clause of the speech. Each of these prepositions uses the word *people* as its object, and all three prepositional phrases modify the word *government.* Discuss how the meaning of each phrase differs. [*Of* shows possession. The people own the government. *By* shows a relationship in which the people empower the government. *For* shows a need fulfilled or service performed. The government serves the people.]

PICTURE THIS

As a brainstorming activity, have students create an idea map with the subject "cows watching an airplane" in the center. Their maps may look something like this:

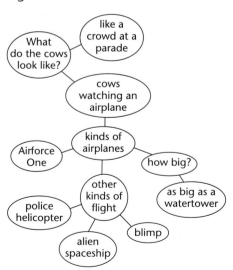

---

476 *The Parts of Speech*

NOTE: Be careful not to confuse a prepositional phrase that begins with *to* (*to town, to her club*) with an infinitive that begins with *to* (*to run, to be seen*). Remember: A prepositional phrase always ends with a noun or a pronoun.

▶ EXERCISE 13 **Identifying Prepositional Phrases**

Identify the <u>prepositional phrase or phrases</u> in each sentence in the following paragraph. Then, underline each <u>preposition</u>.

EXAMPLE **[1] Walt Whitman wrote the very moving poem "O Captain! My Captain!" about Abraham Lincoln.**

1. *about Abraham Lincoln*

[1] <u>In Whitman's poem</u>, the captain directs his ship <u>toward a safe harbor</u>. [2] The captain represents Abraham Lincoln, and the ship is the ship <u>of state</u>. [3] The captain has just sailed his ship <u>through stormy weather</u>. [4] This voyage <u>across rough seas</u> symbolizes the Civil War. [5] <u>On the shore</u>, people joyfully celebrate the ship's safe arrival. [6] One <u>of the ship's crew</u> addresses his captain, "O Captain! my Captain! rise up and hear the bells." [7] Sadly, everyone <u>except the captain</u> can hear the rejoicing. [8] The speaker <u>in the poem</u> says that the captain "has no pulse nor will." [9] The captain has died <u>during the voyage</u>, just as Lincoln died <u>at the end</u> <u>of the Civil War</u>. [10] <u>According to many people</u>, "O Captain! My Captain!" is one <u>of Whitman's finest poems</u>.

PICTURE THIS

You and this cowboy are on night watch. It's a cool, quiet night. The cattle, however, seem extremely interested in the airplane flying over. Their behavior starts you thinking about a tall tale—a humorous, highly improbable story that stretches the facts. To amuse your companion, write a tall tale about the cows watching the airplane. Use five similes expressed in prepositional phrases. To form a simile, use *like* or *as* to show how one thing is similar to another thing. For example: *The cows looked like an attentive movie audience.*

Subjects: cows watching an airplane
Audience: cowboy companion
Purpose: to entertain

Adverb or Preposition?

Some words may be used as either prepositions or adverbs. To tell an adverb from a preposition, remember that a preposition is always followed by a noun or pronoun object.

ADVERB   **The plane circled above.**
PREPOSITION **The plane circled above the field.** [Note the object of the preposition—*field.*]

ADVERB   **Can you come over to my house?**
PREPOSITION **We saw a bald eagle fly over the treetops.** [Note the object of the preposition—*treetops.*]

VISUAL CONNECTIONS
Cows Watching Plane
About the Artist. John Held, Jr. (1889–1958), an American cartoonist, became famous in the 1920s for his classic cartoons that appeared in magazines such as *Harper's Bazaar, Life,* and *Vanity Fair.* He was especially well known for his cartoons that depicted the flappers and jazz musicians in the Roaring Twenties. Held also took up serious painting and wrote several books during the 1930s.

LESSON 5 (pp. 478–480)
THE CONJUNCTION Rule 15d
OBJECTIVE
• To identify coordinating and correlative conjunctions and the words they join

GRAMMAR

ANSWERS
Exercise 14

Sentences will vary. Here are some possibilities:

1. Take it off.
   He threw a rock off the bridge.
2. He crawled across easily.
   The wagon rolled across the bridge.
3. The leaves grow on top, and the roots grow below.
   He put the sacks below the counter.
4. The birds flying above sang sweetly.
   Above the hills, the clouds grew larger.
5. The woman asked the child to put the basket down.
   The turtle crawled down the hill.

THE CONJUNCTION

■ **Independent Practice/ Reteaching** For instruction and exercises, see **Types of Conjunctions** in *Language Skills Practice and Assessment,* p. 47.

■ **Computer Guided Instruction** For additional instruction and practice with conjunctions, see **Lesson 7** in *Language Workshop CD-ROM.*

■ **Practice** To help less-advanced students with additional instruction and practice with conjunctions, see **Chapter 12** in *English Workshop, Second Course,* pp. 111–112.

478

GRAMMAR

478 *The Parts of Speech*

 EXERCISE 14 **Writing Sentences with Adverbs and Prepositions**

Use each of the following words in two sentences, first as an adverb and then as a preposition. Underline the designated word.

EXAMPLE **1.** along
  1. *Do you have to bring your little brother along?*
  Wildflowers were blooming along the riverbank.

1. off **2.** across **3.** below **4.** above **5.** down

The Conjunction

15d. A *conjunction* is a word used to join words or groups of words.

Coordinating conjunctions connect words or groups of words used in the same way.

Coordinating Conjunctions						
and	but	or	nor	for	so	yet

EXAMPLES **Theo or Tyler** [two nouns]
  small but comfortable [two adjectives]
  through a forest and across a river [two prepositional phrases]
  The stars seem motionless, but actually they are moving rapidly through space. [two complete independent clauses]

When *for* is used as a conjunction, it connects groups of words that are sentences. On all other occasions, *for* is used as a preposition.

CONJUNCTION We wrote to the tourist bureau, **for** we
wanted information on places to visit.
PREPOSITION We waited patiently **for** a reply.

NOTE: The conjunction *so* is often overused. Whenever possible, reword a sentence to avoid using *so*.

EXAMPLE You are new, so you'll probably get lost.
Because [*or* Since] you are new, you'll probably get lost.

Correlative conjunctions are pairs of conjunctions that connect words or groups of words used in the same way.

Correlative Conjunctions		
both . . . and	either . . . or	neither . . . nor
whether . . . or	not only . . . but also	

EXAMPLES **Both** horses **and** cattle were brought to North
America by the Spanish. [two nouns]
The student council will meet **not only** on
Tuesday **but also** on Thursday this week. [two
prepositional phrases]
Either leave a message on my answering
machine, **or** call me after 7:00 P.M. [two
complete ideas]

► EXERCISE 15 **Identifying Coordinating and
Correlative Conjunctions**

Identify the conjunctions in the following paragraph as (coordinating) or *correlative*. Be prepared to tell what words or groups of words the conjunctions join.

EXAMPLE [1] The men and women in the picture on the
next page are wearing African clothes.
1. *and—coordinating*

[1] African clothing is fashionable today for both men and women in the United States. [2] People wear not only clothes of African design but also Western-style clothes made of African materials. [3] American women have

QUICK REMINDER

Write the following pairs of sentences on the chalkboard and have students use a coordinating conjunction to combine each pair. Have students identify what is joined by the conjunction in each sentence.

1. Maria loves to take pictures. Joy loves to take pictures. [Maria and Joy love to take pictures. (nouns used as subjects)]
2. Benny is fairly short. Keith is very tall. [Benny is fairly short, but Keith is very tall. (sentences)]
3. Jean plays soccer. Jean coaches her little brother's team. [Jean plays soccer and coaches her little brother's team. (verbs used as predicates)]

MEETING *individual* NEEDS

LEP/ESL

General Strategies. Some students might find *neither . . . nor* and *either . . . or* confusing because the pairs look so much alike. Remind students that the *n* (as in *neither . . . nor*) often marks negative words in both English and Spanish. Explain that *neither . . . nor* implies the negative and *either . . . or* indicates a choice between two possibilities.

OBJECTIVES

- To identify interjections in sentences
- To identify speakers by their dialogue

GRAMMAR

worn modified African headdresses for years, (but) nowadays men are wearing African headgear, too. [4] Men (and) women sometimes wear *kufi* hats, which originated with Muslims. [5] Both women's dresses and women's coats are especially adaptable to African fashions. [6] Many women wear African jewelry (or) scarves. [7] Clothes made of such materials as *kente* cloth from Ghana, *ashioke* cloth from Nigeria, (and) *dogon* cloth from Mali have become quite popular. [8] These fabrics are decorated either with brightly colored printed designs or with stripes. [9] African-inspired clothes usually fit in whether you are at work or at play. [10] African styles are popular, (for) they show appreciation for ancient cultures.

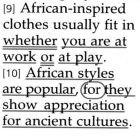

PROGRAM MANAGER

THE INTERJECTION

■ **Independent Practice/ Reteaching** For instruction and exercises, see **Interjections** in *Language Skills Practice and Assessment,* p. 48.

■ **Computer Guided Instruction** For additional instruction and practice with interjections, see **Lesson 8** in *Language Workshop CD-ROM.*

■ **Practice** To help less-advanced students with additional instruction and practice with interjections, see **Chapter 12** in *English Workshop, Second Course,* pp. 111–112.

The Interjection

15e. An *interjection* is a word used to express emotion. It does not have a grammatical relation to other words in the sentence.

EXAMPLES   **Oh!** You surprised me.
Wow! Am I tired!
Well, I did my best.

> EXERCISE 16　**Identifying Interjections**

ANSWERS
Exercise 16

Speakers: Jack of "Jack and the Beanstalk," Baby Bear from "Goldilocks and the Three Bears," Little Red Riding Hood, and the wolf from "The Three Little Pigs"

Some fairy tale characters are meeting to discuss their image. They're worried that the familiar fairy tales make them look stupid or silly. Identify the ten <u>interjections</u> used in the dialogue. Then try to guess who the four fairy tale speakers are.

EXAMPLE　**[1] "Hooray! We're finally getting a chance to tell our side of the stories!"**

　　　　1. *Hooray!*

[1] "<u>Beans</u>! It's not fair what they say. I knew I was taking a giant step that day."

[2] "<u>Well</u>, it's not fair what they say about us, either. Don't you think Papa and Mama saw that little blonde girl snooping around our house?"

[3] "<u>Yeah</u>! And don't you think I intended to buy magic beans, anyway?"

[4] "You guys don't have it as bad as I do. <u>Ugh</u>! How dumb do people think I am? Of course I'd know my own grandmother when I saw her."

[5] "<u>Pooh</u>! I think your cloak was over your eyes, but how about me? I didn't go near those three pigs."

[6] "<u>What</u>! Next you'll probably tell me that I didn't see your brother at Grandmother's house."

[7] "<u>Humph</u>! I don't know what you really saw. It's difficult to tell sometimes in the woods."

[8] "<u>Aw</u>, let's not argue. We've got to put our best feet forward—all the way up the beanstalk if need be."

[9] "<u>Yes</u>! And I want to give people the real story about that kid who broke my bed."

[10] "<u>Great</u>! I'm ready to squeal on those three pigs!"

Determining Parts of Speech

The part of speech of a word is determined by the way the word is used in a sentence. Many words can be used as more than one part of speech.

REVIEWS D–F

OBJECTIVES

- To identify the parts of speech of words in sentences
- To add interjections, conjunctions, prepositions, adverbs, and verbs to sentences

482 *The Parts of Speech*

EXAMPLES **Each** cost three dollars. [pronoun]
Each student baked a cake. [adjective]

The tired shoppers sat **down** for a while. [adverb]
The ball rolled **down** the hill. [preposition]

A member of the crew has spotted **land.** [noun]
The pilot can **land** here safely. [verb]

Well, he seems to have recovered. [interjection]
He doesn't look **well** to me. [adjective]

▶ REVIEW D **Identifying Parts of Speech**

Identify the part of speech of the <u>italicized word</u> in each sentence. Be prepared to explain your answers.

EXAMPLES **1.** The *ship* entered the harbor slowly.
1. *noun* n. = noun   pro. = pronoun   adj. = adjective
                   v. = verb   adv. = adverb
2. Did they *ship* the package to Dee and Seth?
2. *verb*
                   conj. = conjunction   prep. = preposition   itj. = interjection

1. The English test was easy *for* him. **1.** prep.
2. He didn't go to the movies, *for* he wanted to practice on the drums. **2.** conj.
3. It was a steep *climb,* but we made it to the top of the hill. **3.** n.
4. Kimiko and I *climb* the stairs for exercise. **4.** v.
5. *Some* volunteered to sell tickets. **5.** pro.
6. We donated *some* clothes to the rummage sale. **6.** adj.
7. Looking for shells, the girl strolled *along* the shore. **7.** prep.
8. When we went sailing, Raúl and Manuel came *along.* **8.** adv.
9. I lost *my* book report! **9.** pro. [*or* adj.]
10. *My!* This is not a good day! **10.** itj.

▶ REVIEW E **Identifying Parts of Speech**

Identify the part of speech of each italicized word or group of words in the following paragraphs. Be prepared to explain your answers. **See Review D for key to abbreviations.**

MEETING *individual* NEEDS

LEARNING STYLES

Kinetic Learners. You may want to encourage students to play with the parts of speech in much the same way they would piece together the parts of a puzzle. Using colored construction paper, make six sets of cards, one set each for nouns, pronouns, adjectives, verbs, adverbs, and prepositions. Each set of cards (each part of speech) will be a different color. Ask students to take three cards from each set and to create three complete sentences by stringing the parts of speech together appropriately. Students are free to use any extra words, as necessary, but they must make use of all the parts of speech that they select.

EXAMPLE   Dancing may be [1] *easy* for [2] *some*, but I have
[3] *always* had [4] *two* left [5] *feet*.

1. *adjective*   **2.** *pronoun*   **3.** *adverb*
4. *adjective*   **5.** *noun*

      1. adv. **2.** n. **3.** v. **4.** pro. **5.** itj. **6.** adv. **7.** prep.

[1] *Yesterday* after [2] *school*, one of my friends [3] *tried* to
teach [4] *me* some new dance steps. [5] *Well*, I was [6] *so*   **8.** n.
embarrassed I could have hidden [7] *in* the [8] *closet*. My   **9.** v.
feet [9] *seem* to have [10] *minds* of [11] *their* own [12] *and* do   **10.** n.
[13] *not* do what I want them to.   **11.** pro. [or adj.] **12.** conj. **13.** adv.

    "You're [14] *too* tense when you dance, [15] *or* you're try-   **14.** adv.
ing too hard. [16] *You* should [17] *relax* more," my friend   **15.** conj.
told me.   **16.** pro. **17.** v. **18.** itj. **19.** adv.

    [18] *"What!* [19] *How* can I relax?" I groaned. [20] *"No one*   **20.** pro.
[21] *can relax* when his body goes [22] *left* and his feet go   **21.** v.
right!" At that point, I [23] *decided* to give up, but I know I'll   **22.** adv.
try [24] *again* [25] *another* day.   **23.** v. **24.** adv. **25.** adj.

REVIEW F   **Using Different Parts of Speech**

Complete the following poem by adding words that
are the parts of speech called for in the blank spaces.

EXAMPLE   Why [1] *(verb)* Robin all alone?
               [2] *(adverb)* have all the others gone?
               1. *Why sits Robin all alone?*
               2. *Where have all the others gone?*

[1] *(interjection)*, Robin thought her day was just fine.
She [2] *(verb)* to the concert, and there wasn't a line.
[3] *(conjunction)* when she got in and sat herself down,
People were leaving [4] *(preposition)* rows all around.
You can see that Robin looks [5] *(adverb)* dejected;
She thinks that she [6] *(verb)* rejected.
If only she could have the chairs as her friends—
[7] *(interjection!)* —she'd have friends without end.
She sat [8] *(adverb)* and worried and pondered.
Was the problem with her [9] *(conjunction)* the others?
   she wondered.
Then she [10] *(verb)* at her ticket and saw she was late,
So she imagined the concert, and it was just great!

ANSWERS

Review F

Responses will vary. Here are some
possibilities:

  1. Well
  2. went
  3. But
  4. from
  5. extremely
  6. has been
  7. Hooray!
  8. there
  9. or
  10. looked

VISUAL CONNECTIONS

Ideas for Writing. Tell students to imagine that they are the girl
who is sitting in Bonnie Timmon's illustration. Have students write journal
entries explaining why there are so
many chairs and why the girl is alone.
Encourage students to incorporate all
of the parts of speech in their journal
entries.

LESSON 7 *(pp. 484–486)*

REVIEW: POSTTESTS 1 and 2

OBJECTIVES

- To identify verbs, adverbs, prepositions, conjunctions, and interjections
- To identify action, helping, and linking verbs
- To write sentences by using given words as two different parts of speech

GRAMMAR

GRAMMAR

484 *The Parts of Speech*

Review: Posttest 1

A. Identifying Different Parts of Speech

Identify each <u>italicized word or word group</u> in the following sentences as a *verb*, an *adverb*, a *preposition*, a *conjunction*, or an *interjection*. For each verb, indicate whether it is an *action verb*, a *helping verb*, or a *linking verb*. [Note: Keep in mind that correlative conjunctions and some prepositions have more than one word.]

EXAMPLE   **1.** I *am* reading a book *about* baseball cards.
          1. *am—helping verb; about—preposition*

1. a.v./adv.   **1.** We <u>*watched*</u> as the skywriter spelled out the words <u>*carefully*</u>.

2. conj./conj./   **2.** <u>*Both*</u> the dog <u>*and*</u> the cat <u>*are*</u> dirty and need baths.
l.v.

          3. <u>*Whoops*</u>! I dropped my ring <u>*under*</u> the counter.

3. itj./prep.   **4.** <u>*Today*</u> we studied the contributions that ancient

4. adv./prep.   North Africans made <u>*to*</u> mathematics.

5. adv./adv.   **5.** Clever replies <u>*never*</u> occur to me until the situation is <u>*long*</u> past.

6. h.v./prep.   **6.** Sandy <u>*does*</u> not have enough granola <u>*for*</u> breakfast.

7. a.v./prep.   **7.** The girl <u>*tried*</u> again <u>*in spite of*</u> her previous difficulty.

8. itj./conj./   **8.** <u>*Well*</u>, I really want to see <u>*either*</u> Key West <u>*or*</u> the
conj.   Everglades when we go to Florida next summer.

9. adv./h.v.   **9.** <u>*How*</u> <u>*did*</u> the other team win so easily?

10. l.v./conj.   **10.** The beans with rice <u>*tasted*</u> good, <u>*for*</u> we were hungry.

B. Identifying Different Parts of Speech

Identify each <u>italicized word or word group</u> in the following paragraph as a *verb*, an *adverb*, a *preposition*, or a *conjunction*. [Note: Keep in mind that correlative conjunctions and some prepositions have more than one word.]

EXAMPLE   [1] You likely know that Christopher Columbus was a famous explorer, *but* do you know anything *about* his personal life?
          1. *but—conjunction; about—preposition*

484

[11] I've *learned* some interesting facts *about* Christopher Columbus. **[12]** He was born *into* a hard-working Italian family and *learned* how to sail as a boy. **[13]** He *became not only* a master sailor *but also* a mapmaker. **[14]** Although he had *barely* any formal education, he did *study* both Portuguese and Spanish. **[15]** The writings *of* ancient scholars about astronomy and geography *especially* interested him. **[16]** Columbus *apparently had* keen powers of observation. **[17]** These *served* him *well* on his expeditions. **[18]** On his voyages to find a sea route *to* the East Indies, Columbus *was* a determined, optimistic leader. **[19]** He let *neither* doubters *nor* hardships interfere *with* his plans. **[20]** Many people mistakenly think that Columbus was poor when he died in 1506, *but* he was actually *quite* wealthy.

11. v./prep.
12. prep./v.
13. v./conj./conj.
14. adv./v.
15. prep./adv.
16. adv./v.
17. v./adv.
18. prep./v.
19. conj./conj./prep.
20. conj./adv.

GRAMMAR

Review: Posttest 2

Writing Sentences Using Different Parts of Speech

Write two sentences using each of the following words as the parts of speech given in parentheses. Underline the word in the sentence, and write its part of speech after the sentence.

EXAMPLE **1.** over (*adverb* and *preposition*)
  1. *The mob pushed on the statue of the defeated tyrant until they tipped it* over*. (adverb)*
    The horse jumped over *the fence. (preposition)*

1. but (*conjunction* and *preposition*)
2. like (*verb* and *preposition*)
3. run (*noun* and *verb*)
4. well (*adverb* and *interjection*)
5. that (*pronoun* and *adjective*)
6. more (*adjective* and *adverb*)
7. last (*verb* and *adjective*)
8. past (*noun* and *preposition*)
9. near (*verb* and *preposition*)
10. around (*preposition* and *adverb*)

ANSWERS
Review: Posttest 2

Sentences will vary. Here are some possibilities:

1. He liked apples but hated oranges. (conjunction)
   Everyone but the king was asleep. (preposition)

2. I like to watch sunrises. (verb)
   The cloud looked like an elephant. (preposition)

3. We went for a short run this morning. (noun)
   Run three slow laps to warm up. (verb)

4. I wish I could sing well. (adverb)
   Well, I hope you are satisfied! (interjection)

5. That is the way Nancy wants it done. (pronoun)
   Give Charles that orange. (adjective)

6. The dog wanted more food. (adjective)
   I feel more energetic today. (adverb)

7. Our food supply will last for a month. (verb)
   The bus arrived at the station at the last moment. (adjective)

8. History scholars love to study the past. (noun)
   The car went past the driveway. (preposition)

9. If the dog hears us, it will near the fence. (verb)
   The train stopped near the school. (preposition)

10. The executives sat around the conference table. (preposition)
    The child's turn to answer came around again. (adverb)

GRAMMAR

COOPERATIVE LEARNING

Give each student three slips of paper. Ask each student to write a different word and its part of speech on each slip of paper. For example, a student might write *sounds*—verb; *bellows*—noun; and *under*—adverb.

Collect all the papers and redistribute three random words to each student. Then divide the class into groups of four or five. Have each group write a story using the words each person contributes from his or her pieces of paper, making sure each word is used according to the designated part of speech. When they are finished, you may want to have the groups read their stories to the class.

TIMESAVER

Enlarge this chart or have a student copy it onto poster board and put it on the wall. You can save time by referring to the chart as you teach lessons of this chapter, and students can refer to the chart throughout the year when they are writing.

SUMMARY OF PARTS OF SPEECH

Rule	Part of Speech	Use	Examples
14a	noun	names a person, a place, a thing, or an idea	Despite her **fear** of the **dark, Maya** enjoyed her **trip** through **Mammoth Cave.**
14b	pronoun	takes the place of a noun	**I myself** do not know **anyone who** saw **it.**
14c	adjective	modifies a noun or a pronoun	The **last stand-up** comedian, **talented** and **confident**, was **hilarious.**
15a	verb	shows action or a state of being	If we **had arrived** earlier, we **would have seen** many celebrities. We **were** upset. No one **was** there.
15b	adverb	modifies a verb, an adjective, or another adverb	I did **not** answer the last question **correctly.** It was **much more** difficult than the other questions.
15c	preposition	relates a noun or a pronoun to another word	**Because of** the storm the bridge **across** the bay was closed.
15d	conjunction	joins words or groups of words	Teachers **and** students will perform in the talent show. **Either** the principal **or** I will emcee the show.
15e	interjection	expresses emotion	**Ouch!** That hurts! **Aw**, that's too bad.

OBJECTIVE

- To identify direct objects, indirect objects, predicate nominatives, and predicate adjectives in sentences

PROGRAM MANAGER

FOR THE WHOLE CHAPTER

- Review For exercises on chapter concepts, see **Review Form A** and **Review Form B** in *Language Skills Practice and Assessment*, pp. 58–61.

- Assessment For additional testing, see **Grammar Pretests** and **Grammar Mastery Tests** in *Language Skills Practice and Assessment*, pp. 1–8 and pp. 103–110.

16 COMPLEMENTS

Direct and Indirect Objects, Subject Complements

CHAPTER OVERVIEW

This chapter begins by explaining the sentence base and the use of complements to complete the meaning of verbs. Direct and indirect objects, which complete the meaning of action verbs, are covered first. Using action verbs with objects to write an interesting letter is the purpose of the **Writing Application**. The final part of the chapter discusses the use of predicate nominative and predicate adjectives to complete the meanings of linking verbs.

The material in this chapter could be used as a reference when teaching any of the composition chapters. It will be particularly useful with **Chapter 11: "Writing Effective Sentences."**

Diagnostic Test

Identifying Complements

Identify each of the <u>italicized words or word groups</u> in the following sentences as a *direct object*, an *indirect object*, a *predicate nominative*, or a *predicate adjective*.

EXAMPLES **1.** The rancher raised prizewinning *cattle.*
1. *cattle—direct object*

2. The rancher became a rich *man.*
2. *man—predicate nominative*

1. Pilar caught the <u>*ball*</u> and threw it to first base.   **1.** d.o.
2. Your cousin seems <u>*nice*</u>.   **2.** p.a.
3. I'm not the <u>*one*</u> who did that.   **3.** p.n.
4. The sun grew <u>*hotter*</u> as the day went on.   **4.** p.a.
5. Mrs. Sato gave <u>*me*</u> a failing grade.   **5.** i.o.
6. Whoopi Goldberg is <u>*famous*</u> for comedy.   **6.** p.a.
7. Amy's father and mother are both truck <u>*drivers*</u>.   **7.** p.n.

RECOGNIZING COMPLEMENTS Rule 16a

OBJECTIVES

- To identify subjects, verbs, and complements in sentences
- To compose sentences containing complements

USING THE DIAGNOSTIC TEST

You could use **the Diagnostic Test** to determine the amount of reteaching of complements your students need. If students do well on the **Diagnostic Test,** you may want to let them move through the chapter quickly, perhaps working only the **Review** exercises. Stress the **Writing Application, Exercise 8,** and **Picture This,** in which students will be writing original sentences that illustrate the material in the chapter.

PROGRAM MANAGER

RECOGNIZING COMPLEMENTS

- Independent Practice/ Reteaching For instruction and exercises, see **Subject, Verb, and Complement** in *Language Skills Practice and Assessment,* p. 55.

- Computer Guided Instruction For additional instruction and practice with recognizing complements, see **Lesson 34** in *Language Workshop CD-ROM.*

---

488 *Complements*

8. Have you bought your *tickets* yet?   **8.** d.o.
9. Did James ride his new *trail bike* to school today?   **9.** d.o.
10. The irate customer sent the *store manager* a letter of complaint.   **10.** i.o.
11. The nurse gave *Willie* a flu shot.   **11.** i.o.
12. Josh often looks *tired* on Monday mornings.   **12.** p.a.
13. With his calloused hands he cannot feel the *texture* of velvet.   **13.** d.o.
14. My sister's room is always *neater* than mine.   **14.** p.a.
15. Heather, who is new at our school, is the nicest *girl* I know.   **15.** p.n.
16. The Algonquians used *toboggans* to haul goods over snow and ice.   **16.** d.o.
17. Throw *Eric* a screen pass.   **17.** i.o.   **18.** p.n.
18. When left to dry in the sun, plums become *prunes.*
19. Dr. Charles Drew gave *science* a better way to process and store blood.   **19.** i.o.
20. Ms. Rosada will be our Spanish *teacher* this fall.
          20. p.n.

Recognizing Complements

16a.   A *complement* is a word or a group of words that completes the meaning of a verb.

Every sentence has a subject and a verb. Often a verb also needs a complement to make the sentence complete. Without a complement, each of the following subjects and verbs does not make a sentence.

```
                  S       V
INCOMPLETE   Marlene brought [what?]

                  S       V        C
  COMPLETE   Marlene brought sandwiches.

                  S      V
INCOMPLETE   Carlos thanked [whom?]

                  S      V      C
  COMPLETE   Carlos thanked her.
```

                          S   V
INCOMPLETE   **We were** [*what?*]
                          S   V   C
    COMPLETE   **We were hungry.**

As you can see, a complement may be a noun, a pronoun, or an adjective. Complements complete the meanings of verbs in several ways.

EXAMPLES   **Jody painted her room.** [The noun *room* completes the meaning of the verb telling *what* Jody painted.]

My uncle sent me a postcard. [The pronoun *me* and the noun *postcard* complete the meaning of the verb by telling *what* was sent and *to whom* it was sent.]

The Ephron sisters are writers. [The noun *writers* completes the meaning of the verb *are* by identifying the sisters.]

This story is exciting. [The adjective *exciting* completes the meaning of the verb *is.*]

An adverb is never a complement.

    ADVERB   **The dog is outside.** [*Outside* modifies the verb by telling where the dog is.]
COMPLEMENT   **The dog is friendly.** [The adjective *friendly* modifies the subject by telling what kind of dog.]

A complement is never part of a prepositional phrase.

COMPLEMENT   **Benjamin is studying his geography notes.**
    OBJECT OF   **Benjamin is studying for his geography test.**
PREPOSITION

☞ REFERENCE NOTE: For more information on prepositional phrases, see pages 506–509.

▶ EXERCISE 1   **Identifying Subjects, Verbs, and Complements**

Identify the <u>subject</u>, <u>verb</u>, and [complement] in each sentence in the following paragraph. [Remember: A complement is never in a prepositional phrase.]

QUICK REMINDER
Ask students to name the two essential parts of the sentence base [subject and verb]. Then write the following sentences on the chalkboard. Point out that even though each sentence has a subject and a verb, more information is needed. Ask students to complete the sentences and to underline the complements they add.

1. We enjoy ____.
2. Mark admired ____.
3. The story was ____.

MEETING *individual* NEEDS
STUDENTS WITH SPECIAL NEEDS
You may want to provide students with an organizational strategy for **Exercise 1.** List the following steps on the chalkboard and suggest that students follow this sequence in analyzing each sentence in the exercise:

1. Delete the prepositional phrases (as a reminder that essential parts cannot be within a prepositional phrase).
2. Locate the verb.
3. Find the subject.
4. Find the complement that receives the action or renames the subject.

EXAMPLE [1] William Shakespeare was one of the owners of the Globe Theater.
1. *William Shakespeare—subject; was—verb; one—complement*

[1] During Shakespeare's time, <u>plays</u> <u>were</u> a common form of entertainment in England. [2] A great many <u>people</u> <u>watched</u> plays at the most popular playhouse in London—the Globe Theater. [3] <u>Richard</u> and <u>Cuthbert Burbage</u> <u>built</u> the Globe in 1599. [4] In this drawing, <u>you</u> <u>can see</u> many of the differences between the Globe and most modern theaters. [5] The <u>Globe</u> <u>was</u> a building with eight sides. [6] The <u>building</u> <u>enclosed</u> an inner courtyard. [7] The <u>stage</u> <u>was</u> a raised platform at one end of the courtyard. [8] <u>Some</u> of the audience <u>watched</u> the play from seats around the courtyard. [9] Many <u>playgoers</u>, however, <u>did</u> not <u>have</u> seats during a performance. [10] These <u>people</u> <u>filled</u> the courtyard in front of the stage.

The Granger Collection, New York.

▷ EXERCISE 2 **Writing Sentences with Complements**

Write five sentences by adding a different complement to each of the following groups of words.

SUBJECT	VERB
1. men	asked
2. days	are
3. Pam	sent
4. runner	seemed
5. weather	will be

DIRECT OBJECTS AND INDIRECT OBJECTS Rules 16b, 16c

OBJECTIVES

- To identify action verbs and their direct objects in sentences
- To identify direct objects and indirect objects in sentences

Direct Objects and Indirect Objects

The *direct object* and the *indirect object* are the two kinds of complements that complete the meaning of an action verb.

☞ REFERENCE NOTE: For more information about action verbs, see pages 457–459.

Direct Objects

16b. A *direct object* is a noun or a pronoun that receives the action of the verb or shows the result of the action. A direct object tells *what* or *whom* after an action verb.

EXAMPLES Our history class built a **model** of the Alamo.
[The noun *model* shows the result of the action verb *built* and tells *what* the class built.]
Has the freeze destroyed **some** of the crops?
[The pronoun *some* shows the result of the action verb *Has destroyed* and tells *what* the freeze destroyed.]
Dorothea Lange photographed **farmers** in the Midwest during the Depression. [The noun *farmers* receives the action of the verb *photographed* and tells *whom* Dorothea Lange photographed.]

NOTE: A direct object may be compound.

EXAMPLE The man wore a white **beard,** a red **suit,** and black **boots.**

 EXERCISE 3 **Identifying Action Verbs and Direct Objects**

Identify the <u>action verb</u> and the <u>direct object</u> in each of the following sentences.

 PROGRAM MANAGER

DIRECT OBJECTS AND INDIRECT OBJECTS

- **Independent Practice/ Reteaching** For instruction and exercises, see **Direct Objects and Indirect Objects** in *Language Skills Practice and Assessment,* p. 56.
- **Computer Guided Instruction** For additional instruction and practice with direct objects and indirect objects, see **Lesson 35** in *Language Workshop CD-ROM.*
- **Practice** To help less-advanced students with additional instruction and practice with direct objects and indirect objects, see **Chapter 13** in *English Workshop, Second Course,* pp. 115–118.

QUICK REMINDER

Write the following sentences on the chalkboard and have students fill in the blanks:

1. Juanita bought a ____ and a ____.
2. The football player kicked the ____.
3. I gave ____ a ____.

Explain to students that the verbs in the sentences above (*bought, kicked,* and *gave*) are action verbs. All the words students added to the blanks complete the action of the verbs as direct and indirect objects.

GRAMMAR

GRAMMAR

16b

TIMESAVER

To lessen time spent grading papers, you could have students do **Exercise 3** orally. However, you may first want to guide students through the process of finding the verbs and complements in interrogative sentences to prepare them for sentences 5, 7, and 10. Remind students to turn the question into a statement before they attempt to analyze it.

492 *Complements*

EXAMPLE   **1.** Volunteers distributed food to the flood victims.
　　　　　　1. *distributed—food*

1. On the plains the Cheyenne <u>hunted</u> <u>buffalo</u> for food and clothing.
2. We <u>watched</u> a <u>performance</u> of Lorraine Hansberry's *A Raisin in the Sun.*
3. During most of its history the United States <u>has welcomed</u> <u>refugees</u> from other countries.
4. The leading man <u>wore</u> a <u>hat</u> with a large plume.
5. <u>Are</u> you <u>preserving</u> the <u>environment</u>?
6. After the game the coach <u>answered</u> <u>questions</u> from the sports reporters.
7. <u>Did</u> you <u>see</u> her <u>performance</u> on television?
8. The researchers <u>followed</u> the birds' <u>migration</u> from Mexico to Canada.
9. Mayor Fiorello La Guardia <u>governed</u> <u>New York City</u> during the Depression.
10. <u>Have</u> the movie theaters <u>announced</u> the special <u>discount</u> for teenagers yet?

Indirect Objects

16c. An *indirect object* is a noun or a pronoun that comes between the action verb and the direct object and tells *to what* or *to whom* or *for what* or *for whom* the action of the verb is done.

EXAMPLES   **Dad gave the horse an apple.** [The noun *horse* tells *to what* Dad gave an apple.]
　　　　　　Luke showed the class his collection of comic books. [The noun *class* tells *to whom* Luke showed his collection.]
　　　　　　Sarita bought us a chess set. [The pronoun *us* tells *for whom* Sarita bought a chess set.]

An indirect object, like a direct object, is never in a prepositional phrase.

REVIEW A

OBJECTIVE

- To identify direct and indirect objects in sentences within a paragraph

16c

INDIRECT OBJECT	She sent her **mother** some flowers.
OBJECT OF PREPOSITION	She sent some flowers to her **mother.**

NOTE: Like a direct object, an indirect object may be compound.

EXAMPLE Uncle Alphonso bought my **brother** and **me** an aquarium.

 EXERCISE 4   **Identifying Direct Objects and Indirect Objects**

Identify the <u>direct objects</u> and the <u>indirect objects</u> in the following sentences. [Note: Not every sentence has an indirect object.]

EXAMPLE   **1.** They gave us their solemn promise.
     1. *promise—direct object; us—indirect object*

1. They sent <u>me</u> on a wild-goose chase.
2. Gloria mailed the <u>company</u> a <u>check</u> yesterday.
3. The speaker showed the <u>audience</u> the <u>slides</u> of Zimbabwe.
4. Juan would not deliberately tell <u>you</u> and <u>me</u> a <u>lie</u>.
5. The coach praised the <u>students</u> for their school spirit.
6. I sent my <u>cousins</u> some embroidered <u>pillows</u> for their new apartment.
7. The art teacher displayed the students' <u>paintings</u>.
8. Sue's parents shipped <u>her</u> the <u>books</u> and the <u>magazines</u> she had forgotten.
9. Carly and Doreen taught <u>themselves</u> the <u>importance</u> of hard work.
10. In most foreign countries, United States citizens must carry their <u>passports</u> for identification.

 REVIEW A   **Identifying Direct Objects and Indirect Objects**

Identify the <u>direct objects</u> and the <u>indirect objects</u> in the sentences in the following paragraph. [Note: Not every sentence has an indirect object.]

Auditory Learners. It might be easier for some students to hear the direct and indirect objects than it is for them to recognize the objects visually. You could group students together and have them take turns reading aloud the example sentences and the sentences in the exercises.

Kinetic Learners. Ask students to write the following sentences on the chalkboard, to draw arrows from the verbs to the direct objects, and to circle the indirect objects:

1. She wrote me a letter.
2. He gave his dog a bone.
3. Tom brought us the newspaper.
4. Sue sang her sister a lullaby.

    Then tell students to create sentences and to mark the sentences in the same way.

GRAMMAR

GRAMMAR

COOPERATIVE LEARNING

A team race might help reinforce the use of direct and indirect objects. Have teams of four students write as many sentences using direct and indirect objects as possible in four minutes. Have students use the verbs *bought, followed, gave, sent,* and *showed* in their sentences. Award a point for each correct use of a direct object or an indirect object in a complete sentence.

You can continue the game by having the teams choose verbs and write sentences with direct and indirect objects. Again, give the teams a time limit.

WRITING APPLICATION

This assignment gives students practice in writing friendly letters with sentences that contain direct and indirect objects. You may wish to refer students to **Chapter 35: "Letters and Forms"** to review guidelines for letter writing.

WRITING APPLICATION

OBJECTIVE

• To write a descriptive letter containing direct objects and indirect objects

494 *Complements*

EXAMPLE [1] The spring rodeo gives our town an exciting weekend.
1. *weekend—direct object; town—indirect object*

[1] This year Mrs. Perez taught our <u>class</u> many interesting <u>facts</u> about rodeos. [2] She told <u>us</u> <u>stories</u> about the earliest rodeos, which took place more than a hundred years ago. [3] The word *rodeo,* she explained, means "<u>roundup</u>" in Spanish. [4] Mrs. Perez also showed <u>us</u> <u>drawings</u> and <u>pictures</u> of some well-known rodeo performers. [5] The Choctaw roper Clyde Burk especially caught our <u>interest</u>. [6] During Burk's career, the Rodeo Cowboys Association awarded <u>him</u> four world <u>championships</u>. [7] For years, Burk entertained <u>audiences</u> with his roping skill. [8] He also bought and trained <u>some</u> of the best rodeo horses available. [9] This picture shows <u>Burk</u> on his horse Baldy. [10] Burk often gave <u>Baldy</u> <u>credit</u> for his success.

WRITING APPLICATION

Using Direct and Indirect Objects

Writers often use action verbs. Many of these action verbs require direct objects and indirect objects to make a complete statement. Without these objects, sentences are incomplete and cannot express your meaning to your readers.

INCOMPLETE	READER WONDERS
My favorite music store sells.	Sells what?
Mom gave five dollars.	Gave five dollars to whom?

Complete the meanings of the two incomplete statements above by adding a direct object and an indirect object where they are needed.

▶ WRITING ACTIVITY

You've just returned home from an interesting and enjoyable shopping trip. Write a letter to a friend telling about what happened on this trip. Use direct objects and indirect objects in your letter.

Prewriting You may want to write about an actual shopping trip that you've made recently, perhaps to a shopping mall or a flea market. Or you can make up a shopping trip to another country or even another planet. Make a list of what you did, what you saw, and what you bought for whom.

Writing As you write your first draft, think about describing your shopping trip in a way that will interest your friend. Use vivid action verbs and specific direct objects and indirect objects. Be sure to tell when and where your trip took place.

Evaluating and Revising Read over your paragraph. Does it clearly tell why the shopping trip was so interesting and enjoyable? If not, you may want to add or change some details. Be sure that your paragraph follows a consistent and sensible order. For more about organizing ideas in a paragraph, see pages 74–83.

Proofreading Check your paragraph for errors in grammar, punctuation, and spelling. Use a telephone book to check the spelling of names of stores, shopping malls, or shopping centers.

GRAMMAR

CRITICAL THINKING

Analysis. After students have completed their prewriting lists, have them narrow the lists to fit both the interests of their audience and the desired lengths of their letters. This will require analysis of their lists in relationship to their friends' interests and the desired letter length.

PREWRITING

Remind students to choose specific friends to whom they are writing. As they prepare their lists, have them place asterisks (*) beside items that would be of particular interest to the friends.

EVALUATING AND REVISING

You may want to suggest that students put their writing aside for a while before revising it. Explain that professional writers often use this strategy to give them a fresh perspective on whether or not they have clearly communicated their ideas to their audience. Then, have students share their drafts with partners.

GRAMMAR

SUBJECT COMPLEMENTS Rules 16d, 16e

OBJECTIVES

- To identify linking verbs, predicate nominatives, and predicate adjectives in sentences
- To write a radio broadcast by using direct and indirect objects, predicate nominatives, and predicate adjectives

Subject Complements

A *subject complement* completes the meaning of a linking verb and identifies or describes the subject.

☞ REFERENCE NOTE: For more information about linking verbs, see page 461.

EXAMPLES Alice Eng is a dedicated **teacher.** [The noun *teacher* follows the linking verb *is* and identifies the subject *Alice Eng.*]

The lemonade tastes **sour.** [*Sour* follows the linking verb *tastes* and describes the subject *lemonade*—sour lemonade.]

There are two kinds of subject complements—*the predicate nominative* and the *predicate adjective.*

Predicate Nominatives

16d. A *predicate nominative* is a noun or a pronoun that follows a linking verb and identifies the subject or refers to it.

EXAMPLES My aunt's dog is a **collie.** [*Collie* is a predicate nominative that identifies *dog.*]

Enrique is **one** of the best players. [The pronoun *one* follows the linking verb *is* and refers to the subject *Enrique.*]

Like subjects and objects, predicate nominatives never appear in prepositional phrases.

EXAMPLES The prize was a **pair** of tickets to the movies. [The word *pair* identifies the subject *prize*. *Tickets* is the object of the preposition *of*, and *movies* is the object of the preposition *to*.]

NOTE: Predicate nominatives may be compound.

EXAMPLE Hernando de Soto was a **soldier** and a **diplomat.**

PROGRAM MANAGER

SUBJECT COMPLEMENTS

- **Independent Practice/ Reteaching** For instruction and exercises, see **Predicate Nominatives and Adjectives** in *Language Skills Practice and Assessment*, p. 57.

- **Computer Guided Instruction** For additional instruction and practice with subject complements, see **Lesson 36** in *Language Workshop CD-ROM.*

- **Practice** To help less-advanced students with additional instruction and practice with subject complements, see **Chapter 13** in *English Workshop, Second Course*, pp. 119–122.

QUICK REMINDER

Write the following sentences on the chalkboard and have students fill in each blank with three different one-word responses:

1. I am ____.
2. I am a(n) ____.

Explain to students that *am* is a linking verb and they have identified or described the subject by adding nouns, pronouns, or adjectives. Have students label the parts of speech of their complements.

GRAMMAR

- To write a diary entry by using action and linking verbs followed by complements and to classify each complement used

GRAMMAR

▶ EXERCISE 5 **Identifying Predicate Nominatives**

Identify the <u>predicate nominative</u> or <u>nominatives</u> in each of the following sentences.

EXAMPLE **1.** Robert A. Heinlein was one of our country's most important science fiction writers.
1. *one*

1. Before he became a <u>writer</u>, Heinlein had been a naval <u>officer</u> and an <u>engineer</u>.
2. Many of Heinlein's "future history" stories have become <u>classics</u>.
3. Heinlein's novels for young people and adults remain top <u>sellers</u>.
4. Published in 1961, *Stranger in a Strange Land* is a <u>novel</u> still enjoyed by many readers.
5. Heinlein was the <u>winner</u> of several Hugo Awards for his writing.

Predicate Adjectives

16e. A *predicate adjective* is an adjective that follows a linking verb and describes the subject.

EXAMPLES **An atomic reactor is very powerful.** [The adjective *powerful* follows the linking verb *is* and describes the subject *reactor.*]
This ground looks swampy. [The adjective *swampy* follows the linking verb *looks* and describes the subject *ground.*]

NOTE: Predicate adjectives may be compound.

EXAMPLE **A computer can be fun, helpful, and sometimes frustrating.**

▶ EXERCISE 6 **Identifying Predicate Adjectives**

Identify the <u>predicate adjective</u> or <u>adjectives</u> in each of the following sentences.

COMMON ERROR
Problem. Students might use objective-case pronouns as predicate nominatives. Examples include "It's me" and "That is him."

Solution. Refer students to the list of nominative-case pronouns on p. 635. Emphasize that in formal English only the nominative-case pronouns can be used as predicate nominatives. Then provide some correct examples.

GRAMMAR

INTEGRATING THE LANGUAGE ARTS

Grammar and Writing. Ask students to compose an autobiographical paragraph using each type of complement—direct object, indirect object, predicate adjective, and predicate nominative. Students' paragraphs might include information about their families; their favorite foods, music, sports, or books; or their goals in life.

TECHNOLOGY TIP

You could give students practice in identifying complements while familiarizing them with certain word-processing formatting options. When students revise their autobiographical paragraphs, suggest that they double-space, add one-inch margins, and underscore verbs. Students could identify verb and complement types by using the following labels:

1. AV (action verb)
2. LV (linking verb)
3. DO (direct object)
4. IO (indirect object)
5. PA (predicate adjective)
6. PN (predicate nominative)

EXAMPLE   **1.** San Francisco's Chinatown is large and fascinating.
   1. *large, fascinating*

1. The great stone dogs that guard the entrance to Chinatown look a bit <u>frightening</u>.
2. The streets there are <u>crowded</u>, <u>colorful</u>, and <u>full</u> of bustling activity.
3. The special foods at the tearooms and restaurants smell <u>wonderful</u>.
4. To an outsider, the mixture of Chinese and English languages sounds both <u>mysterious</u> and <u>exciting</u>.
5. The art at the Chinese Culture Center is <u>impressive</u>.

Some verbs, such as *look, grow,* and *feel,* may be used as either linking verbs or action verbs.

LINKING VERB   **The sailor felt tired.** [*Felt* is a linking verb because it links the adjective *tired* to the subject *sailor.*]

ACTION VERB   **The sailor felt the cool breeze.** [*Felt* is an action verb because it is followed by the direct object *breeze,* which tells what the sailor felt.]

 EXERCISE 7   **Identifying Linking Verbs and Subject Complements**

Identify the <u>linking verb</u> and the <u>subject complement</u> in each of the following sentences. Then, identify each complement as a *predicate* <u>n</u>*ominative* or a *predicate* <u>a</u>*djective.*

EXAMPLE   **1.** The raincoat looked too short for me.
   1. *looked; short—predicate adjective*

1. My dog <u>is</u> <u>playful</u>.   **1.** p.a.
2. I <u>am</u> the <u>one</u> who called you yesterday.   **2.** p.n.
3. Many public buildings in the East <u>are</u> <u>proof</u> of I. M. Pei's architectural skill.   **3.** p.n.   **4.** p.a.
4. The downtown mall <u>appeared</u> especially <u>busy</u> today.
5. Sally Ride <u>sounded</u> <u>excited</u> and <u>confident</u> during the television interview.   **5.** p.a./p.a.

498

6. The package <u>felt</u> too <u>light</u> to be a book. **6.** p.a.
7. These questions <u>seem</u> <u>easier</u> to me than the ones on the last two tests did. **7.** p.a.
8. The singer's clothing <u>became</u> a <u>symbol</u> that her fans imitated. **8.** p.n.
9. Some poems, such as "The Bells" and "The Raven," <u>are</u> delightfully <u>rhythmical</u>. **9.** p.a.
10. While the mountain lion looked around for food, the fawn <u>remained</u> perfectly <u>still</u>. **10.** p.a.

▶ REVIEW B   **Identifying Subject Complements**

Each of the following sentences has at least one subject complement. Identify each complement as a *predicate nominative* or a *predicate adjective*.

EXAMPLE   **1.** All the food at the Spanish Club dinner was terrific.
            1. *terrific—predicate adjective*

1. These tacos and Juan's fajitas seemed the most <u>popular</u> of the Mexican foods brought to the dinner.
2. The *ensalada campesina,* or peasant salad of Chile, which contained chickpeas, was Rosalinda's <u>contribution</u>.

3. The Ecuadorian tamales not only looked <u>good</u> but also tasted <u>great</u>.
4. The baked fish fillets from Bolivia were <u>spicy</u> and quite <u>appetizing</u>.
5. Peru is <u>famous</u> for its soups, and the shrimp soup was a <u>winner</u>.

REVIEWS B and C

OBJECTIVES

- To identify complements and to classify them as direct objects, indirect objects, predicate nominatives, or predicate adjectives
- To identify verbs and to classify them as action or linking verbs

GRAMMAR

COOPERATIVE LEARNING

Divide the class into heterogeneous groups of four for this activity. Try to include at least one advanced student in each group. Explain to students that they will take turns composing sentences with complements, but that each person's sentence is dependent on the preceding one for information.

For example, the first group member might say "James ate a sandwich." The next member must use the complement as a subject, as in "The sandwich was delicious." In the next sentence, because an adjective cannot be the subject of a sentence, the third member must use the complement to modify the subject, as in "The delicious juice is quite sweet."

If a student creates a sentence such as "The sweet kitten never scratched me," the objective pronoun (*me*) becomes subjective (*I*), and the next sentence could be "I play soccer."

The activity is not an easy one, as students will realize that not all action verbs take objects. Have a recorder in each group write down the sentences, and at the end of ten minutes have each group report to the rest of the class.

GRAMMAR

6. The noodles with mushroom sauce was a <u>specialty</u> of Paraguay.
7. The Spanish cauliflower with garlic and onions was a <u>treat</u> but seemed too <u>exotic</u> for some students.
8. However, the pan of *hallacas*, the national cornmeal dish of Venezuela, was soon <u>empty</u>.
9. *Arroz con coco*, or coconut rice, from Puerto Rico quickly became the most requested <u>dessert</u>.
10. After dinner, all of us certainly felt <u>full</u> and much more <u>knowledgeable</u> about foods from Spanish-speaking countries.

▶ REVIEW C **Identifying Verbs and Complements**

Identify the verbs in the following sentences as <u>*action verbs*</u> or [*linking verbs*] Then, identify the <u>complements</u> as *direct objects*, *indirect objects*, *predicate nominatives*, or *predicate adjectives*.

EXAMPLE **[1] Because they want artistic freedom, many people from other countries become United States citizens.**
1. *want—action verb; freedom—direct object; become—linking verb; citizens—predicate nominative*

1. p.n.

2. p.n./p.n.

3. p.a./p.a.

4. d.o./d.o./ d.o.

5. i.o./d.o.

6. i.o./d.o.

7. p.n.

8. d.o.

9. p.a./p.a.

10. d.o.

[1] Gilberto Zaldivar's story [is] a good <u>example</u>. [2] Zaldivar [was] an <u>accountant</u> and a community theater <u>producer</u> in Havana, Cuba, in 1961. [3] He [became] <u>unhappy</u> and <u>frustrated</u> with the Cuban government's control over the arts. [4] So he <u>left</u> his <u>job</u> and his <u>homeland</u> and <u>started</u> a new <u>life</u> in New York City. [5] The change <u>brought</u> <u>Zaldivar</u> many <u>opportunities</u>. [6] It also <u>gave</u> <u>audiences</u> in the United States a new entertainment <u>experience</u>. [7] Zaldivar [was] a <u>co-founder</u> of the *Repertorio Español* in 1968. [8] This company quickly <u>established</u> a <u>reputation</u> as the country's best Spanish-language theater troupe. [9] Their productions [were] <u>fresh</u> and <u>unfamiliar</u> to audiences. [10] Throughout the years, the company <u>has performed</u> numerous Spanish <u>classics</u> as well as new plays.

REVIEW C

Teaching Note. Some students might identify *plays* as a direct object in the tenth sentence. You could use this opportunity to point out that *as well as* is a compound preposition, which makes *plays* the object of the preposition.

EXERCISE 8 **Using Complements in Speaking**

You're a radio personality, broadcasting live from the grand opening of a record store. Comment on the store, the music it carries, and the customers coming in on the first day of business. Write ten sentences that might be a part of your broadcast. In your sentences, use at least two direct objects, two indirect objects, two predicate nominatives, and two predicate adjectives. Identify the complements you use.

EXAMPLES
1. *The weather is beautiful for the grand opening of Music and More.*
beautiful—predicate adjective
2. *Music and More gives you more music for your money.*
you—indirect object; music—direct object

PICTURE THIS

You're among the hundreds of spectators at this spectacular launch of a space shuttle from the Kennedy Space Center in Florida. As the shuttle zooms out of sight, you sit down to write in your diary. You want to record your

OBJECTIVES
- To identify complements as direct objects, indirect objects, predicate nominatives, or predicate adjectives
- To write specified types of sentences using specified types of complements and to identify each complement used

502 *Complements*

impressions of the launch. Write a paragraph about the liftoff. Use a combination of action verbs and linking verbs. Underline the complements that you use, and be prepared to identify them as *direct objects*, *indirect objects*, *predicate nominatives*, and *predicate adjectives*.

Subject: shuttle launch
Audience: yourself
Purpose: to record an exciting event

Review: Posttest 1

Identifying Complements

Identify each italicized word in the following paragraphs as a *direct object*, an *indirect object*, a *predicate nominative*, or a *predicate adjective*.

EXAMPLES   I enjoy [1] *cooking* but it can be hard [2] *work.*
  1. *cooking—direct object*
  2. *work—predicate nominative*

1. i.o. **2.** d.o.   My dad has been giving [1] *me* cooking [2] *lessons* since
3. p.a.   last summer. At first, I was [3] *reluctant* to tell the guys
4. p.n.   because some of them think that cooking is a girl's [4] *job.*
5. d.o.   But Dad told me to remind them that we guys eat [5] *meals*
           just as often as girls do. He also said that cooking is an ex-
6. p.n.   cellent [6] *way* for us to do our share of the work around
           the house.
7. d.o.   When I began, I could hardly boil [7] *water* without
8. p.a.   fouling up, but Dad remained [8] *patient* and showed [9] *me*
9. i.o.   the correct and easiest ways to do things. For example, did
10. d.o.   you know that water will boil faster if it has a little [10] *salt*
           in it or that cornstarch can make an excellent thickening
11. p.n.   [11] *agent* in everything from batter to gravy?

502

My first attempts tasted **[12]** *awful*, but gradually I've become a fairly good **[13]** *cook*. Probably my best complete meal is chicken **[14]** *stew*. Although stew doesn't require the highest **[15]** *grade* of chicken, a good baking hen will give **[16]** *it* a much better taste. I am always very **[17]** *careful* about picking out the vegetables, too. Our grocer probably thinks that I am too **[18]** *picky* when I demand the best **[19]** *ingredients*. I don't care, though, because when I serve my **[20]** *family* my stew, they say it is their favorite dish.

12. p.a.
13. p.n.
14. p.n.
15. d.o.
16. i.o.
17. p.a.
18. p.a.   19. d.o.   20. i.o.

GRAMMAR

Review: Posttest 2

Writing Sentences with Complements

Write sentences according to the following guidelines. Underline the direct object, the indirect object, or the subject complement in each sentence.

1. a declarative sentence with a direct object
2. a declarative sentence with a predicate nominative
3. an interrogative sentence with a predicate adjective
4. an imperative sentence with an indirect object
5. an exclamatory sentence with a predicate adjective

ANSWERS
Review: Posttest 2

Sentences will vary. Here are some possibilities:

1. Yesterday I sold the <u>car</u>.
2. All of the members of the team were fifteen-year-old <u>girls</u>.
3. Was the apple <u>ripe</u>?
4. Hand <u>me</u> the papers now.
5. Wow, that football game was <u>exciting</u>!

OBJECTIVE

- To identify prepositional, appositive, participial, infinitive, and gerund phrases in sentences

GRAMMAR

CHAPTER OVERVIEW

This chapter begins with a review of verb phrases and prepositional phrases, and the **Writing Application** focuses on the use of prepositional phrases in a story. The remainder of the chapter deals with identifying and using participles, infinitives, gerunds, and appositives.

The information presented can be used in conjunction with any of the composition chapters. In the revision stage of the writing process, students can use knowledge of phrases to combine sentences and subordinate ideas.

GRAMMAR

17 THE PHRASE

Prepositional, Verbal, and Appositive Phrases

Diagnostic Test

Identifying Phrases

In each of the following sentences, identify the <u>italicized phrase</u> as a *prepositional phrase*, a *participial phrase*, an *infinitive phrase*, a *gerund phrase*, or an *appositive phrase*. Do not separately identify a prepositional phrase that is part of a larger phrase.

EXAMPLE   **1.** My brother plans *to marry Maureen in June.*
           1. *to marry Maureen in June—infinitive phrase*

1. ger. phr.   **1.** *Fishing for bass* is my father's favorite pastime.
2. part. phr.   **2.** The seagulls *gliding through the air* looked like pieces of paper caught in the wind.
3. prep. phr.   **3.** The school bus was on time *in spite of the traffic jam*.
4. app. phr.   **4.** Ms. Hoban, *my science teacher*, got married last week.
5. inf. phr.   **5.** There is no time left *to answer your questions*.
6. prep. phr.   **6.** At the carnival, the band played songs *with a lively samba beat*.

7. He tried <u>*to do his best*</u> in the race.   **7.** inf. phr.
8. Nobody seems to be very interested in <u>*going to the fireworks display*</u>.   **8.** ger. phr.
9. Have you seen my cat, <u>*a long-haired Persian with yellow eyes*</u>?   **9.** app. phr.
10. Julio said that he prefers the bike <u>*with all-terrain tires and the wider, more comfortable seat*</u>.   **10.** prep. phr.
11. <u>*Hoping for a new bicycle and a toy robot*</u>, my brother couldn't sleep at all on Christmas Eve.   **11.** part. phr.
12. Rachel talked her friends into <u>*watching that Mariah Carey video*</u>.   **12.** ger. phr.
13. In the United States, citizens have the right <u>*to speak their minds*</u>.   **13.** inf. phr.
14. My aunt's car, <u>*an old crate with a beat-up interior and a rattly engine*</u>, used to belong to my grandfather.   **14.** app. phr.
15. The Mexican artist Diego Rivera enjoyed <u>*painting pictures of children*</u>.   **15.** ger. phr.
16. Last Sunday, we all piled in the car and went <u>*to the beach, the bowling alley, and the mall*</u>.   **16.** prep. phr.
17. The shark <u>*chasing the school of fish*</u> looked like a hammerhead.   **17.** part. phr.
18. Nobody wanted to read the book, <u>*a thick hardback with a faded cover*</u>.   **18.** app. phr.
19. All of the invitations <u>*sent to the club members*</u> had the wrong date on them.   **19.** part. phr.
20. Both the Union and the Confederacy recruited Native Americans <u>*to help them during the Civil War*</u>.   **20.** inf. phr.

GRAMMAR

USING THE DIAGNOSTIC TEST

In evaluating students' writing, you may discover that some students lack an understanding of the use of phrases. Perhaps students are using modifying phrases incorrectly, or perhaps their writing lacks variety. You could use the **Diagnostic Test** to define students' specific strengths and weaknesses. Then have students work individually or in small groups on activities and exercises designed for their particular needs.

GRAMMAR

17a. A *phrase* is a group of related words that is used as a single part of speech and does not contain a verb and its subject.

VERB PHRASE **should have been told** [no subject]
PREPOSITIONAL PHRASE **from my sister and me** [no subject or verb]

NOTE: A group of words that has both a subject and a verb is called a *clause.*

THE PREPOSITIONAL PHRASE Rules 17b–17d
OBJECTIVES
• To identify prepositional phrases
• To identify adjective and adverb phrases and the words they modify

PROGRAM MANAGER

THE PREPOSITIONAL PHRASE

- **Independent Practice/ Reteaching** For instruction and exercises, see **Prepositional Phrases** and **Adjective and Adverb Phrases** in *Language Skills Practice and Assessment,* pp. 65–66.

- **Computer Guided Instruction** For additional instruction and practice with prepositional phrases, see **Lesson 23** in *Language Workshop CD-ROM.*

- **Practice** To help less-advanced students with additional instruction and practice with prepositional phrases, see **Chapter 14** in *English Workshop, Second Course,* pp. 125–130.

QUICK REMINDER

Write the following phrases on the chalkboard or write a few phrases relating to your individual classroom:

1. on the bookcase
2. near Valerie's desk
3. over the world map

Ask students what these phrases are called [prepositional phrases]. Point out that each phrase begins with a preposition and ends with an object. Then have students use these phrases in complete sentences. You could have students share their sentences orally.

506

---

506 *The Phrase*

EXAMPLES   **Leta is watching television.** [*Leta* is the subject of the verb *is watching.*]
           before the train arrived [*Train* is the subject of the verb *arrived.*]

☞ REFERENCE NOTE: For more about clauses, see Chapter 18.

The Prepositional Phrase

17b. A *prepositional phrase* includes a preposition, a noun or a pronoun called the *object of the preposition,* and any modifiers of that object.

EXAMPLES   **The Seine River flows through Paris.** [The noun *Paris* is the object of the preposition *through.*]
           The car in front of us slid into a snowbank. [The pronoun *us* is the object of the preposition *in front of.* The noun *snowbank* is the object of the preposition *into.*]

☞ REFERENCE NOTE: For a list of commonly used prepositions, see page 474.

Any modifier that comes between the preposition and its object is part of the prepositional phrase.

EXAMPLE   **During the stormy night the horse ran off.** [The adjectives *the* and *stormy* modify the object *night.*]

An object of the preposition may be compound.

EXAMPLE   **The dish is filled with raw carrots and celery.** [Both *carrots* and *celery* are objects of the preposition *with.*]

Be careful not to confuse an infinitive with a prepositional phrase. A prepositional phrase always has an object that is a noun or a pronoun. An infinitive is a verb form that usually begins with *to.*

PREPOSITIONAL PHRASE   When we went **to Florida,** we saw the old Spanish fort in Saint Augustine.
INFINITIVE   When we were in Florida, we went **to see** the old Spanish fort in Saint Augustine.

 REFERENCE NOTE: For more about infinitives, see page 522.

▶ EXERCISE 1 **Identifying Prepositional Phrases**

Identify the <u>prepositional phrase or phrases</u> in each numbered sentence in the following paragraph.

EXAMPLE **[1]** Do you recognize the man with a Harlem Globetrotters uniform and a basketball in this picture?

1. *with a Harlem Globetrotters uniform and a basketball; in this picture*

[1] Hubert "Geese" Ausbie was well known <u>for both his sunny smile and his athletic skill</u> <u>during his career</u>. [2] <u>For twenty-five years</u>, Ausbie played <u>on one</u> <u>of the most popular teams</u> <u>in basketball's history</u>. [3] He was a star <u>with the Globetrotters</u>. [4] The all-black team, which was started <u>in 1927</u>, is famous <u>for its humorous performances</u>. [5] But Ausbie discovered that ability must come <u>before showmanship</u>. [6] The combination <u>of skill and humor</u> is what appeals <u>to Globetrotter fans</u> <u>throughout the world</u>. [7] Ausbie, a native <u>of Oklahoma</u>, sharpened his skill <u>on the basketball team</u> <u>at Philander Smith College</u> <u>in Little Rock, Arkansas</u>. [8] While still <u>in college</u>, he tried out <u>for the Globetrotters</u> <u>in 1961</u>. [9] When he retired <u>from the Globetrotters</u>, Ausbie formed a traveling museum <u>of his many souvenirs</u>. [10] His collection includes the autographs <u>of two presidents</u> and boxing gloves <u>from Muhammad Ali</u>.

GRAMMAR

MEETING *individual* NEEDS

LEP/ESL

Asian Languages. In the Japanese and Korean languages, prepositions follow their objects; for example, *in the house* would be *house in.* Also, some languages such as Vietnamese do not always use prepositions. For example, "I went to the train station" would be "I go arrive train station." If your English-language learners are having difficulties with prepositional phrases, ask how they say the phrases in their native languages. Then point out the differences between their usages and English usage.

LEARNING STYLES

Auditory Learners. Have all of the students in your class take turns using the prepositions listed on p. 474 in sentences. You could have each student say his or her sentence and then identify the sentence's prepositional phrase. Be sure to give students the opportunity to listen to the procedure before you call on them to perform. Hearing the prepositions used in sentences should reinforce understanding.

COMMON ERROR

Problem. Some students might use subjective case pronouns as objects of prepositions, especially with compound objects.

Solution. Write the following sentences on the chalkboard and ask students which is correct:

1. Wait for Susie and I.
2. Wait for Susie and me.

Show students that by omitting the first object of the preposition (*Susie*) and the conjunction (*and*), they can determine whether *I* or *me* sounds right. You may also want to review the list of object pronouns in **Chapter 22: "Using Pronouns Correctly."** Then have students write sentences in which object pronouns are used in prepositional phrases.

MEETING *individual* **NEEDS**

LESS-ADVANCED STUDENTS

You may want to simplify **Exercises 2** and **3** and **Review A** by having students identify only the prepositional phrase in each sentence.

The Adjective Phrase

17c. An *adjective phrase* is a prepositional phrase that modifies a noun or a pronoun.

An adjective phrase tells *what kind* or *which one*.

EXAMPLES   Wang Wei was a talented painter **of landscapes.** [The phrase modifies the noun *painter,* telling what kind of painter.]

Mrs. O'Meara is the one **on the left.** [The phrase modifies the pronoun *one,* telling which one Mrs. O'Meara is.]

An adjective phrase always follows the word it modifies. That word may be the object of another prepositional phrase.

EXAMPLES   Sicily is an island **off the coast of Italy.** [The phrase *off the coast* modifies the noun *island.* The phrase *of Italy* modifies the object *coast.*]

More than one adjective phrase may modify the same word.

EXAMPLE   The box **of old magazines in the closet** is full. [The phrases *of old magazines* and *in the closet* modify the noun *box.*]

▶ EXERCISE 2   **Identifying Adjective Phrases**

Each of the following sentences contains two adjective phrases. Identify each <u>adjective phrase</u> and the <u>word it modifies</u>.

EXAMPLE   **1. Megan read a book on the origins of words.**
1. *on the origins—book; of words—origins*

1. Mike's sister Tanya, a real <u>terror</u> <u>with a whale</u> <u>of a temper</u>, shouts "Beans!" whenever something goes wrong.

2. Some <u>words</u> and <u>phrases</u> <u>for the expression</u> <u>of anger</u> have their origin in Latin or Greek.

3. <u>Many</u> of us in English class wanted to discuss how people express their annoyance.
4. Imagine what would happen if <u>everybody</u> with a bad <u>temper</u> in the city had a bad day.
5. We agreed that the best thing to do is to avoid <u>people</u> with chips on their shoulders.

The Adverb Phrase

17d. An *adverb phrase* is a prepositional phrase that modifies a verb, an adjective, or an adverb.

An adverb phrase tells *how, when, where, why,* or *to what extent* (such as *how long, how many,* or *how far*).

EXAMPLES   The snow fell **like feathers.** [The phrase modifies the verb *fell,* telling *how* the snow fell.]
The painting looks strange **over the fireplace.** [The phrase modifies the adjective *strange,* telling *where* the painting looks strange.]
Elaine speaks French well **for a beginner.** [The phrase modifies the adverb *well,* telling *to what extent* Elaine speaks French well.]
Mr. Ortiz has taught school **for sixteen years.** [The phrase modifies the verb phrase *has taught,* telling *how long* Mr. Ortiz has taught.]

An adverb phrase may come before or after the word it modifies.

EXAMPLES   The sportswriter interviewed the coach **before the game.**
Before the game the sportswriter interviewed the coach. [In each sentence the phrase modifies the verb *interviewed.*]

More than one adverb phrase may modify the same word.

EXAMPLE   **On April 24, 1990,** the Hubble Space Telescope was launched **into space.** [Both phrases modify the verb phrase *was launched.*]

GRAMMAR

INTEGRATING THE LANGUAGE ARTS

Grammar and Writing. You may wish to have students use prepositional phrases to write directions to and from destinations of their choice. Encourage students to combine short, choppy sentences and to incorporate a variety of sentence beginnings. Then you could have students volunteer to read their directions aloud and ask the rest of the class to guess the destinations.

GRAMMAR

REVIEWS A and B

OBJECTIVES

- To identify adjective and adverb phrases and the words they modify
- To use adjective and adverb phrases in writing

510 *The Phrase*

▶ EXERCISE 3 **Identifying Adverb Phrases**

In each of the following sentences, identify the <u>adverb phrase</u> and the <u>word or words it modifies</u>.

EXAMPLE **1.** The new restaurant was built over a river.
     1. *over a river—was built*

1. The Bali Hai Restaurant <u>has opened</u> <u>across the road</u>.
2. The food is <u>fantastic</u> <u>beyond belief</u>.
3. Almost everyone <u>has gone</u> <u>to the new place</u>.
4. <u>At the Bali Hai</u> you <u>can eat</u> exotic food.
5. None of the items on the menu are too <u>expensive</u> <u>for most people</u>.
6. They <u>enjoy</u> themselves <u>in the friendly atmosphere</u>.
7. People appear <u>happy</u> <u>with the service</u>.
8. <u>For three weeks</u> the Bali Hai <u>has been crowded</u>.
9. When we went there, we <u>were seated</u> <u>on the patio</u>.
10. <u>Off the river</u> <u>blew</u> a cool breeze.

▶ REVIEW A **Identifying Adjective Phrases and Adverb Phrases**

Identify each prepositional phrase in the sentences in the following paragraph. Then tell whether each phrase is an *adjective phrase* or an *adverb phrase*. Be prepared to tell which word or expression each phrase modifies.

EXAMPLE **[1]** Through old journals, we have learned much about the pioneers.
     1. *Through old journals—adverb phrase; about the pioneers—adjective phrase*

[1] Few of us appreciate the determination of the pioneers who traveled west. [2] The word *travel* comes from the French word *travailler*, which means "to work," and the pioneers definitely worked hard. [3] A typical day's journey began long before dawn. [4] On the trip westward, people rode in wagons like the ones shown on the next page. [5] During the day the wagon train traveled slowly over the mountains and across plains and deserts. [6] Each evening at dusk, the horses were unhitched from the wagons, and tents were pitched around campfires.

ANSWERS

Review A

1. of us (Few)—adjective phrase; of the pioneers (determination)—adjective phrase
2. from the French word *travailler* (comes)—adverb phrase
3. before dawn (began)—adverb phrase
4. On the trip westward (rode)—adverb phrase; in wagons (rode)—adverb phrase; like the ones (wagons)—adjective phrase; on the next page (shown)—adverb phrase
5. During the day (traveled)—adverb phrase; over the mountains (traveled)—adverb phrase; across plains and deserts (traveled)—adverb phrase
6. at dusk (were unhitched)—adverb phrase; from the wagons (were unhitched)—adverb phrase; around campfires (were pitched)—adverb phrase

Worthington Whittredge, *Encampment on the Plains.*
Autry Museum of Western Heritage, Los Angeles.

GRAMMAR

[7] The travelers often established a temporary camp down in a valley for protection from the harsh winter weather. [8] Life in these camps was hard—food was often scarce, and many people never recovered from the hardships. [9] The pioneers who did survive by sheer determination usually continued their journey. [10] When the journey ended, these people worked hard to make homes for their families.

 REVIEW B **Using Adjective and Adverb Phrases**

You and your little brother are in a crowd waiting to get on an elevator. Unlike you, your brother is nervous about riding in an elevator with a large group of people. To distract him, you describe how elevators work and tell him about different elevators that you've seen or ridden. Use this drawing and your own thoughts about elevators to write sentences you might say to your brother. In your sentences use at least five adjective phrases and five adverb phrases, and underline them.

EXAMPLES   **1.** *The elevator has an electric motor for the pulley.*
2. *I liked riding the glass elevator at Dallas's Reunion Tower because I could look around the city.*

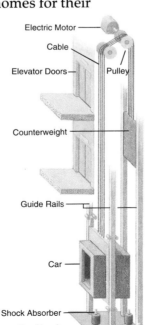

Electric Motor
Cable
Elevator Doors
Pulley
Counterweight
Guide Rails
Car
Shock Absorber

VISUAL CONNECTIONS
Encampment on The Plains

About the Artist. Worthington Whittredge (1820–1910) was an American painter born in Springfield, Ohio. He painted Romantic landscapes and huge canvases of western scenes. He posed as George Washington for Leutze's 1851 painting *Washington Crossing the Delaware.*

7. in a valley (established)—adverb phrase; for protection (established)—adverb phrase; from the harsh winter weather (protection)—adjective phrase

8. in these camps (Life)—adjective phrase; from the hardships (recovered)—adverb phrase

9. by sheer determination (did survive)—adverb phrase

10. for their families (homes)—adjective phrase

REVIEW A
Teaching Note. In Sentence 7, some students may say that the phrase *in a valley* modifies the adverb *down.* Point out that both *down* and *in a valley* modify the verb *established.*

ANSWERS
Review B

Responses will vary. To help students identify whether their phrases are used as adjectives or adverbs, have them draw arrows from the phrases to the words the phrases modify.

WRITING APPLICATION

You may want to advise students to concentrate first on writing down their thoughts about plot and characters for their stories. Details, which are often expressed by the use of prepositional phrases, can be added during revision.

CRITICAL THINKING

Analysis. Remind students to keep their second-grade audience in mind when they are choosing vocabulary for their stories. Suggest that students read books on a second-grade reading list to familiarize themselves with the writing styles and tone.

TIMESAVER

To lessen your grading time, have students help you develop an evaluation scale. For example, the class may decide that the most important aspects of the assignment are interest to the audience, use of prepositional phrases, and use of specific details. Then assign points to each category and use the scale to score the completed stories.

MEETING individual NEEDS

GENERAL STRATEGIES

The publishing stage can offer a creative outlet for students who prefer drawing over writing. Encourage each student to include at least one illustration with his or her story. If some authors do not feel confident about illustrating their stories, they can collaborate with artists in the class.

WRITING APPLICATION

OBJECTIVE

• To write a story that includes adjective and adverb phrases

WRITING APPLICATION

Using Prepositional Phrases in a Story

When you tell a story, you use many details to help your reader picture what happened. Often these details are in prepositional phrases. Adjective phrases tell *what kind* or *which one*. Adverb phrases tell *how, when, where, why,* or *to what extent*.

JUST THE FACTS	The flagship *Revenge* sank.
DETAILS ADDED	The flagship *Revenge* of the Royal Navy sank near the Spanish coast in 1591.

Can you identify the added details as adjective phrases or adverb phrases?

▶ WRITING ACTIVITY

Your class is writing and illustrating a book of original stories. The book will be given to a second-grade class during National Library Week. For the book, write a short story about a search for sunken treasure. In your story, use a variety of adjective and adverb phrases.

Prewriting   Begin by thinking about stories you've read or heard about sunken treasures. Then, write down some details from these real or fictional stories. Next, use your imagination to think of a setting and some characters for your own story. Choose a point of view (first-person or third-person) and start writing.

Writing   As you write your first draft, try to make your story exciting and interesting for second-grade readers. Since you're telling a story, arrange the events in chronological order. Remember to include details in prepositional phrases whenever possible.

Evaluating and Revising   Read the story aloud to a friend or a younger child. Notice what reactions you get from your

LESSON 3 *(pp. 513–518)*

THE PARTICIPLE AND PARTICIPIAL PHRASE Rules 17e, 17f

OBJECTIVES

- To identify participles, participial phrases, and the words they modify
- To write sentences with participial phrases

Verbals and Verbal Phrases **513**

17e

GRAMMAR

GRAMMAR

listener. Does the listener seem interested? Does he or she understand what happens in your story? Have you included enough details to make the story seem real? You may need to cut some details or add some information. New information often can be added easily in prepositional phrases.

 Proofreading and Publishing Check the verbs in your story. Action verbs appeal to most readers. For more about action verbs, see pages 457–458. Also, check to be sure your verb tenses are correct. Publish your story, along with any illustrations for it, in a class book. Your class may want to read the stories aloud to the younger students.

Verbals and Verbal Phrases

A *verbal* is a form of a verb used as a noun, an adjective, or an adverb. There are three kinds of verbals: the *participle*, the *gerund*, and the *infinitive*.

The Participle

17e. A *participle* is a verb form that can be used as an adjective.

There are two kinds of participles—*present participles* and *past participles*.

Present participles end in *–ing*.

EXAMPLES **The news was encouraging.** [*Encouraging*, a form of the verb *encourage*, modifies the noun *news*.]

The horses trotting past were not frightened by the crowd. [*Trotting*, a form of the verb *trot*, modifies the noun *horses*.]

 **PROGRAM MANAGER**

THE PARTICIPLE AND PARTICIPIAL PHRASE

- **Independent Practice/ Reteaching** For instruction and exercises, see **Participles and Participial Phrases** in *Language Skills Practice and Assessment*, p. 67.
- **Computer Guided Instruction** For additional instruction and practice with participles and participial phrases, see **Lesson 24** in *Language Workshop CD-ROM*.
- **Practice** To help less-advanced students with additional instruction and practice with participles and participial phrases, see **Chapter 14** in *English Workshop, Second Course*, pp. 133–134.

 QUICK REMINDER

Write *look* and *take* on the chalkboard and discuss with students how to create present participles and past participles from the verbs [looking, looked; taking, taken].

Then list the following verbs and have students write the present and past participles:

1. burst [bursting, burst]
2. dance [dancing, danced]
3. forget [forgetting, forgotten]
4. lose [losing, lost]

 513

LEP/ESL

Asian Languages. Because some Asian languages such as Vietnamese do not have participles, Asian students might have difficulty identifying and using participles. To clarify the concept, list the verbs *jump, howl, march, polish, iron,* and *trust* on the chalkboard. Ask students to add *–ing* to the first three verbs and *–ed* to the last three verbs and to follow these newly formed participles with nouns. [Possibilities include *jumping frog, howling dog, marching band, polished floor, ironed shirt,* and *trusted friend.*]

LESS-ADVANCED STUDENTS

Because a participle used as an adjective and a participle used in a verb phrase can be easily confused, you may want to simplify **Exercise 4** by identifying for students the verbs in the sentences. You could do the same for **Exercise 5,** or allow students to work together to identify the verbs before trying to locate the participles.

Most past participles end in *–d* or *–ed*. Others are irregularly formed.

EXAMPLES **The police officers searched the abandoned warehouse.** [*Abandoned,* a form of the verb *abandon,* modifies the noun *warehouse.*]
Charlie Parker, known as Bird, was a talented jazz musician. [*Known,* a form of the verb *know,* modifies the noun *Charlie Parker.*]

Do not confuse a participle used as an adjective with a participle used as part of a verb phrase.

PARTICIPLE **Planning their trip, the class learned how to read a road map.**
VERB PHRASE **While they were planning their trip, the class learned how to read a road map.**

PARTICIPLE **Most of the treasure buried by the pirates has never been found.**
VERB PHRASE **Most of the treasure that was buried by the pirates has never been found.**

EXERCISE 4 **Identifying Participles**

Identify the <u>participles used as adjectives</u> in the following sentences. Give the <u>noun or pronoun each participle modifies</u>. Be prepared to identify the participle as a *present participle* or a *past participle*.

EXAMPLE **1.** We heard the train whistling and chugging in the distance.
1. *whistling—train; chugging—train*

1. past/past **1.** <u>Records</u>, <u>cracked</u> and <u>warped</u>, were in the old trunk in the attic.

2. pres. **2.** <u>Shouting</u> loudly, <u>Carmen</u> warned the pedestrian to look out for the car.

3. pres. **3.** The <u>sparkling</u> <u>water</u> splashed in our faces.

4. past/past **4.** The <u>papers,</u> <u>aged</u> and <u>yellowed</u>, were found in the bottom of the file cabinet.

5. past **5.** For centuries the <u>ruins</u> remained there, still <u>undiscovered</u>.

17f

GRAMMAR

6. Carefully <u>painted</u> and <u>decorated</u>, the <u>piñata</u> glittered in the sunlight. **6.** past/past
7. The <u>charging bull</u> thundered across the field. **7.** pres.
8. <u>Cheering</u> and <u>clapping</u>, the <u>fans</u> greeted their team.
9. The <u>children</u>, <u>fidgeting</u> noisily, waited eagerly for recess. **9.** pres.   **8.** pres./pres.
10. Recently <u>released</u>, the <u>movie</u> has not yet come to our local theaters. **10.** past

The Participial Phrase

17f. A *participial phrase* consists of a participle and all of the words related to the participle. The entire phrase is used as an adjective.

A participle may be modified by an adverb and may also have a complement, usually a direct object. A participial phrase includes the participle and all of its modifiers and complements.

EXAMPLES **Seeing itself in the mirror,** the duck seemed bewildered. [The participial phrase modifies the noun *duck*. The pronoun *itself* is the direct object of the present participle *seeing*. The adverb phrase *in the mirror* modifies the present participle *seeing*.]

After a while, we heard the duck **quacking noisily at its own image.** [The participial phrase modifies the noun *duck*. The adverb *noisily* and the adverb phrase *at its own image* modify the present participle *quacking*.]

Then, **disgusted with the other duck,** it pecked the mirror. [The participial phrase modifies the pronoun *it*. The adverb phrase *with the other duck* modifies the past participle *disgusted*.]

A participial phrase should be placed as close as possible to the word it modifies. Otherwise, the sentence may not make sense.

GRAMMAR

COOPERATIVE LEARNING
To give students practice with participial phrases, divide the class into groups of three and seat each group in a small circle. Have each student write a participle on a sheet of paper and pass it to the group member on the right. Tell students to create participial phrases with the participles they receive and to pass the phrases to the right. Finally, have students create sentences from the participial phrases they receive.

Each group should end up with three sentences containing participial phrases. Have groups share their sentences.

515

INTEGRATING THE LANGUAGE ARTS

Grammar and Mechanics. Familiarize students with punctuation rules concerning participial phrases before assigning **Exercise 6**. First, write the following sentences on the chalkboard and underline the participial phrases:

1. <u>Barking loudly</u>, the dogs approached the front door.
2. The books <u>stored in our attic</u> were my great-grandmother's.
3. Uncle José, <u>whistling merrily</u>, just left for work.

Explain to students that a participial phrase at the beginning of a sentence is always followed by a comma (first sentence). When the phrase is in the middle of the sentence and the information it presents is essential to the meaning of the sentence, no commas are needed (second sentence). However, if the phrase contains nonessential information, it is surrounded by commas (third sentence). You could reinforce these rules by discussing the use of commas in **Exercise 5**.

ANSWERS
Exercise 6

Sentences will vary. You could suggest that students vary the position of the participial phrases within the sentences they write. Remind students, however, to place each phrase as close as possible to the word it modifies.

| MISPLACED | **Slithering through the grass,** I saw a snake trimming the hedges this morning. |
| CORRECTED | **Trimming the hedges this morning,** I saw a snake **slithering through the grass.** |

☞ REFERENCE NOTE: For more information about misplaced participial phrases, see pages 671–672.

▶ EXERCISE 5   **Identifying Participial Phrases**

Identify the <u>participial phrases</u> in the following sentences. Give the <u>word or words that each phrase modifies</u>.

EXAMPLE   **1. Myths are wonderful stories passed on from generation to generation.**
    1. *passed on from generation to generation—stories*

1. <u>Noted for her beauty</u>, <u>Venus</u> was sought by all the gods as a wife.
2. <u>Bathed in radiant light</u>, <u>Venus</u> brought love and joy wherever she went.
3. <u>Jupiter</u>, <u>knowing her charms</u>, nevertheless married her to Vulcan, the ugliest of the gods.
4. <u>Mars</u>, <u>known to the Greeks as Ares</u>, was the god of war.
5. <u>Terrified by Ares' power</u>, many <u>Greeks</u> did not like to worship him.
6. They saw both <u>land</u> and <u>people</u> <u>destroyed by him</u>.
7. <u>Observing his path</u>, <u>they</u> said that Ares left blood, devastation, and grief behind him.
8. The <u>Romans</u>, <u>having great respect for Mars</u>, made him one of their three chief deities.
9. They imagined <u>him</u> <u>dressed in shining armor</u>.
10. <u>Mars</u>, <u>supposed to be the father of the founders of Rome</u>, has a <u>planet</u> <u>named after him</u>.

▶ EXERCISE 6   **Writing Sentences with Participial Phrases**

Use each of the following participial phrases in a sentence of your own. Place each phrase as close as possible to the noun or pronoun that it modifies.

REVIEW C

OBJECTIVE

• To combine sentences by using participles and participial phrases

EXAMPLE **1.** standing in line
  1. *Standing in line, we waited twenty minutes for the store to open.*

1. waiting for the bus in the rain
2. passing the store window
3. planning the escape
4. jumping from stone to stone
5. hearing the whistle blow and feeling the train lurch forward

GRAMMAR

▶ REVIEW C **Using Participles and Participial Phrases to Combine Sentences**

You're the sports editor for the school newspaper. A new writer-photographer just turned in these photographs from a district school track-and-field event. She also wrote these captions to go under the photographs. The information is fine, but you want each caption to be only one sentence long. Use participles and participial phrases to combine each set of sentences.

EXAMPLE **1.** Tamara Jackson nears the finish line in the 100-meter dash. She looks happy because she's run her best.
  1. *Looking happy because she's run her best, Tamara Jackson nears the finish line in the 100-meter dash.*

1. In the 100-meter hurdles, Ruth Ann Garcia appears to be leading. She is known for her last-minute bursts of energy.
2. Discus thrower Zack Linquist shifts his weight to his left foot. He twists his body to the right and hurls the discus across the field.

A DIFFERENT APPROACH

Write the following sentence on the chalkboard and have a volunteer explain the unintentional humor of the misplaced modifier.

After playing softball this afternoon, my dog greeted me at the door. [It seems as if the dog played softball.]

Ask students to write five humorous sentences by deliberately misplacing participial phrases. Then have each student choose the sentence he or she likes best to illustrate.

Encourage students to share their sentences and drawings with the class. Ask volunteers to explain how they would change the sentences to make them grammatically correct.

GRAMMAR

ANSWERS
Review C

Responses will vary. Here are some possibilities:

1. Known for her last-minute bursts of energy, Ruth Ann Garcia appears to be leading in the 100-meter hurdles.

2. Shifting his weight to his left foot and twisting his body to the right, Zack Linquist hurls the discus across the field.

517

3. Experienced relay team member Krista Davidson reaches for the baton.

4. Straining every muscle in his body, Dennis Nishimoto clears the crossbar in the pole vault.

5. Favored to win this year's event, Julius McKay shows great promise in the broad jump.

PROGRAM MANAGER

THE GERUND AND THE GERUND PHRASE

- **Independent Practice/ Reteaching** For instruction and exercises, see **Gerunds and Gerund Phrases** in *Language Skills Practice and Assessment,* p. 68.

- **Computer Guided Instruction** For additional instruction and practice with gerunds and gerund phrases, see **Lesson 25** in *Language Workshop CD-ROM.*

- **Practice** To help less-advanced students with additional instruction and practice with gerunds and gerund phrases, see **Chapter 14** in *English Workshop, Second Course,* pp. 135–136.

LESSON 4 *(pp. 518–521)*

THE GERUND AND THE GERUND PHRASE Rules 17g, 17h

OBJECTIVES

- To identify and classify gerunds and gerund phrases
- To write sentences by using gerunds and gerund phrases
- To write a conversation by using gerunds and gerund phrases

3. Relay team member Krista Davidson reaches for the baton. She has much experience in running relay races.

4. In the pole vault, Dennis Nishimoto clears the crossbar. Every muscle in his body strains as he goes over the bar.

5. Julius McKay shows great promise in the broad jump. Most people favor him to win this year's event.

The Gerund

17g. A *gerund* is a verb form ending in *-ing* that is used as a noun.

SUBJECT	**Jogging** can be good exercise.
PREDICATE NOMINATIVE	My favorite hobby is **fishing.**
OBJECT OF PREPOSITION	Lock the door before **leaving.**
DIRECT OBJECT	Did they enjoy **hiking**?

Do not confuse a gerund with a present participle used as part of a verb phrase or as an adjective.

EXAMPLE **Pausing,** the deer **was sniffing** the wind before **stepping** into the meadow. [*Pausing* is a participle modifying *deer,* and *sniffing* is part of the verb phrase *was sniffing. Stepping* is a gerund, serving as the object of the preposition *before.*]

 EXERCISE 7 **Identifying Gerunds**

Find the <u>gerunds</u> in the following sentences. Identify each gerund as a <u>subject</u>, a <u>predicate nominative</u>, a <u>direct object</u>, or an <u>object of a preposition</u>. If a sentence does not contain a gerund, write *none.*

EXAMPLE   **1.** Typing is a useful skill.
           1. *Typing—subject*

1. Why won't that dog stop <u>barking</u>?   **1.** d.o.
2. Dr. Martin Luther King, Jr.'s powerful <u>speaking</u> helped   **2.** s.
   draw attention to the civil rights movement.
3. My sister has always enjoyed horseback <u>riding</u>.   **3.** d.o.
4. In the past, <u>working</u> took up most people's time six
   days a week.   **4.** s.   **5.** none
5. I look forward to a rest after this tiring job is done.
6. Uncle Eli's specialty is <u>barbecuing</u> on the grill.   **6.** p.n.
7. Nobody could stand the child's unceasing whine.   **7.** none
8. The most exciting part of the ceremony will be the
   <u>crowning</u> of the new king.   **8.** p.n.
9. <u>Studying</u> usually pays off in higher scores.   **9.** s.
10. Considering the other choices, Melinda decided on
    <u>walking</u>.   **10.** o.p.

The Gerund Phrase

17h.   A *gerund phrase* consists of a gerund and all the
words related to the gerund.

Because a gerund is a verb form, it may be modified by
an adverb and may have a complement, usually a direct
object. Since a gerund functions as a noun, it may be
modified by an adjective. A gerund phrase includes the
gerund and all of its modifiers and complements.

EXAMPLES   **Having a part-time job** may interfere with your
schoolwork. [The gerund phrase is the subject of
the sentence. The noun *job* is the direct object
of the gerund *having*. The article *a* and the
adjective *part-time* modify *job*.]

The townspeople heard **the loud clanging of
the fire bell.** [The gerund phrase is the direct
object of the verb *heard*. The adjectives *the*
and *loud* and the adjective phrase *of the fire
bell* modify the gerund *clanging*.]

QUICK REMINDER
Write the following sentence on
the chalkboard and underline the
gerunds:

1. <u>Swimming</u> is my favorite sport.
2. My favorite pastime is <u>reading</u>.
3. Do you stretch before <u>running</u>?
4. I also enjoy <u>hiking</u>.

Explain that gerunds are verb
forms ending in *–ing* that function as
nouns.

Ask students to identify which
gerund is used as a direct object
[hiking], a subject [Swimming], the
object of a preposition [running], and a
predicate nominative [reading].

LEARNING STYLES

Visual Learners. Diagram on the
chalkboard the example sentences following **Rule 17g** to illustrate the grammatical functions of gerunds and
gerund phrases. You may want to refer
students to the information about diagraming gerunds in the **Appendix.**

LESS-ADVANCED STUDENTS

You could share with students this clue for identifying gerunds: If a pronoun can be substituted for the word or phrase in question, the word is a gerund or the phrase is a gerund phrase.

Write the following sentences on the chalkboard and have students test the clue:

1. Studying often makes me hungry.
2. Ana likes walking in the rain.
3. Howling loudly, the wind frightened me.

[The first two sentences contain gerunds because pronouns can be substituted: It often makes me hungry; Ana likes it. A pronoun cannot be substituted for *howling loudly*, which is a participial phrase.]

INTEGRATING THE LANGUAGE ARTS

Grammar and Writing. Poetry often uses rhythm, rhyme, and repetition. Gerunds can be useful poetic devices because of their multiple uses as subjects, predicate nominatives, and objects of verbs and prepositions. You may want to brainstorm with the class ideas for poems and to write a poem together. The following poem is one example:

Skating feels like flying.
Why flying?
It's spinning and gliding,
Leaping and soaring,
Looping and twirling,
Whirling and sliding,
Skating is flying.
Why flying?
Skating sets me free!

520

We crossed the stream by **stepping carefully from stone to stone.** [The gerund phrase is the object of the preposition *by.* The adverb *carefully* and the adverb phrases *from stone* and *to stone* modify the gerund *stepping.*]

NOTE: When a noun or a pronoun comes immediately before a gerund, use the possessive form of the noun or pronoun.

EXAMPLES **Michael's** cooking is the best I've ever tasted.
The vultures didn't let anything disturb **their** feeding.

EXERCISE 8 **Identifying Gerund Phrases**

Find the gerund phrases in the following sentences. Identify each phrase as a subject, a predicate nominative, a direct object, or an object of a preposition.

EXAMPLE **1.** The rain interrupted their building of the bonfire.
1. *their building of the bonfire—direct object*

1. Angelo's pleading never influenced his mother's decision. **1.** s.
2. The eerie sound they heard was the howling of the wolves. **2.** p.n.
3. We sat back and enjoyed the slow rocking of the boat. **3.** d.o.
4. The blue jay's screeching at the cat woke us up at dawn. **4.** s.
5. People supported César Chávez and the United Farm Workers by boycotting grapes. **5.** o.p.
6. Our greatest victory will be winning the state championship. **6.** p.n.
7. The frantic darting of the fish indicated that a shark was nearby. **7.** s.
8. She is considering running for class president. **8.** d.o.
9. Ants try to protect their colonies from storms by piling up sand against the wind. **9.** o.p.
10. In his later years, Chief Quanah Parker was known for settling disputes fairly. **10.** o.p.

EXERCISE 9 **Writing Sentences with Gerund Phrases**

Use each of the following gerund phrases in a sentence of your own. Underline the gerund phrase and identify it as a *subject*, a *predicate nominative*, a *direct object*, or an *object of a preposition*.

EXAMPLE **1.** hiking up the hill
1. *Hiking up the hill* took us all morning.—
subject

1. getting up in the morning
2. arguing among themselves
3. refusing any help with the job
4. sharpening my pencil
5. listening to Scott Joplin's ragtime music

EXERCISE 10 **Using Gerunds and Gerund Phrases**

You and a friend see this experimental car at an auto show, and you're amazed by its design. Many of the car's features are unlike anything on the road now. Do you think this design will really work? Will it sell? Write a short conversation between you and your friend about the car design. Make sure that your conversation contains five gerunds or gerund phrases. Underline each gerund or gerund phrase you use.

EXAMPLE **1.** *"Wow! Driving a car like that* would be great!" I said.

GRAMMAR

ANSWERS
Exercise 9

Sentences will vary. Check to see that students use the phrases correctly as gerund phrases because some students might incorrectly use the phrases as participles or incorporate them into verb phrases.

MEETING
individual
NEEDS

STUDENTS WITH SPECIAL NEEDS

To help students get started with **Exercise 10**, brainstorm with them to list gerunds and gerund phrases that they might use in their conversations. You will probably want to relax the conventions of punctuation to allow students to focus on creativity.

ANSWERS
Exercise 10

Responses will vary, but each student's focus should be to incorporate five gerunds or gerund phrases into the conversation. Although you may not want to evaluate the punctuation and capitalization of direct quotations at this time, you could diagnose students' understanding.

GRAMMAR

521

THE INFINITIVE AND INFINITIVE PHRASE Rules 17i, 17j

OBJECTIVES

- To identify and classify infinitives and infinitive phrases
- To use infinitives and infinitive phrases in writing

GRAMMAR

The Infinitive

17i. An *infinitive* is a verb form that can be used as a noun, an adjective, or an adverb. An infinitive usually begins with *to.*

NOUNS   **To install** the ceiling fan took two hours. [*To install* is the subject of the sentence.]
Winona's ambition is **to become** a doctor. [*To become* is a predicate nominative referring to the subject *ambition.*]
Shina likes **to skate** but not **to ski.** [*To skate* and *to ski* are direct objects of the verb *likes.*]

ADJECTIVES   The best time **to visit** Florida is December through April. [*To visit* modifies *time.*]
If you want information about computers, that is the magazine **to read.** [*To read* modifies *magazine.*]

ADVERBS   The gymnasts were eager **to practice** their routines. [*To practice* modifies the adjective *eager.*]
The caravan stopped at the oasis **to rest.** [*To rest* modifies the verb *stopped.*]

NOTE: *To* plus a noun or a pronoun (*to class, to them, to the dance*) is a prepositional phrase, not an infinitive. Be careful not to confuse infinitives with prepositional phrases beginning with *to.*

INFINITIVE   I want **to go.**
PREPOSITIONAL PHRASE   I want to go **to town.**

 EXERCISE 11   **Identifying Infinitives**

Identify the <u>infinitive</u> in each sentence in the following paragraphs.

EXAMPLE   [1] June and I decided to be friends the first time we met.
1. *to be*

[1] After school, June and I like <u>to walk</u> home together. [2] Usually, we go to my house or her house <u>to listen</u> to

tapes. [3] Sometimes I get up <u>to dance</u> to the music, but June never does. [4] It's hard for me <u>to sit</u> still when a good song is playing. [5] June finally told me that she had never learned how <u>to dance</u>.

[6] "Do you want me <u>to show</u> you some steps?" I asked.

[7] "I'm ready <u>to try</u>," she answered.

[8] I decided <u>to start</u> with some simple steps. [9] After doing my best <u>to teach</u> her for three weeks, I finally gave up. [10] It's a good thing that June doesn't plan <u>to become</u> a dancer.

The Infinitive Phrase

17j. An *infinitive phrase* consists of an infinitive and its modifiers and complements.

An infinitive may be modified by an adjective or an adverb; it may also have a complement. The entire infinitive phrase may act as an adjective, an adverb, or a noun.

EXAMPLES **The crowd grew quiet to hear the speaker.** [The infinitive phrase is an adverb modifying the adjective *quiet*. The noun *speaker* is the direct object of the infinitive *to hear*.]

Peanuts and raisins are good snacks to take on a camping trip. [The infinitive phrase is an adjective modifying *snacks*. The adverb phrase *on a camping trip* modifies the infinitive *to take*.]

To lift those weights takes a lot of strength. [The infinitive phrase is a noun used as the subject of the sentence. The noun *weights* is the direct object of the infinitive *to lift*.]

▶ EXERCISE 12 **Identifying Infinitive Phrases**

Most of the sentences in the following paragraph contain an infinitive phrase. Identify each <u>infinitive phrase</u> and tell whether it is a *noun*, an *adjective*, or an *adverb*. If there is no infinitive phrase in a sentence, write *none*.

MEETING *individual* NEEDS

LEP/ESL

General Strategies. Infinitives in some languages such as Spanish and French are marked by a suffix, while English infinitives are not. Also, some languages such as Japanese and Vietnamese do not have infinitives. You may want to give students extra help with additional oral and written practice similar to **Exercise 12.** Use sentences about topics that interest students.

LESS-ADVANCED STUDENTS

To simplify **Exercise 12,** have students identify the infinitive phrases without classifying them as nouns, adjectives, or verbs.

ADVANCED STUDENTS

You could have students research a list of familiar quotations that use infinitive phrases. Then have students create a poster with their favorite quotations. The display could serve as a model to show the class how infinitive phrases are used effectively in writing.

COOPERATIVE LEARNING

You may want to have your students play a game that will introduce them to a variety of original infinitives. Divide the class into groups of three. Each group will need a dictionary and ten blank cards.

Tell each group to use a dictionary to find ten unusual verbs. Then have the group members write sentences using each verb in an infinitive phrase, one to a card. Have students write the meaning of the phrase on the back of each card. (Example: The fire alarm forced us to *scud* outside.—"to move quickly")

Then pair the groups to have them define each other's infinitive phrases. Score one point for each correct answer. The group with the most points wins.

ANSWERS

Exercise 14

Sentences will vary. As this exercise might prove difficult for students, you could write some or all of the following examples on the chalkboard:

1. Pedro has already passed the test <u>to become a lifeguard</u>.
2. Now he is learning <u>to ride horses</u>.
3. <u>To write and direct a play</u> is one of his goals.
4. He is always eager <u>to listen to friends' problems</u>.
5. I think he will be an asset for any camp <u>to hire as a counselor</u>.

EXAMPLE [1] **Taking care of your bicycle is the best way to make it last longer.**
      1. *to make it last longer—adjective*

1. n.
2. adv.
3. n.
4. adj.
5. none
6. adv.
7. adv.
8. n.
9. none
10. adj.

[1] My aunt taught me <u>to take care of my bicycle</u>. [2] We used machine oil <u>to lubricate the chain</u>. [3] She told me <u>to place a drop of oil on each link</u>. [4] Then she showed me the valve <u>to fill the inner tube</u>. [5] Using a hand pump, we added air to the back tire. [6] We were careful <u>not to put in too much air</u>. [7] Next, we got out wrenches <u>to tighten some bolts</u>. [8] My aunt warned me <u>not to pull the wrench too hard</u>. [9] Overtightening can cause as much damage to bolts as not tightening them enough. [10] When we finished, I thanked my aunt for taking the time <u>to give me tips about taking care of my bicycle</u>.

EXERCISE 13 **Writing Sentences with Infinitive Phrases** Sentences will vary; students should correctly identify phrases as nouns, adjectives, or adverbs.

Use each of the following infinitive phrases in a sentence of your own. Underline the infinitive phrase and identify it as a *noun*, an *adjective*, or an *adverb*.

EXAMPLE **1.** to leave school early on Tuesday
      1. *The principal gave me permission to leave school early on Tuesday.—adjective*

1. to give the right answers
2. to go home after school
3. to run after the bus
4. to read the entire book over the weekend
5. to spend the night at my cousin's house

EXERCISE 14 **Using Infinitives and Infinitive Phrases**

A friend of yours has an opportunity to work at a summer camp as an assistant group leader. The application has been approved, but the camp director wants to know more about your friend. Because you're a good writer, your friend asks you for a letter of recommendation. You decide to make a list of your friend's interests, habits, and good points before beginning to write the letter. Write five sentences that you might include in your letter about your friend. In each sentence, use an infinitive or an infinitive phrase, and underline it.

EXAMPLE **1.** *Pedro likes* <u>*to collect baseball cards.*</u>

▶ REVIEW D **Identifying Verbals and Verbal Phrases**

Each of the following sentences contains at least one verbal or verbal phrase. Identify each <u>verbal or verbal phrase</u> as a *gerund*, a *gerund phrase*, an *infinitive*, an *infinitive phrase*, a *participle*, or a *participial phrase*.

EXAMPLE **1.** Visiting Cahokia Mounds State Historic Site in Illinois is a wonderful experience.
1. *Visiting Cahokia Mounds State Historic Site in Illinois—gerund phrase*

1. The Cahokia were a Native American people who built a <u>highly developed</u> civilization in North America more than one thousand years ago. **1.** part. phr.
2. <u>Noting the importance of the Cahokia</u>, the United Nations Educational, Scientific, and Cultural Organization (UNESCO) set aside Cahokia Mounds as a World Heritage Site. **2.** part. phr.
3. After <u>studying the site</u>, archaeologists were able <u>to make a sketch like the one below of the ancient city</u>. **3.** ger. phr./ inf. phr.
4. The city was destroyed long ago, but the <u>remaining</u> traces of it show how huge it must have been. **4.** part.
5. This <u>thriving</u> community had a population of about 20,000 sometime between A.D. 700 and A.D. 1500. **5.** part.

LESSON 6 *(pp. 526–529)*

APPOSITIVES AND APPOSITIVE PHRASES Rules 17k, 17l

OBJECTIVES

- To identify appositives and appositive phrases and the words they identify
- To combine a variety of prepositional, verbal, and appositive phrases in writing

6. You can see that the people chose or were required <u>to build their houses mostly inside the stockade wall</u>. **6.** inf. phr.   **7.** inf. phr.
7. It's still possible <u>to see many of the earthen mounds</u>.
8. The historic site includes about sixty-eight <u>preserved</u> mounds, which were used mainly for ceremonial activities. **8.** part.   **9.** ger. phr.
9. <u>Seeing the 100-foot-high Monks Mound</u> is exciting.
10. The mound was built as the place for the city's ruler <u>to live</u> and <u>to govern</u>. **10.** inf./inf.

Appositives and Appositive Phrases

17k. An *appositive* is a noun or a pronoun placed beside another noun or pronoun to identify or explain it.

Appositives are often set off from the rest of the sentence by commas. However, when an appositive is necessary to the meaning of the sentence or is closely related to the word it refers to, no commas are necessary.

EXAMPLES   The cosmonaut **Yuri Gagarin** was the first person in space. [The noun *Yuri Gagarin* identifies the noun *cosmonaut*.]

The explorers saw a strange animal, **something** with fur and a bill like a duck's. [The pronoun *something* refers to the noun *animal*.]

John James Audubon, an **artist** and a **naturalist**, is famous for his paintings of American birds in their habitats. [The nouns *artist* and *naturalist* explain the noun *John James Audubon*.]

17l. An *appositive phrase* consists of an appositive and its modifiers.

EXAMPLES **Officer Webb, one of the security guards, apprehended the burglar.** [The adjective phrase *of the security guards* modifies the appositive *one.*]

Black Hawk, a famous chief of the Sauk Indians, fought hard for the freedom of his people. [The article *a*, the adjective *famous*, and the adjective phrase *of the Sauk Indians* modify the appositive *chief.*]

EXERCISE 15 Identifying Appositives and Appositive Phrases

Identify the <u>appositives or appositive phrases</u> in the following sentences. Give the <u>word or words each appositive or appositive phrase identifies or explains.</u>

EXAMPLE **1. My dog, the mutt with floppy ears, can do tricks.**
   1. *the mutt with floppy ears—dog*

1. <u>Tacos</u>, <u>tamales</u>, and <u>enchiladas</u>, <u>some of the most popular Mexican dishes</u>, are served here.
2. This <u>color</u>, <u>midnight blue</u>, is just what I've been looking for.
3. Two <u>men</u>, <u>a truck driver and a sailor</u>, helped my father push the car off the road.
4. I'll have a <u>sandwich</u>, <u>tuna salad on rye bread</u>, please.
5. Miguel has the same <u>class</u>, <u>American history</u>, this afternoon.
6. <u>Barbara Jordan</u>, <u>one of my heroes</u>, was a strong champion of both civil and human rights.
7. Shelley asked everyone where her <u>friend</u> <u>Bianca</u> had gone.
8. Somebody reported the <u>hazard</u>, <u>a pile of trash containing broken bottles</u>, to the police.
9. Be sure to bring the exact <u>change</u>, <u>fifty cents</u>.
10. They sang the <u>song</u> <u>"I've Been Working on the Railroad"</u> over and over all the way down the path.

527

REVIEW E

OBJECTIVE

• To identify and classify verbals and appositives

528 *The Phrase*

▶ REVIEW E   **Identifying Verbals and Appositives**

Find all the <u>verbals and appositives</u> in the sentences in the following paragraph. Identify each word as an *appositive,* an *infinitive,* a *gerund,* or a *participle.*

EXAMPLE   [1] Skating on the sidewalk, my little brother Shawn tried to do some acrobatics, and that put an end to his playing for a while.

   1. *Skating—participle; Shawn—appositive; to do—infinitive; playing—gerund*

1. ger./inf.
2. part./part.
3. part./inf.

4. ger./inf.
5. part./part.

6. app./ger.
7. part./part.

8. ger./inf.

9. app./inf.

10. inf./part.

[1] Instead of <u>falling</u> on the soft ground, Shawn managed <u>to hit</u> right on the sidewalk. [2] The concrete, <u>broken</u> and <u>crumbling</u>, cut him in several places on his legs and elbows. [3] We heard his <u>piercing</u> wail all the way up at our house, and my mother and I rushed <u>to see</u> what had happened. [4] By the time we got to him, the cuts had already started <u>bleeding</u>, and he was struggling <u>to get</u> his skates off. [5] <u>Bending</u> down, Mom pulled off the skates and dabbed at the <u>seeping</u> red cuts and scrapes. [6] Shawn, a brave little <u>boy</u> usually, could not keep from <u>crying</u>. [7] Mom carried Shawn to the house, and I followed with his skates, <u>scratched</u> and <u>scraped</u> almost as badly as he was. [8] After <u>cleaning</u> Shawn's cuts, Mom decided <u>to take</u> him to the emergency clinic. [9] The doctor, a young <u>intern</u>, said that she would have <u>to close</u> one of the cuts with stitches. [10] When we got home, Mom said that she hoped Shawn had learned <u>to be</u> more careful, but <u>knowing</u> Shawn, I doubt it.

PICTURE THIS

You are "warming up" with the students in one of the pictures on the next page. Or you're preparing for some other activity that you like to do. A beginner at the activity is watching you and has asked for your help. Write a short paragraph telling the beginner how to prepare for the

PICTURE THIS

Remind students of the importance of chronological order to explain a process. You could suggest that students prewrite by listing the steps involved in the activities they've chosen. During the revision stage, have students work in pairs to check carefully for the inclusion of all important steps.

OBJECTIVES

- To identify prepositional, participial, gerund, infinitive, and appositive phrases
- To use prepositional, verbal, and appositive phrases in writing

Review: Posttest 1   **529**

activity. In your paragraph, use at least one adjective phrase, one adverb phrase, two verbal phrases (participial, gerund, or infinitive), and one appositive phrase.

Subject: "warming up" for an activity
Audience: a beginner
Purpose: to inform

Review: Posttest 1

Identifying Prepositional, Verbal, and Appositive Phrases

Identify each italicized phrase in the following paragraphs as *prepositional*, *participial*, *gerund*, *infinitive*, or *appositive*. Do not separately identify a prepositional phrase that is part of a larger phrase.

EXAMPLES   After [1] *giving me my allowance,* my father
             warned me [2] *not to spend it all in one place.*
             1. *giving me my allowance*—gerund
             2. *not to spend it all in one place*—infinitive

GRAMMAR

GRAMMAR

GRAMMAR

GRAMMAR

1. app.
2. inf.
3. ger.
4. prep.
5. part.
6. inf.
7. ger.

8. part.

9. inf.
10. prep.

11. app.
12. prep.

13. ger.
14. prep.
15. app.
16. prep.
17. ger.

18. app.

19. part.

20. inf.

Gina, [1] *my best friend since elementary school,* and I decided [2] *to go to the mall after school yesterday.* Gina suggested [3] *taking the back way* so that we could jog, but I was wearing sandals [4] *instead of my track shoes,* so we just walked. Along the way we saw Cathy [5] *sitting on her front porch* and asked her if she wanted [6] *to join us.* She was earning a little spending money by [7] *baby-sitting her neighbor's children,* though, and couldn't leave.

[8] *Walking up to the wide glass doors at the mall,* Gina and I looked in our purses. We both had a few dollars and our student passes, so we stopped [9] *to get a glass of orange juice* while we checked what movies were playing. None [10] *of the four features* looked interesting to us. However, Deven Bowers, [11] *a friend from school and an usher at the theater,* said that there would be a sneak preview [12] *of a new adventure film* later, and we told him we'd be back then.

Since stores usually do not allow customers to bring food or drinks inside, Gina and I gulped down our orange juice before [13] *going into our favorite dress shop.* We looked [14] *through most of the sale racks,* but none of the dresses, [15] *all of them formal or evening gowns,* appealed to us. A salesclerk asked if we were shopping [16] *for something special.* After [17] *checking with Gina,* I told the clerk we were just looking, and we left.

We walked past a couple of shops—[18] *the health food store and a toy store*—and went into Record World. [19] *Seeing several cassettes by my favorite group,* I picked out one. By the time we walked out of Record World, I'd spent all my money, so we never did get [20] *to go to the movie that day.*

Review: Posttest 2

Writing Sentences with Prepositional, Verbal, and Appositive Phrases

Write ten sentences, using one of the following phrases in each sentence. Follow the directions in parentheses.

EXAMPLE   **1.** to write a descriptive paragraph (*use as an infinitive phrase that is the predicate nominative in the sentence*)

1. *Our assignment for tomorrow is to write a descriptive paragraph.*

1. after the game (*use as an adverb phrase*)
2. instead of your good shoes (*use as an adjective phrase*)
3. in one of Shakespeare's plays (*use as an adjective phrase*)
4. going to school every day (*use as a gerund phrase that is the subject in the sentence*)
5. living in a small town (*use as a gerund phrase that is the object of a preposition*)
6. walking through the empty lot (*use as a participial phrase*)
7. dressed in authentic costumes (*use as a participial phrase*)
8. to drive a car for the first time (*use as an infinitive phrase that is the direct object in the sentence*)
9. the best athlete in our school (*use as an appositive phrase*)
10. my favorite pastime (*use as an appositive phrase*)

GRAMMAR

ANSWERS
Posttest 2

Sentences will vary. Here are some possibilities:

1. We had a snack after the game.
2. I insisted that Vanessa borrow your sandals instead of your good shoes.
3. Iago is a character in one of Shakespeare's plays.
4. Going to school every day takes time away from my many hobbies.
5. She compared living in the city to living in a small town.
6. Walking through the empty lot, Vi heard a kitten mewing.
7. Dressed in authentic costumes, our tribal council presented the award.
8. Eunice tried to drive a car for the first time.
9. Pasqual, the best athlete in our school, was awarded an academic scholarship.
10. Baking, my favorite pastime, makes my family happy too.

GRAMMAR

OBJECTIVE

- To identify independent clauses and subordinate clauses in sentences and to classify them as adjective clauses, adverb clauses, or noun clauses

PROGRAM MANAGER

FOR THE WHOLE CHAPTER

- **Review** For exercises on chapter concepts, see **Review Form A** and **Review Form B** in *Language Skills Practice and Assessment,* pp. 82–85.

- **Assessment** For additional testing, see **Grammar Pretests** and **Grammar Mastery Tests** in *Language Skills Practice and Assessment,* pp. 1–8 and pp. 103–110.

GRAMMAR

CHAPTER OVERVIEW

This chapter defines and discusses the independent clause, the three types of subordinate clauses, and related terms. Subordinate clauses are classified as adverb clauses, adjective clauses, or noun clauses according to their uses in sentences. In the **Writing Application**, students are asked to use adjective clauses to write informative paragraphs.

Learning about clauses should help students to subordinate ideas and to add variety to their writing. Therefore, this chapter may be integrated with any of the composition chapters.

GRAMMAR

18 THE CLAUSE

Independent and Subordinate Clauses

Diagnostic Test

Identifying Independent and Subordinate Clauses

Identify each italicized clause in the following sentences as an *independent clause* or a *subordinate clause*. Indicate whether each italicized subordinate clause is used as an *adjective*, an *adverb*, or a *noun*.

EXAMPLES **1.** The customer thumbed through the book, but *it didn't seem to interest her.*
      1. *independent clause*

      2. Anyone *who gets a high score on this test* will not have to take the final exam.
      2. *subordinate clause—adjective*

  1. *After it had been snowing for several hours*, we took our sleds out to Sentry Hill. **1.** adv.

  2. The ring *that I lost at the beach last summer* had belonged to my great-grandmother. **2.** adj.

3. If he doesn't get here soon, *I'm leaving*.
4. Do you know *who she is*?   **4.** n.
5. I have not seen Shawn *since the football game ended last Saturday night*.   **5.** adv.
6. *In the morning they gathered their belongings and left* before the sun rose.
7. Nobody knew *that Derrick had worked out the solution*.   **7.** n.
8. *The Hopi and the Zuni built their homes out of adobe*, which is sun-dried earth.
9. My dad says never to trust strangers *who seem overly friendly*.   **9.** adj.
10. *That he had been right* became obvious as the problem grew worse.   **10.** n.
11. Julio knew the right answer *because he looked it up in the dictionary*.   **11.** adv.
12. Today's assignment is to write a three-paragraph composition on *how a bill becomes a law*.   **12.** n.
13. On our vacation we visited my dad's old neighborhood, *which is now an industrial park*.   **13.** adj.
14. *Mr. Johnson told us* that in the late 1800s, at least one fourth of all the cowboys in the West were African Americans.
15. Did you get the message *that your mother called*?   **15.** adj.
16. Tranh raked up the leaves *while his father stuffed them into plastic bags*.   **16.** adv.
17. The Spanish Club sang several Mexican American *corridos*, which are ballads, and *they were a hit*.
18. We will be over *as soon as Sandy finishes his lunch*.   **18.** adv.
19. That is the man *whose dog rescued my sister*.   **19.** adj.
20. Free samples were given to *whoever asked for them*.   **20.** n.

| **18a.** | A *clause* is a group of words that contains a verb and its subject and is used as a part of a sentence. |

Every clause has a subject and a verb. However, not every clause expresses a complete thought.

GRAMMAR

USING THE DIAGNOSTIC TEST

In evaluating students' writing, you may discover that some students are unaware of how to achieve syntactical maturity. You could use the **Diagnostic Test** to assess students' understanding of independent and subordinate clauses. Then have students work individually or in small groups on activities and exercises designed for their particular needs.

GRAMMAR

LESSON 2 (pp. 534–538)

THE INDEPENDENT CLAUSE AND THE SUBORDINATE CLAUSE Rules 18b, 18c

OBJECTIVES

- To identify the subjects and verbs of independent clauses and subordinate clauses
- To identify independent and subordinate clauses
- To write sentences with independent and subordinate clauses

534

GRAMMAR

534   *The Clause*

SENTENCE   Writers gathered at the home of Gertrude Stein when she lived in Paris.

                            S   V

CLAUSE   Writers gathered at the home of Gertrude Stein. [complete thought]

                            S   V

CLAUSE   when she lived in Paris [incomplete thought]

There are two kinds of clauses: the *independent clause* and the *subordinate clause.*

The Independent Clause

18b.   An *independent* (or *main*) *clause* expresses a complete thought and can stand by itself as a sentence.

                      S   V

EXAMPLES   **The sun set an hour ago.** [This entire sentence is an independent clause.]

                      S   V

            Jean Merrill wrote *The Pushcart War,* and

                 S   V

            Ronni Solbert illustrated the book. [This sentence contains two independent clauses.]

                             S V

            After I finished studying, I went to the movies. [This sentence contains one independent clause and one subordinate clause.]

▶ EXERCISE 1   **Identifying Subjects and Verbs in Independent Clauses**

Identify the <u>subject</u> and <u>verb</u> in each numbered, italicized independent clause in the following paragraph.

EXAMPLE   Before she left for college, [1] *my sister read the comics in the newspaper every day.*
          1. *sister—subject; read—verb*

[1] *She told me* that *Jump Start* was one of her favorites. Since she liked it so much, [2] *I made a point of reading it, too.* [3] *The comic strip was created* by this young man, *Robb Armstrong, who lives and works in Philadelphia.* [4] *Jump Start features an African American police officer named Joe and his wife, Marcy, who is a nurse.* If you aren't familiar with the strip, [5] *you may not recognize Joe and Marcy standing behind their creator.*

Jump Start reprinted by permission of United Feature Syndicate, Inc.

The Subordinate Clause

18c. A *subordinate* (or *dependent*) *clause* does not express a complete thought and cannot stand alone as a sentence.

A word such as *that, what,* or *since* signals the beginning of a subordinate clause.

EXAMPLES   **that** I wanted

     what she saw

     since most plants die without light

The meaning of a subordinate clause is complete only when the clause is attached to an independent clause.

EXAMPLES   The store did not have the video game **that I wanted.**

536 *The Clause*

> The witness told the police officers **what she saw.**
> **Since most plants die without light,** we moved our houseplants closer to the window.

Sometimes the word that begins a subordinate clause is the subject of the clause.

EXAMPLES

$\overset{\text{S} \quad \text{V}}{\text{}}$

The animals **that are in the game preserve** are protected from hunters.

$\overset{\text{S} \quad \text{V}}{\text{}}$

Can you tell me **who wrote** "America the Beautiful"?

EXERCISE 2 Identifying Independent and Subordinate Clauses

Identify each of the following groups of words as an *independent clause* or a *subordinate clause*.

EXAMPLE 1. as I answered the telephone
1. *subordinate clause*

1. we memorized the lyrics   1. ind. cl.
2. as they sat on the back porch   2. sub. cl.
3. if no one is coming   3. sub. cl.
4. my sister was born on Valentine's Day   4. ind. cl.
5. which everyone enjoyed   5. sub. cl.
6. the flood destroyed many crops   6. ind. cl.
7. the singer wore a silk scarf   7. ind. cl.
8. when the lights were flickering   8. sub. cl.
9. since the first time we talked   9. sub. cl.
10. that the lion's cage was empty   10. sub. cl.

EXERCISE 3 Identifying Subordinate Clauses and Their Subjects and Verbs

Identify the <u>subordinate clause</u> in each of the following sentences. Give the <u>subject</u> and the (verb) of each subordinate clause.

MEETING *individual* NEEDS

LESS-ADVANCED STUDENTS

General Strategies. The primary objective in focusing on the subordinate clause is not for students to memorize linguistic labels but for students to distinguish a complete sentence from an incomplete one. You may want to introduce **Exercise 2** as a class activity. Write the word groups on the chalkboard as listed in the exercises. Discuss with the class which features make each word group a complete or incomplete sentence. Students should benefit from hearing the process repeated.

TIMESAVER

To simplify the evaluation of **Exercise 2,** have students list the sentence numbers that contain subordinate clauses. The numbers [2, 3, 5, 8, 9, 10] are easy to check by scanning.

536

EXAMPLE　**1.** My report is about the plague that spread across Europe in the fourteenth century.

　　1. *that spread across Europe in the fourteenth century; subject—that; verb—spread*

1. In 1347, trading ships arrived at the Mediterranean island of Sicily from Caffa, <u>which was a port city on the Black Sea</u>.
2. <u>When the sailors went ashore</u>, many of them carried a strange illness.
3. No medicine could save the stricken sailors, <u>who died quickly and painfully</u>.
4. <u>Since it originated in the Black Sea area</u>, the plague was called the Black Death.
5. People <u>who traveled between cities in Europe</u> unknowingly carried the disease with them.
6. Millions of people became sick and died <u>as the plague spread from Sicily across Europe</u>.
7. On this map, you can trace <u>how quickly the plague spread</u>.
8. The terrified survivors thought <u>that the world was coming to an end</u>.
9. No one is sure of the total number of people <u>who died from the dreaded plague</u>.
10. <u>Since medicine offers new ways for controlling plague</u>, the spread of this disease is unlikely today.

GRAMMAR

COMMON ERROR

Problem. Students sometimes use too many subordinate clauses as modifiers.

Solution. Point out that an adverb, an adjective, or a brief phrase often can replace a subordinate clause. Write these sentences on the chalkboard:

1. My house has a door that is red.
2. We live in the house that is near the lot that is used for parking.

Ask students to revise the sentences by changing each subordinate clause to an adjective.

[**1.** My house has a red door.
2. We live in the house that is near the parking lot.]

Then ask students to count the words saved in the two sentences [six] and to say which version they prefer. [Most students will prefer the shorter versions.]

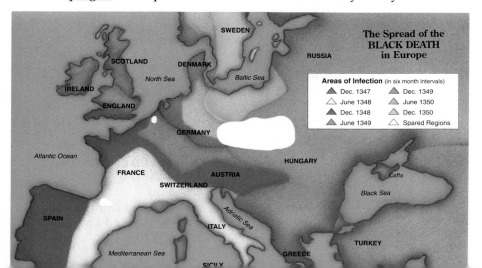

The Spread of the
BLACK DEATH
in Europe

Areas of Infection (in six month intervals)

▲ Dec. 1347　　▲ Dec. 1349
△ June 1348　　△ June 1350
▲ Dec. 1348　　▲ Dec. 1350
△ June 1349　　△ Spared Regions

SWEDEN · RUSSIA · SCOTLAND · DENMARK · North Sea · Baltic Sea · IRELAND · ENGLAND · GERMANY · Atlantic Ocean · HUNGARY · FRANCE · AUSTRIA · SWITZERLAND · Caffa · Black Sea · SPAIN · Adriatic Sea · ITALY · TURKEY · Mediterranean Sea · GREECE · SICILY

LESSON 3 *(pp. 538–544)*

THE ADJECTIVE CLAUSE Rule 18d

OBJECTIVES

- To identify adjective clauses, the relative pronouns they begin with, and the antecedents of the pronouns
- To write a brief report with sentences that include adjective clauses

ANSWERS

Exercise 4

Sentences will vary, but students should correctly identify the subjects and verbs in the independent clauses and subordinate clauses. You might want to remind students to use commas after introductory adverb clauses.

PROGRAM MANAGER

THE ADJECTIVE CLAUSE

- **Independent Practice/ Reteaching** For instruction and exercises, see **Adjective Clauses** in *Language Skills Practice and Assessment,* p. 79.
- **Computer Guided Instruction** For additional instruction and practice with the adjective clause, see **Lesson 29** in *Language Workshop CD-ROM.*
- **Practice** To help less-advanced students with additional instruction and practice with the adjective clause, see **Chapter 15** in *English Workshop, Second Course,* pp. 145–146.

538 *The Clause*

 EXERCISE 4   **Writing Sentences with Independent and Subordinate Clauses**

Write a sentence by adding an independent clause to each subordinate clause. Draw one line under the <u>subject</u> and two lines under the <u>verb</u> of each clause.

EXAMPLES **1.** who came late
1. *Anica is the volunteer who came late.*
2. as the horn blared
2. *As the horn blared, I was running out the door.*

1. when the <u>ice</u> <u>melts</u>
2. if my <u>teacher</u> <u>approves</u>
3. since <u>you</u> <u>insist</u>
4. when <u>they</u> <u>act</u> silly
5. <u>who</u> <u>borrowed</u> my notes
6. as <u>she</u> <u>began</u> to shout
7. when <u>we</u> <u>danced</u> on stage
8. <u>who</u> <u>gave</u> the report
9. since <u>I</u> <u>sleep</u> soundly
10. that <u>I</u> <u>bought</u> yesterday

The Adjective Clause

Like an adjective or an adjective phrase, an adjective clause may modify a noun or a pronoun.

ADJECTIVE	the **blonde** woman
ADJECTIVE PHRASE	the woman **with blonde hair**
ADJECTIVE CLAUSE	the woman **who has blonde hair**

ADJECTIVE	a **steel** bridge
ADJECTIVE PHRASE	a bridge **of steel**
ADJECTIVE CLAUSE	a bridge **that is made of steel**

18d. An *adjective clause* is a subordinate clause that modifies a noun or a pronoun.

An adjective clause usually follows the word it modifies and tells *which one* or *what kind.*

EXAMPLES Ms. Jackson showed slides **that she had taken in Egypt.** [The adjective clause modifies the noun *slides,* telling *which* slides.]
Helen Keller was a remarkable woman **who met the challenge of being both blind and deaf.** [The

GRAMMAR

GRAMMAR

538

adjective clause modifies the noun *woman,* telling *what kind* of woman.]

The ones whose flight was delayed spent the night in Detroit. [The adjective clause modifies the pronoun *ones,* telling *which* ones.]

Relative Pronouns

An adjective clause is usually introduced by a *relative pronoun.*

Relative Pronouns
that   which   who   whom   whose

A **relative pronoun** relates an adjective clause to the word the clause modifies.

EXAMPLES   Leonardo da Vinci was the artist **who painted the *Mona Lisa.*** [The relative pronoun *who* begins the adjective clause and relates to the noun *artist.*]

Everything **that could be done** was done. [The relative pronoun *that* begins the adjective clause and relates to the pronoun *everything.*]

Sometimes a relative pronoun is preceded by a preposition that is part of the adjective clause.

EXAMPLES   Have you read the book **on which the movie is based**?

The young actor **to whom I am referring** is Fred Savage.

In addition to relating a subordinate clause to the rest of the sentence, a relative pronoun also has a function in the subordinate clause.

EXAMPLES   Is this the tape **that is on sale**? [*That* relates the subordinate clause to the word *tape* and also functions as the subject of the subordinate clause.]

QUICK REMINDER

Write the following sentence pairs on the chalkboard and have students combine the sentences using the relative pronouns in parentheses. Ask students to underline the adjective clauses in their sentences.

1. I sat by a girl. Her mother won the Pulitzer Prize (whose) [I sat by a girl whose mother won the Pulitzer Prize.]
2. This is the tree. It was struck by lightning. (that) [This is the tree that was struck by lightning.]
3. Anna is the dancer. She injured her ankle. (who) [Anna is the dancer who injured her ankle.]

MEETING *individual* NEEDS

LEP/ESL

Spanish. In Spanish, clauses generally do not end in verbs. For example, in an English sentence such as "I like the book that Maria is reading," the Spanish speaker will often invert the subject and the verb in the adjective clause. You might give students a list of sentences in which the adjective clause ends in a verb form, and emphasize the subject-verb order. Suggest that students practice reading the sentences aloud.

LEARNING STYLES

Visual Learners. You could display a chart listing the functions and characteristics of adjective clauses. Use the following headings: *Kinds of Clause, Function, Words that Introduce the Clause,* and *Examples.* Students can refer to the chart as they work through the exercises in this segment. As adverb clauses and noun clauses are introduced, add them to the chart.

He is a friend **on whom you can always depend.**
[*Whom* relates the subordinate clause to the word *friend* and functions as the object of the preposition *on.*]

An adjective clause may be introduced by a ***relative adverb,*** such as *when* or *where.*

EXAMPLES This is the spot **where we caught most of the fish.**
The time period **when dinosaurs ruled** lasted millions of years.

In some cases, the relative pronoun or adverb can be omitted.

EXAMPLES We haven't seen the silver jewelry **(that** *or* **which) she brought back from Mexico.**
Do you remember the time **(when** *or* **that) the dog caught the skunk?**

▶ EXERCISE 5 **Identifying Adjective Clauses**

Identify the <u>adjective clause</u> in each of the following sentences. Give the (relative pronoun) and the <u>word that the relative pronoun refers to.</u>

EXAMPLE **1.** Our friends have a canary that is named Neptune.
1. *that is named Neptune; that—canary*

1. Proverbs are <u>sayings (that) usually give advice.</u>
2. Trivia questions have been organized into <u>games (that) have become quite popular.</u>
3. A <u>black hole,</u> (which) <u>results after a star has collapsed,</u> can trap energy and matter.
4. A special award was given to the <u>student</u> (whose) <u>work had improved most.</u>
5. <u>Frances Perkins,</u> (who) <u>served as secretary of labor,</u> was the first woman to hold a Cabinet position.
6. The <u>problem</u> (that) <u>worries us now</u> is the pollution of underground sources of water.

GRAMMAR

CRITICAL THINKING

Synthesis. The omission of the relative pronoun or relative adverb can be confusing to some students. To show that omitting such words often makes sentences more readable and more like spoken English, read the following two sentences aloud and ask which sounds better:

1. I like the haircut that you got yesterday.
2. I like the haircut you got yesterday.

[Most students will prefer the second sentence.] Offer similar sentences to show students how to supply the missing relative pronouns or adverbs when analyzing these sentences. Then, ask students to write several sentences in which the relative pronouns or adverbs are omitted.

7. We enjoyed the poems of <u>Gwendolyn Brooks</u>, (who) <u>for years has been poet laureate of Illinois</u>.
8. In *Walden*, Henry David Thoreau shared <u>ideas</u> (that) <u>have influenced many</u>.
9. <u>Athena</u>, (who) <u>ranked as an important Greek deity</u>, protected the city of Athens.
10. A friend is a <u>person</u> (whom) <u>you can trust</u>.

WRITING APPLICATION

Using Adjective Clauses in Writing a Specific Definition

When you write, you use adjective clauses much as you would use adjectives and adjective phrases. Just as adjective phrases are longer than single-word adjectives, adjective clauses are usually longer than phrases. Because adjective clauses are longer, they can describe more and be more specific.

ADJECTIVE	a **large** building
ADJECTIVE PHRASE	a building **of enormous height**
ADJECTIVE CLAUSE	a building **that towers above all the others**

 **WRITING ACTIVITY**

Sometimes, people misunderstand each other because they aren't thinking of the same meanings for words. For example, what *you* think is a "good" report card may not be the same as what your *parents* think is a "good" report card. Write a paragraph defining one of the people or things listed below or another term that you choose. Use at least four adjective clauses. Underline the clauses you use.

a clean room	a loyal friend	a fun weekend
a good teacher	an ideal pet	a good-looking outfit

WRITING APPLICATION
You may want to remind students that a definition usually has two parts. First, it identifies the large group, or class, that the subject belongs to. Then it tells how the subject is different from all other members of its class.

CRITICAL THINKING
Analysis. Remind students to keep the interests of the audience in mind when they select specific details to use in their definitions. Not all people are interested in the same things. The details selected should vary according to the audience's interests.

EVALUATING AND REVISING

Ask students to check their writing for unnecessary adjective clauses. In addition, students should make sure they have not used circular definition, that is, using a word to define itself, as in the following sentence: "A kind person is someone who acts with kindness."

TECHNOLOGY TIP

Encourage students to use a desktop publishing program, if available, to compile their definitions into a class dictionary. Depending on the capabilities of available programs, suggest that students experiment with layout and design. For example, they could vary the typeface, import graphics as illustrations, and create columns.

---

542 *The Clause*

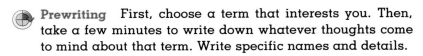 **Prewriting** First, choose a term that interests you. Then, take a few minutes to write down whatever thoughts come to mind about that term. Write specific names and details.

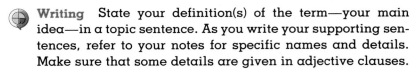 **Writing** State your definition(s) of the term—your main idea—in a topic sentence. As you write your supporting sentences, refer to your notes for specific names and details. Make sure that some details are given in adjective clauses.

Evaluating and Revising Read over your paragraph. Would your reader understand your definition? Would he or she agree with it? Remember that all details in your paragraph should relate to your definition. If they do not, you may need to add, cut, or revise some information. Count the relative pronouns or relative adverbs you've used. That number will tell you how many adjective clauses your paragraph has.

Proofreading and Publishing As you proofread your paragraph, pay attention to spelling and capitalization. Be sure to capitalize proper nouns and proper adjectives. For more about capitalization, see Chapter 25. You and your classmates may enjoy comparing different definitions of the same term. You could also gather the definitions together to create a class dictionary.

EXERCISE 6 **Identifying Adjective Clauses**

Identify the <u>adjective clause</u> in each of the following sentences. Give the (relative pronoun or relative adverb) and the <u>word that the pronoun refers to.</u>

EXAMPLE **1.** Crispus Attucks was an African American patriot who was killed during the Boston Massacre.
1. *who was killed during the Boston Massacre; who—patriot*

1. Coco Chanel is the <u>woman</u> for(whom)the perfume is <u>named</u>.
2. Here is the concert <u>hall</u>(where)we heard the great <u>cello player Pablo Casals</u>.
3. The cello, when played by Pablo Casals, is an <u>instrument</u> to(which)<u>I could listen for hours</u>.
4. <u>Ella Fitzgerald</u>,(who)<u>started singing in New York City</u>, is famous throughout the world.
5. The English playwright Christopher Marlowe wrote of Helen of Troy, "Was this the <u>face</u>(that)<u>launched a thousand ships</u>?"
6. Anita was one of the <u>sopranos</u>(who)<u>sang in the chorus</u>.
7. In the play *My Fair Lady*, Eliza Doolittle, a poor flower merchant, becomes a <u>woman</u>(whom)<u>everyone admires</u>.
8. The Kinderhook was the <u>creek</u> in(which)<u>we found the shells</u>.
9. <u>Janet Flanner</u>,(who)<u>wrote dispatches from Paris</u>, used the pen name Genêt.
10. The <u>astronauts</u>, to(whom)<u>travel in the space shuttle is routine</u>, must always keep in shape.

▶ EXERCISE 7   **Using Adjective Clauses**

Go fly a kite! That's what you and the rest of the participants in this year's Smithsonian Kite Festival in Washington, D.C., did. Now that you're back home, your teacher would like you to tell the class about your experiences. Write a brief report about kites or a short story about your experience at the festival. You might want to describe how to make a kite and fly it. Or you might tell about an event that happened at the festival. In your report, include five adjective clauses and underline them. You can use the picture and the diagram on the following page, as well as your own experiences and your imagination, to help you write.

EXAMPLE   **1.** *The kite <u>that I flew</u> looks like the one in the middle of this picture.*

ANSWERS
Exercise 7

Paragraphs will vary, but students should incorporate five adjective clauses. As a check for misplaced modifiers, you could have students draw arrows from the adjective clauses to the nouns or pronouns they modify.

THE ADVERB CLAUSE Rule 18e

OBJECTIVE

- To identify adverb clauses, the subordinating conjunctions that introduce them, and their subjects and verbs
- To write sentences with adverb clauses
- To write paragraphs using adverb clauses

PROGRAM MANAGER

THE ADVERB CLAUSE

- **Independent Practice/ Reteaching** For instruction and exercises, see **Adverb Clauses** in *Language Skills Practice and Assessment,* p. 80.
- **Computer Guided Instruction** For additional instruction and practice with the adverb clause, see **Lesson 30** in *Language Workshop CD-ROM.*
- **Practice** To help less-advanced students with additional instruction and practice with the adverb clause, see **Chapter 15** in *English Workshop, Second Course,* pp. 147–148.

✏ QUICK REMINDER

Write the following sentences on the chalkboard. Have students rewrite each sentence to switch the position of each adverb clause and independent clause.

1. Because he wants everyone to play, the coach uses the second string. [The coach uses the second string because he wants everyone to play.]
2. I sit patiently on the bench until it is my turn to go into the game. [Until it is my turn to go into the game, I sit patiently on the bench.]

Explain that by occasionally switching the positions of the clauses, students can add variety to their writing. They will be eliminating repetitive sentence patterns that might seem boring to their readers.

544

544 *The Clause*

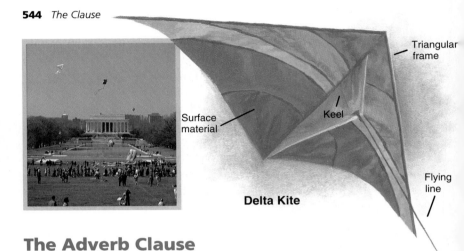

Triangular frame

Surface material

Keel

Flying line

Delta Kite

The Adverb Clause

Unlike an adverb or an adverb phrase, an adverb clause has a subject and a verb.

ADVERB	You may sit **anywhere.**
ADVERB PHRASE	You may sit **in any chair.**
ADVERB CLAUSE	You may sit **wherever you wish.** [*You* is the subject, and *wish* is the verb.]

18e. An *adverb clause* is a subordinate clause that modifies a verb, an adjective, or an adverb.

An adverb clause tells *where, when, how, why, to what extent,* or *under what condition.*

EXAMPLES **You may sit wherever you wish.** [The adverb clause modifies the verb *may sit,* telling *where* you may sit.]

When winter sets in, many animals hibernate. [The adverb clause modifies the verb *hibernate,* telling *when* many animals hibernate.]

My new friend and I talk as if we've known each other for a long time. [The adverb clause modifies the verb *talk,* telling *how* my new friend and I talk.]

Because the weather was hot, the cool water felt good. [The adverb clause modifies the adjective *good,* telling *why* the water felt good.]

Gabrielle can type faster **than I can.** [The adverb clause modifies the adverb *faster,* telling *to what extent* Gabrielle can type faster.]

If it does not rain tomorrow, we will go to Crater Lake. [The adverb clause modifies the verb *will go,* telling *under what condition* we will go to Crater Lake.]

Notice in these examples that an adverb clause does not always follow the word it modifies. When an adverb clause begins a sentence, it is usually followed by a comma.

☞ REFERENCE NOTE: For more information about using commas with adverb clauses, see page 753.

Subordinating Conjunctions

An adverb clause is introduced by a *subordinating conjunction*—a word that shows the relationship between the adverb clause and the word or words that the clause modifies.

Common Subordinating Conjunctions			
after	as though	since	when
although	because	so that	whenever
as	before	than	where
as if	how	though	wherever
as long as	if	unless	whether
as soon as	in order that	until	while

☞ REFERENCE NOTE: The words *after, as, before, since,* and *until* are also commonly used as prepositions. See page 474.

▶ EXERCISE 8   **Identifying Adverb Clauses**

Identify the |adverb clause| in each of the following sentences. In each clause, circle the (subordinating conjunction,) and underline the <u>subject</u> once and the <u>verb</u> twice.

GRAMMAR

MEETING *individual* **NEEDS**

LEP/ESL

General Strategies. Most languages have structures similar to adverb clauses; however, often the order of the subject and the verb is inverted. You may want to have students use the **Common Subordinating Conjunctions** list to practice saying and writing sentences with adverb clauses. Emphasize the subject-verb pattern that is most common in English by having students identify the subject and the verb of each clause they write.

ADVANCED STUDENTS

To help students see how they can use adverb clauses to clarify idea relationships and to increase coherence in paragraphs, write this paragraph on the chalkboard:

Last year we visited several antique shops. We were looking for an old radio to use in the spring play. We came to a small shop. We were sure it didn't have what we wanted. It had one radio—just the one we needed.

Ask students to revise the sentences and to use adverb clauses to subordinate some of the ideas. [Here is one possible revision: Last year, while we were looking in antique shops for an old radio to use in the spring play, we came to a small shop. Although we were sure it didn't have what we wanted, it had just the radio we needed.]

GRAMMAR

EXAMPLE **1.** Although they lived in different regions of North America, Native American children all across the continent enjoyed playing similar kinds of games.

1. (Although) they <u>lived</u> *in different regions of North America*

1. These children used mainly natural objects in games (since) there <u>were</u> no toy <u>stores</u>.
2. Most Native American children played darts with large feathers (as) these Arapaho <u>children</u> <u>are doing</u>.
3. (If) you <u>look</u> closely at the tree, you can see their target, a hole in the trunk.
4. These children are throwing goose feathers attached to bones, but they also used wild turkey feathers (whenever) they <u>could find</u> them.

5. (Although) they <u>played</u> many kinds of games, Native Americans in the Southwest especially liked kickball races.
6. The children made balls out of such materials as wood and tree roots (before) they <u>started</u> playing.
7. (After) snow <u>had fallen</u>, Seneca children raced small handmade "snow boats."
8. Pine cones were used in many games (because) they <u>were</u> so easy to find.
9. You can picture some children playing catch with pine cones (while) others <u>had</u> cone-throwing contests.
10. Games gave the children practice in skills they would need (when) they <u>became</u> adults.

VISUAL CONNECTIONS

Ideas for Writing. Ask students to invent and describe a game using a common object that most people would not think of as a toy. Have students use adverb clauses in explaining how the game is played. When the descriptions are finished, have students underline the adverb clauses and draw lines from the clauses to the words they modify.

You may want to let students choose one or more of the games that are feasible to try out in the classroom. This activity will show students how important it is to be clear and precise when writing instructions.

EXERCISE 9   **Writing Sentences with Adverb Clauses**

Add an adverb clause to each of the following sentences. Write the entire sentence. Circle the subordinating conjunction, and underline the subject of each adverb clause once and the verb twice.

EXAMPLE   **1. The movie finally ended.**
1. (After) we spent three hours in the theater, the movie finally ended.

1. Most of the members of the Drama Club auditioned for the play.
2. Erica speaks three languages.
3. We prepared moussaka, a Greek dish with lamb and eggplant, for our Cooking Club's international supper.
4. The Goldmans have visited Acapulco several times on vacation.
5. Jill daydreams in class.

EXERCISE 10   **Using Adverb Clauses**

Mark Twain's ambition as a boy was to be a steamboat pilot. By the time he was a young man, Twain had served as an apprentice on several steamboats. In *Life on the Mississippi,* Twain tells about his ambition. He begins by writing, "When I was a boy, . . ." Then he goes on to list his childhood ambitions: to be a circus clown, to join a minstrel show, and to be a pirate. Yet even as a child, Twain knew that his "permanent ambition" was to be a steamboat pilot. Write a short paragraph telling about your own ambition or ambitions. In your paragraph, use at least five adverb clauses. Like Twain, you could begin one sentence with the subordinate conjunction *when.* You may want to refer to the list of Common Subordinating Conjunctions on page 545. Be prepared to identify all of the adverb clauses in your paragraph.

EXAMPLE   **1. *When I was a little girl, I wanted to be a doctor.***

ANSWERS
Exercise 9

Sentences will vary, but students should correctly identify the subordinating conjunction, the subject, and the verb of each adverb clause they add to an existing sentence. Remind students to use commas after introductory adverb clauses.

MEETING *individual* NEEDS

AT-RISK STUDENTS
The activity suggested in **Exercise 10** could give you the opportunity to work with students individually to help them identify their abilities to achieve their ambitions. Sometimes students focus on their limitations and do not look for their strong points. You could help students recognize their talents and strengths by having them list the assets that make it possible for them to reach their goals.

ANSWERS
Exercise 10

Responses will vary. You could suggest that, as a prewriting strategy, students freewrite about their ambitions and then go back and add adverb clauses after they have their ideas down on paper.

TIMESAVER
For easier grading, you may want to have students underline the adverb clauses in their paragraphs in **Exercise 10.**

OBJECTIVE
- To identify and classify noun clauses
- To write a descriptive paragraph using adjective clauses, adverb clauses, and noun clauses

GRAMMAR

PROGRAM MANAGER

THE NOUN CLAUSE

■ **Independent Practice/ Reteaching** For instruction and exercises, see **Noun Clauses** in *Language Skills Practice and Assessment,* p. 81.

■ **Computer Guided Instruction** For additional instruction and practice with the noun clause, see **Lesson 31** in *Language Workshop CD-ROM.*

■ **Practice** To help less-advanced students with additional instruction and practice with the noun clause, see **Chapter 15** in *English Workshop, Second Course,* pp. 149–150.

QUICK REMINDER

Remind students that noun clauses and adjective clauses may begin with the same words (*that, which, who, whom, whoever,* and others), but the clauses function differently.

Write the following sentences on the chalkboard, and have students explain the function of the clause in each sentence:

1. He whom we serve eats well. [The adjective clause modifies the pronoun *He* and tells *which* one.]
2. We know whom we serve. [The noun clause tells *what* we know and functions as a direct object.]

548

GRAMMAR

548 *The Clause*

The Noun Clause

18f. A *noun clause* is a subordinate clause used as a noun.

A noun clause may be used as a subject, a complement (predicate nominative, direct object, indirect object), or an object of a preposition.

SUBJECT	**That Felicia is angry** is obvious.
PREDICATE NOMINATIVE	Three dollars was **what he offered.**
DIRECT OBJECT	The judges determined **who won.**
INDIRECT OBJECT	The sheriff gave **whoever volunteered** a flashlight.
OBJECT OF A PREPOSITION	We agreed with **whatever he said.**

Common Introductory Words for Noun Clauses

who	whoever	which
whom	whomever	whichever
what	whatever	that

The word that introduces a noun clause often has another function within the clause.

EXAMPLES **Give a free pass to whoever asks for one.** [The introductory word *whoever* is the subject of the verb *asks.* The entire noun clause is the object of the preposition *to.*]

Did anyone tell him what he should do? [The introductory word *what* is the direct object of the verb *should do*—*he should do what.* The entire noun clause is the direct object of the verb *did tell.*]

Their complaint was that the milk smelled sour. [The word *that* introduces the noun clause but has no other function in the clause. The noun clause is the predicate nominative identifying the subject *complaint.*]

REVIEWS A and B

OBJECTIVE

• To identify adjective, adverb, and noun clauses

The Subordinate Clause **549**

18f

GRAMMAR

GRAMMAR

EXERCISE 11 — Identifying and Classifying Noun Clauses

Identify the <u>noun clause</u> in each of the following sentences. Tell whether the noun clause is a <u>subject</u>, a <u>predicate nominative</u>, a <u>direct object</u>, an <u>indirect object</u>, or an <u>object of a preposition</u>.

EXAMPLE
   1. We couldn't find what was making the noise in the car.
   1. *what was making the noise in the car—direct object*

1. <u>Whatever you decide</u> will be fine with us.   **1.** s.
2. <u>Whoever takes us to the beach</u> is my friend for life.   **2.** s.
3. Do you know <u>what happened to the rest of my tuna sandwich</u>?   **3.** d.o.
4. Stuart is looking for <u>whoever owns that red bicycle</u>.   **4.** o.p.
5. Checking our supplies, we discovered <u>that we had forgotten the flour</u>.   **5.** d.o.
6. The worst flaw in the story is <u>that it doesn't have a carefully developed plot</u>.   **6.** p.n.
7. No, these results are not <u>what we had planned</u>.   **7.** p.n.
8. The painter gave <u>whatever spots had dried</u> another coat of primer.   **8.** i.o.
9. At lunch, my friends and I talked about <u>what we should do as our service project</u>.   **9.** o.p.
10. <u>That Coretta Scott King spoke for peace</u> surprised no one.   **10.** s.

REVIEW A — Identifying Adjective, Adverb, and Noun Clauses

Identify each <u>subordinate clause</u> in the following quotations as an <u>adjective</u>, an <u>adverb</u>, or a <u>noun</u>.

1. Look <u>before you leap</u>.
                Old Proverb   **1.** adv.
2. Do not be afraid of light,
You <u>who are a child of night</u>.
         Langston Hughes, "Song"   **2.** adj.

MEETING *individual* NEEDS

LEP/ESL

General Strategies. To help students understand that noun clauses function as nouns, point out that a simple noun or pronoun can be substituted for a noun clause. Usually, the word *it* can be substituted. As an example, write the following sentence on the chalkboard, cross out the noun clause, and replace it with *it*:

    <u>That Josh won the match</u> surprised everyone. [It surprised everyone.]

    Encourage students to use this technique of substituting as they complete **Exercise 11**.

COOPERATIVE LEARNING

Divide the class into groups of three, and give each group a set of five or more index cards that you have prepared in advance. Each card should have a noun clause that could be used as a subject, a direct object, a predicate nominative, an indirect object, or an object of a preposition. (Not all noun clauses can be used in all five ways, but those starting with *whatever* and *whoever* seem to work well; for example, you could use *whatever moves, whoever answers,* and *whoever gets there first.*)

    Give the groups ten minutes to write sentences that use the clauses on their cards in all five ways. At the end of ten minutes, have the groups read their sentences aloud. Award one point for each correct sentence.

AMENDMENTS TO SELECTIONS
Description of change: excerpted
Rationale: to focus on the concept of subordinate clauses presented in this chapter

549

MEETING individual NEEDS

ADVANCED STUDENTS

Challenge students to explain why some clauses that follow prepositions are considered noun clauses and why others are considered adjective clauses. Such an explanation could prove useful for the rest of the class when completing **Reviews A** and **B** and the **Posttest.**

[Students might suggest that an adjective tells *which, what kind,* or *how many;* a noun tells *who* or *what.* Students might discover that in a noun clause, the relative pronoun usually functions as the subject or the direct object of the clause, while in an adjective clause, the relative pronoun or relative adverb is generally part of a modifying phrase.]

AMENDMENTS TO SELECTIONS
Description of change: excerpted
Rationale: to focus on the concept of subordinate clauses presented in this chapter

---

3. adj.   **3.** You gain strength, courage and confidence by every experience <u>in which you really stop to look fear in the face</u>.

> Eleanor Roosevelt, *You Learn by Living*

4. n.   **4.** <u>What I have to say</u> will come from my heart, and I will speak with a straight tongue.

> Chief Joseph, "An Indian's Views of Indian Affairs"

5. adj.   **5.** For every man <u>who lives without freedom</u>, the rest of us must face the guilt.

> Lillian Hellman, *Watch on the Rhine*

▶ REVIEW B   **Identifying Subordinate Clauses**

Each sentence in the following paragraph contains a subordinate clause. Identify each <u>subordinate clause</u> as an *adjective clause,* an *adverb clause,* or a *noun clause.*

EXAMPLE   **[1]** The Museum of Appalachia, which is in Norris, Tennessee, is a re-created pioneer village.
   1. *which is in Norris, Tennessee—adjective clause*

1. adv.   [1] <u>If you've ever wanted to step into the past</u>, you'll like this museum. [2] You can see many pioneer crafts and

tools <u>that are still used at the museum</u>. [3] For example, the men on the left are splitting shingles with tools <u>that were used in their boyhood</u>. [4] Two other men show <u>how plowing was done before the development of modern equipment</u>. [5] I think <u>that the 250,000 pioneer tools and other items on display will amaze you</u>. [6] <u>What some visitors like to do</u> is to tour the village's log buildings and then take a rest. [7] <u>While they're resting</u>, they can often find some mountain music to listen to. [8] Notice the different instruments <u>that the musicians are playing</u>. [9] The fiddler on the right performs at the museum's Homecoming, <u>which is a yearly fall event</u>. [10] At Homecoming, you might even meet the museum's founder, John Rice Irwin, <u>who grew up in the Appalachian Mountains</u>.

2. adj.
3. adj.
4. n.
5. n.
6. n.
7. adv.
8. adj.
9. adj.
10. adj.

GRAMMAR

PICTURE THIS

Recently, a multinational group of researchers surprised the world with an announcement. They had developed a device that would allow people to travel back in time.

At the United Nations, world leaders agreed that the device should be used by time travelers for recording information and exploring only. Travelers would neither participate in nor try to change events in the past. Upon returning to the present, travelers would make a full report of their findings to the appropriate UN committee.

You were selected from a large group of volunteers to represent the United States in the first time-travel mission. You've just landed at your destination—San Francisco, California, in 1851. You step out of your time machine into the scene shown on the next page. You're struck by how different everything is, especially the buildings, clothing, and methods of transportation. Before exploring the 1800s any further, you decide to sit down and record your first impressions in your log. Write a paragraph or two describing this place and time. In your

COOPERATIVE LEARNING

You may wish to allow students to work cooperatively in groups of three to identify the subordinate clauses in **Review B.** Suggest that one member be responsible for finding the clauses, another member for identifying the parts of speech, and another for justifying the answers.

PICTURE THIS

Suggest that students focus on those things in the pictures that fascinate them or that have changed the most over the years. Have students consider what the members of the UN committee would be most interested in and what other people of the present time would care most about. On the basis of what students see in the pictures, ask them what they can conclude about the daily life and the social customs of the people who lived in San Francisco in 1851.

GRAMMAR

LESSON 6 (pp. 552–554)

REVIEW: POSTTESTS 1 and 2

OBJECTIVE

- To identify independent and subordinate clauses
- To classify subordinate clauses as nouns, adjectives, or adverbs
- To write sentences with independent and subordinate clauses

---

552 *The Clause*

log entry, use a variety of clauses. These should include at least three adjective clauses, four adverb clauses, and three noun clauses.

Subject: San Francisco in 1851
Audience: yourself and the members of the United Nations Committee for the Preservation of North American History
Purpose: to record your observations for use in a future report; to inform

The Granger Collection, New York.

Review: Posttest 1

Identifying Independent and Subordinate Clauses

Identify each italicized clause in the following paragraphs as an *independent clause* or a *subordinate clause*. Tell whether each italicized subordinate clause is a *noun*, an *adjective*, or an *adverb*.

VISUAL CONNECTIONS

Exploring the Subject. The city we now call San Francisco began as a Spanish colony in 1776. For many years it was an isolated trading outpost frequented mainly by fur trappers, explorers, and whalers. In 1821, California became a province of Mexico, and the San Francisco Bay was a Mexican port of entry. During the Mexican War (1846–1848), the area was claimed as a U.S. territory. The name *San Francisco* was officially recorded in 1847. The city was incorporated in 1850. The gold rush of 1849 brought fortune hunters from all over the world, and San Francisco has thrived ever since.

MEETING *individual* NEEDS

STUDENTS WITH SPECIAL NEEDS

Because of the length and format of **Review: Posttest 1**, some students might easily lose their places. You could adapt the activity by providing index cards or rulers for students to use as horizontal guides. The guides will help students concentrate on one line at a time.

GRAMMAR

GRAMMAR

EXAMPLES   When my mother got a new job, [1] *we had to move to another town.*
1. *independent clause*

[2] *When my mother got a new job,* we had to move to another town.
2. *subordinate clause—adverb*

I didn't want to move [1] *because I didn't want to transfer to another school*. This is the fourth time [2] *that I have had to change schools*, and every time I've wished [3] *that I could just stay at my old school*. [4] *As soon as I make friends in a new place*, I have to move again and leave them behind. Then at the new school [5] *I am a stranger again*.   **1.** adv.   **2.** adj.   **3.** n.   **4.** adv.

We lived in our last house for three years, [6] *which is longer than in any other place*. [7] *since I was little*. [8] *Living there so long*, I had a chance to meet several people [9] *who became good friends of mine*. My best friends, Chris and Marty, said [10] *that they would write to me*, and I promised to write to them, too. However, the friends [11] *that I've had before* had promised to write, but [12] *after a letter or two we lost touch.* [13] *Why this always happens* is a mystery to me.   **6.** adj.   **7.** adv.   **9.** adj.   **10.** n.   **11.** adj.   **13.** n.

I dreaded having to register at my new school two months [14] *after the school year had begun*. By then, everyone else would already have made friends, and [15] *I would be an outsider*, [16] *as I knew from past experience*. There are always some students who bully and tease [17] *whoever is new at school* or anyone else [18] *who is different*. Back in elementary school I would get angry and upset [19] *when people picked on me*. Since then, I've learned how to fit in and make friends in spite of [20] *whatever anyone does to hassle me or make me feel uncomfortable*.   **20.** n.   **14.** adv.   **16.** adv.   **17.** n.   **18.** adj.   **19.** adv.

Everywhere [21] *that I've gone to school*, some students always are friendly and offer to show me around. [22] *I used to be shy*, and I wouldn't take them up on their invitations. Since they didn't know [23] *whether I was shy or being unfriendly*, they soon left me alone. Now [24] *whenever someone is friendly to me at a new school or in a new neighborhood*, I fight down my shyness and act friendly myself. It's still hard to get used to new places and new people, but [25] *it's a lot easier with a little help from new friends.*   **21.** adj.   **23.** n.   **24.** adv.

LESS-ADVANCED STUDENTS

You may want to simplify **Review: Posttest 2** by rewording the instructions so there is only one requirement for each sentence.

ANSWERS
Review: Posttest 2

Sentences will vary. Here are some possibilities:

1. I like salads of all kinds.
2. Although I eat many other kinds of food, I like salads best.
3. I especially enjoy salads that have several kinds of sprouts.
4. My sister Tara is the person with whom I most enjoy fixing salads.
5. When Tara and I visit the supermarket, I go to the produce section first.
6. When Tara can't find me near her, she always knows the place where she can find me.
7. Tara knows what I like.
8. What she knows is that I like salads and all the fixings.
9. Sometimes she may get tired of hearing me talk about what I'd most like to have for the next meal.
10. What I'd like tonight is a mixed salad that has bronzeleaf lettuce, red cabbage, and raisins.

Review: Posttest 2

Writing Sentences with Independent and Subordinate Clauses

Write your own sentences according to the following instructions. Underline the subordinate clauses.

EXAMPLE **1.** a sentence with an independent clause and an adjective clause
1. *I am going to the game with Guido, who is my best friend.*

1. a sentence with an independent clause and no subordinate clauses
2. a sentence with an independent clause and one subordinate clause
3. a sentence with an adjective clause that begins with a relative pronoun
4. a sentence with an adjective clause in which a preposition precedes the relative pronoun
5. a sentence with an introductory adverb clause
6. a sentence with an adverb clause and an adjective clause
7. a sentence with a noun clause used as a direct object
8. a sentence with a noun clause used as a subject
9. a sentence with a noun clause used as the object of a preposition
10. a sentence with a noun clause and either an adjective clause or an adverb clause

DIAGNOSTIC TEST

OBJECTIVE

- To classify sentences as simple, compound, complex, or compound-complex

PROGRAM MANAGER

FOR THE WHOLE CHAPTER

- Review For exercises on chapter concepts, see **Review Form A** and **Review Form B** in *Language Skills Practice and Assessment,* pp. 96–99.
- Assessment For additional testing, see **Grammar Pretests** and **Grammar Mastery Tests** in *Language Skills Practice and Assessment,* pp. 1–8 and pp. 103–110.

19 SENTENCE STRUCTURE

The Four Basic Sentence Structures

Diagnostic Test

Identifying the Four Kinds of Sentence Structure

Identify each of the following sentences as *simple, compound, complex,* or *compound-complex.*

EXAMPLE **1.** We bought a new computer program that helps with spelling and grammar.
     1. *complex*

1. Christina wanted to go to the dance, but she had to baby-sit. **1.** cd.
2. When the rabbit saw us, it ran into the bushes. **2.** cx.
3. In 1967, Thurgood Marshall became the first African American named to the U.S. Supreme Court. **3.** simp.
4. You can either buy a new bicycle tire or fix the old one. **4.** simp.
5. Yoko said that this would be the shortest route, but I disagree. **5.** cd.-cx.

CHAPTER OVERVIEW

This chapter builds on material in **Chapter 18: "The Clause."** It covers each of the four types of sentence structure individually and includes a mixed review. In the **Writing Application** students are asked to use a variety of sentence structures in writing messages.

Material in this chapter can be used with any of the composition chapters but will be especially helpful with **Chapter 11: "Writing Effective Sentences."**

USING THE DIAGNOSTIC TEST

The results of the **Diagnostic Test** will tell you which students can identify the four kinds of sentence structure but will not show whether students can use them in their writing. You may wish to give a writing assignment in addition to the test or to use existing writing samples as an aid in evaluation.

6. There was no way that we could tell what had really happened. **6.** cx.
7. Yes, that seems to me like the right answer to the first problem. **7.** simp.
8. Mercedes Rodriguez of Miami, Florida, entered and won the Ms. Wheelchair America contest. **8.** simp.
9. Do you know who wrote this note and left it on my desk? **9.** cx.
10. I'm not sure what you mean, but I think I agree. **10.** cd.-cx.
11. Nobody is worried about that, for it will never happen. **11.** cd.
12. Whatever you decide will be fine with me. **12.** cx.
13. Is the movie that we want to see still playing in theaters, or is it available on videocassette? **13.** cd.-cx.
14. Rammel knew the plan, and he assigned each of us a part. **14.** cd.
15. Amphibians and some insects can live both on the land and in the water. **15.** simp.
16. The detectives searched for the woman who had been wearing a blue beret, but there weren't any other clues. **16.** cd.-cx.
17. The tornado cut across the edge of the housing development yesterday morning, and seven homes were destroyed. **17.** cd.
18. By July of 1847, the Mormons had reached the Great Salt Lake valley. **18.** simp.
19. Before the game started, all the football players ran out onto the field, and everyone cheered. **19.** cd.-cx.
20. My father stopped to help the family whose car had broken down on the highway. **20.** cx.

Sentences may be classified according to *structure*—the kinds and the number of clauses they contain. The four kinds of sentences are *simple, compound, complex,* and *compound-complex.*

☞ REFERENCE NOTE: Sentences may also be classified according to purpose. See pages 422–423.

THE SIMPLE SENTENCE Rule 19a

OBJECTIVE

- To identify subjects and verbs in simple sentences

19a

The Simple Sentence

19a. A *simple sentence* has one independent clause and no subordinate clauses.

	S	V

EXAMPLES   The **hairstylist gave** Latrice a new look.

	S	V

Ernesto has volunteered to organize the recycling campaign.

A simple sentence may have a compound subject, a compound verb, or both.

EXAMPLES   **Beth Heiden** and **Sheila Young won** Olympic medals. [compound subject]

Lawrence caught the ball but then **dropped** it. [compound verb]

The **astronomer** and her **assistant studied** the meteor and **wrote** reports on their findings. [compound subject and compound verb]

☞ REFERENCE NOTE: For more information about compound subjects and compound verbs, see pages 418–420.

▶ EXERCISE 1   **Identifying Subjects and Verbs in Simple Sentences**

Identify the <u>subjects</u> and the <u>verbs</u> of the following simple sentences. [Note: Some sentences have compound subjects or compound verbs.]

EXAMPLE   **1.** Throughout history, people have invented and used a variety of weapons.
    1. *people—subject; have invented, used—verbs*

1. To protect themselves from such weapons, <u>warriors</u> in battle <u>needed</u> special equipment.
2. Some <u>warriors</u> <u>used</u> shields of wood or animal hides.

PROGRAM MANAGER

THE SIMPLE SENTENCE

- **Independent Practice/ Reteaching** For instruction and exercises, see **Simple Sentences** in *Language Skills Practice and Assessment,* p. 91.

- **Computer Guided Instruction** For additional instruction and practice with simple sentences, see **Lesson 37** in *Language Workshop CD-ROM.*

- **Practice** To help less-advanced students with additional instruction and practice with simple sentences, see **Chapter 16** in *English Workshop, Second Course,* pp. 153–154.

✔ QUICK REMINDER

Emphasize that in a simple sentence the subject must do the action of the verb. Write the following patterns on the chalkboard and have students use them to compose four original sentences:

1. single subject and a single verb [Bob rode his bicycle all summer.]
2. compound subject and a single verb [My dog and my cat ran to meet me.]
3. single subject and a compound verb [Tarika picked a whole basket of raspberries and ate them all.]
4. compound subject and a compound verb [Li and Tim came over and helped me with my math project.]

You may want to have students add adjectives, adverbs, and phrases to one of their sentences to show that a simple sentence is not necessarily short.

MEETING *individual* NEEDS

LEP/ESL

General Strategies. To illustrate the relationships of subjects and verbs in simple sentences, draw the following tree diagrams for students:

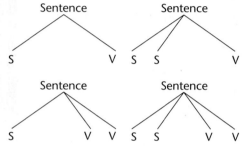

You could point to the different parts of the diagram as you discuss the types of simple sentences, and students can use the diagrams to analyze sentences.

3. In ancient Assyria, <u>soldiers</u> <u>wore</u> leather armor reinforced with bronze.
4. By 1800 B.C., the <u>Greeks</u> <u>had made</u> the first metal armor out of bronze.
5. Later, the <u>Romans</u> <u>manufactured</u> strong iron armor and <u>designed</u> special equipment, such as shin guards.
6. Before and during the Middle Ages, European <u>knights</u> and <u>foot soldiers</u> often <u>dressed</u> in shirts of chain mail.
7. <u>You</u> <u>can see</u> the tiny steel links of the chains in this close-up drawing.

helmet

shoulder piece

8. Compared with chain mail, <u>suits</u> of steel armor <u>gave</u> better protection and therefore <u>became</u> more popular.
9. <u>Helmets</u> and shoulder <u>pieces</u> like these <u>protected</u> a knight's head and neck.
10. To protect his legs and feet, a <u>knight</u> <u>wore</u> greaves and sollerets into battle.

greave (shin guard)

solleret (shoe)

OBJECTIVES

- To identify subjects, verbs, and conjunctions in compound sentences
- To distinguish between compound sentences and compound subjects and compound verbs

The Compound Sentence

19b. A *compound sentence* has two or more independent clauses but no subordinate clauses.

The independent clauses are usually joined by a coordinating conjunction: *and, but, for, nor, or, so,* or *yet.*

EXAMPLES   According to legend, **Betsy Ross made** our first flag, but **there is little evidence of this.** [two independent clauses joined by the conjunction *but*]

The whistle blew, the drums rolled, and the crowd cheered. [three independent clauses, the last two joined by the conjunction *and*]

☞ REFERENCE NOTE: For more information about independent clauses, see page 534.

NOTE: Do not confuse a compound sentence with a simple sentence that contains a compound subject, a compound verb, or both.

SIMPLE
SENTENCE   **Alberto** and **Jared increased** their speed and **passed** the other runners. [compound subject and compound verb]

COMPOUND
SENTENCE   **Alberto led** half the way, and then **Jared took** the lead. [two independent clauses]

The independent clauses in a compound sentence may also be joined by a semicolon.

EXAMPLE   Many mathematical **concepts originated** in North Africa; the ancient **Egyptians used** these concepts in building the pyramids.

PROGRAM MANAGER

THE COMPOUND SENTENCE

- **Independent Practice/ Reteaching** For instruction and exercises, see **Compound Sentences** and **Compound Sentence Parts** in *Language Skills Practice and Assessment,* pp. 92–93.

- **Computer Guided Instruction** For additional instruction and practice with compound sentences, see **Lesson 37** in *Language Workshop CD-ROM.*

- **Practice** To help less-advanced students with additional instruction and practice with compound sentences, see **Chapter 16** in *English Workshop, Second Course,* pp. 153–154.

✔ QUICK REMINDER

Remind students that a compound sentence can include compound subjects and verbs. Write the following sentences on the chalkboard and have students identify them as simple or compound:

1. Helen and Leila went to the movies, and afterwards they walked and talked for a while. [compound]
2. In the volleyball game, Karina was the most valuable player, so she won the trophy. [compound]
3. Her books and papers were out in the rain all night, and they got soaked. [compound]
4. Elisha and her brother ate dinner and washed the dishes. [simple]

MEETING *individual* NEEDS

STUDENTS WITH SPECIAL NEEDS

Some students may not be able to distinguish among the four basic sentence structures. You may want to have students focus on identifying subjects and verbs of simple sentences until they have mastered that task.

LEP/ESL

General Strategies. To illustrate relationships among subjects, verbs, and coordinating conjunctions in compound sentences, you could draw the following tree diagrams:

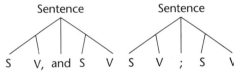

Sentence   Sentence

S   V, and   S   V   S   V   ;   S   V

Be sure to point out the mandatory conjunction or semicolon in these structures.

LESS-ADVANCED STUDENTS

Have students write simple sentences on individual note cards or slips of paper. Then have students make another set of cards with a comma and a coordinating conjunction on each card. They should also make a few cards with a semicolon on each card. Then have pairs of students use the cards to build compound sentences.

When they write the sentences, students may want to pick a theme so the sentence cards can be related in such a way as to produce a story.

☞ **REFERENCE NOTE:** For more information on using semicolons in compound sentences, see pages 759–760.

▶ EXERCISE 2   **Identifying Subjects, Verbs, and Conjunctions in Compound Sentences**

Each of the sentences in the following paragraph is a compound sentence. Identify the <u>subject</u> and the <u>verb</u> in the independent clauses in each sentence. Then, give the [coordinating conjunction] or the (mark of punctuation) that joins the independent clauses.

EXAMPLE   [1] Many strange things happen backstage during a performance, but the audience usually does not know about them.
1. *things—subject; happen—verb; audience—subject; does know—verb; but*

[1] The <u>director</u> of a theater-in-the-round <u>visited</u> our class, [and] <u>we</u> <u>listened</u> to his stories for almost an hour. [2] According to him, the <u>workers</u> in charge of properties <u>are</u> usually alert and careful, [yet] <u>they</u> still <u>make</u> mistakes sometimes. [3] For example, in one production of *Romeo and Juliet*, the <u>character</u> Juliet <u>prepared</u> to kill herself with a dagger, [but] there <u>was</u> no <u>dagger</u> on the stage. [4] <u>Audiences</u> at theaters-in-the-round <u>can</u> also <u>be</u> a problem, [for] <u>they</u> <u>sit</u> very close to the stage. [5] <u>Members</u> of the audience often <u>set</u> things on stage tables, [or] <u>they</u> <u>hang</u> their coats on the actors' coatracks. [6] Sometimes these <u>actions</u> <u>are overlooked</u> by the stagehands, [and] the <u>results</u> <u>can be</u> very challenging for the actors. [7] For example, the main <u>clue</u> in one mystery play <u>was</u> a scarf left lying on the stage floor, [but] the <u>audience</u> <u>had gathered</u> on the stage during intermission. [8] After the intermission, the <u>detective</u> in the play <u>found</u> three scarves instead of one, [yet] <u>he</u> <u>could</u> not <u>show</u> any surprise. [9] During another mystery drama, a <u>spectator</u> <u>became</u> too involved in the play; <u>he</u> <u>leaped</u> up on the stage and <u>tackled</u> the villain. [10] <u>Directors</u> <u>cannot</u> always <u>predict</u> the reactions of the audience, [nor] <u>can</u> <u>they</u> always <u>control</u> the audience.

EXERCISE 3

Distinguishing Between Compound Sentences and Compound Subjects and Compound Verbs

Identify the <u>subject</u>(s) and the <u>verb</u>(s) in each sentence in the following paragraph. Then, tell whether the sentence is a *simple sentence* or a *compound sentence*.

EXAMPLE   [1] African American actors and actresses performed in many early Hollywood movies.

     1. *actors, actresses—subjects; performed—verb; simple sentence*

     [2] Hattie McDaniel, for example, made many films, yet she is best known for her role in *Gone with the Wind.*

     2. *Hattie McDaniel—subject; made—verb; she—subject; is—verb; compound sentence*

[1] Over the years, African American <u>performers</u> <u>have</u> **1. s.s.** <u>earned</u> much acclaim and <u>won</u> a number of Academy Awards. [2] <u>Hattie McDaniel</u> in 1939 and <u>Sidney Poitier</u> **2. s.s.** in 1963 <u>were</u> the first black performers to win Oscars. [3] More recently, <u>Lou Gossett, Jr.</u>, and <u>Denzel Washing-</u> **3. s.s.** <u>ton</u> <u>played</u> supporting roles as military men and <u>won</u> Academy Awards for their performances. [4] Another <u>win-</u> **4. c.s.** <u>ner</u>, Whoopi Goldberg, first <u>gained</u> fame as a stand-up comic; then <u>she</u> <u>went</u> on to make several hit movies. [5] <u>Critics</u> <u>praised</u> her perfor- **5. c.s.** mance in *The Color Purple,* and in 1991, <u>she</u> <u>won</u> an Academy Award for playing this funny character in *Ghost.*

GRAMMAR

COMMON ERROR

Problem. Students frequently make errors in punctuating compound sentences, which results in run-on sentences.

Solution. Give students the following working formulas and stress that these rules are for compound sentences only:

1. Combine sentences by using a comma plus *and, or, but, nor, yet, for,* or *so.* (I bought the steaks for the party, and he grilled them.)

2. Combine sentences by using a semicolon with no coordinating conjunction. (I bought the steaks for the party; he grilled them.)

VISUAL CONNECTIONS

Exploring the Subject. In *Ghost,* Whoopi Goldberg plays Oda Mae Brown, a woman who makes her living by pretending she can talk with spirits of the dead. She is completely surprised when the ghost of a banker (Patrick Swayze) begins to talk to her in an effort to save his girlfriend (Demi Moore).

PROGRAM MANAGER

THE COMPLEX SENTENCE

- **Independent Practice/ Reteaching** For instruction and exercises, see **Complex Sentences** in *Language Skills Practice and Assessment,* p. 94.
- **Computer Guided Instruction** For additional instruction and practice with complex sentences, see **Lesson 38** in *Language Workshop CD-ROM.*
- **Practice** To help less-advanced students with additional instruction and practice with complex sentences, see **Chapter 16** in *English Workshop, Second Course,* pp. 155–156.

QUICK REMINDER

Remind your students that although subordinate clauses contain subjects and verbs, they don't make sense by themselves. Put the following clauses on the chalkboard and ask students what they mean:

1. Because I don't like it
2. When I get home
3. That I was glad

[Students should see that the clauses don't make sense.]

Have students add independent clauses to make these clauses complete sentences.

GRAMMAR

---

562 *Sentence Structure*

The Complex Sentence

19c. A *complex sentence* has one independent clause and at least one subordinate clause.

EXAMPLE   When I watch Martha Graham's performances, I feel like studying dance.

    Independent Clause   **I feel** like studying dance

    Subordinate Clause   When **I watch** Martha Graham's performances

EXAMPLE   Some of the sailors who took part in the mutiny on the British ship *Bounty* settled Pitcairn Island.

    Independent Clause   **Some** of the sailors **settled** Pitcairn Island

    Subordinate Clause   **who took** part in the mutiny on the British ship *Bounty*

EXAMPLE   In *Gone with the Wind,* when Scarlett is faced with near-starvation, she makes a promise that she never will be hungry again.

    Independent Clause   In *Gone with the Wind,* **she makes** a promise

    Subordinate Clause   when **Scarlett is faced** with near-starvation

    Subordinate Clause   that **she** never **will be** hungry again

Notice in the examples above that a subordinate clause can appear at the beginning, in the middle, or at the end of a complex sentence.

 REFERENCE NOTE: For more information about independent and subordinate clauses, see pages 534–548.

> EXERCISE 4

Identifying Independent Clauses and Subordinate Clauses in Complex Sentences

Identify each of the clauses in the following sentences as *independent* or *subordinate*. Be prepared to give the subject and the verb of each clause. [Note: Two sentences have more than one subordinate clause.]

EXAMPLES
1. China is a largely agricultural country that has a population of more than one billion people.
1. *China is a largely agricultural country—independent; that has a population of more than one billion people—subordinate*

2. Although my brother bought one of those old coins for his collection, it was nearly worthless.
2. *Although my brother bought one of those old coins for his collection—subordinate; it was nearly worthless—independent*

1. The detective show appeared on television for several weeks before it became popular with viewers. **1.** show appeared/it became
2. Most of the albums that my parents have from the 1970s are sitting in the corner of the basement behind the broken refrigerator. **2.** most are sitting/parents have
3. Richard E. Byrd is but one of the explorers who made expeditions to Antarctica. **3.** Richard E. Byrd is/who made
4. As studies continued, many important facts about nutrition were discovered. **4.** studies continued/facts were discovered
5. A group of popular singers, who donated their time, recorded a song that made people aware of the problems in Ethiopia. **5.** group recorded/who donated/that made
6. The Hawaiian ruler who wrote the famous song "*Aloha Oe*" ("Farewell to Thee") was Queen Liliuokalani. **6.** ruler was/who wrote
7. After we have prepared our report on the history of computers, we may be able to go to the basketball game. **7.** we have prepared/we may be

MEETING *individual* NEEDS

LEARNING STYLES

Visual Learners. You may want to refer to the **Appendix: "Diagraming Sentences"** to give students a visual model of the structure of complex sentences. The sections **Subordinate Clauses** and **Complex Sentences** give explanations and examples. To give students practice, you could have them do **Exercises 9** and **11** in **"Diagraming Sentences."**

COOPERATIVE LEARNING
Divide the class into mixed-ability groups to practice creating sentences with different structures. Tell students that each group's task is to create a series of four sentences all related to the same topic. The first student in each group begins by stating a simple sentence on the topic of his or her choice. The second student then provides a compound sentence on the same subject. The third student contributes a subordinate clause, and the fourth student provides an independent clause to make a complex sentence.

Have groups repeat the process three more times, exchanging tasks each time so that each student has a chance to choose a topic and to create each kind of sentence structure.

OBJECTIVES
- To classify clauses in compound-complex sentences as independent or subordinate
- To use simple, compound, complex, and compound-complex sentences in writing a description

PROGRAM MANAGER

THE COMPOUND-COMPLEX SENTENCE

- **Independent Practice/ Reteaching** For instruction and exercises, see **Compound-Complex Sentences** in *Language Skills Practice and Assessment,* p. 95.

- **Computer Guided Instruction** For additional instruction and practice with compound-complex sentences, see **Lesson 38** in *Language Workshop CD-ROM.*

- **Practice** To help less-advanced students with additional instruction and practice with compound-complex sentences, see **Chapter 16** in *English Workshop, Second Course,* pp. 155–156.

QUICK REMINDER

To show the progression of growth in sentence structure, build a compound-complex sentence for your students. Begin with a simple sentence, add a second independent clause, and then add a subordinate clause. Here is an example of this process:

1. John went to a ski resort on Monday.
2. John went to a ski resort on Monday, and he enrolled in an expert skier's class.
3. John went to a ski resort on Monday, and he enrolled in an expert skier's class because he wanted to win the big race on Saturday.

Ask your students to create compound-complex sentences by following your model.

564

---

564 *Sentence Structure*

8. <u>Although few students or teachers knew about it</u>, <u>a group of sociologists visited our school to study the relationship between classroom environment and students' grades</u>. **8.** students, teachers knew/group visited
9. <u>While the stage crew was constructing the sets</u>, <u>the performers continued their rehearsal</u>, <u>which went on into the night</u>. **9.** crew was constructing/performers continued/which went
10. <u>Although she had polio as a child</u>, <u>Wilma Rudolph became a top American Olympic athlete</u>. **10.** she had/ Wilma Rudolph became

The Compound-Complex Sentence

19d. A *compound-complex sentence* has two or more independent clauses and at least one subordinate clause.

EXAMPLE Yolanda began painting only two years ago, but already she has been asked to hang one of her paintings at the art exhibit that is scheduled for next month.

Independent Clause	**Yolanda began** painting only two years ago
Independent Clause	already **she has been asked** to hang one of her paintings at the art exhibit
Subordinate Clause	**that is scheduled** for next month

EXAMPLE I have read several novels in which the main characters are animals, but the novel that I like best is *Animal Farm.*

Independent Clause	**I have read** several novels
Independent Clause	the **novel is** *Animal Farm*

Subordinate Clause   in which the main

                    S   V
                  characters are animals

                      S V
Subordinate Clause   that **I like** best

EXAMPLE When Bill left, he locked the door, but he forgot to turn off the lights.

                      S   V
Independent Clause **he locked** the door

                      S   V
Independent Clause **he forgot** to turn off the lights

                          S   V
Subordinate Clause When **Bill left**

NOTE: To show how the parts of a compound-complex sentence are related, be sure to use marks of punctuation correctly.

▷ EXERCISE 5 **Identifying Clauses in Compound-Complex Sentences**

Identify each of the clauses in the following sentences as *independent* or *subordinate*.

EXAMPLE **1.** When they returned from their vacation, they collected their mail at the post office, and they went to the supermarket.
        1. *When they returned from their vacation—subordinate; they collected their mail at the post office—independent; they went to the supermarket—independent*

1. Before we conducted the experiment, we asked for permission to use the science lab, but the principal insisted on teacher supervision of our work.
2. Inside the old trunk up in the attic, which is filled with boxes and toys, we found some dusty photo albums; and one of them contained pictures from the early 1900s.
3. We told them that their plan wouldn't work, but they wouldn't listen to us.

LEP/ESL

General Strategies. You may want to give the following definitions:
compound—two
complex—tied together like a knot.
      Draw a picture of a knot on the chalkboard to reinforce meaning.

LEARNING STYLES

Kinetic Learners. Supply students with an unpunctuated list of independent clauses, coordinating conjunctions, and subordinate clauses. Have students write each item on a separate card and then combine the items in different ways to create compound-complex sentences. For example:
The boy loved to sing
He won a contest
who lived next door
and
      These items could be combined as "The boy who lived next door loved to sing, and he won a contest." Students should write each of the new sentences they create, add punctuation, and then exchange papers to check that each sentence is compound-complex. Students could share a few of their sentences with the class.

GRAMMAR

REVIEW (p. 567)

OBJECTIVE

- To identify sentences as simple, compound, complex, or compound-complex

566   *Sentence Structure*

4. Every expedition that had attempted to explore that region had vanished without a trace, yet the young adventurer was determined to map the uncharted jungle because he couldn't resist the challenge.

5. The smoke, which grew steadily thicker and darker, billowed through the dry forest; and the animals ran ahead of it as the fire spread quickly.

PICTURE THIS

While on vacation, you borrow the family video camera and head for the seashore. There you find this amazing scene. At first you hide quietly and watch. Then, you decide to capture the scene on film. Back home, you show your tape to a TV reporter, who wants to run your story on the news as soon as possible. But first, you need a short description of how you made the film. Write a paragraph about your experience at the seashore. In your paragraph, use at least one simple sentence, one compound sentence, one complex sentence, and one compound-complex sentence.

Subject: unicorns by the sea
Audience: television viewers
Purpose: to inform viewers about what you saw

PICTURE THIS

Because students are asked to write an eyewitness account of this picture for a news story, remind them that news stories traditionally answer the questions posed by the words *who, what, when, where, why,* and *how*—the *5W-How?* questions.

Some students may not relate to the rural setting or the subject matter of the painting. You may want to allow these students to base their accounts on a more familiar image, such as one involving an urban scene.

VISUAL CONNECTIONS
Unicorns (Legend—Sea Calm)

About the Artist. Arthur Davies (1862–1928), a native of New York City, was a painter of the romantic school. His paintings, like this one called *Unicorns (Legend—Sea Calm),* often feature imaginary people and creatures. Mr. Davies was one of a group of artists who set up the Armory show in New York City in 1913, which introduced modern art to Americans.

566

Arthur B. Davies, *Unicorns (Legend—Sea Calm),* (c. 1806). The Metropolitan Museum of Art, Bequest of Lizzie P. Bliss, 1931.

A DIFFERENT APPROACH

Have students make a reference chart such as the one below to use as they do the **Review:**

The Compound-Complex Sentence **567**

GRAMMAR

 REVIEW

Identifying the Four Kinds of Sentence Structure

Identify each sentence in the following paragraphs as *simple, compound, complex,* or *compound-complex.*

EXAMPLE   [1] If he had not practiced, Amleto Monacelli of Venezuela could not have become a champion bowler.

   1. *complex*

1. cd.-cx.

[1] People who are learning a new sport begin by mastering basic skills, and they usually are very eager. [2] After people have practiced basic skills for a while, they usually progress to more difficult moves. [3] At this point a beginner is likely to become discouraged, and the temptation to quit grows strong. [4] One of the most common problems that beginners face is coordination; another is muscular aches and pains. [5] If a beginner is not careful, muscles can be injured, yet the strenuous activity usually strengthens the muscle tissues. [6] When enough oxygen reaches the warmed-up muscles, the danger of injury lessens, and the muscles grow in size. [7] At the same time, coordination grows, along with confidence.

2. cx.

3. cd.

4. cd.-cx.

5. cd.-cx.

6. cd.-cx.

7. simp.

[8] The hours of practice that a beginner puts in usually result in rewarding improvements. [9] As a rule, learning something new takes time and work, or it would not seem worthwhile. [10] In sports, as in most other activities, persistence and patience often pay off.

8. cx.

9. cd.

10. simp.

Kinds of Sentence Structure	Independent Clauses	Subordinate Clauses
Simple	1	0
Compound	2 or more	0
Complex	1	1 or more
Compound-Complex	2 or more	1 or more

Tell students to count the subject-verb pairs in each sentence, to decide which sets are independent and which are subordinate, and then to refer to the chart as they classify the sentences.

GRAMMAR

WRITING APPLICATION

Using Compound, Complex, and Compound-Complex Sentences

In writing and in speech, people use all kinds of sentences to express their thoughts and feelings. Simple sentences are

WRITING APPLICATION

The writing assignment gives students an opportunity to use the various sentence structures in a situation that might occur in real life. You may want to have them take a few minutes to visualize the situation before they begin writing any notes.

CRITICAL THINKING

Analysis. To help students determine what they should include in their messages, have them list all of the questions their parents might ask. Then students must determine which questions are most important to their parents and limit their messages to those items. Limiting a brief message to those items that must be communicated to a parent or guardian to resolve a problem requires analysis of information.

EVALUATING AND REVISING

One way to help students evaluate the effectiveness of their messages is to pair students and let them role-play. Each student should pretend to be the parent of the other student and listen to the message. Ask each student to be sure that the message is clear and that it answers parental questions. Give students time to revise their messages if necessary.

568

best used to express single ideas. To describe more complicated ideas and to show relationships between them, use compound, complex, and compound-complex sentences.

SIMPLE SENTENCES	Yesterday I visited my friend Amy. Then I went to Willa's house. We practiced our dance routine.
COMPOUND-COMPLEX SENTENCE	After I visited my friend Amy yesterday, I went to Willa's house, and we practiced our dance routine.

▶ WRITING ACTIVITY

You missed your ride home after school, so you went to a friend's house. No one is at your home now. But you know you should call and leave a message on the answering machine. Write out the message that you will leave. Use a variety of sentence structures.

Prewriting   First, decide what will be in your message. You probably will want to tell where you are and why you are there. Explain why you missed your ride. And you should tell when you'll be home or should make arrangements to be picked up. Make notes about all of these details.

Writing   Use your notes to write your first draft. As you write, remember that your message must be short but clear and informative. Think about how you can combine ideas.

Evaluating and Revising   Read your message aloud and listen to how it sounds. Are your explanations and plans complete? Do they sound logical? Check to be sure that you've used a variety of sentence structures. If you need to combine sentences, review pages 368–377.

Proofreading   Read over your message again, checking for errors in grammar, spelling, and punctuation. For more about punctuating compound sentences, see pages 745–746 and 759–760. For more on using commas with subordinate clauses, see pages 747–748 and 752–753.

REVIEW: POSTTESTS 1 and 2

OBJECTIVES

- To identify the four kinds of sentence structure
- To write simple, compound, complex, or compound-complex sentences as directed

Review: Posttest 1

Identifying the Four Kinds of Sentence Structure

Identify each sentence in the following paragraphs as *simple*, *compound*, *complex*, or *compound-complex*.

EXAMPLE **[1] When my grandmother came to visit, she taught us how to make our own holiday ornaments.**
       1. *complex*

[1] Last year my grandmother came to stay with us from the middle of December until my brother's birthday in January. [2] While we were getting out the holiday decorations, Mom and Grandma told us all about how people used to make their own decorations. [3] Mom said that she remembered making beautiful decorations and that it used to be a lot of fun, so we decided to try making some of our own.

[4] My dad, my brother, and I drove out to the woods to gather pine cones. [5] We had forgotten to ask what size to get, and since Dad had never made decorations, he didn't know. [6] We decided to play it safe and get all different sizes, which was easy to do because there were pine cones everywhere. [7] My brother picked up all the hard little ones, and my dad and I threw a bunch of medium and big ones into the trunk of the car. [8] When Mom and Grandma saw how many we had, they laughed and said we had enough to decorate ten houses.

[9] First we sorted the cones; the little hard ones went into one pile, and the bigger ones into another. [10] Dad and I painted the little ones silver, and Mom and Grandma painted stripes, dots, and all sorts of other designs on them. [11] Then we tied strings to the tops of the cones; and later, when we put them up, they made great ornaments.

[12] We painted the bigger pine cones all different colors and glued on cranberries and beads, which made each

1. simp.
2. cx.
3. cd.-cx.
4. simp.
5. cd.-cx.
6. cx.
7. cd.
8. cx.
9. cd.
10. cd.
11. cd.-cx.
12. cx.

570 *Sentence Structure*

13. cd.

14. simp.

15. simp.

16. cd.

17. cd.

18. simp.

19. cd.-cx.

20. simp.

cone look like a miniature fir tree. [13] We saved some smaller ones for the dining room table, and we put most of the others all around the house. [14] My brother took some to school, too.

[15] Besides the pine-cone decorations, we made some strings to decorate the mantel. [16] My mom got needles and a spool of heavy thread out of her sewing basket, and we strung the rest of the cranberries on six-foot lengths of the thread.

[17] Mom and Grandma cut several more long pieces of thread, and we used them to make strings of popcorn, just like our strings of cranberries. [18] We left some of the popcorn strings white, painted the others different colors, and hung them around the living room and dining room.

[19] Decorating was even more fun than usual, and I think that the whole house looked prettier, too, with all our homemade ornaments. [20] From now on, we're going to make decorations every year.

TIMESAVER

For **Review: Posttest 2,** you may want to have students highlight independent clauses in one color and subordinate clauses in another color.

ANSWERS

Review: Posttest 2

Sentences will vary. Here are some possibilities:

1. Jan and Mike went to the dance.
2. Emilia sang and danced at the talent show.
3. I wanted to go to the show, but he wanted to stay home.
4. Alan can play tennis after school, or he can run track.
5. The car that we bought last year is already causing us trouble.
6. The man who is wearing the red shirt is my uncle.
7. As soon as the rabbit saw me, it hopped away.
8. The cicadas in the trees were so loud that they almost deafened me.
9. After we came home, I rode the horse that belongs to my neighbor.
10. When we went to the baseball game, John ate too much popcorn, and we had to leave early.

Review: Posttest 2

Writing a Variety of Sentence Structures

Write your own original sentences according to the following instructions.

EXAMPLE **1.** a compound sentence with two independent clauses joined by *and*

1. *My mother usually gives us tacos for supper once a week, and she makes the best tacos in the world.*

1. a simple sentence with a compound subject
2. a simple sentence with a compound verb
3. a compound sentence with two independent clauses joined by *but*

4. a compound sentence with two independent clauses joined by *or*
5. a complex sentence with a subordinate clause that begins with *that*
6. a complex sentence with a subordinate clause that begins with *who*
7. a complex sentence with a subordinate clause at the beginning of the sentence
8. a complex sentence with a subordinate clause at the end of the sentence
9. a complex sentence with two subordinate clauses
10. a compound-complex sentence

GRAMMAR

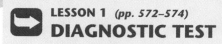
OBJECTIVES

- To identify verbs that agree with their subjects
- To identify pronouns that agree with their antecedents

PROGRAM MANAGER

FOR THE WHOLE CHAPTER

- **Review** For exercises on chapter concepts, see **Review Form A** and **Review Form B** in *Language Skills Practice and Assessment,* pp. 131–133.

- **Assessment** For additional testing, see **Usage Pretests** and **Usage Mastery Tests** in *Language Skills Practice and Assessment,* pp. 115–120 and pp. 191–198.

USAGE

CHAPTER OVERVIEW

This chapter deals with agreement of subjects and verbs and of pronouns and antecedents. After a review of grammatical number, the textbook takes up the idea of subject-verb agreement and discusses prepositional phrases, indefinite pronouns, compound subjects, collective nouns, sentences in unusual order, and *don't* and *doesn't.* The last part of the chapter is concerned with agreement of pronouns and antecedents.

Students can use the rules and examples to solve specific problems they encounter in proofreading their writing. You can also use the chapter for initial teaching of the concepts to English-language learners and for general review for the whole class.

USAGE

20 AGREEMENT

Subject and Verb, Pronoun and Antecedent

Diagnostic Test

A. Identifying Verbs That Agree with Their Subjects

In each of the following sentences, if the italicized verb agrees with its subject, write C. If the italicized verb does not agree with its subject, write the correct form of the verb.

EXAMPLES **1.** The answers to that question *don't* make sense.
1. C

2. Ms. Suarez, our gym teacher, *don't* know what happened.
2. *doesn't*

1. are **1.** When *is* Bill's parents coming to pick us up?
2. doesn't **2.** Mr. Epstein said that it *don't* look like rain today.

572

3. Neither of the bar mitzvahs ~~have~~ been scheduled for next month. **3. has**
4. Everyone who wears eyeglasses *is* having vision tests today. **4. C**
5. My baseball bat and my catcher's mitt ~~was~~ back in my room. **5. were**
6. Neither Ésteban nor Tina ~~have~~ tried out yet for the play. **6. has**
7. All of our guests *have* been to Fort Worth's Japanese Garden. **7. C**
8. ~~Don't~~ the team captain plan to put her into the game before it's over? **8. Doesn't**
9. One of the men ~~have~~ decided that he will get his car washed. **9. has**
10. The Bill of Rights ~~give~~ American citizens the right to worship where they please. **10. gives**

B. Identifying Pronouns That Agree with Their Antecedents

In each of the following sentences, if the italicized pronoun agrees with its antecedent, write C. If the italicized pronoun does not agree with its antecedent, write the correct form of the pronoun.

EXAMPLES **1.** One of the does was accompanied by *her* fawn.
    1. C
  2. Each of the boys brought *their* permission slip.
    2. *his*

11. Have all of the winners taken *their* science fair projects home? **11. C**
12. Everyone going to the concert should bring ~~their~~ own food and lawn chair. **12. his or her**
13. Many of the buildings had green ribbons on ~~its~~ windows for the Saint Patrick's Day Parade. **13. their**
14. Neither Stephanie nor Marilyn had worn ~~their~~ gym suit to class. **14. her**

USAGE

USING THE DIAGNOSTIC TEST

If you notice that some students are having problems with agreement in their compositions, you can use the **Diagnostic Test** to pinpoint error patterns and specific strengths and weaknesses. **Part A** assesses students' understanding of subject-verb agreement, and **Part B** assesses understanding of pronoun-antecedent agreement. Assess students' responses to help you determine which rules of agreement they need to review.

USAGE

OBJECTIVE

• To classify nouns and pronouns by number

USAGE

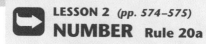 **QUICK REMINDER**

Write the following list of words on the chalkboard and have students classify each as either singular or plural:

1. him [singular]
2. everybody [singular]
3. many [plural]
4. you [singular or plural]
5. them [plural]

MEETING *individual* **NEEDS**

General Strategies. Some speakers do not use plural forms under certain circumstances. If other words in a sentence clearly indicate plurality, as in "I have about a million baseball card," the use of the plural form of *card* is considered optional. You can help students by pointing this out and encouraging them to proofread carefully for plurals.

574

USAGE

574 *Agreement*

15. Every dog in the show had a numbered tag hanging from ∧*their* collar. **15.** its [or his or her]
16. Someone in the scout troop camped near poison ivy and has gotten it all over ∧*themselves.*
17. Only a few of the carpenters had brought tools with *them* to the job. **16.** herself [or himself] **17.** C
18. My dog was among the contest winners that had ∧*its* pictures taken. **18.** their
19. According to the teacher, both of those titles should have lines drawn underneath ∧*it.* **19.** them
20. That Ray Charles song is familiar, but I can't remember *its* title. **20.** C

Number

Number is the form of a word that indicates whether the word is singular or plural.

20a. When a word refers to one person, place, thing, or idea, it is **singular** in number. When a word refers to more than one, it is **plural** in number.

SINGULAR	book	woman	fox	I	he	each
PLURAL	books	women	foxes	we	they	few

ORAL PRACTICE 1 **Classifying Nouns and Pronouns by Number**

Read the following expressions aloud. Tell whether each noun or pronoun is <u>singular</u> or <u>plural</u>.

1. The lion yawns. **1.** sing.
2. The cubs play. **2.** pl.
3. No one stays. **3.** sing.
4. The refugees arrive. **4.** pl.
5. She wins. **5.** sing.
6. The play opens. **6.** sing.
7. Everyone goes. **7.** sing.
8. All applaud. **8.** pl.

LESSON 3 *(pp. 575–578)*

AGREEMENT OF SUBJECT AND VERB Rules 20b, 20c

OBJECTIVES

- To identify verbs that agree in number with their subjects
- To identify subjects and verbs that agree in number

Agreement of Subject and Verb **575**

20 a–b

 EXERCISE 1 **Classifying Nouns and Pronouns by Number**

Classify each word as *singular* or *plural*.

EXAMPLE **1.** cat
 1. *singular*

1. rodeos — **1.** pl.
2. band — **2.** sing. or pl.
3. they — **3.** pl.
4. I — **4.** sing.
5. many — **5.** pl.
6. igloo — **6.** sing.
7. geese — **7.** pl.
8. we — **8.** pl.
9. friends — **9.** pl.
10. it — **10.** sing.

Agreement of Subject and Verb

20b. A verb agrees with its subject in number.

(1) Singular subjects take singular verbs.

EXAMPLES The **car comes** to a sudden stop. [The singular verb *comes* agrees with the singular subject *car.*]
On that route the **plane flies** at a low altitude. [The singular verb *flies* agrees with the singular subject *plane.*]

(2) Plural subjects take plural verbs.

EXAMPLES Many **senators oppose** the new tax bill. [The plural verb *oppose* agrees with the plural subject *senators.*]
Again and again, the **dolphins leap** playfully. [The plural verb *leap* agrees with the plural subject *dolphins.*]

NOTE: Generally, nouns ending in *s* are plural (*candles, ideas, neighbors, horses*), and verbs ending in *s* are singular (*sees, writes, speaks, carries*). For guidelines on forming plurals, see pages 806–810.

USAGE

 PROGRAM MANAGER

AGREEMENT OF SUBJECT AND VERB

- **Independent Practice/ Reteaching** For instruction and exercises, see **Subject-Verb Agreement** and **Agreement of Subject and Verb** in *Language Skills Practice and Assessment,* pp. 125–126.

- **Computer Guided Instruction** For additional instruction and practice with agreement of subject and verb, see **Lesson 10** in *Language Workshop CD-ROM.*

- **Practice** To help less-advanced students with additional instruction and practice with agreement of subject and verb, see **Chapter 17** in *English Workshop, Second Course,* pp. 159–160.

 QUICK REMINDER

Write these two nonsense sentences on the chalkboard:

1. The shink (*grimp* or *grimps*) the vork. [grimps]
2. The shinks (*grimp* or *grimps*) the vork. [grimp]

Ask students to select the correct "verb" and to explain how they were able to make the correct choices. [Answers may vary, but the basic idea is that students recognized the subject-verb-object pattern of the sentences and knew how to choose verbs that agree with the subjects in number.] Point out that not all sentences are as obvious as these, but the same rule applies in all sentences.

USAGE

575

LEP/ESL

General Strategies. Some English-language learners may be confused by the meaning of the word *agreement*. They might expect that when the subject ends in *s,* the verb must also end in *s.* It may be helpful to emphasize that *agreement* means that a singular subject requires a singular verb, ordinarily one ending in *s.* Point out that *singular* starts with *s* and singular verbs usually end in *s.*

COMMON ERROR

Problem. Many students think the *–ing* word is the only verb in verb phrases, and they forget to check the helping verb to make sure it agrees with the subject in number.

Solution. One way to help solve this problem is to emphasize that an *–ing* word can never be the main verb of a sentence. If students find an *–ing* word, they should make it a habit to look for the helping verb.

INTEGRATING THE LANGUAGE ARTS

Vocabulary Link. Some words are plural in form and meaning, but many people use them as though they were singular. Some common words of this type are *media, data, criteria,* and *phenomena.* Ask students to look in a dictionary to find the singular forms of these words [*medium, datum, criterion,* and *phenomenon*]. Remind students to make sure they use plural verbs with plural subjects of sentences.

USAGE

---

576 *Agreement*

The first auxiliary (helping) verb in a verb phrase must agree with its subject.

EXAMPLES **He is building** a bird feeder.
They are building a bird feeder.

Does anyone know the answer?
Do any **students know** the answer?

NOTE: The pronouns *I* and *you* take plural verbs.

EXAMPLES **I walk** to school.
Do you walk to school?
EXCEPTION **I am walking** to school.

EXERCISE 2 **Identifying Verbs That Agree in Number with Their Subjects**

Choose the form of the <u>verb</u> in parentheses <u>that agrees with the given subject</u>.

EXAMPLE **1.** it (*is, are*)
1. *is*

1. this (<u>*costs*</u>, *cost*)
2. Chinese lanterns (*glows,* <u>*glow*</u>)
3. the swimmer (<u>*dives*</u>, *dive*)
4. we (*considers,* <u>*consider*</u>)
5. the men (*was,* <u>*were*</u>)
6. she (<u>*asks*</u>, *ask*)
7. these (*needs,* <u>*need*</u>)
8. those tacos (*tastes,* <u>*taste*</u>)
9. that music (<u>*sounds*</u>, *sound*)
10. lessons (*takes,* <u>*take*</u>)

EXERCISE 3 **Identifying Verbs That Agree in Number with Their Subjects**

For each sentence in the following paragraph, choose the <u>correct form of the verb</u> in parentheses.

EXAMPLE **[1]** *(Do, Does)* you like rap music?
1. *Do*

[1] The rapper KRS-One (<u>*is*</u>, *are*) one of my favorite performers. [2] In fact, his picture (<u>*is*</u>, *are*) hanging in my room. [3] As you can see, KRS's face (<u>*reflects*</u>, *reflect*) his

positive attitude. [4] KRS (*encourages*, *encourage*) people to think for themselves. [5] Many performers (*believes*, *believe*) in using rap music to improve people's lives and to end violence.

hip *hop*

Prepositional Phrases Between Subjects and Verbs

20c. The number of a subject is not changed by a prepositional phrase following the subject.

NONSTANDARD	The lights on the Christmas tree creates a festive atmosphere.
STANDARD	The **lights** on the Christmas tree **create** a festive atmosphere.
NONSTANDARD	The distance between the two posts for the clothesline are eight feet.
STANDARD	The **distance** between the two posts for the clothesline **is** eight feet.

☞ REFERENCE NOTE: For a discussion of standard and nonstandard English, see pages 394 and 682.

EXERCISE 4 **Identifying Subjects and Verbs That Agree in Number**

Identify the <u>subject</u> in each sentence. Choose the form of the <u>verb</u> in parentheses <u>that agrees with the subject</u>.

EXAMPLE **1.** The houses on my block (*has, have*) two stories.
1. *houses—subject; have*

USAGE

VISUAL CONNECTIONS
Exploring the Subject. Many commentators have compared rap music to traditional oral literature of past ages. Have students read "The Cremation of Sam McGee" by Robert W. Service, a poem about a gold prospector in the Klondike region of the Yukon Territory. Ask students to compare this poem to rap songs. How are they similar? [They both rhyme, both deal with a moral lesson, and both tell a story.] How are they different? [Rap tends to deal with urban themes and present-day issues; the poem deals with gold prospecting in the frozen north a long time ago.]

COMMON ERROR
Problem. Many students tend to make the verb agree with the object of a preposition rather than with the subject of a sentence.

Solution. Write several sentences on the chalkboard that follow the pattern: subject, prepositional phrase, predicate. Include both the singular and plural forms of the verb (The trees in the park [lose, loses] their leaves). Point out to students that if they read the sentence with the prepositional phrase removed, it will be easier to determine which form of the verb is correct [lose].

USAGE

577

OBJECTIVE

- To identify subjects and verbs that agree in number when the subject is an indefinite pronoun

USAGE

578 *Agreement*

1. The <u>launch</u> of a space shuttle (*<u>attracts</u>, attract*) the interest of people throughout the world.
2. The <u>thermos bottle</u> in the picnic basket (*<u>is</u>, are*) filled with apple juice.
3. My favorite <u>collection</u> of poems (*<u>is</u>, are*) *Where the Sidewalk Ends.*
4. <u>People</u> in some states (*observes, <u>observe</u>*) the fourth Friday in September as Native American Day.
5. The starving <u>children</u> of the world (*needs, <u>need</u>*) food and medicine.
6. The <u>cucumbers</u> in my garden (*grows, <u>grow</u>*) very quickly.
7. <u>Koalas</u> in the wild and in captivity (*eats, <u>eat</u>*) only eucalyptus leaves.
8. The <u>principal</u> of each high school (*<u>awards</u>, award*) certificates to honor students.
9. <u>Stories</u> about Hank Aaron and Willie Mays always (*makes, <u>make</u>*) me want to play baseball.
10. The <u>house</u> beside the city park (*<u>is</u>, are*) where my grandfather was born.

Indefinite Pronouns

Some pronouns do not refer to a definite person, place, thing, or idea and are therefore called *indefinite* pronouns.

20d. The following indefinite pronouns are singular: *anybody, anyone, each, either, everybody, everyone, neither, nobody, no one, one, somebody, someone.*

Pronouns like *each* and *one* are frequently followed by prepositional phrases. Remember that the verb agrees with the subject of the sentence, not with a word in a prepositional phrase.

EXAMPLES **Everyone was invited** to the celebration.
Either of the answers **is** correct.

USAGE

PROGRAM MANAGER

INDEFINITE PRONOUNS

- **Independent Practice/ Reteaching** For instruction and exercises, see **Agreement with Indefinite Pronouns** in *Language Skills Practice and Assessment,* p. 127.

- **Computer Guided Instruction** For additional instruction and practice with agreement with indefinite pronouns, see **Lesson 11** in *Language Workshop CD-ROM.*

- **Practice** To help less-advanced students with additional instruction and practice with agreement of indefinite pronouns, see **Chapter 17** in *English Workshop, Second Course,* pp. 163–166.

QUICK REMINDER

Write the following sentences on the chalkboard and have students choose the correct form of the verb for each sentence:

1. Either of the books (has, have) interesting information. [has]
2. Everyone in our class (is, are) writing a story. [is]
3. Neither of my brothers (play, plays) soccer. [plays]

Explain to students that the indefinite pronouns *either, everyone,* and *neither* are singular and need singular verbs.

One of the tapes **belongs** to Sabrena.
Someone in the stands **has been waving** at us.

20e. The following indefinite pronouns are plural: *both, few, many, several.*

EXAMPLES **Both** of the apples **are** good.
Few of the guests **know** about the surprise.
Many of the students **walk** to school.
Several of the members **have** not **paid** their dues.

20f. The following indefinite pronouns may be either singular or plural: *all, any, most, none, some.*

The number of the subject *all, any, most, none* or *some* is determined by the number of the object in the prepositional phrase following the subject. If the subject refers to a singular object, the subject is singular. If the subject refers to a plural object, the subject is plural.

EXAMPLES **All** of the fruit **looks** ripe. [*All* refers to the singular object *fruit.*]
All of the pears **look** ripe. [*All* refers to the plural object *pears.*]

Some of the equipment **has been stored** in the garage. [*Some* refers to the singular object *equipment.*]
Some of the supplies **have been stored** in the garage. [*Some* refers to the plural object *supplies.*]

▶ EXERCISE 5 **Identifying Subjects and Verbs That Agree in Number**

Identify the <u>subject</u> in each of the following sentences. Choose the form of the <u>verb</u> in parentheses <u>that agrees with the subject</u>.

EXAMPLE 1. Each of the marchers (*was, were*) carrying a sign protesting apartheid.
1. *Each—subject; was*

USAGE

LEARNING STYLES

Auditory Learners. Have students practice saying these additional examples to use with **Rule 20f:** *Is any* of the watermelon gone? *Are any* of the watermelons gone? *Most* of the watermelon *is* gone. *Most* of the watermelons *are* gone. *None* of the watermelon *is* gone. *None* of the watermelons *are* gone.

Choral reading should be particularly helpful for auditory learners.

Visual Learners. You may want to have students write out the sentences in **Exercise 5** and highlight the indefinite pronoun and verb in each sentence. You could model the process on the chalkboard by using colored chalk to underscore subjects and verbs in sample sentences.

COMMON ERROR

Problem. The pronouns *everybody* and *everyone* cause problems because they're singular in form but plural in meaning in the sense that they imply more than one person.

Solution. Have students associate the word *each* with *everyone* and *everybody.* Have them practice saying "each and everyone" and "each and everybody," until they think of these phrases whenever they hear *everyone* or *everybody.* Since most students will know that *each* takes a singular verb, this procedure might help them to remember that *everyone* and *everybody* are both singular.

USAGE

579

REVIEW A

OBJECTIVE

- To proofread a paragraph for subject-verb agreement

580 *Agreement*

1. <u>All</u> of my friends (*has*, <u>*have*</u>) had the chicken pox.
2. <u>Everyone</u> at the party (<u>*likes*</u>, *like*) the hummus dip.
3. <u>Both</u> of Fred's brothers (*celebrates*, <u>*celebrate*</u>) their birthdays in July.
4. <u>Some</u> of my baseball cards (*is*, <u>*are*</u>) valuable.
5. <u>None</u> of those rosebushes ever (*blooms*, <u>*bloom*</u>) in February.
6. <u>Several</u> of those colors (<u>*do*</u>, *does*) not appeal to me.
7. <u>Many</u> of Mrs. Taniguchi's students (*speaks*, <u>*speak*</u>) fluent Japanese.
8. <u>Nobody</u> in the beginning painting classes (<u>*has*</u>, *have*) displayed work in the annual art show.
9. <u>Most</u> of the appetizers on the menu (*tastes*, <u>*taste*</u>) delicious.
10. <u>One</u> of Georgia O'Keeffe's paintings (<u>*shows*</u>, *show*) a ram's skull.

> REVIEW A

Proofreading a Paragraph for Subject-Verb Agreement

Many of the sentences in the following paragraph contain errors in agreement of subject and verb. If the verb agrees with its subject, write *C*. If the verb does not agree with its subject, write the correct form of the verb. [Note: Some sentences have more than one verb.]

EXAMPLES   [1] One of the best-known prehistoric monuments in the world stand in a field in Britain.
     1. *stands*

     [2] Everybody today calls the monument Stonehenge, and thousands of people visits it each year.
     2. *C; visit*

[1] All of the visitors to Stonehenge ~~wants~~ to know why the structure was built. [2] The huge rocks at Stonehenge almost ~~seems~~ to challenge tourists and scientists alike to uncover their mysteries. [3] Most people easily recognize the monument as it looks in the photograph on the next page. [4] However, nobody ~~are~~ sure how Stonehenge

ANSWERS

Review A

1. want; C
2. seem
3. C; C
4. is; C

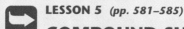
COMPOUND SUBJECTS Rules 20g–20i

OBJECTIVE

• To choose verbs that agree in number with compound subjects

looked long ago. [5] Some of the archaeologists studying the site ~~believes~~ that the drawing below shows how the old Stonehenge looked. [6] Notice that few of the stones ~~remains~~ in their original places. [7] Many visitors to Stonehenge assume that ancient druids built the monument. [8] Most scientists, though, ~~says~~ it was built longer ago— perhaps four thousand years ago. [9] After seeing Stonehenge, few doubt that the stones ~~weighs~~ as much as fifty tons. [10] Of course, nearly everyone ~~seem~~ to have a theory about how these stones were set in place and what they were used for, but no one knows for sure.

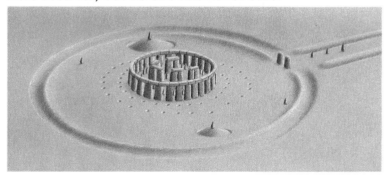

USAGE

Compound Subjects

20g. Subjects joined by *and* usually take a plural verb.

The following compound subjects joined by *and* name more than one person or thing and take plural verbs.

EXAMPLES **Antonia Brico** and **Sarah Caldwell are** famous conductors. [Two persons are conductors.]
Last year a **library** and a **museum were built** in our town. [Two things were built.]

5. believe; C; C
6. C; remain
7. C; C
8. say; C
9. C; weigh
10. seems; C; C; C

PROGRAM MANAGER

COMPOUND SUBJECTS

■ **Independent Practice/ Reteaching** For instruction and exercises, see **Agreement with Compound Subjects** in *Language Skills Practice and Assessment,* p. 128.

■ **Computer Guided Instruction** For additional instruction and practice with agreement with compound subjects, see **Lesson 11** in *Language Workshop CD-ROM.*

■ **Practice** To help less-advanced students with additional instruction and practice with agreement with compound subjects, see **Chapter 17** in *English Workshop, Second Course,* pp. 169–170.

QUICK REMINDER

Write the following sentences on the chalkboard and have students choose the correct verb:

1. Tom and Luís (<u>sit</u>, sits) on the sofa.
2. Tom or Luís (sit, <u>sits</u>) on the sofa.
3. The red purse and the blue one (is, <u>are</u>) mine.
4. The red purse or the blue one (<u>is</u>, are) mine.

continued on next page

USAGE

5. The bicycle and the book bag (was, <u>were</u>) found here.

6. The bicycle or the book bag (<u>was</u>, were) found here.

LEP/ESL

General Strategies. The agreement rules for compound subjects depend on an understanding of the constructions *either . . . or* and *neither . . . nor*. English-language learners often have trouble with the meanings of these constructions. You can help by substituting more familiar forms. For example, *Neither Miami nor Jacksonville* could be paraphrased as *Not Miami and not Jacksonville. Either Mrs. Gomez or Mr. Ming* could be rewritten as *Mrs. Gomez or Mr. Ming.*

A DIFFERENT APPROACH

Point out to students that **Rule 20g** (p. 581) isn't limited to only two elements in a compound subject. Sometimes a series of three or more elements, with *and* before the last element, makes up a compound subject. Example: Sunglasses, backpacks, canteens, and boots are essential for hiking on this trail.

TIMESAVER

You can save time grading papers if you have your students do **Exercise 6** orally instead of in writing. You can call on students who may be having trouble to check their comprehension, and you can give guided practice in how to choose the correct verb if students make errors.

USAGE

A compound subject that names only one person or thing takes a singular verb.

EXAMPLES   The **captain** and **quarterback** of the team **is** Lyle. [One person is both the captain and the quarterback.]

Chicken and dumplings is a favorite Southern dish. [Chicken and dumplings is one dish.]

EXERCISE 6   **Choosing Verbs That Agree in Number with Compound Subjects**

Indicate whether the compound subject in each of the following sentences is <u>*singular*</u> or <u>*plural*</u>. Choose the form of the <u>verb that agrees with the compound subject.</u>

EXAMPLE   **1.** Cleon and Pam (*is, are*) here.
1. *plural—are*

1. pl.   **1.** March and April (*is,* <u>*are*</u>) windy months.

2. pl.   **2.** My mother and the mechanic (*is,* <u>*are*</u>) discussing the bill.

3. pl.   **3.** Monica Seles and Jennifer Capriati (*plays,* <u>*play*</u>) in the finals today.

4. sing.   **4.** Red beans and rice (<u>*is*</u>, *are*) my favorite Cajun dish.

5. pl.   **5.** (*Does,* <u>*Do*</u>) Carla and Jean take dancing lessons?

6. pl.   **6.** (*Is,* <u>*Are*</u>) the knives and forks in the drawer?

7. pl.   **7.** English and science (*requires,* <u>*require*</u>) hours of study.

8. sing.   **8.** (<u>*Here's*</u>, *Here are*) our star and winner of the meet.

9. pl.   **9.** Where (*is,* <u>*are*</u>) the bread and the honey?

10. pl.   **10.** (*Does,* <u>*Do*</u>) an Austrian and a German speak the same language?

20h.   Singular subjects joined by *or* or *nor* take a singular verb.

EXAMPLES   A **pen** or a **pencil is needed** for this test. [Either one is needed.]

Neither **Miami** nor **Jacksonville is** the capital of Florida. [Neither one is the capital.]

▶ EXERCISE 7

Choosing Verbs That Agree in Number with Compound Subjects

Choose the form of the <u>verb</u> in parentheses <u>that agrees</u> <u>with the compound subject</u> in each of the following sentences.

EXAMPLE   **1.** Neither Theo nor Erin (*has, have*) learned the Jewish folk dance *Mayim, Mayim.*
          1. *has*

1. Either Mrs. Gomez or Mr. Ming (<u>*delivers*</u>, *deliver*) the welcome speech on the first day of school.
2. Our guava tree and our fig tree (*bears*, <u>*bear*</u>) more fruit than our entire neighborhood can eat.
3. Tuskegee Institute or Harvard University (<u>*offers*</u>, *offer*) the best courses in Francine's field.
4. Armadillos and anteaters (*has*, <u>*have*</u>) tubular mouths and long sticky tongues for catching insects.
5. Either the president or the vice-president of the class (<u>*calls*</u>, *call*) roll every morning.
6. Sarah's report on Booker T. Washington and Sam's report on Quanah Parker (*sounds*, <u>*sound*</u>) interesting.
7. Red and royal blue (*looks*, <u>*look*</u>) nice in this bedroom.
8. Bridge or canasta (<u>*is*</u>, *are*) my favorite card game.
9. Neither my sister nor my brother (<u>*mows*</u>, *mow*) the lawn without protesting.
10. The tulips and the daffodils (*blooms*, <u>*bloom*</u>) every April.

20i. When a singular subject and a plural subject are joined by *or* or *nor*, the verb agrees with the subject nearer the verb.

EXAMPLES   Neither the **director** nor the **players were** on time for rehearsal. [The verb agrees with the nearer subject, *players.*]
            Neither the **players** nor the **director was** on time for rehearsal. [The verb agrees with the nearer subject, *director.*]

USAGE

USAGE

REVIEW B

OBJECTIVE

- To choose verbs that agree in number with their subjects in a paragraph

Whenever possible, avoid this kind of construction by revising the sentence. For instance, the second example above could be revised in the following way.

Both the players and the director were late for rehearsal.

▶ EXERCISE 8   **Choosing Verbs That Agree in Number with Compound Subjects**

Choose the form of the <u>verb</u> in parentheses <u>that agrees with the compound subject</u> in each of the following sentences.

EXAMPLE   **1.** Both Tyrone and Derrick (*is, are*) going to the Hammer concert.
            1. *are*

1. Either Sylvia or her brothers (*washes, <u>wash</u>*) the kitchen floor each Saturday morning.
2. This bread and this cereal (*contains, <u>contain</u>*) no preservatives or dyes.
3. Either the students or the teacher (*<u>reads</u>, read*) aloud during the last ten minutes of each class period.
4. The heavy rain clouds and the powerful winds (*indicates, <u>indicate</u>*) that a hurricane is approaching.
5. Neither the seal nor the clowns (*catches, <u>catch</u>*) the ball that the monkey throws into the circus ring.

▶ REVIEW B   **Choosing Verbs That Agree in Number with Their Subjects**

Choose the form of the <u>verb</u> in parentheses <u>that agrees with its subject</u> in each sentence in the following paragraph.

EXAMPLE   [1] Breads, such as *pan dulce,* and other baked goods (*sells, sell*) well at the Mexican American bakery shown on the next page.
            1. *sell*

[1] The wonderful smells at the bakery (*invites, <u>invite</u>*) hungry customers. [2] Children and their parents (*enjoys,*

OBJECTIVES

- To write sentences with collective nouns
- To choose verbs that agree in number with their subjects
- To use *doesn't* with singular subjects
- To use *doesn't* and *don't* correctly in sentences

enjoy) choosing and tasting the baked treats. [3] Display cases and bowls *(holds, hold)* the fresh breads and pastries. [4] Cinnamon rolls with powdered toppings and braided breads *(goes, go)* quickly. [5] Either an *empanada* or some giant biscuits *(are, is)* likely to be someone's breakfast. [6] Pumpkin or sweet potato *(is, are)* often used to fill the *empanadas.* [7] Most children really *(likes, like)* volcano-shaped pastries known as *volcanes.* [8] Raisin bars or a *pañuelo (makes, make)* a special after-lunch treat. [9] Bakeries like this one *(prepares, prepare)* mainly traditional Mexican American breads. [10] But holidays and special occasions *(calls, call)* for extra-fancy treats.

Other Problems in Agreement

20j. Collective nouns may be either singular or plural.

A *collective noun* is singular in form but names a group of persons, animals, or things.

Common Collective Nouns			
army	club	fleet	public
assembly	committee	flock	swarm
audience	crowd	group	team
class	family	herd	troop

USAGE

20j

QUICK REMINDER

Write the following sentences on the chalkboard. Ask students to choose the correct form of the verb in parentheses (underscored). You may want to have volunteers explain why choosing the right verb in each sentence is a challenge.

1. The team (is, are) putting on their helmets. [Team refers to individuals and needs a plural verb.]
2. In that tree (live, lives) two squirrels. [The subject follows the verb.]
3. She (doesn't, don't) play tennis. [Incorrect usage is reinforced orally.]

USAGE

USAGE

MEETING *individual* NEEDS

LEP/ESL

General Strategies. An oral drill can help clear up confusion about the use of *don't* and *doesn't.* Read aloud a few sentences that have the same pattern, exaggerating the italicized words.

1. I used to live in Texas, but *I don't* anymore.
2. Lionel used to play video games, but *he doesn't* anymore.
3. Our teams used to win all the games, but *they don't* anymore.

Go slowly and shake your head to emphasize negation when you say *don't* and *doesn't.* When students understand the pattern, let them volunteer their own sentences.

ANSWERS
Exercise 9

Responses will vary. Here are some possibilities:

1. This *committee* supports the bill to raise taxes.
   That *committee* agree to disagree.
2. The *fleet* sails majestically into the harbor.
   The *fleet* scatter as enemy ships attack.
3. The *flock* of geese is migrating south.
   A *flock* of geese are fighting over the food thrown to them.
4. The *audience* applauds the young soloist.
   The *audience* are divided in their response.
5. That *group* meets on Wednesdays.
   That *group* have a dozen different opinions.

586

---

586 *Agreement*

USAGE

A collective noun takes a singular verb when the noun refers to the group as a unit. A collective noun takes a plural verb when the noun refers to the individual parts or members of the group.

EXAMPLES   The science **class is taking** a field trip to the planetarium. [The class as a unit is taking a field trip.]
Today, the science **class are working** on their astronomy projects. [The members of the class are working on various projects.]

The **family has moved** to Little Rock, Arkansas. [The family as a unit has moved.]
The **family have been** unable to agree on where to spend their next vacation. [The members of the family have different opinions.]

▷ EXERCISE 9   **Writing Sentences with Collective Nouns**

Select five collective nouns. Use each noun as the subject of two sentences. In the first sentence, make the subject singular in meaning, so that it takes a singular verb. In the second sentence, make the subject plural in meaning, so that it takes a plural verb.

EXAMPLE   **1.** *The softball team is practicing some new plays.*
The softball team are wearing new uniforms.

20k.   A verb agrees with its subject, not with its predicate nominative.

EXAMPLES
                 S   V   PN
The best **time** to visit **is** weekday mornings.

              S   V   PN
Weekday **mornings are** the best time to visit.

20l.   When the subject follows the verb, find the subject and make sure the verb agrees with it. The subject usually follows the verb in sentences beginning with *here* or *there* and in questions.

EXAMPLES   Here **is** my **seat.**
           Here **are** our **seats.**

           There **is** an exciting **ride** at the fair.
           There **are** exciting **rides** at the fair.

           Where **is** the **bread**?
           Where **are** the **loaves** of bread?

           Does he know them?
           Do they know him?

The contractions *here's, there's,* and *where's* contain the verb *is* and should be used with only singular subjects.

NONSTANDARD   There's the books.
   STANDARD   There **are** the **books.**
   STANDARD   There**'s** the **book.**

☞ REFERENCE NOTE: For more information about contractions, see pages 783–784.

▶ EXERCISE 10   **Choosing Verbs That Agree in Number with Their Subjects**

Choose the form of the <u>verb</u> in parentheses <u>that agrees with the subject</u> in each of the following sentences.

EXAMPLE   **1.** There (*is, are*) many new students this year.
          1. *are*

1. The audience (<u>*loves*</u>, *love*) the mime performance.
2. (*Here's,* <u>*Here are*</u>) the Natalie Cole tapes I borrowed.
3. The club (<u>*sponsors*</u>, *sponsor*) a carwash each March.
4. Andy's gift to Janelle (<u>*was*</u>, *were*) two roses.
5. Here (*is,* <u>*are*</u>) the letters I have been expecting.
6. The public (*differs,* <u>*differ*</u>) in their opinions on the referendum.
7. The map shows that (*there's,* <u>*there are*</u>) seven countries in Central America.
8. The tennis team usually (<u>*plays*</u>, *play*) every Saturday morning.
9. His legacy to us (<u>*was*</u>, *were*) words of wisdom.
10. Where (*is,* <u>*are*</u>) the limericks you wrote?

USAGE

USAGE

🌀 **A DIFFERENT APPROACH**
In sentences in which the subject follows the verb, students can learn to identify the subject by inverting the order of the subject and verb and substituting the word *someplace* for the words *here, there,* and *where.* For example, "Where is my seat?" becomes "My seat is someplace."

⚡ **TIMESAVER**
You can save time in class and save time grading papers by having students do **Exercise 10** orally. You can assess where students are having difficulty and provide guided practice in identifying the correct verb as they do the exercise.

INTEGRATING THE LANGUAGE ARTS

Usage and Speaking. Most people use contractions frequently in speech, but in writing, contractions are usually reserved for an informal style. Contractions can weaken and detract from some expressions. For example, President Kennedy's famous "Ask not what your country can do for you . . ." seems much more powerful than "Don't ask what your country can do for you." You may want to point this out to your students and encourage them to choose words carefully to achieve the exact effect they want to create in their writing and speaking.

CRITICAL THINKING

Analysis. Tell students the use of *do* as a support for yes/no questions and negation is relatively new in the English language. In Shakespeare's time, the usual way to ask a yes/no question was to put the verb first in the sentence: Want you some pie? Negative statements were formed by adding *not* after the verb: I want not any pie. Write those two examples of sixteenth-century usage on the chalkboard, and have students copy them and write the modern usage next to them. Tell them there is a general belief that changes in language always simplify grammar. Ask students if they think the modern form is simpler or more complicated. [Some students will say "Want you some pie" is simpler than "Do you want some pie," and "I want not any pie" is simpler than "I don't want any pie."]

588

---

588 *Agreement*

20m. The contractions *don't* and *doesn't* must agree with their subjects.

Use *don't* with plural subjects and with the pronouns *I* and *you*.

EXAMPLES These **gloves don't** fit.
I don't like that song.
You don't have enough money to buy that.

Use *doesn't* with other singular subjects.

EXAMPLES The **music box doesn't** play.
She doesn't like cold weather.
It doesn't matter.

 ORAL PRACTICE 2   **Using *Doesn't* with Singular Subjects**

Read the following sentences aloud. Pay particular attention to the agreement of *doesn't* with the singular subject in each sentence.

1. It doesn't look like a serious wound.
2. She doesn't call meetings often.
3. One doesn't interrupt a speaker.
4. He doesn't play records loudly.
5. Doesn't the television set work?
6. Doesn't Oktoberfest start Saturday?
7. She doesn't play basketball.
8. Fido doesn't like his new dog food.

EXERCISE 11   **Using *Doesn't* and *Don't* Correctly**

Complete each sentence by inserting the correct contraction, *doesn't* or *don't*.

EXAMPLE   **1.** ___ they go to our school?
     1. *Don't*

1. ___ anyone in the class know any facts about Susan B. Anthony? **1.** Doesn't

20m

2. Kareem Abdul-Jabbar ____ play professional basketball anymore. **2. doesn't**
3. They ____ have enough people to form a softball team. **3. don't**
4. Pearl and Marshall ____ need to change their schedules. **4. don't**
5. It ____ hurt to practice the piano an hour a day. **5. doesn't**
6. ____ the Japanese celebrate spring with a special festival? **6. Don't**
7. Those snow peas ____ look crisp. **7. don't**
8. Hector ____ win every track meet; sometimes he places second. **8. doesn't**
9. ____ anyone know the time? **9. Doesn't**
10. He ____ know the shortest route from Dallas to Peoria. **10. doesn't**

USAGE

▶ EXERCISE 12   **Using *Doesn't* and *Don't* Correctly in Sentences**

What do you see when you look at these two images? Do they seem to play tricks on your eyes? These images give your brain false clues. We call such misleading images *optical illusions*. Write five sentences about what you think you see or don't see in each image. Use *doesn't* or *don't* correctly in each sentence.

EXAMPLE   **1. *I see the goblet, but I don't see the two faces.***

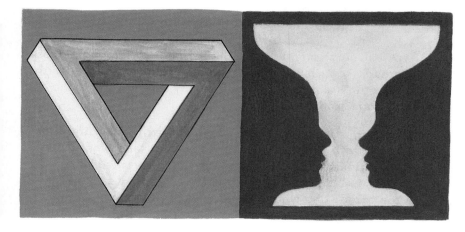

ANSWERS
Exercise 12

Responses will vary. Each sentence should be complete and should use either *doesn't* with a singular subject or *don't* with plural subjects, *I*, or *you*.

USAGE

WRITING APPLICATION

The assignment gives students an opportunity to write a report for an audience of other students. It specifies that they should use at least five collective nouns in reference to clubs and organizations in the school. Since the **Writing** section tells students to begin with a main idea statement, you may want to review the concept of a main idea statement in **Chapter 3: "Learning About Compositions."**

CRITICAL THINKING

Analysis. In order to determine each club's contribution to the parade, students will have to analyze each club to determine its unique features. For example, clubs might have uniforms, a mascot, or equipment they can carry. Point this out to students as they analyze each organization.

WRITING

You may want to review with the class the features of a report, such as the main idea statement, the logical organization, the development with specific details, and the conclusion.

590

WRITING APPLICATION

Using Verbs That Agree in Number with Collective Nouns

People and animals are often gathered in groups. Therefore, when you write about them, you frequently use collective nouns. Should you use a singular verb or a plural verb with a collective noun? Figuring out which verb form to use can be tricky. Use a singular verb when the noun refers to the group as a unit. Use a plural verb when the noun refers to the individual parts or members of the group.

GROUP AS A UNIT | The scout troop wants to be in the parade.
MEMBERS OF GROUP | The troop haven't asked their parents for permission yet.

How might you revise the second sentence above to make it clearer?

▶ WRITING ACTIVITY

You are on the committee in charge of organizing your school's participation in the local Thanksgiving Day Parade. Write a brief report about the committee's plans, which you will read at the next student council meeting. Use at least five collective nouns in your report.

Prewriting Write down the names of some clubs or organizations that might be in the parade. What might these groups contribute to the parade? Think about collective nouns to use in your report. You may want to refer to the list on page 585.

Writing Use your notes to help you write your first draft. Begin with a main idea statement that tells other student council members what progress your committee has made. Then, tell about some of the groups that have asked to be in the parade and what those groups are planning to do.

OBJECTIVES
- To proofread sentences for subject-verb agreement
- To proofread a paragraph for subject-verb agreement

 Evaluating and Revising As you read over your report, ask yourself these questions:

- Is it clear what kind of parade is planned?
- Is it clear what groups are involved?
- Have I included important details?
- Do the committee's plans sound logical?

Revise any parts of the report that are unclear. Check to be sure that you've used five collective nouns and the correct verbs with them.

 Proofreading Carefully read your report again. Check for possible sentence fragments and run-on sentences. For more about these kinds of sentence problems, see pages 361–366. Be sure that you've followed the rules in this chapter for subject-verb agreement.

USAGE

PROOFREADING
   After careful proofreading, students can publish their reports by reading them to small groups.

USAGE

 REVIEW C
Proofreading Sentences for Subject-Verb Agreement

Most of the following sentences contain errors in agreement of subject and verb. If a sentence is correct, write C. If a sentence contains an error in agreement, write the correct form of the verb.

EXAMPLE **1.** There is a man and a woman here to see you.
        1. *are*

1. Leilani and Yoshi doesn't know how to swim. **1.** don't
2. Carrots are my favorite vegetable. **2.** C
3. The Seminoles of Florida sews beautifully designed quilts and jackets. **3.** sew
4. Here's the sweaters I knitted for you. **4.** (Here) are
5. Each of these ten-speed bicycles cost more than one hundred dollars. **5.** costs
6. The soccer team always celebrate each victory with a pizza party. **6.** celebrates

7. C   **7.** The wheelchair division of the six-mile race was won by Randy Nowell.

8. flies   **8.** The flock of geese ~~fly~~ over the lake at dawn.

9. C   **9.** Doesn't that Thai dish with chopped peanuts taste good?

10. C   **10.** Where's the bus schedule for downtown routes?

▶ REVIEW D

Proofreading a Paragraph for Subject-Verb Agreement

Some sentences in the following paragraph contain errors in agreement of subject and verb. If a sentence is correct, write *C*. If a sentence contains an error in agreement, write the correct form of the verb.

EXAMPLE   [1] Doesn't these neon signs light up the night sky with color?
     1. *Don't*

1. has [*or* C]   [1] The public ~~have~~ been fascinated with neon lights
2. (There) are   since they were introduced in the 1920s. [2] ~~There's~~ neon lights in large and small cities all over the world. [3] Times
3. are   Square in New York City and Tokyo's Ginza district ~~is~~ two
4. C   places famous for their neon lights. [4] Some of today's neon signs are very large and creative. [5] All of the signs
5. are   shown below ~~is~~ used in advertising. [6] But nowadays you
6. C   can also see neon decorations and sculptures. [7] Our sci-
7. is   ence class ~~are~~ learning how neon
8. are   lights work. [8] Neon lights ~~is~~ made from hollow glass tubes filled with
9. C   neon gas. [9] An electric current shot through the tube makes the
10. C   gas glow. [10] The diagrams on the next page clearly show the action of a neon light.

USAGE

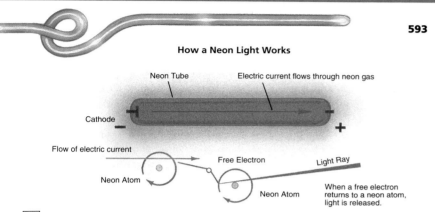

How a Neon Light Works

Neon Tube

Electric current flows through neon gas

Cathode

− +

Flow of electric current

Neon Atom

Free Electron

Light Ray

Neon Atom

When a free electron returns to a neon atom, light is released.

593

▶ EXERCISE 13 **Using Correct Subject-Verb Agreement**

Your class is making up a trivia game, and you're supposed to contribute five geography questions. You've decided to ask questions about the Great Lakes. Use the information from this map and this chart to write five questions about the Great Lakes. In your questions, use one collective noun, one subject following a verb, and one indefinite pronoun. Be sure to provide answers to your questions.

EXAMPLE   1. *What are the names of the five lakes known as the Great Lakes?* [Ontario, Erie, Michigan, Huron, Superior]
2. *Both of these lakes border New York. What are they?* [Ontario, Erie]

USAGE

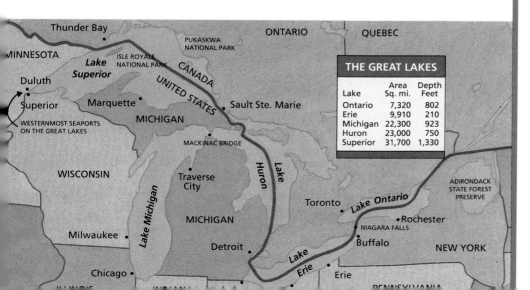

Thunder Bay · ONTARIO   QUEBEC

PUKASKWA NATIONAL PARK

MINNESOTA   ISLE ROYALE NATIONAL PARK   CANADA

Lake Superior

Duluth   UNITED STATES

Superior   Marquette ·   · Sault Ste. Marie

WESTERNMOST SEAPORTS ON THE GREAT LAKES   MICHIGAN

MACKINAC BRIDGE

WISCONSIN   Traverse City   Lake Huron

Milwaukee ·   Lake Michigan   MICHIGAN

Toronto ·   Lake Ontario

· Rochester

NIAGARA FALLS

Detroit ·   · Buffalo   NEW YORK

Chicago ·   Lake Erie   Erie ·

ADIRONDACK STATE FOREST PRESERVE

THE GREAT LAKES		
Lake	Area Sq. mi.	Depth Feet
Ontario	7,320	802
Erie	9,910	210
Michigan	22,300	923
Huron	23,000	750
Superior	31,700	1,330

⚡ **TIMESAVER**
For **Exercise 13**, you may want to have students bracket and label in their sentences a collective noun, a subject following a verb, and an indefinite pronoun. This will not only make grading faster, but will enable you to tell at a glance which concepts students are not grasping.

ANSWERS
Exercise 13

Answers may vary. Each student's questions should contain one collective noun, one subject following a verb, and one indefinite pronoun. It should be possible to answer questions with information contained in the map and chart, and answers should be provided.

👁 **VISUAL CONNECTIONS**
Exploring the Subject. The Great Lakes, along with the St. Lawrence Seaway, form the largest system of lakes in the world. A ship can sail from Duluth, Minnesota, at the head of Lake Superior, to the Atlantic Ocean over 2,300 miles away.

All of the Great Lakes except Lake Michigan are partly in both Canada and the United States. Treaties allow citizens of both countries complete access to all of the international lakes, and the border between the two countries is the longest unfortified border in the world.

You can help your students memorize the names of the Great Lakes by teaching them a simple mnemonic. Each letter of the word *homes* stands for the name of one of the Great Lakes: Huron, Ontario, Michigan, Erie, and Superior.

USAGE

OBJECTIVES

- To proofread sentences for pronoun-antecedent agreement
- To identify antecedents and write pronouns that agree with them
- To write a five-sentence pep talk using pronouns correctly

PROGRAM MANAGER

AGREEMENT OF PRONOUN AND ANTECEDENT

- **Independent Practice/ Reteaching** For instruction and exercises, see **Agreement of Pronoun and Antecedent** in *Language Skills Practice and Assessment,* p. 130.

- **Computer Guided Instruction** For additional instruction and practice with other problems in agreement of pronoun and antecedent, see **Lesson 13** in *Language Workshop CD-ROM.*

- **Practice** To help less-advanced students with additional instruction and practice with agreement of pronoun and antecedent, see **Chapter 17** in *English Workshop, Second Course,* pp. 175–176.

QUICK REMINDER

Write the words *he, she, it,* and *they* in a column on the chalkboard. In a second column write *Maria, book, babies,* and *Patrick.* Ask students to copy the lists and to label each column according to the part of speech it contains [first column—*pronoun;* second column—*noun*]. Then ask students to draw lines to connect each pronoun to the noun that agrees with it [he— Patrick, she—Maria, it—book, they— babies].

---

594 *Agreement*

Agreement of Pronoun and Antecedent

A pronoun usually refers to a noun or another pronoun, called its *antecedent.* Whenever you use a pronoun, make sure that it agrees with its antecedent.

☞ REFERENCE NOTE: For more information about antecedents, see page 436.

20n. A pronoun agrees with its antecedent in number and gender.

Some singular personal pronouns have forms that indicate gender. Masculine pronouns (*he, him, his*) refer to males. Feminine pronouns (*she, her, hers*) refer to females. Neuter pronouns (*it, its*) refer to things (neither male nor female) and sometimes to animals.

EXAMPLES **Bryan** lost **his** book.
Dawn lent **her** book to Bryan.
The **book** had Dawn's name written inside **its** cover.

The antecedent of a personal pronoun can be another kind of pronoun, such as *each, neither,* or *one.* To determine the gender of a personal pronoun that refers to one of these other pronouns, look in the phrase that follows the antecedent.

EXAMPLES **Each** of the men put on **his** hard hat.
Neither of those women got what **she** ordered.

Some antecedents may be either masculine or feminine. When referring to such antecedents, use both the masculine and the feminine forms.

EXAMPLES **No one** on the committee gave **his or her** approval.
Everybody in the class wanted to know **his or her** grade.

Sometimes, using *his or her* to refer to an indefinite pronoun is awkward or confusing. In such cases, use the plural form.

AWKWARD   **When the singer walked out onto the stage, everyone clapped his or her hands.**

CLEAR   **When the singer walked out onto the stage, everyone clapped their hands.**

Even when used correctly, the *his or her* construction sounds awkward to many people. To avoid using *his or her*, try to rephrase the sentence, using a plural pronoun and antecedent.

EXAMPLES   **Everyone in the club paid his or her dues.**
All of the club members paid their dues.

Each of the mechanics uses his or her own tools.
The mechanics use their own tools.

(1) A singular pronoun is used to refer to *anybody, anyone, each, either, everybody, everyone, neither, nobody, no one, one, someone,* **or** *somebody.*

EXAMPLES   **Everybody will have an opportunity to express his or her opinion.**
Each of the birds built its own nest.

(2) A singular pronoun is used to refer to two or more singular antecedents joined by *or* **or** *nor.*

EXAMPLES   **Julio or Van will bring his football.**
Neither the mother nor the daughter had forgotten her umbrella.

NOTE: Although rules (1) and (2) are often disregarded in conversation, they should be followed in writing.

(3) A plural pronoun is used to refer to two or more antecedents joined by *and.*

EXAMPLES   **My mother and father send their regards.**
My dog and cat never share their food.

MEETING *individual* **NEEDS**

LEARNING STYLES

Visual Learners. To help students see the relationship of pronouns to antecedents, write on the chalkboard some of the examples under **Rule 20n.** Then draw an arrow from the pronoun in each sentence to the antecedent of the pronoun.

INTEGRATING THE LANGUAGE ARTS

Usage and Vocabulary. Ask your students to find *antecedent* in the dictionary and to read its etymology. The word consists of two parts, both from Latin. *Ante–* means "before" and *cedent,* derived from *cedere,* means "to go." Ask students how the etymology of the word can help them remember its meaning as applied in grammar. [An *antecedent* usually comes before the pronoun that refers to it.]

Usage and Writing. Students may be unfamiliar with certain pronoun constructions in situations when the gender of the antecedent isn't clear. For example, they may see *he/she* or *(s)he* used in some publications. You can explain to them that gender-neutral constructions are a relatively recent development in the history of the English language. Usage hasn't fully been settled, but the prevailing trend seems to be the one described in the textbook.

Literature Link. If it is available in your literature textbook or library, ask your students to read the poem "Silver" by Walter de la Mare. In this poem the moon is referred to as *she* rather than *it*. Lead your students in a discussion about why de la Mare might have chosen to do this. What effect does this usage have on the poem? [It carries out the personification that begins with "the moon/Walks the night." It makes the moon seem like a friend that turns everything into beautiful silver.]

COOPERATIVE LEARNING
You may want to allow your students to work in pairs on **Exercise 14.** Both students should be able to explain their answers for all of the items.

USAGE

 REFERENCE NOTE: For more information on the correct usage and spelling of the pronouns *its, their,* and *your,* see pages 690, 696, and 699.

 EXERCISE 14 **Proofreading Sentences for Pronoun-Antecedent Agreement**

Many of the following sentences contain errors in agreement of pronoun and antecedent. If the sentence is correct, write *C*. If the sentence contains an error in agreement, write the <u>antecedent</u> and the correct form of the pronoun.

EXAMPLE   **1.** Everyone in my English class has to give their oral report on Friday.
      1. *Everyone—his or her*

1. Either <u>Don or Buddy</u> will be the first to give ~~their~~ report.   **1.** his
2. Several <u>others</u>, including me, volunteered to give ~~mine~~ first.   **2.** theirs
3. <u>Everybody</u> else in class wanted to put off giving ~~their~~ report as long as possible.   **3.** his or her
4. Last year my friend Sandy and I figured out that waiting to give our reports was worse than actually giving them.   **4.** C
5. I am surprised that more <u>people</u> didn't volunteer to give ~~his or her~~ reports first.   **5.** their
6. <u>Someone</u> else will be third to give ~~their~~ report; then I will give mine.   **6.** his or her
7. A few <u>others</u> in my class are going to try to get out of giving ~~his or her~~ reports at all.   **7.** their
8. However, my teacher, Mrs. Goldenburg, said that <u>anyone</u> who does not give an oral report will get an "incomplete" as ~~their~~ course grade.   **8.** his or her
9. <u>Most</u> of us wish that ~~he or she~~ did not have to give an oral report at all.   **9.** we
10. Since <u>no one</u> can get out of giving ~~their~~ report, though, I'd rather get it over with as soon as possible.   **10.** his or her

Agreement of Pronoun and Antecedent **597**

EXERCISE 15 ### Identifying Antecedents and Writing Pronouns That Agree with Them

Complete each of the following sentences by inserting a pronoun that agrees with its antecedent. Identify the <u>antecedent</u>.

EXAMPLE **1.** Ann and Margaret wore ____ cheerleader uniforms.
   1. *their—Ann and Margaret*

1. The <u>trees</u> lost several of ____ branches in the storm. **1.** their
2. <u>Each</u> of the early Spanish missions in North America took pride in ____ church bell. **2.** its
3. Anthony, do you know whether <u>anyone</u> else has turned in ____ paper yet? **3.** his or her
4. <u>Many</u> in the mob raised ____ voices in protest. **4.** their
5. The <u>creek</u> and the <u>pond</u> lost much of ____ water during the drought. **5.** their
6. <u>One</u> of my uncles always wears ____ belt buckle off to one side. **6.** his
7. No <u>person</u> should be made to feel that ____ is worth less than someone else. **7.** he or she
8. <u>None</u> of the dogs had eaten all of ____ food. **8.** their
9. A <u>few</u> of our neighbors have decided to fence ____ backyards. **9.** their
10. <u>Grant Hill</u> and <u>Scottie Pippen</u> looked forward to ____ chance to play basketball during the 1996 Olympics. **10.** their

REVIEW E ### Proofreading Sentences for Pronoun-Antecedent Agreement

Many of the following sentences contain errors in agreement of pronoun and antecedent. If the sentence is correct, write *C.* If the sentence contains an error in agreement, write the <u>antecedent</u> and the correct form of the pronoun.

EXAMPLE **1.** Each of the president's Cabinet officers gave their advice about what to do.
   1. *Each—his or her*

USAGE

USAGE

TIMESAVER

You can save some time grading papers by having students do **Exercise 15** orally. You can use students' mistakes as opportunities for guided practice or additional instruction.

A DIFFERENT APPROACH

You may want to consider using **Review E** as an assessment of how well your students can detect problems in pronoun-antecedent agreement. It covers all of the major areas in which problems are likely to occur.

1. their   **1.** <u>All</u> of the nation's presidents have had ˰his own Cabinets, or groups of advisers.

2. C   **2.** Shortly after taking office, presidents appoint the members of their Cabinets.

3. his or her   **3.** <u>Everyone</u> appointed to the Cabinet is an expert in ˰their field.

4. their   **4.** <u>George Washington</u> and <u>John Adams</u> met regularly with ˰his advisers.

5. his   **5.** <u>Neither</u> had more than five people in ˰their Cabinet.

6. C   **6.** The Cabinet received its name from James Madison, the fourth president.

7. C   **7.** Congress and the president have used their power over the years to create new government agencies.

8. her   **8.** In 1979, <u>Shirley M. Hufstedler</u> took ˰their place on the Cabinet as the first Secretary of Education.

9. his   **9.** <u>Neither</u> President Reagan nor President Bush created a new post in ˰their Cabinet.

10. its   **10.** The Cabinet's <u>meeting room</u> now has more than fifteen chairs around ˰their large table.

PICTURE THIS

Lucy never gives Charlie Brown much help. As you can see in the comic strip on the next page, all she has to offer him to inspire their team is a useless personal pronoun. Luckily, you're on the baseball team, too. Help Charlie Brown give the other players a pep talk. Write five sentences that you might say to the team. In at least three of your sentences, use pronouns with Charlie Brown, Lucy, or other team members as antecedents. In your other sentences, use two of the following pronouns: *anybody*, *each*, *everybody*, *nobody*, *someone*.

Subject: pep talk
Audience: your baseball team
Purpose: to inspire the team to play better

USAGE

PICTURE THIS

You may want to suggest to your students that they write first drafts in which they concentrate on ideas and not on pronouns. After they've written the drafts, encourage students to go back through them and carefully revise sentences as necessary to make sure they use the pronouns specified in the assignment. Let students work in pairs or groups of three for revision to make sure they satisfy the requirements of the assignment.

In evaluating the final products, you probably will want to concentrate on how effective the writing is as a pep talk. You can have students number their pronouns to save you time in grading.

Peanuts reprinted by permission of United Feature Syndicate, Inc.

USAGE

VISUAL CONNECTIONS

Exploring the Subject. Charles M. Schulz began drawing his *Peanuts* cartoon strip in 1950. Since then, Charlie Brown, Lucy, Snoopy (arguably the most famous dog in the world), Linus, and other characters have delighted readers of all ages. The cartoon has given rise to a rather large industry, producing books, toys, clothing, television shows, movies, and even a hit Broadway musical (*You're a Good Man, Charlie Brown*). Charlie Brown and the rest of the *Peanuts* gang have won the hearts of people all over the world.

USAGE

OBJECTIVES

- To identify verbs that agree with their subjects
- To identify pronouns that agree with their antecedents

600 *Agreement*

Review: Posttest

A. Identifying Verbs That Agree with Their Subjects

In each of the following sentences, if the italicized verb agrees with its subject, write C. If the italicized verb does not agree with its subject, write the correct form of the verb.

EXAMPLES **1.** The people on the bus *have* all been seated.
1. C
2. The fish, bass and perch mostly, *has* started feeding.
2. *have*

1. has
1. The swarm of bees *have* deserted its hive.
2. take
2. My spelling lessons and science homework sometimes *takes* me hours to finish.
3. doesn't
3. Somebody *don't* approve of the new rule.
4. C
4. Neither Danny Glover nor Morgan Freeman *stars* in tonight's movie.
5. has
5. The mice or the cat *have* eaten the cheese.
6. are
6. There *is* probably a few children who don't like strawberries.
7. like
7. Most of the guests *likes* the inn's Irish soda bread.
8. C
8. Both of those varsity players *exercise* for an hour each day.
9. are
9. Evenings *is* the best time to visit her.
10. Don't
10. *Doesn't* those children still take piano lessons?

B. Identifying Pronouns That Agree with Their Antecedents

In each of the following sentences, if the italicized pronoun agrees with its antecedent, write C. If the italicized pronoun does not agree with its antecedent, write the correct form of the pronoun.

EXAMPLES   **1.** Either of the men could have offered *their* help.

           1. *his*

          2. Both of the flowers had spread *their* petals.

          2. *C*

11. Why doesn't somebody raise ~~their~~ hand and ask for directions?   **11.** his or her

12. One of the birds lost most of ~~their~~ tail feathers.   **12.** its

13. Sol sold *his* last ticket to Heather.   **13.** C

14. The old tennis court has weeds growing in ~~their~~ nets.   **14.** its

15. The Smithsonian's National Museum of the American Indian had closed ~~their~~ doors for the day.   **15.** its

16. I don't understand how chameleons sitting on a green leaf or a bush change *their* color.   **16.** C

17. Each of these tests has ~~their~~ own answer key.   **17.** its

18. These girls can choose ~~her~~ own materials from the supply room.   **18.** their

19. Stan or Ethan will bring ~~their~~ guitar.   **19.** his

20. Álvar Núñez Cabeza de Vaca and Fray Junípero Serra suffered great hardships in ~~his~~ explorations of the New World.   **20.** their

USAGE

USAGE

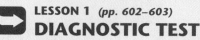
DIAGNOSTIC TEST

OBJECTIVES

- To use the past and past participle forms of verbs
- To make tenses of verbs consistent

PROGRAM MANAGER

FOR THE WHOLE CHAPTER

- **Review** For exercises on chapter concepts, see **Review Form A** and **Review Form B** in *Language Skills Practice and Assessment,* pp. 144–147.

- **Assessment** For additional testing, see **Usage Pretests** and **Usage Mastery Tests** in *Language Skills Practice and Assessment,* pp. 115–120 and pp. 191–198.

USAGE

CHAPTER OVERVIEW

This chapter will help students to use verbs correctly and consistently. After a brief explanation of the principal parts of verbs, the chapter gives rules, examples, and exercises for regular and irregular verbs. A section on tenses follows, with an explanation of conjugation of verbs and a rule and an exercise emphasizing consistency of tense. In a section on special problems with verbs, *sit/set, lie/lay,* and *rise/raise* are treated. In the **Writing Application,** students will use different verb forms and tenses to write poems.

You can refer to the material in this chapter when teaching any of the composition chapters, as using verbs correctly is important to every kind of writing.

USAGE

21 USING VERBS CORRECTLY

Principal Parts, Regular and Irregular Verbs

Diagnostic Test

A. Using the Past and Past Participle Forms of Verbs

For each of the following sentences, give the correct form (past or past participle) of the verb in parentheses.

EXAMPLE **1. We don't know why it (*take*) them so long.**
1. *took*

1. lay
2. risen
3. went
4. written
5. broken

1. The cat (*lie*) down in front of the warm fire.
2. Since the storm began, the river has (*rise*) four feet.
3. Did you see which way they (*go*)?
4. I have (*write*) for tickets to the Alvin Ailey Dance Theater's next performance.
5. Two runners on our track team have (*break*) the school record for the mile run.

6. When the manager unlocked the door, a mob of shoppers (*burst*) into the store to take advantage of the sale.   **6.** burst
7. Larry washed his wool sweater in hot water, and it (*shrink*).   **7.** shrank
8. The witness said that she (*see*) the blue truck run through the red light.   **8.** saw
9. Look in the oven to see if the cake has (*rise*) yet.   **9.** risen
10. Everyone should be in class after the bell has (*ring*).   **10.** rung
11. Sitting Bull (*name*) his son Crowfoot.   **11.** named
12. Jeanette carefully (*lay*) her coat across the back of the chair.   **12.** laid
13. By late December the pond has usually (*freeze*) hard enough to skate on.   **13.** frozen
14. Several of us (*choose*) to visit the Amish community in Pennsylvania.   **14.** chose
15. So far, Dena has (*swim*) fifteen laps around the pool.   **15.** swum

B. Making Tenses of Verbs Consistent

For each of the following sentences, write the italicized verb in the correct tense.

EXAMPLE   **1.** He looked out the window and *sees* the storm approaching.
   1. *saw*

16. Jan was late, so she ~~decides~~ to run the rest of the way.   **16.** decided
17. The man at the gate ~~takes~~ our tickets and said that we were just in time.   **17.** took
18. My uncle often travels in the Far East and ~~brought~~ me fascinating souvenirs.   **18.** brings
19. After Sarah told me about the book of Yiddish folk sayings, I ~~buy~~ a copy.   **19.** bought
20. The waitress brought my order and ~~asks~~ me if I wanted anything else.   **20.** asked

USAGE

USING THE DIAGNOSTIC TEST

Use the **Diagnostic Test** to identify the areas in which students have problems. For further diagnosis, you could provide several sample paragraphs with errors in verb usage for students to proofread. Because students may do well on the test but still have problems in their writing, it would be helpful to evaluate samples of students' writing for correct verb usage.

MEETING *individual* NEEDS

STUDENTS WITH SPECIAL NEEDS

Because reading and writing are difficult for some students, you may want to administer the **Diagnostic Test** to them orally. Throughout the chapter you could also adapt the exercises to be done orally so that students can concentrate on verb usage rather than struggle with the difficult task of writing.

USAGE

REGULAR AND IRREGULAR VERBS
Rules 21b, 21c

OBJECTIVES

- To pronounce and use the past and past participle forms of regular verbs
- To pronounce and use the past and past participle forms of irregular verbs

The Principal Parts of a Verb

The four basic forms of a verb are called the *principal parts* of the verb.

21a. The principal parts of a verb are the *base form*, the *present participle*, the *past*, and the *past participle.*

Notice that the present participle and the past participle require helping verbs (forms of *be* and *have*).

BASE FORM	PRESENT PARTICIPLE	PAST	PAST PARTICIPLE
work	(is) working	worked	(have) worked
sing	(is) singing	sang	(have) sung

EXAMPLES I **sing** in the school Glee Club.
We **are singing** at the music festival tonight.
Mahalia Jackson **sang** gospels at Carnegie Hall.
We **have sung** all over the state.

NOTE: Some teachers refer to the base form as the infinitive. Follow your teacher's directions in labeling these words.

Regular Verbs

21b. A *regular verb* forms its past and past participle by adding *–d* or *–ed* to the base form.

BASE FORM	PRESENT PARTICIPLE	PAST	PAST PARTICIPLE
use	(is) using	used	(have) used
suppose	(is) supposing	supposed	(have) supposed
attack	(is) attacking	attacked	(have) attacked

PROGRAM MANAGER

REGULAR AND IRREGULAR VERBS

- **Independent Practice/ Reteaching** For instruction and exercises, see **Regular Verbs** and **Irregular Verbs** in *Language Skills Practice and Assessment,* pp. 139–140.

- **Computer Guided Instruction** For additional instruction and practice with regular and irregular verbs, see **Lesson 14** in *Language Workshop CD-ROM.*

- **Practice** To help less-advanced students with additional instruction and practice with regular and irregular verbs, see **Chapter 18** in *English Workshop, Second Course,* pp. 179–184.

QUICK REMINDER

Write the following sentences on the chalkboard and have students supply the correct forms of the underscored base forms:

1. Yesterday I <u>find</u> a silver dollar. [found]
2. Every time I've gone swimming this summer I <u>practice</u> my diving. [have practiced]
3. There was a big flood yesterday when the dam <u>burst</u>. [burst]
4. I want to <u>eat</u> some spinach. [eat]

• To use correct verb forms

Avoid the following common errors when forming the past or past participle of regular verbs:

1. leaving off the *–d* or *–ed* ending

NONSTANDARD She use to work in the library.
STANDARD She **used** to work in the library.

NONSTANDARD Who was suppose to bring the decorations?
STANDARD Who was **supposed** to bring the decorations?

2. adding unnecessary letters

NONSTANDARD A swarm of bees attackted us in the orange grove.
STANDARD A swarm of bees **attacked** us in the orange grove.

NONSTANDARD Fortunately, no one in the boating accident drownded.
STANDARD Fortunately, no one in the boating accident **drowned.**

☞ REFERENCE NOTE: For a discussion of standard and nonstandard English, see pages 394 and 682.

▶ ORAL PRACTICE 1   **Using the Past and Past Participle Forms of Regular Verbs**

Read each of the following sentences aloud, stressing the italicized verbs.

1. She has *crossed* this street many times on the way to school.
2. The raccoon *visited* our camp almost every morning last summer.
3. Ryan and Annie *repaired* the engine in less than an hour.
4. Scientists have *discovered* that birds use the sun as a compass.
5. Some people say that Stone Age surgeons in Peru *operated* on the brain.

USAGE

USAGE

MEETING *individual* NEEDS

LEP/ESL

General Strategies. Students may not realize that a past verb form that they hear every day is spelled with a *–d* or an *–ed*. This confusion arises because proficient English speakers often barely pronounce the *d* sound or even pronounce it as a *t* sound. Point out this discrepancy between spelling and pronunciation and have students pay particular attention to these forms as they do **Oral Practice 1.**

6. Alexandra and Anthony have *baked* Bavarian pretzels for the party.
7. The actors *leaped* across the stage to catch the falling door.
8. Sylvia has *used* her computer every day this week.

> **EXERCISE 1** **Using Past and Past Participle Forms of Regular Verbs**

You're an archaeologist in the year 2993. You want to know what life was like in the United States a thousand years ago. While digging for clues, you discover these objects. What are they? What were they used for? Write a brief report about possible uses for these items. (Of course, you really know what these common items are, but imagine yourself as the future scientist.) In your report, use five past forms and five past participle forms of regular verbs. Underline each past and past participle form you use.

EXAMPLE **1.** *I have decided that people used this device to teach their children how to count.*

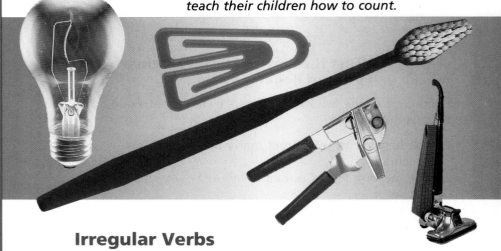

Irregular Verbs

21c. An *irregular verb* forms its past and past participle in some other way than by adding *–d* or *–ed* to the base form.

ANSWERS
Exercise 1

Responses will vary. To help students see the objects in a fresh way, encourage the students to forget what they know about the functions of the articles and to concentrate only on what they see. They could start by writing down the visual features and then use clustering to see where it might lead them in imagining uses for the objects. Point out that it will probably be easiest to concentrate first on writing their ideas and then to check verb forms.

An irregular verb forms its past and past participle by

- changing vowels *or* consonants
- changing vowels *and* consonants
- making no changes

BASE FORM	PAST	PAST PARTICIPLE
ring	rang	(have) rung
make	made	(have) made
go	went	(have) gone
bring	brought	(have) brought
burst	burst	(have) burst

Avoid the following common errors when forming the past or past participle of an irregular verb:

1. using the past form with a helping verb

NONSTANDARD   Carlos has went to the shopping mall.
STANDARD   Carlos **went** to the shopping mall.

or

STANDARD   Carlos **has gone** to the shopping mall.

2. using the past participle form without a helping verb

NONSTANDARD   I seen all of her movies.
STANDARD   I **have seen** all of her movies.

3. adding *–d* or *–ed* to the base form

NONSTANDARD   The right fielder throwed the ball to the shortstop.
STANDARD   The right fielder **threw** the ball to the shortstop.

NOTE: If you are not sure about the principal parts of a verb, look in a dictionary. Entries for irregular verbs give the principal parts of the verb.

The irregular verbs in each of the groups in the charts on the next three pages form their past and past participle in a similar way.

INTEGRATING THE LANGUAGE ARTS

Usage and Dictionary Skills. Point out to students that when they have questions about the principal parts of verbs, they can look the verbs up in a dictionary. Explain that the entry word in a dictionary is the present form and that the past, past participle, and present participle forms are listed following the entry word. For example, if they look up *sing,* they will find *sang, sung,* and *singing* listed following *sing.* Have each student choose two or three irregular verbs to look up in a dictionary. Then the student should write each verb's principal parts.

MEETING *individual* NEEDS

LESS-ADVANCED STUDENTS

As students work through the exercises in this chapter, have them make lists of irregular verbs that are problematic for them. They could make charts with the base, past, and past participle forms of these verbs and keep the charts in their notebooks for reference when they are completing writing assignments.

COMMON IRREGULAR VERBS			
GROUP I: Each of these irregular verbs has the same form for its past and past participle.			
BASE FORM	**PRESENT PARTICIPLE**	**PAST**	**PAST PARTICIPLE**
bring	(is) bringing	brought	(have) brought
build	(is) building	built	(have) built
buy	(is) buying	bought	(have) bought
catch	(is) catching	caught	(have) caught
feel	(is) feeling	felt	(have) felt
find	(is) finding	found	(have) found
get	(is) getting	got	(have) got *or* gotten
have	(is) having	had	(have) had
hold	(is) holding	held	(have) held
keep	(is) keeping	kept	(have) kept
lay	(is) laying	laid	(have) laid
lead	(is) leading	led	(have) led
leave	(is) leaving	left	(have) left
lend	(is) lending	lent	(have) lent
lose	(is) losing	lost	(have) lost
make	(is) making	made	(have) made
meet	(is) meeting	met	(have) met
pay	(is) paying	paid	(have) paid
say	(is) saying	said	(have) said
sell	(is) selling	sold	(have) sold
send	(is) sending	sent	(have) sent
sit	(is) sitting	sat	(have) sat
spend	(is) spending	spent	(have) spent
spin	(is) spinning	spun	(have) spun
stand	(is) standing	stood	(have) stood
swing	(is) swinging	swung	(have) swung
teach	(is) teaching	taught	(have) taught
tell	(is) telling	told	(have) told
think	(is) thinking	thought	(have) thought
win	(is) winning	won	(have) won

COMMON IRREGULAR VERBS			
GROUP II:	— Each of these irregular verbs has a different form for its past and past participle.		
BASE FORM	PRESENT PARTICIPLE	PAST	PAST PARTICIPLE
begin	(is) beginning	began	(have) begun
bite	(is) biting	bit	(have) bitten *or* bit
blow	(is) blowing	blew	(have) blown
break	(is) breaking	broke	(have) broken
choose	(is) choosing	chose	(have) chosen
come	(is) coming	came	(have) come
do	(is) doing	did	(have) done
draw	(is) drawing	drew	(have) drawn
drink	(is) drinking	drank	(have) drunk
drive	(is) driving	drove	(have) driven
eat	(is) eating	ate	(have) eaten
fall	(is) falling	fell	(have) fallen
fly	(is) flying	flew	(have) flown
freeze	(is) freezing	froze	(have) frozen
give	(is) giving	gave	(have) given
go	(is) going	went	(have) gone
grow	(is) growing	grew	(have) grown
know	(is) knowing	knew	(have) known
lie	(is) lying	lay	(have) lain
ride	(is) riding	rode	(have) ridden
ring	(is) ringing	rang	(have) rung
rise	(is) rising	rose	(have) risen
run	(is) running	ran	(have) run
see	(is) seeing	saw	(have) seen
shake	(is) shaking	shook	(have) shaken
sing	(is) singing	sang	(have) sung
sink	(is) sinking	sank	(have) sunk
speak	(is) speaking	spoke	(have) spoken
steal	(is) stealing	stole	(have) stolen
swim	(is) swimming	swam	(have) swum

(continued)

COOPERATIVE LEARNING

Conjugating verbs to a rhythmic beat can help students remember the forms. Divide the class into groups of three or four students with mixed levels of ability. Assign each group ten irregular verbs and have the groups prepare rhythmic, oral presentations that include the present, past, and past participle forms of the verbs. Students can ignore the present participles. The presentations can be poems, songs, stories, or recitations, and students can use movement to keep the beat or to act out their verbs. Even if students just chant the verb forms, they should do it to some form of beat or rhythm.

USAGE

INTEGRATING THE LANGUAGE ARTS

Literature Link. If the selections are available in your literature textbook or library, have students read and discuss Sylvia Plath's "Mushrooms" and Ernest Lawrence Thayer's "Casey at the Bat." Then have them list the regular and irregular verbs used in each poem. Ask students the following questions:

1. Which author relies more on verbs to describe the scene? [Plath]
2. In which poem do verbs vary more in form? ["Mushrooms"]
3. What conclusions can be drawn about the authors' uses of verbs in these poems? [Thayer uses simple, direct verb forms to create action and comedy; Plath uses more variety in verb forms for greater complexity, and this encourages several levels of interpretation.]

COMMON IRREGULAR VERBS			
GROUP II (*continued*)			
take	(is) taking	took	(have) taken
tear	(is) tearing	tore	(have) torn
throw	(is) throwing	threw	(have) thrown
wear	(is) wearing	wore	(have) worn
write	(is) writing	wrote	(have) written
GROUP III:	Each of these irregular verbs has the same form for its base form, past, and past participle.		
BASE FORM	**PRESENT PARTICIPLE**	**PAST**	**PAST PARTICIPLE**
burst	(is) bursting	burst	(have) burst
cost	(is) costing	cost	(have) cost
cut	(is) cutting	cut	(have) cut
hit	(is) hitting	hit	(have) hit
hurt	(is) hurting	hurt	(have) hurt
let	(is) letting	let	(have) let
put	(is) putting	put	(have) put
read	(is) reading	read	(have) read
set	(is) setting	set	(have) set
spread	(is) spreading	spread	(have) spread

ORAL PRACTICE 2

Using the Past and Past Participle Forms of Irregular Verbs

Read each of the following sentences aloud, stressing the italicized verb.

1. Ray Charles *has written* many popular songs.
2. Leigh *did* everything the instructions said.
3. She *knew* the best route to take.
4. Maria Tallchief *chose* a career as a dancer.
5. He *ate* chicken salad on whole-wheat bread for lunch.
6. The monkey *had stolen* the food from its brother.
7. Felipe and Tonya *sang* a duet in the talent show.
8. The shy turtle *came* closer to me to reach the lettuce I was holding.

USAGE

USAGE

TIMESAVER
You might organize a team of several students who have demonstrated mastery of regular and irregular verb forms to correct the exercises in this lesson and to provide tutoring for those students having difficulty.

▶ EXERCISE 2   **Using the Past and Past Participle Forms of Verbs**

For each of the following sentences, give the correct form (past or past participle) of the verb in parentheses.

EXAMPLE   **1. Nobody knew why he (*do*) that.**
　　　　　1. *did*

1. Did you say that the telephone (*ring*) while I was in the shower?   **1. rang**
2. The outfielder (*throw*) the ball to home plate.   **2. threw**
3. Diana Nyad (*swim*) sixty miles from the Bahamas to Florida.   **3. swam**
4. Uncle Olaf has (*ride*) his new snowmobile up to the remote mountain cabin.   **4. ridden**
5. The librarian has (*choose*) a book by Jose Aruego.   **5. chosen**
6. The bean seedlings and the herbs have (*freeze*) in the garden.   **6. frozen**
7. After she finished the race, she (*drink*) two glasses of water.   **7. drank**
8. He (*tell*) me that *waffle, coleslaw,* and *cookie* are words that came from Dutch.   **8. told**
9. We had (*drive*) all night to attend my sister's college graduation exercises.   **9. driven**
10. Marianne (*sit*) quietly throughout the discussion.   **10. sat**

▶ EXERCISE 3   **Using Correct Verb Forms**

For each of the sentences in the following paragraph, give the correct form (past or past participle) of the verb in parentheses.

EXAMPLE   **[1] Have you (*read*) about the Underground Railroad?**
　　　　　1. *read*

[1] Mr. Tucker, our history teacher, (*write*) the words   **1. wrote**
Underground Railroad on the chalkboard. [2] Then he (*draw*)   **2. drew**
black lines on a map to show us where the Underground Railroad ran. [3] What strange tracks this railroad must   **3. had**
have (*have*)! [4] The lines even (*go*) into the Atlantic Ocean.   **4. went**

5. left

6. rode

7. run

8. gained

9. came

10. said

[5] As you may imagine, this map (*leave*) the class very confused. [6] But then Mr. Tucker explained that no one actually (*ride*) on an underground railroad. [7] The railroad was really a secret network to help slaves who had (*run*) away. [8] Between 1830 and 1860, thousands of slaves (*gain*) their freedom by traveling along the routes marked on this map. [9] The name *Underground Railroad* (*come*) from the use of railroad terms as code words. [10] Mr. Tucker (*say*) that hiding places were called "stations" and that people who helped slaves were called "conductors."

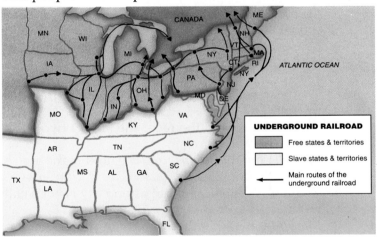

REVIEW A

Proofreading Sentences for Correct Verb Forms

Many of the following sentences contain incorrect verb forms. If the sentence is correct, write *C*. If the sentence has an incorrect verb form, write the correct form.

EXAMPLES **1.** Carmen gave me a menu from the new downtown restaurant.
1. *C*
2. I had spoke to my parents last week about trying this restaurant.
2. *had spoken*

1. drove

2. sat

1. My big brother Mark drived us there in Mom's car.
2. We sit down, and the waiter brought our menus.

![MEETING *individual* NEEDS]

LEP/ESL

General Strategies. In **Reviews A** and **B** students will be exposed to incorrect verb forms. It is better for English-language learners to be exposed only to correct forms, especially when reading. To prevent confusion, use one of the following techniques:

1. Change the sentences to fill-in-the-blank form and give just the base forms and no helping verbs.
2. Tell students which sentences in each review are correct.
3. Have students fill in the correct verb forms as you read the sentences aloud at normal speed.

3. When we arrived at the restaurant, I ~~runned~~ ahead   **3.** ran
of everyone to tell the hostess we needed five seats.

4. Have you ever drunk water with lemon slices in
the glasses?   **4.** C

5. Dad chose the ravioli.   **5.** C

6. My little sister Emilia ~~taked~~ two helpings of salad.   **6.** took

7. The waiter ~~bringed~~ out our dinners on a huge tray.   **7.** brought

8. Mark ~~give~~ me a taste of his eggplant parmigiana.   **8.** gave

9. Emilia ~~stealed~~ a bite of my lasagna.   **9.** stole

10. Dad ~~telled~~ the waiter that the food was delicious.   **10.** told

📗 REVIEW B   **Proofreading Sentences for Correct
Verb Forms**

Some of the following sentences contain incorrect verb
forms. If the sentence is correct, write *C*. If the sentence
has an incorrect verb form, write the correct form.

EXAMPLES   **1.** Mario has lent me his copy of *Journey to the
Center of the Earth.*

   1. *C*

   2. I thinked I had a copy of this famous novel.
   2. *thought*

1. During the 1800s, Jules Verne wrote many scientific
adventure tales.   **1.** C

2. Back then, readers ~~founded~~ his stories amazing.   **2.** found

3. Some people believe that he ~~seen~~ into the future.   **3.** saw

4. For example, in some novels he ~~telled~~ about space
exploration and boats that traveled underwater.   **4.** told

5. These books fascinated readers in the days before
space travel and submarines!   **5.** C

6. Verne ~~lead~~ a quiet life but had incredible adventures
in his imagination.   **6.** led

7. He ~~gived~~ the world some wonderful stories.   **7.** gave

8. Some inventors of modern rockets have said that
they read Verne's stories.   **8.** C

9. Some of his books, such as *20,000 Leagues Under the
Sea*, have been made into great movies.   **9.** C

10. People have ~~gave~~ Verne the title "Father of Modern
Science Fiction."   **10.** given

USAGE

USAGE

LESSON 3 *(pp. 614–618)*

VERB TENSE Rules 21d, 21e

OBJECTIVES

- To proofread a paragraph to make the verb tense consistent
- To write a conversation that contains each of the six verb tenses

PROGRAM MANAGER

VERB TENSE

- **Independent Practice/ Reteaching** For instruction and exercises, see **Verb Tense** and **Understanding Verb Tense** in *Language Skills Practice and Assessment,* pp. 141–142.

- **Computer Guided Instruction** For additional instruction and practice with verb tense, see **Lesson 15** in *Language Workshop CD-ROM.*

- **Practice** To help less-advanced students with additional instruction and practice with verb tense, see **Chapter 18** in *English Workshop, Second Course,* pp. 185–186.

USAGE

 QUICK REMINDER

Write the following sentences on the chalkboard and have students convert the verbs to the verb tenses specified:

1. Lee runs faster than anyone else in his class. (past) [Lee ran . . .]
2. Sol is a lifeguard at the beach. (future) [Sol will be . . .]
3. Tyrone wants to be a doctor. (present perfect) [Tyrone has wanted . . .]
4. The adhesive glue really holds 50 pounds of weight. (past perfect) [The adhesive glue had really held . . .]
5. The space telescope costs over a billion dollars. (future perfect) [The space telescope will have cost . . .]

USAGE

614 *Using Verbs Correctly*

Verb Tense

21d. The *tense* of a verb indicates the time of the action or state of being expressed by the verb.

Every verb has six tenses.

Present	Past	Future
Present Perfect	Past Perfect	Future Perfect

This time line shows how the six tenses are related to one another.

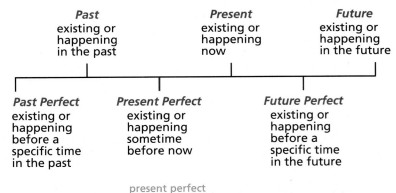

EXAMPLES

present perfect
Melissa **has saved** her money, and now she

present
has enough for a guitar.

past perfect
The scouts **had hiked** five miles before they

past
stopped for lunch.

future perfect
The executive **will have seen** the report by

future
next week and **will make** a decision then.

Listing all the forms of a verb in the six tenses is called *conjugating* a verb.

CONJUGATION OF THE VERB *WRITE*

PRESENT TENSE

SINGULAR	PLURAL
I write	we write
you write	you write
he, she, *or* it writes	they write

PAST TENSE

SINGULAR	PLURAL
I wrote	we wrote
you wrote	you wrote
he, she, *or* it wrote	they wrote

FUTURE TENSE

SINGULAR	PLURAL
I will (shall) write	we will (shall) write
you will write	you will write
he, she, *or* it will write	they will write

PRESENT PERFECT TENSE

SINGULAR	PLURAL
I have written	we have written
you have written	you have written
he, she, *or* it has written	they have written

PAST PERFECT TENSE

SINGULAR	PLURAL
I had written	we had written
you had written	you had written
he, she, *or* it had written	they had written

FUTURE PERFECT TENSE

SINGULAR	PLURAL
I will (shall) have written	we will (shall) have written
you will have written	you will have written
he, she, *or* it will have written	they will have written

NOTE: The helping verb *shall* can be used in the second person (*you*) and third person (*he, she, it, they*), as well as in the first person.

USAGE

MEETING *individual* NEEDS

LEP/ESL

General Strategies. Although English-language learners tend to use the present tense excessively, they do not always learn the rules governing its use. Explain that proficient English speakers use the present for customary or habitual actions. (Every Saturday we do the laundry. On Christmas Day we always wake up early. Our school puts on a play in April.) Words that are often used with the present tense are *sometimes, usually, often,* and *seldom.*

USAGE

Consistency of Tense

21e. Do not change needlessly from one tense to another.

When writing about events that take place in the present, use verbs in the present tense. Similarly, when writing about events that occurred in the past, use verbs in the past tense.

INCONSISTENT	When we were comfortable, we begin to do our homework. [*Were* is past tense, and *begin* is present tense.]
CONSISTENT	When we **are** comfortable, we **begin** to do our homework. [Both *are* and *begin* are present tense.]
CONSISTENT	When we **were** comfortable, we **began** to do our homework. [Both *were* and *began* are past tense.]
INCONSISTENT	Suddenly the great door opened, and an uninvited guest comes into the dining hall. [*Opened* is past tense, and *comes* is present tense.]
CONSISTENT	Suddenly the great door **opens** and an uninvited guest **comes** into the dining hall. [Both *opens* and *comes* are present tense.]
CONSISTENT	Suddenly the great door **opened** and an uninvited guest **came** into the dining hall. [Both *opened* and *came* are past tense.]

▶ EXERCISE 4 **Proofreading a Paragraph to Make the Verb Tense Consistent**

Read the following paragraph and decide whether it should be rewritten in the present or past tense. Then, change the <u>verb forms</u> to make the verb tense consistent.

EXAMPLE   [1] At my grandparents' house, I wake up before anyone else and quietly grabbed the fishing pole and head for the pond.

1. *At my grandparents' house, I wake up before anyone else and quietly grab the fishing pole and head for the pond.*

   or

   At my grandparents' house, I woke up before anyone else and quietly grabbed the fishing pole and headed for the pond.

[1] Across the water, I <u>saw</u> the ripples. [2] "I have to catch some fish," I <u>say</u> to myself. [3] I <u>threw</u> my lure near where I <u>see</u> the ripples and <u>reeled</u> in the line. [4] The fish <u>don't</u> <u>seem</u> interested. [5] I <u>saw</u> more ripples and <u>throw</u> the line in the water again. [6] "I have a strike!" I <u>shout</u> to the trees around me. [7] As I <u>reeled</u> in the line, a beautiful trout <u>jumps</u> out of the water and <u>spit</u> out the hook. [8] Discouraged, I <u>go</u> back to the house. [9] Grandpa <u>was sitting</u> at the kitchen table with a bowl of hot oatmeal for me. [10] I <u>say</u>, "Oh well, maybe tomorrow we'll have fresh trout for breakfast."

USAGE

PICTURE THIS

You are the scientist who built the huge robot shown on the next page. Now you're testing how well it works. To test its ability to understand speech, you decide to question the robot. You take notes while your assistant asks the robot a series of questions. Write down the conversation between your assistant and the robot. In your notes, use sentences with each of the six verb tenses—present, past, future, present perfect, past perfect, and future perfect. Be sure to use quotation marks around the speakers' exact words. Also, start a new paragraph each time the speaker changes.

Subject: conversation between a robot and a scientist
Audience: yourself and your assistant
Purpose: to record the robot's responses to speech

USAGE

SPECIAL PROBLEMS WITH VERBS

OBJECTIVES

- To pronounce and choose the correct forms of *sit* and *set* and to identify direct objects
- To pronounce and choose the correct forms of *lie* and *lay* and to identify direct objects

618 *Using Verbs Correctly*

Special Problems with Verbs

Sit and *Set*

(1) The verb *sit* means "to rest in an upright, seated position." *Sit* seldom takes an object.

(2) The verb *set* means "to put (something) in a place." *Set* usually takes an object. Notice that *set* has the same form for the base form, past, and past participle.

BASE FORM	PRESENT PARTICIPLE	PAST	PAST PARTICIPLE
sit (rest)	(is) sitting	sat	(have) sat
set (put)	(is) setting	set	(have) set

EXAMPLES   **Let's sit under the tree.** [no object]
Let's set the bookcase here. [Let's set what? *Bookcase* is the object.]

Special Problems with Verbs **619**

The tourists **sat** on benches. [no object]
The children **set** the dishes on the table. [The children set what? *Dishes* is the object.]

We **had sat** down to eat when the telephone rang. [no object]
We **have set** the reading lamp beside the couch. [We have set what? *Lamp* is the object.]

▶ ORAL PRACTICE 3   **Using the Forms of *Sit* and *Set***

Read each of the following sentences aloud, stressing the italicized verb.

1. Let's *sit* down here.
2. Look at the dog *sitting* on the porch.
3. Our teacher *set* a deadline for our term projects.
4. I'd like to *sit* on top of an Aztec pyramid and watch the sun rise.
5. I have always *sat* in the front row.
6. Please *set* the carton down inside the doorway.
7. Where did I *set* my book on judo?
8. After I *set* the mop in the closet, I *sat* down to rest.

▶ EXERCISE 5   **Choosing the Forms of *Sit* and *Set***

For each of the following sentences, choose the <u>correct verb</u> in parentheses. If the verb you choose is a form of *set*, identify its <u>object</u>.

EXAMPLE   **1.** Please (*sit, set*) the serving platter on the table.
           1. *set; object—platter*

1. Will you (<u>*sit*</u>, *set*) down here?
2. Aaron asked to (*sit*, <u>*set*</u>) the <u>table</u> for our Passover celebration.
3. Jamyce (*sat*, <u>*set*</u>) down her <u>notebook</u> on the kitchen counter.
4. I have been (<u>*sitting*</u>, *setting*) here all day.
5. (*Sit*, <u>*Set*</u>) the fine <u>crystal</u> in the china cabinet.

USAGE

USAGE

619

Visual Learners. Have students make collages of pictures that illustrate the verbs *sit/set, lie/lay,* and *rise/raise.* Students could look in magazines for pictures of people performing the actions of the verbs, arrange their pictures on poster board, and write under each picture a sentence using the appropriate verb.

620 *Using Verbs Correctly*

6. The referee is (*sitting, setting*) the <u>ball</u> on the fifty-yard line.
7. The kitten cautiously (<u>sat</u>, *set*) down beside the Great Dane.
8. Alex had to (<u>sit</u>, *set*) and catch his breath after joining in the Greek chain dance.
9. Let's (*sit*, <u>set</u>) <u>that</u> aside until later.
10. They have been (<u>sitting</u>, *setting*) there for fifteen minutes without saying a word to each other.

Lie and *Lay*

(1) The verb *lie* means "to rest," "to recline," or "to be in a place." *Lie* never takes an object.

(2) The verb *lay* means "to put (something) in a place." *Lay* usually takes an object.

BASE FORM	PRESENT PARTICIPLE	PAST	PAST PARTICIPLE
lie (rest)	(is) lying	lay	(have) lain
lay (put)	(is) laying	laid	(have) laid

EXAMPLES

The cows **are lying** in the shade. [no object]
The servers **are laying** extra napkins beside every plate for the barbecue. [The servers are laying what? *Napkins* is the object.]

The deer **lay** very still while the hunters passed by. [no object]
The soldiers **laid** a trap for the enemy. [The soldiers laid what? *Trap* is the object.]

Rip Van Winkle **had lain** asleep for twenty years. [no object]
The lawyer **had laid** the report next to her briefcase. [The lawyer had laid what? *Report* is the object.]

ORAL PRACTICE 4 **Using the Forms of *Lie* and *Lay***

Read each of the following sentences aloud, stressing the italicized word.

1. Don't *lie* in the sun until you put on some sunscreen.
2. You shouldn't *lay* your papers on the couch.
3. The lion had been *lying* in wait for an hour.
4. The senator *laid* her notes aside after her speech.
5. I have *lain* awake, listening to Spanish flamenco music on the radio.
6. She has *laid* her books on the desk.
7. At bedtime, Toshiro *lies* down on a futon.
8. The exhausted swimmer *lay* helpless on the sand.

EXERCISE 6 **Using the Forms of *Lie* and *Lay***

Complete each of the following sentences by supplying the correct form of *lie* or *lay*. If the verb you use is a form of *lay*, identify its <u>object</u>.

EXAMPLE **1.** Leo _____ the disk next to the computer.
    1. *laid; object—disk*

1. After the race, Michael Andretti _____ his <u>helmet</u> on the car. **1.** laid
2. My dad was _____ down when I asked him for my allowance. **2.** lying
3. We _____ down some club <u>rules</u>. **3.** laid
4. Have you ever _____ on a water bed? **4.** lain
5. Rammel had _____ his <u>keys</u> beside his wallet. **5.** laid
6. My cat loves to _____ in the tall grass behind our house. **6.** lie
7. My brother left his clothes _____ on the floor until they began to smell. **7.** lying
8. Yesterday that alligator _____ in the sun all day. **8.** lay
9. Lim Sing's great-grandfather _____ railroad <u>track</u> in the United States. **9.** laid
10. The newspaper had _____ in the yard until the sun faded it. **10.** lain

USAGE

USAGE

USAGE

622 *Using Verbs Correctly*

▶ REVIEW C   **Writing Sentences Using the Forms of *Sit* and *Set* and *Lie* and *Lay***

When your neighbors went on vacation, they asked if you would "pet-sit" their animals. At the time, this sounded like an easy way to earn extra spending money. But you've really earned your money taking care of these three beasts! You've discovered that they can be very wild and stubborn. Write ten sentences about your "pet-sitting" experiences. Use a different verb from the list in each of your sentences.

lies	lay (past form of *lie*)	sat
have laid	set	laid
was sitting	were lying	setting
had set		

EXAMPLE   **1.** *Mr. Whiskers lay in Scruffy's food dish every morning.*

Rise and *Raise*

(1) The verb *rise* means "to go up" or "to get up." *Rise* never takes an object.

(2) The verb *raise* means "to lift up" or "to cause (something) to rise." *Raise* usually takes an object.

BASE FORM	PRESENT PARTICIPLE	PAST	PAST PARTICIPLE
rise (go up)	(is) rising	rose	(have) risen
raise (lift up)	(is) raising	raised	(have) raised

EXAMPLES My neighbors **rise** very early in the morning. [no object]

Every morning they **raise** their shades to let the sunlight in. [They raise what? *Shades* is the object.]

The full moon **rose** slowly through the clouds last night. [no object]
The cheering crowd **raised** banners and signs over their heads, welcoming the troops home. [The crowd raised what? *Banners* and *signs* are the objects.]

The senators **have risen** from their seats to show respect for the chief justice. [no object]
The wind **has raised** a cloud of dust. [The wind has raised what? *Cloud* is the object.]

▶ ORAL PRACTICE 5 **Using the Forms of *Rise* and *Raise***

Read each of the following sentences aloud, stressing the italicized verb.

1. The reporters *rise* when the president enters the room.
2. Students *raise* their hands to be recognized.
3. They *have raised* the curtain for the first act of the play.
4. Alex Haley *rose* to fame with his book *Roots*.
5. The sun *was rising* over the mountains.
6. The old Asian elephant slowly *rose* to its feet.
7. Who *had risen* first?
8. Two of the Inuit builders *raised* the block of ice and set it in place.

ADVANCED STUDENTS

You may want to have students develop rules for using additional verb pairs that frequently cause problems, such as *learn/teach* and *leave/let*. Ask students to write explanations of each of the verbs and to include sentences as examples of the correct usage. Then have the students present the material to the rest of the class.

624 *Using Verbs Correctly*

▶ EXERCISE 7 **Choosing the Forms of *Rise* and *Raise***

For each of the following sentences, choose the <u>correct verb</u> in parentheses. If the verb you choose is a form of *raise*, identify its <u>object</u>.

EXAMPLE **1.** Please (*raise, rise*) your hand when you want to speak.
1. *raise; object—hand*

1. The steam was (*rising, raising*) from the pot of soup.
2. That discovery (*rises, raises*) an interesting <u>question</u> about the Algonquian people of Canada.
3. The child's fever (*rose, raised*) during the night.
4. The sun (*rises, raises*) later each morning.
5. The teacher will call only on students who (*rise, raise*) their <u>hands</u>.
6. We must (*rise, raise*) the <u>flag</u> before school begins.
7. The student body's interest in this subject has (*risen, raised*) to new heights.
8. The kite has (*risen, raised*) above the power lines.
9. My father promised to (*rise, raise*) my <u>allowance</u> if I pull the weeds.
10. The art dealer (*rose, raised*) the <u>price</u> of the painting by Frida Kahlo.

▶ EXERCISE 8 **Using the Forms of *Rise* and *Raise***

Complete each sentence in the following paragraphs by supplying the correct form of *rise* or *raise*.

EXAMPLE [1] Have you ever ____ before dawn?
1. *risen*

1. rose

2. rose

3. risen

4. raised

5. rise

[1] We girls ____ early to start our hike to Lookout Mountain. [2] From our position at the foot of the mountain, it looked as though it ____ straight up to the skies. [3] But we had not ____ at daybreak just to look at the high peak. [4] We ____ our supply packs to our backs and started the long climb up the mountain. [5] With every step we took, the mountain seemed to ____ that much higher. [6] Finally, after several hours, we reached the

OBJECTIVES

- To choose the correct forms of *sit* and *set, lie* and *lay,* and *rise* and *raise*
- To proofread a paragraph for correct verb forms
- To choose correct forms of irregular verbs
- To use correct forms of irregular verbs in a letter

Special Problems with Verbs **625**

summit and ____ a special flag that we had brought for the occasion. [7] When our friends at the foot of the mountain saw that we had ____ the flag, they knew that all of us had reached the top safely. [8] They ____ their arms and shouted.

    [9] Our friends' shouts were like an applause that seemed to ____ from the valley below. [10] Then we felt glad that we had ____ early enough to climb to the top of Lookout Mountain.

6. raised

7. raised

8. raised

9. rise

10. risen

> **REVIEW D**
>
> ### Choosing the Forms of *Sit* and *Set, Lie* and *Lay,* and *Rise* and *Raise*

Each of the following sentences has at least one pair of verbs in parentheses. Choose the <u>correct verb</u> from each pair. Be prepared to explain your choices.

EXAMPLE   **1.** The audience (*sat, set*) near the stage.
          1. *sat*

1. To study solar energy, our class (*sit, <u>set</u>*) a solar panel outside the window of our classroom.
2. Since I have grown taller, I have (*rose, <u>raised</u>*) the seat on my bicycle.
3. Mr. DeLemos (*lay, <u>laid</u>*) the foundation for the new Vietnamese Community Center.
4. (*Sit, <u>Set</u>*) the groceries on the table while I start dinner.
5. The water level of the stream has not (*<u>risen</u>, raised*) since last summer.
6. Will you (*lie, <u>lay</u>*) the grass mats on the sand so that we can (*<u>lie</u>, lay*) on them?
7. We (*<u>sat</u>, set*) under a beach umbrella so that we wouldn't get sunburned.
8. When the sun (*<u>rises</u>, raises*), I often have trouble (*sitting, <u>setting</u>*) aside my covers and getting up.
9. He left his collection of Isaac Bashevis Singer stories (*<u>lying</u>, laying*) on the table.
10. The crane (*rose, <u>raised</u>*) the steel beam and carefully (*sat, <u>set</u>*) it into place.

USAGE

▶ REVIEW E

Proofreading a Paragraph for Correct Verb Forms

Some sentences in the following paragraph contain incorrect forms of the verbs *sit* and *set, lie* and *lay,* and *rise* and *raise.* If the sentence is correct, write *C.* If the sentence has an incorrect verb form, write the correct form.

EXAMPLES [1] We rose early for our journey to Havasu Canyon.
1. C
[2] I laid awake for hours thinking about the trip.
2. *lay*

[1] I helped Dad ~~sit~~ our bags in the car, and we headed for Havasu Canyon. [2] The canyon, which lies in northern Arizona, is home of the Havasupai Indian Reservation. [3] At the canyon rim, a Havasupai guide helped me up onto a horse and ~~rose~~ the stirrups so that I could reach them. [4] After we rode horses eight miles to the canyon floor, I was tired from ~~setting~~. [5] Yet I knew I must ~~sit~~ a good example for my younger brother and not complain. [6] As you can see, the trail we took was fairly narrow and lay along the side of a steep, rocky wall. [7] We watched the sun ~~raise~~ high and hot as we rode through this beautiful canyon. [8] I thought about ~~laying~~ down when we reached the village of Supai. [9] Still, I quickly raised my hand to join the next tour to Havasu Falls. [10] When we arrived, I was ready to ~~lay~~ under the spray of the waterfall pictured on the next page.

USAGE

▶ REVIEW F   **Choosing Correct Verb Forms**

Each of the following sentences has at least one pair of verbs in parentheses. Choose the <u>correct verb</u> from each pair.

EXAMPLE   **1.** Josh (*catched, caught*) seven fish this morning.
                1. *caught*

1. Buffy Sainte-Marie has (*sang*, <u>*sung*</u>) professionally for more than twenty years.
2. Have you (*began*, <u>*begun*</u>) your Scottish bagpipe lessons yet?
3. Cindy Nicholas was the first woman who (<u>*swam*</u>, *swum*) the English Channel both ways.
4. When the baby sitter (*rose*, <u>*raised*</u>) her voice, the children (<u>*knew*</u>, *knowed*) it was time to behave.
5. After we had (*saw*, <u>*seen*</u>) all of the exhibits at the county fair, we (<u>*ate*</u>, *eat*) a light snack and then (<u>*went*</u>, *go*) home.
6. The egg (<u>*burst*</u>, *bursted*) in the microwave oven.
7. He (*lay*, <u>*laid*</u>) his lunch money on his desk.
8. The loud noise (*breaked*, <u>*broke*</u>) my concentration.
9. We (<u>*sat*</u>, *set*) through the movie three times because Cantinflas is so funny.
10. We had (*rode*, <u>*ridden*</u>) halfway across the desert when I began to wish that I had (<u>*brought*</u>, *brung*) more water.

USAGE

USAGE

▶ REVIEW G   **Identifying Correct Verb Forms**

Each sentence in the following paragraph has a pair of verbs in parentheses. Choose the <u>correct verb</u> from each pair.

EXAMPLE   [1] Have you ever (*saw, seen*) an animal using a tool?
           1. *seen*

[1] I had (*thought*, *thinked*) that only humans use tools. [2] However, scientists have (*spended*, *spent*) many hours watching wild animals make and use tools. [3] Chimpanzees have been (*saw, seen*) using twigs to catch insects. [4] They (*taken*, *took*) their sticks and poked them into termite holes. [5] In that way, they (*catched*, *caught*) termites. [6] I've been (*telled*, *told*) that some finches use twigs to dig insects out of cracks in tree bark. [7] Sea otters have (*broke*, *broken*) open shellfish by banging them against rocks. [8] You may have (*knew*, *known*) that song thrushes also use that trick to get snails out of their shells. [9] Some animals have (*builded*, *built*) things, using their gluelike body fluids to hold objects together. [10] For example, scientists watched as tailor ants (*spread*, *spreaded*) their sticky film on leaves to hold them together.

▶ REVIEW H   **Using the Forms of Verbs**

You've always enjoyed riding bicycles. Now you have a chance to help out in your uncle's bicycle repair shop. On your first day there, your uncle gives you a copy of a chart. He tells you to use it to check over every bicycle brought in. Write a letter to a friend, telling about your job at the shop. Use the chart on the next page to describe some of the things that you do when you check a bicycle. In your letter, use the past or past participle forms of ten verbs from the list of Common Irregular Verbs on pages 608–610. Underline these ten verbs.

EXAMPLE   **1.** *One man <u>brought</u> in an old bicycle, and I <u>spent</u> all morning fixing the brakes.*

ANSWERS
Review H

Letters will vary. Have students review the lists of common irregular verbs before they begin writing, and have each student list ten or fifteen that could possibly be used in the letter. Have students write their letters and work with partners to revise and proofread the letters.

OBJECTIVE

• To write a short narrative poem that includes at least ten irregular verbs

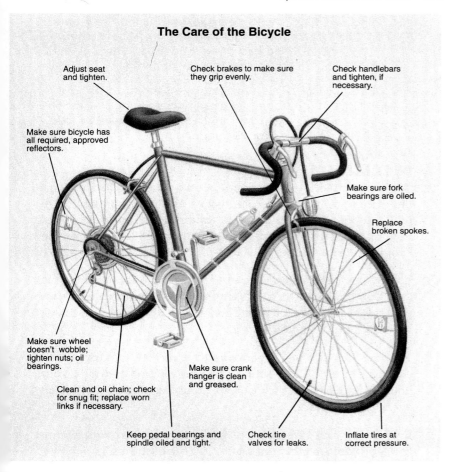

The Care of the Bicycle

Adjust seat and tighten.

Check brakes to make sure they grip evenly.

Check handlebars and tighten, if necessary.

Make sure bicycle has all required, approved reflectors.

Make sure fork bearings are oiled.

Replace broken spokes.

Make sure wheel doesn't wobble; tighten nuts; oil bearings.

Clean and oil chain; check for snug fit; replace worn links if necessary.

Make sure crank hanger is clean and greased.

Keep pedal bearings and spindle oiled and tight.

Check tire valves for leaks.

Inflate tires at correct pressure.

USAGE

 VISUAL CONNECTIONS
Related Expression Skills.
You may want to have students work together to think of verbs that are onomatopoeic to describe actions and sounds of riding a bicycle. [Possible answers include *whiz, buzz, clank, zoom, whir, huff,* and *puff.*] After the class has composed a list of verbs, ask the students to create poems or journal entries that incorporate as many words from the list as possible.

USAGE

WRITING APPLICATION

Using Different Verb Forms and Tenses in a Poem

When you write a story, you use verbs to tell what is happening, has happened, or will happen to your characters. To help your readers understand the order of events, you use different verb forms.

CRITICAL THINKING

Application. Tell students that they should apply their knowledge of prewriting processes and of the elements of a story to plan their narrative poems. Each student should consider audience and purpose and then define a character or characters, setting, tone, conflict, and resolution.

WRITING APPLICATION

"Modern Adventures" is a broad topic. You may want to have a brainstorming session with the class to help students define what specific topics they think would be appropriate to write about. Remind students that their work will be more engaging if they write about adventures that interest them. Possible topics might include things they have done themselves, events they have heard about, or adventures they have imagined.

INCORRECT FORM AND INCONSISTENT TENSE	The huge explosion shaked the whole town. Julie ran to the window when she heard the loud noise. She will want to see what was happening.
CORRECT FORM AND CONSISTENT TENSE	The huge explosion **shook** the whole town. Julie **ran** to the window when she **heard** the loud noise. She **wanted** to see what **was** happening.

▶ WRITING ACTIVITY

You've decided to enter a local poetry contest. The theme of the contest is "Modern Adventures." Write a short narrative poem (a poem that tells a story) about a modern adventure. In your poem use at least ten verbs from the list of Common Irregular Verbs on pages 608–610.

Prewriting First, you'll need to pick an adventure story to tell. You could tell a true story or an imaginary one. After you select a story, jot down some specific details that you want to include in your poem.

Writing As you write your rough draft, try to express the excitement of the adventure. You may want to divide your poem into rhymed stanzas. Each stanza could tell a different event of your story.

Evaluating and Revising Ask a friend to read your poem. Is the adventure story easy to follow? Is it interesting? If not, you may want to add, delete, or revise some details. If your poem is a ballad or other traditional type of poem, be sure that the rhythm and rhyme follow that poetic form. Does your poem contain enough sensory details? For more about sensory details, see page 66.

Proofreading Use your textbook to check the spelling of the irregular verbs in your poem. Be sure that you've used ten irregular verbs from the list. And check to see that the forms are correct and the tenses are consistent.

REVIEW: POSTTEST

OBJECTIVES

- To use the past and past participle forms of verbs
- To choose the correct forms of *lie* and *lay, sit* and *set,* and *rise* and *raise* in sentences
- To make tenses of verbs consistent

Review: Posttest

A. Using the Past and Past Participle Forms of Verbs

For each of the following sentences, give the correct form (past or past participle) of the verb in parentheses.

EXAMPLES   **1. The deer (*run*) right in front of our car.**
1. *ran*

2. Her dog has (*run*) away from home.
2. *run*

1. She (*buy*) several boxes decorated with colorful Amish designs. **1. bought**
2. Have you (*write*) your history report yet? **2. written**
3. I don't think I should have (*eat*) that last handful of sunflower seeds. **3. eaten**
4. Our teacher (*tell*) us that the ukulele is a musical instrument from Hawaii. **4. told**
5. She is the nicest person I have ever (*know*). **5. known**
6. When the medicine finally began to work, his fever (*break*). **6. broke**
7. That phone has (*ring*) every five minutes since I got home. **7. rung**
8. Earl thought and thought, but the answer never (*come*) to him. **8. came**
9. If that had happened to me, I would have (*freeze*) with fear. **9. frozen**
10. Through the murky depths the whales (*sing*) to one another. **10. sang**
11. The coach (*give*) us all a pep talk before the game. **11. gave**
12. We knew that it would start to rain soon because the crickets had (*begin*) chirping. **12. begun**
13. That job shouldn't have (*take*) you all day. **13. taken**
14. The waiter (*bring*) us couscous, a popular North African dish. **14. brought**
15. Though it had (*fall*) from the top of the tree, the baby squirrel was all right. **15. fallen**

USAGE

USAGE

B. Choosing the Forms of *Lie* and *Lay, Sit* and *Set,* and *Rise* and *Raise* in Sentences

For each of the following sentences, choose the <u>correct verb</u> in parentheses.

EXAMPLE   **1.** My cat (*lies, lays*) around the house all day.
       1. *lies*

16. We had to wait for the drawbridge to (<u>*rise*</u>, *raise*) before we could sail out to the bay.
17. (*Sit,* <u>*Set*</u>) that down in the chair, will you?
18. The treasure had (*lay,* <u>*lain*</u>) at the bottom of the sea for more than four hundred years.
19. While (<u>*sitting*</u>, *setting*) on the porch, Nashota read a folk tale about Coyote, the trickster.
20. Look on the other side of any logs (<u>*lying*</u>, *laying*) in the path to avoid stepping on a snake.

C. Making Tenses of Verbs Consistent

For each of the following sentences, write the italicized verb in the correct tense.

EXAMPLE   **1.** My father looked at his watch and *decides* that it was time to leave.
       1. *decided*

21. Marjorie's sister refused to give us a ride in her car, and then she ~~*asks*~~ us to lend her some money for gas. **21.** asked
22. He says he's sorry, but he ~~*didn't*~~ mean it. **22.** doesn't
23. The pine trees grow close together and ~~*had*~~ straight trunks. **23.** have
24. When the show ended, we ~~*get*~~ up to leave, but a crowd had already gathered. **24.** got
25. Several mechanics worked on my aunt's car before one of them finally ~~*finds*~~ the problem. **25.** found

OBJECTIVE

- To identify the correct forms of pronouns in sentences

PROGRAM MANAGER

FOR THE WHOLE CHAPTER

■ **Review** For exercises on chapter concepts, see **Review Form A** and **Review Form B** in *Language Skills Practice and Assessment,* pp. 157–158.

■ **Assessment** For additional testing, see **Usage Pretests** and **Usage Mastery Tests** in *Language Skills Practice and Assessment,* pp. 115–120 and pp. 191–198.

22 USING PRONOUNS CORRECTLY

Nominative and Objective Case Forms

USAGE

CHAPTER OVERVIEW

Following the **Diagnostic Test,** this chapter presents definitions and models of the three cases of personal pronouns. The lesson on the nominative case covers subject and predicate nominatives. The objective case is explained through definitions and models of direct objects, indirect objects, and objects of prepositions. A lesson on special pronoun problems explains standard usage of *who* and *whom* and discusses the use of pronouns with appositives.

The **Writing Application** gives students a chance to concentrate on using pronouns correctly in writing. You can adapt these assignments to your students' needs.

Diagnostic Test

Identifying Correct Forms of Pronouns

For each of the following sentences, identify the <u>correct pronoun</u> in parentheses.

EXAMPLE   **1. When I got home, a package was waiting for (*I, me*).**
    1. *me*

1. Just between you and (*I, <u>me</u>*), I think he's wrong.
2. I don't know (*who, <u>whom</u>*) I'll invite to the dance.
3. We saw (*they, <u>them</u>*) at a Mardi Gras parade in New Orleans.
4. The winners in the contest were Amelia and (<u>*I*</u>, *me*).
5. The wasp flew in the window and bit (*he, <u>him</u>*) on the arm.

OBJECTIVE

- To identify personal pronouns and their cases

6. Elton and (*she, her*) will give reports this morning.
7. The two scouts who have earned the most merit badges are Angelo and (*he, him*).
8. Several people in my neighborhood helped (*we, us*) boys clear the empty lot and measure out a baseball diamond.
9. Nina usually sits behind Alex and (*I, me*) on the bus every morning.
10. My father and (*he, him*) are planning to go into business together.
11. We thought that we'd be facing (*they, them*) in the finals.
12. May I sit next to Terence and (*he, him*)?
13. The tour guide showed Kimberly and (*she, her*) some Japanese *raku* pottery.
14. My aunt once gave (*me, I*) two dolls made from corn husks.
15. Did you know that it was (*I, me*) who called?
16. Corey's mother and my father said that (*we, us*) boys could go on the field trip.
17. Our friends asked (*we, us*) if we had ever been to San Francisco's Chinatown.
18. Invite (*she, her*) and the new girl in our class to the party.
19. Do you know (*who, whom*) received the award?
20. The best soloists in the band are (*they, them*).

Case

Case is the form of a noun or a pronoun that shows its use in a sentence. There are three cases:

- nominative
- objective
- possessive

USING THE DIAGNOSTIC TEST

If students are having problems with pronoun usage in their writing, you may want to administer this **Diagnostic Test.** The results will give you a feel for how familiar your students are with the conventions governing the use of nominative and objective pronouns.

USAGE

PROGRAM MANAGER

CASE

- **Independent Practice/ Reteaching** For instruction and exercises, see **Case Forms** in *Language Skills Practice and Assessment,* p. 151.

- **Computer Guided Instruction** For additional instruction and practice with pronoun case, see **Lessons 17** and **18** in *Language Workshop CD-ROM.*

- **Practice** To help less-advanced students with additional instruction and practice with pronoun case, see **Chapter 19** in *English Workshop, Second Course,* pp. 193–194.

The form of a noun is the same for both the nominative and the objective cases. For example, a noun used as a subject (nominative case) will have the same form when used as an indirect object (objective case).

NOMINATIVE CASE **The singer received a standing ovation.**
[subject]
OBJECTIVE CASE **The audience gave the singer a standing ovation.** [indirect object]

A noun changes its form for the possessive case, usually by adding an apostrophe and an *s*.

POSSESSIVE CASE **Many of the singer's fans waited outside the theater.**

☞ REFERENCE NOTE: For more about possessive pronouns, see pages 437, 817, 821, and 823.

Unlike nouns, most personal pronouns have different forms for all three cases.

PERSONAL PRONOUNS		
SINGULAR		
NOMINATIVE CASE	**OBJECTIVE CASE**	**POSSESSIVE CASE**
I	me	my, mine
you	you	your, yours
he, she, it	him, her, it	his, her, hers, its
PLURAL		
NOMINATIVE CASE	**OBJECTIVE CASE**	**POSSESSIVE CASE**
we	us	our, ours
you	you	your, yours
they	them	their, theirs

NOTE: Some teachers prefer to call possessive pronouns (such as *my, your,* and *our*) adjectives. Follow your teacher's directions in labeling possessive forms.

USAGE

USAGE

USAGE

USAGE

The Far Side cartoon by Gary Larson is reprinted by permission of Chronicle Features, San Francisco, CA. All rights reserved.

"So, then . . . Would that be 'us the people' or 'we the people?'"

▶ EXERCISE 1   **Identifying Personal Pronouns and Their Cases**

Each of the sentences in the following paragraph contains at least one <u>personal pronoun</u>. Identify each pronoun and give its case. nom. = nominative obj. = objective poss. = possessive

EXAMPLE   [1] Uncle Theo gave us this book about rock stars of the 1950s and 1960s.
    1. *us—objective*

1. nom./obj.
2. nom./nom.
3. nom./obj.

4. nom.

5. nom.
6. poss.

[1] Why don't <u>you</u> sit down and look through the book with Clarence and <u>me</u>? [2] <u>We</u> want to see what pictures <u>it</u> has of the great African American rock singers. [3] <u>I</u> also look forward to reading more about <u>them</u>! [4] The contributions <u>they</u> made to rock-and-roll affected popular music all over the world. [5] The stars in the pictures on the next page look so different from the performers <u>we</u> have today. [6] That's Chuck Berry doing <u>his</u> famous "duckwalk." [7] These three women were known as the Supremes, and

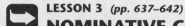
NOMINATIVE CASE Rules 22a, 22b

OBJECTIVES

- To read aloud sentences that have pronouns as subjects
- To identify and use pronouns in the nominative case as subjects and as predicate nominatives

they had twelve number-one songs. [8] The woman in the middle may look familiar; she is Diana Ross. [9] Fans also liked this male vocal group, the Four Tops, and other groups like them that harmonized. [10] Of course, we can't forget Little Richard, known for his wild piano playing.

7. nom.
8. nom.
9. obj.
10. nom./ poss.

USAGE

The Nominative Case

22a. A subject of a verb is in the nominative case.

EXAMPLES   **I** like classical music. [*I* is the subject of *like.*]
He and **she** sold tickets. [*He* and *she* are the subjects of *sold.*]
They called while **we** were away. [*They* is the subject of *called. We* is the subject of *were.*]

QUICK REMINDER

Write the following sentences on the chalkboard and ask students if any sound incorrect:

1. Me want to go home.
2. Tom and me want to go home.
3. Her got pretty shoes.
4. Cherysse and her both got pretty shoes.

Most students will say that numbers 1 and 3 sound incorrect, while numbers 2 and 4 sound all right. Point out that all four sentences incorrectly use objective pronouns as subjects. Have students substitute nominative pronouns for the objective pronouns in the sentences.

USAGE

637

LESS-ADVANCED STUDENTS

Students may have trouble learning the conventions governing nominative pronouns because they don't recognize when a word acts as a subject. Use **Oral Practice 1** to help students recognize subjects and verbs. As each sentence is read aloud, call on a volunteer to identify the subject and the verb. For stronger reinforcement, have students write out the identifications. Be sure students realize that a compound subject can consist of just nouns, just pronouns, or a mixture of the two.

LEP/ESL

Spanish. Because most Spanish personal pronouns have the same form for both the nominative and objective cases, as in "She spoke to she," or "They spoke to they," Spanish speakers are unaccustomed to making a distinction when they speak in their native language. Have students practice saying aloud the sentences for the written exercises as well as those for the oral exercises. Oral repetition will help students establish a correct nominative-objective system for personal pronouns.

⚡ TIMESAVER

To save time grading papers and to provide reinforcement in recognizing standard usage, have students correct each other's papers as answers are read aloud for **Exercises 2** and **3**.

638

To help you choose the correct pronoun in a compound subject, try each form of the pronoun separately.

EXAMPLE: **Candida and (*me, I*) like to dance.**
           ***Me* like to dance.**
           ***I* like to dance.**
ANSWER: **Candida and I like to dance.**

▶ ORAL PRACTICE 1   **Using Pronouns as Subjects**

Read the following sentences aloud, stressing the italicized pronouns.

1. *He* and *she* collect seashells.
2. My grandmother and *I* are painting the boat.
3. Both *they* and *we* were frightened.
4. Did Alicia or *she* answer the phone?
5. *We* are giving a fashion show.
6. *You* and *I* will stay behind.
7. Were *he* and *she* on the Old Spanish Trail?
8. My parents and *they* are good friends.

▶ EXERCISE 2   **Choosing Personal Pronouns Used as Subjects**

Choose appropriate personal pronouns for the blanks in the following sentences. Use a variety of pronouns, but do not use *you* or *it*.   Responses will vary. All pronouns should be in the nominative case.

EXAMPLE   1. ____ and ____ will have a debate.
          1. *We, they*

1. Yesterday she and ____ went shopping.
2. Our cousins and ____ are ready for the race.
3. Neither ____ nor J. B. saw the zydeco band perform.
4. ____ and Lim Sing have copies of the book.
5. When are ____ and ____ coming?
6. Everyone remembers when ____ won the big game.
7. Someone said that ____ and ____ are finalists.
8. Did you or ____ ride in the hot-air balloon?

9. Both ____ and ____ enjoyed the stories about African American cowboys in the Old West.
10. Has ____ or Eduardo seen that movie?

22b. A *predicate nominative* is in the nominative case.

A *predicate nominative* follows a linking verb and explains or identifies the subject of the verb. A personal pronoun used as a predicate nominative follows a form of the verb *be* (*am, is, are, was, were, be,* or *been*).

EXAMPLES   **The last one to leave was he.** [*He* follows the linking verb *was* and identifies the subject *one.*]
Do you think it may have been they? [*They* follows the linking verb *may have been* and identifies the subject *it.*]

To help you choose the correct form of a pronoun used as a predicate nominative, remember that the pronoun could just as well be used as the subject in the sentence.

EXAMPLE   **The fastest runners are she and I.** [predicate nominatives]
She and I are the fastest runners. [subjects]

☞ REFERENCE NOTE: For more information about predicate nominatives, see page 496.

NOTE: Expressions such as *It's me, That's her,* and *It was them* are accepted in everyday speaking. In writing, however, such expressions are generally considered nonstandard and should be avoided.

EXERCISE 3   **Identifying Personal Pronouns Used as Predicate Nominatives**

For each of the following sentences, identify the <u>correct personal pronoun</u> in parentheses.

EXAMPLE   **1.** It was (*I, me*) at the door.
          1. *I*

1. We hoped it was (*her,* <u>she</u>).
2. That stranger thinks I am (<u>she</u>, *her*).

COMMON ERROR
Problem. Because students frequently hear people use objective rather than nominative pronouns in compound subjects and in predicate nominatives, the incorrect usage may sound correct to them.

Solution. Tell students that they can rely on their ear if they strip the sentence so that only one pronoun remains as the subject. (Sample: "Tami and me worked hard" is stripped to become "Me worked hard." Replace *me* with *I.*) To test predicate nominative pronouns, suggest flipping the pronoun so that it's in front of the verb. (Sample: "The singer was her" flipped becomes "Her was the singer." Replace *her* with *she.*) As a reminder you might post the rule "Check your pronoun: Strip it or flip it." Working as a class or in small groups, students can practice stripping and flipping sentences in **Exercises 2** and **3.**

INTEGRATING THE LANGUAGE ARTS
Literature Link. Have each student find a poem from his or her literature book in which the poet has used first-person pronouns. Possible selections are "Mother to Son" by Langston Hughes or "Grandmother Ling" by Amy Ling. Ask students to rewrite the poems by substituting third-person singular forms for the first-person pronouns. Have volunteers read the old versions and the new versions aloud. Discuss how the implications and force of the message are altered when feelings and impressions are presented as a report about someone who has them rather than spoken as if coming directly from the heart and mind of the speaker.

REVIEW A

OBJECTIVE

- To identify personal pronouns in the nominative case

A DIFFERENT APPROACH

To give practice with predicate nominatives, have each student write five questions in which Dr. Watson asks Sherlock Holmes about the identity of a murderer. Have students exchange papers with partners to write Holmes's reply by using predicate nominative pronouns. Sample exchanges:

Watson: Could the murderer have been Professor Johnson?

Holmes: No, I do not believe it could have been he.

Watson: Do you think it was the mayor, Mrs. Murdock?

Holmes: I am certain it was not she.

Partners should review their responses together to make sure they employed standard English usage. Students might want to read their dialogues aloud with British accents.

INTEGRATING THE LANGUAGE ARTS

Usage and Writing. Although pronoun predicate nominatives are considered standard usage, they usually sound stilted or awkward to most native speakers of American English. Tell students that to make their writing flow more smoothly, they can rewrite sentences by using pronoun predicate nominatives as subjects. For example, in **Review A**, the third sentence would read "They are the *Mona Lisa* and the *Last Supper*," and the ninth sentence could be rewritten as "He was also the inventor of the diving bell and the battle tank."

640

---

640 *Using Pronouns Correctly*

3. Luckily, it was not (*them*, *they*) in the accident.
4. It could have been (*she*, *her*) that he called.
5. Everyone believed it was (*we*, *us*).
6. It might have been (*him*, *he*), but I'm not sure.
7. Our opponents could have been (*them*, *they*).
8. I thought it was (*they*, *them*) from whom you bought the Cherokee basket.
9. If the singer had been (*her*, *she*), I would have gone to the concert.
10. Was that Claudia or (*she*, *her*) who brought the Chinese egg rolls?

▶ REVIEW A   **Identifying Personal Pronouns in the Nominative Case**

Each sentence in the following paragraph contains a pair of personal pronouns in parentheses. Choose the <u>correct pronoun</u> from each pair.

EXAMPLE   [1] (*We*, *Us*) think of Leonardo da Vinci mostly as an artist.
            1. *We*

[1] (*Me*, *I*) think you probably have seen some paintings by this Italian Renaissance master. [2] (*Him*, *He*) painted two works that are particularly famous. [3] The *Mona Lisa* and the *Last Supper* are (*they*, *them*). [4] In science class (*we*, *us*) were surprised by what our teacher said about Leonardo. [5] (*Her*, *She*) said that he was also a brilliant inventor. [6] My friend Jill and (*me*, *I*) were amazed to hear that Leonardo

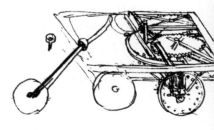

Case **641**

invented a flying machine that looked like a helicopter. [7] Look at the propellers on the flying machine that (*he*, *him*) drew in 1488. [8] (*Me*, *I*) was also impressed by his drawing of a spring-driven car. [9] The inventor of the diving bell and the battle tank was (*him*, *he*), too. [10] Scientists have studied Leonardo's ideas, and (*them*, *they*) have made models of many of his drawings.

WRITING APPLICATION

Using Pronouns in a Letter to a Magazine

The difference between the rules of spoken English and written English can be confusing. For example, the language you hear spoken at home and in your community determines what sounds "right" to you. But sometimes what *sounds* right is actually a nonstandard usage. To communicate effectively with a wide range of people, you need to learn the rules of standard English.

NONSTANDARD   Ernie and me respect Mr. Ray's decision.
STANDARD   Ernie and I respect Mr. Ray's decision.

▶ WRITING ACTIVITY

A national magazine has asked its readers to send in letters telling about the people they respect the most. A prize will be given to the person who writes the best letter. You decide to enter the contest. Write a letter to the magazine, telling about the person you most respect. You want your writing to appeal to many people, so be sure the pronouns you use follow the rules of standard English.

Prewriting   Begin by thinking about a person you respect. This could be someone you know (such as a family member, a teacher, or a friend). Or it could be someone you have

WRITING APPLICATION
  If students have trouble choosing someone to write about, have them list the achievements and qualities they would most like to have themselves. Then they can brainstorm lists of persons who could act as role models.

  Have students look at the letters column in several national magazines and discuss the style of the published letters. Students should see that while the letters are not highly formal, they do tend to avoid slang and nonstandard usage.

CRITICAL THINKING
  Synthesis. In the **Writing Application,** students are asked to present reasons why they respect the persons they are writing about and to support their opinions with facts. In bringing these parts together to create well-organized and convincing letters, students will be synthesizing information.

LESSON 4 *(pp. 642–647)*
THE OBJECTIVE CASE Rules 22c–22e

OBJECTIVES

- To use pronouns as direct objects, indirect objects, and objects of prepositions
- To read aloud sentences that contain pronouns as direct objects, indirect objects, and objects of prepositions

---

EVALUATING AND REVISING

Have students work with partners to review each other's work and specifically look for pronoun usage. They should comment on whether the writer mixes the use of pronouns and the use of the person's name effectively. Discuss how using only pronouns often makes the reader lose track of who is being discussed. On the other hand, repeating a name constantly can be awkward and boring.

THE OBJECTIVE CASE

- **Independent Practice/ Reteaching** For instruction and exercises, see **Direct and Indirect Objects** and **Objects of Prepositions** in *Language Skills Practice and Assessment,* pp. 153–154.

- **Computer Guided Instruction** For additional instruction and practice with the objective case, see **Lesson 18** in *Language Workshop CD-ROM.*

- **Practice** To help less-advanced students with additional instruction and practice with the objective case, see **Chapter 19** in *English Workshop, Second Course,* pp. 197–200.

---

642 *Using Pronouns Correctly*

heard or read about (perhaps an author or a scientist). Choose one person to write about. Then, make some notes on why you respect that person.

Writing   As you write your first draft, include only the most convincing details from your list. Think about how you want to group these details and how they will fit in your letter. Throughout your letter, use personal pronouns so that you don't keep repeating proper names.

Evaluating and Revising   As you read over your letter, imagine that you are a magazine editor. Ask yourself these questions:

- Is it clear why the writer respects the person?
- Has the writer supported all opinions with facts?

Mark any places where more information would be helpful. Delete any unnecessary information. Then, check to be sure that all pronoun antecedents are clear. (For more about antecedents, see pages 436 and 594–596.)

Proofreading and Publishing   Recopy your letter following the business letter format on pages 901–906. Check the spellings of all proper names and places. Make sure that all pronouns are used according to the rules of standard English. You and your classmates could display your letters on a Person-of-the-Week bulletin board. You also might want to send a copy of your letter to the person you wrote about.

The Objective Case

22c.   A *direct object* is in the objective case.

A *direct object* follows an action verb and tells *who* or *what* receives the action of the verb.

642

EXAMPLES   **Evan surprised them.** [*Them* tells *whom* Evan surprised.]
Uncle Ramón took me to the rodeo. [*Me* tells *whom* Uncle Ramón took.]
The ranger guided us to the camp. [*Us* tells *whom* the ranger guided.]

To help you choose the correct pronoun in a compound direct object, try each form of the pronoun separately in the sentence.

EXAMPLE: **We met Tara and (*she, her*) at the video arcade.**
We met *she* at the video arcade.
We met *her* at the video arcade.
ANSWER: **We met Tara and her at the video arcade.**

☞ REFERENCE NOTE: For more information about direct objects, see page 491.

▶ EXERCISE 4   **Choosing Pronouns Used as Direct Objects**

Choose appropriate pronouns for the blanks in the following sentences. Use a variety of pronouns, but do not use *you* or *it*.   Responses will vary. All pronouns should be in the objective case.

EXAMPLE   **1.** The teacher helped ＿＿ with the assignment.
1. *us*

1. All five judges have chosen ＿＿ and ＿＿ as the winners.
2. They asked Ms. Shore and ＿＿ for permission.
3. Rita said that she can usually find Alberto and ＿＿ at your house.
4. Did you know Jarvis and ＿＿?
5. The guide directed ＿＿ to New York City's Little Italy neighborhood.
6. Aunt Aggie took ＿＿ and ＿＿ to the zoo.
7. Rochelle told my sister and ＿＿ about the Freddie Jackson concert.
8. Should we call Mark and ＿＿?
9. Do you remember ＿＿ and ＿＿?
10. The dog chased Adam and ＿＿.

QUICK REMINDER

Remind students that objective pronouns receive the action of verbs or act as objects of prepositions. Write the following sentences on the chalkboard. Have students identify the objective pronouns and tell how they are used.

1. Cecelia left me there for two hours. [*me*—direct object]
2. Raphael gave her his jacket. [*her*—indirect object]
3. As soon as we got the package, we passed it on to them. [*it*—direct object; *them*—object of preposition]

MEETING *individual* NEEDS

LEP/ESL

General Strategies. To help English-language learners perform well on **Exercises 4** and **5**, give them the option of making small pronoun charts such as the one on p. 635 that they can refer to as they work. If they feel ready to sort out the forms in their heads without using a chart, encourage them to do so.

MEETING *individual* NEEDS

LEARNING STYLES

Visual Learners. Some students may find it helpful to visualize objective pronouns as followers. Write on the chalkboard several sentences that use objective pronouns (perhaps the example sentences for each rule). Draw an arrow from the verb or preposition to the objective pronoun. Then write out several nonstandard usages such as "Us boys went first" or "Ella and him walked home." Draw arrows to show that in nonstandard usage, the objective case leads rather than follows.

22d. An ***indirect object*** is in the objective case.

An *indirect object* comes between an action verb and a direct object and tells *to whom or what* or *for whom or what*.

EXAMPLES   Coach Mendez gave **them** a pep talk. [*Them* tells *to whom* Coach Mendez gave a pep talk.]
His mother built **him** a footlocker. [*Him* tells *for whom* his mother built a footlocker.]
The science teacher gave **us** posters of the solar system. [*Us* tells *to whom* the teacher gave posters.]

To help you choose the correct pronoun in a compound indirect object, try each form of the pronoun separately in the sentence.

EXAMPLE: Our neighbor gave Kristen and (*I, me*) a job for the summer.
Our neighbor gave *I* a job for the summer.
Our neighbor gave *me* a job for the summer.

ANSWER: Our neighbor gave Kristen and **me** a job for the summer.

☞ REFERENCE NOTE: For more information about indirect objects, see pages 492–493.

▶ ORAL PRACTICE 2   **Using Pronouns as Direct Objects and Indirect Objects**

Read the following sentences aloud, stressing the italicized pronouns.

1. The hot lentil soup burned Ahmad and *me*.
2. Li showed Raúl and *her* the new kite.
3. The stray dog followed *her* and *him* all the way to school.
4. Did you expect *us* or *them*?
5. The doctor gave *her* and *me* flu shots.
6. Carol helped Sarah and *him* with their chores.
7. Have you seen the Romanos or *them*?
8. After supper Mrs. Karras gave *us* some baklava for dessert.

22d

EXERCISE 5

Using Personal Pronouns as Indirect Objects

These photographs show the changing face of Abraham Lincoln, sixteenth President of the United States. He was the first president to have a beard. There's a legend that Lincoln grew his beard after receiving a letter from a young girl. She suggested that Lincoln would look better if he had one. He grew a beard in 1860 and kept it the rest of his life. Do you agree with the girl? Does Lincoln look better with a beard? Write five sentences about what you think of the change. In each sentence, use a personal pronoun as an indirect object. Use at least three different personal pronouns. Underline the indirect object in each of your sentences.

EXAMPLES
1. *A beard gives him an important look.*
2. *Lincoln should have written her a letter saying he didn't want a beard.*

ANSWERS
Exercise 5

Sentences will vary. Here are some possibilities:

1. Judging from the pictures, I feel the girl gave him good advice.
2. When you showed me the picture of Lincoln without a beard, I was surprised.
3. The beard gives him a more mature look.
4. I wonder if Lincoln ever gave her any thanks for the suggestion.
5. I wonder if Lincoln ever wrote her a letter about growing the beard.

COOPERATIVE LEARNING

Students may need reminding that they use pronouns constantly, whether or not they identify them as such. Put students into teams. Provide a variety of books, magazines, and newspapers, and set up an objective-pronoun scavenger hunt. The winning team will record the most examples of objective pronouns from the publications in the established time. Remind them that *you* and *it* may be in the objective case, depending on usage. You might let students use highlighters to mark examples from newspapers and magazines. Offer double credit if a team identifies whether the usage illustrates **Rule 22c, 22d,** or **22e.**

INTEGRATING THE LANGUAGE ARTS

Usage and Listening. To strengthen students' recognition of pronouns, have them listen as you read each sentence in **Oral Practice 3** aloud. Then ask a volunteer to identify the objective pronoun(s) in each sentence. For further practice, have students name the nominative case of the pronoun.

USAGE

22e. An *object of a preposition* is in the objective case.

The *object of a preposition* is a noun or a pronoun that follows a preposition. Together, the preposition, its object, and any modifiers of that object make a *prepositional phrase.*

EXAMPLES
to **Lee**	in an **hour**	like red **clay**
without **me**	near **her**	except **them**
for **him**	by **us**	next to **us**

☞ REFERENCE NOTE: For a list of prepositions, see page 474. For more discussion of prepositional phrases, use pages 506–509.

A pronoun used as the object of a preposition should always be in the objective case.

EXAMPLES When did you mail the package to **them**? [*Them* is the object of the preposition *to.*]
Are you still planning to go to the movies with **us**? [*Us* is the object of the preposition *with.*]
The reward money was divided equally between **him** and **her.** [*Him* and *her* are the objects of the preposition *between.*]

▷ ORAL PRACTICE 3 **Using Pronouns as Objects of Prepositions**

Read the following sentences aloud, stressing the italicized words.

1. The safari continued *without her* and *me.*
2. Everyone *except us* saw the Navajo rugs.
3. We stood *beside* their families and *them* during the ceremony.
4. Do you have any suggestions *for* Jalene or *me*?
5. The clowns talked *to* Claire and *him.*
6. Give this *to* either your father or *her.*
7. With the help *of* Juan and *her,* we built a fire and set up camp.
8. There was a spelling bee *between us* and *them.*

LESSON 5 (pp. 647–652)
SPECIAL PRONOUN PROBLEMS

OBJECTIVES
- To read aloud sentences that contain *who* and *whom*
- To identify correct forms of pronouns
- To use personal pronouns in a journal entry

22e

 EXERCISE 6 **Choosing Pronouns Used as Objects of Prepositions**

Choose appropriate pronouns for the blanks in the following sentences. Use a variety of pronouns, but do not use *you* or *it*. Responses will vary. All pronouns should be in the objective case.

EXAMPLE   **1.** We could not find all of ____.
  1. *them*

1. The teacher read to André and ____ a saying by Confucius about friendship.
2. I made an appointment for ____ and you.
3. There are some seats behind Lusita and ____.
4. No one except Patrice and ____ was studying.
5. I couldn't have done it without you and ____.
6. Why didn't you speak to Christie and ____?
7. Our team has played basketball against the Jets and ____.
8. I was near you and ____ during the parade.
9. Just between you and ____, I think our chances are good.
10. Did you go with ____ to the Fall Harvest Festival at the Ozark Folk Center?

Special Pronoun Problems

Who and *Whom*

The pronoun *who* has different forms in the nominative and objective cases. *Who* is the nominative form; *whom* is the objective form.

NOTE: In spoken English, the use of *whom* is becoming less common. In fact, when you are speaking, you may correctly begin any question with *who* regardless of the grammar of the sentence. In written English, however, you should distinguish between *who* and *whom*. *Who* is used as a subject or a predicate nominative, and *whom* is used as an object.

PROGRAM MANAGER

SPECIAL PRONOUN PROBLEMS

- **Independent Practice/Reteaching** For instruction and exercises, see *Who* and *Whom* and **Pronouns with Appositives** in *Language Skills Practice and Assessment,* pp. 155–156.
- **Computer Guided Instruction** For additional instruction and practice with special pronoun problems, see **Lesson 19** in *Language Workshop CD-ROM.*
- **Practice** To help less-advanced students with additional instruction and practice with special pronoun problems, see **Chapter 19** in *English Workshop, Second Course,* pp. 201–204.

QUICK REMINDER

Write the following sentences on the chalkboard and have students determine if the underlined pronoun is used as a subject or an object:

1. <u>Whom</u> did you follow? [object]
2. I didn't know <u>who</u> was coming. [subject]
3. <u>Who</u> is the new captain? [subject]
4. From <u>whom</u> did you get the answer? [object]
5. Anyone <u>who</u> has read the book has enjoyed it. [subject]

Ask students what conclusion they can draw about the use of *who* and *whom*. [*Who* is a nominative case pronoun; *whom* is an objective case pronoun.]

USAGE

647

MEETING *individual* NEEDS

LEP/ESL

Spanish. In Spanish *who* does not change form when used as an object, so Spanish-speaking students do not have a first-language context for this concept. You may want to have students practice reading aloud sentences in which *who* and *whom* are used correctly. You could also have students work in pairs to create original sentences using *who* and *whom.* After you check for correct usage, suggest that students read the sentences aloud for reinforcement.

STUDENTS WITH SPECIAL NEEDS

Oral practices can be useful in teaching some students to develop an ear for recognizing standard and non-standard usage. Recording the oral practices provides a set of model sentences for students to hear repeatedly without their having to struggle to read aloud.

648 *Using Pronouns Correctly*

When you are choosing between *who* or *whom* in a subordinate clause, follow these steps:

STEP 1:	Find the subordinate clause.
STEP 2:	Decide how the pronoun is used in the clause—as subject, predicate nominative, object of the verb, or object of a preposition.
STEP 3:	Determine the case of the pronoun according to the rules of standard English.
STEP 4:	Select the correct form of the pronoun.

EXAMPLE:	Do you know (*who, whom*) they are?
STEP 1:	The subordinate clause is (*who, whom*) *they are.*
STEP 2:	In this clause, the subject is *they,* the verb is *are,* and the pronoun is the predicate nominative: *they are* (*who, whom*).
STEP 3:	A pronoun used as a predicate nominative should be in the nominative case.
STEP 4:	The nominative form is *who.*
ANSWER:	Do you know **who** they are?

EXAMPLE:	Isaac Bashevis Singer, (*who, whom*) I admire, wrote interesting books.
STEP 1:	The subordinate clause is (*who, whom*) *I admire.*
STEP 2:	In this clause, the subject is *I,* and the verb is *admire.* The pronoun is the direct object of the verb: *I admire* (*who, whom*).
STEP 3:	A pronoun used as a direct object should be in the objective case.
STEP 4:	The objective form is *whom.*
ANSWER:	Isaac Bashevis Singer, **whom** I admire, wrote interesting books.

ORAL PRACTICE 4 **Using *Who* and *Whom* Correctly**

Read the following sentences aloud, stressing the italicized pronouns.

1. Our team needs a pitcher *who* can throw curve balls.
2. For *whom* do the gauchos in Argentina work?
3. The gauchos work for ranch owners *who* often live in other parts of the world.

4. Dr. Martin Luther King, Jr., was a man *whom* we honor.
5. Is he the new student to *whom* this locker belongs?
6. The Inuit, *who* are sometimes called Eskimos, live along the northern coast of Labrador.
7. *Who* won the speech contest?
8. *Whom* did they suggest for the job?

Pronouns with Appositives

Sometimes a pronoun is followed directly by a noun that identifies the pronoun. Such a noun is called an *appositive.* To help you choose which pronoun to use before an appositive, omit the appositive and try each form of the pronoun separately.

EXAMPLE: **(We, Us) cheerleaders practice after school.**
   [*Cheerleaders* is the appositive identifying the pronoun.]
   ***We* practice after school.**
   ***Us* practice after school.**
ANSWER: **We cheerleaders practice after school.**

EXAMPLE: **The coach threw a party for (we, us) players.**
   [*Players* is the appositive identifying the pronoun.]
   The coach threw a party for *we*.
   The coach threw a party for *us*.
ANSWER: **The coach threw a party for us players.**

☞ REFERENCE NOTE: For more information about appositives, see page 526.

▶ EXERCISE 7   **Identifying Correct Forms of Pronouns**

For each of the following sentences, choose the <u>correct pronoun</u> in parentheses.

1. (*Who*, Whom) selected the new team captain?
2. (*We*, Us) students are having a carnival to raise money.
3. The head nurse gave (we, *us*) volunteers a tour of the new hospital wing.

USAGE

USAGE

OBJECTIVES

- To choose correct forms of pronouns and to identify their uses
- To write sentences employing standard English pronoun usage

4. Did you know that (*we*, *us*) girls are going to the concert?
5. From (*who*, *whom*) did you order the food?

▶ REVIEW B   **Identifying Correct Forms of Pronouns**

For each of the following sentences, identify the <u>correct pronoun</u> in parentheses. Then, tell whether the pronoun is used as the *subject, predicate nominative, direct object, indirect object,* or *object of a preposition.*

EXAMPLE   **1. Say hello to (*she*, *her*) and Anna.**
              1. her—object of a preposition

1. Tulips surround (*we*, *us*) during May in Holland, Michigan. **1.** d.o.
2. The audience clapped for Rudy and (*he*, *him*). **2.** o.p.
3. The best singer in the choir is (*she*, *her*). **3.** p.n.
4. The officer gave (*we*, *us*) girls a ride home. **4.** i.o.
5. I wrote a short story about my great-grandpa and (*he*, *him*) last week. **5.** o.p.
6. Daniel and (*me*, *I*) read a book about Pelé, the great soccer player. **6.** s.
7. Last year's winner was (*he*, *him*). **7.** p.n.
8. To (*who*, *whom*) did you send invitations? **8.** o.p.
9. Please tell me (*who*, *whom*) the girl in the yellow dress is. **9.** p.n.
10. (*We*, *Us*) sisters could help Dad with the dishes. **10.** s.

▶ REVIEW C   **Identifying Personal Pronouns and Their Uses**

Each sentence in the following paragraph contains at least one personal pronoun. Identify each <u>personal pronoun</u> and tell whether it is used as the *subject, predicate nominative, direct object, indirect object,* or *object of a preposition.*

EXAMPLE   **[1] I enjoy watching Edward James Olmos in movies and television shows because he always plays such interesting characters.**
              1. I—subject; he—subject

MEETING *individual* **NEEDS**

LESS-ADVANCED STUDENTS
Students may be able to choose the correct pronoun in a sentence but have difficulty identifying its grammatical function. You may want to limit the focus in **Reviews B–D** by asking students only to distinguish between objective and nominative pronoun forms. Offer multisensory reinforcement of the cases by drawing boxes labeled "nominative" and "objective" on the chalkboard. Have students come forward to write correct responses for **Reviews B** and **C** in the appropriate box.

[1] The cowboy in this picture from the movie *The Ballad of Gregorio Cortez* is <u>he</u>. [2] In the movie, <u>he</u> plays an innocent man hunted by Texas Rangers. [3] The film will give <u>you</u> a good idea of Olmos's acting talents. [4] After I saw <u>him</u> in this movie, <u>I</u> wanted to know more about <u>him</u>. [5] A librarian gave <u>me</u> a book of modern biographies. [6] <u>I</u> read that Olmos's father came from Mexico but that the actor was born in Los Angeles. [7] Growing up, Olmos faced the problems of poverty and gang violence, but <u>he</u> overcame <u>them</u>. [8] Before becoming a successful actor, <u>he</u> played baseball, sang in a band, and moved furniture. [9] In 1978, Olmos's role in the play *Zoot Suit* gave <u>him</u> the big break <u>he</u> needed in show business. [10] Later, the movie *Stand and Deliver*, in which <u>he</u> played math teacher Jaime Escalante, earned <u>him</u> widespread praise.

1. p.n.
2. s.
3. i.o.
4. d.o./ s./o.p.
5. i.o.
6. s.
7. s./d.o.
8. s.
9. i.o. /s.
10. s./ i.o.

▶ REVIEW D   **Using Correct Forms of Personal Pronouns**

Oh, no! Not *another* test on Friday! You were absent from school all last week, and you're just beginning to catch up. Somehow, you've got to convince your teacher to let you take the test next week. Write ten sentences stating your reasons why the teacher should postpone giving you the test. In your sentences, use at least five personal pronouns in the nominative case and five in the objective case. Underline each personal pronoun you use and be prepared to identify how each is used.

EXAMPLE   **1.** *I was sick last week, and studying for another test would give me eye strain.*

USAGE

USAGE

651

OBJECTIVES

- To proofread for standard English pronoun usage
- To choose correct nominative and objective pronouns in sentences and in a paragraph

652 *Using Pronouns Correctly*

PICTURE THIS

Some students might have trouble relating to the rural setting of the picture or to the idea of home-baked goods. Let students know that at the turn of the century, berry picking could have been an important source of food or income for some children and their families, although the outing pictured here is probably recreational.

You may want to have students underline all their pronouns and then work with partners in the revision and proofreading stages.

PICTURE THIS

You're a member of this berry-picking party in Massachusetts in 1873. While you're picking berries, everyone talks about all the delicious treats you'll make from the berries. When your bucket is full, you sit down in the shade to relax. You take your journal out of your lunch basket and begin jotting down some notes to help you remember the day. Write a journal entry about berry picking and your plans for this bucket of ripe berries. In your paragraph, use at least five personal pronouns in the nominative case and five in the objective case.

Subject: berry picking
Audience: yourself
Purpose: to record your experience; to plan

Review: Posttest

A. Proofreading for Correct Forms of Pronouns

Most of the following sentences contain at least one pronoun that has been used incorrectly. Identify each of these incorrect pronouns, and then give its correct form. If the sentence is correct, write C.

EXAMPLE   **1. The teacher told Derek and I a funny story.**
    1. *I—me*

1. That announcer always irritates my father and ˄I.   **1.** me
2. The winners of the science fair were Felicia and he.   **2.** C
3. To ˄who did you and Marie send flowers?   **3.** whom
4. ˄Us teammates have to stick together, right?   **4.** We
5. Aunt Ida bought ˄we boys some boiled peanuts.   **5.** us
6. Coach Johnson said he was proud of Ling and ˄I.   **6.** me
7. Is he the person ˄who we met at Dan's party?   **7.** whom
8. We split the pizza between ˄he and ˄I.   **8.** him/me
9. My grandmother and ˄me enjoy the English custom of having afternoon tea.   **9.** I
10. The little boy asked Neil and him for help.   **10.** C

B. Identifying Correct Forms of Personal Pronouns

For each sentence in the following paragraph, choose the correct pronoun from the pair in parentheses.

EXAMPLE   **[1] Mrs. Lang gave (*we*, *us*) third-period students a list of good books for summer reading.**
    1. *us*

[11] Beth and (*I*, *me*) plan to read the first five books on Mrs. Lang's list soon. [12] We asked (*she*, *her*) for some more information about them. [13] (*She*, *Her*) said that *The Man Who Was Poe* is by Avi. [14] The author of *The True Confessions of Charlotte Doyle* is also (*he*, *him*). [15] We probably will like Avi's books because (*they*, *them*) combine fiction and history. [16] Both of (*we*, *us*) want to read *Where the Lilies Bloom* by Vera and Bill Cleaver, too. [17] Together, the two of (*they*, *them*) have written sixteen books for young readers. [18] The first book (*I*, *me*) am going to read is *Jacob Have I Loved* by Katherine Paterson. [19] But Beth said that *A Gathering of Days* by Joan W. Blos will be the first book for (*she*, *her*). [20] Mrs. Lang told Beth and (*I*, *me*) that our summer reading project is a good idea.

USAGE

DIAGNOSTIC TEST

OBJECTIVES

- To revise sentences by using the correct form of modifiers
- To revise sentences by correcting misplaced and dangling modifiers

PROGRAM MANAGER

FOR THE WHOLE CHAPTER

- **Review** For exercises on chapter concepts, see **Review Form A** and **Review Form B** in *Language Skills Practice and Assessment,* pp. 170–173.

- **Assessment** For additional testing, see **Usage Pretests** and **Usage Mastery Tests** in *Language Skills Practice and Assessment,* pp. 115–120 and pp. 191–198.

CHAPTER OVERVIEW

The first part of this chapter covers the correct use of adjectives and adverbs including the distinction between *good* and *well*, the use of comparatives and superlatives, and the avoidance of double negatives. The second part deals with the correct placement of modifying phrases and clauses in sentences. The **Writing Application** asks students to place modifying phrases and clauses correctly in a friendly letter.

The correct use of modifiers is essential for clear writing. Therefore, you may want to integrate this chapter with the revision stage of writing assignments.

23 USING MODIFIERS CORRECTLY

Comparison and Placement

Diagnostic Test

A. Using the Correct Forms of Modifiers

The following sentences contain errors in the use of modifiers. Identify the error in each sentence. Then, revise the sentence, using the correct form of the modifier.

EXAMPLE **1.** I never get to have no fun.
1. *never, no—I never get to have any fun.*

1. Of all the characters in the movie *Robin Hood,* the one played by Morgan Freeman is the ~~most funniest~~. **1.** funniest
2. Alan thinks that this dessert tastes ~~gooder~~ than the others. **2.** better
3. I ~~couldn't~~ hardly believe she said that. **3.** could
4. Yoshi is the ~~tallest~~ of the twins. **4.** taller
5. The movie made me ~~curiouser~~ about Spanish settlements in the Philippines. **5.** more curious
6. The movie doesn't cost much, but I ~~don't have no~~ money. **6.** don't have any [*or* have no]

7. They offer so many combinations that I don't know which one I like ∧~~more~~. **7.** most
8. The house on Drury Avenue is the one we like the ∧~~bestest~~. **8.** best
9. There's nothing I like to eat for supper ~~more~~ better than barbecued chicken.
10. Why doesn't the teacher give us questions that are ∧~~more easier~~? **10.** easier

B. Correcting Misplaced and Dangling Modifiers

Each of the following sentences contains a misplaced or dangling modifier in italics. Revise each sentence so that it is clear and correct.   **Revisions will vary.**

EXAMPLE **1.** *Waiting at the curb for the bus,* a car splashed water on me.
   1. *While I was waiting at the curb for the bus, a car splashed water on me.*

11. ∧*Looking* in her purse, two French francs and one Italian lira were all she found. **11.** When she looked
12. The library∧has several books about dinosaurs~~in our school~~. **12.** in our school
13. ∧*Sleeping soundly,* Howard woke his father∧~~when supper was ready~~. **13.** When supper was ready, /,who was sleeping soundly.
14. The book ~~is not in the library~~ *that I wanted to read*∧ **14.** is not in the library.
15. Aunt Lucia sent away a coupon∧for a free recipe book~~in a magazine~~. **15.** in a magazine
16. ∧*Alarmed,* a sudden gust of wind swept through the camp and battered our tent. **16.** We were alarmed when
17. *Left alone for the first time in his life,* a loud sound in the night scared my little brother∧ **17.** , who had been left alone for the first time in his life.
18. *After* ∧*eating* all their food, we put the cats outside. **18.** they ate
19. *Often slaughtered for their tusks,* many African nations prohibit the hunting of elephants∧ **19.** , which are often slaughtered for their tusks.
20. *Sitting in the bleachers,* ∧the outfielder∧~~caught~~ the ball right in front of us. **20.** we saw/catch

655

OBJECTIVE

• To use *good* and *well* correctly in speaking and in writing

 **PROGRAM MANAGER**

GOOD AND *WELL*

■ **Independent Practice/ Reteaching** For instruction and exercises, see *Good* and *Well* in *Language Skills Practice and Assessment,* p. 163.

■ **Computer Guided Instruction** For additional instruction and practice with *good* and *well,* see **Lesson 21** in *Language Workshop CD-ROM.*

■ **Practice** To help less-advanced students with additional instruction and practice with *good* and *well,* see **Chapter 21** in *English Workshop, Second Course,* pp. 223–224.

✔ QUICK REMINDER

Write the following sentences on the chalkboard. Have students fill in the blanks with *good* or *well.*

1. I can't roller-skate very _____. [well]
2. You can skate as _____ as I can. [well]
3. Maybe we both need a _____ teacher. [good]

Remind students that *good* modifies a noun or a pronoun and *well* modifies a verb.

---

656 Using Modifiers Correctly

656 *Using Modifiers Correctly*

Good and *Well*

23a. Use *good* to modify a noun or a pronoun. Use *well* to modify a verb.

EXAMPLES **Whitney Houston's voice sounded very good to me.** [*Good* modifies the noun *voice.*]
Whitney Houston sang the national anthem very well. [*Well* modifies the verb *sang.*]

Good should never be used to modify a verb.

NONSTANDARD **Paula does good in all her school subjects.**
STANDARD **Paula does well in all her school subjects.**
[*Well* modifies the verb *does.*]

NONSTANDARD **The mariachi band can play good.**
STANDARD **The mariachi band can play well.**
[*Well* modifies the verb *can play.*]

Well can be used as an adjective meaning "in good health" or "healthy."

EXAMPLES **Rammel feels well today.** [Meaning "in good health," *well* modifies the noun *Rammel.*]

☞ REFERENCE NOTE: For more about *good* and *well,* see page 687.

 ORAL PRACTICE   **Using *Well* Correctly**

Read the following sentences aloud, stressing the modifier *well.*

1. Everyone did *well* on the test.
2. We work *well* together.
3. Do you sing as *well* as your sister does?
4. I can't water-ski very *well.*
5. How *well* can you write?
6. All went *well* for the Korean gymnastics team.
7. Our class pictures turned out *well.*
8. The freshman goalie can block as *well* as the senior.

COMPARISON OF MODIFIERS Rule 23b

OBJECTIVES

- To form the degrees of comparison of modifiers correctly
- To write sentences using the comparative form of modifiers correctly

Comparison of Modifiers **657**

23a

▶ EXERCISE 1 **Using *Good* and *Well* Correctly**

Use *good* or *well* to complete each of the following sentences correctly.

EXAMPLE **1.** We danced ____ at the recital.
1. *well*

1. Melba did not run as ____ during the second race. **1.** well
2. The casserole tasted ____ to us. **2.** good
3. How ____ does she play the part? **3.** well
4. Everyone could hear the huge Swiss alphorn very ____ when the man played it. **4.** well
5. He certainly looks ____ in spite of his illness. **5.** well
6. I gave them directions as ____ as I could. **6.** well
7. The children behaved very ____. **7.** well
8. Bagels with cream cheese always taste ____ to him. **8.** good
9. The debate did not go as ____ as we had hoped. **9.** well
10. How ____ the pool looks on such a hot day! **10.** good

Comparison of Modifiers

A *modifier* describes or limits the meaning of another word. The two kinds of modifiers—adjectives and adverbs—may be used to compare things. In making comparisons, adjectives and adverbs take different forms. The specific form that is used depends upon how many syllables the modifier has and how many things are being compared.

ADJECTIVES   This building is **tall.** [no comparison]
This building is **taller** than that one. [one compared with another]
This building is the **tallest** one in the world. [one compared with many others]

ADVERBS   I ski **frequently.** [no comparison]
I ski **more frequently** than she does. [one compared with another]
Of the three of us, I ski **most frequently.** [one compared with two others]

USAGE

PROGRAM MANAGER

COMPARISON OF MODIFIERS

- **Independent Practice/ Reteaching** For instruction and exercises, see **Comparison of Modifiers** in *Language Skills Practice and Assessment,* p. 164.

- **Computer Guided Instruction** For additional instruction and practice with comparison of modifiers, see **Lesson 20** in *Language Workshop CD-ROM.*

- **Practice** To help less-advanced students with additional instruction and practice with comparison of modifiers, see **Chapter 20** in *English Workshop, Second Course,* pp. 207–210.

QUICK REMINDER

Write the following sentences on the chalkboard. Have students decide which choice offered in parentheses completes each sentence correctly.

1. Which star is the (brightest, most bright)? [brightest]
2. Your message is (importanter, more important) than mine. [more important]
3. What is the (prettiest, most pretty) song? [prettiest]

You may want to remind students that the number of syllables in the modifier can help determine whether to add *–er/–est* or *more/most.*

USAGE

657

USAGE

23b. The three degrees of comparison of modifiers are *positive, comparative,* and *superlative.*

POSITIVE	COMPARATIVE	SUPERLATIVE
weak	weaker	weakest
proudly	more proudly	most proudly
likely	less likely	least likely
bad	worse	worst

Regular Comparison

(1) Most one-syllable modifiers form their comparative and superlative degrees by adding *–er* and *–est.*

POSITIVE	COMPARATIVE	SUPERLATIVE
near	nearer	nearest
bright	brighter	brightest
brave	braver	bravest
dry	drier	driest

👉 **REFERENCE NOTE:** For guidelines on how to spell words when adding *–er* or *–est,* see pages 803–805.

(2) Some two-syllable modifiers form their comparative and superlative degrees by adding *–er* and *–est.* Other two-syllable modifiers form their comparative and superlative degrees by using *more* and *most.*

POSITIVE	COMPARATIVE	SUPERLATIVE
simple	simpler	simplest
healthy	healthier	healthiest
clearly	more clearly	most clearly
often	more often	most often

23b

When you are not sure about which way a two-syllable modifier forms its degrees of comparison, look up the word in a dictionary.

(3) Modifiers that have three or more syllables form their comparative and superlative degrees by using *more* and *most.*

POSITIVE	COMPARATIVE	SUPERLATIVE
important	more important	most important
creative	more creative	most creative
happily	more happily	most happily
accurately	more accurately	most accurately

EXERCISE 2 **Forming the Degrees of Comparison of Modifiers**

Give the forms for the comparative and superlative degrees of the following modifiers.

EXAMPLE **1.** long
      1. *longer; longest*

1. slow
2. cautiously
3. early
4. thankful
5. possible
6. short
7. easy
8. confident
9. seriously
10. loyal

(4) To show decreasing comparisons, all modifiers form their comparative and superlative degrees with *less* and *least.*

POSITIVE	COMPARATIVE	SUPERLATIVE
safe	less safe	least safe
expensive	less expensive	least expensive
often	less often	least often
gracefully	less gracefully	least gracefully

USAGE

INTEGRATING THE LANGUAGE ARTS

Usage and Dictionary Skills. By having students look up the word *gentle,* you may want to demonstrate how a dictionary indicates degrees of comparison. Point out the *–er* and *–est* endings, and indicate that the comparative form is *gentler* and the superlative form is *gentlest.* Remind students that if the comparative and superlative forms are not listed in a dictionary, they usually are formed by adding *more* and *most.*

Usage and Spelling. Before assigning **Exercise 2,** you may want to review the following spelling rule:

    For words ending in *–y* preceded by a consonant, change the *–y* to *i* before any suffix that does not begin with *i.*

    Illustrate the rule by writing *happy, happier,* and *happiest* on the chalkboard.

ANSWERS
Exercise 2

1. slower; slowest
2. more cautiously; most cautiously
3. earlier; earliest
4. more thankful; most thankful
5. more possible; most possible
6. shorter; shortest
7. easier; easiest
8. more confident; most confident
9. more seriously; most seriously
10. more loyal; most loyal

USAGE

659

ANSWERS

Exercise 3

Responses will vary. You may want to remind students to use dictionaries to check any comparative and superlative forms they are unsure of.

INTEGRATING THE LANGUAGE ARTS

Literature Link. Initiate a brief discussion of the importance of word choice to poets. Explain that because of poetry's condensed form and because poets use words to create images, word choice is particularly important. If your literature textbook contains the selection, have students read "The Secret Heart" by Robert P. Tristram Coffin, and ask them why they think the poet uses the superlative form *stillest* in the third line. [Students might say that the superlative form indicates that this hour of the night differs from any other hour, thus making it special. The use of *stillest* also sets the mood of quiet and peace.]

REVIEW A

OBJECTIVE

• To form the comparative and superlative degrees of modifiers

 EXERCISE 3 **Using Comparison Forms of Adjectives**

Just look up in any big city and you'll see skyscrapers. They've towered over cities since the 1930s. Skyscrapers have been built all over the world, but the tallest ones are in the United States. The chart below contains information about seven skyscrapers. Use this information to write five sentences comparing these skyscrapers. Use three comparative and two superlative forms of adjectives. Also, make one of your sentences a decreasing comparison, using *less* or *least*. Underline the adjectives you use.

EXAMPLES
1. *The Empire State Building is <u>taller</u> than the John Hancock Center.*
2. *Of the seven buildings, the Pittsburgh Plate Glass Building has the <u>least</u> number of stories.*

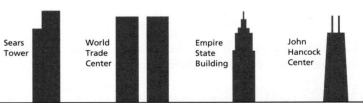

SOME INTERESTING SKYSCRAPERS		
Building	Height	Year Completed
Sears Tower, Chicago, IL	110 stories (1,454 feet)	1974
World Trade Center, New York City, NY	110 stories (1,350 feet)	1976
Empire State Building, New York City, NY	102 stories	1931
John Hancock Center, Chicago, IL	100 stories	1969
Chrysler Building, New York City, NY	77 stories	1930
One Liberty Place, Philadelphia, PA	61 stories	1987
Pittsburgh Plate Glass, Pittsburgh, PA	40 stories	1983

LESSON 4 *(pp. 661–665)*

USE OF COMPARATIVE AND SUPERLATIVE FORMS Rules 23c–23e

OBJECTIVES

- To proofread for the correct use of the comparative and superlative forms
- To revise sentences by using the correct forms of comparison
- To write sentences by using comparisons

23c

Irregular Comparison

Some modifiers do not form their comparative and superlative degrees by using the regular methods.

POSITIVE	COMPARATIVE	SUPERLATIVE
far	farther	farthest
good	better	best
well	better	best
many	more	most
much	more	most

 REVIEW A **Forming the Comparative and Superlative Degrees of Modifiers**

Give the forms for the comparative and superlative degrees of the following modifiers.

EXAMPLE **1. wasteful**
1. *more (less) wasteful; most (least) wasteful*

1. sheepish
2. simply
3. much
4. surely
5. gracious
6. quick
7. weary
8. easily
9. many
10. tasty
11. furious
12. enthusiastic
13. suddenly
14. frequently
15. generous
16. hot
17. good
18. well
19. bad
20. old

Use of Comparative and Superlative Forms

23c. Use the comparative degree when comparing two things. Use the superlative degree when comparing more than two.

COMPARATIVE   The second problem is **harder** than the first.
Luisa can perform the gymnastic routine **more gracefully** than I.
Of the two tape players, this one costs **less**.

USAGE

ANSWERS
Review A

1. more (less) sheepish; most (least) sheepish
2. more (less) simply; most (least) simply
3. more (less); most (least)
4. more (less) surely; most (least) surely
5. more (less) gracious; most (least) gracious
6. quicker (less quick); quickest (least quick)
7. wearier (less weary); weariest (least weary)
8. more (less) easily; most (least) easily
9. more (less); most (least)
10. tastier (less tasty); tastiest (least tasty)
11. more (less) furious; most (least) furious
12. more (less) enthusiastic; most (least) enthusiastic
13. more (less) suddenly; most (least) suddenly
14. more (less) frequently; most (least) frequently
15. more (less) generous; most (least) generous
16. hotter (less hot); hottest (least hot)
17. better (worse); best (worst)
18. better (worse); best (worst)
19. worse (better); worst (best)
20. older (less old); oldest (least old)

USAGE

USAGE

USAGE

SUPERLATIVE	Mount Everest is the world's **highest** mountain peak.
	This is the **most valuable** coin in my collection.
	Of the three dogs, that one barks the **least**.

Avoid the common mistake of using the superlative degree to compare two things.

NONSTANDARD	Of the two plans, this is the best one.
STANDARD	Of the two plans, this is the **better** one.

NONSTANDARD	Felicia is the youngest of the two girls.
STANDARD	Felicia is the **younger** of the two girls.

▶ EXERCISE 4 **Proofreading for Correct Use of Comparative and Superlative Forms**

Some sentences in the following paragraph contain incorrect uses of comparative and superlative forms. For each incorrect form, give the correct form. If a sentence is correct, write *C*.

EXAMPLE **[1]** My family spends the most time preparing for Cinco de Mayo than any other family on our block.
 1. *the most—more*

1. harder
2. C
3. best
4. liveliest

5. most
6. C

7. best

8. most beautiful

9. fancier
10. C

[1] My parents work even‸more hard than I do to prepare for the holiday. [2] But I get more excited about the parade and festivals. [3] I think Cinco de Mayo is the ‸bestest holiday of the year. [4] At least it's the‸more lively one in our San Antonio neighborhood. [5] Of all the speakers each year, my father always gives the‸more stirring speech about the history of the day. [6] Cinco de Mayo celebrates Mexico's most important victory over Napoleon III of France. [7] For me, the‸better part of the holiday is singing and dancing in the parade. [8] I get to wear the ‸beautifulest dresses you've ever seen. [9] They're even ‸more fancy than the ones worn by the girls in the picture on the next page. [10] Although these white dresses are certainly pretty, they are also less colorful than mine.

23d. Include the word *other* or *else* when comparing a member of a group with the rest of the group.

NONSTANDARD   Jupiter is larger than any planet in the solar system. [Jupiter is one of the planets in the solar system and cannot be larger than itself.]

STANDARD   Jupiter is larger than any **other** planet in the solar system.

NONSTANDARD   Roland can keyboard faster than anyone in his computer class. [Roland is one of the students in his computer class and cannot keyboard faster than himself.]

STANDARD   Roland can keyboard faster than anyone **else** in his computer class.

23e. Avoid using double comparisons.

A ***double comparison*** is the use of both *–er* and *more* (*less*) or both *–est* and *most* (*least*) to form a degree of comparison. For each degree, comparisons should be formed in only one of these two ways, not both.

NONSTANDARD   The Asian elephant is more smaller than the African elephant.

STANDARD   The Asian elephant is **smaller** than the African elephant.

USAGE

USAGE

663

USAGE

COOPERATIVE LEARNING

Divide the class into groups of four and have each group compose a story. Give each student a slip of paper with three modifiers written on it. Each group is to work as a team to create a story that includes each of the modifiers—a total of twelve for the group. Encourage students to use the comparative and superlative forms when appropriate. Story ideas include a space launch to Mars, an athletic contest between rival schools, a political debate, an unusual Halloween or holiday party, or the arrival of unexpected guests at a family reunion. The groups could read or dramatize their stories.

TIMESAVER

In exercises requiring revisions such as **Exercise 5**, ask students to underscore their revisions. The underscoring should simplify your grading.

NONSTANDARD	Ribbon Falls, in Yosemite National Park, is the most beautifulest waterfall I have ever seen.
STANDARD	Ribbon Falls, in Yosemite National Park, is the **most beautiful** waterfall I have ever seen.

EXERCISE 5   **Using the Degrees of Comparison Correctly**

Most of the following sentences contain incorrect forms of comparison. Revise each incorrect sentence, using the correct form. If a sentence is correct, write *C*.

EXAMPLE   **1.** It's the most homeliest dog in the world.
1. *It's the homeliest dog in the world.*

1. other
1. Juanita, the pitcher, is worse at bat than any∧ member of the team.

2. The ~~most~~ largest ancient cliff dwellings in Arizona are in Navajo National Monument.

3. That modern sculpture is the ~~most~~ strangest I've ever seen.

4. more
4. After watching the two kittens for a few minutes, Rudy chose the∧~~most~~ playful one.

5. This morning was ~~more~~ sunnier than this afternoon.

6. worse
6. Your cough sounds ∧~~worser~~ today.

7. C
7. The music on this album is better for dancing than the music on that one.

8. other
8. New York City has a larger population than any∧city in the United States.

9. Karl likes German sauerkraut ~~more~~ better than Korean kimchi.

10. C
10. She was the most talented singer in the show.

EXERCISE 6   **Using Comparisons Correctly in Sentences**

You've been elected president of a new student organization, the We Care Club. Five committees—Environment,

OBJECTIVES

- To eliminate double negatives in sentences
- To use the correct forms of negative words to write a news report

Health, Education, Society, and Family and Friends—were created at the club's first meeting. Now you must appoint committee chairpersons. To help you decide, you're jotting down your thoughts about some possible candidates. Write five sentences comparing the people you consider worthy of each position. In each of your sentences, include the word *other* or *else*. Be sure to avoid double comparisons.

EXAMPLE   **1.** *Ray Hampton understands health issues better than anyone else in our school.*

The Double Negative

23f. Avoid using double negatives.

A *double negative* is the use of two negative words to express one negative idea.

Common Negative Words			
barely	never	none	nothing
hardly	no	no one	nowhere
neither	nobody	not (–n't)	scarcely

NONSTANDARD	We don't have no extra chairs.
STANDARD	We have **no** extra chairs.
STANDARD	We **don't** have any extra chairs.

NONSTANDARD	He couldn't hardly talk.
STANDARD	He **could hardly** talk.

EXERCISE 7   **Correcting Double Negatives**

Revise each of the following sentences, eliminating the double negative.   Revisions will vary.

ANSWERS
Exercise 6

Responses will vary. Here are some possibilities:

1. Mary is more concerned about preventing air pollution than anyone else in the club is.

2. Felipe reads more newspaper and magazine articles about health issues than any other club member.

3. Sue wants to be a teacher; she is more knowledgeable about educational issues than any other student in the school.

4. Juan is more aware of social issues than any other student is.

5. Charles has a larger family than any other student in the club.

PROGRAM MANAGER

THE DOUBLE NEGATIVE

- **Independent Practice/Reteaching** For instruction and exercises, see **Double Negatives** in *Language Skills Practice and Assessment,* p. 166.

- **Computer Guided Instruction** For additional instruction and practice, see **Lesson 21** in *Language Workshop CD-ROM.*

- **Practice** To help less-advanced students, see **Chapter 20** in *English Workshop, Second Course,* pp. 211–212.

QUICK REMINDER

Write the following sentences on the chalkboard. Have students tell which are correct.

1. I don't have no paper.
2. I have no paper.
3. I don't have any paper.

[The second and third sentences are correct.]

Explain to students that the first sentence incorrectly uses a double negative (*don't* and *no*).

MEETING *individual* NEEDS

LEP/ESL

General Strategies. Some students may have difficulty avoiding double negatives. In Spanish, for example, double and triple negatives are sometimes used in the same sentence. Acknowledge the correctness of this usage in students' own languages, but stress that double negatives should be avoided in English.

PICTURE THIS

If possible, tape several radio traffic reports for students to listen to before they write. Remind students of the importance of including specific times and places because many commuters listen to traffic reports to plan their routes to and from work.

---

666 *Using Modifiers Correctly*

EXAMPLE **1.** We don't hardly have time to relax.
1. *We hardly have time to relax.*

1. has   **1.** Josie‿hasn't never been to Tennessee.
2. could **2.** Because of the heavy rain, we‿couldn't scarcely find our way home.
3. a   **3.** He never had‿no problem with public speaking.
         4. The athletes don't hardly have a break between events.
         5. The authorities don't allow no passenger cars on Michigan's popular Mackinac Island.
6. anything **6.** By the time I had made sandwiches for everyone else, I didn't have‿nothing left for me.
7. anyone **7.** I never listen to‿no one who gossips.
8. any   **8.** Your answer doesn't make‿no difference to me.
9. ever   **9.** Don't‿never say *not* and *scarcely* together.
10. has   **10.** The goalie‿doesn't have no excuse.

PICTURE THIS

You're the traffic reporter for a local radio station. From the station's helicopter, you give brief, live reports on rush hour traffic. It's almost 5:30 P.M., and this is how the freeway looks. Write a news report about the traffic. In

REVIEWS B and C

OBJECTIVES

- To revise sentences to eliminate the misuse of modifiers
- To proofread a paragraph to correct the misuse of modifiers

your report, use at least five of the common negative words listed on page 665. Be sure to avoid using any double negatives.

Subject: traffic report
Audience: radio listeners
Purpose: to inform motorists of traffic conditions

▶ REVIEW B   **Using Modifiers Correctly**

Most of the following sentences contain errors in the use of modifiers. Revise each incorrect sentence, eliminating the error. If a sentence is correct, write C.

EXAMPLE   **1.** We don't never stay after school.
            1. *We never stay after school.*

1. Which did you like best—the book or the movie?   **1.** better
2. Gina has more ideas for the festival than anyone.   **2.** else
3. The Suez Canal is ~~more~~ longer than the Panama Canal.
4. I can't hardly reason with her.   **4.** can
5. Jean and Dominic work good as a team.   **5.** well
6. Benita's bruise looks worse today than it did yesterday.   **6.** C   **7.** haven't said anything [*or* have said nothing]
7. They haven't said nothing to us about it.
8. Of the two singers, Natalie Cole has the best voice.   **8.** better
9. Which has better sound, your stereo or mine?   **9.** C
10. The cast performed extremely well.   **10.** C

▶ REVIEW C   **Proofreading for Correct Use of Modifiers**

Revisions of sentence 10 may vary.

Most of the following sentences contain errors in the use of modifiers. If a sentence contains an error, give the correct form of the modifier. If a sentence is correct, write C.

PLACEMENT OF MODIFIERS Rule 23g

OBJECTIVES

- To revise sentences to correct misplaced prepositional phrases, misplaced and dangling participial phrases, and misplaced adjective clauses
- To write sentences with introductory participial phrases
- To proofread a passage for misplaced and dangling modifiers

---

668 *Using Modifiers Correctly*

EXAMPLE **1.** Of the three programs, the one on Japanese plays was the more interesting.
  1. *more—most*

1. Before the program, I~~didn't hardly know~~ anything about Japanese theater. **1.** hardly knew
2. I learned that Japanese theater is much~~more old~~ than theater in many other countries. **2.** older
3. *No* and *Kabuki* are the two ~~most~~ best-known kinds of Japanese drama.
4. Dating from the Middle Ages, *no* is different from any form of Japanese theater. **4.** other
5. *No* plays, which are narrated in an ancient language, are performed more slowly than *Kabuki* plays. **5.** C
6. *No* plays are seen ~~lesser~~ often than the more modern *Kabuki* plays. **6.** less
7. In the West, we don't have ~~no~~ theater like Japan's *Bugaku* for the Imperial Court. **7.** any
8. I was more interested in Japan's puppet theater, the *bunraku*, than anyone in my class. **8.** else
9. Puppet theater performers have a ~~more~~ harder job than other theater performers.
10. I~~didn't never know~~ that it takes three people to operate one puppet. **10.** never knew

Placement of Modifiers

Notice how the meaning of the following sentence changes when the position of the phrase *from Canada* changes.

The professor **from Canada** gave a televised lecture on famous writers. [The phrase modifies *professor.*]
The professor gave a televised lecture on famous writers **from Canada.** [The phrase modifies *writers.*]
The professor gave a televised lecture **from Canada** on famous writers. [The phrase modifies *gave.*]

PROGRAM MANAGER

PLACEMENT OF MODIFIERS

- **Independent Practice/ Reteaching** For instruction and exercises, see **Misplaced Prepositional Phrases, Misplaced and Dangling Participial Phrases,** and **Misplaced Adjective Clauses** in *Language Skills Practice and Assessment,* pp. 167–169.

- **Computer Guided Instruction** For additional instruction and practice, see **Lesson 22** in *Language Workshop CD-ROM.*

- **Practice** To help less-advanced students, see **Chapter 20** in *English Workshop, Second Course,* pp. 213–218.

QUICK REMINDER

Write the following sentences on the chalkboard and have students revise them. Remind students to place modifying phrases and clauses as close as possible to the words they modify.

1. Snarling and growling, I tried to help the injured dog. [I tried to help the injured dog that was snarling and growling.]
2. Ms. Smith returned to work after a long vacation on Monday. [Ms. Smith returned to work on Monday after a long vacation.]

USAGE

USAGE

23g. Place modifying words, phrases, and clauses as close as possible to the words they modify.

A modifier that seems to modify the wrong word in a sentence is called a *misplaced modifier.* A modifier that does not clearly modify another word in a sentence is called a *dangling modifier.*

MISPLACED My aunt has almost seen all of the documentaries directed by Camille Billops.
CORRECT My aunt has seen **almost** all of the documentaries directed by Camille Billops.

DANGLING While vacationing in Mexico, snorkeling was the most fun.
CORRECT **While vacationing in Mexico,** we had the most fun snorkeling.

EXERCISE 8 **Correcting Errors with Modifiers**

Revise each incorrect sentence to eliminate the misplaced or dangling modifier in italics. You may need to add, delete, or rearrange words. If a sentence is correct, write *C.*

EXAMPLE **1.** *Surprised,* the finish line was only fifty yards away!
1. *I was surprised that the finish line was only fifty yards away!*

1. Both Dr. Albert Sabin and Dr. Jonas Salk succeeded in *almost* developing polio vaccines at the same time.   **1.** almost
2. Kristi Yamaguchi won a gold medal in the 1992 Olympics, *which was for figure skating.*   **2.** In the 1992 Olympics,
3. *Looking out the airplane window,* the volcano seemed ready to erupt.   **3.** I saw a/that
4. *As a new student,* the teacher introduced me to my classmates.   **4.** To my classmates/as a new student.
5. *Before eating supper,* your hands must be washed.   **5.** you must wash
6. *Recognized as the first U.S. woman to earn an international pilot's license,* Bessie Coleman dreamed of starting a flying school for African Americans.   **6.** C
7. *Hot and tired,* cold water was what the team needed.   **7.** hot and tired

USAGE

USAGE

CRITICAL THINKING

Analysis and Synthesis. To correct misplaced modifying phrases or clauses, students must first carefully analyze each sentence. You may want to suggest the following procedure for sentence analysis:

1. Find the simple subject and the simple predicate of the main clause.
2. Identify any objects or subject complements.
3. Bracket all modifying phrases and clauses and determine what word or words they modify in the sentence.

Students can synthesize the information and revise the sentences by placing the modifying phrases or clauses near the words they modify.

TIMESAVER

Because most of the exercises in this lesson focus on revising, grading these papers can be labor-intensive. You may want to have students check papers by working in small groups or in pairs. For some groups you might need to suggest revisions. You could let other groups work independently and ask you questions only when they are uncertain about a response.

8. in that old shoebox

8. Did you look ᴧfor the black-and-white photographs taken by Grandfather? ~~in that old shoebox?~~

9. From Canine

9. ᴧMy uncle got a guide dog ~~from Canine Assistants~~ Assistants *that could open cabinets, pull a wheelchair, and go for help.*

10. ~~Thrilled, my sister's~~ ᴧface lit up when she saw her present. 10. My sister was thrilled, and her

Prepositional Phrases

A *prepositional phrase* begins with a preposition and ends with a noun or a pronoun.

☞ REFERENCE NOTE: For more information about prepositions, see pages 474–477. For more discussion of prepositional phrases, see pages 475–476 and 506–509.

A prepositional phrase used as an adjective should be placed directly after the word it modifies.

MISPLACED	This book describes Nat Turner's struggle for freedom **by Judith Berry Griffin.**
CORRECT	This book **by Judith Berry Griffin** describes Nat Turner's struggle for freedom.

A prepositional phrase used as an adverb should be placed near the word it modifies.

MISPLACED	Spanish explorers discovered gold along the river that runs near my house **during the 1500s.**
CORRECT	**During the 1500s,** Spanish explorers discovered gold along the river that runs near my house.
CORRECT	Spanish explorers discovered gold **during the 1500s** along the river that runs near my house.

Avoid placing a prepositional phrase where it can modify either of two words. Place the phrase so that it clearly modifies the word you intend it to modify.

MISPLACED	Emily said **in the morning** it might get colder. [Does the phrase modify *said* or *might get?*]
CORRECT	Emily said it might get colder **in the morning.** [The phrase modifies *might get.*]
CORRECT	**In the morning** Emily said it might get colder. [The phrase modifies *said.*]

EXERCISE 9 **Correcting Misplaced Prepositional Phrases**

Find the misplaced prepositional phrases in the following sentences. Then, revise each sentence, placing the phrase near the word it modifies. Revisions may vary.

EXAMPLE **1.** I read that a satellite was launched in the news today.
　　　　　1. *I read in the news today that a satellite was launched.*

1. The nature photographer told us about filming a herd of water buffalo in class today. **1.** In class today
2. The quick steps of the Texas clog-dancing teams amazed us on the wooden stage. **2.** on the wooden stage
3. The robotic mannequins drew a huge crowd in the futuristic window display. **3.** in the futuristic window display
4. Many people watched the Fourth of July fireworks in their cars. **4.** in their cars
5. For my history report, I read three magazine articles on the Statue of Liberty. **5.** on the Statue of Liberty,
6. My aunt has promised me on Saturday that she will take me to the symphony. **6.** on Saturday.
7. There is one gymnast who can tumble as well as vault on our gymnastics team. **7.** on our gymnastics team
8. That man bought the rare painting of Pocahontas with the briefcase. **8** with the briefcase
9. The model posed gracefully in front of the statue in the designer gown. **9.** in the designer gown
10. We saw the trapeze artist swinging dangerously through our field binoculars. **10.** Through our field binoculars

Participial Phrases

A *participial phrase* consists of a verb form—either a present participle or a past participle—and its related words. A participial phrase modifies a noun or a pronoun.

 REFERENCE NOTE: For more information about participial phrases, see pages 515–516. For guidelines on using commas with participial phrases, see pages 747–748 and 753.

COMMON ERROR

Problem. Misplaced and dangling modifiers often occur in the early drafts of writing assignments when students write hurriedly and add information to the ends of sentences as afterthoughts.

Solution. Ask students to work in pairs to edit each other's papers and to look specifically for the logical order and closeness of each modifier to the word modified. Students should circle any dangling or misplaced modifier and draw an arrow to the correct placement in the paper.

USAGE

INTEGRATING THE LANGUAGE ARTS

Usage and Mechanics. Students may have trouble with comma placement as they revise sentences. Therefore, you may want to write the following rule and example sentences on the chalkboard. Remind students that a nonessential phrase adds information that isn't needed to understand the meaning of the sentence. *Rule:* Use commas to set off nonessential participial phrases.

1. Excited about the beautiful autumn day, Monica went hiking.
2. The dew on the grass, sparkling in the morning sun, looked like diamonds.

USAGE

ANSWERS
Exercise 10

Sentences will vary, but be sure that students place participial phrases near the nouns and pronouns they modify. Remind students to use a comma after introductory participial phrases.

Like a prepositional phrase, a participial phrase should be placed as close as possible to the word it modifies.

MISPLACED   Bandits chased the stagecoach **yelling wildly.**
CORRECT   **Yelling wildly,** bandits chased the stagecoach.

MISPLACED   The vase was lying on the floor **broken into many pieces.**
CORRECT   The vase, **broken into many pieces,** was lying on the floor.

To correct a dangling participial phrase, supply a word that the phrase can modify, or change the phrase to a clause.

DANGLING   **Jogging down the sidewalk,** my ankle was sprained.
CORRECT   **Jogging down the sidewalk,** I sprained my ankle.
CORRECT   I sprained my ankle **when I was jogging down the sidewalk.**

DANGLING   **Dressed in warm clothing,** the cold was no problem.
CORRECT   **Dressed in warm clothing,** we had no problem with the cold.
CORRECT   **Since we were dressed in warm clothing,** the cold was no problem.

EXERCISE 10   **Correcting Misplaced and Dangling Participial Phrases**

Revise each incorrect sentence to eliminate the misplaced or dangling modifier. You may need to add, delete, or rearrange words. If a sentence is correct, write C.

EXAMPLE   1. Dressed in our clown costumes, the police officer waved and smiled.
     1. *Seeing us dressed in our clown costumes, the police officer waved and smiled.*

1. Standing on the dock, the boat didn't look seaworthy⊙ to the sailors. **1. the sailors thought**   **2. Exploring the old house,**
2. Pat found a secret passage, exploring the old house.
3. Having brought in plenty of firewood, the cabin soon warmed up, and we fell asleep.   **3. After we**

 4. ~~Wanting~~ to see more of Mexico City, our vacation
    grew from one to two weeks. **4.** Because we wanted
 5. Questioned by reporters, the governor's view on the
    matter ~~became~~ clear. **5.** governor made his
 6. Suffering from blisters, the runner's chance of
    winning was slight. **6.** Because she was   **7.** As I was
 7. Reading a book, my cat crawled into my lap.
 8. The old suit hanging in the closet would make the
    perfect costume for the play. **8.** C
 9. Balancing precariously on the wire, ~~the tricks that~~
    the tightrope walker performed ~~were~~ amazing. **9.** tricks.
10. Exhausted after hiking in the Florida Everglades, a
    tall, cool glass of water ~~was a welcome sight.~~
                                  10. we welcomed the sight of

Adjective Clauses

An *adjective clause* is a subordinate clause that modifies a
noun or a pronoun. Most adjective clauses begin with a
relative pronoun—*that, which, who, whom,* or *whose.*

👉 REFERENCE NOTE: For more information about adjective clauses,
see pages 538–540. For more information about punctuating
adjective clauses, see pages 747–748.

Like an adjective phrase, an adjective clause should be
placed directly after the word it modifies.

MISPLACED   His parents traded an old television for a new
             tape recorder **that they no longer wanted.** [Did
             his parents no longer want a new tape recorder?]
CORRECT   His parents traded an old television **that they no
             longer wanted** for a new tape recorder.

MISPLACED   The book was about insects **that we read.** [Did
             we read the insects?]
CORRECT   The book **that we read** was about insects.

▶ EXERCISE 11 **Correcting Misplaced Adjective Clauses**

Find the misplaced adjective clauses in the following sentences. Then, revise each sentence, placing the clause
near the word it modifies. Revisions may vary. Misplaced adjective
                                clauses are underscored.

COOPERATIVE LEARNING
An often-successful reteaching
strategy is to reverse a process. You
might want to use this reversal strategy
by having students write sentences
that purposefully include misplaced
modifiers. Have students work in pairs
to create sentences with misplaced
prepositional phrases, misplaced participial phrases, dangling participial
phrases, and misplaced adjective
clauses. Then, have the groups
exchange sentences to correct the misplaced modifiers.

OBJECTIVE

• To proofread sentences for misplaced and dangling modifiers

USAGE

USAGE

674 *Using Modifiers Correctly*

EXAMPLE **1.** I retyped the first draft on clean paper which I had corrected.

  1. *I retyped the first draft, which I had corrected, on clean paper.*

1. The boy is from my school ~~that won the contest~~. **1.** that won the contest

2. We tiptoed over the ice ~~in our heavy boots~~, which had begun to crack. **2.** In our heavy boots

3. The jade sculpture was by a famous Chinese artist ~~that my cousin broke~~. **3.** that my cousin broke

4. We sometimes play soccer in one of the parks ~~on nice days~~ that are near the school. **4.** On nice days

5. Did that telethon ~~achieve its goal~~ that was on for thirty-six hours? **5.** achieve its goal?

6. Nisei Week ~~is in August~~, which is celebrated by Japanese Americans in Los Angeles. **6.** , is in August.

7. The friendly man ~~said hello to my mother~~, whose name I can't remember. **7.** , said hello to my mother.

8. The sweater ~~belongs to my best friend~~ that has a V-shaped neck. **8.** belongs to my best friend.

9. My married sister has the flu ~~who lives in Ohio~~. **9.** who lives in Ohio

10. The documentary ~~was filmed in several countries~~ which will be broadcast in the fall. **10.** , was filmed in several countries.

▶ REVIEW D **Proofreading for Misplaced and Dangling Modifiers**

Most sentences in the following paragraph contain misplaced or dangling modifiers. They may be words, prepositional phrases, participial phrases, or adjective clauses. Revise each sentence that contains a misplaced or dangling modifier. If a sentence is correct, write C.

EXAMPLE **[1]** Living in cold and treeless areas, snow houses are built by some Native Arctic people.

  1. *Living in cold and treeless areas, some Native Arctic people build snow houses.*

[1] You've probably seen pictures of houses built of snow on television. [2] Knowing that these houses are igloos, other facts about them may be new to you. [3] At one time, the word *igloo*, which means "shelter,"

ANSWERS

Review D

Revisions will vary. Here are some possibilities:

1. You've probably seen pictures on television of houses built of snow.

2. Although you know that these houses are igloos, other facts about them may be new to you.

3. C

674

OBJECTIVE

- To revise sentences so that modifiers are used correctly

applied to all types of houses. [4] However, *igloo* has come to mean houses now built of snow. [5] Used only during the winter, large blocks of snow are stacked together in building igloos. [6] Adapting to their environment long ago, snow houses provided protection against the bitter cold. [7] Look at this drawing, which shows three steps in the building of an igloo. [8] First, blocks are cut by the builders of snow. [9] Arranged in a circle about ten feet across, the builders slant the blocks inward. [10] The finished igloo that you see is dome-shaped and has a hole at the top.

REVIEW E   **Using Modifiers Correctly**

In each of the following sentences, a modifier is used incorrectly. The mistake may result from (1) a confusion of *good* and *well*, (2) an incorrect comparison, (3) the use of a double negative, or (4) a misplaced or dangling modifier. Revise each sentence so that it is clear and correct.

Revisions may vary.

EXAMPLE   **1.** This is the most interesting of the two articles.
          1. *This is the more interesting of the two articles.*

1. During last night's concert, the singing group ~~was protected~~ from being swarmed ~~by guards.~~   **1.** guards protected

---

4. Now, however, *igloo* has come to mean "a house built of snow."

5. Used only during the winter, igloos are built of large blocks of snow stacked together.

6. Adapting to their environment long ago, the native people built snow houses for protection against the bitter cold.

7. C

8. First, blocks of snow are cut by the builders.

9. The builders arrange the blocks in a circle about ten feet across and slant them inward.

10. C

MEETING *individual* NEEDS

LESS-ADVANCED STUDENTS

To simplify **Review E**, you may want to identify the type of error in each sentence:

1. misplaced prepositional phrase
2. misplaced participial phrase
3. double negative
4. misplaced adjective clause
5. incorrect comparison
6. misplaced participial phrase
7. misplaced adjective clause
8. incorrect comparison
9. dangling participial phrase
10. incorrect comparison

USAGE

REVIEW E

Teaching Note. Explain to students that moving a misplaced modifier closer to the word it modifies may not be the best revision tactic. Instead, a sentence may need to be reworded for clarity. Write the following revisions of sentence 1 on the chalkboard to show students that the second revision is clearer:

1. During last night's concert, the singing group was protected by guards from being swarmed.

2. During last night's concert, guards protected the singing group from being swarmed.

USAGE

WRITING APPLICATION

In the writing activity, students are asked to use modifiers in letters about their sports activities. You may want to let students who have no interest in sports write about any extracurricular activities in which they're involved.

676

USAGE

676 *Using Modifiers Correctly*

2. , which performed most of their old hits as well as several new tunes,

2. The group played before an extremely enthusiastic crowd, ~~performing most of their old hits as well as several new tunes.~~

3. Years ago the singers wore strange costumes and makeup so that fans ~~couldn't~~ hardly tell what their faces looked like.   **3. could**

4. ~~Bored,~~ these gimmicks no longer appealed to the fans after a while.   **4. bored**

5. They finally chose the ~~most~~ simply tailored look of the two they had considered.   **5. more**   **6. the fans barely noticed**

6. Charmed by the group's new look, a change in their singing style ~~was barely noticed by the fans.~~

7. Few fans could tell the first time they appeared in public after changing their style ~~how nervous the singers were.~~   **7. how nervous the singers were**

8. "That was the ~~most~~ scariest performance of my career," one singer remarked.   **9. Because of the hearty**

9. Cheering ~~heartily,~~ the singers' fears were relieved.

10. Both the concert and the picnic did exceptionally ~~good~~ at raising funds.   **10. well**

WRITING APPLICATION

Placing Modifying Phrases and Clauses Correctly

Have you ever put together a jigsaw puzzle? Each piece must fit in the right place. If the pieces don't fit properly, the picture appears jumbled. You can think of a sentence as a jigsaw puzzle. The words in the sentence—including any modifying phrases and clauses—are the puzzle pieces. For the sentence to make sense, the words must go in the right places.

MISPLACED   The fans supported the batter cheering and singing.

CORRECT   Cheering and singing, the fans supported the batter.

What kind of picture do you get from the first sentence? from the second sentence?

▶ WRITING ACTIVITY

You've just received a letter from a favorite aunt who is a professional athlete. She wants to hear about your sports activities and any sports events you've participated in or seen in person or on television. Write a letter to your aunt, telling her about sports you have been playing and watching. You may also want to make some predictions about upcoming events. Be sure to place modifying phrases and clauses correctly.

Prewriting You'll first need to choose a sports activity or event to write about. You may write about your own experiences in a school or community sport or about a sports event you've seen. Or you may use your imagination. You could look at the sports section of a newspaper for some ideas. Before you begin writing, make notes about the activity or event you find most interesting.

Writing As you write your first draft, try to include specific details that will interest your aunt. Organize your letter so that the details are clear and logical. Be sure to place modifying phrases and clauses as close as possible to the words they modify.

Evaluating and Revising Read over your finished letter. Is it interesting and lively? If not, revise it by adding more adjectives, adverbs, and action verbs to improve your descriptions. Underline all of the prepositional phrases, participial phrases, and adjective clauses. Check to make sure that they are correctly placed near the words they modify.

Proofreading Check your letter for errors in spelling and punctuation, especially in the address, salutation, and closing. For guidelines on correctly capitalizing and punctuating these parts of a personal letter, see pages 726, 739, and 754–755.

USAGE

CRITICAL THINKING

Evaluation. With the help of students, develop a set of criteria for evaluating the writing activity. The criteria could be used by students for peer grading. You may want to include the following items:

1. appropriateness for audience
2. clear and logical organization
3. interesting presentation
4. correct use of modifiers
5. proper form

USAGE

LESSON 7 *(pp. 678–679)*
REVIEW: POSTTEST

OBJECTIVES
- To revise sentences by using correct forms of modifiers
- To revise sentences to correct misplaced and dangling modifiers

Review: Posttest

A. Using the Correct Forms of Modifiers

Most of the sentences in the following paragraphs contain errors in the use of modifiers. Identify each error; then, revise the sentence, using the correct form of the modifier. If a sentence is correct, write *C*.

EXAMPLE [1] I didn't want to live nowhere else.
1. *didn't, nowhere—I didn't want to live anywhere else.*

1. most
2. C
3. other
4. better
5. any
6. better
7. else
8. most
9. best
11. C
13. is hardly anything
15. more

[1] The ∧wonderfull~~est~~ place in the whole world is my grandmother's house. [2] We used to live there before we got an apartment of our own. [3] Since her house is bigger than any∧house in the neighborhood, we all had plenty of room. [4] Grandma was glad to have us stay because my dad can fix things so that they're ∧~~gooder~~ than new. [5] He plastered and painted the walls in one bedroom so that I wouldn't have to share a room∧~~no~~ more with my sister. [6] I don't know which was ∧~~best~~—having so much space of my own or having privacy from my sister.

[7] My grandmother can sew better than anybody∧can. [8] She taught my sister and me how to make the∧beautifull~~est~~ clothes. [9] She has three sewing machines and my mother has one, but I like Grandma's oldest one∧~~better~~. [10] We started with the ~~more~~ simpler kinds of stitches. [11] After we could do those, Grandma showed us fancier stitches and sewing tricks. [12] For instance, she taught us to wrap thread behind buttons we sew on, so that they will be ~~more~~ easier to button. [13] We learned how to make dresses, skirts, blouses, and all sorts of other things, until now there∧~~isn't hardly nothing~~ we can't make.

[14] I was sad when we left Grandma's house, but I like our new apartment ~~more~~ better than I thought I would. [15] Luckily, we moved to a place near my grandmother's, and after school I can go over there or go home—whichever I want to do∧~~most~~.

B. Correcting Misplaced and Dangling Modifiers

Each of the following sentences contains a misplaced or a dangling modifier. Revise each sentence so that it is clear and correct.   **Revisions may vary.**

EXAMPLE **1.** Tearing away his umbrella, Mr. Pérez became drenched in the storm.
   1. *Tearing away his umbrella, the storm drenched Mr. Pérez.*

16. Our math teacher told us˄that she had been a nurse⊙ ~~yesterday.~~ **16.** yesterday   **17.** In class,
17. ˄We read a story written by Jade Snow Wong⊙~~in class.~~
18. ~~Destroyed by the fire,~~ the man looked sadly at the charred house˄ **18.** that was destroyed by fire.
19. After˄~~missing~~ the school bus, my mother gave me a ride in the car. **19.** I missed
20. ˄The fox escaped from the hounds pursuing it⊙~~with a crafty maneuver.~~ **20.** With a crafty maneuver,
21. ˄~~Walking~~ through the park, the squirrels chattered at me. **21.** As I walked
22. The cook ~~will win a new oven~~ that makes the best German potato salad˄ **22.** will win a new oven.
23. The squid ~~fascinated the students~~ preserved in formaldehyde˄ **23.** fascinated the students.
24. ˄~~Keeping~~ track of the race with binoculars, the blue car with a yellow roof pulled into the lead. **24.** As we kept
25. ˄We watched the snow pile up in drifts⊙~~inside our warm house.~~ **25.** Inside our warm house,

USAGE

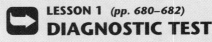

DIAGNOSTIC TEST

OBJECTIVE

• To identify and correct errors in usage

FOR THE WHOLE CHAPTER

■ **Review** For exercises on chapter concepts, see **Review Form A** and **Review Form B** in *Language Skills Practice and Assessment,* pp. 184–187.

■ **Assessment** For additional testing, see **Usage Pretests** and **Usage Mastery Tests** in *Language Skills Practice and Assessment,* pp. 115–120 and pp. 191–198.

CHAPTER OVERVIEW

This chapter treats common problems in usage in alphabetical order and gives guidelines for standard English with examples.

Some of the problems treated involve correctly distinguishing between words that sound similar but have different meanings such as *affect/effect, than/then, their/there/they're,* and *your/you're.* Other rules and examples illustrate differences between standard and nonstandard usage, such as *ain't,* that do not affect meaning but that can affect the impression one makes. Finally, some expressions are treated that are acceptable in informal English but that should be avoided in formal speech or writing, such as *how come.*

In the **Writing Application,** students are asked to employ standard English usage in writing and presenting speeches.

24 A GLOSSARY OF USAGE

Common Usage Problems

Diagnostic Test

Identifying and Correcting Errors in Usage

One sentence in each of the following sets contains an error in usage. Choose the letter of the <u>sentence that contains an error</u>. Then revise the sentence, using standard English.

EXAMPLE **1. a.** I rode a unicycle.
b. Everyone came except Michael.
c. What are the side affects of this medicine?
1. c. *What are the side effects of this medicine?*

1. a. They bought themselves new pens.
b. The balloon ~~busted~~. **1.** burst
c. Use less flour.
2. a. She did not feel well.
b. Leo ought to help us.
c. Armando ~~hisself~~ bought that. **2.** himself

3. **a.** Jerome could of come.   **3. have**
   b. This book has fewer pages.
   c. He sang well.
4. **a.** We had already been there.
   b. She feels alright now.   **4. all right**
   c. We looked everywhere for him.
5. **a.** He behaved badly.
   b. She felt badly about being late.   **5. bad**
   c. There is no talking between classes.
6. **a.** We saved ten dollars between the four of us.
   b. Bring a salad when you come.   **6. among**
   c. The chair broke.
7. **a.** She set down.   **7. sat**
   b. This news may affect his decision.
   c. They left less milk for me.
8. **a.** I cannot go unless I finish my work first.
   b. Your my friend.   **8. You're**
   c. She laid the packages on the table.
9. **a.** My father use to play the piano.   **9. used**
   b. We have a long way to go.
   c. Yesterday I read in the newspaper that Jesse Jackson is in town.
10. **a.** I know how come she left.   **10. why**
    b. It's windy.
    c. He likes this kind of movie.
11. **a.** I am somewhat hungry.
    b. Will you learn me how to ski?   **11. teach**
    c. Do as the leader does.
12. **a.** She looks as though she is exhausted.
    b. Meet me outside of the building.
    c. He wrote the letter and mailed it.
13. **a.** The reason that he works is that he wants to save money for a trip.
    b. Your backhand has improved somewhat.
    c. Their are not enough chairs.   **13. There**
14. **a.** I just bought those shoes.
    b. This here ride is broken.
    c. Try to relax.

USAGE

USING THE DIAGNOSTIC TEST

If you notice that some students are having problems with usage in their compositions, this test will provide information about each student's ability to recognize common usage problems and to generate standard formal usage. After reviewing their performance, you may decide to have students selectively work on the specific expressions or on clusters of problems with which they have difficulty. For example, items 5, 10, and 15 involve differences between formal and informal English. You might have students who are fluent in standard English concentrate on such items while you emphasize problems with standard usage for other students.

USAGE

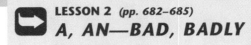

PROGRAM MANAGER

A, AN—BAD, BADLY

■ **Independent Practice/ Reteaching** For instruction and exercises, see **Common Usage Problems A** in *Language Skills Practice and Assessment,* p. 179.

■ **Computer Guided Instruction** For additional instruction and practice with common usage problems, see **Lesson 63** in *Language Workshop CD-ROM.*

■ **Practice** To help less-advanced students with additional instruction and practice with common usage problems, see **Chapter 21** in *English Workshop, Second Course,* pp. 221–222.

QUICK REMINDER

Write *all ready* and *already* on the chalkboard. As you read the following sentences aloud to students, have them write one of the two forms for each sentence:

1. When I got there, she was already gone.
2. When I got there, she was all ready to go.

Point out to students that although *all ready* and *already* sound the same, they have different spellings and different meanings. When students are writing, they need to distinguish between the forms to follow standard usage.

682

15. **a.** I am real happy. **15.** very
    b. Let's study now and go outside later.
    c. They're new in school.
16. **a.** Take the report when you go.
    b. She might have gone.
    c. Mr. Bennigan ~~he~~ is my English teacher.
17. **a.** We worked for a hour. **17.** an
    b. She accepted your invitation.
    c. They can hardly see the sign.
18. **a.** Where do you study?
    b. Divide the tasks ~~among~~ the two of us. **18.** between
    c. If he had been there, I would have seen him.
19. **a.** You should have come.
    b. Less sugar is needed.
    c. ~~It's~~ pedal is stuck. **19.** Its
20. **a.** He likes these kinds of ties.
    b. It looks like a rabbit. **20.** rose
    c. The submarine slowly ~~raised~~ to the surface.

This chapter contains an alphabetical list of common problems in English usage. You will notice throughout the chapter that some examples are labeled *standard* or *nonstandard.* **Standard English** is the most widely accepted form of English. It is used in *formal* situations, such as in speeches and compositions for school, and in *informal* situations, such as in conversation and everyday writing. **Nonstandard English** is language that does not follow the rules and guidelines of standard English.

REFERENCE NOTE: For more discussion of standard and nonstandard English, see page 394.

a, an Use *a* before words beginning with a consonant sound. Use *an* before words beginning with a vowel sound.

EXAMPLES   He did not consider himself **a** hero.
Market Avenue is **a** one-way street.
An oryx is a large antelope.
We waited in line for **an** hour.

accept, except *Accept* is a verb that means "to receive." *Except* may be either a verb or a preposition. As a verb, *except* means "to leave out" or "to exclude"; as a preposition, *except* means "other than" or "excluding."

EXAMPLES   I **accept** your apology.
Some students will be **excepted** from this assignment.
Mark has told all his friends **except** Diego.

affect, effect *Affect* is a verb meaning "to influence." *Effect* used as a verb means "to bring about." Used as a noun, *effect* means "the result of some action."

EXAMPLES   His score on this test will **affect** his final grade.
Bo and Anica's hard work **effected** a solution to the problem.
The **effects** of the medicine were immediate.

ain't Avoid this word in speaking and writing; it is nonstandard English.

all ready, already *All ready* means "completely prepared." *Already* means "previously."

EXAMPLES   The mechanic checked the engine parts to make sure they were **all ready** for assembly.
We have **already** served the refreshments.

all right Used as an adjective, *all right* means "unhurt" or "satisfactory." Used as an adverb, *all right* means "well enough." *All right* should always be written as two words.

EXAMPLES   Your work is **all right**. [adjective]
Linda fell off the horse, but she is **all right**. [adjective]
You did **all right** at the track meet. [adverb]

a lot *A lot* should always be written as two words.

EXAMPLE   Her family donated **a lot** of money to the Red Cross.

USAGE

MEETING *individual* NEEDS

LEP/ESL

General Strategies. English-language learners need to hear you pronounce *a* and *an* so that they will notice these words in the correct speech around them. Tell them that *a* is frequently pronounced as *uh,* the last sound in the word *America:* "I'd like *uh* tomato." *An* is often pronounced as *'n,* almost as though it has no vowel at all: "I'd like *'n* apple." First, pronounce slowly, and then pronounce at normal speed. Have students repeat after you.

AT-RISK STUDENTS

Students might enjoy the old saying, "*Ain't* ain't a word because it ain't in the dictionary." Point out that while *ain't* is in most modern dictionaries, it is non-standard English, and its use is very noticeable to speakers of standard English. Tell students it will be useful to them to practice substituting *isn't* or *aren't* for *ain't* so it will feel natural to them in situations such as job interviews that call for standard usage.

COMMON ERROR

Problem. Often, *effect* and *except* are used incorrectly as verbs in both speaking and writing.

Solution. The verb forms of *effect* and *except* are rare, so suggest to students that in most cases they can "Stick with the *a* for action," and use *affect* and *accept* as verbs.

USAGE

ADVANCED STUDENTS

Students who have good vocabularies may be familiar with other possible confusions with *a lot,* such as the homonym verb *allot* and the merchandising unit of a *lot.* Challenge students to write an additional entry to this glossary explaining these usages and providing an example of correct usage for each term.

A DIFFERENT APPROACH

To inspire students to use alternatives for the overused *a lot,* bring in a copy of *An Exaltation of Larks* by James Lipton. This illustrated book lists traditional names for groups of animals, such as a "pride of lions." Lipton then coins a series of modern group names such as a "slouch of models" or a "wince of dentists." Have students work in small groups to come up with collective terms for numerous items or groupings in their world—books, teachers, homework, music videos, and so on.

NOTE: Many writers overuse *a lot.* Whenever you run across *a lot* as you revise your own writing, try to replace it with a more exact word or phrase.

EXAMPLE   The Spaniards explored a lot of North America and South America.
The Spaniards explored vast areas [or *millions of square miles*] of North America and South America.

among   See **between, among.**

anywheres, everywheres, nowheres, somewheres   Use these words without the final *s.*

EXAMPLE   I didn't go **anywhere** [not *anywheres*] yesterday.

as   See **like, as.**

as if   See **like, as if, as though.**

at   Do not use *at* after *where.*

NONSTANDARD   Where is it at?
STANDARD   Where is it?

bad, badly   *Bad* is an adjective. *Badly* is an adverb.

EXAMPLES   The fish tastes **bad.** [*Bad* modifies the noun *fish.*]
The boy's wrist was sprained **badly.** [*Badly* modifies the verb *was sprained.*]

NOTE: In informal usage the expression "feel badly" has become acceptable, though ungrammatical, English.

INFORMAL   Marcia felt badly about her low grade.
FORMAL   Marcia felt **bad** about her low grade.

▶ EXERCISE 1   **Identifying Correct Usage**

Choose the <u>correct word or expression</u> from the pair in parentheses in each of the following sentences.

EXAMPLE   **1.** Korea has been in the news (*alot, a lot*) in recent years.
1. *a lot*

1. South Korea occupies the lower half of (<u>a</u>, *an*) peninsula between China and Japan.
2. According to an old Korean saying, you are never out of sight of mountains (*anywheres*, <u>*anywhere*</u>) in Korea.
3. The 1988 Olympic games in Seoul had a dramatic (*affect*, <u>*effect*</u>) on Korea's world image.
4. I looked on a map to find out where Korea's Lotte World (<u>*is*</u>, *is at*).
5. That unique cultural and athletic showcase is (*a*, <u>*an*</u>) attraction to visitors in Seoul.
6. Many Koreans come to the United States to join family members who (*all ready*, <u>*already*</u>) live here.
7. In Korea girls practice on their neighborhood swings so that they won't perform (*bad*, <u>*badly*</u>) in swinging contests during *Tano*, a spring festival.
8. Most boys hope they do (*allright*, <u>*all right*</u>) in *Tano* wrestling matches.
9. In 1446, King Sejong the Great required the Korean people to use a new alphabet, which scholars and government officials readily (<u>*accepted*</u>, *excepted*).
10. Even if you (*ain't*, <u>*aren't*</u>) interested in dancing, you'd probably enjoy watching the lively Korean folk dancers shown here.

USAGE

USAGE

VISUAL CONNECTIONS
Exploring the Subject. If you have students who are familiar with Korean culture and customs, you could ask them if they would like to share their knowledge with the class. Some students may have participated in folk-dancing groups and will be able to explain the difference between folk dancing and ordinary dancing. [Folk dancing is most often group dancing with traditional music and steps associated with a particular region or culture.]

OBJECTIVE

• To identify correct usage

QUICK REMINDER

Write the following sentences on the chalkboard. Ask students which ones sound like a newspaper account and which ones might be remarks made at a ballgame.

1. He had ought never to of let that ball get away.
2. The cheering could have been heard on the other side of the city.
3. They needed the ref to bust up that fight.
4. There was scarcely time to sit down between the next two scoring plays.

[2 and 4, newspaper report; 1 and 3, remarks at game]

Have students rewrite sentences 1 and 3 in standard English.
[**1.** He ought never to have let that ball get away. **3.** They needed the referee to break up that fight.]

686

USAGE

686 *A Glossary of Usage*

because See **reason . . . because.**

between, among Use *between* when referring to two things at a time, even though they may be part of a group containing more than two.

> EXAMPLES In homeroom, Carlos sits **between** Bob and me.
> Some players practice **between** innings. [Although a game has more than two innings, the practice occurs only between any two of them.]

Use *among* when referring to a group rather than to separate individuals.

> EXAMPLES We saved ten dollars **among** the three of us. [As a group the three saved ten dollars.]
> There was disagreement **among** the fans about the coach's decision. [The fans are thought of as a group.]

bring, take *Bring* means "to come carrying something." *Take* means "to go carrying something." Think of *bring* as related to *come* and of *take* as related to *go.*

> EXAMPLES **Bring** your skateboard when you come to my house this weekend.
> Please **take** these letters to the post office when you go.

bust, busted Avoid using these words as verbs. Use a form of either *burst* or *break.*

> EXAMPLES The balloon **burst** [not *busted*] when it touched the ceiling.
> The vase **broke** [not *busted*] when I dropped it.

could of Do not write *of* with the helping verb *could.* Write *could have.* Also avoid *ought to of, should of, would of, might of,* and *must of.*

> EXAMPLE Reva **could have** [not *could of*] played the piano.

Of is also unnecessary with *had*.

EXAMPLE   If I **had** [not *had of*] seen her, I would have said hello.

doesn't, don't *Doesn't* is the contraction of *does not*. *Don't* is the contraction of *do not*. Use *doesn't,* not *don't,* with *he, she, it, this, that,* and singular nouns.

EXAMPLES   He **doesn't** [not *don't*] know how to swim.
The price **doesn't** [not *don't*] include tax.

effect See **affect, effect.**

everywheres See **anywheres,** etc.

except See **accept, except.**

fewer, less *Fewer* is used with plural words. *Less* is used with singular words. *Fewer* tells "how many"; *less* tells "how much."

EXAMPLES   We have **fewer** tickets to sell than we thought.
These plants require **less** water.

good, well *Good* is always an adjective. Never use *good* as an adverb. Instead, use *well.*

NONSTANDARD   Nancy sang good at the audition.
STANDARD   Nancy sang **well** at the audition.

Although *well* is usually an adverb, *well* may also be used as an adjective to mean "healthy."

EXAMPLE   He didn't look **well** after eating the entire pizza all by himself.

NOTE: *Feel good* and *feel well* mean different things. *Feel good* means "to feel happy or pleased." *Feel well* means "to feel healthy."

EXAMPLES   I felt **good** [*happy*] when I got an A on my report.
He did not feel **well** [*healthy*] yesterday.

REFERENCE NOTE: For more information about the differences between *good* and *well,* see page 656.

USAGE

MEETING *individual* **NEEDS**

USAGE

had of See **could of.**

had ought, hadn't ought Unlike other verbs, *ought* is not used with *had.*

NONSTANDARD Eric had ought to help us; he hadn't ought to have missed our meeting yesterday.

STANDARD Eric **ought to** help us; he **oughtn't to have** missed our meeting yesterday.

or

Eric **should** help us; he **shouldn't have** missed our meeting yesterday.

hardly, scarcely The words *hardly* and *scarcely* convey negative meanings. They should never be used with another negative word.

EXAMPLES I **can** [not *can't*] **hardly** read your handwriting.

We **had** [not *hadn't*] **scarcely** enough food for everyone.

☞ REFERENCE NOTE: For more examples of double negatives, see page 665.

▶ EXERCISE 2 **Identifying Correct Usage**

Choose the <u>correct word or expression</u> from the pair in parentheses in each sentence.

EXAMPLE **1.** When you come to my house, (*bring, take*) that interesting book about U.S. presidents.
1. *bring*

1. Theodore Roosevelt must have (<u>*felt good*</u>, *felt well*) about having the teddy bear named for him.
2. The letter *S* in Harry S Truman's name (*don't,* <u>*doesn't*</u>) stand for anything.
3. William Henry Harrison served as president (<u>*fewer*</u>, *less*) days than any other president.
4. Herbert Hoover (*could of,* <u>*could have*</u>) kept his presidential salary, but he gave it to charity.

A Glossary of Usage   **689**

5. A president who (*doesn't*, *don't*) throw the first ball of the baseball season breaks a tradition started in 1910.
6. Both Theodore Roosevelt and Franklin Roosevelt were presidents of the United States; (*between*, *among*) them, they served a total of twenty years in office.
7. Abraham Lincoln's ability to write (*well*, *good*) led to his success in politics.
8. Woodrow Wilson believed that countries (*had ought*, *ought*) to work together in the League of Nations.
9. I (*can hardly*, *can't hardly*) imagine a president training horses, but Ulysses S. Grant did.
10. When Zachary Taylor went to the White House, he (*brought*, *took*) his old war horse with him.

▶ REVIEW A   **Correcting Errors in Usage**

Each sentence in the following paragraph contains at least one error in usage. Identify each error and write the correct form.

EXAMPLE   **1.** Between the various Native American peoples, there were alot of stories about mythological figures.
   1. *Between—Among; alot—a lot*

1. The Creek people believed that goblins, giants, and dwarfs effected their lives bad.   **1. affected/badly**

Wood engraving by Michael McCurdy.

2. The Micmacs believed that a enormous being named Glooskap created humans and animals everywheres.
2. an/ everywhere

3. This picture shows how humans busted into life because of Glooskap's magic.   **3. burst**

A DIFFERENT APPROACH
Have students write two sample sentences for each expression that they get wrong in **Review A.** If many students do poorly on the review, you might create a new practice exercise by using the students' sentences.

VISUAL CONNECTIONS
Exploring the Subject. The Micmacs are one tribe of the Algonquian Native Americans from the Northeast woodlands who feature Glooskap in their myths. Details may vary from one tribe's version to another, but all Algonquians tell stories about Glooskap's adventures in which he uses his super-human powers and size to create the natural world as well as its animal and human inhabitants. One collection of these tales is *How Glooskap Outwits the Ice Giants,* retold by Howard Norman.

USAGE

USAGE

689

HE, SHE, THEY—LIKE, AS IF, AS THOUGH

OBJECTIVES

- To write a passage correctly using the possessive pronoun *its* and the contraction *it's*
- To identify correct usage
- To use standard English in a report

4. The other animals don't appear to think that Glooskap's new creations are ~~allright~~. **4. all right**
5. The Tehuelche people of South America tell the story of Elal, a hero who brought fire to where the people were ~~at~~.
6. When the Mayas heard the thunderous approach of their god Chac, they knew he was ~~taking~~ rain to their fields. **6. bringing**
7. The Pawnee people on the plains ~~couldn't~~ hardly help noticing where the stars were. **7. could**
8. They told stories about Morning Star, who fought ~~good~~ and defeated star monsters. **8. well**
9. One sad Tewa story is about Deer Hunter, who ~~had~~ ought to have ~~excepted~~ the death of his wife, White Corn Maiden. **9. accepted**
10. Her death ~~busted~~ Deer Hunter's heart, causing him to disobey the laws of his people. **10. broke**

he, she, they Do not use an unnecessary pronoun after a noun. This error is called the ***double subject***.

NONSTANDARD	Nancy Lopez she is a famous professional golfer.
STANDARD	Nancy Lopez is a famous professional golfer.

hisself *Hisself* is nonstandard English. Use *himself*.

EXAMPLE   Ira bought **himself** [not *hisself*] a lavender polka-dot tie.

how come In informal situations, *how come* is often used instead of *why*. In formal situations, *why* should always be used.

INFORMAL	I don't know how come she's not here.
FORMAL	I don't know **why** she is not here.

its, it's *Its* is a personal pronoun in the possessive form. *It's* is a contraction of *it is* or *it has*.

EXAMPLES   **Its** handle is broken. [possessive pronoun]
It's a hot day. [contraction of *it is*]
It's been a good trip. [contraction of *it has*]

USAGE

PROGRAM MANAGER

HE, SHE, THEY—LIKE, AS IF, AS THOUGH

- **Independent Practice/ Reteaching** For instruction and exercises, see **Common Usage Problems C** in *Language Skills Practice and Assessment*, p. 181.

- **Computer Guided Instruction** For additional instruction and practice, see **Lesson 64** in *Language Workshop CD-ROM*.

- **Practice** To help less-advanced students, see **Chapter 21** in *English Workshop, Second Course*, pp. 225–226.

QUICK REMINDER

Write the following sentences on the chalkboard and have students choose the correct word in parentheses (correct usage is underlined):

1. The bird fell out of (its, it's) nest.
2. (It's, Its) easy to see from here.
3. (Its, It's) been cold here all week.

Remind students that *it's* is a contraction for *it is* or *it has*. Have them try each sentence with those phrases to see if either of them makes sense. If not, then *its* is the correct choice.

PICTURE THIS

From your bedroom window, you see this amazing sight. The house across the street is lifting off into space! Up until now, the house has appeared to be perfectly normal. However, you have wondered about the house's new owners. You're excited and want to tell your friends all about the liftoff. You decide to jot down your impressions so that you won't forget anything later. Write a page of notes about the house and its strange liftoff. In your notes, use the possessive form *its* five times. Also, use the contraction *it's* (meaning "it is" or "it has") five times.

Subject: a house that lifts off into space
Audience: friends
Purpose: to record details and thoughts; to inform

THE MYSTERIES OF HARRIS BURDICK by Chris Van Allsburg. Copyright © 1984 by Chris Van Allsburg. Reprinted by permission of Houghton Mifflin Company. All rights reserved.

USAGE

PICTURE THIS

Remind students that when they are taking notes they do not have to use full sentences. Have them take a minute to look at the picture and feel the strangeness of the situation before they begin writing. Suggest that they mention visual details, discuss their reactions, and speculate about possible causes for the liftoff. You may want to have them underline each use of *its* and *it's*.

For a model of how to use sensory and factual details to create a clear picture, refer students to **A Student Model** by Alyssa Reynolds on p. 177.

VISUAL CONNECTIONS

About the Artist. Born in Grand Rapids, Michigan, in June 1949, American artist Chris Van Allsburg is the author and illustrator of *The Polar Express* and other children's books dealing with imaginative, mysterious situations. He has received numerous awards, including the American Library Association Caldecott Medal in 1982 and 1986 and the Regina Medal in 1993. Many of Van Allsburg's works have the dreamlike, fantastic quality depicted here. He achieves this by manipulating light and shade to give the illusion of depth.

USAGE

USAGE

kind, sort, type The words *this, that, these,* and *those* should agree in number with the words *kind, sort,* and *type.*

EXAMPLES Whitney likes **this kind** of music.
Those kinds of math problems are easy.

kind of, sort of In informal situations, *kind of* and *sort of* are often used to mean "somewhat" or "rather." In formal English, *somewhat* or *rather* is preferred.

INFORMAL He seemed kind of embarrassed by our compliments.
FORMAL He seemed **somewhat** embarrassed by our compliments.

learn, teach *Learn* means "to acquire knowledge." *Teach* means "to instruct" or "to show how."

EXAMPLES I am **learning** how to use this computer.
My father is **teaching** me how to use this computer.

less See **fewer, less.**

lie, lay See page 620.

like, as In informal situations, the preposition *like* is often used instead of the conjunction *as* to introduce a clause. In formal situations, *as* is preferred.

EXAMPLE I looked up several words in my dictionary, **as** [not *like*] the teacher had suggested.

☞ REFERENCE NOTE: For more information about clauses, see Chapter 18.

like, as if, as though In informal situations, the preposition *like* is often used for the compound conjunction *as if* or *as though.* In formal situations, *as if* or *as though* is preferred.

EXAMPLES They acted **as if** [not *like*] they hadn't heard him.
You looked **as though** [not *like*] you knew the answer.

▶ EXERCISE 3   **Identifying Correct Usage**

Choose the <u>correct word or expression</u> from the pair in parentheses in each of the following sentences.

EXAMPLE   **1.** I'd like to know (*how come, why*) folk tales about animals that play tricks have always been popular.
   1. *why*

1. People all over the world enjoy stories about a creature that outsmarts (*it's*, <u>*its*</u>) enemies.
2. (*These kind*, <u>*These kinds*</u>) of stories are known as trickster tales.
3. In the tales of Native Americans of the Southwest, (<u>*Coyote*</u>, *Coyote he*) is a trickster who causes disorder and confusion.
4. In one story, Coyote (*kind of*, <u>*somewhat*</u>) playfully scatters stars across the sky.
5. In South American tales, the trickster Fox talks (*like*, <u>*as though*</u>) he is clever, but he really isn't.
6. Fox doesn't even understand (*how come*, <u>*why*</u>) a vulture beats him in a tree-sitting contest.
7. Our teacher (*learned*, <u>*taught*</u>) us about Brer Rabbit, a famous trickster in African American folklore.
8. Brer Rabbit gets (<u>*himself*</u>, *hisself*) into a lot of trouble trying to trick Brer Fox.
9. In a funny tale from India, a monkey and a (<u>*crocodile*</u>, *crocodile they*) play tricks on each other.
10. Just (<u>*as*</u>, *like*) Aesop's tortoise defeats the hare, Toad wins a race against Donkey in a Jamaican tale.

▶ EXERCISE 4   **Using Standard English in a Report**

As a Career Day project, you interviewed a crane operator at a construction site. The operator explained how the different parts of a boom crane work and gave you the drawing shown on the next page. The operator also talked about the hard work involved in moving construction materials. Write a brief report for your classmates, telling how a crane works and what its operator does. Use the

USAGE

TIMESAVER
Have students do **Exercise 3** as a pretest, and put the correct answers on the chalkboard after all students have finished. Have students independently study the glossary entries of missed items. Then have each student include two examples of correct usage for those targeted items in the reports for **Exercise 4**.

USAGE

ANSWERS
Exercise 4

Reports will vary. You may want to have students underline the glossary entries they use. Have students work with partners to review draft reports, checking both for standard usage and for clarity.

693

OBJECTIVE

• To identify correct usage

PROGRAM MANAGER

MIGHT OF, MUST OF— TRY AND

■ **Independent Practice/ Reteaching** For instruction and exercises, see **Common Usage Problems D** in *Language Skills Practice and Assessment,* p. 182.

■ **Computer Guided Instruction** For additional instruction and practice with common usage problems, see **Lesson 65** in *Language Workshop CD-ROM.*

■ **Practice** To help less-advanced students with additional instruction and practice with common usage problems, see **Chapter 21** in *English Workshop, Second Course,* pp. 225–226.

QUICK REMINDER

Write on the chalkboard the following statement:

I kind of wish I would of tried harder but I never got off of my chair when I should of so I wasn't the winner of any prizes.

Read the sentence aloud once. Then go through erasing all of the *of*'s except the last one. Have students write in necessary changes. [I rather wish I had tried harder but I never got off my chair when I should have. . . .]

694

---

694 *A Glossary of Usage*

drawing below, your memories of cranes you've seen, and your own storytelling abilities to write the report. In your report, use standard English to demonstrate any five of these glossary entries:

he, she, they	kind of, sort of
hisself	learn, teach
how come	lie, lay
its, it's	like, as
kind, sort, type	like, as if

EXAMPLE *"This type of crane is fun but sometimes scary to operate," Mr. Arlen said.*

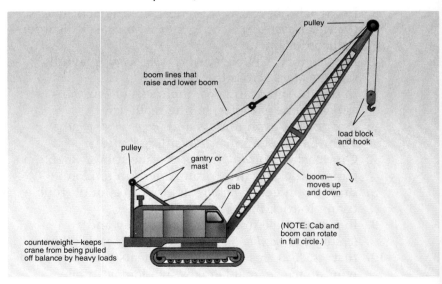

might of, must of See **could of.**

nowheres See **anywheres,** etc.

of Do not use *of* with other prepositions such as *inside, off,* and *outside.*

EXAMPLES He quickly walked **off** [not *off of*] the stage.
She waited **outside** [not *outside of*] the school.
What is **inside** [not *inside of*] this large box?

ought to of See **could of.**

real In informal situations, *real* is often used as an adverb meaning "very" or "extremely." In formal situations, *very* or *extremely* is preferred.

INFORMAL	My mother is expecting a real important telephone call.
FORMAL	My mother is expecting a **very** important telephone call.

reason . . . because In informal situations, *reason . . . because* is often used instead of *reason . . . that.* In formal situations, use *reason . . . that,* or revise your sentence.

INFORMAL	The reason I did well on the test was because I had studied hard.
FORMAL	The **reason** I did well on the test was **that** I had studied hard.

or

I did well on the test **because** I had studied hard.

rise, raise See pages 622–623.

scarcely, hardly See **hardly, scarcely**

should of See **could of.**

sit, set See pages 618–619.

some, somewhat Do not use *some* for *somewhat* as an adverb.

NONSTANDARD	My math has improved some.
STANDARD	My math has improved **somewhat.**

somewheres See **anywheres,** etc.

sort See **kind, sort, type.**

sort of See **kind of, sort of.**

take See **bring, take.**

teach See **learn, teach.**

USAGE

USAGE

COMMON ERROR

Problem. *There, their,* and *they're* are frequently misused in writing.

Solution. Tell students to keep these tips in mind when trying to decide which form to use:

1. Look for the *here* in *there* when you mean a place (as in *over there*) or when you mean the impersonal expression *there is.*
2. Look for the *heir* in *their* when you are talking about possession.
3. If you can substitute *they are,* use *they're.*

A DIFFERENT APPROACH

Use a quiz-show format to reinforce standard usage of *there/their/they're.* Pass out index cards. Have students write sentences using one of the three forms on each card. Collect the cards and give them to one student who will act as moderator.

Provide three students who will be contestants with three cards labeled *there, their,* and *they're.* For each round, the moderator reads aloud a sentence from one of the index cards. Contestants compete to see who can first flash the card showing the form used in the sentence. After five rounds, have the winner compete against two new opponents. Continue until all students have had a chance to participate.

696

---

than, then *Than* is a conjunction; *then* is an adverb.

> EXAMPLES Margo is a faster runner **than** I am.
> First we went to the bookstore. **Then** we went to the library.

that See **who, which, that.**

that there See **this here, that there.**

their, there, they're *Their* is the possessive form of *they. There* is used to mean "at that place" or to begin a sentence. *They're* is a contraction of *they are.*

> EXAMPLES **Their** team won the game.
> We are planning to go **there** during spring vacation.
> **There** were twenty people at the party.
> **They're** the best players on the team.

theirself, theirselves *Theirself* and *theirselves* are nonstandard English. Use *themselves.*

> EXAMPLE They bought **themselves** [not *theirself* or *theirselves*] a telescope.

them *Them* should not be used as an adjective. Use *those.*

> EXAMPLE Karen gave you **those** [not *them*] cassettes yesterday.

this here, that there The words *here* and *there* are unnecessary after **this** and **that.**

> EXAMPLE Do you like **this** [not *this here*] shirt or **that** [not *that there*] one?

this kind, sort, type See **kind,** etc.

try and In informal situations, *try and* is often used instead of *try to.* In formal situations, *try to* should be used.

> INFORMAL Try and be on time for the party.
> FORMAL **Try to** be on time for the party.

▶ EXERCISE 5   **Identifying Correct Usage**

Choose the <u>correct word or expression</u> from the pair in parentheses in each of the following sentences.

EXAMPLE   **1.** Athletes find the physical and mental
challenges of their sports (*real, very*) exciting.
1. *very*

1. Yosemite Park Ranger Mark Wellman discovered new strengths (*inside of,* <u>*inside*</u>) himself when he climbed El Capitan.
2. Wellman, paralyzed from the waist down, was anxious to (*try and,* <u>*try to*</u>) climb the 3,595-foot rock.
3. In this picture, Wellman strains (<u>*somewhat*</u>, *some*) as he climbs the granite peak in 1989.

4. The reason Wellman was strong enough for the climb is (*because,* <u>*that*</u>) he had trained for a year.
5. Like Wellman, many people are able to swim, hike, cycle, and canoe in spite of (*there,* <u>*their*</u>) disabilities.
6. (*Them,* <u>*Those*</u>) newer, lighter, easier-to-use wheelchairs have helped many people enjoy a wider variety of sports activities.
7. Nowadays, national and state parks offer more services for physically challenged people (<u>*than*</u>, *then*) they used to offer.
8. (*This here,* <u>*This*</u>) magazine story lists dozens of sports organizations for athletes who have disabilities.

USAGE

VISUAL CONNECTIONS
Exploring the Subject. You may want to tell students that few persons have ever achieved what Mark Wellman has. Climbing the sheer rock face is considered an acid test even for able-bodied rock climbers. In 1991, Wellman succeeded in becoming the first paraplegic to scale Yosemite's other giant, Half Dome.

LESSON 6 *(pp. 698–704)*
USE TO, USED TO—YOUR, YOU'RE

OBJECTIVE
• To identify correct usage

PROGRAM MANAGER

USE TO, USED TO—YOUR, YOU'RE

- **Independent Practice/ Reteaching** For instruction and exercises, see **Common Usage Problems E** in *Language Skills Practice and Assessment,* p. 183.

- **Computer Guided Instruction** For additional instruction and practice with common usage problems, see **Lesson 65** in *Language Workshop CD-ROM.*

- **Practice** To help less-advanced students with additional instruction and practice with common usage problems, see **Chapter 21** in *English Workshop, Second Course,* pp. 227–228.

QUICK REMINDER
Write the following sentence on the chalkboard, and have students identify and correct the usage errors:

My uncle which was in Japan told me about something called a tsunami; a tsunami is where there's a giant tidal wave who can destroy entire villages.

If students have difficulty identifying the errors, let them know that all errors involve words that begin with *wh–*. [Possible correction: My uncle who was in Japan told me about something called a tsunami; a tsunami is a giant tidal wave that can destroy entire villages.]

USAGE

698

USAGE

698   *A Glossary of Usage*

9. You (*might of, might have*) heard of the National Wheelchair Basketball Association, which sponsors teams and organizes tournaments.
10. Other athletes pride (*themselves, theirselves*) on being able to play wheelchair tennis.

use to, used to   Be sure to add the *d* to *use. Used to* is the past form.

> EXAMPLE   We **used to** [not *use to*] live in Phoenix, Arizona.

way, ways   Use *way,* not *ways,* in referring to a distance.

> EXAMPLE   They still had a long **way** [not *ways*] to go.

well   See **good, well.**

when, where   Do not use *when* or *where* incorrectly in writing a definition.

> NONSTANDARD   In bowling, a "turkey" is when a person rolls three strikes in a row.
>
> STANDARD   In bowling, a "turkey" is rolling three strikes in a row.

where   Do not use *where* for *that.*

> EXAMPLE   I read in our newspaper **that** [not *where*] Monica Seles won the tennis tournament.

who, which, that   The relative pronoun *who* refers to people only; *which* refers to things only; *that* refers to either people or things.

> EXAMPLES   Kim is the only one **who** got the right answer. [person]
> My bike, **which** has ten speeds, is for sale. [thing]
> He is the one person **that** can help you. [person]
> This is the ring **that** I want to buy. [thing]

who's, whose   *Who's* is the contraction of *who is* or *who has. Whose* is the possessive form of *who.*

EXAMPLE **Who's** keeping score?
Who's been using my typewriter?
Whose baseball glove is this?

without, unless Do not use the preposition *without* in place of the conjunction *unless*.

EXAMPLE My mother said that I can't go to the game **unless** [not *without*] I finish my homework first.

would of See **could of.**

your, you're *Your* is the possessive form of *you*. *You're* is the contraction of *you are*.

EXAMPLES **Your** dinner is on the table.
You're one of my closest friends.

EXERCISE 6 **Identifying Correct Usage**

Choose the <u>correct word or expression</u> from the pair in parentheses in each sentence.

EXAMPLE **1.** I (*use, used*) to know the names of all thirty-three state birds.
     1. *used*

1. You may have read (*where,* <u>*that*</u>) some states have the same state birds.
2. The mockingbird, (*who,* <u>*which*</u>) mimics other birds, is the state bird of Texas, Mississippi, Arkansas, Tennessee, and Florida.
3. "Mimicking" is (*when a person or an animal imitates another,* <u>*imitating a person or an animal*</u>).
4. (*Your,* <u>*You're*</u>) probably familiar with New Mexico's state bird, the roadrunner, from cartoons.
5. My grandfather, (<u>*who's*</u>, *whose*) a fisherman, often hears the loud calls of Minnesota's state bird, the common loon.
6. The bluebird, state bird of Missouri and New York, (*use,* <u>*used*</u>) to come around our house.

MEETING *individual* **NEEDS**

STUDENTS WITH SPECIAL NEEDS

Some students may confuse *where* and *were* in writing. Involve students in writing a glossary entry that identifies the grammatical function of each word and that gives sample sentences showing each form used correctly.

COMMON ERROR

Problem. Students may confuse *who's* and *whose* and *your* and *you're*.

Solution. Suggest a substitution test to determine which form to use. If *who is* fits the sentence, use *who's*; if it doesn't, use *whose*. If *you are* can be substituted, use *you're*; if it can't, use *your*. Remind students that one general rule governs all these cases: If you can substitute a pronoun plus *is* or *are*, use the apostrophe form.

REVIEW B

OBJECTIVE

• To correct errors in usage

VISUAL CONNECTIONS
Related Expression Skills.
Call on students to give examples of baseball chatter—the kind of encouraging talk coaches and fellow players engage in during a game. Record some examples on the chalkboard and have students rewrite them in formal English. For example: "Ain't no batter" might become "You don't know how to bat!" or "Look alive, you should of had that!" might be "Wake up, you should have caught that!" Discuss how informal expressions are more appropriate than formal expressions for a situation such as a ballgame. People who grow up speaking only standard English may have to learn to speak nonstandard English to adapt to some social situations. The people with the greatest social advantage are those who feel comfortable with both standard and nonstandard English.

MEETING
individual
NEEDS

LESS-ADVANCED STUDENTS

Students may feel overwhelmed at having to identify and also to correct the errors in **Review B.** To encourage success, have students work in small groups. To help reinforce learning, have students locate the glossary entry for each correction that is made. At the end of the period or the next day, have students work the exercise independently. The results will help you gauge retention and learning.

700

7. The spunky bird on this baseball player's cap represents both a state and a team quite (*good, well*).
8. (*Without, Unless*) I'm mistaken, you can guess what state claims the Baltimore oriole.
9. It travels a long (*way, ways*) between its summer and winter homes.
10. Would you (*of, have*) guessed that the cardinal is the official bird of the most states?

▶ REVIEW B   **Correcting Errors in Usage**

Most of the following sentences contain an error in usage. If a sentence contains an error, identify the error and write the correct form. If a sentence is correct, write *C*.

EXAMPLE   **1.** It was pirate Jean Laffite which established an early settlement on Texas' Galveston Island.
1. *which—who (or that)*

1. Since ancient times, pirates ~~they~~ have terrorized the world's seas.
2. Bands of pirates ^use to build fortified hide-outs from which they attacked ships. **2.** used
3. I once read ^~~where~~ the Roman general Julius Caesar was captured by pirates. **3.** that
4. My history teacher ^~~learned~~ my class about pirates who disrupted shipping along the North African coast. **4.** taught

5. As you may have seen in movies, these pirates preyed upon African, European, and American ships. **5.** C

6. During the 1600s and 1700s, pirates lived off ~~of~~ the South American coast.

7. One of these pirates, Sir William Kidd, was a ~~real~~ dangerous cutthroat on the Caribbean Sea. **7.** very

8. You may be surprised to learn that two other fearsome pirates were women. **8.** C

9. Anne Bonny and Mary Read attacked and robbed ~~alot~~ of ships on the Caribbean. **9.** a lot

10. You may think that piracy is a thing of the past, but ~~its~~ still going on in some parts of the world. **10.** it's

WRITING APPLICATION

Using Formal Standard English in a Speech

Listen closely to the speech of a professional radio or TV broadcaster. Then, listen to the conversations of people around you. You'll likely discover quite a difference. On the air, broadcasters use formal standard English to set a serious, businesslike tone. In casual conversation, most people frequently use informal, sometimes even nonstandard, English.

Which of the following sounds like a real newscast?

NEWSCAST 1: At today's press conference, the mayor he was real optimistic about the new recycling program. According to him, if our town had started recycling last year, we could of saved more than $75,000 in landfill and disposal costs. The mayor admitted that recycling ain't a cure-all for our budget problems. But he stressed that these kind of savings takes some of the burden off of the backs of taxpayers.

USAGE

USAGE

Ask volunteers to read aloud the two newscasts as the other students listen with their books closed. Then ask which version sounds more professional. Have students look at the texts of the newscasts to offer details of usage to support their conclusions.

When students are ready to give their speeches, spend some time discussing effective oral presentation. Play a brief tape of a professional newscast. Point out that professionals speak clearly to make their meaning clear and they time their pauses to add emphasis.

You could also refer students to the material on **Speaking Expressively,** pp. 864–865, in **Chapter 30: "Speaking."** The pointers given there on effective speaking will be useful for both taped and live presentations.

CRITICAL THINKING

Analysis. Suggest that students structure their speeches by analyzing cause and effect. They can use the following format:

Topic: Choose a topic. (Example: recycling)

Effect: State one specific problem within the topic. (Example: Packaging wastes an enormous amount of energy and natural resources in its manufacture and then gluts landfills when it is thrown away.)

Cause: List two or three specific factors or causes of the problem. (Examples: Aluminum soft drink cans are thrown away after a single use, and bulky plastic packages aren't biodegradable.)

Action: Identify one or two specific actions that will cause a lessening of the harmful effect—that is, things that can be done to help cut down or solve the problem. (Examples: Recycle all your aluminum cans. Choose products packaged in recycled paper rather than in plastic.)

NEWSCAST 2: At today's press conference, **the mayor** was **extremely** optimistic about the new recycling program. According to him, if our town had started recycling last year, we **could have** saved more than $75,000 in landfill and disposal costs. The mayor admitted that recycling **isn't** a cure-all for our budget problems. But he stressed that **this kind** of savings takes some of the burden **off** the backs of taxpayers.

Written in standard, formal English, Newscast 2 sounds more professional and more believable.

WRITING ACTIVITY

A local radio station is sponsoring a speech contest for Earth Day. To enter, contestants must write a speech about an environmental issue. The speech should be no more than three minutes long. The winner gets to read his or her speech on the air. Write a speech for the contest. Use only formal English in your speech.

Prewriting You'll need to choose a specific topic about the environment. Is there an issue that you are especially concerned about? You might brainstorm some ideas with friends or family. You may wish to discuss one of the following subjects: local recycling efforts, pollution, endangered animals, or rain forests. When you've selected a topic, jot down some notes about it. List not only facts and information you've read or heard about the topic but also your feelings about it. Then, make an informal outline of what you want to say.

Writing Use your notes from the prewriting activities as you write the first draft of your speech. You'll want to have an introduction that catches people's attention. Make the main point of your speech very clear in a thesis statement early in your speech. Then, discuss each supporting point in a paragraph or two. Restate your main point in your conclusion. Time your speech to be sure it's no longer than three minutes.

REVIEW C

OBJECTIVE

- To revise sentences by correcting errors in usage

 Evaluating and Revising   Ask a friend to listen to your speech and to time it. Is the speech clear, informative, and (if you want it to be) persuasive? Did your listener hear any informal English? Review the rules and guidelines of standard English given in this chapter. Make any necessary corrections in usage. If your speech is too long, you'll need to cut or revise some information.

 Proofreading and Publishing   Read the speech to yourself and look for errors in subject-verb agreement. For more about subject-verb agreement, see pages 575–588. Be sure that you don't have any dangling or misplaced modifiers. For more on these, see pages 668–677. Publish your speech by recording it and playing it back for your class. If Earth Day is near, you could ask to read your speech at an Earth Day event.

▶ REVIEW C   **Revising Sentences by Correcting Errors in Usage**

Revise the sentences in the following paragraph to correct each error in usage. [Note: A sentence may contain more than one error.]

EXAMPLE   **[1] Our vacation along the Pan American Highway was real interesting.**
1. *real—very* (or *extremely*)

[1] My parents were ~~already~~ to leave as soon as school was out. [2] Mom and Dad planned the trip ~~theirselves~~ so that we'd see ~~alot~~ of country. [3] The Pan American Highway, as the map on the next page shows, runs ~~among~~ North America and South America. [4] Like a bridge, this ~~here~~ highway connects the two continents. [5] ~~Like~~ you can see, Laredo, Texas, is one of the terminals for the highway. [6] That's ~~how come~~ we went to Laredo first.

1. all ready

2. themselves/ a lot

3. through

5. As

6. why

USAGE

USAGE

OBJECTIVE

• To identify and correct errors in usage

USAGE

VISUAL CONNECTIONS

Exploring the Subject. Ask students to find the dotted lines near Panama on the map. Let them know that that section of the highway is not completed, and travelers go by ship from Panama to Colombia or Venezuela. If any students have traveled on the highway, invite them to share information about their experiences.

MEETING *individual* NEEDS

STUDENTS WITH SPECIAL NEEDS

Because some students may find it very difficult to isolate usage errors, identify for them which sentence in each set needs correcting in **Review: Posttest.** For reinforcement, have them list the glossary entry heading that applies to each sentence.

704

---

704 *A Glossary of Usage*

[7] I enjoyed visiting the towns and seeing the countryside deep inside ~~of~~ Mexico. [8] If you follow along on the map,
8. then you'll notice that we ~~than~~ drove through Central America. [9] We crossed the Panama
9. there Canal to get to Colombia; ~~their~~ we enjoyed touring the capi-
10. have tal, Bogotá. [10] We couldn't ~~of~~ stayed in Venezuela and Chile any longer because both Mom and Dad had to get back to work.

Review: Posttest

Identifying and Correcting Errors in Usage

One sentence in each of the following sets contains an error in usage. Choose the letter of the <u>sentence that contains an error.</u> Then revise the sentence, using standard English.

EXAMPLE   **1. a.** The chicken tastes bad.
      b. Where is the book at?
      c. There was agreement among the five dancers.
      1. *b. Where is the book?*

  1. a. Bring your notes when you come.
     b. The dish ~~busted~~. **1. broke**
     c. He could have danced.
  2. a. I drew an apple.
     b. The cold affects the plant.
     c. We are ~~already~~ to go. **2. all ready**

3. **a.** Manuel feels ~~alright~~ today.   **3.** all right
    b. She went everywhere.
    c. We have fewer chairs than we need.
4. **a.** They danced ~~good~~ at the party.   **4.** well
    b. If I had sung, you would have laughed.
    c. You ought to help.
5. **a.** It's cold.
    b. He made it ~~hisself~~.   **5.** himself
    c. Its knob is broken.
6. **a.** Teach me the song.
    b. That story is ~~kind of~~ funny.   **6.** somewhat [*or* rather]
    c. The dog lay down.
7. **a.** Mr. Barnes is here.
    b. I know why he left.
    c. ~~This~~ kinds of bikes are expensive.   **7.** These
8. **a.** These taste like oranges.
    b. Sing as she does.
    c. She might ~~of~~ moved.   **8.** have
9. **a.** Please come inside the house.
    b. I am ~~real~~ happy.   **9.** very
    c. The reason she laughed was that your dog
       looked funny.
10. **a.** I looked for the book, but someone must ~~of~~
       misplaced it.   **10.** have
    b. Your forehand has improved somewhat.
    c. He sings better than I do.
11. **a.** Your coat is beautiful.
    b. You're a fast runner.
    c. I cannot leave ~~without~~ I wash the dishes first.   **11.** unless
12. **a.** She is the student ~~which~~ plays the violin.   **12.** who [*or* that]
    b. We only have a short way to go.
    c. We read in our newspaper that a new store is
       opening in the mall.
13. **a.** I ~~use~~ to read mysteries.   **13.** used
    b. Set that crate down here.
    c. This hat is old.
14. **a.** I gave you ~~them~~ books.   **14.** those
    b. They bought themselves new shirts.
    c. There is the cat.

USAGE

INTEGRATING THE LANGUAGE ARTS

Usage and Writing. Remind students that while the glossary may look long, virtually no one has to worry about every entry. In fact, most people have just a few usage errors that show up frequently. Have students use their results on exercises in this unit to develop personal *Watch Out* lists that they can use when proofreading their writing or when preparing formal speeches.

15. a. Sit down.
    b. They're smiling.
    c. ~~There~~ team is good.   **15.** Their
16. a. Gail did not feel well.
    b. Have ~~a~~ orange.   **16.** an
    c. You invited everyone except Cai.
17. a. I ~~raised~~ at 8:00 this morning.   **17.** rose
    b. Sunscreen lessens the effects of the sun's rays.
    c. We already read the book in class.
18. a. You did all right.
    b. They went ~~nowheres~~.   **18.** nowhere
    c. He looks as if he has lost something.
19. a. Nancy's ankle was hurt ~~bad~~.   **19.** badly
    b. The funds were divided among the three cities.
    c. The pipe burst.
20. a. I ~~cannot~~ hardly dance.   **20.** can
    b. Warm days make me feel good.
    c. It's pretty.
21. a. He must be somewhere.
    b. I can scarcely ride this bike.
    c. The reason I like him is ~~because~~ he is kind.   **21.** that
22. a. We have fewer shelves than we need.
    b. Those kinds of shirts are warm.
    c. This morning I ~~laid~~ in bed too long.   **22.** lay
23. a. Latoya always lays her books on the couch.
    b. Learn how to play this game.
    c. Do ~~like~~ he does.   **23.** as
24. a. They are inside ~~of~~ the house.
    b. I will have a sandwich.
    c. He set the chair down.
25. a. ~~Their~~ my cats.   **25.** They're
    b. Do you need those books?
    c. This house has fourteen rooms.

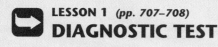

LESSON 1 *(pp. 707–708)*
DIAGNOSTIC TEST
OBJECTIVE
- To proofread sentences for correct capitalization

PROGRAM MANAGER

FOR THE WHOLE CHAPTER

■ **Review** For exercises on chapter concepts, see **Review Form A** and **Review Form B** in *Language Skills Practice and Assessment,* pp. 218–221.

■ **Assessment** For additional testing, see **Mechanics Pretests** and **Mechanics Mastery Tests** in *Language Skills Practice and Assessment,* pp. 203–210 and pp. 275–282.

25 CAPITAL LETTERS

Rules for Capitalization

Diagnostic Test

Proofreading Sentences for Correct Capitalization

Each of the following sentences contains at least one error in capitalization. Correct the errors by changing capitals to lowercase letters or lowercase letters to capitals.
Words that should be lowercased or capitalized are underscored.
EXAMPLE   **1. The Maxwells enjoyed visiting the southwest, particularly the alamo in San Antonio.**
    1. *Southwest; Alamo*

1. Is <u>dr</u>. Powell's office at Twenty-<u>First</u> <u>street</u> and Oak <u>drive</u>?
2. On <u>labor</u> <u>day</u> we went to Three Trees State Park.
3. We invited <u>aunt</u> Mae and my cousins to go with us.
4. Our junior high school had a much more successful carnival than Lakeside <u>junior</u> <u>high</u> <u>school</u> did.
5. Did you know that the folk tale "<u>cinderella</u>," which is included in *<u>grimm's</u> <u>fairy</u> <u>tales</u>,* is similar to a tale from ninth-century <u>china</u>?
6. Abe's cousin joined the Peace <u>corps</u> and lived in a small village on the west coast of <u>africa</u>.

CHAPTER OVERVIEW

This chapter gives rules for capitalizing the first words of sentences, the pronoun *I*, the interjection *O*, proper nouns, proper adjectives, course names, and titles.

Examples are given of what to capitalize when writing about history, politics, geography, religions, and astronomy.

This chapter could be referred to in connection with any writing assignment in which students are unsure of what should be capitalized.

MECHANICS

MECHANICS

USING THE DIAGNOSTIC TEST

If you have some students who are having problems with capitalization in their writing, the **Diagnostic Test** can help you to identify particular areas in which students need instruction and practice. The test assesses mastery of all the rules of capitalization that are given in this chapter. You can assess students' responses to determine which rules students need to review.

PROGRAM MANAGER

FIRST WORDS, THE PRONOUN *I*, THE INTERJECTION *O*

■ **Independent Practice/ Reteaching** For instruction and exercises, see **Using Capital Letters A** in *Language Skills Practice and Assessment,* p. 214.

■ **Computer Guided Instruction** For additional instruction and practice with using capital letters, see **Lesson 57** in *Language Workshop CD-ROM.*

■ **Practice** To help less-advanced students with additional instruction and practice with capital letters, see **Chapter 22** in *English Workshop, Second Course,* pp. 231–232 and pp. 241–242.

708 *Capital Letters*

7. No fish live in the Great <u>salt</u> <u>lake</u> in Utah.
8. I found out that I could save money by shopping at Al's <u>discount</u> <u>city</u>.
9. We have studied Japanese <u>Culture</u> and the <u>shinto</u> religion.
10. This semester I have English, American <u>History</u>, Spanish, and Industrial Arts I in the afternoon.
11. On <u>saturday</u> and <u>sunday</u>, my mother and <u>i</u> are going to a family reunion in the town where she grew up.
12. The Robinsons live near <u>route</u> 41 not far from Memorial Parkway on the <u>South</u> side of town.
13. At our Wednesday <u>Night</u> meeting, the <u>reverend</u> Terry Witt gave a talk on the beliefs of Lutherans.
14. We salute you, <u>o</u> Caesar!
15. Did you know that <u>thursday</u> was named after the Norse <u>God</u> Thor?
16. The <u>Winter</u> air chilled the scouts to the bone.
17. Dale Evans and Roy Rogers always sang "Happy <u>trails</u> to <u>you</u>" at the end of their television programs.
18. Thurgood Marshall was the first <u>african</u> <u>american</u> appointed to the Supreme <u>court</u>.
19. My <u>Uncle</u> served in the U.S. Army during the Vietnam <u>war</u>.
20. The American <u>revolution</u> took place toward the end of the Age of Enlightenment in the 1700s.

Capital letters are used to

■ mark the beginnings of sentences
■ distinguish proper nouns from common nouns
■ indicate other words that deserve special attention

25a. Capitalize the first word in every sentence.

EXAMPLES **M**ore and more people are discovering the benefits of exercise. **D**aily workouts at the gymnasium or on the running track strengthen the heart.

The first word of a sentence that is a direct quotation is capitalized even if the quotation begins within a sentence.

EXAMPLE   In his *Sacred Meditations,* Francis Bacon states, "**K**nowledge is power."

Traditionally, the first word in a line of poetry is capitalized.

> **H**old fast to dreams
> **F**or if dreams die
> **L**ife is a broken-winged bird
> **T**hat cannot fly.
>
> Langston Hughes, "Dreams"

NOTE: Some modern poets and writers do not follow this style. When you are quoting, follow the capitalization used in the source of the quotation.

☞ **REFERENCE NOTE:** For more about using capital letters in quotations, see pages 773–774.

25b.   Capitalize the pronoun *I.*

EXAMPLES   They took my lover's tallness off to war,
Left me lamenting. Now **I** cannot guess
What **I** can use an empty heart–cup for.
Gwendolyn Brooks, "The Sonnet–Ballad"

25c.   Capitalize the interjection *O.*

The interjection *O* is most often used on solemn or formal occasions. It is usually followed by a word in direct address.

EXAMPLES   **O** our Mother the Earth, **O** our Father the Sky,
Your children are we, and with tired backs
We bring you the gifts you love.
from a traditional song of the Tewa people

Protect us in the battle, **O** great Athena!

MECHANICS

MEETING *individual* **NEEDS**

LEP/ESL

General Strategies. It could be useful for your English-language learners to have a chart of properly formed upper-case letters visible in the classroom when they work on this chapter. Because they see so much variation in handwriting in the United States, English-language learners may be uncertain about how to form the cursive capitals.

STUDENTS WITH SPECIAL NEEDS

To prevent the sheer number of rules of capitalization from overwhelming some students, you may want to teach only the rules pertaining to situations that occur frequently in everyday writing. You could eliminate the rules pertaining to situations that occur only occasionally. Have students identify the rule that corresponds to each capitalization error in the sentences you have them correct.

MECHANICS

AMENDMENTS TO SELECTIONS
Description of change: excerpted
Rationale: to focus on the use of capitalization presented in this chapter

OBJECTIVES
- To use capitalization correctly in an original paragraph
- To correct sentences by capitalizing words

PROGRAM MANAGER

PROPER NOUNS

- **Independent Practice/ Reteaching** For instruction and exercises, see **Using Capital Letters B** in *Language Skills Practice and Assessment,* p. 215.

- **Computer Guided Instruction** For additional instruction and practice with using capital letters, see **Lesson 58** in *Language Workshop CD-ROM.*

- **Practice** To help less-advanced students with additional instruction and practice with capital letters, see **Chapter 22** in *English Workshop, Second Course,* pp. 231–236.

QUICK REMINDER

Write the following words and phrases on the chalkboard. Have students copy them and capitalize the words that should be capitalized. (Letters that should be capitalized are underlined.)

1. supermarket
2. the smoky mountains
3. sesame seeds
4. afghanistan
5. forty-fifth street
6. thursday
7. alphabet
8. oregano
9. martian
10. vietnam

SELECTION AMENDMENT
Description of change: excerpted
Rationale: to focus on the use of capitalization presented in this chapter

---

The interjection *oh* requires a capital letter only at the beginning of a sentence.

> Oh, I wish I could tell you how lonely I felt.
> Rudolfo A. Anaya, *Tortuga*

Otherwise, *oh* is not capitalized.

EXAMPLE   **We felt tired but, oh, so victorious.**

EXERCISE 1   Correcting Sentences by Capitalizing Words

Most of the following sentences contain errors in capitalization. If a sentence is correct, write C. If there are errors in the use of capitals, identify the <u>word or words that should be changed</u>.

EXAMPLE   **1. Save us, o Poseidon, on this stormy sea.**
          1. o—O

1. If i need a ride, i will give you a call.
2. Loretta is spending her vacation in Maine, but <u>Oh</u>, how she would like to visit Paris.
3. Ana exclaimed, "<u>oh</u> no, I left my backpack on the bus!"
4. Please accept these gifts, <u>o</u> Lord.
5. Have I told you that my grandmother teaches karate?
   5. C

25d. Capitalize proper nouns.

A *common noun* names one of a group of persons, places, or things. A *proper noun* names a particular person, place, or thing.

☞ REFERENCE NOTE: For more about common and proper nouns, see pages 433–435.

A common noun is capitalized only when it begins a sentence or is part of a title. A proper noun is always capitalized.

COMMON NOUNS	PROPER NOUNS
athlete	Florence Griffith Joyner
river	Nile
month	February
team	Los Angeles Dodgers

Some proper nouns consist of more than one word. In these names, short prepositions (those of fewer than five letters) and articles (*a, an, the*) are not capitalized.

EXAMPLES   **Statue of Liberty, Alexander the Great**

(1) Capitalize the names of persons.

EXAMPLES   **Alice Walker, Franklin Chang-Diaz, Ms. Sandoz**

(2) Capitalize geographical names.

TYPE OF NAME	EXAMPLES	
Towns, Cities	Jamestown San Diego	Montreal St. Louis
Counties, States	Cook County Georgia	Orange County New Hampshire
Countries	Germany Mexico	Japan New Zealand
Islands	Wake Island Isle of Wight	Attu Molokai
Bodies of Water	Lake Erie Tampa Bay	Kentucky River Indian Ocean
Forests, Parks	Sherwood Forest Palmetto State Park	Yellowstone National Park
Streets, Highways	Madison Avenue Interstate 75	Route 44 West Fourth Street

MECHANICS

NOTE: In a hyphenated street number, the second part of the number is not capitalized.

EXAMPLE   **East Seventy-eighth Street**

MEETING *individual* **NEEDS**

LEP/ESL

General Strategies. English-language learners could have difficulty identifying words that should be capitalized because the students may not be familiar with the English names of people, places, buildings, and so on. You might want to pair students with English-proficient speakers who can act as informants as needed.

INTEGRATING THE LANGUAGE ARTS

Mechanics and Writing. To reinforce the rules for capitalizing geographical names, ask students to write informative paragraphs describing dream trips they would like to make.

Have students tell why they would like to make the trips. Students should include the names of any places they would have to pass through to get to their destinations. If possible, have maps of the world, North America, the United States, and your state for students to consult.

MECHANICS

TYPE OF NAME	EXAMPLES	
Mountains	Mount Washington Big Horn Mountains	Sawtooth Range Pikes Peak
Continents	Europe North America	Asia Africa
Regions	Middle East New England	the North the Midwest

NOTE: Words such as *north, east,* and *southwest* are not capitalized when they indicate direction.

EXAMPLES   flying **s**outh for the winter
northeast of Atlanta

☞ **REFERENCE NOTE:** Some proper nouns, common nouns, titles, and other words are commonly abbreviated. For guidelines on capitalizing abbreviations, see page 739.

▶ EXERCISE 2   **Writing a Paragraph Using Capitalization Correctly**

After visiting this wax museum, you decide to open one of your own. Write a paragraph telling where you'd locate your museum, what you'd name it, and what figures—real, fictional, or imaginary—you'd like to display in it.

EXAMPLE   *I'd open the Waikiki Wax Museum in Waikiki Beach, Hawaii. In it I'd display figures of people from Hawaii's history. One would be Queen Liliuokalani, the last queen of the Hawaiian Islands.*

ANSWERS
Exercise 2

Paragraphs will vary. Point out to students how simple and direct the example is. Encourage them to be similarly direct and simple in their writing. Finished paragraphs should demonstrate correct usage of capital letters.

(3) Capitalize the names of planets, stars, and other heavenly bodies.

EXAMPLES   **Jupiter, Saturn, Sirius, the Milky Way, the Big Dipper**

NOTE: The word *earth* is not capitalized unless it is used along with the names of other heavenly bodies. The words *sun* and *moon* are not capitalized.

EXAMPLES   Water covers more than 70 percent of the surface of the earth.
Mercury and Venus are closer to the sun than Earth is.

(4) Capitalize the names of teams, organizations, businesses, institutions, and government bodies.

TYPE OF NAME	EXAMPLES	
Teams	**Detroit Pistons**	**Pittsburgh Pirates**
	Seattle Seahawks	**Southside Raiders**
Organizations	**African Studies Association**	
	Future Farmers of America	
	National Football League	
Businesses	**General Cinema Corporation**	
	Levi Strauss Associates	
	Kellogg Company	
Institutions	**Cary Memorial Hospital**	
	Hillcrest Junior High School	
	Antioch College	
Government Bodies	**Air National Guard**	
	Department of Agriculture	
	Governor's Council on Equal Opportunity	

NOTE: The word *party* following the name of a political party is usually not capitalized. Some writers, however, do capitalize it in such cases. Either way is correct.

EXAMPLE   **Democratic party** [*or* Party]

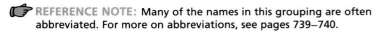 REFERENCE NOTE: Many of the names in this grouping are often abbreviated. For more on abbreviations, see pages 739–740.

 INTEGRATING THE LANGUAGE ARTS

Mechanics and Dictionary Skills. Explain to students that acronyms are abbreviations made up of the first letters of several words. They are written in all capital letters (FBI, UCLA). Some acronyms eventually enter common usage as words and then are no longer written with capital letters. Have students look up the following words in a dictionary and report on their origins as acronyms:

1. radar [radio detecting and ranging]
2. sonar [sound navigation and ranging]
3. scuba [self-contained underwater breathing apparatus]
4. laser [light amplification by stimulated emission of radiation]

713

TECHNOLOGY TIP

Most word-processing programs have search features that are particularly useful for correcting a recurring word that has been incorrectly left lowercase or uppercase in a composition. Some programs allow the user to enter a word in the search mode and to specify that the first letter of the word is either uppercase or lowercase. Others will find every instance of the word, regardless of whether it begins with an uppercase or lowercase letter.

(5) Capitalize the names of historical events and periods, special events, and calendar items.

TYPE OF NAME	EXAMPLES	
Historical Events	Revolutionary War Battle of Bunker Hill	Crusades Yalta Conference
Historical Periods	Great Depression Paleozoic Era	Middle Ages Renaissance
Special Events	World Series Olympic Games	Oklahoma State Fair Cannes Film Festival
Calendar Items	Friday October	Memorial Day Fourth of July

NOTE: The name of a season is not capitalized unless it is part of a proper name.

EXAMPLES   the last day of summer
the Oak Ridge Winter Carnival

(6) Capitalize the names of nationalities, races, and peoples.

EXAMPLES   **Greek, Asian, African American, Caucasian, Hispanic, Lakota Sioux**

NOTE: The words *black* and *white* may or may not be capitalized when they refer to races.

EXAMPLE   The first edition of the first black [*or* Black] newspaper, *Freedom's Journal,* was published on Friday, March 16, 1827.

(7) Capitalize the names of religions and their followers, holy days, sacred writings, and specific deities.

TYPE OF NAME	EXAMPLES	
Religions and Followers	Christianity Zen Buddhism	Muslim Amish

MECHANICS

TYPE OF NAME	EXAMPLES	
Holy Days	Lent Easter	Ramadan Passover
Sacred Writings	Koran Talmud	the Bible New Testament
Specific Deities	God Allah	Holy Spirit Jehovah

NOTE: The word *god* is not capitalized when it refers to a god of ancient mythology. The names of specific gods, however, are capitalized.

EXAMPLE   The trickster **g**od in many Native American tales is called **C**oyote.

(8) Capitalize the names of buildings and other structures.

EXAMPLES   **W**orld **T**rade **C**enter, **G**olden **G**ate **B**ridge, **S**hubert **T**heater, **P**laza **H**otel, **H**oover **D**am, **E**iffel **T**ower

 EXERCISE 3   **Correcting Sentences by Capitalizing Words**

Identify the <u>words that should be capitalized</u> in each of the following sentences. If a sentence is correct, write C.

EXAMPLE   **1.** Towering over the surrounding countryside, the san esteban mission is visible for miles.
   1. *San Esteban Mission*

1. The mission sits atop a sandstone mesa in <u>valencia county</u>, <u>new</u> <u>mexico</u>.
2. Near San Esteban is the <u>pueblo</u> village of <u>acoma</u>, which is fifty-four miles west-southwest of <u>albuquerque</u>.
3. Almost one thousand years old, <u>acoma</u> is believed to be the oldest continuously inhabited community in the <u>united</u> <u>states</u>.

COMMON ERROR

Problem. Students capitalize the word *god* when it is not naming a specific deity.

Solution. Point out that when the word *god* is used as a name for a specific deity, it is capitalized. Otherwise it is not. In determining correct usage of the word *god,* have them apply the test: Is it used as a name?

AT-RISK STUDENTS

You may want to obtain copies of different kinds of application forms such as applications for jobs, schools, and driver's licenses. Have students fill them out, and then check for correct use of capital letters. Point out that standard usage will often be important to the people evaluating these types of applications.

VISUAL CONNECTIONS
Related Expression Skills.
You may want to have students sketch missions like the San Esteban mission pictured here. Ask each student to research the people who have lived in Acoma and to write one to three interesting facts about the Acoma culture inside his or her mission drawings. Remind students to be aware of their use of capitalization when writing their facts. Have students share their findings with the class. You may want to display the drawings on a bulletin board.

4. In the seventeenth and eighteenth centuries, the <u>spanish</u> established dozens of <u>catholic</u> missions in <u>new</u> <u>mexico</u>.
5. The main purpose of the missions was to spread <u>christianity</u> among the native peoples, but the outposts also served political and military purposes.
6. This photo of San <u>esteban</u>, which was built between 1629 and 1651, shows the type of mission architecture that developed in that region of the <u>united</u> <u>states</u>.
7. Adobe, a sandy clay commonly used in construction throughout the <u>southwest</u>, covers all the outside surfaces of the building.
8. The building's design is based on the design of churches in central <u>mexico</u>.
9. Those churches, in turn, are regional variations of church buildings in <u>spain</u>.
10. Thus, <u>san</u> <u>esteban</u>, like other <u>new</u> <u>mexican</u> missions, combines various elements of three cultures: <u>native</u> <u>american</u>, <u>mexican</u>, and <u>spanish</u>.

MECHANICS

REVIEWS A–D

OBJECTIVES

- To identify and to give examples of common nouns and proper nouns
- To use capital letters correctly
- To correct sentences by capitalizing words

(9) Capitalize the names of monuments and awards.

TYPE OF NAME	EXAMPLES	
Monuments	Washington Monument Statue of Liberty	Vietnam Veterans Memorial
Awards	Academy Award Pulitzer Prize	Newbery Medal Purple Heart

(10) Capitalize the names of trains, ships, airplanes, and spacecraft.

TYPE OF NAME	EXAMPLES	
Trains	*Silver Rocket*	*Orient Express*
Ships	USS *Nimitz*	*Santa Maria*
Airplanes	*Spirit of St. Louis*	*Air Force One*
Spacecraft	*Apollo 11*	*Columbia*

(11) Capitalize the brand names of business products.

EXAMPLES   **Nike** shoes, **Buick** station wagon, **Wrangler** jeans
[Notice that the names of the types of products are not capitalized.]

REVIEW A   Common Nouns and Proper Nouns

For each proper noun, give a corresponding common noun. For each common noun, give a proper noun.

EXAMPLES   **1.** Independence Hall   **2.** city
             1. *building*   **2.** *San Francisco*

1. mountain range
2. Oprah Winfrey
3. historical event
4. river
5. North Dakota
6. Ethiopia
7. Lincoln Memorial
8. spacecraft
9. cereal
10. Environmental Protection Agency

MEETING *individual* NEEDS

LEP/ESL

General Strategies. Because the name for a specific geographic feature such as *Pacific Ocean* is different in different languages, students may not recognize English names. For **Reviews A–D**, you could check to see if students recognize the geographic names. Use a map to point out places students do not recognize. Ask students to share the names in other languages for geographic features.

STUDENTS WITH SPECIAL NEEDS

Review A might be very confusing for students with reading difficulties. To simplify the task, you could arrange the entries in two columns, one for common nouns and one for proper nouns.

ANSWERS

Review A

Nouns will vary. Be sure that proper nouns have capital letters and that common nouns do not. Here are some possible answers:

1. Rocky Mountains
2. actress
3. Civil War
4. Mississippi
5. state
6. country
7. monument
8. *Enterprise*
9. Wheatena
10. government agency

MECHANICS

MECHANICS

▶ REVIEW B   **Using Capital Letters Correctly**

Correct each of the following expressions, using capital letters as needed.   Words that should be capitalized are underscored.

EXAMPLE   **1.** a member of the peace corps
1. *a member of the Peace Corps*

1. decisions of the <u>united</u> <u>states</u> <u>supreme</u> <u>court</u>
2. the <u>apaches</u> of the <u>southwest</u>
3. <u>boulder</u> <u>dam</u>
4. the <u>tomb</u> of the <u>unknown</u> <u>soldier</u>
5. 512 <u>west</u> <u>twenty</u>-fourth <u>street</u>
6. pictures of <u>saturn</u> sent by *voyager* 2
7. the <u>hawaiian</u> island named <u>maui</u>
8. the <u>great</u> <u>lakes</u>
9. <u>monday</u>, <u>april</u> 29
10. the <u>stone</u> <u>age</u>

▶ REVIEW C   **Correcting Sentences by Capitalizing Words**

Identify the <u>words that should be capitalized</u> in each of the following sentences.

EXAMPLE   **1.** Imagine how many flowers it must take to cover just one of these floats for the rose parade!
1. *Rose Parade*

1. I don't have plans for <u>new</u> <u>year's</u> <u>eve</u> yet, but <u>i</u> know where <u>i'll</u> be on <u>new</u> <u>year's</u> <u>day</u>.
2. Watching the <u>rose</u> <u>parade</u> on TV is a <u>new</u> <u>year's</u> <u>day</u> tradition in my family.
3. The parade takes place each year in <u>pasadena</u>, <u>california</u>, which is northeast of <u>los</u> <u>angeles</u>.
4. The parade is sponsored by the <u>pasadena</u> <u>tournament</u> of <u>roses</u> <u>association</u>.
5. Did you know that the name *pasadena* comes from a <u>ojibwa</u> expression meaning "valley town"?
6. That's a fitting name for a town overlooking a valley at the base of the <u>san</u> <u>gabriel</u> <u>mountains</u>.

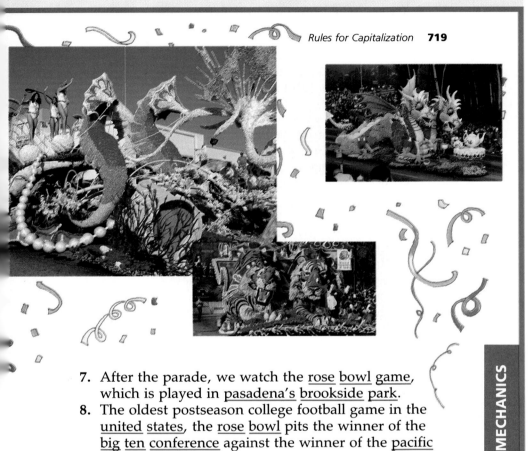

MECHANICS

VISUAL CONNECTIONS
Ideas for Writing. Have your students write brief descriptions of their favorite parades, live or televised. Have each student tell where the parade was, when it was held, what kinds of floats were in it, and what people rode in it. After students have finished their rough drafts, have them exchange papers with partners to proofread for capitalization errors. Have volunteers share their descriptions with the class.

7. After the parade, we watch the <u>rose</u> <u>bowl</u> <u>game</u>, which is played in <u>pasadena's</u> <u>brookside</u> <u>park</u>.
8. The oldest postseason college football game in the <u>united</u> <u>states</u>, the <u>rose</u> <u>bowl</u> pits the winner of the <u>big</u> <u>ten</u> <u>conference</u> against the winner of the <u>pacific</u> <u>ten</u> <u>conference</u>.
9. New <u>year's</u> <u>day</u> is nearly always bitterly cold in <u>cleveland</u>, where we live.
10. Yet by the end of the game, we feel as though we've started the new year off with a mini-vacation in <u>california</u>.

▶ REVIEW D **Correcting Sentences by Capitalizing Words**

Correct the <u>words that should be capitalized</u> in each of the following sentences.

EXAMPLE **1.** our class visited abraham lincoln's home in springfield, illinois.
1. *Our; Abraham Lincoln's; Springfield; Illinois*

PROPER ADJECTIVES, COURSE NAMES

Rules 25e, 25f

OBJECTIVES

- To correct sentences by capitalizing proper nouns and proper adjectives
- To use capital letters correctly

PROPER ADJECTIVES, COURSE NAMES

- **Independent Practice/ Reteaching** For instruction and exercises, see **Using Capital Letters C** in *Language Skills Practice and Assessment,* p. 216.

- **Computer Guided Instruction** For additional instruction and practice with capital letters, see **Lesson 58** in *Language Workshop CD-ROM.*

- **Practice** To help less-advanced students with additional instruction and practice with capital letters, see **Chapter 22** in *English Workshop, Second Course,* pp. 241–242.

QUICK REMINDER

Write the following sentences on the chalkboard and have students copy the sentences, capitalizing letters correctly. (Letters to be capitalized are underscored.)

1. james is taking government, science, english, and health.

2. joan is taking government I, science II, english II, and health.

1. the federal aviation administration regulates airlines only in the united states and not throughout the world.
2. when she was a child, ethel waters lived in chester, pennsylvania.
3. the sacred muslim city of mecca is located in saudi arabia.
4. in chicago, the sears tower and the museum of science and industry attract many tourists.
5. we watched the minnesota twins win the world series in 1991.
6. the valentine's day dance is always the highlight of the winter.
7. several of my friends bought new adidas shoes at the big sporting goods sale in the mall.
8. the citywide food pantry is sponsored and operated by protestants, catholics, and jews.
9. the second-place winners will receive polaroid cameras.
10. jane bryant quinn writes a magazine column on money management.

25e. Capitalize proper adjectives.

A *proper adjective* is formed from a proper noun and is almost always capitalized.

PROPER NOUN	PROPER ADJECTIVE
China	Chinese doctor
Rome	Roman army
Islam	Islamic culture
King Arthur	Arthurian legend

 EXERCISE 4

Correcting Sentences by Capitalizing Proper Nouns and Proper Adjectives

Capitalize the proper nouns and proper adjectives in each of the following sentences.

EXAMPLE   **1.** A finnish architect, eliel saarinen, designed a number of buildings in the detroit area.
          1. *Finnish; Eliel Saarinen; Detroit*

1. The <u>alaskan</u> wilderness is noted for its majestic beauty.
2. The <u>syrian</u> and <u>israeli</u> leaders met in <u>geneva</u>.
3. The <u>european</u> cities I plan to visit someday are <u>paris</u> and <u>vienna</u>.
4. Our <u>american</u> literature book includes <u>hopi</u> poems and <u>cheyenne</u> legends.
5. The <u>south</u> <u>american</u> rain forests contain many different kinds of plants and animals.
6. Maria has watched two <u>shakespearean</u> plays on television.
7. Did you see the exhibit of <u>african</u> art at the library?
8. Our program will feature <u>irish</u> and <u>scottish</u> folk songs.
9. The language most widely spoken in <u>brazil</u> is <u>portuguese</u>.
10. Several <u>baptist</u> leaders agreed with the ruling of the <u>supreme</u> <u>court</u>.

25f. Do *not* capitalize the names of school subjects, except languages and course names followed by a number.

EXAMPLES   I have tests in **English, Latin,** and **m**ath.
           You must pass **Art I** before taking **Art II.**

▶ EXERCISE 5   **Using Capital Letters Correctly**

Correct each of the following expressions, using capital letters as needed. Words that should be capitalized are underscored.

1. a lesson in <u>spanish</u>
2. report for <u>english</u> II
3. a program on <u>chinese</u> customs
4. problems in <u>geometry</u> I
5. studying <u>german</u>, chemistry, and <u>government</u> II

MECHANICS

MECHANICS

LEP/ESL

General Strategies. To help English-language learners recognize proper adjectives, explain that proper adjectives often end in *–n* and are formed by adding *–n* or *–an* to proper nouns. Point out examples of this in **Exercise 4.**

TECHNOLOGY TIP

If your students use style- or grammar-checking features on computers, remind students that these programs, although useful, do make mistakes. Advise students to double-check everything these computer features question.

MEETING *individual* NEEDS

LEP/ESL

General Strategies. For **Review E,** it might be helpful to discuss the differences among *trace, route, trail, highway, parkway,* and *path.*

722 *Capital Letters*

▶ REVIEW E

Correcting Sentences by Capitalizing Proper Nouns and Proper Adjectives

Capitalize the <u>proper nouns</u> and <u>proper adjectives</u> in each of the following sentences.

EXAMPLE   **1. The natchez trace developed from a series of trails made long before hernando de soto explored the area in 1540.**
1. *Natchez Trace; Hernando de Soto*

1. As the map shows, the <u>natchez</u> <u>trace</u> linked the present-day cities of <u>natchez</u>, <u>mississippi</u>, and <u>nashville</u>, <u>tennessee</u>.
2. From <u>natchez</u> the 450-mile route ran northeast between the <u>big</u> <u>black</u> <u>river</u> and the <u>pearl</u> <u>river</u>.

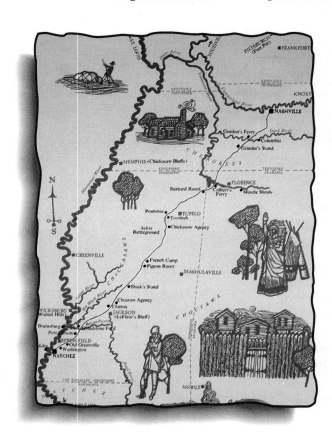

3. Turning east a few miles north of <u>tupelo</u>, it crossed the <u>tennessee</u> <u>river</u> near <u>muscle</u> <u>shoals</u>, <u>alabama</u>, and then headed into <u>tennessee</u>.

4. Among the peoples living along the trail were the <u>natchez</u>, the <u>chickasaw</u>, the <u>choctaw</u>, and the <u>cherokee</u>.

5. Finding no gold or silver in the area, the <u>spanish</u> explorers turned their attention to what is now the <u>u.s.</u> <u>southwest</u>.

6. At the conclusion of the <u>french</u> and <u>indian</u> <u>war</u> (1754–1763), <u>france</u> was forced to give most of its territory east of the <u>mississippi</u> <u>river</u> to <u>great</u> <u>britain</u>.

7. Near the time of the <u>louisiana</u> <u>purchase</u> of 1803, the <u>natchez</u> <u>trace</u> was improved for use by mail and military wagons traveling to the <u>west</u>.

8. Traffic along the trail increased steadily until the 1830s, when regular steamboat service provided a less dangerous, more comfortable means of travel on the <u>mississippi</u> <u>river</u>.

9. Today a modern highway, named the <u>natchez</u> <u>trace</u> <u>parkway</u>, follows the general route of the ancient path.

10. In an effort to reclaim history, volunteers with the <u>natchez</u> <u>trace</u> <u>trail</u> <u>conference</u> are carving out a hiking trail the entire length of the parkway.

MECHANICS

WRITING APPLICATION

Using Capital Letters Correctly in an Essay

The use of a capital letter or a lowercase letter at the beginning of a word can greatly alter the word's meaning. If a word in a sentence is capitalized or lowercased incorrectly, the sentence may not make sense.

WRITING APPLICATION
After each student has selected a person to write about, encourage him or her to include in the biography an incident in which the subject has been involved. A short narrative of a person's actions in a certain situation can be a good way to illustrate the character traits the student admires.

MECHANICS

CONFUSING   We used the heavy-duty Jack at Ben's garage to lift my brother's mustang. [The meaning of the sentence is *We used the strong person at Ben's garage to lift my brother's horse.*]

CLEAR   We used the heavy-duty jack at Ben's Garage to lift my brother's Mustang. [The meaning of the sentence is *We used the equipment at Ben's auto repair shop to lift my brother's car.*]

CRITICAL THINKING

Analysis. Students may list more information in the prewriting stage than they can use in their essays. Suggest that their main ideas focus on why they admire the individuals they are writing about. Then, have students analyze the information they have listed and decide what supports their main ideas and what is irrelevant and should be left out.

MECHANICS

MECHANICS

▶ WRITING ACTIVITY

Your class is putting together a booklet of biographical sketches on the most-admired people in your community. Each student in your class will contribute one biography. Write a short essay about someone you admire. The person can be a friend, a family member, or someone you have never met. In your essay, use capital letters and lowercase letters correctly to help your readers understand precisely what you mean.

Prewriting Brainstorm to develop a list of people you admire. Then look over your list, and choose the person you admire most. Jot down information about his or her background (such as date and place of birth, upbringing, schooling, and talents), personality traits (such as honesty, courage, creativity, and a good sense of humor), and major achievements. In the case of someone you know, you may wish to interview him or her to gather additional information. Finally, organize your information in an outline.

Writing Begin your essay with a sentence or two that catches your audience's attention and identifies your subject. Using your notes and outline, write your first draft. In your conclusion, sum up the points you've made, or restate the main idea in your introduction.

Evaluating and Revising Reread your paper to make sure you've clearly shown why you admire this person. Did you give enough information about him or her, and is the information correct? Add, delete, or rearrange information to make your essay clearer and more interesting.

TITLES Rule 25g

OBJECTIVES
- To correct sentences by capitalizing words
- To write a letter in which proper nouns and proper adjectives are used and correctly capitalized

Proofreading and Publishing   Read over your essay again, looking for any errors in grammar, punctuation, or spelling. Pay special attention to your use of capital letters and lowercase letters. Then, photocopy your paper or input it on a computer. With your classmates, create a booklet of your compositions. You may also wish to include photographs or sketches of the people you've written about. Invite other classes, friends, neighbors, and family members to read your booklet.

25g.   Capitalize titles.

(1) Capitalize the title of a person when it comes before a name.

EXAMPLES   There will be a short address by **G**overnor Halsey.
Report to **L**ieutenant Engstrom, please.
Does **M**s. Tam know **D**r. Politi?
This is the church in which the **R**everend Henry Ward Beecher preached.
How many terms did **P**resident Theodore Roosevelt serve?

NOTE: Capitalize a title used alone or following a person's name only when you want to emphasize the position of someone holding a high office.

EXAMPLES   Will the **S**ecretary of **L**abor hold a news conference this afternoon?
The **s**ecretary of our scout troop has the measles.

The crowd grew quiet as the **R**abbi rose to speak at the town meeting.
Is he the **r**abbi at the new synagogue on the corner?

PROGRAM MANAGER

TITLES
- **Independent Practice/ Reteaching** For instruction and exercises, see **Using Capital Letters D** in *Language Skills Practice and Assessment*, p. 217.
- **Computer Guided Instruction** For additional instruction and practice with capital letters, see **Lesson 57** in *Language Workshop CD-ROM*.
- **Practice** To help less-advanced students with additional instruction and practice with capital letters, see **Chapter 22** in *English Workshop, Second Course*, pp. 239–240.

QUICK REMINDER
Write the following sentences on the chalkboard and have students correct them by capitalizing words. (Letters to be capitalized are underscored.)
1. I was taught how to play the harmonica by uncle archie.
2. My uncle archie taught me to play the harmonica.
3. Yes, doctor brown will attend.
4. We had to take sylvester to the doctor this morning.

RULE 25 g (1)
Application of this rule will depend largely on the writer's intent. If the writer's purpose is to show special respect to someone holding a high office, the title should be capitalized. Otherwise the title should be lowercase.

MECHANICS

MECHANICS

A title used alone in direct address is usually capitalized.

EXAMPLES   Is the patient resting comfortably, **Nurse?**
What is your name, **Sir** [*or* sir]?

(2) Capitalize a word showing a family relationship when the word is used before or in place of a person's name.

EXAMPLES   I received a letter from **A**unt Christina and **U**ncle Garth.
When will **M**om and **D**ad be home?

Do not capitalize a word showing a family relationship when a possessive comes before the word.

EXAMPLE   Angela's **m**other and my **a**unt Daphne coach the softball team.

(3) Capitalize the first and last words and all important words in titles and subtitles of books, magazines, newspapers, poems, short stories, historical documents, movies, television programs, works of art, and musical compositions.

Unimportant words in titles include

- prepositions of fewer than five letters (such as *at, of, for, from, with*)
- coordinating conjunctions (*and, but, for, nor, or, so, yet*)
- articles (*a, an, the*)

☞ REFERENCE NOTE: For a list of prepositions, see page 474.

NOTE: An article (*a, an,* or *the*) before a title is not capitalized unless it is the first word of the title or subtitle.

EXAMPLES   Is that the late edition of the *Chicago Sun-Times*?
I read an interesting story in *The New Yorker.*

TYPE OF NAME	EXAMPLES	
Books	*Dust Tracks on a Road* *River Notes: The Dance of the Herons*	
Magazines	*Sports Illustrated* *Woman's Day*	*Latin American Literary Review*
Newspapers	*The Boston Globe*	*St. Petersburg Times*
Poems	"Refugee Ship" "Mother to Son"	"With Eyes at the Back of Our Heads"
Short Stories	"The Tell-Tale Heart" "Gorilla, My Love"	"My Wonder Horse" "Uncle Tony's Goat"
Historical Documents	Bill of Rights Treaty of Ghent	Emancipation Proclamation
Movies	*Stand and Deliver*	*Back to the Future*
Television Programs	*The Wonder Years* *A Different World*	*FBI: The Untold Stories*
Works of Art	*Mona Lisa*	*Bird in Space*
Musical Compositions	*West Side Story* *Rhapsody in Blue*	"Unforgettable" "On Top of Old Smoky"

► EXERCISE 6 **Correcting Sentences by Capitalizing Words**

Most of the following sentences contain words that should be capitalized. Correct the words requiring capitals. If a sentence is correct, write C. Optional capitalization is indicated with a double underscore.

1. During Woodrow Wilson's term as president of the united states, sheep grazed on the front lawn of the White House.
2. When my aunt Inez visited Mexico, she met several of grandmother Villa's brothers and sisters for the first time.
3. All of these pronunciations are correct according to *the american heritage dictionary*.
4. Some of the gods in greek mythology have counterparts in ancient asian and egyptian cultures.

MECHANICS

OBJECTIVES
- To correct sentences by capitalizing words
- To proofread sentences for correct capitalization

728 *Capital Letters*

5. Did you hear <u>commissioner</u> of <u>education</u> <u>smathers'</u> speech recommending a longer school day?
6. Was Carrie Fisher in *return of the jedi*?
7. After the secretary read the minutes, the treasurer reported on the club's budget. **7.** C
8. Elizabeth Speare wrote *the witch of blackbird pond*.
9. My older brother subscribes to *field and stream*.
10. The first politician to make a shuttle flight was <u>senator</u> Jake Garn of Utah.

TIMESAVER

Allow students to complete **Reviews F–H** in class. After they have completed the reviews, let students work in groups of three or four to compare and correct their work. For each error, have students identify the rule and write a sentence using the rule correctly. Groups can also check the revisions.

▶ REVIEW F **Correcting Sentences by Capitalizing Words**

Correct the <u>words requiring capitals</u> in each of the following sentences.

1. The <u>andersons</u> hosted an exchange student from <u>argentina</u>.
2. The <u>king ranch</u> in <u>texas</u> is larger than <u>rhode island</u>.
3. At <u>rand community college</u>, <u>ms</u>. <u>epstein</u> is taking three courses: <u>computer programming</u> I, <u>japanese</u>, and <u>english</u>.
4. The sixth day of the week, <u>friday</u>, is named for the <u>norse</u> goddess of love, <u>frigg</u>.
5. The <u>christian</u> holiday of <u>christmas</u> and the <u>jewish</u> holiday of <u>hanukkah</u> are both celebrated in <u>december</u>.
6. My uncle <u>ronald</u> was stationed in the <u>south pacific</u> when he was an ensign.
7. The <u>liberty bell</u>, on display in <u>independence hall</u> in <u>philadelphia</u>, was rung to proclaim the <u>boston tea party</u> and to announce the first public reading of the <u>declaration</u> of <u>independence</u>.
8. Is your mother still teaching an art appreciation class at the <u>swen parson gallery</u>?
9. In the 1920s, <u>zora neale hurston</u> and <u>countee cullen</u> were both active in the movement known as the <u>harlem renaissance</u>.
10. I walk to the <u>eagle</u> supermarket each <u>sunday</u> to buy a copy of the *<u>miami herald</u>* and a quart of <u>tropicana</u> orange juice.

► REVIEW G

Proofreading Sentences for Correct Capitalization

Each of the following sentences contains at least one error in capitalization. Correct the errors by supplying or omitting capitals as necessary. Words that should be lowercased or capitalized are underscored.

1. president Roosevelt's saturday talks from the white house were broadcast on the radio.
2. In History class, we learned about these suffragists: elizabeth cady stanton, susan b. anthony, and lucretia c. mott.
3. In April the cherry blossom festival will be celebrated by a Parade through the heart of the City.
4. The 1996 summer olympics were held in atlanta.
5. The rio grande, a major river of north america, forms the Southwestern border of Texas.
6. jane addams, an American Social Reformer who co-founded hull house in chicago, was awarded the 1931 nobel peace prize.
7. Many of the countries of europe are smaller than some states in our country.
8. William Least Heat-Moon began his journey around America, which he tells about in his book *blue highways*, in the southeast.
9. Can we have a surprise Birthday party for uncle Victor, mom?
10. The panama canal connects the atlantic ocean and the pacific ocean.

► REVIEW H

Proofreading Sentences for Correct Capitalization

Each of the following sentences contains at least one error in capitalization. Correct the errors by supplying or omitting capitals as necessary. Words that should be lowercased or capitalized are underscored.

EXAMPLE 1. The south african vocal group Ladysmith Black Mambazo sings *a capella*—that is, without instrumental accompaniment.
1. *South African*

MECHANICS

MECHANICS

1. Ladysmith's music is based on the work songs of black <u>south</u> <u>african</u> miners.   **1. [or Black]**
2. In a sense, their music is the <u>south</u> African version of the <u>american</u> blues, which grew out of the work songs of African <u>americans</u>.
3. In 1985, <u>ladysmith</u> was featured on two songs on <u>paul</u> <u>simon's</u> album *<u>graceland</u>*.
4. Those two songs, "<u>homeless</u>" and "<u>diamonds</u> on the <u>soles</u> of <u>her</u> <u>shoes</u>," helped to make the album an enormous hit; it even won a Grammy <u>award</u>.
5. To promote the album, Ladysmith and <u>simon</u> toured the United <u>states</u>, <u>europe</u>, and <u>south</u> America.
6. Most of Ladysmith's songs are in the performers' native language, <u>zulu</u>.
7. Even people who don't understand the <u>Lyrics</u> enjoy the music's power and beauty.
8. Ladysmith has also appeared in <u>eddie</u> <u>murphy's</u> movie *<u>coming</u> to <u>america</u>*, in the famous <u>Music</u> <u>Video</u> *<u>moonwalker</u>*, and on the television shows *Sesame <u>street</u>* and *<u>the</u> Tonight <u>show</u>*.
9. The group's exposure to <u>american</u> music is reflected in two songs on its 1990 album, *<u>two</u> <u>worlds</u>, <u>one</u> <u>heart</u>*.
10. One song is a gospel number, and the other adds elements of <u>Rap</u> music to <u>ladysmith's</u> distinctive sound.

PICTURE THIS

It's 1899. You're aboard this ship, sailing from Seattle, Washington, to Nome, Alaska, where gold was discovered last September. Using the map, write a letter home, telling your family about your trip so far. You may wish to tell about your fellow passengers, the towns and islands you've passed or visited, or the specific things you've seen. You may also wish to tell about your plans. Are you going to Alaska to strike it rich in the goldfields? Do you

---

MECHANICS

PICTURE THIS

Have students take a few minutes to visualize themselves on this ship in the nineteenth century. Suggest that students, especially the girls, could be characters of the opposite gender, as roles for women were much more limited in 1899. Have students proofread their letters carefully for correct capitalization.

aim to start a business? Perhaps you want to be a law officer. Of course, you could be simply looking for adventure. In your letter, use at least five proper nouns and five
proper adjectives.

Subject: sailing to the goldfields in Alaska
Audience: your family
Purpose: to tell about your journey

MEETING *individual* NEEDS

LEP/ESL

General Strategies. If students are completely unfamiliar with Alaska and the gold rush there, it may be hard for them to engage their imaginations in the writing assignment. Allow students to choose waterways in areas more familiar to them and to pick their historical periods.

VISUAL CONNECTIONS

Related Expression Skills. Have your students use a map or an atlas to route a voyage from their homes to Nome, Alaska, by ship. If they are inland, they must list states and cities through which they must travel to arrive at the waterway where they will board ship. Ask students to identify the ocean they will sail and the major ports they will pass on their voyage. You may want them to draw maps and to list and label states, cities, ports, and oceans.

MECHANICS

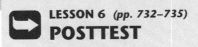

POSTTEST

OBJECTIVE

• To proofread sentences and paragraphs for correct capitalization

MEETING *individual* NEEDS

LEP/ESL

General Strategies. Many English-language learners are hesitant at first to use the pronoun *I* because they find it difficult to pronounce. You could give a demonstration of its pronunciation. Say the word very slowly so that students can view the positions your mouth takes as you articulate it; let your voice drop at the end. Finish by saying the word at normal speed in a sentence.

MECHANICS

MECHANICS

732   *Capital Letters*

Review: Posttest

A. Proofreading Sentences for Correct Capitalization Words that should be lowercased or capitalized are underscored. Optional capitalization is indicated with a double underscore.

Each of the following sentences contains at least one error in capitalization. Correct the errors by changing capitals to lowercase letters or lowercase letters to capitals.

EXAMPLE   **1.** The shubert Theater is located at 225 West Forty-Fourth Street in New York.
   1. *Shubert; Forty-fourth*

1. The planet <u>mars</u> was named for the <u>roman</u> <u>God</u> of war.
2. In <u>History</u> class we memorized the <u>Capitals</u> of all the states.
3. Uncle Dave owns one of the first <u>honda</u> <u>Motorcycles</u> that were sold in <u>north</u> America.
4. My cousin gave me a terrific book, <u>*rules*</u> *of the* <u>*game*</u>, which illustrates the rules of all sorts of games.
5. Rajiv Gandhi, who was then the <u>prime</u> <u>minister</u> of India, visited Washington, <u>d.c.</u>, in June of 1985.
6. The Indus <u>river</u> flows from the Himalaya <u>mountains</u> to the Arabian <u>sea</u>.
7. The writings and television appearances of <u>dr.</u> Carl Sagan have increased public interest in <u>Science</u>.
8. In the afternoons <u>i</u> help Mrs. Parkhurst deliver the *Evening Independent*, a local <u>Newspaper</u>.
9. Many people have left <u>Northern</u> states and moved to the <u>south</u> and <u>west</u>.
10. The <u>Writers</u> Ernest Hemingway, an <u>american</u>, and Robert Service, a <u>canadian</u>, served in the <u>red</u> <u>cross</u> during World <u>war</u> I.
11. Could you please tell me how to get to the <u>chrysler</u> <u>Factory</u> on <u>highway</u> 21 and <u>riverside</u> <u>road</u>?
12. For <u>father's</u> <u>day</u>, let's buy Dad a new power saw.
13. In 1978, the <u>president</u> of <u>egypt</u> and the <u>prime</u> <u>minister</u> of <u>israel</u> shared the <u>nobel</u> <u>peace</u> <u>prize</u>.

14. After we read "<u>fire</u> and <u>ice</u>" by Robert Frost, <u>i</u> wanted to read more of the <u>Poet's</u> work.
15. When <u>i</u> ate <u>Supper</u> at Cam's house, <u>i</u> tried *nuoc mam*, a <u>vietnamese</u> fish sauce.

B. Proofreading Paragraphs for Correct Capitalization

Words that should be lowercased or capitalized are underscored. Optional capitalization is indicated with a double underscore.

Proofread the following paragraphs, adding or omitting capital letters as necessary.

EXAMPLE   [1] The national park service celebrated its seventy-fifth Anniversary in 1991.
   1. *National Park Service; anniversary*

[16] The <u>national</u> <u>park</u> <u>service</u> was set up as a <u>Bureau</u> of the <u>department</u> of the <u>interior</u> on <u>august</u> 15, 1916. [17] However the beginnings of today's system of <u>National</u> parks go back to 1872, when <u>congress</u> established Yellowstone <u>national</u> <u>park</u> in <u>idaho</u>, <u>montana</u>, and <u>wyoming</u>. [18] In 1906, <u>president</u> Theodore Roosevelt signed the Antiquities <u>act</u>, which authorized the <u>president</u> to declare <u>spanish</u> missions and ancient <u>native</u> <u>american</u> villages as monuments. [19] Of the more than three hundred areas now under the <u>Agency's</u> protection, the one located farthest <u>North</u> is Noatak <u>national</u> <u>preserve</u> in northern Alaska. [20] Farthest east is the Buck Island National Monument on <u>st</u>. Croix, in the <u>u</u>.<u>s</u>. Virgin <u>islands</u>. [21] One park is both the farthest <u>South</u> and the farthest west: the <u>national</u> <u>park</u> of <u>american</u> Samoa, in the South <u>pacific</u>.

[22] Continuing to expand its services to visitors, the <u>national</u> <u>park</u> <u>service</u> in 1991 began compiling a computerized directory of the 3,500,000 <u>civil</u> <u>war</u> <u>Soldiers</u>. [23] The <u>Directory</u> will eventually be installed at all twenty-eight <u>civil</u> <u>war</u> sites maintained by the <u>national</u> <u>park</u> <u>service</u>. [24] It should be popular with the 11,000,000 people who visit those <u>Sites</u> each year. [25] Historians estimate that one half of all <u>americans</u> have <u>Relatives</u> who fought in the <u>civil</u> War, and the question visitors ask most often is, "<u>did</u> my <u>Great</u>-great-grandfather fight here?"

MECHANICS

MECHANICS

MECHANICS

SUMMARY STYLE SHEET

Names of Persons

Lupe Serrano	a ballet dancer
Neil A. Armstrong	an astronaut
Martin Luther King, Jr.	a civil rights leader

Geographical Names

Twenty-second Street	a one-way street
Salt Lake City	a city in Utah
in the East, Northwest	traveling east, northwest
Denmark	a country in Europe
Philippine Islands	a group of islands
Pacific Ocean	the largest ocean
Redwood National Park	a park in California
Blue Ridge Mountains	camping in the mountains

Names of Heavenly Bodies

Mars, Pluto, Uranus, Earth	the surface of the earth
North Star	a bright star

Names of Organizations, Businesses, Institutions, Government Bodies

Clarksville Computer Club	the members of the club
Eastman Kodak Company	employed by the company
Pine Bluff High School	a large high school
Department of Transportation	a department of government

Names of Historical Events and Periods, Special Events, Calendar Items

Boston Tea Party	an afternoon tea party
Stone Age	at the age of fourteen
National Chess Tournament	an annual tournament
Memorial Day	a national holiday

Names of Nationalities, Races, Religions

Japanese	a nationality
Caucasian	a race
Christianity	a religion
God	a god of Greek mythology

(continued)

SUMMARY STYLE SHEET *(continued)*

Names of Buildings, Monuments, Awards

the John Hancock Building	an insurance building
Aladdin Motel	a motel in Miami
Mount Rushmore National Memorial	a national monument
Pulitzer Prize	winning a prize

Names of Trains, Ships, Airplanes, Spacecraft

Golden Arrow	a train
Andrea Doria	a ship
Spirit of St. Louis	an airplane
Apollo 11	a spacecraft

Brand Names

Timex watch	a digital watch
Huffy bicycle	a ten-speed bicycle

Names of Languages, School Subjects

English, German, French, Spanish	a native language
Algebra I, Science II, Art 101	algebra, science, art

Titles

Governor Martinez	a former governor
the President of the United States	the president of the club
Grandfather Bennett	my grandfather
Thank you, Grandfather.	
The War of the Worlds	a book
People Weekly	a magazine
The Dallas Morning News	a newspaper
"Casey at the Bat"	a poem
"The Gift of the Magi"	a short story
Declaration of Independence	a historical document
West Side Story	a play, a movie
The Cosby Show	a television program
American Gothic	a painting
"The Star-Spangled Banner"	a national anthem

MECHANICS

TECHNOLOGY TIP

There are video and computer games available that move students closer to achieving a given goal each time they correctly capitalize a word. If you have access to such games, they can be useful learning tools for students.

MECHANICS

DIAGNOSTIC TEST

OBJECTIVE

• To insert end marks, commas, semicolons, and colons as needed in sentences

FOR THE WHOLE CHAPTER

■ **Review** For exercises on chapter concepts, see **Review Form A** and **Review Form B** in *Language Skills Practice and Assessment,* pp. 234–235.

■ **Assessment** For additional testing, see **Mechanics Pretests** and **Mechanics Mastery Tests** in *Language Skills Practice and Assessment,* pp. 203–210 and pp. 275–282.

CHAPTER OVERVIEW

This chapter allows students to review and build on past knowledge of punctuation. The first part of the chapter discusses end marks and abbreviations. Then comma rules are presented, followed by rules for the use of semicolons and colons. The **Writing Application** asks students to write letters and use punctuation to clarify meaning.

This chapter can be a valuable resource throughout the year, especially during the proofreading stage of writing assignments. Explain to students that a familiarity with the information in this chapter can help them add variety and clarity to their writing.

MECHANICS

26 PUNCTUATION

End Marks, Commas, Semicolons, Colons

Correcting Sentences by Adding End Marks, Commas, Semicolons, and Colons

Write the following sentences, inserting end marks, commas, semicolons, and colons as needed.

EXAMPLE **1.** Have you seen our teacher Ms. O'Donnell today

1. *Have you seen our teacher, Ms. O'Donnell, today?*

1. Cortez Peters, the world's fastest typist, can type 250 words per minute, and he has won thirteen international typing contests.

2. We made a salad with the following vegetables from our garden: lettuce, cucumbers, and cherry tomatoes.

3. Running after the bus, Dr. Sloan tripped and fell in a puddle.

736

END MARKS Rules 26a–26e

OBJECTIVE

- To correct paragraphs by adding the proper end marks to sentences

4. My first pet, which I got when I was six, was a beagle. I named it Bagel. **4. ;** [*or* .]
5. Come in, Randy, and sit down.
6. The soft, subtle colors of this beautiful Navajo rug are produced from natural vegetable dyes.
7. Well, I do know John 3:16 by heart.
8. Does anyone know where the crank that we use to open the top windows is? **9.** ^ [*or* C]
9. The chickens clucked, and the ducks squawked; however, the dogs didn't make a sound.
10. Now I recognize her! She's in my math class. **10.** . [*or* !]
11. Wow! That's the longest home run I've ever hit. **11. !** [*or* .]
12. After the rain stopped, the blue jays hopped around the lawn in search of worms.
13. Wasn't President John F. Kennedy assassinated in Dallas, Tex., on November 22, 1963?
14. Soy sauce, which is made from soybeans, flavors many traditional Chinese and Japanese foods.
15. Everybody had told her, of course, that she couldn't succeed if she didn't try.
16. Preparing for takeoff, the huge jetliner rolled slowly toward the runway.
17. In one of the barns, we found an old butter churn.
18. Did you see the highlights of the Cinco de Mayo Fiesta on the 6:00 news?
19. Her address is 142 Oak Hollow Blvd., Mendota, CA 93640.
20. To get a better view of the fireworks, Josh and I rode our bikes to Miller's Hill.

PROGRAM MANAGER

END MARKS

- **Independent Practice/ Reteaching** For instruction and exercises, see **Using End Marks** in *Language Skills Practice and Assessment,* p. 225.

- **Computer Guided Instruction** For additional instruction and practice, see **Lesson 50** in *Language Workshop CD-ROM.*

- **Practice** To help less-advanced students, see **Chapter 23** in *English Workshop, Second Course,* pp. 245–246.

MECHANICS

End Marks

An *end mark* is a mark of punctuation placed at the end of a sentence. The three kinds of end marks are the *period,* the *question mark,* and the *exclamation point.*

LEP/ESL

General Strategies. When an English-language learner makes an error in punctuation, it may be the result of transfer from his or her native language system. For example, the question mark may take several different forms:

1. Spanish—¿Where is Bill?
2. Farsi—Where is Bill ؟ (Farsi is spoken in Iran, Afghanistan, Pakistan, southern Russia, and India.)
3. Arabic—؟Where is Bill?
4. Greek—Where is Bill; (The question mark in Greek looks like the English semicolon.)

LEARNING STYLES

Auditory Learners. It may be easier for some students to hear the differences in the sentence types than to recognize them visually. Give students oral examples of each type, and have students identify each sentence type and its proper end mark.

QUICK REMINDER

Have each student write a question, a statement, an exclamation, a request, and a command. Each sentence should have an appropriate end mark. You may want to write the following examples on the chalkboard:

1. Why are you smiling? (question)
2. He enjoys reading. (statement)
3. What a great game! (exclamation)
4. Please sit down. (request)
5. Close that window. (command)

Point out to students that the period and the exclamation point are sometimes interchangeable, depending on the emotion expressed.

MECHANICS

738

MECHANICS

26a. Use a period at the end of a statement.

EXAMPLES   One of the figure skaters was Sonja Henie.
"I live in a world of such beautiful stories that I have to write one every now and then."
from an interview with Pearl Crayton

26b. Use a question mark at the end of a question.

EXAMPLES   What is the capital of Canada?
Did Gordon Parks write *The Learning Tree*?

26c. Use an exclamation point at the end of an exclamation.

EXAMPLES   What an exciting time we had!
Wow! What a view!

26d. Use a period or an exclamation point at the end of a request or a command.

EXAMPLES   Please give me the scissors. [a request]
Give me the scissors! [a command]

EXERCISE 1   Using End Marks

In the following paragraphs, sentences have been run together without end marks. Identify the <u>last word</u> of every sentence, and supply the proper end mark. [Note: The paragraphs contain a total of ten sentences.]

EXAMPLE   1. Can you imagine what life was like in Abraham Lincoln's time
1. *time?*

In New Salem Park, Illinois, you will find a reproduction of the little village of New Salem, just as it was when Abraham Lincoln lived <u>there</u>.A visit to this village reveals that life in Lincoln's time was harder than it is <u>today</u>.

The cabin of the Onstats is not a reproduction but, instead, is the original cabin where Lincoln spent many hours.In that living room, on that very floor, young Abe studied with Isaac Onstat.It was the cabin's only room.

Across the way hangs a big kettle once used by Mr. Waddell for boiling wool.Mr. Waddell, the hatter of the village, made hats of wool and fur.

Do any of you think that you'd like to go back to those days?What endurance those people must have had!Could we manage to live as they did?

26e. Use a period after most abbreviations.

TYPES OF ABBREVIATIONS	EXAMPLES
Personal Names	Pearl S. Buck W.E.B. DuBois
Titles Used with Names	Mr. Mrs. Ms. Jr. Sr. Dr.
States	Ky. Fla. Tenn. Calif.

NOTE: A two-letter state abbreviation without periods is used only when it is followed by a ZIP Code. Both letters of the abbreviation are then capitalized.

EXAMPLE   Austin, **TX** 78741

TYPES OF ABBREVIATIONS	EXAMPLES
Times	A.M. P.M. B.C. A.D.
Addresses	St. Rd. Blvd. P.O. Box
Organizations and Companies	Co. Inc. Corp. Assn.

NOTE: Abbreviations for government agencies and some widely used abbreviations are written without periods. Each letter of the abbreviation is capitalized.

EXAMPLES   UN, FBI, PTA, NAACP, PBS, CNN, YMCA, VHF

If you're not sure whether to use periods with abbreviations, look in a dictionary.

MECHANICS

COMMON ERROR

Problem. All states can be abbreviated two different ways—one with a period and one without. Therefore, many students punctuate state abbreviations incorrectly in their writing.

Solution. Display the following list used by the United States Postal Service and remind students not to use periods with these abbreviations. Students can refer to the list throughout the year.

AL	Alabama	NV	Nevada
AK	Alaska	NH	New
AZ	Arizona		Hampshire
AR	Arkansas	NJ	New Jersey
CA	California	NM	New Mexico
CO	Colorado	NY	New York
CT	Connecticut	NC	North
DE	Delaware		Carolina
FL	Florida	ND	North
GA	Georgia		Dakota
HI	Hawaii	OH	Ohio
ID	Idaho	OK	Oklahoma
IL	Illinois	OR	Oregon
IN	Indiana	PA	Pennsylvania
IA	Iowa	RI	Rhode Island
KS	Kansas	SC	South
KY	Kentucky		Carolina
LA	Louisiana	SD	South Dakota
ME	Maine	TN	Tennessee
MD	Maryland	TX	Texas
MA	Massachusetts	UT	Utah
MI	Michigan	VT	Vermont
MN	Minnesota	VA	Virginia
MS	Mississippi	WA	Washington
MO	Missouri	WV	West Virginia
MT	Montana	WI	Wisconsin
NE	Nebraska	WY	Wyoming

MECHANICS

OBJECTIVE

• To add the appropriate end marks in sentences

A DIFFERENT APPROACH

To give students practice in using end marks and abbreviations, try a team game. Divide the class into five teams. Specify a kind of sentence and a specific type of abbreviation to be used in that sentence. You could combine the following types:

Kind of Sentence	Abbreviation
statement	proper name
question	title with name
exclamation	state
request	address
command	organization/ company
	time
	unit of measure

Team members may confer for fifteen seconds; then each team must send a member to the chalkboard to write the sentence. Give a point for the correct sentence type, end mark, and abbreviation. Continue the procedure by having teams rotate members sent to the chalkboard.

CRITICAL THINKING

Analysis and Synthesis. End marks let readers know whether the writer is making a statement, asking a question, or expressing strong feelings. Write the following sentences on the chalkboard:

1. I made the highest grade.
2. I made the highest grade?
3. I made the highest grade!

Ask students to analyze and explain how the purpose of the sentence changes according to the end mark used. Then have students use the model on the chalkboard to develop original sentences. This synthesis should demonstrate whether they have mastered the correct use of end punctuation.

MECHANICS

MECHANICS

740

740 *Punctuation*

Abbreviations for units of measure are usually written without periods. However, you should use a period with the abbreviation *in.* (for *inch*) to prevent confusing it with the word *in.*

EXAMPLES   cm, kg, ml, oz, lb, ft, yd, mi

NOTE: When an abbreviation with a period ends a sentence, another period is not needed. However, a question mark or an exclamation point is used as needed.

EXAMPLES   This is my friend, J. R.
Have you met Nguyen, J. R.?

REVIEW A   **Correcting Sentences by Adding End Marks**

Write the following sentences, adding end marks where they are needed.

EXAMPLE   **1.** Look at the beautiful costume this Japanese actor is wearing
1. *Look at the beautiful costume this Japanese actor is wearing!*

1. The picture reminds me of our visit to Little Tokyo last year.
2. Have you ever heard of Little Tokyo?

LESSON 3 *(pp. 741–758)*
COMMAS Rules 26f–26l

OBJECTIVES

- To correct sentences by adding commas to separate items in a series and to separate two or more adjectives preceding a noun
- To correct compound sentences by adding commas

26f

3. It's a Japanese neighborhood in Los Angeles, Calif., bordered by First St., Third St., Alameda St., and Los Angeles St. 3. ⊙/⊙/⊙/⊙
4. Some friends of ours who live in Los Angeles, Mr. and Mrs. Albert B. Cook, Sr., and their son, Al, Jr., introduced us to the area. 4. ⊙/⊙
5. They met our 11:30 A.M. flight from Atlanta, Ga., and took us to lunch at a restaurant in the Japanese Plaza Village. 5. ⊙/⊙/⊙
6. Later we stopped at a bakery for *mochigashi*, which are Japanese pastries, and then we visited the Japanese American Cultural and Community Center on San Pedro St.
7. Outside the center is a striking abstract sculpture by Isamu Noguchi, who created the stone sculpture garden at the UNESCO headquarters in Paris, France.
8. Next door is the Japan America Theater, which stages a wide variety of works by both Eastern and Western artists.
9. Soon, it was time to head for the Cooks's home, at 6311 Oleander Blvd. where we spent the night. 9. ⊙
10. What a great afternoon we had exploring Japanese culture!

Commas

A *comma* is used to separate words or groups of words so that the meaning of a sentence is clear.

Items in a Series

26f. Use commas to separate items in a series.

Words, phrases, and clauses in a series are separated by commas to show the reader where one item in the series ends and the next item begins.

MECHANICS

PROGRAM MANAGER

COMMAS

- **Independent Practice/ Reteaching** For instruction and exercises, see **Commas with Items in a Series, Commas with Compound Sentences, Commas with Nonessential Elements, Uses of Commas,** and **Other Uses of Commas** in *Language Skills Practice and Assessment,* pp. 226–230.

- **Computer Guided Instruction** For additional instruction and practice with commas, see **Lessons 46–49** in *Language Workshop CD-ROM.*

- **Practice** To help less-advanced students with additional instruction and practice with commas, see **Chapter 23** in *English Workshop, Second Course,* pp. 247–258.

QUICK REMINDER

Commas not only give the reader a natural break but also make sense of complicated sentences. Write the following sentences on the chalkboard without commas and have students suggest where commas should be added:

1. We need to find out what time we play[,] which uniform we wear[,] and which bus we board.
2. We play our first game at noon[,] but the bus leaves at 9:00.
3. By the way[,] you're the first batter.
4. Amelia[,] our team's best hitter[,] bats next.
5. Running for home plate[,] Amelia tripped and fell.

MECHANICS

- To correct sentences by adding commas to set off nonessential phrases and clauses, appositives and appositive phrases, words in direct address, parenthetical expressions, and introductory phrases and clauses
- To correct dates, addresses, and letter parts by adding commas
- To write a paragraph by using end marks and commas correctly
- To write a journal entry by using all types of end marks and by using commas in compound sentences and to separate items in a series

MEETING *individual* NEEDS

STUDENTS WITH SPECIAL NEEDS

Some students may have difficulty taking in too many new concepts at one time. The numerous rules of comma usage presented in this lesson might be frustrating if presented all together. Be prepared to spend ample time on each rule before proceeding to the next one.

LESS-ADVANCED STUDENTS

Students will probably be familiar with the use of commas to separate single-word items in series, but they may not be familiar with their use to separate phrases and clauses in series. You may want to review **Chapter 17: "The Phrase"** and **Chapter 18: "The Clause"** and to give additional examples of phrases and clauses in series.

MECHANICS

MECHANICS

742 *Punctuation*

WORDS IN A SERIES
Barbecue, hammock, canoe, and *moccasin* are four of the words that the English language owes to American Indians. [nouns]
Always stop, look, and listen before crossing railroad tracks. [verbs]
In the early morning, the lake looked cold, gray, and calm. [adjectives]
PHRASES IN A SERIES
Tightening the spokes, checking the tire pressure, and oiling the gears, Carlos prepared his bike for the race. [participial phrases]
We found seaweed in the water, on the sand, under the rocks, and later in our shoes. [prepositional phrases]
Clearing the table, washing the dishes, and putting everything away took almost an hour. [gerund phrases]
CLAUSES IN A SERIES
We didn't know where we were going, how we would get there, or when we would arrive. [subordinate clauses]
The lights dimmed, the curtain rose, and the orchestra began to play. [short independent clauses]

NOTE: Only *short* independent clauses in a series may be separated by commas. Independent clauses in a series are usually separated by semicolons.

Use a comma before the *and* joining the last two items in a series so that the meaning will be clear.

UNCLEAR   Luanne, Zack and I are going riding. [Is Luanne being addressed, or is she going riding?]

CLEAR   Luanne, Zack, and I are going riding. [Three people are going riding.]

If all items in a series are joined by *and* or *or,* do not use commas to separate them.

EXAMPLES   I voted for Corey **and** Mona **and** Ethan.
For your report you may want to read Jean Toomer's *Cane* **or** Ralph Ellison's *Invisible Man* **or** Richard Wright's *Native Son.*

EXERCISE 2

Correcting Sentences by Adding Commas

Insert commas where they are needed in each series in the following sentences.

EXAMPLE **1.** On their expedition, the explorers took with them 117 pounds of potatoes 116 pounds of beef and 100 pounds of fresh vegetables.

          1. *117 pounds of potatoes, 116 pounds of beef, and 100 pounds of fresh vegetables*

1. Carlos and Anna and I made a piñata filled it with small toys and hung it from a large tree.
2. The four states that have produced the most U.S. presidents are Virginia Ohio Massachusetts and New York.
3. The school band includes clarinets trumpets tubas saxophones trombones flutes piccolos and drums.
4. Most flutes used by professional musicians are made of sterling silver fourteen-carat gold or platinum.
5. We know what we will write about where we will find sources and how we will organize our reports.
6. Squanto became an interpreter for the Pilgrims showed them how to plant corn and stayed with them throughout his life.
7. Sylvia Porter wrote several books about how to earn money and how to spend it borrow it and save it.
8. Last summer I read *The Lucky Stone A Wizard of Earthsea Barrio Boy* and *A Wrinkle in Time.*
9. The San Joaquin kit fox the ocelot the Florida panther and the red wolf are only some of the endangered mammals in North America.
10. I want to visit Thailand Nepal China and Japan.

26g. Use a comma to separate two or more adjectives that come before a noun.

EXAMPLES An Arabian horse is a fast, beautiful animal.
Many ranchers depended on the small, tough, sure-footed mustang.

MECHANICS

A team race may help reinforce comma use with words, phrases, and clauses in series. Have teams of four students each write in five minutes as many sentences using commas in series as possible. To help them begin, list the following examples on the chalkboard:

Word Series
1. Red, gold, and blue were her colors.
2. She was tall, gentle, and graceful.

Phrase Series
1. The water came over the tub, onto the floor, and under the door.
2. Counting the money, writing checks, and making deposits took four hours.

Clause Series
1. We asked who he was, where he was going, and when he was leaving.
2. The runners took their marks, the gun sounded, and the race began.

Award a point for each correct use of a comma in series.

MECHANICS

Sometimes the final adjective in a series is closely linked to the noun. When the adjective and the noun are linked in such a way, do not use a comma before the final adjective.

EXAMPLE   Training a frisky colt to become a gentle, dependable riding horse takes great patience.

Notice in this example that no comma is used between *dependable* and *riding* because the words *riding horse* are closely connected.

If you aren't sure whether the final adjective and the noun are linked, use this test. Insert the word *and* between the adjectives. If *and* makes sense, use a comma. In the example, *and* makes sense between *gentle* and *dependable*. *And* doesn't make sense between *dependable* and *riding*.

A comma should never be used between an adjective and the noun immediately following it.

INCORRECT   Mary O'Hara wrote a tender, suspenseful, story about a young boy and his colt.
CORRECT   Mary O'Hara wrote a tender, suspenseful story about a young boy and his colt.

▶ EXERCISE 3   **Correcting Sentences by Adding Commas**

Write the following sentences, adding commas where they are needed.

EXAMPLE   **1.** A squat dark wood-burning stove stood in one corner.
   1. *A squat, dark wood-burning stove stood in one corner.*

1. They made a clubhouse in the empty‚unused storage shed.
2. This book describes the harsh‚isolated lives of pioneer women in Kansas.
3. What a lovely‚haunting melody that tune has!

26h

4. Charlayne Hunter-Gault's skillful͵probing interviews have made her a respected broadcast journalist.
5. The delicate͵colorful wings of the hummingbird vibrate up to two hundred times each second.

Compound Sentences

26h. Use a comma before *and, but, or, nor, for, so,* or *yet* when it joins independent clauses.

EXAMPLES The musical comedy began as an American musical form, **and** its popularity has spread throughout the world.
I enjoyed *The King and I,* **but** *Oklahoma!* is still my favorite musical.

When the independent clauses are very short, the comma before *and, but,* or *or* may be omitted.

EXAMPLES Oscar Hammerstein wrote the words and Richard Rodgers wrote the music.
I'm tired but I can't sleep.
The cat can stay inside or it can go out.

A comma is always used before *nor, for, so,* or *yet* joining independent clauses.

EXAMPLES We will not give up, **nor** will we fail.
Everyone seemed excited, **for** it was time to begin.
No one else was there, **so** we left.
The water was cold, **yet** it looked inviting.

NOTE: Don't be misled by a simple sentence with a compound verb. A simple sentence has only one independent clause.

SIMPLE SENTENCE WITH COMPOUND VERB : Margo likes golf but doesn't enjoy archery.

COMPOUND SENTENCE : Margo likes golf, but she doesn't enjoy archery. [two independent clauses]

MECHANICS

MEETING individual NEEDS

LEP/ESL

General Strategies. Comma placement is not universal throughout the world. Three languages that use the comma without a linking word to join coordinate independent clauses are Turkish, Dutch, and Arabic. Students who speak these languages may use comma splices such as "My hometown is not large, it is very pretty." When you correct such comma splices, acknowledge that you may be asking students to change rules they have already mastered.

LEARNING STYLES

Visual Learners. To help students distinguish between a compound sentence and a simple sentence with a compound verb, write the following sentence pairs on the chalkboard:

1. Fred loves to eat yet hates meat. Fred loves to eat, yet he hates meat.
2. Pam swims often and jogs daily. Pam swims often, and she jogs daily.
3. Maria reads books but sees no movies.
   Maria reads books, but she sees no movies.

Underline the subjects with one color of chalk and underline the verbs with another color. Circle the comma in each compound sentence and emphasize that compound sentences have two independent clauses, each of which has a subject and a verb.

MECHANICS

COOPERATIVE LEARNING

You may wish to use this activity with the study of a piece of literature. Write each of the coordinating conjunctions—*and, but, or, not, for, so,* and *yet*—on an index card, creating a set of seven cards. Then make a duplicate set. Divide the class into two teams and give each team a set of cards. The object is for the teams to use each word in at least one compound sentence about a specific piece of literature or its author. Each sentence must have the subject and the verb identified and the comma used correctly.

At the end of ten minutes, have each team read its sentences aloud. Award a point for correct identification of each subject and each verb and for correct comma usage before the conjunction.

☞ REFERENCE NOTE: For more about compound sentences, see pages 559–560. For more about simple sentences with compound verbs, see page 557.

▶ EXERCISE 4 **Correcting Compound Sentences by Adding Commas**

For each of the following sentences, identify the two words that should be separated by a comma. Include the comma. If a sentence is correct, write *C.*

EXAMPLE **1. Have you read this article or do you want me to tell you about it?**
1. *article, or*

1. Human beings must study to become <u>architects‸yet</u> some animals build amazing structures by instinct.

2. The male gardener bower bird builds a complex <u>structure‸and</u> he decorates it carefully to attract a mate.

3. This bird constructs a dome-shaped garden in a small <u>tree‸and</u> underneath the tree he lays a carpet of moss covered with brilliant tropical flowers.

4. Then, he gathers twigs and arranges them in a three-foot-wide circle around the display. **4. C**

5. Tailor ants might be called the ant world's high-rise <u>workers‸for</u> they gather leaves and sew them around tree twigs to make nests like those shown here.

26i

6. These nests are built in tropical trees,and they may be one hundred feet or more above the ground.
7. Adult tailor ants don't secrete the silk used to weave the leaves together,but they squeeze it from their larvae.
8. The female European water spider builds a waterproof nest under water,and she stocks the nest with air bubbles.
9. This air supply is very important,for it allows the spider to hunt underwater.
10. The water spider lays her eggs in the waterproof nest,and they hatch there.

Interrupters

26i. Use commas to set off an expression that interrupts a sentence.

(1) Use commas to set off a nonessential participial phrase or a nonessential subordinate clause.

A *nonessential* (or *nonrestrictive*) phrase or clause adds information that isn't needed to understand the meaning of the sentence. Such a phrase or clause can be omitted without changing the main idea of the sentence.

NONESSENTIAL PHRASES   The spider web, **shining in the morning light,** looked like sparkling lace.
Harvard College, **founded in 1636,** is the oldest college in the United States.

NONESSENTIAL CLAUSES   Kareem Abdul-Jabbar, **who retired from professional basketball in 1989,** holds several NBA records.
Joshua eventually overcame his acrophobia, **which is the abnormal fear of being in high places.**

INTEGRATING THE LANGUAGE ARTS

Mechanics and Library Skills. Have each student use various library resources (encyclopedias, biographies, the *Readers' Guide to Periodical Literature,* and *Who's Who*) to find three names with which other students might be unfamiliar. Have students exchange these names with partners who will research each person named and write two descriptive sentences about him or her. One of the sentences should contain a nonessential phrase, and one should contain a nonessential clause. The more obscure the name, the more the partner must search for information. Only as a last resort should students divulge sources.

When all sentences have been written, have partners check to see that commas have been used to set off nonessential phrases and clauses.

MECHANICS

MECHANICS

COOPERATIVE LEARNING

To give students extra practice punctuating phrases and clauses, separate the class into groups of three to four students. Give each group five blank note cards, and ask the group members to write a phrase or a clause on each card. You could write the following examples on the chalkboard:

1. who found a million dollars
2. which made her pause
3. with no one else in sight
4. looking around carefully
5. that she discovered

Have the groups exchange their sets of cards and use the clauses from their acquired sets to write a correctly punctuated story. You may want to have one member of each group read the group's story to the rest of the class.

TIMESAVER

As students complete the exercises in this chapter, suggest that students use a different-colored ink for the punctuation. The different color will make the punctuation more visually striking and easier to grade.

Do not set off an *essential* (or *restrictive*) phrase or clause. Since such a phrase or clause tells *which one(s)*, it cannot be omitted without changing the meaning of the sentence.

ESSENTIAL PHRASES All farmers **growing the new hybrid corn** should have a good harvest. [Which farmers?]
The discoveries **made by Einstein** have changed the way people think about the universe. [Which discoveries?]

ESSENTIAL CLAUSES The book **that you recommended** is not in the library. [Which book?]
Often, someone **who does a good deed** gains more than the person **for whom the deed is done.** [Which someone? Which person?]

NOTE: A clause beginning with *that* is usually essential.

REFERENCE NOTE: For more information about participial phrases, see pages 515–516. For more about subordinate clauses, see pages 535–548.

EXERCISE 5 **Using Commas in Sentences with Nonessential Phrases or Clauses**

Write the following sentences, adding commas to set off the nonessential phrases or clauses. If a sentence is correct, write C.

EXAMPLE 1. My favorite performer is Gloria Estefan who is the lead singer with the Miami Sound Machine.
1. *My favorite performer is Gloria Estefan, who is the lead singer with the Miami Sound Machine.*

1. Estefan, badly injured in a bus accident in 1990, made a remarkable comeback the following year.
2. The accident, which occurred on March 20, 1990, shattered one of her vertebrae and almost severed her spinal cord.

3. The months of physical therapy required after the accident were painful for the singer. **3.** C
4. Yet less than a year later‸performing in public for the first time since the accident‸she sang on the American Music Awards telecast January 28, 1991.
5. On March 1 of that year‸launching a yearlong tour of Japan, Europe, and the United States‸she and the band gave a concert in Miami.
6. Estefan‸who was born in Cuba‸came to the United States when she was two years old.
7. Her family‸fleeing the Cuban Revolution‸settled in Miami‸where she now lives with her husband, Emilio, and their son, Nayib.
8. The album released to mark her successful comeback is titled *Into the Light*. **8.** C
9. It contains twelve songs‸including the first one written by the singer after the accident.
10. Appropriately, that song‸inspired by a fragment that Emilio wrote as Gloria was being taken to surgery‸is titled "Coming Out of the Dark."

(2) Use commas to set off an appositive or an appositive phrase that is nonessential.

EXAMPLES   My best friend, **Nancy,** is studying ballet.
We're out of our most popular flavor, **vanilla.**
Nancy, **my best friend,** has won a dance
   scholarship.
The Rio Grande, **one of the major rivers of
North America,** forms the border between
Texas and Mexico.

   Do not set off an appositive that tells *which one(s)* about the word it identifies. Such an appositive is essential to the meaning of the sentence.

EXAMPLES   My ancestor **Alberto Pazienza** immigrated to
the United States on the ship *Marianna.* [Which
ancestor? Which ship?]

👉 REFERENCE NOTE: For more on appositives, see pages 526–527.

MECHANICS

COMMON ERROR

Problem. Many students will omit the comma that should follow an appositive. This is a particular problem if the appositive identifies the subject, and the verb directly following the appositive makes the sentence sound complete. (For example, "Marta, our goalie was named the most valuable player" should read "Marta, our goalie, ...")

Solution. Make a large sentence strip of a sentence containing an appositive phrase. Cut the strip in two places and remove the appositive phrase to show students that the sentence can stand alone without the phrase. Emphasize that when the phrase is reinserted, it must be set off from the sentence with commas. Suggest that students underline or highlight appositive phrases in their written work to make sure the phrases are set off with commas.

MECHANICS

TIMESAVER

You may wish to have students read aloud the sentences in **Exercise 6,** inserting the commas as needed.

A DIFFERENT APPROACH

To give students practice in using commas in direct address, have each student write an imaginary dialogue between two famous people, living or dead. To provide ideas, suggest NFL quarterbacks, TV and movie stars, explorers, politicians, artists, singers, inventors, or writers.

Before having the pairs trade their papers to check for correct comma usage, have each pair read their dialogues and leave out the names in direct address, as if the dialogues were scenes from a play. Have students try to guess who the famous speakers are.

---

750 *Punctuation*

 EXERCISE 6   **Using Commas in Sentences to Set Off Appositives and Appositive Phrases**

Write the sentences that require commas. Insert the commas. If a sentence is correct, write *C*.

EXAMPLE **1.** The dog a boxer is named Brindle.
         1. *The dog, a boxer, is named Brindle.*

1. The composer Mozart wrote five short piano pieces when he was only six years old.   **1.** C
2. Katy Jurado, the actress, has appeared in many fine films.
3. Harper Lee, author of *To Kill a Mockingbird,* is from Alabama.
4. The card game canasta is descended from mah-jongg, an ancient Chinese game.
5. Jupiter, the fifth planet from the sun, is so large that all the other planets in our solar system would fit inside it.
6. The main character in many of Agatha Christie's mystery novels is the detective Hercule Poirot.   **6.** C
7. The writing of Elizabeth Bowen, an Irish novelist, shows her keen, witty observations of life.
8. Charlemagne, the king of the Franks in the eighth and ninth centuries, became emperor of the Holy Roman Empire.
9. Chuck Yeager, an American pilot, broke the sound barrier in 1947.
10. Artist Effie Tybrec, a Sioux from South Dakota, decorates plain sneakers with elaborate beadwork.

(3) Use commas to set off words used in direct address.

EXAMPLES **Mrs. Clarkson,** this package is addressed to you.
          Do you know, **Elena,** when the next bus is due?

EXERCISE 7   **Using Commas in Sentences to Set Off Words in Direct Address**

Write the following sentences, adding commas to set off the words in direct address.

EXAMPLE   **1.** Are you hungry Jan or have you had lunch?
          1. *Are you hungry, Jan, or have you had lunch?*

1. Ms. Wu,will you schedule me for the computer lab tomorrow?
2. Have you signed up for a baseball team yet,Aaron?
3. Your time was good in the hurdles,Juanita,but I know you can do better.
4. Wear sturdy shoes,girls; those hills are hard on the feet!
5. Run,Susan; the bus is pulling out!

(4) Use commas to set off a parenthetical expression.

A *parenthetical expression* is a side remark that adds information or relates ideas.

EXAMPLES   The president said**,** **of course,** that he was
          deeply disappointed.
          In my opinion, the movie was too violent.
          I will invite Samantha**, I think.**

Commonly Used Parenthetical Expressions		
after all	generally speaking	nevertheless
at any rate	on the other hand	of course
by the way	I believe (hope,	on the contrary
for example	suppose, think)	however
for instance	in my opinion	therefore

Some of these expressions are not always used as interrupters. Use commas only when the expressions are parenthetical.

EXAMPLES   What**, in your opinion,** is the best solution?
          [parenthetical]
          I have faith **in your opinion.** [not parenthetical]

          Traveling by boat may take longer**, however.**
          [parenthetical]
          However you go, it will be a delightful trip. [not parenthetical]

MECHANICS

MECHANICS

751

LEARNING STYLES

Auditory Learners. Some students might be able to hear parenthetical expressions more easily than they can spot them on a page. You may wish to read aloud the examples from this section of the chapter. Then read the examples without the parenthetical expressions. Students should recognize that the sentences do not need the parenthetical expressions in order to make sense. Stress that parenthetical expressions always interrupt the flow of the sentence and that this interruption indicates the use of commas.

You may want to allow students to do **Exercise 8** orally.

COMMON ERROR

Problem. Many students fail to add commas after introductory phrases or clauses and inadvertently create sentences that are difficult to understand.

Solution. To demonstrate to students how important the placement of commas can be after introductory phrases and clauses, write the following incorrect sentence on the chalkboard:

After eating my cat takes a nap.

Ask students to think of similar sentences with introductory phrases or clauses that demonstrate the need for commas and to write these examples on the chalkboard. Have students check their writing for similar comma omissions.

---

752 *Punctuation*

 EXERCISE 8 **Using Commas in Sentences to Set Off Parenthetical Expressions**

Write each of the following sentences, using commas to set off the parenthetical expression.

EXAMPLE **1.** Mathematics I'm afraid is my hardest subject.
1. *Mathematics, I'm afraid, is my hardest subject.*

1. The posttest‚of course‚covered material from the entire chapter.
2. Your subject should‚I think‚be limited further.
3. *Cilantro*‚by the way‚is the Spanish name for the herb coriander.
4. Flying‚however‚will be more expensive than driving there in the car.
5. After all‚their hard work paid off.

Introductory Words, Phrases, and Clauses

26j. Use a comma after *yes, no,* or any mild exclamation such as *well* or *why* at the beginning of a sentence.

EXAMPLES **Yes,** I understand the problem.
Well, I think we should ask for help.

26k. Use a comma after an introductory phrase or clause.

Prepositional Phrases

A comma is used after an introductory prepositional phrase if the phrase is long or if two or more phrases appear together.

EXAMPLES **Underneath the moss-covered rock,** we found a shiny, fat earthworm.
At night in the desert, the temperature falls rapidly.

If the introductory prepositional phrase is short, a comma may or may not be used.

EXAMPLE **In the morning,** [or In the morning] **we'll tour the Caddo burial mounds.**

Verbal Phrases

A comma is used after a participial phrase or an infinitive phrase that introduces a sentence.

PARTICIPIAL PHRASE **Forced onto the sidelines by a sprained ankle, Carlos was restless and unhappy.**

INFINITIVE PHRASE **To defend the honor of King Arthur's knights, Sir Gawain accepted the Green Knight's challenge.**

Adverb Clauses

An adverb clause may be placed at various places in a sentence. When it begins the sentence, the adverb clause is followed by a comma.

EXAMPLES **When March came, the huge ice pack began to melt and break up.**

Because I had a sore throat, I could not audition for the school play.

☞ REFERENCE NOTE: For more about prepositional phrases, see pages 506–509. For more about verbal phrases, see pages 515–523. For more about adverb clauses, see pages 544–545.

▶ EXERCISE 9   **Using Commas in Sentences with Introductory Phrases or Clauses**

If a sentence needs a comma, identify the <u>word it should follow</u>, and add the comma. If a sentence is correct, write C.

EXAMPLE   **1. Patented in 1883 Matzeliger's lasting machine, which attached the sole of a shoe to its upper part, revolutionized the shoe industry.**

1. *1883,*

MECHANICS

MECHANICS

VISUAL CONNECTIONS

Related Expression Skills.
Where does the Postal Service get its ideas for stamps? Some ideas come from political-interest groups. Others come from ordinary citizens. You may want to have an interested team of students choose a subject, design a stamp, and compose a convincing letter to the selection committee—the committee of stamp collectors, lay people, and celebrities appointed by the Postmaster General. Address the letter to:

> The Citizen's Stamp Advisory
> Committee, Stamp Management
> U.S. Postal Service
> 475 L'Enfant Plaza S.W.
> Washington, D.C. 20260

Remind students to proofread for comma usage.

You may want to tell students that a person cannot be commemorated until he or she has been dead for more than ten years. One exception is U.S. presidents, who can be commemorated as soon as they die.

1. Issued in <u>1991</u>,this stamp honoring inventor Jan Matzeliger is part of the U.S. Postal Service's Black Heritage series.

2. Since the Postal Service began issuing the series in <u>1978</u>,the stamps have become popular collectors' items.

3. Originally picturing only government officials or national <u>symbols</u>,U.S. stamps now feature a wide variety of people, items, and events.

4. As stamps became more <u>varied</u>,stamp collecting became even more popular.

5. Because stamps portray our country's <u>culture</u>,they fascinate many people.

6. In the United States <u>alone</u>,more than twenty million people enjoy stamp collecting. **6.** ⋀ [*or* C]

7. To attract <u>collectors</u>,the Postal Service produces limited numbers of special stamps.

8. Collectors can always look forward to adding new stamps because new designs are issued often. **8.** C

9. To keep their collections from becoming too <u>bulky</u>⋀ many collectors concentrate on a single topic.

10. With their treasures safely in <u>albums</u>,collectors enjoy examining their first stamps as well as their most recent ones.

Conventional Situations

26l. Use commas in certain conventional situations.

(1) Use commas to separate items in dates and addresses.

261

EXAMPLES   The delegates to the Constitutional Convention signed the Constitution on September 17, 1787, in Philadelphia, Pennsylvania.

Each year the Kentucky Derby is held in Louisville, Kentucky, on the first Saturday in May.

Passover begins on Wednesday, April 14, this year.

My grandparents' address is 6448 Higgins Road, Chicago, IL 60607.

Notice that a comma separates the last item in a date or in an address from the words that follow it. However, a comma does *not* separate a month and a day (*April 14*), a house number and a street name (*6448 Higgins Road*), or a state abbreviation and a ZIP Code (*IL 60607*). A comma also does not separate a month and a year if no day is given (*June 1992*).

NOTE: If a preposition is used between items of an address, a comma is not necessary.

EXAMPLE   He lives at 144 Smith Street **in** Moline, Illinois.

(2) Use a comma after the salutation of a friendly letter and after the closing of any letter.

EXAMPLES   Dear Aunt Margaret,
Sincerely yours,
Yours truly,

EXERCISE 10   **Correcting Dates, Addresses, and Parts of a Letter by Adding Commas**

Write the following items, inserting commas as needed.

1. 11687 Montana Avenue⸱Los Angeles⸱CA 90049
2. Dresser Road at North First Street in Lynchburg⸱ Virginia
3. from December 1⸱1991⸱to March 15⸱1992
4. Dear Joanne⸱
5. Sincerely yours⸱

MECHANICS

 **INTEGRATING THE LANGUAGE ARTS**

Mechanics and Writing. As a culminating activity for this lesson, you may wish to have students write letters to students who will be eighth-graders next year. Have your students tell what they like best and least about being eighth-graders. Ask each student to include at least one sentence that uses commas in each of the following ways: to separate phrases or clauses in a series, to separate adjectives before a noun, to separate independent clauses that are joined by a conjunction, to set off an expression that interrupts a sentence, and to set off an introductory phrase or clause. Students may need to review **Chapter 35: "Letters and Forms"** before beginning this activity.

MECHANICS

755

MECHANICS

> **EXERCISE 11** **Writing a Paragraph Using End Marks and Commas Correctly**

Using the graph below, write a paragraph comparing the television viewing patterns of women, men, teenagers, and children. Remember to use commas and end marks where they are needed.

EXAMPLE   *According to the graph, fewer men than women watch regular network programs between 7:00 P.M. and 11:00 P.M.*

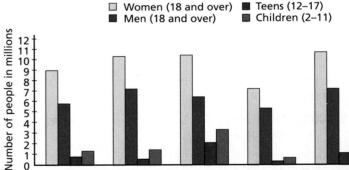

Audience Composition by Selected Program Type[1]

Source: Nielsen Media Research, 1990 Nielsen Report on Television.

☐ Women (18 and over)   ■ Teens (12–17)
■ Men (18 and over)   ■ Children (2–11)

[1]All figures are estimated for the period Nov. 1989.
[2]Multiweekly viewing.

> **REVIEW B** **Correcting Sentences by Adding End Marks and Commas**

Write the following sentences, adding end marks and commas as needed. If a sentence is correct, write C.

EXAMPLE   **1.** I moved from Canton Ohio to Waco Texas in 1985

   1. *I moved from Canton, Ohio, to Waco, Texas, in 1985.*

1. At the corner of Twelfth St. and Park Ave., I ran into an old friend.
2. Have you ever made the long, tiring climb to the head of the Statue of Liberty, Alan?
3. Oh, by the way, remind Geraldine to tell you what happened yesterday.
4. To prepare for her role in that movie, the star observed lawyers at work during a trial.
5. Turtles, crocodiles, alligators, frogs, and dolphins must breathe air in order to survive.
6. His new address is 6731 Wilcox Blvd., Hartford, CT 06101.
7. Junko Tabei, one of a team of Japanese women, reached the summit of Mount Everest in 1975.
8. Students who are late must bring a note from home. **8.** C
9. Will the twenty-first century begin officially on January 1, 2000, or on January 1, 2001, Sarah?
10. What a great fireworks display that was!

▶ REVIEW C **Correcting a Paragraph by Adding End Marks and Commas**

Write the sentences from the following paragraph, adding end marks and commas where they are needed.

EXAMPLE **[1] Have you ever played chess**
    1. *Have you ever played chess?*

[1] To beginners and experts alike, chess is a complex, demanding game. [2] It requires mental self-discipline, intense concentration, and dedication to long hours of practice. [3] Displaying those qualities, the Raging Rooks of Harlem tied for first place at the 1991 National Junior High Chess Championship, which was held in Dearborn, Mich. [4] Competing against the Rooks were sixty teams from all across the U.S. [5] The thirteen- and fourteen-year-old Rooks attended New York City Public School 43. [6] When they returned to New York after the tournament, they were greeted by Mayor David Dinkins. [7] Becoming media

celebrities‸they appeared on television and were interviewed by local newspapers and national news services⊙ [8] Imagine how proud of them their friends and families must have been! [9] The Rooks' coach‸Maurice Ashley‸ wasn't surprised that the team did so well in the tournament⊙ [10] After all‸the twenty-five-year-old Ashley is a senior master of the game‸and his goal is to become the first African American grandmaster⊙

PICTURE THIS

Who's that famous person being honored with a ticker-tape parade? Why, it's none other than you! Write a journal entry about the parade. Tell when and where the parade is taking place, and what you've done to receive such an honor. In addition to these concrete details, record your feelings about the experience. Be sure that you use all three types of end marks. Also, use commas to separate items in a series and to help join independent clauses in a compound sentence.

Subject: being honored with a ticker-tape parade
Audience: yourself at some later date
Purpose: to record information and express your feelings

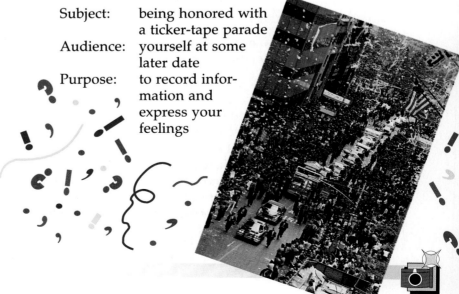

PICTURE THIS

You may want to give students a checklist so they can be sure to include in their writing journal entries all the punctuation requirements. You could use the following list:

1. periods as end marks
2. question marks
3. exclamation points
4. commas to separate items in a series
5. commas to join independent clauses in a compound sentence

MEETING *individual* NEEDS

AT-RISK STUDENTS

Students with low self-esteem may have difficulty thinking of themselves as the center of attention in a ticker-tape parade. You may want to work individually with students to help them acknowledge talents they have or goals they might aspire to.

SEMICOLONS Rules 26m–26o

OBJECTIVE

- To correct sentences by using semicolons and commas

Semicolons

A *semicolon* is used primarily to join independent clauses that are closely related in meaning.

26m. Use a semicolon instead of a comma between independent clauses when they are not joined by *and, but, or, nor, for, so,* or *yet.*

EXAMPLES   On our first trip to Houston I wanted to see the Astrodome; my little brother wanted to visit the Johnson Space Center.
Our parents settled the argument for us; they took us to both places.

Use a semicolon rather than a period between independent clauses only when the ideas in the clauses are closely related.

EXAMPLE   I called Leon. He will be here in ten minutes.
I called Leon; he will be here in ten minutes.

NOTE: Very short independent clauses without conjunctions may be separated by commas.

EXAMPLE   The leaves whispered, the brook gurgled, the sun beamed brightly.

26n. Use a semicolon between independent clauses joined by a conjunctive adverb or a transitional expression.

A *conjunctive adverb* or a *transitional expression* shows how the independent clauses that it joins are related.

EXAMPLES   Mary Ishikawa decided not to stay at home; **instead,** she went to the game.
English was Louise's most difficult subject; **accordingly,** she gave it more time than any other subject.
The popular names of certain animals are misleading; **for example,** the koala bear is not a bear.

PROGRAM MANAGER

SEMICOLONS

- **Independent Practice/ Reteaching** For instruction and exercises, see **Using Semicolons** and **Understanding Semicolons** in *Language Skills Practice and Assessment,* pp. 231–232.
- **Computer Guided Instruction** For additional instruction and practice with semicolons, see **Lesson 49** in *Language Workshop CD-ROM.*
- **Practice** To help less-advanced students with additional instruction and practice with semicolons, see **Chapter 23** in *English Workshop, Second Course,* pp. 261–262.

QUICK REMINDER

Write the following sentences on the chalkboard and omit the semicolons. Ask students to add a semicolon to each sentence.

1. I wanted to go to a movie[;] Mia wanted to watch TV.
2. I decided not to argue with her[;] besides, I was low on money.
3. We saw a comedy, a mystery, and a game show[;] and I enjoyed them all.

You may want to point out that the sentences illustrate **Rules 26m– 26o.**

MECHANICS

CRITICAL THINKING

Synthesis. Write the following sentence on the chalkboard:

The first room contained grand old clocks and a beautifully carved piano; and antique dolls, a hat collection, and women's fans were in the next room.

Have a student read the sentence aloud. Then erase the semicolon after *piano* and replace it with a comma. Students should recognize that with the comma, instead of the semicolon, the sentence is not easily understood. Have students work alone or in pairs to create similar sentences that would be confusing if commas were used instead of semicolons.

MECHANICS

MECHANICS

760 *Punctuation*

Commonly Used Conjunctive Adverbs

accordingly	furthermore	instead	nevertheless
besides	however	meanwhile	otherwise
consequently	indeed	moreover	therefore

Commonly Used Transitional Expressions

as a result	for example	for instance	that is
in addition	in other words	in conclusion	in fact

NOTE: When a conjunctive adverb or a transitional expression *joins* clauses, it is preceded by a semicolon and followed by a comma. When it *interrupts* a clause, however, it is set off by commas.

EXAMPLES   You are entitled to your opinion; however, you can't ignore the facts.
You are entitled to your opinion; you can't, however, ignore the facts.

26o. Use a semicolon rather than a comma before a coordinating conjunction to join independent clauses that contain commas.

EXAMPLES   A tall, slender woman entered the large, drafty room; and a short, slight, blonde woman followed her.
We will practice Act I on Monday, Act II on Wednesday, and Act III on Friday; and on Saturday we will rehearse the entire play.

 EXERCISE 12   **Correcting Sentences by Adding Semicolons and Commas**

Write the following sentences, adding semicolons and commas as needed.

EXAMPLE   **1.** The gym is on the ground floor the classrooms are above it.
1. *The gym is on the ground floor; the classrooms are above it.*

760

OBJECTIVE

• To correct sentences by adding colons

1. Scientists have explored almost all areas of the earth; they are now exploring the floors of the oceans.
2. Some scientists predict the development of undersea cities; however, other scientists question this prediction.
3. St. Augustine, Florida, was the first European settlement in the United States; the Spanish founded it in 1565.
4. Mike Powell set a world's record for the long jump in 1991; his leap of 29 feet and 4 1/2 inches beat Bob Beamon's 1968 record by two inches.
5. Some reptiles like a dry climate; others prefer a wet climate.
6. Many of today's office buildings look like glass boxes; they appear to be made entirely of windows.
7. In April 1912, a new, "unsinkable" ocean liner, the *Titanic*, struck an iceberg in the North Atlantic; as a result, roughly 1,500 persons lost their lives.
8. The *Titanic* carried nearly 2,200 passengers and crew; it had enough lifeboats to accommodate less than half of them, however.
9. The tragedy brought stricter safety regulations for ships; for example, the new laws required that ships carry more lifeboats.
10. Today's shipwrecks can produce a different kind of tragedy; if a large oil tanker is wrecked, for instance, the spilled oil damages beaches and kills wildlife.

Colons

26p. Use a colon before a list of items, especially after expressions like *as follows* or *the following.*

EXAMPLES Minimum equipment for camping is as follows: bedroll, utensils for cooking and eating, warm clothing, sturdy shoes, jackknife, and rope.

Beyond talent lie all the usual words: discipline, love, luck, but, most of all, endurance.

James Baldwin, from *The Writer's Chapbook*

QUICK REMINDER

Write the following sentences on the chalkboard and omit the colons. Ask students to add a colon to each sentence.

1. The list of items for the test is as follows[:] two pencils, a pad of paper, and your notes from class.
2. She reminded the first-grader of the rules for crossing streets[:] Stop, look, and listen before you cross.
3. He followed Ben Franklin's advice[:] "A penny saved is a penny earned."
4. The school was divided into two classes[:] seventh and eighth grades.

PROGRAM MANAGER

COLONS

■ **Independent Practice/ Reteaching** For instruction and exercises, see **Using Colons** in *Language Skills Practice and Assessment,* p. 233.

■ **Computer Guided Instruction** For additional instruction and practice with colons, see **Lessons 49** and **55** in *Language Workshop CD-ROM.*

■ **Practice** To help less-advanced students with additional instruction and practice with colons, see **Chapter 23** in *English Workshop, Second Course,* pp. 263–264.

MECHANICS

MECHANICS

LESS-ADVANCED STUDENTS

Some students may confuse the colon and the semicolon or think that they are interchangeable. Tell your class that ordinarily a colon indicates what the writer wants to emphasize, whereas a semicolon helps the reader avoid confusion.

You may want to make and display a poster illustrating the uses of the colon and the semicolon. Students can refer to the poster throughout the year.

COMMON ERROR

Problem. Some students will make the error of using a colon between a verb and a series of items.

Solution. Remind students that a colon is *not* used between a verb and a series of items. Then write the following sentences on the chalkboard:

1. I have the following classes: math, English, and history.
2. My classes are as follows: math, English, and history.
3. My classes are math, English, and history.

Point out that the first two sentences need colons, but that a colon in the third sentence would be incorrect because it would come between the verb and the series of items. Have students look for this error in their writing.

26q. Use a colon before a statement that explains or clarifies a preceding statement.

When a list of words, phrases, or subordinate clauses follows a colon, the first word of the list is lowercase. When an independent clause follows a colon, the first word of the clause begins with a capital letter.

EXAMPLES   My opinion of beauty was clearly expressed by Margaret Wolfe Hungerford in *Molly Baun***:** "Beauty is in the eye of the beholder."
All books are divisible into two classes**:** the books of the hour, and the books of all time.

John Ruskin, *Of Kings' Treasuries*

26r. Use a colon in certain conventional situations.

(1) Use a colon between the hour and the minute.

EXAMPLES   11**:**30 P.M.
4**:**08 A.M.

(2) Use a colon after the salutation of a business letter.

EXAMPLES   Dear Ms. Gonzalez**:**
Dear Sir or Madam**:**
To Whom It May Concern**:**

(3) Use a colon between chapter and verse in biblical references and between titles and subtitles.

EXAMPLES   Matthew 6**:**9–13
"Easter**:** Wahiawa, 1959"

▶ EXERCISE 13   **Correcting Sentences by Adding Colons**

Write each of the following sentences, inserting a colon as needed.

EXAMPLE   1. In Ruth 1 16, Ruth pledges her loyalty to Naomi, her mother-in-law.
1. *In Ruth 1:16, Ruth pledges her loyalty to Naomi, her mother-in-law.*

MECHANICS

1. During the field trip our teacher pointed out the following trees:sugarberry, papaw, silver bell, and mountain laurel.
2. The first lunch period begins at 11:00 A.M.
3. This is my motto:Laugh and the world laughs with you.
4. Using a recipe from *Miami Spice:The New Florida Cuisine,* we made barbecue sauce.
5. The artist showed me how to obtain one common flesh tone:Mix yellow, white, and a little red.

 REVIEW D

Correcting a Paragraph by Adding End Marks, Commas, Semicolons, and Colons

Write the following paragraph, adding end marks, commas, semicolons, and colons where they are needed.
Optional punctuation marks are underscored.

EXAMPLE   **[1] Acadiana La isn't a town it's a region**
            1. *Acadiana, La., isn't a town; it's a region.*

[1] Known as Cajun Country,the region includes the twenty-two southernmost parishes of Louisiana.[2] Did you know that the word *Cajun* is a shortened form of *Acadian?*[3] Cajuns are descended from French colonists who settled along the Bay of Fundy in what is now eastern Canada; they named their colony Acadie.[4] After the British took over the area,they deported nearly two thirds of the Acadians; in 1755,many families were separated.[5] Some Acadians took refuge in southern Louisiana's isolated swamps and bayous.[6] They didn't remain isolated, however,because the Cajun dialect blends elements of the following languages:French,English,Spanish,German,and a variety of African and Native American languages.[7] In 1847 the American poet Henry Wadsworth Longfellow described the uprooting of the Acadians in *Evangeline,*a long narrative poem that inspired Joseph Rusling Meeker to paint *The Land of Evangeline,*which is shown on the next page.[8] Today most people associate Cajun culture with hot,spicy foods and lively fiddle and accordion music.

MECHANICS

Mechanics and Speaking. This activity should reinforce the use of colons and give students practice in speaking before a group. First, have students select quotations that they like. If they need help, refer them to Bartlett's *Familiar Quotations* or *Poor Richard's Almanac.* Next, have them write sentences containing the quotations, such as the following one: I'll never forget Patrick Henry's stirring words: "Give me liberty, or give me death."

Have each student write his or her sentence on the chalkboard, read it, and tell why he or she chose that quotation. Check sentences for correct colon usage.

If your school has morning announcements, you might have a student present a quotation each week in a "Quotation of the Week" feature.

REVIEW D

Teaching Note. In sentence 4, a semicolon could correctly be placed either before or after the prepositional phrase *in 1755.*

MECHANICS

WRITING APPLICATION

OBJECTIVE

- To write a persuasive business letter by using correct punctuation and by following the rules of business correspondence

VISUAL CONNECTIONS
The Land of Evangeline

About the Artist. Joseph Rusling Meeker (1827–1889) first depicted the tranquil scenery of the Louisiana swamps and bayous during wartime. Meeker worked as a portrait painter until the Civil War, when he served with the Federal forces in the South. It was during this period of violent devastation that he painted images of serenity and calm.

WRITING APPLICATION

This assignment gives students practice in writing persuasive business letters and in using their knowledge of end marks, commas, semicolons, and colons. You may wish to refer to **Chapter 35: "Letters and Forms"** to review guidelines for writing letters.

MECHANICS

764 *Punctuation*

[9] Remembering their tragic history, Cajuns sum up their outlook on life in the following saying, *Lâche pas la patate* ("Don't let go of the potato"). [10] What a great way to tell people not to lose their grip!

The Saint Louis Art Museum. Gift of Mrs. W.P. Edgerton, by exchange.

WRITING APPLICATION

Using Punctuation to Make Your Meaning Clear

Punctuation marks haven't always been a part of writing. Ancient Roman texts, like other ancient writings, were hard to read because the words ran together.

EXAMPLE   *SENATUSPOPULUSQUEROMANUS*

Later, Romans began using dots to separate the words.

EXAMPLE   *MAGNO • ET·INVICTO • ACSUPER*

These dots were helpful, but readers still had no way to know where one sentence ended and the next began.

As reading and writing became more widespread, certain practices became standard. Writers left spaces between words and used marks of punctuation to show pauses between ideas. These conventions, which are still followed, made writing easier to read and understand.

▶ WRITING ACTIVITY

A local radio station is sponsoring a contest to select items to put in a time capsule. To enter the contest, write a business letter suggesting one item to include in the time capsule, which will be buried for one hundred years. In your letter, use punctuation marks correctly and follow the rules of business correspondence.

Prewriting List tangible items (ones you can touch) that show what life in the 1990s is like in the United States. Next, choose the item you think would give people in the 2090s the clearest picture of life today. Finally, make up a name, address, and call letters for the radio station.

Writing As you draft your letter, keep in mind that a business letter calls for a businesslike tone. Explain *why* the item you're suggesting should be included in the time capsule. Keep your letter brief, and stick to the point.

Evaluating and Revising To evaluate your letter, ask yourself the following questions:

- Does the item I suggested truly reflect my culture?
- Is the letter easy to follow?
- Is the tone suitable for the form?
- Have I used standard English to present my ideas clearly and reasonably?

Based on your answers to these questions, revise your letter to make it clearer and easier to follow.

Proofreading and Publishing Proofread your letter carefully, paying special attention to your use of end marks, commas, semicolons, and colons. Make sure that you have followed the proper form for a business letter. (Look on

MECHANICS

? CRITICAL THINKING

Analysis. After students have completed their prewriting lists, have each student select the item most representative of today's society. This will require analysis of their lists by comparing 1990s society with differences they project for the 2090s.

TECHNOLOGY TIP

You may want to suggest that, if possible, students graphically enhance their letters. They could create their own letterheads, or they could create graphic designs of their items. For example, if a student chose a mountain bike, he or she could search for an example of a bicycle in clip art and enhance it to better resemble the actual bike. Students could also use graphic-arts programs, if available, to create original drawings.

MECHANICS

MEETING *individual* NEEDS

LESS-ADVANCED STUDENTS
You may want to simplify the **Review: Posttest** by indicating the kind of punctuation that is needed in each sentence. If commas are needed in a sentence, you could tell students how many are needed.

ADVANCED STUDENTS
You could have students create paragraphs without punctuation, similar to those in the **Review: Posttest.** Encourage students to review the chapter and to include as many different uses as possible for commas, semicolons, and colons. Then you could ask students to exchange paragraphs and to add the punctuation. Or you could have students use their paragraphs to tutor peers who need additional review.

766 *Punctuation*

pages 901–906 for information about writing business letters.) Then, input your letter on a computer or photocopy it. Compare it with those of your classmates. The class could vote on what ten items they would choose to put in a time capsule.

Review: Posttest

Correcting Sentences by Adding End Marks, Commas, Semicolons, and Colons

Write the following paragraphs, inserting end marks, commas, semicolons, and colons as needed.

EXAMPLE **[1]** Did I ever tell you how our washing machine which usually behaves itself once turned into a foaming monster

1. *Did I ever tell you how our washing machine, which usually behaves itself, once turned into a foaming monster?*

[1] "Oh, no! The basement is full of soapsuds," my younger sister Sheila yelled. [2] When I heard her, I could tell how upset she was. [3] Her voice had that tense, strained tone that I know so well. [4] To see what had alarmed her, I ran down to the basement. [5] Imagine the following scene: The washing machine, the floor, and much of my sister were completely hidden in a thick, foamy flow of bubbles. [6] I made my way gingerly across the slippery floor, fought through the foam, and turned off the machine.

[7] This, of course, merely stopped the flow. [8] Sheila and I now had to clean up the mess, for we didn't want Mom and Dad to see it when they got home. [9] We mopped up soapsuds, we sponged water off the floor, and

we dried the outside of the washing machine. [10] After nearly an hour of steady effort at the task, we were satisfied with our work and decided to try the washer.

[11] Everything would have been fine if the machine had still worked; however, it would not even start. [12] Can you imagine how upset we both were then? [13] Thinking things over, we decided to call a repair shop.

[14] We frantically telephoned Mr. Hodges, who runs the appliance-repair business nearest to our town. [15] We told him the problem and asked him to come to 21 Crestview Drive, Ellenville, as soon as possible.

[16] When he arrived a few minutes after 4:00, Mr. Hodges inspected the machine, asked us a few questions, and said that we had no real problem. [17] The wires had become damp; they would dry out if we waited a day before we tried to use the machine again.

[18] Surprised and relieved, we thanked Mr. Hodges and started toward the stairs to show him the way out. [19] He stopped us, however, and asked if we knew what had caused the problem with the suds. [20] We didn't want to admit our ignorance, but our hesitation gave us away. [21] Well, Mr. Hodges suggested that from then on we measure the soap, instead of just pouring it into the machine.

[22] Looking at the empty box of laundry powder, I realized what had happened. [23] It was, I believe, the first time Sheila had used the washing machine by herself; she hadn't followed the instructions on the box.

[24] This incident occurred on November 10, 1992, and we have never forgotten it. [25] Whenever we do the laundry now, we remember the lesson we learned the day the washer overflowed.

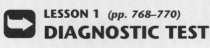

DIAGNOSTIC TEST

OBJECTIVE

• To proofread and revise sentences for the correct use of quotation marks, underlining (italics), apostrophes, hyphens, parentheses, and dashes

PROGRAM MANAGER

FOR THE WHOLE CHAPTER

■ **Review** For exercises on chapter concepts, see **Review Form A** and **Review Form B** in *Language Skills Practice and Assessment,* pp. 251–253.

■ **Assessment** For additional testing, see **Mechanics Pretests** and **Mechanics Mastery Tests** in *Language Skills Practice and Assessment,* pp. 203–210 and pp. 275–282.

CHAPTER OVERVIEW

This chapter covers underlining (italics), quotation marks, apostrophes, hyphens, parentheses, and dashes. It could serve as a useful reference in the proofreading stage of writing assignments. The first part of the chapter explains the use of underlining (italics) for titles and for words and letters referred to as such. Next is a section on the use of quotation marks and on capitalizing and punctuating quotations. The next section explains the use of apostrophes in possessives, contractions, and plurals; and, finally, the use of hyphens, parentheses, and dashes is explained in the final lesson. The chapter closes with a **Writing Application** that asks students to use quotations in a report based on actual interviews.

MECHANICS

27 PUNCTUATION

Underlining (Italics), Quotation Marks, Apostrophes, Hyphens, Parentheses, Dashes

Diagnostic Test

A. Proofreading Sentences for the Correct Use of Quotation Marks and Underlining (Italics)

Each of the following sentences contains at least one error in the use of quotation marks or underlining (italics). Write each sentence correctly.

EXAMPLE **1.** Marcella asked, "Did you read Robert Frost's poem Nothing Gold Can Stay in class?"
1. *Marcella asked, "Did you read Robert Frost's poem 'Nothing Gold Can Stay' in class?"*

1. Uncle Ned reads the <u>Wall Street Journal</u> every day.
2. "Fill in all the information on both sides of the form," the secretary said.
3. How many times have you seen the movie of Margaret Mitchell's novel <u>Gone with the Wind</u>?

4. Many of the students enjoyed the humor and irony in O. Henry's short story "The Ransom of Red Chief."
5. My little sister asked, "Why can't I have a hamster?"
6. Please don't sing "I've Been Working on the Railroad."
7. Last summer my older sister played in a band on a Caribbean cruise ship named <u>Bright Coastal Star</u>.
8. "Read James Baldwin's essay "Autobiographical Notes," and answer both of the study questions," the teacher announced.
9. Dudley Randall's poem "Ancestors" questions why people always seem to believe that their ancestors were aristocrats.
10. "That artist," Mr. Russell said, "was influenced by the Cuban painter Amelia Pelaez del Casal."

B. Proofreading Sentences for the Correct Use of Apostrophes, Hyphens, Parentheses, and Dashes

Each of the following sentences contains at least one error in the use of apostrophes, hyphens, parentheses, or dashes. Write each sentence correctly. Hyphens are indicated by the ∧ symbol.

EXAMPLE   1. Alices mother said shes read that tomatoes are native to Peru.
       1. *Alice's mother said she's read that tomatoes are native to Peru.*

11. Marsha is this year's captain of the girls' basketball team.
12. Susan B. Anthony (1820–1906) worked to get women the right to vote in the United States.
13. I'd never heard of a Greek bagpipe before, but Mr. Karras played one during the folk festival.
14. We couldn't have done the job without ~~you're~~ help.   14. your
15. He's strict about being on time.
16. On my older brother's next birthday, he will turn twenty-one.
17. We'd have forgotten to turn off the computer if Maggie hadn't reminded us.

USING THE DIAGNOSTIC TEST

The **Diagnostic Test** contains two parts. **Part A** focuses on the correct use of underlining (italics) and quotation marks. You may wish to use **Part A** to determine if students need a review before writing literary analyses, research reports, or stories containing dialogue.

Part B asks students to correct sentences by adding apostrophes, hyphens, parentheses, or dashes. You may wish to use **Part B** prior to writing assignments that may require these punctuation marks. For instance, a descriptive essay is likely to include examples of possession such as *my sister's room.*

MECHANICS

MECHANICS

UNDERLINING (ITALICS) Rules 27a, 27b

OBJECTIVE

- To identify words that should be underlined (italicized) in sentences

18. The recipe said to add two eggs, a teaspoon of salt, and one-quarter cup of milk.
19. My mother's office is on the twenty-second floor.
20. Our dog—he's a giant schnauzer—is gentle and very well behaved. **20.** dash/dash

Underlining (Italics)

Italics are printed letters that lean to the right, such as *the letters in these words.* In your handwritten or typewritten work, indicate italics by underlining. If your work were to be printed for publication, the underlined words would appear in italics. For example, if you were to write

Born Free is the story of a lioness that became a pet.

the printed version would look like this:

> *Born Free* is the story of a lioness that became a pet.

NOTE: If you use a personal computer, you may be able to set words in italics yourself. Most word-processing software and many printers are capable of producing italic type.

27a. Use underlining (italics) for titles of books, plays, periodicals, works of art, films, television programs, record albums, long musical compositions, trains, ships, aircraft, and spacecraft.

TYPE OF TITLE	EXAMPLES	
Books	*Storyteller* *Barrio Boy*	*A Wrinkle in Time*
Plays	*The Piano Lesson* *Macbeth*	*Visit to a Small Planet*
Periodicals	*Hispanic* *USA Today*	*The New York Times*

QUICK REMINDER

Write the following list on the chalkboard:

Book: Lust for Life
Play: An Ideal Husband
Movie: Rear Window
Painting: Christina's World
Magazine: Newsweek
Newspaper: Chicago Tribune
TV Show: Biography

Ask students what they notice about how you wrote the titles [underlining]. Have students write three sentences using at least one title in each sentence.

RULE 27a

Individual newspapers and magazines may have a house style that affects punctuation of titles. For example, some publications use quotation marks instead of italics for movie titles.

NOTE: The article *the* before the title of a magazine or a newspaper is neither italicized nor capitalized when it is written within a sentence.

EXAMPLE My parents subscribe to **the** *San Francisco Chronicle.*

TYPE OF TITLE	EXAMPLES	
Works of Art	*The Thinker* *The Last Supper*	*American Gothic* *Bird in Space*
Films	*Stand and Deliver* *Casablanca*	*Do the Right Thing*
Television Programs	*Life Goes On* *In Living Color*	*Wall Street Week*
Record Albums	*Unforgettable* *No Fences*	*Into the Light* *Man of Steel*
Long Musical Compositions	*Don Giovanni* *A Sea Symphony*	*The Four Seasons* *Peer Gynt* suite
Ships	*Calypso* *Pequod*	USS *Nimitz* *Queen Elizabeth 2*
Trains	*Orient Express* *City of New Orleans* *Garden State Special*	
Aircraft	*Enola Gay* *Spruce Goose*	*Spirit of St. Louis*
Spacecraft	*Apollo 12* *Voyager I*	USS *Enterprise* *Sputnik II*

☞ REFERENCE NOTE: For examples of titles that are not italicized but are enclosed in quotation marks, see page 778.

27b. Use underlining (italics) for words, letters, and figures referred to as such.

EXAMPLES What is the difference between the words *affect* and *effect*?
Don't forget to drop the final *e* before you add *–ing* to that word.
Is the last number a *5* or an *8*?

MECHANICS

LESS-ADVANCED STUDENTS

Because some students have difficulty distinguishing between titles that should be underlined (italicized) and those that should be placed in quotation marks, you could teach **Rules 27a** and **27l** (p. 778) together. Directly compare the two lists of rules, using an overhead projector. Point out that titles that are underlined (italicized) name longer works or works that are whole. Titles in quotation marks usually name shorter works or portions of works.

On an overhead projector, present a scrambled list of items covered by these two rules. Show one item at a time. As each item is uncovered, have students call out either "italics" or "quotation marks."

◆ **COMMON ERROR**

Problem. Students write unclear sentences because they fail to incorporate **Rule 27b** into their writing.

Solution. Write the following sentence on the chalkboard:

She forgot an and wrote other.

Show students that when they underline (italicize) *an* and *other,* the sentence is easier to read. Write the following rule on the chalkboard and have students use it to proofread their written work: If you see the words *the word, the letter,* or *the figure* before a word, letter, or figure—or if you could add this phrase to the sentence without changing the meaning—then underline (italicize) the word, letter, or figure.

MECHANICS

LESSON 3 *(pp. 772–780)*

QUOTATION MARKS Rules 27c–27l

OBJECTIVES

- To revise sentences by adding capital letters, commas, end marks, and quotation marks
- To write a news article using quotation marks and proper punctuation for each quotation

 EXERCISE 1   **Using Underlining (Italics) in Sentences**

Write and underline the <u>words that should be italicized</u> in each of the following sentences.

EXAMPLE   **1. Have you read The Call of the Wild?**
   1. *The Call of the Wild*

1. The magazine rack held current issues of <u>National Wildlife</u>, <u>Time</u>, <u>Hispanic</u>, <u>Jewish Monthly</u>, and <u>Sports Illustrated</u>.
2. Sometimes I forget to put the first <u>o</u> in the word <u>thorough</u>, and by mistake I write <u>through</u>.
3. The final number will be a medley of excerpts from George Gershwin's opera <u>Porgy and Bess</u>.
4. Jerry Spinelli won the Newbery Medal for his book <u>Maniac Magee</u>, which is about an unusual athlete.
5. Picasso's painting <u>Guernica</u> is named for a Spanish town that was destroyed by German planes during the Spanish Civil War.
6. My father reads the <u>Chicago Sun-Times</u> because he likes Carl Rowan's column.
7. The first battle between ironclad ships took place between the <u>Monitor</u> and the <u>Merrimac</u> in 1862.
8. The 1989 Irish movie <u>My Left Foot</u> celebrates the accomplishments of a writer and artist who has severe disabilities.
9. The plays <u>Les Misérables</u> and <u>Cats</u> were hits on Broadway and are now on national tours.
10. Janice finally found her mistake; the <u>4</u> was in the wrong column.

Quotation Marks

 27c. Use quotation marks to enclose a *direct quotation*—a person's exact words.

Be sure to place quotation marks both before and after a person's exact words.

LEP/ESL

General Strategies. One way to help students perform well on **Exercise 1** is to tell them which of the many proper nouns are names of people and, therefore, will not require underlining. A lack of familiarity with names and titles could hinder students, even if they clearly understand the rules for underlining (italics).

PROGRAM MANAGER

QUOTATION MARKS

- **Independent Practice/ Reteaching** For instruction and exercises, see **Direct and Indirect Quotations, Setting Off Quotations, Punctuating Dialogue,** and **Other Uses of Quotation Marks** in *Language Skills Practice and Assessment,* pp. 242–245.
- **Computer Guided Instruction** For additional instruction and practice, see **Lessons 53** and **54** in *Language Workshop CD-ROM.*
- **Practice** To help less-advanced students, see **Chapter 24** in *English Workshop, Second Course,* pp. 269–272.

MECHANICS

27 c—e

EXAMPLES   "Has anyone in the class swum in the Great Salt
            Lake?" asked Ms. Estrada.
            "I swam there last summer," said Peggy Ann.

Do not use quotation marks for an ***indirect quotation***—a rewording of a direct quotation.

DIRECT QUOTATION	Kaya asked, "What is your inter-pretation of the poem?"
INDIRECT QUOTATION	Kaya asked for my interpretation of the poem.
DIRECT QUOTATION	As Barbara Jordan said in her keynote address to the Democratic National Convention in 1976, "We are willing to suffer the discomfort of change in order to achieve a better future."
INDIRECT QUOTATION	Barbara Jordan said that people will put up with the discomfort of change to have a better future.

27d. A direct quotation begins with a capital letter.

EXAMPLES   Brandon shouted, "Let's get busy!"
            Abraham Lincoln said, "Those who deny free-
            dom to others deserve it not for themselves."

27e. When the expression identifying the speaker
interrupts a quoted sentence, the second part of
the quotation begins with a small letter.

EXAMPLES   "What are some of the things," asked Mrs.
            Perkins, "that the astronauts discovered on
            the moon?"
            "One thing they found," answered Gwen, "was
            that the moon is covered by a layer of dust."
            "Gee," Angelo added, "my room at home is a
            lot like the moon, I guess."

Notice in the examples above that each part of a divided
quotation is enclosed in a set of quotation marks. In addition, the interrupting expression is followed by a comma.

MECHANICS

QUICK REMINDER

Write the following conversation on the chalkboard without punctuation and have students add punctuation:

"Did you find the books I left in your locker?" Maria asked me.

"Yes, and I returned them to the library," I said, "but I didn't get them there on time."

"Then I guess I'll have to pay the fine next time I check something out," answered Maria.

MEETING *individual* **NEEDS**

LEP/ESL

General Strategies. Students some-times make mistakes using the verbs *said* and *told,* resulting in sentences such as "He said me, 'Look out!'" Give the following examples of how these verbs differ and draw attention to the idea that *told* usually takes an indirect object:

1. He said, "Look out!" (He told me to look out.)
2. Maria said, "This is a good book." (Maria told us that this is a good book.)

MECHANICS

SELECTION AMENDMENT
Description of change: excerpted
Rationale: to focus on the use of punctuation presented in this chapter

MEETING *individual* NEEDS

AT-RISK STUDENTS

Students will be more motivated if they can see the relevance of the material to their lives. They may view direct quotations as something they will use only in a school setting—in quoting material for research papers and in writing compositions with dialogue. Tell students that they may find a need to properly use direct and indirect quotations when they submit a letter with a job application, have a problem with a bill, or need to file a complaint to a utility company, a work supervisor, or a union.

MECHANICS

MECHANICS

When the second part of a divided quotation is a sentence, it begins with a capital letter.

EXAMPLE "Any new means of travel is exciting," remarked Mrs. Perkins. "Space travel is no exception."

Notice that a period, not a comma, follows the interrupting expression.

▶ EXERCISE 2 **Correcting Sentences by Adding Capital Letters and Punctuation**

Revise the following sentences by supplying <u>capital letters</u> and marks of punctuation as needed. If a sentence is correct, write C.

EXAMPLE **1.** I think, Phil said, that the Yoruba people of Nigeria are fantastic artists.
1. *"I think," Phil said, "that the Yoruba people of Nigeria are fantastic artists."*

1. Ella exclaimed, "this helmet mask is one of the most amazing things I've ever seen!"
2. Mr. Faulkner told the class that the mask weighs eighty pounds and is five feet tall.   **2.** C
3. "Don't you think," asked Earl, "the figures must have been difficult to carve?"
4. "Just look at all the detail," Marcia said. "it's a beautiful piece of sculpture, but I can't imagine wearing it."
5. Lou explained that the mask was designed to honor the Yoruba people.   **5.** C

774

27f. A direct quotation is set off from the rest of the sentence by a comma, a question mark, or an exclamation point, but not by a period.

EXAMPLES "I've just finished reading a book about Narcissa Whitman," Alyssa said.
"Was she one of the early settlers in the Northwest?" asked Delia.
"What an adventure!" exclaimed Iola.

27g. A period or a comma is always placed inside the closing quotation marks.

EXAMPLES Ramón said, "Hank Aaron was a better player than Babe Ruth because he hit more home runs in his career."
"But Hank Aaron never hit sixty homers in one year," Paula responded.

27h. A question mark or an exclamation point is placed inside the closing quotation marks when the quotation itself is a question or an exclamation. Otherwise, it is placed outside.

EXAMPLES "Is the time difference between Los Angeles and Chicago two hours?" asked Ken. [The quotation is a question.]
Linda exclaimed, "I thought everyone knew that!" [The quotation is an exclamation.]
What did Jade Snow Wong mean in her story "A Time of Beginnings" when she wrote, "Like the waves of the sea, no two pieces of pottery art can be identical"? [The sentence, not the quotation, is a question.]
I'm angry that Mom said, "You are not allowed to stay out past 10 P.M. on Friday night"! [The sentence, not the quotation, is an exclamation.]

When both the sentence and the quotation at the end of the sentence are questions (or exclamations), only one

MECHANICS

MECHANICS

SELECTION AMENDMENT
Description of change: excerpted
Rationale: to focus on the use of punctuation presented in this chapter

question mark (or exclamation point) is used. It is placed inside the closing quotation marks.

EXAMPLE Did Elizabeth Barrett Browning write the poem that begins with "How do I love thee?"

▶ EXERCISE 3 **Correcting Sentences by Adding Capital Letters and Punctuation**

Revise the following sentences by supplying <u>capitals</u> and marks of punctuation as needed.

EXAMPLE **1.** Why she asked can't we leave now
1. *"Why," she asked, "can't we leave now?"*

1. "Mom, will you take us to the soccer field?"asked Libby.
2. "Please hold my backpack for a minute, Dave,"Josh said. "I need to tie my shoelace."
3. Cary asked,"What is pita bread?"
4. Did Alison answer,"It's a round, flat Middle Eastern bread"?
5. "Run! Run!"cried the boys."a tornado is headed this way!"

27i. When you write dialogue (conversation), begin a new paragraph each time you change speakers.

EXAMPLE "No," I answered, "I do not fish for carp. It is bad luck."
"Do you know why?" he asked and raised an eyebrow.
"No," I said and held my breath. I felt I sat on the banks of an undiscovered river whose churning, muddied waters carried many secrets.
"I will tell you a story," Samuel said after a long silence, "a story that was told to my father . . ."

Rudolfo A. Anaya, *Bless Me, Ultima*

27j. When a quotation consists of several sentences, place quotation marks at the beginning and at the end of the whole quotation.

COMMON ERROR

Problem. When writing dialogue, many students fail to begin new paragraphs when they change speakers.

Solution. Write the following dialogue on the chalkboard without beginning any new paragraphs:

"Did you finish that book yet?" I asked. "No, and if I ever do," said Tarika, "it'll be a miracle. It's very boring." "Well then," I told her, "maybe you should take it back to the library."

Have students rewrite the dialogue by adding paragraph breaks. Point out that it is easier to tell who is speaking when a new paragraph starts with each change of speaker.

SELECTION AMENDMENT
Description of change: excerpted
Rationale: to focus on the use of punctuation presented in this chapter

EXAMPLE   **"Memorize all your lines for Monday. Have someone at home give you your cues. Enjoy your weekend!" said Ms. Goodwin.**

▶ EXERCISE 4   **Correcting Paragraphs by Adding Punctuation**

Revise the following paragraphs by adding commas, end marks, and quotation marks where necessary.

EXAMPLE   **[1] Which would you rather use, a pencil or a pen asked Jody**

1. **"Which would you rather use, a pencil or a pen?" asked Jody.**

[1] "Gordon, do you ever think about pencils?" Annie asked.

[2] "I'm always wondering where I lost mine," Gordon replied.

[3] "Well," said Annie, "let me tell you some of the things I learned about pencils."

[4] "Okay," Gordon said, "I love trivia."

[5] "People have used some form of pencils for a long time," Annie began. [6] "The ancient Greeks and Romans used lead pencils. [7] However, pencils as we know them weren't developed until the 1500s, when people started using graphite."

[8] "What's graphite?" asked Gordon.

[9] "Graphite is a soft form of carbon," Annie explained, "that leaves a mark when it's drawn over most surfaces."

[10] "Thanks for the information, Annie," Gordon said. "Now, do you have a pencil I can borrow?"

27k. Use single quotation marks to enclose a quotation within a quotation.

EXAMPLES   **"I said, 'The quiz will cover Unit 2 and your special reports,'" repeated Mr. Allyn.**
"What Langston Hughes poem begins with the line 'Well, son, I'll tell you: / Life for me ain't been no crystal stair'?" Carol asked.

INTEGRATING THE LANGUAGE ARTS

Literature Link. If your literature textbook contains the selection, have students read and discuss Toni Cade Bambara's "Raymond's Run." Refer them to a few lines of dialogue in which the characters are clearly differentiated.

Point out that much of the story is told by narration, and ask why the author might have chosen to include the direct quotations. [The direct quotations give the reader a direct and immediate experience of the characters' personalities. The quotations add a dimension not possible to achieve through description and narration.]

SELECTION AMENDMENT
Description of change: excerpted
Rationale: to focus on the use of punctuation presented in this chapter

INTEGRATING THE LANGUAGE ARTS

Mechanics and Writing. Have students create guides they can keep in their notebooks to use for reference when punctuating titles in their writing. List on the chalkboard all the categories of titles in the examples for **Rules 27a** and **27l**. Have the class brainstorm other categories to add to the list. Then alphabetize the list and designate beside each category whether it requires italics or quotation marks. Have students copy the list and illustrate their guides with pictures or icons if they like.

27l. Use quotation marks to enclose titles of short works such as short stories, poems, articles, songs, episodes of television programs, and chapters and other parts of books.

TYPE OF TITLE	EXAMPLES
Short Stories	"Raymond's Run" "The Rule of Names" "The Tell-Tale Heart"
Poems	"Mother to Son" "The Road Not Taken" "Calling in the Cat"
Articles	"Free Speech and Free Air" "How to Sharpen Your Knife" "Marriage in the '90s"
Songs	"La Bamba" "Amazing Grace" "The Streets of Laredo"
Episodes of Television Programs	"Heart of a Champion" "The Trouble with Tribbles" "An Englishman Abroad"
Chapters and Other Parts of Books	"Learning About Reptiles" "English: Origins and Uses" "Creating a Federal Union"

REFERENCE NOTE: For examples of titles that are italicized, see page 771.

EXERCISE 5 **Correcting Sentences by Adding Quotation Marks**

Revise the following sentences by supplying quotation marks as needed.

EXAMPLE **1.** We sang Greensleeves for the assembly.
1. *We sang "Greensleeves" for the assembly.*

1. Has anyone read the story To Build a Fire? asked the teacher.

OBJECTIVE

• To correct sentences by adding punctuation and capital letters

271

2. "I have," said Eileen. "It was written by Jack London."
3. Do you know the poem "To Make a Prairie"?
4. Our chorus will sing "When You Wish upon a Star" at the recital.
5. In the chapter "Workers' Rights," the author discusses César Chávez's efforts to help migrant workers.

▶ REVIEW A **Correcting Sentences by Adding Punctuation and Capital Letters**

Revise the following sentences by adding **marks** of punctuation and capital letters as needed. If a sentence is correct, write C.

EXAMPLE **1.** Did you read the article about runner Jackie Joyner-Kersee in USA Weekend Lynn asked.
1. *"Did you read the article about runner Jackie Joyner-Kersee in <u>USA Weekend</u>?" Lynn asked.*

1. Won't you stay pleaded Wynnie there will be music and refreshments later.
2. Hey, Jason, said Chen, you play the drums like an expert!
3. The girls asked whether we needed help finding our campsite.
4. Elise, do you know who said The only thing we have to fear is fear itself asked the teacher.
5. What a wonderful day for a picnic exclaimed Susan.
6. I've read Connie said that Thomas Jefferson loved Italian food and ordered pasta from Italy.
7. When President Lincoln heard of the South's defeat, he requested that the band play Dixie.
8. The latest issue of National Geographic has a long article on rain forests.
9. What can have happened to Francine this time, Tina? Didn't she say I'll be home long before you're ready to leave? Justin asked.
10. Langston Hughes's Dream Deferred is a thought-provoking poem.

MECHANICS

ANSWERS
Review A

1. "Won't you stay?" pleaded Wynnie. "There will be music and refreshments later."
2. "Hey, Jason," said Chen, "you play the drums like an expert!"
3. C
4. "Elise, do you know who said, 'The only thing we have to fear is fear itself'?" asked the teacher.
5. "What a wonderful day for a picnic!" exclaimed Susan.
6. "I've read," Connie said, "that Thomas Jefferson loved Italian food and ordered pasta from Italy."
7. When President Lincoln heard of the South's defeat, he requested that the band play "Dixie."
8. The latest issue of <u>National Geographic</u> has a long article on rain forests.
9. "What can have happened to Francine this time, Tina? Didn't she say, 'I'll be home long before you're ready to leave'?" Justin asked.
10. Langston Hughes's "Dream Deferred" is a thought-provoking poem.

MECHANICS

LESSON 4 *(pp. 780–786)*
APOSTROPHES Rules 27m–27r
OBJECTIVES
- To supply apostrophes for possessive nouns
- To form singular possessives and plural possessives
- To use apostrophes in a letter
- To correct sentences by adding apostrophes

PICTURE THIS

To help students get started, point out that in a crowd of spectators, students could expect to find people of different ages and different walks of life, with many different reasons for being there. Remind students to answer the *5W-How?* questions (*Who? What? When? Where? Why?* and *How?*) in their articles.

Students' articles will vary but should include correctly punctuated and capitalized quotes from five observers. The articles should be easy to understand, informative, and appropriate for a newspaper.

MECHANICS

MECHANICS

780 *Punctuation*

PICTURE THIS

You are a newspaper reporter covering this year's hot-air balloon race. While watching the balloons lift off, you interview some of the people in the crowd around you. You want to use their comments in your news story. For that reason, you quickly write down each speaker's exact words. Write a short article about the balloon liftoff. In your article, quote at least five observers of this event. Use quotation marks and proper punctuation for each quotation.

Subject: hot-air balloon liftoff
Audience: newspaper readers
Purpose: to inform

Apostrophes

An *apostrophe* is used to form the possessive case of nouns and some pronouns, to indicate in a contraction where letters have been omitted, and to form some plurals.

Possessive Case

The *possessive case* of a noun or a pronoun shows ownership or relationship.

OWNERSHIP	RELATIONSHIP
Sandra's boat	an **hour's** time
Mother's job	**Julio's** father
your book	**everyone's** choice

27m. To form the possessive case of a singular noun,
add an apostrophe and an –*s*.

EXAMPLES   **a dog's collar
a moment's notice
one dollar's worth
Charles's typewriter**

NOTE: A proper name ending in *s* may take only an apostrophe
to form the possessive case if the addition of *'s* would
make the name awkward to pronounce.

EXAMPLES   Marjorie Kinnan Rawlings' novels
Hercules' feats
Buenos Aires' population

EXERCISE 6 Supplying Apostrophes for Possessive Nouns

Write each <u>noun that should be in the possessive case</u> in
the following sentences, and add the apostrophe.

EXAMPLE   **1. The dogs leash is made of nylon.
1. *dog's***

1. That <u>trucks</u> taillights are broken.
2. The judges were impressed with <u>Veronicas</u> project.
3. Last <u>weeks</u> travel story was about Mindanao, the
   second largest island of the Philippines.
4. <u>Matthias</u> dream is to have a palomino.   **4. Matthias's**
5. Please pack your <u>mothers</u> books.

27m

MECHANICS

MECHANICS

MECHANICS

ANSWERS

Exercise 7

1. boys' boots
2. women's careers
3. friends' comments
4. three days' homework
5. girls' parents
6. Joneses' cabin
7. men's shoes
8. children's games
9. cities' mayors
10. oxen's yokes

27n. To form the possessive case of a plural noun ending in *s*, add only the apostrophe.

EXAMPLES   students' records   doctors' opinions
         citizens' committee   Haines' invitations

To form the possessive case of a plural noun that does not end in *s*, add an apostrophe and an –*s*.

EXAMPLES   women's suits   geese's noise
         mice's tracks   children's voices

NOTE: Do not use an apostrophe to form the *plural* of a noun.

INCORRECT   The passenger's showed their tickets to the flight attendant.

CORRECT   The **passengers** showed their tickets to the flight attendant. [plural]

CORRECT   The flight attendant checked the **passengers'** tickets. [plural possessive]

▶ EXERCISE 7   **Forming Plural Possessives**

Give the correct possessive form for each of the following plural expressions.

EXAMPLE   **1.** artists paintings
          1. *artists' paintings*

1. boys boots
2. women careers
3. friends comments
4. three days homework
5. girls parents
6. Joneses cabin
7. men shoes
8. children games
9. cities mayors
10. oxen yokes

27o. Do not use an apostrophe with possessive personal pronouns.

EXAMPLES   These keys are **yours,** not **mine.**
         Are these tapes **ours** or **theirs**?
         His pantomime was good, but **hers** was better.

27p. To form the possessive case of some indefinite pronouns, add an apostrophe and an –*s*.

27 n–q

EXAMPLES everyone's opinion
no one's fault
somebody's umbrella

 REFERENCE NOTE: For more about possessive personal pronouns, see page 635. For information about indefinite pronouns used as adjectives, see page 442.

EXERCISE 8 **Forming Singular Possessives and Plural Possessives**

Form the singular possessive and the plural possessive of each of the following nouns.

EXAMPLE **1.** citizen
1. *citizen's; citizens'*

1. book	**4.** mouse	**7.** elephant	**9.** school
2. puppy	**5.** calf	**8.** tooth	**10.** family
3. donkey	**6.** hero		

Contractions

27q. To form a contraction, use an apostrophe to show where letters have been omitted.

A *contraction* is a shortened form of a word, a figure, or a group of words. The apostrophe in a contraction indicates where letters or numerals have been left out.

Common Contractions			
I am	I'm	they had	they'd
1993	'93	where is	where's
let us	let's	we are	we're
of the clock	o'clock	he is	he's
she would	she'd	you will	you'll

The word *not* can be shortened to *n't* and added to a verb, usually without changing the spelling of the verb.

MECHANICS

MECHANICS

COMMON ERROR

Problem. Because some contractions and possessive pronouns sound alike (*who's/whose; it's/its; you're/your; they're/their; there's/theirs*), students confuse them in writing.

Solution. Make a list of confusing contraction/possessive pronoun pairs. Suggest that students apply this test: Read all contractions and all possessive pronouns as if they were two words. If the expanded phrase makes sense, then the word should have an apostrophe because it is a contraction.

INTEGRATING THE LANGUAGE ARTS

Mechanics and Letter Writing. Before students begin **Exercise 9**, you may wish to have them review the material on letter writing in **Chapter 35: "Letters and Forms."**

After students have completed their rough drafts, have them exchange letters with partners. Partners can double-check each other's mechanics and give each other feedback on whether the letters are clear and understandable. Encourage them to suggest ways of making the letters more interesting.

ANSWERS
Exercise 9

Letters will vary. Before students begin writing, lead a class discussion about the pictures on p. 785. Have students share observations about the pictures and any other relevant information they may have from their reading or experience. All letters should follow the proper form for letter writing and should refer to the pictures accompanying the exercise.

MECHANICS

784

EXAMPLES			
is not . . . . isn't		has not . . . . hasn't	
are not . . . . .aren't		have not. . . . . . haven't	
does not . . doesn't		had not. . . . . . . hadn't	
do not . . . . . . don't		should not . . shouldn't	
was not . . . . wasn't		would not . . .wouldn't	
were not. . weren't		could not . . . . .couldn't	

EXCEPTIONS: will not . . . . . **won't**   cannot . . . . . **can't**

Do not confuse contractions with possessive pronouns.

CONTRACTIONS	POSSESSIVE PRONOUNS
It's snowing. [*It is*] **It's** been a long time. [*It has*]	**Its** front tire is flat.
Who's next in line? [*Who is*] **Who's** been helping you? [*Who has*]	**Whose** idea was it?
You're a good friend. [*You are*]	**Your** writing has improved.
They're not here. [*They are*]	**Their** dog is barking.
There's only one answer. [*There is*]	This trophy is **theirs**.

EXERCISE 9   **Using Apostrophes in a Letter**

You're having a great time, spending your vacation on a relative's ranch in Argentina. The ranch hands, called *gauchos*, are fascinating people, and you're eager to tell your best friend about them. Using pictures that you've taken and notes that you've made, write a letter to your friend, telling about the gauchos on the ranch. (These pictures and notes appear on the next page.) In your letter, use six apostrophes to form the possessive case of nouns and four apostrophes to form contractions. Circle each apostrophe in your letter.

EXAMPLE   *Dear Larry,*
  Greetings from Argentina! You'd love it here! The gauchos in these pictures work on my uncle's ranch.

27r

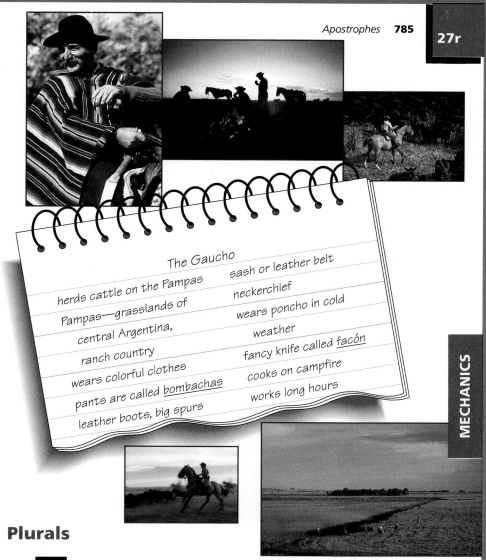

The Gaucho

herds cattle on the Pampas	sash or leather belt
Pampas—grasslands of central Argentina, ranch country	neckerchief
	wears poncho in cold weather
wears colorful clothes	fancy knife called <u>facón</u>
pants are called <u>bombachas</u>	cooks on campfire
leather boots, big spurs	works long hours

Plurals

27r. Use an apostrophe and an *–s* to form the plurals of letters, numerals, and symbols, and of words referred to as words.

EXAMPLES   The word has two *d*'s, not one.
Your *2*'s look like *5*'s.
Jazz became quite popular in the 1920's.
Don't use *&*'s in place of *and*'s.

MECHANICS

MECHANICS

COMMON ERROR

Problem. Students may fail to use an apostrophe to form the plurals of letters, numerals, signs, and words referred to as words.

Solution. Point out that without the apostrophes, some plural constructions would be unclear. Write the following sentences on the chalkboard:

1. My teacher couldn't read the <u>is</u> in my paper.
2. My teacher couldn't read the <u>i's</u> in my paper.

Students should be able to see that *i's* could easily be misread as *is* without the apostrophe.

785

HYPHENS, PARENTHESES, AND DASHES Rules 27s–27v

OBJECTIVES

- To hyphenate numbers and fractions
- To write sentences with parentheses
- To write sentences with dashes

MECHANICS

PROGRAM MANAGER

HYPHENS, PARENTHESES, AND DASHES

- **Independent Practice/ Reteaching** For instruction and exercises, see **Using Hyphens** in *Language Skills Practice and Assessment,* p. 250.

- **Computer Guided Instruction** For additional instruction and practice with using hyphens, parentheses, and dashes, see **Lesson 56** in *Language Workshop CD-ROM.*

QUICK REMINDER

Write the following sentences without the hyphens, dashes, and parentheses, and have students add punctuation where needed:

1. Sylvia's sister had her twenty-first birthday yesterday.
2. The movie (the one at the Square) starts at 7:00.
3. I saw Robin—that's him over there now—at the museum last weekend.
4. I think I'll need—oh, Mary, here we are—about three more.

786

---

786 *Punctuation*

MECHANICS

NOTE: In your reading, you may notice that an apostrophe is not always used in forming these four kinds of plurals. Nowadays, many writers omit the apostrophe if the plural meaning is clear without it. However, to make sure that your writing is clear, always use an apostrophe.

EXERCISE 10 Correcting Sentences by Adding Apostrophes

Write the correct form of each <u>item that requires an apostrophe</u> in the following sentences.

EXAMPLE 1. Do you know what youre doing?
1. *you're*

1. The girls <u>didnt</u> say when <u>theyd</u> be back.
2. <u>Lets</u> find out when the next game is.
3. My cousin Dorothy usually gets all <u>As</u> and <u>Bs</u> on her report card.
4. It <u>isnt</u> correct to use <u>&s</u> in your compositions.
5. Many of the scores on the spelling test were in the <u>80s</u> and <u>90s</u>.
6. They <u>cant</u> come with us; <u>theyre</u> studying.
7. <u>Theyll</u> meet us later, if <u>its</u> all right to tell them where <u>were</u> going.
8. <u>Whos</u> signed up for the talent show?
9. <u>Dont</u> those <u>2s</u> look like <u>zs</u> to you?
10. Your capital <u>Ls</u> and <u>Fs</u> are hard to tell apart.

Hyphens

27s. Use a hyphen to divide a word at the end of a line.

EXAMPLES How long had the new bridge been under construction before it was opened?
You can probably find the answer in the almanac in the library.

27
s–t

When dividing a word at the end of a line, remember the following rules:

(1) Divide a word only between syllables.

INCORRECT Lisa wrote her science report on the tyra-
nnosaurs, the largest meat-eating dinosaurs.
CORRECT Lisa wrote her science report on the tyran-
nosaurs, the largest meat-eating dinosaurs.

(2) Do not divide a one-syllable word.

INCORRECT The fans stood and sang while the band played the school song.
CORRECT The fans stood and sang while the band played
the school song.

(3) Divide an already hyphenated word at a hyphen.

INCORRECT I went to the fair with my sister and my brother-in-law.
CORRECT I went to the fair with my sister and my brother-
in-law.

(4) Do not divide a word so that one letter stands alone.

INCORRECT On their way to Chicago last week, they stayed o-
vernight in Cincinnati.
CORRECT On their way to Chicago last week, they stayed
overnight in Cincinnati.

27t. Use a hyphen with compound numbers from *twenty-one* to *ninety-nine* and with fractions used as adjectives.

EXAMPLES thirty-five students
one-half cup of milk
forty-eighth state

When a fraction is a noun, do not use a hyphen.

EXAMPLE **two thirds** of the earth's surface

MECHANICS

MEETING *individual* NEEDS

LEP/ESL

General Strategies. Students sometimes do not know how to divide an English word into syllables, and this problem leads students to hyphenate improperly at the end of a line. Let students know that there are rules for the division of words (one vowel *sound* per syllable; divide between a double consonant) and that they can always check in a dictionary for correct word divisions.

MECHANICS

TECHNOLOGY TIP

Because most computer programs simply move words that are too long to the next line or automatically insert hyphens to divide words, students may question the purpose of studying the rules for hyphens. Point out that in order to proofread computer-generated text accurately and in order to be able to write by hand when computers are not available, students need to know the rules for dividing words.

MECHANICS

MECHANICS

REVIEWS B and C

OBJECTIVES

- To form contractions
- To add apostrophes, hyphens, and underlining

 EXERCISE 11   Hyphenating Numbers and Fractions

Write the following expressions, inserting hyphens as needed. If an expression is correct, write *C*.   Hyphens are indicated by the ⌃ symbol.

EXAMPLE   **1.** thirty one days
          1. *thirty-one*

1. a two‿thirds majority
2. one half of the coconut   **2.** C
3. one hundred thirty‿five pages
4. Forty‿second Street
5. twenty‿two Amish quilts

 REVIEW B   **Forming Contractions**

Form a contraction of each of the following pairs of words.

1. will not **1.** won't	8. should not **8.** shouldn't	15. we are **15.** we're
2. there is **2.** there's	9. let us **9.** let's	16. I am **16.** I'm
3. who will **3.** who'll	10. I have **10.** I've	17. had not **17.** hadn't
4. they are **4.** they're	11. you are **11.** you're	18. she is **18.** she's
5. who is **5.** who's	12. does not **12.** doesn't	19. you will **19.** you'll
6. are not **6.** aren't	13. he would **13.** he'd	20. could not **20.** couldn't
7. it is **7.** it's	14. has not **14.** hasn't	

 REVIEW C   **Adding Apostrophes, Hyphens, and Underlining**

Write the following sentences, inserting apostrophes, hyphens, and underlining as needed.   Hyphens are indicated by the ⌃ symbol.

EXAMPLE   **1.** Isnt the preface to that edition of ⌃ Frankenstein twenty four pages long?
          1. *Isn't the preface to that edition of Frankenstein twenty-four pages long?*

1. There's where they live.
2. Who'll go with me to next week's showing of the French film <u>Small Change</u>?
3. The Lockwood sisters' golden retriever is named Storm.

4. One third of Holly's allowance goes into the bank.
5. From Fifty‑third Street down to Forty‑fifth, there are ninety‑seven businesses.
6. Twenty‑six student council members (more than a two‑thirds majority) voted to change the school song.
7. Shelly said that she's always wanted to read Maya Angelou's book <u>I Know Why the Caged Bird Sings</u>.
8. If two thirds of the class has a score below seventy‑five, we'll all have to retake the test.
9. Let's find out more about the recovery of Henry VIII's flagship, the <u>Mary Rose</u>.
10. Ninety‑seven years ago my great-grandparents left Scotland for the United States.

Parentheses

27u. Use parentheses to enclose material that is added to a sentence but is not considered of major importance.

EXAMPLES Mohandas K. Gandhi **(1869–1948)** led India's struggle for independence from British rule.
Mrs. Matsuo served us the sushi **(sōo′shē)** that she had prepared.

Material enclosed in parentheses may range from a single word or number to a short sentence. A short sentence in parentheses may stand by itself or be contained within another sentence.

EXAMPLES Fill in the order form carefully. **(Do not use pencil.)**
My great-uncle Chester **(he's Grandma's brother)** will stay with us during the holidays.

NOTE: Too many parenthetical expressions in a piece of writing can distract readers from the main idea. Keep your meaning clear by limiting the number of parenthetical expressions you use.

MECHANICS

COOPERATIVE LEARNING
Tell students that good writing is smooth writing; having too many parenthetical expressions interrupts the flow of ideas. Have students work in groups of three or four to write five sentences that contain too many parenthetical expressions. Then have the groups exchange papers and rewrite the sentences to make them smoother without losing any of the information in the parentheses.

MECHANICS

CRITICAL THINKING

Analysis. When students work **Exercises 12** and **13**, they have to analyze sentences to identify the parenthetical elements that are to be set off by either parentheses or dashes. Tell students that they can apply this test: identify the main idea in each of the sentences, and then analyze whether or not the basic meaning changes when the rest of the sentence is removed. If the meaning does not change, then students will know they have identified a parenthetical element, and they need to set it off with parentheses or dashes.

MECHANICS

MECHANICS

790

 EXERCISE 12   **Writing Sentences with Parentheses**

For each of the following sentences, insert parentheses where they are needed. Be sure not to enclose any words or marks of punctuation that do not belong inside the parentheses.

EXAMPLE   **1.** One of the most popular pets is the house cat *Felis cattus.*
      1. *One of the most popular pets is the house cat* **(Felis cattus).**

1. The old fort (it was used during the Civil War) has been rebuilt and is open to the public.
2. Most of Yellowstone National Park (the oldest national park in the United States) is in Wyoming.
3. The writer Langston Hughes (1902–1967) is best known for his poetry.
4. Alligators use their feet and tails to dig water holes (also called "gator holes") in marshy fields.
5. On the Sabbath we eat braided bread called challah (pronounced khä′lə).

Dashes

Many words and phrases are used *parenthetically;* that is, they break into the main thought of a sentence. Most parenthetical elements are set off by commas or parentheses.

EXAMPLES   The tomato**,** **however,** is actually a fruit, not a vegetable.
      The outcome **(which candidate would be elected governor?)** was in the hands of the voters.

☞ REFERENCE NOTE: For more about using commas with parenthetical expressions, see page 751. For more about using parentheses, see page 789.

Sometimes parenthetical elements demand a stronger emphasis. In such instances, a dash is used.

REVIEW D

OBJECTIVE

• To correct sentences by adding punctuation

27v. Use a dash to indicate an abrupt break in thought or speech.

EXAMPLES   Ms. Alonzo—she just left—will be one of the judges of the talent show.
"Right over here—oh, excuse me, Mr. Mills—you'll find the reference books," said the librarian.

▶ EXERCISE 13   **Writing Sentences with Dashes**

For each of the following sentences, insert dashes where they are needed.

EXAMPLE   **1.** Paul Revere he imported hardware made beautiful jewelry and utensils.
    1. *Paul Revere—he imported hardware—made beautiful jewelry and utensils.*

1. A beautiful grand piano‸it was once played by Chopin‸was on display in the museum.

1. dash/dash

2. "I'd like the red‸no, give me the blue‸cycling shorts," said Josh.

2. dash/dash

3. Frederic Remington‸artist, historian, and lover of the frontier‸painted the West as it really was.

3. dash/dash

4. On July 7, 1981, Sandra Day O'Connor‸she's the first woman associate justice‸was nominated to the U.S. Supreme Court.

4. dash/dash

5. Cheryl wondered aloud, "Where in the world‸oh, my poor Muffy‸could that hamster be?"

5. dash/dash

▶ REVIEW D   **Correcting Sentences by Adding Punctuation**

Write the following sentences, supplying punctuation marks where needed. If a sentence is correct, write *C*.

EXAMPLE   **1.** Stans going to the Washingtons Birthday cele bration in Laredo, Texas Teresa said.
    1. *"Stan's going to the Washington's Birthday cele-bration in Laredo, Texas," Teresa said.*

COOPERATIVE LEARNING

Divide the class into mixed-ability groups of three or four students each. Have them look through magazines, newspapers, or books to find examples of parenthetical elements set off by commas, dashes, and parentheses. (Each group should find at least three examples from each category.)

Have students discuss the punctuation usage, and have them decide what conclusions they can draw about when to use commas, parentheses, or dashes. [Answers may vary, but most students will deduce that when parenthetical elements have a close logical relationship to the main idea of the sentence, commas are used. When the logical relationship of the parenthetical element to the rest of the sentence is more remote, dashes or parentheses are used.]

TECHNOLOGY TIP

Some students might want to do **Review D** on a computer. Be sure to point out that standard keyboards on computers and typewriters do not contain a key for the dash. Instead, dashes are keyed by using two hyphens without any spacing before, between, or after them.

MECHANICS

ANSWERS

Review D

1. "Some say that Laredo's festivities are the country's biggest celebration of Washington's birthday," Juan said. "Isn't that surprising?"

2. "No; not really," said Frank. "The city's large Hispanic population chose to honor George Washington, whom they consider a freedom fighter."

3. "But," Teresa said, "the citizens also have great respect for Washington's abilities as a leader."

4. Juan said that the annual celebration began back in the 1800's. [*or* C]

5. "Do you know they've extended the birthday party to both sides of the Texas-Mexico border?" Teresa asked.

6. "That's right," Juan said. "The citizens of Nuevo Laredo in Mexico really enjoy the celebration, too."

7. "Just look at the colorful costumes in these pictures!" exclaimed Teresa. "Can you tell what famous couple these people are portraying?"

8. Mrs. Serrano—she's Juan's aunt who lives in Houston—has gone to the celebration in Laredo for the past twenty-two years.

9. "The <u>Laredo Morning Times</u> reported today that a jalapeño-eating contest was part of this year's celebration," Angie added.

10. In honor of Washington's birthday (February 22), three fourths of our class read the book <u>Washington</u> by William Jay Jacobs.

MECHANICS

MECHANICS

792

---

1. Some say that Laredos festivities are the countrys biggest celebration of Washingtons birthday Juan said Isnt that surprising

2. No, not really said Frank The citys large Hispanic population chose to honor George Washington, whom they consider a freedom fighter

3. But Teresa said the citizens also have great respect for Washingtons abilities as a leader

4. Juan said that the annual celebration began back in the 1800s.

5. Do you know theyve extended the birthday party to both sides of the Texas-Mexico border Teresa asked.

6. Thats right Juan said the citizens of Nuevo Laredo in Mexico really enjoy the celebration, too

7. Just look at the colorful costumes in these pictures exclaimed Teresa Can you tell what famous couple these people are portraying

WRITING APPLICATION

OBJECTIVE

- To interview five people and to write a report containing correctly punctuated direct quotations

8. Mrs. Serrano she's Juans aunt who lives in Houston has gone to the celebration in Laredo for the past twenty two years.
9. The Laredo Morning Times reported today that a jalapeño-eating contest was part of this years cele bration Angie added.
10. In honor of Washingtons birthday February 22, three fourths of our class read the book Washington by William Jay Jacobs.

WRITING APPLICATION

Using Quotations in Interviews

When you read an interview in a newspaper or magazine, how do you know exactly what was said? Usually, publishers print the questions and answers of an interview in a very clear format.

EXAMPLE   *Juan Bruce-Novoa:* How do you perceive your
role as a writer?
Rolando Hinojosa-Smith: My role is to write and then to try to get the stuff published; in the meantime, I keep writing.

from *Chicano Authors*

Reporters and other interviewers like Juan Bruce-Novoa often use a tape recorder to help them accurately report what was said and to have a permanent record of the interview.

If you were writing a report on Hinojosa-Smith and wanted to use material from the interview above, you would need to quote information from the source material.

EXAMPLE   An interviewer asked Hinojosa-Smith how he saw his role as a writer. The author replied, "My role is to write and then to try to get the stuff published; in the meantime, I keep writing."

MECHANICS

WRITING APPLICATION
In this **Writing Application** assignment, students are asked to conduct interviews and to write reports based on those interviews. The idea is to give students an opportunity to apply to a writing assignment what they have learned about punctuating and capitalizing direct quotations.

CRITICAL THINKING
Synthesis. Before students can begin writing their reports, they must synthesize the information they have gathered into an orderly format. For example, students must decide what to quote from the interviews. Remind students that the main idea must go in the first paragraph, and the material quoted from the interviews should support the main idea.

SELECTION AMENDMENT
Description of change: excerpted
Rationale: to focus on the use of punctuation presented in this chapter

MECHANICS

793

Notice how Hinojosa-Smith's exact words are enclosed in quotation marks. In general, you should follow two rules when using information from source materials.

- When you use someone else's ideas, give him or her credit.
- When you use someone else's words, quote them accurately.

▶ WRITING ACTIVITY

Your class is taking a survey of people's reading habits. Think of five questions you could ask about when and what people read. Then, use these questions to interview at least five people. Based on the information you gather, write a brief report about people and their reading habits. In your report, use quotation marks and correct punctuation to quote people's exact words.

Prewriting First, think of questions to ask. These questions could be about what people read, and how often, when, and why they read. Avoid asking questions that can be answered with a simple *yes* or *no*. Next, select at least five people to interview (perhaps friends, family members, or neighbors). Record the name, age, and occupation of each person. As you conduct your interviews, write down or tape-record what people say. If you want to tape the interview, be sure to ask the interviewee for permission to do so. Think about what reading habits the people you interviewed have in common. For example, you may find that most of them read magazines. Perhaps your survey group's reading habits can be organized by the age or gender of your interviewees. Jot down some notes to help you organize your information.

Writing In the first paragraph of your rough draft, include a statement that summarizes the main idea of your project and findings. Then, use people's answers to your survey questions to support your main idea. Clearly identify each person that you quote.

PREWRITING

Have students work in small groups to review each other's interview questions to ensure that the questions are sufficiently open-ended. You may want to have the groups brainstorm on different angles they could use to focus their interviews. The following questions are examples:

1. For VCR owners: How have your reading habits changed since you got a VCR?
2. For adults: How have changes in the economy affected the amount of time you have for reading?
3. For athletes: How does your reading pattern vary between the on-season and the off-season for your sport?

REVIEW: POSTTESTS A and B

OBJECTIVES

- To correct sentences by adding underlining (italics) and quotation marks
- To correct sentences by adding apostrophes, hyphens, parentheses, and dashes

Evaluating and Revising After you've finished your rough draft, take another look at your main idea. Does the body of your report support that idea? If not, revise your main idea. Add, cut, or rearrange details to present your findings clearly. What, if any, conclusions can you draw about the reading habits of the people you interviewed? State your conclusions in the last paragraph of your report.

Proofreading As you proofread your report, check your notes to be sure that you've spelled people's names correctly. Pay special attention to the use of apostrophes to show possessive cases of nouns and pronouns. Finally, be sure that you've put quotation marks around direct quotations and that you've correctly capitalized and punctuated all quotations.

Review: Posttest

A. Proofreading Sentences for the Correct Use of Quotation Marks and Underlining (Italics)

Each of the following sentences requires underlining (italics), quotation marks, or both. Write each sentence correctly.

EXAMPLE **1.** Ted, can you answer the first question? Ms. Simmons asked.

      1. *"Ted, can you answer the first question?" Ms. Simmons asked.*

1. The best chapter in our vocabulary book is the last one, "More Word Games."
2. "I answered all the questions," Todd said, "but I think that some of my answers were wrong."
3. <u>Star Wars</u> was more exciting on the big movie screen than it was on our small television set.

MEETING *individual* NEEDS

LESS-ADVANCED STUDENTS

To assist students with **Review: Posttest A,** you may want to list the following guide on the chalkboard:

1. Look for words that are a direct quotation. Copy the sentence and insert quotation marks. Pay attention to where other punctuation marks go.
2. Look for words, letters, and figures used as words, letters, and figures. They need to be underlined (italicized). If you can add the phrase *the word, the letter,* or *the figure,* and it makes sense, you need to underline (italicize).
3. Go back to look for words that are titles. Decide what the title refers to (a book, a newspaper, a submarine, and so forth). Use clues in the sentence to help you. Think about whether the item is long/whole or short/part; if the former is true, underline (italicize) it; if the latter is true, put quotation marks around it.

4. Mr. Washington asked Connie, "Which flag also included the slogan ＂Don't Tread on Me?"

5. There is a legend that the band on the <u>Titanic</u> played the hymn ＂Nearer My God to Thee＂ as the ship sank into the icy sea.

6. ＂Play the Freddie Jackson tape again, Sam,＂ Rebecca called from her room.　　**6.** [*or* <u>Freddie Jackson</u>]

7. Wendy wrote an article called ＂Students, Where Are You?＂ for our local newspaper, the <u>Morning Beacon</u>.

8. In the short story ＂Thank You, M'am＂ by Langston Hughes, a woman helps a troubled boy.

9. "Can I read <u>Treasure Island</u> for my book report?" Carmine asked.

10. Every Christmas Eve my uncle recites ＂The Night Before Christmas＂ for the children in the hospital.

B. Proofreading Sentences for the Correct Use of Apostrophes, Hyphens, Parentheses, and Dashes

Each of the following sentences contains at least one error in the use of apostrophes, hyphens, parentheses, or dashes. Write each sentence correctly.　Hyphens are indicated by the ～ symbol.

EXAMPLE　　**1.** Ive been thinking about rivers names that come from Native American words.

　　　　　1. *I've been thinking about rivers' names that come from Native American words.*

11. Boater's on the Missouri River may not know that *Missouri* means "people of the big canoes."　**11.** Boaters

12. Have you heard the song about the South's famous Shenandoah River?

13. The committee voted to help keep the walkway ～clean along the Connecticut River.　**13.** clean

14. I can't remember ～I wonder how many people have this same problem ～how many *i*s are in the word *Mississippi*.　**14.** dash/dash

---

MECHANICS

MECHANICS

15. Everybody's favorite tour stop was Mount Vernon, George Washington's home overlooking the Potomac River.
16. Don't you remember ~~they're~~ story about catching twenty-two fish in the Arkansas River? **16. their**
17. Three fourths of the class couldn't pronounce the name *Monongahela* until we broke it into syllables (Mo-non-ga-he-la).
18. His painting of the Mohawk River was good, but her's was better. **18. hers**
19. Ricardo's guidebook the one he ordered last month states that the Suwannee is one of Florida's major rivers. **19. dash/dash**
20. She's lived in Massachusetts for thirty-one years but has never before seen the Merrimack River.

MECHANICS

MECHANICS

28 SPELLING

Improving Your Spelling

Good Spelling Habits

As your vocabulary grows, you may have difficulty spelling some of the new words. You can improve your spelling by using the following methods.

1. *Pronounce words correctly.* Pronouncing words carefully can often help you to spell them correctly.

> EXAMPLES athlete: ath•lete [not *ath • e • lete*]
> probably: prob•a•bly [not *pro • bly*]
> library: li•brar•y [not *li • bar • y*]

2. *Spell by syllables.* When you have trouble spelling long words, divide them into syllables. A *syllable* is a word part that can be pronounced by itself. Learning to spell the syllables of a word one at a time will help you master the spelling of the whole word.

> EXAMPLES gymnasium: gym•na•si•um [four syllables]
> representative: rep•re•sent•a•tive [five syllables]

3. *Use a dictionary.* When you are not sure about the spelling of a word, look in a dictionary. A dictionary will also tell you the correct pronunciations and syllable divisions of words.

4. *Keep a spelling notebook.* The best way to master words that give you difficulty is to list the words and review them frequently. Divide each page of a notebook into four columns.

COLUMN 1 Write correctly the words you frequently misspell.

COLUMN 2 Write the words again, dividing them into syllables and marking the accents. (If you are not sure how to do this, use a dictionary.)

COLUMN 3 Write the words again, circling the parts that give you trouble.

COLUMN 4 Jot down any comments that may help you remember the correct spelling.

EXAMPLE

Correct Spelling	Syllables and Accents	Trouble Spot	Comments
escape	es•cape'	es̲c̲ape	Pronounce correctly.
calendar	cal'•en•dar	calend(a)r	Think of days marked on the calendar.
casually	cas'•u•al•ly	casua(lly)	Study rule 28e.

5. *Proofread for careless spelling errors.* Whenever you write, proofread your paper for errors in spelling. By slowly rereading what you have written, you can correct careless errors such as uncrossed *t*'s, undotted *i*'s, and crossed *l*'s.

MECHANICS

CHAPTER OVERVIEW

This chapter is intended to provide additional instruction for students who discover spelling problems in proofreading their writing. The first part of the chapter gives five methods students can use to improve their spelling. The chapter then presents a series of basic spelling rules and a discussion of seventy-four homonyms that are often confused. Further information on usage of some of these homonyms can be found in **Chapter 24: "A Glossary of Usage."**

PROGRAM MANAGER

GOOD SPELLING HABITS

- **Independent Practice/ Reteaching** For instruction and exercises, see **Proofreading for Spelling Errors** in *Language Skills Practice and Assessment,* p. 259.

- **Computer Guided Instruction** For additional instruction and practice with good spelling habits, see **Lesson 59** in *Language Workshop CD-ROM.*

- **Practice** To help less-advanced students with additional instruction and practice with good spelling habits, see **Chapter 25** in *English Workshop, Second Course,* pp. 281–282.

MECHANICS

OBJECTIVES
- To spell words with *ie* and *ei* and words with *–cede, –ceed,* and *–sede* correctly
- To spell words with prefixes and suffixes

PROGRAM MANAGER

SPELLING RULES

- **Independent Practice/Reteaching** For instruction and exercises, see **Using Spelling Rules** and **Adding Prefixes and Suffixes** in *Language Skills Practice and Assessment,* pp. 260–261.

- **Computer Guided Instruction** For additional instruction and practice with using spelling rules and adding prefixes and suffixes, see **Lesson 59** in *Language Workshop CD-ROM.*

- **Practice** To help less-advanced students with additional instruction and practice with using spelling rules and adding prefixes and suffixes, see **Chapter 25** in *English Workshop, Second Course,* pp. 281–286.

QUICK REMINDER

Read aloud the sentence below. Have students tell you the spelling of each word as you write the sentence on the chalkboard.

After my neighbor and I declared peace, she gave me a piece of pie that weighed at least a ton.

Ask students to recall the rhyme that helps in spelling words with *ie* and *ei*. [*I before e,* except after *c,* or when sounded like *a,* as in *neighbor* and *weigh.*]

MECHANICS

800 *Spelling*

Spelling Rules

ie and *ei*

28a. Except after *c,* write *ie* when the sound is long *e.*

EXAMPLES achieve believe chief field piece
ceiling conceit deceit deceive receive

EXCEPTIONS either leisure neither
protein seize weird

28b. Write *ei* when the sound is not long *e.*

EXAMPLES foreign forfeit height heir their
freight neighbor reign veil weigh

EXCEPTIONS ancient conscience efficient
friend mischief patience

▶ EXERCISE 1 **Spelling Words with *ie* and *ei***

The following paragraph contains ten words with missing letters. Add the letters *ie* or *ei* to spell each numbered word correctly.

EXAMPLE **Many people know [1] th____r signs in the Chinese zodiac.**
1. *their*

My [1] n__ei__ghbor, Mrs. Yee, told me about the Chinese zodiac signs. Not all Chinese people [2] bel__ie__ve in the zodiac. My parents don't, and [3] n__ei__ther do I, but I do think it's interesting. The Chinese zodiac is an [4] anc__ie__nt set of twelve-year cycles named after different animals. According to Mrs. Yee, the [5] ch__ie__f traits in your personality come from your animal sign. At first, I thought this notion was a bit [6] w__ei__rd, but it's not hard to understand. For example, a tiger is supposed to [7] s__ei__ze opportunities [8] f__ie__rcely. That description perfectly fits my brother's [9] fr__ie__nd Mike Chen, who was born in 1974. Mrs. Yee showed me a chart like the one on this page so that I could figure out the signs of all [10] __ei__ght members of my family.

RAT	OX	TIGER	RABBIT	DRAGON	SNAKE
1972, 1984, 1996	1973, 1985, 1997	1974, 1986, 1998	1975, 1987, 1999	1976, 1988, 2000	1965, 1977, 1989
HORSE	SHEEP	MONKEY	ROOSTER	DOG	BOAR
1966, 1978, 1990	1967, 1979, 1991	1968, 1980, 1992	1969, 1981, 1993	1970, 1982, 1994	1971, 1983, 1995

–cede, –ceed, and –sede

28c. The only word ending in –*sede* is *supersede.* The only words ending in –*ceed* are *exceed, proceed,* and *succeed.* Most other words with this sound end in –*cede.*

EXAMPLES   con**cede**   inter**cede**   pre**cede**   re**cede**   se**cede**

⏵ EXERCISE 2   **Proofreading Misspelled Words Ending in –*cede*, –*ceed*, and –*sede***

The following sentences contain five misspelled words ending in –*cede, –ceed,* and –*sede.* Identify the errors and spell the words correctly.

EXAMPLE   **1. The guitarist could not procede until the electricity came back on.**
   1. *procede—proceed*

1. Clarence Leo Fender succeeded in changing the music business in the 1950s.   **1. succeeded**
2. He improved the design of electric guitars, which quickly superceded acoustic guitars in popular music.
   2. superseded

MEETING *individual* NEEDS

STUDENTS WITH SPECIAL NEEDS

Some students have difficulty with spelling. You might try the following game to motivate students. Divide the class into teams of five or six students each. Have a spelling bee, but instead of having a student spell the whole word, he or she names only one letter. The first student names the first letter, the second student names the second letter, and so on. If a student misses a letter, the word is assigned to the next team, until the word is correctly spelled.

LESS-ADVANCED STUDENTS

You may want to have less-advanced students omit **Rule 28c** from their study. These are words students will seldom, if ever, have occasion to use.

LEARNING STYLES

Auditory Learners. Encourage students to spell and pronounce new or problem words aloud as they practice writing the words.

3. The success of Fender's invention probably ~exceeded~ his wildest dreams.   **3. exceeded**
4. Music critics ~consede~ that a new era began with the invention of the electric guitar.   **4. concede**
5. Concerts that ~preceeded~ Fender's invention were not nearly as loud as modern ones.   **5. preceded**

Adding Prefixes

A *prefix* is a letter or group of letters added to the beginning of a word to change its meaning.

EXAMPLES   dis + honest = **dis**honest
un + selfish = **un**selfish
pre + arrange = **pre**arrange

28d.   When adding a prefix to a word, do not change the spelling of the word itself.

EXAMPLES   mis + spell = **mis**spell   il + logical = **il**logical
over + see = **over**see   in + exact = **in**exact

▶ EXERCISE 3   **Spelling Words with Prefixes**

Spell each of the following words, adding the prefix given.

EXAMPLE   **1.** un + wrap
1. *unwrap*

1. immigrate
1. im + migrate

2. re + settle
2. resettle

3. uncertain
3. un + certain

4. il + legal
4. illegal

5. semi + circle
5. semicircle

Adding Suffixes

A *suffix* is a letter or group of letters added to the end of a word to change its meaning.

EXAMPLES   care + less = care**less**
comfort + able = comfort**able**
walk + ed = walk**ed**

INTEGRATING THE LANGUAGE ARTS

Literature Link. Tell students that once they know the meanings of prefixes, they can figure out new words if parts of the words are familiar. In "The Day the Dam Broke" James Thurber's humor is partly achieved by Thurber's use of elegant English to describe a hilarious, embarrassing scene. If your literature textbook contains it, have students read the story and list words they find that contain prefixes. Using the context of the sentences and their understanding of prefixes, students should see if they can determine the meanings of the words.

A DIFFERENT APPROACH

Have students write sentences with the words in **Exercises 3, 4,** and **5.** To generate interest in the activity, have students brainstorm topics of current interest to write about. Explain to the class that an important way of retaining spelling is using new or problem words in context.

28e. When adding the suffix *–ly* or *–ness* to a word, do not change the spelling of the word itself.

EXAMPLES   slow + ly = slow**ly**   dark + ness = dark**ness**
usual + ly = usual**ly**   eager + ness = eager**ness**
shy + ly = shy**ly**   shy + ness = shy**ness**

EXCEPTIONS   For words that end in *y* and have more than one syllable, change the *y* to *i* before adding *–ly* or *–ness.*
happy + ly = happ**ily**   lazy + ness = laz**iness**

28f. Drop the final silent *e* before a suffix beginning with a vowel.

EXAMPLES   line + ing = lin**ing**
desire + able = desir**able**
approve + al = approv**al**

EXCEPTIONS   Keep the final silent *e*
  ■ in a word ending in *ce* or *ge* before a suffix beginning with *a* or *o:*
    notice + able = noticeable
    courage + ous = courageous
  ■ in *dye* before *–ing: dyeing*
  ■ in *mile* before *–age: mileage*

28g. Keep the final silent *e* before a suffix beginning with a consonant.

EXAMPLES   hope + less = hope**less**
care + ful = care**ful**
awe + some = awe**some**
love + ly = love**ly**
nine + ty = nine**ty**
amuse + ment = amuse**ment**

EXCEPTIONS   nine + th = nin**th**
argue + ment = arg**ument**
true + ly = tr**uly**
judge + ment = judg**ment**
whole + ly = whol**ly**
awe + ful = aw**ful**

INTEGRATING THE LANGUAGE ARTS

Mechanics and Writing. If students are having problems finding misspelled words as they proofread, suggest they go over their work backwards. Tell students to pay attention to each word and to circle any they are uncertain about. After they have gone over their papers, they should check each circled word in a dictionary.

QUICK REMINDER

Write the following list of words on the chalkboard and have students divide the words into syllables. Remind students that this is a way to break difficult words into more-manageable parts to figure out their spellings.

1. dictionary [dic • tion • ar • y]
2. laboratory [lab • o • ra • to • ry]
3. congratulations [con • grat • u • la • tions]
4. engineering [en • gi • neer • ing]
5. manipulation [ma • nip • u • la • tion]
6. temperament [tem • per • a • ment]
7. advertisement [ad • ver • tise • ment]
8. acquaintance [ac • quaint • ance]

ANSWERS
Exercise 4

1. naturally
2. adorable
3. surely
4. dryness
5. teasing
6. luckily
7. tuneful
8. traceable
9. confinement
10. advantageous

A DIFFERENT APPROACH

Word games can help students learn to spell. Give students phrases of two or three words and have students make as many other words of four or more letters as they can by using letters from the phrases. Allow them to use dictionaries. The class could compete in teams.

Encourage students to play other word games, including crossword puzzles, word-searches, and manufactured games.

MECHANICS

804

---

804 *Spelling*

EXERCISE 4   **Spelling Words with Suffixes**

Spell each of the following words, adding the suffix given.

EXAMPLE   **1.** hope + ful
            1. *hopeful*

1. natural + ly   5. tease + ing   9. confine + ment
2. adore + able   6. lucky + ly   10. advantage + ous
3. sure + ly   7. tune + ful
4. dry + ness   8. trace + able

28h. For words ending in *y* preceded by a consonant, change the *y* to *i* before any suffix that does not begin with *i*.

EXAMPLES   cry + ed = **cried**   duty + ful = **dutiful**
            easy + ly = **easily**   cry + ing = **crying**

28i. For words ending in *y* preceded by a vowel, keep the *y* when adding a suffix.

EXAMPLES   pray + ing = **praying**   pay + ment = **payment**
            obey + ed = **obeyed**   boy + hood = **boyhood**

EXCEPTIONS   day—**daily**   lay—**laid**   pay—**paid**   say—**said**

28j. Double the final consonant before a suffix beginning with a vowel if the word

(1) has only one syllable or has the accent on the last syllable

and

(2) ends in a single consonant preceded by a single vowel.

EXAMPLES   sit + ing = **sitting**   occur + ed = **occurred**
            swim + er = **swimmer**   begin + er = **beginner**
            drop + ed = **dropped**   forbid + en = **forbidden**

Otherwise, the final consonant is usually not doubled before a suffix beginning with a vowel.

REVIEW A

OBJECTIVE

- To identify and correct misspelled words

**28
h–j**

EXAMPLES   sing + er = singer   final + ist = finalist
             speak + ing = **speaking**   center + ed = **centered**

NOTE: In some cases, the final consonant may or may not be doubled.

       EXAMPLES   cancel + ed = canceled   *or*   cancelled
                 travel + er = traveler   *or*   traveller

       Most dictionaries list both of these spellings as correct. When you are not sure about the spelling of a word, it is best to check in a dictionary.

▶ EXERCISE 5   **Spelling Words with Suffixes**

Spell each of the following words, adding the suffix given.

EXAMPLE   **1.** study + ed
               1. *studied*

1. tiny + est
2. trim + ing
3. carry + ed
4. pity + ful
5. display + ed
6. destroy + ing
7. refer + al
8. jog + er
9. submit + ing
10. win + er

▶ REVIEW A   **Proofreading for Misspelled Words**

Most of the following sentences contain a spelling error. Identify and correct each error. If a sentence is correct, write *C.*

EXAMPLE   **1.** The man shown on the next page is not Sam Houston or Jim Bowie, but he is a certifyed Texas hero.
            1. *certifyed—certified*

1. This industryous blacksmith is William Goyens.   **1.** industrious
2. In 1820, he moved from North Carolina to Texas, where he succeded in several businesses.   **2.** succeeded
3. Goyens acheived his greatest fame as a negotiator with the Comanche and the Cherokee peoples.   **3.** achieved
4. He easily made freinds with the Native Americans who traded in the small town of Nacogdoches.   **4.** friends

MECHANICS

INTEGRATING THE LANGUAGE ARTS

Mechanics and Dictionary Skills. Because dictionaries sometimes give more than one spelling for a word, you may want to allow time in class for students to become familiar with the dictionaries they use. Have students study the introductory material that explains the policy regarding multiple spellings. For example, the first spelling given is usually the one most commonly used. If two spellings are joined by the word *or,* both may be equally correct.

ANSWERS
Exercise 5
1. tiniest
2. trimming
3. carried
4. pitiful
5. displayed
6. destroying
7. referral
8. jogger
9. submitting
10. winner

A DIFFERENT APPROACH
Students can practice proofreading for misspelled words by working with partners on current writing assignments. Have students exchange drafts of writing assignments for your class or for another class. Their task is to list words they are uncertain about and to check the words in a dictionary.

MECHANICS

FORMING THE PLURALS OF NOUNS

- **Independent Practice/ Reteaching** For instruction and exercises, see **Spelling the Plurals of Nouns** in *Language Skills Practice and Assessment*, p. 262.

- **Computer Guided Instruction** For additional instruction and practice with spelling the plurals of nouns, see **Lesson 60** in *Language Workshop CD-ROM*.

- **Practice** To help less-advanced students with additional instruction and practice with spelling the plurals of nouns, see **Chapter 25** in *English Workshop, Second Course*, pp. 287–290.

QUICK REMINDER

Write the following sentences on the chalkboard. Ask students to write the sentences, to change the underlined words to their plural forms, and to change verbs as necessary.

1. The radio was so loud that the sheriff heard an echo outside the igloo. [The radios were so loud that the sheriffs heard echoes outside the igloos.]

2. The alto served the soprano a baked potato on the patio. [The altos served the sopranos baked potatoes on the patios.]

Tell students that by learning a few rules they can master the spelling of plural nouns.

806

OBJECTIVE

- To correctly spell the plural forms of nouns

806 *Spelling*

5. Later, he assisted the Mexican government and then the Texas army in makking peace with their Native American neighbors. **5.** making

6. General Sam Houston asked Goyens to interceed on behalf of the settlers. **6.** intercede

7. Because of Goyens's efforts, the Comanches and the Cherokees agreed to remain on peaceful terms with the settlers. **7.** peaceful

8. In addition to negotiating peace treaties, Goyens studyed law to protect his own and others' freedoms. **8.** studied

9. People started coming to him with their legal problems, and he unselfishly tried to help them. **9.** C

10. William Goyens was truely an important force in shaping Texas history. **10.** truly

Forming the Plurals of Nouns

28k. For most nouns, add –*s*.

SINGULAR	desk	idea	shoe	friend	camera	Wilson
PLURAL	desk**s**	idea**s**	shoe**s**	friend**s**	camera**s**	Wilson**s**

28l. For nouns ending in *s*, *x*, *z*, *ch*, or *sh*, add –*es*.

SINGULAR	gas	fox	waltz	inch	dish	Suarez
PLURAL	gas**es**	fox**es**	waltz**es**	inch**es**	dish**es**	Suarez**es**

▶ EXERCISE 6   **Spelling the Plural Forms of Nouns**

Spell the plural form of each of the following nouns.

EXAMPLE   **1.** right
          1. *rights*

1. dish_∧ **1. es**   5. skyscraper_∧ **5. s**   9. Gómez_∧ **9. es**
2. plumber_∧ **2. s** 6. march_∧ **6. es**   10. tax_∧ **10. es**
3. candle_∧ **3. s** 7. parade_∧ **7. s**
4. watch_∧ **4. es** 8. republic_∧ **8. s**

28m. For nouns ending in *y* preceded by a vowel, add –*s*.

SINGULAR	decoy	highway	alley	Riley
PLURAL	decoy**s**	highway**s**	alley**s**	Riley**s**

28n. For nouns ending in *y* preceded by a consonant, change the *y* to *i* and add –*es*.

SINGULAR	army	country	city	pony	ally	daisy
PLURAL	arm**ies**	countr**ies**	cit**ies**	pon**ies**	all**ies**	dais**ies**

EXCEPTIONS **For proper nouns, add –*s*.**
Brady—Brady**s**   Murphy—Murphy**s**

28o. For some nouns ending in *f* or *fe*, add –*s*. For others, change the *f* or *fe* to *v* and add –*es*.

SINGULAR	belief	thief	sheriff	knife	giraffe
PLURAL	belief**s**	thie**ves**	sheriff**s**	kni**ves**	giraffe**s**

NOTE: When you are not sure about how to spell the plural of a noun ending in *f* or *fe*, look in a dictionary.

28p. For nouns ending in *o* preceded by a vowel, add –*s*.

SINGULAR	radio	patio	stereo	igloo	Matteo
PLURAL	radio**s**	patio**s**	stereo**s**	igloo**s**	Matteo**s**

28q. For nouns ending in *o* preceded by a consonant, add –*es*.

SINGULAR	tomato	potato	echo	hero
PLURAL	tomato**es**	potato**es**	echo**es**	hero**es**

MECHANICS

MEETING
individual
NEEDS

LEP/ESL

General Strategies. Students will often not notice –*s* endings on plurals when reading or listening and, in turn, will fail to produce them in speaking and writing. A good way to heighten students' awareness of –*s* endings is to have students read aloud a portion of text that contains many plurals and to have them pronounce after you whenever they miss an –*s*. When you pronounce, use normal sounds such as the *z* sound in *tomatoes*.

MECHANICS

EXCEPTIONS For musical terms and proper nouns, add –*s.*

alto—alto**s**   soprano—soprano**s**

Tejano—Tejano**s**   Nakamoto—Nakamoto**s**

NOTE: To form the plural of some nouns ending in *o* preceded by a consonant, you may add either –*s* or –*es.*

SINGULAR	domino	mosquito	banjo	flamingo
PLURAL	domino**s**	mosquito**s**	banjo**s**	flamingo**s**
	or	*or*	*or*	*or*
	domino**es**	mosquito**es**	banjo**es**	flamingo**es**

When you are in doubt about the way to form the plural of a noun ending in *o* preceded by a consonant, check the spelling in a dictionary.

28r. The plural of a few nouns is formed in irregular ways.

SINGULAR	ox	goose	foot	tooth	woman	mouse
PLURAL	ox**en**	g**ee**se	f**ee**t	t**ee**th	w**o**men	m**i**ce

▶ EXERCISE 7   **Spelling the Plurals of Nouns**

Spell the plural form of each of the following nouns. [Note: A word may have more than one correct plural form.]

EXAMPLE   **1.** volcano

              1. *volcanoes or volcanos*

1. monkey	5. hoof	9. cargo
2. trophy	6. proof	10. woman
3. Massey	7. palomino	
4. diary	8. child	

28s. For most compound nouns, form the plural of the last word in the compound.

SINGULAR	bookshelf	push-up	sea gull	ten-year-old
PLURAL	bookshel**ves**	push-up**s**	sea gull**s**	ten-year-old**s**

MECHANICS

COOPERATIVE LEARNING

After students have completed **Exercise 7**, organize them into groups of five. Their challenge is to use the singular forms of the words in **Exercise 7** to create paragraphs. Encourage them to be as outlandish as possible while still making some sense. If you are pressed for time, you may have them write numbered sentences instead of paragraphs. Have groups exchange papers to rewrite the sentences by changing the words to plurals.

ANSWERS

Exercise 7

1. monkeys

2. trophies

3. the Masseys

4. diaries

5. hoofs *or* hooves

6. proofs

7. palominos

8. children

9. cargoes *or* cargos

10. women

28t. For compound nouns in which one of the words is modified by the other word or words, form the plural of the word modified.

SINGULAR brother-in-law maid of honor eighth-grader
PLURAL brothers-in-law maids of honor eighth-graders

28u. For some nouns the singular and the plural forms are the same.

SINGULAR AND PLURAL trout sheep Sioux deer moose

28v. For numbers, letters, symbols, and words used as words, add an apostrophe and –s.

EXAMPLES The product of two **4's** is twice the sum of four **2's.**
Notice that the word *committee* has two **m's,** two **t's,** and two **e's.**
Write **$'s** before, not after, amounts of money.
This composition contains too many **so's** and **and's.**

NOTE: In your reading you may notice that some writers do not use apostrophes to form the plurals of numbers, capital letters, symbols, and words used as words.

EXAMPLES Their music is as popular today as it was in the **1970s.**
When dividing, remember to write **R**s before the remainders in the quotients.

However, using an apostrophe is never wrong. Therefore, it is best always to use the apostrophe.

Spelling Numbers

28w. Spell out a number that begins a sentence.

EXAMPLE **Fifteen thousand** people went to see the Milton Nascimento concert.

A DIFFERENT APPROACH
Have students work in small groups to generate lists of the plurals of the last names of students in the class. Students may need to refer to the rules in this lesson to complete the activity. After each group has a complete list, go over it and make certain each name is correct.

As an alternative to this activity, provide telephone books or other directories and have groups list twenty-five names and their plurals.

MECHANICS

MECHANICS

INTEGRATING THE LANGUAGE ARTS

Literature Link. Authors often use misspelling and nonstandard grammar to create dialects for characters. Mark Twain is a master of dialect, and his story "The Celebrated Jumping Frog of Calaveras County" provides an excellent example. The first narrator speaks in an elevated style, which creates a sharp contrast to Simon Wheeler's mining-camp dialect. If your literature textbook contains Twain's story, have students read it to find at least five examples of the use of misspellings to indicate dialect.

ANSWERS
Review B

1. Sioux
2. basketballs
3. Japanese
4. sons-in-law
5. *i*'s
6. car pools
7. major generals
8. sit-ups
9. handfuls
10. 1900's *or* 1900s

REVIEWS B and C

OBJECTIVE

• To spell and use the plural forms of nouns correctly

28x. Within a sentence, spell out numbers that can be written in one or two words. Use numerals for other numbers.

EXAMPLES   Do you have **two** nickels for **one** dime?
In all, **fifty-two** people attended the family reunion.
More than **160** people were invited.

 NOTE: If you use several numbers, some short and some long, write them all the same way. Usually, it is better to write them all as numerals.

INCORRECT   We sold eighty-six tickets to the first dance and 121 tickets to the second dance.
CORRECT   We sold 86 tickets to the first dance and 121 tickets to the second dance.

28y. Spell out numbers used to indicate order.

EXAMPLE   **Our team came in third** [not *3rd*] in the regional track meet.

▶ REVIEW B   **Spelling the Plurals of Nouns**

Spell the plural form of each of the following nouns.

EXAMPLE   **1.** editor in chief
1. *editors in chief*

1. Sioux
2. basketball
3. Japanese
4. son-in-law
5. *i*
6. car pool
7. major general
8. sit-up
9. handful
10. 1900

▶ REVIEW C   **Using Plurals of Nouns**

You and your friends are creating word games for a party on Saturday night. You've decided to write tongue twisters and challenge your friends to read them aloud. Write the plural forms of the following five pairs of words. Then, use words with similar consonant sounds to create hard-to-say sentences. Your tongue-twisting sentences can be silly or serious.

WORDS OFTEN CONFUSED

OBJECTIVE

- To spell correctly words that are often confused

EXAMPLE   **1.** tooth—train
            1. *teeth—trains*
             *Twyla tickled three tigers' teeth on two trains
to Timbuktu this Thursday.*

1. donkey—dash
2. O'Reilly—raspberry
3. moose—mother-in-law
4. potato—patio
5. fox—finch

Words Often Confused

People frequently confuse the words in each of the following groups. Some of these words are *homonyms.* Their pronunciations are the same, but their meanings and spellings are different. Others have the same or similar spellings.

accept	[verb] *to receive with consent; to give approval to* In 1964, Dr. Martin Luther King, Jr., *accepted* the Nobel Prize for peace.
except	[verb] *leave out from a group;* [prep.] *other than; but* We were *excepted* from the assignment. Everyone will be there *except* Ruben.
advice	[noun] *a recommendation about a course of action* Good *advice* may be easy to give but hard to follow.
advise	[verb] *to recommend a course of action; to give advice* I *advise* you to continue your music lessons if you can.

MECHANICS

MECHANICS

QUICK REMINDER

Have students listen as you read each sentence below. Then have students write the sentences as you read them slowly.

1. No one <u>except</u> my <u>counselor</u> thinks I should <u>choose</u> my <u>clothes</u>.
2. It's unusual to <u>advise</u> someone to <u>lead</u> a life of <u>peace</u>.
3. The <u>weather</u> will be <u>quite</u> cold <u>through</u> Monday.

Go over the correct spellings of the underscored words.

MEETING *individual* NEEDS

LEP/ESL

General Strategies. If available, software that teaches spelling can be very helpful for English-language learners. Pair them with English-proficient speakers who can model pronunciation, an integral part of spelling ability.

LESS-ADVANCED STUDENTS

You may want to have students concentrate on learning to spell words they will use often. For example, they may never use words such as *formally* or *formerly* in their writing.

812 *Spelling*

affect	[verb] *to influence; to produce an effect upon* The explosion of Krakatoa *affected* the sunsets all over the world.
effect	[noun] *the result of an action; consequence* The phases of the moon have an *effect* on the tides of the earth's oceans.
all ready	*all prepared* The players are *all ready* for the big game.
already	*previously* Our class has *already* taken two field trips.
all right	[adjective] *satisfactory;* [adverb] *satisfactorily* [*All right* must be written as two words. The spelling *alright* is not acceptable.] Was my answer *all right?* Maria did *all right* in the track meet.

EXERCISE 8   **Using Words Often Confused**

From the choices in parentheses, select the <u>correct word or words</u> for each of the following sentences.

EXAMPLE   **1.** Anh and her family are (*all ready, already*) to celebrate Tet, the Vietnamese New Year.
   1. *all ready*

1. Do you think my work is (<u>*all right*</u>, *alright*)?
2. The (*affect*, <u>*effect*</u>) of the victory was startling.
3. The scientists were (<u>*all ready*</u>, *already*) to watch the launching of the rocket.
4. Whose (<u>*advice*</u>, *advise*) are you going to take?
5. The coach (*advices*, <u>*advises*</u>) us to stick to the training rules.
6. Why did you (*accept*, <u>*except*</u>) Carla from the rule?
7. Her weeks of practice have finally (<u>*affected*</u>, *effected*) her game.

8. Juan has (*all ready*, *already*) learned how to water-ski.
9. Most of the rebels were offered a full pardon and (*accepted*, *excepted*) it, but the leaders were (*accepted*, *excepted*) from the offer.
10. Gabriel took my (*advice*, *advise*) and visited the home of Frederick Douglass in Washington, D.C.

altar	[noun] *a table for a religious ceremony* The *altar* was covered with lilies.
alter	[verb] *to change* The outcome of the election may *alter* the mayor's plan.
all together	*everyone or everything in the same place* The director called us *all together* for one final rehearsal.
altogether	*entirely* He is *altogether* pleased with his victory.
brake	[noun] *a stopping device* Can you fix the *brake* on my bicycle?
break	[verb] *to fracture; to shatter* A high-pitched noise can *break* glass.
capital	*a city; the seat of a government* Olympia is the *capital* of Washington.
capitol	*building; statehouse* Where is the *capitol* in Albany?
choose	[verb; present tense, rhymes with *whose*] *to select* Will you *choose* speech or art as your elective next year?
chose	[verb; past tense, rhymes with *grows*] *selected* Sara *chose* a red pen, not a blue one.

MECHANICS

MECHANICS

A DIFFERENT APPROACH

Memory tricks such as the following ones can be helpful for some students:

1. *all right*—If it's not *all right,* it's all wrong.
2. *dessert*—When this is served, we often want two (two *s*'s).
3. *hear*—We do this with our ears.
4. *piece*—A pie contains this.
5. *stationery*—People used to buy this from a stationer.
6. *stomach*—His stomach aches.
7. *weird*—We are weird.

Frank & Ernest reprinted by permission of Newspaper Enterprise Association, Inc.

EXERCISE 9   Using Words Often Confused

From the choices in parentheses, select the correct word or words for each of the following sentences.

EXAMPLE
1. Mr. Conway said he (*choose, chose*) teaching as a career because he wants to help young people.
   1. *chose*

1. The building with the dome is the (*capital, capitol*).
2. By working (*all together, altogether*), we can succeed.
3. Because she loved dramatics, Alice (*choose, chose*) a difficult part in the school play.
4. Be careful not to (*brake, break*) those dishes.
5. That book is (*all together, altogether*) too complicated for you to enjoy.
6. The candles on the (*altar, alter*) of the synagogue glowed beautifully.
7. Why did you (*choose, chose*) that one?
8. A car without a good emergency (*brake, break*) is a menace.
9. Will Carrie's accident (*altar, alter*) her plans to go canoeing on the Buffalo Fork River in Arkansas?
10. Tallahassee is the (*capital, capitol*) of Florida.

clothes	*wearing apparel* One can learn a lot about a historical period by studying its styles of *clothes.*
cloths	*pieces of fabric* You'll find some cleaning *cloths* in the drawer.

coarse	[adjective] *rough; crude* The beach is covered with *coarse* brown sand.
course	[noun] *path of action; unit of study or route* [also used in the expression *of course*] If you follow that *course,* you'll succeed. My mother is taking a *course* in accounting. The wind blew the ship slightly off its *course.* You know, of *course,* that I'm right.
consul	*a representative of a government in a foreign country* Who is the American *consul* in Cairo?
council	*a group of people who meet together* The mayor called a meeting of the city *council.*
councilor	*member of a council* The *councilors* discussed several issues.
counsel	[noun] *advice;* [verb] *to give advice* When choosing a career, seek *counsel* from your teachers. Ms. Jiménez *counseled* me to pursue a career in teaching.
counselor	*one who advises* Who is your guidance *counselor?*
desert	[noun] *a dry, sandy region* The Sahara is the largest *desert* in Africa.
desert	[verb] *to abandon; to leave* Most dogs will not *desert* a friend in trouble.
dessert	[noun] *the final course of a meal* Fruit salad is my favorite *dessert.*

MECHANICS

INTEGRATING THE LANGUAGE ARTS

Mechanics and Dictionary Skills. Some dictionaries have sections in the front matter that tell the history of spelling. If such dictionaries are available, you may want to have students read this material and report to the class three new things they learn.

MECHANICS

CRITICAL THINKING

Analysis. Pair students with partners for a game of Spelling Algebra. Assign partners pairs of homonyms and have them write one or two sentences using both words. Then have teams read their sentences aloud, but have them substitute the algebraic terms *x* and *y* for the homonyms. The class must figure out what the words are. For example:

1. All the members *x* the girl whose parents were away were able to *y* the invitation to the party. [except, accept]

2. My dog didn't *x* me when I said, "Come *y*." [hear, here]

---

816 *Spelling*

EXERCISE 10   **Using Words Often Confused**

From the choices in parentheses, select the <u>correct word</u> or words for each of the following sentences.

EXAMPLE   **1. Egypt, of (*course, coarse*), is an ancient country in northeastern Africa.**
1. *course*

1. The student (<u>council</u>, *counsel*) voted to have "A Night on the Nile" as its dance theme.
2. In this photograph, many shoppers at an Egyptian market wear Western (<u>clothes</u>, *cloths*).

3. Some, however, wear traditional garments, including (*clothes*, <u>cloths</u>) called *kaffiyehs* wrapped around their heads.
4. In ancient Egypt, pharaohs didn't always follow the advice of their (*councilors*, <u>counselors</u>).
5. The surfaces of some famous Egyptian monuments look (<u>coarse</u>, *course*) from years of exposure to wind and sand.
6. In my geography (*coarse*, <u>course</u>), I learned that Nubians make up the largest minority group in Egypt's population.
7. The American (<u>consul</u>, *council*) in Cairo welcomed the vice-president to Egypt.
8. Camels didn't (<u>desert</u>, *dessert*) their owners when they crossed the Egyptian (<u>desert</u>, *dessert*).

9. Figs, grapes, and dates have long been popular (*deserts*, *desserts*) in Egypt.
10. In Cairo, the confused tourists looked to their tour director for (*council*, *counsel*).

formally	*with dignity; according to strict rules or procedures* The mayor delivered the speech *formally*.
formerly	*previously; in the past* Adele Zubalsky was *formerly* the principal of the school.
hear	[verb] *to perceive sounds by ear* Dogs can *hear* sounds that people can't hear.
here	[adverb] *in this place* The treasure is buried *here*.
its	[possessive form of *it*] Mount Fuji is noted for *its* beauty.
it's	[contraction of *it is* or *it has*] *It's* a good idea to open a savings account. *It's* been a long time since I last saw you.
lead	[verb, present tense, rhymes with *feed*] *to go first; to be a leader* A small town in New Hampshire often *leads* the nation in filing its election returns.
led	[verb, past tense of *lead*] *went first* Mr. Tanaka *led* the scout troop back to camp.
lead	[noun, rhymes with *red*] *a heavy metal* Many fishing nets are weighted with *lead* to hold them on the sea bottom.

MECHANICS

INTEGRATING THE LANGUAGE ARTS

Mechanics and Dictionary Skills. Some dictionaries contain reference material on learning to spell correctly. Have students study this material in dictionaries from home, school, or public libraries. If they find any rules or tips that are not included in the textbook, students could share them with the class.

818 *Spelling*

loose	[adjective, rhymes with *moose*] *not securely attached; not fitting tightly*
	If the knot is too *loose*, the piñata will fall out of the tree.
lose	[verb, present tense, rhymes with *whose*] *to suffer loss*
	Vegetables *lose* some of their vitamins when they are cooked.

 EXERCISE 11   **Using Words Often Confused**

From the choices in parentheses, select the <u>correct word or words</u> for each of the following sentences.

EXAMPLE   **1.** Mary Beth didn't (*loose, lose*) her Southern accent even after she moved to Boston.
1. *lose*

1. According to Ethan's map, (*its*, <u>*it's*</u>) a long way from (*hear*, <u>*here*</u>) to the park.
2. The ancient Chinese, Greeks, and Romans used (<u>*lead*</u>, *led*) in their coins.
3. If you don't wait (*hear*, <u>*here*</u>), we may (*loose*, <u>*lose*</u>) you in the crowd.
4. Before the club takes up new business, the secretary (<u>*formally*</u>, *formerly*) reads the minutes of the previous meeting.
5. (*Its*, <u>*It's*</u>) too bad that the oak tree has lost (<u>*its*</u>, *it's*) leaves.
6. Didn't you (<u>*hear*</u>, *here*) me, Charlotte? Come over (*hear*, <u>*here*</u>) now!
7. The Yankees were ten runs behind, and it seemed certain that they were going to (*loose*, <u>*lose*</u>).
8. Steffi Graf (*lead*, <u>*led*</u>) in the first games of the tennis match.
9. My mother told me that our new neighbor, Mr. Brown, was (*formally*, <u>*formerly*</u>) a colonel in the U.S. Army.
10. That (<u>*loose*</u>, *lose*) bolt can cause trouble.

passed	[verb, past tense of *pass*] *went by* The people in the car waved as they *passed* us.
past	[noun] *that which has gone by;* [preposition] *beyond* Some people long to live in the *past*. They walked *past* the dozing guard.
peace	*security and quiet order* We are striving for *peace* and prosperity.
piece	*a part of something* Some people can catch fish with a pole, a *piece* of string, and a bent pin.
plain	[adjective] *simple, common, unadorned;* [noun] *a flat area of land* The actors wore *plain* costumes. What is the difference between a prairie and a *plain?*
plane	[noun] *a tool; an airplane; a flat surface* The *plane* is useful in the carpenter's trade. Four single-engine *planes* are in the hangar. In geometry class we learned how to measure the angles of *planes* such as squares and triangles.
principal	[noun] *the head of a school;* [adjective] *main or most important* The *principal* of the school is Mr. Arimoto. What are the *principal* exports of Brazil?
principle	[noun] *a rule of conduct; a main fact or law* Judge Rios is a woman of high *principle*. We discussed some of the basic *principles* of democracy.

MECHANICS

MECHANICS

MECHANICS

COMMON ERROR

Problem. Students have trouble finding in dictionaries the spellings of words they don't know how to spell.

Solution. Tell students that certain sounds can be spelled in various ways. For example, the *r* sound is spelled differently in *run, wrong,* and *rhyme.* Some dictionaries provide lists of the various spellings for particular sounds. Have students work in groups of mixed abilities to make charts of the spellings of sounds. Have them start with the sound of *k,* which can be spelled *k, c, ck,* or *ch.* They can then continue with all the consonant and vowel sounds that can be spelled various ways. Students could keep the charts in their notebooks for reference.

MECHANICS

---

820 *Spelling*

quiet	[adjective] *still and peaceful; without noise* A *quiet* room is needed for concentrated study.
quite	[adverb] *wholly or entirely; to a great extent* Winters in New England can be *quite* severe.

▶ EXERCISE 12 **Using Words Often Confused**

From the choices in parentheses, select <u>the correct word</u> for each of the following sentences.

EXAMPLE **1.** Summer (*passed, past*) by too quickly!
1. *passed*

1. In some Filipino villages, you can still find (*plain*, *plane*), practical houses built on bamboo stilts.
2. The summer was not (*quiet*, *quite*) over before the beginning of school brought a (*quiet*, *quite*) household once more.
3. This is a main (*principal*, *principle*) in mathematics.
4. On July 11, 1991, the moon (*passed*, *past*) between the earth and the sun, causing a total solar eclipse.
5. A (*plain*, *plane*) is a useful tool.
6. Save me a (*peace*, *piece*) of that blueberry pie.
7. Have you heard that the new (*principal*, *principle*) used to be a student here?
8. You can learn much from (*passed*, *past*) experience.
9. After the long war came a long period of (*peace*, *piece*).
10. Cattle were grazing over the (*plain*, *plane*).

shone	[verb, past tense of *shine*] *gleamed; glowed* The Navajo jeweler polished the silver-and-turquoise ring until it *shone.*
shown	[verb, past participle of *show*] *revealed* A model of the new school will be *shown* to the public next week.

stationary	[adjective] *in a fixed position* Most of the furnishings of a space capsule must be *stationary*.
stationery	[noun] *writing paper* I need a new box of *stationery*.

than	[conjunction used for comparisons] The Amazon River is longer *than* the Mississippi River.
then	[adverb] *at that time* If the baby is awake by four o'clock, we will leave *then*.

their	[possessive form of *they*] *Their* team seems very skillful.
there	[adverb] *at or in that place;* [also used to begin a sentence] Go *there* in the fall when the leaves are turning. *There* were no objections.
they're	[contraction of *they are*] *They're* rehearsing for a production of *A Soldier's Story*.

threw	[verb, past tense of *throw*] *cast; tossed* Our relief pitcher *threw* nine strikes in succession.
through	[preposition] The ship went *through* the series of locks in the Panama Canal.

▶ EXERCISE 13   **Using Words Often Confused**

From the choices in parentheses, select the <u>correct word</u> for each of the following sentences.

MECHANICS

TECHNOLOGY TIP
You may want to discuss the use of spell-checker features for students who use word-processing programs. Explain how the feature works: The computer will query any spellings that are not in its dictionary, and it will suggest alternative spellings. Remind students, though, of the danger of depending entirely on computers for spelling. Most spell-checker programs will not question sentences such as "Their having a good time at there family reunion." Discuss the responsibilities of careful proofreading in addition to the use of spell-checker features.

MECHANICS

MECHANICS

EXAMPLE **1.** (*There, Their*) are some truly amazing tunnels used for transportation throughout the world.
1. *There*

1. Take a good look at the workers in this photograph because (*their*, <u>*they're*</u>) part of history.
2. (<u>*Their*</u>, *They're*) labor helped create a tunnel under the English Channel to link England with France.
3. A documentary about the tunnels through the Alps will be (*shone*, <u>*shown*</u>) at the library.
4. Huge exhaust fans were constructed to move the (<u>*stationary*</u>, *stationery*) air in the Holland Tunnel in New York.
5. To run railroad lines all across the United States, workers had to dig many tunnels (*threw*, <u>*through*</u>) mountains.
6. Used to blast tunnels in mountainsides, explosives (<u>*threw*</u>, *through*) enormous boulders into the air.
7. The warm sun (<u>*shone*</u>, *shown*) bright on the snowy top of Mont Blanc, but in the mountain's tunnel it was dark and chilly.
8. We rode the underground, or subway, into London, where I bought some (*stationary*, <u>*stationery*</u>).
9. Boston's subway is older (<u>*than*</u>, *then*) New York City's subway.
10. In Paris, we took the subway, called the *métro*, to the Eiffel Tower and (*than*, <u>*then*</u>) to the Louvre museum.

MECHANICS

VISUAL CONNECTIONS
Exploring the Subject. In 1802, Napoleon approved a project to build a tunnel under the English Channel. The project was proposed again in 1830 and finally attempted in 1975. Success came on October 30, 1990, when the British and the French met deep under the Channel. They had encountered numerous engineering problems, including having to use huge batteries to power the boring machines, having to remove massive amounts of muck, and having to deal with water leaks as powerful as hail. The end result is the longest undersea tunnel in the world, and it is called the Chunnel.

822

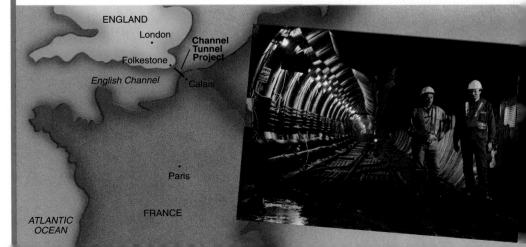

ENGLAND
London
Channel Tunnel Project
Folkestone
English Channel
Calais
Paris
ATLANTIC OCEAN
FRANCE

to	[preposition; also part of the infinitive form of a verb] Marco Polo began his trip *to* China in 1271. Do you know how *to* make tortillas?
too	[adverb] *also; more than enough* We have lived in Iowa and in Alaska, *too.* It is *too* cold for rain today.
two	*cardinal number between one and three* She borrowed *two* dollars from me.
weak	[adjective] *not strong; feeble* The patient is too *weak* to have visitors.
week	[noun] *seven days* Your pictures of Josh's bar mitzvah will be ready in about a *week.*
weather	[noun] *condition of the air or atmosphere* The *weather* is hot and humid.
whether	[conjunction] *if* Jessica wondered *whether* she should go.
who's	[contraction of *who is* or *who has*] *Who's* representing the yearbook staff? *Who's* read today's newspaper?
whose	[possessive form of *who*] *Whose* report are we hearing today?
your	[possessive form of *you*] *Your* work in math is improving.
you're	[contraction of *you are*] *You're* right on time!

MECHANICS

▶ EXERCISE 14 **Using Words Often Confused**

From the choices in parentheses, select the <u>correct word</u> <u>or words</u> for each of the following sentences.

 INTEGRATING THE LANGUAGE ARTS

Literature Link. Lewis Carroll's "The Walrus and the Carpenter" is a good selection to use to illustrate the variety of ways that vowel sounds can be spelled in English. If your literature textbook contains it, have students study Carroll's poem. Challenge them to find the two verses in which the three end-rhyming sounds are all spelled differently. [The stanza beginning with line 37 rhymes *said, head,* and *bed.* The stanza beginning with line 79 rhymes *blue, do,* and *view.*]

You may wish to extend this activity by having students find other poems that have rhymes with different spellings. Students could read the poems to the class and write the spellings on the chalkboard.

MECHANICS

INTEGRATING THE LANGUAGE ARTS

Mechanics and Writing. Students who are interested in writing rhyming poetry or song lyrics might find rhyming dictionaries useful for finding words that rhyme and for learning how to spell the words. You could bring one or several dictionaries to class or have students find them in libraries.

TECHNOLOGY TIP

You may want to point out that some word-processing programs have rhyming dictionaries. Students can indicate the words they need rhymes for, determine how many syllables they wish to rhyme, and let the computer suggest possible words.

REVIEW D

OBJECTIVE

- To identify and correct misspelled words

824 *Spelling*

EXAMPLE   **1.** (*Your, You're*) class gets to visit Minnehaha Park in Minneapolis.
       1. *Your*

1. Jason felt (*weak, week*) after skiing all day in the Sangre de Cristo Mountains of New Mexico.
2. (*Weather, Whether*) we'll go or not depends on the (*weather, whether*).
3. (*Whose, Who's*) books are you carrying?
4. Find out (*whose, who's*) going if you can.
5. Learning (*to, too, two*) roll carved sticks for the Korean game of *yut* wasn't (*to, too, two*) difficult.
6. (*Your, You're*) off your course, captain.
7. We took (*to, too, two*) (*weaks, weeks*) for our trip.
8. The (*weather, whether*) was cloudy in Miami, Florida.
9. Would you enjoy a trip (*to, too, two*) Mars, Flo?
10. Aren't you using (*your, you're*) compass?

▶ REVIEW D   **Proofreading for Misspelled Words**

The following paragraph contains ten spelling errors. Identify and correct each error.

EXAMPLE   **[1]** Anne Shirley, here portrayed by actress Megan Fallows, found a pieceful life and a loving family on Prince Edward Island.
       1. *pieceful—peaceful*

1. shown   **[1]** Does the island's scenery shone in the picture on the next page appeal to you? **[2]** My family enjoyed the green
2. week   hillsides and rugged seashore during our two weak vacation there last summer. **[3]** Prince Edward Island is quite
3. it's   a beautiful spot, and its Canada's smallest province. **[4]** Everyone who lives there calls the island PEI, and now
4. too   I do, to. **[5]** During our visit, the weather was pleasant, so
5. led   I lead my parents all over PEI on foot. **[6]** We walked to
6. capital   several places of interest in Charlottetown, the capitol. **[7]** I
7. choose   got to chose our first stop, and I selected the farmhouse that's the setting for the novel *Anne of Green Gables*. **[8]** That
8. whose   novel's main character, Anne Shirley, is someone who's ideas I admire. **[9]** Walking around "The Garden Province,"

VISUAL CONNECTIONS

Exploring the Subject. L. M. Montgomery, author of *Anne of Green Gables,* was a Canadian author who grew up on Prince Edward Island. She wrote seven other novels about the character Anne Shirley, and they are known for their pleasing descriptions of nature. Through her novels, the climate, landscapes, beaches, bays, and harbors of this island in the Gulf of St. Lawrence off the east coast of Canada come to life for the reader.

we passed many farms; the ∧principle crop is potatoes. **9.**
[10] Take my∧advise, and visit Prince Edward Island if you principal
get the chance.

10. advice

50 Commonly Misspelled Words

ache	cough	guess	once	though
again	could	half	ready	through
always	country	hour	said	tired
answer	doctor	instead	says	tonight
blue	does	knew	shoes	trouble
built	don't	know	since	wear
busy	early	laid	straight	where
buy	easy	meant	sugar	which
can't	every	minute	sure	whole
color	friend	often	tear	women

250 Spelling Words

As you study the following words, pay particular attention to the letters in italics. These letters generally cause the greatest difficulty in correctly spelling the words.

abandon	actually	appearance
absolutely	advertisement	application
acceptance	against	appreciation
accidentally	aisle	approach
accommodate	amount	argument
accompany	analysis	article
accomplish	anticipate	assistance
achieve	anxiety	authority
acquaintance	apology	awful
acquire	apparent	basis

MECHANICS

MECHANICS

825

MEETING *individual* NEEDS

LEP/ESL

General Strategies. If possible, let English-language learners put accent marks over the stressed syllables of the words in the **250 Spelling Words** list. If students stress syllables correctly when speaking, they will recognize the words more readily in print. Recognition will lead to better spelling.

826 *Spelling*

beginning	description	guardian
believe	desirable	gymnasium
benefit	despair	hatred
boundary	develop	height
bouquet	diamond	heroine
bulletin	difficulties	hesitate
business	disappointment	humorous
cancel	discipline	ignorance
capacity	discussion	imagination
careless	distinction	immediately
carrier	distribution	incidentally
ceiling	doctrine	individual
challenge	duplicate	inferior
choice	economic	initial
choir	eighth	inspiration
chorus	eligible	intelligence
circuit	embarrass	interfere
colonel	engineering	interrupt
column	enthusiasm	involve
coming	eventually	jealous
commercial	exactly	judgment
committees	exaggerate	knowledge
competition	excellent	laboratory
completely	existence	leisure
conceive	experience	lengthen
condemn	experiment	license
congratulations	explanation	lieutenant
conscience	fascinating	loneliness
conscious	favorite	majority
control	February	manufacture
convenience	finally	marriage
courteous	flu	mechanical
criticism	forty	medieval
cylinder	fourth	military
dealt	friendliness	mourn
decision	generally	multiplication
defense	governor	muscular
definite	grammar	mystery
definition	gratitude	naturally
describe	guarantee	necessary

nickel
nonsense
numerous
obvious
occasionally
occurrence
opinion
opponent
opportunity
orchestra

originally
paid
parallel
parliament
patience
performance
personal
personality
persuade
philosopher

picnicking
planned
pleasant
possess
precede
preferred
prejudice
privilege
probably
procedure

professor
pursuit
qualified
realize
receipt
recognize
recommend
referring
regularly
relieve

repetition
research
response
restaurant
rhythm
satisfied
saucer
schedule
scissors
sense

sentiment
separate
sergeant
shepherd
similar
solemn
source
souvenir
sponsor
straighten

subscription
success
sufficient
suggest
suppress
surprise
surround
suspense
suspicion
tailor

temperament
tendency
theory
therefore
thorough
tobacco
tonsils
tradition
tragedy
transferred

tries
truly
unanimous
unnecessary
unsatisfactory
until
useful
using
utilized
vacuum

variety
various
vein
view
villain
violence
warrant
weird
wholly
writing

MECHANICS

MECHANICS

827

PROGRAM MANAGER

FOR THE WHOLE CHAPTER

■ **Computer Guided Instruction Review** For additional instruction and practice with concepts often used as indicators of verbal skills on standardized tests, see the **Core Lessons** in *Language Workshop CD-ROM.*

■ **Practice** To help less-advanced students who need additional practice with concepts and activities related to this chapter, see specific relevant topics in *English Workshop, Second Course.*

■ **Assessment/Practice** To help students practice marking standardized test answers and as an answer sheet for the **Grammar and Usage Tests** on pp. 844–846 and **Mechanics Tests** on pp. 854–857, see the **Standardized Test Answer Sheet** in *Language Skills Practice and Assessment,* p. 287.

CHAPTER OVERVIEW

This chapter provides application and review of aspects of grammar, usage, and mechanics that cause students difficulty. Since this chapter concentrates attention on areas of greatest concern, you may find it useful as a diagnostic test; judging by student scores, you can decide which topics need the most attention.

29 CORRECTING COMMON ERRORS

Key Language Skills Review

This chapter reviews key skills and concepts that pose special problems for writers.

■ Sentence Fragments and Run-on Sentences
■ Subject-Verb and Pronoun-Antecedent Agreement
■ Verb Forms
■ Pronoun Forms
■ Comparison of Modifiers
■ Misplaced and Dangling Modifiers
■ Capitalization
■ Punctuation—Commas, End Marks, Colons, Semicolons, Quotation Marks, and Apostrophes
■ Spelling
■ Standard Usage

Most of the exercises in this chapter follow the same format as the exercises found throughout the grammar, usage, and mechanics sections. You will notice, however, that two sets of review exercises are presented in standardized test formats. These exercises are designed to provide you with practice not only in solving usage and mechanics problems but also in dealing with these kinds of problems on such tests.

EXERCISE 1
OBJECTIVE

- To revise sentence fragments by adding a subject or verb or by attaching the fragment to a complete sentence

EXERCISE 2
OBJECTIVE

- To identify and correct run-on sentences

EXERCISE 1 Correcting Sentence Fragments

Most of the following groups of words are sentence fragments. If a word group is a sentence fragment, correct it by adding or deleting words to make a complete sentence or by attaching it to a complete sentence. You may need to change the punctuation and capitalization, too. If a word group is already a complete sentence, write *S*.

EXAMPLE **1. The movie about Cleopatra.**
1. *The movie about Cleopatra is playing downtown.*

1. Answered the telephone politely.
2. An armadillo's covering of bony plates like armor.
3. Because Alan prefers volleyball to any other team sport.
4. After the first winter snow.
5. Someone gave the museum those photographs of settlers in the Ozarks.
6. When she returns to the house this afternoon.
7. Delivering the package with postage due.
8. The recycling center now accepting magazines and catalogs.
9. Moved here from Germany so that she could study at the institute.
10. The kitten walked across the computer keyboard.

EXERCISE 2 Correcting Run-on Sentences

Correct each of the following run-on sentences by making two separate sentences or by combining the two parts of the run-on sentence to make one complete sentence.

Answers will vary. Sample responses are given.

EXAMPLE **1. Sign language, or manual speech, is not new, in fact, it has a long history.**
1. *Sign language, or manual speech, is not new; in fact, it has a long history.*

1. Some people may think that manual speech dates from this century^the beginnings of manual speech go much further back. **1., but**

ANSWERS
Exercise 1

Answers will vary. Accept reasonable responses. The following are models of possible answers.

1. Daniel answered the telephone politely.
2. An armadillo's covering of bony plates is like armor.
3. Because Alan prefers volleyball to any other team sport, he plans to organize a local league.
4. After the first winter snow, many people buy snow shovels.
5. S
6. When she returns to the house this afternoon, Cora will repair her sister's tricycle.
7. The mail carrier was delivering the package with postage due.
8. The recycling center is now accepting magazines and catalogs.
9. Evelyn moved here from Germany so that she could study at the institute.
10. S

MEETING *individual* NEEDS

LEP/ESL

Since they sometimes overuse one method of revising run-ons, you may wish to give students practice in correcting run-on sentences in a variety of ways. Remind students that good writing uses a variety of sentence structures, and encourage students to find the method of revision that works best for the particular run-on. Some run-ons are better as separate sentences, and others are better as one sentence joined by a comma and coordinating conjunction.

CORRECTING COMMON ERRORS

![icon] **COOPERATIVE LEARNING**

To give students additional practice in checking for sentence fragments and run-on sentences, take a passage from your students' literature textbook or a passage from a magazine or newspaper article and revise the passage so that it contains no punctuation. Organize students into small groups and give each group a copy of the revised passage.

Have each group replace the punctuation in the passage. The groups should not change the wording of the passage, but they should use correct punctuation to avoid run-ons and fragments as well as any awkward shifts of voice or tense within a sentence. Groups can check their results against the original text.

830 *Correcting Common Errors*

2. An Italian physician played an important role in the development of manual speech. I had never heard of him.

3. His name was Girolamo Cardano, he lived during the sixteenth century. 3. , and

4. Cardano proposed the theory that people unable to hear could learn to associate written symbols with objects or actions. he thought that people who could not hear or speak could then use such symbols to communicate. 5. , and

5. In the 1700s, Abbé Charles Michel de L'Epée opened the first free school for people with impaired hearing. he devised a manual sign version of spoken French.

6. In 1778, Samuel Heinicke began a school in Germany for people unable to hear. it was the first such school to receive government recognition.

7. The first school in the United States for those unable to hear was founded in 1817. its founder was Thomas Hopkins Gallaudet, a minister from Philadelphia.

8. Laurent Clerc was the first deaf person to teach other deaf people in a school in the United States. in 1816 he came to the United States to help Gallaudet found the Hartford School for the Deaf.

9. Gallaudet University is in Washington, D.C. it is still the world's only liberal arts college for people who are deaf or hard of hearing.

10. Today, American Sign Language is used by at least 500,000 people in the United States and Canada. it is the fourth most common language in the United States.

▶ EXERCISE 3 **Correcting Sentence Fragments and Run-on Sentences**

The following groups of words contain fragments, run-ons, and complete sentences. Identify each group of words by writing *F* for a fragment, *R* for a run-on, or *S* for a complete sentence. If a word group is a sentence fragment, correct it by adding or deleting words to make a complete sentence.

EXERCISE 4

OBJECTIVE

- To identify and correct sentence fragments and run-on sentences

Correct each of the run-ons by making it into two separate sentences or by using a comma and a coordinating conjunction. You may also need to change the punctuation and capitalization. Answers will vary. Sample responses are given.

EXAMPLE **1.** The old truck drove very slowly up the hill, a long line of cars followed it.
  1. *R—The old truck drove very slowly up the hill. A long line of cars followed it.*

1. One of the most famous photographs taken during World War II shows soldiers raising the U.S. flag at Iwo Jima.
2. I hope to travel to Asia someday, I want to climb the Himalayas.
3. To uproot the stumps of the trees we cut down in the front yard.
4. Some kinds of spiders, such as the bolas spider, that do not make webs.
5. Played a variety of music from different countries for the dancers.
6. To say no to Robin was hard.
7. Into the forest and across the valley they rode it took until sundown to reach the camp.
8. When a cicada comes out of the ground.
9. My mother's favorite movie is about the composer Mozart, I can't remember its title.
10. Sirius, which is the brightest star that can be seen from Earth at night.

EXERCISE 4 — **Correcting Sentence Fragments and Run-on Sentences**

The following paragraph contains sentence fragments, run-on sentences, and complete sentences. First, identify each numbered item by writing *F* for a fragment, *R* for a run-on, or *S* for a complete sentence. Then, revise the paragraph to correct the fragments and run-ons.

EXAMPLE [1] The history of food a delicious subject.
  1. *F—The history of food is a delicious subject.*

ANSWERS

Exercise 3

1. S
2. R—I hope to travel to Asia someday, for I want to climb the Himalayas.
3. F—They worked hard to uproot the stumps of the trees we cut down in the front yard.
4. F—Some kinds of spiders, such as the bolas spider, do not make webs.
5. F—The quartet played a variety of music from different countries for the dancers.
6. S
7. R—Into the forest and across the valley they rode. It took until sundown to reach the camp.
8. F—When a cicada comes out of the ground, it usually climbs a tree and sheds its skin.
9. R—My mother's favorite movie is about the composer Mozart. I can't remember its title.
10. F—Sirius is the brightest star that can be seen from Earth at night.

CORRECTING COMMON ERRORS

CORRECTING COMMON ERRORS

831

ANSWERS
Exercise 4

Revisions will vary. Accept reasonable responses. Sample responses are given.

There have been many milestones in the history of food production. The development of canned food is one of the most important. Because canned goods fill our stores today, most people generally take these goods for granted. The story of canned goods begins in the 1700s with Lazzaro Spallanzani. His experiments in preserving food were some of the earliest to succeed. Other early experimenters preserved vegetables, fruit, and meat in glass bottles. They used processes in which the bottles of food were heated to very high temperatures. Bottles were later replaced with containers made of tin-plated iron. Heating the containers of food kills the bacteria that cause food to spoil, as Louis Pasteur discovered in the mid-1800s. The development of this process, now called pasteurization, made eating canned food safer, and the eventual invention of the can opener made it easier!

CORRECTING COMMON ERRORS

CORRECTING COMMON ERRORS

832 *Correcting Common Errors*

1. R
2. F
3. S
4. R

5. S

6. F
7. F
8. S

9. F
10. R

[1] There have been many milestones in the history of food production, the development of canned food is one of the most important. [2] Because canned goods fill our stores today. [3] Most people generally take these goods for granted. [4] The story of canned goods begins in the 1700s with Lazzaro Spallanzani his experiments in preserving food were some of the earliest to succeed. [5] Other early experimenters preserved vegetables, fruit, and meat in glass bottles. [6] Using processes in which the bottles of food were heated to very high temperatures. [7] Bottles later replaced with containers made of tin-plated iron. [8] Heating the containers of food kills the bacteria that cause food to spoil. [9] As Louis Pasteur discovered in the mid-1800s. [10] The development of this process, now called pasteurization, made eating canned food safer the eventual invention of the can opener made it easier!

▶ EXERCISE 5 **Identifying Verbs That Agree in Number with Their Subjects**

For each of the following sentences, choose the form of the verb in parentheses that agrees with the subject.

EXAMPLE **1.** (*Do, Does*) you know much about cloud formations?
1. *Do*

1. Learning about clouds (*help, helps*) you predict the weather.
2. Some of the books I used in my report about weather (*give, gives*) detailed information about clouds.
3. Water droplets and ice crystals (*form, forms*) clouds.
4. Many of us (*like, likes*) to look for faces and familiar shapes in clouds overhead.
5. One of the most common types of clouds (*is, are*) the cumulonimbus rain cloud.
6. People often (*call, calls*) these clouds thunderstorm clouds.
7. Clouds of this kind (*produce, produces*) tornadoes and hail at times.

EXERCISE 6
OBJECTIVE
- To correct sentences with errors in subject-verb agreement

8. My friends Jeffrey and Kate (*don't*, *doesn't*) remember the name of cloud formations that look like wisps of cotton.
9. Several of these cirrus clouds (*was*, *were*) in the sky yesterday.
10. Stratus clouds, which often produce drizzle, (*look*, *looks*) like smooth sheets.

EXERCISE 6 **Proofreading Sentences for Correct Subject-Verb Agreement**

Most of the following sentences contain errors in subject-verb agreement. If a verb does not agree with its subject, give the correct form of the verb. If a sentence is correct, write C.

EXAMPLE **1.** Spanish explorers and missionaries is important in New Mexico's history.
       1. *are*

1. Spanish missions throughout New Mexico attracts many tourists nowadays.   1. attract
2. Some of these missions has been in continuous use for centuries.   2. have
3. Two missions especially interests me.   3. interest
4. I can't decide whether the Mission of San Agustin de Isleta or the Mission of San Miguel of Santa Fe are my favorite.   4. is
5. Both of these missions date from the early seventeenth century.   5. C
6. Each of them have survived damage caused by fires and centuries of wear.   6. has
7. Antique objects and priceless art lends their beauty to the missions.   7. lend
8. One of the most noteworthy features of the Santa Fe mission is a bell.   8. C
9. The bell, which was brought to Santa Fe in the 1800s, were cast in 1356 in Spain.   9. was
10. Churches in Spain and Mexico was home to the bell before it was brought to New Mexico.   10. were

A DIFFERENT APPROACH
You might want to take a few minutes before having your students complete **Exercises 5** and **6** to examine the relationship of subjects and verbs. Write the following lists of subjects and verbs on the chalkboard or display them on a large piece of paper. Ask the class to duplicate the lists on paper and to draw lines connecting the subjects to their verbs.

SUBJECT	VERB
dog	race
squirrel	stop
runners	climbs
buses	trots

Students should explain their choices. Or you may prefer to ask them to write an original sentence for each subject-verb combination.

As further review, you may ask students to supply the verb form that is in agreement if you combine two of the subjects (for example, *runners* and *buses*). [Possible answers might be *go*, *travel*, *run*.]

Then, ask students what happens if an indefinite pronoun is introduced and the original subject becomes part of a prepositional phrase (for example, *One of the runners* or *Many of the buses*). [Students should realize that the pronoun becomes the subject and the verb must agree with it in number. Some may remember the rule that the subject of a sentence cannot be part of a prepositional phrase.]

EXERCISE 7
OBJECTIVE

• To select pronouns that agree with their antecedents

EXERCISE 8
OBJECTIVE

• To correct errors in pronoun-antecedent agreement

CORRECTING COMMON ERRORS

COMMON ERROR

Problem. Students may use masculine pronouns to refer to both men and women. Until recent years, it was common practice to do so, but that usage is avoided now because it seems to ignore or exclude females.

Solution. One way to deal with this problem is to switch from singular to plural usage since plural pronouns don't have gender. To illustrate this solution, write the following sentence on the chalkboard and ask students to suggest ways to revise it to avoid the generic use of masculine pronouns:

Every student should complete *his* own assignment. [Possible revisions: "Students should complete their own assignments," or "Everyone should complete his or her own assignment."]

A DIFFERENT APPROACH

To help you quickly evaluate the nature of difficulties students may be having with pronoun-antecedent agreement, you might want to use this strategy: For **Exercises 7** and **8**, have students bracket the antecedent (or antecedents) and then label it (or them) as singular or plural. Then, have students circle the pronoun given in the sentence and label it as singular or plural. Typically, the primary difficulty is that the student does not recognize the correct antecedent and thus does not match the pronoun to it in number.

834

---

834 *Correcting Common Errors*

▶ EXERCISE 7 **Identifying Pronouns That Agree with Their Antecedents**

For each of the following sentences, choose the pronoun or pair of pronouns in parentheses that agrees with its antecedent or antecedents.

EXAMPLE 1. The horse and mule walked toward (*its, their*) owner.
1. *their*

1. Did your uncle or your father take (*his, their*) fishing license to the pier?
2. Does one of the coats have Kim's initials on (*their, its*) label?
3. Everyone has had (*his or her, their*) turn to play in the game.
4. Ms. Torres and Ms. Lawrence accepted (*her, their*) Community Appreciation Certificates.
5. Anyone may recite (*his or her, their*) poem during the program tonight.
6. Did David or Tim put (*his, their*) jacket on?
7. Neither of my twin stepbrothers has had (*his, their*) first haircut.
8. After careful consideration, each of the women cast (*their, her*) vote.
9. The first grade and the second grade will be taking (*its, their*) field trip tomorrow.
10. Neither Ramona nor Isabel recalled (*her, their*) dream from the night before.

▶ EXERCISE 8 **Proofreading Sentences for Correct Pronoun-Antecedent Agreement**

Most of the following sentences contain errors in agreement of pronoun and antecedent. Identify each incorrect pronoun, and supply the correct form or forms. If the sentence is correct, write C.

EXAMPLE 1. Tintin, whose adventures spanned the globe, traveled with their dog, Snowy.
1. *their—his*

EXERCISE 9

OBJECTIVE
• To write correct verb forms

1. The Belgian cartoonist Georges Remi created the comic strip character Tintin in the 1920s and set ~~their~~ first adventures in the Soviet Union.   1. his
2. Everybody in class who had read Tintin stories had ~~their~~ favorite tales of the adventurous reporter.   2. his or her
3. Both of this character's closest companions, Captain Haddock and Professor Cuthbert Calculus, help ~~his~~ friend Tintin.   3. their   4. his
4. Each of these men has ~~their~~ own unusual characteristics.
5. Thomson and Thompson, detectives who look alike, add ~~his~~ own silliness to Tintin's travels.   5. their
6. Several of the students said that ~~he or she~~ had read the comic strip.   6. they
7. Which one of the seven girls remembered to bring ~~their~~ own copy of *Tintin in Tibet*?   7. her
8. Julia showed us her drawing of Tintin's dog, Snowy. 8. C
9. My grandparents still have some of ~~his or her~~ old Tintin books.   9. their
10. Did *Tintin's Travel Diaries* inspire James or Reginald to keep ~~their~~ own travel diary during the summer? 10. his

CORRECTING COMMON ERRORS

▶ EXERCISE 9   **Writing Correct Verb Forms**

For each of the following sentences, fill in the blank with the correct past or past participle form of the verb given before the sentence.

EXAMPLE   **1.** *draw*   Kevin has _____ a Japanese pagoda.
1. *drawn*

1. hiked **1.** *hike*   Most of the club members have _____ on the Appalachian Trail.
2. known **2.** *know*   I have _____ the Katsanos family for years.
3. stolen **3.** *steal*   Can you believe that Jean Valjean was put in prison because he had _____ a loaf of bread?
4. tried **4.** *try*   The baby giraffe _____ to stand immediately after its birth.
5. spun **5.** *spin*   The car _____ around twice on the wet road.
6. built **6.** *build*   My dad and my sister _____ a workbench.
7. made **7.** *make*   Who _____ this delicious Irish soda bread?

CORRECTING COMMON ERRORS

EXERCISE 10
OBJECTIVE
• To correct errors in use of verb forms

EXERCISE 11
OBJECTIVE
• To proofread sentences for correct verb forms

General Strategies. Point out to students that when they have questions about the principal parts of verbs, they can often find the answers in a dictionary. Tell them that the base forms of verbs are listed as entry words and that the past, past participle, and present participle forms of irregular verbs are usually given in the entries. For example, if students look up *drive,* they will find *drive, drove,* and *driven.* As practice, have each student look up three irregular verbs and find the verbs' principal parts in the dictionary entries.

CRITICAL THINKING
Analysis. Have each student listen to five friends or relatives to make notes on which verbs are used most often. Suggest that students each choose one person to analyze each day for a school week. Tell each student to keep a log, to list all the verbs that occur in each conversation, and to categorize the verbs as regular or irregular. Students can then conclude the assignment by writing summaries about how people speak, including information about verb choices and correctness. (You might mention to students that this observation and documentation practice is commonly used by linguists who study the ways people actually use language and the ways languages change over time and in different regions.)

836 *Correcting Common Errors*

8. *swim*   Our team has _____ in pools this size, but we
   8. swum   prefer Olympic-size pools.
9. *suppose* Gary was _____ to rent a funny movie for us
   9. supposed to watch tonight.
10. *shake*   The wet puppy _____ itself and got water all
    10. shook   over Phuong's dress.

EXERCISE 10 **Proofreading for Correct Past and Past Participle Verb Forms**

If a sentence contains an incorrect verb form, write the correct form. If a sentence is correct, write *C.*

EXAMPLE   **1. Have you ever saw a sundial?**
           1. *seen*

1. I have read Anne Frank's *The Diary of a Young Girl.*   1. C
2. The song that Ann and Brian sang ~~use~~ to be popular in the 1950s.   2. used   3. began
3. Caitlin ~~begun~~ swimming lessons around the age of six.
4. Ben ~~perform~~ that routine for the judges last year.   4. performed
5. The lizard ~~done~~ its best to catch the fly, but the fly flew away unharmed.   5. did [*or* had done]
6. Have you ~~wrote~~ a letter recently?   6. written
7. The performer ~~telled~~ jokes and stories while he danced.   7. told
8. Excited about her new idea, Marie ~~gived~~ up on her first plan.   8. gave
9. Is it true the winner actually ~~run~~ backward in the race?   9. ran
10. Did you know that Bill "Bojangles" Robinson made up the word *copacetic,* which means "fine" or "excellent"?   10. C

EXERCISE 11 **Proofreading for Correct Past and Past Participle Verb Forms**

If a sentence contains an incorrect verb form, write the correct form. If a sentence is correct, write *C.*

EXAMPLE   **1. I have took several lessons in aikido.**
           1. *taken*

1. Aikido, a Japanese system of self-defense, has ~~interest~~ me for some time.   1. interested

2. A month ago, I ~~begun~~ lessons at a local martial arts studio. **2. began**

3. Every time I have ~~went~~ to class, I have been nervous, but I am finally becoming more confident. **3. gone**

4. Our instructor has ~~teached~~ us that the Japanese word *aikido* means "the way of blending energy." **4. taught**

5. He ~~sayed~~ that I can "accept" an attacker's energy and blend my own energy with it to redirect the attack away from myself. **5. said**

6. Today in class, I saw how redirecting an opponent's energy really works. **6. C**

7. The aikido holds and movements I ~~choosed~~ played off my opponent's strength. **7. chose**

8. I ~~maked~~ each of these movements without using any unnecessary force. **8. made**

9. My opponent lunged at me, but he ~~losed~~ his footing when I redirected his energy. **9. lost**

10. My instructor said that attackers are usually ~~throwed~~ off balance by such movements because they expect a person under attack to use force to fight back. **10. thrown**

CORRECTING COMMON ERRORS

CORRECTING COMMON ERRORS

▶ EXERCISE 12 **Identifying Correct Pronoun Forms**

For the following sentences, choose the correct form of each pronoun in parentheses.

EXAMPLE **1.** The new rules do not apply to any of (*us, we*) eighth-graders.
1. *us*

1. Please give (*her, she*) the sequins for the costume.
2. The new paramedics at the stadium are (*they, them*).
3. Sasha and (*he, him*) are good at trivia games.
4. Coach Mendoza adjusted the parallel bars for Paul and (*me, I*).
5. The usher showed (*us, we*) to our seats.
6. My sister and (*me, I*) will help Dad paint our house this summer.
7. A friend of ours sent (*us, we*) a new book of short stories by a popular Venezuelan author.

A DIFFERENT APPROACH

For review and practice of pronoun use, create flashcards that state the number, person, and form of a pronoun on one side and the corresponding pronoun on the reverse side. (For example, a flashcard description might read "First-person Singular—Subject Form," and on the other side, the pronoun *I*.) Prepare twelve cards, one for each subject and object pronoun form. (For *you* and *it*, you can include all the combinations on the descriptive side of the card. Be sure to include the gender of third-person pronouns in your descriptions.)

Show the descriptive sides of the cards and let student volunteers name the correct pronouns. Then, to increase students' understanding of how these pronouns are used, have student teams compose sentences with the pronouns replaced with blanks. Let other student teams then attempt to give the description of the type of pronoun, followed by an identification of the pronoun that would have to go into the blank to complete the sentence. (For example, "The librarian helped Manuel and me by giving _____ a key to the lock." The answer would be described as "First-person Plural—Object Form" and the pronoun itself would be *us*.)

838 *Correcting Common Errors*

8. The retirement home where Brad's grandmother lives impressed (*him, he*).
9. Did you give the oranges and apples to (*them, they*) for the picnic?
10. The first ones to arrive in the morning are almost always (*she and I, her and me*).

▶ EXERCISE 13 **Identifying Correct Pronoun Forms**

For each of the following sentences, choose the correct form of the pronoun in parentheses.

EXAMPLE   **1. Facts about First Ladies interest (*me, I*).**
          1. *me*

1. Hillary Rodham Clinton wrote a book called *It Takes a Village: And Other Lessons Children Teach Us;* last week she autographed copies for (*us, we*).
2. James and (*I, me*) were surprised to learn that Lucy Hayes was the first president's wife to earn a college degree.
3. It was (*her, she*) who was nicknamed Lemonade Lucy.
4. The school librarian gave (*him, he*) an article about Grace Coolidge, who taught children with hearing impairments.
5. Jack showed Eric, Heather, and (*me, I*) a picture of Mrs. Coolidge with Helen Keller.
6. Tell (*them, they*) about Martha Washington's role as hostess of the new nation.
7. The artist who painted the portrait of the elegant Elizabeth Monroe could have been (*him, he*).
8. In his report on Edith Wilson, Nathaniel said that (*she, her*) sewed clothes to send to soldiers during World War I.
9. When she was a delegate to the United Nations, Eleanor Roosevelt championed human rights and worked to secure (*they, them*) for all people.
10. With (*she, her*) as chairperson, the United Nations' Human Rights Commission drafted the Universal Declaration of Human Rights.

EXERCISE 14
OBJECTIVE
- To select correct forms of regular and irregular modifiers

EXERCISE 15
OBJECTIVE
- To identify and correct errors in the use of double comparisons and double negatives

 EXERCISE 14   **Choosing Correct Regular and Irregular Modifiers**

Choose the correct form of the modifier in parentheses in each of the following sentences.

EXAMPLE   **1.** *The Fantasticks* is Jorge's (*favorite, favoritest*) musical.
           1. *favorite*

1. *The Fantasticks* has had the (*longer, longest*) run of any musical in New York City.
2. In fact, it is the (*oldest, older*) continuously running musical in the United States.
3. My aunt says that the performance she saw at New York's Sullivan Street Playhouse in 1996 was the (*better, best*) show of any she'd ever seen.
4. She told me that *The Fantasticks* was created by one of the (*most talented, talentedest*) teams of writers for the stage—Tom Jones and Harvey Schmidt.
5. Jones and Schmidt have also written other musicals, but *The Fantasticks* is generally considered to be their (*popularest, most popular*) one.
6. Have you ever seen a musical with a character called something (*more strange, stranger*) than The Man Who Dies?
7. The play has both serious and funny songs; many people like the funny songs (*best, better*).
8. The Handyman, who appears only during the play's intermission, has one of the (*most odd, oddest*) roles in modern theater.
9. The students who put on our school's production of *The Fantasticks* performed (*good, well*).
10. If the play ever comes to your town, you might find it (*more, most*) enjoyable to see than a movie.

 EXERCISE 15   **Correcting Double Comparisons and Double Negatives**   Revisions may vary. Sample responses are given.

For each of the following sentences, identify the incorrect modifier. Then, give the correct form of the modifier.

CORRECTING COMMON ERRORS

CORRECTING COMMON ERRORS

TECHNOLOGY TIP

Have students check for proper grammar and usage in their writing by using a grammar-checking program. Grammar-checking programs will readily catch a number of mistakes, including double negatives and nonstandard use of modifiers such as *beautifulest* or *popularer*.

ANSWERS
Exercise 16

Revisions may vary. Sample responses are given.

1. My dad said we are going to the beach today. [*or* Today, my dad said we are going to the beach.]
2. Using their new microscope, the children could see the bacteria.
3. Richard saw on the bulletin board the announcement for the book sale.
4. We watched the chameleon change color to a bright green, concealing itself among the leaves.
5. I gave my friends flowers that I had picked along the roadside.

840

EXERCISE 16
OBJECTIVE
• To correct misplaced modifiers

840   *Correcting Common Errors*

EXAMPLE   **1.** Some of the most prettiest candles are made of beeswax.
1. *most prettiest—prettiest*

1. one **1.** We wanted to rent a movie but couldn't find ~~none~~ that we all wanted to see.
2. Both Ted and I are learning Spanish, but I am ~~more~~ shyer about speaking it than he is.
3. anywhere **3.** Kim never wanted to go ~~nowhere~~ near the icy rapids.
4. safe **4.** People in cars are less ~~safer~~ when they do not wear seat belts.
5. anybody **5.** We volunteered to help with the preschool art classes because there wasn't ~~nobody~~ else who had the time.
6. common **6.** Of all the kinds of trees in our neighborhood, which do you think is the least ~~commonest~~?
7. Moose are the ~~most~~ largest members of the deer family.
8. ever **8.** Don't ~~never~~ use the elevator if a building is on fire.
9. could **9.** Carrie ~~couldn't~~ scarcely walk after she broke her toe.
10. Kudzu is a Japanese vine that grows ~~more~~ faster than many other plants.

EXERCISE 16   **Revising Sentences to Correct Misplaced Modifiers**

Each of the following sentences contains a misplaced modifier. Revise each sentence to correct the error.

EXAMPLE   **1.** Bathing in the mud, the photographer snapped several photographs of the elephants.
1. *The photographer snapped several photographs of the elephants bathing in the mud.*

1. My dad said today we are going to the beach.
2. The children could see the bacteria using their new microscope.
3. Richard saw the announcement for the book sale on the bulletin board.
4. Changing color to a bright green, we watched the chameleon conceal itself among the leaves.
5. I gave flowers to my friends that I had picked along the roadside.

EXERCISE 17
OBJECTIVE
• To correct misplaced and dangling modifiers

EXERCISE 18
OBJECTIVE
• To identify correct usage

Grammar and Usage **841**

EXERCISE 17 **Revising Sentences to Correct Misplaced and Dangling Modifiers**

Each of the following sentences contains an error in the use of modifiers. Revise each sentence to correct the error.

EXAMPLE **1.** Growing in the root cellar, my aunt found a red mushroom.
1. *My aunt found a red mushroom growing in the root cellar.*

1. I read a book about how the Egyptian pyramids were built yesterday.
2. While making lunch for the visitors, the stove caught on fire.
3. The children played in the puddle with no boots on.
4. Don announced at the meeting he will be asking for volunteers.
5. Running to catch the bus, several books fell out of his backpack.
6. Wobbling, the crowd anxiously watched the tightrope walker.
7. My sister described the giraffe she had seen during our flight back to the United States.
8. Tired of the drought, the rain was greeted with loud cheers.
9. Sparkling in the sunlight, the mockingbird showed no interest in the sapphire ring.
10. While walking along the shoreline, a large, black fossilized shark's tooth caught my eye.

EXERCISE 18 **Identifying Correct Usage**

Choose the correct word or words in parentheses in each of the following sentences.

EXAMPLE **1.** About (*a, an*) hour before sunrise, the dam almost (*burst, busted*).
1. *an, burst*

1. (*Doesn't, Don't*) the long-term (*affects, effects*) of global warming concern you?

ANSWERS
Exercise 17

Answers may vary.

1. Yesterday I read a book about how the Egyptian pyramids were built.
2. The stove caught on fire while I was making lunch for the visitors.
3. The children with no boots on played in the puddle.
4. At the meeting, Don announced he will be asking for volunteers.
5. Several books fell out of his backpack as he ran to catch the bus.
6. The crowd anxiously watched the wobbling tightrope walker.
7. During our flight back to the United States, my sister described the giraffe she had seen.
8. Tired of the drought, the farmers greeted the rain with loud cheers.
9. The mockingbird showed no interest in the sapphire ring sparkling in the sunlight.
10. While I was walking along the shoreline, a large, black fossilized shark's tooth caught my eye.

CORRECTING COMMON ERRORS

CORRECTING COMMON ERRORS

841

CORRECTING COMMON ERRORS

CORRECTING COMMON ERRORS

MEETING individual NEEDS

ADVANCED STUDENTS

Some students will benefit from exposure to errors in usage not covered in **Exercises 18** and **19.** Have students review manuals of style such as Strunk and White's *The Elements of Style.* Encourage students to identify additional rules concerning errors in usage that might help them or their classmates.

Students can then present the rules they discover by providing examples or explanations of them. These rules and the explanations students have provided can be collected in a notebook, indexed, and updated continually for use as a reference work by their class and future classes.

EXERCISE 19
OBJECTIVE

• To correct errors in usage

2. There (*use to, used to*) be (*fewer, less*) people jogging in my neighborhood.
3. (*Without, Unless*) we have permission, I don't think we ought to (*bring, take*) Dad's new CD player to the beach tomorrow.
4. Marshall (*would of, would have*) gone to the park, but (*then, than*) he changed his mind.
5. We had a difficult time choosing (*between, among*) the two puppies playing together (*inside, inside of*) the large basket.
6. My clarinet playing has improved (*some, somewhat*), but I really (*had ought, ought*) to practice more.
7. Everyone (*accept, except*) John thinks the weather will be (*alright, all right*) for our walk in the park.
8. I (*try and, try to*) go to all of my aunt's softball games because her team plays so (*good, well*).
9. (*Who's, Whose*) going to sleep outside with so many of (*them, those*) mosquitoes around?
10. Randy talks (*like, as if*) he has to ride his bike a long (*way, ways*) on his paper route.

▶ EXERCISE 19 **Correcting Errors in Usage**

Each of the following sentences contains an error in usage. Identify and correct each error.

EXAMPLE **1.** Patrick did so good at the spelling bee that he qualified for the national contest.
1. *good—well*

1. bad **1.** If the tuna-fish salad tastes badly, don't eat any more of it.
2. teach **2.** My stepsister said she would learn me how to play the piano.
3. take **3.** Please bring these vegetables to your grandmother when you visit her this Friday.
4. that **4.** I read where a waterspout is the name for a tornado that occurs over a lake or an ocean.
5. who **5.** The cartoonist which works for our newspaper has a [or that] wonderful sense of humor.

6. The *ruble* is‸an unit of currency used in Russia and
   Tajikistan.   6. a
7. A friendly rivalry arose‸between all of the members
   of the soccer team.   7. among
8. Late last night, Jack saw a light shining‸somewheres
   across the river.   8. somewhere
9. Mr. Catalano said that the smallest dinosaurs‸weren't
   scarcely larger than chickens.   9. were
10. I knew that we should‸of brought the umbrella with
    us when we left the house today.   10. have

▶ EXERCISE 20 **Correcting Errors in Usage**

Each of the following sentences contains an error in usage.
Identify and correct each error.

EXAMPLE   **1.** Our class has all ready read about the life of
               José Luis Muñoz Marín (1898–1980).
          1. *all ready—already*

1. Where was Muñoz Marín born ‸at?
2. I read in this here biography that he was born in
   San Juan, the capital of Puerto Rico.
3. For more‸then a quarter of a century, Muñoz Marín
   was Puerto Rico's chief political leader.   3. than
4. He worked to help Puerto Ricans build better lives
   for‸theirselves.   4. themselves
5. ‸Like Muñoz Marín himself discovered, he had been
   born at a major turning point in the history of his
   country.   5. As
6. He must‸of been very popular, for he was elected
   governor four times.   6. have
7. When I read his biography, I learned‸how come he
   founded the Popular Democratic Party.   7. why
8. John F. Kennedy was the president‸which awarded 8. who
   Muñoz Marín the Presidential Medal of Freedom.   [*or that*]
9. ‸Its fascinating to think of Muñoz Marín's being both
   a poet and a politician.   9. It's
10. Did you know that‸their is a U.S. postage stamp
    featuring Muñoz Marín?   10. there

GRAMMAR AND USAGE TEST: Section 1
OBJECTIVES

- To practice responses similar to those required on standardized tests of mastery of language skills and concepts
- To select from among given choices the phrasing that is most grammatically correct and best completes the sentence

TEACHING NOTE

Using the Grammar and Usage Tests. You may prefer to have students regard the **Grammar and Usage Tests** as review exercises instead of using them as practice in standardized test taking. If so, have students number blank sheets of paper and write their answers there instead of filling in the **Standardized Test Answer Sheet** provided in *Language Skills Practice and Assessment,* p. 287.

CORRECTING COMMON ERRORS

CORRECTING COMMON ERRORS

844 *Correcting Common Errors*

Grammar and Usage Test: Section 1

DIRECTIONS Read the paragraph below. For each numbered blank, select the word or group of words that best completes the sentence. Indicate your response by shading in the appropriate oval on your answer sheet.

EXAMPLE

The word *organic* (1) "of or related to living things."

1. (A) it means
   (B) meant
   (C) is meaning
   (D) means

SAMPLE ANSWER 1. Ⓐ Ⓑ Ⓒ ●

Scientists (1) study the prehistoric world (2) carbon dating to determine the age of organic materials such as wood and bone. All living things absorb carbon-14 from the environment into (3) tissues. An organism that has died (4) carbon-14 because (5) no longer takes in air and food. Carbon-14 that was previously absorbed into the organism's tissues (6) at a specific rate. Knowing the rate of breakdown, scientists measure the amount of carbon-14 in an organism's remains to determine how much time (7) since the organism died. Scientists cannot use carbon dating to determine the age of organic material (8) is (9) about 120,000 years, because carbon-14 (10) down and becomes untraceable after that long a time.

1.B 1. (A) which
  (B) who
  (C) whom
  (D) what

2.B 2. (A) they use
  (B) use
  (C) uses
  (D) used

3.D 3. (A) its
  (B) his or her
  (C) they're
  (D) their

4.C 4. (A) doesn't absorb no more
  (B) don't absorb no more
  (C) doesn't absorb any more
  (D) don't absorb any more

5.C 5. (A) he
  (B) she
  (C) it
  (D) they

6.B 6. (A) it decays
  (B) decays
  (C) decay
  (D) were decaying

7.D 7. (A) passes
  (B) is passing
  (C) have passed
  (D) has passed

8.A 8. (A) that
  (B) what
  (C) who
  (D) whom

844

TEACHING NOTE

Using the Grammar and Usage Tests. A Standardized Test Answer Sheet that students may use for this **Grammar and Usage Test** is provided in *Language Skills Practice and Assessment,* p. 287.

Grammar and Usage **845**

9.B **9.** (A) more old then
     (B) older than
     (C) more older than
     (D) older then

10.D **10.** (A) busts
      (B) busted
      (C) has busted
      (D) breaks

Grammar and Usage Test: Section 2

DIRECTIONS Either part or all of each of the following sentences is underlined. Using the rules of standard written English, choose the answer that most clearly expresses the meaning of the sentence. If there is no error, choose A. Indicate your response by shading in the appropriate oval on your answer sheet.

EXAMPLE
1. The first Cuban-born woman to become a U.S. Army officer was Mercedes O. Cubria, <u>whom</u> served in the Women's Army Corps.

   (A) whom
   (B) who
   (C) that
   (D) which

SAMPLE ANSWER 1. Ⓐ ● Ⓒ Ⓓ

1.D **1.** In basketball, one kind of illegal dribbling <u>is when</u> a player stops dribbling and then begins dribbling again.

   (A) is when
   (B) is that
   (C) is because
   (D) occurs when

2.C **2.** Karen's sandwich is <u>more tastier than</u> the one I brought.

   (A) more tastier than
   (B) more tastier then
   (C) tastier than
   (D) tastier then

3.B **3.** <u>Tonya said she had seen a hummingbird at her feeder in the mall today.</u>

   (A) Tonya said she had seen a hummingbird at her feeder in the mall today.
   (B) In the mall today, Tonya said she had seen a hummingbird at her feeder.
   (C) Tonya said in the mall today she had seen a hummingbird at her feeder.
   (D) Tonya said in the mall today at her feeder she had seen a hummingbird.

4.C **4.** Have the Glee Club and they set down to discuss the program?

    (A) Have the Glee Club and they set
    (B) Have the Glee Club and them sat
    (C) Have the Glee Club and they sat
    (D) Has the Glee Club and they sat

5.D **5.** For years, Matthew Henson accompanied Robert Peary on expeditions, together, in 1908, they set out to reach the North Pole.

    (A) expeditions, together, in 1908, they set
    (B) expeditions; together, in 1908, they setted
    (C) expeditions, together, in 1908, them setted
    (D) expeditions. Together, in 1908, they set

6.B **6.** The reason you should wear a helmet is because it can prevent head injuries.

    (A) is because it
    (B) is that it
    (C) is that they
    (D) is when it

7.B **7.** A dedicated and creative teacher, Anne Sullivan learned Helen Keller how to communicate effectively.

    (A) learned
    (B) taught
    (C) was learning
    (D) teached

8.A **8.** Between Josh and him lay the exhausted puppy.

    (A) him lay
    (B) he lay
    (C) him laid
    (D) him has laid

9.D **9.** The treasure that was buried in the abandoned mine.

    (A) The treasure that was buried in the abandoned mine.
    (B) The treasure found buried in the abandoned mine.
    (C) The treasure buried in the abandoned mine.
    (D) The treasure was buried in the abandoned mine.

10.B **10.** Peering behind the bookcase, a secret passage was discovered by the detective.

    (A) Peering behind the bookcase, a secret passage was discovered by the detective.
    (B) Peering behind the bookcase, the detective discovered a secret passage.
    (C) The detective discovered a secret passage peering behind the bookcase.
    (D) While peering behind the bookcase, a secret passage was discovered by the detective.

EXERCISE 21 **Correcting Errors in Capitalization**

Each of the following groups of words contains at least one capitalization error. Correct the errors either by changing capital letters to lowercase letters or by changing lowercase letters to capital letters.

EXAMPLE   **1.** central avenue in albuquerque, New mexico
           1. *Central Avenue in Albuquerque, New Mexico*

1. venus and jupiter
2. my Aunt Jessica
3. wednesday morning
4. the Jewish holiday hanukkah
5. thirty-fifth street
6. the stone age
7. nobel peace prize
8. Minute maid® orange juice
9. spanish, earth science, and algebra I
10. secretary of state warren christopher

EXERCISE 22 **Correcting Errors in Capitalization**

Each of the following sentences contains errors in capitalization. Correct the errors either by changing capital letters to lowercase letters or by changing lowercase letters to capital letters.

EXAMPLE   **1.** many african americans lived and worked in the western United states after the civil war.
           1. *Many African Americans lived and worked in the western United States after the Civil War.*

1. one of the most remarkable people from that era is bill pickett, who was born on December 5, 1870.
2. His Father worked on ranches near austin, texas, and pickett grew up watching cowhands work.
3. Pickett began performing rodeo tricks at County fairs, and in 1905, he joined the 101 wild west show in the region then called the oklahoma territory.
4. With this show, Pickett toured the united states, south america, canada, and great britain.

QUICK REMINDER
Write the following proper nouns on the chalkboard and ask students to correct capitalization errors:

1. Pacific ocean [Ocean]
2. lions club [Lions Club]
3. Locust avenue [Avenue]
4. spanish olive [Spanish]
5. a North Pole Marker [marker]
6. president Clinton [President]
7. uncle Wilson [Uncle]
8. her Grandmother [grandmother]
9. an organization Treasurer [treasurer]
10. the Miltonville wintertime Fair [Wintertime]

5. i wish i could have seen all the cowboys, cowgirls, horses, buffalo, and longhorn cattle that were part of the show!
6. Pickett portrayed himself in a 1923 silent movie called *the bull-dogger.*
7. Pickett, who died in 1932, was later inducted into the national rodeo cowboy hall of fame.
8. in 1977, the university of oklahoma press published a biography, *bill pickett, bulldogger,* written by colonel bailey c. hanes.
9. a bronze statue of Bill Pickett was dedicated at the fort worth cowtown coliseum in 1987.
10. The Bill Pickett invitational rodeo, which tours all over the united states, draws rodeo talent from around the nation.

EXERCISE 23 **Correcting Sentences by Adding Commas**

Each of the following sentences lacks at least one comma. Write the word that comes before each missing comma, and add the comma.

EXAMPLE
1. When the Spanish brought the first horses to North America the lives of many American Indians changed.
   1. *America,*

1. Native peoples bred the Spanish horses and developed ponies that could survive on the stubby, coarse grass of the Great Plains.
2. These hardy ponies may not have been considered as beautiful as the Spanish horses, but they were faster, stronger, and smarter.
3. Because horses were so highly valued, they came to signify status and wealth.
4. These ponies, which were useful in the daily activities of American Indians, were also ridden into battle.
5. Before riding into a battle, Crow warriors painted symbolic designs on themselves and on their ponies.

MEETING *individual* NEEDS

LEARNING STYLES

Visual Learners. You may want to help students visualize some of the uses of commas by showing examples of comma usage. On the chalkboard, draw six columns. Label the columns *independent clauses, nonessential clauses, introductory elements, interrupters, items in a series,* and *conventions (dates and addresses).* Work with students to generate examples to go in each column. Write the examples under the appropriate headings on the chalkboard.

You may then want to assign **Exercise 23** for homework and go over the answers with students in class. Survey the class for error patterns and review those rules of comma usage that seem to give students problems.

EXERCISE 24
OBJECTIVE
- To correct sentences by adding commas and end marks

Mechanics **849**

6. These designs might show that the rider possessed "medicine power," had been on successful horse raids, or had lost someone special to him.
7. Colors, not just designs, had special meanings.
8. The color blue, for example, represented wounds; red, which symbolized courage and bravery, represented bloodshed.
9. Often painted on the pony's flanks or under its eyes, white clay stripes indicated the number of horses a warrior had captured.
10. Among the Plains Indians, warriors who disgraced their enemies by tapping them at close range earned horizontal stripes called "coup" marks.

▶ EXERCISE 24 **Using End Marks and Commas Correctly**

The following sentences need end marks and commas. Write the word or number that comes before each missing end mark or comma, and add the proper punctuation.

EXAMPLE **1.** Did you sign up for the class trip to Washington Baltimore and Roanoke
1. *Washington, Baltimore, Roanoke?*

1. What, for instance, would you suggest doing to improve wheelchair access to the theater?
2. Well, I was standing on the ladder, but I still couldn't reach the apples.
3. Marta, a friend of mine, always recycles her aluminum cans and newspapers.
4. When I draw with pastels, charcoal, or chalk, I'm careful to wash my hands before touching anything else.
5. Watch out for the falling tree branch!
6. Is the Spanish Club meeting scheduled for today or tomorrow, Lee?
7. Adela wrote one letter on May 19, 1997, and another on October 5, 1997.
8. Mr. N. Q. Galvez, Ms. Alma Lee, and Dr. Paul M. Metz spoke at the nutrition seminar last week.

CORRECTING COMMON ERRORS

CORRECTING COMMON ERRORS

COOPERATIVE LEARNING
To review the use of end marks and commas, have students write short, informative paragraphs about topics that interest them. Tell students that their paragraphs should include at least one question and one exclamation. Then, pair students and have them dictate their paragraphs to each other. When they have finished, have the pairs compare their use of commas and end marks in both the original and the dictated version of each paragraph. If there are any discrepancies, have students decide cooperatively which version is correct.

COMMON ERROR

Problem. Some students confuse the colon and the semicolon or think they are interchangeable.

Solution. Explain the different functions of these two punctuation marks. Tell students that a colon is a kind of pointer to something that a writer wants to emphasize. A semicolon provides clarity (in setting off a list with internal commas) or accentuates a close relationship between two independent clauses.

EXERCISE 25
OBJECTIVE
• To correct sentences by adding colons and semicolons

EXERCISE 26
OBJECTIVE
• To correct sentences by adding capital letters and punctuation

---

850 *Correcting Common Errors*

9. What a great idea that is!
10. My friends and I like to hike in the mountains, water-ski on the lake, and jog along the park trails.

▶ EXERCISE 25 **Using Semicolons and Colons Correctly**

The following sentences lack necessary colons and semicolons. Write the word or numeral that comes before and after each missing punctuation mark, and add the proper punctuation.

EXAMPLE   **1.** Friday is the day for the band concert all of my family is attending.
1. *concert; all*

1. I put bread in the oven at 4:15 it should be done soon.
2. We have been keeping the highway clean for three years; naturally, no one in the club litters, no matter where he or she is.
3. My brother's favorite movie is *Homeward Bound: The Incredible Journey.*
4. We gathered driftwood, shells, and rocks; but we also needed sand, glass, and paint for the sculpture.
5. My stepsister Sarah, who is deaf, uses the following electronic devices: a doorbell that makes the lights flicker, a telephone that converts speech to written words, and a television with closed captioning.

▶ EXERCISE 26 **Correcting Sentences by Adding Quotation Marks, Other Marks of Punctuation, and Capital Letters**

Revise the following sentences by supplying capital letters and marks of punctuation as needed.

EXAMPLE   **1.** Diane asked where is Denali National Park?
1. *Diane asked, "Where is Denali National Park?"*

1. Natalie Merchant is my favorite singer said Stephen but I haven't heard her newest song yet.
2. Aunt Caroline exclaimed what a beautiful garden you have!

3. To block some of the traffic noise Russell commented the city should plant some trees along this street.
4. The first episode of that new television series is called Once upon a Twice-Baked Potato.
5. Did you see that Francis asked. That player bumped the soccer ball into the goal with his heel
6. Beverly asked why doesn't Janet want to be president of the club?
7. I'll go with you Dee said that sack of birdseed will be too heavy for you to carry back by yourself.
8. I just finished reading the chapter titled Noah Swims Alone, and I really enjoyed it Shawn said.
9. Did Stephanie actually yell I'm out of here before she left the room asked Joel.
10. You've Got a Friend is one of the songs in the movie *Toy Story* Jonathan said.

EXERCISE 27 Proofreading a Dialogue for Correct Punctuation

In the following dialogue, correct any errors in the use of quotation marks and other marks of punctuation. Also, correct any errors in the use of capitalization, and begin a new paragraph each time the speaker changes.

EXAMPLES   [1] Guess what! Henry exclaimed This Saturday I'm going with my youth group to work on a Habitat for Humanity project
[2] What is Habitat for Humanity Lynn asked

1. *"Guess what!" Henry exclaimed. "This Saturday I'm going with my youth group to work on a Habitat for Humanity project."*
2. *"What is Habitat for Humanity?" Lynn asked.*

[1] It's an organization that renovates and builds houses for people who are poor and do not own homes Henry replied. [2] Oh, now I remember Lynn said. Many volunteers help with the work, right [3] Yes that's true Henry answered and the people who will live in the houses also help with the renovating or building of these houses

ANSWERS
Exercise 26

1. "Natalie Merchant is my favorite singer," said Stephen, "but I haven't heard her newest song yet." [*or* "Natalie Merchant is my favorite singer," said Stephen. "But I haven't heard her newest song yet."]
2. Aunt Caroline exclaimed, "What a beautiful garden you have!"
3. "To block some of the traffic noise," Russell commented, "the city should plant some trees along this street."
4. The first episode of that new television series is called "Once upon a Twice-Baked Potato."
5. "Did you see that?" Frances asked. "That player bumped the soccer ball into the goal with his heel!"
6. Beverly asked, "Why doesn't Janet want to be president of the club?"
7. "I'll go with you," Dee said. "That sack of birdseed will be too heavy for you to carry back by yourself."
8. "I just finished reading the chapter titled 'Noah Swims Alone,' and I really enjoyed it," Shawn said.
9. "Did Stephanie actually yell, 'I'm out of here!' before she left the room?" asked Joel.
10. "'You've Got a Friend' is one of the songs in the movie *Toy Story*," Jonathan said.

ANSWERS

Exercise 27

1. "It's an organization that renovates and builds houses for people who are poor and do not own homes," Henry replied.

2. "Oh, now I remember," Lynn said. "Many volunteers help with the work, right?"

3. "Yes, that's true," Henry answered, "and the people who will live in the houses also help with the renovating or building of these houses." [*or* "Yes, that's true," Henry answered. "And the people who will live in the houses also help with the renovating or building of these houses."]

4. "Are they required to help paint, hammer, and do whatever else needs to be done?" Lynn asked.

5. "Yes, and over an extended period of time, they also pay back the building costs," Henry explained.

6. Lynn asked, "Isn't it expensive to build a house?"

7. "Well," Henry responded, "it does take a lot of money, but volunteer labor, donated construction materials, and skillful management keep the cost of building affordable."

8. "How long has Habitat for Humanity existed, and who started it?" Lynn asked.

9. "Our youth group leader told us that Millard and Linda Fuller started Habitat for Humanity in Georgia in 1976," Henry replied.

10. "Hey, I think I'll go with you to work on the building project," Lynn said.

---

[4] Are they required to help paint hammer and do whatever else needs to be done? Lynn asked. [5] Yes, and over an extended period of time, they also pay back the building costs Henry explained.

[6] Lynn asked Isn't it expensive to build a house [7] Well Henry responded it does take a lot of money, but volunteer labor, donated construction materials, and skillful management keep the cost of building affordable.

[8] How long has Habitat for Humanity existed, and who started it Lynn asked [9] Our youth group leader told us that Millard and Linda Fuller started Habitat for Humanity in Georgia in 1976 Henry replied

[10] Hey, I think I'll go with you to work on the building project Lynn said.

EXERCISE 28 Correcting Sentences by Adding Apostrophes

Write the correct form of each word that requires an apostrophe in the following sentences. If a sentence is already correct, write *C*.

EXAMPLE 1. Didnt the womens team win the tournament last year, too?
1. *Didn't, women's*

1. They're looking for Rodney's bucket of seashells that he gathered at the beach.
2. It's anybody's guess who will win!
3. I'm glad you enjoyed staying at the Caldwells' cabin last weekend.
4. If you help me wash my car this afternoon, I will help you wash yours tomorrow.   4. C
5. Isn't ten dollars' worth going to be enough?
6. I haven't a clue about that.
7. Charles Dickens's "A Christmas Carol" is a story you'll really enjoy.   7. [*or* Dickens']
8. The men's clothing shop is closed today.
9. Let's go swimming next Wednesday.
10. Tonya's recipes are always a hit at the church's annual cookoff.

EXERCISE 29
OBJECTIVE

• To correct spelling errors

EXERCISE 30
OBJECTIVE

• To distinguish and choose correctly between words often confused

Mechanics **853**

▶ EXERCISE 29 **Correcting Spelling Errors**

If a word in the following list is spelled incorrectly, write the correct spelling. If a word is correctly spelled, write C.

EXAMPLE   **1.** superceed
            1. *supersede*

1. fryed	8. casualy	15. ageing
2. receed	9. disfigureing	16. measurment
3. brief	10. mother-in-laws	17. denys
4. wifes	11. dimmer	18. ratioes
5. tempoes	12. sliegh	19. sheeps
6. Lopezs	13. reciept	20. tablescloth
7. freewayes	14. mishapen	

▶ EXERCISE 30 **Using Words Often Confused**

For each of the following sentences, select the correct word or words from the choices in parentheses.

EXAMPLE   **1.** My brother's (*advise, advice*) is usually good.
            1. *advice*

1. When will you hear (*whether, weather*) your poem has been (*accepted, excepted*) for publication?
2. We have (*all ready, already*) planned the field trip.
3. Do you think we will need to (*alter, altar*) our plans?
4. If you could (*choose, chose*) any place in the world to visit, where would you go?
5. Did the town (*counsel, council, consul*) meet today?
6. I'd rather experience the (*piece, peace*) and quiet of the beach (*then, than*) the noise and crowds of the city.
7. (*Its, It's*) good manners to hold the door open for anyone (*whose, who's*) hands are full.
8. The floats (*shown, shone*) brightly in the sunlight as the parade (*passed, past*) by our house.
9. If the (*whether, weather*) is bad, will that (*effect, affect*) our party, or are we having the party indoors?
10. Before turning in plastic bags for recycling, we reuse them (*to, too, two*) or three times.

CORRECTING COMMON ERRORS

ANSWERS
Exercise 29

1. fried
2. recede
3. C
4. wives
5. tempos
6. Lopezes
7. freeways
8. casually
9. disfiguring
10. mothers-in-law
11. C
12. sleigh
13. receipt
14. misshapen
15. aging
16. measurement
17. denies
18. ratios
19. sheep
20. tablecloths

MEETING *individual* **NEEDS**

Auditory Learners. Students might benefit from intentionally mispronouncing and then pronouncing correctly a list of the words often confused that are used in **Exercise 30.** Students could then mispronounce the words to exaggerate the spelling differences between these homonyms. Exaggerating the spelling differences aloud may help students recall the distinctions in spelling and meaning between the pairs of words.

CORRECTING COMMON ERRORS

Special Needs. Students may feel overwhelmed by the task of proofreading whole sentences or passages for an unknown number of errors. To help students succeed, suggest that they proofread each sentence in isolation (such as by covering with a blank sheet of paper the sentences below the sentence they are reading).

TEACHING NOTE

Using the Mechanics Tests. A Standardized Test Answer Sheet that students may use for these **Mechanics Tests** is provided in *Language Skills Practice and Assessment,* p. 287.

MECHANICS TEST: Section 1
OBJECTIVE

• To demonstrate mastery by selecting answers that show correct capitalization, punctuation, and spelling

Mechanics Test: Section 1

DIRECTIONS   Each numbered item below contains an underlined group of words. Choose the answer that shows the correct capitalization, punctuation, and spelling of the underlined part. If there is no error, choose answer D (Correct as is). Indicate your response by shading in the appropriate oval on your answer sheet.

EXAMPLE

Thank you very [1] much, Mr. and Mrs. Fernandez for a great visit.

1. (A) much Mr. and Mrs. Fernandez,
   (B) much, Mr. and Mrs. Fernandez,
   (C) much Mr. and Mrs. Fernandez;
   (D) Correct as is

SAMPLE ANSWER 1. (A) ● (C) (D)

1201 Palm Circle
[1] Jacksonville Fla. 32201
[2] April 11 1997

[3] Dear Mr. and Mrs. Fernandez,

I am so glad that you and Pedro invited me to stay at your home this [4] past weekend, I had a great time. The [5] whether I think was perfect for the activities you planned. The [6] picnic lunches volleyball games, and boat rides were so much fun! I especially enjoyed going fishing in your boat [7] *the ugly duckling.*

Next weekend my parents are going to have a barbecue party to celebrate [8] my aunt Jessicas birthday. If you would like to join us this coming [9] Saturday at 5:30 P.M. please give us a call sometime this week.

[10] Sincerely yours,

Todd Grinstead

854

1. A **1.** (A) Jacksonville, FL 32201
(B) Jacksonville Fla 32201
(C) Jacksonville FL 32201
(D) Correct as is

2. C **2.** (A) April, 11 1997
(B) April Eleventh 1997
(C) April 11, 1997
(D) Correct as is

3. D **3.** (A) Dear Mr. and Mrs. Fernandez:
(B) Dear Mr and Mrs Fernandez:
(C) Dear Mr. And Mrs. Fernandez,
(D) Correct as is

4. B **4.** (A) passed weekend; I had
(B) past weekend; I had
(C) passed weekend, I had
(D) Correct as is

5. C **5.** (A) whether, I think was
(B) weather, I think was
(C) weather, I think, was
(D) Correct as is

6. C **6.** (A) picnic lunchs,
(B) picnic lunchs
(C) picnic lunches,
(D) Correct as is

7. B **7.** (A) *the Ugly Duckling.*
(B) *The Ugly Duckling.*
(C) "The Ugly Duckling."
(D) Correct as is

8. C **8.** (A) my Aunt Jessica's
(B) my Aunt Jessicas'
(C) my aunt Jessica's
(D) Correct as is

9. B **9.** (A) Saturday, at 5:30 P.M.
(B) Saturday at 5:30 P.M.,
(C) Saturday, at 5:30 PM.,
(D) Correct as is

10. D **10.** (A) Sincerely yours',
(B) Sincerly yours,
(C) Sincerely yours:
(D) Correct as is

- To demonstrate mastery by selecting answers that show correct capitalization, punctuation, and spelling

856 *Correcting Common Errors*

Mechanics Test: Section 2

DIRECTIONS   Each of the following sentences contains an underlined word or group of words. Choose the answer that shows the correct capitalization, punctuation, and spelling of the underlined part. If there is no error, choose answer D (Correct as is). Indicate your response by shading in the appropriate oval on your answer sheet.

EXAMPLE

1. King Louis Philippe of France created the <u>foreign legion</u> in 1831.
   - (A) Foreign Legion
   - (B) Foriegn Legion
   - (C) foriegn legion
   - (D) Correct as is

SAMPLE ANSWER   1. ● Ⓑ Ⓒ Ⓓ

1. C   1. My music teacher, <u>Mrs. O'Henry will sing two solos</u> at our school's talent show.
   - (A) Mrs. O'Henry, will sing two soloes
   - (B) Mrs. O'Henry will sing two soloes
   - (C) Mrs. O'Henry, will sing two solos
   - (D) Correct as is

2. C   2. "Do we have enough pickets to build the <u>fence,"</u> asked Michelle.
   - (A) fence"
   - (B) fence"?
   - (C) fence?"
   - (D) Correct as is

3. A   3. Last Friday <u>my sister-in-laws</u> nephew stopped by.
   - (A) my sister-in-law's
   - (B) my sister's-in-law
   - (C) my sister-in-laws'
   - (D) Correct as is

4. C   4. The short story <u>Over the Fence is about three oxen</u> and a frog.
   - (A) 'Over the Fence' is about three oxes
   - (B) 'Over The Fence' is about three oxen
   - (C) "Over the Fence" is about three oxen
   - (D) Correct as is

5. D   5. Turn left on <u>Ninety-eighth Street</u>.
   - (A) Ninty-eighth Street
   - (B) Ninety-Eighth Street
   - (C) Ninety-eighth street
   - (D) Correct as is

6. B **6.** Roberto Clemente twice <u>lead the Pittsburgh Pirates</u> to victory in the World Series.

(A) lead The Pittsburgh Pirates
(B) led the Pittsburgh Pirates
(C) led the Pittsburgh pirates
(D) Correct as is

7. A **7.** "How many of you," asked <u>Mr. Reynolds "have</u> seen a painting by the young Chinese artist <u>Wang Yani?"</u>

(A) Mr. Reynolds, "have
(B) Mr. Reynolds," have
(C) Mr. Reynolds, "Have
(D) Correct as is

8. C **8.** <u>Those who studied for the test</u> of course, did better than those who did not.

(A) Those, who studied for the test,
(B) Those, who studied for the test
(C) Those who studied for the test,
(D) Correct as is

9. B **9.** "Did you <u>say that "it's time to go?"</u> asked Raul.

(A) say, that 'it's time to go'?"
(B) say that it's time to go?"
(C) say that 'It's time to go'?"
(D) Correct as is

10. C **10.** My younger sister excels in the following <u>classes Art II, social studies,</u> and English.

(A) classes art II, social studies,
(B) classes, Art II, Social Studies,
(C) classes: Art II, social studies,
(D) Correct as is

CORRECTING COMMON ERRORS

CORRECTING COMMON ERRORS

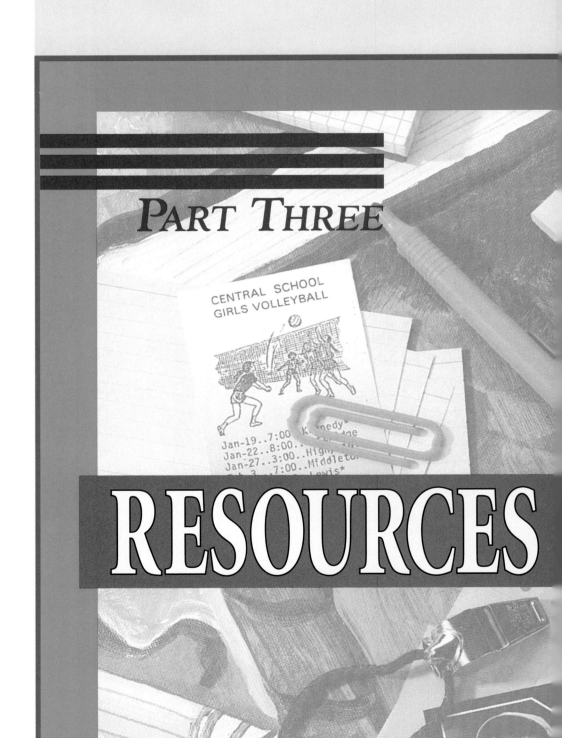

PART THREE

RESOURCES

CENTRAL SCHOOL
GIRLS VOLLEYBALL

Jan-19..7:00..Kennedy*
Jan-22..8:00..
Jan-27..3:00..High...
Jan-27..3:00..Middleto...
...3...7:00...Lewis*

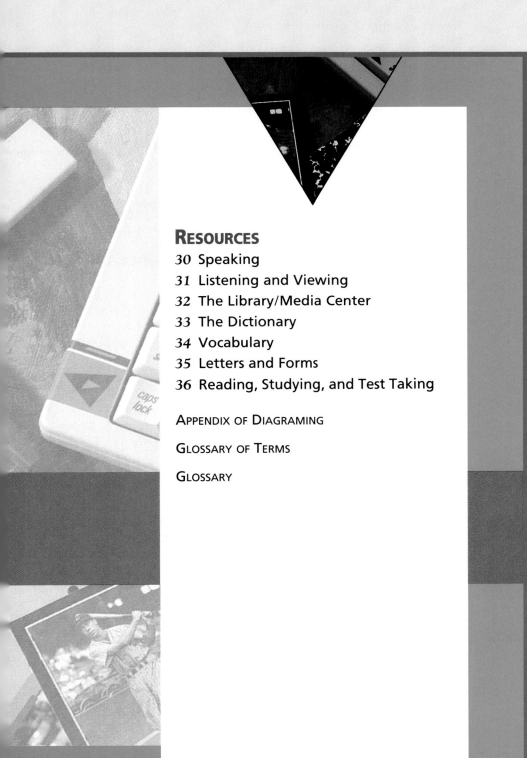

RESOURCES

PART THREE: RESOURCES

The following **Teaching Resources** booklets contain materials that may be used with this part of the Pupil's Edition.

- *Academic and Workplace Skills*
- *Portfolio Assessment* (for Chs. 30, 31)
- *Practice for Assessment in Reading, Vocabulary, and Spelling* (for Ch. 34)

OBJECTIVES

- To communicate a telephone message effectively
- To give clear directions or instructions
- To make social introductions
- To prepare and give a speech
- To write an announcement for an event

PROGRAM MANAGER

SPEAKING

- **Independent Practice/ Reteaching** For additional practice and reinforcement, see **Variety in Speaking, Nonverbal Communication, Impromptu Speaking, Speaking on the Telephone, Giving Directions, Practicing and Delivering a Speech, Planning an Announcement,** and **Cooperative Learning Through Discussion** in *Academic and Workplace Skills,* pp. 1–8.

- **Assessment/Reflection** To assess student work and evaluate progress, see **Portfolio Forms** in *Portfolio Assessment,* pp. 31–33.

- **Review** For exercises on chapter concepts, see **Review Form A** and **Review Form B** in *Academic and Workplace Skills,* pp. 9–12.

CHAPTER OVERVIEW

This chapter enables students to apply the skills developed for composition to other communication activities—impromptu speaking, speaking on the telephone, giving directions, and making introductions. It also leads students through the steps necessary to prepare and deliver speeches using methods similar to those for planning compositions. Instructions are provided for making announcements, introducing presentations, and participating in group discussions. The chapter concludes with instruction in planning and delivering oral interpretations of literature.

30 SPEAKING

Skills and Strategies

Whether you are speaking at school or in the workplace, you can be a more effective communicator if you consider

- your purpose (What are you trying to say?)
- your topic (What are you speaking about?)
- your audience (Who are your listeners?)

The Communication Cycle

Communication takes teamwork. First, a speaker communicates feelings or ideas to listeners. Then the listeners respond to the speaker's message. This response is called *feedback.*

Listeners may respond to a speaker by a *verbal* response, using words (such as "I see what you mean"). Or a listener could make *nonverbal* responses without using any words (such as by applauding).

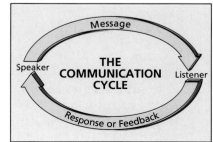

- To introduce a speaker
- To participate in a group discussion
- To prepare and present an oral interpretation of a literature selection

Nonverbal Communication

Along with words, or verbal signals, you can communicate many meanings with nonverbal signals.

NONVERBAL COMMUNICATION	
NONVERBAL SIGNALS	**EXAMPLES**
Gestures or motions	thumbs up or nodding head (meaning agreement or encouragement), shrugging (uncertainty), shaking head (disagreement)
Facial expressions	smiling, raising an eyebrow, smirking, frowning, grimacing, pouting, or grinning (meanings vary with each situation)
Body language	turning away (rejection), stroking the chin (puzzlement), crossing arms on chest (reluctance, uncertainty)
Sounds	laughing, groaning, giggling (meanings vary with each situation)

Speaking Informally

Impromptu Speaking

Sometimes you need to speak to a group of people without having time to prepare what you want to say. This is called an *impromptu speech.* Remember the following points.

1. *Consider your purpose.* (Are you trying to inform your audience? Do you want to persuade them?)
2. *Consider your topic.* (What are the main ideas you need to say? Do you have time to add details that support or explain your main points?)
3. *Consider your audience.* (Does what you're saying suit the time, place, and audience you're speaking to?)

RESOURCES

QUICK REMINDER

For impromptu speeches, write on the chalkboard several related topics such as billboards, nutritional labels, clothing tags, and warning labels. Select a topic and explain to students that you are going to give a one-minute, spur-of-the-moment talk about it. After you finish, ask volunteers to select from the other topics and to give short speeches. Explain to students that this kind of impromptu speaking is one of the informal methods they will study.

MEETING *individual* NEEDS

LEP/ESL

General Strategies. Some English-language learners go through years of school without the opportunity to speak their first languages in the classroom. Ask students to give presentations both in English and in their first languages, adjusting their style as appropriate. This language presentation also allows English-proficient speakers an opportunity to appreciate and understand linguistic differences.

TIMESAVER

When you assign impromptu speeches, you can reduce your workload by asking students to think of topics for speeches.

RESOURCES

TECHNOLOGY TIP

When students make telephone calls, they may have to leave messages on answering machines. Remind students that when they leave recorded messages, they need to identify themselves clearly, give their telephone numbers, and keep their messages brief.

A DIFFERENT APPROACH

Suggest to students that, after they are introduced to someone, they make every effort to use that person's name in the ensuing conversation. Repeating a name will help them remember that person's name. Because people like to be addressed by name, doing this will also increase your students' sociability.

PREPARING A SPEECH

Many students find that the hardest part of preparing a speech is selecting a topic. Students sometimes discount their own experiences. Suggest to students that hobbies and personal experiences often make excellent topics.

Speaking Socially

In most social situations, you can be effective in communicating if you remember to speak clearly and politely.

Speaking on the Telephone

1. Call people at times which are convenient for them.
2. Identify yourself and state your reason for calling.
3. Be polite. Keep your call to a reasonable length.

Giving Instructions or Directions

1. Divide directions into clear, understandable steps.
2. Tell your listener the steps, in order.
3. Check to be sure your listener understands.

Making Social Introductions

1. Be confident. Introduce yourself to others.
2. When introducing others, identify them by name.
3. When you are introducing others, it is customary to speak first to

   - a person of higher job status
   - an older person before a younger person
   - the person you know best

Speaking Formally

Preparing a Speech

A *formal speech* is one given at an arranged time and place. This allows you to prepare carefully beforehand.

Planning Your Speech

When preparing your speech, you will need to consider your purpose, choose a subject, narrow your subject to a limited topic, and gather and arrange your information. See the composition chapters of this textbook for other suggestions.

The following chart shows some common types of speeches, arranged according to their purpose.

IDENTIFYING YOUR PURPOSE		
PURPOSE	**DESCRIPTION OF SPEECH**	**EXAMPLES OF SPEECH TITLES**
To inform	gives facts or explains how to do something	What Makes an Airplane Fly How to Make Your Home a Safer Place
To persuade	attempts to change listeners' opinion or attempts to get listeners to act	Why Getting Suntans May Be a Bad Idea Why Students Should Learn CPR
To entertain	relates an amusing story or incident	My First Experience with Riding a Bicycle

Considering Your Audience

When you plan your speech, you also need to consider your audience's needs and interests.

THINKING ABOUT YOUR AUDIENCE		
QUESTIONS ABOUT AUDIENCE	**EVALUATION**	**YOUR SPEECH WILL NEED**
What does your audience already know about this subject?	very little	to provide background details to inform your listeners about your topic
	a little	to include at least some background detail
	a lot	to focus only on interesting points about the topic
How interested will your audience be in this subject?	very interested	to maintain your listeners' interest
	mildly interested	to stick to parts of the topic your listeners are most interested in
	uninterested	to convince your listeners that this topic is important

CRITICAL THINKING

Synthesis. You may wish to involve your class in a brainstorming session to discover other suitable topics. Ask them to make lists of current issues that are discussed in the news. As students name topics, help them see how current problems relate to each other. For example, failure to recycle aluminum cans not only wastes money but also leads to shortened lives for city landfills.

CONSIDERING YOUR AUDIENCE

You may wish to discuss with your class additional factors that affect audience response. These factors include age, sex, cultural background, educational level, and group membership.

RESOURCES

RESOURCES

COMMON ERROR

Problem. Students often read their extemporaneous speeches from notes. Reading results in speeches that are inflexible in presentation and seem dull because the vocal delivery lacks spontaneity.

Solution. Stress to your students that the extemporaneous method of delivery is intended to encourage spontaneity and to allow flexibility in presentation. Encourage students to become familiar with their material by practicing. However, suggest that they avoid memorizing their speeches word-for-word.

MEETING *individual* NEEDS

LEARNING STYLES

Visual Learners. You might suggest that students use their outlines to develop visual means of presentation. Visuals such as charts, diagrams, outlines, or illustrations shared with the audience become integral parts of speeches and keep students from relying on notes.

COMMON ERROR

Problem. When it is their turn to speak, inexperienced speakers often reveal their reluctance with inappropriate facial expressions and body language.

Solution. Remind students that how they look before they begin to speak influences how the audience will respond. Speaking occasions begin the moment students rise from their chairs.

Organizing Your Speech Notes

The most common type of speech is an ***extemporaneous speech.*** *Extemporaneous* comes from Latin words meaning "from the time." When you give an extemporaneous speech, you prepare an outline of your main points. Then you make note cards for each main point. When you give your speech, you talk directly to the audience just as you would in an impromptu speech. But with an extemporaneous speech, you have prepared your speech and you can refer to your note cards whenever you need to remember your main points.

HOW TO MAKE SPEECH NOTE CARDS
1. Write each main idea on a separate note card.
2. Make a special note card for anything that you plan to read word for word (such as a quotation or a series of dates or statistics that's too hard to memorize).
3. Include a special note card to indicate when to show a chart, diagram, model, or other visual materials.
4. Number your completed cards to keep them in order.

Giving Your Speech

Speaking Expressively

When you speak effectively, you use your voice and your gestures to help convey your meaning to your listeners. Here are some pointers to use when you are speaking.

1. *Stand confidently.* Stand up straight and look alert.
2. *Act naturally.* Use facial expressions and gestures that reflect what you're saying.
3. *Speak clearly.* Speak loudly so that everyone can hear you clearly. Pronounce your words carefully.
4. *Look at your audience.* When you speak, look directly at members of your audience and speak to them directly.

5. *Use variety when you speak.* Use a normal variety of voice patterns as you speak. These are clues that help your audience understand what points you want to emphasize.

- *Volume:* Be loud enough to be heard, but strengthen or soften your tone for emphasis.
- *Pitch:* Use the normal rise and fall of your voice to highlight various ideas.
- *Stress:* Emphasize important words as you speak.
- *Rate:* Speak at a comfortable, relaxed pace.

Speaking Before an Audience

It's normal to feel nervous about speaking in front of an audience. However, you can use the following suggestions to help you stay in control.

1. *Be prepared.* Organize your material carefully and practice using your note cards and any visuals you plan to use during your speech.
2. *Practice your speech.* Each time you rehearse, pretend you're actually giving your speech.
3. *Focus on your purpose.* Think about how you want your speech to affect your audience.

Special Speaking Situations

Making Announcements

When you make an announcement, your main goal is to provide information. Follow these guidelines.

1. When you write your announcement, be brief but include all the most important details.
2. To give your announcement, get your audience's attention and then say your message slowly and clearly.

RESOURCES

A DIFFERENT APPROACH
Each person hears his or her voice differently from how the rest of the world hears it. Because sound vibration from a speaker's vocal cords affects hearing, speakers often think they are using more vocal variety than they actually are. Encourage more variety by having students record and listen to their speeches. Have them exaggerate their use of volume, pitch, stress, and rate.

COMMON ERROR
Problem. When speakers make announcements, they sometimes omit pieces of vital information.

Solution. Encourage your students to construct and use checklists when making announcements.

RESOURCES

Making an Introduction to a Presentation

An introduction is often given before a speaker's presentation or before a short performance. An introduction gets the audience's attention. It also gives an audience background information to explain details about the performance or presentation. This introduction may include information about the speaker or the subject of a speech. Or, it might include background information about a dramatic work, the actors, or the author of the work being presented.

Group Discussions

Setting a Purpose

In many of your classes and in future work situations, you will work with others in groups to accomplish a specific purpose. This purpose may be

- to discuss and share ideas
- to cooperate in group learning
- to solve a problem
- to arrive at a decision or make a recommendation to a larger group or committee

Once your group decides on a purpose, find out how much time will be allowed and identify what you'll need to accomplish within the time limit.

Group Roles in Cooperative Learning

Everyone involved in a group discussion has a specific role. Each role has special responsibilities. For example, your group may choose a chairperson to help keep the discussion moving smoothly. Someone else may be chosen as the secretary or reporter (or recorder), with the responsibility of taking notes during the discussion.

Usually, a group establishes an *agenda,* or outline of the order of topics to follow in a discussion. The agenda

RESOURCES

RESOURCES

may be decided by the chairperson, or it may be decided by the entire group.

A Chairperson's Responsibilities

1. Announce the topic and establish an agenda.
2. Follow the agenda.
3. Encourage each member to participate.
4. Help group members stay on track and avoid disagreements.

A Secretary's or Reporter's Responsibilities

1. Take notes about important information.
2. Prepare a final report.

A Participant's Responsibilities

1. Take an active part in the discussion.
2. Ask questions and listen attentively to others.
3. Cooperate and share information.

Oral Interpretation

Oral interpretation is more like acting in a play than giving a speech. When you perform an oral interpretation, you read a piece of literature expressively to your listeners. You use facial expressions, vocal techniques, and body language to interpret and express the basic meaning of the literary work.

Selecting or Adapting Material

When you are choosing material for an oral interpretation, you usually know the purpose, audience, and occasion for your presentation. You'll also need to think about the length of time allowed for your presentation.

Here are suggestions for finding a literary work for an oral interpretation. You could use a poem, especially one that tells a story (such as an epic poem) or that has a speaker (using the word *I* or featuring a conversation between two characters.) You could use a short story, or a

 INTEGRATING THE LANGUAGE ARTS

Literature Link. Reader's theater allows students to develop skills in oral interpretation and awareness of drama. You might have students adapt short stories for dramatic presentation. Possibilities include "The Treasure of Lemon Brown" by Walter Dean Myers, "The Open Window" by Saki, and "The Devil and Daniel Webster" by Stephen Vincent Benét. Then divide your class into groups and have each group read one story. If a story has several small parts, some students could read more than one part. After the groups have familiarized themselves with their stories, they can take turns performing for each other.

Another possible activity for oral interpretation is a poetry reading. Narrative poetry, especially when it contains dialogue, is effective when read aloud by more than one person. For example, many episodes from Longfellow's "The Song of Hiawatha" are suitable for such group reading.

RESOURCES

RESOURCES

part of a story, that has a beginning, a middle, and an end and that has one or more characters who talk during the story. Or you could use part of a play, such as a scene between two characters.

You may be able to find just the right piece of literature that's already the perfect length. But often, you need to shorten a work. This shortened version is called a *cutting*.

HOW TO MAKE A CUTTING

1. Follow the story line in time order.
2. Cut dialogue tags such as *she whispered sadly.* Instead, use these clues to tell you how to act out the characters' words.
3. Cut parts that don't contribute to the portion of the story you are telling.

You may need to introduce your interpretation to set the scene, tell something about the author of the piece of literature you're presenting, or describe some important events that have already taken place in the story.

Presenting an Oral Interpretation

After you've decided on a piece to present, you'll need to prepare a *reading script.* A reading script is usually typed (double-spaced). It can then be marked to help you with your interpretive reading. For example, you can underline words you want to emphasize.

Rehearse your presentation several different ways until you are satisfied that you have chosen the most effective way to interpret the passage. Use your voice so that it suits your meaning. Vary your body movements and your voice to show that you are portraying different characters and to show important character traits.

 COMPUTER NOTE: Use a word-processing program to prepare your script. You can use bold, italic, or underline formatting to show emphasis or to indicate notes to yourself.

PRESENTING AN ORAL INTERPRETATION

Students should be encouraged to hold their reading scripts high enough to read them without bobbing their heads up and down, but not so high that their faces are concealed.

Review

▶ EXERCISE 1 **Practicing Telephone Speaking Situations**

For each of the following situations, explain what you would say to be polite but clear.

1. A salesperson calls while your mother is taking a nap. You don't want to wake her.
2. You're calling the public library to find out if they have issues of *The New York Times* from May of 1991.
3. You're calling your dentist to cancel an appointment.
4. You've dialed the wrong telephone number.

▶ EXERCISE 2 **Giving Directions**

Provide directions for each of the following situations.

1. Give a new neighbor directions to the nearest mall.
2. An out-of-town guest staying at your home needs directions to the nearest restaurant.
3. You're on the yearbook committee. The next meeting is at your house. A member asks you for directions.
4. Direct a new student to the cafeteria.

▶ EXERCISE 3 **Making Social Introductions**

Tell what you might say when making an introduction under each of the following circumstances.

1. You're visiting a friend's house. Your friend's uncle answers the door. Introduce yourself.
2. You're at a school dance. Your date is from another school. [a] Introduce your date to one of your friends. [b] Introduce your date to the chaperon.
3. Your mother comes to pick you up from a new friend's house. Introduce your friend to your mother.

RESOURCES

ANSWERS
Exercise 1

Responses will vary. Here are some possibilities:

1. This is her son (daughter), _____. My mother is taking a nap. Could I ask her to call you back later? Would you like to leave a name and phone number?
2. Hello, this is _____. I'm working on a homework assignment. Could you tell me if you have back issues of *The New York Times* from May of 1991?
3. Hi, this is _____. I have an appointment for tomorrow, but something has come up. Could I please reschedule it?
4. Hello, this is _____. May I speak to _____? Oh, please excuse me. I must have dialed the wrong number.

ANSWERS
Exercise 2

Answers will vary. Students should divide their directions into clear, understandable steps. After going through the steps, they should check to make sure the listeners understand the steps, repeating any that are unclear.

ANSWERS
Exercise 3

Responses will vary. Here are some possibilities:

1. Hi, I'm _____'s friend _____.
2a. _____, I'd like you to meet my date, _____. She (he) goes to Glenview Junior High. _____, I'd like you to meet my friend _____.
b. Mr. (Ms.)_____, I'd like you to meet my date, _____. She (he) goes to Glenview Junior High. _____, I'd like you to meet our chaperon, Mr. (Ms.) _____.
3. Mom, I'd like you to meet _____. _____, this is my mom, Mrs. _____.

RESOURCES

869

STUDENTS WITH SPECIAL NEEDS

Some students may have trouble with the numerous instructions in **Exercise 4.** They may need a step-by-step presentation of instructions, especially when the assignment is detailed. Rewrite the instructions using a numbered list of steps. Have students check off each step as they complete it. Be sure to add a step for practicing the speech, and give students opportunities for practice before their final presentations.

ANSWERS
Exercise 7

Discussions will vary. Groups should determine their specific purposes and decide who will be chairperson and secretary. The success of the discussion should be gauged by how well students fulfill the responsibilities associated with being a chairperson, secretary, or participant.

ANSWERS
Exercise 8

Interpretations will vary. Students should prepare suitable introductions for their selections, make cuttings that meet the time limit and retain narrative coherence, prepare reading scripts by using underlining and slashes for emphasis, and deliver the material by using variations in voice and body language to convey different characters.

870 *Speaking*

▶ EXERCISE 4 **Preparing and Giving a Speech**

Choose a topic for a two- to three-minute speech to your English class. Prepare note cards for your speech. Include a visual, such as a chart, diagram, time line, or drawing. Then, give your speech to the class, following the guidelines on pages 864–865 for speaking effectively.
Speeches will vary. Use the Speaking Expressively pointers to assess students' speeches.

▶ EXERCISE 5 **Making an Announcement**

Write an announcement for a real or imaginary event. Be brief but include all important details. **Announcements should include the date, time, place, and type of event, and any special instructions.**

▶ EXERCISE 6 **Introducing a Speaker**

Prepare an introduction for the speaker of your choice. The speaker can be a sports star, a famous actor or musician, a politician, or your favorite author. **Introductions should describe what the speaker does, what the speech addresses, or why the speaker is interested in the subject.**

▶ EXERCISE 7 **Conducting a Group Discussion**

Select a group chairperson to lead a discussion on a topic assigned by your teacher or one of your own choosing. Establish an agenda and determine how much time you will have for discussion. The purpose for the discussion is to decide on a list of findings about this topic to be presented to the class.

▶ EXERCISE 8 **Presenting an Oral Interpretation**

Prepare a three-minute oral interpretation to present to your class. Select a portion of a short story, a scene from a play, or a section of a novel that contains a scene for one or two characters. Prepare a reading script. Write a brief introduction.

LISTENING AND VIEWING *(pp. 871–880)*

OBJECTIVES
- To listen to instructions for details and sequences
- To prepare interview questions
- To listen critically and take lecture notes
- To identify common persuasive techniques
- To identify and analyze personal television viewing habits

31 LISTENING AND VIEWING

Strategies for Listening and Viewing

Hearing is not the same as listening, and seeing is not the same as viewing. When you hear and see, you detect sounds and images. But both listening and viewing are active processes that require you to think about what you hear and see.

Listening with a Purpose

Keeping your purpose in mind as you listen helps you to become a more effective listener. You hear things differently depending on what you are listening for. For example, if you listen to your friends talking, you may only pay enough attention to follow the topic. But if you listen to directions to a new friend's house, you will probably need to pay closer attention in order to find your way. Common purposes for listening are

- for enjoyment or entertainment
- to gain information
- to understand information or an explanation
- to evaluate or form an opinion

PROGRAM MANAGER

LISTENING AND VIEWING

■ **Independent Practice/ Reteaching** For additional practice and reinforcement, see **Listening for Information, Interviewing, Critical Listening, Lectures and Note-taking, Methods of Persuasion,** and **Critical Viewing** in *Academic and Workplace Skills,* pp. 17–22.

■ **Assessment/Reflection** To assess student work and evaluate progress, see **Portfolio Forms** in *Portfolio Assessment,* pp. 28–30.

■ **Review** For exercises on chapter concepts, see **Review Form A** and **Review Form B** in *Academic and Workplace Skills,* pp. 23–24.

CHAPTER OVERVIEW

This chapter reviews effective listening techniques by leading students through the skills of listening with a purpose, listening for details, listening to instructions, and listening politely. The LQ2R study method is explained, and students are shown how to conduct interviews. Students are then introduced to critical listening skills and are instructed in how to take lecture notes. Finally, students are instructed in how to understand persuasive techniques used by speakers and how to become more critically analytical of their television viewing habits.

RESOURCES

RESOURCES

871

QUICK REMINDER

Have students imagine that they received the following message over the telephone: "Hello. This is Dr. Ford's receptionist. Would you remind your mother that she has a dental appointment at 3:00 tomorrow? If she can't make it, have her call me." Ask students what other information they would need to ask in order to relay the message effectively. [The caller's telephone number is missing.]

MEETING *individual* **NEEDS**

LEP/ESL

General Strategies. English-language learners may have difficulties with many listening skills because they are unfamiliar with the English language. You might want to record some exercises so that students could repeat anything they missed as often as needed. You could also allow small groups to confer about the topics and to use visuals as memory cues.

COMMON ERROR

Problem. Listeners can jump to conclusions about a speaker's message based on nothing more than the speaker's appearance or style of delivery.

Solution. Remind students that first impressions shouldn't be everything. Tell them to make a conscious effort to disregard superficial aspects of appearance or delivery and to focus on the content of the message.

Listening for Information

Listening for Details

When you listen for information, you need to listen for details that answer the basic *5W-How?* questions: *Who? What? When? Where? Why?* and *How?* For example, when you are asked to take messages on the telephone, you will need to get important details from the caller, such as

- the caller's name
- the caller's message
- whom the call is for
- the caller's telephone number

Listening to Instructions

Usually, instructions are made up of a series of steps. When you listen to instructions, be sure you understand all the steps you will need to follow.

1. *Listen for the order of steps.* Identify words that tell you when each step ends and the next one begins, such as *first, second, next, then,* and *last.*
2. *Identify the number of steps in the process.* If the instructions are long and complicated, take notes.
3. *Visualize each step.* Imagine yourself actually performing the action. Try to get a mental image of what you should be doing at every step in the process.
4. *Review the steps.* When the speaker is finished, be sure you understand the instructions.

Listening and Responding Politely

To complete the communication cycle, the listener must respond to the speaker. Here's how to respond politely.

1. *Respect the speaker.* Show respect for the speaker's cultural, racial, and religious background. Be tolerant of individual differences.

2. *Don't interrupt.* Pay attention, and save your questions or comments until the speaker has finished.
3. *Keep an open mind.* Be aware of how your own point of view affects the way you judge others' opinions.
4. *Don't judge too soon.* Wait to hear the speaker's whole message before you make judgments.
5. *Ask appropriate questions.* Use a voice loud enough for all to hear. For better understanding, summarize or paraphrase the speaker's point you are questioning.
6. *Use polite, effective gestures.* They should help you emphasize your point and be appropriate to the situation.

Using the LQ2R Method

The LQ2R study method is especially helpful when you are listening to a speaker who is giving information.

L   *Listen* carefully to material as it is being presented.

Q   *Question* yourself as you listen. Make a list, mentally or in your notes, of questions that occur to you.

R   *Recite* mentally the answers to your questions as you discover them, or jot down notes as you listen.

R   *Relisten* as the speaker concludes the presentation. Major points may be summed up or listed again.

Conducting an Interview

An *interview* is a special listening situation. An interview usually takes place between two people, an interviewer and the person being interviewed (called the *interviewee*). The purpose of an interview is to gather information.

Before the Interview
- Decide what information you most want to know.
- Make a list of questions.
- Make an appointment and be on time.

RESOURCES

COOPERATIVE LEARNING
Ask your students to use the LQ2R study method in one of their classes (yours or another teacher's). Later, divide your class into groups of five. Members of the groups should take turns reporting their success in applying the LQ2R method. Each group should then compile a list of the difficulties they encountered and share them with the entire class.

CONDUCTING AN INTERVIEW
Tell your class that many experienced interviewers make it a habit to write brief thank-you notes. Ask the class why this might be desirable. [It creates goodwill in case a follow-up interview is needed; it helps the interviewer remember the interviewee's name.]

RESOURCES

INTEGRATING THE LANGUAGE ARTS

Literature Link. In addition to speeches, essays that are read aloud make useful listening exercises. When an essay is read, students should listen to discover the purpose of the essay, the main ideas or opinions developed, the method the writer uses to support these ideas or opinions, and the tone the writer adopts. You might have students volunteer to read aloud essays such as Fabiola Cabeza de Baca's "The Pioneer Women" and Ann Petry's "Go On or Die."

CRITICAL THINKING

Application. Read a short poem to the class such as Robert Frost's "The Road Not Taken." Ask students to paraphrase the poem and then ask them to write about experiences in their lives that correspond to the experiences of the poet. Those students who wish to share their experiences with the class can be invited to do so.

During the Interview
- Be polite and be patient. Give the interviewee time to answer each question.
- When you ask a question, listen to the answer. If you're not sure you understand, ask questions.
- If you are planning to quote the person directly, it is best to ask permission first.
- Respect the interviewee's opinion. You may ask the other person to explain an opinion, but be polite even if you disagree.
- Conclude by thanking the interviewee.

After the Interview
- Review your notes and write a summary while you still remember the interview clearly.

 COMPUTER NOTE: If you put your interview notes into a computer file, you can keep your notes open on one half of the screen while you write your draft on the other half.

Critical Listening

Critical listening means analyzing and interpreting a speaker's message. You can't remember every word a speaker says. But if you listen critically, you can find the parts of the speaker's message that are most important.

HOW TO LISTEN CRITICALLY	
Find main ideas.	What are the most important points? Listen for clue words a speaker might use, such as *major, main, most important,* or similar words.
Identify significant details.	What dates, names, or facts does the speaker use to support the main points of the speech? What kinds of examples or explanations are used to support the main ideas?

(continued)

HOW TO LISTEN CRITICALLY *(continued)*	
Distinguish between facts and opinions.	A fact is a statement that can be proved to be true. An opinion is a belief or a judgment about something. It cannot really be proved.
Identify the order of organization.	What order is the speaker using to arrange the ideas—time sequence, spatial order, order of importance?
Note comparisons and contrasts.	Are some details compared or contrasted with others?
Understand cause and effect.	Do some events that the speaker refers to relate to or affect other events?
Predict outcomes and draw conclusions.	What can you reasonably conclude from the facts and evidence you have gathered from the speech?

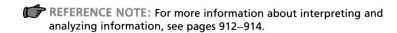 **REFERENCE NOTE:** For more information about interpreting and analyzing information, see pages 912–914.

Taking Lecture Notes

When you listen to a speaker, don't just rely on your memory. Taking notes helps you remember information. For example, write key words or phrases the speaker says. You can also use *paraphrasing* and *summarizing*.

Paraphrasing. When you *paraphrase* material, you express it in your own words. As you listen, translate complex terms that the speaker uses into your own words and write your paraphrase in your notes. Use what you already know or your own experience to help you translate the ideas.

Summarizing. When you *summarize,* you write only the speaker's main points. Write these points in your notes.

MEETING *individual* **NEEDS**

LEARNING STYLES

General Strategies. Give students ample opportunities to develop the note-taking styles that work best for them. Auditory learners may only need to record key words, while visual learners may need complete notes as study guides.

A DIFFERENT APPROACH
Students will be more conscientious about taking notes if they can see the advantages of doing so. If you plan to quiz students over a lecture, you might announce in advance that they will be permitted, while taking the quiz, to consult any notes they have taken.

RESOURCES

RESOURCES

TIMESAVER

Advertisements and commercials provide many sources of persuasive techniques. Have your students assist you in collecting persuasive materials for discussion by listing three advertisements or commercials that they feel are especially persuasive. Use the lists for a class discussion about the persuasive devices used by the advertisers.

COOPERATIVE LEARNING

Make students aware that advertisers use words to create positive or negative emotional appeal. *Natural, old-fashioned,* and *love* are words used to create a positive emotional appeal, while *rat, garbage,* and *disease* have a negative appeal. Have students work in groups of five or six to brainstorm for words with both positive and negative appeal. Allow sufficient class time to discuss the lists.

CRITICAL THINKING

Analysis. As students examine common persuasive techniques, you might want to have them analyze some of the persuasive influences the mass media exerts on society. For example, when television news reports mention the economy, statistics aren't always as powerful as people are. Reporters select "plain folks" to tell how the economic situation affects them or they use interviews with experts to explain the consequences. Have students examine and discuss these and other aspects of the mass media that affect and influence our lives.

Understanding Persuasive Techniques

As a listener, you should be aware of the purpose of the speaker. Many times, speakers (including those on television or radio) have a specific purpose in mind for you, their listener. The speaker's purpose may be:

- to inform you
- to entertain or amuse you
- to persuade you

If the speaker intends to give you information, his or her methods will include techniques for expressing facts or details clearly and accurately. The methods of a speaker who wants to entertain or amuse you will include techniques for performing interesting or comic material. A speaker who wants to persuade you may use one of the following persuasive techniques.

COMMON PERSUASIVE TECHNIQUES USED BY SPEAKERS	
TECHNIQUE	**EXPLANATION**
Bandwagon	Those who use this technique urge you to "jump on the bandwagon" by suggesting that you should do or believe something because everyone (or everyone admirable or worthwhile) is doing it.
Testimonial	Experts or famous people sometimes give a personal "testimony" about a product or idea. However, the person offering the testimonial may not really know much about that particular product or idea.
"Plain folks"	Ordinary people (or people who pretend to be ordinary) are often used to persuade others. People tend to believe others who seem to be similar to themselves.
Emotional appeals	This technique uses words that appeal to your emotions rather than to your ability to reason.

Becoming a Critical Viewer

You probably know that one part of being a critical reader is evaluating what and how you read. But did you know that you can do the same type of thing when you view television? As a critical viewer, you should ask questions and make judgments about your TV viewing habits.

What Do You Watch, and Why?

When you evaluate your viewing habits, you should question more than the quality of the programs you watch. You should also assess the amount of your television viewing and the kinds of programs you select. These guidelines will help you to evaluate your television habits.

1. *Be selective.* Pay attention to how much of your viewing you actually *choose* to see and how much is "couch-potato" time. Do you watch anything that happens to be on while you are in the room? For every program you actively choose to watch, think about why you chose that program and rejected others.
2. *Evaluate what you see.* Develop *criteria,* or objective standards, for judging various kinds of TV programs. To generate your criteria, consider these questions:
   - Is the program's purpose to entertain, to inform, or to persuade?
   - How well does the program accomplish its purpose?
   - Who is the intended audience, the targeted age group? (Advertisements provide a clue.)
   - How effective is the script, or spoken part, of the program? What makes it excellent or poor?
   - How effective are the visuals? the sound effects or music? What standards can you use to measure them?
   - How effective are the actors? the participants? the moderator?
   - What reasons can you give for making your evaluations?

COOPERATIVE LEARNING

Divide your class into five groups and assign each group a different television show to evaluate. Or, if you wish, you might allow students to suggest shows that they want to evaluate, with you holding the right of approval for any proposed show. The purpose of this activity is to have students gain practice and support for using the list of criteria suggested for critical viewing. In general, students often have difficulty articulating what they see as engaging about specific features of the programs that they watch. The practice, in a group, of establishing and applying specific criteria for evaluation will help students when they attempt to complete **Exercise 6** and **Exercise 7** individually.

Instruct each group to prepare and present a report evaluating the group's chosen or assigned program. You may want to have the group present a "panel report" to the class, with each student taking a specific area of evaluation, as presented in item 2. For example, one student could identify the purpose of the television program and assess how well it accomplishes that purpose; a second student could report on the intended audience of the program and how people of that particular audience are targeted by the advertising accompanying the program or characters portrayed on the show; a third student could report on the script of the program and what makes this script good or bad; a fourth student could report on the visuals, sound effects, or music used in the show; and a fifth student could report on the quality of performance of the actors or the moderator and participants who are prominently featured on the show.

3. *Ask yourself questions.* Don't accept what you see and hear uncritically. Ask yourself questions that relate to the type of program you are watching. For example, for a news program, ask: Is this worth my time? What am I learning? Are both sides of a controversial issue presented? How can I tell if this is a fact or someone's opinion? For a talk show, ask: Can I learn something worthwhile from this program? Does the subject affect the lives of many people, or is it just designed to shock or excite the audience? Does the program present any solutions to the situations described?

To sharpen your viewing skills, practice applying the guidelines above on programs you seldom or never watch. When you have done this several times with new programs, you will be ready to critically examine your favorite programs and your viewing habits.

Review

▶ EXERCISE 1 **Listening to Instructions**

Your teacher will read aloud a set of instructions or directions. When the teacher has finished, write the details of the instructions or directions from memory. Then the teacher will reread the instructions and ask you to check the accuracy of what you remembered.

▶ EXERCISE 2 **Listening Accurately**

Practice listening accurately by making up three information statements and a question about each one, similar to the following numbered examples. The object of the game is to answer all the questions correctly without having to hear the statement read a second time. Pause about five seconds after each question to allow the listeners time to write their answers. Check your listeners' answers to determine how accurately they listened.

RESOURCES

ANSWERS
Exercise 1

Answers may vary according to the directions selected. Students should list the steps in chronological order and should use signal words such as *first, second, next,* and *last.*

ANSWERS
Exercise 2

Responses will vary. Students should invent statements similar to those offered in the exercise. Suggest that students use resource materials as sources for some or all of their questions.

RESOURCES

878

1. Here is a series of numbers: *8, 3, 4, 9, 2.* What is the third number? **1. 4**
2. Here is the order of pairs: first, Elvin and Randall; then Carmen and Andrea; last, Vo and Darla. What group is Andrea in? **2. second**
3. The Mohawk River is in the state of New York, the Brazos River is in Texas, and the Snake River is in Idaho. Where is the Mohawk River? **3. New York**

EXERCISE 3 **Preparing Interview Questions**

Think of a person that you admire and would like to interview. For example, you might imagine an athletic hero, an elected official, a movie star, or someone that you think is admirable or knowledgeable. Prepare ten questions that you would like to ask that person in an interview. **Responses will vary. Questions should indicate some preliminary knowledge of the person to be interviewed.**

EXERCISE 4 **Listening Critically**

Listen to a short speech presented by your teacher in class. Take brief notes. Then, answer these questions.

1. What do you think is the speaker's purpose? Does the speaker intend to inform, entertain, or persuade you?
2. What are the main ideas expressed in the speech?
3. What details are used to support the main points in the speech? Identify several supporting details.
4. Identify one fact and one opinion from the speech. What reasons are given to support the opinion?
5. Draw a conclusion about the ideas presented in the speech. Did you find the speech convincing? Explain why or why not.

EXERCISE 5 **Recognizing Persuasive Techniques**

Identify the kind of persuasive technique used in each of the following items.

1. "Be a part of the fitness generation. Try the health drink that everyone's talking about."
2. "My opponent for governor is a friend of only the rich."

RESOURCES

ANSWERS
Exercise 4

Answers may vary according to the speech selected but should be consistent with the content of the speech. Selections such as **"Use It Again and Again and Again"** (p. 256) or **"Ban Dogs from Trails?"** (p. 271) are possible speeches for this exercise.

RESOURCES

ANSWERS
Exercise 5

Answers may vary.

1. bandwagon
2. "plain folks"
3. "plain folks"
4. testimonial

ANSWERS
Exercise 6

Students' answers will vary depending on the television program chosen, but should contain specific responses to each of the four questions listed.

ANSWERS
Exercise 7

Students' answers will vary. However, students should provide specific details about the program as identified in the questions listed. Students should be able to discuss their reviews with others, as noted.

---

3. "As a housewife just like you, I know a good value when I see one. Try Snowy White detergent. It keeps my family looking good for less money."
4. "Superior Motor Oil is a winner. And, as a member of the Super Bowl champion team, I should know something about winning."

EXERCISE 6 Keeping a Viewing Log

Keep a log of your television viewing for one week. Include the name, day, and time of the program; the amount of time you watched; the type of program; and the number of commercials.

1. Add up the amount of time you spent viewing. Multiply the total by fifty-two to find out how much time you spend watching TV during a year.
2. Add up the programs of each type that you watched. What types of programs do you prefer?
3. Multiply the number of commercials by fifty-two. How many commercials do you see per year?
4. Compare your viewing time per week and your program preferences with those of your classmates.

EXERCISE 7 Writing a Television Review

You are the television reporter for your local newspaper. Your assignment is to review a half-hour comedy or drama. In your review of the program, be sure to include
- the name of program, the time, the date, and the channel
- the type of program, the program's purpose, and the intended audience
- a brief plot summary
- your evaluation (based on the questions in the guidelines on pages 877–878) of the plot, the acting, and the show as a whole

Share your review with your classmates, and compare your evaluation with others who reviewed or watched the same program.

THE LIBRARY/MEDIA CENTER *(pp. 881–888)*

OBJECTIVES

- To locate specific information in an excerpt from the *Readers' Guide*
- To arrange titles of fiction books in library shelf order
- To use the card catalog or the online catalog to find specific information
- To identify reference material to use in finding specific information
- To explore the purposes and uses of various sections of a newspaper

32 THE LIBRARY/ MEDIA CENTER

Finding and Using Information

The best place to look for information is in the library, or media center. To make the most of a library's resources, whether that library is at school, in your community, or in the workplace, you must understand what kinds of information exist and how that information is arranged and classified.

The Arrangement of a Library

Libraries give a number and letter code—a *call number*— to each book. The call number tells you how the book has been classified and where to find it in the library. Most school libraries use the Dewey decimal system to classify and arrange nonfiction books according to their subjects.

Biographies are often placed in a separate section of the library. They are arranged in alphabetical order according to the subjects' last names. If there are several books about the same person, the biographies are then arranged according to the last names of the authors.

PROGRAM MANAGER

THE LIBRARY/MEDIA CENTER

- **Independent Practice/ Reteaching** For additional practice and reinforcement, see **Online and Card Catalog, The *Readers' Guide,*** and **Special Reference Works** in *Academic and Workplace Skills,* pp. 29–32.

- **Review** For exercises on chapter concepts, see **Review Form A** and **Review Form B** in *Academic and Workplace Skills,* pp. 33–34.

CHAPTER OVERVIEW

This chapter covers organization of the library, arrangement of books by the Dewey Decimal System, use of the card catalog or online catalog, the parts of a book, use of the *Readers' Guide,* contents of specific reference books, and uses for sections of a newspaper. You may want to refer students to this chapter throughout the year, especially in conjunction with **Chapter 10: "Writing a Research Report."**

RESOURCES

RESOURCES

QUICK REMINDER

Ask students to think of a favorite novel and the author who wrote it. List several of their choices on the chalkboard: title, author's first name, and author's last name.

Have the class determine how these books would be shelved in the fiction section of the library and number the titles as students volunteer the order. You may need to remind students that novels are arranged alphabetically by author's last name, and that if there are two or more books by one author, then they are arranged alphabetically by title (main words).

MEETING *individual* **NEEDS**

LEARNING STYLES

Visual Learners. You may want to have students work as a group to develop a floor plan of the school library. Individuals could be responsible for making maps of the various sections. Then they could work as a group to put the map on a poster. Have them label the sections and possibly list what the sections contain. You could post this in your classroom and offer one to be put up in the school library.

In most libraries, books of fiction are located in one specific section. The books are arranged alphabetically by the authors' last names. Books by the same author are arranged alphabetically by the first word of their titles.

Types of Card Catalogs

To find the book you want, look up the call number in the library's card catalog. There are two types of catalogs: the online catalog and the traditional card catalog.

The *online catalog* is stored on a computer. To find the book you want, type in the title, author, or subject of the book. The computer will display the results of the search information on the computer screen.

Search Results from Online Catalog	
Author:	Ashabranner, Brent K., 1921–
Title:	Still a nation of immigrants/Brent Ashabranner; photographs by Jennifer Ashabranner.
Edition:	1st ed.
Published:	New York: Cobblehill Books/Dutton, ©1993.
Description:	ix, 131 p.: ill.; 24 cm.
LC Call No.:	JV6455 .A892 1993
Dewey No.:	325.7320 ASH
ISBN:	0525651306
Notes:	Includes bibliographical references (p. 127–128) and index.
Subjects:	United States—Emigration and immigration—Juvenile literature.
	Immigrants—United States—Juvenile literature.
	United States—Emigration and immigration.
	Immigrants.

The traditional *card catalog* is a cabinet of small drawers containing cards. These cards list books by title, author, and subject. Fiction books have a title card and an author card. Nonfiction books also have a subject card. A *"See"* or *"See also"* card tells you where to find additional information on a subject.

INFORMATION IN THE CARD CATALOG

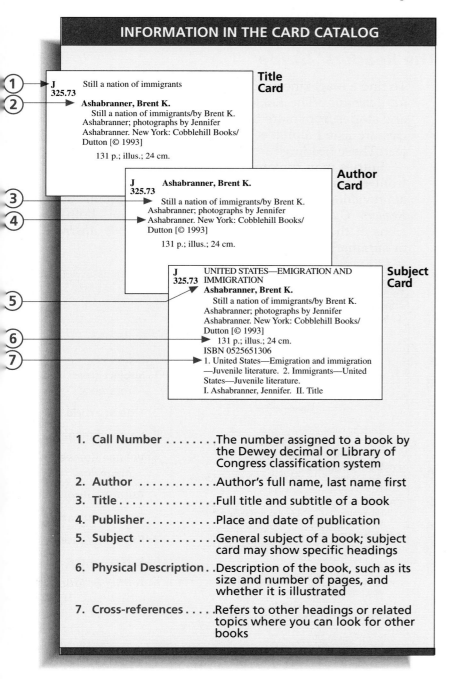

1. **Call Number** . . . . The number assigned to a book by the Dewey decimal or Library of Congress classification system

2. **Author** . . . . Author's full name, last name first

3. **Title** . . . . Full title and subtitle of a book

4. **Publisher** . . . . Place and date of publication

5. **Subject** . . . . General subject of a book; subject card may show specific headings

6. **Physical Description** . . Description of the book, such as its size and number of pages, and whether it is illustrated

7. **Cross-references** . . . . Refers to other headings or related topics where you can look for other books

RESOURCES

TECHNOLOGY TIP

If your school library has an online catalog, demonstrate its use and give students time to locate information using it. You might suggest that students keep notecards with instructions explaining how to locate books using the online catalog.

INTEGRATING THE LANGUAGE ARTS

Literature Link. You may want to ask students to write the titles and authors of their favorite novels. Explain how to locate the authors' names in the card catalog and how to search for more books by the same authors.

Other students may be interested in biographies and autobiographies. Suggest books from the following list: *Silent Dancing: A Partial Remembrance of a Puerto Rican Childhood* by Judith Ortiz Cofer, *The Diary of a Young Girl* by Anne Frank, *I Know Why the Caged Bird Sings* by Maya Angelou, *Nisei Daughter* by Monica Sone, and *Woodsong* by Gary Paulsen.

RESOURCES

MEETING *individual* NEEDS

ADVANCED STUDENTS

Have small groups of students prepare oral reports about libraries. Possible topics include the history of public libraries in the United States, services offered by public libraries, library careers, nonprint media, and famous libraries.

CRITICAL THINKING

Analysis. Have students analyze the way you have arranged the books in your classroom. If your class library is extensive, students could prepare a floor plan detailing the arrangement. You could also challenge students to devise a more useful arrangement.

Using Reference Materials

The *Readers' Guide*

To find a magazine article, use the *Readers' Guide to Periodical Literature*. The *Readers' Guide* indexes articles, poems, and stories from more than one hundred magazines. Articles are listed alphabetically both by author and by subject. These headings are printed in boldface capital letters.

Entries may contain abbreviations. Use the key at the front of the *Readers' Guide* to find the meaning of these abbreviations. The printed and online versions of the *Readers' Guide* provide the same information. Both versions of the *Readers' Guide* sometimes provide **abstracts,** or summaries, of the articles.

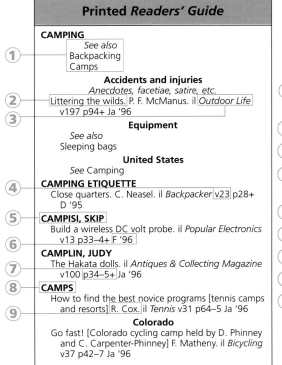

Printed *Readers' Guide*

CAMPING

① *See also*
Backpacking
Camps

Accidents and injuries
Anecdotes, facetiae, satire, etc.
② Littering the wilds. P. F. McManus. il *Outdoor Life*
③ v197 p94+ Ja '96

Equipment
See also
Sleeping bags

United States
See Camping

④ **CAMPING ETIQUETTE**
Close quarters. C. Neasel. il *Backpacker* v23 p28+
D '95

⑤ **CAMPISI, SKIP**
Build a wireless DC volt probe. il *Popular Electronics*
⑥ v13 p33–4+ F '96

CAMPLIN, JUDY
⑦ The Hakata dolls. il *Antiques & Collecting Magazine*
v100 p34–5+ Ja '96

⑧ **CAMPS**
How to find the best novice programs [tennis camps
⑨ and resorts] R. Cox. il *Tennis* v31 p64–5 Ja '96

Colorado
Go fast! [Colorado cycling camp held by D. Phinney
and C. Carpenter-Phinney] F. Matheny. il *Bicycling*
v37 p42–7 Ja '96

① Subject cross-reference
② Title of article
③ Name of magazine
④ Volume number of magazine
⑤ Author entry
⑥ Date of magazine
⑦ Page reference
⑧ Subject entry
⑨ Author of article

Result of Online Search of *Readers' Guide*

AUTHOR:	Neasel, Carla.
TITLE:	Close quarters.
SOURCE:	Backpacker v. 23 (Dec. '95) p. 28+ il.
STANDARD NO:	0277-867X
DATE:	1995
RECORD TYPE:	art
CONTENTS:	feature article
SUBJECT:	Camping etiquette.

COMPUTER NOTE: If you store the notes from your library research in a computer file, you can rearrange the notes to follow the same order as your outline. Then you won't have to search through piles of paper or to scroll through your file until you find the notes that correspond to the points you're discussing.

Special Information Sources

The *vertical file* is a special file containing up-to-date materials such as pamphlets, newspaper clippings, or government, business, and educational information.

Microforms are reduced-size photographs of pages from various publications. The two most common kinds of microforms are *microfilm* (a roll or reel of film) and *microfiche* (a sheet of film). A special projector enlarges the images to a readable size.

Many libraries use computers to research reference sources. Collections of information are stored on CD-ROMs or diskettes for easy retrieval. Some libraries are linked to *online databases.* These databases store all types of information. Libraries that are linked to the *Internet,* an international network of computers, have access to thousands of information sources. You search for a specific topic by typing a *keyword* or key phrase. Ask your librarian for help in wording your search requests and in using the Internet.

RESOURCES

LESS-ADVANCED STUDENTS

If possible, take students to the library, show them the location of the *Readers' Guide,* and explain its use. Point out authors, subjects, article and periodical titles, clarification of title meaning (in brackets), volume and page numbers, and abbreviations. Identify at least one reference to an article that is held in the library collection. Have students find the reference and then find the article.

STUDENTS WITH SPECIAL NEEDS

Learning to use reference material without prior library training will prove difficult for some students. They will need hands-on practice in the library to reinforce the instruction given in the classroom. If your time is limited, consider having students who are advanced in their research skills serve as guides to the library or as research assistants for students who might be overwhelmed by the material available.

RESOURCES

Reference Works

Most libraries devote a section entirely to reference works. These materials (books, magazines, newspapers, CD-ROMs, and databases) contain information on many subjects.

REFERENCE WORKS	
TYPE	**CONTENT DESCRIPTION**
ENCYCLOPEDIAS *Collier's Encyclopedia* *Compton's Encyclopedia* *The World Book Multimedia Encyclopedia*™	■ multiple volumes ■ articles arranged alphabetically by subject ■ contain general information ■ may have index or annuals
GENERAL BIOGRAPHICAL REFERENCES *Current Biography Yearbook* *Dictionary of American Biography* *Biography Index* (database) *Webster's New Biographical Dictionary*	■ information about birth, nationality, and major accomplishments of outstanding people
SPECIAL BIOGRAPHICAL REFERENCES *American Men & Women of Science* *Contemporary Authors*® *on CD-ROM* *Mexican American Biographies*	■ information about people noted for accomplishments in various fields or for membership in specific groups
ATLASES *Atlas of World Cultures* *National Geographic Atlas of the World*	■ maps and geographical information
ALMANACS *The Information Please Almanac, Atlas and Yearbook* *The World Almanac and Book of Facts*	■ up-to-date information about current events, facts, statistics, and dates

(continued)

REFERENCE WORKS *(continued)*	
TYPE	CONTENT DESCRIPTION
BOOKS OF QUOTATIONS Bartlett's *Familiar Quotations*	■ famous quotations indexed or grouped by subject
BOOKS OF SYNONYMS *Roget's International Thesaurus* *Webster's New Dictionary of Synonyms*	■ lists of more vivid or more exact words to express ideas
LITERARY REFERENCES *Granger's Index to Poetry* *Short Story Index* *Subject Index to Poetry*	■ information about various works of literature

Newspapers

A daily newspaper has a variety of reading materials in its various sections. Newspaper writers write for different purposes. Readers, like you, read the newspaper for purposes of your own. The following chart shows contents that you may find in a typical newspaper.

WHAT'S IN A NEWSPAPER?		
WRITER'S PURPOSE/ TYPE OF WRITING	READER'S PURPOSE	READING TECHNIQUE
to inform news stories sports	to gain knowledge or information	Ask yourself the *5W-How?* questions (page 29).
to persuade editorials comics reviews ads	to gain knowledge; to make decisions; or to be entertained	Identify points you agree or disagree with. Find facts or reasons the writer uses.
to be creative or expressive comics columns	to be entertained	Identify ways the writer interests you or gives you a new viewpoint or ideas.

RESOURCES

INTEGRATING THE LANGUAGE ARTS

Library Skills and Writing. When students are working on composition structure and focusing on main idea, they may want to include quotations in their writing for emphasis. One reference book about literature that may be very helpful is Bartlett's *Familiar Quotations.* Students can use it when they want to know the author of a quotation, the work in which a quotation appears, the complete or correct version of a partial quotation, and quotations on specific subjects by various authors. Explain to students that if they are writing papers or speeches, they can look their topics up in the index and see what published authors have had to say about their subjects.

CRITICAL THINKING

Analysis. As you study the various media available in the library, you might want to have students analyze the effects of the mass media in society. Start by having students define *media* and then have them brainstorm to discover how the mass media affect people's everyday decisions. For example, you could discuss how the various media educate, inform, persuade, entertain, and solve problems, as well as homogenize thinking and foster reliance on their authority.

RESOURCES

ANSWERS
Exercise 1

1. *Gorilla, My Love* by Toni Cade Bambara
2. "The Hakata Dolls"; *Antiques & Collecting Magazine*
3. Titles will vary.
4. atlas, encyclopedia
5. vertical file

ANSWERS
Exercise 2

1. Newspaper sections chosen will vary.
2. Students should list the article selected and answer the *5W-How?* questions about it.
3. Selections and opinions will vary.
4. Comics chosen will vary.
5. Advertisements and purchase decisions will vary.

Review

▶ EXERCISE 1 **Using the Library**

Answer the following questions to review your understanding of the library and its resources.

1. Which of the following fiction books would be shelved first: *Barrio Boy*, by Ernesto Galarza, or *Gorilla, My Love*, by Toni Cade Bambara?
2. Using the *Readers' Guide* sample on page 884, find the title of an article by Judy Camplin about Hakata dolls. What magazine printed this article?
3. Using the card catalog or online catalog, find a book about your favorite hobby. Write the title, the author's name, and the call number.
4. Tell which reference work you might use to find information about the climate and landforms of Antarctica.
5. Tell where to find a pamphlet about air pollution printed by the U.S. Environmental Protection Agency.

▶ EXERCISE 2 **Exploring the Newspaper**

Using a copy of the Sunday newspaper from home or your library, answer the following questions.

1. What part of the newspaper do you read first? Explain whether you read it for information or entertainment.
2. Find one article that gives you information about an event in world news, sports, or entertainment. In this article, find the answers to the *5W-How?* questions (*Who? What? Where? When? Why? How?*).
3. Identify the topic of an editorial or a letter to the editor on the editorial pages. Do you agree or disagree with the writer's opinion? Explain.
4. Find one comic that you think was intended to persuade you. Find another comic that you think was intended just for fun. Explain your choice.
5. Find an ad that makes you want to buy the item shown. What, in the ad, influences you most?

OBJECTIVES

- To use a dictionary to find alternate spellings, part-of-speech labels, and usage labels for words
- To use a dictionary to check for capitalization and syllabication of words

PROGRAM MANAGER

THE DICTIONARY

- **Independent Practice/ Reteaching** For additional practice and reinforcement, see **Types of Dictionaries, Pronunciation and the Dictionary, Etymologies, Usage Labels,** and **Alternate Spellings** in *Academic and Workplace Skills,* pp. 37–41.

- **Review** For exercises on chapter concepts, see **Review Form A** and **Review Form B** in *Academic and Workplace Skills,* pp. 42–45.

33 THE DICTIONARY

Types and Contents

Types of Dictionaries

There are many types of dictionaries. Each type contains different kinds of information. However, all dictionaries contain certain general features.

TYPES OF DICTIONARIES		
TYPE AND EXAMPLE	NUMBER OF WORDS	NUMBER OF PAGES
Unabridged *Webster's Third New International Dictionary*	460,000	2,662
College/Abridged *Merriam-Webster's Collegiate Dictionary, Tenth Edition*	160,000	1,600
School *The Lincoln Writing Dictionary*	35,000	932
Paperback *The Random House Dictionary*	74,000	1,056

CHAPTER OVERVIEW

This chapter briefly covers types of dictionaries and the kinds of information found in dictionaries. You could refer students to this chapter when they are revising or proofreading writing assignments.

QUICK REMINDER

Ask students to list the different ways a dictionary can be used. [Students might say that a dictionary can be used to find the proper or preferred spelling of a word; to check capitalization, syllabication, pronunciation, and usage of a word; to find the etymology or definition of a word; to find synonyms or antonyms for a word.]

RESOURCES

RESOURCES

MEETING individual NEEDS

LEP/ESL

General Strategies. English-language learners might not use some of the English sounds in their native languages. Therefore, you will need to familiarize students with the sounds that diacritical marks represent before students can use dictionaries to check pronunciation.

You may want to read the pronunciation key of the classroom dictionary into a tape recorder and to have students look at the pronunciation key as they listen to the tape. Encourage students to stop the tape periodically and to reproduce the sounds out loud.

STUDENTS WITH SPECIAL NEEDS

You may want to enlarge a less-complicated dictionary entry and to give each student a copy. If possible, reproduce the same entry on an overhead transparency. As you explain each aspect of the model entry, have students use highlighters or colored pencils to identify the different kinds of information found in the entry.

LESS-ADVANCED STUDENTS

It may be helpful to make and display a chart listing all of the abbreviations that students might encounter in dictionary entries. Include those used in etymologies and usage labels.

SELECTION AMENDMENT
Description of change: excerpted and annotated
Rationale: to focus on the content of a dictionary entry as presented in this chapter

890

A SAMPLE ENTRY

From *Webster's New World College Dictionary*, Third Edition. Copyright © 1996, 1994, 1991, 1988 by Simon & Schuster, Inc. Reprinted by permission of Macmillan USA, a Simon & Schuster Macmillan Company.

1. **Entry word.** The entry word shows the correct spelling of a word and how it is divided into syllables. The entry word may also tell whether the word is capitalized and provide alternate spellings.
2. **Pronunciation.** The pronunciation of a word is shown by the use of accent marks and either phonetic respellings or *diacritical marks* (special symbols placed above the letters). A pronunciation key is provided as a guide to diacritical marks or phonetic symbols.
3. **Part-of-speech labels.** These labels (usually in abbreviated form) indicate how the entry word should be used in a sentence. Some words may be used as more than one part of speech. In this case, a part-of-speech label is provided before each definition.
4. **Other forms.** These may show spellings of plural forms of nouns, tenses of verbs, or the comparative forms of adjectives and adverbs.
5. **Etymology.** The *etymology* is the origin and history of a word. It tells how the word (or its parts) entered the English language.

6. **Examples.** Phrases or sentences may demonstrate how the defined word is to be used.
7. **Definitions.** If there is more than one meaning, definitions are numbered or lettered.
8. **Special usage labels.** These labels identify words that have special meanings or are used in special ways in certain situations.
9. **Related word forms.** These are alternate forms of the entry word, usually created by adding suffixes or prefixes.
10. **Synonyms and antonyms.** Sometimes synonyms and antonyms are listed at the end of a word entry.

COMPUTER NOTE: A spell-checking program highlights unfamiliar letter combinations, often finding proper nouns and special terms. Some programs allow you to add words and thus create your own user dictionary.

Review

▶ EXERCISE 1   **Finding Alternate Spellings for Words**

Use your dictionary to find an alternate spelling for each of the following words. Tell if one spelling is <u>preferred</u> or more common. **Answers may vary according to the dictionary used. These are from *Webster's New World College Dictionary*, Third Edition.**

1. <u>anapest</u> **1.** anapaest
2. <u>abridgment</u> **2.** abridgement
3. <u>likable</u> **3.** likeable
4. <u>savior</u> **4.** saviour
5. ameba **5.** <u>amoeba</u>

▶ EXERCISE 2   **Using the Dictionary to Check for Capitalization**

Look up the following words in a dictionary and explain when they are and are not capitalized. Your dictionary may not give capitalized uses for all the words.

RESOURCES

ANSWERS
Exercise 2

Answers may vary according to the dictionary used. These are from *Webster's New World College Dictionary*, Third Edition:

1. *Cupid*—Roman god of love; *cupid*—a representation of Cupid as a winged cherub
2. *West*—the western part of a continent or country, the part of a church opposite the altar, or any usage following *the; west*—the direction to the left of a person facing north
3. *Revolutionary*—of the American Revolution; *revolutionary*—of a revolution in a government, or bringing about great change
4. *Senate*—the upper house of the U.S. legislature, a similar body in other countries, the governing council in a college or university, or the building where a senate meets; *senate*—a council of elders, the supreme council of the ancient Roman state, or a lawmaking assembly
5. *Democrat*—a member of the Democratic Party; *democrat*—one who believes in government by the people

RESOURCES

EXERCISE 3

Teaching Note. You may want to explain to students that some dictionaries indicate where a word can and cannot be acceptably divided at the end of a line. For example, the vertical lines in the second and fifth words indicate places where the words should not be divided at the ends of lines. Encourage students to check their classroom dictionaries for such information.

INTEGRATING THE LANGUAGE ARTS

Literature Link. If the selection is available in your library or literature textbook, have students read and discuss an excerpt from "Flowers for Algernon" by Daniel Keyes. Then have them use dictionaries to correct the misspelled words in one of Charlie's progress reports.

When students have completed the proofreading exercise, discuss how the misspelled words contribute to the effect of the story. [The misspellings help to illustrate Charlie's mental handicap, and the improvements in spelling over time illustrate the effectiveness of Charlie's treatments.]

COOPERATIVE LEARNING

Divide the class into groups of three, and have each group create a dictionary of slang words. (If the members of a group have a common interest—a sport or hobby—they might want to create a dictionary of jargon specific to that interest.) You will probably want to specify the number of entries and the type of information needed in each entry. Encourage creativity (illustrations, a clever cover, or an unusual format).

1. cupid
2. west
3. revolutionary
4. senate
5. democrat

▶ EXERCISE 3   **Dividing Words into Syllables**

Divide the following words into syllables. Use the same method to show syllable division that your dictionary uses.   Answers may vary according to the dictionary used.
These are from *Webster's New World College Dictionary,* Third Edition.

1. endurance   **1.** en·dur·ance
2. underdog   **2.** un|der·dog
3. junior   **3.** jun·ior
4. socialize   **4.** so·cial·ize
5. flexible   **5.** flex·i|ble

▶ EXERCISE 4   **Finding Part-of-Speech Labels**

Look up each of the following words in a dictionary. Give all the parts of speech listed for each word.
n. = noun   v. = verb   adj. = adjective   adv. = adverb

1. fuss   **1.** n./v.
2. incline   **2.** v./n.
3. corner   **3.** n./v./adj.
4. smooth   **4.** adj./v./adv./n.
5. smirk   **5.** v./n.

▶ EXERCISE 5   **Finding Usage Labels**   Answers may vary according to the dictionary used.
These are from *Webster's New World College Dictionary,* Third Edition.

If your college or unabridged dictionary lists special usage labels for entry words, look up the following words. Write the usage label(s) given for the word or for any of its meanings. If your dictionary has no labels, write *none.*

1. noise   **1.** colloquial/electronics/ now rare
2. glitzy   **2.** colloquial
3. quarter   **3.** astronomy/football/basketball/soccer/ heraldry/nautical/mechanics
4. mixture   **4.** chemistry
5. dude   **5.** western slang/slang

OBJECTIVES

- To define words by using context clues
- To select synonyms to complete sentences
- To select antonyms for specific words
- To define words by using roots, prefixes, and suffixes
- To add suffixes to words

PROGRAM MANAGER

VOCABULARY

- **Independent Practice/ Reteaching** For additional practice and reinforcement, see **Context Clues, Using Context Clues, Multiple Meanings in Dictionary Entries, Synonyms and Antonyms, Base Words and Prefixes, Base Words and Suffixes,** and **Learning New Words** in *Academic and Workplace Skills,* pp. 49–56.

- **Reinforcement/Reteaching** For additional instruction and exercises, see **Vocabulary Masters 1–10** in *Practice for Assessment in Reading, Vocabulary, and Spelling,* pp. 11–20.

- **Review** For exercises on chapter concepts, see **Review Form A** and **Review Form B** in *Academic and Workplace Skills,* pp. 57–60.

34 VOCABULARY

Learning and Using New Words

You probably encounter many new words every day through conversations, the media, class discussions, and your readings. To acquire a large vocabulary, you should try to recognize clues to the meanings of unfamiliar words. Learning the meanings of frequently used word parts is also helpful in building your vocabulary. By practicing methods shown in this chapter, you can increase your knowledge of words and expand your vocabulary.

Developing a Word Bank

An effective way to increase your vocabulary is by starting a word bank. When you encounter an unfamiliar word, enter the word and its definition in a section of your notebook. Then, write a sentence or phrase to illustrate how each word is used. Check the definition and pronunciation of an unfamiliar word in your dictionary.

CHAPTER OVERVIEW

This chapter discusses the concepts of context clues, synonyms, antonyms, word roots, prefixes, and suffixes as tools students can use to increase their vocabularies. Because the exercises require students to use dictionaries, you may want to review the information on looking up words in **Chapter 33: "The Dictionary."**

RESOURCES

RESOURCES

COMPUTER NOTE: You can also create a vocabulary file on your computer. Add new words to the end of the file. Then, use your word-processing program's Sort command to arrange the words in alphabetical order.

QUICK REMINDER

Give students practice using context clues by writing the following sentences on the chalkboard and asking students to guess the meaning of each underlined word. Have students share their definitions and explain which sentence clues helped them determine their answers.

1. Roaring with excitement, the <u>exuberant</u> crowd cheered as the defensive end intercepted the pass and scored the winning touchdown. [*Exuberant* means "high-spirited"; *excitement, cheered,* and *winning touchdown* are clues.]

2. Because she was uncertain about getting her mother's permission to go to the party, Rhea's acceptance was <u>tentative</u>. [*Tentative* means "not firmly decided"; *uncertain* is the clue.]

MEETING *individual* NEEDS

STUDENTS WITH SPECIAL NEEDS

To help students recognize context clues, give them copies of the example sentences from the **Using Context Clues** chart and the sentences from **Exercise 1.** Have students bracket and highlight the context clues in the sentences. You could guide students through this process in a few of the sentences. Then have students work independently on the rest as you circulate to offer assistance.

Learning New Words from Context

Most of the words you encounter are used in combination with other words. The *context* of a word means the words that surround it in a sentence and the whole situation in which the word is used. These surrounding words often provide valuable clues to meaning. Context clues provide meaning in a variety of ways.

USING CONTEXT CLUES	
TYPE OF CLUE	**EXPLANATION**
Definitions and restatements	Look for words that define the term or restate it in other words. • Toshio's ambition is to *circumnavigate* —or sail around—the world.
Examples	Look for examples used in context that reveal the meaning of an unfamiliar word. • People use all sorts of *conveyances* such as cars, bicycles, rickshaws, airplanes, boats, and space shuttles.
Comparisons	Look for clues that indicate an unfamiliar word is similar to a familiar word or phrase. • Those *glaciers* were like huge ice cubes.
Contrast	Look for clues that indicate an unfamiliar word is opposite in meaning to a familiar word or phrase. • Don has become quite *apprehensive,* unlike Irene, who has always been easygoing.
Cause and effect	Look for clues that indicate an unfamiliar word is related to the cause or the result of an action, feeling, or idea. • Because the clouds looked *foreboding,* we decided to cancel the picnic.

Choosing the Right Word

Since many words have several meanings, you must look at *all* the definitions given for a word. When you meet an unfamiliar word, think about its context. Then, determine the definition that best fits the context.

Some dictionaries include sample contexts to indicate a word's various meanings. Compare the sample contexts given in the dictionary with the context of a new word to make sure you've found the meaning that fits.

Synonyms and Antonyms

A *synonym* is a word that means nearly the same thing as another word. However, words that are synonyms rarely have *exactly* the same meaning. Two words may have the same **denotation,** or dictionary definition, but different **connotations,** or suggested meanings.

The dictionary may list several synonyms for a word. To help you distinguish between synonyms, some dictionaries give **synonym articles**—brief explanations of a word's synonyms and how they differ in meaning. The more often you meet a word in different contexts, the better you will be able to determine its meaning.

The **antonym** of a word is a word with the opposite meaning. Knowing the antonym of a word will often help you understand the first word's meaning. A dictionary sometimes lists antonyms at the end of a word entry.

Using Word Parts

English words can be classified into two main groups: those that cannot be divided into parts and those that can. Words that cannot be divided into parts are called **base words.** *Plate, grind,* and *large* are examples of base words.

CRITICAL THINKING

Analysis. Frequently, students learn new words from context in song lyrics. Have students work in pairs to write down song lyrics they know. Then tell students to analyze the lyrics for new vocabulary words. (Remind students that the lyrics should be appropriate for use in the classroom.) You may want to have students bring tapes to class to share examples of word meanings inferred from context in songs.

COMMON ERROR

Problem. Students might use general, imprecise words in their writing.

Solution. Organize students into groups of three or four with varying levels of ability in each group. Have them use dictionaries and thesauruses to brainstorm lists of synonyms for the words *said, great,* and *a lot.* You could also have students make lists for other words. After lists are completed, each student should make a copy to refer to when writing.

INTEGRATING THE LANGUAGE ARTS

Literature Link. Edgar Allan Poe's style in "The Raven" is marked by his control of atmosphere and tone. One element contributing to the dark, foreboding atmosphere is Poe's use of words that are rich in connotations.

If your literature textbook contains it, have students read "The Raven" to identify and evaluate Poe's word choice in creating the somber, frightening tone. You may want to discuss the differences in "midnight dreary" and another phrase with a similar denotation, such as "dark night." Have students read the poem aloud to better identify imagery rich in connotation.

MEETING individual NEEDS

LEP/ESL

General Strategies. If English-language learners have very limited English vocabularies, you may want to order *The Oxford Picture Dictionary* and workbook. The book presents colorful illustrations of 2,400 words in scenes where they are most likely to occur. Editions come in English/English or English and one other language: Spanish, Chinese, Japanese, Korean, Vietnamese, Cambodian, or Navajo.

896

---

896 *Vocabulary*

Words that can be divided into parts, like *overhear, reception,* and *denial,* are made up of **word parts.** The three types of word parts are

- roots
- prefixes
- suffixes

The **root** is the foundation a word is built on. It carries the word's core meaning, and prefixes and suffixes are added to it. A **prefix** is added before a root; a **suffix** is added after a root. For example, in the word *inflexible, in–* is the prefix, *–flex–* is the root, and *–ible* is the suffix.

WORD	PREFIX	ROOT	SUFFIX
predictable	pre–	–dict–	–able
interpersonal	inter–	–person–	–al
disagreement	dis–	–agree–	–ment

Knowing the meanings of word parts can help you figure out the meanings of many unfamiliar words.

COMMONLY USED PREFIXES		
PREFIXES	MEANINGS	EXAMPLES
anti–	against, opposing	antiwar, anticlimax
bi–	two	bimonthly, bilingual
co–	with, together	coexist, codependent
de–	away, from, off, down	debone, debug
extra–	beyond, outside	extralegal, extraordinary
fore–	before, front part of	forehead, foreshadow
hyper–	over, excessive	hypercritical, hypersensitive
inter–	between, among	interpersonal, interact
mis–	badly, not, wrongly	misbehave, misfortune
non–	not	nonprofit, nonsense
over–	above, excessive	overstate, overhead
post–	after, following	postwar, postgraduate
pre–	before	prepayment, preexist

(continued)

COMMONLY USED PREFIXES *(continued)*		
PREFIXES	MEANINGS	EXAMPLES
re—	back, again	rebuild, reclaim
semi—	half, partly	semiannual, semiprecious
sub—	under, beneath	submarine, substandard
trans—	across, beyond	transplant, transpacific
un—	not, reverse of	unlock, uneven

 REFERENCE NOTE: For guidelines on spelling when adding prefixes, see page 802.

COMMONLY USED SUFFIXES		
SUFFIXES	MEANINGS	EXAMPLES
NOUNS		
—ance, —ancy	act, quality	admittance, constancy
—ence	act, condition	conference, excellence
—ity	state, condition	reality, sincerity
—ment	result, action	judgment, fulfillment
—tion	action, condition	rotation, selection
—ty	quality, state	safety, certainty
VERBS		
—ate	become, cause	captivate, activate
—en	make, become	deepen, soften
—fy	make, cause	identify, simplify
—ize	make, cause to be	socialize, motorize
ADJECTIVES		
—able	able, likely	readable, lovable
—esque	in the style of, like	picturesque, statuesque
—ible	able, likely	flexible, digestible
—ous	characterized by	dangerous, furious
ADVERB		
—ly	in a (certain) way	urgently, rigidly

REFERENCE NOTE: For guidelines on spelling when adding suffixes, see pages 802–805.

MEETING *individual* NEEDS

LEARNING STYLES

Kinetic Learners. Have each student make four note cards in each of three different categories: prefixes, suffixes, and base words or word roots. Have students color-code the cards—for example, blue for prefixes, green for suffixes, and red for base words and word roots.

Students can find suffixes and prefixes in the lists in the textbook. Base words and word roots can be found by looking up specific prefixes in dictionaries. The prefixes will always be attached to something, and that something will usually be a base word or word root.

Next, have students combine their cards to see how many words they can create. Have them make lists of their combinations. Finally, have students check in dictionaries to see how many of their combinations are actually words.

TIMESAVER

To save time grading papers, have students exchange and check each other's papers as you go over the answers to the exercises with the whole class.

TECHNOLOGY TIP

If students have access to word-processing software with an electronic dictionary, they can check the denotations of the words in **Exercise 2** more quickly.

ANSWERS
Exercise 2

Answers may vary. Have students write the definition for each synonym, and have them explain why they feel the connotation of each word they chose is the most appropriate for the sentence.

Review

▶ EXERCISE 1   **Using Context Clues**

Use context clues to choose the word or phrase that best fits the meaning of each italicized word.

a. drinks
b. lack of concern
c. knowledge
d. drifter
e. kindness
f. transformation
g. myths
h. someone who starts a business

1. Leslie Marmon Silko uses Native American *lore,* or teachings, in her writing.   **1. c**   **2. e**
2. We should encourage *compassion* rather than cruelty.
3. They have a variety of *beverages,* such as milk, juice, iced tea, and water.   **3. a**
4. Jim Bob's *metamorphosis* was so complete that we barely recognized him.   **4. f**
5. Since Pilar disliked working for others, she decided to become an *entrepreneur.*   **5. h**

▶ EXERCISE 2   **Selecting Synonyms to Complete Sentences**

For each sentence below, write the synonym you have selected that best fits the sentence. Use a dictionary to learn the exact meaning of each synonym.

1. My black jacket is made of a new (*fabricated, imitation, synthetic*) material.
2. Some medieval artists had a special (*fashion, technique, system*) for making stained-glass windows.
3. Although the lawyer stayed within the law, she relied on (*guile, trickery, fraud*) to win the case.
4. Under the new government, many of the citizens were (*robbed, deprived, dismantled*) of their rights.
5. You can imagine how (*ridiculous, shaming, humiliating*) it was to drop my tray of food in the cafeteria line.

EXERCISE 3   **Selecting Antonyms for Specific Words**

For each numbered word below, write the letter of the correct antonym. Use a dictionary if necessary.

1. frustrate	1. d	a. tiny	
2. contemptible	2. h	b. dawn	
3. colossal	3. a	c. ornamental	
4. impertinent	4. g	d. satisfy	
5. upbraid	5. j	e. wordiness	
6. twilight	6. b	f. biased	
7. brevity	7. e	g. courteous	
8. neutral	8. f	h. admirable	
9. functional	9. c	i. orderly	
10. random	10. i	j. praise	

EXERCISE 4   **Using Prefixes to Define Words**

For each of the following words, give the prefix used and its meaning. Then give the meaning of the whole word. Use a dictionary if necessary.

1. biannual   1. *bi* – (two)   6. transatlantic   6. *trans* – (across)
2. misfire   2. *mis* – (wrongly)   7. interstate   7. *inter* – (between, among)
3. antiviral   3. *anti* – (against)   8. postnatal   8. *post* – (after)
4. preheat   4. *pre* – (before)   9. deform   9. *de* – (away from, down)
5. nondairy   5. *non* – (not)   10. subnormal   10. *sub* – (under)

EXERCISE 5   **Adding Suffixes to Words**

Add the suffix in parentheses to each of the following words. Then give the meaning of the new word and its part of speech. Use a dictionary if necessary. [Hint: The spelling of some words changes when a suffix is added.]   n. = noun   v. = verb   adj. = adjective

1. appease (*–ment*)   1. n.   6. defense (*–ible*)   6. adj.
2. Roman (*–esque*)   2. adj.   7. envy (*–ous*)   7. adj.
3. change (*–able*)   3. adj.   8. haste (*–en*)   8. v.
4. civil (*–ize*)   4. v.   9. defy (*–ance*)   9. n.
5. beauty (*–fy*)   5. v.   10. employ (*–able*)   10. adj.

RESOURCES

ANSWERS
Exercise 4

Definitions of words will vary. Here are some possibilities:
1. twice a year
2. to fail to ignite properly
3. able to stop the growth of a virus
4. to heat beforehand
5. containing no milk
6. crossing or spanning the Atlantic
7. between or among states
8. immediately after birth
9. to impair the form of
10. below normal

ANSWERS
Exercise 5

Definitions of words will vary according to the dictionary used. Here are some possibilities:
1. appeasement—the policy of giving in to demands of an aggressive power to keep the peace
2. Romanesque—style of architecture, painting, sculpture, and so forth based on the Roman style
3. changeable—able to be changed
4. civilize—to refine habits or manners
5. beautify—to adorn or make beautiful
6. defensible—able to be defended, protected, or justified
7. envious—characterized by envy
8. hasten—to become faster, accelerate
9. defiance—the act of resisting authority
10. employable—able to be employed

RESOURCES

899

PROGRAM MANAGER

LETTERS AND FORMS

■ **Independent Practice/ Reteaching** For additional practice and reinforcement, see **Addressing an Envelope, Informal Letters, The Parts of a Business Letter, The Request or Order Letter, The Complaint or Adjustment Letter,** and **Filling Out Forms** in *Academic and Workplace Skills,* pp. 63–68.

■ **Review** For exercises on chapter concepts, see **Review Form A** and **Review Form B** in *Academic and Workplace Skills,* pp. 69–72.

CHAPTER OVERVIEW

This chapter covers informal or personal letters, and it also explains the parts of a business letter and the correct way to address envelopes. Types of business letters presented include the request or order letter, the complaint or adjustment letter, and the appreciation or commendation letter. The discussion of tone in **How to Write Effective Business Letters** integrates with the skills developed in **Chapter 12: "English: Origins and Uses."**

QUICK REMINDER

Draw the outlines of an envelope and a piece of stationery on the chalkboard. Have students give you directions for filling in the envelope address and arranging the parts of a letter.

Have the class tell you what material to include, where to place it, and how to punctuate it. If necessary, review this information.

RESOURCES

RESOURCES

35 LETTERS AND FORMS

Style and Contents

The personal letters you write are an important way of communicating to others your ideas, updates on events in your life, or your feelings. You may also need to write occasional business letters or to fill out printed forms. For each of these, you can improve your effectiveness in communicating if you follow a few simple guidelines.

Addressing an Envelope

Whether you're writing a personal letter or a business letter, you'll need to address an envelope. On your envelope, put your own address in the top left-hand corner. Place the name and address of the person to whom you are writing in the center of the envelope. Make sure all addresses are correct and include ZIP Codes. Use standard two-letter postal abbreviations for states, such as *IA* for Iowa and *NM* for New Mexico.

COMPUTER NOTE: Most word-processing programs have standard document styles from which to choose. Many programs allow you to create a custom style that you can store and use again.

Writing Informal or Personal Letters

Sometimes an informal letter is the best way to communicate a personal message. Informal or personal letters may include thank-you letters, invitations, or letters of regret.

Thank-you Letters. These are letters that you send to tell someone that you appreciate his or her taking time, trouble, or expense to do something for you. Always respond promptly, and try to say something in your letter in addition to thanking the person. You might mention that you are aware of the person's effort, or tell why the person's gift is special to you.

Invitations. In an informal invitation, include specific information about the occasion, the time and place, and any other special details your guest might need to know (such as that everyone is expected to bring a friend, dress casually, or donate food).

Regrets. A letter of regret is written to inform someone that you will not be able to accept an invitation. You should especially respond in writing to invitations that include the letters *R.S.V.P.* (in French, an abbreviation for "please reply").

Writing Business Letters

The Appearance of a Business Letter

- Use unlined $8\frac{1}{2}'' \times 11''$ paper.
- Type your letter if possible (single-spaced, leaving an extra line between paragraphs). Otherwise, neatly write the letter by hand, using black or blue ink. Check for typing errors and misspellings.
- Center your letter on the paper with equal margins on the sides and at the top and bottom.

RESOURCES

MEETING *individual* NEEDS

LEP/ESL

General Strategies. Many English-language learners will need extra practice with the abbreviations used in addresses because the terms will be unfamiliar to them. You might make a reference chart with common abbreviations. Include both the long and short abbreviations for states and abbreviations for address words, titles, and company names. Explain how each is used on an envelope and in a letter.

STUDENTS WITH SPECIAL NEEDS

Some students might have difficulty visualizing the standard forms and components of each of the different types of letters. Before teaching this chapter, collect examples of different types of letters. Use names of real people and familiar places to arouse students' interest. Provide copies in handbook form, or display them on a poster. Discuss similarities and differences in the letters. Have writing paper and envelopes available so students can practice their skills.

A DIFFERENT APPROACH

Once students have mastered personal-letter format, you may want to encourage them to be creative. They can design thank-you notes and invitations with colored pens by drawing pictures and designs for the cards. This activity may appeal particularly to visual learners. Encourage students to write and create their own letters and cards.

RESOURCES

LESS-ADVANCED STUDENTS

You may want to teach only one type of business letter to less-advanced students. If you choose to teach the letter of request, you could find out what reports students are writing in their other classes and help them send letters for any information they need.

ADVANCED STUDENTS

Students could combine their persuasive abilities with their letter-writing skills by writing letters to the editor. Have students use the **Framework for a Persuasive Paper** on p. 275 to plan their letters. Emphasize the need to use an acceptable form and a respectful tone in the letter.

- Use only one side of the paper. If your letter won't fit on one page, leave a one-inch margin at the bottom of the first page, and carry over at least two lines onto the second page.

These guidelines apply whether you are writing a personal letter to a business or are writing a letter as a workplace employee.

The Parts of a Business Letter

The six parts of a business letter are

    (1) the heading
    (2) the inside address
    (3) the salutation
    (4) the body
    (5) the closing
    (6) the signature

Block Style

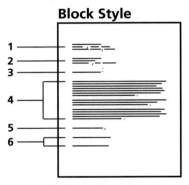

The six parts of a business letter are usually arranged on the page in one of two styles. In the *block form* of a business letter, every part of the letter begins at the left margin, and paragraphs are not indented. In the *modified block form*, the heading, the closing, and your signature are placed to the right of the center of the page. However, the other parts of the letter begin at the left margin, and paragraphs are indented.

Modified Block Style

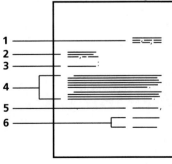

The Heading. The heading usually has three lines:

- your street address
- your city, state, and ZIP Code
- the date the letter was written

The Inside Address. The inside address gives the name and address of the person or company you are writing. If you're directing your letter to someone by name, use a courtesy title (such as *Mr., Ms.,* or *Mrs.*) or a professional title (such as *Dr.* or *Professor*) in front of the person's name. After the person's name, include the person's business title.

The Salutation. The salutation is your greeting. If you are writing to a specific person, begin with *Dear,* followed by a courtesy title or a professional title and the person's name.

The Body. The body is the main part of your letter. This is where you state your message. If your letter contains more than one paragraph, leave a blank line between paragraphs.

The Closing. You should end your letter politely. To close a business letter, use a standard phrase such as *Sincerely, Yours truly,* or *Respectfully yours.*

The Signature. Sign your name in ink below the closing. Type or print your name neatly just below your signature.

HOW TO WRITE EFFECTIVE BUSINESS LETTERS

- *Use a polite, respectful, professional tone.* A courteous letter is much more effective than a rude one.
- *Use standard English.* Avoid slang, contractions, and abbreviations. Informal language that might be acceptable in a telephone conversation or personal letter is not usually acceptable for a business letter.
- *Get to the point.* State the reason for your letter clearly and promptly. Be polite, but don't ramble.
- *Include all necessary information.* Be sure your reader can understand why you wrote and what you are asking.

RESOURCES

COOPERATIVE LEARNING
Organize the class into pairs for letter writing. Assign each pair a topic for a business or an informal letter. Some possibilities include a personal letter describing the interests of the writers to a class in another state, a business letter suggesting television programming changes, a business letter explaining why an old product is better than the company's newer version, and a personal letter to a visiting team explaining how to locate the school gym. After students have finished, have the pairs exchange letters and write letters in response to the first letters.

When students write business letters to request information from several sources, they can simplify the task by using computers. Many word-processing programs have well-designed business letter templates included. Students need only type in the correct information. They could further simplify the operation by planning the bodies of their letters with all the different recipients in mind. Then, they could change the inside address and salutation for each letter. Remind students to proofread each letter carefully and to use the preview command, if available, to see how the letter will look.

A DIFFERENT APPROACH

To discuss uses of business letters, ask students to describe on slips of paper specific situations that call for business letters. Choose several interesting suggestions and discuss them with the class.

Types of Business Letters

The Request or Order Letter

In a request letter, you write to ask for information about a product or service or to request sample materials. In an order letter, you ask for something specific, such as a free brochure advertised in a magazine or an item of merchandise that is listed in a catalog when you don't have a printed order form.

Here is the body of a sample request letter. The writer is asking a state tourism board to send travel information.

> My family is planning a two-week vacation in Wyoming in July. We'd like to visit Yellowstone National Park, Jackson Lake, and Grand Teton National Park. Please send me any information—free brochures, pamphlets, or maps—that might help us on the trip. We would be interested in any information about attractions, such as museums or natural rock or cavern formations, that lie on our route.
>
> We'll be driving down from Bozeman in a large camper, so we would also appreciate a list of campsites and fees.

When you are writing a request or order letter, remember the following points.

1. Clearly state your request.
2. If you are requesting information, enclose a self-addressed, stamped envelope.
3. Make your request well in advance of the time you need it.
4. If you want to order something, include all important information. Give the size, color, brand name, or any other specific information. If there are costs involved, add the amount correctly.

The Complaint or Adjustment Letter

If an error has been made or you have a specific complaint, you may write a complaint or adjustment letter.

Here is the body of a sample adjustment letter.

---

387 Mountain Lane
Bozeman, MT 59715
May 25, 1998

Vargas Pool Supply
600 West Main, Suite 100
Cheyenne, WY 82001

Dear Sir or Madam:

    On April 30, I ordered a pair of green, heavy-duty swim fins with adjustable straps. In your spring catalog, these fins are item number 820. This morning, however, I received a big, yellow, inflatable sea serpent, which I am returning to you. Please exchange the sea serpent for the swim fins.
    Thank you for your help.

        Sincerely yours,

        Paula Kotran

        Paula Kotran

When you are writing a complaint or adjustment letter, remember these points.

1. Register your complaint as soon as possible.
2. Be sure to mention specifics. Necessary details might include the following:
   - why you are unhappy (with the product or service)
   - how you were affected (lost time or money)
   - what solution you believe will correct the problem
3. Keep the tone of your letter calm and courteous.

CRITICAL THINKING

Evaluation. You may want to collect a variety of business letters to show on an overhead projector. Have students evaluate the letters using the guidelines in **How to Write Effective Business Letters** on p. 903.

COMMON ERROR

Problem. Students may have difficulty achieving the correct tone in their business letters.

Solution. Emphasize to students that most business letters will be received by busy people who need straightforward but complete presentations of the writers' intentions. Tell the students to pretend they work in the order or complaint department of the businesses they wrote to and that they are now the recipients of the letters. Then have them read over and revise their letters with this opposite perspective in mind.

RESOURCES

RESOURCES

INTEGRATING THE LANGUAGE ARTS

Literature Link. Writing a letter by assuming the role of a character in a story can help students relate personally to literature. One popular literary theme is personal transformation. Ask each student to think of a novel or story that shows a character who changes, to pretend to be that character, and to write a letter to another character in the story explaining the transformation. For example, a student who has read Charles Dickens's *A Christmas Carol* could pretend to be Scrooge and could write a letter to Bob Cratchit to explain his changed feelings and beliefs.

COMPLETING PRINTED FORMS

You may want to assemble a folder of forms for your students. You could include camp enrollments, job applications, magazine subscriptions, surveys, order blanks, school forms, contest entries, driver's license applications, social security card applications, and even test forms. Have copies available for students to complete. Discuss unique formats and special requests. (Often forms require unusual date or name placements or use specialized vocabulary.)

The Appreciation or Commendation Letter

You write an appreciation or commendation letter to express appreciation, gratitude, or praise for a person, group, or organization. State exactly why you are pleased.

Here is the body of a sample appreciation letter.

> I am writing this letter to thank all of you at the Water Control Board for your help with our team project. The information we gained firsthand on our tour of the facilities was very helpful to our research efforts.
>
> We realize how busy you are with the duties of your work, so the time and patience you gave to our group is sincerely appreciated.
>
> Thanks again for all your help.

Completing Printed Forms

Printed forms differ. However, if you follow a few standard guidelines, you should be able to fill out most forms accurately and completely.

HOW TO FILL OUT FORMS

1. Look over the entire form before you begin.
2. Take note of any special instructions, such as "Please print clearly," or "Use a pencil."
3. Read each item carefully.
4. Supply all the information requested. You may want to indicate that some information requested does not apply to you. In this case, you might use a dash or the symbol N/A, which means "not applicable."
5. When you're finished, proofread your form to make sure you didn't leave any blanks. Also, check for errors and correct them neatly.

Review

▶ EXERCISE 1 **Writing an Informal Letter**

Write an informal letter for one of the following situations, or make up your own situation.

1. You're recovering from the flu. Your friend bought you a book of jokes to read and dropped it off along with your homework assignments.
2. You have been invited to a classmate's going-away party but cannot attend because you will be out of town with your family.
3. You are planning a surprise birthday party for your best friend. Write an invitation letter that includes all the information your guests will need to know.

▶ EXERCISE 2 **Writing a Business Letter**

Write a business letter for one of the situations below and address an envelope for your letter. Make up any details you may need to complete your letter. (Do not mail the letter.)

1. You'd like to order a video game from Computer Games, Inc., 104 Centre Street, Seattle, Washington 98109. The catalog description of the game is too brief, and you want a complete description before you place an order. Make up a name for the video game, or use a brand name you know.
2. Write a letter to the editor of your local newspaper complaining about the lack of news coverage about a recent community event. Explain why you think the newspaper should have covered the event and how this problem can be avoided in the future.
3. Write a letter of appreciation or commendation to a school official or community leader, expressing your thanks for a job well done.

ANSWERS
Exercise 1

Answers will vary.

Students should follow the guidelines for the types of letters they have chosen and include information relevant to the situations. If students choose to make up their own situations, you might have them include short notes to you describing the purposes of their letters.

ANSWERS
Exercise 2

Letters will vary. However, the parts of the letter should follow the placement guidelines for one of the two styles of business letters (the block form or the modified block form). The tone should be professional and polite. The writer should use standard English, get to the point quickly, and include all necessary information. Letters should include details relevant to the situation. Envelopes should be legible, and the information should be complete and placed correctly.

RESOURCES

RESOURCES

36 READING, STUDYING, AND TEST TAKING

Using Skills and Strategies

Good grades are usually the result of good reading skills and efficient study habits. In this chapter are strategies for making your reading, studying, and test-taking skills more effective. These strategies will help you earn better grades, finish homework on time, and be prepared for tests—without agony the night before.

Planning a Study Routine

Be realistic when you schedule your study time, and stick to your plan. Here are some suggestions:

1. *Know your assignments.* Write down the assignments you have and their due dates. Be sure you understand the instructions for each assignment.
2. *Make a plan.* Break large assignments into small steps. Keep track of when you should be finished with each step.
3. *Concentrate when you study.* Select an appropriate time and a place where you can focus your attention only on your assignment.

LESSON 1 *(pp. 909–924)*

IMPROVING READING AND STUDY SKILLS

OBJECTIVES

- To choose appropriate reading rates
- To apply the SQ3R method
- To analyze details in a passage
- To draw conclusions and to make inferences

Improving Reading and Study Skills

Reading and Understanding

If you read with a purpose, you will find it much easier to remember what you read. Three of the most common purposes for reading are

- to find specific details
- to find main ideas
- to understand and remember

As you read different materials, adjust your rate of reading to suit your purpose.

READING RATES ACCORDING TO PURPOSE		
READING RATE	PURPOSE	EXAMPLE
Scanning	Reading for specific information or details	Looking for poems written by Hispanic authors in your literature book
Skimming	Reading for main points or important ideas	Reviewing chapters in your science book for key concepts the night before a test
Reading for mastery	Reading closely to understand and remember	Reading a chapter in your history book in order to write a report on the material

Writing to Learn

Writing can help you in the process of learning. You can use your writing to help you organize your thoughts, analyze a problem, record your observations, and plan your work. The following chart shows some of the ways that writing can help you learn.

PROGRAM MANAGER

IMPROVING READING AND STUDY SKILLS

- **Independent Practice/ Reteaching** For additional instruction and exercises, see **Scanning and Skimming, Keeping a Learning Log, Using SQ3R, Reading for the Main Idea, Identifying Relations Among Details, Drawing Conclusions, Analyzing a Graph, Taking Notes, Outlines, Paraphrases,** and **Summaries** in *Academic and Workplace Skills,* pp. 75–85.

 QUICK REMINDER

Write the following categories on the chalkboard:

1. a magazine
2. a novel
3. a chapter in a textbook
4. a catalogue
5. a driver's manual

Have students identify the purpose for reading each of these types of materials. Then have students tell which reading method they would use with each category: scanning, skimming, or reading for mastery. [Answers will vary according to students' purposes.]

RESOURCES

RESOURCES

- To interpret graphic information
- To analyze personal note-taking methods
- To identify classifications
- To apply visual organization
- To paraphrase a poem

LEP/ESL

General Strategies. Unless students are provided hands-on experience with word-processing programs, the information under **Using Word-Processing Tools for Writing** will be largely irrelevant. A field trip either to the school's computer lab or to a nearby facility (perhaps a community college) will prove invaluable. Students should be guided individually through the simple procedure of opening a new file and naming it, creating a short document and saving it, and printing out a hard copy.

TECHNOLOGY TIP

For prewriting on computers, have students try invisible writing. Before they begin, have them turn down the brightness knobs until letters no longer appear on the screen. This will enable students to enter ideas freely without thinking about grammar, usage, or mechanics. After they enter their ideas in this way, students can go back and revise.

TYPE OF WRITING	PURPOSE	EXAMPLE
Freewriting	To help you focus your thoughts	Writing for two minutes to plan an essay for a take-home test
Autobiographies	To help you examine important events in your life	Writing about an event that showed you the value of a good friend
Diaries	To help you recall your impressions and feelings	Writing about your reaction to an idea in your textbook
Journals and Learning Logs	To help you record your observations, ideas, descriptions, solutions, and questions	Jotting down a few questions to raise during a class discussion of an assigned reading
	To help you define or analyze information, or to propose a solution	Recording your findings as you conduct a science experiment

Using Word-Processing Tools for Writing

A word processor or a computer word-processing program can help you plan, draft, and edit your writing. These tools can make every step of the writing process easier.

Prewriting.   Your rough notes, ideas, or outlines can be revised without having to be copied or retyped.

Writing First Drafts.   You can write, revise, and rearrange as often as you want. At any time, you can use the printer to produce a hard copy, or printout.

Evaluating.   You can make "What if?" revisions. Just save a copy of your document and type in your changes. If you don't like the revisions, you still have the original.

Revising. You can easily make changes and print clean copies without having to repeat steps.

Proofreading. Some word processors have a spell-checking feature, and some even have features that evaluate sentence structure and punctuation.

Publishing. Publishing is easy to do with a word processor. It's simple to print a final copy or even multiple copies with your printer.

Using the SQ3R Reading Method

SQ3R is the name of a reading method developed by an educational psychologist, Francis Robinson. The SQ3R reading method includes five simple steps.

S *Survey* the entire study assignment. Glance quickly at the headings, subheadings, terms printed in boldface and in italics, and all charts, outlines, illustrations, and summaries.

Q *Question* yourself. Make a list of questions that you want to be able to answer after you have read the selection.

R *Read* the material carefully to find answers to your questions. Take notes as you read.

R *Recite* in your own words answers to each question.

R *Review* the material by rereading quickly, looking over your questions, and recalling the answers.

You can use the SQ3R method to turn routine assignments into interesting and active reading sessions. When you respond actively to what you are reading, you are more likely to remember what you have read.

RESOURCES

Interpreting and Analyzing What You Read

Every essay, article, or textbook chapter that you read organizes ideas in a pattern that relates them to one another. Interpreting and analyzing these relationships will help you think critically about what you read.

Stated Main Idea. When you look for the main idea of a passage, you are trying to identify the writer's most important point. The main idea may be stated, meaning that the author clearly expresses the major point. A main idea that is stated directly can often be found in one specific sentence.

Implied Main Idea. The main idea may not be stated directly but might be implied, or suggested. You may have to figure out an implied main idea by analyzing the meaning of the details in the passage to decide what overall meaning these details combine to express.

HOW TO FIND THE MAIN IDEA
■ Skim the passage to decide what topic the sentences have in common.
■ Identify what topic the whole passage is about.
■ Identify what the passage says about the topic.
■ State the meaning of the passage in your own words.
■ Review the passage. If you have correctly identified the main idea, all the details will support it.

 REFERENCE NOTE: For additional information on finding the main idea, whether stated or implied, see pages 62–64.

Reading to Find Relationships Among Details

When you are looking for the meaning of a reading passage, you'll need to understand how the details in the passage are related to the main idea and to each other.

FINDING RELATIONSHIPS AMONG DETAILS	
Identify specific details.	Which of the details answer questions such as *Who? What? When? Where? Why?* and *How? (5W-How?* questions)?
Distinguish between fact and opinion.	What can be proved true or false? What expresses a personal belief or attitude?
Identify similarities and differences.	Are there any details that are shown to be similar to or different from one another?
Understand cause and effect.	Do earlier events influence later ones?
Identify an order of organization.	In what kind of order are the details arranged— chronological order, spatial order, order of importance, or some other pattern?

Reading Passage

Garrett Morgan was a famous African American inventor. He was born in 1877 in Kentucky. Raised on a farm, he attended school only through the sixth grade. Later, he moved to Ohio, where he started a sewing-machine repair shop and then a garment business.

His hard work made him prosperous. Reportedly the first black man in Cleveland to own a car, Morgan may have invented the modern traffic signal in response to his experiences in driving. He sold his patent to the General Electric Company for $40,000.

Sample Analysis

DETAIL: When and where was Morgan born?
ANSWER: *He was born in 1877 in Kentucky.*

FACT: Did Morgan receive a formal education?
ANSWER: *No. He only finished the sixth grade.*

TIME ORDER: What did Morgan do after opening a sewing-machine repair shop?
ANSWER: *He started a garment business.*

COMMON ERROR

Problem. Students may fail to identify the relationships among details when they read textbook material.

Solution. Have students copy the **Finding Relationships Among Details** chart onto note cards. Provide the class with copies of a nonfiction passage and have students apply the five strategies as they read the passage. Students should mark and annotate their copies. They can use the sample annotations on the passage about Garrett Morgan as a model. Have students keep their note cards handy so they can refer to the note cards when working on other material.

RESOURCES

RESOURCES

Another of Morgan's inventions was the Safety Hood. This device, patented in 1914, originally was made of a helmet and a long breathing tube lined with material to cool and filter incoming air. A separate tube with a valve prevented the return of contaminated air.

Wearing the Safety Hood, a firefighter could breathe clear air for fifteen to twenty minutes. One fire chief from Akron, Ohio, claimed that two of his men wearing Safety Hoods could be more effective in stopping fires than a whole company of firefighters without them.

In 1916, an explosion in Cleveland trapped workers deep in an underground tunnel. The tunnel was filled with deadly gases, and no one could enter. Morgan and his brother arrived, put on Safety Hoods, and—one by one—carried out all of the injured workers. The city of Cleveland rewarded Morgan's heroism with a medal made of solid gold.

During World War I, when American soldiers were exposed to poisonous chlorine gas, Morgan's Safety Hood was updated, becoming the modern gas mask. Over the years, Morgan's inventions have saved countless lives.

CAUSE AND EFFECT: What experience may have led Morgan to invent the traffic signal?
ANSWER: *Driving one of the first cars in Cleveland may have given him experience with traffic problems.*

DIFFERENCE: How did Morgan's Safety Hood provide fresh, breathable air?
ANSWER: *In a tube, incoming air was cooled and filtered, while contaminated air was kept out by a separate tube with a valve.*

OPINION: What did one expert say about Morgan's invention?
ANSWER: *A fire chief said that Morgan's Safety Hood made a few firefighters more effective than a whole company of firefighters without this equipment.*

Applying Reasoning Skills to Your Reading

To think critically about what you read, you evaluate and interpret evidence and facts that you gather from your

RESOURCES

RESOURCES

reading. You may draw *conclusions,* meaning that you make decisions based on clearly expressed facts and evidence.

Or you may make *inferences,* meaning that you make decisions based on evidence that is only hinted at or implied in what you have read.

For example, based on your analysis of the reading passage on pages 913–914, you might draw the following conclusions or inferences about the character of Garrett Morgan.

> **Garrett Morgan was financially successful.**
> **(Evidence: He owned businesses and a car, and he sold his traffic signal patent for $40,000.)**
>
> **Garrett Morgan's inventions benefited the human race.**
> **(Evidence: Two of Morgan's major inventions—the traffic signal and the Safety Hood—were safety devices.)**

A *valid conclusion* is a conclusion that is based on facts, evidence, or logic. An *invalid conclusion,* however, is not based on logical reasoning and is not grounded on facts or evidence. For example, it is invalid to conclude that Garrett Morgan's prosperity was the result of family wealth. This conclusion is not consistent with facts stated in the reading passage. The reading passage states that Garrett Morgan grew up on a farm and that he only attended school through the sixth grade.

HOW TO DRAW CONCLUSIONS	
Gather all the evidence.	What facts or details have you learned about the subject?
Evaluate the evidence.	What do the facts and details you have gathered tell you about the subject?
Make appropriate connections and draw reasonable conclusions.	What can you reasonably conclude from the evidence that you have gathered and evaluated?

RESOURCES

CRITICAL THINKING

Analysis. To give them practice in analyzing the process of drawing conclusions, have students find texts of speeches that interest them. Have students identify the conclusions drawn in the speeches and have them list the supporting evidence. Then students should analyze the evidence to determine whether or not it logically leads to the conclusions.

RESOURCES

Creating graphs and charts is relatively easy with computers. Encourage students to use computers to generate graphics to use when they make speeches. Emphasize how much clearer a speaker's ideas can be when visuals are used. For example, on newscasts the camera switches from a commentator to a list of the main points being made. Students can use graphics ranging from simple lists to complicated graphs to make their speeches more effective.

Reading Graphics and Illustrations

Many of the materials that you read—from textbooks to magazine articles—include visuals such as diagrams, maps, graphs, and illustrations. These visuals make information clearer and easier to understand.

When you read a paragraph filled with detailed information, it is often difficult to understand and remember its meaning. Graphs or diagrams make detailed information much easier to understand. Graphics and illustrations help you understand relationships among sets of facts. For example, the bar graph below shows the final medal standings from the 26th Summer Olympics in 1996.

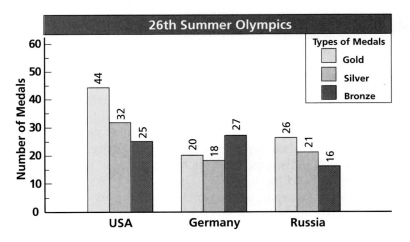

From this graph you can quickly compare the number and the kinds of medals won by three different countries.

Suppose you were a television anchorperson reporting on the Olympics. Information about the medal standings would be very difficult for a viewer to understand quickly. However, if you showed a graph at the same time as you reported the information, it would be easier for the viewer to understand. For example, by looking at the chart, the viewer can immediately see who won the most or the fewest bronze medals.

Graphs such as the one on page 916 help you understand information more easily because you can actually see relationships between the data.

Applying Study and Reading Strategies

As you compare study and reading strategies, you will see that they are simply different ways of organizing and handling information. There are a variety of study and reading strategies. Some of the most common are

- taking notes
- classifying
- organizing information visually
- outlining
- paraphrasing
- summarizing
- memorizing

Taking Notes

If you take careful notes whenever you read or listen to a lecture, your information will already be organized for you when you study, take tests, or write reports.

HOW TO TAKE STUDY NOTES
1. Set off the main subjects as headings in your notes. In a lecture, listen for key words and phrases, such as *first, most important,* or *therefore,* that often introduce main ideas. In a textbook, chapter headings and subheadings usually indicate main topics.
2. Use abbreviations and summarize material in your own words.
3. Note important examples that can help you recall the main ideas.
4. Review your notes soon after you have taken them to be sure you have included all important details.

RESOURCES

COOPERATIVE LEARNING
You may wish to assign **Applying Study and Reading Strategies** as a cooperative-learning activity. Organize students into groups of seven and assign one of the seven methods to each member. When they have completed their studies, have members of different teams who worked on the same topics meet to master their topics. Each original group should then reconvene, with each expert presenting his or her special topic.

MEETING *individual* NEEDS

LEP/ESL

General Strategies. Note taking, especially for lectures, can prove difficult and frustrating. It is especially difficult to control the listening experience when the student cannot ask the speaker to slow down. In addition, because students may be confronting unfamiliar vocabulary, it is often difficult for them to follow what they are hearing. They may try to record the lecture verbatim, resulting in further frustration. To provide practice and reinforcement for this skill, have students work with peer tutors in interview or dictation situations.

RESOURCES

Look at the following example. A careful student might take these study notes about the reading passage on pages 913–914. The notes include the main points of the passage. They are grouped with headings that identify the key ideas.

> *Garrett Morgan*
>
> *Biography*
> - *Famous African American inventor*
> - *Born 1877 in Kentucky*
> - *Grew up on farm; only finished 6th grade*
> - *Moved to Ohio*
> - *Started sewing-machine repair shop, then garment shop*
>
> *Achievements*
> - *Made money with his work*
> - *Possibly first black man in Cleveland with own car*
> - *Invented modern traffic signal*
> - *Invented the Safety Hood, patented in 1914*
> - *Saved men trapped in tunnel; given gold medal*
> - *WWI—Safety Hood became gas mask; saved lives*

Classifying

Classification is a way to organize items by arranging them into categories. When you make an outline, you are using classification. You decide which ideas fit together under each heading. In order to decide which group an item belongs in, you identify relationships among the items.

MEETING *individual* NEEDS

LEP/ESL

General Strategies. Some students may have difficulty understanding the explanation of *classification*. To make the concept more accessible, organize students into mixed-ability groups of five or six. Ask the groups to make lists of all the ways they can classify their members. When they finish, the groups should report to the class and explain the categories they chose. You may want to explain that classifying is a way of showing how people, things, or events relate to each other.

EXAMPLE   **What do the following items have in common?**
          pancakes, oatmeal, bacon, eggs, cereal
ANSWER   **They are common breakfast foods.**

You also use classifying when you identify patterns. For example, look at the following sequence of numbers.

What's the next number in the series?

1   3   2   4   3   _____?_____

ANSWER   To the first number, 2 is added. This addition produces *3*, the second number. From this number, *1* is subtracted. To the next number, *2* is added. From the fourth number, *1* is subtracted. The pattern is "add 2, subtract 1." Therefore, you should add two to the fifth number, and the next number in the series would be *5*.

Organizing Information Visually

Mapping, diagramming, and charting are techniques that allow you to organize new information so that it is visually presented. This makes the ideas easier to understand.

For example, the passage that follows compares and contrasts the two kinds of elephants.

> African and Asian elephants have interesting differences. The African elephant lives on the continent of Africa in areas south of the Sahara. The average African bull elephant is almost eleven and a half feet tall and weighs about six tons. The African elephant has dark gray skin and ears four feet wide, long enough to cover its shoulders. Its forehead forms a smooth curve, and its tusks grow to a length of six to eight feet. The Asian, or Indian, elephant, however, lives in India and in many parts of Southeast Asia. The

RESOURCES

A DIFFERENT APPROACH

You may want to make further examples of number-sequence problems available to students. Test-preparation books are a good source. Model one or two examples and then have students work through others.

MEETING *individual* **NEEDS**

LEARNING STYLES

Visual Learners. Some students find it helpful to use color to organize information. Give students copies of the passage comparing the African elephant and the Asian elephant and have them sort the information in the paragraph by using two highlighters. For example, have students use yellow to highlight information pertaining to the African elephant and blue to highlight information about the Asian elephant.

RESOURCES

average Asian bull elephant is smaller, standing nine to ten feet tall and weighing about four tons. Its skin is light gray and its ears are only half the width of the African elephant's. The Asian elephant has two humps on its forehead, and its tusks grow to only four or five feet in length. Many have no tusks at all.

AFRICAN ELEPHANT	ASIAN ELEPHANT
lives in Africa, south of the Sahara	lives in India and Southeast Asia
average bull $11\frac{1}{2}$ feet tall	average bull 9 to 10 feet tall
weighs about 6 tons	weighs about 4 tons
dark gray skin	light gray skin
ears 4 feet wide	ears 2 feet wide
tusks 6 to 8 feet long	tusks 4 to 5 feet long

Outlining

An *outline* helps organize important ideas and information. When you make an outline, you group ideas in an organized pattern that makes their order and their relationship to one another clear.

You might make a formal outline, with Roman numerals for headings and capital letters for subheadings. Or, you might use an informal outline form to help you organize information more quickly.

FORMAL OUTLINE FORM

I. Main Point
  A. Supporting Point
    1. Detail
      a. Information or detail

INFORMAL OUTLINE FORM

Main Idea
  Supporting detail
  Supporting detail
  Supporting detail

Paraphrasing

Paraphrasing is a good way to check your understanding of what you read. A *paraphrase* is a restatement of someone else's ideas in your own words. When you paraphrase, you translate complex or poetic ideas into your own words so that they are easier to understand. Your written paraphrase will usually be about the same length as the original. In language arts classes, you may be asked to paraphrase a short passage, such as a poem. Here is an example.

> Desert Noon
> *by Elizabeth Coatsworth*
>
> When the desert lies
> Pulsating with heat
> And even rattlesnakes
> Coil among the roots of the mesquite
> And the coyotes pant at the waterholes—
>
> Far above,
> Against the sky,
> Shines the summit of San Jacinto,
> Blue-white and cool as a hyacinth
> With snow.

Here is a possible paraphrase of the poem.

> The speaker in this poem is observing a desert scene. The heat rising from the ground causes the image of the desert to waver. It's so hot that even the rattlesnakes aren't moving; they're just lying in the shade at the base of desert trees. Coyotes show signs of thirst as they go to places where they usually find water.
>
> By contrast, a mountain, San Jacinto, rises high above the desert, framed by the sky. The top of the mountain is blue and white with snow. It looks cool, like an early spring flower poking through the snow.

INTEGRATING THE LANGUAGE ARTS

Study Skills and Mechanics. You may want to remind students that while paraphrased material does not contain direct quotations from the original source, credit for the ideas is still given to the original writer. If words or phrases from the original source are used verbatim, they must be enclosed in quotation marks.

RESOURCES

RESOURCES

922 *Reading, Studying, and Test Taking*

Use the following guidelines when you write a paraphrase.

HOW TO PARAPHRASE

1. Read the selection carefully before you begin.
2. Be sure you understand the main idea of the selection. Look up unfamiliar words in a dictionary.
3. Determine the tone of the selection. (What is the attitude of the writer toward the subject of the selection?)
4. Identify the speaker in fictional material. (Is the poet or a character within the selection speaking?)
5. Write your paraphrase in your own words. Shorten long sentences or stanzas and use your own, familiar vocabulary, but follow the same order of ideas used in the selection.
6. Check to be sure that your paraphrase expresses the same ideas as the original.

You will paraphrase often when you write a research report. In order to avoid *plagiarism,* make sure that you cite the source that you paraphrase. You should always give credit to the person whose ideas you use.

REFERENCE NOTE: For more about crediting your sources in research reports, see pages 339–342.

Summarizing

A *summary* is a brief restatement of a piece of writing. Like a paraphrase, a summary expresses the ideas of a passage in your own words. However, a summary condenses the original material, presenting only the most important points.

Writing a summary requires critical thinking. You analyze the material that you are condensing. Then you draw conclusions about what should be included in the summary and what can be left out.

HOW TO SUMMARIZE

1. Skim the selection.
2. Reread the passage closely and look for the main ideas and supporting details.
3. Write your summary in your own words. Include only the writer's main ideas and most important supporting points.
4. After you write your draft, evaluate and revise your summary, checking to see that you have covered the most important points. Make sure that the information is clearly expressed. Also be sure that the reader can follow your ideas.

Here's a sample summary of the reading passage found on pages 326–328.

> Tropical rain forests are being destroyed. In minutes, a chain saw can cut down a tree that it will take the rain forest 500 years to replace. After the loggers cut the trees, the forest is burned to clear the land for agriculture. When the rain forest is burned, the top coating of ash is rich. The soil underneath, however, is very poor. Soon, crops use it up or rain washes it away, and then desperate farmers try to burn more forest to clear more land.
>
> Losing the rain forests also means trouble for our air. We need trees to absorb carbon dioxide. We also need trees because they recycle oxygen and moisture. When forests are cleared, there are fewer trees to produce oxygen. Also, when the trees are burned, the carbon dioxide that's in them is released into the air. The extra carbon dioxide traps the heat from the sun. The sun's rays enter the atmosphere but can't get out. This process could cause a rise in the global temperature and a change in the world's weather.

INTEGRATING THE LANGUAGE ARTS

Literature Link. To give students practice in summarizing a story and to help them distinguish between summary and evaluation, use the following activity. If the selection is contained in your literature textbook, have students read and discuss Howard Fast's "The First Rose of Summer." Then have each student write a review that includes one paragraph of summary and one paragraph of evaluation. The first paragraph should tell the main points but omit the details. The evaluation paragraph should judge the story by telling why the student would or would not recommend it to a friend.

RESOURCES

RESOURCES

IMPROVING TEST-TAKING SKILLS

OBJECTIVE

- To analyze essay questions

LEARNING STYLES

Kinetic Learners. Suggest that students move around when they are memorizing. For example, a student who is memorizing a poem might want to find a quiet place to walk back and forth while reciting the material aloud. The need to refer to notes should gradually lessen. By connecting the movement with the material, the student should later be able to remember the feeling and hence recapture the words.

IMPROVING TEST-TAKING SKILLS

- **Independent Practice/Reteaching** For additional practice and reinforcement, see **Taking Objective Tests, Reasoning and Logic Questions, Analogy Questions, Short Answer Questions,** and **Essay Test Questions** in *Academic and Workplace Skills,* pp. 86–90.

---

924 *Reading, Studying, and Test Taking*

Memorizing

Sometimes, you have to memorize information. If you practice in frequent, short, focused sessions, you are more likely to remember the information. Follow these guidelines to memorize material more efficiently.

HOW TO MEMORIZE	
Memorize only the most important information.	Whenever possible, condense the material you need to remember.
Rehearse the material in different ways.	Copy the material by hand. Recite the material out loud.
Invent memory games.	Form a word from the first letters of important terms, or make up rhymes to help you remember facts and details.

Improving Test-Taking Skills

Preparing for Different Kinds of Tests

It's natural to feel nervous before an important test. However, you can channel your nervous energy in order to do well on the test. Your attitude is the key.

HOW TO PREPARE FOR A TEST
Plan for success. Think of all the things you can do to improve your performance. Know what material will be covered on the test, and make a practical plan to take notes, study, and review the material.
Be confident. If you have studied thoroughly, you know you are prepared. During the test, pay attention only to reading and answering the questions.
Keep trying. Know that you can constantly plan and improve your study effectiveness.

There are two basic types of test questions: *objective* and *essay* questions. Certain strategies can help you prepare for these types of questions.

Objective Tests

Objective test questions appear in many forms. Types of questions include multiple-choice, true/false, matching, reasoning or logic, analogy, and short-answer questions. Objective questions measure your ability to recall and apply specific information, such as dates, names, terms, or definitions. Most objective test questions have only one answer that is scored as correct. For this reason, they are also called *limited-response* or *limited-answer tests.*

You can prepare for objective tests by reviewing the specific information that the test is supposed to cover. The study skills listed earlier in this chapter help you prepare for objective tests.

HOW TO STUDY FOR OBJECTIVE TESTS

1. Answer the study questions in your textbook. Review class notes to identify important terms or facts.
2. Study the information in more than one form. For example, you may be responsible for labeling a map or diagram. Make an unlabeled version and then practice identifying areas on the map.
3. Practice and repeat factual information. Note which items you have difficulty with, and review them.
4. If possible, review all the terms once more, shortly before the actual test.

For each type of objective test, you may have to adapt your study strategies a little. For example, if your test will include defining key terms, then use flashcards as you study. If problem solving is included, work out practice problems and then check your answers with your textbook.

QUICK REMINDER

Write the following list of analogies on the chalkboard and have students identify the one that doesn't fit. Have students explain their reasoning.

1. willow: tree
2. humus: soil
3. sedan: car
4. bowl: plate
5. shirt: clothes

[Number 4 doesn't fit. In all the other analogies in this set, the second item names a category that the first item is part of. A bowl is not a type of plate.]

MEETING individual NEEDS

LEP/ESL

General Strategies. One way to introduce the material on test taking is through class discussion. How do students feel about taking tests? What kinds of past experiences contribute to these feelings? What do students consider a fair way of testing knowledge and understanding of a topic? Expressing opinions and having them validated is important for students.

A DIFFERENT APPROACH

To provide practice using the strategies under **Objective Tests**, have students bring material from other classes on which they are soon to be tested. Have students work in pairs to apply the study techniques. Have students evaluate what they learned about studying.

AT-RISK STUDENTS

Some students may show antipathy to studying test-taking methods because testing has so often been an unpleasant experience for them. It may be helpful to act as if you are giving them inside information by revealing the secrets of doing well on tests. Point out that test-taking skills are, in fact, one element of success in school.

When you take an objective test, scan the test before you begin. Notice how many items there are on the test and decide how you can budget your time for each item.

Here are some strategies that are effective in handling specific kinds of objective test questions.

Multiple-Choice Questions. Multiple-choice questions require you to select a correct answer from among a number of choices.

EXAMPLE **1.** Garrett Morgan's design for the Safety Hood was later used to develop
  A the crash helmet.
  B the welding mask.
  Ⓒ the gas mask.
  D the construction worker's safety helmet.

HOW TO ANSWER MULTIPLE-CHOICE QUESTIONS	
Read the question or statement carefully.	■ Make sure you understand the key question or statement before examining the choices. ■ Look for words such as *not* or *always* that will limit the correct answers.
Read all the choices before selecting an answer.	■ Eliminate choices that you know are incorrect. ■ Think carefully about the remaining choices and select the one that makes the most sense.

True/False Questions. True/false questions ask you to determine whether a specific, given statement is true or false.

EXAMPLE **1.** Ⓣ F In the medal tallies in the 26th Summer Olympics, the United States won a greater number of medals than either Germany or Russia.

HOW TO ANSWER TRUE/FALSE QUESTIONS	
Read the statement carefully.	■ The whole statement is false if any part of it is false.
Look for word clues.	■ Words such as *always* or *never* limit a statement.

Matching Questions. Matching questions ask you to match the items in one list with the items in another list.

Directions: Match the item in the left-hand column with its description in the right-hand column.

  C 1. weight of African bull elephant   **A** about 4 tons

  B 2. height of Asian bull elephant   **B** 9 to 10 feet

  D 3. height of African bull elephant   **C** about 6 tons

  A 4. weight of Asian bull elephant   **D** $11\frac{1}{2}$ feet

HOW TO ANSWER MATCHING QUESTIONS	
Read the directions carefully.	Sometimes you won't use all the items listed in one column. Other times items may be matched up to more than one item.
Scan the columns to identify related items.	Match items you know first. Then evaluate items you are less sure about.
Complete the rest of the matching.	Make your best educated guess on remaining items.

Reasoning or Logic Questions. These questions may test your reasoning abilities more than your knowledge of a specific subject. Reasoning or logic questions often

MEETING *individual* NEEDS

STUDENTS WITH SPECIAL NEEDS

Some students suffer from severe test anxiety and are unable to do their best work in a test situation. Some signs of test anxiety are trembling hands, expressions of fear, self-belittling, preoccupation with unrelated tasks, or watching what others do instead of tackling the test itself. You may want to have a class discussion about test anxiety. Ask students to share their strategies for overcoming nervousness. In particular, you may want to suggest that students remember to take deep breaths and to relax as they exhale. Point out that learning to deal with test anxiety can help students cope with other stressful situations outside class.

RESOURCES

LESS-ADVANCED STUDENTS

Standardized answer sheets may be intimidating to some students. You may wish to provide students with scoring sheets to fill in. Have students practice to find out how hard to press their pencils. (Answers should not press through the paper and should not be impossible to erase.) Give students the following reminders:

1. Fill in only one answer per question.
2. Erase carefully and completely.
3. Make sure there are no stray marks on the score sheet before handing it in.

Tell students that standardized tests are usually graded by machine. Two answers on one line or one answer and one partially erased answer will register as an error.

appear on standardized tests. They often ask you to identify the relationship between several items (usually words, pictures, or numbers).

Reasoning questions might ask you to identify a pattern in a number sequence (for example: 14, 35, 49, 84—these are multiples of the number 7). Or you might be asked to predict the next item in a visual sequence. Look at the following example.

What comes next?

1 2 3 4

In this sequence of three drawings, a different square is missing each time from a box of four squares. Therefore, the last drawing in the series should show a square missing in the only position that had not yet been shown with a missing square.

HOW TO ANSWER REASONING OR LOGIC QUESTIONS	
Be sure you understand the instructions.	Reasoning or logic questions are often multiple-choice. On some tests, however, you may need to fill in a blank, complete a number sequence, or even draw a picture.
Analyze the relationship implied in the question.	Look at the question carefully to gather information about the relationship of the various items you are given.
Draw reasonable conclusions.	Evaluate the relationship of the items to decide your final answer.

Analogy Questions. Analogy questions are special reasoning and logic questions that measure your ability to analyze relationships between words. Analogy questions ask you to recognize the relationship between two words and to identify a pair of words with a similar relationship.

EXAMPLE   **1. Directions: Select the appropriate pair of words to complete the analogy.**

DRIVER : CAR :: _____

   A engine : truck
   B food : stomach
   Ⓒ sailor : boat
   D family : house

Analogies may also appear as fill-in-the-blank questions.

EXAMPLE   **2. Directions: Complete the following analogy.**

STANZA : POEM :: chapter : ___*book*___

HOW TO ANSWER ANALOGY QUESTIONS	
Analyze the first pair of words.	▪ Reason out the relationship between the first two items. (Using Example 1, the relationship between a car and a driver is that a car is controlled by a driver.)
Express the analogy in sentence or question form.	▪ The first example on this page could be read as "A *driver* controls a *car*, just as . . . (what other pair of items among the choices given?)."
Find the best available choice to complete the analogy.	▪ With multiple-choice analogies, select the pair of words that has the same type of relationship between them as the original pair. ▪ For fill-in-the-blank analogies, you are often given one word of the second pair of items, and you are expected to supply the final word. (In Example 2, a *stanza* is a part of a *poem;* a *chapter* is part of a *book*.)

A DIFFERENT APPROACH

If students have difficulty with reasoning or logic questions on standardized tests, make test-preparation books available in class. You may want to use information from the books to prepare sample test questions. Model the correct procedure for selecting the answers.

RESOURCES

A DIFFERENT APPROACH

Have students work independently with the **Analogy Examples** chart to generate one example of each type of analogy. Each student should write the first pair of words in each analogy and exchange lists with a partner. Students will then complete their partners' analogies by writing the second pair of words and identifying the type of each analogy. Students can discuss their solutions by using sentences to express the analogies.

The following chart shows you a few of the most common types of analogy relationships. Many other types of analogies are possible, because there are many ways that any two things can be related.

ANALOGY EXAMPLES	
TYPE OF ANALOGY	EXAMPLE
A word to its synonym	FLAT : SMOOTH :: bumpy : rough
A word to its antonym	MOIST : DRY :: sweet : sour
A thing to its cause	COLD : ICE :: heat : fire
A thing to its effect	BLEACH : WHITENESS :: dye : color
A part of something to the whole thing	TWIG : BRANCH :: finger : hand
A whole thing to a part of that thing	BOOK : PAGES :: melody : notes
A thing as part of a category it belongs to	RECLINER : CHAIR :: loveseat : sofa
A thing to a characteristic of that thing	PILLOWS : SOFT :: diamonds : hard
A thing to its use	EARS : HEAR :: nose : smell
An action to the person who performs the action	WRITING : AUTHOR :: cooking : chef
A person who performs an action to the action performed	ARCHITECT : DESIGNING :: farmer : planting
A location to a related location	MONTREAL : CANADA :: Paris : France

Short-Answer Questions. Short-answer questions require you to show your knowledge in short, precise answers that you write out yourself. Some short-answer questions (such as fill-in-the-blank questions) can be answered with one or a few words. Other types of short-answer questions require you to write a full response, usually one or two sentences.

EXAMPLE   What were Garrett Morgan's two most famous inventions, and how were they useful?

ANSWER   *Garrett Morgan's two most famous inventions were the Safety Hood and the traffic signal. The Safety Hood made it safer for firefighters and rescue workers to do their jobs, and the traffic signal reduced accidents at intersections.*

HOW TO RESPOND TO SHORT-ANSWER QUESTIONS

Read the question carefully.	Some questions have more than one part, and you will have to include an answer to each part to receive full credit.
Plan your answer.	Briefly decide what you need to include in the answer.
Be as specific as possible in your answers.	Give a complete, precise answer.
Budget your time.	Begin by answering those questions you are certain about. Return later to the questions you are less sure about.

Essay Tests

Essay tests measure your understanding of material you have learned. You are required to write a paragraph or more to answer an essay question.

HOW TO STUDY FOR ESSAY TESTS

1. Read your textbook carefully.
2. Make an outline, identifying the main points and important details.
3. Try making up your own essay questions and practice writing out the answers.
4. Evaluate and revise your practice answers. Check your notes and textbook for accuracy and the composition section of this textbook for help in writing.

COOPERATIVE LEARNING
You may want to have students work in groups of four or five to write tests. Have each group work with a textbook they are currently using to prepare a list of eight key terms or concepts on which they might be tested. Then have students use the information to write two of each of the following types of objective test questions:

1. matching
2. multiple choice
3. short answer
4. true-false

RESOURCES

RESOURCES

931

A DIFFERENT APPROACH

To assist students in understanding the **Essay Test Questions** chart, have each student dictate two sample questions to illustrate each of the key verbs. Then have students explain how they would go about answering the questions.

There are several steps you should take before you begin an essay test. You should quickly scan the questions. How many essay questions are you expected to answer? Are you allowed to choose from several items? Which of them do you think you can answer best? After you have determined these issues, plan how much time to spend on each answer, and stay on this schedule.

Read the question carefully. You may be asked for an answer that contains several parts.

Pay attention to important terms in the question. Essay questions on tests usually require specific responses. Each task is expressed with a verb. Become familiar with the key verbs and what type of response each one calls for.

ESSAY TEST QUESTIONS		
KEY VERB	TASK	SAMPLE QUESTION
argue	Take a viewpoint on an issue and give reasons to support this opinion.	Argue whether or not students who receive good grades should be excused from routine homework assignments.
analyze	Take something apart to see how each part works.	Analyze the major effects of the destruction of the rain forests.
compare	Point out likenesses.	Compare Carmen Maymi and Herman Badillo as famous Puerto Ricans.
contrast	Point out differences.	Contrast Travis's life in *Old Yeller* with a typical routine of a modern teenager.
define	Give specific details that make something unique.	Define the term *symbiosis* as it is used in biology.

(continued)

ESSAY TEST QUESTIONS *(continued)*		
KEY VERB	TASK	SAMPLE QUESTION
demonstrate (also illustrate, present, show)	Provide examples to support a point.	Demonstrate the importance of the ozone layer to the world's weather.
describe	Give a picture in words.	Describe incidents from "A Walk to the Jetty" that Jamaica Kincaid recalls as she prepares to leave her home.
discuss	Examine in detail.	Discuss the term *passive resistance.*
explain	Give reasons.	Explain the popularity of Winston Churchill during World War II.
identify	Point out specific characteristics.	Identify the types of poetic meter.
interpret	Give the meaning or significance of something.	Interpret the impact of the discovery of penicillin.
list (also outline or trace)	Give all steps in order or all details about a subject.	List the events that led to the landing of an American on the moon.
summarize	Give a brief overview of the main points.	Summarize the myth of Prometheus the fire-bringer.

RESOURCES

Take a moment to use prewriting strategies. After considering the key verbs in the question, write notes or a rough outline on scratch paper to help you decide what you want to say and how you want to say it.

CRITICAL THINKING

Analysis. Have students study the tips at the end of **Essay Tests** and discuss the tips in terms of the writing process. Ask students the following questions.

Answers will vary.

1. In what ways will prewriting be helpful? [Students can plan and order their ideas.]
2. What problems might arise if prewriting is omitted? [Less important matters may receive more attention than important matters due to time or space problems.]
3. What possible pitfalls might students encounter in writing essay answers? [Responses will vary, but time problems may occur if students don't prewrite.]
4. In what ways does this answering process differ from composition writing? [Writing, evaluating, and revising need to be done simultaneously for an essay test, but not for a composition.]

RESOURCES

Allow time to evaluate and revise after you write your essay. While you are writing your essay, you won't have time to edit very much. However, as soon as you finish, look over what you have written. You can check for simple errors as well as for omission of important points. Make sure you have answered every part of each question.

QUALITIES OF A GOOD ESSAY ANSWER

- The essay is well organized.
- The main ideas and supporting points are clearly expressed.
- The sentences are complete and well written.
- There are no distracting errors in spelling, punctuation, or grammar.

Review

EXERCISE 1   **Choosing an Appropriate Reading Rate**

Identify the reading rate that best fits each of the following situations.

1. You are reading the instructions to a new game so you will understand how to teach several of your friends to play the game.   **1. for mastery**
2. You are looking through current issues of *National Geographic* to find articles about ancient temples in Southeast Asia.   **2. scanning**   **3. skimming**
3. You need to write an outline of the main points in a history chapter about the Industrial Revolution.
4. You are reading a short story by Gabriel García Márquez, knowing you are expected to discuss the meaning of it in tomorrow's English class.   **4. for mastery**
5. You are trying to find in your history book the date of John F. Kennedy's assassination.   **5. scanning**

RESOURCES

▶ EXERCISE 2   **Applying the SQ3R Reading Method**

Use the SQ3R method while reading a magazine article or a textbook chapter that you need to read for a class. List at least five questions while you are reading. Then write a brief answer to each one.

▶ EXERCISE 3   **Reading: Analyzing Details in a Passage**

Answer the following questions about the reading passage on pages 913–914.

1. What are two facts or details about Garrett Morgan (other than those facts and details already noted in the sample analysis)?
2. What was Morgan's contribution to traffic safety?
3. What two types of businesses did Morgan start while he lived in Ohio?
4. What happened in Cleveland in 1916 that helped Morgan's invention become recognized as a life-saving device?
5. Why was Morgan's Safety Hood important during World War I?

▶ EXERCISE 4   **Reading: Drawing Conclusions and Making Inferences**

Using the reading passage on pages 913–914, identify the evidence or the reasoning that you might need to use in making the following inferences or in drawing the following conclusions.

1. Garrett Morgan knew a great deal about practical engineering.
2. Garrett Morgan gained knowledge on his own that he used in his inventions.
3. Garrett Morgan and his brother were men of considerable strength and stamina.
4. Garrett Morgan was considered a hero by the city of Cleveland.

ANSWERS
Exercise 2

Students' questions and answers will vary, but the questions should be relevant to the magazine articles or textbook chapters they chose to read.

ANSWERS
Exercise 3

1. Answers will vary, but each should consist of two facts not noted in the sample analysis.
2. Garrett Morgan invented the first modern traffic signal.
3. While in Ohio, Garrett Morgan started a sewing machine repair business and a garment shop.
4. Garrett Morgan and his brother wore Safety Hoods and rescued thirty-two workers trapped by deadly gasses from an explosion in the Lake Erie tunnel. The brothers saved the workers' lives and became heroes.
5. During World War I, Morgan's Safety Hood protected soldiers from poisonous chlorine fumes.

ANSWERS
Exercise 4

1. To invent the traffic signal and the safety hood, Garrett Morgan had to know a great deal about practical engineering.
2. Because Garrett Morgan attended school only through the sixth grade, he must have gained knowledge on his own that he used in his inventions.
3. They carried workmen out of the tunnel one by one.
4. The city of Cleveland awarded Morgan a medal after he and his brother saved the injured workers in the tunnel.

RESOURCES

▶ EXERCISE 5 **Reading: Interpreting Graphic Information**

Using the graph on page 916, answer the following questions.

1. How many gold medals did the United States win in the 26th Summer Olympics? **1.** 44
2. What is the difference between the number of medals won by the United States and by Germany? **2.** 36
3. Which nation won the most bronze medals? **3.** Germany
4. Which nation won the most silver medals? **4.** USA
5. What is the difference between the number of medals won by Germany and by Russia? **5.** 2

▶ EXERCISE 6 **Analyzing Your Note-Taking Method**

For one day, take notes in all of your classes by using the techniques suggested on page 917. Write a paragraph, comparing and contrasting your usual method and this new method. Be sure to address these points: How are the two methods similar? How are they different? Which works better? Why?

▶ EXERCISE 7 **Identifying Classifications**

For each of the following groups, identify the category.

1. peso, franc, dollar, rupee, yen **1.** money
2. barley, wheat, oats, rice, millet **2.** grain
3. Benjamin Franklin, Thomas Paine, Paul Revere, George Washington, Benedict Arnold

   3. leaders of American Revolution
4. Lake Superior, Lake Michigan, Lake Huron, Lake Erie, Lake Ontario **4.** Great Lakes
5. gila monster, alligator, grass snake, tortoise **5.** reptiles

▶ EXERCISE 8 **Reading: Applying Visual Organization**

After reading the following paragraph, make a chart or other visual representation of its contents. Use your graphic to answer the numbered questions.

ANSWERS

Exercise 6

Paragraphs will vary, but they should show that students have used the note-taking methods outlined in the textbook and then have compared and contrasted those methods carefully with their usual methods.

The Nile River and the Congo River are two of the great rivers of the world. Both are vital waterways to their home continent, Africa. For example, electricity is generated from power plants built on each river.

The Nile flows mostly through desert country. The Nile has a total length of over 4,000 miles and is located in east and northeast Africa. The Nile's main branches are the White Nile, originating at Lake Victoria, and the Blue Nile, beginning at Lake Tana. The Nile gains about 21 percent of its total volume from the Atbara River, another of its important tributaries. The mouth of the Nile is the Mediterranean Sea. The Congo, with a total length of 2,900 miles, is located in central Africa. It originates between the nations of Zaire and Zambia, and flows through warm, wet lands. Its mouth is at the Atlantic Ocean.

1. Where are the Nile and Congo Rivers located?
2. What is the total length of the Nile River? of the Congo River?
3. Where is the mouth of the Congo River?
4. What is the difference between the lands through which the Nile and the Congo flow?

▶ EXERCISE 9   **Reading: Paraphrasing a Poem**

Read the following short poem by Robert Frost. Then write a paraphrase of the poem.

A Time to Talk
by Robert Frost

When a friend calls to me from the road
And slows his horse to a meaning walk,
I don't stand still and look around
On all the hills I haven't hoed,
And shout from where I am, "What is it?"

RESOURCES

ANSWERS
Exercise 8

Students' charts will vary. Here is a possibility:

NILE	CONGO
vital African waterway	same
harnessed for electricity	same
flows through desert country	flows through warm, wet lands
4,000 miles long	2,900 miles long
located in east and northeast Africa	located in central Africa
originates at Lake Victoria (White Nile) and Lake Tana (Blue Nile) 21% of volume from the Atbara River	originates between Zaire and Zambia
mouth at the Mediterranean Sea	mouth at the Atlantic Ocean

1. The Nile is located in east and northeast Africa. The Congo is located in central Africa.
2. The Nile River is more than 4,000 miles long. The Congo River is 2,900 miles long.
3. The mouth of the Congo River is on the Atlantic Ocean.
4. The Nile flows mostly through desert, while the Congo flows through warm, wet lands.

ANSWERS
Exercise 9

Students' paraphrases will vary. Here is a sample paraphrase of the poem:

The speaker in the poem is saying that if a friend comes by while he is working, he will take the time for a friendly conversation, even if he still has a lot of work to do.

RESOURCES

> No, not as there is a time to talk.
> I thrust my hoe in the mellow ground,
> Blade-end up and five feet tall,
> And plod: I go up to the stone wall
> For a friendly visit.

▶ EXERCISE 10   **Analyzing Essay Questions**

Identify the <u>key verb(s)</u> in each of the following essay questions. Do not write an essay answer. Just state briefly what task you would need to do to answer the question.

1. <u>Compare</u> the populations and physical sizes of Tokyo, Mexico City, and New York City.
2. <u>Analyze</u> the effect of the narrator on the message of Isaac Bashevis Singer's story "Zlateh the Goat."
3. While many people consider television a waste of time, others consider it important for the modern world. They point out its potential for educating and informing citizens. <u>Argue</u> your opinion about the value of television. Be sure to use specific examples.
4. <u>Describe</u> how to print a document on one of your school's computers.
5. <u>Compare and contrast</u> a violin and a viola.
6. <u>Summarize</u> how courts settle disputes in the United States.
7. <u>Demonstrate</u> the historical importance of the March on Washington on August 28, 1963.
8. <u>Trace</u> the path of blood circulation through the human heart.
9. <u>Define</u> the type of humor represented in the writings of Mark Twain and O. Henry.
10. Stonehenge—located on the Salisbury Plain in Wiltshire, England—has fascinated scientists, archaeologists, and historians for centuries. <u>Identify</u> some of the characteristics of Stonehenge that make it so fascinating.

ANSWERS
Exercise 10

1. Point out likenesses in the populations and physical sizes of the three cities.
2. First, determine the story's message. Then take apart the narrator's role in the story to see how that role affects the message.
3. Decide which viewpoint you want to take and support it with reasons and specific examples.
4. Give a picture in words of the steps involved in printing a document.
5. Point out the likenesses and differences between a violin and a viola.
6. Give a brief overview of the main points of how courts settle disputes.
7. Provide examples to show how the march was historically important.
8. Give in order all the steps that blood circulation follows through the human heart.
9. Give specific details that make the humor of Mark Twain and O. Henry unique.
10. Point out specific characteristics of Stonehenge.

DIAGRAMING SENTENCES

A *sentence diagram* is a picture of how the parts of a sentence fit together. It shows how the words in the sentence are related.

Subjects and Verbs (pages 409–423)

To diagram a sentence, first find the simple subject and the verb (simple predicate), and write them on a horizontal line. Then separate them with a vertical line.

EXAMPLES   The reporter dashed to the fire.

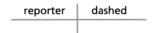

Have you been studying?

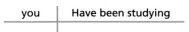

Notice that a diagram shows the capitalization but not the punctuation of a sentence.

Understood Subjects (page 423)

To diagram an imperative sentence, place the understood subject *you* in parentheses on the horizontal line.

EXAMPLE   Listen to the beautiful music.

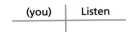

 EXERCISE 1   **Diagraming Simple Subjects and Verbs**

Diagram only the simple subjects and the verbs in the following sentences.

EXAMPLE   **1.** Midas is a character in Greek mythology.

1. Midas ruled the kingdom of Phrygia.
2. One of the gods gave Midas the power to turn anything into gold.
3. Soon this gift became a curse.
4. Do you know why?
5. Read the story of King Midas in a mythology book.

Compound Subjects (page 418)

EXAMPLE   **Vines** and **weeds** grew over the old well.

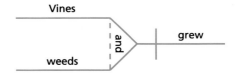

Compound Verbs (pages 419–420)

EXAMPLE   We ran to the corner and barely caught the bus.

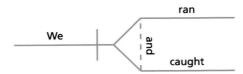

Compound Subjects and Compound Verbs (page 372)

EXAMPLE   **Ken** and **LaDonna dived** into the water and **swam** across the pool.

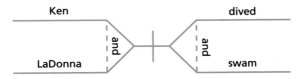

▶ EXERCISE 2   **Diagraming Simple Subjects and Verbs**

Diagram the simple subjects and the verbs in the following sentences.

EXAMPLE   **1. Nikki and Chris chopped the cilantro and added it to the salsa.**

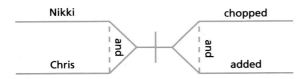

1. Mr. Carrington collects aluminum cans and returns them for recycling.
2. The students and the faculty combined their efforts and defeated the proposal.
3. The plane circled above the landing field but did not descend.
4. Pencil and paper are needed for tomorrow's math assignment.
5. Rita Moreno and her costar prepared for the scene.

Adjectives and Adverbs (pages 445–448 and 469–472)

Both adjectives and adverbs are written on slanted lines below the words they modify. Notice that possessive pronouns are diagramed in the same way adjectives are.

Adjectives (pages 445–448)

EXAMPLE   **bright** star   **a special** person   **her favorite** class

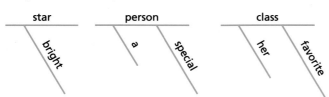

Two or more adjectives joined by a connecting word are diagramed this way:

EXAMPLE   **a lovely** and **quiet** place

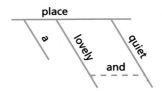

EXERCISE 3   **Diagraming Adjectives**

Diagram the following groups of words.

1. mighty warrior
2. long, exciting movie
3. short and funny story

4. my final offer
5. the slow but persistent turtle

Adverbs (pages 469–472)

EXAMPLES   studies **hard**   does **not** exercise **daily**

When an adverb modifies an adjective or another adverb, it is placed on a line connected to the word it modifies.

EXAMPLES   **extremely** strong wind   tried **rather** hard

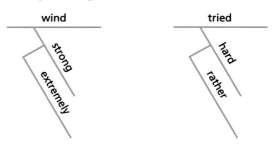

EXERCISE 4   **Diagraming Adverbs**

Diagram the following groups of words.

1. answered quickly
2. listened quite intently
3. dangerously sharp curve
4. never plans very carefully
5. may possibly happen

 REVIEW A   **Diagraming Sentences That Contain Adjectives and Adverbs**

Diagram the following sentences.

1. The shutters rattled quite noisily.
2. We are definitely leaving tomorrow.
3. The anxious motorist drove much too far.
4. Our turn finally came.
5. The new car had not been damaged badly.

Objects (pages 491–493)

Direct Objects (page 491)

A direct object is diagramed on the horizontal line with the subject and verb. A vertical line separates the direct object from the verb. Notice that this vertical line does not cross the horizontal line.

EXAMPLE   **The rain cleaned the street.**

Compound Direct Objects (page 491)

EXAMPLE   We sold **lemonade** and **oranges.**

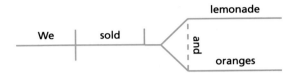

Indirect Objects (pages 492–493)

To diagram an indirect object, write it on a short horizontal line below the verb. Connect the indirect object to the verb by a slanted line.

EXAMPLE   The artist showed **me** his painting.

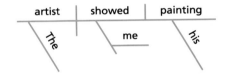

Compound Indirect Objects (page 493)

EXAMPLE   The company gave **Jean** and **Corey** summer jobs.

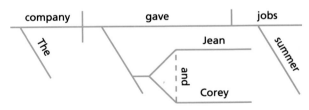

 EXERCISE 5   **Diagraming Sentences That Contain Direct Objects and Indirect Objects**

Diagram the following sentences.

1. Placido Domingo signed photographs and programs.
2. Cara's sister taught her the rules.
3. The cashier handed the children balloons.
4. The judges awarded Jelisa and Rae the prizes.
5. Snow gives motorists and pedestrians trouble.

Subject Complements (pages 496–497)

A subject complement is placed on the horizontal line with the simple subject and the verb. The subject complement comes after the verb and is separated from it by a line slanting toward the subject. This slanted line shows that the complement refers to the subject.

Predicate Nominatives (page 496)

EXAMPLE   William Least Heat-Moon is an **author.**

Compound Predicate Nominatives (page 496)

EXAMPLE   The contestants are **Joan** and **Dean.**

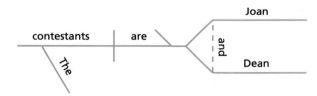

Predicate Adjectives (page 497)

EXAMPLE   The river looked **deep.**

Compound Predicate Adjectives (page 497)

EXAMPLE   This Chinese soup tastes **hot** and **spicy**.

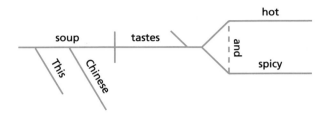

▶ EXERCISE 6   **Diagraming Sentences That Contain Subject Complements**

Diagram the following sentences.

1. Is Freddie Jackson your favorite singer?
2. The air grew cold and damp.
3. Sir Francis Drake was a brave explorer.
4. The chimpanzees seemed tired but happy.
5. My shoes looked worn and dusty.

▶ REVIEW B   **Diagraming Sentences That Contain Complements**

Diagram the following sentences.

1. Her mother was a motorcycle mechanic.
2. Don and Maria rehearsed their parts.
3. The Gypsies' origin remains mysterious and strange.
4. The girls made themselves bracelets and necklaces.
5. My favorite Mexican foods are tamales and tacos.

Phrases (pages 505–527)

Prepositional Phrases (pages 506–509)

Prepositional phrases are diagramed below the word they modify. Write the preposition that introduces the phrase on a line slanting down from the modified word. Then, write the object of the preposition on a horizontal line extending from the slanting line.

Adjective Phrases (page 508)

EXAMPLES   paintings **by famous artists**

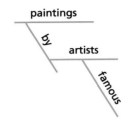

cloth **from Costa Rica and Guatemala**

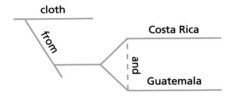

Adverb Phrases (page 509)

EXAMPLES   walked **along the road**

went **with Hollis and Dave**

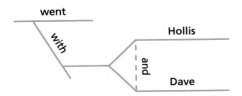

When a prepositional phrase modifies the object of another prepositional phrase, the diagram looks like this:

EXAMPLE   camped on the side **of a mountain**

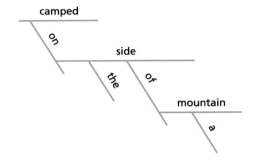

▶ EXERCISE 7   **Diagraming Prepositional Phrases**

Diagram the following word groups.

1. invited to the celebrations
2. a glimpse of the famous ruler
3. one of the people in the room
4. read about the Vietnamese and their history
5. drove to a village near Paris

▶ REVIEW C   **Diagraming Sentences That Contain Prepositional Phrases**

Diagram the following sentences.

1. The number of whales is decreasing.
2. Hundreds of animal species are being protected by concerned citizens.
3. Citrus fruits are grown in California and Florida.
4. Many historic events have been decided by sudden changes in the weather.
5. The defeat of the debate team resulted from a lack of preparation.

Verbals and Verbal Phrases (pages 513–523)

Participles and Participial Phrases (pages 513–516)

Participles are diagramed in the same way that other adjectives are.

EXAMPLE   José comforted the **crying** baby.

Participial phrases are diagramed as follows:

EXAMPLE   **Shaking the manager's hand,** Teresa accepted her new job.

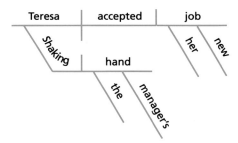

Notice that the participle has a direct object (*the manager's hand*), which is diagramed in the same way that the direct object of a main verb is.

Gerunds and Gerund Phrases (pages 518–520)

EXAMPLES   I enjoy **swimming.** [gerund used as direct object]

Being slightly ill is no excuse for **missing two days of baseball practice.** [Gerund phrases used as subject and as object of preposition. The first gerund has a subject complement (*ill*); the second gerund has a direct object (*days*).]

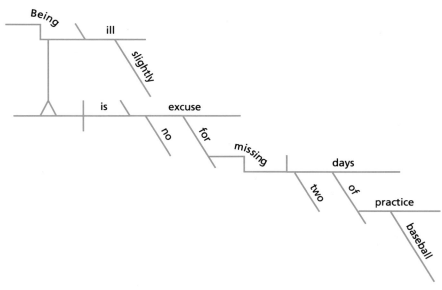

Infinitives and Infinitive Phrases (pages 522–523)

EXAMPLES **To write** is her ambition. [infinitive used as subject]

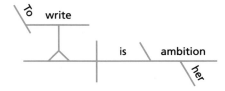

He was the first one **to solve that tricky problem.** [infinitive phrase used as adjective]

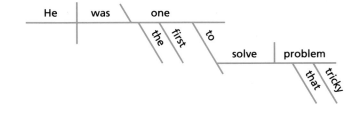

Marge was hoping **to go with us.** [infinitive phrase used as direct object]

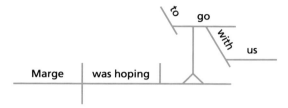

She called **to invite us over.** [infinitive phrase used as adverb]

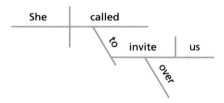

▶ EXERCISE 8   **Diagraming Sentences That Contain Verbal Phrases**

Diagram the following sentences.

1. Taking that shortcut will cut several minutes off the trip.
2. I want to watch *Nova* tonight.
3. That is my cat licking its paws.
4. Did they stop to ask directions?
5. Checking the time, Wynetta rushed to the gym.

Appositives and Appositive Phrases (pages 526–527)

To diagram an appositive or an appositive phrase, write the appositive in parentheses after the word it explains.

EXAMPLES   Our cousin **Iola** is a chemical engineer.

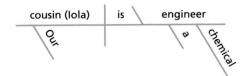

Bill Cosby, **the popular TV star,** is also the author of a best-selling book.

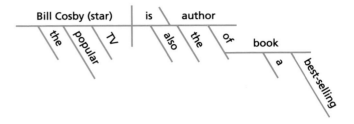

Subordinate Clauses (pages 535–548)

Adjective Clauses (pages 538–540)

Diagram an adjective clause by connecting it with a broken line to the word it modifies. Draw the broken line between the relative pronoun and the word that it relates to. [Note: The words *who, whom, whose, which,* and *that* are relative pronouns.]

EXAMPLES   The grades **that I got last term** pleased my parents.

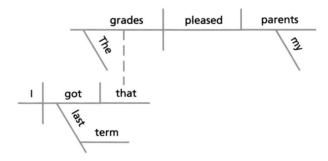

Adverb Clauses (pages 544–545)

Diagram an adverb clause by using a broken line to connect the adverb clause to the word it modifies. Place the subordinating conjunction that introduces the adverb clause on the broken line.

EXAMPLE   **When I got home from school,** I ate an apple.

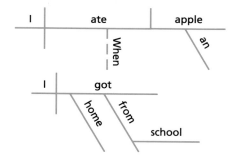

Noun Clauses (page 548)

Diagram a noun clause by connecting it to the independent clause with a solid line.

EXAMPLES   Olivia knew **what she wanted.** [The noun clause is the direct object of the independent clause. The word *what* is the direct object in the noun clause.]

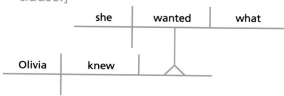

When the introductory word of the noun clause does not have a specific function in the noun clause, the sentence is diagramed in this way:

EXAMPLE   The problem is **that they lost the map.** [The noun clause is the predicate nominative of the independent clause. The word *that* has no function in the noun clause except as an introductory word.]

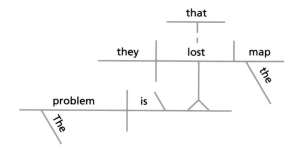

> **EXERCISE 9** **Diagraming Sentences That Contain Subordinate Clauses**

Diagram the following sentences.

1. The test that we took on Friday was hard.
2. If I had not studied Thursday night, I could not have answered half the questions.
3. Our teacher announced what would be on the test.
4. Several friends of mine were not paying attention when the teacher gave the assignment.
5. My friends who did not know what to study are worried now about their grades.

Sentences Classified According to Structure (pages 556–565)

Simple Sentences (page 557)

EXAMPLE **Tracy is building a birdhouse in industrial arts class.** [one independent clause]

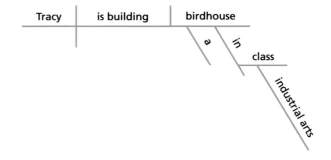

Compound Sentences (pages 559–560)

The second independent clause in a compound sentence is diagramed below the first and is joined to it by a coordinating conjunction.

EXAMPLE   Darnell threw a good pass, but Clay did not catch
it. [two independent clauses]

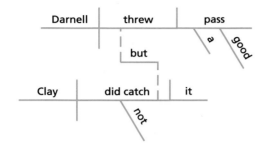

▶ EXERCISE 10   **Diagraming Compound Sentences**

Diagram the following compound sentences.

1. I want a motorboat, but Jan prefers a sailboat.
2. The bus stopped at the restaurant, and all of the
   passengers went inside.
3. Our club is very small, but it is growing.
4. Shall we meet you at the station, or will you take
   a taxi?
5. In Arizona the temperature is often high, but the
   humidity always remains low.

Complex Sentences (page 562)

EXAMPLE   Before they left the museum, Lester and Jessica
visited the exhibit of masks from Nigeria and the
Ivory Coast. [one subordinate clause and one
independent clause]

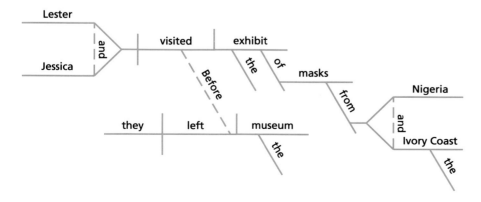

☞ REFERENCE NOTE: See pages 952–953 for more information on diagraming the three different kinds of subordinate clauses—adjective clauses, adverb clauses, and noun clauses.

▶ EXERCISE 11   **Diagraming Complex Sentences**

Diagram the following complex sentences.

1. One book that has won a Pulitzer Prize is *Pilgrim at Tinker Creek.*
2. Invite whomever you wish.
3. The satellite will be launched if the weather remains good.
4. The knight in black armor fought whoever would challenge him.
5. Alexander the Great, who conquered most of the known world, died at the age of thirty-three.

Compound-Complex Sentences (pages 564–565)

EXAMPLE   Hamako, whose mother is a musician, studies piano, but her cousin Akio prefers to play tennis. [two independent clauses and one subordinate clause]

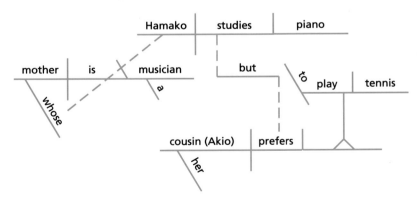

▶ REVIEW D   **Diagraming Sentences**

Diagram the following sentences.

1. Diego Rivera and Rufino Tamayo were two important Mexican artists of this century.

2. Mom wanted to fly to Utah, but Dad and I wanted to drive there.
3. Our new neighbors, the Chens, come from Taiwan, which is an island off the coast of China.
4. When I returned to the store, the purple shirt had been sold, so I bought the blue one.
5. For my report, I wrote about Katherine Anne Porter and Eudora Welty, two Southern authors.

Glossary of Terms

A

Abstract noun An abstract noun names an idea, a feeling, a quality, or a characteristic. (See page 435.)

Action verb An action verb is a verb that expresses physical or mental action. (See page 457.)

Adjective An adjective is a word used to modify a noun or a pronoun. (See page 445.)

Adjective clause An adjective clause is a subordinate clause that modifies a noun or a pronoun. (See page 538.)

Adjective phrase An adjective phrase is a prepositional phrase that modifies a noun or a pronoun. (See page 508.)

Adverb An adverb is a word used to modify a verb, an adjective, or another adverb. (See page 469.)

Adverb clause An adverb clause is a subordinate clause that modifies a verb, an adjective, or an adverb. (See page 544.)

Adverb phrase An adverb phrase is a prepositional phrase that modifies a verb, an adjective, or an adverb. (See page 509.)

Agreement Agreement refers to the correspondence, or match, between grammatical forms. For example, the number and person of a subject and verb, and the number and gender of a pronoun and its antecedent, should always agree, or match. (See Chapter 20.)

Aim An aim is one of the four basic purposes, or reasons, for writing. (See pages 7 and 22.)

Antecedent An antecedent is a noun to which a pronoun refers. (See page 436.)

Antonym The antonym of a word is a word with the opposite meaning of that word. (See page 895.)

Appositive An appositive is a noun or a pronoun placed beside another noun or pronoun to identify or explain it. (See page 526.)

Appositive phrase An appositive phrase is made up of the appositive and its modifiers. (See page 526.)

Article *A, an,* and *the* are the most frequently used adjectives and are called articles. *A* and *an* are **indefinite articles.** Each indicates that a noun refers to one of a general group. *The* is a **definite article.** It indicates that a noun refers to someone or something in particular. (See page 446.)

Audience An audience is the person(s) who reads or listens to what the writer or speaker says. (See page 33.)

B

Base form One of the four principal parts of a verb. (See page 604.)

Body The body of a composition is one or more paragraphs that state and develop the composition's main points. (See page 108.)

Brainstorming Brainstorming is a technique for finding ideas by saying what comes to mind in response to a word without stopping to judge what's said. (See page 27.)

Business letter A business letter is a formal letter written to request something, complain or seek the correction of a problem, or express appreciation. (See page 901.)

C

Call number A call number is a number and letter code a library assigns to a book to tell how the book has been classified and where it has been placed on the shelves. (See page 881.)

Card catalog The library's card catalog is a cabinet or electronic database that contains listings of books by title, author, and subject. (See page 882.)

Case Case is the form of a noun or pronoun that shows its use in a sentence. (See page 634.)

Chronological order Chronological order is a way of arranging details in a paragraph or composition according to when events or actions take, or have taken, place. (See page 75.)

Classification Classification is a strategy of development in which a writer looks at a subject as it relates to other subjects in a group. (See page 79.)

Clause A clause is a group of words that contains a verb and its subject and is used as part of a sentence. (See page 533.)

Cliché A cliché is a vague and overused expression. (See page 399.)

Clustering Clustering, or **webbing,** is a technique for finding writing ideas and gathering information by breaking a large subject into its smaller parts, creating a visual map of the writer's thoughts. (See page 28.)

Coherence Coherence, in a paragraph or composition, is a quality achieved when all the ideas are clearly arranged and connected. (See page 71.)

Collective noun A collective noun is a word that names a group. (See page 433.)

Colloquialism A colloquialism is a colorful, widely used expression of conversational language. (See page 396.)

Common noun A common noun names any one of a group of persons, places, or things and is not capitalized unless it begins a sentence. (See page 433.)

Comparative degree Comparative degree is the form a modifier takes when comparing two things. (See page 661.)

Complement A complement is a word or group of words that completes the meaning of a verb. (See page 488.)

Complex sentence A complex sentence has one independent clause and at least one subordinate clause. (See page 562.)

Compound noun A compound noun is two or more words used together as a single noun. (See page 432.)

Compound sentence A compound sentence has two or more independent clauses but no subordinate clauses. (See page 559.)

Compound subject A compound subject consists of two or more subjects that are joined by a conjunction and have the same verb. (See page 418.)

Compound verb A compound verb consists of two or more verbs or verb phrases that are joined by a conjunction and have the same subject. (See page 419.)

Compound-complex sentence A compound-complex sentence contains two or more independent clauses and at least one subordinate clause. (See page 564.)

Conclusion A conclusion reinforces the main idea and brings the composition to a definite close. (See page 110.)

Conclusion A conclusion is a decision reached by reasoning from clearly expressed facts and evidence found in a reading passage or other materials. It may be **valid** or **invalid.** (See page 915.)

Concrete noun A concrete noun names an object that can be perceived by one or more of the senses. (See page 435.)

Conjunction A conjunction is a word used to join words or groups of words. **Coordinating conjunctions** connect words or groups of words used in the same way. **Correlative conjunctions** also connect words used in the same way and are always used in pairs. (See page 478.)

Connotation The connotation of a word is the meaning, association, or emotion suggested by a word. (See page 895.)

Context The context of a word includes the surrounding words and the way the word is used. (See page 894.)

Contraction A contraction is a shortened form of a word, a figure, or a group of words. (See page 783.)

Creative writing Creative writing is writing that aims at creating literature: stories, poems, songs, and plays. (See page 7.)

Declarative sentence A declarative sentence makes a statement and is followed by a period. (See page 422.)

Demonstrative pronoun A demonstrative pronoun points out a person, a place, a thing, or an idea. (See page 440.)

Denotation The denotation of a word is its direct, plainly expressed meaning—the meaning a dictionary lists. (See page 895.)

Description Description is a strategy of development in which a writer uses sensory details to describe something. (See page 74.)

Dialect A dialect is a distinct version or variety of a language used by a particular group of people. Dialects of a language may differ from one another in vocabulary, grammar, and pronunciation. A dialect may be **regional** or **ethnic.** (See page 392.)

Dialogue Dialogue consists of the words that characters say in a story. (See page 202.)

Direct object A direct object is a noun or a pronoun that receives the action of the verb or shows the result of the action. It tells *what* or *whom* after an action verb. (See page 491.)

Direct quotation A direct quotation is a person's exact words and is enclosed in quotation marks. (See page 772.)

Double negative A double negative is the use of two negative words to express one negative idea. (See page 665.)

Early plan An early plan, sometimes called an **informal outline,** is a writer's rough plan for a composition in which he or she groups and orders information. (See page 97.)

End marks An end mark is a punctuation mark that is placed at the end of a sentence to indicate the purpose of the sentence. (See page 737.)

Essay test An essay test is a test that requires a student to think carefully about material learned and to express his or her understanding of that material, in writing, in an organized way. (See page 931.)

Essential clause/Essential phrase An essential (or **restrictive**) clause or phrase is necessary to the meaning of a sentence. (See page 748.)

Evaluating Evaluating is the stage in the writing process in which a writer goes over a draft, making judgments about its strengths and weaknesses in content, organization, and style. (See pages 6 and 43.)

Evaluation Evaluation is a strategy of development in which a writer makes judgments about a subject in an attempt to determine its value. (See page 82.)

Example An example is a specific instance, or illustration, of a general idea. (See page 68.)

Exclamatory sentence An exclamatory sentence shows excitement or expresses strong feeling and is followed by an exclamation point. (See page 423.)

Expository writing. *See* Informative writing.

Expressive writing Expressive writing is writing that aims at expressing a writer's feelings and thoughts. (See page 7.)

F

Fact A fact is something that can be checked and proved to be true by concrete information. (See page 67.)

Feedback Feedback is the listener's response to a speaker's message. (See page 860.)

Figure of speech A figure of speech is a word or a group of words that has a meaning other than its literal one. (See page 165.)

5W-How? questions The *5W-How?* questions—*Who? What? Where? When? Why? How?*—are questions a writer uses to collect information about a subject. (See page 29.)

Formal outline A formal outline is a highly structured, clearly labeled writing plan. It has a set pattern, using letters and numbers to label main headings and subheadings. (See page 99.)

Formal speech A formal speech is carefully prepared and given at an arranged time and place. (See page 862.)

Freewriting Freewriting is a technique for finding ideas in which the writer writes whatever pops into his or her head without regard to form. **Focused freewriting,** or **looping,** is a technique in which a writer focuses on one word or phrase from his or her original freewriting and uses it to start freewriting again. (See page 25.)

G

Gerund A gerund is a verb form ending in *–ing* that is used as a noun. (See page 518.)

Gerund phrase A gerund phrase contains a gerund and all the words related to the gerund. (See page 519.)

H

Homonyms Homonyms are words that are spelled differently and that mean different things, but are pronounced alike. (See page 811.)

I

Imperative sentence An imperative sentence gives a command or makes a request and is followed by either a period or an exclamation point. (See page 423.)

Impromptu speech An impromptu speech is a short speech made on the spur of the moment, with little or no time for development or preparation of ideas. (See page 861.)

Indefinite pronoun An indefinite pronoun refers to a person, a place, or a thing that is not specifically named. (See page 442.)

Independent clause An independent (or **main**) clause expresses a complete thought and can stand by itself as a sentence. (See page 534.)

Indirect object An indirect object is a noun or pronoun that comes between a transitive verb and its direct object and tells *to whom* or *for whom* the action of the verb is done. (See page 492.)

Indirect quotation An indirect quotation is a rewording or paraphrasing of something a person has said. (See page 773.)

Infinitive An infinitive is a verb form, usually preceded by *to,* that can be used as a noun, an adjective, or an adverb. (See page 522.)

Infinitive phrase An infinitive phrase consists of an infinitive and its modifiers and complements. (See page 523.)

Informative writing Informative writing is writing that aims at conveying information or explaining something. (See page 7.)

Instructions Instructions are a form of writing in which a writer explains how to use or do something. (See page 228.)

Intensive pronoun An intensive pronoun emphasizes a noun or another pronoun. (See page 438.)

Interjection An interjection is a word used to express emotion. It has no grammatical relation to other words in the sentence. (See page 480.)

Interrogative pronoun An interrogative pronoun introduces a question. (See page 440.)

Interrogative sentence An interrogative sentence asks a question and is followed by a question mark. (See page 423.)

Interview An interview is a special listening situation with the specific purpose of gathering information that usually takes place between two people, an interviewer and the person being interviewed (called the *interviewee*). (See page 873.)

Intransitive verb An intransitive verb expresses action (or tells something about the subject) without passing the action from a doer to a receiver. (See page 459.)

Introduction An introduction begins a composition and should catch the reader's interest and present the main idea. (See page 104.)

Irregular verb An irregular verb is a verb that forms its past and past participle in some other way than by adding *–d* or *–ed* to the infinitive form. (See page 606.)

Jargon Jargon consists of words and phrases that have special meanings for particular groups of people. (See page 400.)

Linking verb A linking verb links, or connects, the subject with a noun, a pronoun, or an adjective in the predicate. (See page 461.)

Main idea A main idea is the idea around which a paragraph or composition is organized. (See pages 62 and 97.)

Metaphor A metaphor is a figure of speech that directly compares two things without using the word *like* or *as*. A metaphor says that something *is* something else. (See page 165.)

Modifier A modifier describes or limits the meaning of another word. (See page 657.)

Narration Narration is a strategy of development in which a writer relates events or actions over a period of time. (See page 75.)

Nonessential clause/Nonessential phrase A nonessential (or **nonrestrictive**) clause or phrase adds information that is not needed to understand the meaning of the sentence. It is set off by commas. (See page 747.)

Noun A noun is a word used to name a person, a place, a thing, or an idea. (See page 430.)

Noun clause A noun clause is a subordinate clause used as a noun. (See page 548.)

Number Number is the form of a word that indicates whether the word is singular or plural. (See page 574.)

O

Object An object receives the action of a transitive verb. (See page 459.)

Object of the preposition The noun or pronoun that ends a prepositional phrase is the object of the preposition that begins the phrase. (See page 506.)

Objective test An objective test is a test that may contain multiple-choice, true/false, matching, reasoning or logic, analogy, or short-answer questions. (See page 925.)

Opinion An opinion is a belief or attitude. (See page 261.)

Oral interpretation Oral interpretation is an expressive presentation of a literary work to an audience. (See page 867.)

Order of importance Order of importance is a way of arranging details in a paragraph or composition according to the details' levels of importance. (See page 82.)

P

Paraphrase A paraphrase is a restatement of someone's ideas in different words. (See pages 875 and 921.)

Parenthetical expression A parenthetical expression is a side remark that adds information or relates ideas. (See page 751.)

Participial phrase A participial phrase contains a participle and all of the words related to the participle. (See page 515.)

Participle A participle is a verb form that can be used as an adjective. (See page 513.)

Personal letter A personal letter is an informal letter in which a writer might thank someone for something, invite someone to a particular event or occasion, or reply to an invitation he or she has received. (See page 901.)

Personal narrative A personal narrative is a form of writing in which an author explores and shares the meaning of an experience that was especially important to him or her. (See Chapter 4.)

Personal pronoun A personal pronoun refers to the one speaking (*first person*), the one spoken to (*second person*), or the one spoken about (*third person*). (See page 437.)

Personification Personification is a figure of speech in which human characteristics are given to nonhuman things. (See page 166.)

Persuasive essay A persuasive essay is a form of writing in which a writer supports an opinion and tries to persuade an audience. (See Chapter 8.)

Persuasive writing Persuasive writing is writing that aims at persuading people to change their minds about something or to act in a certain way. (See page 7.)

Phrase A phrase is a group of related words that is used as a single part of speech and does not contain a verb and its subject. (See page 505.)

Plot The plot is the series of events in a story that follow each other and cause each other to happen. The plot centers on a **conflict,** or problem, that the main character faces. (See page 198.)

Point of view Point of view is the vantage point, or position, from which a writer tells a story. (See page 200.)

Positive degree Positive degree is the form of a modifier when only one thing is being described. (See page 658.)

Predicate The predicate is the part of a sentence that says something about the subject. The **simple predicate,** or **verb,** is the main word or group of words within the **complete predicate.** The complete predicate is composed of the main verb and its modifiers. (See page 413.)

Predicate adjective A predicate adjective is an adjective that follows a linking verb and describes the subject. (See page 497.)

Predicate nominative A predicate nominative is a noun that follows a linking verb and identifies the subject or refers to it. (See page 496.)

Prefix A prefix is a letter or group of letters added to the beginning of a word to change its meaning. (See page 802.)

Preposition A preposition is a word used to show the relationship of a noun or a pronoun to some other word in the sentence. (See page 474.)

Prepositional phrase A prepositional phrase is a group of words beginning with a preposition and ending with a noun or a pronoun. (See page 506.)

Prewriting Prewriting is the first stage in the writing process. In this stage, a writer thinks and plans, figures out what to write about, collects ideas and details, and makes a plan for presenting ideas. (See pages 6 and 24.)

Principal parts of a verb The principal parts of a verb are the verb's forms: the *base form,* the *present participle,* the *past,* and the *past participle.* (See page 604.)

Pronoun A pronoun is a word used in place of a noun or more than one noun. (See page 436.)

Proofreading Proofreading is the stage of the writing process in which a writer carefully reads a revised draft to correct mistakes in grammar, usage, and mechanics. (See pages 6 and 50.)

Proper adjective A proper adjective is formed from a proper noun and begins with a capital letter. (See page 448.)

Proper noun A proper noun names a particular person, place, thing, or idea and is always capitalized. (See page 433.)

Publishing Publishing is the last stage of the writing process. In this stage, a writer makes a final, clean copy of a paper and shares it with an audience. (See pages 6 and 51.)

Purpose Purpose is the reason for writing or speaking: to express yourself; to be creative; to entertain; to explain, inform, or explore; or to persuade. (See page 33.)

R

Reflexive pronoun A reflexive pronoun refers to the subject and directs the action of the verb back to the subject. (See page 438.)

Regular verb A regular verb is a verb that forms its past and past participle by adding *–d* or *–ed* to the base form. (See page 604.)

Relative pronoun A relative pronoun introduces a subordinate clause and relates an adjective clause to the word that the clause modifies. (See pages 440 and 539.)

Research report A research report is a form of writing in which a writer presents factual information that he or she has discovered through exploration and research. (See Chapter 10.)

Revising Revising is the stage of the writing process in which a writer goes over a draft, making changes in its content, organization, and style in order to improve it. (See pages 6 and 43.)

Run-on sentence A run-on sentence is two or more complete sentences run together as one. (See page 364.)

S

Sentence A sentence is a group of words that contains a subject and a verb and expresses a complete thought. (See page 406.)

Sentence base The sentence base consists of the subject and the verb of a sentence. (See page 417.)

Sentence fragment A sentence fragment is a part of a sentence that does not express a complete thought. (See pages 361 and 406.)

Setting The setting is where and when a story takes place. (See page 197.)

Simile A simile is a figure of speech that compares two basically unlike things, using the word *like* or *as*. (See page 165.)

Simple sentence A simple sentence has one independent clause and no subordinate clauses. (See page 557.)

Slang Slang consists of made-up words and old words used in new ways. (See page 396.)

Spatial order Spatial order is a way of arranging details in a paragraph or composition by ordering them according to how they are spaced—nearest to farthest, left to right, and so on. (See page 74.)

Statement of opinion A statement of opinion is a sentence in which a writer clearly states a topic and his or her opinion about it. (See page 262.)

Stringy sentence A stringy sentence is a sentence that has too many independent clauses, often strung together with words like *and* or *but*. (See page 378.)

Subject The subject is the part of a sentence that tells whom or what the sentence is about. The **simple subject** is the main word or group of words within the **complete subject.** The complete subject consists of the simple subject and its modifiers. (See page 409.)

Subject complement A subject complement completes the meaning of a linking verb and identifies or describes the subject. (See page 496.)

Subordinate clause A subordinate (or **dependent**) clause does not express a complete thought and cannot stand alone as a sentence. (See page 535.)

Subordinating conjunction A subordinating conjunction is a word that shows the relationship between an adverb clause and the word or words that the clause modifies. (See page 545.)

Suffix A suffix is a letter or group of letters added to the end of a word to change its meaning. (See page 802.)

Summary A summary is a restatement, in shortened form, of the main points of a passage, a speech, etc. (See pages 875 and 922.)

Superlative degree Superlative degree is the form a modifier takes when comparing more than two things. (See page 661.)

Supporting sentences Supporting sentences are sentences in a paragraph or composition that give specific details or information to support the main idea. (See page 66.)

Syllable A syllable is a word part that can be pronounced by itself. (See page 798.)

Synonym A synonym is a word that has a meaning similar to but not exactly the same as another word's. (See page 895.)

T

Tense The tense of a verb indicates the time of the action or state of being expressed by the verb. (See page 614.)

Topic sentence A topic sentence is the sentence that expresses the main idea of a paragraph. (See page 63.)

Transitional words and phrases Transitional words and phrases connect ideas in a paragraph or composition by showing how ideas and details are related. (See page 71.)

Transitive verb A transitive verb is an action verb that expresses an action directed toward a person or thing. (See page 459.)

U

Unity Unity, in a paragraph or composition, is a quality achieved when all the sentences or paragraphs work together as a unit to express or support one main idea. (See page 69.)

V

Verb A verb is a word used to express an action or a state of being. (See page 457.)

Verb phrase A verb phrase consists of a main verb preceded by at least one **helping verb,** or **auxiliary verb.** (See page 464.)

Verbal A verbal is a form of a verb used as a noun, an adjective, or an adverb. (See page 513.)

W

"What if?" questions Asking "What if?" questions is a creative thinking technique that can help a writer draw upon imagination to explore ideas for writing. (See page 31.)

Word bank A word bank is a writer's storehouse of words that he or she can use in writing. (See pages 164 and 893.)

Writer's journal A writer's journal is a written record of a person's experiences, feelings, questions, and thoughts. (See page 25.)

Writing Writing is the stage in the writing process in which a writer puts his or her ideas into sentences and paragraphs, following a plan for presenting the ideas. (See pages 6 and 41.)

Writing process The writing process is the series of stages or steps that a writer goes through to develop ideas and to communicate them clearly in a piece of writing. (See pages 6 and 22.)

Glossary

This glossary is a short dictionary of words found in the professional writing models in this textbook. The words are defined according to their meanings in the context of the writing models.

Pronunciation Key

Symbol	Key Words	Symbol	Key Words
a	asp, fat, parrot	b	bed, fable, dub, ebb
ā	ape, date, play, break, fail	d	dip, beadle, had, dodder
ä	ah, car, father, cot	f	fall, after, off, phone
e	elf, ten, berry	g	get, haggle, dog
ē	even, meet, money, flea, grieve	h	he, ahead, hotel
i	is, hit, mirror	j	joy, agile, badge
ī	ice, bite, high, sky	k	kill, tackle, bake, coat, quick
		l	let, yellow, ball
ō	open, tone, go, boat	m	met, camel, trim, summer
ô	all, horn, law, oar	n	not, flannel, ton
○○	look, pull, moor, wolf	p	put, apple, tap
̄○○	ooze, tool, crew, rule	r	red, port, dear, purr
y○̄○	use, cute, few	s	sell, castle, pass, nice
y○○	cure, globule	t	top, cattle, hat
oi	oil, point, toy	v	vat, hovel, have
ou	out, crowd, plow	w	will, always, swear, quick
u	up, cut, color, flood	y	yet, onion, yard
₩r	urn, fur, deter, irk	z	zebra, dazzle, haze, rise
ə	a in ago	ch	chin, catcher, arch, nature
	e in agent	sh	she, cushion, dash, machine
	i in sanity	th	thin, nothing, truth
	o in comply	*th*	then, father, lathe
	u in focus	zh	azure, leisure, beige
ər	perhaps, murder	ŋ	ring, anger, drink

Abbreviation Key

adj.	adjective	*prep.*	preposition
adv.	adverb	*vi.*	intransitive verb
n.	noun	*vt.*	transitive verb
pl.	plural		

A

a·fi·cio·na·do [ə fish'ə nä'dō] *n.* A person who likes, knows about, and devotedly pursues some interest or activity.

ail·ment [āl'mənt] *n.* An illness.

a·larm·ist [ə lärm'ist] *adj.* Of or like a person who spreads exaggerated reports of danger.

am·bi·tion [am bish'ən] *n.* A strong desire to succeed.

au·to·bi·o·graph·i·cal [ôt'ō bī'ə graf'i kəl] *adj.* About one's own life story.

a·verse [ə vʉrs'] *adj.* Unwilling or not inclined; opposed (to).

B

bade [bad] *vt.* Commanded.

bar·ren [bar'ən] *adj.* Empty.

be·moan [bē mōn'] *vt.* To feel sorry about something.

bi·zarre [bi zär'] *adj.* Very odd or out of the ordinary; unexpected and unbelievable.

Brown·ing [brou̇n'iŋ], **Elizabeth Barrett** *n.* (1806–1861) An English poet.

Brown·ing [brou̇n'iŋ], **Robert** *n.* (1812–1889) An English poet.

C

Car·roll [kar'əl], **Lewis** *n.* (1832–1898) An English writer.

clab·ber [klab'ər] *n.* Thick, sour milk.

clad [klad] *adj.* Dressed or clothed.

con·scious·ly [kän'shəs lē] *adv.* Done with a knowledge or awareness of.

con·ser·va·tion·ist [kän'sər vā'shən ist] *n.* A person who promotes the preservation of natural resources.

con·vey [kən vā'] *vt.* To communicate.

co-op [kō'äp'] *n.* Short for **cooperative**; an apartment house, store, society, or other organization owned and operated by those who use its facilities or buy its goods.

cov·ey [kuv'ē] *n.* A small flock of birds.

D

de·but [dā byo͞o'] *n.* An introduction to the public, as of an actor; a career's beginning.

de·fi·ance [dē fī'əns] *n.* The act of openly challenging an opposition.

dell [del] *n.* A small valley.

de·pict [dē pikt'] *vt.* To describe.

Dick·ens [dik'ənz], **Charles** *n.* (1812–1870) The English writer who wrote *Oliver Twist* and *A Christmas Carol.*

doff [däf] *vt.* To take off one's hat in greeting.

drove [drōv] *n.* A great number of something, such as people or animals.

E

eaves·drop·per [ēvz'dräp ər] *n.* One who listens secretly to others' conversations.

El·ling·ton [el'iŋ tən], **Duke** *n.* (1899–1974) A U.S. jazz musician, bandleader, and composer.

en·hance [en hans'] *vt.* To improve the quality of.

ep·i·dem·ic [ep'ə dem'ik] *n.* The quick spreading of a disease.

F

flat [flat] *n.* An area of level land.

flush [flush] *vt.* To drive out game birds from their cover.

G

gas plate [gas plāt] *n.* A small, portable stove.

gran·deur [grän'jər] *n.* Magnificence.

gru·el·ing [grōō'əl iŋ] *adj.* Extremely harsh and exhausting.

H

half nel·son [haf nel'sən] *n.* A type of wrestling hold.

haugh·ty [hôt'ē] *adj.* Showing too much pride in oneself.

hum·ding·er [hum'diŋ'ər] *n.* A slang word for a person or thing of excellence.

I

ice·box [īs'bäks'] *n.* An insulated box that holds ice for keeping foods cold.

in·flu·en·za [in'flōō en'zə] *n.* A contagious viral disease.

in·or·di·nate·ly [in ôr'də nit lē] *adv.* Excessively.

in·tact [in takt'] *adj.* Untouched; kept whole and uninjured.

L

Le·o·pold [lē'ə pōld'], **Aldo** *n.* (1887–1948) A U.S. naturalist, one of only one hundred trained foresters working for the U.S. Forest Service in 1909; he later became a private forestry and wildlife consultant.

M

mag·ma [mag'mə] *n.* Molten rock within the earth.

Mag·na Car·ta [mag'nə kär'tə] *n.* The document that King John of England was forced to sign in 1215, giving civil and political rights to the people.

Mar·shal [mär'shəl], **Bob** *n.* (1942–) The first recreation chief of the U.S. Forest Service. He has worked to preserve lands.

mel·an·chol·y [mel'ən käl'ē] *n.* Sadness and gloom.

met·a·phor·i·cal [met'ə fôr'i kəl] *adj.* Not meant to be taken literally.

Milne [miln], **A(lan) A(lexander)** *n.* (1882–1956) An English playwright and novelist.

Mil·ton [mil'tən], **John** *n.* (1608–1674) The English poet who wrote *Paradise Lost*.

mi·nor·i·ty [mī nôr'ə tē] *n.* Less than half of a group.

Muir [myōōr], **John** *n.* (1838–1914) The naturalist who worked to make Yosemite a national park and gained support from Theodore Roosevelt for 148,000,000 acres for forest reserves.

mul·ti·tude [mul'tə tōōd] *n.* A large number of people or things.

mu·tant [myōō'tənt] *adj.* Of or produced by a sudden change in some inheritable characteristic in a plant or animal.

my·col·o·gist [mī käl'ə jist] *n.* A person who studies fungi.

P

per·ti·nent [pur'tə nənt] *adj.* Having to do with the matter at hand.

phi·los·o·phy [fə läs'ə fē] *n.* The love of or search for wisdom or knowledge.

pig·eon·hole [pij'ən hōl'] *v.* To categorize or classify.

poised [poizd] *vi.* Balanced.

pro·to·zo·an [prōt'ō zō'ən] *n.* A member of the animal subkingdom Protozoa. Protozoans are usually single-celled and microscopic and are either water-dwelling or parasitic organisms.

pul·sate [pul'sāt'] *v.* To throb or move rhythmically; quiver.

pur·ga·tive [pur'gə tiv] *n.* A substance that causes a bowel movement.

Q

quell [kwel] *vt.* To quiet or put an end to.

R

roil [rɔil] *vt.* To stir up; to agitate; to move turbulently.

room · er [ro͞om'ər] *n.* A person who lives in a rented room.

S

schoon · er [sko͞on'ər] *n.* A ship with two or more masts.

scle · ro · ti · um [skli rō'shē əm] *n.* In various fungi, a hardened mass of threads that stores food material and can remain dormant for long periods.

sem · i · pro · fes · sion · al [sem'i prə fesh'ə nəl] *adj.* Engaged in for pay but not as a full-time occupation.

shale [shāl] *n.* Fine-grained, layered rock, formed by the hardening of clay, mud, or silt.

slack [slak] *adj.* Loose.

sock · dol · a · ger [säk däl'ə jər] *n.* Something outstanding.

sphere [sfir] *n.* Something round; a ball.

sphe · roid [sfir'oid] *n.* An object that is almost but not completely round.

spore [spōr] *n.* A small reproductive organ associated with many non-flowering plants (such as fungi, mosses, or ferns), with bacteria, and with some protozoans.

stoop [sto͞op] *n.* A small porch with steps.

strick · en [strik'ən] *adj.* Affected by something upsetting.

sub · tle · ty [sut"l tē] *n.* The condition of not being obvious.

syc · a · more [sik'ə môr'] *n.* A kind of maple tree with yellow flowers.

T

tas · sel [tas'əl] *n.* A group of strings hanging from the knot where they are tied together.

Ten · ny · son [ten'i sən] **Alfred** *n.* (1808–1892) An English poet.

ter · res · tri · al [tə res'trē əl] *adj.* Of or relating to the earth.

tin · ker [tink'ər] *n.* A person who makes minor repairs.

tongue [tuŋ] *n.* A language.

top · ple [täp'əl] *vt.* To cause to fall over.

tou · can [to͞o'kan'] *n.* A fruit-eating bird of tropical America, character-ized by its large beak and bright colors.

tour · ni · quet [tʉr'ni kit] *n.* A device, such as a bandage twisted about a limb, to control bleeding.

trend [trend] *n.* A current style.

tu · mult [to͞o'mult'] *n.* Noisy uproar of a crowd.

Twain [twān], **Mark** *n.* (1835–1910) American humorist and writer.

U

un · con · scious · ly [un kän'shəs lē] *adv.* Done without a knowledge or awareness of.

un · heed · ed [un hēd'id] *adv.* Not having attention being paid.

un · sur · passed [un sər past'] *adj.* Not outdone; best.

V

ver · min [vʉr'mən] *n. pl.* Various harmful bugs or small animals that are difficult to control.

vis · age [viz'ij] *n.* The face and its expressions.

viv · id · ly [viv'id lē] *adv.* Done in a clear or realistic way.

W

writh · ing [rīth'iŋ] *vi.* Squirming or twisting of the body.

Index

D

INDEX

INDEX

E

F

INDEX

M

INDEX

INDEX

P

INDEX

INDEX

INDEX

INDEX

Acknowledgments

For permission to reprint copyrighted material, grateful acknowledgment is made to the following sources:

Andrews and McMeel: From "Chapter 9: Use It Again . . . and Again . . . and Again . . ." from *50 Simple Things Kids Can Do to Save the Earth* by The Earth Works Group. Copyright © 1990 by John Javna.

Atheneum Books for Young Readers, an imprint of Simon & Schuster: From *Rockhound Trails* by Jean Bartenbach. Copyright © 1977 by Jean Bartenbach.

Ballantine Books, a division of Random House, Inc.: From "WHAT TO DO IN A WILDERNESS MEDICAL EMERGENCY" from *Dave Barry's Only Travel Guide You'll Ever Need* by Dave Barry. Copyright © 1991 by Dave Barry.

Susan Bergholz Literary Services, New York: From *Bless Me Ultima* by Rudolfo A. Anaya. Copyright © 1972 by Rudolfo A. Anaya. Published by Warner Books in hardcover and mass market editions; originally published by TQS Publications, Berkeley, CA. All rights reserved. From "Salomon's Story" from *Tortuga* by Rudolfo A. Anaya. Copyright © 1979 by Rudolfo A. Anaya. Published by University of New Mexico Press, Albuquerque, NM. All rights reserved.

Boy Scouts of America: From "Are There Martians on Mars?" from "A Home on the Martian Range" by Scott Stuckey from *Boy's Life,* July 1990. Copyright © 1990 by Boy Scouts of America.

Gwendolyn Brooks: From "The Sonnet-Ballad" from *Blacks* by Gwendolyn Brooks. Copyright © 1987 by Gwendolyn Brooks. Published by The David Company. Reissued by Third World Press, 1991. "Robert, Who Is Often a Stranger to Himself" from *Bronzeville Boys and Girls* by Gwendolyn Brooks. Copyright © 1956 by Gwendolyn Brooks Blakely.

Curtis Brown Ltd.: From "Strange and Terrible Monsters of the Deep" by William Wise from *Boy's Life,* February 1978. Copyright © 1978 by The Boy Scouts of America.

Juan Bruce-Novoa and University of Texas Press, Inc.: From *Chicano Authors: Inquiry by Interview* by Juan Bruce-Novoa. Copyright © 1980 by Juan Bruce-Novoa.

Children's Television Workshop: From "Paradise Lost" by Elizabeth Vitton from *3–2–1 Contact,* December 1990, pp. 7–9. Copyright © 1990 by Children's Television Workshop, New York, NY. All rights reserved.

Cobblestone Publishing, Inc., 7 School Street, Peterborough, NH 03458: From "Energy: Powering a Nation" by Laurel Sherman from *Cobblestone,* vol. 11, no. 10, October 1990. Copyright © 1990 by Cobblestone Publishing, Inc.

Coffee House Press: From "Part I: Emile" from *Brazil Maru* by Karen Tei Yamashita. Copyright © 1992 by Karen Tei Yamashita.

Ruth Cohen, Inc., on behalf of Lensey Namioka: From "The All-American Slurp" by Lensey Namioka from *Visions,* edited by Donald R. Gallo. Copyright © 1987 by Lensey Namioka. Published by Delacorte Press.

Coward-McCann, Inc.: "Desert Noon" from *Compass Rose* by Elizabeth Coatsworth. Copyright 1929 by Coward-McCann, Inc.; copyright renewed © 1957 by Elizabeth Coatsworth.

Stanley Crouch: From "The Duke's Blues" by Stanley Crouch from *The New Yorker,* April 19 & May 6, 1996, p. 158. Copyright © 1996 by Stanley Crouch.

Crown Publishers Inc.: "Travel Tip: How to Use Chopsticks" from *Dave Barry Does Japan* by Dave Barry. Copyright © 1992 by Dave Barry.

Kent Dannen: From "Ban Dogs from Trails?" by Kent Dannen from *Dog Fancy,* June 1988. Copyright © 1988 by Kent Dannen.

DC Comics: Superman Trademark slogan. ™ DC Comics. All rights reserved.

E. L. Doctorow: Unpublished quotation by E. L. Doctorow. Copyright © 1993 by E. L. Doctorow.

Doubleday, a division of Bantam Doubleday Dell Publishing Group, Inc.: "Tuesday, 4 April, 1944" (Retitled: "Becoming a Journalist") and from "March 7, 1944" from *Anne Frank: The Diary of a Young Girl* by Anne Frank. Copyright 1952 by Otto H. Frank.

Dutton Signet, a division of Penguin Books USA Inc.: From "The Letter" from *Max Perkins, Editor of Genius* by A. Scott Berg. Copyright © 1978 by A. Scott Berg.

Paul S. Eriksson, Publisher: From a journal entry by Mary Garfield from *Small Voices* by Josef and Dorothy Berger.

Farrar, Straus & Giroux, Inc.: From *A Wind in the Door* by Madeleine L'Engle. Copyright © 1974 by Crosswicks, Ltd.

HarperCollins Publishers, Inc.: "Jimmy Jet and His TV Set" from *Where the Sidewalk Ends* by Shel Silverstein. Copyright © 1974 by Evil Eye Music, Inc.

HarperCollins Publishers Limited: From *Survive the Savage Sea* by Dougal Robertson. Copyright © 1973 by Dougal Robertson.

Highlights for Children, Inc., Columbus, OH: From "Billy Mills" by Della A. Yannuzzi from *Highlights for Children,* January 1990. Copyright © 1990 by Highlights for Children, Inc. From "Pictures of the Poor" by Elsa Marston from *Highlights for Children,* September 1990. Copyright © 1990 by Highlights for Children, Inc.

Hill & Wang, a division of Farrar, Straus & Giroux, Inc.: "Thank You, M'am" from *Short Stories* by Langston Hughes. Copyright © 1996 by Ramona Bass and Arnold Rampersad.

International Creative Management, Inc.: From "On the Ball" from *Five Seasons* by Roger Angell. Copyright © 1972 by Roger Angell.

Stephen King: From "Everything You Need to Know About Writing Successfully in Ten Minutes" by Stephen King from *The Writer's Handbook,* edited by Sylvia K. Burack. Copyright © 1990 by Stephen King.

Alfred A. Knopf, Inc.: From "Along the Colorado" from *The Secret Worlds of Colin Fletcher* by Colin Fletcher. Copyright © 1989 by Colin Fletcher. From "Dream Deferred" ("Harlem"), from "Dreams," and from "Song" from *Collected Poems* by Langston Hughes. Copyright © 1994 by the Estate of Langston Hughes. From "Mother to Son" from *Selected Poems* by Langston Hughes. Copyright 1926 by Alfred A. Knopf, Inc.; copyright renewed 1954 by Langston Hughes. "Alta Weiss" from *Baseball: An Illustrated History,* narrative by Geoffrey C. Ward, based on a documentary filmscript by Geoffrey C. Ward and Ken Burns. Copyright © 1994 by Baseball Film Project, Inc.

Nedra Newkirk Lamar: "Does a Finger Fing?" by Nedra Newkirk Lamar.

Larry Leonard: Quotation by Jean Auel from "Jean Auel" by Larry Leonard from *On Being a Writer,* edited by Bill Strickland. Copyright © 1984 by Larry Leonard.

Ray Lincoln Literary Agency, Elkins Park House, 107–B, Elkins Park, PA: From "The Big Bang" from *Mount St. Helens: A Sleeping Volcano Awakens* by Marian T. Place. Copyright © 1981 by Marian T. Place.

Liveright Publishing Corporation: From "An Interview with Ann Petry" from *Interviews with Black Writers,* edited by John O'Brien. Copyright © 1973 by Liveright Publishing Corporation.

Sterling Lord Literistic, Inc.: From "The Log Jam" from *River Notes: The Dance of Herons* by Barry Holstun Lopez. Copyright © 1979 by Barry Holstun Lopez.

Los Angeles Times Syndicate: From "Get Eco-logical" from "Earth SOS" from *Seventeen Magazine,* April 1991. Copyright © 1991 by Seventeen Magazine. Distributed by the Los Angeles Times Syndicate. From "Disaster Hits Home" by Jennifer Cohen from *Seventeen Magazine,* March 1990. Copyright © 1990 by Seventeen Magazine. Distributed by the Los Angeles Times Syndicate.

David Low: From "Winterblossom Garden" by David Low from *Ploughshares,* vol. 8, no. 4, 1982. Copyright © 1982 by David Low.

Macmillan USA, a Simon & Schuster Macmillan Company: Entry "large" and "Pronunciation Key" from *Webster's New World College Dictionary*, Third Edition. Copyright © 1996, 1994, 1991, 1988 by Simon & Schuster Inc. From "Zion National Park/Utah" from *National Park Guide* by Michael Frome. Copyright © 1991 by Simon & Schuster Inc.

Anne McCaffrey and agent, Virginia Kidd: From "The Smallest Dragonboy" by Anne McCaffrey. Copyright © 1973 by Anne McCaffrey. First appeared in *Science Fiction Tales.*

National Council of Teachers of English: "A Letter to Gabriela, A Young Writer" by Pat Mora from *English Journal,* vol. 79, no. 5, September 1990. Copyright © 1990 by the National Council of Teachers of English. From "Joyce Carol Thomas" from *Speaking for Ourselves,* compiled and edited by Donald R. Gallo. Copyright © 1990 by the National Council of Teachers of English.

National Geographic World, the official magazine for Junior Members of the National Geographic Society: From "Animal Body Talk" from *National Geographic World,* no. 175, March 1990. Copyright © 1990 by National Geographic Society.

Nielsen Media Research: Chart, "Audience Composition by Selected Program Type (Average Minute Audience)" from *1990 Nielsen Report on Television* by Nielsen Media Research. Copyright © 1990 by Nielsen Media Research.

Omni: From "Road Warrior" by Bob Berger from *Omni,* March 1990. Copyright © 1990 by Omni Publications International, Ltd. From "Making Fun" by A.J.S. Rayl from *Omni,* November 1990. Copyright © 1990 by Omni Publications International, Ltd.

Pantheon Books, a division of Random House, Inc.: From "The Sound of Flutes" by Henry Crow Dog from *The Sound of Flutes and Other Indian Legends,* edited by Richard Erdoes. Text copyright © 1976 by Richard Erdoes.

Popular Science Magazine: From "Water World" by Tony Reichhardt from *Popular Science,* February 1996, p. 70. Copyright © 1996 by Times Mirror Magazines Inc. Distributed by Los Angeles Times Syndicate.

Byron Preiss Visual Publications, Inc.: From "A Cautionary Tale" from *A Kid's Guide to How to Save the Planet* by Billy Goodman, illustrated by Paul Meisel. Copyright © 1990 by Byron Preiss Visual Publications, Inc.

Gail Provost: Quote by Ellen Goodman from "Ellen Goodman" by Gary Provost from *On Being a Writer,* edited by Bill Strickland. Copyright © 1981 by Gary Provost.

Random House, Inc.: From *I Know Why the Caged Bird Sings* by Maya Angelou. Copyright © 1969 by Maya Angelou. From *Gorilla, My Love* by Toni Cade Bambara. Copyright © 1966 by Toni Cade Bambara.

School Library Journal: From a book review by Kathleen Odean on the book *Lyddie* by Katherine Paterson from *School Library Journal,* vol. 37, no. 2, February 1991. Copyright © 1991 by School Library Journal.

Photo Credits

Abbreviations used: (t) top, (c) center, (b) bottom, (l) left, (r) right, (bckgd) background, (bdr) border.

COVER: Ralph J. Brunke Photography

TABLE OF CONTENTS: Page vii(t), Lois Ellen Frank/Westlight; vii(c), Craig Aurness/Westlight; vii(b), Mark Wagoner/Picturesque; viii, The Kobal Collection; ix(t), Culver Pictures; ix(b), Brown Brothers; xii, Walter Chandoha; xv(t), François Gohier/Photo Researchers; xv(b), Sturgis McKeever/National Audubon Society/Photo Researchers; xvii, Bettmann Archives; xxi, Jerry Wachter/Focus on Sports; xxiii, Obremski/The Image Bank; xxiv(l), Pictorial Press Limited/Star File; xxiv(r), Michael Ochs Archives; xxviii, Wide World Photos; xxxi, James Newberry; xxxii, HRW Photo by John Langford; xxxiv, Courtesy of Pat Mora.

INTRODUCTION: Page 4, Comstock; 5, HRW photo by Russell Dian; 6, Will McIntyre/Tony Stone Images; 7, M. Durrance/Photo Researchers.

CHAPTER 1: Page 19, AP/Wide World Photos; 26, The Bettmann Archive; 29, Gerry Ellis/Ellis Nature Photography; 30, Nawrocki Stock Photography; 35, Laurence Parent; 39, Culver Pictures; 40(bl), Don & Pat Valenti/Tony Stone Images ; 40(cl), Skjold/Nawrocki Stock Photo; 40(cr), T. Rosenthal/Superstock; 40(br), Myrleen Ferguson Cate/PhotoEdit; 42, S. Vidler/Superstock; 45(l), (r), Benjamin Mendlowitz; 47, George Holton/Photo Researchers; 49, Frank Lane Agency/Bruce Coleman Inc.; 51(l), Jeff Schultz/AlaskaStock Images; 51(r), Greg Martin/AlaskaStock Images.

CHAPTER 2: Page 56(t), Lois Ellen Frank & Craig Aurness/Westlight; 56(b), Mark Wagoner/Picturesque; 57, Lois Ellen Frank & Craig Aurness/Westlight; 58, Victor Duran © Sylvia Duran Sharnoff; 60, © Sylvia & Stephen Sharnoff; 63, D. Sprague/WeatherStock; 64, T. Murphy/SuperStock; 65, Bill Bachman/Photo Researchers; 67, David Weintraub/Photo Researchers; 70, HRW Collection; 71(l), Anne Marie Weber/Adventure Photo; 71(r), David Hiser/Photographers Aspen; 73, UPI/Bettmann Newsphotos; 76, AP/Wide World Photos; 80, Mary Gow; 81(l), Gerad Lacz/Peter Arnold; 81(r), Mike & Moppet Reed/Animals Animals; 82, AKG London.

CHAPTER 3: Page 90, Luis Castaneda/The Image Bank; 102(l), Gamma Liaison; 102(r), The Kobal Collection; 103, Walt Disney Pictures/The Kobal Collection; 105, Courtesy of HarperCollins; 107(t), NASA; 107(b), Archive Photos; 111(bl), (br), Roy Britt/WeatherStock; 112(l), Brunskill/Bob Thomas Sports Photography;

112(r), The Bettmann Archive; 114, Dennis O'Conner II/Paul Bardagjy Photography.

CHAPTER 4: Page 119, Culver Pictures; 121, UPI/Bettmann; 124(l), Fukuhara, Inc./Westlight; 124(r), James Newberry; 124(inset), U.S. Forest Service; 126(l), AP/Wide World Photos; 126(r), AP/Wide World Photos; 127, Adrienne T. Gibson/Animals Animals; 132, Rick Stewart/Allsport; 134, James Newberry; 148(cr), Brown Brothers; 149(t), NASA; 149(bl), Globe Photos; 149(br), Ken Regan/Camera 5.

CHAPTER 5: Page 155, James Newberry; 158(tl), Smith/Gamma Liaison; 158(tr), Rivera Collection/Superstock; 158(bl) HRW photo by Peter Van Steen; 158(br), P. R. Productions/SuperStock; 159, Walter Chandoha; 160, Al Grillo/AlaskaStock; 162, P. R. Dunn; 165, HRW photo by Eric Beggs; 169, HRW photo by Lance Schriner; 171, Library of Congress; 175, Park Street; 178, Courtesy of Ray Young Bear; 179, John Running/Black Star; 181, James Newberry; 182(l), Walter Chandoha; 182(r), HRW photo by Eric Beggs; 183, A. Cosmos Blank/Photo Researchers.

CHAPTER 6: Page 195, Tom Bean/Tony Stone Images; 197, both images Nawrocki Stock Photo; 212, Courtesy of Pat Mora; 220, James Newberry.

CHAPTER 7: Page 233, HRW photo by Pat Dunn; 240, courtesy of Sterling Publishing Co.; 242, 243, Walter Chandoha; 249, HRW photo by Peter Van Steen; 253, James Newberry.

CHAPTER 8: Page 263, Tim Davis/Duomo; 265, James Newberry; 270, Archives Division, Texas State Library; 272, Kent & Donna Dannen; 275, James Newberry; 283(l), Rick Reinhard/Impact Visuals; 283(r), John Harrington/Black Star; 284, James Newberry; 287(b), James Newberry.

CHAPTER 9: Page 300(tl), HRW photo by Eric Beggs; 303, Paul J. Sutton/Duomo Photography; 309, Mark Antman/The Image Works; 310, Toris Von Wolfe/Everett Collection, Inc.; 316, Kathleen Carr/Index Stock; 321, Archive Photos; 323(cl), Peter Fetters/Matrix; 323(c), Nawrocki Stock Photo; 323(c), Lawrence Barns/Black Star; 323(cr), Nawrocki Stock Photo; 323(bc), Theo Westenberger/Sygma; 323(br), Ken Regan/Camera 5.

CHAPTER 10: Page 326, Gary Braasch/Tony Stone Images; 327, Randall Hyman; 331, Park Street; 334, François Gohier/Photo Researchers; 336(l), HRW Photo by John Langford; 336(r), John Griffin/The Image Works; 338(t), Sturgis McKeever/National Audubon Society/Photo Researchers; 338(b), James Newberry; 346(l),

Archive Photos; 346(c), Sipa Press; 346(r), Sygma; 347(l)(c), HRW photo by Peter Van Steen; 347(r), HRW Photo by Sam Dudgeon; 348, Everett Collection, Inc.; 349, AP/Wide World Photos; 355, ©1965 by Elizabeth Borton de Trevino. Courtesy of Farrar, Straus & Giroux.

CHAPTER 11: Page 361, Carol Boone; 362(l), Culver; 363, UPI/Bettmann; 366, Jim Corwin/ Tony Stone Images; 367, Francis Le Guen/Sygma; 368(l), Paramount Studios/SuperStock; 368(r), Sygma; 370, Frederic Lewis/American Stock; 372, John Cancalosi/Natural Selection; 376(l), D. Done/SuperStock; 376(r), M. Thonig/ H. Armstrong Roberts; 377(tl), Luis Castaneda/ The Image Bank; 377(c), Nick Nicholson/ The Image Bank; 380, Bettmann Archive.

CHAPTER 12: Page 400, Paramount Studios/ SuperStock.

CHAPTER 13: Page 413, Ronald C. Modra/ Sports Illustrated ©Time, Inc.; 416, Bridgeman Art Library/Art Resource; 421, Courtesy of the Austin American-Statesman.

CHAPTER 14: Page 431, National Anthropological Archives/National Museum of Natural History/ Smithsonian Institution; 435, G. Ahrens/ H. Armstrong Roberts; 441, Henry J. Kokojan/ The Stockhouse; 445, Courtesy of Concord Jazz; 452(l), Ken Dequaine/Third Coast Stock Source; 452(r), David A. Jentz/Third Coast Stock Source.

CHAPTER 15: Page 458, Nin Berman/Sipa Press; 463(all), Scott Newton; 466, Cotton Coulson/ Woodfin Camp & Associates; 473(l), P. B. Kaplan/ Photo Researchers; 473(r), Frank Schreider/Photo Researchers; 477, *Cows Watching Plane*, John Held, Jr., Courtesy of Illustration House, Inc.; 480, Gwendolen Cates/Sygma; 483, Bonnie Timmons/ The Image Bank.

CHAPTER 16: Page 494, Professional Rodeo Cowboys Association; 499, Phillip Kretchmar/The Image Bank; 501, NASA.

CHAPTER 17: Page 507, Jerry Wachter/Focus on Sport; 517(l), (r), © David Madison 1996; 518(t), Pat Caruso/Sportschrome East/West; 518(c), © David Madison 1996; 518(b), Mitchell R. Reibel/Sportschrome East/West; 529 (all) James Newberry.

CHAPTER 18: Page 544, John Neubauer/ Uniphoto Picture Agency; 550(all), Museum of Appalachia; 552(r), Nawrocki Stock Photo.

CHAPTER 19: Page 558, Musee de l'Armée, Paris/Art Resource; 561, Paramount/Shooting Star.

CHAPTER 20: Page 577, © Mark Seliger; 581, Robert Harding Picture Library; 585, HRW photo by Eric Beggs; 592(l), Craig Aurness/Westlight; 592(c), Rob Atkins/The Image Bank; 592(r), Obremski/The Image Bank.

CHAPTER 21: Page 606(all), HRW photos by Eric Beggs; 618, Steven Guarnaccia/The Image Bank; 622(l), Alexandra Buxbaum/Nawrocki Stock Photo; 622(c), Nawrocki Stock Photo; 622(r), Zephyr Pictures/Nawrocki Stock Photo; 626, Steve Allen/Peter Arnold, Inc.; 627, Jerry Jacka/Jerry Jacka Photography.

CHAPTER 22: Page 636, Nawrocki Stock Photo; 637(tl), Michael Ochs Archives; 637(tr), Michael Ochs Archives; 637(c), Pictorial Press Limited/ Star File; 637(br), Michael Ochs Archives; 640(t), Biblioteca Ambrosiana, Milan; 640(b), Bibliothèque Nationale, Paris; 645(l), Library of Congress; 645(cl), The Lincoln Museum, Fort Wayne, Indiana, a part of Lincoln National Corporation; 645(cr),(r), Library of Congress; 651, Collector's Showcase; 652, Nawrocki Stock Photo.

CHAPTER 23: Page 663, Craig Aurness/ Westlight; 666, Uniphoto, Inc.

CHAPTER 24: Page 685, Cameramann International, Inc.; 697, Chris Falkenstein; 700, Al Tielemans/Duomo.

CHAPTER 25: Page 712, Andrew A. Wagner; 716, Sandak, Inc.; 719(tl), Andy Caulfield/The Image Bank; 719(tr), Paul Nehrenz/The Image Bank; 719(b), Andy Caulfield/The Image Bank; 722, Courtesy of McGraw-Hill; 731, Ross Alistair/SuperStock.

CHAPTER 26: Page 740, Mike Powers; 746, Kjell B. Sandved/Photo Researchers, Inc.; 754, U.S. Postal Service; 758, Wide World Photos.

CHAPTER 27: Page 774(br), Collection of the Newark Museum, Purchase 1985, The Members' Fund; 780, Dr. E. R. Degginger/Color-Pic, Inc.; 785(tl), Robert Frerck/Woodfin Camp & Associates; 785(tc),(tr),(bl),(br), Loren McIntyre/Woodfin Camp & Associates; 792(all), Michael Sullivan/TexaStock.

CHAPTER 28: Page 806, Courtesy of Hendrick-Long Publishing Co.; 816, H. Gruyaert/Magnum Photos; 822, R. Gaillardi/Gamma Liaison; 825(l), Richard Sullivan/Shooting Star; 825(r), G. Hunter/SuperStock.

ILLUSTRATION CREDITS

Brian Battles—112, 113, 114, 165, 252, 416, 494, 511, 525, 558, 581, 593, 629, 731, 746, 754, 889

Kate Beetle—259

Kim Behm—15, 123

Linda Blackwell—171, 209

Keith Bowden—ix, xxix, 98, 148, 332, 384, 386, 537, 599, 612, 694, 704, 822

Paul Casale—14

Rondi Collette—64, 220, 232, 233, 239, 240, 326, 327, 328, 370, 421, 589

Chris Ellison—204, 207, 208, 544

Richard Erickson—62, 242, 243, 265

Janice Fried—x, 152, 153, 490, 719

Tom Gianni—366, 494

John Hanley—211, 372

Mary Jones—268

Linda Kelen—xiii, 68, 256, 257, 258, 383, 389, 398, 399

Susan Kemnitz—xiv, 290, 291, 318

Tatjana Krizmanic—224–225

Rich Lo—xxiii, 355, 592–593

Judy Love—xi, 8, 12, 13, 186–187, 188, 189, 190, 191, 192, 295, 296, 298, 546, 675

Richard Murdock—69, 156, 157, 801

Jack Scott—401

Steve Shock—vi, xxvi–xxvii, 20, 93, 94–95

Chuck Solway—521

Troy Thomas—xvi, xvii, 380

Nancy Tucker—80

Acknowledgments

For permission to reprint copyrighted material in the Annotated Teacher's Edition, grateful acknowledgment is made to the following sources:

Algonquin Books of Chapel Hill: From *Daughters of Memory* by Janis Arnold. Copyright © 1991 by Janis Arnold.

Harcourt Brace & Company: From "Little Gidding" from *Four Quartets* by T. S. Eliot. Copyright 1943 by T. S. Eliot; copyright renewed © 1971 by Esme Valerie Eliot.

Will Hobbs: From "Bringing Your Words to Life" by Will Hobbs from *R & E Journal,* Spring 1996. Copyright © 1996 by Will Hobbs.

People Weekly: From "Hell on Wheels" from the "Up Front" section of *People Weekly,* vol. 36, no. 10, September 16, 1991. Copyright © 1991 by People Weekly.

School Library Journal: From a book review by Kathleen Odean on the book *Lyddie* by Katherine Paterson from *School Library Journal,* vol. 37, no. 2, February 1991. Copyright © 1991 by School Library Journal.

Gary Soto: From "October" from *The Elements of San Joaquin* by Gary Soto. Copyright © 1977 by Gary Soto.

The Estate of Igor Stravinsky: Quotation by Igor Stravinsky from *Saturday Review,* November 9, 1957.

Ray A. Young Bear: From "Grandmother" from *Winter of the Salamander* by Ray A. Young Bear. Copyright © 1980 by Ray Young Bear.

PHOTO CREDITS *(Annotated Teacher's Edition)*

Abbreviations used: (t) top, (c) center, (b) bottom, (1) left, (r) right, (bckgd) background, (bdr) border

COVER: Ralph J. Brunke Photography

TABLE OF CONTENTS: T8(t)(r), Lois Ellen Frank & Craig Aurness/Westlight; (b), Mark Wagoner/ Picturesque; T9, The Kobal Collection; T10(t), Culver Pictures; (b), Brown Brothers; T13, Walter Chandoha; T16, Sturgis McKeever/National Audubon Society/Photo Researchers, Inc.; T18(br), Bettmann Archive; T22, Jerry Wachter/Focus on Sports; T24, Obremski/The Image Bank; T25(bl), Pictorial Press Limited/Star File; (br), Michael Ochs Archives; T31, James Newberry; T32, HRW Photo by John Langford; T34, Courtesy of Pat Mora.

PROFESSIONAL ESSAYS: Page T36-T77, border by M. Angelo/Westlight; T36(t), Dennis Carlyle Darling; T36(c), (b), T37(tl), Larry Ford; T37(tr), J. Alexander Newberry; T37(cl), Larry Ford; T37(cr), Dennis Carlyle Darling; T37(bl), (br), James Newberry; T38, T39, T42, Dennis Carlyle Darling; T45, T47, T48, Larry Ford; T51, Dennis Carlyle Darling; T53, T55, Larry Ford; T57, Dennis Carlyle Darling; T62, T65, J. Alexander Newberry; T66, Courtesy of Judith Irvin; T67, James Newberry; T68, Courtesy of Joyce Armstrong Carrol; T69, James Newberry; T72, Jonathan Lock, T73; Larry Ford.

ILLUSTRATION CREDITS: *(Annotated Teacher's Edition)*

Jane Thurmond Design— Page 13A, 61A, 103A, 131A, 165A, 201A, 247A, 283A, 32lA, 361A, 405A, 420A, 440A

Front Matter Design—Maeder Design

Edd Patton—Page T39, T40, T41, T44, T46, T49, T50, T53, T54, T57, T58, T59, T60, T61, T63, T64, T66, T67, T69, T71, T72, T74, T75, T76, T77

Icons—Leslie Kell, Mike Krone